Visit classzone.com and get connected

Online resources for students and parents

***ClassZone* resources are linked together and provide instruction, practice, and learning support.**

eEdition Plus ONLINE

This interactive version of the text encourages students to explore mathematics.

eWorkbook

Interactive practice, correlated to the text, provides support for key concepts and skills.

@HomeTutor

This interactive tutorial reinforces key skills and helps students prepare for tests.

Chapter–Based Support

State test practice, quizzes, vocabulary support, activities, and examples help students succeed.

Now it all clicks!™

McDougal Littell

McDougal Littell

GEORGIA Middle School MATHEMATICS

Course 2

McDougal Littell

GEORGIA Middle School

MATHEMATICS

Course 2

Ron Larson
Laurie Boswell
Timothy D. Kanold
Lee Stiff

Complete listing of

Georgia Performance Standards
for Grade 7 Mathematics

on pages G1–G3
at the back of the book

A DIVISION OF HOUGHTON MIFFLIN COMPANY
Evanston, Illinois • Boston • Dallas

GEORGIA Middle School Mathematics

About Course 2

The focus of the early chapters in *Georgia Course 2* is on rational numbers and their operations, equations and inequalities. You will build your understanding of these concepts using models, such as algebra tiles, number lines, and verbal models. You will also apply your skills to problem-solving situations and use estimation to check reasonableness. Topics from math strands, such as real number properties, geometric formulas, and averages, are introduced early in the course and then integrated and expanded upon throughout.

Later chapters in *Georgia Course 2* include topics such as linear equations and their graphs, properties of right triangles, geometric transformations, and probability. The number and variety of problems, ranging from basic to challenging, give you the practice you need to develop your math skills.

Every lesson in *Georgia Course 2* has both skill practice and problem solving, including multi-step problems. These types of problems often appear on standardized tests and cover a wide variety of math topics. To help you prepare for standardized tests, *Georgia Course 2* provides instruction and practice on standardized test questions in many formats—multiple choice, short response, extended response, and so on. Technology support for course content and standardized test preparation is available at classzone.com.

Georgia Middle School Mathematics Course 2, along with its accompanying *Georgia Active Learning Textbook Course 2,* provide you with the skills you need to master the Georgia Performance Standards for Grade 7 Mathematics.

ISBN-13: 978-0-618-80052-0
ISBN-10: 0-618-80052-2 123456789—DWO— 10 09 08 07 06

Internet Web Site: http://www.mcdougallittell.com

About the Authors

Ron Larson is a professor of mathematics at Penn State University at Erie, where he has taught since receiving his Ph.D. in mathematics from the University of Colorado. Dr. Larson is well known as the author of a comprehensive program for mathematics that spans middle school, high school, and college courses. Dr. Larson's numerous professional activities keep him in constant touch with the needs of teachers and supervisors. He closely follows developments in mathematics standards and assessment.

Laurie Boswell is a mathematics teacher at The Riverside School in Lyndonville, Vermont, and has taught mathematics at all levels, elementary through college. A recipient of the Presidential Award for Excellence in Mathematics Teaching, she was also a Tandy Technology Scholar. She served on the NCTM Board of Directors (2002–2005), and she speaks frequently at regional and national conferences on topics related to instructional strategies and course content.

Timothy D. Kanold is the superintendent of Adlai E. Stevenson High School District 125 in Lincolnshire, Illinois. Dr. Kanold served as a teacher and director of mathematics for 17 years prior to becoming superintendent. He is the recipient of the Presidential Award for Excellence in Mathematics and Science Teaching, and a past president of the Council for Presidential Awardees in Mathematics. Dr. Kanold is a frequent speaker at national and international mathematics meetings.

Lee Stiff is a professor of mathematics education in the College of Education and Psychology of North Carolina State University at Raleigh and has taught mathematics at the high school and middle school levels. He served on the NCTM Board of Directors and was elected President of NCTM for the years 2000–2002. He is a recipient of the W. W. Rankin Award for Excellence in Mathematics Education presented by the North Carolina Council of Teachers of Mathematics.

Advisers and Reviewers

Georgia Curriculum Advisers and Reviewers

Michele Borror Long
Mathematics Teacher
LaGrange High School
LaGrange, GA

Georgia Advisers and Reviewers

Sandye Ashley
Mathematics Teacher
Rome Middle School
Rome, GA

Sally Asnip
Mathematics Teacher
McCleskey Middle School
Marietta, GA

Brian Butera
Mathematics Department Chair
Whitewater Middle School
Fayetteville, GA

Tiffany Comer
Mathematics Department Chair
Griffin Middle School
Smyrna, GA

Tina Conner
Mathematics Department Chair
Mundy's Mill Middle School
Jonesboro, GA

Michael Fox
Mathematics Teacher
Hightower Trail Middle School
Marietta, GA

Michelle Frost
Mathematics Teacher
Samuel M. Inman Middle School
Atlanta, GA

Veletta Gebert
Mathematics Department Chair
Marietta Middle School
Marietta, GA

Mesha Greene
Mathematics Teacher
Sandtown Middle School
Atlanta, GA

Susan Hall
Mathematics Department Chair
Rising Star Middle School
Fayetteville, GA

Barbara Harrell
Mathematics Department Chair
Woodstock High School
Woodstock, GA

Brian Jackson
Mathematics Department Chair
Northwestern Middle School
Alpharetta, GA

Carolyn Jones
Mathematics Department Chair
Fayette Middle School
Fayetteville, GA

Jayne Lewis
Mathematics Teacher
LaGrange High School
LaGrange, GA

Ruth Keenan
Mathematics Department Chair
J.C. Booth Middle School
Peachtree City, GA

Christine Morgan
Mathematics Department Chair
Avondale Middle School
Avondale Estates, GA

Sherry Nance
Mathematics Department Chair
Mundy's Mill Middle School
Jonesboro, GA

Michael Phillips
Mathematics Teacher
Stephenson Middle School
Stone Mountain, GA

Lynn Ridgeway
Mathematics Supervisor
Fayette County Schools
Fayetteville, GA

Audrey Smith
Mathematics Teacher
Camp Creek Middle School
College Park, GA

Celeta Thomas
Mathematics Department Chair
North Clayton Middle School
College Park, GA

Gina Tindall
Mathematics Department Chair
Dutchtown Middle School
Hampton, GA

National Advisers and Reviewers

Susanne Artiñano
Bryn Mawr School
Baltimore, MD

Lisa Barnes
Bishop Spaugh Academy
Charlotte, NC

Beth Bryan
Sequoyah Middle School
Oklahoma City, OK

Judy Carlin
Brown Middle School
McAllen, TX

Kathryn Chamberlain
McCarthy Middle School
Chelmsford, MA

Jennifer Clark
Mayfield Middle School
Oklahoma City, OK

Judith Cody
Deady Middle School
Houston, TX

Lois Cole
Pickering Middle School
Lynn, MA

Louis Corbosiero
Pollard Middle School
Needham, MA

Linda Cordes
Paul Robeson Middle School
Kansas City, MO

James Cussen
Candlewood Middle School
Dix Hills, NY

Kristen Dailey
Boardman Center Middle School
Boardman, OH

Sheree Daily
Canal Winchester Middle School
Canal Winchester, OH

Linda Dodd
Argentine Middle School
Kansas City, KS

Melanie Dowell
Raytown South Middle School
Raytown, MO

Margarita Figueredo
Cummings Middle School
Brownsville, TX

Donna Foley
Chelmsford Middle School
Chelmsford, MA

Rhonda Foote
Maple Park Middle School
North Kansas City, MO

Shannon Galamore
Clay-Chalkville Middle School
Pinson, AL

Tricia Highland
Moon Area Middle School
Moon Township, PA

Lisa Hiracheta
Irons Junior High School
Lubbock, TX

Deborah Kebe
Canal Winchester Middle School
Canal Winchester, OH

Cas Kyle
Richard A. Warren Middle School
Leavenworth, KS

Jill Leone
Twin Groves Junior High School
Buffalo Grove, IL

Wendy Loeb
Twin Groves Junior High School
Buffalo Grove, IL

Melissa McCarty
Canal Winchester Middle School
Canal Winchester, OH

Myrna McNaboe
Immaculate Conception
East Aurora, NY

Deb Mueth
St. Aloysius School
Springfield, IL

Kay Neuse
Wilson Middle School
Plano, TX

Barbara Nunn
Broward County Schools
Fort Lauderdale, FL

Louise Nutzman
Sugar Land Middle School
Sugar Land, TX

Clarise Orise
Tafolla Middle School
San Antonio, TX

Jan Rase
Moreland Ridge Middle School
Blue Springs, MO

Angela Richardson
Sedgefield Middle School
Charlotte, NC

James Richardson
Booker T. Washington Middle School
Mobile, AL

Dan Schoenemann
Raytown Middle School
Kansas City, MO

Tom Scott
Duval County Public Schools
Jacksonville, FL

Gail Sigmund
Charles A. Mooney Middle School
Cleveland, OH

Reginald Taylor
Ryan Middle School
Houston, TX

Dianne Walker
Traverse City Central High School
Traverse City, MI

Wonda Webb
William H. Atwell Middle School
and Law Academy, Dallas, TX

Stacey Wood
Cochrane Middle School
Charlotte, NC

Karen Young
Murchison Elementary School
Pflugerville, TX

Georgia Course 2 Overview

Number and Operations

Pre-Course Review

- divisibility tests, 761
- decimal operations, 764, 769–770
- fraction operations, 765, 768
- whole number estimation, 766, 771

Course 2 Content

- powers and exponents, 19, 202, 208, 726
- order of operations, 8, 19
- fraction and decimal estimation, 238, 247, 260, 265
- scientific notation, 212
- prime factorization, 176
- integer operations, 63–77
- write between fractions, decimals, and percents, 255, 359
- rational number operations, 233, 238, 243, 247, 260, 265
- rational and irrational numbers, 475
- ratios, 343
- percent of change, 366–370

Algebra

Pre-Course Review

Course 2 builds on work students have done in earlier grades with Algebra topics such as patterns, equations, and functions.

Course 2 Content

- evaluate variable expressions, 13, 469
- use formulas, 32, 142, 375, 482, 521
- identity and inverse properties, 63, 73
- commutative and associative properties, 83
- distributive property, 88
- write expressions and equations, 13, 26, 134
- solve equations, 26, 117, 122, 129, 293, 298, 303, 469
- graph equations, 598, 606, 622
- solve inequalities, 148, 154, 318, 324
- graph inequalities, 629
- functions, 583, 739
- slope of a line, 612
- solve proportions, 348, 354, 447
- operations on polynomials, 721–734

Geometry and Measurement

Pre-Course Review

- units of time, 778
- converting customary units, 779
- converting metric units, 780
- converting between metric and customary units, 781

Course 2 Content

- perimeter and area, 32, 142, 312, 521, 527
- scale models, 348
- classify angles, 403–411
- classify polygons, 411–420
- identify congruent and similar figures, 427, 447
- transformations, 433–447
- Pythagorean theorem, 482–487
- special right triangles, 493
- trigonometric ratios, 500
- circles, 312, 527
- classify and sketch solids, 534

Data Analysis and Probability

Pre-Course Review

- Venn diagrams and logical reasoning, 785
- reading data displays, 782–784

Course 2 Content

- mean, median, and mode, 77, 272
- make and interpret data displays, 3, 588, 649, 654, 659
- appropriate data displays, 659
- find outcomes, 670–680
- find probability and odds, 381, 685,

Problem Solving

Pre-Course Review

- make a model, 786
- draw a diagram, 787
- guess, check, and revise, 788
- work backward, 789
- make a list or table, 790
- look for a pattern, 791
- break into parts, 792
- solver a simpler problem, 793
- use a Venn diagram, 794

Course 2 Content

Problem solving is integrated throughout the course with a section of problem solving exercises in every lesson. The following problem solving features also occur throughout. For examples see:

- short response exercises, 17, 25, 36, 41, 50
- extended response exercises, 7, 20, 25, 36, 108
- choose a strategy exercises, 24, 87, 133
- Mixed Review of Problem Solving, 25, 44, 82, 101
- Brain Games, 43, 100, 139

Variables and Equations

Evaluating Expressions, p. 13
$5 + 6(t)$

Chapter 1 Highlights

STUDENT HELP

- Homework Help, 5, 10, 15, 21, 28, 34, 40
  At classzone.com: @HomeTutor, Online Quiz, eWorkbook, Hints and Homework
- Reading and Vocabulary, 2, 3, 8, 13, 14, 19, 26, 27, 32, 33, 37, 38, 45
- Notetaking, 8, 20, 32, 33, 38
- Avoid Errors, 4, 19

★ ASSESSMENT

- Multiple Choice, 6, 7, 10, 11, 16, 17, 18, 21, 22, 24, 28, 29, 30, 34, 35, 36, 40, 41, 43
- Short Response, 6, 11, 17, 22, 25, 30, 36, 41, 44
- Extended Response, 7, 22, 25, 36, 44
- Writing, 11, 17, 30, 35, 41
- Open-Ended, 6, 7, 11, 17, 25, 30, 35, 44

PROBLEM SOLVING

- Real Life Examples, 3, 4, 9, 13, 15, 20, 27, 33, 34, 39
- Mixed Review of Problem Solving, 25, 44
- Multi-Step Problems, 4, 5, 11, 17, 22, 25, 28, 30, 36, 39, 42, 44
- Challenge, 7, 11, 18, 23, 30, 36, 42, 43

Integer Operations

Ordering Integers, p. 57
−154, −86, 0, 90, 115

Chapter 2 Highlights

Solving Equations and Inequalities

Getting Ready

Using Area Formula, p. 144
Total area = $lw + r$

Chapter 3 Highlights

STUDENT HELP

- Homework Help, 119, 124, 131, 136, 145, 150, 156
  At classzone.com: @HomeTutor, Online Quiz, eWorkbook, Hints and Homework
- Reading, Vocabulary, and Notetaking, 114, 117, 118, 122, 123, 129, 130, 134, 142, 143, 148, 149, 154, 155, 161
- Avoid Errors, 118, 123, 130

★ ASSESSMENT

- Multiple Choice, 119–121, 124, 125, 131, 133, 134, 136, 137, 139, 143–147, 151–153, 156, 157, 158, 159
- Short or Extended Response, 120, 126, 132, 133, 138, 141, 146, 147, 153, 158, 160
- Writing, 121, 126, 128, 133, 137, 146, 152, 157
- Open-Ended, 121, 125, 132, 137, 141, 145, 151, 152, 157, 160

PROBLEM SOLVING

- Real Life Examples, 118, 123, 129, 134, 135, 143, 144, 150, 155
- Mixed Review of Problem Solving, 141, 160
- Multi-Step Problems, 121, 125, 133, 138, 141, 147, 152, 157, 160
- Challenge, 121, 126, 133, 138, 139, 147, 153, 158, 159

Factors, Fractions, and Exponents

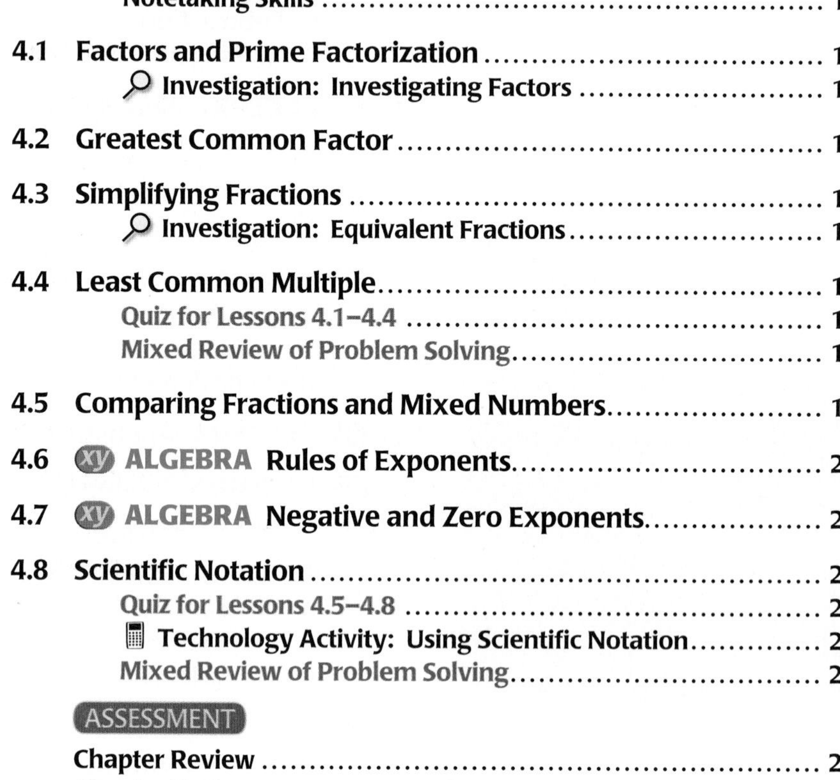

Least Common Multiples, p. 197

3, 6, 9, (12)

4, 8, (12)

Chapter 4 Highlights

STUDENT HELP

- Homework Help, 178, 183, 189, 194, 200, 204, 210, 214
  At classzone.com: @HomeTutor, Online Quiz, eWorkbook, Hints and Homework
- Reading and Vocabulary, 174, 176, 181, 187, 192, 198, 202, 208, 212, 220
- Notetaking, 189, 202, 203, 208, 209, 212
- Avoid Errors, 176, 181, 182, 193, 203, 204, 209, 214

★ ASSESSMENT

- Multiple Choice, 179, 184, 185, 190, 191, 194, 195, 196, 199, 200, 201, 205, 206, 207, 210, 211, 213, 214, 215, 217
- Short Response, 179, 180, 184, 191, 195, 197, 201, 206, 211, 216, 219
- Extended Response, 180, 191, 197, 219
- Writing, 180, 185, 191, 195, 201, 216
- Open-Ended, 180, 184, 185, 194, 200, 205, 219

PROBLEM SOLVING

- Real Life Examples, 176, 182, 187, 192, 199, 208, 212, 213
- Mixed Review of Problem Solving, 197, 219
- Multi-Step Problems, 176, 180, 181, 182, 185, 191, 193, 195, 197, 198, 199, 201, 206, 211, 216, 219
- Challenge, 180, 185, 191, 196, 201, 207, 211, 217

Rational Number Operations

Getting Ready

Subtracting Decimals, p. 263
time (sec) = 58.01 − 55.48

Chapter 5 Highlights

STUDENT HELP

- Homework Help, 235, 240, 245, 249, 257, 262, 267, 274
  At classzone.com: @HomeTutor, Online Quiz, eWorkbook, Hints and Homework
- Reading and Vocabulary, 232, 233, 234, 238, 243, 247, 248, 249, 255, 260, 265, 272, 280
- Notetaking, 233, 243, 247, 257, 265, 266, 272
- Avoid Errors, 234, 239, 244, 266, 273

★ ASSESSMENT

- Multiple Choice, 236, 237, 240, 241, 242, 245, 246, 250, 251, 252, 258, 259, 262, 263, 264, 267, 268, 273, 274, 276, 278
- Short Response, 237, 242, 246, 251, 254, 264, 268, 269, 276, 279
- Extended Response, 251, 254, 259, 277, 279
- Writing, 237, 241, 251, 259, 264, 268, 271, 275
- Open-Ended, 241, 254, 259, 276, 279

PROBLEM SOLVING

- Real Life Examples, 234, 239, 244, 249, 256, 260, 261, 262, 265, 272, 273
- Mixed Review of Problem Solving, 254, 279
- Multi-Step Problems, 237, 242, 246, 251, 254, 257, 259, 261, 264, 269, 276, 279
- Challenge, 237, 242, 246, 252, 259, 264, 269, 277, 278

6 Multi-Step Equations and Inequalities

Using Circumference Formula, p. 313
$423.9 \text{ ft} = \pi d$

Chapter 6 Highlights

STUDENT HELP

★ ASSESSMENT

PROBLEM SOLVING

Ratio, Proportion, and Percent

Using Percent Equation, p. 375
$a = 26.7\% \cdot 2000$

Chapter 7 Highlights

Polygons and Transformations

Finding Angle Measures, p. 408
$2(m\angle 1) = 135°$

Chapter 8 Highlights

Real Numbers and Right Triangles

Using Irrational Numbers, p. 477

$$s = \sqrt{\frac{95}{0.019}}$$

Chapter 9 Highlights

STUDENT HELP

- Homework Help, 472, 477, 484, 489, 495, 503
  At classzone.com: @HomeTutor, Online Quiz, eWorkbook, Hints and Homework
- Reading and Vocabulary, 468, 469, 471, 475, 482, 487, 493, 500, 509
- Notetaking, 482, 493, 494, 500
- Avoid Errors, 476, 488, 501

★ ASSESSMENT

- Multiple Choice, 470, 472, 473, 474, 478, 479, 483, 484, 485, 486, 489, 491, 496, 497, 503, 505
- Short Response, 473, 486, 492, 497, 506, 508
- Extended Response, 480, 492, 505, 508
- Writing, 473, 479, 480, 486, 490, 497, 504
- Open-Ended, 479, 485, 492, 497, 505, 508

PROBLEM SOLVING

- Real Life Examples, 471, 477, 483, 487, 493, 495, 502
- Mixed Review of Problem Solving, 492, 508
- Multi-Step Problems, 492, 508, 474, 476, 480, 486, 488, 491, 492, 494, 495, 497, 505, 508
- Challenge, 474, 480, 486, 491, 497, 505, 506

Measurement, Area, and Volume

Area of Circles, p. 528
$A = 2\pi(15)^2$

Chapter 10 Highlights

STUDENT HELP

- Homework Help, 523, 529, 536, 545, 550, 557, 563
  At classzone.com: @HomeTutor, Online Quiz, eWorkbook, Hints and Homework
- Reading and Vocabulary, 520, 521, 522, 527, 534, 535, 539, 542, 548, 554, 556, 561, 567, 569
- Notetaking, 521, 522, 527, 543, 544, 548, 550, 554, 555, 561, 562, 567
- Avoid Errors, 528, 554

★ ASSESSMENT

- Multiple Choice, 523, 524, 525, 526, 529, 530, 532, 537, 538, 545, 546, 547, 550, 551, 556, 558, 559, 564, 565, 566
- Short Response, 530, 541, 547, 552, 559, 565, 568
- Extended Response, 526, 541, 559, 568
- Writing, 526, 531, 537, 547, 552, 559
- Open-Ended, 525, 537, 541, 547, 568

PROBLEM SOLVING

- Real Life Examples, 522, 528, 543, 544, 556, 563
- Mixed Review of Problem Solving, 541, 568
- Multi-Step Problems, 523, 526, 528, 531, 535, 538, 541, 547, 549, 552, 556, 559, 565, 568
- Challenge, 526, 532, 538, 547, 552, 559, 566

CHAPTER 11

Linear Equations and Graphs

Using Intercepts, p. 607
$4x + 2y = 8$

Chapter 11 Highlights

STUDENT HELP

- Homework Help, 585, 590, 600, 608, 614, 624, 631
  At classzone.com: @HomeTutor, Online Quiz, eWorkbook, Hints and Homework
- Reading and Vocabulary, 582, 583, 584, 588, 593, 598, 606, 612, 618, 622, 627, 629, 630, 636
- Notetaking, 600, 606, 607, 612, 614, 622, 630
- Avoid Errors, 583, 599, 600, 613

★ ASSESSMENT

- Multiple Choice, 585–587, 592, 593, 595, 596, 597, 600, 602, 603, 608, 609, 615, 616, 617, 624, 625, 626, 632, 633
- Short Response, 587, 592, 597, 602, 605, 609, 616, 625, 633, 635
- Extended Response, 605, 609, 617, 626, 633, 635
- Writing, 587, 592, 596, 609, 616, 625, 632
- Open-Ended, 587, 592, 605, 616, 626, 633, 635

PROBLEM SOLVING

- Real Life Examples, 584, 588, 589, 593, 599, 607, 612, 623, 631
- Mixed Review of Problem Solving, 605, 635
- Multi-Step Problems, 584, 585, 587, 588, 589, 592, 594, 597, 599, 602, 605, 606, 607, 609, 617, 623, 626, 627, 628, 630, 633, 635
- Challenge, 587, 592, 597, 603, 609, 617, 626, 633, 634

Unit 4: Advanced Algebra Topics

Data Analysis and Probability

Box-and-Whisker Plots, p. 654

$$\text{median} = \frac{1377 + 1385}{2}$$

Chapter 12 Highlights

STUDENT HELP

- Homework Help, 651, 656, 661, 672, 677, 682, 687, 697
  At classzone.com: @HomeTutor, Online Quiz, eWorkbook, Hints and Homework
- Reading and Vocabulary, 648, 649, 654, 659, 667, 670, 675, 680, 682, 685, 686, 690, 694, 701, 704
- Notetaking, 660, 671, 676, 681, 690, 695, 696
- Avoid Errors, 650, 660, 661

★ ASSESSMENT

- Multiple Choice, 651, 652, 653, 656, 657, 658, 662, 663, 672, 673, 674, 677, 678, 679, 683, 684, 688, 689, 695, 697, 700
- Short Response, 652, 657, 663, 664, 669, 674, 678, 684, 688, 699, 703
- Extended Response, 658, 669, 674, 679, 699, 703
- Writing, 653, 658, 663, 673, 678, 684, 689, 699
- Open-Ended, 657, 662, 669, 697

PROBLEM SOLVING

- Real Life Examples, 649, 650, 654, 655, 659, 660, 671, 675, 676, 680, 682, 685, 687, 695, 696
- Mixed Review of Problem Solving, 669, 703
- Multi-Step Problems, 649, 653, 657, 659, 660, 664, 669, 670, 672, 674, 678, 684, 689, 691, 698, 703
- Challenge, 653, 658, 664, 674, 679, 684, 689, 699, 700

CHAPTER 13

Unit 4: Advanced Algebra Topics

Polynomials and Functions

Evaluating Polynomials, p. 720
$-16t^2 + 88t + 2$

Chapter 13 Highlights

STUDENT HELP

- Homework Help, 719, 723, 728, 736, 741
  At classzone.com: @HomeTutor, Online Quiz, eWorkbook, Hints and Homework
- Reading and Vocabulary, 716, 717, 721, 726, 734, 735, 739, 748
- Notetaking, 727, 728, 734
- Avoid Errors, 717, 722, 723, 739, 741

★ ASSESSMENT

- Multiple Choice, 719, 720, 724, 725, 729, 730, 736, 737, 738, 740, 742, 744, 745
- Short Response, 720, 725, 730, 732, 737, 743, 747
- Extended Response, 725, 730, 732, 744, 747
- Writing, 720, 725, 730, 737, 743
- Open-Ended, 724, 731, 732, 737, 743, 747

PROBLEM SOLVING

- Real Life Examples, 718, 723, 727, 735, 739
- Mixed Review of Problem Solving, 732, 747
- Multi-Step Problems, 720, 722, 725, 730, 732, 738, 740, 745, 747
- Challenge, 720, 725, 730, 731, 738, 745

Contents of Student Resources

McDougal Littell

GEORGIA Middle School MATHEMATICS

Course 2

1 Variables and Equations

Before

In previous courses you've . . .

- Compared quantities
- Performed operations on numbers

Now

In Chapter 1 you'll study . . .

- 1.1 Interpreting graphs
- 1.2 Order of operations
- 1.3 Variable expressions
- 1.4 Powers and exponents
- 1.5 Equations and solutions
- 1.6 Familiar formulas
- 1.7 Problem solving

Why?

So you can solve real-world problems about . . .

- volcanoes, p. 3
- cliff diving, p. 22
- tiger beetles, p. 35
- parachuting, p. 36

at classzone.com

- Mountain Climbing Substitution Race, p. 14
- Powers and Exponents, p. 19
- Perimeter and Area, p. 35

Get-Ready Games

Review Prerequisite Skills by playing *Vacation Views* and *Next Stop.*

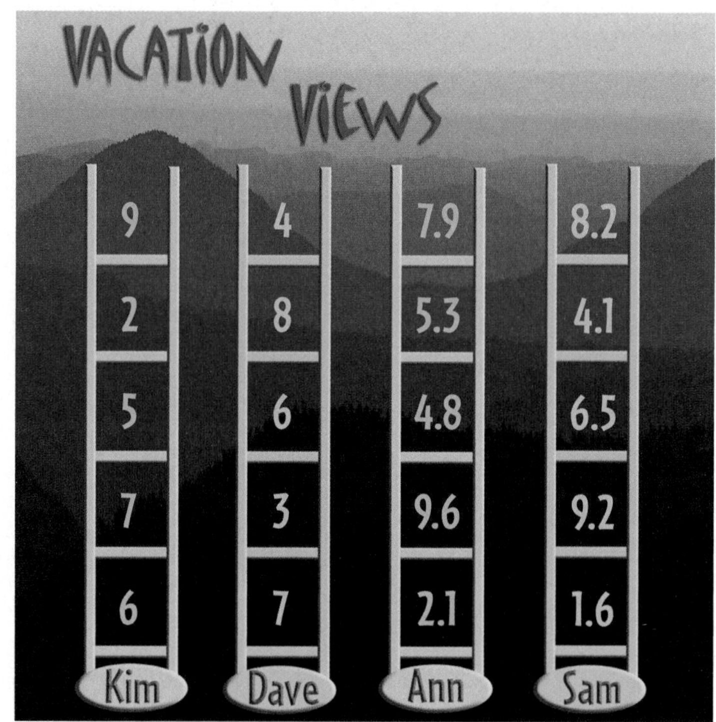

Skill Focus: Finding the sums of whole numbers and decimals

On a family vacation trip, the first stop is a mountain lookout tower. The four ladders lead to the top of the tower. Which child gets to the top first?

- Find the sum of the numbers on the rungs of each ladder.
- The ladder with the least sum is where the fastest person climbs.

NEXT STOP

			Place value
	415.79		Tens
410 M	420 U	430 E	?
	19.45		Ones
17 D	18 A	19 N	?
	8.178		Hundredths
8.16 A	8.17 T	8.18 H	?
	589.63		Tenths
589.6 C	589.7 R	589.8 S	?
	627.4		Hundreds
600 L	700 E	899 N	?

5575

Skill Focus: Rounding and identifying place value

Help the kids figure out what the next stop is on the family trip by solving the puzzle.

- Each number has been rounded to one of its digits. Select the answer that shows the number rounded correctly.
- On the right, write each letter below the place value it was rounded to.
- Put letters in correct place value order to figure out the next stop.

Stop and Think

1. **CRITICAL THINKING** List the names in *Vacation Views* from who gets to the top first to who gets there last (the least sum to the greatest). Whose name is first on this list?
2. **WRITING** In *Next Stop*, a student thinks that the result of rounding 8.178 is 8.17 because the last digit is removed. What is wrong with the student's reasoning?

1 Getting Ready

Review Prerequisite Skills

REVIEW WORDS
- **whole number,** *p. 759*
- **sum,** *p. 764*
- **difference,** *p. 764*
- **product,** *p. 768*
- **quotient,** *p. 770*

VOCABULARY CHECK

Copy and complete using a review word from the list at the left.

1. When you add two numbers, the result is called the _?_.
2. When you multiply two numbers, the result is called the _?_.
3. When you split up an amount into equal parts, the result is called the _?_.

SKILL CHECK

Write the place value of the red digit. ***(p. 759)***

4. 26.10
5. 45.901
6. 139.07
7. 6.394

Find the sum, difference, product, or quotient.

8. $12.7 - 9.4$ ***(p. 764)***
9. $17.8 + 26.3$ ***(p. 764)***
10. $9.64 + 6.36$ ***(p. 764)***
11. $20.24 - 16.5$ ***(p. 764)***
12. 1.3×3 ***(p. 769)***
13. $9.6 \div 6$ ***(p. 770)***
14. You are shopping for new clothes. If you have $75.00 and buy a pair of jeans for $37.75, how much money do you have left? ***(p. 767)***

@HomeTutor Prerequisite skills practice at classzone.com

Notetaking Skills — Keeping a Notebook

In each chapter you will learn a new notetaking skill. In Chapter 1 you will apply the strategy of keeping a notebook to Example 3 on p. 20.

Your math notebook is an important tool for learning and reviewing the topics of this course. Here are some tips for organizing your notes. Organize your notes in the same way for each lesson.

Start with the date and topic.

September 7 Decimals

To add decimals, line up the decimal points.

Copy examples shown in class.

Example: Adding Decimals

$$\begin{array}{r} 23.40 \\ +\ 36.15 \\ \hline 59.55 \end{array}$$

1.1 Interpreting Graphs

Before You compared quantities.

Now You'll use graphs to analyze data.

Why? So you can make conclusions about data, as in Example 1.

k8pe-0101-0001-h

KEY VOCABULARY

- **bar graph,** *p. 3*
- **data,** *p. 3*
- **frequency table,** *p. 4*
- **histogram,** *p. 4*

Volcanoes The *bar graph* at the right shows the number of historically active volcanoes in four countries. Which country has the most historically active volcanoes?

A **bar graph** is a type of graph in which the lengths of bars are used to represent and compare *data* in categories. **Data** are facts, numbers, or numerical information.

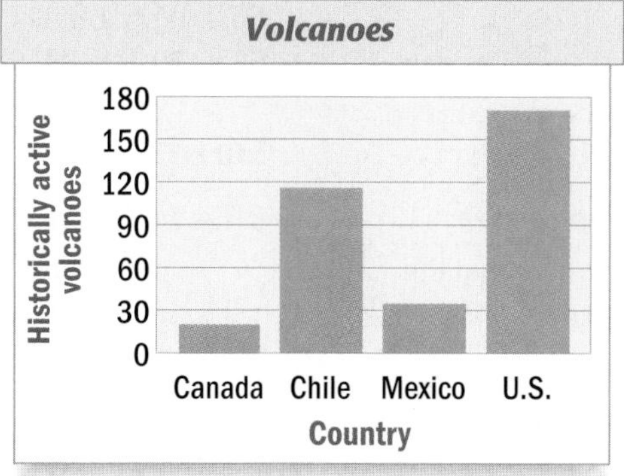

k8pe-0101-0001-t

EXAMPLE 1 Interpreting a Bar Graph

Use the bar graph above about volcanoes. Answer the question or explain why you can't answer the question using the graph.

a. Which country has the most historically active volcanoes?

b. Which country has the most volcanic eruptions in a given year?

SOLUTION

a. The vertical axis in the bar graph is labeled *Historically active volcanoes*, so the tallest bar represents the country with the most historically active volcanoes. Because the United States has the tallest bar, it has the most historically active volcanoes.

b. Having more historically active volcanoes doesn't necessarily mean having more eruptions, so you can't answer this question from the bar graph.

READING MATH

Read carefully to make sure you don't misinterpret the graph. Just because the U.S. has the most active volcanoes of the countries shown does not mean it has the most in the world.

✓ GUIDED PRACTICE for Example 1

Use the bar graph above about historically active volcanoes.

1. About how many more historically active volcanoes does Chile have than Mexico?

2. Which country has the least number of historically active volcanoes?

3. About how many historically active volcanoes do Canada, Mexico, and the U.S. have altogether?

Histograms A large set of data values can be grouped into intervals in a **frequency table**. The *frequency* of data in an interval is the number of values in the interval. You can graph data organized in equal intervals in a **histogram**, where the height of each bar indicates its frequency.

EXAMPLE 2 Making a Frequency Table

Roller Coasters The data show the heights, in meters, of some of the tallest roller coasters in the world. Make a frequency table of the data.

66.4, 94.5, 68.3, 115, 62.5, 97, 66.4, 126.5, 63.4, 74.7, 63.4, 70.1, 66.4, 64.9, 63.7, 79, 63.4, 63.1, 62.5, 61.9, 71.6

SOLUTION

AVOID ERRORS
Make sure that the intervals do not overlap.

STEP 1 **Choose** intervals of equal size for the data. The intervals should include numbers from 61.9 to 126.5.

STEP 2 **Tally** the data in each interval. Use tally marks to record each occurrence of a height in its interval.

STEP 3 **Write** the frequency for each interval by totaling the tally marks.

Height (m)	*Tally*	*Frequency*
60–69.9	~~IIII~~ ~~IIII~~ III	13
70–79.9	IIII	4
80–89.9		0
90–99.9	II	2
100–109.9		0
110–119.9	I	1
120–129.9	I	1

EXAMPLE 3 Making a Histogram

Make a histogram of the data in the frequency table above.

STEP 1 **Draw** and label the horizontal and vertical axes. Start the vertical scale at 0 and end at a point greater than 13. Use equal increments.

STEP 2 **Draw** a bar to represent the frequency of each interval. The bars of neighboring intervals should touch.

STEP 3 **Write** a title for the histogram.

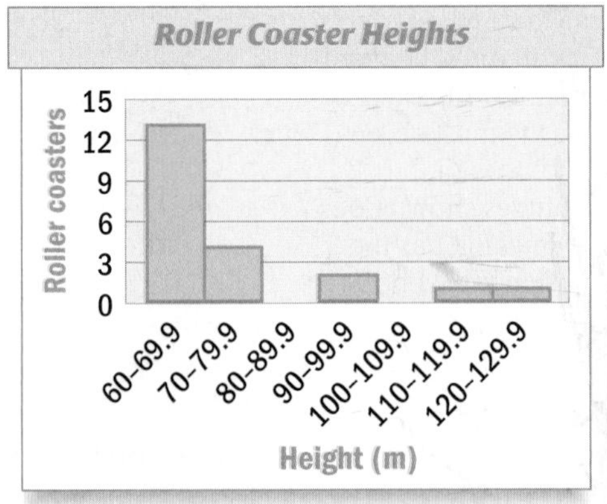

✓ GUIDED PRACTICE for Examples 2 and 3

4. **What If?** Using the data from Example 2, make a new frequency table using 6 intervals. Then make a histogram from your frequency table.

1.1 EXERCISES

HOMEWORK KEY

★ = **STANDARDIZED TEST PRACTICE** Exs. 13, 14, 18, 21, 22, and 36

○ = **HINTS AND HOMEWORK HELP** for Exs. 3, 5, 7, 13, 15 at classzone.com

SKILL PRACTICE

1. **VOCABULARY** Copy and complete: A histogram is a graph that shows data that are divided into equal _?_.

2. **VOCABULARY** Copy and complete: The lengths of bars are used to represent and compare data in categories in a _?_.

INTERPRETING A GRAPH Use the bar graph. It shows the number of businesses at a mall by category.

SEE EXAMPLE 1 on p. 3 for Exs. 3–6

3. Which category has the greatest number of businesses?

4. Which category has the least number of businesses?

5. About how many more shoe stores are there than jewelry stores?

6. Can you tell from the graph which category of businesses uses the most floor space in the mall? Why or why not?

SEE EXAMPLE 2 on p. 4 for Ex. 7

7. **MULTI-STEP PROBLEM** The data show the numbers of hours 30 students in a class spent on the Internet in a week.

   4, 2.5, 5.7, 1.8, 3.7, 5.4, 5.5, 11.6, 3.7, 6.5, 2, 10, 0.5, 4.5, 5, 9.5, 2.1, 4.5, 7.5, 2.5, 8, 1, 9, 4.2, 8, 7, 3, 7, 5, 6

   a. **Make a Frequency Table** Make a frequency table of the data. Use 0–1.9 as the first interval.

   b. **Make a Frequency Table** Make a frequency table of the data. Use 0–2.9 as the first interval.

   c. **Compare** Does the frequency table in part (a) or part (b) give a clearer representation of the data? *Explain* your reasoning.

SEE EXAMPLE 3 on p. 4 for Exs. 8–9

8. **ERROR ANALYSIS** Jack used the intervals 0–2, 2–4, 4–6, 6–8, and 8–10 to make a histogram. Describe the error Jack made.

9. **GRAPHING DATA** The frequency table shows when new states were added to the United States. Make a histogram of the data.

Year	1787–1836	1837–1886	1887–1936	1937–1986
States	25	13	10	2

10. **CHALLENGE** *Explain* why a frequency table and a histogram aren't appropriate to show the data: 1, 23, 97, 184, 551, 2097, 9143 and 12,221.

PROBLEM SOLVING

11. **GUIDED PROBLEM SOLVING** The table shows the numbers of movies released in the United States from 1998 through 2003. Use a bar graph to help you describe how the data have changed from year to year.

Year	Movies
1998	357
1999	438
2000	502
2001	477
2002	473
2003	492

a. **Choose** intervals for the scale for a bar graph.

b. **Make** a bar graph.

c. **Compare** the values for different years to describe how they've changed.

MEDIA In Exercises 12–14, use the triple bar graph. It shows how many U.S. high schools (per 100 schools) have the given media activities.

SEE EXAMPLE 1 on p. 3 for Exs. 12–14

12. Which of the given media did the greatest number of schools offer in each of the 3 years?

13. ★ **SHORT RESPONSE** Which of the media saw the most growth from 1991 to 2002? *Explain* how you can tell that from the graph.

14. ★ **MULTIPLE CHOICE** In 1998, how did the number of high schools with newspapers compare to the number of high schools with radio or TV stations?

Ⓐ About $\frac{1}{4}$ as many had newspapers

Ⓑ About $\frac{1}{2}$ as many had newspapers

Ⓒ About twice as many had newspapers

Ⓓ About 4 times as many had newspapers

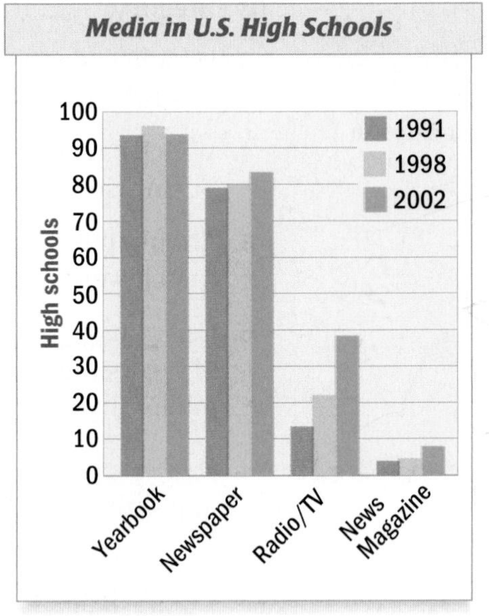

HURRICANES In Exercises 15–17 the histogram shows the numbers of hurricanes in the Atlantic Ocean from 1950 through 1999.

15. How many years of data does this graph show?

16. Can you determine the number of hurricanes in the Atlantic Ocean in 1965? *Explain.*

17. Can you use the histogram to predict the number of hurricanes in 2000–2009? Why or why not?

18. ★ **OPEN-ENDED MATH** Give an example of a set of data that can be graphed with a bar graph but not with a histogram.

19. **REASONING** You are looking for data on high tides. Is it easier to find the exact number of high tides between 2:00 A.M. and 2:59 A.M. last year from a frequency table or a histogram? *Explain.*

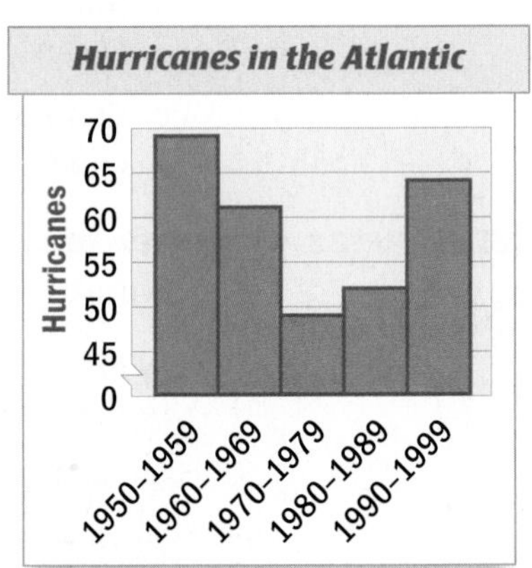

20. ◆ **MULTIPLE REPRESENTATIONS** The data show the average numbers of meteors that fall per hour during 39 annual meteor showers. For example, in the first meteor shower, an average of 60 meteors fall each hour.

60, 4, 1, 5, 5, 1, 40, 4, 5, 20, 2, 15, 8, 6, 21, 15, 20, 30, 3, 15, 10, 62, 25, 26, 50, 12, 20, 12, 15, 30, 10, 10, 20, 12, 12, 60, 10, 12, 20

a. **Frequency Table** Make a frequency table of the data. Use intervals of 10 starting with 0–9.

b. **Histogram** Make a histogram of the data from your frequency table.

c. **Compare** Compare the displays. *Discuss* one thing that is easier to tell about the data from each display.

Meteor shower

21. ★ **OPEN-ENDED MATH** You want to collect data about the pets owned by students in your class. What data would you collect to make a bar graph? Could you use the same data to make a histogram? *Explain* your reasoning.

22. ★ **EXTENDED RESPONSE** The data below are the number of medals the United States won in each of the Winter Olympic Games as of 2002.

4, 7, 12, 4, 9, 11, 7, 10, 6, 7, 8, 10, 12, 8, 6, 11, 13, 13, 34

a. Create a histogram of the data with intervals of 5 and a second histogram with intervals of 10.

b. Which histogram gives a clearer picture of how many medals you can expect the U.S. to win in future Winter Olympics? What might account for the 34 medals?

23. **CHALLENGE** Use the graph at the right. *Describe* how the data changed during the years shown. What might explain the rapid growth in sales of DVD players? What might cause the growth to slow down in the future? *Explain* your reasoning.

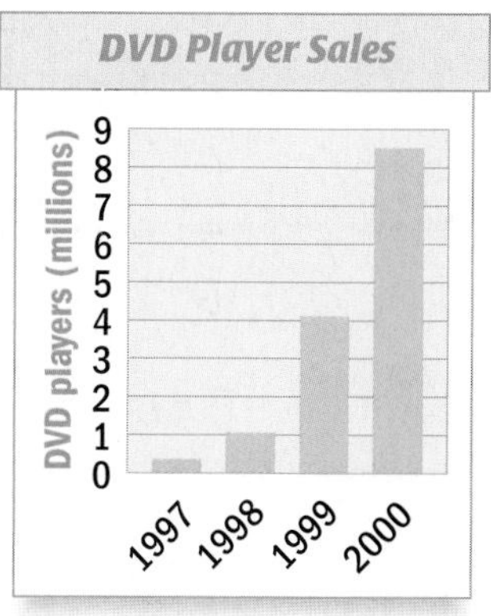

MIXED REVIEW

Get-Ready

Prepare for Lesson 1.2 in Exs. 24–27

Evaluate the expression. *(p. 764)*

24. $38 + 15 + 29$ **25.** $25 - 2 - 6$ **26.** $6.4 - 3.8 - 1.6$ **27.** $1.8 + 1.7 + 2.8$

Find the product or quotient.

28. 34×4 *(p. 769)* **29.** 6×15 *(p. 769)* **30.** $140 \div 20$ *(p. 770)* **31.** $84 \div 7$ *(p. 770)*

32. 7×36 *(p. 769)* **33.** 19×8 *(p. 769)* **34.** $155 \div 5$ *(p. 770)* **35.** $92 \div 4$ *(p. 770)*

36. ★ **MULTIPLE CHOICE** Round 453.571 to the nearest tenth. *(p. 760)*

Ⓐ 453.57 Ⓑ 453.6 Ⓒ 450 Ⓓ 500

1.2 Order of Operations

Before	You performed operations on numbers.
Now	You'll use order of operations to evaluate numerical expressions.
Why?	So you can find total costs, as in the aquarium visit in Example 3.

KEY VOCABULARY
- **numerical expression,** *p. 8*
- **evaluate,** *p. 8*
- **order of operations,** *p. 8*
- **verbal model,** *p. 9*

Visiting an Aquarium You and four friends visit an aquarium, but only three of you go to the movie at the aquarium. What is the total cost of the visit? You will find the total cost of the visit using the prices in the table on the right in Example 3 and applying the *order of operations.*

Aquarium Prices	
Admission	$13.50
Sea Lion show	Free
Movie	$8.00

A **numerical expression** consists of numbers and operations. To find the value of a numerical expression is to **evaluate** it. When a numerical expression has more than one operation, use a set of rules called the **order of operations**.

KEY CONCEPT *For Your Notebook*

Order of Operations

To evaluate an expression that has more than one operation:

1. Evaluate expressions inside grouping symbols.
2. Multiply and divide from left to right.
3. Add and subtract from left to right.

EXAMPLE 1 Using the Order of Operations

Evaluate the expression $7 + 16 \div 4 \times 2$.

$7 + 16 \div 4 \times 2 = 7 + 4 \times 2$	**Divide 16 by 4.**
$= 7 + 8$	**Multiply 4 by 2.**
$= 15$	**Add 7 and 8.**

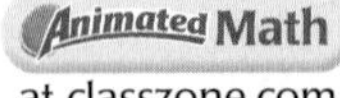
at classzone.com

INTERPRET SYMBOLS
You can express multiplication by using parentheses or the symbols • or ×.
$3(4) = 12$
$3 \cdot 4 = 12$
$3 \times 4 = 12$

✓ **GUIDED PRACTICE** for Example 1

Evaluate the expression.

1. $14 - 6 \div 2 + 12$ **2.** $20 - 7 \times 2 + 1$ **3.** $2 \cdot 13 - 2 \cdot 7$

Grouping Symbols The most common grouping symbols are parentheses ( ), brackets [ ], and fraction bars.

EXAMPLE 2 Using Grouping Symbols

a. $(14 + 6) \cdot 8 = 20 \cdot 8$ — **Add inside parentheses first.**

$= 160$ — **Then multiply.**

b. $\frac{9 \times 8}{4 + 8} = \frac{72}{4 + 8}$ — **Evaluate numerator.**

$= \frac{72}{12}$ — **Evaluate denominator.**

$= 6$ — **Divide.**

c. $45 \div [63 \div (56 \div 8)] = 45 \div [63 \div 7]$ — **Divide inside the innermost set of grouping symbols.**

$= 45 \div 9$ — **Divide inside brackets.**

$= 5$ — **Divide.**

Animated Math at classzone.com

ANOTHER WAY
You can express division using either ÷ or a fraction bar. To evaluate an expression with a fraction bar, evaluate the numerator and the denominator before you divide.

Verbal Model When you solve a problem, it may help to write a **verbal model**. Use symbols for operations, and use words to label necessary information.

EXAMPLE 3 Using a Verbal Model

To find the total cost of the visit to the aquarium described on the previous page, you can use a verbal model to write and evaluate an expression.

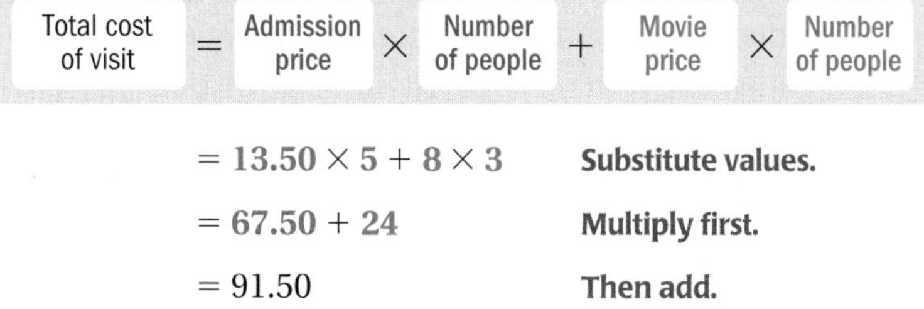

Total cost of visit
=
Admission price
×
Number of people
+
Movie price
×
Number of people

$= 13.50 \times 5 + 8 \times 3$ — **Substitute values.**

$= 67.50 + 24$ — **Multiply first.**

$= 91.50$ — **Then add.**

▶ **Answer** The total cost of the visit is $91.50.

REVIEW DECIMALS
Need help with decimal operations? See pp. 764, 769, and 770.

✓ GUIDED PRACTICE for Examples 2 and 3

Evaluate the expression.

4. $35 \div (9 - 4)$

5. $3 \cdot [(11 - 1) \div 5]$

6. $\frac{45 + 19}{2 \times 8}$

7. What If? Suppose 50 students go to the aquarium and movie in Example 3. It costs $35 to park their school bus. Use a verbal model to write and evaluate an expression for the total cost of their visit.

1.2 EXERCISES

HOMEWORK KEY

★ = **STANDARDIZED TEST PRACTICE** Exs. 3, 25, 36, 37, 38, 39, and 51

○ = **HINTS AND HOMEWORK HELP** for Exs. 5, 7, 9, 11, 37 at classzone.com

SKILL PRACTICE

1. **VOCABULARY** Use the order of operations to list, in order, the steps needed to evaluate the following expression: $8 + 2 \times 5 - 4$.

2. **VOCABULARY** Copy and complete: A(n) _?_ consists of numbers and operations.

SEE EXAMPLES 1 AND 2 on pp. 8–9 for Exs. 3–24

3. ★ **MULTIPLE CHOICE** In what order should the operations be performed to evaluate the expression $2 \times 4 - 6 \div 3 + 1$?

   (A) $\times, \div, -, +$ (B) $\times, -, \div, +$ (C) $\times, \div, +, -$ (D) $\times, +, -, \div$

USING ORDER OF OPERATIONS **Evaluate the expression.**

4. $12 - 10 + 4$
5. $7 + 3 - 2 + 4$
6. $18 + 6 \div 3 \times 2$
7. $16 - 6 + 2 \times 4$
8. $26 - 15 + 8 \div 2$
9. $18 \div (8 + 4 - 9)$
10. $\frac{8 + 2}{5 - 3}$
11. $\frac{16}{7 - 3}$
12. $8 \times [6 \div (5 - 3)]$
13. $120 \div [(6 + 2) \cdot 3]$
14. $9 \div \left[3 \cdot \left(\frac{5}{3} + \frac{4}{3}\right)\right]$
15. $3 \cdot \left(\frac{7}{2} + \frac{1}{2}\right)$
16. $(1.5 - 0.5) \times 2$
17. $4 + 3.9 \div 1.3$
18. $9.4 + 4.2 \div 6$
19. $6 \times (2.4 - 0.4 + 3)$
20. $7.8 \times (5 + 2)$
21. $8.4 \div (21 - 14)$
22. $3 \cdot (12 - 5) + \frac{23 - 9}{7}$
23. $\frac{41 - 2(3 + 4)}{(36 \div 4)}$
24. $\frac{62 - (3 + 4)}{3 + (4 \times 2)}$

25. ★ **MULTIPLE CHOICE** Which operation should be performed first when finding *the sum of twenty and the quotient of eighteen and six*?

   (A) $20 + 18$ (B) $18 \div 6$ (C) $20 + 6$ (D) $20 \div 6$

26. **ERROR ANALYSIS** Describe and correct the error made in the solution.

$$\begin{aligned} 3 \times 3 + 63 \div 9 &= 9 + 63 \div 9 \\ &= 72 \div 9 \\ &= 8 \end{aligned}$$

NUMBER SENSE **Insert parentheses to make the statement true.**

27. $5 \cdot 2 + 3 - 8 = 17$
28. $12 \div 6 + 4 - 7 = 4$
29. $13 - 5 \times 8 - 6 = 3$
30. $7 - 2 \times 3 + 12 = 27$
31. $12 \div 3 \times 4 + 1 = 20$
32. $24 \div 10 - 3 + 1 = 3$

CHALLENGE **Copy and complete the statement using one of the operations +, −, ×, and ÷, and one set of parentheses to obtain the greatest possible value of the expression.**

33. 12 _?_ 4 + 2
34. 15 _?_ 5 − 2
35. 12 + 9 _?_ 3

PROBLEM SOLVING

SEE EXAMPLE 3 on p. 9 for Exs. 36–40

36. ★ **MULTIPLE CHOICE** Your friend pledges \$10 to you for a fundraising walk and \$.25 for each mile you walk. You walk 6 miles. Which expression could you use to find your friend's contribution?

(A) $10 + 0.25(6)$ (B) $6 \times (10 + 0.25)$ (C) $10(6) + 0.25$ (D) $10(6)(0.25)$

37. ★ **WRITING** You buy 3 notebooks at \$2 each and 4 pens at \$1.50 each. *Explain* how to find the total cost.

38. ★ **SHORT RESPONSE** Your school softball team has 25 members. The school contributes \$30 toward each \$40 uniform. Write and evaluate a verbal model to find how much money the team needs to raise to buy uniforms for every member. Is more than one model possible? *Explain.*

39. ★ **OPEN-ENDED MATH** Write a verbal model and an expression for a real-world problem whose answer is 25. Use at least three operations.

40. **MULTI-STEP PROBLEM** Liz and Ty are baking for the school bake sale. Liz makes 5 batches of 3 dozen cookies, and Ty makes 4 batches of 4 dozen cookies.

a. **Verbal Model** Write a verbal model for the total number of cookies baked.

b. **Evaluate** Evaluate the expression.

c. **Extend** Liz and Ty decide to make packages of three cookies. Write and evaluate an expression to find the number of packages they can make.

41. **CHALLENGE** To make the statement below true, copy and complete using one or more of the operators $\times$, $\div$, $-$, and $+$: $8 \underline{?} 6 \underline{?} 3 \underline{?} 7 \underline{?} 1 = 5$

42. **CHALLENGE** Your sister is 14 years old. Your brother is 10 years less than twice your sister's age. Your cousin is half of your brother's age. Write and evaluate an expression to find your cousin's age.

MIXED REVIEW

Prepare for Lesson 1.3 in Exs. 43–46

Grapes cost \$2 per pound. How much does the given amount cost? *(p. 772)*

43. 2 pounds 44. 3 pounds 45. 0.5 pounds 46. 0.25 pounds

Find the product. Simplify if possible. *(p. 768)*

47. $8 \times \frac{5}{24}$ 48. $3 \times \frac{2}{7}$ 49. $4 \times \frac{5}{12}$ 50. $6 \times \frac{3}{8}$

51. ★ **MULTIPLE CHOICE** You buy groceries costing \$13.48. How much change should you receive if you pay with a \$20 bill? *(p. 767)*

(A) \$7.52 (B) \$7.48 (C) \$6.62 (D) \$6.52

GOAL
Use a calculator to evaluate numerical expressions with decimals.

1.2 Using Order of Operations

EXAMPLE **You and three friends are ordering a pizza. The cost of the pizza is $15.90, but you have a coupon for $1.50 off. How much should each of you pay if you want to divide the total cost equally?**

SOLUTION

$$\text{Cost per person} = \frac{\text{Price of a pizza} - \text{Coupon}}{\text{Number of friends} + \text{Yourself}}$$ **Write a verbal model.**

$$= \frac{15.90 - 1.50}{3 + 1}$$ **Substitute.**

To find the cost per person, use the order of operations. Use parentheses to separate expressions that should be grouped together.

Keystrokes	**Display**
(15.90 − 1.50) ÷ (3 + 1) =	3.6

▶ **Answer** Each person should pay $3.60 for the pizza.

PRACTICE **Use a calculator to evaluate the expression.**

1. $62 + 7 \times 6.4$
2. $8.32 - 9 \div 2$
3. $6.8 \div 4 + 15.9 \div 3$
4. $36.2 - 4.3 \cdot 5$
5. $\frac{14 + 11}{4 + 1}$
6. $\frac{20 - 3.5}{10.3 - 7}$
7. $\frac{10}{3.8 + 1.2}$
8. $\frac{17.7 - 13.7}{0.2 + 4.8}$
9. **SNACKS** You buy 3 bags of snack mix for $1.49 each, 2 boxes of raisins for $1.79 each, and lemonade for $2.39. Find the total cost using the expression $3 \cdot 1.49 + 2 \cdot 1.79 + 2.39$.
10. **CLOTHING** You buy 3 T-shirts at $9.99 each, a pair of sneakers for $44.89, a hat for $10.59, and a pair of socks at a cost of 4 pairs for $8.60. Find the total cost.
11. **MUSIC** You pick out 2 CDs for $12.99 each, 3 CDs for $9.49 each, and a CD for $15.97. At the register, you find out that, when you buy 5 CDs, you get the sixth CD for half off. Find the total cost if you get the least expensive CD for half off. Round to the nearest cent.

1.3 Variables and Expressions

Before You evaluated numerical expressions.

Now You'll write and evaluate variable expressions.

Why? So you can find total distances traveled, as in Example 1.

KEY VOCABULARY

- **variable,** *p. 13*
- **variable expression,** *p. 13*

A **variable** is a symbol, usually a letter, that represents one or more numbers. A **variable expression** consists of numbers, variables, and operations. To evaluate a variable expression, substitute a number for each variable. Then find the value of the numerical expression.

You can write the product of a number and a variable by writing the number next to that variable. For example, you can write $5 \cdot n$ as $5n$.

EXAMPLE 1 Using a Variable Expression

Hot Air Balloons You are riding in a hot air balloon. After traveling 5 miles, the balloon speed changes to 6 miles per hour. So, the total distance traveled is *original distance + speed • time,* which is $5 + 6t$, where t is the number of hours traveled at 6 mi/h.

READING
The speed 6 mi/h is read "six miles per hour."

What is the total distance you travel if the balloon moves at this speed for 1 hour? for 2 hours?

SOLUTION

STEP 1 **Write** hours traveled t.	STEP 2 **Substitute** for t in the expression $5 + 6t$.	STEP 3 **Evaluate** to find total distance.
1	$5 + 6(1)$	11
2	$5 + 6(2)$	17

▶ **Answer** If the balloon travels at 6 miles per hour for 1 hour, you travel a total of 11 miles. After 2 hours you travel a total of 17 miles.

✓ GUIDED PRACTICE for Example 1

What If? Use the information above about hot air balloons.

1. If you travel at 6 miles per hour for 3 hours, what is the total distance?
2. If you travel at 6 miles per hour for $\frac{1}{2}$ hour, what is the total distance?
3. If you travel at 3 miles per hour for 2 hours, what is the total distance?

EXAMPLE 2 Evaluating Variable Expressions

Evaluate the expression when $x = 8$ and $y = 2$.

a. $3x - 5y = 3(8) - 5(2)$ — **Substitute 8 for x and 2 for y.**

$= 24 - 10$ — **Multiply.**

$= 14$ — **Subtract.**

b. $5(x + y) = 5(8 + 2)$ — **Substitute 8 for x and 2 for y.**

$= 5(10)$ — **Add.**

$= 50$ — **Multiply.**

Animated Math at classzone.com

Writing Expressions Many words and phrases suggest mathematical operations. The following common words and phrases indicate addition, subtraction, multiplication, and division.

Addition	*Subtraction*	*Multiplication*	*Division*
plus	minus	times	divided by
the sum of	the difference of	the product of	the quotient of
increased by	decreased by	multiplied by	separate into equal parts
total	fewer than	of	
more than	less than	twice	
added to	subtracted from		

EXAMPLE 3 Translating Verbal Phrases

READING
Order is important when translating subtraction and division expressions. The *difference of a number and 6* means $n - 6$, not $6 - n$. The *quotient of a number and 10* means $n \div 10$, not $10 \div n$.

Verbal Phrase	**Variable Expression**
The sum of a number and 9	$n + 9$
The difference of a number and 21	$n - 21$
The product of 6 and a number	$6n$
The quotient of 48 and a number	$\frac{48}{n}$
One third of a number	$\frac{1}{3}n$

Animated Math at classzone.com

✓ GUIDED PRACTICE for Examples 2 and 3

Evaluate the expression when $a = 12$ and $b = 3$.

4. $9a$ **5.** ab **6.** $b(a - 6)$ **7.** $\frac{6a}{a - b}$

Write the phrase as a variable expression using x.

8. a number increased by 15 **9.** 8 times a number

EXAMPLE 4 Writing and Evaluating an Expression

 **Heart Rate** To measure your heart rate, count the number of heartbeats n in 15 seconds. Then multiply by 4 to find your heart rate in beats per minute.

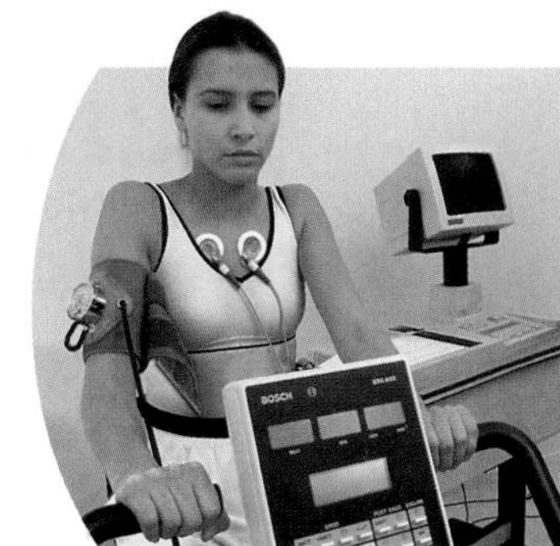

a. Use n to write an expression for heart rate in beats per minute.

b. After exercising, you count 24 beats in 15 seconds. Find your heart rate.

SOLUTION

a. The phrase *multiply by* suggests multiplication. So, multiply the number of heart beats n by 4.

▶ **Answer** A variable expression for heart rate in beats per minute is $4n$.

b. Substitute 24 for n in the expression $4n$ to find your heart rate.

$$4n = 4(24) = 96$$

▶ **Answer** Your heart rate is 96 beats per minute.

 **GUIDED PRACTICE** for Example 4

10. Savings You have \$25 saved. You save \$4 more per week for n weeks. Write and evaluate an expression for your total savings after 8 weeks.

1.3 EXERCISES

HOMEWORK KEY

★ = **STANDARDIZED TEST PRACTICE** Exs. 22, 44, 45, 47, 48, and 63

○ = **HINTS AND HOMEWORK HELP** for Exs. 7, 11, 15, 19, 43 at classzone.com

SKILL PRACTICE

VOCABULARY **Copy and complete the statement.**

1. $3t - 4$ is a(n) _?_ expression and $5 + 13$ is a(n) _?_ expression.
2. A(n) _?_ is a symbol, usually a letter, that represents one or more numbers.

EVALUATING EXPRESSIONS **Evaluate the expression for the given value(s) of the variable(s).**

SEE EXAMPLE 2 on p. 14 for Exs. 3–12

3. $4x - 5, x = 7$
4. $10n + 115, n = 9$
5. $3(c - d), c = 12, d = 7$
6. $4(f + g), f = 10, g = 6$
7. $7p + 6q, p = 3, q = 1.5$
8. $8a - 3b, a = 3, b = 8$
9. $3x + 4y, x = 6, y = 2.5$
10. $6r + 4q, q = 6, r = 5$
11. $\frac{d + 10}{c - d}, c = 14, d = 8$
12. $\frac{50 - s}{p + 3}, p = 6, s = 5$

SEE EXAMPLE 1 on p. 13 for Ex. 13

13. **ERROR ANALYSIS** Describe and correct the error made in evaluating $5 + 4 \cdot x$ when $x = 7$.

$$\begin{aligned} 5 + 4 \cdot x &= 5 + 4 \cdot 7 \\ &= 9 \cdot 7 \\ &= 63 \end{aligned}$$

TRANSLATING VERBAL PHRASES Write the phrase as a variable expression. Let *x* represent the variable.

SEE EXAMPLE 3 on p. 14 for Exs. 14–21

14. two fifths of a number
15. a number subtracted from 10
16. 12 increased by a number
17. the quotient of a number and 7
18. the sum of a number and 11
19. a number decreased by 15
20. 8 times a number
21. the product of a number and 22

22. ★ **MULTIPLE CHOICE** Which values make the expression $x \cdot [4 + (y \div 5)]$ have a value of 18?

(A) $x = 10, y = 20$ (B) $x = 3, y = 30$ (C) $x = 2, y = 50$ (D) $x = 3, y = 10$

REASONING Evaluate the expression when $x = 2.4$ and $y = 8$. Then tell whether swapping the values of *x* and *y* will *increase, decrease,* or *not change* the value of the expression. *Explain* your reasoning.

23. $7x + 2y$
24. $10(x + y)$
25. $5xy$
26. $x(y - 2)$
27. $4x - y$
28. $7.2y \div x$
29. $\frac{3y}{x}$
30. $x - \frac{y}{4}$

EVALUATING EXPRESSIONS Evaluate the expression when $x = 1.05$, $y = 7$, and $z = 0.65$. Round to the nearest hundredth.

31. $\frac{5(3x + 2z + 0.14)}{xy + z}$
32. $\frac{2x - 4y - 41.6 + 2z}{y - 5z}$
33. $\frac{5y + 3z + x}{x + 2yz}$

CHALLENGE Tell whether there is a whole number *x* that will make the statement true. If so, find the value of *x*.

34. $2x + 4 = 4$
35. $x \div 9 = 9 \div x$
36. $8 - 5x = 8 + 5x$
37. $4 + x = 3x$

PROBLEM SOLVING

SEE EXAMPLE 1 on p. 13 for Exs. 38–39

BICYCLES Evaluate the expression $9t$ to find how many miles you go if you ride your bike for *t* hours at 9 miles per hour.

38. How far do you go if you ride your bike for 2 hours?

39. How far do you go if you ride your bike for $3\frac{1}{2}$ hours?

SEE EXAMPLE 4 on p. 15 for Ex. 40

40. **GUIDED PROBLEM SOLVING** You buy a hat for \$8 and rent videos for \$3.80 each. How much do you spend altogether if you rent 5 videos?

a. Write a variable expression for the cost to rent *m* videos.

b. Add the cost of the hat to this expression.

c. Evaluate the expression for $m = 5$.

SEE EXAMPLE 4
on p. 15
for Exs. 41–44

41. TELEVISION You watch x thirty-minute TV shows and y sixty-minute TV shows in one week, but you don't watch z three-minute commercial breaks during the shows. Write a variable expression representing the total number of minutes you spend watching television that week.

42. NUTRITION Rice has 13 grams of protein per serving, beans have 15 grams per serving, and an orange has 2 grams per serving. Write a variable expression for the total grams of protein in x servings of rice, y servings of beans, and z oranges.

43. MOVIES At the movies, popcorn costs \$2.75 and drinks cost \$2.50. Write an expression to find the change you will receive from \$20 if you buy p popcorns and d drinks. Find your change from \$20 if you treat 3 people to popcorn and 4 people to drinks.

44. ★ SHORT RESPONSE A personal CD player costs \$35 and CDs cost \$15 each. Write an expression to represent the total cost of the CD player and n CDs. How much will you spend for a personal CD player and 4 CDs? Will you spend twice as much for 8 CDs? *Explain.*

45. ★ MULTIPLE CHOICE You are saving money to buy a bike that costs \$152.88. You want to buy the bike in n weeks by saving the same amount of money each day. How much money should you save each day?

Ⓐ $\frac{152.88(7)}{n}$ Ⓑ $\frac{152.88}{7n}$ Ⓒ $\frac{152.88n}{7}$ Ⓓ $\frac{152.88}{n}$

46. MEASUREMENT The vine shown below grows the same distance every week. Measure the vine's current length in centimeters. Write a variable expression for the length of the vine w weeks from now. Then estimate the vine's length in centimeters 19 weeks from now.

47. ★ OPEN-ENDED MATH *Describe* a real-world situation that can be modeled by the expression $98 - 8d$. Choose one reasonable value for d and evaluate the expression. Then choose one unreasonable value for d and *explain* why it is unreasonable.

48. ★ WRITING An Internet music club offers unlimited downloads for \$14.85 per month. Another club offers downloads for \$.99 per song. Write an expression for the difference in cost between a 2 month subscription and the purchase of n downloaded songs. *Explain* what it means when the expression has a value of zero.

READING *IN* MATH **Read the information below for Exercises 49–51.**

Ice Sculptures Ice sculptures can be beautiful additions to special parties and large celebrations. The sculptures can last a surprisingly long time indoors. After 4 to 6 hours, the sculpture will begin to lose its detail. To melt an entire 122 cm thick ice sculpture would take about 192 hours at room temperature. It melts at a constant rate of about 0.6 cm in one hour.

49. Estimate How much does the sculpture described above melt in 3 hours? In 6 hours?

50. Write and Evaluate Write and evaluate an expression for how long it would take a sculpture y centimeters thick to melt if it melts at the same rate. Then evaluate when $y = 64$ cm. Round to the nearest hour.

51. Reasoning What factors might affect the melting rate of the ice sculpture?

52. CHALLENGE Jim's car gets 18 miles per gallon in city traffic and 26 miles per gallon on the highway. He has 22 gallons of gasoline in his tank and is going on a trip.

a. Write an expression for the amount of gas Jim uses driving h highway miles and c city miles.

b. Can Jim make a 480 mile trip with 90 miles of city traffic without buying more gasoline? *Explain* your reasoning.

53. CHALLENGE The population of Amesville can be represented by $6800 - 120x$, and the population of Boomville can be represented by $4200 + 80x$, where x is the number of years after 2006. In how many years will the population of the two towns be equal? What will the population of each town be in the year 2030?

MIXED REVIEW

Prepare for Lesson 1.4 in Exs. 54–62

Evaluate the expression. *(p. 8)*

54. $12 \cdot 3 + 14$

55. $93 - 74 \div 2$

56. $16 + 6 \cdot 3 \div 2 - 7$

57. $6 \times (6 - 4) \div 3$

58. $38 - 56 \div 8$

59. $24 \cdot 5 + 18$

60. $12 + 9 \cdot 8 \div 4 - 2$

61. $5 \times (7 + 3) \div 10$

62. $45 + 20 \div 5$

63. ★ **MULTIPLE CHOICE** You buy 5 notebooks. Each notebook costs \$1.65. How much do you pay for all 5 notebooks? *(p. 772)*

Ⓐ \$.33 Ⓑ \$1.65 Ⓒ \$6.65 Ⓓ \$8.25

1.4 Powers and Exponents

Before	You evaluated numerical and variable expressions.
Now	You'll evaluate expressions with powers.
Why?	So you can calculate speed, as in Ex. 61.

KEY VOCABULARY
- **power,** *p. 19*
- **exponent,** *p. 19*
- **base,** *p. 19*

Waterfall A stone falls over the edge of a cliff next to a waterfall. The stone hits the water 5 seconds later. How tall is the cliff?

You will find the height of the cliff in Example 3 using an expression with a *power*. A **power** is a product made of repeated factors. The **exponent** tells how many times the **base** is used as a factor.

Base — Exponent

$$b^8 = \underbrace{b \cdot b \cdot b \cdot b \cdot b \cdot b \cdot b \cdot b}_{}$$

Power — *b* is a factor 8 times.

EXAMPLE 1 Reading Powers

AVOID ERRORS
Make sure that you write 4^2 and not $4 \cdot 2$.

Power	Repeated Multiplication	Description in Words
4^2	$4 \cdot 4$	4 to the *second power*, or 4 *squared*
9^3	$9 \cdot 9 \cdot 9$	9 to the *third power*, or 9 *cubed*
y^5	$y \cdot y \cdot y \cdot y \cdot y$	*y* to the *fifth power*

EXAMPLE 2 Evaluating a Power

Evaluate five cubed.

$5^3 = 5 \cdot 5 \cdot 5$ **Write 5 as a factor 3 times.**

$= 125$ **Multiply.**

at classzone.com

✓ GUIDED PRACTICE for Examples 1 and 2

Write the product as a power.

1. $7 \times 7 \times 7 \times 7 \times 7 \times 7$ **2.** $10 \cdot 10 \cdot 10 \cdot 10$ **3.** $w \cdot w$

Describe the power in words and then evaluate.

4. 6^3 **5.** 2^5 **6.** 13^2 **7.** 3^1

Order of Operations When you evaluate expressions with powers, evaluate any powers before multiplying or dividing.

KEY CONCEPT *For Your Notebook*

Order of Operations

1. Evaluate expressions inside grouping symbols.
2. Evaluate powers.
3. Multiply and divide from left to right.
4. Add and subtract from left to right.

EXAMPLE 3 Using a Power

Cliff Height To find the height of the cliff from the previous page, use the expression $16t^2$, the distance in feet that an object falls in t seconds after it begins to fall.

$16t^2 = 16(5)^2$	**Substitute 5 for *t*.**
$= 16(25)$	**Evaluate the power.**
$= 400$	**Multiply.**

▶ **Answer** The height of the cliff is 400 feet.

TAKE NOTES
In your notes, you may want to label each example that you copy with a title so that you can tell what it is about.

EXAMPLE 4 Using the Order of Operations

Evaluate the expression.

a. $(6 - 4)^3 + 3 - 2^2 = 2^3 + 3 - 2^2$	**Evaluate inside grouping symbols.**
$= 8 + 3 - 4$	**Evaluate powers.**
$= 7$	**Add and subtract from left to right.**
b. $3.3 \cdot (7 + 1)^2 \div 4^2 = 3.3 \cdot 8^2 \div 42$	**Evaluate inside grouping symbols.**
$= 3.3 \cdot 64 \div 16$	**Evaluate powers.**
$= 13.2$	**Multiply and divide from left to right.**

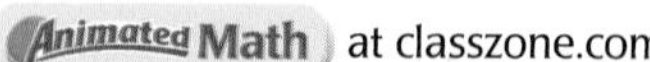

at classzone.com

✓ GUIDED PRACTICE for Examples 3 and 4

Evaluate the expression.

8. $(5 - 2)^3 - 7 + 4^3$ **9.** $12.3 + (4 + 2)^2 - 2^4$ **10.** $7^3 + 24 \div (7 - 6)^4$

11. What If? Suppose the falling stone in Example 3 took 8 seconds to hit the water. Evaluate the expression to find the height of the cliff.

1.4 EXERCISES

HOMEWORK KEY

★ = **STANDARDIZED TEST PRACTICE**
Exs. 37, 54, 56, 58, 59, 63, and 73

○ = **HINTS AND HOMEWORK HELP**
for Exs. 3, 9, 21, 25, 53 at classzone.com

SKILL PRACTICE

1. **VOCABULARY** Write a power and label the base and the exponent.

2. **VOCABULARY** Using the order of operations, what should you do first before evaluating powers?

SEE EXAMPLE 1 on p. 19 for Exs. 3–5

READING POWERS Write the product as a power and describe it in words.

3. $9 \cdot 9 \cdot 9 \cdot 9 \cdot 9$
4. $3 \cdot 3 \cdot 3$
5. $n \cdot n \cdot n \cdot n \cdot n \cdot n$

EVALUATING A POWER Evaluate the power.

SEE EXAMPLE 2 on p. 19 for Exs. 6–18

6. three squared
7. eleven cubed
8. one to the ninth
9. 2^6
10. 5^5
11. 0^7
12. 6^1
13. 11^2
14. 2^7
15. 10^3
16. 1^8
17. 20^2

18. **ERROR ANALYSIS** Describe and correct the error made in evaluating 7^2.

$$7^2 = 7 \times 2 = 14 \quad \times$$

ALGEBRA Evaluate the expression when $g = 4$.

SEE EXAMPLE 3 on p. 20 for Exs. 19–24

19. $g^4 \div 16$
20. $(3 + g)^3$
21. $(3g)^2 - 25$
22. $(g - 1)^5 \div 9$
23. $2 \times (g + 2)^3$
24. $(2g + 3)^2 + 12$

USING THE ORDER OF OPERATIONS Evaluate the expression.

SEE EXAMPLE 4 on p. 20 for Exs. 25–36

25. $(2 + 1)^4 \div 9 - 4$
26. $48 \div (9 - 7)^3$
27. $(5 \times 3)^2 - 4$
28. $(2 \times 5)^2 + 9$
29. $500 \div (12 - 7)^1$
30. $6 \times 18 \div 3^2$
31. $(9 - 7)^5 + 17$
32. $108 \div (5 + 1)^2$
33. $9^2 - 3^3$
34. $(8 - 5)^3 - 6.2 \times 3$
35. $\frac{3}{4} \times 4 + 6^2 \div 9$
36. $10.7 - 0.8 + 4^4 \div 2^3$

Animated Math at classzone.com

37. ★ **MULTIPLE CHOICE** Which operation should be done last when evaluating $5^3 - 2^4 \div 4$?

   (A) Find 5^3 (B) Find 2^4 (C) Subtract (D) Divide

COMPARING VALUES Copy and complete the statement using <, >, or =.

38. $3^2 \underline{?} 2^3$
39. $5^4 \underline{?} 4^5$
40. $10^1 \underline{?} 1^{10}$
41. $\left(\frac{1}{4}\right)^4 \underline{?} \left(\frac{1}{3}\right)^4$
42. $\left(\frac{5}{2}\right)^1 \underline{?} \left(\frac{2}{5}\right)^5$
43. $\left(\frac{1}{4}\right)^3 \underline{?} \left(\frac{1}{2}\right)^6$

ALGEBRA **Evaluate the expression when $a = 2$, $b = 4$, and $c = 5$.**

44. $a^3 b^2 + 4.2$

45. $5.9 \times (c - a)^3$

46. $2 \cdot (b + 2)^2 \div (3a)$

47. **LOOK FOR A PATTERN** Evaluating $2^1, 2^2, 2^3, 2^4, 2^5, 2^6, 2^7$, and 2^8 gives the sequence 2, 4, 8, 16, 32, 64, 128, and 256. Find the pattern with the ones' digits. Predict the ones' digit in 2^{14}.

48. **LOOK FOR A PATTERN** Evaluate $3^1, 3^2, 3^3, 3^4, 3^5, 3^6, 3^7$, and 3^8. Predict the ones' digit in 3^{15}. *Justify* your reasoning.

49. **LOOK FOR A PATTERN** Evaluate $4^1, 4^2, 4^3, 4^4, 4^5$, and 4^6. Predict the ones' digit in 4^{24}, and in 4^{87}. *Justify* your reasoning.

CHALLENGE **Find the value of x.**

50. $3^x = 9^4$

51. $6^{10} = 36^x$

52. $4^x = 64^3$

PROBLEM SOLVING

SEE EXAMPLE 3 on p. 20 for Exs. 53–55

53. **GEOMETRY** The *area* of a square is s^2, where s is the length of one side of the square. Find the area of a square that has a side length of 17 inches.

54. ★ **MULTIPLE CHOICE** The *volume* of a cube is s^3, where s is the length of one side of the cube. A cube has a side length of 14 centimeters. What is the volume of the cube in cubic centimeters?

(A) 42 (B) 196 (C) 1400 (D) 2744

55. **MULTI-STEP PROBLEM** At Kaunolo in Hawaii, divers jump from a platform on top of a cliff 82 feet above the water. At time t seconds, a diver has fallen $16t^2$ feet.

  a. Does a diver reach the surface of the water in 2 seconds? *Explain* your reasoning.

  b. How much lower would a diver be after 3 seconds than after 2 seconds? *Explain.*

56. ★ **SHORT RESPONSE** *Describe* how to find the value of 3^9 using the fact that $3^8 = 6561$. *Explain* your reasoning.

57. **LOOK FOR A PATTERN** Write an expression for the nth number of the sequence of numbers 1, 4, 9, 16, ...

58. ★ **MULTIPLE CHOICE** Joe puts $1275 into a retirement account that earns interest so that the account has two times the value every 15 years. What expression represents the amount of money in the account after 45 years?

(A) 1275×2^2 (B) 1275×2^3 (C) 1275×2^{15} (D) 1275×2^{45}

59. ★ **WRITING** *Explain* why $4x^2 < (4x)^2$ for $x \neq 0$.

60. **FOOTBALL** The season attendance at your school's football games is 1000 people one year. For each of the next 3 years, the attendance is double the previous year's attendance. Write an expression with a power that shows the season attendance at the football games after 3 years.

61. **INLINE SKATING** An inline skater is at the top of a hill. The hill is 30 feet long and is angled such that the speed of a skater going down the hill doubles every 6 feet. A skater is going 3 miles per hour after the first 6 feet. What is the speed of the skater when the skater reaches the bottom of the hill?

62. **MULTIPLE REPRESENTATIONS** At an archeological dig, the lead scientist decides that the dig should be organized by repeatedly dividing the square area into four smaller squares as shown.

Stage 1

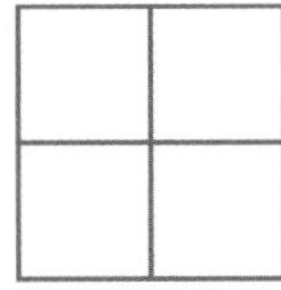
Stage 2

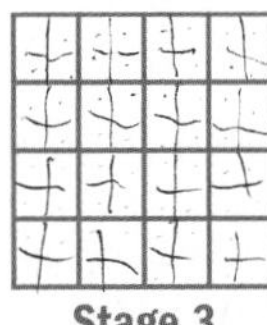
Stage 3

a. **Make a Table** Make a table that shows the number of squares at each stage from the 1st stage through the 6th stage.

b. **Write an Expression** Write an expression as a power for the number of squares in the dig at the 7th stage.

c. **Write a Description** How many squares are along each side of the dig at the 7th stage? If the whole dig is 64 feet on a side, what is the side length of each individual square at the 7th stage?

63. ★ **EXTENDED RESPONSE** On an ostrich farm a single breeding pair hatches 30 eggs per season. These hatchlings will form breeding pairs the following season. Each new breeding pair will hatch about 30 eggs per season. How many breeding pairs would be on the farm after 1 breeding season, assuming all survive? after 2 seasons? after n seasons? *Explain* your answer.

64. **EVALUATING POWERS** Some powers of 11 read the same forward and backward. For example $11^1 = 11$, $11^2 = 121$. What is the smallest n such that 11^n does *not* read the same forward and backward?

65. **REASONING** Evaluate 7^4, 7^3, 7^2, and 7^1. Based on this pattern, what is the value of 7^0? *Predict* the value of x^0, where x is a whole number greater than 0. *Explain* your reasoning.

66. **CHALLENGE** The personal computers of the early 1980s had 64 kilobytes of memory. Today they have more than one gigabyte of memory. Use the table. Write, as a power, the number of bytes of memory that personal computers of the early 1980s had.

Name	*Bytes*
Kilobyte	2^{10}
Megabyte	2^{20}
Gigabyte	2^{30}

MIXED REVIEW

CHOOSE A STRATEGY Use a strategy from the list to solve the following problem. *Explain* your choice of strategy.

67. You have 3 shirts and 2 pairs of pants that you are packing for a trip. You can wear each shirt with each pair of pants. How many different outfits are possible?

Problem Solving Strategies
- Draw a Diagram (p. 787)
- Make a List (p. 790)
- Look for a Pattern (p. 791)

Get-Ready

Prepare for Lesson 1.5 in Exs. 68–71

Evaluate the expression when $x = 3$ and $y = 9$. *(p. 13)*

68. $5x - 12$ **69.** $6x - y$ **70.** $\frac{y}{x} + 20$ **71.** $\frac{45}{x} - 2$

72. PARTY ATTENDANCE The histogram shows the times the people arrived at a party. How many people attended. *(p. 3)*

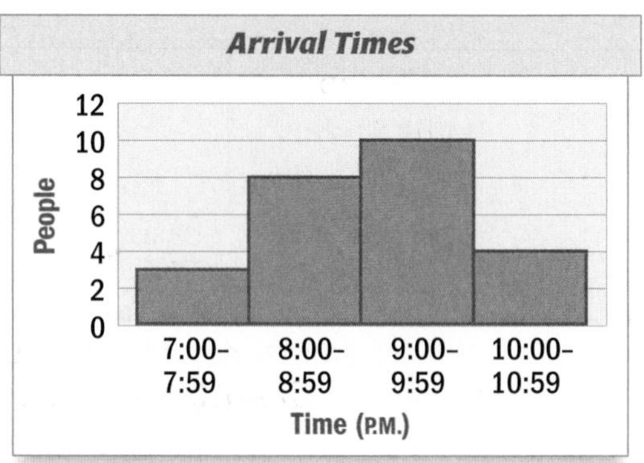

73. ★ MULTIPLE CHOICE Use the histogram. How many people arrived between 9:00 P.M. and 10:59 P.M.? *(p. 3)*

Ⓐ 4 Ⓑ 14

Ⓒ 21 Ⓓ 25

QUIZ for Lessons 1.1–1.4

HOME RUNS In Exercises 1–2, use the table at the right. It shows the record number of home runs hit in a single season by position as of 2005. *(p. 3)*

Position	Home Runs
Catcher	42
1st base	69
Pitcher	9
2nd base	42
Shortstop	57
3rd base	48
Outfield	71

1. Make a bar graph that displays the data.

2. How many more home runs is the record for outfield than for pitcher?

Evaluate the expression. *(p. 8)*

3. $21 - 2 \cdot 7$ **4.** $8 \times 10 - 40 + 25$ **5.** $24 - (9 + 7) \div 4$

6. $(3 + 1)^2 - 1^5$ **7.** $10^4 \div 5^3$ **8.** $3^4 + 7 \cdot 5$

9. PLANTS A plant is 14 inches tall and grows 4 inches each year. Another plant is 8 inches tall and grows 6 inches each year. Write a variable expression for each plant's height in x years. Then evaluate the expressions to find the heights in 5 years. *Compare* the results. *(p. 13)*

Evaluate the expression for the given value of the variable. *(p. 19)*

10. $5a - 3 + 7$ when $a = 4$ **11.** $8 + b + 4 \cdot 11$ when $b = 3$

12. $2 \cdot z^4 \div 8$ when $z = 4$ **13.** $(9 - x)^5 \cdot 3 - 16$ when $x = 7$

MIXED REVIEW *of Problem Solving*

Lessons 1.1–1.4

1. **MULTI-STEP PROBLEM** Muntz metal is an alloy of copper and zinc. A sample of Muntz metal has a volume of 15 cubic centimeters. The volume of the copper in the sample is x cubic centimeters. The mass of this copper is 80.1 grams.

   a. Write an expression in terms of x for the volume of zinc in the sample.

   b. Use the fact that 1 cubic centimeter of zinc has a mass of 7.1 grams to write an expression in terms of x for the total mass of the sample.

   c. What is the sample's total mass if the volume of its copper is 9 cubic centimeters? Show your calculations.

2. **EXTENDED RESPONSE** The frequency table shows the heights of 30 students.

Height (inches)	*Frequency*
54–55.9	1
56–57.9	2
58–59.9	4
60–61.9	5
62–63.9	7
64–65.9	6
66–67.9	3
68–69.9	2

   a. Make a histogram of the data shown in the frequency table.

   b. Which height interval has the most students?

   c. Can you use the histogram to determine the number of students who are between 60 and 65 inches tall? *Explain.*

3. **GRIDDED ANSWER** The expression $16t^2$ is used to find the distance in feet that an object has fallen t seconds after being dropped. When dropping a rock off of a 512 foot cliff, how many more feet does it fall in 4 seconds than in 3 seconds?

4. **EXTENDED RESPONSE** You are participating in a 20 mile fundraising walk. People can contribute a certain amount per mile that you walk or just make a fixed contribution. The fixed individual contributions that you collected total $150. The per mile contributions total $15 per mile.

   a. Write an expression for the amount of money you raise if you walk the entire 20 miles.

   b. How much will you raise if you complete the walk?

   c. How far will you have to walk to raise $300?

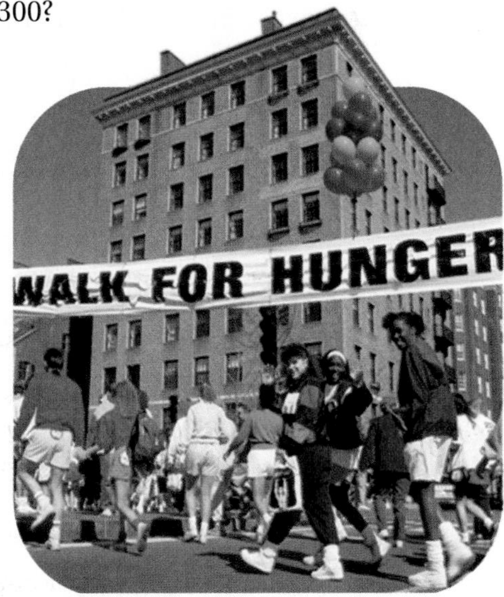

5. **SHORT RESPONSE** Your car's fuel gauge is broken. The car can go 22 miles on one gallon of gasoline. You start a trip with 13 gallons of gasoline, and you want to always have at least two gallons in the tank. What is the farthest you should drive before stopping for more gasoline? *Explain.*

6. **OPEN-ENDED** Consider the expression $3 + 18 \div 3 + 3 \times 5 + 3$. Find at least six values for the expressions that result from inserting one pair of parentheses. For one of these expressions, write a real-world problem that can be modeled by the expression. Show your calculations.

1.5 Equations and Solutions

Before You wrote and evaluated variable expressions.
Now You'll write and solve equations using mental math.
Why? So you can find unknown measures, as in Ex. 47.

KEY VOCABULARY
- **equation,** *p. 26*
- **solution,** *p. 26*
- **solving an equation,** *p. 26*

ACTIVITY

You can use algebra tiles to solve equations.

In an *equation*, the quantities on each side of the equal sign have the same value. The algebra tile model below represents the equation $x + 2 = 6$.

=

STEP 1 With how many 1-tiles should you replace the x-tile so that the quantities on both sides of the equal sign have the same value? *Explain.*

STEP 2 What value of x makes the equation $x + 2 = 6$ a true statement?

Make a model to represent the equation. Then tell what value of x makes the equation a true statement.

1. $x + 3 = 8$ **2.** $x + 4 = 5$ **3.** $6 + x = 10$

An **equation** is a mathematical sentence formed by placing an equal sign (=) between two expressions.

A **solution** of a variable equation is a number that you can substitute for a variable to make the equation true. Finding all the solutions of an equation is called **solving an equation**.

EXAMPLE 1 Using Mental Math to Solve Equations

Solve the equation using mental math.

a. $15 - n = 4$ **b.** $8x = 32$ **c.** $r \div 12 = 4$

SOLUTION

To solve an equation using mental math, think of the equation as a question.

a. 15 minus **what number** equals 4? $15 - \mathbf{11} = 4$, so $n = 11$.

b. 8 times **what number** equals 32? $8(\mathbf{4}) = 32$, so $x = 4$.

c. **What number** divided by 12 equals 4? $\mathbf{48} \div 12 = 4$, so $r = 48$.

EXAMPLE 2 Checking Solutions

Tell whether the value of the variable is a solution of $n - 8 = 20$.

a. $n = 12$

b. $n = 28$

SOLUTION

Substitute for n and then simplify.

a. $n - 8 = 20$

$12 - 8 \stackrel{?}{=} 20$

$4 \neq 20$

▶ **Answer** 12 is not a solution.

b. $n - 8 = 20$

$28 - 8 \stackrel{?}{=} 20$

$20 = 20$

▶ **Answer** 28 is a solution.

READING

The $\stackrel{?}{=}$ symbol means *are these values equal?* The $\neq$ symbol means *is not equal to.*

EXAMPLE 3 Writing an Equation

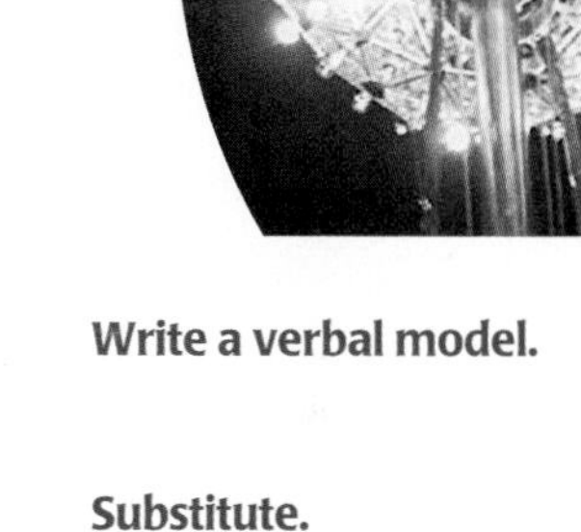

Times Square The Times Square New Year's Eve Ball drops a total of 77 feet in 60 seconds. After 54 seconds it has dropped 69 feet. How many more feet will it drop?

SOLUTION

You can use a verbal model to write an equation. Let d represent the distance left to drop.

Total distance ball drops	=	Distance ball has dropped	+	Distance left to drop	**Write a verbal model.**
77	=	69	+	d	**Substitute.**
77	=	69	+	**8**	**Use mental math.**

▶ **Answer** Because $d = 8$, the ball will drop 8 more feet.

Check You can check your answer by finding the sum of 8 and 69.

$8 + 69 \stackrel{?}{=} 77$

$77 = 77$ ✓

✓ GUIDED PRACTICE for Examples 1, 2, and 3

Solve the equation using mental math.

1. $5x = 45$
2. $16 + n = 21$
3. $t \div 6 = 9$

Tell whether the value of the variable is a solution of the equation.

4. $a + 9 = 16$; $a = 7$
5. $88 \div y = 8$; $y = 8$
6. $7n = 13$, $n = 2$
7. **Laundry** Julie has $9 to wash her clothes at the laundromat. Each load costs $1.75 to wash and $1.25 to dry. How many loads can she do?

EXAMPLE 4 Standardized Test Practice

Heights Cesar, Luis, and Marco are brothers. The difference of Cesar's and Marco's heights is 5 inches. Luis is 3 inches taller than Cesar. Marco is 50 inches tall. How tall is Luis?

Ⓐ 47 inches Ⓑ 52 inches Ⓒ 55 inches Ⓓ 58 inches

ELIMINATE CHOICES
Luis is taller than Cesar and Cesar is taller than Marco, who is 50 inches tall. So, you can eliminate choice A.

SOLUTION

STEP 1 **Write** and solve an equation to find Cesar's height.

Cesar's height	−	Marco's height	= 5	**Write a verbal model.**
c	−	50	= 5	**Substitute 50 for Marco's height.**
55	−	50	= 5	**Use mental math.**

Cesar is 55 inches tall.

STEP 2 **Use** Cesar's height to find Luis's height. Add: $55 + 3 = 58$.

▶ **Answer** Luis is 58 inches tall. The correct answer is D. Ⓐ Ⓑ Ⓒ Ⓓ

✓ GUIDED PRACTICE for Example 4

8. **What If?** In Example 4, suppose Luis is 3 inches taller than Marco, Cesar is 50 inches tall, and the difference of Cesar's and Marco's height is 5 inches. How tall is Luis?

1.5 EXERCISES

HOMEWORK KEY
★ = **STANDARDIZED TEST PRACTICE** Exs. 25, 48, 49, 50, 51, and 65
○ = **HINTS AND HOMEWORK HELP** for Exs. 3, 11, 19, 21, 45 at classzone.com

SKILL PRACTICE

VOCABULARY **Copy and complete the statement.**

1. The process of finding all possible values that make a mathematical sentence true is _?_.
2. A(n) _?_ is a mathematical sentence formed by placing an equal sign between two expressions.

SEE EXAMPLE 1 on p. 26 for Exs. 3–18

SOLVING EQUATIONS **Solve the equation using mental math.**

3. $9 + p = 31$	4. $y - 10 = 34$	5. $7x = 77$	6. $56 \div k = 8$
7. $z + 8 = 19$	8. $6m = 48$	9. $c - 16 = 13$	10. $51 \div k = 3$
11. $\frac{32}{n} = 16$	12. $26 - r = 17$	13. $10y = 150$	14. $7 + x = 31$
15. $z - 5 = 12$	16. $6x = 42$	17. $22 \div c = 11$	18. $3 + a = 19$

Animated Math at classzone.com

CHECKING SOLUTIONS **Tell whether the given value is a solution.**

SEE EXAMPLE 2 on p. 27 for Exs. 19–26

19. $35 - x = 21; x = 16$
20. $75 \div x = 5; x = 15$
21. $7x = 84; x = 14$
22. $x + 29 = 42; x = 13$
23. $15 + b = 28; b = 13$
24. $37 - d = 14; d = 21$

25. ★ **MULTIPLE CHOICE** Which of the following is a solution of $63 \div x = 9$?

(A) 6 (B) 7 (C) 9 (D) 54

26. **ERROR ANALYSIS** A student says that a solution of $5 \div x = 10$ is 2. *Explain* why the student's solution is incorrect.

TRANSLATING EQUATIONS **Write the equation as a question in words. Then solve the equation.**

27. $24 \div t = 8$
28. $t + 8 = 24$
29. $24t = 8$
30. $\frac{t}{24} = 8$

IDENTIFYING SOLUTIONS **Tell which of the given values is a solution of the equation.**

31. $3x + 6 = x + 12; x = 1, 2, 3$
32. $2x - 7 = x + 1; x = 8, 9, 10$
33. $8 - 4x = 4x; x = 0, 1, 2$
34. $2x - 4.5 = x \div 2; x = 3, 4, 5$
35. $5x + 1 = x + 17; x = 3, 4, 5$
36. $12 - 3x = 3x; x = 0, 1, 2$

CHALLENGE **Find the value of *x* that makes the equation true.**

37. $[(x + 3) \cdot 4 - 7] \div 3 = 3$
38. $[(x + 3) \cdot 3 - 6] \div 5 = 3$
39. $[(x - 2) \cdot 6 - 2] \div 5 = 2$
40. $[(x - 2) \cdot 5 + 8] \div 4 = 2$

CHALLENGE **Solve the equation.**

41. $\frac{x - 8}{6} = 12$
42. $\frac{71 - x}{7} = 8$
43. $\frac{x + 6}{9} = 5$
44. $\frac{64 - x}{4} = 10$

PROBLEM SOLVING

SEE EXAMPLE 3 on p. 27 for Exs. 45–47

45. **RAINFALL** The greatest recorded rainfall in the United States in a 24 hour period is 43 inches. At your location, 14 inches has already fallen in 7 hours. Write an equation to find how much more rain needs to fall in the next 17 hours to equal the record. Then solve the equation.

46. **MEASUREMENT** Write and solve an equation to find the number of feet f in 3600 inches.

47. **ELEPHANTS** A baby elephant at the Bronx Zoo would get on a scale only with its mother. The zoo weighed the mother as 5033 pounds. They weighed the mother and the baby together as 5396 pounds. Write and solve an equation to find the weight of the baby elephant.

SEE EXAMPLE 3 on p. 27 for Exs. 48–49

48. ★ **WRITING** *Explain* how you can tell if 5 is a solution of $4x = 20$.

49. ★ **MULTIPLE CHOICE** You are writing invitations to a party. It takes you four minutes to complete each invitation. What is the equation for finding x, the number of invitations you can complete in one hour?

(A) $\frac{4}{x} = 60$ (B) $\frac{x}{4} = 60$ (C) $4x = 60$ (D) $x - 4 = 60$

SEE EXAMPLE 4 on p. 28 for Ex. 50

50. ★ **SHORT RESPONSE** Your town's fireworks show lasted 20 minutes. The total cost was \$25,000. Use a verbal model to write and solve an equation to find the cost per minute. What is the cost of a show at the same rate per minute that lasts twice as long? *Explain* your answer.

51. ★ **OPEN-ENDED MATH** *Describe* a situation that can be modeled by $\frac{x}{9} = 13$. Then solve the equation.

52. **MARATHON** To qualify for the Boston Marathon, Maria needs to run a qualifying time of 3 hours 40 minutes or less. Her best time so far is 4 hours 5 minutes. Write and solve an equation to find the fewest minutes by which Maria must improve her time to qualify.

53. **VOLUNTEERING** You want to volunteer 200 total hours at a zoo. After 5 weeks, you have worked 80 hours. Write and solve an equation to find how many hours you will work per week over the remaining 8 weeks.

54. **CONSECUTIVE NUMBERS** Consecutive numbers are numbers that follow one after another, such as 1, 2, and 3. The sum of two consecutive numbers divided by 3 is 71. What are the two numbers?

55. **CHALLENGE** Joe had a box of gumballs. He gave half of them to Antowain, one sixth to Shaniqua, and one fourth to Naresh. He has 4 left. How many gumballs did Joe have before he gave some away?

56. **CHALLENGE** Jen has $\frac{4}{5}$ as much money as Bob. Tim has \$50 more than Jen. Rita has \$150, which is \$35 more than Bob. How much money does Tim have?

MIXED REVIEW

Prepare for Lesson 1.6 in Exs. 57–60

Evaluate the expression when $y = 8$. *(p. 13)*

57. $7y + 17$ 58. $(36 - 24) \cdot y$ 59. $y \cdot 4 + 20 \cdot y$ 60. $19 - 2y$

Estimate the sum or difference. *(p. 766)*

61. $8748 - 3109$ 62. $876 + 622$ 63. $144 + 89 + 791$ 64. $178 - 43 - 78$

65. ★ **MULTIPLE CHOICE** What is the value of $(20 + 4^3) \div 6$? *(p. 19)*

(A) 6 (B) 14 (C) $30\frac{2}{3}$ (D) 2304

INVESTIGATION

Use before Lesson 1.6

GOAL
Develop formulas for finding the areas of rectangles and squares.

MATERIALS
- square tiles

1.6 Modeling Area

You can use square tiles to find the *areas* of rectangles and squares.

EXPLORE **Find the area of a 5-unit by 3-unit rectangle.**

STEP 1 Use square tiles to make a rectangle with side lengths of 5 units and 3 units.

1 unit
1 unit
One square unit

STEP 2 The *area* of the rectangle is equal to the number of square unit tiles that cover it. Count the square tiles to find the area of the rectangle.

width = 3 units
length = 5 units

PRACTICE

1. Use square tiles to make rectangles that have the dimensions given in the table. Copy and complete the table.

Dimensions	*Length*	*Width*	*Number of square tiles*	*Area of rectangle*
3 by 4	?	?	?	?
4 by 4	?	?	?	?
5 by 6	?	?	?	?
3 by 3	?	?	?	?

DRAW CONCLUSIONS

2. **WRITING A FORMULA** Write a variable equation to find the area of a rectangle and explain what each variable represents.

3. **WRITING A FORMULA** Write a different equation to find the area of a square and explain what each variable represents.

4. **REASONING** Area is measured in square units. Perimeter is the distance around a figure. Is perimeter measured in square units? Why or why not?

1.6 Variables in Familiar Formulas

Before You evaluated variable expressions.
Now You'll use formulas to find unknown values.
Why? So you can calculate distances, as in Ex. 31.

KEY VOCABULARY
- **formula,** *p. 32*
- **perimeter,** *p. 32*
- **area,** *p. 32*

A **formula** is an equation that relates two or more quantities such as *perimeter*, length, and width. The **perimeter** of a figure is the sum of the lengths of its sides. The amount of surface the figure covers is called its **area**.

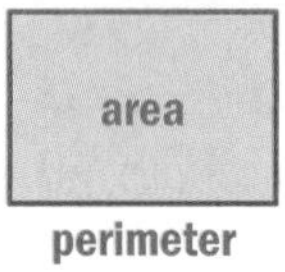

Perimeter is measured in linear units such as feet. Area is measured in square units such as square feet, written as ft^2. You may have found the formula for area in the Investigation on p. 31.

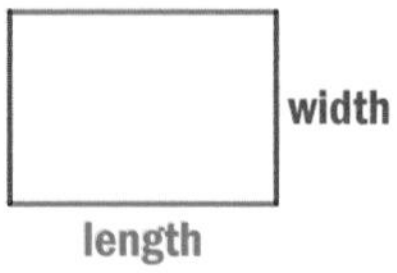

KEY CONCEPT — *For Your Notebook*

Perimeter and Area Formulas

	Diagram	Perimeter	Area
Rectangle	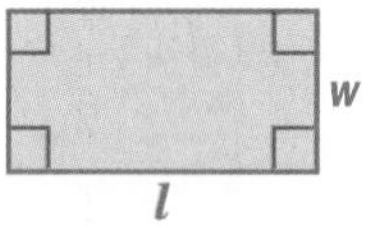	$P = l + w + l + w$ or $P = 2l + 2w$	$A = lw$
Square	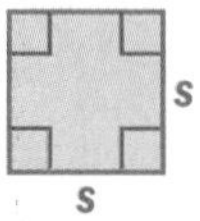	$P = 4s$	$A = s^2$

EXAMPLE 1 Finding Perimeter and Area

Find the perimeter and area of the rectangle.

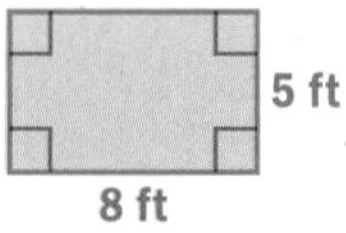

READING
The mark ⌉ tells you that an angle is a right angle, which measures 90°.

SOLUTION

Find the perimeter.

$P = 2l + 2w$	**Write formula.**
$= 2(8) + 2(5)$	**Substitute.**
$= 26$	**Multiply, then add.**

Find the area.

$A = lw$	**Write formula.**
$= (8)(5)$	**Substitute.**
$= 40$	**Multiply.**

▶ **Answer** The perimeter is 26 feet, and the area is 40 square feet.

EXAMPLE 2 Finding Side Length

 **Find the side length of a square with an area of 81 square feet.**

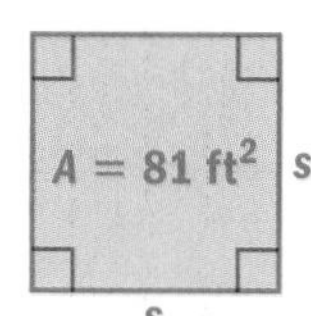

$A = s^2$	Write formula for area of a square.
$81 = s^2$	Substitute 81 for *A*.
$9 = s$	Use mental math: $9^2 = 81$.

▸ **Answer** The side length of the square is 9 feet.

Distance Formula Another useful formula is the distance formula. You can use the distance formula to find distance traveled.

KEY CONCEPT *For Your Notebook*

Distance Formula

Words The distance traveled *d* is the product of the rate *r* and the time *t*.

Algebra $d = r \cdot t$, or $d = rt$

Numbers $d = 45 \frac{\text{miles}}{\cancel{\text{hour}}} \cdot 3 \cancel{\text{hours}} = 135$ miles

EXAMPLE 3 Using the Distance Formula

Rabbits A rabbit is running at a rate of 26.4 feet per second. How far does the rabbit travel in 5 seconds?

SOLUTION

VOCABULARY
In the formula $d = rt$, the rate *r* is the speed of travel.

$d = r \cdot t$	Write distance formula.
$= 26.4 \cdot 5$	Substitute 26.4 for *r* and 5 for *t*.
$= 132$	Multiply.

▸ **Answer** The rabbit travels 132 feet in 5 seconds.

✓ **GUIDED PRACTICE** for Examples 1, 2, and 3

Find the perimeter and area of the figure.

1. rectangle: $l = 25$ in., $w = 14$ in.

2. square: $s = 7$ in.

Find the side length of the figure.

3. rectangle: $A = 91$ cm^2, $l = 13$ cm, $w =$ __?__

4. square: $A = 100$ yd^2, $s =$ __?__

5. Distance How far does a car travel in 2 hours at a rate of 40 mi/h?

Rewriting the Distance Formula You can write the distance formula in different forms to find rate or time. Use $t = \frac{d}{r}$ to find the time and $r = \frac{d}{t}$ to find the rate.

EXAMPLE 4 Standardized Test Practice

Running Times How long will it take a rabbit to travel 264 feet at a rate of 22 feet per second?

Ⓐ 0.083 sec Ⓑ 12 sec

Ⓒ 286 sec Ⓓ 5808 sec

ELIMINATE CHOICES
Since 264 feet is more than 22 feet, 0.083 seconds is unreasonable. So, you can eliminate choice A.

SOLUTION

$t = \frac{d}{r}$ **Write distance formula.**

$= \frac{264}{22}$ **Substitute 264 for *d* and 22 for *r*.**

$= 12$ **Divide.**

▶ **Answer** It will take a rabbit 12 seconds to travel 264 feet. The correct answer is B. Ⓐ Ⓑ Ⓒ Ⓓ

GUIDED PRACTICE for Example 4

6. **Running Speeds** How fast is a rabbit running if it travels 192 feet in 8 seconds?

1.6 EXERCISES

HOMEWORK KEY

★ = **STANDARDIZED TEST PRACTICE** Exs. 20, 23, 28, 32, 33, 34, and 42

○ = **HINTS AND HOMEWORK HELP** for Exs. 3, 9, 13, 15, 27 at classzone.com

SKILL PRACTICE

1. **VOCABULARY** Describe the difference between area and perimeter.
2. **VOCABULARY** Write the three forms of the distance formula.

FINDING PERIMETER AND AREA **Find the perimeter and area of the figure.**

SEE EXAMPLE 1 on p. 32 for Exs. 3–7

3. 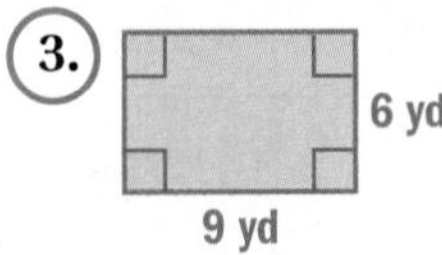

4. 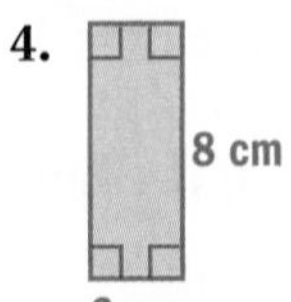

5. 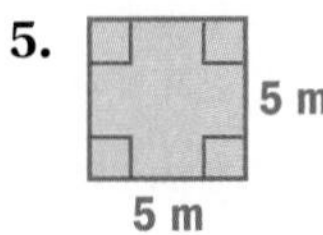

6. 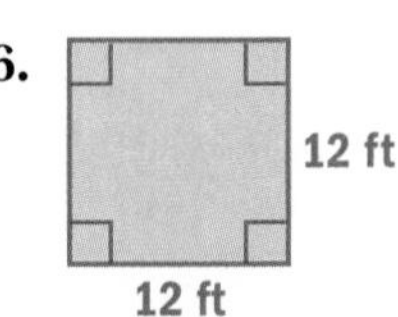

7. **ERROR ANALYSIS** Describe and correct the error made in finding the area.

$A = s^2$
$= 4^2$
$= 16$ meters

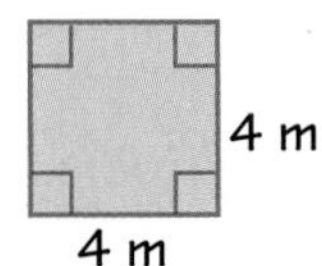

ALGEBRA **Find the unknown value.**

SEE EXAMPLES 1 AND 2 on pp. 32–33 for Exs. 8–13

8. square: $A = 36\text{ yd}^2$, $s = \underline{\ ?\ }$
9. square: $P = 24$ m, $s = \underline{\ ?\ }$
10. square: $A = 144\text{ ft}^2$, $s = \underline{\ ?\ }$
11. square: $A = \underline{\ ?\ }$, $s = 18$ in.
12. rectangle: $A = \underline{\ ?\ }$, $l = 17$ m, $w = 9$ m
13. rectangle: $A = 88\text{ in.}^2$, $l = \underline{\ ?\ }$, $w = 8$ in.

USING FORMULAS **Use the distance formula to find the unknown value.**

SEE EXAMPLES 3 AND 4 on pp. 33–34 for Exs. 14–19

14. $d = 36$ km, $r = \underline{\ ?\ }$, $t = 4$ h
15. $d = \underline{\ ?\ }$, $r = 0.5$ mi/min, $t = 10$ min
16. $d = \underline{\ ?\ }$, $r = 7$ mi/h, $t = 1.5$ h
17. $d = 40$ ft, $r = 5$ ft/sec, $t = \underline{\ ?\ }$
18. $d = 130$ mi, $r = 65$ mi/h, $t = \underline{\ ?\ }$
19. $d = 75$ ft, $r = \underline{\ ?\ }$, $t = 5$ sec

20. ★ **MULTIPLE CHOICE** Which pair of dimensions for a rectangle does *not* yield a perimeter of 16 feet?

Ⓐ 1 ft by 7 ft Ⓑ 2 ft by 8 ft Ⓒ 3 ft by 5 ft Ⓓ 4 ft by 4 ft

COMPOSITE FIGURES **Find the perimeter and area of the figure.**

21.

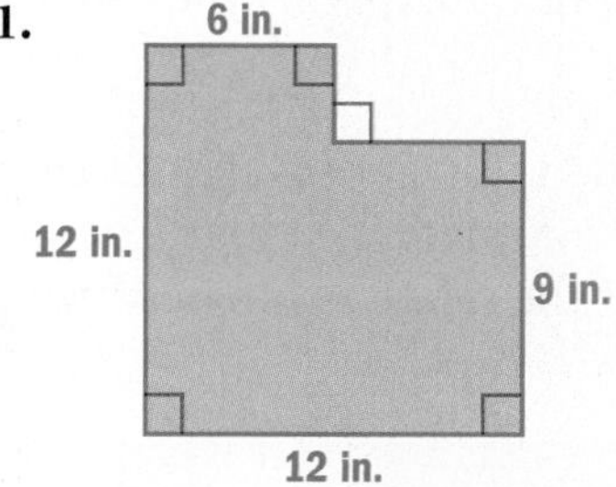

22.

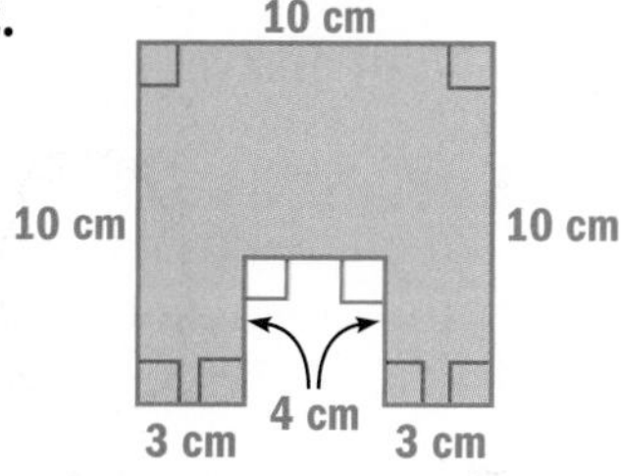

Animated Math at classzone.com

23. ★ **OPEN-ENDED MATH** Give the dimensions of 6 rectangles, 3 with a perimeter of 24 centimeters and 3 with an area of 24 square centimeters.

24. **FINDING SIDE LENGTHS** A rectangle has an area of 60 square inches and a perimeter of 38 inches. Find the length and width of the rectangle.

25. **CHALLENGE** A rectangular box has a length of 10 centimeters, a width of 6 centimeters, and a height of 5 centimeters. Find the area of all six sides.

PROBLEM SOLVING

SEE EXAMPLE 4 on p. 34 for Ex. 26

26. **TIGER BEETLES** A tiger beetle runs 210 centimeters in 4 seconds. How fast is the beetle running?

27. **MEASUREMENT** To convert from degrees Celsius C to degrees Fahrenheit F, you can use the formula $F = \frac{9}{5}C + 32$. Convert 20°C to degrees Fahrenheit.

28. ★ **WRITING** *Describe* how to find the width of a rectangle when you know its area and length.

29. **ESTIMATION** The driving distance between Dallas and Houston is 240 miles. Suppose a car travels at an average rate of 55 miles per hour. Estimate the time it takes to travel from Houston to Dallas.

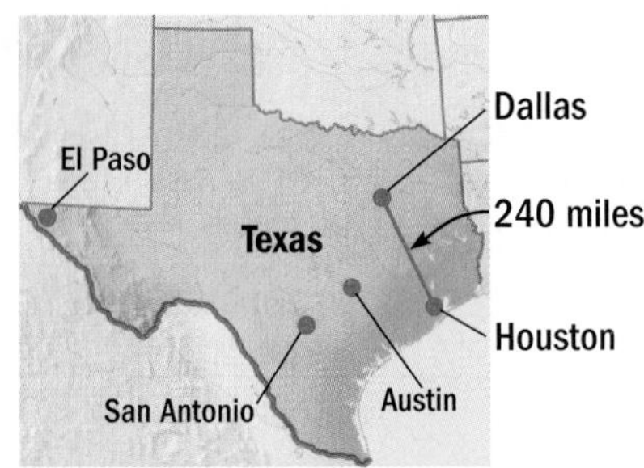

30. **MEASUREMENT** Write a formula for converting meters to centimeters in words and in symbols.

31. **PARACHUTING** A parachutist falls for 2 minutes at a speed of 13 feet per second. How far does the parachutist fall during this time?

32. ★ **MULTIPLE CHOICE** You drive 50 miles per hour for 1 hour 30 minutes. Which expression can be used to find how many miles you travel?

Ⓐ 50×130 Ⓑ 50×90 Ⓒ 50×1.5 Ⓓ $50 \div 90$

33. ★ **SHORT RESPONSE** A train travels from New York to Philadelphia to Washington, D.C., a total of 226 miles. It travels 1 hour 13 minutes, makes one stop, and continues for 1 hour 44 minutes. Find the average speed of the train to the nearest mile per hour. *Explain* how you found your answer.

34. ★ **EXTENDED RESPONSE** The table shows information about two rectangular swimming pools. Copy and complete the table. *Compare* the dimensions of the two pools. What is the relationship between their areas? Their perimeters?

	Length	Width	Area	Perimeter
Pool A	60 ft	22 ft	?	?
Pool B	?	44 ft	5280 ft^2	?

35. **CHALLENGE** Your rectangular yard is twice as long as it is wide. You fenced in the yard using 240 feet of fencing. You want to fertilize your yard. Each bag of fertilizer covers 2000 square feet. How many bags should you buy? *Justify* your answer.

MIXED REVIEW

Get-Ready

Prepare for Lesson 1.7 in Exs. 36–37

Describe the pattern. Then draw the next figure. *(p. 791)*

36. ● ●● ●● ●● ●●●● ●●●●

37.  

Solve the equation using mental math. *(p. 26)*

38. $8x = 72$

39. $g - 19 = 37$

40. $\frac{y}{3} = 10$

41. $m + 21 = 52$

42. ★ **MULTIPLE CHOICE** Which improper fraction is equal to $4\frac{3}{8}$? *(p. 762)*

Ⓐ $\frac{20}{8}$ Ⓑ $\frac{32}{8}$ Ⓒ $\frac{35}{8}$ Ⓓ $\frac{43}{8}$

1.7 A Problem Solving Plan

Before	You used problem solving strategies to solve problems.
Now	You'll use a problem solving plan to solve problems.
Why?	So you can predict future events, as in Ex. 30.

KEY VOCABULARY

- **unit analysis,** *p. 39*

Triathlon You and a friend decide to compete in a triathlon. You both swim 200 meters, bike 10 kilometers, and then run 2 kilometers.

The table shows your speeds for swimming in meters per minute, and biking in kilometers per minute. Who has the better total time after these two stages?

	Swimming (m/min)	Biking (km/min)
You	76.9	0.43
Friend	82.6	0.41

EXAMPLE 1 Understanding and Planning

To solve the triathlon problem, you need to make sure you understand the problem. Then make a plan for solving the problem.

READ AND UNDERSTAND

What do you know?

The table displays your speeds for each stage.

You both swim 200 meters and bike 10 kilometers.

What do you want to find out?

Who has the better total time for swimming and biking?

MAKE A PLAN

How can you relate what you know to what you want to find out?

Find each of your swimming and biking times. You can organize this information in a table.

Find each of your total times and then compare these times.

You will solve the problem in Example 2.

✓ GUIDED PRACTICE for Example 1

1. Which formula would you use to find swimming and running times? *Explain* your reasoning.

   A. $distance = rate \cdot time$ **B.** $time = \frac{distance}{rate}$ **C.** $rate = \frac{distance}{time}$

EXAMPLE 2 Solving and Looking Back

Carry out the plan from Example 1. Check the answer.

SOLVE THE PROBLEM

Use the formula $time = \frac{distance}{rate}$.

	Swimming	Biking
You	$t = \frac{d}{r}$ $= \frac{200}{76.9}$ ≈ 2.60 min	$t = \frac{d}{r}$ $= \frac{10}{0.43}$ ≈ 23.26 min
Friend	$t = \frac{d}{r}$ $= \frac{200}{82.6}$ ≈ 2.42 min	$t = \frac{d}{r}$ $= \frac{10}{0.41}$ ≈ 24.39 min

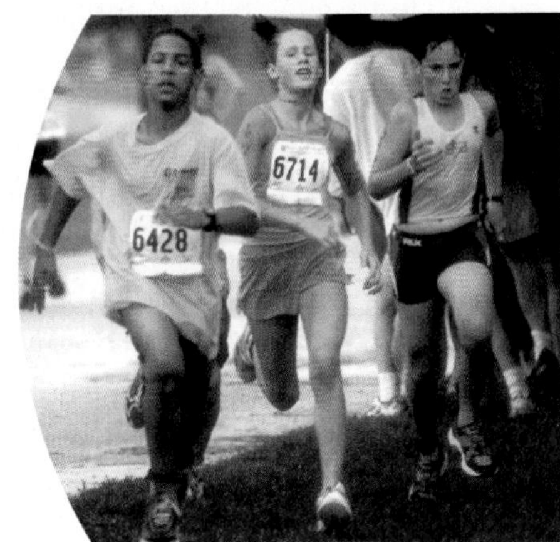

READING
The symbol $\approx$ means *is approximately equal to.*

Add to find the total time.

You $2.60 + 23.26 = 25.86$ min

Friend $2.42 + 24.39 = 26.81$ min

▶ **Answer** You have the better total time after the two stages.

Animated Math at classzone.com

LOOK BACK

Does your answer make sense?

You swim slower than your friend, so your swimming time should be greater. You bike faster than your friend, so your biking time should be less. So the calculations are reasonable.

✓ GUIDED PRACTICE for Example 2

2. **What If?** Suppose in Example 2 that your friend biked at a rate of 0.44 km/min. Who had the better total time after two stages?

KEY CONCEPT *For Your Notebook*

A Problem Solving Plan

1. **Read and Understand** Read the problem carefully. Identify the question and any important information.
2. **Make a Plan** Decide on a problem solving strategy.
3. **Solve the Problem** Use the strategy to answer the question.
4. **Look Back** Check that your answer is reasonable.

Unit Analysis You can use **unit analysis** to evaluate expressions with units of measure and to check that your answer uses the correct units.

For example, when you find the product of rate (miles per hour) and time (hours), the units for distance will be in miles: $\frac{\text{miles}}{\cancel{\text{hour}}} \cdot \cancel{\text{hour}} = \text{miles}$.

EXAMPLE 3 Using a Problem Solving Plan

City Blocks In parts of New York City, the blocks between avenues are called *long blocks*. There are 4 long blocks per mile. Blocks between streets are called *short blocks*. There are 20 short blocks per mile. You walk 40 short blocks and 6 long blocks. How many miles do you walk?

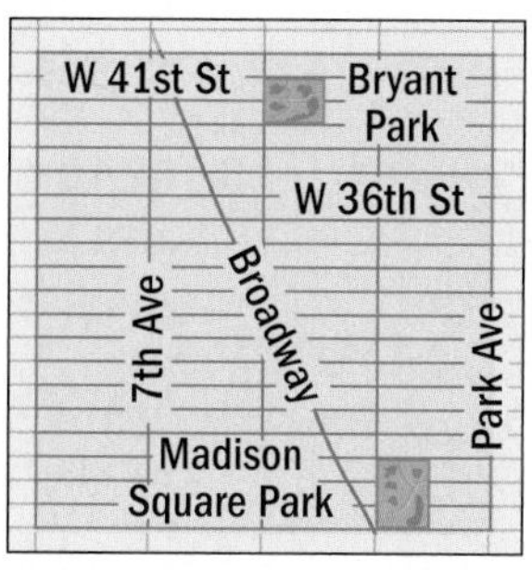

SOLUTION

REVIEW PROBLEM SOLVING STRATEGIES
Need help with problem solving strategies? See pp. 786–795.

Read and Understand You walk 40 short blocks and 6 long blocks. There are 20 short blocks per mile and 4 long blocks per mile. You are asked to find how many miles you walk.

Make a Plan Convert short blocks to miles and long blocks to miles using unit analysis. Then add to find the total miles.

Solve the Problem Because 20 short blocks equal one mile, you can multiply the number of short blocks by $\frac{1 \text{ mile}}{20 \text{ short blocks}}$ to convert to miles.

$$40 \cancel{\text{ short blocks}} \times \frac{1 \text{ mile}}{20 \cancel{\text{ short blocks}}} = 2 \text{ miles}$$

You can convert long blocks to miles by multiplying by $\frac{1 \text{ mile}}{4 \text{ long blocks}}$.

$$6 \cancel{\text{ long blocks}} \times \frac{1 \text{ mile}}{4 \cancel{\text{ long blocks}}} = 1.5 \text{ miles}$$

Animated Math at classzone.com

▶ **Answer** You walk a total of $2 + 1.5 = 3.5$ miles.

Look Back Check your answer by drawing a diagram.

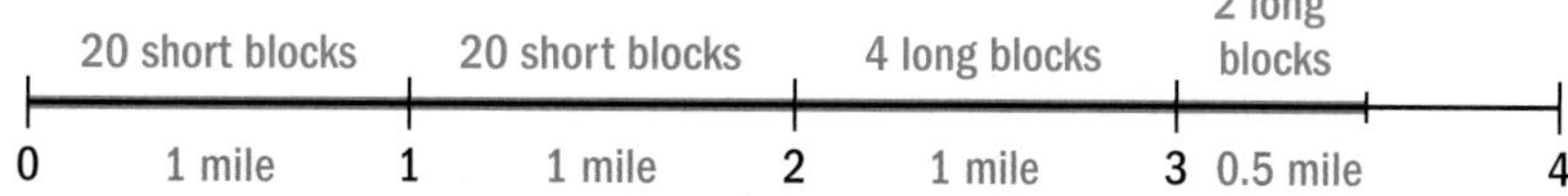

From the diagram you can see that 40 short blocks are 2 miles and 6 long blocks are 1.5 miles, which totals 3.5 miles. So, your answer checks.

✓ GUIDED PRACTICE for Example 3

3. **What If?** In Example 3, how many miles do you walk if you walk 50 short blocks and 12 long blocks?

1.7 EXERCISES

HOMEWORK KEY ★ = **STANDARDIZED TEST PRACTICE** Exs. 8, 17, 18, 21, 22, and 42

○ = **HINTS AND HOMEWORK HELP** for Exs. 3, 5, 7, 17, 19 at classzone.com

SKILL PRACTICE

1. **VOCABULARY** List the four steps of the problem solving plan.

2. **VOCABULARY** Copy and complete: You can use _?_ to evaluate expressions with units of measure and to check for the correct units.

SEE EXAMPLE 1 on p. 37 for Exs. 3–4

3. **READ AND UNDERSTAND** A customer bought a lunch that cost \$3.99 and a drink that cost \$.99. The customer paid with a \$10 bill. You are the cashier. Identify what you know and what you need to find out.

4. **MAKE A TABLE** You have a handful of quarters, nickels, and dimes that totals 75 cents. Make a table listing all possible combinations.

SEE EXAMPLE 2 on p. 38 for Exs. 5–6

5. **LOOK BACK** The cost of a ticket to a baseball game is \$10. The cost of a hot dog is \$2. Matt goes to the game and has 3 hot dogs. One of your friends says that Matt spent \$16. *Explain* how to check the answer.

6. **ERROR ANALYSIS** Daniel can take 96 photos on a 5 day trip. He takes 45 photos in 2 days. He wants to take an equal number of photos each of the last 3 days. *Describe* and correct the error in the solution.

> ✗ $\frac{96}{3} = 32$
> Daniel can take 32 pictures each day.

SEE EXAMPLE 3 on p. 39 for Ex. 7

7. **USING A PLAN** You are selling bags of microwavable popcorn as a fundraiser. Each bag costs \$2. A neighbor wants to buy 5 bags. Use the verbal model to find out how much money the neighbor will give you.

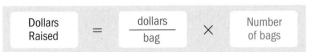

$$\text{Dollars Raised} = \frac{\text{dollars}}{\text{bag}} \times \text{Number of bags}$$

8. ★ **MULTIPLE CHOICE** Which represents the 15th arrow in the pattern?

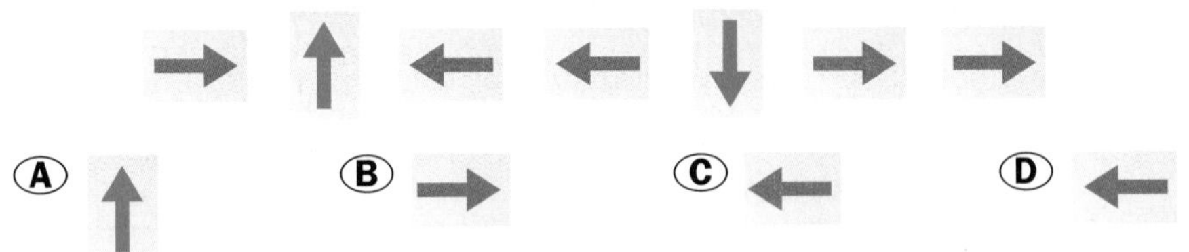

Ⓐ ↑ Ⓑ → Ⓒ ← Ⓓ ←

9. **IDENTIFYING UNNECESSARY INFORMATION** You buy 3 packs of pens for \$12. Each pack of pens contains 12 pens. How much does each pack of pens cost? Identify the unnecessary information in this problem.

LOOK FOR A PATTERN Complete the pattern.

10. $7x^2, 15x^2, 23x^2,$ _?_ , _?_

11. $81x, 78x^2, 75x^3, 72x^4,$ _?_ , _?_

CHALLENGE What are the next three numbers? Describe the rule.

12. 11, 7, 14, 10, 20, 16, . . .

13. 7, 20, 46, 98, 202, 410, . . .

14. 1.5, 1.5, 3, 4.5, 7.5, 12, . . .

PROBLEM SOLVING

15. **GUIDED PROBLEM SOLVING** A monorail ride at an amusement park has 5 cars in each train, and each car can hold 4 passengers. In one hour, 900 people can ride the monorail. How many trains run in one hour?
   a. Write a verbal model of the problem.
   b. Use the model to find the number of trains that run in one hour.
   c. Check your answer.

16. **MUSIC** You practice piano for 50 minutes each weekday and for 40 minutes on each weekend day. How many hours per week do you practice?

17. ★ **SHORT RESPONSE** You pay $15 a ticket for 4 tickets and a service charge of $2 for every ticket after the second one. You are charged $64 for this order. *Describe* a way to check that this is the correct price.

SEE EXAMPLE 3 on p. 39 for Exs. 18–23

18. ★ **MULTIPLE CHOICE** You are trying to earn 4000 points in a computer game. In the first round you get 1540 points. In the next round you get 780 points. How many more points do you need?

   (A) 760 (B) 1680 (C) 1760 (D) 2680

19. **BICYCLE RACE** A Tour de France bicycle race covered 3462 kilometers in 21 days. Riders traveled 3152 kilometers during the first 19 racing days and 160 kilometers the next day. How long was the ride on the last day?

20. **SALES** During a 4 week period, a salesperson at a photography studio wants to sell photography packages worth a total of $16,000. What does the sales amount need to be in week 4 to reach the $16,000 goal?

Week	1	2	3	4
Sales	$1240	$3720	$5980	?

21. ★ **MULTIPLE CHOICE** You are making lasagna for 30 people at a shelter. You need 8 ounces of mozzarella cheese to make enough for 10 people. You have 12 ounces. How many more ounces do you need?

   (A) 0 (B) 4 (C) 12 (D) 24

22. ★ **WRITING** Is there enough information to answer the question? *Explain* how to solve the problem, or tell what information is needed.

   Amanda has sold magazine subscriptions worth $330 for a school fundraiser. If she reaches a total of $500, she wins a gift certificate. How many more subscriptions does she need to sell to reach $500?

23. **HOMEWORK** You need to read 60 pages for English and 20 pages for History by Friday. You have read 16 pages on Monday. How much do you need to read each day to complete the assignment on time?

24. **SAVING** Fran is saving for a printer that costs $210. Her mom will pay $120. Fran makes $6 an hour baby-sitting. Use the problem solving plan to find how many hours she needs to baby-sit to earn enough to buy the printer.

25. **GUESS, CHECK, AND REVISE** You know you have 15 coins in your pocket, 5 of them are nickels, and the rest are dimes and quarters. The total amount is $2.30. How many dimes do you have? How many quarters?

26. **VENN DIAGRAMS** There are 48 students on the track team, 16 on the wrestling team, and 117 on neither team. There are 171 students total. How many students are on both teams? Solve using a Venn Diagram.

27. **MAKE A TABLE** Your school talent show allows people to sign up for 3 or 5 minute acts. There is one minute between acts. The talent show has 15 acts and lasts for 79 minutes. How many 3 minute acts are there?

28. **GARDEN** You have 28 yards of fencing and want to construct a rectangular garden with the largest possible area with whole number dimensions. Find the side lengths of the largest garden. What is its area?

29. **NUMBER SENSE** The product of two numbers is 104. Their difference is 5. Find the two numbers.

30. **BASKETBALL** The table shows the numbers of people who attended Women's National Basketball Association (WNBA) games from 2000 through 2004. *Describe* a strategy to predict the attendance for WNBA games in 2005. Use your strategy to predict the 2005 attendance.

Year	2000	2001	2002	2003	2004
Attendance	2,322,429	2,323,161	2,391,972	2,100,630	1,898,077

31. **USE A DIAGRAM** John lives 1.2 miles west of the library and his school is 0.6 miles east of the library on the same road. The distance between the school and the post office is twice the distance between John's home and school. How far is John's home from the post office using the diagram below? Suppose the post office is west of John's home. How far from John's home would the post office be then?

32. **SOLVE A SIMPLER PROBLEM** At summer camp, 12 campers in a group each shake hands with every other camper once as they introduce themselves. How many handshakes occur?

PROBLEM SOLVING
Need help with problem solving strategies? See p. 793.

33. **CHALLENGE** Bill's house is third in a row of 12 houses. There are 5 houses between Chris's house and Audrey's house, and 2 between Chris's house and Bill's house. How many houses are between Audrey's house and the first house? *Explain* how you found your answer.

MIXED REVIEW

Get-Ready

Prepare for Lesson 2.1 in Exs. 34–37

Complete the statement using < or >. *(p. 759)*

34. 23.2 _?_ 23 **35.** 0.5 _?_ 5 **36.** 0.1 _?_ 0.01 **37.** 1.4 _?_ 4.1

Evaluate the expression. *(p. 8)*

38. $7 + 4 \times 3 - 6$ **39.** $24 \div (2 \times 4) - 3$

Find the perimeter and area of the figure. *(p. 32)*

40. a 16 inch by 3 inch rectangle **41.** a square with a 237-foot side

42. ★ **MULTIPLE CHOICE** Which of the following is the standard form of $4 \times 10{,}000 + 5 \times 1000 + 7 \times 10$? *(p. 759)*

(A) 457 (B) 45,007 (C) 45,070 (D) 45,700

QUIZ *for Lessons 1.5–1.7*

Solve the equation using mental math. *(p. 26)*

1. $h + 12 = 21$ **2.** $22 - y = 8$ **3.** $54 = 6x$ **4.** $\frac{108}{r} = 9$

5. **VIDEO GAMES** You have $24 to spend on video game rentals. Each rental costs $3. How many video games can you rent? *(p. 26)*

6. **GEOMETRY** Find the perimeter and area of a rectangle 14 feet by 11 feet. *(p. 32)*

7. **DRIVING** On the highway you drive at a speed of 55 miles per hour for 3 hours. How far do you drive? *(p. 32)*

8. **EXERCISE** You plan to exercise 200 minutes over 5 days. The first four days you exercise 45 minutes, 30 minutes, 20 minutes, and 1 hour. Use a problem solving plan to find the number of minutes you need to exercise on the fifth day to meet your goal. *(p. 37)*

Brain Game

What's Happening?

Scott, John, Annie, and Rebecca are each doing a different activity (debate, art club, student council, or tutoring). Who is doing what?

- Annie is not going to student council or to art club.
- Rebecca and Scott are not members of the student council.
- Annie and Rebecca do not tutor.

MIXED REVIEW *of Problem Solving*

Lessons 1.5–1.7

1. **MULTI-STEP PROBLEM** The table shows the times it took to complete two parts of a triathlon.

	Run 10 kilometers	*Swim 1000 meters*
Renee	48.5 min	22.4 min
Beth	47.6 min	22.8 min

   a. Who completed the two events in less time?

   b. Find each rate for running and swimming. Who swam faster? Who ran faster?

   c. Renee and Beth also biked 10 kilometers. Renee's rate was 0.46 kilometers per minute and Beth's rate was 0.44 kilometers per minute. Who completed the three events in less time?

2. **GRIDDED ANSWER** A store has 10 pairs of black shoes and three times as many pairs of brown shoes as black. There are 10 more pairs of sandals than black shoes. What is the combined number of pairs of sandals and shoes?

3. **SHORT RESPONSE** An ice cream shop offers week-long specials when you purchase a large ice cream cake. They offer a free small ice cream cake every fifth week, a free pint of ice cream every sixth week, and a free ice cream cone every third week. How many times in one year will they offer all three deals in the same week if they offer all three the first week of the year? *Explain* how you found your answer.

4. **GRIDDED ANSWER** One ton of gravel will fill 16 cubic feet of space. Marcus wants to cover a driveway that is 12 feet wide and 60 feet long with 4 inches of gravel. The formula for volume of a rectangular solid is $V = lwh$. How many tons of gravel should he order?

5. **SHORT RESPONSE** *Describe* two methods for finding the area of the figure below.

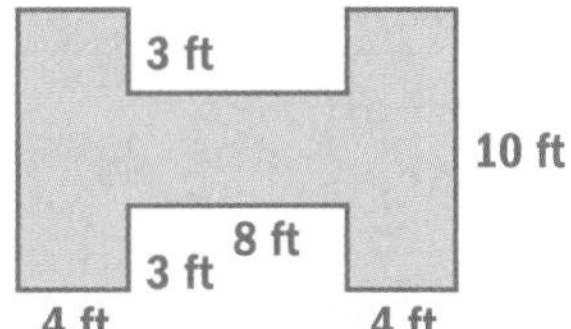

6. **OPEN-ENDED** Write a verbal model to describe the cost of going to the movies assuming you want to buy food and drinks for yourself and 2 friends.

7. **SHORT RESPONSE** The area of the rectangle is 120 square centimeters. Write an equation you can use to find the width w. Then solve the equation for w.

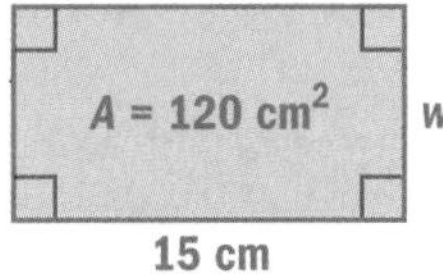

8. **EXTENDED RESPONSE** You are planting a rectangular garden and want to separate the garden area from the rest of your yard with a wooden border. You have 2 pieces of wood that are each 16 feet long. You want to build the border with sides of integer foot length.

   a. List all possible dimensions (length and width) of the garden border that you can build by cutting your 2 pieces of wood.

   b. Find the area of each rectangle in your list.

   c. Which of the dimensions in your list would give the garden the largest area?

   d. *Describe* the difference in appearance between the rectangles with the largest area and the smallest area.

1 CHAPTER REVIEW

@HomeTutor
classzone.com
Vocabulary Practice

REVIEW KEY VOCABULARY

- bar graph, *p. 3*
- data, *p. 3*
- frequency table, histogram, *p. 4*
- numerical expression, *p. 8*
- evaluate, *p. 8*
- order of operations, *p. 8*
- verbal model, *p. 9*
- variable, variable expression, *p. 13*
- power, exponent, base, *p. 19*
- equation, solution, *p. 26*
- solving an equation, *p. 26*
- formula, *p. 32*
- perimeter, area, *p. 32*
- unit analysis, *p. 39*

VOCABULARY EXERCISES

1. You can graph data organized in a frequency table using a(n) _?_.
2. _?_ is the amount of surface covered by a figure.
3. To evaluate an expression that has more than one operation, use the _?_.
4. A power has an exponent and a(n) _?_.

REVIEW EXAMPLES AND EXERCISES

1.1 Interpreting Graphs pp. 3–7

EXAMPLE

The bar graph displays the number of times each country has won the World Cup in soccer. How many more times has Italy won than England?

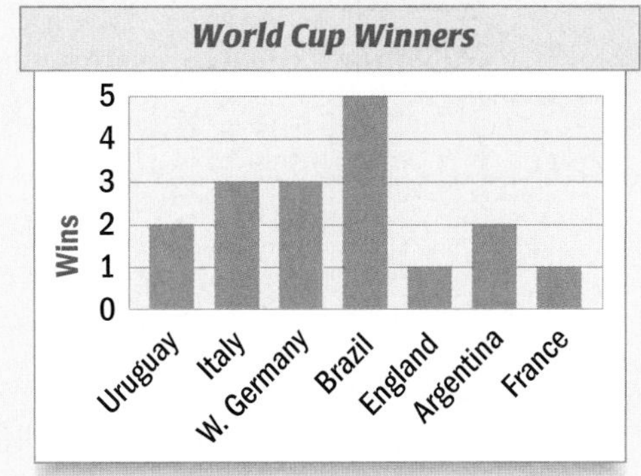

SOLUTION

Italy has won the World Cup 3 times and England once. Italy has won 2 more times.

EXERCISES

Volunteering Use the table that shows the number of volunteers at a local animal shelter.

Age Group	Volunteers
15–24	24
25–34	30
35–44	31
45–54	30
55–64	27
65+	23

SEE EXAMPLE 2 on p. 4 for Exs. 5–6

5. Which age group has the most volunteers? Which age group has the fewest volunteers?
6. Can you determine the number of volunteers who are teenagers? *Explain.*

1.2 Order of Operations

pp. 8–11

EXAMPLE

Evaluate the expression $5 + 12 \cdot 5 \div 4$.

$5 + 12 \cdot 5 \div 4 = 5 + 60 \div 4$ **Multiply 12 by 5.**

$= 5 + 15$ **Divide 60 by 4.**

$= 20$ **Add 5 and 15.**

EXERCISES

Evaluate the expression.

SEE EXAMPLES 1, 2, AND 3 on pp. 8–9 for Exs. 7–10

7. $16 + 5 \times 3 + 8$

8. $40 \div [(14 + 6) \cdot 2]$

9. $10 + \frac{60}{31 - 26}$

10. Electricians An electrician charges \$50 to come to your house plus \$40 per hour of work. To find how much the electrician charges for 2 hours of work, evaluate the expression $50 + 40 \cdot 2$.

1.3 Variables and Expressions

pp. 13–18

EXAMPLE

Evaluate the expression when $x = 6$ and $y = 5$.

$4x - 3y = 4(6) - 3(5)$ **Substitute 6 for x and 5 for y.**

$= 24 - 15$ **Multiply.**

$= 9$ **Subtract.**

EXERCISES

Evaluate the expression when $x = 4$ and $y = 9$.

SEE EXAMPLES 1, 2, AND 3 on p. 14 for Exs. 11–21

11. $\frac{xy}{3x}$

12. $\frac{y + 19}{x + 3}$

13. $5y - 6x$

14. $3xy - xy$

15. $\frac{x + y}{y - x}$

16. $\frac{x + y}{2xy}$

17. $4x + 6y$

18. $5xy + \frac{9x}{y}$

Write the phrase as a variable expression using n.

19. the sum of a number and 12

20. one fifth of a number

21. Clothes You are saving money to buy two sweaters. Each one costs \$28.50. You have saved \$20. To find out how much more money you need to save, translate *20 less than the product of 2 and 28.5* into an expression and then evaluate.

1.4 Powers and Exponents

pp. 19–24

EXAMPLE

Evaluate the expression.

$(5 - 2)^2 + 7 - 2^2 = 3^2 + 7 - 2^2$ **Evaluate inside grouping symbols.**

$= 9 + 7 - 4$ **Evaluate powers.**

$= 12$ **Add and subtract from left to right.**

EXERCISES

Evaluate the power.

SEE EXAMPLES 2 AND 4 on pp. 19–20 for Exs. 22–29

22. 15^2 **23.** 4^5 **24.** 10^4 **25.** 9^4

Evaluate the expression.

26. $(5 + 4)^2 \div 3$ **27.** $5 \cdot (6 - 3)^5 + 45$ **28.** $[10 + (4 \times 2)^3] \div 2$

29. Icicles An icicle falls from the roof of a building. It hits the ground in 3 seconds. Use the expression $16t^2$ to find the distance in feet that the icicle falls in t seconds to find the height of the building.

1.5 Equations and Solutions

pp. 26–30

EXAMPLE

Solve the equation $18 - n = 13$ using mental math.

To solve a simple equation using mental math, you can think of the equation as a question.

18 minus **what number** equals 13? $18 - 5 = 13$, so $n = 5$.

EXERCISES

Solve the equation using mental math.

SEE EXAMPLES 1, 2, AND 3 on pp. 26–27 for Exs. 30–36

30. $7b = 56$ **31.** $\frac{84}{x} = 12$ **32.** $98 - t = 35$

Tell whether the value of the variable is a solution of the equation.

33. $t + 11 = 30; t = 29$ **34.** $48 \div k = 12; k = 4$ **35.** $8m = 68, m = 8$

36. River Speed A log travels 50 feet down a river in 20 seconds. After 15 seconds it has traveled 40 feet. How many more feet will it travel in the remaining 5 seconds?

1.6 Variables in Familiar Formulas

pp. 32–36

EXAMPLE

Find the length and perimeter of the rectangle. Its area is 54 square feet.

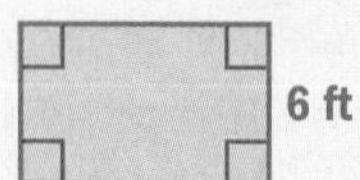

For area use the formula $A = lw$.

$A = lw$	**Write formula.**
$54 = l(6)$	**Substitute.**
$9 = l$	**Use mental math.**

For perimeter use the formula $P = 2l + 2w$.

$P = 2l + 2w$	**Write formula.**
$= 2(9) + 2(6)$	**Substitute.**
$= 30$	**Multiply, then add.**

▶ **Answer** The length is 9 feet and the perimeter is 30 feet.

EXERCISES

Find the unknown value for the rectangle or square.

SEE EXAMPLES 1 AND 3 on pp. 32–33 for Exs. 37–39

37. rectangle: $P = 56$ cm, $l = 12$ cm, $w =$ __?__

38. square: $A = 121\text{ ft}^2$, $s =$ __?__

39. **Cars** A car travels at an average rate of 50 miles per hour for 3 hours. How far does it travel?

1.7 A Problem Solving Plan

pp. 37–42

EXAMPLE

You need 3 pitcherfuls to fill a 5-gallon aquarium with a pitcher. How many trips will you need to fill a 55-gallon aquarium with the same pitcher?

Read and Understand and Make a Plan Find how many times as great the capacity of the larger tank is than the smaller tank. Compare using division. Then multiply that number by 3, because it takes 3 pitcherfuls to make 5 gallons.

Solve the Problem $\frac{55\text{ gal}}{5\text{ gal}} \cdot 3\text{ trips} = 11 \cdot 3\text{ trips}$

$= 33\text{ trips}$

▶ **Answer** You need 33 pitcherfuls to fill the larger aquarium.

EXERCISES

SEE EXAMPLE 3 on p. 39 for Ex. 40

40. **Sugar** You like 2 teaspoons of sugar in an 8-ounce glass of iced tea. How much sugar should you add to a 36-ounce thermos of iced tea?

1 CHAPTER TEST

@HomeTutor
classzone.com
Chapter Test Practice

Evaluate the expression.

1. $20 + 12 \div 4$
2. $6 \times 5 - 20 \div 2$
3. $(3 + 7) \div 5 + 10$
4. $(2 + 3)^4 \div 5$
5. $10^2 - 3^4 + 22$
6. $(11 - 5)^4 - 300 \div 12$

Solve the equation using mental math.

7. $17 - t = 5$
8. $9n = 72$
9. $49 \div b = 7$
10. $21 + a = 27$

Tell whether the value of the variable is a solution of the equation.

11. $z + 2 = 15; z = 13$
12. $65 \div y = 16; y = 4$
13. $11x = 45; x = 4$

ALGEBRA Find the unknown value for the variable.

14. square: $A = 64$ yd^2, $s =$ __?__
15. square: $P = 44$ m, $s =$ __?__
16. rectangle: $A =$ __?__, $l = 12$ m, $w = 9$ m
17. rectangle: $A = 128$ in.^{2}, $l =$ __?__, $w = 8$ in.

SPORTS In a survey, 3000 people in Japan were asked about their participation in ten sports. The results for four sports are in the table.

Sport	*Participants*
Gymnastics	1002
Bowling	996
Jogging	807
Swimming	717

18. Make a bar graph of the data.

19. Is it possible to make a histogram of the data? *Explain.*

20. **PLUMBING** A plumber charges a flat rate of \$25 plus an additional \$55 for each hour of work. To find how much money the plumber makes in 5 hours at one location, evaluate the expression $25 + 55 \cdot 5$.

21. **FRUIT** You are buying 3 apples and 4 oranges for a fruit salad. The cost of one apple is x dollars. The cost of one orange is y dollars. Write a variable expression to represent the cost of 3 apples and 4 oranges. If one apple costs \$.75 and one orange costs \$.50, what is the total cost?

22. **HORSES** A horse travels at a rate of 30 feet per second. How far does the horse travel in 4 seconds?

23. **COURT AREA** The lengths and widths of three types of courts are listed in the table. Find the area of each court. Which court has the largest area? Which court has the smallest area?

Court	*Length*	*Width*
Squash	32 feet	21 feet
Tennis	78 feet	27 feet
Racquetball	40 feet	20 feet

24. **PARK** A rectangular park that is 90 feet long and 60 feet wide needs to be planted with sod. A roll of sod covers 1 square yard. Use a problem solving plan to find how many rolls of sod are needed to cover the park.

1 ★ Standardized TEST PREPARATION

SHORT RESPONSE QUESTIONS

Scoring Rubric

Full Credit
- solution is complete and correct

Partial Credit
- solution is complete but errors are made, *or*
- solution is without error, but incomplete

No Credit
- no solution is given, *or*
- solution makes no sense

PROBLEM

The cost for admission to an ice skating rink is \$10. The cost of a pretzel is \$1.25 and a drink is \$2. You go skate at the rink and buy three pretzels and two drinks. Write and evaluate a variable expression to find the cost of your trip to the ice skating rink. *Justify* your answer.

Below are sample solutions to the problem. Read each solution and the comments in blue to see why the sample represents full credit, partial credit, or no credit.

SAMPLE 1: Full Credit Solution

This reasoning is the key to choosing the correct problem solving plan.

To find the total cost of the trip to the ice skating rink, let p be the number of pretzels and d be the number of drinks. An expression for the total cost of the trip is

The variable expression is written correctly.

$$10 + 1.25p + 2d.$$

Substitute the number of pretzels and drinks into the expression.

$$10 + 1.25p + 2d = 10 + 1.25(3) + 2(2)$$
$$= 10 + 3.75 + 4$$
$$= 17.75$$

The answer is correct.

The cost of admission, three pretzels, and two drinks is \$17.75.

SAMPLE 2: Partial Credit Solution

The reasoning and process are correct.

An expression for the cost of the trip to the ice skating rink is

$$10 + 1.25p + 2d$$

where p is the number of pretzels and d is the number of drinks. Substitute the number of pretzels and drinks into the expression.

The student substitutes for the wrong variable in this step.

$$10 + 1.25p + 2d = 10 + 1.25(2) + 2(3)$$
$$= 10 + 2.50 + 6$$
$$= 18.50$$

The answer is incorrect.

The cost of admission, three pretzels, and two drinks is \$18.50.

SAMPLE 3: Partial Credit Solution

The student did not write a variable expression.

The answer is correct, but it is not justified.

$$10 + 1.25(3) + 2(2) = 10 + 3.75 + 4$$
$$= 17.75$$

The cost of admission, three pretzels, and two drinks is \$17.75.

SAMPLE 4: No Credit Solution

The expression is wrong.

The answer is incorrect.

$$10 + 1.25 + 2 = 13.25$$

The cost of the trip to the ice skating rink is \$13.25.

PRACTICE Apply the Scoring Rubric

Score the solution to the problem below as *full credit, partial credit,* or *no credit. Explain* your reasoning.

PROBLEM Entrance to a science center costs \$14 for adults and \$10 for children. Write and evaluate a variable expression to find the cost for 3 adults and 6 children to enter the science center. *Justify* your answer.

1. An expression for the cost to enter the science center is $14a + 10c$.

Substitute the number of adults and children into the expression.

$$14a + 10c = 14(6) + 10(3)$$
$$= 84 + 30$$
$$= 114$$

The cost for 3 adults and 6 children to enter the science center is \$114.

2. Let a be the number of adults and c be the number of children. An expression for the cost to enter the science center is $14a + 10c$.

Substitute the number of adults and children into the expression.

$$14a + 10c = 14(3) + 10(6)$$
$$= 42 + 60$$
$$= 102$$

The cost for 3 adults and 6 children to enter the science center is \$102.

1 ★ Standardized TEST PRACTICE

SHORT RESPONSE

1. The perimeter of a rectangular field is 500 feet. The field is 100 feet wide. How long is the field? Draw a diagram. *Explain* how you found your answer.

2. Sita leaves at 8:30 A.M. and drives at an average speed of 55 miles per hour. She reaches her destination at 11:30 A.M. How many miles does Sita travel? *Explain* how you found your answer.

3. Rajiv and Angela shared a roll of tickets at an amusement park. Angela took half of the tickets and used 15 of them. Now she has 30 tickets. How many tickets were on the original roll? *Explain* how you found your answer.

4. You want to collect data about the heights of students in your class. What data would you collect to make a histogram? Could you use the same data to make a bar graph? *Explain* your reasoning.

5. Diego plans to use tiles like the one shown below to tile his rectangular kitchen floor. The floor measures 24 feet by 15 feet. If there are 20 tiles per box, how many boxes must he buy? *Explain* your reasoning.

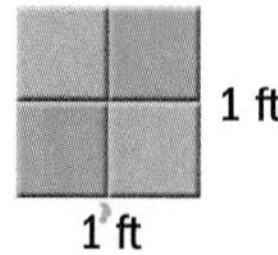

6. You have a total of 12 nickels, dimes, and quarters in your pocket. You know 3 of the coins are dimes and the total amount is $1.15. How many nickels do you have? How many quarters?

7. Tran, Silvio, Eva, Carla, and Tim are all different heights. Eva is taller than Carla and Tran. Tim is shorter than Tran but taller than Carla. Silvio is the tallest of the group. Put the students in order from tallest to shortest.

8. It takes 56 minutes to travel 7 miles in rush hour traffic on some city streets. In similar traffic, how long should it take to travel 4.5 miles? *Justify* your answer.

9. Jason was paid $8 per hour and got paid $52. Use a verbal model to write and solve an equation to find how many hours Jason worked. *Explain* how you found the verbal model.

10. A rectangular yard has a width of 40 yards and a length of 50 yards. A house takes up 45 feet on one side of the yard. How much fencing is needed to fence in the yard? Draw a diagram to support your answer.

11. You do 2 hours of yard work each day for 4 days and earn $6 per hour. Then you go to the movies and buy a $7 ticket and four $2 fountain drinks for you and your friends. Use the problem solving plan to find how much money you have left.

12. Lezlie has 25 students in her literature class, 29 students in her math class, 11 students in both classes, and 49 in neither class. If all of these students make up Lezlie's grade, how many are in her grade? Draw a diagram to support your answer.

13. The area of a rectangle is 27 square meters. *Explain* how you can find the length of the rectangle if its width is 3 meters. What is the length of the rectangle?

14. Tomo can read 12 pages per hour and Umi can read 14 pages per hour. How much longer will it take Tomo to read a book that is 420 pages long? *Explain* your solution process.

15. Insert grouping symbols into the expression $8 + 5 \times 3 - 2$ to make it equal to 37. Insert grouping symbols into the expression to make it equal to 13. *Justify* your answers.

MULTIPLE CHOICE

16. How many more mums than tulips are in the garden?

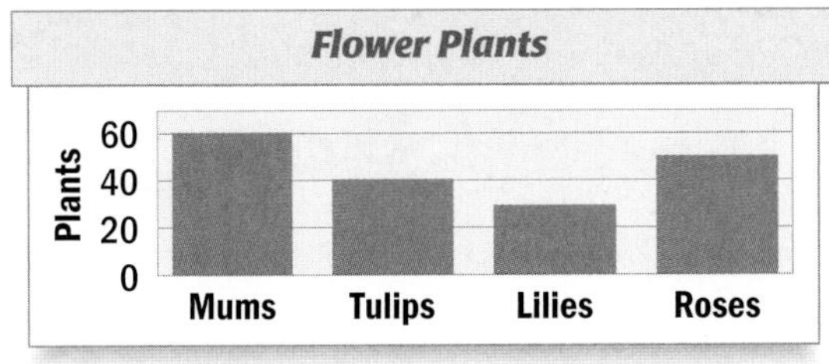

Ⓐ 10 Ⓑ 20

Ⓒ 30 Ⓓ 40

17. What is the value of the expression $8x - 4y$ when $x = 4$ and $y = 6$?

Ⓐ 8 Ⓑ 16

Ⓒ 32 Ⓓ 38

GRIDDED ANSWER

18. What is the value of the expression $2 \cdot 6 - 10 \div 2$?

19. What is the value of the expression $(6 - 2)^2 - 8 + 3^3$?

20. Nikki is driving at a rate of 50 miles per hour. How many hours will it take her to travel 275 miles?

21. A package of 8 computer disks costs \$10, and a package of 15 disks costs \$16.50. How many dollars will you save on 60 disks if you buy packages of 15 instead of packages of 8?

22. Each week Sheila makes \$40 babysitting, spends \$25 at the mall, and spends \$8 at the movies. Sheila saves the rest of her money. How much money, in dollars, has Sheila saved after 5 weeks?

EXTENDED RESPONSE

23. Bud's truck gets about 15 miles per gallon in city traffic and 24 miles per gallon on the highway. He is leaving for his uncle's house, which is 350 miles away. He sees that he has driven 75 miles in city traffic since filling up his 20 gallon tank. Bud knows the first 30 miles of his trip will be in city traffic, but after that he will be on the highway. Should Bud expect to reach his uncle's house without buying gas? *Explain* your reasoning and show your calculations.

24. The results of a poll are shown at the right.

a. Use the data to make a frequency table using the following 4 intervals: *0–1 day, 2–3 days, 4–5 days,* and *6–7 days.*

b. Use your frequency table to create a histogram of the data.

c. How many people polled use a computer more than once a week? Which data display is more helpful when answering that question? *Explain.*

How many days a week do you use a computer at home?

6	4	2	1	7	3
5	3	0	1	2	2
5	7	6	4	2	3
1	3	2	3	2	

25. Ahmad, Betty, Cory, and Deb each live in a different color house. Betty doesn't live in the red house. Neither Cory nor Deb lives in the white house or the green house. Ahmad doesn't live in the yellow or green house. Deb doesn't live in the yellow house. Who lives in which house?

2 Integer Operations

Before

In previous chapters you've . . .

- Performed operations on whole numbers
- Evaluated expressions

Now

In Chapter 2 you'll study . . .

- 2.1 Integers
- 2.2 Adding integers
- 2.3 Subtracting integers
- 2.4 Multiplying integers
- 2.5 Dividing integers
- 2.6 Number properties
- 2.7 The distributive property
- 2.8 The coordinate plane

Why?

So you can solve real-world problems about . . .

- space shuttles, p. 60
- dinosaurs, p. 72
- diving, p. 73

Math

at classzone.com

- Adding Integers, p. 66
- Multiplying Integers, p. 74
- The Coordinate Plane, p. 97

Get-Ready Games

Review Prerequisite Skills by playing *Four in a Row.*

Skill Focus: Multiplying whole numbers

FOUR IN A ROW

MATERIALS

- 2 Answer Cards
- 24 Expression Cards
- 24 Markers

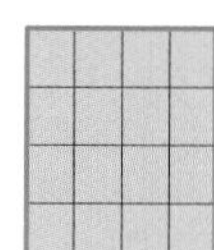

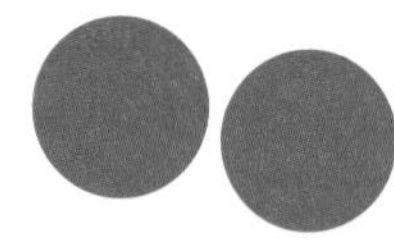

HOW TO PLAY Fill in your Answer Card with 16 of the 24 answers given below. Place the Expression Cards face down in a pile. On each turn follow the steps on the next page.

168	196	240	315	338	342
352	361	405	414	418	441
516	522	529	595	720	792
832	851	918	961	975	1020

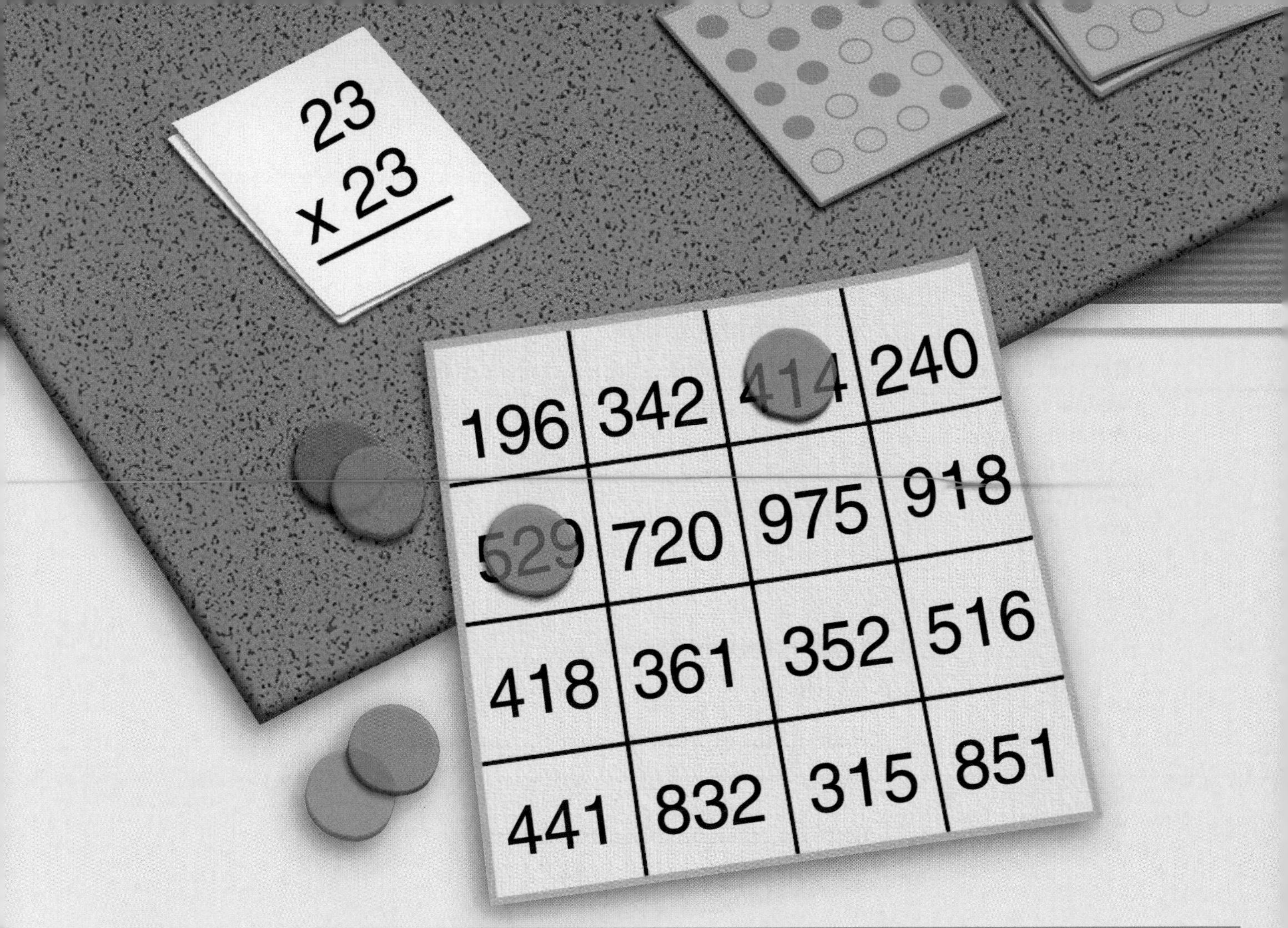

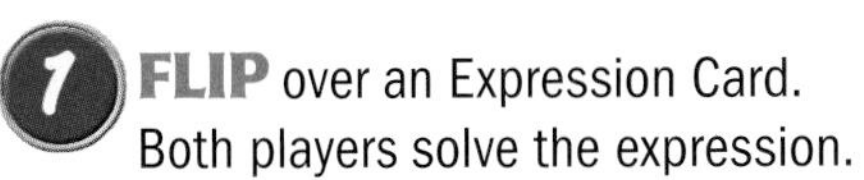

FLIP over an Expression Card. Both players solve the expression.

LOOK for the answer on your Answer Card. If you find it, place a marker over the answer.

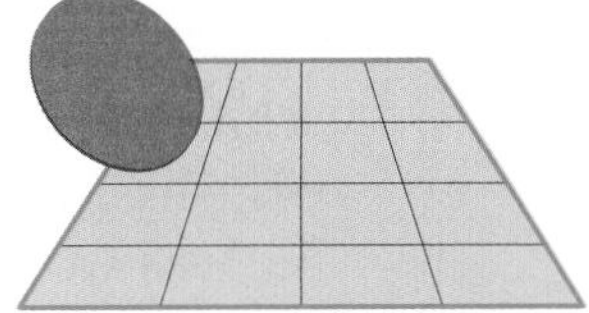

HOW TO WIN Mark 4 answers in a row across, up and down, or diagonally.

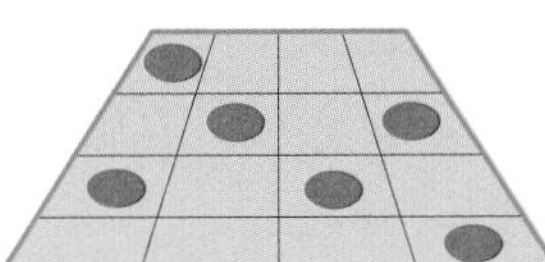

Stop and Think

1. **CRITICAL THINKING** **How many ways can you get 4 answers in a row on your card?**
2. **CRITICAL THINKING** **How many squares can you mark without winning?**

2 Getting Ready

Review Prerequisite Skills

REVIEW WORDS
- **variable,** *p. 13*
- **variable expression,** *p. 13*
- **perimeter,** *p. 32*
- **area,** *p. 32*

VOCABULARY CHECK

Copy and complete using a review word from the list at the left.

1. A symbol that represents one or more numbers is called a(n) _?_.

2. The measure of the surface enclosed by a figure in a plane is its _?_.

SKILL CHECK

Round the decimal to the nearest whole number. *(p. 760)*

3. 10.61 **4.** 134.7 **5.** 0.25 **6.** 12.86

Evaluate the expression. *(p. 8)*

7. $32 - 27 + 14$ **8.** $4 \cdot 12 \div 6$ **9.** $6 + 34 \div 2$

Evaluate the expression when $s = 4$ and $t = 16$. *(p. 13)*

10. $(t - 9) + s$ **11.** $s(t - 5)$ **12.** $\frac{1}{4}t - 4$

Solve the equation using mental math. *(p. 26)*

13. $3x = 39$ **14.** $x - 6 = 12$ **15.** $x + 13 = 17$

@HomeTutor Prerequisite skills practice at classzone.com

Notetaking Skills Including Vocabulary Notes

In each chapter you will learn a new notetaking skill. In Chapter 2 you will apply the strategy of including vocabulary notes on p. 89.

When you write down new vocabulary words, you should also write examples of how they are used. Label the examples with the new words.

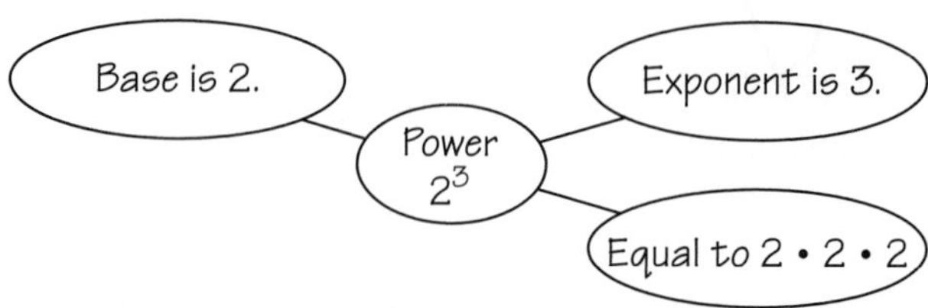

5^2 is read "five squared"

5^3 is read "five cubed"

5^4 is read "five to the fourth power"

As you work through Chapter 2, label examples of new vocabulary in your notes.

2.1 Integers and Absolute Value

Before	You studied whole numbers.
Now	You'll study integers.
Why?	So you can order elevations, as in Example 1.

KEY VOCABULARY

- **integers,** *p. 57*
- **negative integers,** *p. 57*
- **positive integers,** *p. 57*
- **absolute value,** *p. 58*
- **opposites,** *p. 58*

Geography The Global Positioning System (GPS) can be used to determine elevations. The table shows the lowest elevations of several countries. Which country in the table has the lowest elevation?

Lowest Elevations	
Country	***Elevation (m)***
United States	−86
Canada	0
China	−154
Bolivia	90
Czech Republic	115

Each number in the table is an *integer*. The following numbers are **integers**.

$$\ldots, -5, -4, -3, -2, -1, 0, 1, 2, 3, 4, 5, \ldots$$

Negative integers are less than 0. They lie *to the left* of 0 on a number line. **Positive integers** are greater than 0. They lie *to the right* of 0 on a number line. Zero is neither positive nor negative. When you use a number line to compare numbers, numbers increase as you move to the right.

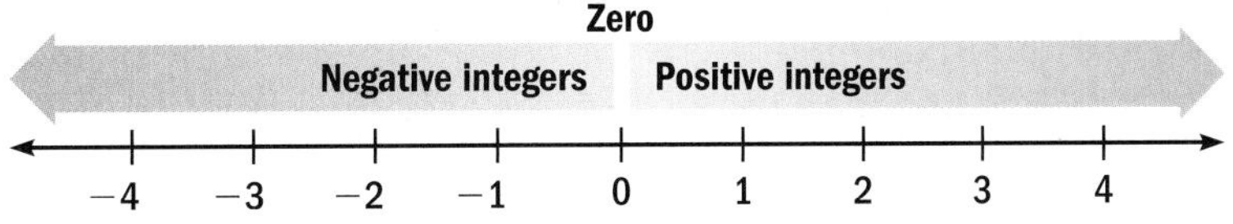

EXAMPLE 1 Graphing and Ordering Integers

To find which country in the table above has the lowest elevation, graph each integer on a number line.

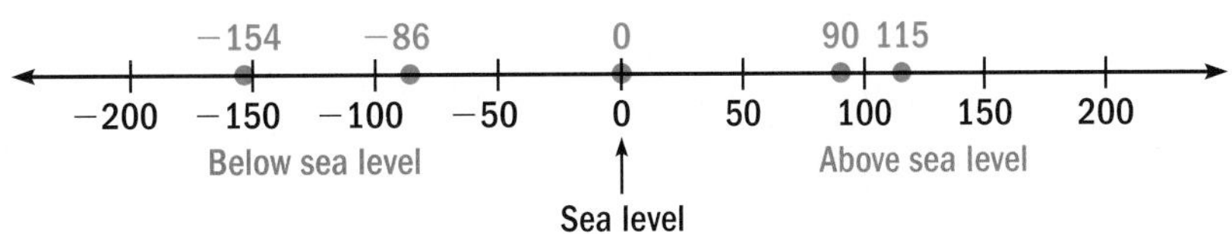

▶ **Answer** China has the lowest elevation, at −154 meters.

✓ GUIDED PRACTICE for Example 1

Order the integers from least to greatest.

1. −7, 2, −1, 0, −2 **2.** 9, −4, 12, −11, −1 **3.** 0, −99, 44, −60, 16

Absolute Value The **absolute value** of a number is the distance between the number and zero on a number line. The absolute value of a number n is written as $|n|$. The absolute value of 0 is 0.

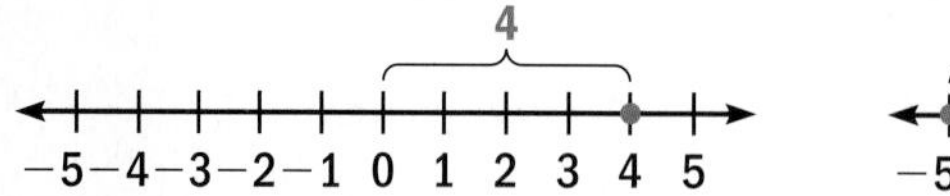

The distance between 4 and 0 is 4. So, $|4| = 4$.

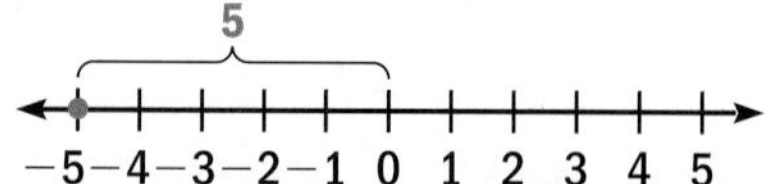

The distance between −5 and 0 is 5. So, $|-5| = 5$.

EXAMPLE 2 Finding Absolute Value

Eyeglasses An eyeglass prescription is given as a positive or negative number. A prescription for a person who is farsighted is positive. A prescription for a person who is nearsighted is negative. The greater the absolute value, the stronger the prescription. Which prescription is stronger, −3 or 2?

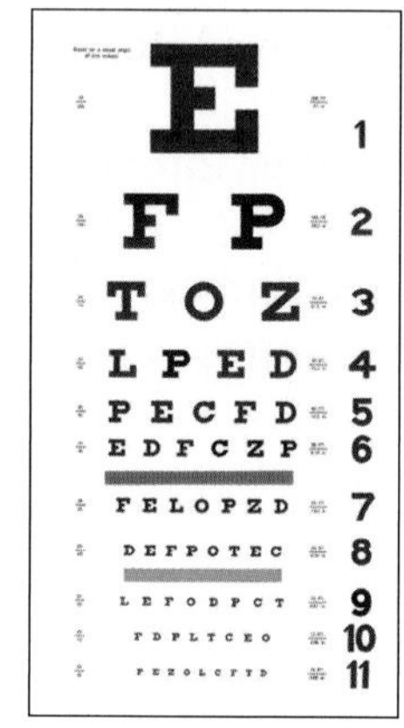

SOLUTION

$|-3| = 3$ and $|2| = 2$.

▸ **Answer** The prescription of −3 is stronger because $3 > 2$.

READING
The integer −2 can be read "negative 2" or "the opposite of 2."

Opposites Two numbers are **opposites** if they have the same absolute value but different signs. Opposites are the same distance from 0 on a number line but on opposite sides of 0. The opposite of 0 is 0.

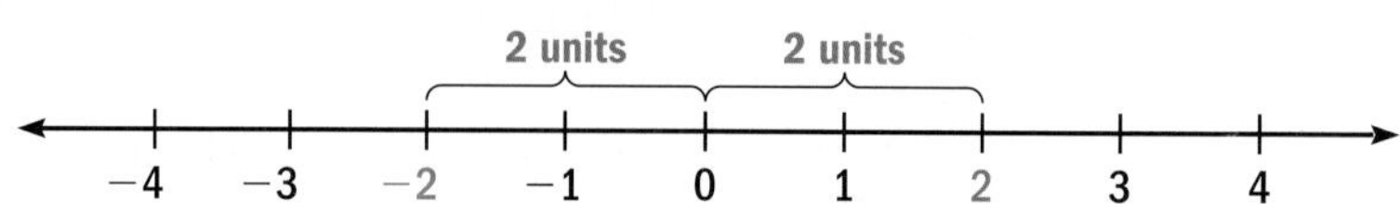

−2 and 2 are *opposites.*

EXAMPLE 3 Finding Opposites

Write the opposite of the integer.

a. 5 — The opposite of 5 is −5.

b. −12 — The opposite of −12 is 12.

c. $|-9|$ — Because $|-9| = 9$, the opposite of $|-9|$ is −9.

✓ GUIDED PRACTICE for Examples 2 and 3

Write the absolute value and the opposite of the integer.

4. −16 **5.** 140 **6.** −1 **7.** 0

2.1 EXERCISES

HOMEWORK KEY

★ = **STANDARDIZED TEST PRACTICE** Exs. 15, 46, 47, 50, and 59

○ = **HINTS AND HOMEWORK HELP** for Exs. 3, 13, 17, 19, 45 at classzone.com

SKILL PRACTICE

VOCABULARY **Copy and complete the statement.**

1. The _?_ of a number is its distance from zero on a number line.
2. Two integers are _?_ if their sum is zero.

COMPARING INTEGERS **Copy and complete the statement with < or >.**

SEE EXAMPLE 1 on p. 57 for Exs. 3–16

3. 4 _?_ −6
4. −12 _?_ 1
5. −9 _?_ −2
6. 0 _?_ −5
7. 5 _?_ −5
8. −17 _?_ 2
9. 34 _?_ −29
10. −20 _?_ −14

ORDERING INTEGERS **Use a number line to order the integers from least to greatest.**

11. 5, −10, 15, 27, −20, 13
12. 120, 62, 0, −56, 74, −130
13. 64, −12, 18, 59, −20, 44
14. 278, 121, −301, 262, −155

15. ★ **MULTIPLE CHOICE** Which list orders the integers from least to greatest?

(A) −1, −6, −12, −34 (B) −1, −12, −34, −6

(C) −34, −12, −6, −1 (D) −34, −6, −12, −1

16. **ERROR ANALYSIS** A student was asked to order the integers 3, 1, 0, −9, −2, and 5 from least to greatest. Describe and correct the error in the solution.

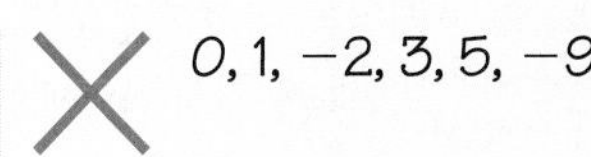

SEE EXAMPLES 2 AND 3 on p. 57 for Exs. 17–20

ABSOLUTE VALUE **Write the absolute value and the opposite of the integer.**

17. 19
18. −8
19. −740
20. 1327

READING VERBAL EXPRESSIONS **Match the integer expression with the verbal expression.**

21. $-|7|$ A. the opposite of negative seven

22. $|-7|$ B. the opposite of the absolute value of seven

23. $-|-7|$ C. the absolute value of negative seven

24. $-(-7)$ D. the opposite of the absolute value of negative seven

SIMPLIFYING EXPRESSIONS **Simplify the expression.**

25. $|-32|$
26. $-|9|$
27. $-|29|$
28. $-(-5)$
29. $-(-81)$
30. $-|-17|$
31. $-|-3|$
32. $-(-(-4))$

COMPARING VALUES **Copy and complete the statement with <, >, or =.**

33. $|4|$ _?_ $|-4|$
34. $|-6|$ _?_ $-|6|$
35. $-|-9|$ _?_ $-(-9)$
36. $|-2|$ _?_ $-(-2)$

ORDERING INTEGERS Order the numbers from least to greatest.

37. $-28, -(-73), |-65|, |95|, -|47|$

38. $|-19|, -74, -|12|, -(-56), -|-58|$

39. $-|6|, -8, -(-5), -14, |-1|$

40. $|38|, -37, -|-42|, -(-29), |-49|$

CHALLENGE Tell whether the statement is *always, sometimes,* or *never* true. *Justify* your answer.

41. The absolute value of a number x is greater than or equal to x.

42. The opposite of a number y is greater than or equal to y.

43. The absolute value of a number z is less than the opposite of z.

PROBLEM SOLVING

ELEVATION In Exercises 44 and 45, use the table at the right showing elevations of lakes.

Lakes	Elevation (ft)
Jones Lake	−30
Silver Lake	90
Gieselmann Lake	−162
Seneca Lake	445
Craigs Pond	0

SEE EXAMPLE 1 on p. 57 for Exs. 44–45

44. Which lake is at a lower elevation, Gieselmann Lake or Silver Lake?

45. Arrange the lakes in order from least to greatest elevation.

46. ★ **SHORT RESPONSE** What numbers have opposites that are the same as their absolute values? What numbers have opposites that are different from their absolute values? Use examples to support your answer.

47. ★ **MULTIPLE CHOICE** The Java Trench in the Indian Ocean lies 7725 meters below sea level. Which number represents this elevation in meters?

Ⓐ -7725 Ⓑ $-(-7725)$ Ⓒ $|-7725|$ Ⓓ $|7725|$

48. LAUNCH COUNTDOWN Put the following activities for a shuttle launch in the order in which they occur. "T−5 minutes" means 5 minutes before liftoff.

Count	Activity
T–5 minutes	Pilot starts auxiliary power units.
T+7 seconds	Shuttle clears launch tower, and control switches to the Mission Control Center.
T–2 hours, 55 minutes	Flight crew departs for launch pad.
T–6 seconds	Main engine starts.
T–0	Liftoff.

Animated Math at classzone.com

49. NUMBER SENSE A is a point on a number line halfway between -11 and 5. B is a point halfway between A and 3. What point on the number line is B?

50. ★ **WRITING** *Explain* why no value of x makes the equation $|x| = -8$ true.

51. **REASONING** Suppose $|a| < |b|$. What are the possible relationships between a and b?

52. **MULTI-STEP PROBLEM** The bar graph shows the quarterly earnings at a store in four quarters of one year.

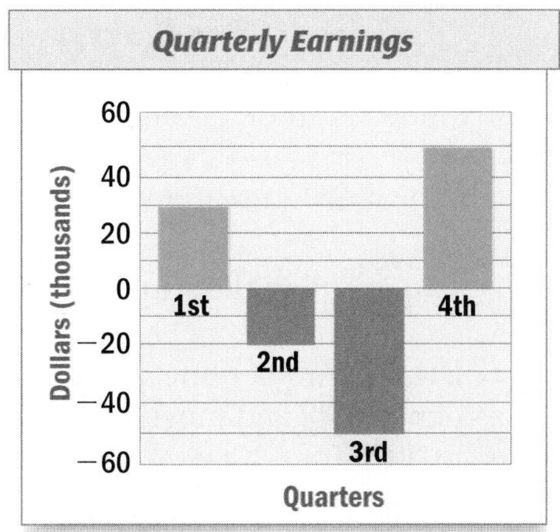

   a. Which quarters showed gains? Write a positive integer to represent these earnings.

   b. Which quarters showed losses? Write a negative integer to represent these earnings.

   c. Did the gains balance the losses? Did the store make a profit for the year? *Explain* your reasoning.

Kaya

53. **BOILING POINTS** The table below shows the substances in a solution and their boiling points in degrees Celsius. Order the substances from lowest boiling point to highest boiling point. If you heat the solution, which substance will you expect to be left at the end of the heating? *Explain* your reasoning.

Solution	*Ethanol*	*Water*	*Propanol*	*Methanol*
Boiling Point	$\|-78\|$	$-(-100)$	97	$\|-65\|$

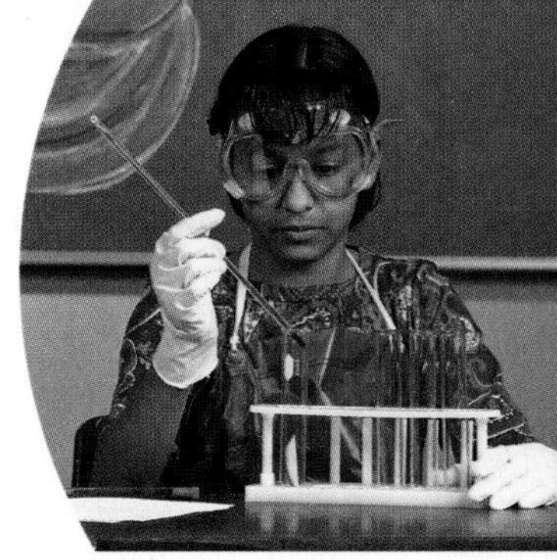

54. **CHALLENGE** A newspaper reports these changes in the price of a stock during a 5 month period: -1, -8, $+2$, -4, and $+6$. The stock price ended at \$35 in the fifth month. Use a number line to show the price of the stock at the beginning of the 5 month period.

MIXED REVIEW

Prepare for Lesson 2.2 in Exs. 55–57

Evaluate the expression when $a = 8$ and $b = 2$. *(p. 13)*

55. $a + 6$

56. $b + 15$

57. $5 + a + b$

58. Patty needs to read a 238 page book in 6 days. By the end of the first day she has read 68 pages. How many pages does she need to read each of the remaining days to finish the book on time? *(p. 37)*

59. ★ **MULTIPLE CHOICE** You have \$118. You earn \$10 an hour doing yard work for a neighbor. How much money do you have if you work for 3 hours? *(p. 772)*

   Ⓐ \$30   Ⓑ \$88   Ⓒ \$148   Ⓓ \$418

INVESTIGATION

Use before Lesson 2.2

GOAL
Model integer addition on a number line.

MATERIALS
- pencil
- paper

2.2 Adding Integers

You can model addition of integers by using a number line.

EXPLORE **Find the sum $-15 + 11$.**

STEP 1 **Draw** a number line, place a pencil at 0, and move 15 units to the left to show -15.

STEP 2 **Move** 11 units to the right to show the sum of -15 and 11.

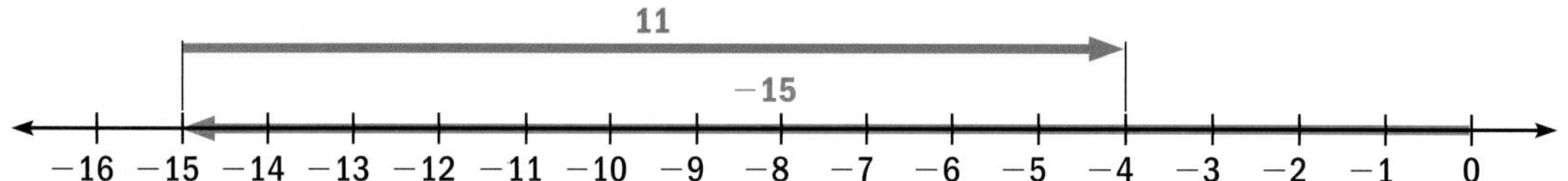

STEP 3 The final position is -4. So, $-15 + 11 = -4$.

PRACTICE **Write an addition expression to represent the figure. Then evaluate the expression.**

1.

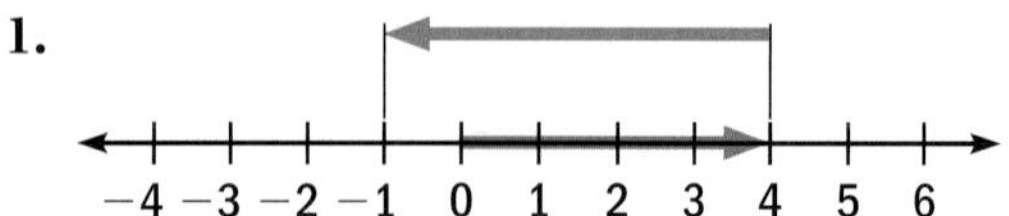

2.

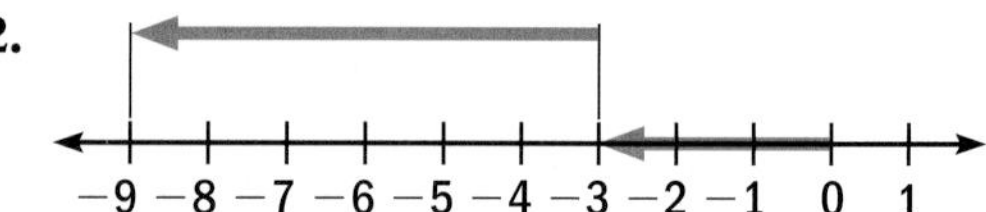

Use a number line to find the sum.

3. $-7 + (-14)$
4. $20 + (-25)$
5. $-10 + 15$
6. $-7 + (-33)$
7. $11 + (-13)$
8. $-23 + 5$
9. $-18 + (-12)$
10. $16 + (-17)$

DRAW CONCLUSIONS

11. The sum of two positive integers is always positive. What is the sign of the sum of two negative integers? *Explain* your answer using a number line.

12. **REASONING** How can you predict the sign of the sum of a positive integer and a negative integer before you add the numbers?

13. **WRITING** Write the steps you use to evaluate $25 + (-13) + 5 + (-20)$. Then evaluate the expression.

2.2 Adding Integers

Before You added whole numbers.
Now You'll add integers.
Why? So you can find total scores, as in Ex. 57.

KEY VOCABULARY
- **integer,** *p. 57*
- **absolute value,** *p. 58*
- **additive identity,** *p. 64*
- **additive inverse,** *p. 64*
- **sum,** *p. 764*

You can use a number line to add integers.

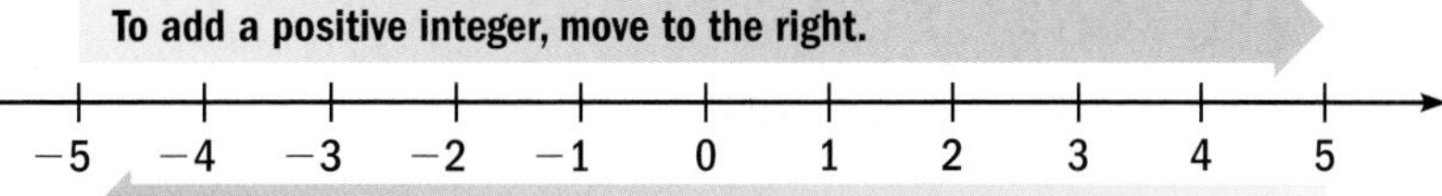

EXAMPLE 1 Adding Integers Using a Number Line

Use a number line to find the sum.

a. $5 + (-8)$ **b.** $-6 + 10$ **c.** $-4 + (-3)$

a. Start at 0. Move **5** units to the right. Then move **8** units to the left.

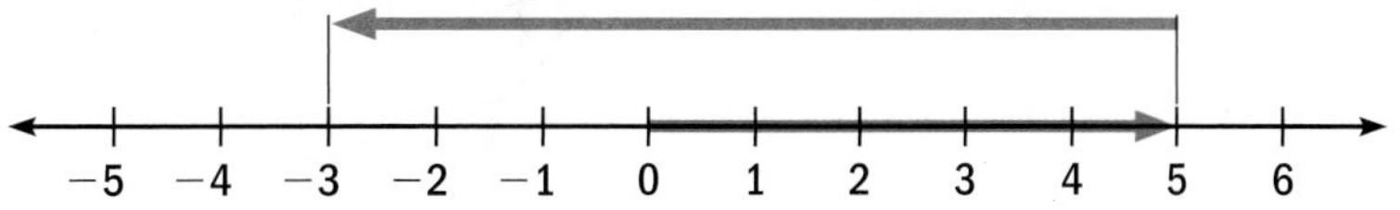

▸ **Answer** The final position is -3. So, $5 + (-8) = -3$.

b. Start at 0. Move **6** units to the left. Then move **10** units to the right.

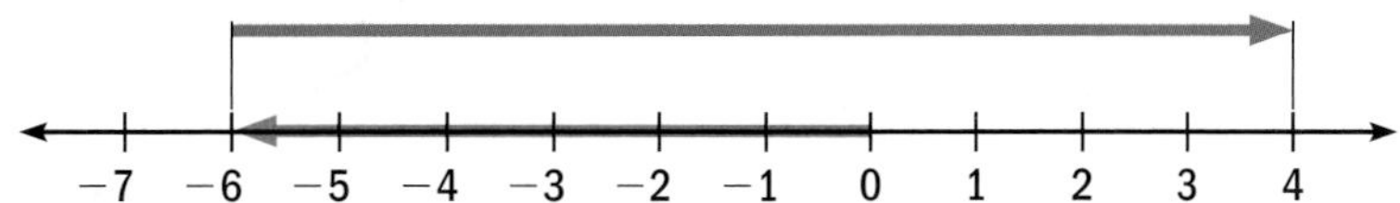

▸ **Answer** The final position is 4. So, $-6 + 10 = 4$.

c. Start at 0. Move **4** units to the left. Then move **3** units to the left.

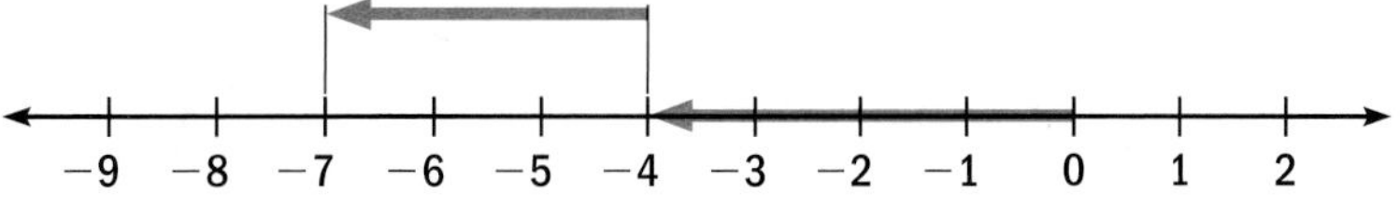

▸ **Answer** The final position is -7. So, $-4 + (-3) = -7$.

✓ GUIDED PRACTICE for Example 1

1. Use a number line. Find $-8 + 4$.
2. Find $-1 + (-6)$.

KEY CONCEPT — For Your Notebook

Adding Integers

You can add integers without using a number line by following these rules.

Same sign

Add the absolute values and use the common sign.

Different signs

Subtract the lesser absolute value from the greater absolute value. Use the sign of the number with the greater absolute value.

EXAMPLE 2 Adding Integers

Find the sum $-12 + 4$.

$-12 + 4 = -8$ ← **Different signs, so subtract $|4|$ from $|-12|$.**

↑ **Use sign of number with greater absolute value.**

Check Use a number line to find the sum.

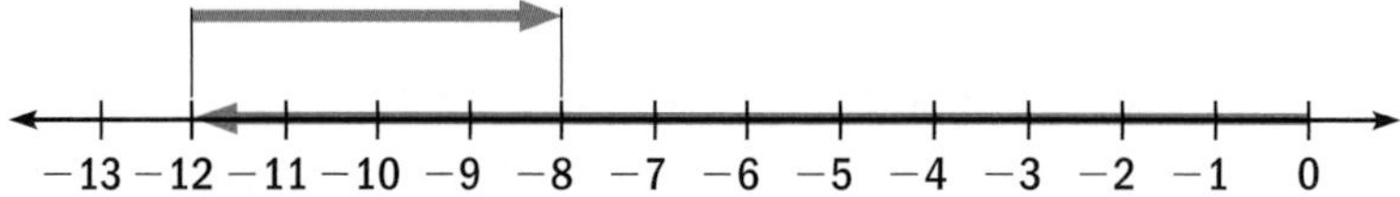

KEY CONCEPT — For Your Notebook

Addition Properties

Identity Property of Addition

Words The sum of a number and the **additive identity**, 0, is the number.

Numbers $-3 + 0 = -3$ **Algebra** $a + 0 = a$

Inverse Property of Addition

Words The sum of a number and its **additive inverse**, or opposite, is 0.

Numbers $5 + (-5) = 0$ **Algebra** $a + (-a) = 0$

EXAMPLE 3 Adding More Than Two Integers

Find the sum using the order of operations.

$(-7 + 7) + (-8) + (-5) = \mathbf{0} + (-8) + (-5)$	**Inverse property of addition**
$= -8 + (-5)$	**Identity property of addition**
$= -13$	**Same sign, so sum has common sign**

EXAMPLE 4 Adding More Than Two Integers

School Fair Your class has a fair to raise money for a field trip. The table shows the incomes and expenses for the fair. How much money was raised?

Games	\$750
Display tables	\$625
Donations	\$36
Advertising	−\$16
Decorations	−\$60
Game rentals	−\$500

ANOTHER WAY
You can also add the numbers in order from left to right or look for compatible numbers, such as 750 and −500, to make the calculation easier.

SOLUTION

First, add the positive integers. Then add the negative integers.

$$750 + 625 + 36 + (-16) + (-60) + (-500) = 1411 + (-576)$$
$$= 835$$

▶ **Answer** Your class raised \$835.

✓ GUIDED PRACTICE for Examples 2, 3, and 4

Find the sum. Identify any addition properties you use.

3. $-20 + (-15)$
4. $18 + 0 + (-54)$
5. $300 + 111 + (-44) + (-256)$
6. $-230 + (-512) + 178 + 94$
7. **What If?** Suppose in Example 4 that games made \$825 and the decorations cost \$100. How much money did your class raise?

2.2 EXERCISES

HOMEWORK KEY
★ = **STANDARDIZED TEST PRACTICE** Exs. 11, 36, 53, 54, 56, and 65
◯ = **HINTS AND HOMEWORK HELP** for Exs. 3, 9, 13, 17, 53 at classzone.com

SKILL PRACTICE

1. **VOCABULARY** Copy and complete: To add two integers with the same sign, add the __?__ and use the common sign.

ADDING WITH A NUMBER LINE **Use a number line to find the sum.**

SEE EXAMPLE 1 on p. 63 for Exs. 2–10

2. $-6 + 8$
3. $-3 + (-9)$
4. $5 + (-7)$
5. $-4 + 4$
6. $-2 + (-1)$
7. $-10 + (-9)$
8. $-3 + 7$
9. $7 + (-5)$
10. **ERROR ANALYSIS** Describe and correct the error made in finding the sum of −8 and 5.

✗ $-8 + 5 = -13$

SEE EXAMPLES 2, 3, AND 4 on pp. 64–65 for Exs. 11–23

11. ★ **MULTIPLE CHOICE** Evaluate $-8 + 3$.

(A) -11 (B) -5 (C) 5 (D) 11

ADDING INTEGERS **Find the sum. Identify any addition properties you use.**

12. $42 + (-23)$	(13.) $-63 + (-49)$	14. $-93 + (-16)$
15. $25 + (-25)$	16. $0 + (-82)$	(17.) $98 + (-128)$
18. $-9 + 9 + (-14)$	19. $-12 + 9 + (-5)$	20. $20 + (-15) + (-22)$
21. $-12 + (-25) + 8$	22. $-21 + (-15) + (-25)$	23. $-17 + 8 + 16$

Animated Math at classzone.com

EVALUATING EXPRESSIONS **Evaluate when $a = -13$, $b = 24$, and $c = -27$.**

24. $a + b$	25. $b + c$	26. $-b + c$	27. $a + (-b)$
28. $a + \lvert c \rvert$	29. $b + \lvert a \rvert$	30. $\lvert a \rvert + \lvert c \rvert$	31. $\lvert c \rvert + \lvert b \rvert$

ALGEBRA **Evaluate $x + (-478)$ using the given value of x.**

32. $x = 806$	33. $x = -729$	34. $x = \lvert -349 \rvert$	35. $x = -\lvert -521 \rvert$

36. ★ **OPEN-ENDED MATH** Name two integers with the same sign that have a sum of -28. Name two integers with different signs that have a sum of -28.

REASONING **Tell whether the sum of the two integers is *always*, *sometimes*, or *never* negative. *Justify* your answer.**

37. two negative integers	38. two positive integers
39. a positive integer and a negative integer	40. a negative integer and zero

MENTAL MATH **Solve the equation using mental math.**

41. $-92 + k = 102$	42. $-6 = x + (-7)$	43. $-9 = 5 + j$	44. $-81 + b = -90$

CHALLENGE **Find the value(s) of x that make the equation true.**

45. $\lvert x \rvert + (-13) = 29$	46. $\lvert x \rvert + (-45) = -12$	47. $-123 + \lvert x \rvert = -98$

PROBLEM SOLVING

CHEMISTRY **A proton has a charge of $+1$, and an electron has a charge of -1. Find the sum of the charges.**

48. Sodium: 11 protons, 10 electrons	49. Chlorine: 17 protons, 17 electrons
50. Oxide: 8 protons, 10 electrons	51. Phosphorus: 15 protons, 12 electrons

52. **ELEVATORS** You enter an elevator on the sixth floor. The elevator goes up 3 floors and then down 5 floors, where you exit. Write and evaluate an addition expression to find the floor on which you exit.

53. ★ **MULTIPLE CHOICE** A bank statement for January is shown. What is the sum of the transactions in this month?

Ⓐ −$30 Ⓑ $30

Ⓒ $20 Ⓓ $90

Central Savings	
January 5	+$25
January 6	−$30
January 15	+$35

54. ★ **WRITING** You want to add a positive integer and a negative integer. How do you choose the sign of your answer? *Explain.*

55. **MULTI-STEP PROBLEM** The classic Mexican period began around 200 B.C. and lasted for 1100 years. The classic Greek period began in 500 B.C. and lasted for 200 years.

a. About what year did the classic Mexican period end?

b. About what year did the classic Greek period end?

c. About how many years after the classic Greek period ended did the classic Mexican period end?

Classical Mexican art

SEE EXAMPLE 4 on p. 65 for Ex. 56–57

56. ★ **SHORT RESPONSE** A football team gained 7 yards on the first play, lost 9 yards on the second play, and gained 6 yards on the third play. To get a first down, they must gain 10 yards in 4 plays. How many yards must they gain on the fourth play to get a first down? *Explain* your reasoning.

57. **MINIATURE GOLF** *Par* is the number of strokes considered necessary to get the ball in the hole. A player's score for each hole is the number of strokes above or below par. The total score is the sum of the scores for each hole. Is Jill's score for the first 8 holes *above par, under par,* or *at par*? What score does she need next to be at par for the first 9 holes?

HOLE	1	2	3	4	5	6	7	8	9	OUT
PAR	4	5	3	3	5	4	3	5	3	35
Jill	0	+1	−2	−1	0	+1	+2	+1	?	

58. **CHALLENGE** Does $|x + y| = |x| + |y|$ if x and y are both positive? both negative? What if x is positive and y is negative? *Explain.*

MIXED REVIEW

Get-Ready Prepare for Lesson 2.3 in Exs. 59–62

Find the opposite of the number. *(p. 57)*

59. 34 **60.** 187 **61.** −2321 **62.** −4650

Order the integers from least to greatest. *(p. 57)*

63. −2479, 1802, 2479, −1802 **64.** −346, −125, −921, 724, 128

65. ★ **MULTIPLE CHOICE** In what order should the operations be performed in the expression $3 + 7 \times 4 \div 2 - 6$? *(p. 8)*

Ⓐ ×, −, ÷, + Ⓑ +, ×, ÷, − Ⓒ ×, ÷, +, − Ⓓ +, −, ×, ÷

2.3 Subtracting Integers

Before You added integers.
Now You'll subtract integers.
Why? So you can find lengths of time, as in Ex. 49.

KEY VOCABULARY
- **integer,** *p. 57*
- **opposite,** *p. 58*
- **difference,** *p. 764*

ACTIVITY

You can use patterns to discover a rule for subtracting integers.

STEP 1 **Copy** the table below. In the second column, write the answer to the subtraction problem. Use a pattern to find the differences involving negative integers.

STEP 2 **Complete** the addition problem in the third column so the sum is equal to the number in the difference column.

Subtraction Problem	Difference	Addition Problem
$3 - 3$	0	$3 + (-3)$
$3 - 2$	?	$3 + ?$
$3 - 1$	?	$3 + ?$
$3 - 0$	?	$3 + ?$
$3 - (-1)$	?	$3 + ?$
$3 - (-2)$	?	$3 + ?$
$3 - (-3)$	?	$3 + ?$

STEP 3 **Tell** how the second number in the addition problems relates to the second number in the subtraction problems.

STEP 4 **Describe** how to use addition to subtract integers.

In the activity above, you may have observed that when you subtract integers you can write the expression as an addition expression and then use the rules for adding integers.

KEY CONCEPT *For Your Notebook*

Subtracting Integers

Words To subtract an integer, add its opposite.

Numbers $3 - 7 = 3 + (-7) = -4$
$2 - (-6) = 2 + 6 = 8$

Algebra $a - b = a + (-b)$
$a - (-b) = a + b$

EXAMPLE 1 Subtracting Integers

a. $-56 - (-9) = -56 + 9$ — **Add the opposite of −9.**

$= -47$ — **Add.**

b. $-14 - 21 = -14 + (-21)$ — **Add the opposite of 21.**

$= -35$ — **Add.**

EXAMPLE 2 Evaluating a Variable Expression

Evaluate $15 - a - b$ when $a = 24$ and $b = -36$.

$15 - a - b = 15 - 24 - (-36)$ — **Substitute 24 for *a* and −36 for *b*.**

$= 15 + (-24) + 36$ — **Add the opposite of 24 and of −36.**

$= -9 + 36$ — **Add 15 and −24.**

$= 27$ — **Add −9 and 36.**

EXAMPLE 3 Standardized Test Practice

Oceanography The SOFAR (*SO*und *F*ixing *A*nd *R*anging) channel is a layer of water in the oceans, as shown at the right, that allows sounds to travel extremely long distances. What is the vertical height of the SOFAR channel?

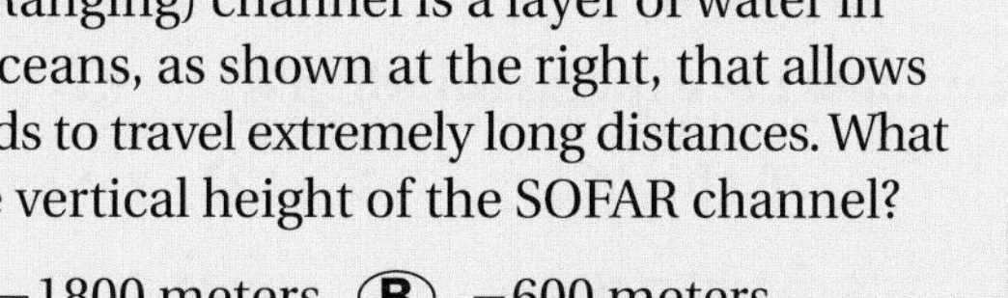

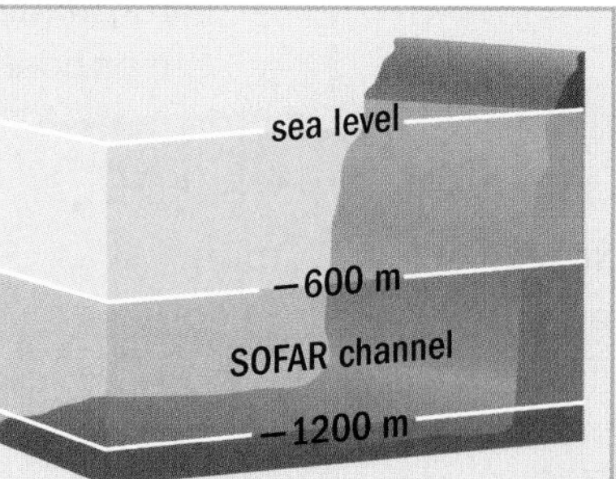

Ⓐ −1800 meters Ⓑ −600 meters

Ⓒ 600 meters Ⓓ 1800 meters

ELIMINATE CHOICES

A height is always a positive number. So, you can eliminate choices A and B.

SOLUTION

The height is the difference of the upper and lower elevations.

Vertical height $= -600 - (-1200)$ — **Write subtraction statement.**

$= -600 + 1200$ — **Add the opposite of −1200.**

$= 600$ — **Add.**

▶ **Answer** The height of the SOFAR channel is 600 meters. The correct answer is C. Ⓐ Ⓑ Ⓒ Ⓓ

GUIDED PRACTICE for Examples 1, 2, and 3

Evaluate the expression.

1. $15 - 41$

2. $-16 - 8$

3. $a - b - (-6);\ a = 8,\ b = -15$

4. Distance What is the difference in elevation between 4 feet above sea level and 30 feet below sea level?

2.3 EXERCISES

HOMEWORK KEY

★ = **STANDARDIZED TEST PRACTICE**
Exs. 27, 36, 43, 47, 48, and 60

○ = **HINTS AND HOMEWORK HELP**
for Exs. 5, 13, 19, 25, 43 at classzone.com

SKILL PRACTICE

VOCABULARY **Write the verbal phrase as a numerical expression.**

1. The difference of negative two and six
2. The difference of the opposite of five and the opposite of three

SUBTRACTING INTEGERS **Find the difference.**

SEE EXAMPLE 1 on p. 69 for Exs. 3–18

3. $5 - 12$ **4.** $6 - (-16)$ **5.** $-11 - (-7)$

6. $-13 - 12$ **7.** $-14 - (-14)$ **8.** $11 - (-6)$

9. $9 - 17$ **10.** $-18 - (-12)$ **11.** $-20 - 7$

12. $32 - 40$ **13.** $28 - (-16)$ **14.** $-39 - (-13)$

15. $-5 - (-5) - (-5)$ **16.** $8 - 2 - 6 - 10$ **17.** $-52 - (-18) - 37$

18. **ERROR ANALYSIS** Describe and correct the error made in finding the difference between the opposite of 12 and 5.

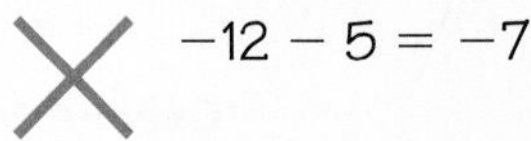

ALGEBRA **Evaluate the expression when $a = -9$, $b = 18$, and $c = -4$.**

SEE EXAMPLE 2 on p. 69 for Exs. 19–27

19. $a - 6$ **20.** $b - c$ **21.** $a - c$ **22.** $14 - a - b$

23. $a - b - c$ **24.** $c - a - b$ **25.** $a + b - c$ **26.** $c - a + b$

27. ★ **MULTIPLE CHOICE** Evaluate the expression $-c + 2a - b$ when $a = 5$, $b = -9$, and $c = 3$.

Ⓐ −2 Ⓑ 4 Ⓒ 16 Ⓓ 22

SOLVING EQUATIONS **Use mental math to solve the equation.**

28. $35 - x = 45$ **29.** $-32 - x = -37$ **30.** $-49 = 50 - x$ **31.** $x - 11 = -3$

32. $-56 = x - 52$ **33.** $-36 = x - 24$ **34.** $16 = 12 - x$ **35.** $64 - x = -37$

36. ★ **OPEN-ENDED MATH** Give an example of two integers with the same sign that have a difference of −9. Give an example of two integers with different signs that have a difference of −9.

37. **REASONING** Are the expressions $x - y$ and $y - x$ always opposites? *Explain* your reasoning.

CHALLENGE **Copy and complete the statement using *always, sometimes,* or *never. Justify* your reasoning.**

38. A positive number minus a negative number is _?_ negative.

39. A negative number minus a negative number is _?_ positive.

PROBLEM SOLVING

SEE EXAMPLE 3 on p. 69 for Exs. 40, 43

40. **GUIDED PROBLEM SOLVING** Find the distances between the bird and the boat, the boat and the reef, and the bird and the reef.

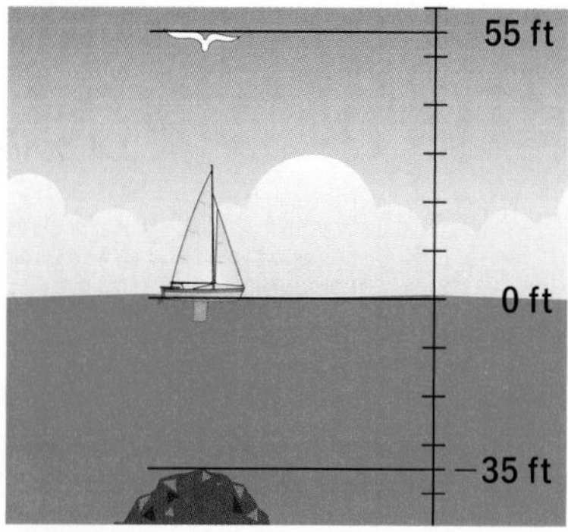

a. Identify which elevation is greater for each situation above.

b. Subtract the lesser elevation from the greater elevation.

c. Answer the original question by completing each statement.

The bird is __?__ feet above the boat.

The boat is __?__ feet above the reef.

The bird is __?__ feet above the reef.

GAME SHOW Bobby Joe is on a game show and has −400 points. He has one question left. Find his total score after the given scenario.

41. He answers the question incorrectly and loses 600 points.

42. He answers the question correctly and gains 600 points.

43. ★ **MULTIPLE CHOICE** A whale that is 660 feet below sea level rises up and breaches out of the water to a height of 32 feet above sea level. What is the vertical distance the whale travels?

Ⓐ −628 feet Ⓑ 628 feet

Ⓒ 660 feet Ⓓ 692 feet

44. **REASONING** *Explain* how you can find the distance between the points on the number line using subtraction.

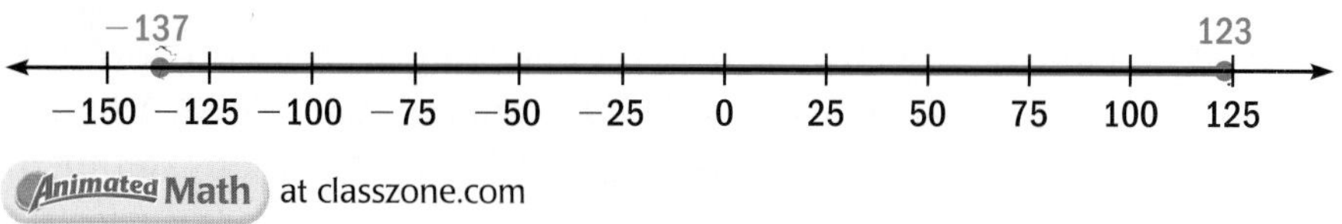

at classzone.com

TEMPERATURES In Exercises 45–47, use the given table.

45. How much colder is Alaska's coldest temperature than Kentucky's?

46. How much colder is Colorado's coldest temperature than Mississippi's?

47. ★ **SHORT RESPONSE** Which two states have the greatest difference in coldest temperatures? Which two states have the least difference in coldest temperatures? *Justify* your answer.

Coldest Recorded Temperatures

State	*Temperature*
Alaska	−80°F
Colorado	−61°F
Kentucky	−37°F
Mississippi	−19°F

48. ★ **WRITING** *Explain* why you add an integer's opposite when you are subtracting integers.

49. **DINOSAURS** The table shows the ranges of three dinosaur periods during the Mesozoic Era. Which period lasted 64 million years? About what fraction of the three periods did that period last?

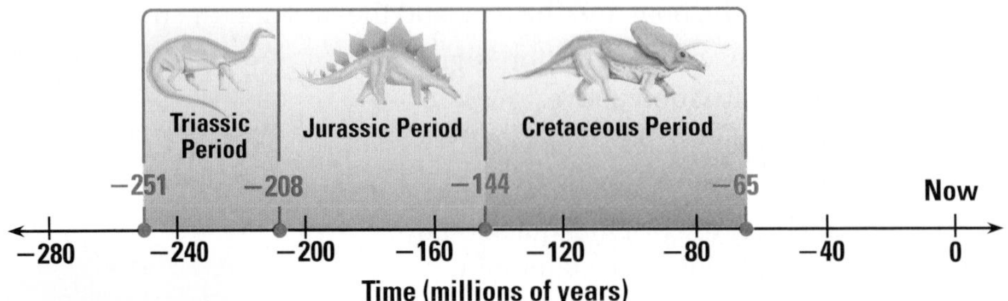

READING *IN* MATH **Read the information below for Exercises 50–52.**

Lunar Temperatures The Moon has no atmosphere, which results in the Moon experiencing extreme temperatures. During the day, it can reach a high temperature of 265°F. At night, the temperature can reach a low of −170°F. The highest temperature ever recorded on Earth is 136°F and the lowest temperature recorded on Earth is −129°F.

50. **Compare** What is the difference between the high temperatures on the Moon and on Earth?

51. **Compare** What is the difference between the low temperatures on the Moon and on Earth?

52. **Interpret** What is the range of temperatures on the Moon? How does this compare with the range of temperatures on Earth? *Explain* how the lack of an atmosphere might cause the greater range of temperatures on the Moon.

53. **CHALLENGE** Craig had \$150 in his checking account on April 1. He wrote 3 checks in April, one for \$47 and another for \$63. He did not record the amount of the third check. He received a statement stating that he overdrew his account by \$23. What was the amount on the third check that he wrote?

MIXED REVIEW

Prepare for Lesson 2.4 in Exs. 54–56

Evaluate the expression. ***(p. 19)***

54. $5^3 + (21 \cdot 7) - 6$

55. $6^2 \cdot (4 - 2) \div 18$

56. $(12 - 4) \cdot (9 - 1)^2$

Solve the equation using mental math. ***(p. 26)***

57. $v + 5 = 13$

58. $7w = 42$

59. $12 - x = 9$

60. ★ **MULTIPLE CHOICE** What is the sum $11 + (-9)$? ***(p. 63)***

Ⓐ −20 Ⓑ −2 Ⓒ 2 Ⓓ 20

2.4 Multiplying Integers

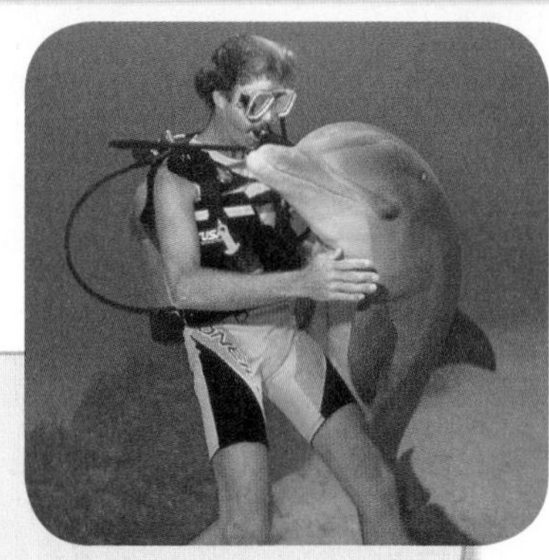

Before	You added and subtracted integers.
Now	You'll multiply integers.
Why?	So you can find positions of objects, as in Example 1.

KEY VOCABULARY

- **integer,** *p. 57*
- **multiplicative identity,** *p. 74*
- **product,** *p. 768*

Diving A diver is swimming downward to explore a coral reef. The diver's depth is changing by -2 feet per second. The diver started at sea level. What is the diver's position relative to sea level after 10 seconds? after 30 seconds?

To find the position, you can multiply integers. When you multiply integers, the sign of the product depends on the signs of the factors.

KEY CONCEPT *For Your Notebook*

Multiplying Integers

Words	Numbers
Same Sign The product of two integers with the same sign is positive.	$4 \cdot 2 = 8$ $-3 \cdot (-7) = 21$
Different Sign The product of two integers with different signs is negative.	$4 \cdot (-2) = -8$ $-3 \cdot 7 = -21$

EXAMPLE 1 Multiplying Integers

a. To find the diver's position relative to sea level after 10 seconds, use the distance formula $d = rt$.

$d = rt$ — **Write the distance formula.**

$d = -2(10)$ — **Substitute -2 for r and 10 for t.**

$d = -20$ — **Different signs, so product is negative.**

▸ **Answer** The diver's position relative to sea level is -20 feet.

b. Find the diver's position relative to sea level after 30 seconds.

$d = rt$ — **Write the distance formula.**

$d = -2(30)$ — **Substitute -2 for r and 30 for t.**

$d = -60$ — **Different signs, so product is negative.**

▸ **Answer** The diver's position relative to sea level is -60 feet.

Properties You can use the following properties when multiplying.

KEY CONCEPT *For Your Notebook*

Multiplication Properties

Multiplication Property of Zero

Words The product of a number and 0 is 0.

Numbers $-4 \cdot 0 = 0$ **Algebra** For any value of a, $a \cdot 0 = 0$.

Identity Property of Multiplication

Words The product of a number and the **multiplicative identity**, 1, is the number.

Numbers $4(1) = 4$ **Algebra** For any value of a, $a(1) = a$.

EXAMPLE 2 Multiplying Two or More Integers

AVOID ERRORS
If a product has an even number of negative factors, it is positive. If a product has an odd number of negative factors, it is negative.

a. $-1(6) = -6$ Different signs, so product is negative.

b. $-8(-2) = 16$ Same sign, so product is positive.

c. $-15(0) = 0$ Product of an integer and 0 is 0.

d. $4(-10)(-12) = -40(-12)$ Multiply from left to right.

$= 480$ Multiply.

EXAMPLE 3 Evaluating an Expression with Integers

Evaluate $a^2 + 3b$ when $a = -5$ and $b = -11$.

$a^2 + 3b = (-5)^2 + 3(-11)$ Substitute -5 for a and -11 for b.

$= 25 + 3(-11)$ Evaluate the power.

$= 25 + (-33)$ Multiply.

$= -8$ Add.

at classzone.com

✓ GUIDED PRACTICE for Examples 1, 2, and 3

1. **What If?** In Example 1, what is the diver's position relative to sea level after 13 seconds?

Find the product.

2. $-1(4)$
3. $7(0)$
4. $-6(-11)$
5. $-1(-12)(-9)$

Evaluate the expression when $a = 3$, $b = -4$, and $c = -8$.

6. $ac - b$
7. $ac + b$
8. $a^2 + bc$
9. $ab - c^2$

2.4 EXERCISES

HOMEWORK KEY

★ = **STANDARDIZED TEST PRACTICE** Exs. 40, 56, 58, 59, and 66

○ = **HINTS AND HOMEWORK HELP** for Exs. 5, 17, 25, 31, 55 at classzone.com

SKILL PRACTICE

1. **VOCABULARY** Copy and complete: The product of a positive integer and a negative integer is a _?_ integer.

2. **VOCABULARY** Copy and complete: The product of two integers with the same sign is _?_.

MULTIPLYING INTEGERS Find the product. Identify any properties you use.

SEE EXAMPLES 1 AND 2 on pp. 73–74 for Exs. 3–23

3. $-4(-7)$ 4. $0(-9)$ 5. $-3(6)$ 6. $8(-5)$
7. $-6(7)$ 8. $-1(-17)$ 9. $0(-13)$ 10. $-4(-11)$
11. $9(-2)$ 12. $3(-5)$ 13. $-15(-12)$ 14. $1(-32)$
15. $-1(-2)(-3)$ 16. $2(-4)(5)$ 17. $10(-9)(-3)$ 18. $-7(-9)(-6)$
19. $-2(5)(-6)$ 20. $6(-4)(12)$ 21. $-8(-7)(-5)$ 22. $12(0)(-45)$

23. **ERROR ANALYSIS** Describe and correct the error made in finding the product of -8 and -12.

✗ $-8(-12) = -96$

EVALUATING EXPRESSIONS Evaluate the expression when $x = -9$, $y = -7$, and $z = -4$.

SEE EXAMPLE 3 on p. 74 for Exs. 24–35

24. xy 25. y^2 26. $2xyz$ 27. $-3z^2$
28. $-x(-x)$ 29. $z(-y^2)$ 30. $3xy - yz$ 31. $x + 2y^2 - z$
32. $x^2 + y$ 33. $z - y^2$ 34. $[x + (-x)y]^2$ 35. $xz^2 - (-y)^2z$

USING ABSOLUTE VALUE Find the product.

36. $-12 \cdot |11|$ 37. $-7(-8) \cdot |-4|$ 38. $10(-4) \cdot |13|$ 39. $|8| \cdot |-14| \cdot 3$

40. ★ **MULTIPLE CHOICE** What is the value of the expression $-4(-8) \cdot |-3|$?

Ⓐ -96 Ⓑ -36 Ⓒ 12 Ⓓ 96

MENTAL MATH Use mental math to solve the equation.

41. $2x = -8$ 42. $-21y = 63$ 43. $-5(-4)z = -80$ 44. $-4a = -20$
45. $130 = -13b$ 46. $6(-8)k = -96$ 47. $-36 = 9a$ 48. $7(-3)m = -21$

49. **REASONING** Does $(-3)^2$ equal -3^2? *Explain* your reasoning.

CHALLENGE What are the next three numbers of the sequence? Write a rule using the variable n for the nth number in the list.

50. $-2, 4, -6, 8, \ldots$ 51. $5, 10, 15, 20, \ldots$ 52. $-3, 9, -27, 81, \ldots$

PROBLEM SOLVING

SEE EXAMPLE 1 on p. 73 for Ex. 53

53. FINDING DEPTH A coin is tossed off a boat into the ocean. The coin's depth changes by −8 inches per second. Determine the depth of the coin 12 seconds after it hits the water.

54. BANKING You have \$500 in a savings account. Over a 2 month period, you make 9 withdrawals of \$30 each. What is your new balance?

55. VIDEO GAME David is playing a video game. If he falls into a pit, he loses 125 points. He has 400 points before he falls into 5 pits. Write and evaluate an expression to find how many points he now has.

56. ★ SHORT RESPONSE A coconut falls 64 feet from a palm tree. The equation $h = -16t^2 + 64$ gives the height h, in feet, of the coconut after falling for t seconds. Evaluate the equation when t equals 1, 2, and 3 seconds. After how many seconds does the coconut hit the ground?

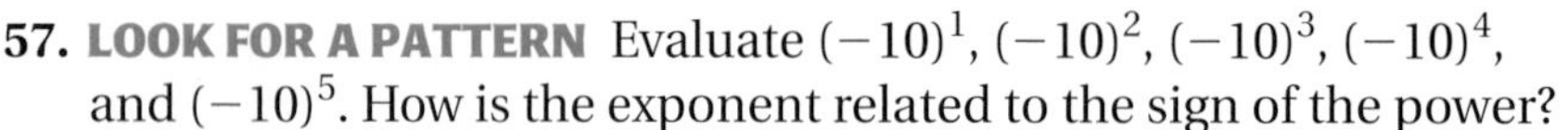

57. LOOK FOR A PATTERN Evaluate $(-10)^1$, $(-10)^2$, $(-10)^3$, $(-10)^4$, and $(-10)^5$. How is the exponent related to the sign of the power?

58. ★ WRITING When multiplying integers other than zero, explain why the product is negative when there is an odd number of negative factors. Why is it positive when there is an even number of negative factors?

59. ★ MULTIPLE CHOICE When you multiply an integer less than 1 and an integer less than −1, the product is which of the following?

(A) less than zero (B) greater than zero

(C) less than or equal to zero (D) greater than or equal to zero

60. STOCK MARKET Your uncle owns 25 shares of stock A, 45 shares of stock B, and 60 shares of stock C. In one day, the price per share changed by +56¢ for stock A, −\$2 for stock B, and −56¢ for stock C. Find the total change, in dollars, of the value of your uncle's stock.

61. CHALLENGE Mount Everest is 8850 meters tall. The temperature falls at a rate of 1°C per 100 meters. The base is at an elevation of 5400 meters and its temperature is −3°C. Write and evaluate an expression to find the temperature at the top of the mountain. What is the temperature?

MIXED REVIEW

Get-Ready

Prepare for Lesson 2.5 in Exs. 62–65

Find the quotient. If necessary, round to the nearest thousandth. *(p. 770)*

62. 75 ÷ 5.5 **63.** 0.85 ÷ 12 **64.** 3.4 ÷ 17 **65.** 6.32 ÷ 7

66. ★ MULTIPLE CHOICE What is the side length of a square with a perimeter of 64 feet? *(p. 32)*

(A) 4 feet (B) 8 feet (C) 16 feet (D) 252 feet

2.5 Dividing Integers

Before You added, subtracted, and multiplied integers.

Now You'll divide integers.

Why? So you can find means of profits, as in Ex. 38.

KEY VOCABULARY

• **mean,** *p. 78*

You will use the rules for dividing integers to find an average temperature in Example 2. Because division is the opposite of multiplication, these rules are similar to the rules for multiplying integers.

KEY CONCEPT *For Your Notebook*

Dividing Integers

Words	Numbers	
Same Sign The quotient of two integers with the same sign is positive.	$\frac{12}{6} = 2$	$\frac{-12}{-6} = 2$
Different Sign The quotient of two integers with different signs is negative.	$\frac{12}{-6} = -2$	$\frac{-12}{6} = -2$
Zero The quotient of 0 and any nonzero integer is 0.	$\frac{0}{12} = 0$	$\frac{0}{-12} = 0$

EXAMPLE 1 Dividing Integers

a. $\frac{-40}{-8} = 5$ **Same sign, so quotient is positive.**

b. $\frac{-14}{2} = -7$ **Different signs, so quotient is negative.**

c. $\frac{36}{-9} = -4$ **Different signs, so quotient is negative.**

d. $\frac{0}{-7} = 0$ **Dividend is 0 so quotient is 0.**

AVOID ERRORS

You cannot divide a number by 0. Any number divided by 0 is *undefined.*

✓ GUIDED PRACTICE for Example 1

Find the quotient, if possible.

1. $\frac{-33}{11}$ **2.** $\frac{-25}{-5}$ **3.** $\frac{0}{-4}$

4. $\frac{72}{-9}$ **5.** $\frac{-36}{18}$ **6.** $\frac{-28}{0}$

The **mean** of a data set is the sum of the values divided by the number of values.

$$\textbf{mean} = \frac{\textbf{sum of values}}{\textbf{number of values}}$$

EXAMPLE 2 Finding a Mean

Temperatures One of the coldest places on Earth is the Russian town of Verkhoyansk, located near the Arctic Circle. Find the mean of the average high temperatures during winter in Verkhoyansk. Use the data in the table.

Winter Temperatures				
Month	Dec	Jan	Feb	Mar
Average High	−41°F	−40°F	−48°F	−18°F

SOLUTION

STEP 1 **Find** the sum of the temperatures.

$$-41 + (-40) + (-48) + (-18) = -147$$

STEP 2 **Divide** the sum by the number of temperatures. $\frac{-147}{4} = -36.75$

▶ **Answer** The mean of the temperatures is about −37°F.

EXAMPLE 3 Evaluating Expressions

Evaluate the expression when $a = -24$, $b = 8$, and $c = -4$.

SOLUTION

a. $\frac{a}{b} = \frac{-24}{8}$ **Substitute values.**

$= -3$ **Different signs, so quotient is negative.**

b. $\frac{ab}{c} = \frac{-24 \cdot 8}{-4}$ **Substitute values.**

$= \frac{-192}{-4}$ **Multiply.**

$= 48$ **Same sign, so quotient is positive.**

✓ GUIDED PRACTICE for Examples 2 and 3

Find the mean of the data.

7. −16, 17, 8, −23, −31

8. 0, −4, −10, 4, 11, −9, −13

9. Evaluate $\frac{a}{bc}$ when $a = -42$, $b = -3$, and $c = 7$.

2.5 EXERCISES

HOMEWORK KEY

★ = **STANDARDIZED TEST PRACTICE** Exs. 34, 39, 41, 42, 44, and 54

○ = **HINTS AND HOMEWORK HELP** for Exs. 9, 11, 15, 21, 39 at classzone.com

SKILL PRACTICE

1. **VOCABULARY** Copy and complete: To find the _?_ of three numbers, add them and divide the sum by three.

SEE EXAMPLE 1 on p. 77 for Exs. 2–13

DIVIDING INTEGERS **Find the quotient if possible.**

2. $\frac{-44}{4}$ 3. $\frac{0}{-7}$ 4. $\frac{-81}{-9}$ 5. $\frac{50}{-10}$

6. $\frac{-49}{-7}$ 7. $\frac{-28}{2}$ 8. $\frac{36}{-4}$ (9.) $\frac{-19}{-1}$

10. $\frac{-66}{-11}$ (11.) $\frac{-27}{0}$ 12. $\frac{-9}{6}$ 13. $\frac{-6}{-30}$

SEE EXAMPLE 2 on p. 78 for Exs. 14–17

FINDING A MEAN **Find the mean of the data.**

14. −12, 5, −9, 10, 16, −8, −2, 8

(15.) 4, −3, −8, 7, −1, 4, −2, −9, −1

16. −18, 14, 16, −24, 31, −8, −19

17. −38, 32, 41, −45, 39, −21, −24

SEE EXAMPLE 3 on p. 78 for Exs. 18–25

ALGEBRA **Evaluate the expression when $x = 18$, $y = -12$, and $z = -6$.**

18. $\frac{y}{z}$ 19. $\frac{x}{z}$ 20. $\frac{xz}{y}$ (21.) $\frac{z^2}{y}$

22. $\frac{x}{y+z}$ 23. $\frac{x-yz}{x}$ 24. $\frac{x^2+y}{z}$ 25. $\frac{y-z^2}{y}$

ORDER OF OPERATIONS **Evaluate the expression.**

26. $2 + 3(-4) \div 6$ 27. $5 + 6 \cdot 8 \div 4 - 3$ 28. $12 \div 3 + 3 \cdot (-4)$ 29. $16 + 8(-2) - 4$

30. $7 - 10 \div 2$ 31. $5 \cdot 6 - 2(6) \div 4$ 32. $-14 - 6 \div 2 + 7$ 33. $7 \cdot 3 - 12 \div 6$

34. ★ **MULTIPLE CHOICE** You multiply the quotient of a negative integer and a positive integer by −1. What is the sign of the product?

(A) negative (B) positive (C) zero (D) can't be determined

35. **WHICH ONE DOESN'T BELONG?** Suppose that $a > 0$ and $b > 0$. Which expression's sign is different from the others?

A. $-a \cdot (-b)$ **B.** $b \div (-a)$ **C.** $-ab$ **D.** $a \div (-b)$

36. **ERROR ANALYSIS** On three SCUBA dives, John once reached a depth of 85 feet below sea level, and twice reached a depth of 95 feet below sea level. Describe and correct the error made in finding the mean of the depths.

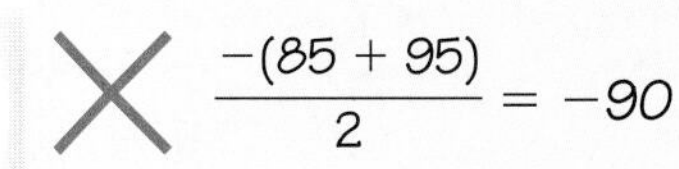

37. **CHALLENGE** Use the number line shown to determine the sign of the quotient $\frac{a-b}{ab}$. *Explain* your reasoning.

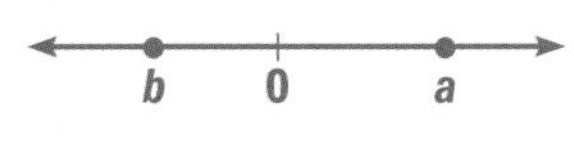

PROBLEM SOLVING

SEE EXAMPLE 2 on p. 78 for Exs. 38–40

38. **GUIDED PROBLEM SOLVING** Will opened a musical instrument shop. The table shows his profits for the first three months. Find his mean profit for these months.

Month	Profit
October	−\$172
November	−\$203
December	\$157

   a. Add the profits.

   b. Count the number of months given.

   c. Divide the sum in part (a) by the number in part (b).

39. ★ **MULTIPLE CHOICE** Over a 6 month period a bookstore has earnings of \$400, −\$76, −\$139, \$526, \$650, and −\$17. What is the mean of the monthly earnings for the 6 months?

   (A) \$224 (B) \$268.80 (C) \$301.33 (D) \$361.60

40. **TEMPERATURES** The temperatures during a 5 day period in Center City were −19°F, −14°F, −8°F, 13°F, and 18°F. What was the mean temperature for these 5 days?

41. ★ **SHORT RESPONSE** The table shows the temperatures in Fairbanks, Alaska during a 5 day period. Find the mean. Suppose the temperature on Tuesday was 5°F lower than shown. How would this affect the mean? *Explain* your reasoning.

Day	Mon	Tues	Wed	Thu	Fri
Temperature	−8°F	−1°F	−6°F	−21°F	−31°F

42. ★ **WRITING** Is the mean of a set of negative numbers *always, sometimes,* or *never* negative? *Explain* your reasoning, and include examples.

43. **BASKETBALL** In 3 basketball games, a player records the statistics shown in the table. Find the mean of each of the categories. *Explain* why there is at least one actual value above and below the mean for each category.

Points	18	26	19
Assists	3	6	3
Rebounds	13	14	6

44. ★ **EXTENDED RESPONSE** The table shows your test scores for 5 tests. You can use integers to find the mean of these scores quickly. Begin by choosing an integer close to what you think the mean might be. In this case, try 85.

   a. Find the difference between each test score and 85. For scores less than 85, record the difference as negative. Complete the third column of the table.

   b. What is the mean of the differences? Look for groups of numbers that are opposites to make your calculation easier.

   c. Use your answer to part (b) to adjust the "close to mean" that you started with. What is the exact mean of all the test scores?

Test	Score	Difference
1	81	?
2	83	?
3	92	?
4	88	?
5	79	?

45. **TEMPERATURE CONVERSION** The natural habitat of reindeer is the Arctic tundra. The mean temperature during the winter in the Arctic tundra is $-34°C$. You can convert degrees Celsius C to degrees Fahrenheit F by using the formula $F = \frac{9}{5}C + 32$. What is the mean temperature in degrees Fahrenheit?

46. **REASONING** Is it possible to work backward from the mean in Exercise 45 to determine the high and low winter temperatures? *Explain* your reasoning.

47. **CHALLENGE** The mean of five daily high temperatures is $-2°F$. Four of the temperatures are shown. Find the fifth temperature.

$-4°F$ $-6°F$ $3°F$ $-1°F$

MIXED REVIEW

Prepare for Lesson 2.6 in Exs. 48–50

Find the sum. *(p. 63)*

48. $2 + (-4) + 5$
49. $[2 + (-4)] + 5$
50. $2 + (-4 + 5)$

Write the product as a power. *(p. 19)*

51. $5 \cdot 5 \cdot 5 \cdot 5 \cdot 5$
52. $8 \cdot 8 \cdot 8 \cdot 8 \cdot 8 \cdot 8$
53. $b \cdot b \cdot b \cdot b$

54. ★ **MULTIPLE CHOICE** What is the value of $6(-8)(-2)$? *(p. 73)*

Ⓐ -96 Ⓑ -4 Ⓒ 16 Ⓓ 96

QUIZ *for Lessons 2.1–2.5*

Copy and complete the statement with < or >. *(p. 57)*

1. $-8 \ \underline{?} \ 8$
2. $0 \ \underline{?} \ -14$
3. $-20 \ \underline{?} \ |-30|$
4. $|-7| \ \underline{?} \ 5$

Find the sum, difference, product, or quotient.

5. $-6 + 1$ *(p. 63)*
6. $-20 + (-10)$ *(p. 63)*
7. $-4 - (-3)$ *(p. 68)*
8. $\frac{36}{-9}$ *(p. 77)*
9. $-6(-8)$ *(p. 73)*
10. $-12(4)$ *(p. 73)*
11. $\frac{-48}{-8}$ *(p. 77)*
12. $-11 - 8$ *(p. 68)*

Find the mean of the data. *(p. 77)*

13. $-9, -15, 16, 4, 2, -10, 8, 20$
14. $-10, 6, -11, -6, -7, 3, -4, 1, 1$

15. **GRAVITY** You drop a ball out of a window that is 144 feet above the ground. The equation $h = -16t^2 + 144$ gives the height h, in feet, of the ball after falling for t seconds. Find the height of the ball after 1, 2, and 3 seconds. After how many seconds does the ball hit the ground? *(p. 73)*

MIXED REVIEW *of Problem Solving*

Lessons 2.1–2.5

1. **MULTI-STEP PROBLEM** The table shows the earnings and expenses for the theater club during the year.

Event	Earnings	Expenses
Fall play	\$500	\$800
Winter play	\$800	\$600
Musical	\$1500	\$900
Spring play	\$600	\$700

   a. For which events did the club earn more than it spent?

   b. Write a positive or negative integer for the profit for each event.

   c. What was the theater club's profit during the year?

2. **SHORT RESPONSE** A rock is dropped from a height of 256 feet above the ground. The equation $h = -16t^2 + 256$ gives the rock's height h, in feet, above the ground after falling for t seconds.

   a. Evaluate the equation when t equals 3, 4, and 5 seconds.

   b. *Describe* the position of the rock relative to its starting height and to the ground for the values of t in part (a).

3. **SHORT RESPONSE** A fish shop advertises that its large size shrimp averages 16 shrimp per pound. You count the number of shrimp in 4 different pounds that you buy and find the following: 5 shrimp under average, 6 shrimp over average, 1 shrimp over average, and 2 shrimp under average. Is the advertisement accurate? *Explain* your reasoning.

4. **OPEN-ENDED** Choose a positive integer x and a negative integer y that are 12 units apart on the number line. Write numerical expressions of the form $|x - y|$ and $|y - x|$. Evaluate both expressions to show that either one can be used to represent the distance between the integers.

5. **EXTENDED RESPONSE** The table shows golf scores for eight students. Par for the course is 72.

Player	Score	Player	Score
Elliot	84	Irma	72
Louisa	76	Petra	65
Chad	68	Frank	70
Mark	71	Rosalinda	74

   a. Copy the table and add columns that show how many strokes above or below par each player was. Use negative numbers to represent scores below par.

   b. Who had the lowest score? *Explain.*

   c. Was the mean score *above* or *below* par?

6. **SHORT RESPONSE** The table shows a runner's time for each mile of a 2 mile race for 2 races.

Race	1st Mile	2nd Mile
Race 1	6 min 45 sec	7 min 32 sec
Race 2	6 min 49 sec	7 min 27 sec
Difference	?	?

   a. Copy and complete the table by finding the difference between the runner's time in race 1 and race 2.

   b. Based on part (a), did the runner's overall time increase or decrease from race 1 to race 2? *Explain.*

2.6 Number Properties

Before You evaluated expressions.
Now You'll use properties to evaluate expressions.
Why? So you can find total distance traveled, as in Example 1.

KEY VOCABULARY
- **sum,** *p. 764*
- **product,** *p. 768*
- **identity property of addition,** *p. 63*
- **inverse property of addition,** *p. 63*
- **identity property of multiplication,** *p. 73*

You can use the commutative properties of addition and multiplication to easily evaluate expressions using mental math.

KEY CONCEPT *For Your Notebook*

The Commutative Property

	Addition	Multiplication
Words	You can add numbers of a sum in any order.	You can multiply factors of a product in any order.
Numbers	$3 + (-8) = -8 + 3$	$5(-6) = -6(5)$
Algebra	$a + b = b + a$	$ab = ba$

EXAMPLE 1 Using the Commutative Property

Tour Biking You are going on a 400 mile bike trip. You plan to cycle at an average speed of 12 miles per hour for 7 hours a day. Can you complete the trip in 5 days?

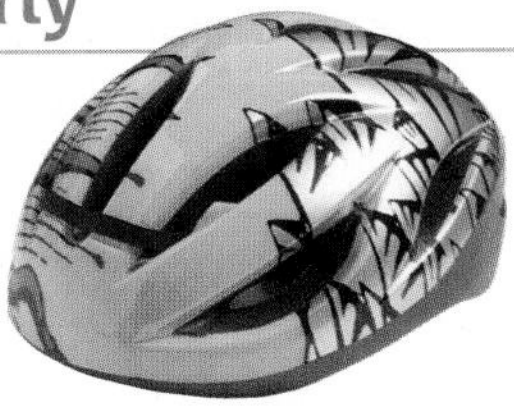

SOLUTION

Write a verbal model to find the total distance you can cycle in 5 days.

Total distance = Average speed • Hours per day • Number of days

$= 12 \cdot 7 \cdot 5$ **Substitute known values.**

$= 12 \cdot 5 \cdot 7$ **Commutative property of multiplication**

$= 60 \cdot 7$ **Multiply.**

$= 420$ **Multiply.**

The unit for the result is miles. $\frac{\text{miles}}{\cancel{\text{hour}}} \cdot \frac{\cancel{\text{hours}}}{\cancel{\text{day}}} \cdot \cancel{\text{days}} = \text{miles}$

▸ **Answer** Because 400 miles is less than the 420 miles you can cycle in 5 days, you can complete the trip in 5 days.

Properties and Subtraction Subtracting a number is the same as adding its opposite. So you can rewrite subtraction expressions using the commutative property of addition to simplify them.

EXAMPLE 2 Using the Commutative Property

SIMPLIFY COMPUTATIONS

When deciding what numbers to add or multiply first, look for pairs whose sum or product ends in zero, because multiples of 10 are easier to work with.

$-54 + 35 - 16 = -54 + 35 + (-16)$	**Change subtraction to addition.**
$= -54 + (-16) + 35$	**Commutative property of addition**
$= -70 + 35$	**Add −54 and −16.**
$= -35$	**Add −70 and 35.**

✓ GUIDED PRACTICE for Examples 1 and 2

1. **What If?** Suppose in Example 1 you only want to bike for 6 hours a day at an average speed of 14 miles per hour. Can you complete the trip in 6 days?

Use the commutative property to evaluate the expression.

2. $4 \cdot (-9) \cdot 25$
3. $-13 + 34 - 7$
4. $\frac{3}{7} + \left(8 + \frac{4}{7}\right)$

Associative Properties You can also use the associative properties of addition and multiplication to evaluate expressions more easily using mental math.

KEY CONCEPT *For Your Notebook*

The Associative Property

	Addition	**Multiplication**
Words	Changing the grouping of numbers will not change their sum.	Changing the grouping of factors will not change their product.
Numbers	$(2 + 3) + 4 = 2 + (3 + 4)$	$(7 \cdot 4) \cdot 5 = 7 \cdot (4 \cdot 5)$
Algebra	$(a + b) + c = a + (b + c)$	$(ab)c = a(bc)$

EXAMPLE 3 Using the Associative Property

REVIEW ADDING FRACTIONS

Grouping fractions can make adding them easier. For help adding fractions with common denominators, see p. 765.

$\frac{3}{5} + \left(\frac{2}{5} + 3\right) = \left(\frac{3}{5} + \frac{2}{5}\right) + 3$	**Associative property of addition**
$= \frac{5}{5} + 3$	**Add fractions.**
$= 1 + 3$	**Write $\frac{5}{5}$ as 1.**
$= 4$	**Add.**

EXAMPLE 4 Using the Associative Property

VOCABULARY
Commute means change locations. *Associate* means group together. These words can help you remember which property is which.

$5 \cdot (11 \cdot 2) = 5 \cdot (2 \cdot 11)$	**Commutative property of multiplication**
$= (5 \cdot 2) \cdot 11$	**Associative property of multiplication**
$= 10 \cdot 11$	**Multiply inside grouping symbols.**
$= 110$	**Multiply.**

✓ GUIDED PRACTICE for Examples 3 and 4

Use properties to evaluate the expression.

5. $18 + (-34 + 12)$ **6.** $\frac{4}{5} + \left(8 + \frac{1}{5}\right)$ **7.** $12\left(6 \cdot \frac{1}{12}\right)$ **8.** $\frac{5}{6}\left(3 \cdot \frac{6}{5}\right)$

Evaluate the expression using mental math.

9. $4\left(\frac{1}{4} \cdot 23\right)$ **10.** $-2(46 \cdot 50)$ **11.** $[-21 \cdot (-29)] \cdot 0$ **12.** $10(-6)\left(\frac{1}{10}\right)$

2.6 EXERCISES

HOMEWORK KEY
★ = **STANDARDIZED TEST PRACTICE** Exs. 22, 44, 45, 48, and 54
○ = **HINTS AND HOMEWORK HELP** for Exs. 7, 13, 17, 23, 41 at classzone.com

SKILL PRACTICE

VOCABULARY Match the equation with the property it illustrates.

1. $(x + 9) + 1 = x + (9 + 1)$
2. $12(1) = 12$
3. $8a = a \cdot 8$
4. $-16 + 0 = -16$
5. $(5 \cdot 7)y = 5(7y)$
6. $-24 + a = a + (-24)$

A. Identity property of addition
B. Commutative property of multiplication
C. Commutative property of addition
D. Associative property of multiplication
E. Associative property of addition
F. Identity property of multiplication

MENTAL MATH Evaluate the expression using mental math. Identify any property you used.

SEE EXAMPLES 1, 2, 3, AND 4 on pp. 83–85 for Exs. 7–21

7. $17 + 15 + 13$ **8.** $-27 + 43 - 13$ **9.** $5 \cdot (-29) \cdot 2$
10. $-53 + (-27 + 44)$ **11.** $(-39 + 48) + 12$ **12.** $-2(-9 \cdot 50)$
13. $[-4 \cdot (-7)](-5)$ **14.** $[25 \cdot (-7)]4$ **15.** $(-20 \cdot 9) \cdot 5$

USING PROPERTIES Copy and complete the statement using the property indicated.

16. $28 + 65 =$ __?__; commutative **17.** $54 \cdot 16 =$ __?__; commutative
18. $(7 \cdot 3)3 =$ __?__; associative **19.** $4 + (9 + 2) =$ __?__; commutative
20. $5(11 \cdot 2) =$ __?__; commutative **21.** $(8 + 16) + 2 =$ __?__; commutative

SEE EXAMPLES 1, 2, 3, AND 4 on pp. 83–85 for Exs. 22–34

22. ★ **MULTIPLE CHOICE** Which expression is equivalent to $7 + 5 - 17$?

   (A) $7 + 17 - 15$ (B) $17 - 7 + 5$ (C) $7 - 17 + 5$ (D) $7 - 5 + 17$

EVALUATING EXPRESSIONS Evaluate the expression. Show and justify each step.

23. $45 - (-68) - 44$
24. $-57 - 38 - (-57)$
25. $(-26 + 33) + (-4)$
26. $(0.5)(45 \cdot 2)$
27. $\left(\frac{2}{7} + 5\right) + \frac{5}{7}$
28. $\left(\frac{2}{3} \cdot 7\right) \cdot 21$
29. $12 \cdot (7 \cdot 1 \cdot 5)$
30. $-2 \cdot (19 \cdot 15) \cdot 1$
31. $36 + 57 + (-36)$
32. $17 + 0 + (-19)$
33. $24 + (-12 - 8) + 6$
34. $5(7 \cdot 4)(0.25)$

ALGEBRA Simplify the expression.

35. $7 \cdot x \cdot 10$
36. $-67 + [x + (-13)]$
37. $(52 + x) + 18$

38. **ERROR ANALYSIS** Describe and correct the error made in evaluating the expression.

$$15 - (5 + 3) = (15 - 5) + 3$$
$$= 10 + 3$$
$$= 13$$

39. **CHALLENGE** Use the commutative properties of addition and multiplication to write three expressions equivalent to $4 \cdot 8 + 5$.

PROBLEM SOLVING

SEE EXAMPLE 1 on p. 83 for Exs. 40–42

40. **SUPER BOWL** During Super Bowl XXXVI, six New England Patriots rushed the football for 92 yards, 22 yards, 15 yards, 5 yards, 3 yards, and -4 yards. What was the total number of their rushing yards?

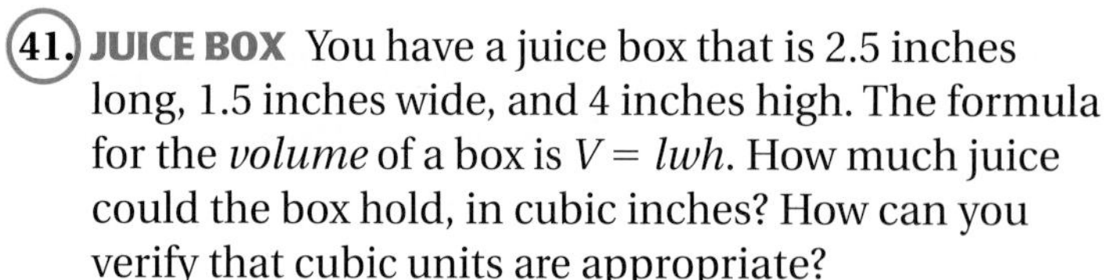

41. **JUICE BOX** You have a juice box that is 2.5 inches long, 1.5 inches wide, and 4 inches high. The formula for the *volume* of a box is $V = lwh$. How much juice could the box hold, in cubic inches? How can you verify that cubic units are appropriate?

42. **PAYCHECK** The table shows the hours you worked during one week. Your hourly wage is \$8 per hour. Write a multiplication model to find the amount you earned for the week. Then find the amount.

Time Card						
Day	Monday	Tuesday	Wednesday	Thursday	Friday	Saturday
Time in	4 P.M.	4 P.M.	did not work	3 P.M.	3 P.M.	11 A.M.
Time out	6 P.M.	6 P.M.		5 P.M.	5 P.M.	1 P.M.

43. **REASONING** Is the expression $-15 + 34 - 44 - 19 + 51$ equivalent to the expression $34 - 19 + 15 - 44 + 51$? *Explain* your reasoning.

44. ★ **WRITING** You need to find the sum of 52, 99, 65, 38, and 11. *Describe* how the commutative and associative properties of addition can help you find the sum using mental math.

45. ★ **SHORT RESPONSE** Show how to use order of operations to simplify the product $25 \cdot 6 \cdot 4 \cdot 7$. *Describe* how the commutative and associative properties of multiplication can help you find the product using mental math. Then find the product.

46. **REASONING** Is division commutative? *Justify* your answer with an example.

47. **SALE PRICE** You are buying 9 yards of fabric that costs $5.25 per yard. You have a coupon for one third off the original price. What is the discount? What is the price of your purchase after the discount?

48. ★ **EXTENDED RESPONSE** *Explain* how a student used the properties of addition to go from the first expression to the second expression below. Use the same method to find the sum of the numbers from 1 to 19. *Describe* how to use this method to find the sum of the numbers from 1 to 99.

$$1 + 2 + 3 + 4 + 5 + 6 + 7 + 8 + 9 = 10 + 10 + 10 + 10 + 5$$
$$= 45$$

49. **CHALLENGE** The shortest side length of a four-sided figure is a feet. The second side is 4 feet longer than the first side. The third side is 8 feet longer than the second side. The fourth side is 6 feet shorter than the third side. Write and simplify an expression to find the perimeter of the figure. Then evaluate when $a = 6$ feet. Find the perimeter.

MIXED REVIEW

Get-Ready

Prepare for Lesson 2.7 in Exs. 50–52

Evaluate the expression. *(p. 8)*

50. $3(12 - 5)$

51. $7(2 + 4)$

52. $2(18 - 14)(8)$

CHOOSE A STRATEGY **Use a strategy from the list to solve the following problem. *Explain* your choice of strategy.**

53. You have two stacking bookcases that are 60 inches tall when stacked on top of each other. If you place them side by side, the difference of their heights is 8 inches. How tall is each bookcase?

Problem Solving Strategies
- Guess, Check, and Revise *(p. 788)*
- Work Backward *(p. 789)*
- Look for a Pattern *(p. 791)*

54. ★ **MULTIPLE CHOICE** What is the value of $18 + (-12) + (-8)$? *(p. 63)*

Ⓐ −38 Ⓑ −2 Ⓒ 2 Ⓓ 38

2.7 The Distributive Property

Before	You used addition and multiplication properties.
Now	You'll use the distributive property.
Why?	So you can find areas, as for murals in Ex. 46.

KEY VOCABULARY
- **distributive property,** *p. 88*
- **terms,** *p. 89*
- **like terms,** *p.89*
- **coefficient,** *p. 89*
- **constant term,** *p. 89*

Architecture A replica of the Parthenon, a temple in ancient Greece, was built in Nashville, Tennessee, in 1897. The diagram below shows the approximate dimensions of two adjacent rooms inside the replica. You can find the total area in two ways as shown in Example 1.

EXAMPLE 1 Finding a Combined Area

Two methods can be used to find the total area of the two rooms.

METHOD 1 **Find** the area of each room, and then find the total area.

$$\text{Area} = 63(44) + 63(98)$$
$$= 2772 + 6174$$
$$= 8946 \text{ square feet}$$

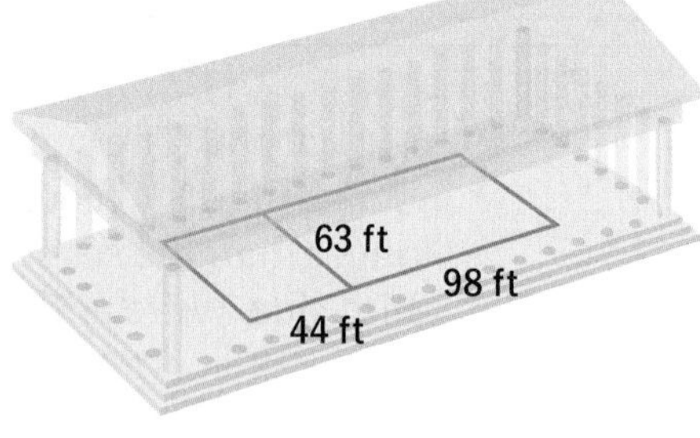

METHOD 2 **Find** the total length, and then multiply by the common width.

$$\text{Area} = 63(44 + 98)$$
$$= 63(142)$$
$$= 8946 \text{ square feet}$$

▸ **Answer** The total area of the two rooms is 8946 square feet.

Example 1 demonstrates the distributive property.

KEY CONCEPT *For Your Notebook*

The Distributive Property

Words You can multiply a number and a sum by multiplying the number by each part of the sum and then adding these products. The same property applies to subtraction.

Algebra $a(b + c) = ab + bc$
$a(b - c) = ab - bc$

Numbers $6(4 + 3) = 6(4) + 6(3)$
$7(8 - 5) = 7(8) - 7(5)$

Distributive Property You can apply the distributive property to expressions with a sum or difference of two or more numbers or variable expressions. Applying the distributive property produces an equivalent expression.

EXAMPLE 2 Using the Distributive Property

a. $-5(x + 10) = -5x + (-5)(10)$ **Distributive property**

$= -5x + (-50)$ **Multiply.**

$= -5x - 50$ **Simplify.**

b. $3[1 - 20 + (-5)] = 3(1) - 3(20) + 3(-5)$ **Distributive property**

$= 3 - 60 + (-15)$ **Multiply.**

$= 3 + (-60) + (-15)$ **Add the opposite of 60.**

$= -72$ **Add.**

✓ GUIDED PRACTICE for Examples 1 and 2

Use the distributive property to find the area of the figure.

1. 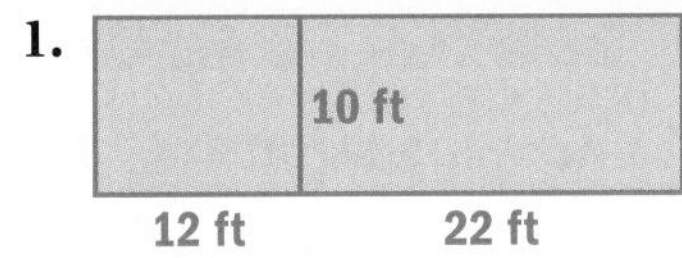

2. 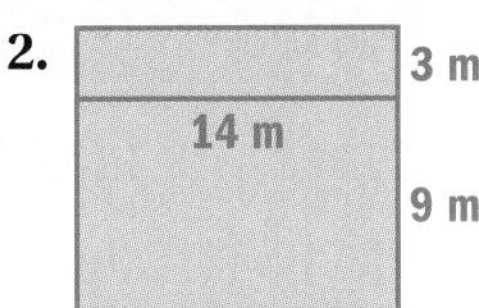

Use the distributive property to evaluate or write an equivalent expression.

3. $-2(5 + 12)$ **4.** $-4(-7 - 10)$ **5.** $2(w - 8)$ **6.** $-8(z + 25)$

Combining Like Terms In an expression, **terms** are separated by addition and subtraction symbols. You can use the distributive property to combine *like terms.* **Like terms** have identical variable parts raised to the same power. In a term, the number multiplied by the variable is the **coefficient** of the variable. A term that has no variable is a **constant term**.

Coefficients are 4 and 8. Constant term is 1.

$4x + 8x + 1$

$4x$ and $8x$ are like terms.

TAKE NOTES
When you add new vocabulary words to your notebook, be sure to include examples of how they are used.

EXAMPLE 3 Combining Like Terms

a. $3x + 4x = (3 + 4)x$ **Distributive property**

$= 7x$ **Add inside grouping symbols.**

b. $-9y + 7y + 5z = (-9 + 7)y + 5z$ **Distributive property**

$= -2y + 5z$ **Add inside grouping symbols.**

EXAMPLE 4 Simplifying an Expression

AVOID ERRORS
Remember that $x = 1 \cdot x$, so x has a coefficient of 1.

a. $2(4 + x) + x = 8 + 2x + x$ — Distributive property

$= 8 + 3x$ — Combine like terms.

b. $-5(3x - 6) + 7x = -15x + 30 + 7x$ — Distributive property

$= -8x + 30$ — Combine like terms.

✓ GUIDED PRACTICE for Examples 3 and 4

Simplify the expression by combining like terms.

7. $2(x + 4) + 3x - 5$ **8.** $5y + 9z - 7 - 3y$ **9.** $-3(6x + 2y) + 22x$

2.7 EXERCISES

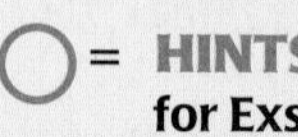

HOMEWORK KEY ★ = STANDARDIZED TEST PRACTICE Exs. 15, 37, 45, 46, 48, 49, and 58

○ = HINTS AND HOMEWORK HELP for Exs. 9, 21, 23, 45 at classzone.com

SKILL PRACTICE

VOCABULARY **Identify the following in the expression $7x - 3y - 6y + x + 2$.**

1. the coefficient of the third term **2.** the coefficient of the fourth term

3. a like term for the second term **4.** a constant term

SEE EXAMPLE 2 on p. 89 for Exs. 5–21

MATCHING EXPRESSIONS **Match the expression with its equivalent expression.**

5. $3(x + 4)$ **6.** $4(x + 3)$ **7.** $2(2x - 6)$ **8.** $x(4 + 9)$

A. $4x - 12$ **B.** $3x + 12$ **C.** $13x$ **D.** $4x + 12$

WRITING EQUIVALENT EXPRESSIONS **Use the distributive property to write a sum that is equivalent to the expression. Then find the sum.**

9. $4(7 + 8)$ **10.** $-7(3 + 2)$ **11.** $3(5 + 6)$

12. $-13(-12 + 9)$ **13.** $6(-5 + 10 + 2)$ **14.** $-4(3 + 6 + -8)$

15. ★ **MULTIPLE CHOICE** Which expression is equivalent to $-3(2x + 4)$?

Ⓐ $-6x + 4$ Ⓑ $-6x + 12$ Ⓒ $-6x - 12$ Ⓓ $-6x - 3$

USING THE DISTRIBUTIVE PROPERTY **Use the distributive property to simplify.**

16. $9(x - 3)$ **17.** $-8(5 - x)$ **18.** $-12(4 + 5 + y)$

19. $19[7 + w + (-2)]$ **20.** $-34(z - 21 - 5)$ **21.** $-2[4 - x + (-7)]$

SEE EXAMPLE 3 on p. 89 for Exs. 22–28

COMBINING LIKE TERMS **Simplify the expression by combining like terms.**

22. $r + 2s + 3r$ **23.** $11w + 9z + 3z + 5w$ **24.** $7a - 2a + 8b - 2b$

25. $3x + 2x + y + 2y - 3$ **26.** $-3x + 2x - 9y - 2x$ **27.** $r + 2s - (-3r) - s$

28. ERROR ANALYSIS Describe and correct the error made in simplifying the expression $4x + 2y - 7y - 2x$.

> ✗ $4x + 2y - 7y - 2x = 4x - 2x + 2y - 7y$
> $= 2x - 5y$
> $= -3xy$

SIMPLIFYING EXPRESSIONS Simplify by combining like terms.

SEE EXAMPLE 4 on p. 90 for Exs. 29–37

29. $5(z + 2z) - 4z$

30. $2(2x + 1) + 3x - 5x$

31. $4(3c - 4) + 2 - 4c$

32. $8d - 2(3d - 5d)$

33. $3(a + 4) + b - 5 - a + 7(b - 3)$

34. $7(y - 1.3) + 2.4 - 5.3y$

35. $3.2(2z - 3x) + 4(1.1y + x) - 2z$

36. $5(x + 2) - 5(y + 3) - 2x + 5y$

37. ★ **MULTIPLE CHOICE** Which expression is equivalent to $5 - 4x + 2(2 - y)$?

Ⓐ $2x + 2y - x$ Ⓑ $9 - 4x - 2y$ Ⓒ $2x + y$ Ⓓ $9 - 2x - 2y$

Animated Math at classzone.com

MENTAL MATH Use the distributive property and mental math to find the product. *Explain* your reasoning.

38. 4(34) **39.** 9(19) **40.** 24(12) **41.** 65(24)

42. REASONING Are $3xy$ and $4yx$ like terms? *Explain* your reasoning.

43. CHALLENGE Simplify the expression $7[6 - 2(x + 3)]$ using the order of operations. Show and justify each step. Then show how to get the same result by first distributing the 7. *Explain* why the second method works.

PROBLEM SOLVING

44. GUIDED PROBLEM SOLVING You are buying three pairs of flip-flops that cost $12.90 each. Use mental math and the distributive property to find the total cost of the flip-flops.

a. Copy and complete: $3(12.90) = 3(13 - \underline{\ ?\ })$.

b. Find the products 3(13) and 3(0.10).

c. Find the difference of the products.

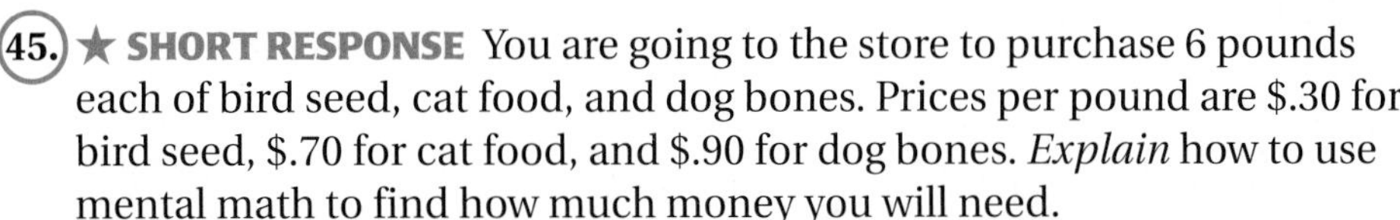

45. ★ **SHORT RESPONSE** You are going to the store to purchase 6 pounds each of bird seed, cat food, and dog bones. Prices per pound are $.30 for bird seed, $.70 for cat food, and $.90 for dog bones. *Explain* how to use mental math to find how much money you will need.

46. ★ **WRITING** Some students have been given permission to paint murals on 5 walls around your school. The walls are each 8 feet tall. The mural widths are 21.5 feet, 35 feet, 27.5 feet, 33.5 feet, and 22.5 feet. *Describe* two methods for finding the total area of the murals. Then find the total area.

SEE EXAMPLE 1
on p. 88
for Exs. 47–49

47. GEOMETRY A floor plan of a house is shown. You want to carpet the family room and the living room. The carpeting you want to use in these two rooms sells for \$3.12 per square foot. How much will the carpet cost?

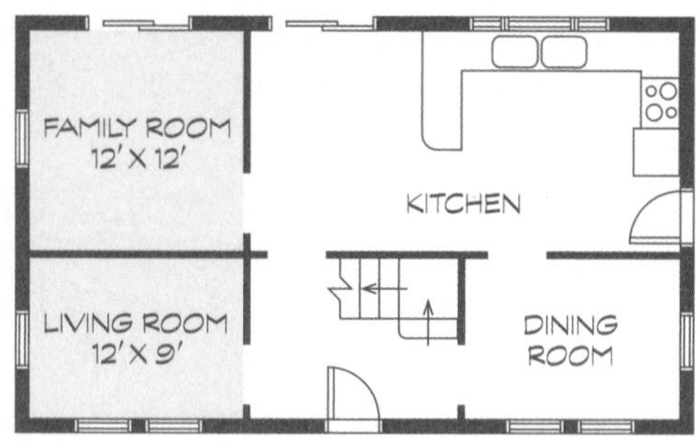

48. ★ MULTIPLE CHOICE Which is an appropriate expression to model the area of a room that is 23 feet by 35 feet?

Ⓐ $20(30 + 5) + 3(20 + 3)$ Ⓑ $30(20 + 3) + 5(20 + 3)$

Ⓒ $35(20 + 3) + 23(30 + 5)$ Ⓓ $35(30 + 5) + 23(20 + 3)$

49. ★ EXTENDED RESPONSE The perimeter of the entire stage, including backstage, is 200 feet. Find the value of x. Show your work. *Explain* two different ways to find the area of the stage. Use either method to find the area.

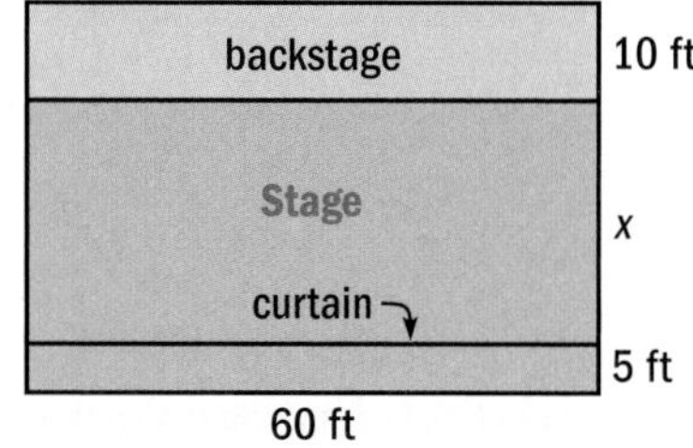

50. EXAMPLES AND NONEXAMPLES *Explain* what you should consider when deciding which expression is easier to evaluate, $8(1000 - 2)$ or $8 \cdot 1000 - 8 \cdot 2$. Give an example of a problem you think is easier to solve using the distributive property and an example you think is more difficult to solve using the distributive property.

51. CHALLENGE You are ordering T-shirts with your school logo. Each T-shirt costs \$7.25. There is a \$25 setup fee for silk screening and a screening charge of \$1.85 per shirt. Write an expression to find the total cost for x T-shirts. What is the total cost for 75 T-shirts? What is the total cost for 170 T-shirts? How does the distributive property apply?

MIXED REVIEW

Prepare for Lesson 2.8 in Exs. 52–53

Use a number line to order the integers from least to greatest. *(p. 57)*

52. −90, 35, 19, −35, 80

53. 70, −20, −90, 0, −100

Evaluate the expression. *(p. 83)*

54. $-5(4 \cdot 17)$

55. $(-23 + 14) - 12$

56. $17 + (3 - 12) + 24(0)$

57. $(-4 \cdot 7) \cdot 25$

58. ★ MULTIPLE CHOICE A package of 8 computer disks costs \$10, and a package of 15 disks costs \$16.50. How much money will you save per disk if you buy a package of 15 instead of a package of 8? *(p. 37)*

Ⓐ \$.15 Ⓑ \$1.25 Ⓒ \$1.50 Ⓓ \$6.50

GOAL
Use a calculator to evaluate expressions.

2.7 Using Integer Operations

EXAMPLE **Use a calculator to evaluate the expression.**

a. $-900{,}018 + (-805{,}560)$ **b.** $\dfrac{-278 \cdot (-640)}{-139}$

SOLUTION

Use the following keystrokes to find your answer.

	Keystrokes	Display
a.	(−) 900018 + (−) 805560 =	−1705578

▶ **Answer** $-900{,}018 + (-805{,}560) = -1{,}705{,}578$

	Keystrokes	Display
b.	(−) 278 × (−) 640 ÷ (−) 139 =	−1280

▶ **Answer** $\dfrac{-278 \cdot (-640)}{-139} = -1280$

PRACTICE **Use a calculator to evaluate the expression.**

1. $18{,}432 + (-46{,}978)$ **2.** $-50{,}215 + 1315$ **3.** $7010 - (-3999)$

4. $-14{,}300 - (-500)$ **5.** $-751 \cdot 2804$ **6.** $-1940 \cdot (-689)$

7. $3336(-198 \cdot 398)$ **8.** $\dfrac{-105{,}638}{-221}$ **9.** $\dfrac{-67{,}771}{671}$

10. **EARTH** The diameter of Earth is about 4 times the diameter of the Moon. The diameter of the Moon is 3476 kilometers. What is the diameter of Earth? Find the difference of the diameter of Earth and the diameter of the Moon.

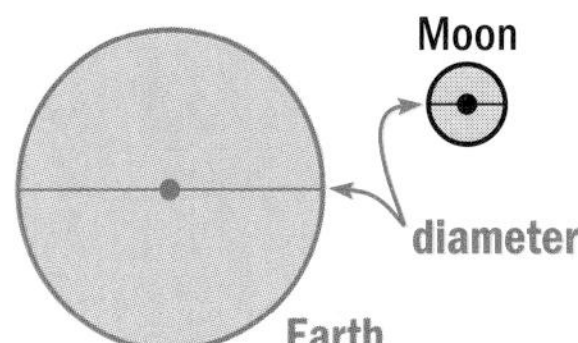

11. **BLUEBERRIES** Blueberries are purchased in a six ounce package and the manufacturer guarantees about 170 blueberries in each package. You purchase three packages of blueberries and count the number of blueberries in each package.
Package 1: 12 blueberries below average
Package 2: 8 blueberries below average
Package 3: 16 blueberries above average
Is the manufacturer's guarantee accurate? *Justify* your reasoning.

2.8 The Coordinate Plane

Before You used number lines.

Now You'll identify and plot points in a coordinate plane.

Why? So you can find patterns in real-world data, as in Ex. 41.

KEY VOCABULARY
- **coordinate plane,** *p. 94*
- ***x*-axis, *y*-axis,** *p. 94*
- **origin,** *p. 94*
- **quadrant,** *p. 94*
- **ordered pair,** *p. 94*
- ***x*- and *y*-coordinates,** *p. 94*

A **coordinate plane** is formed by the intersection of a horizontal number line called the ***x*-axis** and a vertical number line called the ***y*-axis**. The axes meet at the point (0, 0), called the **origin**, and divide the coordinate plane into four **quadrants**.

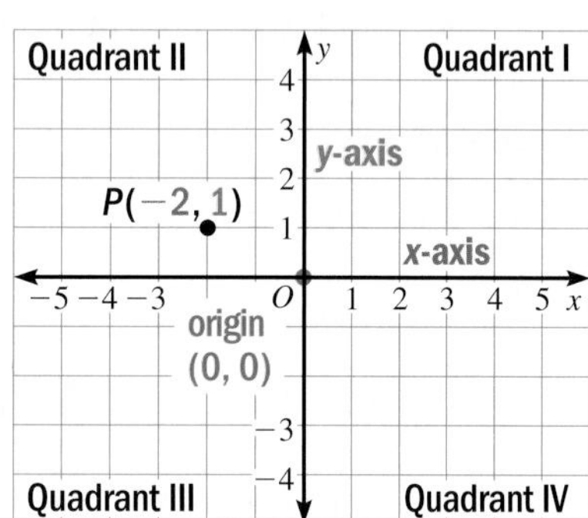

Points in a coordinate plane are represented by **ordered pairs**. The first number is the ***x*-coordinate**. The second number is the ***y*-coordinate**. Point *P* is represented by the ordered pair (−2, 1).

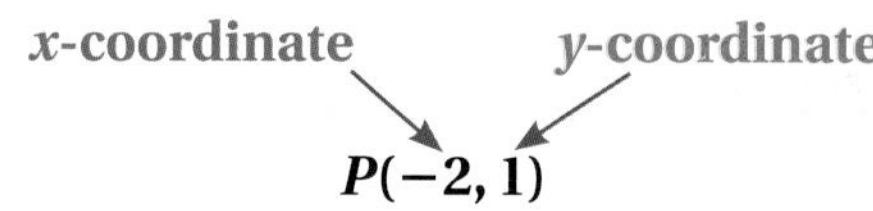

EXAMPLE 1 Naming Points in a Coordinate Plane

Give the coordinates of the point.

a. *A* **b.** *B* **c.** *C*

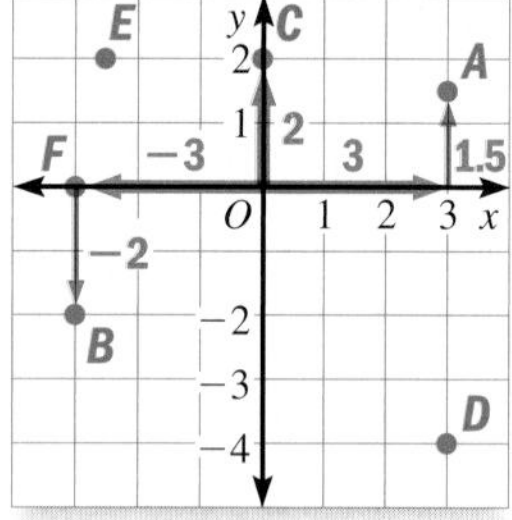

SOLUTION

a. Point *A* is 3 units to the right of the origin and 1.5 units up. So, the *x*-coordinate is 3 and the *y*-coordinate is 1.5. The coordinates of *A* are (3, 1.5).

b. Point *B* is 3 units to the left of the origin and 2 units down. So, the *x*-coordinate is −3 and the *y*-coordinate is −2. The coordinates of *B* are (−3, −2).

c. Point *C* is 2 units up from the origin. So, the *x*-coordinate is 0 and the *y*-coordinate is 2. The coordinates of *C* are (0, 2).

✓ **GUIDED PRACTICE** for Example 1

Use the graph in Example 1. Give the coordinates of the point.

1. *D* **2.** *E* **3.** *F*

EXAMPLE 2 Graphing Points in a Coordinate Plane

Plot the point and describe its location.

a. $A(4, -2)$ **b.** $B(-1, 2.5)$ **c.** $C(0, -3)$

SOLUTION

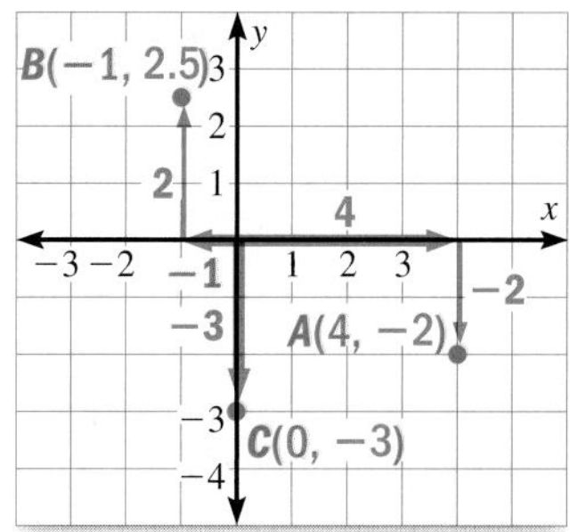

a. Begin at the origin, move 4 units to the right, then 2 units down. Point A lies in Quadrant IV.

b. Begin at the origin, move 1 unit to the left, then 2.5 units up. Point B lies in Quadrant II.

c. Begin at the origin, move 3 units down. Point C lies on the y-axis.

VOCABULARY
Points on the x-axis or y-axis do not lie in any quadrant.

EXAMPLE 3 Solve a Multi-Step Problem

Archaeology On a field trip, students are exploring an archaeological site. They rope off a region to explore as shown. Identify the shape of the region and find its perimeter. The units on the scale are feet.

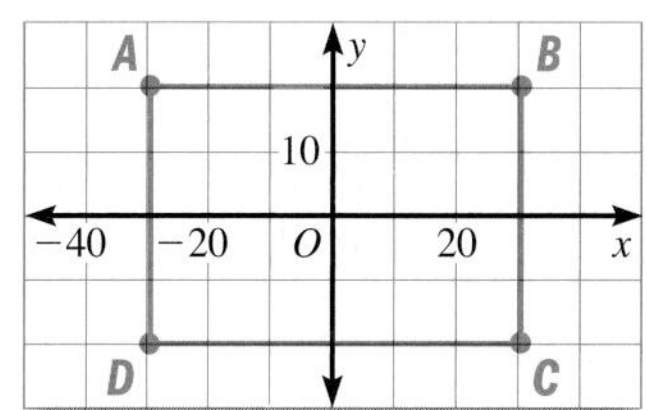

SOLUTION

FINDING DISTANCES
You can find the distance d between two points a and b on a number line. Use the formula $d = |a - b|$.

STEP 1 **Notice** that points A, B, C, and D form a rectangle. Find the coordinates of the vertices.

$$A(-30, 20), B(30, 20), C(30, -20), D(-30, -20)$$

STEP 2 **Find** the *horizontal* distance from A to B to find the length l.

$$l = |\text{ }x\text{-coordinate of } A - x\text{-coordinate of } B|$$
$$= |-30 - 30| = |-60| = 60$$

STEP 3 **Find** the *vertical* distance from A to D to find the width w.

$$w = |y\text{-coordinate of } A - y\text{-coordinate of } D|$$
$$= |20 - (-20)| = |40| = 40$$

STEP 4 **Find** the perimeter: $2l + 2w = 2(60) + 2(40) = 200$.

▸ **Answer** The region's perimeter is 200 units × 10 feet per unit = 2000 feet.

✓ GUIDED PRACTICE for Examples 2 and 3

Plot the point and describe its location.

4. $R(-3, 4)$ **5.** $S(1, -2.5)$ **6.** $T(0.5, 3)$ **7.** $U(-4, 0)$

8. Move points A and B in Example 3 to form a new rectangle. Find the perimeter.

2.8 EXERCISES

HOMEWORK KEY

★ = **STANDARDIZED TEST PRACTICE**
Exs. 28, 36, 38, 41, 42, 46, and 60

○ = **HINTS AND HOMEWORK HELP**
for Exs. 3, 7, 15, 21, 39 at classzone.com

SKILL PRACTICE

1. **VOCABULARY** Draw a coordinate plane and label the x-axis, y-axis, each quadrant, and the origin.

2. **VOCABULARY** Identify the y-coordinate in the ordered pair $(3, -4)$.

NAMING POINTS **Give the coordinates of the point.**

SEE EXAMPLE 1 on p. 94 for Exs. 3–10

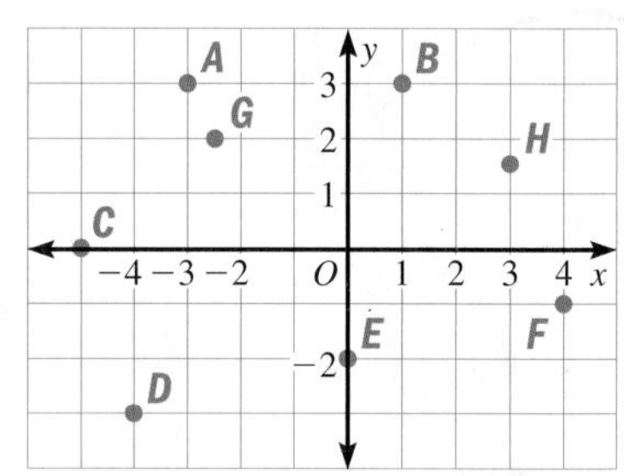

3. A
4. B
5. C
6. D
7. E
8. F
9. G
10. H

PLOTTING POINTS **Plot the point in a coordinate plane and describe its location.**

SEE EXAMPLE 2 on p. 95 for Exs. 11–23

11. $(4, 1)$
12. $(2, -3)$
13. $(-3, 0)$
14. $(-2, -1)$
15. $(-2, 3)$
16. $(3, -1)$
17. $(0, -5)$
18. $(-3, -4)$
19. $(-8.2, 6.1)$
20. $(-0.4, -9.6)$
21. $(2.4, 0)$
22. $(4.3, -1.8)$

23. **ERROR ANALYSIS** Describe and correct the error made in plotting the points $P(2, 3)$ and $Q(1, -1)$.

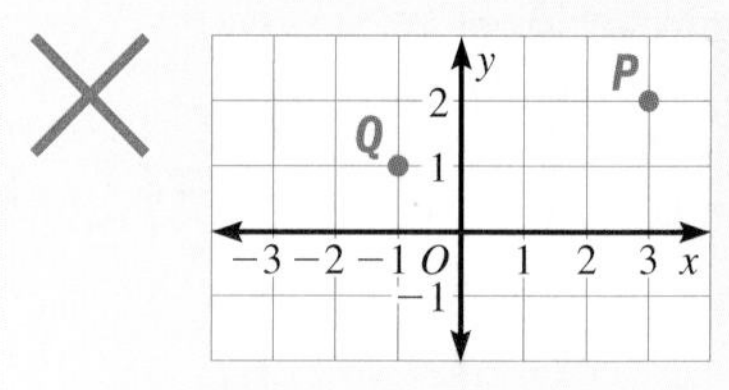

FINDING PERIMETER **Plot and connect the given points. Identify the resulting figure and find its perimeter.**

SEE EXAMPLE 3 on p. 95 for Exs. 24–27

24. $A(-2, 6)$, $B(2, 6)$, $C(2, -6)$, $D(-2, -6)$

25. $E(4, -2)$, $F(4, 3)$, $G(-1, 3)$, $H(-1, -2)$

26. $J(5, 4)$, $K(5, -2)$, $L(-1, -2)$, $M(-1, 4)$

27. $N(-5, 4)$, $O(8, 4)$, $P(8, -1)$, $Q(-5, -1)$

28. ★ **MULTIPLE CHOICE** Which pair of points have x-coordinates that are opposites?

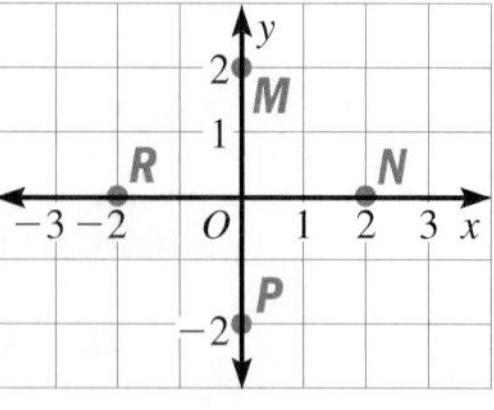

Ⓐ M and N Ⓑ M and P

Ⓒ R and N Ⓓ R and P

GEOMETRY Plot and connect the given points. Find the perimeter and area of the figure formed.

29. $A(1, 1)$, $B(4, 1)$, $C(4, -1)$, $D(-3, -1)$, $E(-3, 1)$, $F(-2, 1)$, $G(-2, 2)$, $H(1, 2)$

30. $J(-4, 1)$, $K(-4, -2)$, $L(0, -2)$, $M(0, 0.5)$, $N(4, 0.5)$, $P(4, 1)$

31. $W\left(-\frac{1}{2}, -7\right)$, $X\left(-\frac{1}{2}, 3\right)$, $Y(2, 3)$, $Z(2, -7)$

FINDING SIDE LENGTH The perimeter and the coordinates of two vertices for a side of a rectangle are given. Find the other side length. Give the possible coordinates for the other vertices of the rectangle.

32. Perimeter = 22 units, $R(4, -5)$, $S(-1, -5)$

33. Perimeter = 36 units, $R(2, 1)$, $S(9, 1)$

34. Perimeter = 68 units, $R(-4, -2)$, $S(10, -2)$

35. CHALLENGE Two vertices of a rectangle are $(-8, 5)$ and $(4, -5)$. The vertices do not share a common side. Find two other vertices that will form a rectangle. Then find the area and perimeter of the rectangle.

PROBLEM SOLVING

36. ★ **MULTIPLE CHOICE** The grid at the right shows the streets of a town. What are the coordinates of the intersection of Eagle Road and Deer Lane?

Ⓐ (2, 3) Ⓑ (3, 2)

Ⓒ (2, 2) Ⓓ (3, 3)

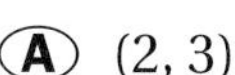

at classzone.com

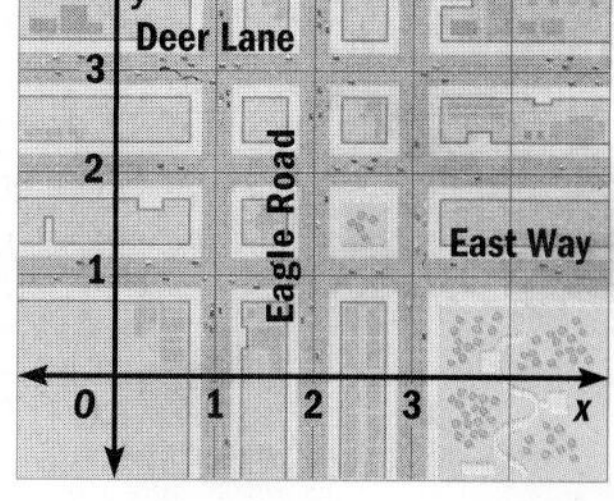

37. SEGMENTS Draw four horizontal or vertical line segments that start at the point $(2, -1)$ and have a length of 6 units. What are the endpoints of the four segments?

38. ★ **OPEN-ENDED MATH** Rectangle $ABCD$ has a length of 8 units and one vertex at $B(2, 5)$. Its other vertices are in other quadrants. Give two sets of possible coordinates of the other three vertices of the rectangle. What are the perimeters and areas in each case?

39. CITY PARK The rectangle with vertices A, B, C, and D represents a city park. The length and width of each small square on the coordinate grid represents 100 feet. Find the distance around the city park.

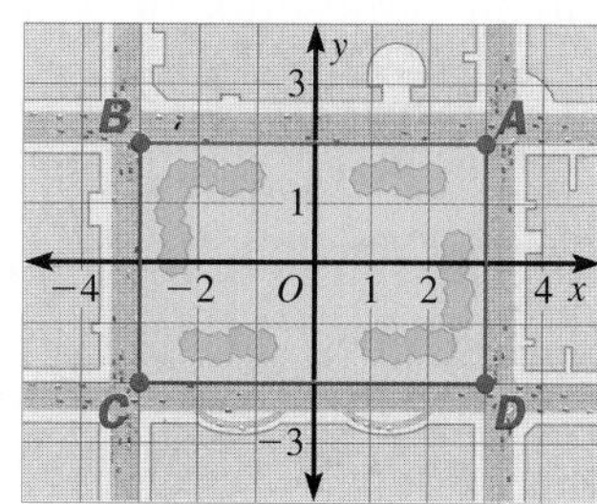

40. **RUNWAYS** Two runways at an airport are shown. Plane 1 needs 1500 meters to take off and plane 2 needs 2500 meters to take off. Planes 1 and 2 are both scheduled to leave on different runways. Which runway will each plane use? What are the coordinates of the point at which each plane takes off, if each starts at the labeled end of its runway?

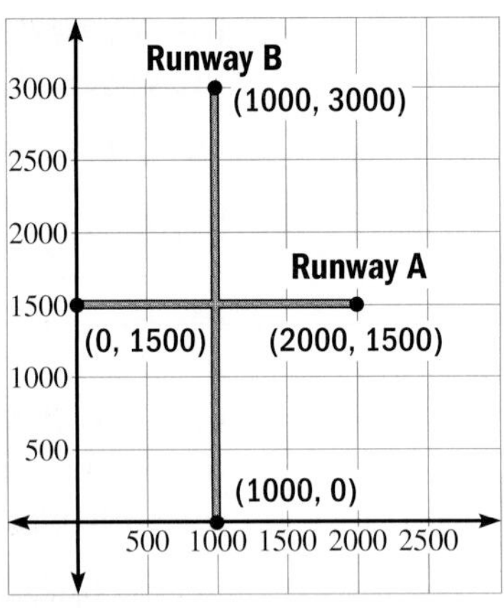

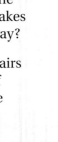

41. ★ **SHORT RESPONSE** The following ordered pairs represent the cost of buying several weights of pineapple from a fruit stand. The x-coordinate represents the number of pounds and the y-coordinate represents the cost.

(1, \$3.50), (2, \$7.00), (3, \$10.50), (4, \$14.00)

Plot the points in a coordinate plane. *Identify* the pattern. *Explain* how to use the pattern to estimate the cost of $2\frac{1}{2}$ pounds of pineapple.

42. ★ **WRITING** On a coordinate plane, sketch a figure with at least 8 sides. Write instructions telling a friend how to draw the figure that you drew. Then have your friend follow your instructions to draw the figure, without looking at your sketch. Compare your friend's drawing with yours. Do they match? How could you improve your instructions?

43. **MULTI-STEP PROBLEM** The table below shows the number of minutes used on a telephone call.

	Length of a call
Jane	10 minutes
Tom	20 minutes
Chris	30 minutes

a. **Calculate** It costs 7 cents per minute to make a phone call using a phone card. Using the table above, find the cost of each of the phone calls.

b. **Graph** Plot the costs you found in part (a) in a coordinate plane, where the x-coordinate represents the length, in minutes, of the call and the y-coordinate represents the total cost of the call, in dollars.

c. **Estimate** Draw a line through the points. Use the line to estimate the cost of a 1 hour call.

44. **FURNITURE** The center of the top of a desk is at the origin of a coordinate plane. Each grid represents 1 inch. The screws, which attach the desk to the frame, are located at $(0, -11)$, $(-8, -11)$, $(-8, 0)$, $(-8, 11)$, $(0, 11)$, $(8, 11)$, $(8, 0)$, and $(8, -11)$. Each screw is 1 inch from the closest edge of the desk. The corner screws are 1 inch from each edge. What is the perimeter of the desk top?

45. TRANSFORMATIONS Copy the figure shown. Move the figure 2 units to the left and 3 units up. Give the new coordinates of A, B, C, D, and E.

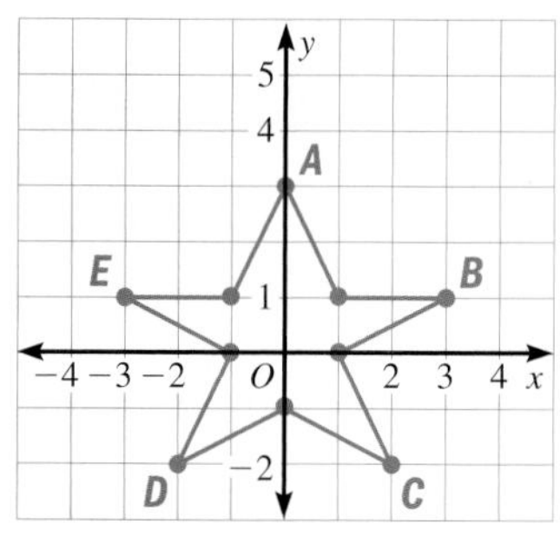

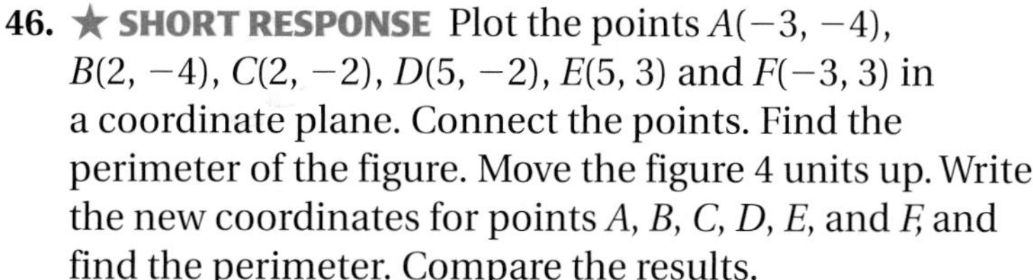

46. ★ SHORT RESPONSE Plot the points $A(-3, -4)$, $B(2, -4)$, $C(2, -2)$, $D(5, -2)$, $E(5, 3)$ and $F(-3, 3)$ in a coordinate plane. Connect the points. Find the perimeter of the figure. Move the figure 4 units up. Write the new coordinates for points A, B, C, D, E, and F, and find the perimeter. Compare the results.

47. GEOMETRY Draw a rectangle that has one vertex in each quadrant. Multiply each coordinate by 2 and draw the resulting figure. Compare the new figure with the original figure and compare their perimeters. What do you find?

48. TRANSFORMATIONS Plot and connect the points (0, 0), (0, 3), (1, 3), (1, 1), (3, 1), and (3, 0) on a coordinate plane. Multiply each coordinate by −2 and draw the resulting figure. *Compare* this figure with the original figure and compare their perimeters. What do you find?

49. GEOMETRY A rectangle has a width of x centimeters and a length of 8 centimeters. Copy and complete the table using this information. Graph the data. Is there a pattern in the graph? *Explain.*

Width x (cm)	1	2	3	4	5	6	7	8
Perimeter P (cm)	?	?	?	?	?	?	?	?

50. CHALLENGE (8, 1), (5, 6), (−5, 0), (−2, −5) are the vertices of a rectangle. Find the area of the rectangle. *Explain* how you found your answer.

MIXED REVIEW

Get-Ready

Prepare for Lesson 3.1 in Exs. 51–53

Solve the equation using mental math. *(p. 26)*

51. $23 - n = 12$ **52.** $x + 9 = 24$ **53.** $14 - y + 6 = 15$

Find the sum. *(p. 63)*

54. $24 + (-9) + (-12)$ **55.** $-14 + 30 + (-17)$ **56.** $-40 + 8 + 12$

Simplify the expression. *(p. 88)*

57. $4(x + 9) - 4$ **58.** $6(y - 6) + 11$ **59.** $-9(z - 2) + z$

60. ★ MULTIPLE CHOICE You are selling candles as a fundraiser for your school's soccer team. You need to sell 35 candles to reach your goal, and you have sold 18 candles. How many more candles do you need to sell? *(p. 767)*

Ⓐ 7 Ⓑ 17 Ⓒ 18 Ⓓ 53

QUIZ for Lessons 2.6–2.8

Evaluate the expression. ***Justify*** **each step.** *(p. 83)*

1. $(19 + 33) + 11$
2. $(25 \cdot 16)(-4)$
3. $5(-4 \cdot 9)$

Simplify the expression. *(p. 88)*

4. $9x + 22x$
5. $3a - 2b + 6 - a$
6. $8(y + 2) - 4y$

In Exercises 7–9, use the coordinate plane. *(p. 94)*

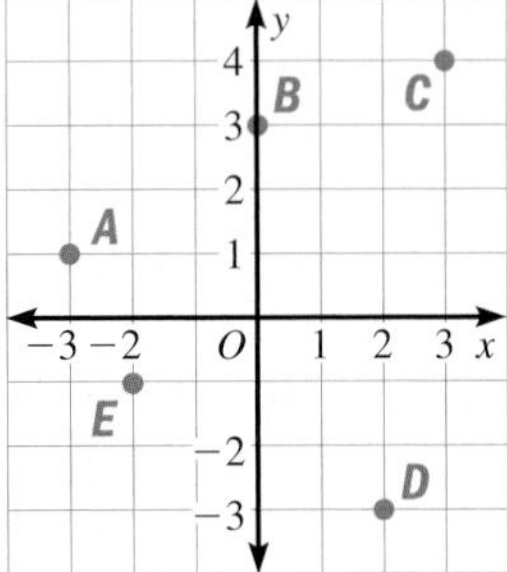

7. Write the coordinates of points *A*, *B*, *C*, *D*, and *E*.
8. Which point lies on the *y*-axis?
9. Which point lies in Quadrant II?

10. **BASKETBALL** In the first basketball game, Joe scored 13 points in the first half and 6 points in the second half. In the second game, he scored 7 points in the first half and 14 points in the second half. How many total points did Joe score? *Explain* how to use properties to find the answer using mental math. *(p. 83)*

Brain Game

Spatial Delivery

Jack delivers balloons in a city. Below is a grid of Jack's city and a list of the deliveries he made today. Copy the diagram on graph paper and plot each stop. How many blocks did Jack travel?

Delivery Stops

Began at Main and State Street

1. E 3rd St. and Main
2. E 3rd St. and N 2nd Ave.
3. E 1st St. and N 2nd Ave.
4. E 1st St. and S 2nd Ave.
5. W 2nd St. and S 3rd Ave.
6. W 3rd St. and S 1st Ave.
7. W 3rd St. and N 2nd Ave.
8. W 1st St. and N 2nd Ave.

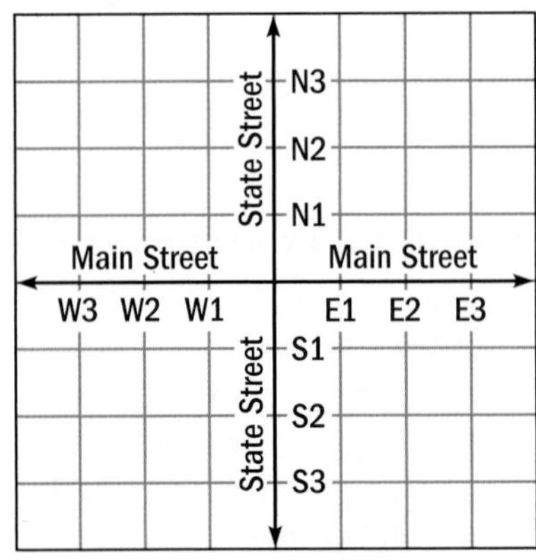

MIXED REVIEW of Problem Solving

STATE TEST PRACTICE
classzone.com

Lessons 2.6–2.8

1. **MULTI-STEP PROBLEM** Use the coordinate plane to answer the questions below.

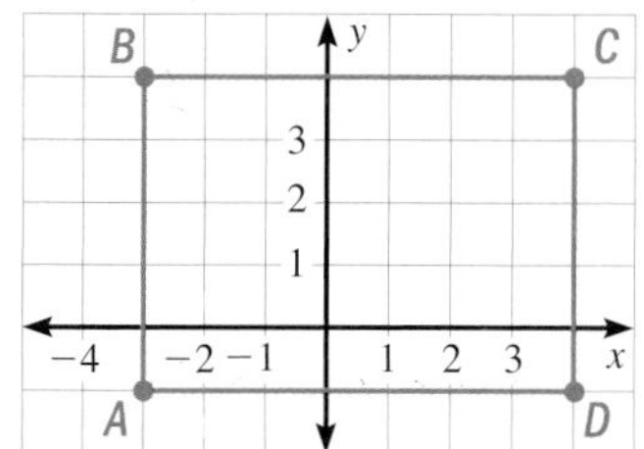

   a. Write and evaluate numerical expressions for the length and width of the rectangle. Then find its area.

   b. Draw a new rectangle that has twice the length and twice the width of the original rectangle. Find the area of the new rectangle.

   c. Does the new rectangle have twice the area of the original rectangle? *Explain.*

2. **GRIDDED ANSWER** You want to buy gifts for 3 friends while on vacation. For each friend you decide to buy a keychain that costs \$3.25, a miniature statue that costs \$7.95, and a postcard that costs \$1. How much money do you spend on gifts for your friends?

3. **SHORT RESPONSE** Olivia is calculating how much paint she needs for one side of a wall that is 6 feet high. The lengths of the sections of the wall are 42 feet, 87 feet, 22 feet, and 29 feet. *Describe* two methods for finding the total area to be painted. *Explain* how the methods are related, and tell which you prefer and why.

4. **SHORT RESPONSE** *Show* and *justify* the steps in simplifying the following expressions. Use the associative and commutative properties.

   a. $(12 + 92) + (-12)$

   b. $-64 + (100 + 64)$

   c. $[10 \times (-2)] \times 50$

   d. $(20 \div 4) \div (-5)$

   e. $(16 - 5) - (-4)$

5. **SHORT RESPONSE** The coordinate grid models the streets of a vacation village. A statue is at the origin of the grid. Each side of a grid square is 100 yards.

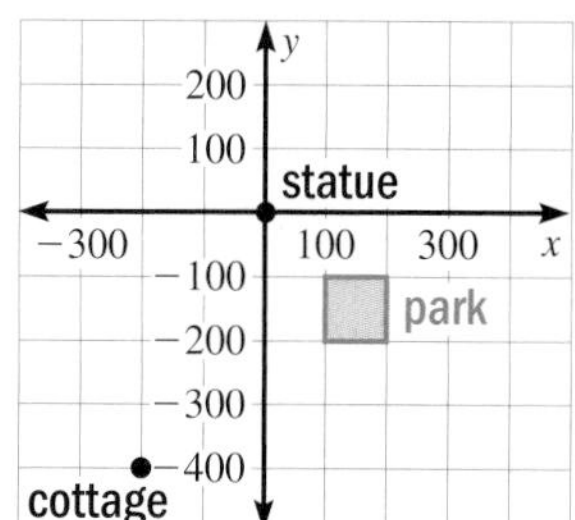

   Paulo wants to walk exactly 2200 yards in 40 minutes every day. Can he do this by walking from his cottage in a single rectangle that encloses or passes the statue and park and ends back at the cottage? If so, tell how and show an example. If not, explain why not.

6. **EXTENDED RESPONSE** You are planning a field trip to a museum. The cost for the bus is \$250. Admission is \$8 per person and lunch is \$5 per person. Write two expressions to find the total cost for x students. What would the cost be if 20 students went on the trip? 25 students? Did you use the distributive property to find your answer? *Explain* why or why not.

7. **OPEN-ENDED** You belong to a group that is selling printed sweatshirts at a fair. Select a cost for buying the sweatshirts, printing the sweatshirts, and any other appropriate expenses. Write an expression for the profit from selling x sweatshirts for \$20 each.

2 CHAPTER REVIEW

@HomeTutor
classzone.com
Vocabulary Practice

REVIEW KEY VOCABULARY

- integer, *p. 57*
- negative integer, *p. 57*
- positive integer, *p. 57*
- absolute value, *p. 58*
- opposite, *p. 58*
- mean, *p. 78*
- distributive property, *p. 88*
- terms, *p. 89*
- like terms, *p. 89*
- coefficient, *p. 89*
- constant term, *p. 89*
- coordinate plane, *p. 94*
- *x*-axis, *y*-axis, *p. 94*
- origin, *p. 94*
- quadrant, *p. 94*
- ordered pair, *p. 94*
- *x*-coordinate, *p. 94*
- *y*-coordinate, *p. 94*

VOCABULARY EXERCISES

1. How many numbers have an absolute value of 15? List them.

2. Copy the expression. List the terms and the coefficients.

$$-6y + 8 - 7x + 17x - 21y$$

3. How many quadrants are in a coordinate plane? Draw a coordinate plane and label each quadrant.

4. A point in a coordinate plane is represented by a(n) __?__.

5. A(n) __?__ is formed by the intersection of a horizontal number line and a vertical number line.

6. The __?__ is the sum of the values divided by the number of values.

REVIEW EXAMPLES AND EXERCISES

2.1 Integers and Absolute Value *pp. 57–61*

EXAMPLE

Write the opposite of the integer.

a. 8 — The opposite of 8 is -8.

b. -3 — The opposite of -3 is 3.

c. $|-22|$ — Because $|-22| = 22$, the opposite of $|-22|$ is -22.

EXAMPLE

Use a number line to order the integers from least to greatest: 2, -8, -6, 4, -1.

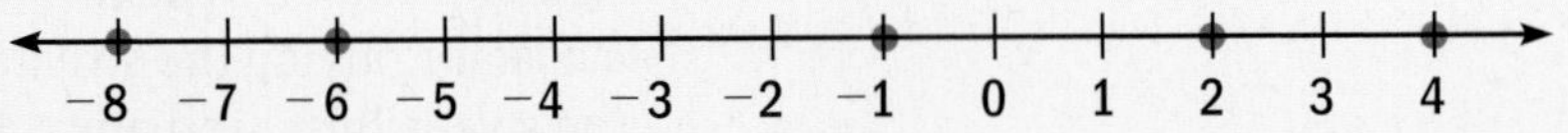

Ordered least to greatest: $-8, -6, -1, 2, 4$

EXERCISES

Order the integers from least to greatest.

SEE EXAMPLES 1, 2, AND 3 on pp. 57–58 for Exs. 7–16

7. −42, 53, 8, −31, −5, 11

8. −56, −102, 98, −58, 114

Write the opposite and the absolute value of the integer.

9. 22 **10.** −13 **11.** −512 **12.** 102

13. −92 **14.** 76 **15.** 147 **16.** −250

2.2 Adding Integers *pp. 63–67*

EXAMPLE

Find the sum −9 + 6.

−9 + 6 = −3 ← **Different signs, so subtract |6| from |−9|.**

Use sign of number with greater absolute value.

Check Use a number line to check.

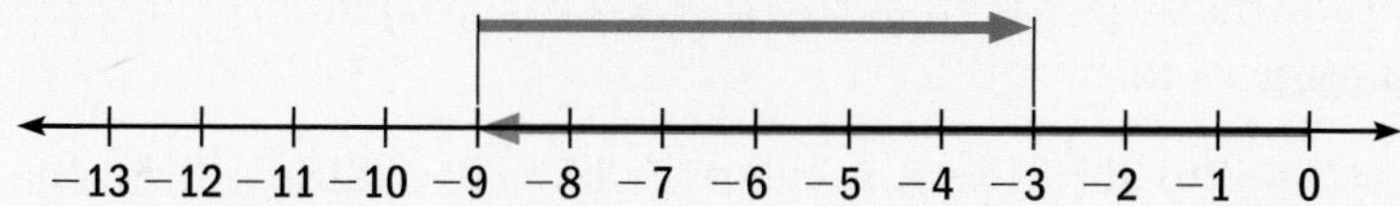

EXERCISES

Find the sum.

SEE EXAMPLE 2 on p. 64 for Exs. 17–28

17. −81 + (−91) **18.** 32 + (−79) **19.** −324 + 500 **20.** −468 + (−196)

21. 752 + (−351) **22.** −96 + (−11) **23.** −246 + 198 **24.** −28 + (−59)

25. −34 + 68 **26.** 471 + (−504) **27.** −101 + (−235) **28.** 97 + (−41)

2.3 Subtracting Integers *pp. 68–72*

EXAMPLE

a. −62 − (−8) = −62 + 8 **Add the opposite of −8.**

= − 54 **Add.**

b. −12 − 43 = −12 + (−43) **Add the opposite of 43.**

= −55 **Add.**

EXERCISES

Find the difference.

SEE EXAMPLE 1 on p. 69 for Exs. 29–36

29. $-29 - 57$ **30.** $62 - (-58)$ **31.** $-43 - (-122)$ **32.** $31 - 108$

33. $88 - (-49)$ **34.** $-56 - (-32)$ **35.** $-50 - 84$ **36.** $61 - 28$

2.4 Multiplying Integers

pp. 73–76

EXAMPLE

a. $-3(5) = -15$ **Different signs, so product is negative.**

b. $-6(-2) = 12$ **Same sign, so product is positive.**

c. $-22(0) = 0$ **Product of an integer and 0 is 0.**

d. $5(-9)(-8) = -45(-8)$ **Multiply from left to right.**

$= 360$ **Multiply.**

EXERCISES

Find the product.

SEE EXAMPLES 1, 2, AND 3 on pp. 73–74 for Exs. 37–49

37. $-6(9)$ **38.** $31(-4)$ **39.** $-9(-23)(0)$ **40.** $-2(-3)(6)(-8)$

Evaluate the expression when $x = -6$, $y = -4$, and $z = -8$.

41. xyz **42.** $9z - 2x$ **43.** $11y - 2xz$ **44.** $2x + 3yz$

45. $2xy - z$ **46.** $3y + 4x$ **47.** $2yz + 3yz$ **48.** $9z - 4xy$

49. Hot Air Balloon A hot air balloon at a height of 110 feet rises for 6 minutes at a rate of 18 feet per minute, then drops 22 feet per minute for 3 minutes. What is the height of the balloon?

2.5 Dividing Integers

pp. 77–81

EXAMPLE

a. $\frac{-96}{-16} = 6$ **Same sign, so quotient is positive.**

b. $\frac{-36}{4} = -9$ **Different signs, so quotient is negative.**

c. $\frac{24}{-4} = -6$ **Different signs, so quotient is negative.**

EXERCISES

Find the quotient.

SEE EXAMPLES 1 AND 2 on pp. 77–78 for Exs. 50–61

50. $\frac{-26}{2}$ **51.** $\frac{-98}{-7}$ **52.** $\frac{-120}{-15}$ **53.** $\frac{63}{-7}$

54. $\frac{-56}{-14}$ **55.** $\frac{-84}{12}$ **56.** $\frac{45}{-9}$ **57.** $\frac{-48}{-16}$

Find the mean of the data.

58. 5, 7, −9, −2, −6, 8, −9, 6

59. 15, −9, 6, −14, −18, 12, 7, 5, −2, 8

60. −11, 15, 26, 12, −8, 0, 1

61. 24, −23, −17, −13, 27, 31, −44, −9

2.6 Number Properties

pp. 83–87

EXAMPLE

$5 \cdot (13 \cdot 4) = 5 \cdot (4 \cdot 13)$ Commutative property of multiplication

$= (5 \cdot 4) \cdot 13$ Associative property of multiplication

$= 20 \cdot 13$ Multiply inside grouping symbols.

$= 260$ Multiply.

EXERCISES

Evaluate the expression using mental math. Name the property or properties used.

SEE EXAMPLES 2 AND 4 on pp. 84–85 for Exs. 62–70

62. $19 - (-58 - 81)$ **63.** $(-28 - 95 + 85) + (-62)$ **64.** $(-45 + 97) - (-45)$

65. $4(19 \cdot 25)$ **66.** $[-54 \cdot (-56)] \cdot 0 \cdot (-17)$ **67.** $(-15 \cdot 5) \cdot (-20)$

68. $(-19 - 56) + 19$ **69.** $12 \cdot 96 \cdot 0 + 3$ **70.** $(-92 + 47) - (-92)$

2.7 The Distributive Property

pp. 88–93

EXAMPLE

a. $3(5 + x) + x = 15 + 3x + x$ Distributive property

$= 15 + 4x$ Combine like terms.

b. $-2(5x - 8) + 4x = -10x + 16 + 4x$ Distributive property

$= -6x + 16$ Combine like terms.

EXERCISES

Use the distributive property to simplify the expression.

SEE EXAMPLES 2, 3, AND 4 on pp. 89–90 for Exs. 71–83

71. $5(12x - 20)$ **72.** $7(9 + 11y)$ **73.** $4(25z - 30)$

74. $12(6y - 4)$ **75.** $9(15 - 12t)$ **76.** $15(4r + 15)$

Simplify the expression by combining like terms.

77. $14x - 3y - 7x + y$ **78.** $4x - 11y + 2(1 - x)$ **79.** $5x + 2y - 9x - 8y$

80. $6a + 2a - 5b - 11a$ **81.** $9(4a - 2b) + 13a + 19b$ **82.** $-2(5 - y) + 11y + 12$

83. Baseball Caps Use mental math and the distributive property to find the total price of 5 baseball caps that cost $16.90 each.

2.8 The Coordinate Plane *pp. 94–100*

EXAMPLE

Give the coordinates of the point.

a. *A* **b.** *B* **c.** *C*

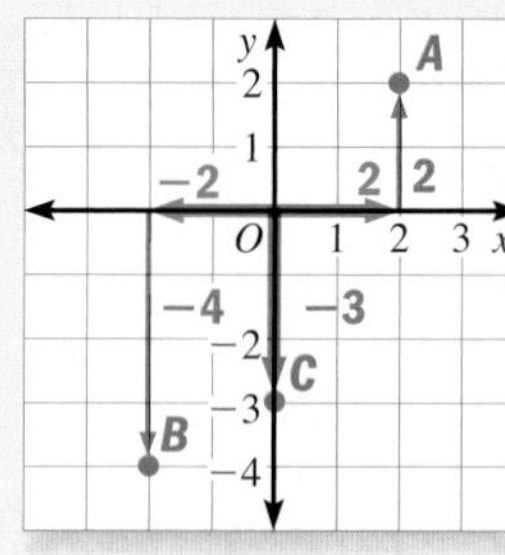

SOLUTION

a. Point *A* is 2 units to the right of the origin and 2 units up. So, the *x*-coordinate is 2 and the *y*-coordinate is 2. The coordinates of *A* are (2, 2).

b. Point *B* is 2 units to the left of the origin and 4 units down. So, the *x*-coordinate is −2 and the *y*-coordinate is −4. The coordinates of *B* are (−2, −4).

c. Point *C* is 3 units down from the origin. So, the *x*-coordinate is 0 and the *y*-coordinate is −3. The coordinates of *C* are (0, −3).

EXERCISES

Give the coordinates of the point.

SEE EXAMPLES 1 AND 3 on pp. 94–95 for Exs. 84–88

84. *A* **85.** *B*

86. *C* **87.** *D*

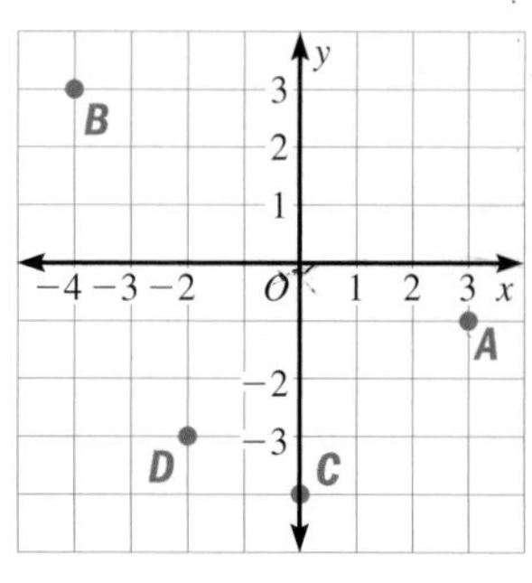

88. Geometry Plot, label, and connect in order the following points in a coordinate plane. Find the perimeter of the figure.

$A(0, 7), B(4, 7), C(4, 4), D(8, 4), E(8, 0), F(0, 0)$

2 CHAPTER TEST

@HomeTutor
classzone.com
Chapter Test Practice

Order the integers from least to greatest.

1. $-9, 8, 14, -11, 0, -1$

2. $123, 87, -59, -12, -111, 22$

Evaluate.

3. $|x|$ when $x = 2$ and when $x = -4$.

4. $-(-x)$ when $x = -1$ and when $x = 7$.

Find the sum or difference.

5. $17 + (-9)$

6. $-8 + (-14)$

7. $-2 + (-21)$

8. $-33 + 26$

9. $1 - 19$

10. $-4 - 17$

11. $10 - (-15)$

12. $-7 - (-18)$

13. $17 + 35 - 3$

14. $-16 + 14 - 12$

15. $11 + (-1 + 32)$

16. $(-26 + 17) + 4$

Find the product or the quotient.

17. $-5(14)$

18. $-12(-20)$

19. $\frac{-152}{-19}$

20. $\frac{-132}{6}$

Evaluate the expression when $a = 3$, $b = -15$, and $c = 15$.

21. $\frac{c}{-a}$

22. $\frac{6b}{2c}$

23. $\frac{c}{-5a}$

24. $\frac{b^2}{a^2}$

Simplify the expression by combining like terms.

25. $3x + 4 - x + 1$

26. $2x - 3y + 5x - (-9y)$

27. $2(9x - 22y) + 4x$

Plot the point in a coordinate plane and describe its location.

28. $(-3, 3)$

29. $(6, 0)$

30. $(-4, -8)$

31. $(5, -2)$

32. TEMPERATURE The following temperatures were taken during a week in December in Nome, Alaska. What is the mean temperature, to the nearest degree?

$-5°F, -8°F, -13°F, -16°F, -8°F, 11°F, 0°F$

33. GROCERIES You are purchasing a loaf of bread for \$2.16, a box of cereal for \$3.25, and two cans of soup for \$.42 each. Write an expression to find the total cost. Then evaluate your expression.

34. ALGEBRA Copy and complete the table for the equation $y = |x|$. Then plot the points on a coordinate plane.

x	-3	-2	-1	0	1	2	3
y	?	?	?	?	?	?	?

Scoring Rubric

Full Credit
- solution is complete and correct

Partial Credit
- solution is complete but errors are made, *or*
- solution is without error, but incomplete

No Credit
- no solution is given, *or*
- solution makes no sense

EXTENDED RESPONSE QUESTIONS

PROBLEM

POOLS A contractor uses a coordinate plane to design a rectangular pool in a backyard. The four corners of the pool are represented by the points *A*, *B*, *C*, and *D*. Find the coordinates of the points. Then find the perimeter and area of the pool if each unit on the graph represents 6 feet.

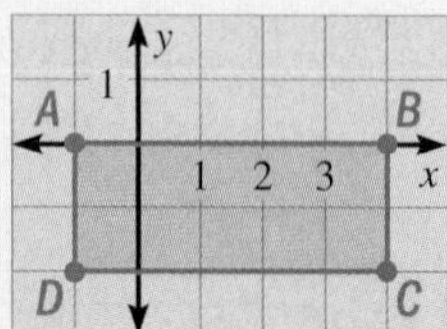

Below are sample solutions to the problem. Read each solution and the comments in blue to see why the sample represents full credit, partial credit, or no credit.

SAMPLE 1: Full Credit Solution

The steps are clearly stated and reflect correct mathematical reasoning.

The coordinates of the points are $A(-1, 0)$, $B(4, 0)$, $C(4, -2)$, and $D(-1, -2)$.

To find the length of the rectangle, find the absolute value of the difference between the *x*-coordinates of *A* and *B*.

The calculations are correct.

Length = | *x*-coordinate of *A* − *x*-coordinate of *B* |
$= |-1 - 4| = |-5| = 5$ units

The width of the rectangle is the *vertical* distance between *A* and *D*. To find this distance, find the absolute value of the difference between the *y*-coordinates of *A* and *D*.

Width = | *y*-coordinate of *A* − *y*-coordinate of *D* |
$= |0 - (-2)| = |2| = 2$ units

Because 1 unit on the graph represents 6 feet, multiply the length and width of the rectangle in the diagram by 6 to find the actual length and width.

Length = 5(6) = 30 feet Width = 2(6) = 12 feet

Find the perimeter and area of the pool.

Perimeter $= 2l + 2w$
$= 2(30) + 2(12)$
$= 84$ feet

Area $= lw$
$= (30)(12)$
$= 360$ square feet

The answer is correct.

The perimeter of the pool is 84 feet and the area of the pool is 360 square feet.

SAMPLE 2: Partial Credit Solution

The coordinates are $A(-1, 0)$, $B(4, 0)$, $C(4, -2)$, and $D(-1, -2)$.

Length $= |x\text{- coordinate of } A - x\text{-coordinate of } B|$
$= |-1 - 4| = |-5| = 5$ units

Width $= |y\text{-coordinate of } A - y\text{-coordinate of } D|$
$= |0 - (-2)| = |2| = 2$ units

Find the perimeter and area of the rectangle.

Perimeter $= 2l + 2w = 2(5) + 2(2) = 14$ units

Area $= lw = (5)(2) = 10$ square units

The steps of the solution reflect correct mathematical reasoning, but the area is incorrectly calculated.

Perimeter $= 14(6) = 84$ feet   Area $= 10(6) = 60$ square feet

The answer is incorrect.

The perimeter of the pool is 84 feet, and the area of the pool is 60 square feet.

SAMPLE 3: No Credit Solution

The given calculations are correct, but the work is incomplete and steps aren't explained. The answer is incorrect.

Perimeter $= 2l + 2w = 2(5) + 2(2) = 14$ Area $= lw = (5)(2) = 10$

The perimeter is 14 feet and the area of the pool is 10 square feet.

PRACTICE Apply the Scoring Rubric

A student's solution to the problem on the previous page is given below. Score the solution as *full credit, partial credit,* or *no credit. Explain* your reasoning. If you choose partial credit or no credit, explain how you would change the solution so that it earns a score of full credit.

1. The coordinates are $A(-1, 0)$, $B(4, 0)$, $C(4, -2)$, and $D(-1, -2)$.

Length $= |x\text{-coordinate of } D - x\text{-coordinate of } C| = |-1 - 4| = |-5| = 5$ units

Width $= |y\text{-coordinate of } B - y\text{-coordinate of } C| = |0 - (-2)| = |2| = 2$ units

Because 1 unit on the graph represents 6 feet, multiply the current length and width by 6 to find the actual length and width. Then find the perimeter and area of the pool.

Length $= 5(6) = 30$ feet   Width $= 2(6) = 12$ feet

Perimeter $= 2l + 2w = 2(30) + 2(12) = 84$ feet

Area $= lw = (30)(12) = 360$ square feet

The perimeter is 84 feet, and the area is 360 square feet.

EXTENDED RESPONSE

1. Your class is planning a field trip to a science center. The cost of the bus is $150. Admission is $8 per person and lunch is $3 per person. Write two expressions to find the total cost for x students. What would the cost be if 18 students went on the trip? 26 students? Did you use the distributive property to find your answer? *Explain* why or why not.

2. The bar graph below shows the earnings at a store for a week.

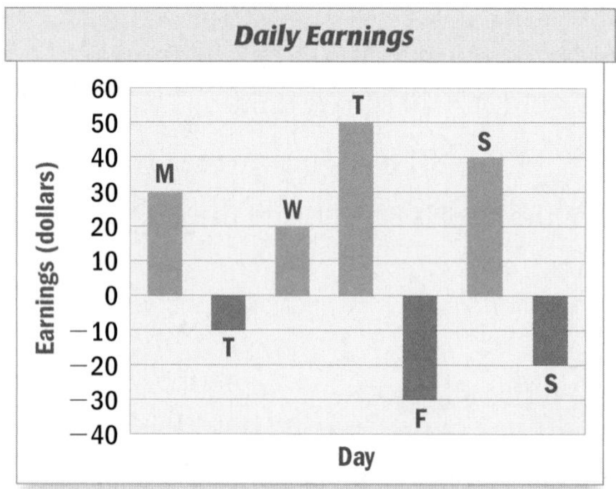

   a. Write a positive or negative integer to represent the earnings for each day.

   b. Order the integers from least to greatest.

   c. Did the store make a profit during the week? *Explain.*

3. One day, the temperature was 5°C at 7 A.M., 68°F at 3 P.M., and 15°C at 6 P.M.

   a. Use the formula $F = \frac{9}{5}C + 32$ to convert the temperature from degrees Celsius to degrees Fahrenheit. Make a line graph of the temperatures data in degrees Fahrenheit.

   b. What was the change in temperature, in degrees Fahrenheit, between 7 A.M. and 3 P.M.? What was the change in temperature, in degrees Fahrenheit, between 3 P.M. and 6 P.M.?

   c. The next day, the changes in temperature between 7 A.M. and 3 P.M. and between 3 P.M. and 6 P.M. were the same as the day before. If the temperature at 7 A.M. was 10°C, what was the temperature at 3 P.M. and 6 P.M., in degrees Fahrenheit?

4. A rectangular garden is plotted in a coordinate plane as shown. Name the ordered pair that represents each vertex. Then find the perimeter and area of the garden if each unit in the coordinate plane represents 5 feet.

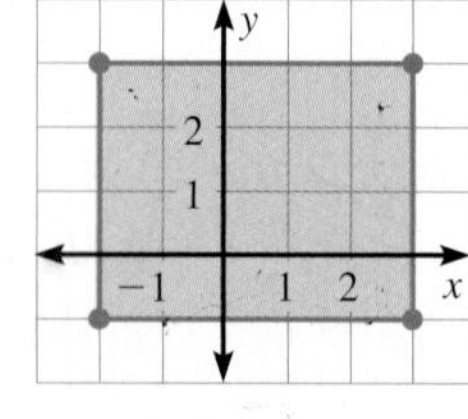

MULTIPLE CHOICE

5. Meg is scuba diving. She ascends to the surface at a rate of 30 feet per minute. After 2 minutes, her position relative to the surface is -15 feet. What was Meg's position when she began her ascent?

Ⓐ -75 ft   Ⓑ -45 ft

Ⓒ 45 ft   Ⓓ 75 ft

6. Which expression is equivalent to $5 - 3x + 4 - 2y - x$?

Ⓐ $2x + 2y - x$ Ⓑ $9 - 4x - 2y$

Ⓒ $2x + y$ Ⓓ $9 - 2x - 2y$

7. What is the value of $20 - a - (-b)$ when $a = 9$ and $b = -6$?

Ⓐ -23 Ⓑ 5

Ⓒ 17   Ⓓ 35

GRIDDED ANSWER

8. What is the mean of the following numbers?

$-6, -4, -1, 3, 6, -2, 5, 7$

9. The high temperature yesterday was -3°F. Today the high temperature was 8°F greater. What was the high temperature today, in degrees Fahrenheit?

10. The height of a flying bird is 30 feet. The bird rises for 5 seconds at a rate of 5 feet per second, and then drops 7 feet per second for 3 seconds. What is the height, in feet, of the bird now?

11. A newspaper reports these weekly changes in the price of a share of stock during a 5 week period: -3, $+4$, $+1$, -2, and $+4$. The share price was \$26 at the end of the fifth week. What was the price of a share of the stock, in dollars, before the 5 week period started?

SHORT RESPONSE

12. *Explain* how the commutative and associative properties of addition can help you find the sum using mental math.

$(57 + 24) + (36 + 83)$

13. Graph the first three points in the table in a coordinate plane. To form a rectangle, what ordered pair must represent point D? Find the length, width, and perimeter of rectangle $ABCD$.

Point	Ordered Pair
A	(−5, 4)
B	(1, 4)
C	(1, −3)
D	(?, ?)

14. Is the opposite of the sum of two numbers equal to the sum of the opposites of the numbers? *Explain.* Use examples to support your answer.

15. During halftime at a football game, your friend goes to the concession stand to buy hamburgers and drinks for everyone. Each hamburger costs \$3.50, and each drink costs \$1.75. Your friend orders 3 hamburgers and 3 drinks. Use the distributive property to write and evaluate an expression for the total amount of money your friend spends.

3 Solving Equations and Inequalities

Before

In previous chapters you've . . .

- Evaluated expressions
- Solved word problems

Now

In Chapter 3 you'll study . . .

- 3.1 One-step equations
- 3.2 More one-step equations
- 3.3 Two-step equations
- 3.4 Writing equations
- 3.5 Geometric formulas
- 3.6 One-step inequalities
- 3.7 More inequalities

Why?

So you can solve real-world problems about . . .

- sea lions, p. 121
- illustrators, p. 132
- biplane rides, p. 152
- DJs, p. 157

at classzone.com

- Algebra Tiles, p. 117
- Solving Two-Step Equations, p. 128
- Inequalities, p. 150

Get-Ready Games

Review Prerequisite Skills by playing *Name that Planet!* and *Planet Pinball.*

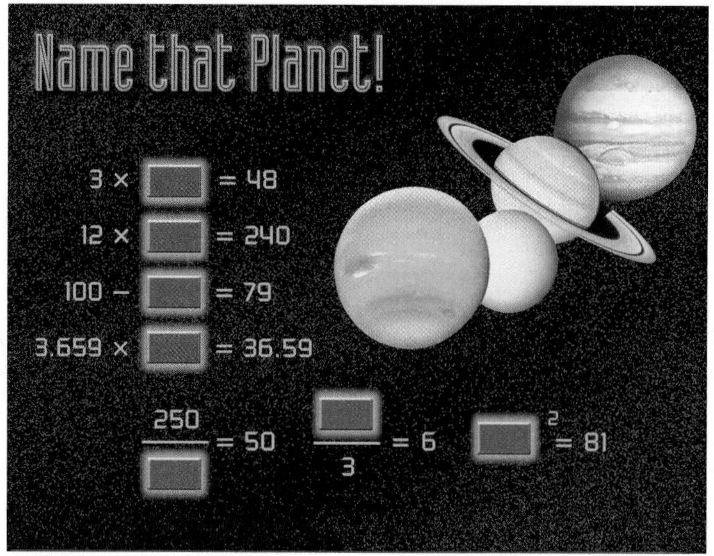

Skill Focus: Solving mental math equations

- Use mental math to find the missing number.
- Match each answer with the corresponding letter of the alphabet. (1 = A, 2 = B, etc.)
- Rearrange the letters to find the name of a planet.

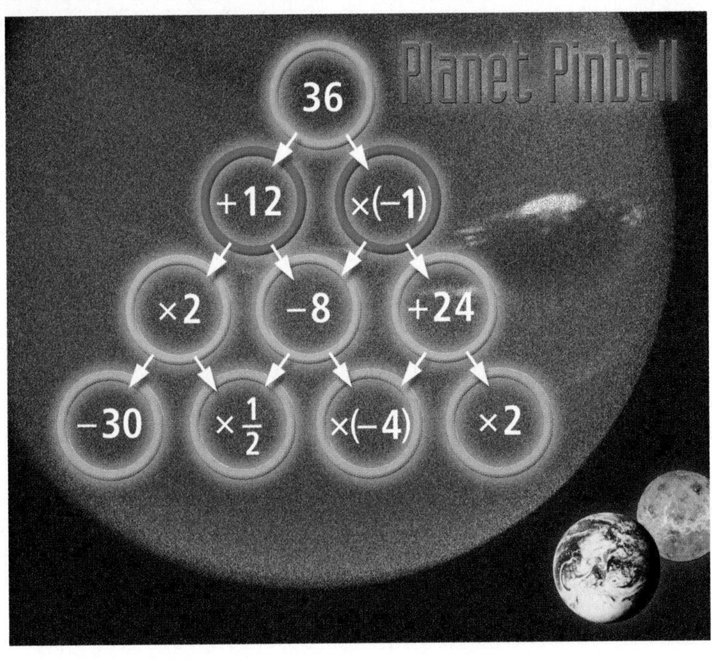

Skill Focus: Operations with integers

Materials: coin

- Both players start at the top planet with 36 points.
- On your turn, toss a coin. If you get heads, go to the planet on the left. If you get tails, go to the planet on the right.
- Perform the operation written on the planet. The result is your current score.
- Take turns moving until both players reach the bottom row.
- The player with the higher score wins.

Stop and Think

1. **WRITING** Without tossing the coin, work with your partner to find the route through the planets in the *Planet Pinball* that gives the highest score. *Explain* how you know you have found the best route.
2. **EXTENSION** Choose another planet name. Write a puzzle like *Name that Planet!* with that name as the solution.

3 Getting Ready

Review Prerequisite Skills

REVIEW WORDS

- **variable,** *p. 13*
- **equation,** *p. 26*
- **solution,** *p. 26*
- **opposite,** *p. 58*
- **like terms,** *p. 89*
- **coefficient,** *p. 89*

VOCABULARY CHECK

Copy and complete using a review word from the list at the left.

1. 5 is the __?__ of −5.

2. In the expression $6x$, 6 is the __?__.

3. A statement with an equal sign between two expressions is a(n) __?__.

4. __?__ have identical variable parts raised to the same power.

SKILL CHECK

Solve the equation using mental math. ***(p. 26)***

5. $x - 1 = 5$ **6.** $x - 2 = 9$ **7.** $4 + x = 12$ **8.** $10 = x + 3$

9. $5x = 20$ **10.** $x \div 3 = 1$ **11.** $x \div 7 = 5$ **12.** $3x = 51$

In Exercises 13–20, evaluate the expression. ***(pp. 63, 68, 73, 77)***

13. $-3 - 2 + 8$ **14.** $3 - 7 + 2 - 1$ **15.** $-2(3 + 1) + 2$ **16.** $8(1 - 4) - 9$

17. $-5 \times 4 + 2$ **18.** $7(3 + 1) \div 2$ **19.** $-8 \div 2 + 4 \times 6$ **20.** $6(2 - 5) \times 3$

21. AIRPLANE SPEED A jet airplane cruises at a speed of 540 mi/h. Write and solve an equation to find how far it travels at that cruising speed in 15 minutes. ***(p. 32)***

@HomeTutor Prerequisite skills practice at classzone.com

Notetaking Skills Organizing Information

In each chapter you will learn a new notetaking skill. In Chapter 3 you will apply the strategy of organizing information to the Key Concept on p. 155.

Sometimes you can organize information in a table to make it easier to understand and remember.

Multiplying Integers

×	Positive	Negative
Positive	+	−
Negative	−	+

INVESTIGATION

Use before Lesson 3.1

GOAL

Solve addition and subtraction equations using algebra tiles.

MATERIALS

• algebra tiles

3.1 Modeling One-Step Equations

You can use algebra tiles to model and solve one-step addition equations and one-step subtraction equations.

x-tile represents the variable x

1-tile represents a positive unit, or 1

−1-tile represents a negative unit, or −1

EXPLORE 1 **Model and solve $x + 3 = 8$.**

STEP 1 **Model** $x + 3 = 8$ using algebra tiles.

STEP 2 **Remove** three 1-tiles from each side so the x-tile is by itself.

STEP 3 **Write** the solution.
The solution of the equation is 5.

PRACTICE

1. Use algebra tiles to model each step below. Draw a picture of each step.

   Step 1 **Model** the equation $x + 5 = 7$.

   Step 2 **Remove** five 1-tiles from each side.

   Step 3 **Find** the solution.

Use algebra tiles to model and solve the equation.

2. $x + 4 = 9$
3. $5 + x = 7$
4. $6 = x + 2$
5. $7 + x = 9$

Continued on next page

Continued from the previous page

When you combine a 1-tile and a −1-tile, the result is zero. This pair of tiles is called a *zero pair* and may be removed from the model.

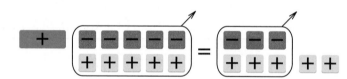

EXPLORE 2 **Model and solve $x - 5 = -3$. Write the equation at each step.**

	Tile Model	Algebra
STEP 1	**Model** $x - 5 = -3$ using algebra tiles.	$x - 5 = -3$
STEP 2	**Add** the same number of 1-tiles to each side to create zero pairs. Add five 1-tiles to each side and then remove zero pairs from each side, to get the x-tile by itself.	$x - 5 + 5 = -3 + 5$
STEP 3	**Write** the solution. The solution is 2.	$x = 2$

at classzone.com

PRACTICE **Use algebra tiles to model and solve the equation. Write the equation at each step.**

6. $x - 3 = 6$

7. $x - 5 = 5$

8. $x + 6 = 2$

9. $8 + x = 1$

10. $x - 4 = -2$

11. $x - 7 = -3$

12. $x + 8 = 4$

13. $x - 3 = -6$

DRAW CONCLUSIONS

14. REASONING Give an example of an equation that requires you to create zero pairs to solve it. How do you know that zero pairs are required?

3.1 Solving Equations Using Addition or Subtraction

Before You solved equations using mental math.

Now You'll solve equations using addition or subtraction.

Why? So you can solve problems, such as finding distances in Example 3.

KEY VOCABULARY

- **equivalent equations,** *p. 117*
- **inverse operation,** *p. 117*

You can model and solve an equation by thinking of the equation as a "balanced" set of numbers, as shown below.

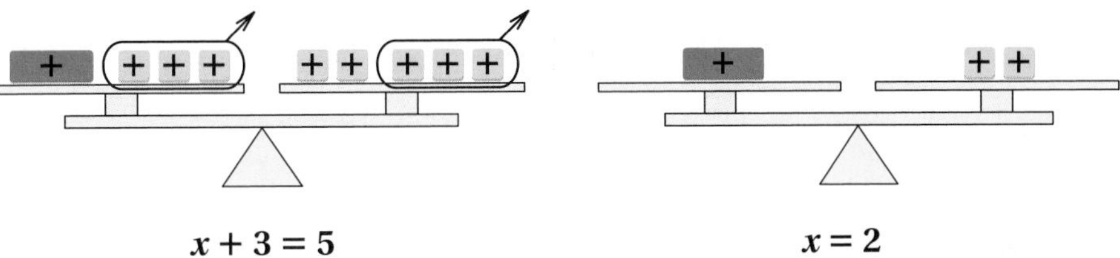

$x + 3 = 5$ $\qquad$ $x = 2$

In the model above, removing three 1-tiles from each side of the scale keeps the scale in balance.

When you perform the same operation on each side of an equation, the result is a new equation that has the same solution. Equations that have the same solution(s) are **equivalent equations**.

You solve an equation by using *inverse operations* to write equivalent equations. An **inverse operation** is an operation that "undoes" another operation. Addition and subtraction are inverse operations.

KEY CONCEPT *For Your Notebook*

Subtraction Property of Equality

Words Subtracting the same number from each side of an equation produces an equivalent equation.

Numbers If $x + 5 = 7$, then $x + 5 - 5 = 7 - 5$.

Algebra If $x + a = b$, then $x + a - a = b - a$.

EXAMPLE 1 Solving an Equation Using Subtraction

$x + 8 = -15$	**Original equation**
$\underline{-8 \quad\; -8}$	**Subtract 8 from each side to undo addition.**
$x \quad = -23$	**Simplify. *x* is by itself.**

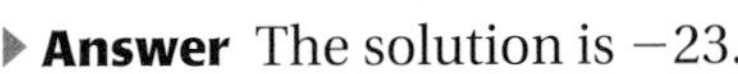

▶ **Answer** The solution is −23.

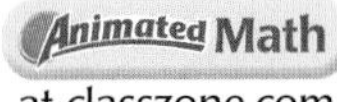

at classzone.com

You can also use the *addition property of equality* to solve an equation.

KEY CONCEPT *For Your Notebook*

Addition Property of Equality

Words Adding the same number to each side of an equation produces an equivalent equation.

Numbers If $x - 2 = 6$, then $x - 2 + 2 = 6 + 2$.

Algebra If $a = b$, then $a + c = b + c$.

EXAMPLE 2 Solving an Equation Using Addition

AVOID ERRORS
You can add or subtract horizontally or vertically to solve equations. Either way, you must remember to perform the same operation on *each* side.

$c - 4.5 = 13$	**Original equation**
$c - 4.5 + 4.5 = 13 + 4.5$	**Add 4.5 to each side to undo subtraction.**
$c = 17.5$	**Simplify. *c* is by itself.**
Check $17.5 - 4.5 \stackrel{?}{=} 13$	**Substitute 17.5 for *c* in original equation.**
$13 = 13$ ✓	

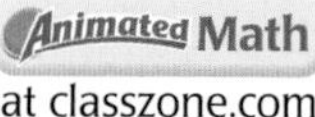

at classzone.com

EXAMPLE 3 Using a Model

Rock Climbing A cliff has a height of about 1500 feet. If you have already climbed 675 feet, how much farther do you have to climb to reach the top?

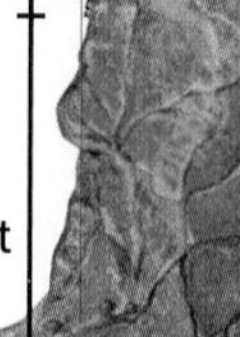

SOLUTION

Use the diagram to help you write an algebraic model. Let x represent the distance left to climb.

$1500 = x + 675$	**Write an algebraic model.**
$1500 - 675 = x + 675 - 675$	**Subtract 675 from each side.**
$825 = x$	**Simplify. *x* is by itself.**

▶ **Answer** You have about 825 feet left to climb.

GUIDED PRACTICE for Examples 1, 2, and 3

Solve the equation. Check your solution.

1. $x + 9 = 20$ **2.** $-10 = 3 + y$ **3.** $m - 14 = -15$ **4.** $2 = z - 6.4$

5. Seashells Lucinda combines her 49 seashells with Jerry's seashells, for a total of 162. Write and solve an addition equation to find how many seashells s Jerry had before their collections were combined.

3.1 EXERCISES

HOMEWORK KEY

★ = **STANDARDIZED TEST PRACTICE**
Exs. 22, 51, 52, 56, 57, and 68

○ = **HINTS AND HOMEWORK HELP**
for Exs. 3, 9, 11, 19, 49 at classzone.com

SKILL PRACTICE

VOCABULARY **Copy and complete the statement.**

1. Addition and subtraction are _?_ operations.
2. Equations that have the same solution(s) are called _?_.

SOLVING EQUATIONS **Solve the equation. Check your solution.**

SEE EXAMPLES 1 AND 2 on pp. 117–118 for Exs. 3–28

3. $x + 10 = 16$
4. $12 = x - 8$
5. $43 = a - 21$
6. $r + 2 = 7$
7. $t - 5 = 2$
8. $z + 9 = 11$
9. $23 = 6 + n$
10. $y - 15 = 9$
11. $13 = d - 27$
12. $24 = 52 + n$
13. $-204 = m - 41$
14. $11 = c + 48$
15. $p + 3.4 = 4.4$
16. $1.76 = a - 2.94$
17. $3.777 + c = 3.977$
18. $x + \frac{1}{2} = \frac{1}{2}$
19. $\frac{2}{3} = d + \frac{1}{3}$
20. $y - \frac{3}{4} = \frac{1}{4}$

21. **ERROR ANALYSIS** Describe and correct the error made in solving the equation.

$$x + 1000 = 5000$$
$$x + 1000 + 1000 = 5000 + 1000$$
$$x = 6000$$

22. ★ **MULTIPLE CHOICE** What is the solution of $-4 + x = 8$?

(A) -12 (B) -4 (C) 4 (D) 12

SOLVING EQUATIONS **Solve the equation. Check your solution.**

23. $m + (-20) = -12$
24. $-2 = b + (-4)$
25. $r - (-36) = 5$
26. $2 + x - 4 = 12$
27. $m - 5 - 9 = 21$
28. $d + 6(3) = -11$

MODELING **Write and solve an equation to model the statement.**

SEE EXAMPLE 3 on p. 118 for Exs. 29–34

29. The sum of a number n and twelve is twenty-five.
30. Thirty-five is the sum of a number n and eight.
31. Three less than a number n is negative sixteen.

GEOMETRY **Write and solve an equation to find the length of the fourth side.**

32. Perimeter = 16 ft

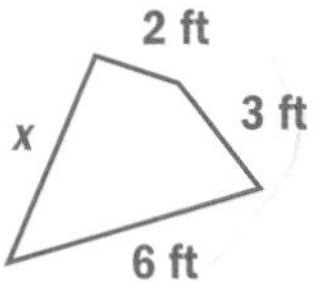

33. Perimeter = 97 cm

24 cm
k
38 cm
16 cm

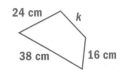

34. Perimeter = 40 m

11 m
7 m
8 m
y

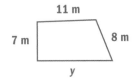

CHOOSE A METHOD **Tell whether you would use *mental math* or *paper and pencil* to solve the equation. Then solve.**

35. $x + 367 = 426$

36. $y + 4 = 6$

37. $m - \frac{8001}{21} = 792$

REASONING **Without solving the equation, decide whether the solution is *positive* or *negative*. *Explain* your reasoning.**

38. $27 + m = 6$

39. $-50 = p - 12$

40. $-10 + y = 5$

SIMPLIFY AND SOLVE **Solve the equation.**

41. $3x - 2x + 8 - 10 = 7$

42. $0.2x + 3.4 + 0.8x = 4$

43. $7.3x + 9 - 6.3x = 12$

CHALLENGE **Find the solutions of the equation.**

44. $|x| - 3 = 14$

45. $|x| + 5 = 25$

46. $|x - 2| = 7$

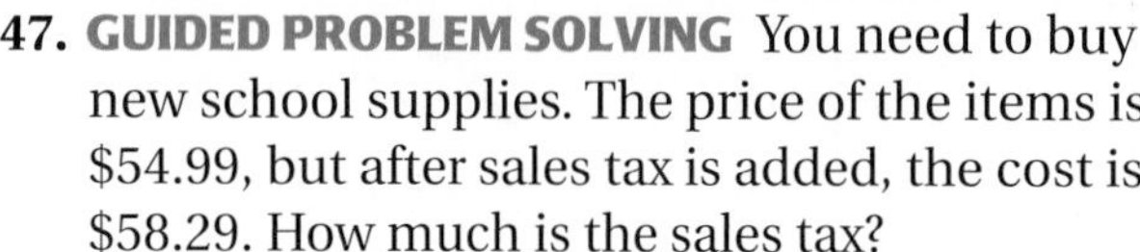

PROBLEM SOLVING

SEE EXAMPLE 3 on p. 118 for Exs. 47–51

47. GUIDED PROBLEM SOLVING You need to buy new school supplies. The price of the items is \$54.99, but after sales tax is added, the cost is \$58.29. How much is the sales tax?

a. Copy and complete the verbal model.

Price + __?__ = Total cost

b. Substitute numbers and variables in the verbal model to write an algebraic model.

c. Solve the algebraic model. Check your solution.

ERROR ANALYSIS **In Exercises 48–50, tell whether the equation correctly represents the situation. If not, correct the equation. Then answer the question.**

48. At 62 inches tall, you are 5 inches taller than your sister. What is your sister's height h? Equation: $62 = h + 5$.

49. The mean temperature for February 4 in Chicago is 3°F below the mean temperature of 29°F for all of February in Chicago. What is the mean temperature t for February 4? Equation: $t - 3 = 29$.

50. An item that usually costs \$2.29 will cost \$1.79 with a coupon. How much is the coupon c worth? Equation: $2.29 - c = 1.79$.

51. ★ MULTIPLE CHOICE Five less than the total number of students x is twenty-four. Which equation represents the statement?

Ⓐ $5 - x = 24$ Ⓑ $24 - 5 = x$ Ⓒ $x + 24 = 5$ Ⓓ $x - 5 = 24$

52. ★ SHORT RESPONSE *Explain* how to use inverse operations to solve an addition or subtraction equation. Give two examples.

READING *IN* MATH **Read the information below for Exercises 53–55.**

Sea Lions Steller sea lions live in the northern Pacific Ocean. Pups are about 45 inches long at birth. Their diet of fish, squid, and octopus help them to grow much larger. Female sea lions reach their full adult size of about 104 inches in seven years. Male sea lions reach their full size of about 128 inches in 12 years. These lengths (and also their weights) make the Steller sea lion the largest of all the eared seals.

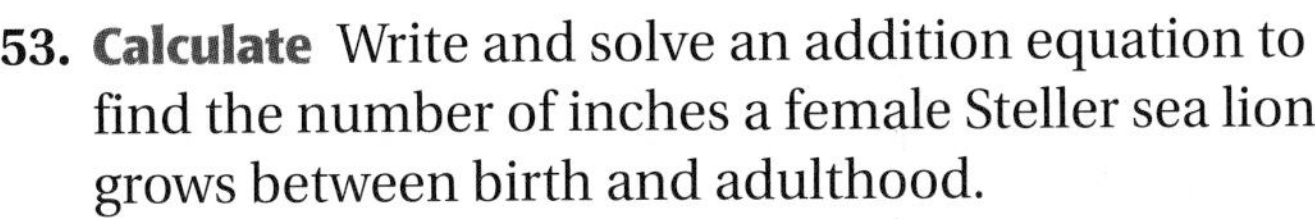

53. Calculate Write and solve an addition equation to find the number of inches a female Steller sea lion grows between birth and adulthood.

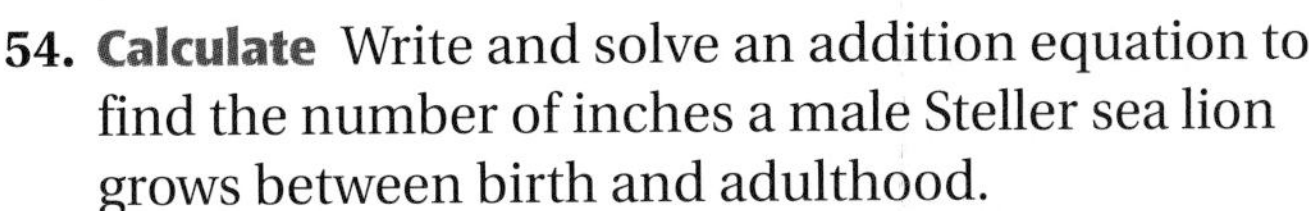

54. Calculate Write and solve an addition equation to find the number of inches a male Steller sea lion grows between birth and adulthood.

55. Predict What is the average growth per year between birth and adulthood for a female and a male Steller sea lion? Round to the nearest inch. After five years, which is longer, a male or a female?

56. ★ **OPEN-ENDED MATH** *Describe* a real-word situation that can be represented by the equation $s + 13 = 55$.

57. ★ **WRITING** *Explain* why $24 = x + 21$ and $27 + x = 30$ are equivalent equations.

58. COST You spent a total of \$11.09 at the store. You bought two bottles of water for \$1.29 each, a magazine for \$3.50, trail mix for \$1.49, and a package of 10 markers for m dollars. Write an addition equation for the situation. (Assume there is no sales tax.) Solve the equation and find the cost of a marker.

59. CHALLENGE The cost b of a book bag is \$3 more than the cost s of a pair of sneakers. The cost of the sneakers is \$6 more than the cost c of a CD, which is \$8 less than the cost t of a T-shirt. The sneakers cost \$18. Write and solve three equations to find the cost of the book bag, the CD, and the T-shirt.

MIXED REVIEW

Get-Ready

Prepare for Lesson 3.2 in Exs. 60–63

Find the product or quotient.

60. 15×1.9 ***(p. 769)*** **61.** 11×13.2 ***(p. 769)*** **62.** $78 \div 19.5$ ***(p. 770)*** **63.** $111.3 \div 3$ ***(p. 770)***

Plot the point in a coordinate plane and describe its location. ***(p. 94)***

64. $P(-2, 5)$ **65.** $Q(5, -2)$ **66.** $R(-2, -5)$ **67.** $S(4.5, 4.5)$

68. ★ **MULTIPLE CHOICE** Which statement is true? ***(p. 19)***

Ⓐ $2^6 < 6^2$ Ⓑ $4^7 < 7^4$ Ⓒ $1^9 > 9^1$ Ⓓ $3^5 > 5^3$

3.2 Solving Equations Using Multiplication or Division

Before You solved equations using addition or subtraction.

Now You'll solve equations using multiplication or division.

Why? So you can find unknown values, such as rows in Exercise 43.

KEY VOCABULARY
- **equivalent equations,** *p. 117*
- **inverse operations,** *p. 117*

ACTIVITY

You can use multiplication to solve equations.

$\frac{x}{2} = 5$ → **Multiply each side by 2.** → $\frac{x}{2} \cdot 2 = 5 \cdot 2$ → **Simplify.** → $x = 10$

Solve the equations.

1. $\frac{y}{5} = 4$ **2.** $\frac{h}{6} = 9$ **3.** $\frac{m}{6} = -3$

4. What operation did you use to solve each division equation? How did you use that operation? Write a rule for solving division equations.

In the activity, you used multiplication to solve equations involving division. Multiplication and division are inverse operations.

KEY CONCEPT *For Your Notebook*

Multiplication Property of Equality

Words Multiplying each side of an equation by the same nonzero number produces an equivalent equation.

Numbers If $\frac{x}{3} = 4$, then $\frac{x}{3} \cdot 3 = 4 \cdot 3$.

Algebra If $a = b$ and $c \neq 0$, then $ac = bc$.

EXAMPLE 1 Solving an Equation Using Multiplication

$\frac{y}{3} = 5$ **Original equation**

$\frac{y}{3} \cdot 3 = 5 \cdot 3$ **Multiply each side by 3 to undo division.**

$y = 15$ **Simplify. *y* is by itself.**

Check $\frac{15}{3} = 5$ ✓ **Substitute 15 for *y* in original equation.**

CHECK ANSWERS
Remember to check your answer by substituting it in the original equation.

You can use division to solve equations involving multiplication.

KEY CONCEPT *For Your Notebook*

Division Property of Equality

Words Dividing each side of an equation by the same nonzero number produces an equivalent equation.

Numbers If $2x = 24$, then $\frac{2x}{2} = \frac{24}{2}$.

Algebra If $a = b$ and $c \neq 0$, then $\frac{a}{c} = \frac{b}{c}$.

EXAMPLE 2 Solving an Equation Using Division

DIVIDING
Need help dividing negatives and decimals? See pp. 70 and 770.

$-2.5x = 20$ **Original equation**

$\frac{-2.5x}{-2.5} = \frac{20}{-2.5}$ **Divide each side by −2.5 to undo multiplication.**

$x = -8$ **Simplify. *x* is by itself.**

EXAMPLE 3 Writing and Solving an Equation

Sports Ninety basketball players show up for a tournament. Write and solve an equation to find how many five-person teams can be formed.

SOLUTION

Let t be the number of five-person teams that can be formed.

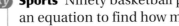

Total number of people = Number per team • Number of teams

$90 = 5t$ **Write an algebraic model.**

$\frac{90}{5} = \frac{5t}{5}$ **Divide each side by 5.**

$18 = t$ **Simplify.**

▶ **Answer** Eighteen five-person teams can be formed.

GUIDED PRACTICE for Examples 1, 2, and 3

Solve the equation. Check your solution.

1. $21 = \frac{x}{9}$ **2.** $\frac{x}{3.5} = 14$ **3.** $9x = 54$ **4.** $48 = -3x$

5. Team Size A teacher divided a class into four teams, with 6 students per team. Write and solve a division equation to find the class size.

3.2 EXERCISES

HOMEWORK KEY

★ = **STANDARDIZED TEST PRACTICE** Exs. 27, 29, 36–39, 44, 47, 52, and 65

○ = **HINTS AND HOMEWORK HELP** for Exs. 5, 9, 13, 21, 45 at classzone.com

SKILL PRACTICE

VOCABULARY **Copy and complete the statement.**

1. To solve $6x = 36$, __?__ each side of the equation by 6.

2. Multiplying each side of an equation by __?__ produces an equivalent equation.

INVERSE OPERATIONS **Describe an inverse operation that will undo the operation.**

SEE EXAMPLES 1 AND 2 on pp. 122–123 for Exs. 3–28

3. Multiplying by 5
4. Dividing by −9
5. Adding −6
6. Subtracting 10
7. Multiplying by −3
8. Subtracting −4

SOLVING EQUATIONS **Solve the equation. Check your solution.**

9. $\frac{p}{2} = 9$
10. $18 = 6g$
11. $3b = 39$
12. $48 = 96z$
13. $\frac{z}{1.8} = 5$
14. $14 = \frac{x}{5}$
15. $44 = 4.4p$
16. $25 = \frac{h}{14}$
17. $14h = 35$
18. $\frac{r}{18} = 12$
19. $12m = -25.2$
20. $7 = \frac{k}{15}$
21. $1368 = 456x$
22. $\frac{h}{6} = -36$
23. $12 = -2z$
24. $-2.4k = 48$
25. $\frac{y}{-1.5} = 21$
26. $-21 = -0.7p$

27. ★ **MULTIPLE CHOICE** What is the solution of $-3 = 0.3a$?

(A) 30 (B) 3 (C) −10 (D) −30

28. **ERROR ANALYSIS** Describe and correct the error made in solving the equation represented by the verbal sentence.

The quotient of a number and the opposite of 7 is 56.

$$\frac{x}{-7} = 56$$
$$\frac{x}{-7} \cdot 7 = 56 \cdot 7$$
$$x = 392$$

29. ★ **MULTIPLE CHOICE** Which operation should you perform to solve the equation represented by the verbal sentence?

The quotient of a number and four is the opposite of two.

(A) Divide each side by 4.
(B) Multiply each side by 4.
(C) Divide each side by −4.
(D) Multiply each side by −4.

SOLVING EQUATIONS **Solve the equation. Explain each step.**

30. $-x = -8$

31. $-b = 12 - 4$

32. $15 - 21 = -n$

33. $\frac{m}{6} = \frac{2}{3}$

34. $\frac{a}{3} = 5\frac{1}{3}$

35. $\frac{t}{4} = 3\frac{1}{6}$

★ **OPEN-ENDED MATH** **Write a multiplication equation and a division equation such that each has the given solution.**

36. -7

37. 2

38. 9

39. -2.5

CHALLENGE **Rewrite the formula so that the indicated variable is by itself.**

40.

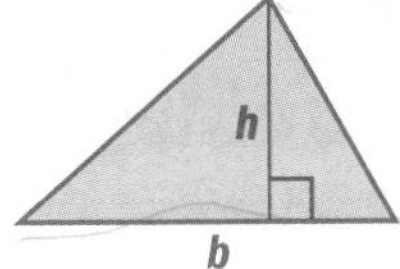

$A = \frac{1}{2}bh$

$b = \underline{\ ?\ }$

41.

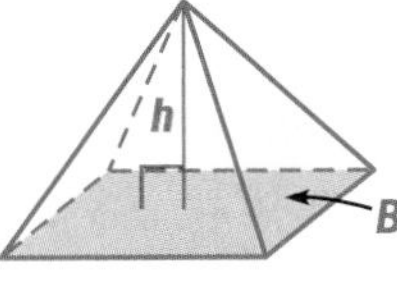

$V = \frac{1}{3}Bh$

$h = \underline{\ ?\ }$

42.

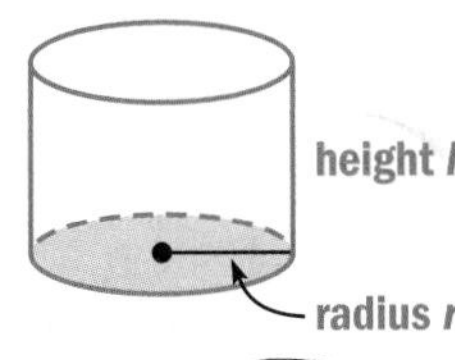

$V = \pi r^2 h$

$h = \underline{\ ?\ }$

PROBLEM SOLVING

SEE EXAMPLE 3 on p. 123 for Exs. 43–46

43. THEATER A movie theater has 1950 seats. Each row has 30 seats. Use the verbal model to write and solve an equation to find how many rows of seats there are.

People in theater = Seats per row • Number of rows

44. ★ **MULTIPLE CHOICE** A pizza shop cuts a pizza into 8 slices. One slice costs \$1.10. Which equation can you use to find the cost x of the whole pizza?

Ⓐ $1.10x = 8$ Ⓑ $8x = 1.10$ Ⓒ $\frac{x}{8} = 1.10$ Ⓓ $x = \frac{1.10}{8}$

45. MOWING LAWNS Your friend charged your neighbors \$56 for mowing their lawn 7 times. Write and solve a multiplication equation to find the amount a your friend charged for mowing the lawn once.

46. MULTI-STEP PROBLEM Joanne drove for three hours at a constant speed r. She traveled a total of 174 miles.

a. **Write an Equation** Write a multiplication equation that represents the situation.

b. **Solve the Equation** Solve the equation to find her speed.

c. **Apply the Result** Can Joanne travel 100 miles farther in two hours at the same speed? *Justify* your answer.

47. ★ **WRITING** *Describe* how algebra tiles could be used as an alternative way to solve Example 3.

WATERFALLS **In Exercises 48–50, use the graph below. Write and solve a multiplication equation for the unknown height. Use the graph to check whether your solution is reasonable.**

48. The height of Angel Falls in Venezuela is 20 times the height of Niagara Falls in Canada and the United States.

49. The height of Comet Falls in Washington is $\frac{1}{5}$ the height of Takkakaw Falls in British Columbia.

50. The height of Skykje Falls in Norway is 1.25 times the height of Feather Falls in California.

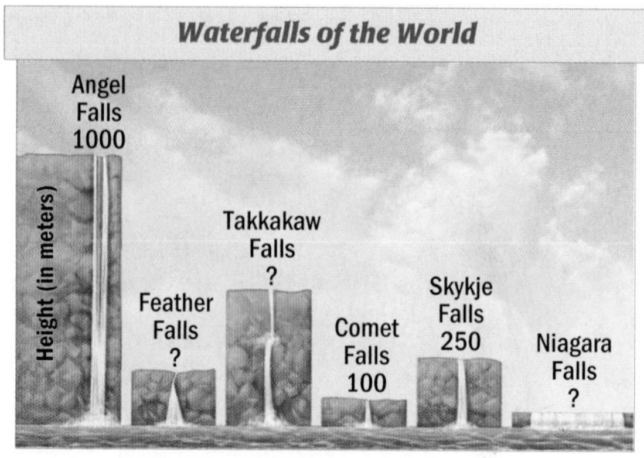

51. **EGG PRODUCTION** About 285 million laying hens produce about 76 billion eggs each year in the United States. About how many eggs does each hen lay in a month? in a week?

52. ★ **EXTENDED RESPONSE** A basketball team plays 20 games and averages 65 points per game. Write a verbal model involving division for finding the total number of points for the season. Write and solve a related equation. The team's goal for next season is to score 5 more points per game for 20 games. *Explain* how to adjust the model to find the total number of points for next season. Then solve.

53. **CHALLENGE** A hardcover book sells for $19.50. The same title in paperback sells for t times the price. The price for 26 paperbacks equals the price for 12 hardcover books. Find the price of one paperback.

54. **CHALLENGE** Find the dimensions of a rectangle whose perimeter is 36 inches and whose length is three times its width.

MIXED REVIEW

Get-Ready

Prepare for Lesson 3.3 in Exs. 55–58

Solve the equation. *(p. 117)*

55. $x + 3 = 12$ **56.** $y - 8 = 4$ **57.** $n - 14 = 325$ **58.** $b + 38 = 9$

Copy and complete the statement with < or >. *(p. 57)*

59. $3 \underline{?} -6$ **60.** $-21 \underline{?} -17$ **61.** $-12 \underline{?} -5$ **62.** $0 \underline{?} -3$

Write the number in standard form. *(p. 759)*

63. twelve thousand forty-eight **64.** five and seventeen thousandths

65. ★ **MULTIPLE CHOICE** A ball is dropped from 80 feet above the ground. Use the equation $h = -16t^2 + 80$ to find the height h of the ball after 2 seconds. *(p. 73)*

(A) 2 ft (B) 16 ft (C) 24 ft (D) 80 ft

INVESTIGATION

Use before Lesson 3.3

GOAL

Use algebra tiles to solve two-step equations.

MATERIALS

- algebra tiles

3.3 Modeling Two-Step Equations

A *two-step equation* is an equation you solve using two operations. You can use algebra tiles to model and solve two-step equations.

EXPLORE 1 **Model and solve $2x + 3 = 7$.**

STEP 1 **Model** the equation $2x + 3 = 7$.

STEP 2 **Remove** three 1-tiles from each side.

STEP 3 **Notice** there are two x-tiles, and the coefficient of x is 2, so divide the remaining tiles on each side into 2 identical groups.

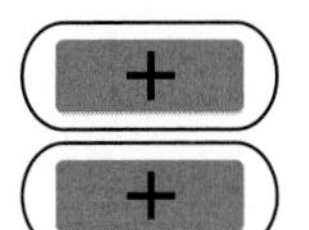

STEP 4 **Compare** one group from each side. One x-tile is equal to two 1-tiles. So, the solution is 2.

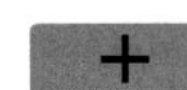

PRACTICE

1. Model each step described below. Draw a picture of each step.

   Step 1 **Use** algebra tiles to model the equation $3x + 1 = 10$.

   Step 2 **Remove** one 1-tile from each side.

   Step 3 **Divide** the remaining tiles into three identical groups.

   Step 4 **Solve** the equation. Then check your solution by substituting in the original equation.

Use algebra tiles to model and solve the equation.

2. $3x + 1 = 7$
3. $2x + 4 = 10$
4. $2x + 3 = 5$
5. $4x + 1 = 9$

Continued on next page

Continued from the previous page

EXPLORE 2

Model and solve $3x - 4 = 5$. Write the equation at each step.

	Tile Model	Algebra
STEP 1		$3x - 4 = 5$

STEP 2 **Add** four 1-tiles to each side. Then remove zero pairs.

$3x - 4 + 4 = 5 + 4$

STEP 3

$\frac{3x}{3} = \frac{9}{3}$

STEP 4

$x = 3$

 at classzone.com

PRACTICE

Use algebra tiles to model and solve the equation. Write the equation at each step.

6. $3x - 6 = 6$ **7.** $2x - 3 = 7$ **8.** $4x + 2 = -10$ **9.** $2x - 5 = -9$

DRAW CONCLUSIONS

10. REASONING *Explain* what kinds of equations are difficult or impossible to solve using algebra tiles. Give an example.

11. WORK BACKWARD Use algebra tiles to write a two-step equation whose solution is 1.

3.3 Solving Two-Step Equations

Before You solved one-step equations.
Now You'll solve two-step equations.
Why? So you can find costs, as for using a pool in Ex. 45.

KEY VOCABULARY
- **equation,** *p. 26*
- **solution,** *p. 26*

Music Club You pay $9.95 to join an Internet music club. You pay $.99 for each song that you download. Your cost for joining and downloading some songs is $17.87. How many songs did you download? Example 1 answers this question using a two-step equation.

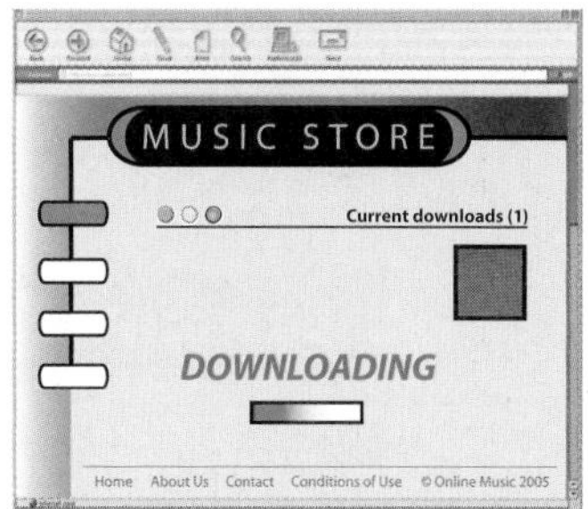

EXAMPLE 1 Solving a Real-World Problem

The model below represents a way of finding how many songs you downloaded. You can use x to represent the number of songs.

Cost to join	+	Cost per song	•	Number of songs	=	Total cost

$9.95 + 0.99x = 17.87$ **Write an algebraic model.**

$-9.95 \qquad -9.95$ **Subtract 9.95 from each side to undo addition.**

$0.99x = 7.92$ **Simplify.**

$\frac{0.99x}{0.99} = \frac{7.92}{0.99}$ **Divide each side by 0.99 to undo multiplication.**

$x = 8$ **Simplify. x is by itself.**

▸ **Answer** You downloaded 8 songs.

✓ GUIDED PRACTICE for Example 1

1. Show how to check the solution in Example 1.

2. **What If?** Suppose the cost to join and download some songs is $26.78. How does this change the equation in Example 1? Find the number of songs.

3. **Film** You pay $35 in dues to a photo club and $10 per roll you have developed. If you spend $225 during the year, how many rolls of film do you have developed? Use $10x + 35 = 225$ and solve for x.

KEY CONCEPT — For Your Notebook

Solving a Two-Step Equation

Some equations require two inverse operations to solve.

$2x + 1 = 5$	**Original equation**
$2x + 1 - 1 = 5 - 1$	**Undo addition or subtraction.**
$2x = 4$	**Simplify.**
$\frac{2x}{2} = \frac{4}{2}$	**Undo multiplication or division.**
$x = 2$	**Simplify.**

EXAMPLE 2 Solving with a Variable in the Numerator

$\frac{x}{2} - 14 = 8$	**Original equation**
$\quad +14 \quad +14$	**Add 14 to each side to undo subtraction.**
$\frac{x}{2} = 22$	**Simplify.**
$\frac{x}{2} \cdot 2 = 22 \cdot 2$	**Multiply each side by 2 to undo division.**
$x = 44$	**Simplify.**

Check $\frac{44}{2} - 14 \stackrel{?}{=} 8$ **Substitute 44 for *x* in original equation.**

$22 - 14 = 8$ ✓

EXAMPLE 3 Solving with a Negative Coefficient

ANOTHER WAY

Remember that you can solve an equation horizontally, as shown here, or vertically, as shown in Example 2.

$8 = 12 - 2x$	**Original equation**
$8 - 12 = 12 - 2x - 12$	**Subtract 12 from each side to undo addition.**
$-4 = -2x$	**Simplify.**
$\frac{-4}{-2} = \frac{-2x}{-2}$	**Divide each side by -2 to undo multiplication.**
$2 = x$	**Simplify.**

✓ GUIDED PRACTICE for Examples 2 and 3

AVOID ERRORS

Recall from Lesson 2.7 that $a = 1 \cdot a$, so a has a coefficient of 1.

Solve the equation. Check your answer.

4. $13 = 11 + \frac{y}{3}$ **5.** $\frac{z}{5} - 3 = 4$ **6.** $-6x + 5 = 23$ **7.** $6 = 16 - a$

8. $10 - 4a = 34$ **9.** $8w - 3 = 21$ **10.** $7x + 3 = 17$ **11.** $\frac{3}{4}m + 1 = 7$

3.3 EXERCISES

HOMEWORK KEY

★ = **STANDARDIZED TEST PRACTICE** Exs. 21, 40, 41, 42, 45, and 51

○ = **HINTS AND HOMEWORK HELP** for Exs. 3, 5, 13, 17, 39 at classzone.com

SKILL PRACTICE

1. **VOCABULARY** Copy and complete: A number that you can substitute for a variable to make an equation true is a(n) _?_ of the equation.

2. **VOCABULARY** Copy and complete: A mathematical sentence formed by placing an equal sign (=) between two expressions is a(n) _?_.

SOLVING EQUATIONS **Solve the equation. Check your answer.**

SEE EXAMPLES 1, 2, AND 3 on pp. 129–130 for Exs. 3–22

3. $2x + 1 = 7$
4. $3y - 4 = 2$
5. $10 - 7z = 3$
6. $15 = -4p + 7$
7. $9 - 2k = 25$
8. $11 = \frac{h}{6} + 8$
9. $\frac{x}{9} - 4 = 5$
10. $6 + 2c = 15$
11. $29 = -5a + 4$
12. $7 + 5b = -23$
13. $100 - 7r = 44$
14. $20 - 6w = 14$
15. $-32 = -17 - \frac{d}{2}$
16. $\frac{c}{3} - 7 = 5.3$
17. $-7 + \frac{z}{4} = 5.2$
18. $\frac{3x}{5} = 12$
19. $\frac{2x}{3} = -8$
20. $-\frac{5m}{2} = 35$

21. ★ **MULTIPLE CHOICE** What is the solution of the equation $21 = 3x + 9$?

Ⓐ -2 Ⓑ 4 Ⓒ 10 Ⓓ 16

22. **ERROR ANALYSIS** Describe and correct the error made in solving the equation.

$$3x - 9 = 18$$
$$3x = 9$$
$$x = 3$$

REASONING **In Exercises 23 and 24, two methods for solving the equation $2(m + 3) = 18$ are shown. *Justify* each step of the solution.**

23.
$$2(m + 3) = 18$$
$$2m + 6 = 18$$
$$2m + 6 - 6 = 18 - 6$$
$$2m = 12$$
$$\frac{2m}{2} = \frac{12}{2}$$
$$m = 6$$

24.
$$2(m + 3) = 18$$
$$\frac{2(m + 3)}{2} = \frac{18}{2}$$
$$m + 3 = 9$$
$$m + 3 - 3 = 9 - 3$$
$$m = 6$$

CHOOSE A METHOD **Use one of the methods in Exercises 23 and 24 to solve. *Explain* your choice of method.**

25. $3(r + 1) = 9$
26. $4 = -1(z + 11)$
27. $6\left(\frac{1}{3} + h\right) = 20$

GEOMETRY **Write and solve equations to find the values of the variables.**

28.

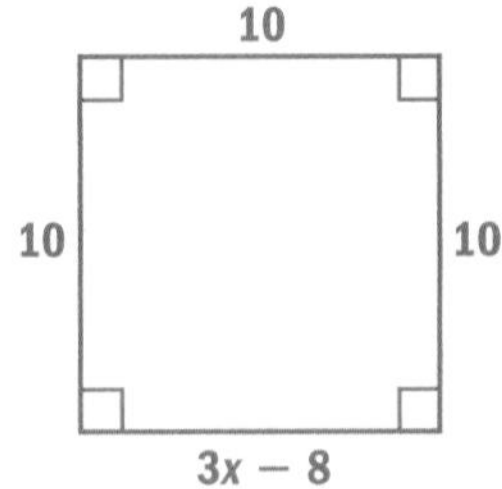

29.

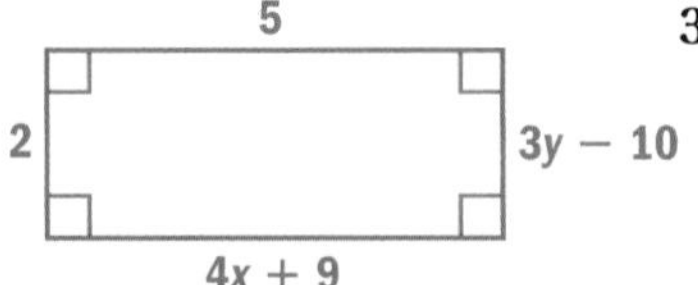

30.

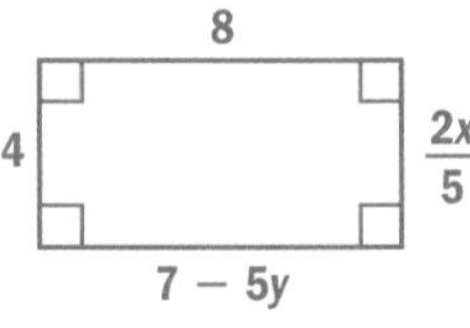

APPLYING PROPERTIES **Solve the equation. *Justify* each step.**

31. $\frac{4h-6}{8}=-3$

32. $\frac{3a+4}{5}=11$

33. $\frac{2w-3}{9}=5$

34. $\frac{2(h+12)}{5}=10$

35. $\frac{2(4t-7)}{3}=-22$

36. $\frac{6(4h+5)}{7}=-6$

37. CHALLENGE The perimeter of a rectangle is found by the formula $P = 2l + 2w$, where l is the length and w is the width.

a. Rewrite this formula with w alone on one side.

b. Rewrite this formula with l alone on one side.

PROBLEM SOLVING

SEE EXAMPLE 1
on p. 129
for Exs. 38–40

38. GUIDED PROBLEM SOLVING You draw illustrations. You charge \$50 per illustration and \$12 per hour to make changes. You get a check for \$198 to pay for three illustrations and changes. How many hours did you spend making changes to the illustrations?

a. Read the problem. What is the main idea? What do you know and what do you need to find?

b. You can use the equation $3(50) + 12n = 198$ to find the number of hours you spent making changes to the illustrations. Why is the value of n the number of hours you spent making changes?

c. Solve the equation and check your answer.

39. WALKING DOGS You earn money by walking dogs in your neighborhood. Each neighbor pays you \$5 per walk and you spend \$4 per week on dog treats. If your goal is to earn \$51 per week, how many walks do you need to do at \$5 each? To answer this question, solve the equation $5w - 4 = 51$.

40. ★ SHORT RESPONSE Students are cleaning up 11 miles of trails in a local park. After an hour, they have cleaned about 3 miles of trails. Solve the two-step equation $3h + 3 = 11$. *Explain* why the value of h is an estimate of the number of hours it will take to finish.

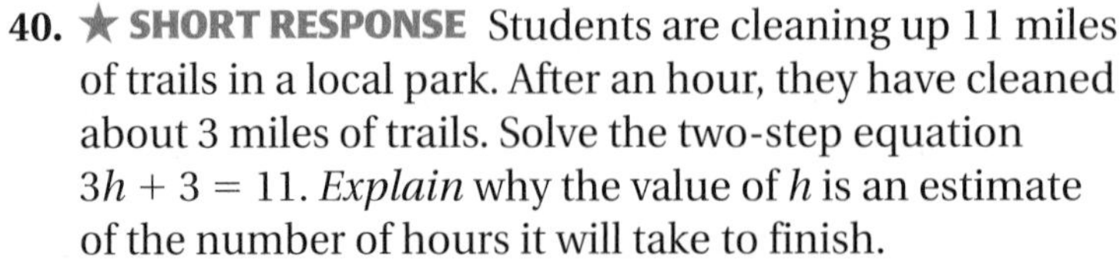

41. ★ OPEN-ENDED MATH *Describe* a real-world situation that can be solved using a two-step equation involving subtraction and multiplication. Write and solve the equation.

42. ★ **WRITING** Jamie is a certified youth soccer referee. After completing a course that cost \$35, she earned \$15 per game. Her profit in the first season was \$280. Which equation should you use to find g, the number of games Jamie worked? *Explain.*

Ⓐ $15g + 35 = 280$ Ⓑ $15g - 35 = 280$

43. **PHONE CARDS** You have \$2.10 remaining on your phone card. You pay 7 cents for each minute of a call and a 75 cent charge for using a pay phone. If you make a call from a pay phone, what is the maximum whole number of minutes that you can talk? (*Hint:* The cost is the sum of the pay phone charge and 7 cents per minute for your call.)

44. **REASONING** Ted has \$12 more than Carla, and Carla has \$8 more than Devon. Together they have \$73. How much money does each person have? Write an equation in terms of D to represent the situation.

45. ★ **EXTENDED RESPONSE** Use the given information about the cost of using the city pool.

a. **Evaluate and Explain** Evaluate the expression $3(40) + 12$. What does the value of the expression represent?

b. **Interpret** Solve the two-step equation $3x + 12 = 100$. What does the answer tell you about the payment plans?

c. **Compare and Contrast** For each payment plan, give one reason why you might choose it.

CITY POOL RATES
SUMMER PASS $100
unlimited visits – including registration
DAY PASS $3
additional $12 registration

46. **CHALLENGE** The length of a rectangle is 5 meters less than twice its width. If each dimension is reduced by 6 meters, the rectangle has a perimeter of 38 meters. What are the dimensions of the original rectangle?

MIXED REVIEW

Prepare for Lesson 3.4 in Exs. 47–49

Solve the equation. Check your answer.

47. $p + 9 = 19$ ***(p. 117)*** 48. $-20 = 4x$ ***(p. 122)*** 49. $\frac{1}{2}y = 24$ ***(p. 122)***

CHOOSE A STRATEGY Use a strategy from the list to solve the following problem. *Explain* your choice of strategy.

50. A running club has six members. The instructor wants each member to race one-on-one against every other member. How many times will each member race? How many races will there be altogether?

Problem Solving Strategies
- Draw a Diagram *(p. 787)*
- Guess, Check, and Revise *(p. 788)*
- Look for a Pattern *(p. 791)*

51. ★ **MULTIPLE CHOICE** Which number is 4.6578 rounded to the tenths' place? ***(p. 760)***

Ⓐ 4.6 Ⓑ 4.66 Ⓒ 4.7 Ⓓ 4.9

3.4 Writing Two-Step Equations

Before You solved two-step equations.
Now You'll solve problems by writing two-step equations.
Why? So you can find additional quantities, as in Example 1.

KEY VOCABULARY
- **equation,** *p. 26*
- **solution,** *p. 26*

You can solve some problems by writing and solving two-step equations. You can use a verbal model to help you write a two-step equation.

EXAMPLE 1 Standardized Test Practice

American Flamingos A zoo currently spends \$1580 to feed its American flamingos. Next year, its budget for feeding the flamingos will be \$2370 and it will cost \$395 to feed each additional flamingo. Which equation can be used to find n, the number of additional flamingos the zoo can buy?

Ⓐ $1580 + 2370 = n$ Ⓑ $2370 = 395n + 1580$

Ⓒ $1580 + 2370 = 395n$ Ⓓ $2370 = n + 395$

ELIMINATE CHOICES
Each additional flamingo costs \$395 to feed. So, you need to multiply the number of flamingos by 395. This eliminates choices A and D.

SOLUTION

Write and solve a two-step equation to find the number of flamingos. Write a verbal model. Let n be the number of additional flamingos.

Budget available = Cost of each new flamingo • Number of new flamingos + Cost of existing flamingos

$2370 = 395n + 1580$	**Write an algebraic model.**
$2370 - 1580 = 395n + 1580 - 1580$	**Subtract 1580 from each side.**
$790 = 395n$	**Simplify.**
$\frac{790}{395} = \frac{395n}{395}$	**Divide each side by 395.**
$2 = n$	**Simplify.**

▶ **Answer** The zoo can buy 2 new flamingos next year. An equation for finding the number of flamingos is $2370 = 395n + 1580$. The correct answer is B. Ⓐ Ⓑ Ⓒ Ⓓ

GUIDED PRACTICE for Example 1

1. **Feeding Costs** It costs a zoo \$1150 this year to feed tortoises. Each new tortoise costs \$575 to feed. A zoo's budget for tortoise food next year is \$2875. How many new tortoises can the zoo buy next year?

EXAMPLE 2 Writing and Solving a Two-Step Equation

The sum of 4 times a number plus −6 is 14. What is the number?

4 times a number and −6 is 14.	**Write a verbal model.**
$4 \cdot n + (-6) = 14$	**Translate.**
$4n - 6 = 14$	**Write equation.**
$4n - 6 + 6 = 14 + 6$	**Add 6 to each side.**
$4n = 20$	**Simplify.**
$\frac{4n}{4} = \frac{20}{4}$	**Divide each side by 4.**
$n = 5$	**Simplify.**

REWRITE SUMS
Remember that adding −6 is the same as subtracting 6.

▸ **Answer** The number is 5.

EXAMPLE 3 Writing and Solving a Two-Step Equation

Reading You want to find how many pages you need to read per week in order to finish several books in six weeks. The books have a total of 1244 pages. You have already read 500 pages. How many pages do you have to read per week?

SOLUTION

Let p be the number of pages to read per week.

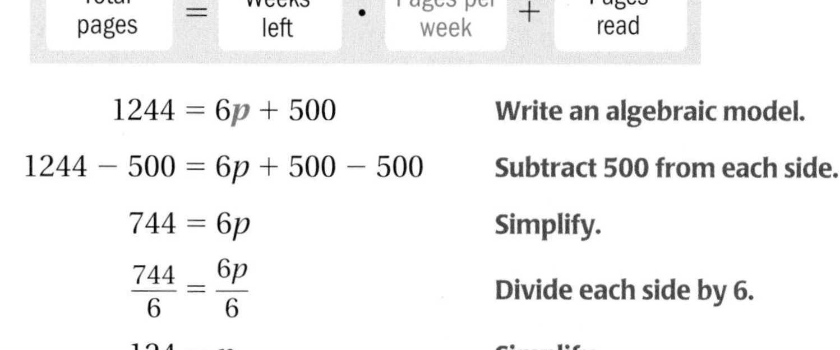

$1244 = 6p + 500$	**Write an algebraic model.**
$1244 - 500 = 6p + 500 - 500$	**Subtract 500 from each side.**
$744 = 6p$	**Simplify.**
$\frac{744}{6} = \frac{6p}{6}$	**Divide each side by 6.**
$124 = p$	**Simplify.**

▸ **Answer** You have to read 124 pages per week.

✓ GUIDED PRACTICE for Examples 2 and 3

2. The difference of six times a number and 9 is −3. What is the number?

3. **What If?** Suppose in Example 3 that you have read 714 pages and have five weeks left. How many pages do you have to read per week?

3.4 EXERCISES

HOMEWORK KEY

★ = **STANDARDIZED TEST PRACTICE**
Exs. 7, 24, 27, 28, 33, 37, and 48

○ = **HINTS AND HOMEWORK HELP**
for Exs. 3, 5, 9, 11, 23 at classzone.com

SKILL PRACTICE

VOCABULARY Copy and complete the statement.

1. You use two inverse operations to solve a(n) _?_.

2. A(n) _?_ model uses symbols for operations and words to label information.

TRANSLATING STATEMENTS Match the statement with the correct equation.

SEE EXAMPLE 2 on p. 135 for Exs. 3–16

3. The sum of 3 and a number is 16. **A.** $3n - 2 = 16$

4. The product of 3 and a number is 16. **B.** $3(2n) = 16$

5. The difference of 3 times a number and 2 is 16. **C.** $3n = 16$

6. The product of 3 and twice a number is 16. **D.** $3 + n = 16$

7. ★ **MULTIPLE CHOICE** The sum of twice a number and 5 is 13. Which equation matches this statement?

(A) $2x + 5 = 13$ (B) $2x - 5 = 13$ (C) $x + 5 = 13$ (D) $5x + 13 = 2$

8. ERROR ANALYSIS Describe and correct the error made in translating the statement into an equation.
The difference of 3 times a number and −2 is 4.

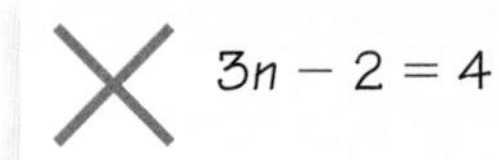

WRITING AND SOLVING TWO-STEP EQUATIONS Translate the statement into an equation. Then solve the equation.

9. The sum of 5 times a number and 4 is 9.

10. Seven subtracted from the quotient of a number and 2 is −6.

11. The sum of −2 times a number and 3.5 is 7.5.

12. The difference of 3 times a number and $-\frac{1}{2}$ is $-\frac{5}{2}$.

13. The absolute value of a number divided by 6 is 4.

14. Two times the absolute value of a number is 8.

15. The sum of the absolute value of a number and 6 is 12.

16. Five less than the product of 2 and the absolute value of a number is 3.

CHALLENGE Translate the statement into an equation. Then solve.

17. The product of a number divided by 5 and 2 is 1.

18. The sum of 2 and 3, plus 3 times a number, is −4.

19. The quotient of −36 and 9 exceeds 4 times a number by 8.

20. The product of 8 squared divided by 16 and a number is 24.

PROBLEM SOLVING

SEE EXAMPLES 1 AND 3 on pp. 134–135 for Exs. 21–29

21. **GUIDED PROBLEM SOLVING** You and your friends decide to have a car wash as a fundraiser for the school chorus. You spend \$15 on supplies and charge \$6 per car. At the end of the day your profit is \$93. How many cars did you and your friends wash?
   a. Write a verbal model.
   b. Translate your verbal model into an algebraic model.
   c. Solve the equation.
   d. Check that your answer is reasonable.

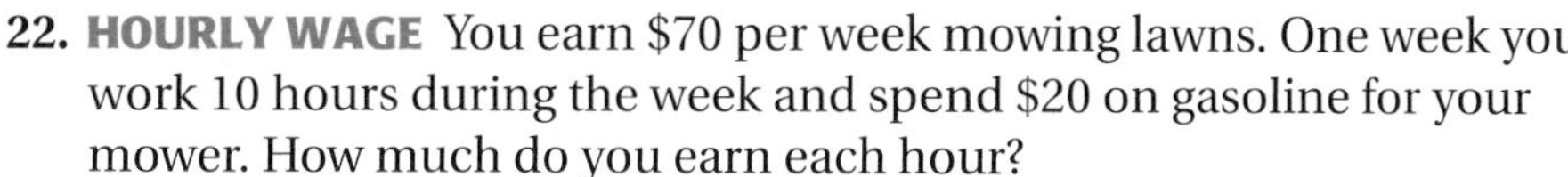

22. **HOURLY WAGE** You earn \$70 per week mowing lawns. One week you work 10 hours during the week and spend \$20 on gasoline for your mower. How much do you earn each hour?

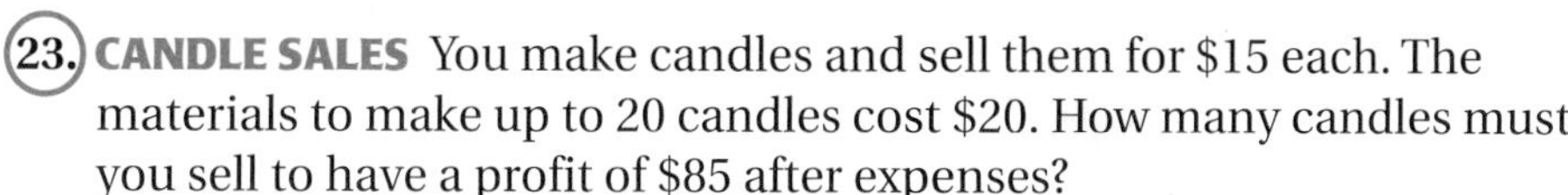

23. **CANDLE SALES** You make candles and sell them for \$15 each. The materials to make up to 20 candles cost \$20. How many candles must you sell to have a profit of \$85 after expenses?

24. ★ **MULTIPLE CHOICE** A bicycle rental shop charges \$5 per hour plus a fee of \$10 each time you rent a bicycle. Which equation can you use to find the number of hours you can rent a bicycle for \$45?

   (A) $5h + 10 = 45$ (B) $10h + 5 = 45$
   (C) $5 + h + 10 = 45$ (D) $15h = 45$

25. **MAGAZINE SUBSCRIPTION** You subscribe to a magazine that costs \$26 yearly. You make an initial payment of \$5 and then make three equal payments. How much is each payment?

26. **RUNNING TIME** How long will it take the dog to be 0.7 mile away from the owner? Use $d = 35t + 0.1$, where d is the distance the dog is from the owner after t hours.

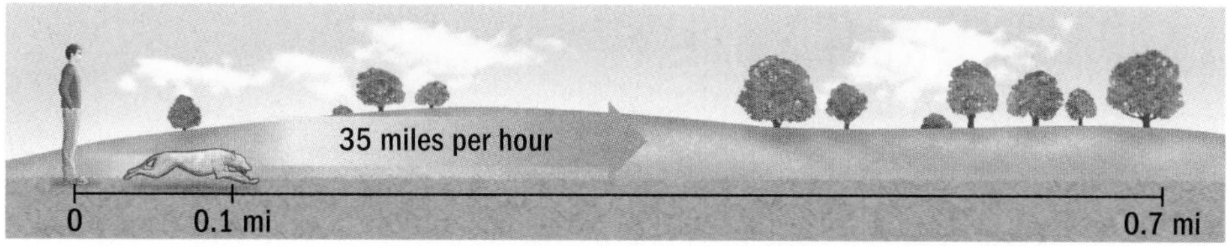

27. ★ **OPEN-ENDED MATH** Write two different two-step equations that both have 8 as a solution.

28. ★ **WRITING** Write a word problem that can be modeled by the equation $5x - 6 = 9$. Interpret the solution in terms of your problem.

29. **RESTAURANT** At a restaurant one day, 60 sandwiches were sold in all, some on rye bread and 28 on white bread. The number of sandwiches sold on rye bread was twice the number sold the day before. How many sandwiches on rye bread were sold the day before?

30. **PARTY SUPPLIES** You need 124 plastic forks for a party. At one store you buy the last 5 boxes, and each box contains 8 forks. At another store you find boxes that each contain 12 forks. How many of these boxes do you need to buy?

31. **SCHOOL FAIR** The senior class at your school made a \$300 profit at the school fair by having a dunk tank. The dunk tank cost \$135 to rent, and the senior class charged \$5 for each person to play. If one third of people who participated were adults, how many adults participated?

32. **GEOMETRY** The sum of the angles of a triangle is 180°. In triangle *ABC*, the measure of angle *A* is 12° greater than the measure of angle *C*, and the measure of angle *B* is 4 times as great as the measure of angle *C*. Write an equation where each angle is expressed in terms of the measure of angle *C*. Find the measure of each angle. Show your work.

33. ★ **SHORT RESPONSE** A taxicab costs \$2 plus an additional \$1.50 for every mile. Your ride cost \$17 before the tip. How many miles did you go? Will it cost twice as much to go twice as far? *Explain.*

REASONING Exercises 34 and 35 are missing information. Tell what information is needed to solve the problems.

34. You jog for 5 minutes and then you run for 20 minutes. For each week after, you jog for 5 minutes, but increase the time that you run. After how many weeks will you be training for a total of 85 minutes?

35. You have a job in which you make \$6 per hour plus tips. You made a total of \$34 yesterday. How much did you make in tips?

36. **GEOMETRY** The length of a rectangle is 15 feet more than three times its width. The perimeter is 94 feet. What is the area of the rectangle?

37. ★ **EXTENDED RESPONSE** The table shows how much it costs to rent videos, including \$5 for snacks. Write an equation for finding the cost of renting *x* videos. *Explain* how you found your equation. Find the cost of renting 12 videos.

Videos	1	2	3	4	5	6
Price	\$8	\$11	\$14	\$17	\$20	\$23

38. **CHALLENGE** Amanda takes her car to the repair shop. The mechanic starts working on her car at 10:30 A.M., takes a 45 minute lunch break, and then continues working into the afternoon. The parts to fix the car cost \$350 and the labor costs \$80 per hour. Amanda pays \$730 in all. At what time does the mechanic finish the work?

MIXED REVIEW

Get-Ready

Prepare for Lesson 3.5 in Exs. 39–41

Find the perimeter and area of the rectangle or square. *(p. 32)*

39. 3 ft, 12 ft

40. 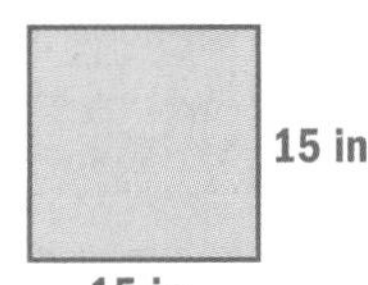

41. 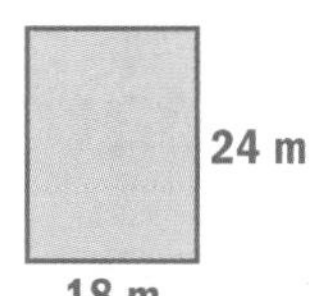

Simplify the expression. *(p. 88)*

42. $3(7 + x) + x$

43. $-2(8x - 3) + 2x$

44. $4x + 9(2x - 5)$

Solve the equation. *(p. 129)*

45. $6 + 4k = 14$

46. $\frac{y}{2} + 7 = -10$

47. $30 = -3a - 9$

48. ★ **MULTIPLE CHOICE** Which value is greatest? *(p. 57)*

Ⓐ $|-7|$ Ⓑ $-|-7|$ Ⓒ $-(-9)$ Ⓓ $-|9|$

QUIZ *for Lessons 3.1–3.4*

Solve the equation.

1. $x - 16 = 8$ *(p. 117)*

2. $8 + x = 3$ *(p. 117)*

3. $19r = 76$ *(p. 122)*

4. $\frac{y}{-1.4} = -5$ *(p. 122)*

5. $3x - 8 = 7$ *(p. 129)*

6. $14 = 2 + \frac{x}{3}$ *(p. 129)*

Translate the statement into an equation. Then solve. *(p. 134)*

7. The sum of 10 times a number and 5 is -15.

8. The difference of 4 times a number and -7 is 39.

9. **BICYCLE** Mary wants to buy a bicycle that costs $280. Her parents agree to pay $100. Mary will save $20 a week. Write and solve an equation to find how long it will take her to save enough money. *(p. 134)*

Brain Game

Behind the Magic

Choose any number. Multiply the number by 2. Add 14. Divide by 2. Subtract the number you started with. Multiply by 3. Your answer is 21.

To figure out why the answer is always 21, let x be the number you choose and write an algebraic expression that shows all of the steps. Then simplify the expression. What is your answer?

GOAL
Use the Internet to search for information necessary to write an equation.

3.4 Searching for Information

EXAMPLE

A class is planning a trip to the Naismith Memorial Basketball Hall of Fame in Springfield, Massachusetts. The class has $310 to spend on admission. There are 35 students in the class. How many adults can they afford to bring?

SOLUTION

Follow these steps to perform a search on the Internet:

STEP 1 **Pick** a search engine.

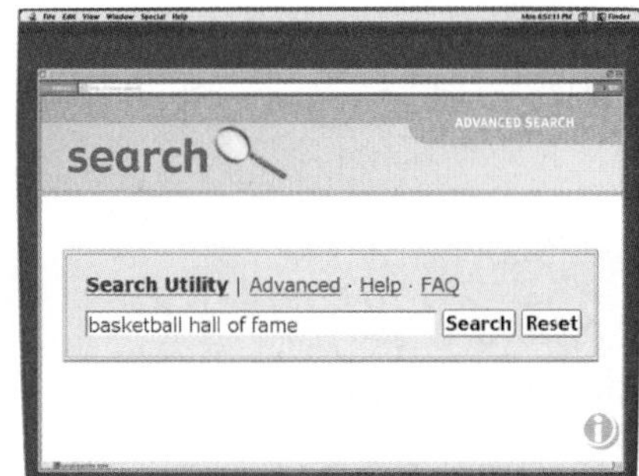

STEP 2 **Type** keywords that cover the topic you would like to search. Then select Search.

STEP 3 **Pick** a site from the results that is likely to have the information you need.

Use the steps described above to find the prices for students and adults. (*Hint:* There are over 35 people going, so the group rates would apply.)

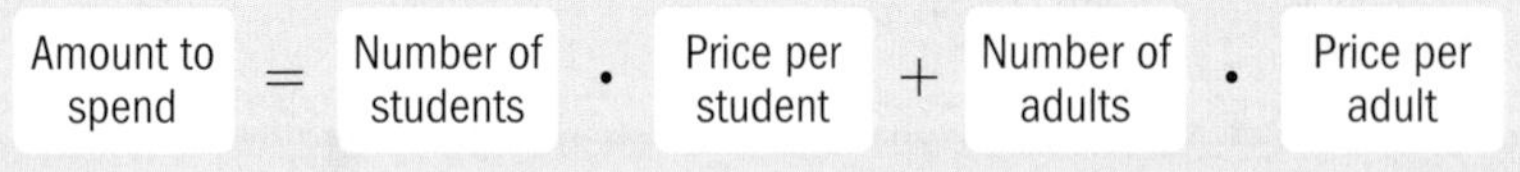

Amount to spend = Number of students • Price per student + Number of adults • Price per adult

PRACTICE **Use the results of your search.**

1. Write and solve an equation to solve the problem in the example.
2. Your class is planning a trip to a museum. Use the Internet to research prices for student and adult tickets at a nearby museum. If your class has $350 to spend on admission, how many adults can you afford to bring?

MIXED REVIEW *of Problem Solving*

Lessons 3.1–3.4

1. **MULTI-STEP PROBLEM** The difference between the height of the CN Tower in Toronto, Canada, and the height of the Empire State building in New York is 565 feet. The height of the CN Tower is 365 feet more than the height of the Sears Tower in Chicago.

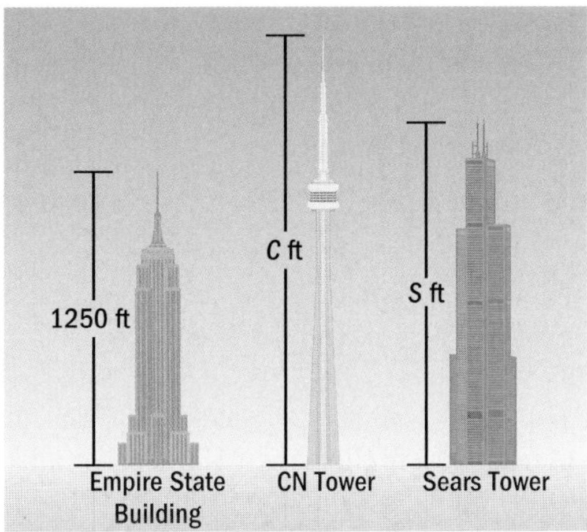

   a. Write a verbal model involving subtraction that can help you find the height of the CN Tower.

   b. Write and solve an equation to find the height of the CN Tower.

   c. Write and solve an addition equation to find the height of the Sears Tower.

2. **SHORT RESPONSE** A football team plays 16 games and averages 93 rushing yards per game. Write a verbal model involving division for finding the total number of rushing yards for the season. Write and solve an algebraic model. The team's goal for next year is to gain 25 more rushing yards per game. *Explain* how to adjust the model to find total rushing yards for next year. Then solve.

3. **OPEN-ENDED** *Describe* a real-world situation that can be modeled by an equation that requires both addition and division to solve. Then write and solve an equation. Show your steps, and write a sentence that describes the solution in the context of the problem.

4. **SHORT RESPONSE** It takes Jesse 60 minutes to drive 20 miles to an interview during rush hour. Use the formula $d = rt$ to find Jesse's average speed. If Jesse can travel half again as fast on the way home, how many minutes will it take him to return home? *Explain* your reasoning.

5. **GRIDDED ANSWER** Jen's truck gets 5 miles per gallon of diesel fuel. Jen will drive 3400 miles to deliver a shipment. If she leaves with a full tank and uses 80 gallons of fuel between each fill-up, how many times will Jen have to stop for fuel on her one-way trip?

6. **GRIDDED ANSWER** Lola traveled from her house to the city library by bus. She took one bus 3 miles. Then she changed buses. The second bus traveled at an average speed of 45 miles per hour. Lola's entire trip covered 18 miles. How many minutes did she spend on the second bus?

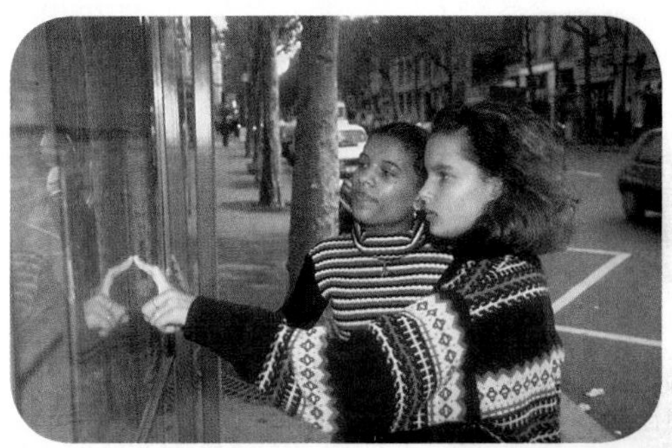

7. **EXTENDED RESPONSE** A rectangle has width x and length $x + 7$. The perimeter is 46 inches.

   a. Sketch and label the rectangle with expressions for its dimensions.

   b. Write and solve an equation to find the dimensions of the rectangle.

   c. What is the area of the rectangle?

   d. Suppose the length and width are each increased to 4 times their original dimensions. What effect does this have on the perimeter and area of the rectangle? *Explain* your reasoning.

3.5 Applying Geometric Formulas

Before You measured rectangles.
Now You'll use formulas for perimeter and area.
Why? So you can find areas, as for exhibits in Example 5.

KEY VOCABULARY
- **base,** *p. 142*
- **height,** *p. 142*

ACTIVITY

You can use a model to find the area of a triangle.

STEP 1 **Copy** the diagram on graph paper.

STEP 2 **Cut** out the three pieces.

STEP 3 **Arrange** the pieces to make two equal-sized triangles.

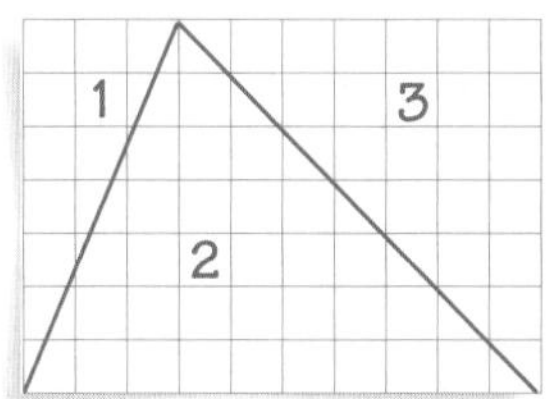

STEP 4 **Compare** the height of triangle 2 to the height of the original rectangle. What is the area of the rectangle? of triangle 2?

STEP 5 **Draw** your own triangle on graph paper so that its longest side is a side of a rectangle and the opposite vertex touches the opposite side of the rectangle. Find its area by following the steps above.

STEP 6 **Write** a formula for the area of a triangle.

To find the area of a triangle, you need to know the *base* and the *height.* Any side of a triangle can be labeled as the triangle's **base**. The perpendicular distance from a base to its opposite vertex is the **height** of a triangle.

KEY CONCEPT *For Your Notebook*

Area and Perimeter of a Triangle

Words The *area* of a triangle is one half the product of its base b and height h.

The *perimeter* of a triangle is the sum of the lengths of all three sides a, b, and c.

Algebra $A = \frac{1}{2}bh$ $P = a + b + c$

Diagram

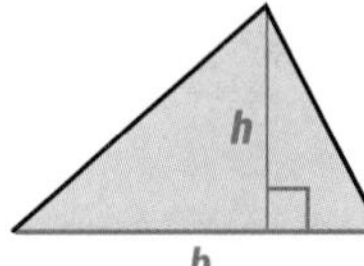

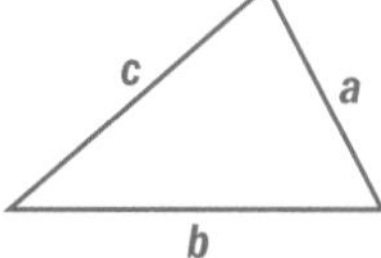

EXAMPLE 1 Finding Area and Perimeter of a Triangle

VOCABULARY
Remember that *perimeter* is measured in linear units, such as feet, and *area* is measured in square units, such as square feet, or ft^2.

Find the area and perimeter of the triangle.

$A = \frac{1}{2}bh$ $\qquad$ $P = a + b + c$

$= \frac{1}{2}(14)(12)$ $\qquad$ $= 13 + 14 + 15$

$= 84 \text{ in.}^2$ $\qquad$ $= 42 \text{ in.}$

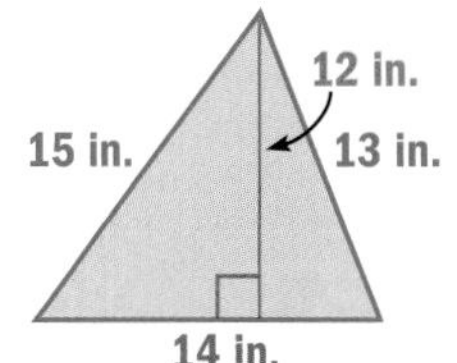

EXAMPLE 2 Finding the Area of a Triangle

Sailboats Find the area of the sail.

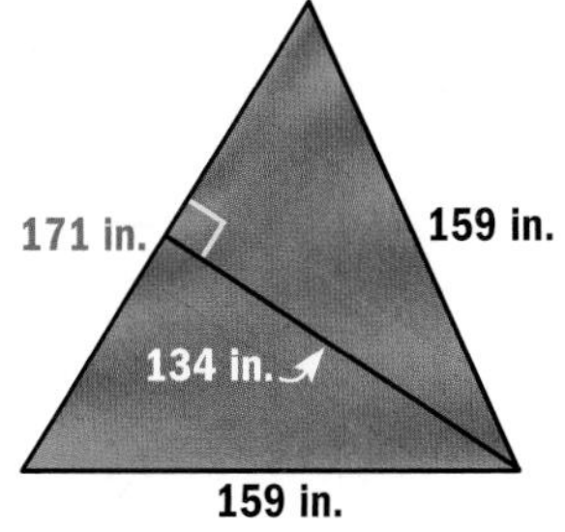

SOLUTION

$A = \frac{1}{2}bh$ **Write area formula.**

$= \frac{1}{2}(171)(134)$ **Substitute values.**

$= 11{,}457$ **Multiply.**

▸ **Answer** The area of the sail is 11,457 square inches.

✓ GUIDED PRACTICE for Examples 1 and 2

1. A triangle's height is 9 inches and its base is 10 inches. Find its area.
2. A triangle's side lengths are 4 feet, 6 feet, and 2.5 feet. Find its perimeter.

Unknown Dimensions Now that you can solve equations, you can use area and perimeter formulas to find unknown dimensions of geometric shapes.

EXAMPLE 3 Standardized Test Practice

Architecture An architect designs a rectangular entryway with an area of 63 square feet and a length of 9 feet. What is the width?

Ⓐ 7 feet Ⓑ 9 feet Ⓒ 16 feet Ⓓ 567 feet

ELIMINATE CHOICES
Since $A = lw$, the length has to be less than 63. So, you can eliminate choice D.

SOLUTION

$A = lw$ **Write area formula.**

$63 = 9w$ **Substitute values.**

$\frac{63}{9} = \frac{9w}{9}$ **Divide each side by 9.**

$7 = w$ **Simplify.**

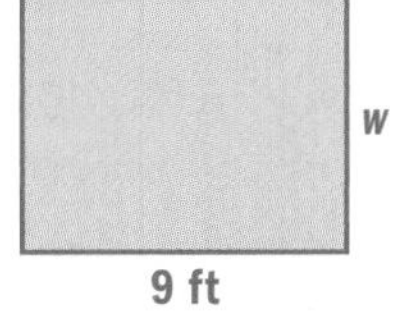

▸ **Answer** The width is 7 feet. The correct answer is A. Ⓐ Ⓑ Ⓒ Ⓓ

EXAMPLE 4 Finding an Unknown Length

The rectangle at the right has a perimeter of 20 inches. Find the length of the rectangle.

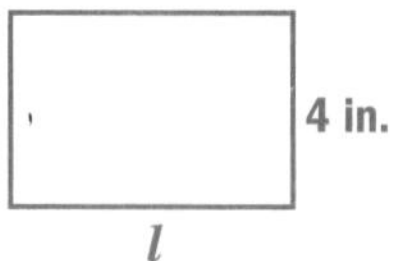

$P = 2l + 2w$	**Write perimeter formula.**
$20 = 2l + 2(4)$	**Substitute 20 for *P* and 4 for *w*.**
$20 = 2l + 8$	**Multiply.**
$20 - 8 = 2l + 8 - 8$	**Subtract 8 from each side.**
$12 = 2l$	**Simplify.**
$\frac{12}{2} = \frac{2l}{2}$	**Divide each side by 2.**
$6 = l$	**Simplify.**

▶ **Answer** The length of the rectangle is 6 inches.

EXAMPLE 5 Using an Area Formula

Zoo Exhibit A polar bear exhibit includes a rectangular pool and rocks. Find the area of the region with rocks.

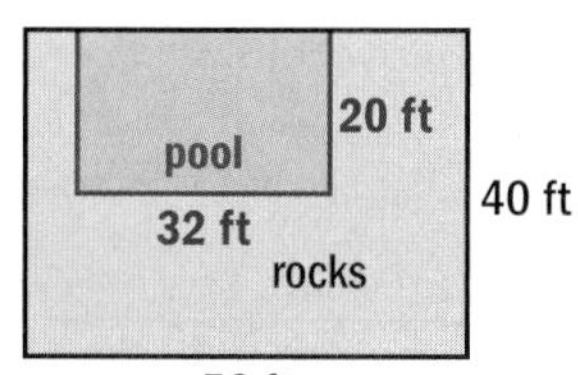

SOLUTION

Let r be the area of the region with rocks.

$40 \cdot 56 = 20 \cdot 32 + r$	
$2240 = 640 + r$	**Write an algebraic model.**
$2240 - 640 = 640 - 640 + r$	**Subtract 640 from each side.**
$1600 = r$	**Simplify.**

at classzone.com

▶ **Answer** The area of the region with rocks is 1600 square feet.

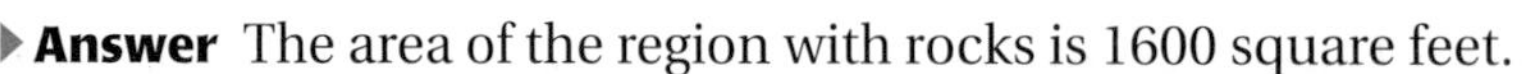

✓ GUIDED PRACTICE for Examples 3, 4, and 5

Find the unknown dimension.

3. Perimeter = 36 feet

8 ft

l

4. Area = 32 mm^2

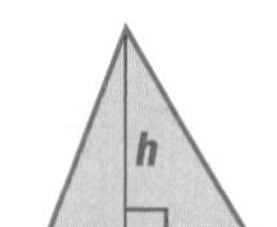

5. Area = 6 in.^{2}

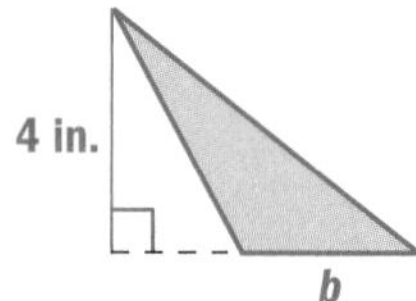

6. What If? In Example 5, suppose the length of the exhibit area was 64 feet instead of 56 feet. Find the area of the region with rocks.

3.5 EXERCISES

HOMEWORK KEY

★ = **STANDARDIZED TEST PRACTICE** Exs. 10, 13–15, 24–27, 33, and 43

○ = **HINTS AND HOMEWORK HELP** for Exs. 3, 5, 7, 9, 27 at classzone.com

SKILL PRACTICE

VOCABULARY **Copy and complete the statement.**

1. In order to find the area of a triangle, you need to know the length of a(n) __?__ and the __?__.

2. The __?__ of a triangle is the sum of the lengths of all three of its sides.

FINDING AREA AND PERIMETER **Find the area and perimeter of the triangle.**

SEE EXAMPLES 1 AND 2 on p. 143 for Exs. 3–6

(3.)

4.

(5.)

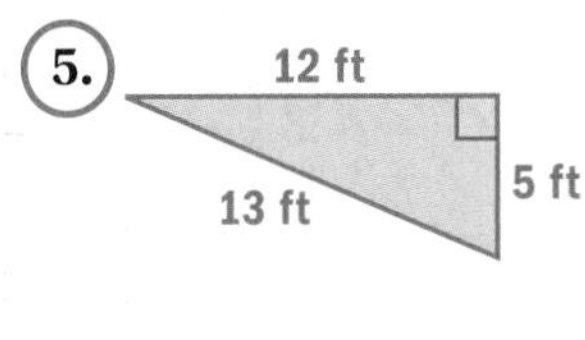

6. **ERROR ANALYSIS** Describe and correct the error made in finding the area of a triangle with a base of 5 inches and a height of 4 inches.

✗ $A = \frac{1}{2}(5 \text{ in.})(4 \text{ in.})$

$A = \frac{1}{2}(20 \text{ in.})$

$A = 10 \text{ in.}$

FINDING DIMENSIONS **Find the unknown dimension.**

SEE EXAMPLES 3 AND 4 on pp. 143–144 for Exs. 7–10

(7.) $A = 18 \text{ ft}^2$

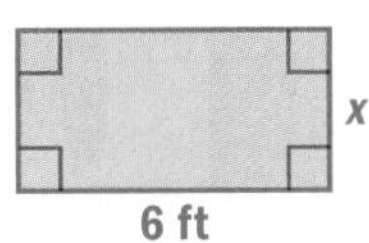

8. $A = 49 \text{ in.}^2$

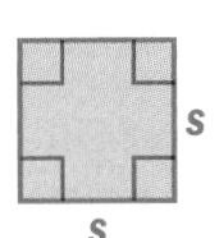

(9.) $P = 60$ m

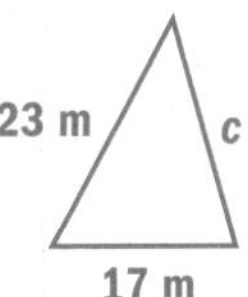

10. ★ **MULTIPLE CHOICE** What is the length, in feet, of a rectangle that has a perimeter of 24 feet and a width of 4 feet?

Ⓐ 4 feet Ⓑ 8 feet Ⓒ 12 feet Ⓓ 32 feet

FINDING COMBINED AREA **Find the area of the figure.**

11.

12.

★ **OPEN-ENDED MATH** **Draw and label two triangles with different dimensions that have the given area.**

13. 36 square feet

14. 20 square inches

15. 9 square meters

USING PERIMETER AND AREA Find the unknown dimension.

16. A rectangle has a perimeter of 146 inches, a length of 49 inches, and a width of $2x$. What is the value of x?

17. A triangle has an area of 36 square meters, a height of 8 meters, and a base of $3y$. What is the value of y?

18. A triangle has an area of 5 square meters and a base of $2x$. What is the height of the triangle in terms of x?

19. A rectangle has an area of 70 square inches and a width of $3.5w$ inches. What is the length of the rectangle in terms of w?

CHALLENGE Find the value of the variable in the rectangular figures, given the area of the shaded region.

20. $A = 16\text{ m}^2$

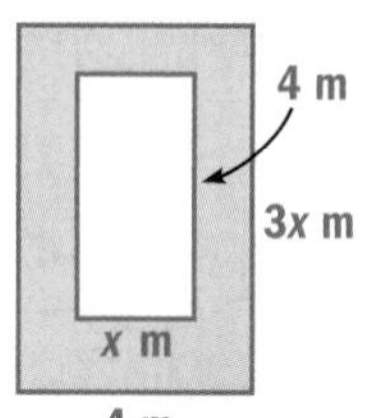

21. $A = 76\text{ cm}^2$

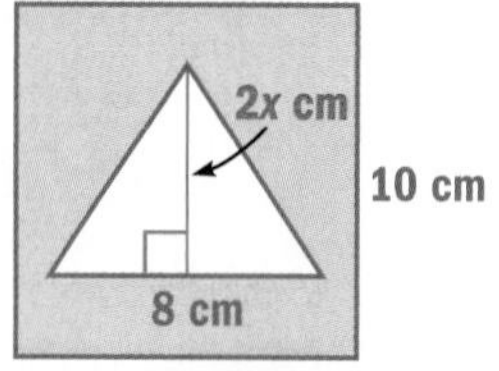

22. $A = 180\text{ ft}^2$

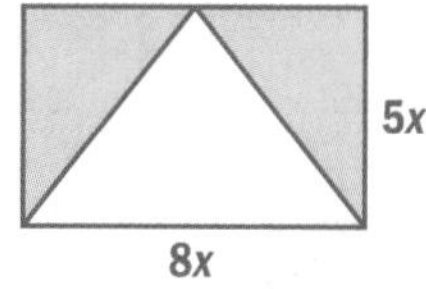

PROBLEM SOLVING

SEE EXAMPLES 3, 4, AND 5 on p. 144 for Exs. 23–27

23. **GUIDED PROBLEM SOLVING** Find the area of the stone patio inside the backyard.
    a. Find the area of the rectangular portion of the patio.
    b. Find the area of the square portion of the patio.
    c. Add the two areas.

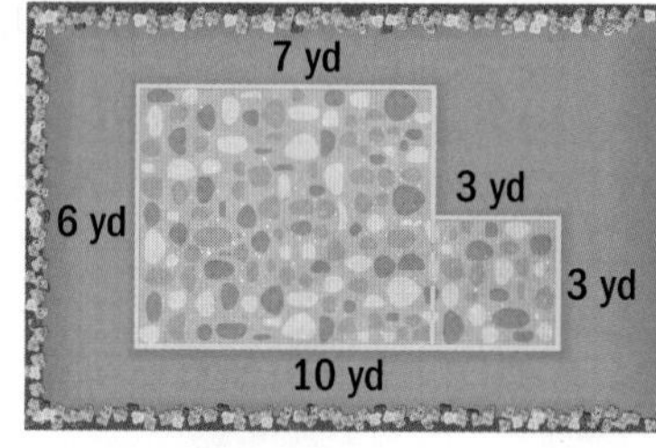

24. ★ **MULTIPLE CHOICE** A rectangular garden has an area of 64 square feet. Its length is 16 feet. Which equation can you use to find the width?

    (A) $16 = 64 - x$ (B) $32 = x + 16$ (C) $16 = 64x$ (D) $64 = 16x$

25. ★ **MULTIPLE CHOICE** What is the length of a rectangular room that is 22 feet wide and has a perimeter of 114 feet?

    (A) 20 feet (B) 25 feet (C) 30 feet (D) 35 feet

26. ★ **WRITING** In Example 2 on page 143, the bottom of the triangle has a length of 159 inches. *Explain* why this is not used as the base.

27. ★ **SHORT RESPONSE** Michelle and Kate share a bedroom that is 18 feet by 14 feet. They want to divide the room so that each sister has half the area. Kate jokingly marks a square with sides 11 feet long in the center of the room. Does Kate have half the area of the room? *Explain.*

28. GEOMETRY Find the area of the regular *hexagon*. All the triangles are congruent.

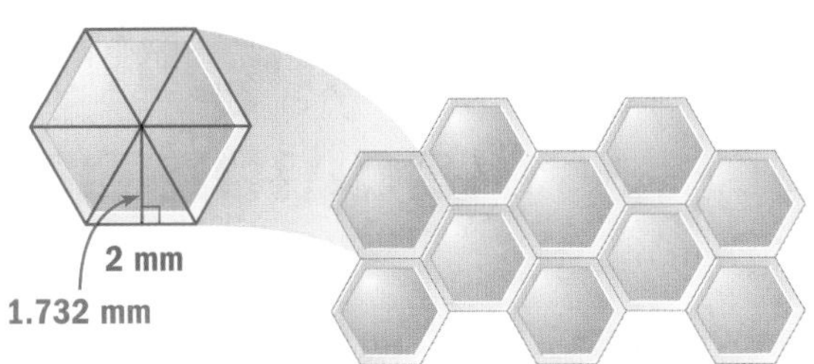

REASONING Draw a triangle with a right angle at *A* on graph paper. Make the lengths of the sides through *A* whole numbers. Find the area. *Describe* how the area of the triangle changes if you change the triangle as described below.

29. Double the height.

30. Double the base.

31. Double both the height and the base.

32. Change its shape, but not its base or height.

33. ★ **EXTENDED RESPONSE** Use the advertisement shown.

a. **Calculate** Find the area of the tent floor.

b. **Estimate** Estimate the dimensions of a rectangular sleeping bag and find its area.

c. **Analyze** Could four sleeping bags fit in the tent without overlapping? *Explain* your reasoning. Include a diagram.

34. WINDOWS A roll of weather stripping for windows is 108 inches long and costs \$4. You need enough to go around three square windows that measure 3 feet on each side and one rectangular window that measures 3 feet by 5 feet. Is \$25 enough money? *Explain.*

35. CHALLENGE The distance between lines *a* and *b* is constant. *Explain* why triangles *VYZ*, *WYZ*, and *XYZ* have the same area.

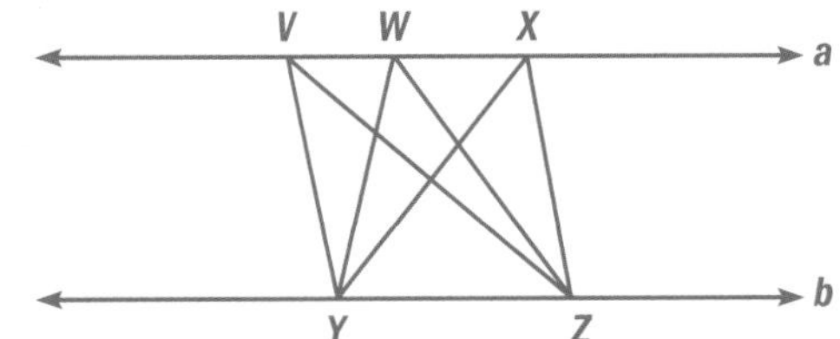

MIXED REVIEW

Prepare for Lesson 3.6 in Exs. 36–38

Find the difference. *(p. 68)*

36. $-18 - 42$

37. $-21 - (-14)$

38. $10 - 15$

Copy and complete the statement with <, >, or =. *(p. 57)*

39. $3 \underline{?} -3$

40. $-5 \underline{?} -6$

41. $-17 \underline{?} -13$

42. $13 \underline{?} |13|$

43. ★ **MULTIPLE CHOICE** What is the value of $6r + 7s$ when $r = 5$ and $s = 2$? *(p. 13)*

Ⓐ 20 Ⓑ 44 Ⓒ 52 Ⓓ 137

3.6 Solving Inequalities Using Addition or Subtraction

Before	You solved equations using addition or subtraction.
Now	You'll solve inequalities using addition or subtraction.
Why?	So you can find a minimum throwing distance, as in Example 3.

KEY VOCABULARY
- **inequality,** *p. 148*
- **solution of an inequality,** *p. 148*
- **equivalent inequalities,** *p. 149*

Disc Golf In a game of disc golf, the target is beyond a pond, the far end of which is 300 feet away. Your first throw travels 134 feet. How long does your second throw have to be in order to clear the pond? You will use an inequality to answer this question in Example 3.

An **inequality**, such as $x \le 6$, is a statement formed by placing an inequality symbol between two expressions. The **solution of an inequality** is the set of numbers that you can substitute for the variable to make the inequality true. To translate sentences into inequalities, look for the following phrases:

Phrase	Symbol
is less than	$<$
is less than or equal to	$\le$
is greater than	$>$
is greater than or equal to	$\ge$

You can graph the solution of an inequality using a number line. When graphing inequalities with $>$ or $<$, use an open circle. When graphing inequalities with $\ge$ or $\le$, use a closed circle.

EXAMPLE 1 Graphing Inequalities

Inequality	Graph	Verbal Phrase
a. $y < 7$	2 3 4 5 6 7 8	All numbers less than 7
b. $q \le 3$	−2 −1 0 1 2 3 4	All numbers less than or equal to 3
c. $x > -5$	−6 −4 −2 0	All numbers greater than −5
d. $h \ge 2\frac{1}{2}$	0 1 2 3	All numbers greater than or equal to $2\frac{1}{2}$

Solving Inequalities When you solve an inequality, you find all solutions of the inequality. Inequalities that have the same solutions are **equivalent inequalities**. You can solve some inequalities by adding or subtracting.

KEY CONCEPT — For Your Notebook

Addition and Subtraction Properties of Inequality

Words Adding or subtracting the same number on each side of an inequality produces an equivalent inequality.

Algebra If $a > b$, then $a + c > b + c$.

If $a > b$, then $a - c > b - c$.

EXAMPLE 2 Solving Inequalities

VOCABULARY
Just as with equations, you can solve inequalities by using *inverse operations* to write equivalent inequalities.

Solve the inequality. Then graph its solution.

a. $x - 5 < 8$ **Original inequality**

$x - 5 + 5 < 8 + 5$ **Add 5 to each side.**

$x < 13$ **Simplify.**

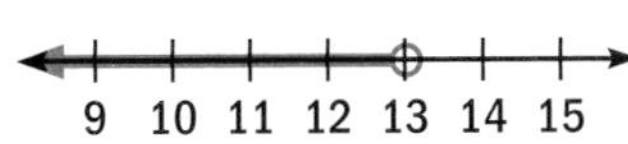

b. $y - 7 \geq -10$ **Original inequality**

$y - 7 + 7 \geq -10 + 7$ **Add 7 to each side.**

$y \geq -3$ **Simplify.**

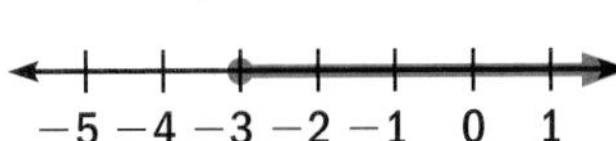

AVOID ERRORS
The graph of $m > 7$ starts just after 7, not at 8, because numbers such as 7.01 are also solutions.

c. $8 + m > 15$ **Original inequality**

$8 - 8 + m > 15 - 8$ **Subtract 8 from each side.**

$m > 7$ **Simplify.**

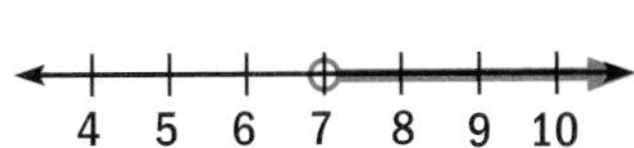

✓ GUIDED PRACTICE for Examples 1 and 2

Graph and write a verbal phrase for the inequality.

1. $z \geq -1$ **2.** $4 > p$ **3.** $k \leq -3.5$ **4.** $m > \frac{1}{2}$

Solve the inequality. Then graph its solution.

5. $x - 3 > -2$ **6.** $6 > t - 1$ **7.** $12 \geq p + 14$

8. $x + 5 < 10$ **9.** $t + 9 \leq 6$ **10.** $-4 < k - 3$

EXAMPLE 3 Writing and Solving an Inequality

Disc Golf Using an inequality, you can find the distance the second throw must travel to clear the pond described on page 148. Let d be the distance of your second throw.

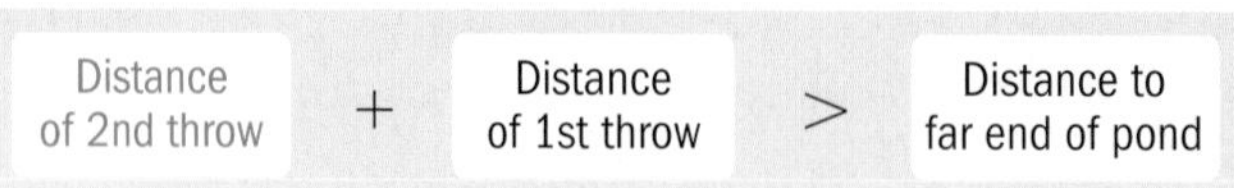

$d + 134 > 300$	**Write an algebraic model.**
$d + 134 - 134 > 300 - 134$	**Subtract 134 from each side.**
$d > 166$	**Simplify.**

at classzone.com

▸ **Answer** Your second throw needs to travel more than 166 feet.

GUIDED PRACTICE for Example 3

11. **What If?** Suppose in Example 3 that your first throw went 155 feet. How far does your second throw have to go to clear the pond?

3.6 EXERCISES

HOMEWORK KEY

★ = **STANDARDIZED TEST PRACTICE** Exs. 20, 25–28, 40, 41, 44, 47, and 60

○ = **HINTS AND HOMEWORK HELP** for Exs. 7, 11, 13, 17, 39 at classzone.com

SKILL PRACTICE

1. **VOCABULARY** Copy and complete: $-4 + x < -6$ and $x < -2$ are _?_.

MATCHING **Match the inequality with its graph.**

SEE EXAMPLE 1 on p. 148 for Exs. 2–10

2. $x < -1$ A. −2 −1 0 1 2

3. $x \le 1$ B. −2 −1 0 1 2

4. $x \ge 1$ C. −2 −1 0 1 2

5. $x > -1$ D. −2 −1 0 1 2

WRITING INEQUALITIES **Write the inequality and the verbal phrase represented by the graph.**

6. −3 −2 −1 0 1 2

7. −10 −5 0 5 10 15

8. −2 −1 0 1 2 3

9. −2 0 2 4 6 8

10. **ERROR ANALYSIS** Describe and correct the error made in graphing $x \geq -6$.

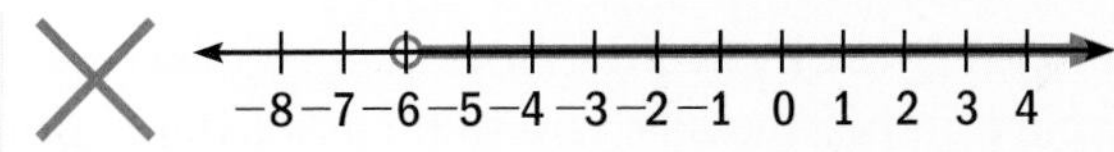

SOLVING INEQUALITIES Solve the inequality. Then graph its solution.

SEE EXAMPLE 2 on p. 149 for Exs. 11–20

11. $12 + p < 7$
12. $k + 4 \leq 11$
13. $n - 6 > 3$
14. $17 + r \geq 25$
15. $-8 \geq m - 19$
16. $-3.5 < w - 9$
17. $5.45 + b < -3.55$
18. $\frac{2}{3} \leq p - 2\frac{1}{3}$
19. $t + \frac{1}{4} > 5$
20. ★ **MULTIPLE CHOICE** Which inequality has 23 for a solution?

   (A) $x - 3 > 20$ (B) $x - 3 \geq 20$ (C) $x - 3 < 20$ (D) $x + 3 \leq 20$

SOLUTIONS Tell which positive integers less than 10 are solutions.

21. $-8 + x \leq 2$
22. $x - 20 > -15$
23. $-10 - x \leq -4$
24. $5 + x \leq 9$

★ **OPEN-ENDED MATH Write two equivalent inequalities for the phrase. Then graph the solution.**

25. all real numbers less than 4
26. all real numbers greater than -10
27. all real numbers greater than 19
28. all real numbers less than -7
29. **REASONING** Are the inequalities $x < 2$ and $2 > x$ equivalent? *Explain.*

CHALLENGE *Describe* the values of x that will make the statement true.

30. $|x| < 3$
31. $|x| > 2$
32. $|x| + 1 \leq 5$
33. $|x| + 1 \geq 7$

In Exercises 34–36, write two verbal sentences that describe the *compound inequality*.

EXTENSION Compound Inequalities

The set of all real numbers greater than or equal to 0 *and* less than 4 can be represented by the following graph.

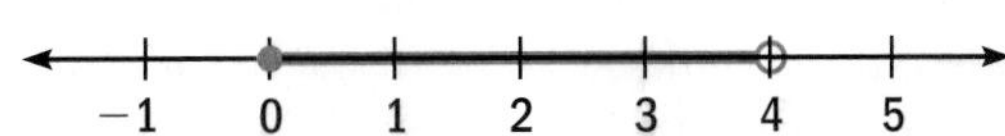

This set of numbers can be written as two inequalities or as a single *compound inequality.*

two inequalities	compound inequality
$0 \leq x$ and $x < 4$	$0 \leq x < 4$

The compound inequality can be read in these two ways:

x is greater than or equal to 0 and x is less than 4.
x is between 0 and 4, including 0.

34. $-2 < y < 1$
35. $7 \leq t < 9$
36. $4 \leq m \leq 11$

PROBLEM SOLVING

SEE EXAMPLE 3 on p. 150 for Exs. 37–39

37. **GUIDED PROBLEM SOLVING** On four tests you scored 90, 85, 98, and 87. To earn a B in math class, you need at least 425 points on five tests. Write and solve an inequality that represents the possible test scores you could get on your fifth test and still get at least a B in the class.

    a. Add your current scores.

    b. Let x represent the fifth score. Write and solve the inequality.

    c. Graph the possible test scores.

38. **BANKING** You have $33.96 in a savings account. At your bank, you must have a minimum balance of $50 in your account to avoid a fee. Write and solve an inequality to represent the amount of money you must deposit in order to equal or exceed the minimum balance.

39. **SKI JUMPING** In a ski jumping competition, the top four jumpers perform as shown. How much farther does the fourth place jumper need to jump in order to place first? Write and solve an addition inequality that describes the situation.

Name	Distance
Cara	57 m
Jason	91.5 m
Marisa	85 m
Mitchell	93.5 m

40. ★ **OPEN-ENDED MATH** Write and solve a real-world problem that can be solved using the inequality $p + 4 < 10$.

41. ★ **WRITING** *Explain* why $x - 3 \geq 10$ and $x \geq 13$ are equivalent inequalities. Then explain why 13 and 20 would be useful values to substitute for x to check the solution.

42. **BIPLANE RIDE** Your family bought your grandmother a biplane ride for her sixtieth birthday. The flight can last up to 1 hour 15 minutes.

    The ride has 10 minutes of corkscrew rolls, 15 minutes of hammerheads, and 30 minutes of over-water flying. Write and solve an addition inequality to find how much time can be used for scenic low-altitude flying without going over the time limit.

43. **RACING** You run a race in 2.5 hours. The record winning time is 1.9 hours. Write and solve an inequality to find the number of minutes you can improve by and break the record.

44. ★ **MULTIPLE CHOICE** The frequency f of the human singing voice is between about 81 hertz and about 1100 hertz. Which statement is *not* true about f?

    Ⓐ $f \geq 81$ Ⓑ $f \leq 1100$ Ⓒ $81 \leq f$ Ⓓ $f \geq 1100$

45. TIGER POPULATION The map shows the tiger population in India around 1900. The population dropped to below 2000 in 1972 but has rebounded since then, increasing by about 2200 animals. Write and solve an inequality to find the number of tigers today. How many whole tiger icons would be on the map today?

Indian Tiger Population, 1900

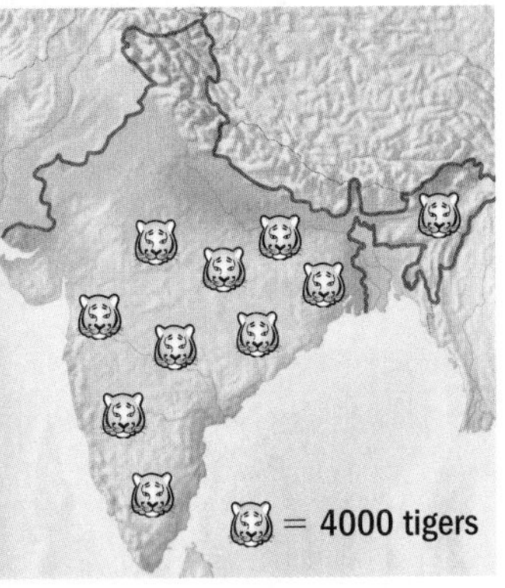

46. ADVERTISING During the first Super Bowl in 1967, a 30 second television commercial cost about \$42,000. In 2005, advertisers paid about \$2.4 million for a 30 second commercial. Assuming those were the least and greatest costs during that period, write two inequalities that together describe the cost c of 30 seconds of commercial time during the Super Bowl from 1967 through 2005.

47. ★ SHORT RESPONSE Lauren can spend at most \$75 at the mall. She plans to buy a backpack on sale for between \$25 and \$35. She'll spend the remaining money on gifts. Let x represent the cost of the gifts. Write and solve an addition equation to find the least amount Lauren will be able to spend on gifts. Repeat this to find the greatest amount Lauren can spend. *Describe* possible values for x using inequalities.

48. CHALLENGE The *triangle inequality theorem* states that the sum of the lengths of any two sides of a triangle is greater than the length of the third side. A side of a triangle is 13 inches. Another side measures 6 inches. What values can the length x of the third side be? *Explain* your reasoning.

MIXED REVIEW

Prepare for Lesson 3.7 in Exs. 49–51

Solve the equation. *(p. 122)*

49. $\frac{x}{6} = -7$ **50.** $4m = 36$ **51.** $-9m = 126$

Find the quotient. *(p. 77)*

52. $\frac{-22}{11}$ **53.** $\frac{0}{3}$ **54.** $\frac{45}{-5}$ **55.** $\frac{-63}{-9}$

56. $\frac{46}{2}$ **57.** $\frac{35}{-7}$ **58.** $\frac{-56}{-4}$ **59.** $\frac{-72}{6}$

60. ★ MULTIPLE CHOICE What is nine and fifty-three thousandths written in standard form? *(p. 759)*

(A) 9.0053 (B) 9.053 (C) 9.53 (D) 953,000

3.7 Solving Inequalities Using Multiplication or Division

Before You solved equations using multiplication or division.

Now You'll solve inequalities using multiplication or division.

Why? So you can find measurements, as in Example 3.

KEY VOCABULARY
- **inequality,** *p. 148*
- **solution of an inequality,** *p. 148*
- **equivalent inequalities,** *p. 149*

Solving inequalities and solving equations have one important difference. Look at what happens when you multiply each side of the inequality $3 > 1$ by -1.

$$3 > 1$$

$$3(-1) \ \underline{?} \ 1(-1)$$

$$-3 < -1$$

You can use a number line to check this.

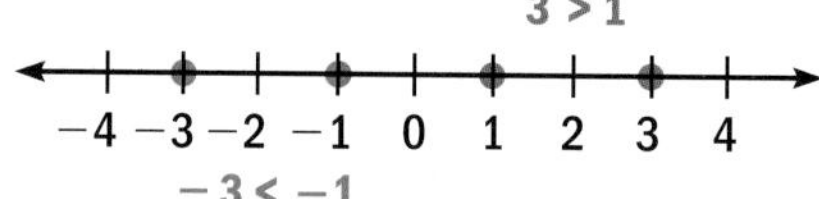

From the number line you know that $-3 < -1$. So when multiplying or dividing each side of an inequality by a negative number, you must *reverse the direction of the inequality symbol.*

KEY CONCEPT — For Your Notebook

Multiplication Properties of Inequality

Words	Algebra
Multiplying by a positive Multiplying each side of an inequality by a *positive* number produces an equivalent inequality.	$4x < 10$ $\left(\frac{1}{4}\right)(4x) < \left(\frac{1}{4}\right)(10)$
Multiplying by a negative Multiplying each side of an inequality by a *negative* number and *reversing the direction of the inequality symbol* produces an equivalent inequality.	$-5x < 10$ $\left(-\frac{1}{5}\right)(-5x) > \left(-\frac{1}{5}\right)(10)$

EXAMPLE 1 Solving an Inequality Using Multiplication

$-\frac{1}{8}n \geq 2$ **Original inequality**

$-8 \cdot \left(-\frac{1}{8}\right)n \leq -8 \cdot 2$ **Multiply each side by −8. Reverse inequality symbol.**

$n \leq -16$ **Simplify.**

KEY CONCEPT — *For Your Notebook*

Division Properties of Inequality

Words	Algebra
Dividing by a positive Dividing each side of an inequality by a *positive* number produces an equivalent inequality.	$2x < 10$ $\frac{2x}{2} < \frac{10}{2}$
Dividing by a negative Dividing each side of an inequality by a *negative* number and *reversing the direction of the inequality symbol* produces an equivalent inequality.	$-5x < 15$ $\frac{-5x}{-5} > \frac{15}{-5}$

TAKE NOTES
You could use a table to organize the information about reversing the inequality symbol.

EXAMPLE 2 Solving an Inequality Using Division

$15 > -3m$ **Original inequality**

$\frac{15}{-3} < \frac{-3m}{-3}$ **Divide each side by −3. Reverse inequality symbol.**

$-5 < m$ **Simplify.**

EXAMPLE 3 Using the Division Property of Inequality

Biology About 15,000 fruit-eating bats live on Barro Colorado Island. Yearly they eat up to 61,440,000 grams of fruit. Write and solve an inequality to find about how many grams g of fruit each bat eats yearly.

SOLUTION

Number of bats • Grams each bat eats ≤ Maximum amount eaten yearly

$15{,}000g \leq 61{,}440{,}000$ **Write an algebraic model.**

$\frac{15{,}000g}{15{,}000} \leq \frac{61{,}440{,}000}{15{,}000}$ **Divide each side by 15,000.**

$g \leq 4096$ **Simplify.**

▶ **Answer** Each bat eats up to 4096 grams of fruit in a year.

READING
Read the problem carefully to decide which inequality symbol to use. Because you know the bats eat "up to" 61,440,000 grams, then you know that the amount they eat is "≤" 61,440,000.

✓ GUIDED PRACTICE for Examples 1, 2, and 3

Solve the inequality.

1. $\frac{t}{6} > 4$
2. $-\frac{1}{2}x \leq 10$
3. $27 > -3t$
4. $9n < 63$

5. **Fruit Bats** A bat that weighs about 25 grams can eat up to 2.5 times its body mass in figs in one night. How many grams g of figs can it eat?

3.7 EXERCISES

HOMEWORK KEY

★ = **STANDARDIZED TEST PRACTICE** Exs. 29, 36, 37, 46, 52, 53, and 67

○ = **HINTS AND HOMEWORK HELP** for Exs. 5, 11, 23, 25, 43 at classzone.com

SKILL PRACTICE

1. **VOCABULARY** Copy and complete: When you multiply both sides of an inequality by a negative number, you need to __?__ the inequality symbol.

2. **VOCABULARY** Copy and complete: Dividing each side of an inequality by a __?__ number makes an equivalent equation.

PROPERTIES OF INEQUALITIES **Tell whether you would reverse the inequality symbol when solving. Write *Yes* or *No*. Do not solve.**

SEE EXAMPLES 1 AND 2 on pp. 154–155 for Exs. 3–29

3. $\frac{1}{3}y < 18$ 4. $-6x \geq 24$ 5. $\frac{m}{-8} > 3$ 6. $2b \leq -14$

MATCHING **Solve the inequality. Match the inequality with the graph of its solution.**

7. $\frac{1}{4}x \leq 8$ 8. $-4x \geq 8$ 9. $4x \geq -8$ 10. $-\frac{1}{4}x \leq 8$

A. −8 −6 −4 −2 0 2

B. −40 −32 −24 −16 −8 0

C. −8 −6 −4 −2 0 2

D. 0 8 16 24 32 40

SOLVING INEQUALITIES **Solve the inequality. Then graph its solution.**

11. $\frac{1}{2}x < 4$ 12. $\frac{m}{-7} \geq 6$ 13. $9 \leq 3z$ 14. $30 > -6p$

15. $\frac{1}{4}x > 1$ 16. $-\frac{1}{7}t \geq -3$ 17. $-\frac{1}{5}b \geq 72$ 18. $\frac{1}{3}d < -33$

19. $4g < 24$ 20. $12 \geq -3s$ 21. $-9c \leq 54$ 22. $5z < -15$

23. $7 > -\frac{1}{8}r$ 24. $-6t \geq 36$ 25. $-39 \leq 13k$ 26. $-\frac{1}{6}a < -54$

ERROR ANALYSIS **Describe and correct the error made in solving the inequality.**

27.

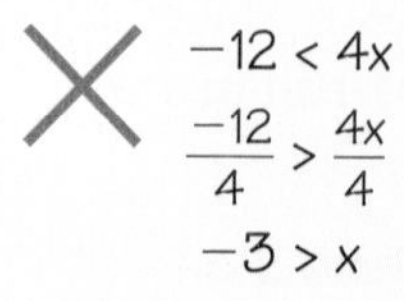

28.

$$-7x \geq 35$$
$$\frac{-7x}{-7} \geq \frac{35}{-7}$$
$$x \geq -5$$

29. ★ **MULTIPLE CHOICE** Which inequality is represented by the graph?

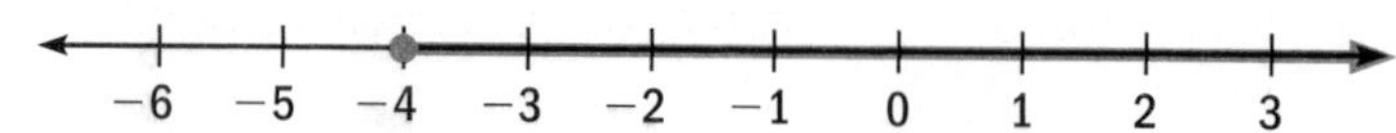

Ⓐ $2x \geq -8$ Ⓑ $3x < -12$ Ⓒ $\frac{1}{2}x > -2$ Ⓓ $\frac{x}{4} \leq -1$

SOLVING INEQUALITIES **Solve the inequality. Then graph its solution.**

30. $12 > 6 - 2x$

31. $4p - 9 \geq -1$

32. $5(5 - 2x) > 15$

33. $8g + 6 < 24$

34. $\frac{8}{3}y + 3 \leq 51$

35. $\frac{5}{6}(a - 12) \leq 20$

36. ★ **MULTIPLE CHOICE** What is the solution of the inequality $-4 > 26 + 2x$?

Ⓐ $x < -15$ Ⓑ $x > -15$ Ⓒ $x \leq 11$ Ⓓ $x < 11$

37. ★ **OPEN-ENDED MATH** Write an inequality where you reverse the inequality symbol to solve. Write another inequality where you do *not* reverse the inequality symbol to solve.

NUMBER SENSE ***Describe*** **all the numbers that satisfy both inequalities.**

38. $\frac{n}{2} < 2$ and $-6n \leq -6$

39. $3n + 4 < 52$ and $4n - 7 > 25$

CHALLENGE **Solve the compound inequality.**

40. $-6 < 2x < 10$

41. $-35 \leq 7x \leq -14$

42. $10 < 5x < 100$

PROBLEM SOLVING

SEE EXAMPLE 3 on p. 155 for Exs. 43–44

43. **DANCE** The student council must pay a disc jockey \$275 to work at a dance. A ticket to the dance costs \$5.50. Write and solve an inequality that gives the numbers of tickets that can be sold to cover the cost of the disc jockey.

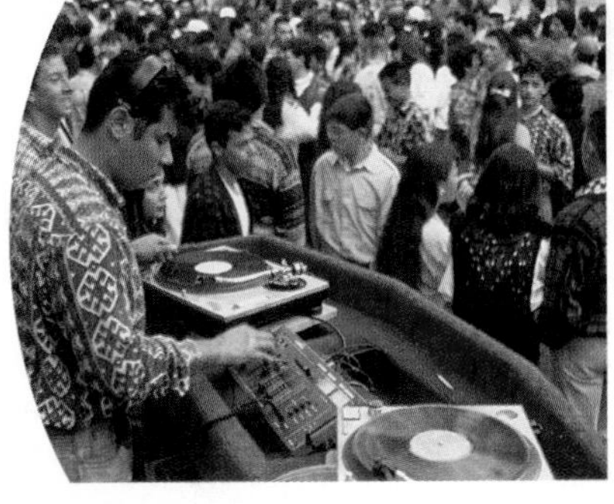

44. **FUNDRAISING** Students are having a car wash. They want to raise at least \$300 for disaster relief work. The profit is \$5 per car. How many cars must they wash?

45. **COMPARE AND CONTRAST** How is solving an inequality similar to solving an equation? How is solving an inequality different from solving an equation?

46. ★ **WRITING** A friend says that the solution of $-x < 0$ is all numbers greater than zero. Do you agree? *Explain.*

47. **MULTI-STEP PROBLEM** An elevator can hold a maximum of 2000 pounds. The average weight of a person is 150 pounds. Let p be the number of people the elevator can hold.

a. Write an inequality involving multiplication that models the situation.

b. Solve the inequality.

c. What does the answer tell you about the number of people who can ride in the elevator?

48. **BORROWING MONEY** You borrow \$200 from your aunt to buy a new surfboard. You pay her back \$12 per week. Write and solve an inequality to find when you will owe her less than \$60.

49. **GEOMETRY** The width of a rectangle is 12 meters and its area is greater than 228 square meters. Write and solve an inequality for the length l.

50. **TICKETS** Concert tickets are sold for \$15 in advance and \$20 at the door. There were 120 advance tickets sold. Write and solve an inequality to find how many tickets must be sold at the door for total ticket revenue to be at least \$4000.

51. **EXAMPLES AND NONEXAMPLES** *Describe* a real-world situation for which you can list all solutions of an inequality and a situation for which you cannot list all solutions of an inequality.

52. ★ **MULTIPLE CHOICE** John has test scores of 75, 84, 88, and 77 on four of his five science tests. He wants to get at least an average of 80 on his five tests. What is the lowest score that John can get on his last test to achieve his goal?

(A) 76 (B) 79 (C) 80 (D) 81

53. ★ **SHORT RESPONSE** Joe has x baseball cards. If he had 6 more than twice as many, he would have more than 20. If he had 10 fewer than three times as many, he would have fewer than 17. Write and solve two inequalities to find how many baseball cards Joe has.

54. **BICYCLE RACING** A professional bicycle racer trains by biking at least 50 miles a day. The racer starts by biking at a rate of 13 miles per hour for 2 hours. Then the racer bikes at a rate of 8 miles per hour. How long does the racer bike at this rate?

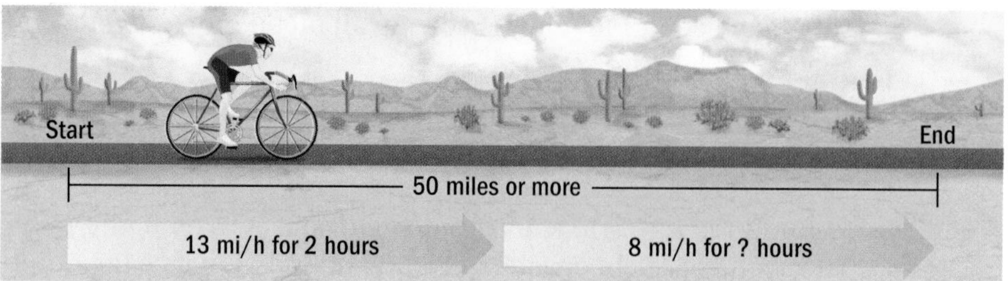

55. **COMPUTER SCREEN** The height of a rectangular computer screen is 20 inches less than twice the width. The perimeter is at least 53 inches. Write and solve an inequality to find the minimum dimensions of the screen if each dimension is an integer.

56. **CHALLENGE** Your neighbor is a real estate agent and earns a \$50 commission for every \$1000 in house sales, rounded to the nearest \$1000. For what range of prices will the neighbor earn a commission between \$4000 and \$5000?

57. **CHALLENGE** Let a, b, c, and d be positive integers. Show that for fractions $\frac{a}{b}$ and $\frac{c}{d}$, if $ad > bc$, then $\frac{a}{b} > \frac{c}{d}$. Use this property to compare the fractions $\frac{3}{5}, \frac{5}{8}, \frac{7}{8}$, and $\frac{9}{11}$. If any of the integers are negative, is the statement still true?

MIXED REVIEW

Prepare for Lesson 4.1 in Exs. 58–60

Test the number for divisibility by 2, 3, 4, 5, 6, 8, 9, and 10. *(p. 761)*

58. 42 59. 26 60. 120

Use mental math to solve the equation. *(p. 26)*

61. $-4x = 0$ 62. $11a = 11$ 63. $z + (-12) = -12$

Solve the inequality. Then graph its solution. *(p. 148)*

64. $c + 7 \leq 11$ 65. $3 < 12 + s$ 66. $x - 12 > 17$

67. ★ **MULTIPLE CHOICE** Which choice shows $2\frac{3}{5}$ written as an improper fraction? *(p. 762)*

Ⓐ $\frac{6}{5}$ Ⓑ $\frac{10}{5}$ Ⓒ $\frac{13}{5}$ Ⓓ $\frac{23}{5}$

QUIZ for Lessons 3.5–3.7

Find the length of each side. *(p. 142)*

1. A rectangle has a perimeter of 30 millimeters and a width of 6 millimeters. Find the length.

2. A triangle has an area of 26 square yards and a height of 4 yards. Find the length of the base.

Solve the inequality. Then graph its solution.

3. $a + 9 \geq -1$ *(p. 148)* 4. $16 > y - 12$ *(p. 148)* 5. $\frac{x}{3} < -3$ *(p. 154)* 6. $-7x > 42$ *(p. 154)*

7. **APPLES** An empty basket weighs 2 pounds. When filled with apples, the basket weighs more than 13 pounds. Write and solve an inequality that represents this situation. What does the variable represent? *(p. 148)*

8. **CALLING CARD** You have \$9.50 with which to recharge your phone card. Write and solve an inequality to find how many minutes you can add to your phone card if each minute costs \$.10. *(p. 154)*

MIXED REVIEW *of Problem Solving*

Lessons 3.5–3.7

1. **MULTI-STEP PROBLEM** Use the figure below. It shows the top of a platform on a stage.

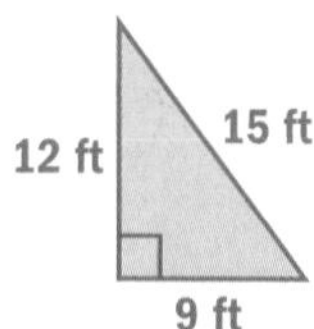

   a. Find the perimeter and area of the platform.

   b. Draw two rectangular surfaces that can be formed using four of these platforms.

   c. Find and compare the perimeter and area of the rectangles to those of the original triangle.

2. **EXTENDED RESPONSE** A rancher wants to use 6000 feet of fence to enclose a rectangular area of a pasture for a horse.

   a. What dimensions give the largest area? What is this area? *Describe* the process you used to find the dimensions.

   b. The rancher decides to build the enclosure using 6000 feet of new fence, but with an existing fence forming one side. What dimensions give the largest area? How much more area does this give the horse compared to the enclosure in part (a)? Show your work.

3. **OPEN-ENDED** Draw two triangular sails that each have an area of 64 square feet.

4. **MULTI-STEP PROBLEM** Use the figures below.

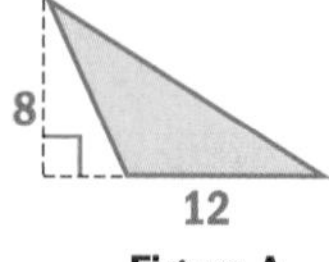

Figure A

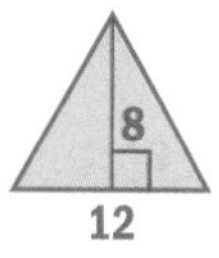

Figure B

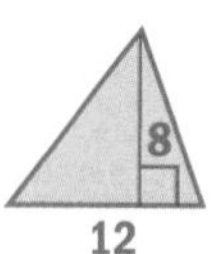

Figure C

   a. Find the area of each triangle.

   b. What do you notice about the areas?

   c. Find the dimensions of two rectangles that have the same area as Figure A.

5. **GRIDDED ANSWER** Mike and his sister Rebecca plan to buy a gift for their parents. Rebecca can contribute up to \$9. Mike can contribute no more than twice the amount his sister can contribute. What is the greatest amount, in dollars, that they can spend altogether on a gift?

6. **SHORT RESPONSE** The Uniform Building Code requires at least 20 square feet of space for each person in a classroom. A classroom is 28 feet long and 18 feet wide. Write and solve an inequality that models the number of people that can be in the classroom legally. *Explain* how to use the solution to find the maximum number of people allowed in the classroom.

7. **EXTENDED RESPONSE** Emma, Frank, and Megan are playing a game. The sum of Emma's score and Frank's score is less than Megan's score.

   a. Write an inequality to represent the situation. Use E, F, and M to represent Emma, Frank, and Megan.

   b. Suppose Frank's score is 30 and Megan's score is 75. *Describe* the number of points Emma has.

   c. If Emma doubles her score on her next turn, could she have more points than Megan? *Explain* your reasoning.

3 CHAPTER REVIEW

@HomeTutor
classzone.com
Vocabulary Practice

REVIEW KEY VOCABULARY

- equivalent equations, *p. 117*
- inverse operation, *p. 117*
- base, height, *p. 142*
- inequality, *p. 148*
- solution of an inequality, *p. 148*
- equivalent inequalities, *p. 149*

VOCABULARY EXERCISES

1. List two pairs of inverse operations. *Explain* why these are called inverse operations.
2. How can two inequalities be equivalent? Give an example of equivalent inequalities.

Copy and complete the statement.

3. Two equations that have the same solution are _?_.
4. A(n) _?_ is a statement formed by placing an inequality symbol between two expressions.

REVIEW EXAMPLES AND EXERCISES

3.1 Solving Equations Using Addition or Subtraction *pp. 117–121*

EXAMPLE

Solve the equation.

$$\begin{aligned} x - 23 &= 9 \\ +23 &\quad +23 \\ \hline x &= 32 \end{aligned}$$

Add 23 to each side. / **Simplify.**

$$\begin{aligned} y + 17.3 &= 68.8 \\ -17.3 &\quad -17.3 \\ \hline y &= 51.5 \end{aligned}$$

Subtract 17.3 from each side. / **Simplify.**

EXERCISES

Solve the equation.

SEE EXAMPLES 1, 2, AND 3 on pp. 117–118 for Exs. 5–14

5. $c + 14 = 3$
6. $y - 31 = 11$
7. $7.7 = s - 4.3$
8. $29 = 40 + p$
9. $b + 3.09 = -5.91$
10. $v + 13 = 29$
11. $t - \frac{3}{7} = \frac{1}{7}$
12. $x + (-5) = -8$
13. $y - 3.9 = 10.9$
14. Last year Marguerite had 12 elm trees in her yard. This year she has 17 elm trees. Write an equation and solve it to find how many elm trees she planted this year.

3.2 Solving Equations Using Multiplication or Division

pp. 122–126

EXAMPLE

Solve the equation.

$\frac{y}{4} = -8$	**Original equation**	$-7x = -56$	**Original equation**
$\frac{y}{4} \cdot 4 = -8 \cdot 4$	**Multiply each side by 4.**	$\frac{-7x}{-7} = \frac{-56}{-7}$	**Divide each side by −7.**
$y = -32$	**Simplify.**	$x = 8$	**Simplify.**

EXERCISES

SEE EXAMPLES 1 AND 2 on pp. 122–123 for Exs. 15–20

Solve the equation.

15. $\frac{m}{3} = 9$ **16.** $\frac{z}{-7} = 23$ **17.** $-5 = \frac{w}{-11}$

18. $-25x = 0$ **19.** $7 = 3.5t$ **20.** $-9.5m = -22.8$

3.3 Solving Two-Step Equations

pp. 129–133

EXAMPLE

Solve the equation.

$3x + 10 = -20$	**Original equation**
$3x + 10 - 10 = -20 - 10$	**Subtract 10 from each side to undo addition.**
$3x = -30$	**Simplify.**
$\frac{3x}{3} = \frac{-30}{3}$	**Divide each side by 3 to undo multiplication.**
$x = -10$	**Simplify.**

EXERCISES

SEE EXAMPLES 1, 2, AND 3 on pp. 129–130 for Exs. 21–27

Solve the equation.

21. $2p - 5 = 13$ **22.** $19 + 8v = 43$ **23.** $\frac{g}{9} + 6 = -2$

24. $\frac{c}{-10} + 26 = 46$ **25.** $-82 = 53 - 5t$ **26.** $-33 = -15t - 12$

27. Ralph is putting pictures in a scrapbook. He puts four pictures on each page and has three pictures left over. If he starts with 55 pictures, write and solve an equation to find how many pages have four pictures on them.

3.4 Writing Two-Step Equations

pp. 134–139

EXAMPLE

A catering company charges \$100 for setup plus \$15 per guest. How many guests can be served within a \$1000 budget?

Setup	+	Cost per guest	•	Number of guests	=	Budget

$100 + 15n = 1000$ **Write an algebraic model.**

$15n = 900$ **Subtract 100 from each side.**

$n = 60$ **Divide each side by 15.**

▸ **Answer** 60 guests can be served within a \$1000 budget.

EXERCISES

SEE EXAMPLES 2 AND 3 on p. 135 for Exs. 28–31

28. The sum of 3 times a number and 6 is 12. What is the number?

29. Four less than 2 times a number is 20. What is the number?

30. Fruit Baskets Your class spends \$26 on supplies for fruit baskets. How many baskets must your class sell at \$7 each to make a profit of \$100?

31. Attendance A small college has 1250 students. There are 30 more women than men. How many women attend the college?

3.5 Applying Geometric Formulas

pp. 142–147

EXAMPLE

Find the height of the triangle. Its area is 21 square inches.

$A = \frac{1}{2}bh$ **Write area formula.**

$21 = \frac{1}{2}(6)(h)$ **Substitute known values.**

$7 = h$ **Solve for *h*.**

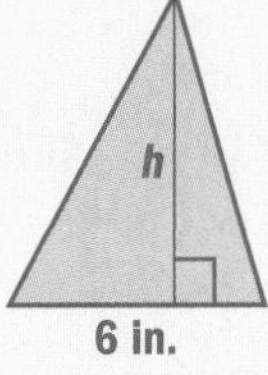

▸ **Answer** The height of the triangle is 7 inches.

EXERCISES

SEE EXAMPLE 4 on p. 144 for Exs. 32 and 33

Find the unknown dimension of the triangle.

32. $b = 10$ cm, $h = 5$ cm, $A = \underline{\ ?\ }$ cm^2

33. $A = 45$ ft^2, $h = 10$ ft, $b = \underline{\ ?\ }$

3.6 Solving Inequalities Using Addition or Subtraction

pp. 148–153

EXAMPLE

Solve the inequality.

$x - 9 \le -4$	Original inequality
$x - 9 + 9 \le -4 + 9$	Add 9 to each side.
$x \le 5$	Simplify.

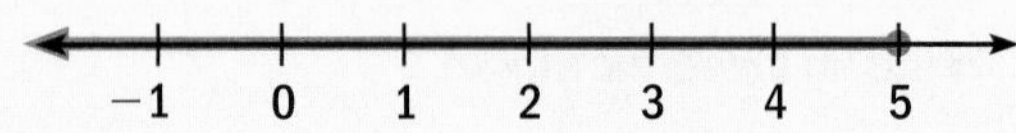

EXERCISES

Solve the inequality. Then graph its solution.

SEE EXAMPLES 2 AND 3 on pp. 149–150 for Exs. 34–42

34. $h - 12 > 12$ **35.** $-4 + k \le 6$ **36.** $7 < 15 + p$ **37.** $d + 11 \ge 5$

38. $m - 10 > 21$ **39.** $b + 13 \le 11$ **40.** $k - 8 \ge 2\frac{1}{2}$ **41.** $p - 2.5 < 7.7$

42. CDs Mary claims that she has at least 50 CDs at home and she just got 4 more for her birthday. Write an inequality for the number of CDs she has now.

3.7 Solving Inequalities Using Multiplication or Division

pp. 154–159

EXAMPLE

Solve the inequality.

$\frac{t}{7} > 2$	Original inequality	$-12k \le 60$	Original inequality
$\frac{t}{7} \cdot 7 > 2 \cdot 7$	Multiply each side by 7.	$\frac{-12k}{-12} \ge \frac{60}{-12}$	Divide each side by −12. Reverse inequality symbol.
$t > 14$	Simplify.	$k \ge -5$	Simplify.

EXERCISES

Solve the inequality.

SEE EXAMPLES 1 AND 2 on pp. 154–155 for Exs. 43–50

43. $\frac{d}{6} \le 34$ **44.** $-\frac{1}{5}x \ge 20$ **45.** $-15b < 60$ **46.** $5c > 25$

47. $-4k \le -36$ **48.** $\frac{2}{3}y > -12$ **49.** $16z < 32$ **50.** $\frac{m}{5} \ge -11$

3 CHAPTER TEST

Solve the equation.

1. $s - 6 = 39$
2. $x + 12 = -2$
3. $14.6 = \frac{k}{2.5}$
4. $24v = 288$
5. $\frac{1}{9} = t + \frac{1}{9}$
6. $-9.8 = \frac{y}{-4.7}$
7. $5b - 7 = 120$
8. $-236 = 29 - 5g$

Translate the statement into an equation. Then solve the equation.

9. A number times 3 subtracted from 20 is -4.
10. The sum of 5 times a number and 14 is 9.

Find the unknown dimension.

11. Perimeter = 62 in.

11 in.

l

12. Area = 72 in.^{2}

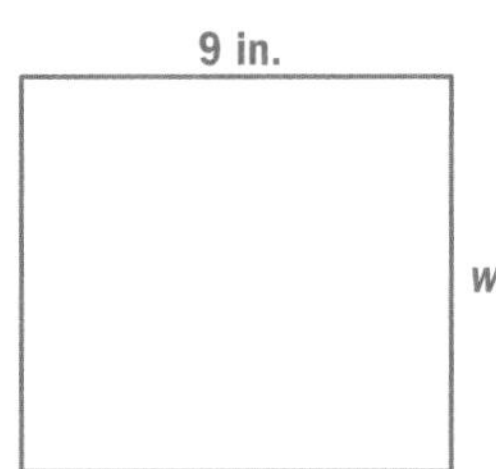

13. Area = 200 cm^2

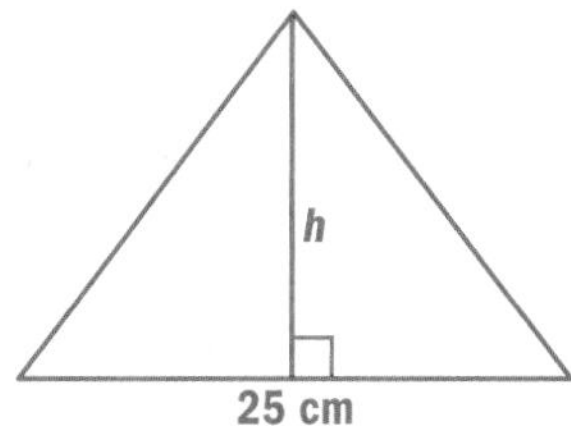

Solve the inequality.

14. $y + 78 < -124$
15. $-8.56 + k \geq 5.32$
16. $-8x < 64$
17. $-\frac{1}{6}x > 5$
18. $3x \leq 12$
19. $m - 9 \leq 19$

20. **HIKING** You go on a 20 mile hike. In the morning you hike 8.3 miles, and by 2:00 P.M. you have hiked 7.5 more miles. Write and solve an equation to find how many miles you have left to hike.

In Exercises 21 and 22, write and solve an equation.

21. **BOOK SALES** A bookstore offers three books in a set for \$21.75. Each book costs the same amount. How much does each book cost?

22. **WEIGHT** A calf weighs 220 pounds. The calf gains about 22 pounds a month. In how many months will the calf weigh 550 pounds?

23. **LUNCH** You and a friend are having lunch together. You can spend no more than \$30 on both meals. The total cost of your friend's meal is \$14.78. Write and solve an inequality to determine how much you can spend on your meal.

24. **FIGURE SKATING** You are taking figure skating lessons. You can rent skates for \$5 per lesson. You can buy skates for \$75. Write and solve an inequality to find the number of lessons for which it is cheaper to buy skates than to rent.

MULTIPLE CHOICE QUESTIONS

If you have difficulty solving a multiple choice problem directly, you may be able to use another approach to eliminate incorrect answer choices and obtain the correct answer.

PROBLEM 1

A bus company charges $75 and an additional $2.50 for each student going on a field trip. The school has $180 set aside for the trip. What are all possible numbers of students that can go on the field trip?

Ⓐ $s \le 20$ Ⓑ $s \le 30$ Ⓒ $s \le 42$ Ⓓ $s \le 72$

METHOD 1

SOLVE DIRECTLY Write a verbal model that represents the situation. Then write and solve an inequality to find all possible numbers of students that can go on the field trip.

STEP 1 Write a verbal model.

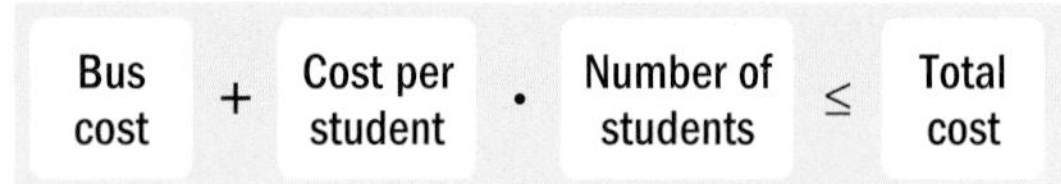

STEP 2 Write and solve an inequality. Let s represent the number of students.

$$75 + 2.5s \le 180$$

$$75 - 75 + 2.5s \le 180 - 75$$

$$2.5s \le 105$$

$$\frac{2.5s}{2.5} \le \frac{105}{2.5}$$

$$s \le 42$$

At most 42 students can go on the field trip.

The correct answer is C. Ⓐ Ⓑ Ⓒ Ⓓ

METHOD 2

ELIMINATE CHOICES In some multiple choice questions, you can identify answer choices that can be eliminated.

First find the amount of money remaining after the bus charge by subtracting the bus charge from the amount of money the school has set aside: $180 - 75 = 105$. There is $105 left for the cost of the students.

- Because $20(2.5) = 50$, which is less than 105, 20 students can attend the field trip.
- Because $30(2.5) = 75$, which is less than 105, 30 students can attend the field trip. So, you can eliminate choice A since $30 > 20$.
- Because $42(2.5) = 105$, 42 students can attend the field trip. So, you can eliminate choice B since $42 > 30$. Because this cost equals $105, more than 42 students will not be able to go.

At most 42 students can go on the field trip.

The correct answer is C. Ⓐ Ⓑ Ⓒ Ⓓ

PROBLEM 2

Matt bought 104 hot dogs for a party. Hot dogs come in packages of 8. How many packages of hot dogs did Matt buy?

Ⓐ 10 Ⓑ 13 Ⓒ 22 Ⓓ 832

METHOD 1

SOLVE DIRECTLY Write a verbal model that represents the situation. Then write and solve an equation to find the number of packages of hot dogs that Will bought.

STEP 1 Write a verbal model.

Hot dogs per package • Number of packages = Number of hot dogs

STEP 2 Write and solve an equation. Let p represent the number of packages of hot dogs.

$$8p = 104$$

$$\frac{8p}{8} = \frac{104}{8}$$

$$p = 13$$

Matt bought 13 packages of hot dogs.

The correct answer is B. Ⓐ Ⓑ Ⓒ Ⓓ

METHOD 2

ELIMINATE CHOICES In some multiple choice questions, you can identify answer choices that can be eliminated.

Because there is more than 1 hot dog in each package, the number of packages of hot dogs must be less than 104. So, you can eliminate choice D.

Think of numbers compatible with 8 on either side of 104. For example, try 80 and 160.

$$80 < 104 < 160$$

$$10 < \frac{104}{8} < 20$$

Because the number of packages is between 10 and 20, you can eliminate choices A and C.

Matt bought 13 packages of hot dogs.

The correct answer is B. Ⓐ Ⓑ Ⓒ Ⓓ

PRACTICE

Explain why you can eliminate the highlighted answer choice.

1. You are stuffing 560 envelopes for a school event. By 1:00 P.M., you have stuffed 140 envelopes. How many envelopes per hour do you need to stuff to finish by 5:00 P.M.?

   × **Ⓐ 4 envelopes** Ⓑ 84 envelopes
   Ⓒ 105 envelopes Ⓓ 420 envelopes

2. Your school earns $1.50 for every T-shirt sold. Find the minimum number of T-shirts you must sell to raise $500.

   Ⓐ 333 Ⓑ 334 Ⓒ 500 × **Ⓓ 750**

3 ★ Standardized TEST PRACTICE

MULTIPLE CHOICE

1. What is the value of n in the equation $n - 34 = -17$?

   (A) -51 (B) -17 (C) 17 (D) 51

2. Which inequality is represented by the graph?

   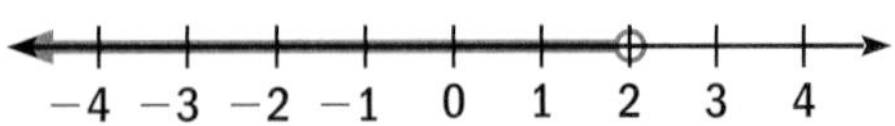

   (A) $x \leq 2$ (B) $x > 2$
   (C) $x < 2$ (D) $x \geq 2$

3. A triangle has an area of 8 square feet. Which measurements *cannot* be the base length b and height h of the triangle?

   (A) $h = 1$ ft, $b = 16$ ft
   (B) $h = 8$ ft, $b = 2$ ft
   (C) $h = 4$ ft, $b = 8$ ft
   (D) $h = 4$ ft, $b = 4$ ft

4. Stores rent space in a mall. The cost to rent Store 58 is $35 per square foot. What is the total rent for the store?

   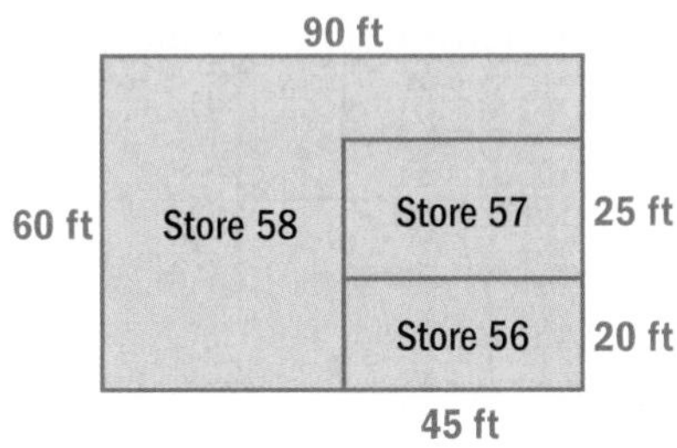

   (A) $39,375 (B) $94,500
   (C) $118,125 (D) $189,000

5. Bob's exam of 21 questions takes 50 minutes. He needs at least 10 minutes for the extended response question. He uses an equal amount of time on all 20 multiple choice problems. What is the greatest number of minutes Bob can spend on one multiple choice problem?

   (A) 1 (B) 2 (C) 3 (D) 4

6. What is the area of the triangle?

   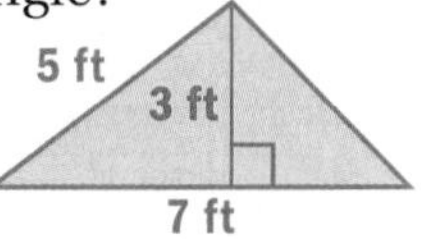

   (A) 7.5 ft^2 (B) 10.5 ft^2
   (C) 21 ft^2 (D) 35 ft^2

7. A rectangle has a perimeter of 54 inches and a width of 8 inches. What is the length of the rectangle?

   (A) 19 inches (B) 26 inches
   (C) 38 inches (D) 46 inches

8. The bill for the repair of a car is $560. The cost of parts is $440. The cost of labor is $40 per hour. Which equation can you use to find the number of hours of labor?

   (A) $40 + 440x = 560$
   (B) $40x + 440 = 560$
   (C) $40(x + 440) = 560$
   (D) $40 + x + 440 = 560$

9. Which equation does *not* have a solution of 8?

   (A) $x - 4 = 4$ (B) $7 + x = 15$
   (C) $x - 4.4 = 3.6$ (D) $x + 6.2 = 1.8$

10. Which inequality is represented by the graph?

    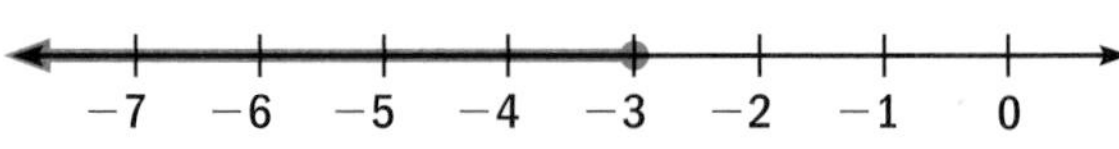

    (A) $-4x \leq 12$ (B) $-15 \leq -5x$
    (C) $21 \leq -7x$ (D) $3x > -9$

11. A gym is 100 feet by 70 feet. Bleachers are along both 100 foot sides of the gym. The bleachers each cover 4 feet of the length of the floor when closed. When open, they cover 9 feet of the length of the floor. What is the difference in playing area of the gym floor between when the bleachers are open and when they are closed?

    (A) 1000 ft^2 (B) 1800 ft^2
    (C) 5200 ft^2 (D) 6600 ft^2

GRIDDED ANSWER

12. What is the value of x in the equation $20 = 3x + 2$?

13. On each weekday that she worked in July, Kate worked 6 hours. She also worked 9 hours on one Saturday. Kate worked 117 hours total in July. How many weekdays did Kate work in July?

14. Rachel has \$60 in savings. If she saves \$5 each week, in how many weeks will she have \$100 in savings?

15. Caleb and Peter hiked for 2 hours, took a break, and then hiked some more. They traveled 10.5 miles at an average speed of 3 miles per hour. For how many hours did Caleb and Peter hike after their break?

SHORT RESPONSE

16. A dog sees a squirrel and begins to chase it. Initially, the squirrel is 46.2 meters from the dog, 25.2 meters from a tree, and directly between the dog and the tree. The dog can run 17 meters per second. The squirrel must reach the tree before the dog does to escape. How fast must the squirrel run? *Justify* your answer mathematically.

17. A person must be at least 18 years old to have a driver's license in North Carolina. Tracy got her license 6 years ago. Write an inequality that expresses Tracy's age. Graph the solution of the inequality on a number line. *Explain* your inequality and your graph. Then use them to explain why Tracy cannot be 19 years old but she can be 30 years old.

EXTENDED RESPONSE

18. Alice bought carpet for two rooms in her house. The floor plan of the rooms is shown here.

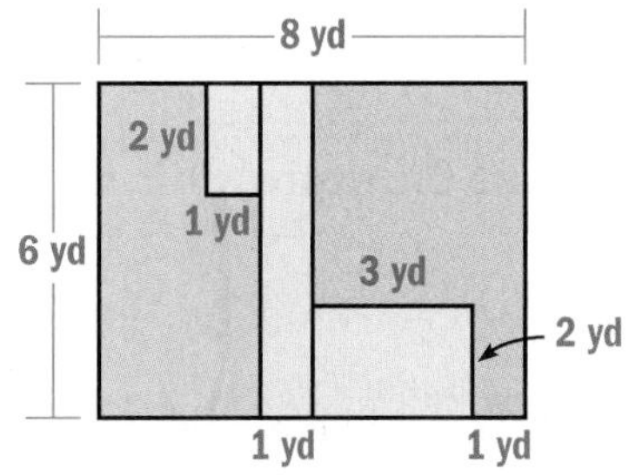

a. Find the area of the room with red carpet and the area of the room with blue carpet.

b. Alice spent \$444 total on carpet. The red carpet cost \$14 per square yard. Find the cost of the blue carpet per square yard.

c. How much would it have cost to buy carpet in blue for both rooms? *Explain* how you found your answer.

19. Paul, Don, and Jeff are raising money to go on a band trip. Each person needs to raise at least \$200 to go on the trip. Paul has raised \$7 more than half as many dollars as Don. Don has raised \$4 less than twice as many dollars as Jeff. Jeff has raised \$85.

a. Write equations that you can use to find the amount of money that each person has raised so far.

b. How much money has each person raised so far?

c. Write and solve inequalities to determine how much more money each person still has to raise.

d. Explain how your inequalities in part (c) would change if each person needed to raise at least \$250.

3 CUMULATIVE REVIEW Chapters 1–3

Evaluate the expression.

1. $8 + 6 \div 2$ *(p. 8)*
2. $15 - 9 \div 3$ *(p. 8)*
3. $3 \times (1.8 + 5 - 0.6)$ *(p. 8)*
4. $9 \times 2^3 - 15$ *(p. 19)*
5. $(2^5 + 8) \cdot 5^2$ *(p. 19)*
6. $(18 \div 6)^3 + (11 - 4)^3$ *(p. 19)*

Solve the equation using mental math. *(p. 26)*

7. $x + 3 = 9$
8. $3w = 33$
9. $24 \div r = 6$
10. $34 - z = 21$

Find the perimeter and area of the rectangle or square. *(p. 32)*

11. length = 12 m, width = 7 m
12. length = 18 cm, width = 14 cm
13. side length = 9 in.
14. length = 13 ft, width = 11 ft

Use a number line to order the integers from least to greatest. *(p. 57)*

15. −15, 16, 1, −5, 4, 8
16. 40, −60, 98, −85, −6, 42

Find the sum or difference.

17. $29 + (-18)$ *(p. 63)*
18. $-8 - 9$ *(p. 68)*
19. $44 - (-11)$ *(p. 68)*

Find the product or quotient.

20. $-5(4)$ *(p. 73)*
21. $-12(-8)$ *(p. 73)*
22. $\frac{42}{-3}$ *(p. 77)*

Evaluate the expression when $a = 4$, $b = -16$, and $c = 12$. *(p. 83)*

23. $\frac{-c}{a}$
24. $\frac{3b}{2c}$
25. $\frac{b}{-4a}$

Simplify the expression by combining like terms. *(p. 88)*

26. $9(3a + 11) - 4$
27. $-8b + 12(7b + 3)$
28. $2c - 8(9c - 5)$

Plot the point in a coordinate plane and describe its location. *(p. 94)*

29. $L(3, -5)$
30. $M(0, -1)$
31. $N(6, 0)$

Solve the equation.

32. $n + 8 = 15$ *(p. 117)*
33. $z + 12 = 3$ *(p. 117)*
34. $4r = -32$ *(p. 122)*
35. $\frac{k}{7} = 5$ *(p. 122)*
36. $8 = 7y - 13$ *(p. 129)*
37. $\frac{a}{6} + 4 = -8$ *(p. 129)*
38. A triangle has an area of 48 square meters and a height of 6 meters. What is the length of its base? *(p. 142)*

Solve the inequality. Then graph its solution.

39. $96 \geq -12 + c$ *(p. 148)*
40. $-\frac{1}{3}x > 4$ *(p. 154)*
41. $-96 < 24h$ *(p. 154)*

HEIGHTS The frequency table shows the heights of 30 students. *(p. 3)*

Height (inches)	*Frequency*
54–55.9	1
56–57.9	2
58–59.9	4
60–61.9	5
62–63.9	7
64–65.9	6
66–67.9	3
68–69.9	2

42. Make a histogram of the data shown in the frequency table.

43. Which height interval has the most students?

44. Can you use the histogram to determine the number of students who are between 60 and 69.9 inches tall? *Explain.*

45. **DOLPHINS** After swimming 22 miles, a dolphin changes direction and swims at a rate of 18 miles per hour. Use the expression $22 + 18t$, where t is the number of hours, to find the total distance traveled by the dolphin after 2.4 more hours. *(p. 13)*

46. **RADIO** You are the disc jockey for a 15 minute radio show at your school. You must leave 3 minutes open for announcements, and you want to play 3 songs. Use the table at the right to determine the 3 songs you can play. *(p. 37)*

Song	A	B	C	D	E
Length (minutes)	6	4	3	5	6

47. **CHECKBOOK** The balance of a checkbook is \$225. There are deposits of \$80 and \$40 and withdrawals of \$100 and \$25. What is the new balance of the checkbook? *(p. 63)*

48. **FALLING ROCK** A rock falls 144 feet from a ledge. The equation $h = -16t^2 + 144$ gives the height h, in feet, of the rock after falling for t seconds. Evaluate the equation when t equals 2.5, 3, and 3.5 seconds. When does the rock hit the ground? What is the actual height of the rock after 3.5 seconds? *(p. 73)*

49. **FUEL** You rent an all-terrain vehicle that has $\frac{5}{8}$ of a tank of fuel. When you are done riding, $\frac{3}{8}$ of a tank is left. Write a verbal model to represent the fraction of a tank of fuel you used. Then write and solve an algebraic model. *(p. 117)*

50. **INTRAMURALS** A college brochure states that 215 students participate in intramural sports. This is one third of the students. How many students attend the college? *(p. 122)*

51. **GROUNDSKEEPING** You need to buy enough bags of grass seed to cover a field that is 300 feet long and 150 feet wide. One bag of seed covers 5000 square feet. How many bags do you need? *(p. 142)*

4 Factors, Fractions, and Exponents

Before

In previous chapters you've . . .

- Multiplied numbers
- Compared integers

Now

In Chapter 4 you'll study . . .

- 4.1 Factors
- 4.2 Greatest common factors
- 4.3 Simplifying fractions
- 4.4 Least common multiples
- 4.5 Comparing fractions
- 4.6 Rules of exponents
- 4.7 Negative exponents
- 4.8 Scientific notation

Why?

So you can solve real-world problems about . . .

- geography, p. 190
- orangutans, p. 199
- bubbles, p. 213

at classzone.com

- Creating a Factor Tree, p. 177
- Simplifying Fractions, p. 186
- Mixed Numbers and Improper Fractions, p. 199

Get-Ready Games

Review Prerequisite Skills by playing *Bicycle Math.*

Skill Focus: Whole number division

BICYCLE MATH

HOW TO PLAY

1. **PICK** the number with each letter that divides evenly into the bold number in the matching fact.

   A 4, 8, 42 **B** 7, 13, 23 **C** 15, 17, 21

2. **USE** the answer for each letter to evaluate the expression below. The value of the expression is the world record bicycle speed in miles per hour, set by Fred Rompelberg in 1995.

   A(B + C) + 30.9

In **1884**, the "safety bicycle," a bicycle resembling the ones we use today, was invented.

A

In 2001, **39,000,000** people in the United States rode a bicycle more than once.

B

In 2002, **189** cyclists competed in the Tour de France.

C

Stop and Think

1. **WRITING** A student thinks that 42 divides evenly into 1884 because 42 divides evenly into 84. *Explain* what is wrong with the student's reasoning.
2. **CRITICAL THINKING** What number will divide evenly into any even number? *Explain.*

4 Getting Ready

Review Prerequisite Skills

REVIEW WORDS

- **power,** *p. 19*
- **base,** *p. 19*
- **exponent,** *p. 19*
- **fraction,** *p. 762*

VOCABULARY CHECK

Copy and complete using a review word from the list at the left.

1. In the expression 2^6, 2 is called the _?_.
2. The expression 3^7 is a(n) _?_ of 3.
3. In the expression 5^4, 4 is called the _?_.

SKILL CHECK

Evaluate the expression. *(p. 19)*

4. $3^2 \cdot 3$
5. $(2 + 3)^2$
6. $4^2 \div 4^2$
7. $(6 - 5)^7$
8. $3^2 + 4 \cdot 5$
9. $12 - 8 \div 2^2$
10. $7^2 - 3^3$
11. $6^2 \div 2^2$

Simplify the expression by combining like terms. *(p. 88)*

12. $7x + 4 - 3x$
13. $-2x + 5x - x$
14. $x + 4 - 12x$
15. $6x - 5 + x$
16. $15y + 9x - 6x - y$
17. $-13y + 8x - 2x + 3y - 10$

Solve the equation. Check your answer. *(p. 129)*

18. $2a + 6 = 14$
19. $8 - 4m = 20$
20. $-7 + 5c = -32$

@HomeTutor Prerequisite skills practice at classzone.com

Notetaking Skills Preview the Chapter

In each chapter you will learn a new notetaking skill. In Chapter 4 you will apply the strategy of previewing the chapter to Example 5 on p. 189.

Skim the content of the chapter you are about to study. If you already know something about the topic, outline what you know in your notes.

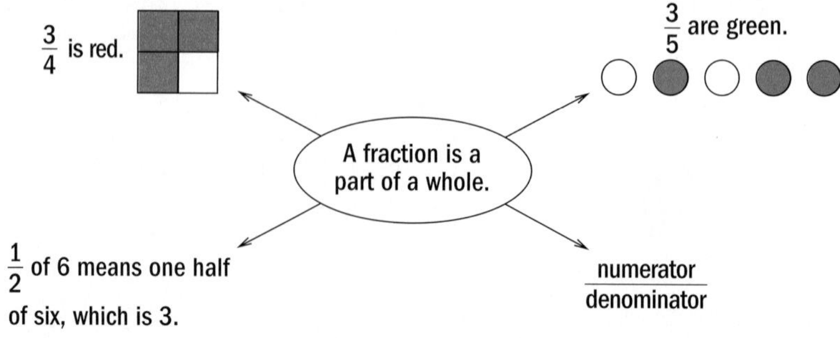

In Chapter 4, you will learn more things about fractions that you can add to your outline.

INVESTIGATION

Use before Lesson 4.1

GOAL
Introduce prime and composite numbers.

MATERIALS
- paper
- colored pencils

4.1 Investigating Factors

A *prime* number is a whole number that has exactly two factors: 1 and itself. A *composite* number has more than two factors. In this activity, you will look at a number pattern attributed to Eratosthenes, a mathematician who lived in Alexandria, Egypt, around 230 B.C.

EXPLORE **Create the Sieve of Eratosthenes with the integers 1 to 60.**

STEP 1 **Write** the whole numbers 1 to 60 in a rectangular array as shown at the right.

1	2	3	4	5	6	7	8	9	10
11	12	13	14	15	16	17	18	19	20
21	22	23	24	25	26	27	28	29	30
31	32	33	34	35	36	37	38	39	40
41	42	43	44	45	46	47	48	49	50
51	52	53	54	55	56	57	58	59	60

STEP 2 **Start** with the number 2. Circle it and cross out every multiple of 2 after 2.

STEP 3 **Move** to the next number that is not crossed out, 3. Circle it and cross out every multiple of 3 after 3.

STEP 4 **Move** to the next number that is not crossed out. Circle it and cross out all other multiples of that number.

STEP 5 **Repeat** Step 4 until every number except 1 is either crossed out or circled.

1	(2)	(3)	~~4~~	5	~~6~~	7	~~8~~	~~9~~	~~10~~
11	~~12~~	13	~~14~~	~~15~~	~~16~~	17	~~18~~	19	~~20~~
~~21~~	~~22~~	23	~~24~~	25	~~26~~	~~27~~	~~28~~	29	~~30~~
31	~~32~~	~~33~~	~~34~~	35	~~36~~	37	~~38~~	~~39~~	~~40~~
41	~~42~~	43	~~44~~	~~45~~	~~46~~	47	~~48~~	49	~~50~~
~~51~~	~~52~~	53	~~54~~	55	~~56~~	~~57~~	~~58~~	59	~~60~~

Skip the numbers that have already been crossed out.

PRACTICE

1. What type of numbers are circled in your array?
2. What type of numbers are crossed out in your array?

DRAW CONCLUSIONS

3. **WRITING** If you continued this process with the numbers 61 to 100, what type of numbers would you expect to be circled? Why?

4.1 Factors and Prime Factorization

Before You multiplied and divided numbers.
Now You'll write the prime factorization of numbers.
Why? So you can find different arrangements of rows and columns, as in Example 1.

KEY VOCABULARY
- **prime number, composite number, prime factorization, factor tree,** *p. 177*
- **monomial,** *p. 178*

Lettering Members of the art club are learning to do calligraphy. Their first project is to make posters to display their new lettering style. A poster will display 36 characters in order: the 26 uppercase letters of the alphabet and the digits 0 through 9.

The art club members want the characters arranged in a rectangular display with the same number of characters in each row. You can use the factors of 36 to determine how many arrangements are possible.

EXAMPLE 1 Writing Factors

In the situation above, how many ways can the art club arrange the 36 characters in a rectangular display with rows of equal length?

SOLUTION

STEP 1 **List** the factors of 36 by writing 36 as a product of two numbers in all possible ways.

1×36 2×18 3×12 4×9 6×6

The factors of 36 are 1, 2, 3, 4, 6, 9, 12, 18, and 36.

STEP 2 **Use** these factors to find all the possible rectangular arrangements of rows and columns.

1×36 2×18 3×12 4×9 6×6

36×1 18×2 12×3 9×4

AVOID ERRORS
Because you are looking for arrangements of rows and columns, 1×36 is different from 36×1. Each product except 6×6 is listed twice.

▸ **Answer** There are nine possible rectangular arrangements.

✓ GUIDED PRACTICE for Example 1

Write all the factors of the number.

1. 20 **2.** 29 **3.** 42 **4.** 57

5. What If? Suppose the poster in Example 1 was to include both uppercase and lowercase letters as well as the digits 0–9. How many ways can the 62 characters be arranged in rows of equal length?

Primes and Composites A **prime number** is a whole number greater than 1 whose only positive factors are 1 and itself. A **composite number** is a whole number greater than 1 that has positive factors other than 1 and itself. The number 1 is neither prime nor composite.

EXAMPLE 2 Identifying Prime and Composite Numbers

Write all the factors of the number and tell whether it is *prime* or *composite.*

Number	Factors	Prime or Composite?
a. 32	1, 2, 4, 8, 16, 32	composite
b. 39	1, 3, 13, 39	composite
c. 43	1, 43	prime
d. 76	1, 2, 4, 19, 38, 76	composite
e. 149	1, 149	prime
f. 121	1, 11, 121	composite

FIND FACTORS

You can use divisibility tests to help find all the factors of a composite number. For help with divisibility tests, see p. 761.

Prime Factorization When you write a whole number as the product of prime numbers, you are writing its **prime factorization**. One way to find the prime factorization of a number is to use a **factor tree**.

EXAMPLE 3 Writing Prime Factorization

Write the prime factorization of 450.

Three factor trees are shown. Notice that each factor tree produces the same prime factorization, differing only in the order of the factors.

450

$30 \cdot 15$

$6 \cdot 5 \cdot 3 \cdot 5$

$2 \cdot 3 \cdot 5 \cdot 3 \cdot 5$

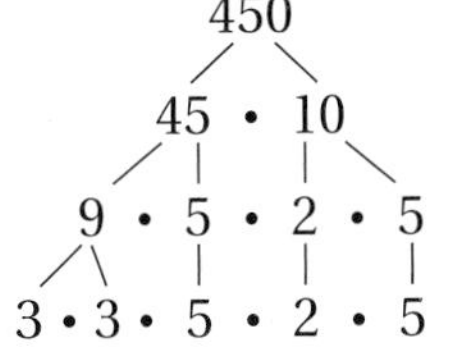

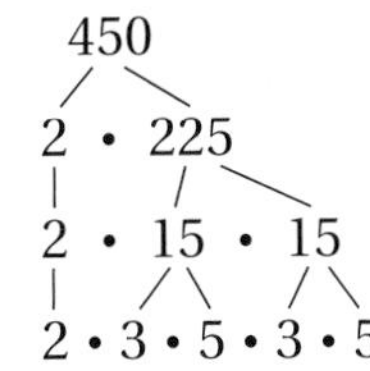

So, $450 = 2 \cdot 3 \cdot 3 \cdot 5 \cdot 5$.

▶ **Answer** Using exponents, the prime factorization of 450 is $2 \cdot 3^2 \cdot 5^2$.

ORDER FACTORS

When writing the prime factorization, write the factors in order from least to greatest.

Animated Math at classzone.com

✓ GUIDED PRACTICE for Examples 2 and 3

Tell whether the number is *prime* or *composite.* If it is composite, write its prime factorization using exponents.

6. 24 **7.** 51 **8.** 73 **9.** 560

Factoring Monomials A **monomial** is a number, a variable, or a product of a number and one or more variables. To factor a monomial means to write the monomial as a product of prime numbers and variables with exponents of 1.

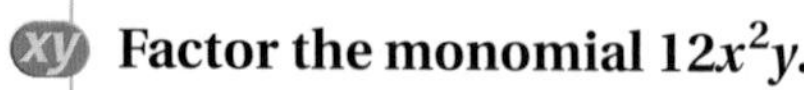

EXAMPLE 4 Factoring a Monomial

Factor the monomial $12x^2y$.

$12x^2y = 2 \cdot 2 \cdot 3 \cdot x^2 \cdot y$ Factor 12.

$= 2 \cdot 2 \cdot 3 \cdot x \cdot x \cdot y$ Write x^2 as $x \cdot x$.

✓ GUIDED PRACTICE for Example 4

Factor the monomial.

10. $3mn$ **11.** $18t^2$ **12.** $14x^2y^3$ **13.** $54w^3z^4$

4.1 EXERCISES

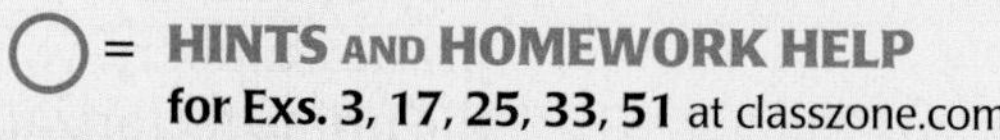

HOMEWORK KEY

★ = STANDARDIZED TEST PRACTICE Exs. 30, 50, 51, 52, 53, 55, and 64

○ = HINTS AND HOMEWORK HELP for Exs. 3, 17, 25, 33, 51 at classzone.com

SKILL PRACTICE

1. VOCABULARY Copy and complete: The only positive factors of a(n) __?__ number are the number itself and one.

2. VOCABULARY What is the prime factorization of a number?

SEE EXAMPLES 1 AND 2 on pp. 176–177 for Exs. 3–18

WRITING FACTORS **Write all the factors of the number.**

3. 18 **4.** 27 **5.** 34 **6.** 41

7. 29 **8.** 64 **9.** 108 **10.** 175

11. 299 **12.** 336 **13.** 400 **14.** 512

IDENTIFYING PRIMES **Tell whether the number is *prime* or *composite*.**

15. 21 **16.** 45 **17.** 59 **18.** 91

USING FACTOR TREES **Copy and complete the factor tree. Then write the prime factorization of the number.**

SEE EXAMPLE 3 on p. 177 for Exs. 19–21

19.

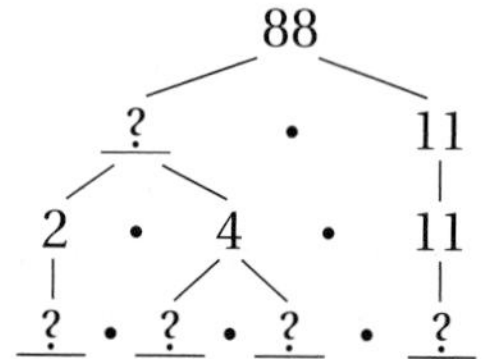

20.

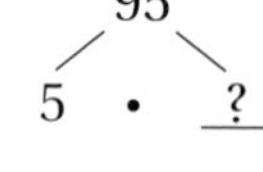

21.

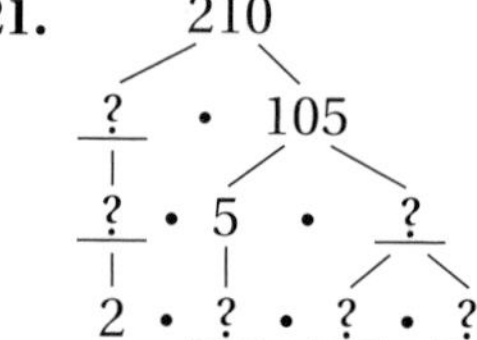

PRIME FACTORIZATION **Write the prime factorization of the number.**

SEE EXAMPLE 3 on p. 177 for Exs. 22–30

22. 28
23. 55
24. 97
25. 96
26. 280
27. 396
28. 1125
29. 2000

30. ★ **MULTIPLE CHOICE** What is the prime factorization of 405?

Ⓐ $9 \cdot 9 \cdot 5$ Ⓑ $3^3 \cdot 5^2$ Ⓒ $3^4 \cdot 5$ Ⓓ $3^3 \cdot 15$

ALGEBRA **Factor the monomial.**

SEE EXAMPLE 4 on p. 178 for Exs. 31–39

31. $15cd$
32. $40pq$
33. $9x^2y$
34. $24g^2h^3$
35. $48n^3m^3$
36. $144n^2m^5$
37. $20ab^4c^2$
38. $99r^3s^2t$

39. **ERROR ANALYSIS** Your friend says that the factored form of the monomial $18x^2y$ is $1 \cdot 3 \cdot 6 \cdot x \cdot y$. Describe and correct your friend's error.

MAKE A LIST **Show how the prime factorization of the number can be used to find all of its factors besides 1 and itself.**

40. 24
41. 56
42. 102
43. 225

REWRITING NUMBERS **Many even numbers are the sum of two primes. For example, $8 = 3 + 5$. Write the number as the sum of two primes.**

44. 10
45. 16
46. 28
47. 30

48. **CHALLENGE** Some numbers have an odd number of factors. For example, the factors of 4 are 1, 2, and 4. Find three more numbers that have an odd number of factors. What do the numbers have in common?

PROBLEM SOLVING

SEE EXAMPLE 1 on p. 176 for Exs. 49–51

49. **GUIDED PROBLEM SOLVING** You are making a quilt out of 120 square patches. What are the two most reasonable rectangular arrangements of the patches for the quilt?

    a. List all of the factors of 120.

    b. List all the pairs of factors from part (a) that have a product of 120. These are the possible arrangements of the patches.

    c. List the two most reasonable arrangements of the patches. *Explain* why the other arrangements are not reasonable.

50. ★ **SHORT RESPONSE** The director of a baseball league must divide 180 players into teams of equal size. List all the possible combinations of number of teams and team sizes of 9 to 50. The director wants an even number of teams. Which two sizes are most reasonable? *Explain.*

51. ★ **MULTIPLE CHOICE** Several teachers at a school are rearranging the desks in their classrooms. Which number of desks *cannot* be arranged in a rectangular arrangement with two or more rows all of equal length?

Ⓐ 20 Ⓑ 23 Ⓒ 25 Ⓓ 27

52. ★ **WRITING** *Explain* how you can create two different factor trees for 540. Do both factor trees result in the same prime factorization?

53. ★ **SHORT RESPONSE** You are in charge of a ring toss game at a school fair. In this game, players try to throw a small ring over a bottle that is in a rectangular display. You have 140 bottles to arrange in equal rows. Can you have 40 equal rows? *Explain.* You are setting the display on a square table that can fit at most 15 bottles across. Which rectangular arrangements of the 140 bottles will fit on the table? *Explain.*

54. **NUMBER SENSE** Name two prime numbers that have a difference of 1. Are there others? *Explain* your reasoning.

55. ★ **EXTENDED RESPONSE** Find dimensions in whole inches.

  a. **Calculate** The area of a rectangle is 24 square inches. Find all possible dimensions of the rectangle. Which dimensions produce the rectangle with the least perimeter?

  b. **Calculate** Repeat step (a) for a rectangle with an area of 36 square inches and a rectangle with an area of 40 square inches.

  c. **Predict** A rectangle has an area of 100 square inches. Without making any calculations, which dimensions produce the rectangle with the least perimeter? *Explain* your reasoning.

56. **GEOMETRY** The *volume* of a box can be found by using the formula Volume = length $\times$ width $\times$ height. A box has a volume of 200 cubic inches. Find all the possible whole-number dimensions of the box.

57. **CHALLENGE** *Twin primes* are prime numbers with a difference of 2. For example, 5 and 7 are twin primes. List five other pairs of twin primes.

58. **CHALLENGE** A *perfect number* is a number that is equal to the sum of all its factors excluding itself. For example, 6 is a perfect number because $6 = 1 + 2 + 3$. Find the next perfect number.

MIXED REVIEW

Get-Ready

Prepare for Lesson 4.2 in Exs. 59–62

Write the product as a power and describe the power in words. *(p. 19)*

59. $n \cdot n \cdot n \cdot n$

60. $r \cdot r \cdot r$

61. $m \cdot m \cdot m \cdot m \cdot m$

62. $i \cdot i \cdot i \cdot i \cdot i \cdot i \cdot i$

CHOOSE A STRATEGY Use a strategy from the list to solve the following problem. *Explain* your choice of strategy.

63. The bookstore at your favorite mall is expanding to include the space adjacent to it, which shares a 25 foot wall. The original store was 20 feet long. The space adjacent to it is 14 feet long. What is the perimeter of the store with the additional space?

Problem Solving Strategies
- Draw a Diagram *(p. 787)*
- Guess, Check, and Revise *(p. 788)*
- Look for a Pattern *(p. 791)*

64. ★ **OPEN-ENDED MATH** Write two inequalities equivalent to $x > 5$. *(p. 154)*

4.2 Greatest Common Factor

Before You found the factors of a number.
Now You'll find the greatest common factor of two or more numbers.
Why? So you can find compatible dimensions, as for pens in Ex. 46.

KEY VOCABULARY
- **common factor,** *p. 181*
- **greatest common factor (GCF),** *p. 181*
- **relatively prime,** *p. 182*

ACTIVITY

The table at the right shows the factors of 24, 20, and 18.

Number	Factors
24	1, 2, 3, 4, 6, 8, 12, 24
20	1, 2, 4, 5, 10, 20
18	1, 2, 3, 6, 9, 18

STEP 1 Which number(s) are factors of 18 and 24?

STEP 2 Which number(s) are factors of 20 and 24?

STEP 3 Which number(s) are factors of 18, 20, and 24?

STEP 4 What is the greatest factor that is in all three lists?

A **common factor** is a whole number that is a factor of two or more nonzero whole numbers. The greatest of the common factors is the **greatest common factor (GCF)**. One way to find the GCF of two or more numbers is to multiply the common prime facors.

VOCABULARY
The GCF is sometimes called the *greatest common divisor* (GCD) because it is the greatest number that divides the given numbers.

EXAMPLE 1 Finding the Greatest Common Factor

Find the greatest common factor of 56 and 84.

SOLUTION

STEP 1 **Write** the prime factorization of each number.

$56 = 2 \times 2 \times 2 \times 7$ $\qquad$ $84 = 2 \times 2 \times 3 \times 7$

STEP 2 **Find** the common prime factors. They are 2, 2, and 7. The GCF of 56 and 84 is the product of these factors.

AVOID ERRORS
2 appears twice in each prime factorization. So it must be used twice when computing the GCF.

▸ **Answer** The GCF of 56 and 84 is $2 \cdot 2 \cdot 7$, or 28.

GUIDED PRACTICE for Example 1

Find the greatest common factor of the numbers.

1. 12, 32 **2.** 42, 60 **3.** 36, 90 **4.** 96, 120

Relatively Prime Numbers Two numbers are **relatively prime** if their greatest common factor is 1. For example, 8 and 15 are relatively prime.

EXAMPLE 2 Identifying Relatively Prime Numbers

Tell whether the numbers 112 and 45 are relatively prime.

SOLUTION

Write the prime factorization of each number. Then look for all the common prime factors.

$112 = 2^4 \cdot 7$ $\qquad 45 = 3^2 \cdot 5$

AVOID ERRORS

Notice that relatively prime numbers are not necessarily prime themselves.

There are no common prime factors. However, two numbers always have 1 as a common factor. So, the GCF is 1.

▸ **Answer** The numbers 112 and 45 are relatively prime.

EXAMPLE 3 Solve a Multi-Step Problem

Pep Rally Students at your school are planning to hand out pep rally packs to support your school's athletic program. The students have 240 bumper stickers, 360 pennants, and 720 pencils. Every pack must have the same contents, and no items should be left over. What is the greatest number of packs that can be made? What will each pack contain?

STEP 1 **Find** the greatest number of pep rally packs by finding the GCF.

$240 = 2^4 \cdot 3 \cdot 5$ $\qquad 360 = 2^3 \cdot 3^2 \cdot 5$ $\qquad 720 = 2^4 \cdot 3^2 \cdot 5$

The common prime factors are 2^3, 3, and 5. The GCF is $2^3 \cdot 3 \cdot 5$, or 120. So, 120 pep rally packs can be made.

STEP 2 **Divide** the number of items by the number of pep rally packs.

$240 \div 120 = 2$ $\qquad 360 \div 120 = 3$ $\qquad 720 \div 120 = 6$

▸ **Answer** The greatest number of pep rally packs is 120. Each pack will contain 2 bumper stickers, 3 pennants, and 6 pencils.

✓ GUIDED PRACTICE for Examples 2 and 3

Tell whether the numbers are relatively prime. If they are not relatively prime, find the GCF.

5. 48, 72 **6.** 124, 128 **7.** 39, 44 **8.** 200, 63

9. What If? In Example 3, suppose the students have 240 bumper stickers and 360 pennants, but only 600 pencils. How many pep rally packs can be made? What items will each pack contain?

GCF of Monomials You can find the greatest common factor of two monomials by factoring the monomials.

EXAMPLE 4 Finding the GCF of Monomials

Find the greatest common factor of $12a^3$ and $9a^2$.

STEP 1 **Write** the prime factorization of each expression.

$12a^3 = 2 \cdot 2 \cdot 3 \cdot a \cdot a \cdot a$ $\qquad$ $9a^2 = 3 \cdot 3 \cdot a \cdot a$

STEP 2 **Find** the common factors, 3 and a^2. The GCF is their product.

▶ **Answer** The GCF of $12a^3$ and $9a^2$ is $3 \cdot a^2$, or $3a^2$.

✓ GUIDED PRACTICE for Example 4

Find the greatest common factor of the monomials.

10. $6x, 18x$ **11.** $6xy, 4xy^2$ **12.** $15y, 9x^2y^2$ **13.** $5xy^3, 10x^2y^2$

4.2 EXERCISES

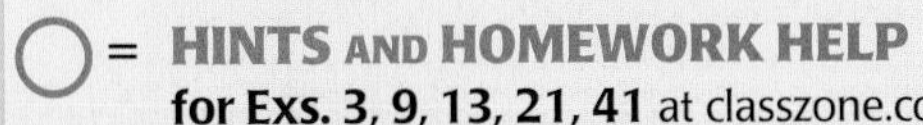

HOMEWORK KEY
★ = **STANDARDIZED TEST PRACTICE** Exs. 20, 30–33, 41, 42, 43, 44, and 57
○ = **HINTS AND HOMEWORK HELP** for Exs. 3, 9, 13, 21, 41 at classzone.com

SKILL PRACTICE

VOCABULARY **Copy and complete the statement.**

1. Six is the _?_ of 12 and 18.

2. Two numbers are _?_ if their GCF is 1.

SEE EXAMPLE 1 on p. 181 for Exs. 3–11

FINDING THE GCF **Find the GCF of the numbers.**

3. 14, 70 **4.** 38, 51 **5.** 24, 196 **6.** 42, 184

7. 3, 9, 27 **8.** 21, 28, 56 **9.** 17, 18, 20 **10.** 24, 36, 180

11. ERROR ANALYSIS Describe and correct the error made in finding the GCF of 140 and 440.

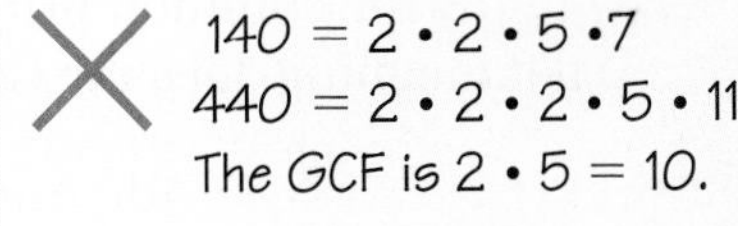

SEE EXAMPLE 2 on p. 182 for Exs. 12–19

RELATIVELY PRIME NUMBERS **Tell whether the numbers are relatively prime. If not, find the GCF.**

12. 5, 16 **13.** 10, 25 **14.** 28, 42 **15.** 55, 72

16. 21, 66 **17.** 18, 216 **18.** 212, 312 **19.** 268, 515

SEE EXAMPLE 4 on p. 183 for Ex. 20

20. ★ **MULTIPLE CHOICE** What is the GCF of $4x^2$ and $6x$?

(A) x (B) $2x$ (C) $4x$ (D) $2x^2$

ALGEBRA Find the GCF of the monomials.

SEE EXAMPLE 4 on p. 183 for Exs. 21–29

21. $3x^2, 9x$
22. $4z^3, 2z^2$
23. $5t^4, 15t^5$
24. $12x^2y^2, 16xy^3$
25. $18rs^2, 30st^2$
26. $15bc^3, 75b^3c$
27. $9t^3, 33t, 27t^4$
28. $12x^2y^3, 42x^3y^2, 36x^2y^3$
29. $63mn, 42m^3, 32n^2$

★ **OPEN-ENDED MATH Find two numbers or monomials with the given GCF.**

30. 16
31. 21
32. $18x^2$
33. $15sc^3$

REASONING Copy and complete the statement using *always, sometimes,* or *never. Explain* your reasoning.

34. The greatest common factor of two numbers is _?_ greater than both of the numbers.
35. The greatest common factor of two numbers is _?_ equal to one of the two numbers.
36. The greatest common factor of two numbers is _?_ prime.
37. The greatest common factor of relatively prime numbers is _?_ 1.

CHALLENGE Describe the pattern and find the next three monomials. What is the GCF of the list of monomials?

38. $5x, 10x^2, 20x^3, \ldots$
39. $4r^2s, 16r^3s^3, 64r^4s^5, \ldots$

PROBLEM SOLVING

SEE EXAMPLE 3 on p. 182 for Exs. 40–42

40. **GUIDED PROBLEM SOLVING** In a youth sports league, 60 girls and 66 boys will be divided into teams. Each team will have an equal number of players and will have the same number of girls. What is the greatest number of teams that can be formed?
    a. Write the prime factorizations of 60 and 66.
    b. What are the common prime factors of the two numbers?
    c. Multiply the common prime factors to find the GCF. What meaning does the GCF have in the situation?

41. ★ **MULTIPLE CHOICE** You must cut four pieces of wood that measure 36 inches, 45 inches, 81 inches, and 108 inches into smaller, equally sized pieces. What is the longest each piece can be so that each piece is the same length?

    (A) 3 in. (B) 9 in. (C) 18 in. (D) 36 in.

42. ★ **SHORT RESPONSE** A florist is making identical bouquets from 360 tulips, 270 roses, and 180 lilies. No flowers should be left over. What is the greatest number of bouquets that the florist can make? What will each bouquet contain? *Explain* your reasoning.

43. ★ **WRITING** Can two even numbers be relatively prime? *Explain* why or why not.

44. ★ **OPEN-ENDED MATH** Name three composite numbers that are relatively prime.

45. **REASONING** *Explain* why any two prime numbers are always relatively prime. Give two examples to justify your reasoning.

46. **MULTI-STEP PROBLEM** A farmer needs to build two adjacent rectangular pens for his sheep as shown. Fence lengths are available in one-foot increments. What is the greatest length x the farmer can make the fence that is shared by the two pens? What are the dimensions of each pen? How many feet of fence are needed to build the two pens?

x ft | $A = 156\text{ ft}^2$ | $A = 204\text{ ft}^2$

47. **REASONING** Three numbers x, y, and z are each multiplied by a constant c. Compare the GCF of x, y, and z to the GCF of cx, cy, and cz. *Explain* your reasoning.

48. **CHALLENGE** *Describe* a process for finding the GCF of two monomials that involves comparing exponents.

MIXED REVIEW

Get-Ready

Prepare for Lesson 4.3 in Exs. 49–52

Write the prime factorization of the number. *(p. 176)*

49. 84   50. 56   51. 39   52. 1260

Solve the equation. *(p. 117)*

53. $-6 + n = 4$ 54. $n + 13 = 5$ 55. $n + 2.7 = 5.7$ 56. $n - 4 = 20$

57. ★ **MULTIPLE CHOICE** What is the area of the triangle at the right? *(p. 142)*

Ⓐ 36 m^2 Ⓑ 54 m^2

Ⓒ 90 m^2 Ⓓ 108 m^2

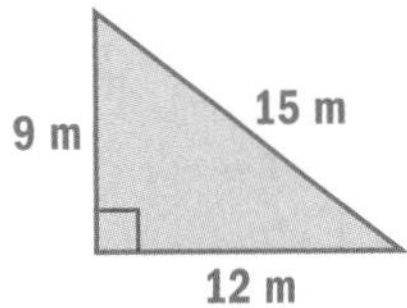

Brain Game

Marble Mystery

You have a bucket full of marbles. If the marbles in the bucket are counted by twos, threes, fives, and sevens, there is exactly one left over each time. What is the fewest number of marbles that could be in the bucket?

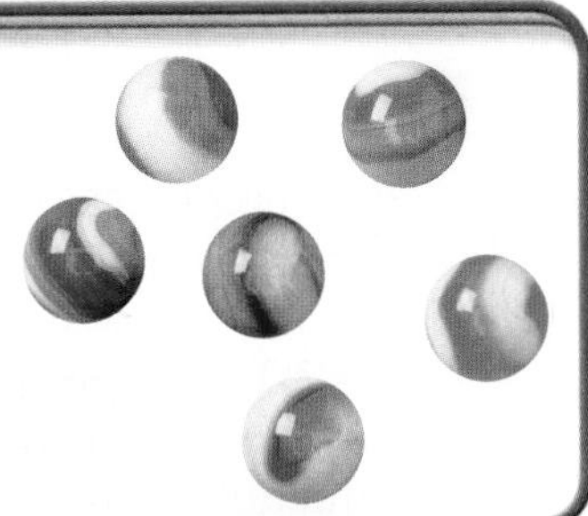

INVESTIGATION

Use before Lesson 4.3

GOAL
Use area models to find equivalent fractions.

MATERIALS
- graph paper
- colored pencils

4.3 Equivalent Fractions

You can use area models to find equivalent fractions that represent the same number.

EXPLORE **Find two fractions equivalent to $\frac{6}{8}$.**

STEP 1 **Draw** a rectangle on a piece of graph paper. Divide the rectangle into 8 equal parts and shade 6 of the parts.

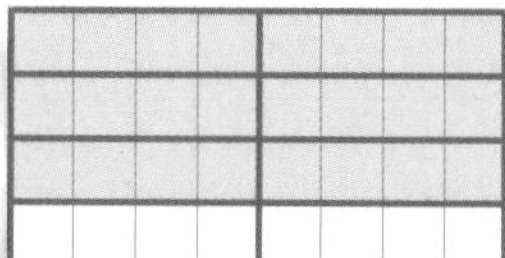

STEP 2 **Look** for other ways of dividing the rectangle into equal parts.

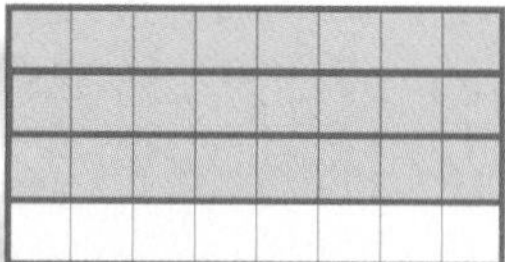

There are 4 parts and 3 are shaded.

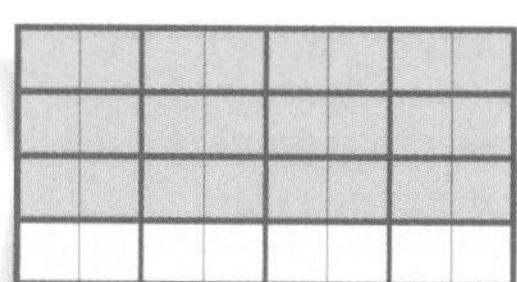

There are 16 parts and 12 are shaded.

STEP 3 **Write** the equivalent fractions.

The fractions $\frac{3}{4}$ and $\frac{12}{16}$ are equivalent to $\frac{6}{8}$.

Animated Math at classzone.com

PRACTICE **Draw a model of the given fraction. Then find two equivalent fractions.**

1. $\frac{4}{6}$ **2.** $\frac{10}{12}$ **3.** $\frac{4}{16}$ **4.** $\frac{10}{16}$

DRAW CONCLUSIONS

5. **WRITING** Look at the fractions in Step 3. How can factoring both the numerator and denominator of a fraction help to write an equivalent fraction?

4.3 Simplifying Fractions

Before You evaluated numerical expressions.
Now You'll simplify fractions.
Why? So you can find fractions of an amount, as in Example 1.

KEY VOCABULARY
- **simplest form,** *p. 187*
- **equivalent fractions,** *p. 187*

A *fraction* is a number of the form $\frac{a}{b}$ $(b \neq 0)$ where a is called the numerator and b is called the denominator. A fraction is in **simplest form** if its numerator and denominator have 1 as their GCF.

Equivalent fractions represent the same number. They have the same simplest form.

EXAMPLE 1 Writing a Fraction in Simplest Form

History One of the Czech Republic's royal coronation jewels is the St. Wenceslas crown. It was made around 1345 and is decorated with 44 spinels, 30 emeralds, 22 pearls, 19 sapphires, and 1 ruby. Write in simplest form the fraction of jewels in the crown that are emeralds.

SOLUTION

Write the fraction of jewels in the crown that are emeralds. Then simplify.

$$\frac{\text{Number of emeralds}}{\text{Total number of jewels in the crown}} = \frac{30}{116}$$

METHOD 1 Find and use the GCF of 30 and 116.

$$30 = 2 \cdot 3 \cdot 5 \qquad 116 = 2^2 \cdot 29$$

The GCF of 30 and 116 is 2.

$\frac{30}{116} = \frac{30 \div 2}{116 \div 2}$ **Divide numerator and denominator by GCF.**

$= \frac{15}{58}$ **Simplify.**

METHOD 2 Use prime factorization.

$\frac{30}{116} = \frac{2 \cdot 3 \cdot 5}{2 \cdot 2 \cdot 29}$ **Write prime factorizations.**

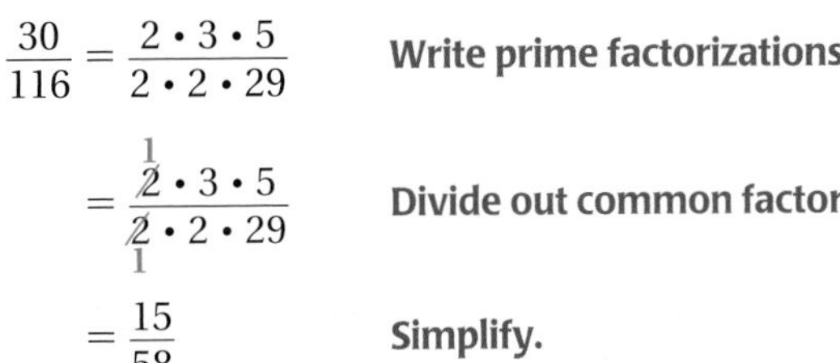

$= \frac{\overset{1}{\cancel{2}} \cdot 3 \cdot 5}{\underset{1}{\cancel{2}} \cdot 2 \cdot 29}$ **Divide out common factor.**

$= \frac{15}{58}$ **Simplify.**

Answer The fraction of jewels that are emeralds is $\frac{15}{58}$.

APPLY PROPERTIES

You can use the identity property of multiplication to understand dividing out common factors.

$$\frac{2 \cdot 3 \cdot 5}{2 \cdot 2 \cdot 29} = \frac{2}{2} \cdot \frac{3 \cdot 5}{2 \cdot 29}$$
$$= 1 \cdot \frac{3 \cdot 5}{2 \cdot 29}$$
$$= \frac{3 \cdot 5}{2 \cdot 29}$$

Sapphire Ruby Pearl Spinel Emerald

✓ GUIDED PRACTICE for Example 1

Use the information from Example 1. Write the fraction of jewels in the crown that are the given jewel. Simplify if possible.

1. pearls **2.** sapphires **3.** spinels

EXAMPLE 2 Identifying Equivalent Fractions

Tell whether the fractions $\frac{3}{8}$ and $\frac{18}{48}$ are equivalent.

SOLUTION

Write each fraction in simplest form.

$\frac{3}{8}$ is in simplest form. $\frac{18}{48} = \frac{18 \div 6}{48 \div 6} = \frac{3}{8}$

▶ **Answer** The fractions have the same simplest form, so they are equivalent.

EXAMPLE 3 Writing Equivalent Fractions

Write two fractions that are equivalent to $\frac{4}{10}$.

SOLUTION

Multiply or divide the numerator and denominator by the same nonzero number.

$\frac{4}{10} = \frac{4 \times 3}{10 \times 3} = \frac{12}{30}$ **Multiply numerator and denominator by 3.**

$\frac{4}{10} = \frac{4 \div 2}{10 \div 2} = \frac{2}{5}$ **Divide numerator and denominator by 2, a common factor of 4 and 10.**

▶ **Answer** The fractions $\frac{12}{30}$ and $\frac{2}{5}$ are equivalent to $\frac{4}{10}$.

OTHER SOLUTIONS
Many other equivalent fractions can be found by multiplying the numerator and denominator by other numbers.

✓ GUIDED PRACTICE for Examples 2 and 3

Tell whether the fractions are equivalent.

4. $\frac{1}{6}, \frac{4}{24}$ **5.** $\frac{3}{7}, \frac{10}{21}$ **6.** $\frac{24}{30}, \frac{4}{6}$ **7.** $\frac{15}{35}, \frac{3}{7}$

Write two fractions that are equivalent to the given fraction.

8. $\frac{8}{16}$ **9.** $\frac{9}{15}$ **10.** $\frac{10}{12}$ **11.** $\frac{21}{24}$

Variable Expressions You can use prime factorization to simplify fractions that contain variable expressions, as you will see in the next example.

EXAMPLE 4 Simplifying a Variable Expression

$\frac{14x}{7xy} = \frac{2 \cdot 7 \cdot x}{7 \cdot x \cdot y}$ Factor numerator and denominator.

$= \frac{2 \cdot \cancel{7}^{1} \cdot \cancel{x}^{1}}{\cancel{7}_{1} \cdot \cancel{x}_{1} \cdot y}$ Divide out common factors.

$= \frac{2}{y}$ Simplify.

EXAMPLE 5 Evaluating a Variable Expression

 **Evaluate the expression $\frac{-4x^3}{2x}$ when $x = 5$.**

$\frac{-4x^3}{2x} = \frac{-1 \cdot 2 \cdot 2 \cdot x \cdot x \cdot x}{2 \cdot x}$ Factor numerator and denominator.

$= \frac{-1 \cdot 2 \cdot \cancel{2}^{1} \cdot \cancel{x}^{1} \cdot x \cdot x}{\cancel{2}_{1} \cdot \cancel{x}_{1}}$ Divide out common factors.

$= -2x^2$ Simplify.

$= -2(5)^2$ Substitute 5 for *x*.

$= -50$ Evaluate powers and simplify.

TAKE NOTES
You may want to add information on simplifying fractions with variable expressions to the outline that you started on page 174.

GUIDED PRACTICE for Examples 4 and 5

Simplify the variable expression. Then evaluate for $x = -2$ and $y = 3$.

12. $\frac{4xy}{6x}$ **13.** $\frac{32x}{8xy}$ **14.** $\frac{2x^3y}{6x}$ **15.** $\frac{5x^2y}{10xy}$

4.3 EXERCISES

HOMEWORK KEY
★ = STANDARDIZED TEST PRACTICE Exs. 21, 48, 49, 50, 51, 52, and 62
○ = HINTS AND HOMEWORK HELP for Exs. 3, 7, 13, 27, 45 at classzone.com

SKILL PRACTICE

VOCABULARY **Copy and complete the statement.**

1. The GCF of the numerator and denominator of a fraction in _?_ is 1.
2. Fractions with the same simplest form are _?_.

WRITING IN SIMPLEST FORM **Write the fraction in simplest form.**

SEE EXAMPLE 1 on p. 187 for Exs. 3–12

3. $\frac{21}{49}$ **4.** $\frac{-9}{72}$ **5.** $\frac{10}{15}$ **6.** $\frac{16}{20}$ **7.** $\frac{-25}{40}$

8. $\frac{-36}{72}$ **9.** $\frac{39}{52}$ **10.** $\frac{18}{27}$ **11.** $\frac{-49}{56}$ **12.** $\frac{33}{121}$

EQUIVALENT FRACTIONS **Tell whether the fractions are equivalent.**

SEE EXAMPLE 2 on p. 188 for Exs. 13–21

13. $\frac{4}{5}, \frac{20}{25}$
14. $\frac{21}{28}, \frac{1}{3}$
15. $\frac{24}{40}, \frac{30}{50}$
16. $\frac{30}{60}, \frac{27}{54}$
17. $\frac{30}{75}, \frac{75}{105}$
18. $\frac{45}{54}, \frac{90}{108}$
19. $\frac{54}{96}, \frac{144}{256}$
20. $\frac{84}{112}, \frac{168}{192}$

21. ★ **MULTIPLE CHOICE** Which pair of fractions are equivalent?

(A) $\frac{6}{10}, \frac{9}{25}$ (B) $\frac{3}{8}, \frac{15}{35}$ (C) $\frac{14}{21}, \frac{12}{18}$ (D) $\frac{2}{5}, \frac{5}{20}$

SEE EXAMPLE 3 on p. 188 for Exs. 22–25

WRITING FRACTIONS **Write two fractions equivalent to the given fraction.**

22. $\frac{45}{90}$
23. $\frac{36}{81}$
24. $\frac{24}{60}$
25. $\frac{48}{140}$

EVALUATING EXPRESSIONS **Write the fraction in simplest form. Then evaluate the expression when $x = 3$ and $y = 5$.**

SEE EXAMPLES 4 AND 5 on p. 189 for Exs. 26–33

26. $\frac{3x}{x^3}$
27. $\frac{2y^2}{-5y}$
28. $\frac{5y}{y^2}$
29. $\frac{4x^4}{24x^3}$
30. $\frac{-18x^2y}{24x}$
31. $\frac{35xy^2}{7x^2y^4}$
32. $\frac{6x^3y^2}{21xy^4}$
33. $\frac{-20x^2y}{8x^4y^3}$

34. **WHICH ONE DOESN'T BELONG?** Which fraction is *not* equivalent to the other fractions?

A. $\frac{180}{320}$ B. $\frac{9}{16}$ C. $\frac{81}{144}$ D. $\frac{14}{25}$

ALGEBRA **Find the value of x that makes the fractions equivalent.**

35. $\frac{x}{140} = \frac{1}{10}$
36. $\frac{x}{5} = \frac{42}{70}$
37. $\frac{8}{18} = \frac{x}{54}$
38. $\frac{36}{78} = \frac{x}{13}$

VARIABLE EXPRESSIONS **Tell whether the expressions are equivalent.**

39. $\frac{4abc}{5ab}, \frac{4c}{5a}$
40. $\frac{3a}{5}, \frac{6a^2}{10a}$
41. $\frac{2a}{3b}, \frac{10a^2b}{15ab^2}$
42. $\frac{7a}{9b}, \frac{21a^4b^3}{27a^5b^4}$

43. **CHALLENGE** The product of the integers from n down to 1 is called *n factorial* and is written $n! = n \cdot (n-1) \cdot (n-2) \cdot \ldots \cdot 1$. Simplify the expression $\frac{12!}{3! \cdot 4!}$.

PROBLEM SOLVING

SEE EXAMPLE 1 on p. 187 for Exs. 44–47

GEOGRAPHY **Write the number of states in the region as a fraction of all the states. Write your answer in simplest form.**

44. Northeast: 9
45. Midwest: 12
46. South: 16
47. West: 13

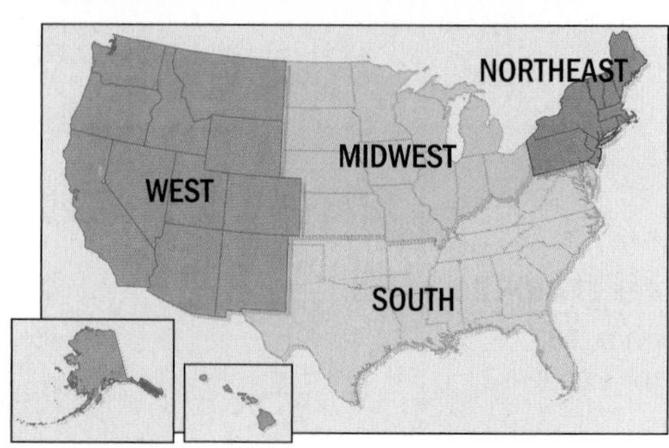

The U.S. Census Bureau divides the 50 states into 4 regions.

48. ★ **MULTIPLE CHOICE** Mr. Wilkens has attended 18 of his daughter's 24 basketball games. What fraction of the games has he *missed*?

Ⓐ $\frac{1}{4}$ Ⓑ $\frac{2}{3}$ Ⓒ $\frac{3}{4}$ Ⓓ $\frac{4}{3}$

49. ★ **SHORT RESPONSE** You buy two dozen eggs. In one carton, 1 egg is broken. In the other, 2 are broken. What fraction of all the eggs are broken? What fraction of all the eggs are unbroken? Write your answers in simplest form. *Explain* your reasoning.

50. ★ **EXTENDED RESPONSE** The table gives information about animals in Peru.

a. **Calculate** Find the fraction of threatened species in each group (mammals, birds, and reptiles). Write your answers in simplest form.

b. **Estimate** Round the number of known bird species to 1500 and the number of threatened bird species to 60. Approximately what fraction of bird species are threatened?

c. **Mental Math** Use mental math and your fraction from part (b) to find which group has the greatest fraction of threatened species and which group has the least. *Explain* your reasoning.

Yellow-faced parrot

Peruvian Animal Species

	Mammals	*Birds*	*Reptiles*
Known	460	1541	360
Threatened	46	64	9

51. ★ **SHORT RESPONSE** Your class of 30 students votes on what type of fundraiser to have this year: a car wash, a fair, or a dance. Eight students choose a car wash and 12 students choose a fair. Find the fraction of students who choose to have a dance. Write your answer in simplest form. *Explain* how you found your answer.

52. ★ **WRITING** If you divide the numerator and denominator of a fraction by a common factor, will the resulting fraction always be in simplest form? *Explain* your reasoning and give an example to justify your answer.

53. **CHALLENGE** Jason believes that if the numerator or the denominator of a fraction is prime, then the fraction is in simplest form. *Explain* why this is not always true.

9/16 30/30

MIXED REVIEW

Get-Ready

Prepare for Lesson 4.4 in Exs. 54–57

Find the GCF of the monomials. *(p. 181)*

54. $4a^5, 14a^2$ 55. $18s^2t^4, 12st$ 56. $3x^3y, 6x^2y^2$ 57. $15a^2b^3, 40a^3b^2$

Use a protractor to draw an angle with the given measure. *(p. 776)*

58. 53° 59. 97° 60. 145° 61. 178°

62. ★ **MULTIPLE CHOICE** Evaluate the expression $-12 + 46 - 18$. *(p. 83)*

Ⓐ −76 Ⓑ 16 Ⓒ 40 Ⓓ 52

4.4 Least Common Multiple

Before	You found the greatest common factor of two numbers.
Now	You'll find the least common multiple of two numbers.
Why?	So you can plan a schedule, as in Example 1.

KEY VOCABULARY
- **multiple,** *p. 192*
- **common multiple,** *p. 192*
- **least common multiple (LCM),** *p. 192*

A **multiple** of a number is the product of the number and any nonzero whole number. A multiple that is shared by two or more numbers is a **common multiple**. The least of the common multiples of two or more whole numbers is the **least common multiple (LCM)**.

EXAMPLE 1 Finding the Least Common Multiple

Animal Clinic A veterinarian at an animal clinic is on call every four days. Today is Saturday, and the veterinarian is on call. In how many more days will the veterinarian be on call on a Saturday again?

SOLUTION

The veterinarian is on call every 4 days. A Saturday occurs every 7 days. Find the least common multiple of 4 and 7.

READING Read the problem above carefully to determine what you know and what you need to find out.

METHOD 1 Use a calendar. Start with a Saturday and circle every 4 days on a calendar. You can see that the veterinarian will be on call on a Saturday in 28 days.

June 29 is 28 days after June 1.

METHOD 2 Make a list.

List the multiples of each number.

Multiples of 4: 4, 8, 12, 16, 20, 24, **28**, 32, . . .

Multiples of 7: 7, 14, 21, **28**, 35, 42, 49, 56, . . .

The least common multiple is the first number that appears in both lists. The LCM of 4 and 7 is 28.

METHOD 3 Use prime factorization.

Write the prime factorization of each number. $4 = 2^2$ $7 = 7$

Circle the greatest power of each prime factor. $4 = \textcircled{2^2}$ $7 = \textcircled{7}$

The LCM of 4 and 7 is the product of the circled numbers: $2^2 \cdot 7 = 28$

▶ **Answer** In 28 days, the veterinarian will be on call on a Saturday.

EXAMPLE 2 Finding the Least Common Multiple

Find the LCM of 32, 96, and 120 using prime factorization.

SOLUTION

AVOID ERRORS
Make sure you circle the greatest power of each prime factor only once in *all* of the prime factorizations. 2^5 occurs in both 32 and 96, but it is only circled once.

STEP 1 **Write** the prime factorization of each number and circle the greatest power of each prime factor.

$$32 = \textcircled{2^5}$$
$$96 = 2^5 \cdot \textcircled{3}$$
$$120 = 2^3 \cdot 3 \cdot \textcircled{5}$$

STEP 2 **Find** the product of the circled factors.

$$2^5 \cdot 3 \cdot 5 = 480$$

▶ **Answer** The LCM of 32, 96, and 120 is 480.

Animated Math at classzone.com

Monomials The factoring method used in Example 2 is also useful for finding the least common multiples of monomials.

EXAMPLE 3 Finding the LCM of Monomials

xy **Find the LCM of $6x^2y$ and $9x^4z$.**

SOLUTION

STEP 1 **Factor** each expression using exponents and circle the greatest power of each factor.

$$6x^2y = \textcircled{2} \cdot 3 \cdot x^2 \cdot \textcircled{y}$$
$$9x^4z = \textcircled{3^2} \cdot \textcircled{x^4} \cdot \textcircled{z}$$

STEP 2 **Find** the product of the circled factors.

$$2 \cdot 3^2 \cdot x^4 \cdot y \cdot z = 18x^4yz$$

▶ **Answer** The LCM of $6x^2y$ and $9x^4z$ is $18x^4yz$.

✓ GUIDED PRACTICE for Examples 1, 2, and 3

1. **What If?** In Example 1, suppose the veterinarian is on call every 3 days. In how many more days will the vet be on call on a Saturday again?

Find the least common multiple of the numbers.

2. 6, 15
3. 4, 20
4. 12, 28
5. 24, 36, and 72

Find the least common multiple of the monomials.

6. $8x^3, 20x^7$
7. $12y^4, 36y^8$
8. $4ab^2, 10a^2b$
9. $6m^3np^2, 8mp^3$

4.4 EXERCISES

HOMEWORK KEY

★ = **STANDARDIZED TEST PRACTICE** Exs. 37, 38–41, 47, 50, 52, and 61

○ = **HINTS AND HOMEWORK HELP** for Exs. 3, 13, 21, 29, 45 at classzone.com

SKILL PRACTICE

VOCABULARY **Copy and complete the statement.**

1. A(n) _?_ of 6 and 9 is 54.

2. The _?_ of 6 and 9 is 18.

LISTING MULTIPLES **Find the LCM of the numbers by listing multiples.**

SEE EXAMPLE 1 on p. 192 for Exs. 3–10

3. 6, 8 **4.** 6, 21 **5.** 8, 10 **6.** 10, 15

7. 18, 36 **8.** 45, 75 **9.** 6, 8, 12 **10.** 3, 6, 15

USING PRIME FACTORIZATION **Find the LCM of the numbers by using prime factorization.**

SEE EXAMPLE 2 on p. 193 for Exs. 11–19

11. 14, 21 **12.** 7, 56 **13.** 15, 55 **14.** 36, 90

15. 42, 105 **16.** 90, 108 **17.** 10, 12, 14 **18.** 16, 20, 40

19. ERROR ANALYSIS Describe and correct the error made in finding the LCM.

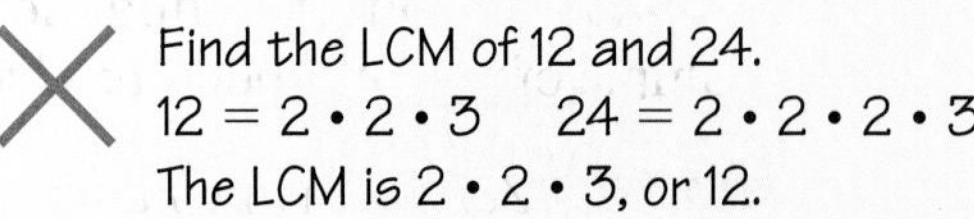

Find the LCM of 12 and 24.
12 = 2 • 2 • 3   24 = 2 • 2 • 2 • 3
The LCM is 2 • 2 • 3, or 12.

SEE EXAMPLES 1 AND 2 on pp. 192–193 for Exs. 20–27

CHOOSE A METHOD **Tell whether you would find the LCM of the numbers by *using mental math, listing multiples* or *using prime factorization.* *Explain* your choice and find the LCM.**

20. 17, 57 **21.** 125, 500 **22.** 8, 16, 32 **23.** 6, 15, 45

24. 30, 75, 100 **25.** 36, 54, 72 **26.** 10, 12, 30, 60 **27.** 21, 42, 63, 105

ALGEBRA **Find the LCM of the monomials.**

SEE EXAMPLE 3 on p. 193 for Exs. 28–36

28. $4x, 16x^3$ **29.** $9y^4, 12y$ **30.** $24t, 60st$

31. $5ab, 7ab^2$ **32.** $7s^3t, 49st^2$ **33.** $4x^3y^3, 18xy^5$

34. $18x^2y, 24x^4y, 30y^7$ **35.** $24c^2d^3, 30c^3d^2, 60c^2d^6$ **36.** $33g^4hk^3, 36g^3h^7k, 45gh^5k^3$

37. ★ **MULTIPLE CHOICE** Which statement is *always* true?

Ⓐ The LCM of two prime numbers is 1.

Ⓑ The LCM of two numbers is greater than or equal to both numbers.

Ⓒ The LCM of two different numbers is the product of the two numbers.

Ⓓ The LCM of a prime number and a composite number is the product of the two numbers.

★ **OPEN-ENDED MATH** **Find a pair of numbers that have the given LCM. *Explain* how you found your answer.**

38. 30 **39.** 70 **40.** 105 **41.** 150

42. **NUMBER SENSE** What is the *least* possible number for which the LCM of the number and 15 is 105? What is the *greatest* number for which the LCM of the number and 15 is 105? *Explain* your reasoning.

43. **CHALLENGE** Could the GCF of two different numbers also be the LCM of those numbers? *Explain.*

PROBLEM SOLVING

SEE EXAMPLES 1 AND 2 on pp. 192–193 for Exs. 44–46

44. **SCHEDULE** Your schedule changes on a three-day rotation. Your math class is the last period of every third day. This week, your math class is on Friday. In how many more school days will you again have math on Friday?

45. **TRAFFIC LIGHTS** One traffic light turns red every 45 seconds. Another traffic light turns red every 60 seconds. Both traffic lights just turned red. In how many seconds will they turn red at the same time again?

46. **CLASS SIZES** A teacher can arrange a class into groups of 2, 5, or 6 students with no one left out. What is the least number of students that the teacher can have in class to do this? *Explain* your reasoning.

47. ★ **WRITING** Could you find the *greatest* common multiple of two numbers? *Explain* your reasoning.

48. **COOKING** Zoe is making lasagna for a family reunion. Her recipe calls for 12 noodles for each batch of lasagna. One box of lasagna noodles contains 14 noodles. What is the least number of batches of lasagna that Zoe can make without having any noodles left over? *Explain.*

49. **REASONING** You are asked to find the LCM of two numbers. One of the numbers is a factor of the other. Is there a shortcut to finding their LCM? *Explain.*

50. ★ **SHORT RESPONSE** You are forming sets of plastic utensils for a party that include one spoon, one fork, and one knife. Spoons come in packs of 24, forks come in packs of 36, and knives come in packs of 20. What is the least number of sets you can make without having any utensils left over? How many packs of each utensil will you need to make the sets? *Explain.*

51. **LOOK FOR A PATTERN** What is the number of the next figure that will be identical to Figure 1 in color and orientation? *Explain.*

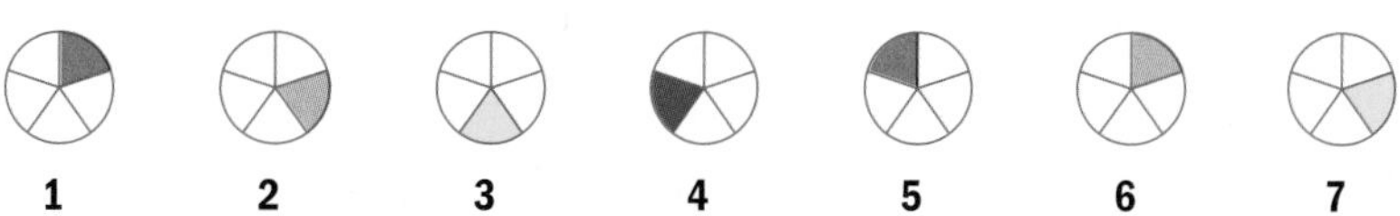

52. ★ **MULTIPLE CHOICE** Becky and Tonya are running laps. Becky runs one lap in 4 minutes. Tonya runs one lap in 3 minutes. They start at 4:00 P.M. from the same point. At which time will they *not* both be at the starting point?

Ⓐ 4:12 P.M. Ⓑ 4:18 P.M. Ⓒ 4:24 P.M. Ⓓ 4:36 P.M.

53. **CHALLENGE** Will swims one pool length in 45 seconds, while Martin swims one length in 40 seconds. The boys start at the same time from the same end of the pool and maintain their pace.

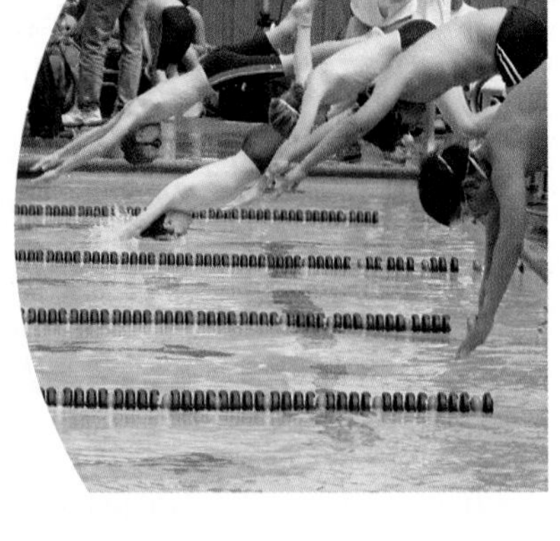

a. When will they both be at their starting place at the same time again? Write your answer in seconds and in minutes.

b. Kyle swims at a constant rate of 75 lengths per hour. Assume Kyle started swimming at the same time from the same end of the pool as Will and Martin. Will Kyle end up at the starting place at the same time as in part (a)? *Explain.*

c. Kyle swims a total of 45 lengths. How many times will Kyle end up at the starting place at the same time as Will and Martin? *Explain* how you found your answer.

MIXED REVIEW

Prepare for Lesson 4.5 in Exs. 54–57

Find the greatest common factor of the numbers. *(p. 181)*

54. 54, 81 55. 18, 125 56. 121, 187 57. 64, 144

Simplify the expression by combining like terms. *(p. 88)*

58. $7x + 9 + 12x + 11 + 2y$ 59. $18x - 2 + 5y + 2 + 3x$

60. **RUNNING** Rebecca ran on her treadmill at 6 miles per hour for one half hour. How many miles did Rebecca run? *(p. 32)*

61. ★ **MULTIPLE CHOICE** What is the prime factorization of 72? *(p. 192)*

(A) $2 \cdot 3 \cdot 12$ (B) $2 \cdot 6^2$ (C) $2^3 \cdot 3^2$ (D) $2^2 \cdot 3^2 \cdot 6$

QUIZ *for Lessons 4.1–4.4*

1. Write the prime factorization of 1620. *(p. 176)*

Find the GCF of the numbers or monomials. *(p. 181)*

2. 24, 90 3. 36, 72, 108 4. $20c^3, 48c^2$ 5. $64m^2, 80m^5$

Find the LCM of the numbers or monomials. *(p. 192)*

6. 88, 99 7. 36, 96 8. $7xy, 21y^3$ 9. $6ab^2, 30ab$

Tell whether the fractions are equivalent. *(p. 187)*

10. $\frac{9}{27}, \frac{60}{180}$ 11. $\frac{39}{91}, \frac{42}{56}$ 12. $\frac{40}{48}, \frac{70}{84}$ 13. $\frac{108}{120}, \frac{189}{210}$

14. **SUPERMARKET** A supermarket gives every tenth customer a coupon and every twenty-fifth customer a gift. Which of the first 200 customers receive both a coupon and a gift? *(p. 176)*

Lessons 4.1–4.4

1. **SHORT RESPONSE** Two fifths of the students at an assembly are girls. Suppose there are between 400 and 500 students at the assembly. What is the *greatest* possible number of girls? the *least* possible number of boys? *Explain* your answers.

2. **SHORT RESPONSE** A company wants to find at least 35 but no more than 40 people to participate in a scientific study. The company wants to be able to divide the people into groups and have between 8 and 10 groups of equal size.
   a. Write the factors of each number from 35 to 40.
   b. How many people should the company find to conduct the study? Is there more than one correct answer? *Explain.*

3. **EXTENDED RESPONSE** Every fourth Saturday, Alana visits her aunt. Alana and a friend want to start playing tennis every third Saturday. She will visit her aunt this coming Saturday and wants to begin playing tennis one of the three following Saturdays.
   a. When should she start playing tennis to postpone the first conflict as long as possible? *Justify* your answer.
   b. In how many weeks will this first conflict occur?
   c. How often after the first conflict will other conflicts occur? *Explain* how you found your answer.

4. **GRIDDED ANSWER** For a neighborhood party, hats are bought in packages of 8 and party favors in packages of 6. After the party, Bo notices that there are no hats or favors left over. There were over 60 people at the party and each guest received exactly one hat and one favor. What is the *least* number of people who could have attended?

5. **MULTI-STEP PROBLEM** The Orb of 1661 is a gold sphere displayed at the Tower of London. It is set with 365 diamonds, 363 cultured pearls, 18 rubies, 9 emeralds, 9 sapphires, and 1 amethyst.
   a. What is the total number of jewels in the Orb of 1661?
   b. Write the fraction of jewels that are emeralds in simplest form.
   c. Jane estimates that about $\frac{3}{4}$ of the jewels in the Orb are *not* emeralds. Do you agree with this estimate? Why or why not?

6. **SHORT RESPONSE** A coin collector will have a complete 50 state quarters collection when the last state quarter (Hawaii) is distributed in 2008. The book below shows one way that the quarters can be arranged in a rectangular pattern. How else could they be arranged in a rectangular pattern? *Describe* a pattern with one less coin in every other row.

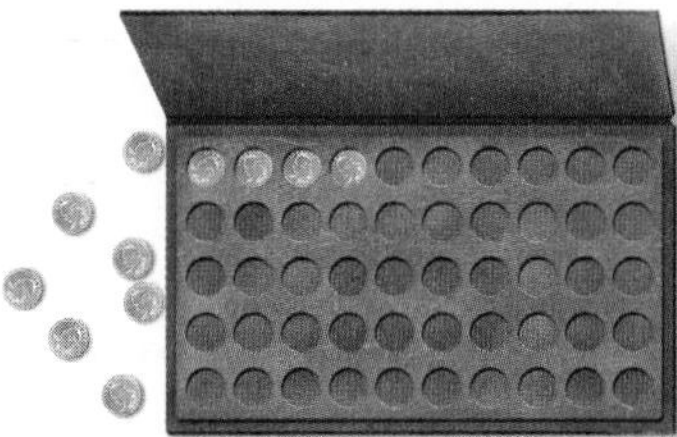

7. **GRIDDED ANSWER** A piece of wood is 56 inches wide and 84 inches long. What is the least number of identical squares it can be divided into so that the entire piece of wood is used?

4.5 Comparing Fractions and Mixed Numbers

Before	You compared and ordered integers.
Now	You'll compare and order fractions and mixed numbers.
Why?	So you can compare statistics, as for sports in Ex. 43.

KEY VOCABULARY
- **least common denominator (LCD),** *p. 198*

You can use models to compare the fractions $\frac{2}{3}$ and $\frac{3}{4}$.

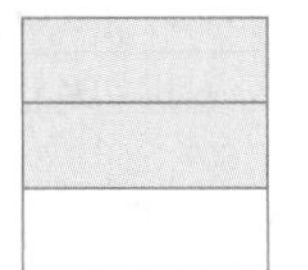

$$\frac{2}{3} = \frac{2 \cdot 4}{3 \cdot 4} = \frac{8}{12} \qquad \frac{3}{4} = \frac{3 \cdot 3}{4 \cdot 3} = \frac{9}{12}$$

In the diagram above, $\frac{8}{12} < \frac{9}{12}$, so $\frac{2}{3} < \frac{3}{4}$.

The **least common denominator (LCD)** of two or more fractions is the least common multiple of the denominators. You can compare fractions by using the least common denominator to write equivalent fractions.

EXAMPLE 1 Comparing Fractions Using the LCD

Compare $\frac{3}{8}$ and $\frac{5}{12}$.

SOLUTION

STEP 1 **Find** the least common denominator of the fractions.
The LCM of 8 and 12 is 24, so the least common denominator is 24.

STEP 2 **Use** the least common denominator to write equivalent fractions.

$$\frac{3}{8} = \frac{3 \cdot 3}{8 \cdot 3} = \frac{9}{24} \qquad \frac{5}{12} = \frac{5 \cdot 2}{12 \cdot 2} = \frac{10}{24}$$

STEP 3 **Compare** the numerators: $9 < 10$, so $\frac{9}{24} < \frac{10}{24}$.

▶ **Answer** Because $\frac{9}{24} < \frac{10}{24}$, you can write $\frac{3}{8} < \frac{5}{12}$.

GUIDED PRACTICE for Example 1

Copy and complete the statement with <, >, or =.

1. $\frac{2}{3} \underline{?} \frac{5}{8}$ **2.** $\frac{2}{4} \underline{?} \frac{15}{20}$ **3.** $\frac{3}{10} \underline{?} \frac{2}{4}$ **4.** $\frac{9}{16} \underline{?} \frac{11}{18}$

Mixed Numbers To compare or order improper fractions and mixed numbers, first write any mixed numbers as improper fractions.

EXAMPLE 2 Standardized Test Practice

What is the order of $4\frac{7}{16}$, $\frac{19}{4}$, and $\frac{35}{8}$ from least to greatest?

Ⓐ $4\frac{7}{16}, \frac{19}{4}, \frac{35}{8}$ Ⓑ $4\frac{7}{16}, \frac{35}{8}, \frac{19}{4}$ Ⓒ $\frac{35}{8}, \frac{19}{4}, 4\frac{7}{16}$ Ⓓ $\frac{35}{8}, 4\frac{7}{16}, \frac{19}{4}$

ELIMINATE CHOICES
Using mental math, you can see that $\frac{19}{4} = \frac{38}{8}$. Because $\frac{38}{8} > \frac{35}{8}$, choice A can be eliminated.

SOLUTION

STEP 1 **Find** the least common denominator of the fractions.
The LCM of 16, 4, and 8 is 16, so the LCD is 16.

STEP 2 **Use** the least common denominator to write equivalent fractions.

$$4\frac{7}{16} = \frac{4 \cdot 16 + 7}{16} = \frac{71}{16} \qquad \frac{19}{4} = \frac{19 \cdot 4}{4 \cdot 4} = \frac{76}{16} \qquad \frac{35}{8} = \frac{35 \cdot 2}{8 \cdot 2} = \frac{70}{16}$$

STEP 3 **Compare** the numerators: 70 < 71, 71 < 76, so $\frac{70}{16} < \frac{71}{16}$ and $\frac{71}{16} < \frac{76}{16}$.

▶ **Answer** From least to greatest, the numbers are $\frac{35}{8}$, $4\frac{7}{16}$, and $\frac{19}{4}$.
The correct answer is D. Ⓐ Ⓑ Ⓒ Ⓓ

EXAMPLE 3 Comparing Mixed Numbers

Orangutans A female orangutan is about $3\frac{3}{7}$ feet tall. A male is about $3\frac{2}{5}$ feet tall. Which of the two orangutans is taller?

ANOTHER WAY
When the whole parts of two mixed numbers are equal, you can just compare the fraction parts. Because $\frac{3}{7} > \frac{2}{5}$, $3\frac{3}{7} > 3\frac{2}{5}$.

SOLUTION

STEP 1 **Write** equivalent fractions using the LCD, 35.

$$3\frac{3}{7} = \frac{24}{7} = \frac{24 \cdot 5}{7 \cdot 5} = \frac{120}{35} \qquad 3\frac{2}{5} = \frac{17}{5} = \frac{17 \cdot 7}{5 \cdot 7} = \frac{119}{35}$$

STEP 2 **Compare** the fractions: $\frac{120}{35} > \frac{119}{35}$, so $3\frac{3}{7} > 3\frac{2}{5}$.

▶ **Answer** The female orangutan is taller.

Animated Math at classzone.com

✓ GUIDED PRACTICE for Examples 2 and 3

Copy and complete the statement with <, >, or =.

5. $\frac{16}{5}$? $3\frac{1}{3}$ **6.** $1\frac{4}{5}$? $\frac{21}{12}$ **7.** $2\frac{2}{3}$? $\frac{17}{6}$

8. Order the numbers $2\frac{7}{9}$, $2\frac{5}{12}$, and $\frac{11}{4}$ from least to greatest.

4.5 EXERCISES

HOMEWORK KEY

★ = **STANDARDIZED TEST PRACTICE** Exs. 24, 29–32, 38, 39, 40, 42, and 52

○ = **HINTS AND HOMEWORK HELP** for Exs. 3, 7, 9, 17, 37 at classzone.com

SKILL PRACTICE

1. **VOCABULARY** Copy and complete: The least common denominator of two fractions is the __?__ of their denominators.

2. **VOCABULARY** *Explain* how to compare fractions using the LCD.

FINDING LCDs Find the LCD of the fractions.

SEE EXAMPLES 1 AND 3 on pp. 198–199 for Exs. 3–15

3. $\frac{1}{2}, \frac{2}{3}$ 4. $\frac{3}{4}, \frac{7}{20}$ 5. $\frac{11}{24}, \frac{5}{6}$ 6. $\frac{5}{12}, \frac{7}{18}$

COMPARING NUMBERS Copy and complete the statement with <, >, or =.

7. $\frac{7}{18} \underline{?} \frac{5}{9}$ 8. $\frac{24}{32} \underline{?} \frac{3}{4}$ 9. $\frac{5}{8} \underline{?} \frac{9}{16}$ 10. $\frac{165}{36} \underline{?} 4\frac{5}{12}$

11. $2\frac{4}{5} \underline{?} \frac{7}{3}$ 12. $\frac{31}{6} \underline{?} 5\frac{2}{12}$ 13. $3\frac{1}{4} \underline{?} \frac{13}{14}$ 14. $\frac{5}{9} \underline{?} \frac{16}{24}$

15. **ERROR ANALYSIS** A classmate says that $\frac{3}{5} < \frac{4}{7}$ because $3 < 4$. Describe and correct your classmate's error.

ORDERING NUMBERS Order the numbers from least to greatest.

SEE EXAMPLE 2 on p. 199 for Exs. 16–24

16. $\frac{1}{2}, \frac{1}{8}, \frac{3}{4}, \frac{5}{16}$ 17. $1\frac{1}{2}, \frac{5}{4}, \frac{11}{6}$ 18. $\frac{5}{3}, \frac{35}{15}, 2\frac{2}{5}, \frac{15}{16}$ 19. $\frac{3}{4}, \frac{5}{9}, 1\frac{1}{3}$

20. $\frac{19}{6}, 3\frac{1}{2}, \frac{11}{4}$ 21. $1\frac{3}{5}, \frac{7}{3}, 2\frac{1}{4}, \frac{19}{12}$ 22. $\frac{15}{4}, 3\frac{2}{3}, \frac{25}{7}$ 23. $\frac{34}{3}, 11\frac{7}{12}, \frac{47}{4}$

24. ★ **MULTIPLE CHOICE** Which list of fractions is in order from least to greatest?

(A) $\frac{12}{18}, \frac{13}{30}, \frac{8}{15}$ (B) $\frac{4}{18}, \frac{9}{15}, \frac{18}{27}$ (C) $\frac{6}{10}, \frac{4}{18}, \frac{16}{24}$ (D) $\frac{7}{11}, \frac{7}{8}, \frac{15}{25}$

MENTAL MATH Copy and complete the statement with <, >, or = by first comparing each fraction to $\frac{1}{2}$.

25. $\frac{25}{50} \underline{?} \frac{37}{74}$ 26. $\frac{17}{30} \underline{?} \frac{10}{33}$ 27. $\frac{23}{100} \underline{?} \frac{19}{36}$ 28. $\frac{105}{210} \underline{?} \frac{13}{27}$

★ **OPEN-ENDED MATH Name a fraction $\frac{a}{b}$ between the given pair, where *a* and *b* are positive integers.**

29. $\frac{1}{3}, \frac{1}{2}$ 30. $\frac{3}{4}, \frac{4}{5}$ 31. $\frac{5}{8}, \frac{2}{3}$ 32. $\frac{3}{5}, \frac{1}{2}$

CHALLENGE Copy and complete the statement with <, >, or =, where $a > b$ and $b > 0$. *Explain* your reasoning.

33. $\frac{a}{b} \underline{?} \frac{b}{a}$ 34. $\frac{1}{a} \underline{?} \frac{1}{b}$ 35. $\frac{a}{a+1} \underline{?} \frac{b}{b+1}$ 36. $\frac{a+1}{a} \underline{?} \frac{b+1}{b}$

PROBLEM SOLVING

SEE EXAMPLE 1 on p. 198 for Ex. 37–39

37. **WALKERS** Sarah walks two thirds mile to school every day. Amy walks five eighths mile to school. Who walks the greater distance to school?

38. ★ **SHORT RESPONSE** During a 30 minute TV show, there are 8 minutes of commercials. During a 2 hour movie, there are 31 minutes of commercials. Which TV program has a greater fraction of commercial time? *Explain.*

39. ★ **MULTIPLE CHOICE** In a class of 32 people, 28 were at school. Which fraction is *less* than the fraction of people in the class who were at school?

Ⓐ $\frac{27}{30}$ Ⓑ $\frac{24}{27}$ Ⓒ $\frac{21}{24}$ Ⓓ $\frac{24}{28}$

40. ★ **WRITING** *Explain* how comparing fractions with like denominators differs from comparing fractions with like numerators.

41. **ELEPHANTS** Which elephant's trunk represents a greater fraction of the elephant's weight? *Explain* how you can answer this question without writing the fractions with a common denominator.

Elephant	*Trunk*
10,000 lb	350 lb
13,200 lb	430 lb

42. ★ **WRITING** In Exercises 25–28, why does it help to compare each number to $\frac{1}{2}$ first? Will this step always work? *Explain.*

43. **CHALLENGE** Teams from California have played in the world championship game of the Little League World Series 20 times and won 5 times. Texas teams have appeared in 7 world championship games and won twice.
   a. Which state has won a greater fraction of their world championship games? What is the fraction?
   b. What is the *least* number of future wins the other state needs in order to have won a *greater* fraction of their games than the fraction in part (a)? *Explain.*

MIXED REVIEW

Get-Ready
Prepare for Lesson 4.6 in Exs. 44–47

Evaluate the power. *(p. 19)*

44. 18^2 45. 10^4 46. 8^5 47. 11^3

Write the prime factorization of the number. *(p. 176)*

48. 336 49. 258 50. 364 51. 483

52. ★ **MULTIPLE CHOICE** What is the area of the figure? *(p. 142)*

Ⓐ 48 ft² Ⓑ 64 ft² Ⓒ 80 ft² Ⓓ 96 ft²

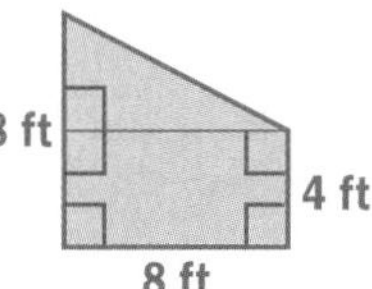

4.6 Rules of Exponents

Before You multiplied and divided numerical expressions.
Now You'll multiply and divide expressions with exponents.
Why? So you can represent large amounts, such as distance in Ex. 89.

KEY VOCABULARY
- **exponent,** *p. 19*
- **power,** *p. 19*

ACTIVITY

Use patterns to discover rules for multiplying powers.

STEP 1 **Copy** and complete the table.

Expression	Expanded Expression	Number of Factors	Product as a Power
$2^2 \cdot 2^4$	$(2 \cdot 2) \cdot (2 \cdot 2 \cdot 2 \cdot 2)$	6	2^6
$3^3 \cdot 3^1$	$(3 \cdot 3 \cdot 3) \cdot 3$	?	$3^?$
$7^2 \cdot 7^3$	?	?	?

STEP 2 **Explain** how the exponents in the first and last columns are related.

Write the product as a single power.

1. $3^4 \cdot 3^3$ **2.** $6^5 \cdot 6^{11}$ **3.** $10^7 \cdot 10^{13}$

As you saw in the activity, you can expand expressions to find their product. The following equation suggests a rule for multiplying powers with the same base.

$$a^4 \cdot a^2 = \underbrace{\overbrace{(a \cdot a \cdot a \cdot a)}^{\text{4 factors}} \cdot \overbrace{(a \cdot a)}^{\text{2 factors}}}_{\text{6 factors}} = a^{4+2} = a^6$$

KEY CONCEPT *For Your Notebook*

Product of Powers Property

Words To multiply powers with the same base, add their exponents.

Algebra $a^m \cdot a^n = a^{m+n}$ **Numbers** $5^6 \cdot 5^3 = 5^{6+3} = 5^9$

EXAMPLE 1 Using the Product of Powers Property

Simplify $x^4 \cdot x^7$.

$x^4 \cdot x^7 = x^{4+7}$ **Product of powers property**

$= x^{11}$ **Add exponents.**

✓ GUIDED PRACTICE for Example 1

Simplify the expression. Write your answer as a power.

1. $4^6 \cdot 4^4$ **2.** $9^8 \cdot 9$ **3.** $a^6 \cdot a^9$ **4.** $c \cdot c^{12} \cdot c^3$

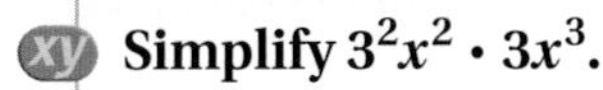

EXAMPLE 2 Using the Product of Powers Property

Simplify $3^2x^2 \cdot 3x^3$.

$3^2x^2 \cdot 3x^3 = (3^2 \cdot 3) \cdot (x^2 \cdot x^3)$ **Use properties of multiplication.**

$= 3^{2+1} \cdot x^{2+3}$ **Product of powers property**

$= 3^3x^5$ **Add exponents.**

$= 27x^5$ **Evaluate the power.**

AVOID ERRORS
Remember that numbers raised to the first power are usually written without an exponent. For example, $3 = 3^1$.

✓ GUIDED PRACTICE for Example 2

Simplify the expression.

5. $10^2s^4 \cdot 10^4s^2$ **6.** $6^3t^5 \cdot 6^2t^8$ **7.** $7x^2 \cdot 7x^4$ **8.** $5^2z \cdot 5z^7 \cdot z^2$

Dividing Powers The following equation suggests a rule for dividing powers with the same base when the exponents are integers.

$$\frac{a^5}{a^3} = \frac{\overbrace{a \cdot a \cdot a \cdot a \cdot a}^{\text{5 factors}}}{\underbrace{a \cdot a \cdot a}_{\text{3 factors}}} = \frac{a \cdot a \cdot \overset{1}{\cancel{a}} \cdot \overset{1}{\cancel{a}} \cdot \overset{1}{\cancel{a}}}{\underset{1}{\cancel{a}} \cdot \underset{1}{\cancel{a}} \cdot \underset{1}{\cancel{a}}} = \overbrace{a \cdot a}^{\text{2 factors}} = a^{5-3} = a^2$$

KEY CONCEPT *For Your Notebook*

Quotient of Powers Property

Words To divide two powers with the same nonzero base, subtract the exponent of the denominator from the exponent of the numerator.

Algebra $\frac{a^m}{a^n} = a^{m-n}$ **Numbers** $\frac{4^7}{4^4} = 4^{7-4} = 4^3$

EXAMPLE 3 Using the Quotient of Powers Property

Simplify the expression. Write your answer as a power.

a. $\frac{x^{12}}{x^7} = x^{12-7}$ — **Quotient of powers property**

$= x^5$ — **Subtract exponents.**

b. $\frac{9^7}{9^3} = 9^{7-3}$ — **Quotient of powers property**

$= 9^4$ — **Subtract exponents.**

EXAMPLE 4 Simplifying Fractions with Powers

AVOID ERRORS

The bases of the powers must be the same to use the product or quotient property. In part (b) of Example 4, you cannot simplify the numerator any further because the bases, x and y, are different.

Simplify the expression.

a. $\frac{y^4 \cdot y}{y^3} = \frac{y^5}{y^3}$ — **Simplify numerator using product of powers property.**

$= y^{5-3}$ — **Quotient of powers property**

$= y^2$ — **Subtract exponents.**

b. $\frac{xy^4}{y^3} = xy^{4-3}$ — **Quotient of powers property**

$= xy$ — **Subtract exponents.**

✓ GUIDED PRACTICE for Examples 3 and 4

Simplify the expression. Write your answer as a power.

9. $\frac{a^6}{a^4}$ **10.** $\frac{10^9}{10^6}$ **11.** $\frac{q^3 \cdot q^5}{q^4}$ **12.** $\frac{a^2b^8}{b^2}$

4.6 EXERCISES

HOMEWORK KEY

★ = **STANDARDIZED TEST PRACTICE** Exs. 31, 54, 88, 90, 91, and 108

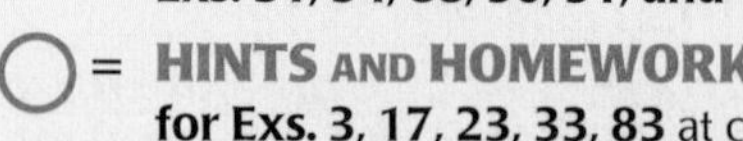

○ = **HINTS AND HOMEWORK HELP** for Exs. 3, 17, 23, 33, 83 at classzone.com

SKILL PRACTICE

VOCABULARY **Copy and complete the statement.**

1. Three is the _?_ of the power 3^4.
2. Seven is the _?_ of the power 4^7.

SIMPLIFYING PRODUCTS **Simplify the product. Write your answer as a power.**

SEE EXAMPLE 1 on p. 203 for Exs. 3–14

3. $4^2 \cdot 4^4$ **4.** $8 \cdot 8^3$ **5.** $a^5 \cdot a^7$ **6.** $b^9 \cdot b^9$

7. $u^7 \cdot u$ **8.** $v^2 \cdot v^{10}$ **9.** $b^9 \cdot b^6$ **10.** $m^{11} \cdot m^8$

11. $3^2 \cdot 3^5$ **12.** $7^2 \cdot 7^2$ **13.** $(-4)^2 \cdot (-4)^3$ **14.** $(-5)^4 \cdot (-5)$

SEE EXAMPLE 2 on p. 203 for Exs. 15–22

SIMPLIFYING EXPRESSIONS **Simplify the product.**

15. $3a^3 \cdot 3a^2$
16. $2y^3 \cdot 2y^2$
17. $3^2x^5 \cdot 3^3x^4$
18. $4a^3b^4 \cdot 4^2a^4b^6$
19. $5x^7 \cdot 5x^9$
20. $7^2b^3 \cdot 7^5b^8$
21. $6^2x^2y \cdot 6x^4y^3$
22. $10c^4 \cdot 10c^2$

SEE EXAMPLES 3 AND 4 on p. 204 for Exs. 23–39

SIMPLIFYING QUOTIENTS **Simplify the quotient. Write your answer as a power.**

23. $\frac{5^8}{5^4}$
24. $\frac{8^7}{8^2}$
25. $\frac{d^8}{d}$
26. $\frac{a^4}{a}$
27. $\frac{w^{15}}{w^9}$
28. $\frac{y^{20}}{y^{18}}$
29. $\frac{(-7)^7}{(-7)^4}$
30. $\frac{(-2)^{13}}{(-2)^3}$

31. ★ **MULTIPLE CHOICE** Which expression is equivalent to $\frac{a^9 \cdot a^6}{a^5}$?

Ⓐ a^3 Ⓑ a^5 Ⓒ a^{10} Ⓓ a^{15}

SIMPLIFYING EXPRESSIONS **Simplify the quotient.**

32. $\frac{p^5q^9}{pq^5}$
33. $\frac{z^6 \cdot z^3}{z^4}$
34. $\frac{3^3m^9}{3^2m^5}$
35. $\frac{5^5n^{15}}{5^3n^{12}}$
36. $\frac{6^4k^5}{6k^3}$
37. $\frac{7^9r^{12}}{7^5r^8}$
38. $\frac{a^{11} \cdot b^7}{a^{10} \cdot b}$
39. $\frac{y^6 \cdot y^{13}}{y^9}$

SEE EXAMPLES 1 AND 4 on pp. 203–204 for Exs. 40–41

ERROR ANALYSIS **Describe and correct the error made in simplifying the expression.**

40. ✗ $2^2 \cdot 2^4 = (2 \cdot 2)^{2+4} = 4^6$

41. ✗ $\frac{x^{20}y^6}{x^5y^3} = x^4y^2$

ALGEBRA **Simplify the expression when $x = 2$, $y = 3$, and $z = 4$. Write your answer as a power.**

42. $\frac{3^x \cdot 3^y}{3^z}$
43. $\frac{(-2)^{2z}}{(-2)^x}$
44. $\frac{(-6)^{2y}}{(-6)^z}$
45. $\frac{2^{2x}}{2^y}$
46. $\frac{5^x \cdot 5^z}{5^y}$
47. $\frac{(-3)^{3y}}{(-3)^z}$
48. $\frac{7^{3z}}{7^{2y}}$
49. $\frac{w^{x+y+z}}{w^{3y}}$
50. $\frac{64a^z}{4a^y}$
51. $\frac{-20b^{2y+z}}{5b^{3x}}$
52. $\frac{12m^{x+y}}{6m^{z-y}}$
53. $\frac{27n^{x+y}}{3n^x}$

54. ★ **OPEN-ENDED MATH** Write three variable expressions that simplify to x^4y^4. Write three variable expressions that simplify to $\frac{2b^3}{5a}$.

NUMBER SENSE **Find the number that correctly completes the equation.**

55. $2^3 \cdot 2^? = 2^{11}$
56. $5^4 \cdot ?^5 = 5^9$
57. $12^3 \cdot ?^{13} = 12^{16}$
58. $3^2 \cdot 3^? = 3^7$
59. $\frac{8^7}{8^?} = 8^3$
60. $\frac{7^4}{7^?} = 7$
61. $\frac{13^?}{13^9} = 13^2$
62. $9^3 \cdot 9^? = 9^{20}$
63. $\frac{6^{14}}{6^?} = 6^6$
64. $\frac{12^?}{12^5} = 12^4$
65. $4^? \cdot 4^7 = 4^{19}$
66. $\frac{11^3}{11^?} = 11^2$

ALGEBRA Write and solve an equation to find the value of x that makes the statement true.

67. $4^{2x} \cdot 4^{x-3} = 4^{12}$
68. $5^{x-3} \cdot 5^{3x} = 5^{13}$
69. $8^{3x+4} \cdot 8^{x} = 8^{12}$
70. $2^{22} = 2^{2x-2} \cdot 2^{4x-6}$
71. $\frac{3^{2x-1}}{3^{x+4}} = 3^3$
72. $7^8 = \frac{7^{3x-2}}{7^x}$
73. $9^2 = \frac{9^{5x}}{9^{x+2}}$
74. $\frac{11^{6x+1}}{11^{3x-7}} = 11^{17}$

EVALUATING EXPRESSIONS Write the expression as a power and evaluate.

75. $(3^2 \cdot 3)^2$
76. $(2^3 \cdot 2^2)^3$
77. $\left(\frac{4^7}{4^5}\right)^2$
78. $\left(\frac{5^8}{5^7}\right)^4$

CHALLENGE Simplify the expression.

79. $4y^3 + \frac{6y^5}{2y^2} - 3y(y^2)$
80. $\frac{9s^4t^2}{3st} + \frac{6s^2t^5}{2t^2} - \frac{s^5t^2}{s^2t}$
81. $\frac{x^{n+1}}{x^n}$

PROBLEM SOLVING

METRIC UNITS In Exercises 82–87, use the table. It shows the number of meters in some metric measures written as powers of ten. Write your answers as powers of 10.

Metric Units	
Unit	**Meters**
yottameter	10^{24}
zettameter	10^{21}
exameter	10^{18}
petameter	10^{15}
terameter	10^{12}
gigameter	10^{9}
megameter	10^{6}
kilometer	10^{3}
decameter	10^{1}

82. How many decameters are in a yottameter?
83. How many kilometers are in a petameter?
84. How many gigameters are in a zettameter?
85. How many terameters are in a yottameter?
86. How many megameters are in an exameter?
87. How many petameters are in a zettameter?
88. ★ **MULTIPLE CHOICE** The product of 1 kilometer and which power of 10 yields 1 exameter? Use the table at the right.

 Ⓐ 10^6 Ⓑ 10^9

 Ⓒ 10^{15} Ⓓ 10^{18}

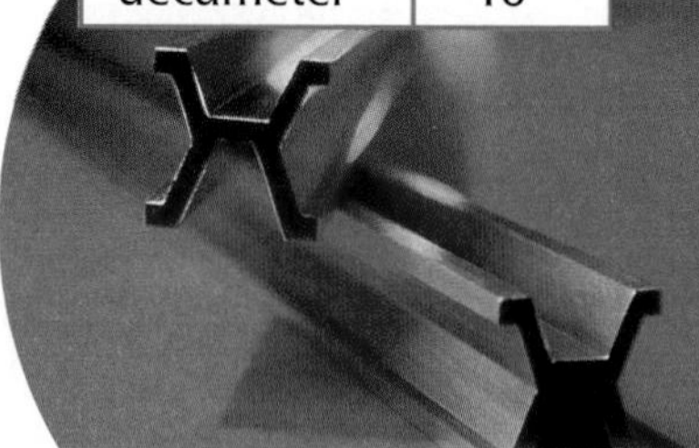
The historical standard platinum iridium meter bar

89. **MULTI-STEP PROBLEM** The distance to the Andromeda Galaxy is 21 quintillion kilometers, which is 21 followed by 18 zeros. Refer to the table above to answer the questions.
 a. How many exameters are in 1 quintillion kilometers?
 b. Use your answer to part (a) to find the number of exameters in 21 quintillion kilometers.
 c. How many gigameters are in 1 exameter?
 d. Use your answers to parts (b) and (c) to find the number of gigameters in 21 quintillion kilometers.

90. ★ **SHORT RESPONSE** *Describe* two ways to evaluate the expression $\frac{6y^{10}}{3y^8}$ when $y = 5$. Evaluate the expression using both methods. Which method do you prefer? Why?

91. ★ **WRITING** *Explain* why it is not necessary to multiply to evaluate powers of 10. Include an example with your answer.

92. **CHECKING REASONABLENESS** It takes you 5^2 seconds to run x feet. If your speed remains constant, is it reasonable to say that it will take you 5^3 seconds to run $5x$ feet? *Justify* your answer.

93. **LAND AREA** A square field has sides of length 3^8 millimeters. Find the area of the field. A larger field has side lengths 9 times those of the smaller field. How many times greater is the area of the large field? *Explain.*

94. **COMPUTERS** A friend tells you that his family first bought a computer in 1979. It had 2^3 KB (kilobytes) of available memory.

   a. Your family's first computer was purchased in 1987 and had 64 times the amount of memory of your friend's. How much memory did your computer have? Express your answer as a power of 2.

   b. A typical computer purchased in 2005 had at least 2^9 MB (megabytes) of memory. A MB is equal to 2^{10} KB. How many times the amount of the memory in your friend's 1979 computer is this? *Explain.*

95. **CHALLENGE** A number x is c followed by b zeros. Another number y, which is smaller than x, is d followed by b zeros. How many times greater is x than y? *Explain* your reasoning.

MIXED REVIEW

Get-Ready

Prepare for Lesson 4.7 in Exs. 96–103

Write the fraction in simplest form. *(p. 187)*

96. $\frac{28xy}{7y}$ 97. $\frac{24x}{18x}$ 98. $\frac{46xyz}{82xy}$ 99. $\frac{25y^2}{145y}$

100. $\frac{36yz}{45xy}$ 101. $\frac{52x^2}{13x^4}$ 102. $\frac{30x^2y}{12xy^2}$ 103. $\frac{6xy}{44xz}$

Use the line plot below. It shows the results of a survey asking people how many hours they read each week. *(p. 782)*

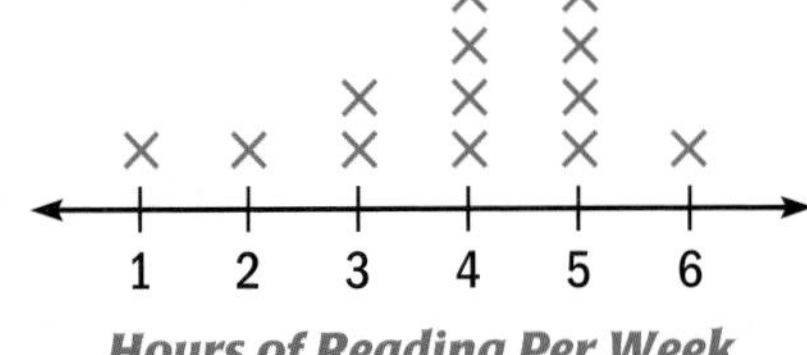

104. How many people completed the survey?

105. How many people read 3 hours or less each week?

106. How many people read more than 4 hours each week?

107. How many more people read 4 hours each week than 6 hours each week?

108. ★ **MULTIPLE CHOICE** What is the greatest common factor of 144, 300, and 240? *(p. 181)*

   (A) 4 (B) 6 (C) 12 (D) 60

4.7 Negative and Zero Exponents

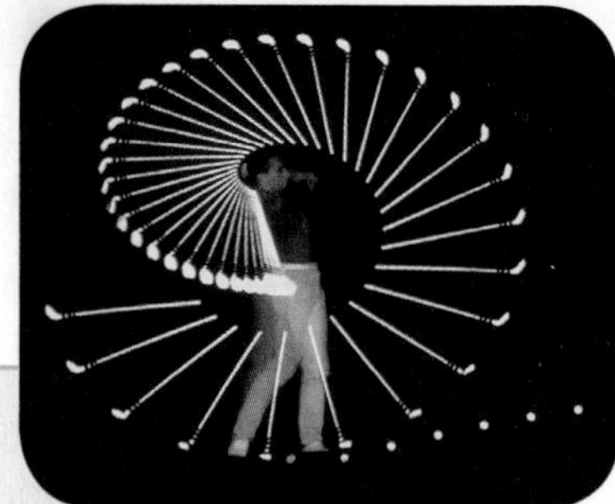

Before	You simplified expressions with positive exponents.
Now	You'll simplify expressions with negative exponents.
Why?	So you can describe very quick events, as the flash in Example 1.

KEY VOCABULARY
- **exponent,** *p. 19*
- **common factor,** *p. 181*

You have seen two ways to evaluate expressions involving division of powers. Compare the results of the two methods when the denominator contains the greater power.

Divide out common factors.

$$\frac{x^5}{x^7} = \frac{\cancel{x}^1 \cdot \cancel{x}^1 \cdot \cancel{x}^1 \cdot \cancel{x}^1 \cdot \cancel{x}^1}{\cancel{x}_1 \cdot \cancel{x}_1 \cdot \cancel{x}_1 \cdot \cancel{x}_1 \cdot \cancel{x}_1 \cdot x \cdot x} = \frac{1}{x^2}$$

Quotient of powers property

$$\frac{x^5}{x^7} = x^{5-7} = x^{-2}$$

So $\frac{1}{x^2} = x^{-2}$. This suggests the following definition for negative exponents.

KEY CONCEPT *For Your Notebook*

Negative Exponents

Words For any integer n and any number $a \neq 0$, a^{-n} is equal to $\frac{1}{a^n}$.

Algebra $a^{-n} = \frac{1}{a^n}$

Numbers $2^{-3} = \frac{1}{2^3}$

EXAMPLE 1 Using a Negative Exponent

Strobes The picture of the golf ball was taken using a strobe light. Each flash of the strobe light lasted about 1 microsecond. How can you write this time in seconds as a power of ten?

SOLUTION

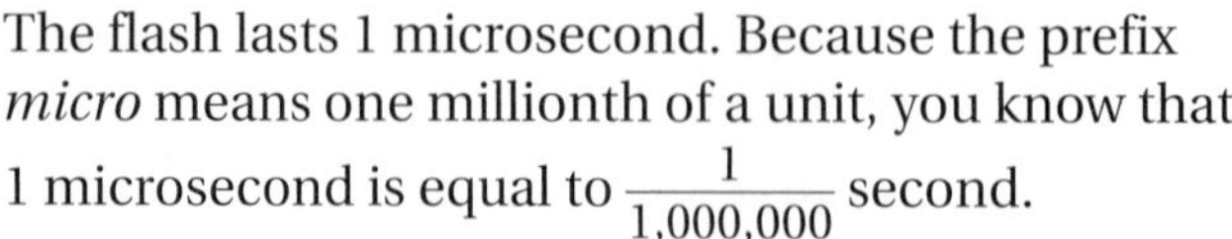

The flash lasts 1 microsecond. Because the prefix *micro* means one millionth of a unit, you know that 1 microsecond is equal to $\frac{1}{1{,}000{,}000}$ second.

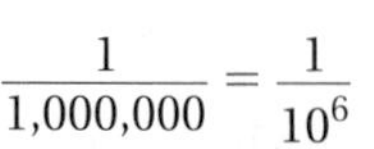

$\frac{1}{1{,}000{,}000} = \frac{1}{10^6}$ **Write 1,000,000 as 10^6.**

$= 10^{-6}$ **Definition of negative exponent**

▸ **Answer** One flash of the strobe light lasts about 10^{-6} second.

EXAMPLE 2 Evaluating a Numerical Expression

Evaluate the expression.

$5^2 \cdot 5^{-5} = 5^{2+(-5)}$ **Product of powers property**

$= 5^{-3}$ **Simplify.**

$= \frac{1}{5^3}$ **Definition of negative exponent**

$= \frac{1}{125}$ **Evaluate the power.**

KEY CONCEPT *For Your Notebook*

Zero Exponents

Words For any number $a \neq 0$, a^0 is equal to 1.

Algebra $a^0 = 1$ **Numbers** $2^0 = 1$

EXAMPLE 3 Simplifying Variable Expressions

Simplify. Write the expression using only positive exponents.

AVOID ERRORS
In expressions such as $-2n^0$ and $4n^{-5}$, the exponent is applied only to the variable, not to the coefficient. $-2n^0 \neq -2^0 \cdot n^0$

a. $-2n^0 = -2 \cdot n^0$ **Zero exponent applies only to *n*.**

$= -2 \cdot 1$ **Definition of zero exponent**

$= -2$ **Multiply.**

b. $\frac{8x^{-3}}{x} = \frac{8 \cdot x^{-3}}{x^1}$ **Exponent applies only to *x*.**

$= 8 \cdot x^{-3-1}$ **Quotient of powers property**

$= 8 \cdot x^{-4}$ **Simplify.**

$= \frac{8}{x^4}$ **Definition of negative exponent**

Animated Math at classzone.com

✓ GUIDED PRACTICE for Examples 1, 2, and 3

1. **What If?** In Example 1, suppose the flash of a light lasted about one thousandth of a second. Write this time in seconds as a power of 10.

Evaluate the expression.

2. 7^{-2}
3. $(-2)^{-5}$
4. $6 \cdot 6^{-3}$
5. $10^{-5} \cdot 10^5$

Simplify. Write the expression using only positive exponents.

6. $-6m^{-1}$
7. $b^2 \cdot b^{-2}$
8. $\frac{5x^4}{x^{-7}}$
9. $\frac{10a^{-3}}{a^4}$

4.7 EXERCISES

HOMEWORK KEY
★ = **STANDARDIZED TEST PRACTICE** Exs. 20, 37, 43, and 52
○ = **HINTS AND HOMEWORK HELP** for Exs. 3, 5, 13, 15, 39 at classzone.com

SKILL PRACTICE

VOCABULARY Copy and complete the statement.

1. The power x^0 is equal to _?_.
2. The power x^{-h} is equal to _?_.

EVALUATING EXPRESSIONS Evaluate the expression.

SEE EXAMPLES 1 AND 2 on pp. 208–209 for Exs. 3–11

3. 3^{-4}
4. 12^0
5. -2^{-4}
6. $(-4)^{-3}$
7. $(-6)^{-2} \cdot (-6)^0$
8. $-2 \cdot 2^{-6}$
9. $-5^4 \cdot 5^{-8}$
10. $9^0 \cdot 9^{-2}$
11. **ERROR ANALYSIS** Describe and correct the error made in evaluating 5^{-3}.

$$5^{-3} = (-5)(-5)(-5) = -125$$

SIMPLIFYING EXPRESSIONS Simplify. Write the expression using only positive exponents.

SEE EXAMPLE 3 on p. 209 for Exs. 12–20

12. $m^{-9} \cdot m^5$
13. $x^5 \cdot x^{-5}$
14. $9n^{-3}$
15. $c^{-1} \cdot c^{-2} \cdot c^{-4}$
16. $b^3 \cdot b^{-4} \cdot b^{-5}$
17. $\frac{4z^{-2}}{z^4}$
18. $\frac{a^{-5}}{a^8}$
19. $\frac{18r^{-6}}{3r^3}$
20. ★ **MULTIPLE CHOICE** Simplify the expression $\frac{-3x^{-4}}{x^2}$.

Ⓐ $\frac{-3}{x^6}$ Ⓑ $-3x^6$ Ⓒ $\frac{-3}{x^{-6}}$ Ⓓ $\frac{-3x}{x^6}$

MENTAL MATH Find the missing exponent.

21. $(4x^5)^? = 1$
22. $15a^? = \frac{15}{a^8}$
23. $y^? \cdot y^4 = \frac{1}{y}$
24. $\frac{x^{-3}}{x^?} = \frac{1}{x^{13}}$
25. $\frac{5x^?}{x^{-5}} = 5x^3$
26. $(2y^8)^? = 1$
27. $9b^? = \frac{9}{b^7}$
28. $a^6 \cdot a^? = \frac{1}{a^2}$

REASONING Copy and complete the statement using *always, sometimes,* or *never*. *Explain* your reasoning.

29. A power with an exponent of zero is _?_ positive.
30. A power with a positive base and a negative exponent is _?_ negative.
31. A power with a negative base and a positive exponent is _?_ positive.
32. A power with an integer base and a negative exponent can _?_ be written as a fraction.

CHALLENGE Simplify. Write the expression using only positive exponents.

33. $c^{-1} \cdot (b^2c)^{-2}$
34. $\frac{x^6y^4}{(x^3y^{-4})^{-2}}$
35. $(2t)^{-3} \cdot 4t^3 \cdot (4t^{-3})^0$

PROBLEM SOLVING

SEE EXAMPLES 1 AND 3 on pp. 208–209 for Exs. 36–37

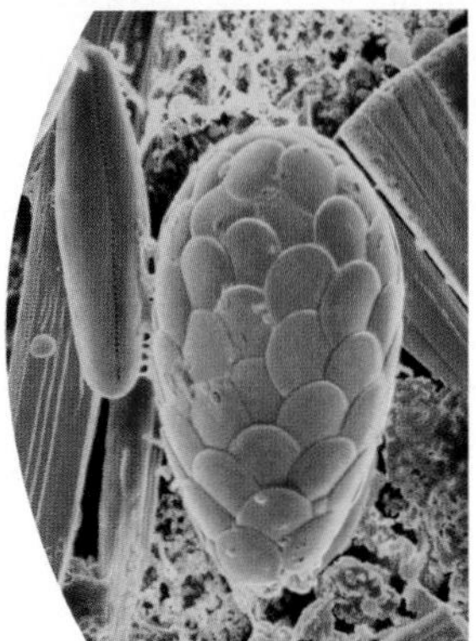
Single-celled alga

36. **BIOLOGY** Phytoplankton are tiny plants that live in the ocean. One type has a length of about 0.2 micrometer. A micrometer is 10^{-6} meter. What part of a meter is this phytoplankton? Use a positive exponent to write your answer.

37. ★ **SHORT RESPONSE** The time it takes a decaying radioactive substance to be reduced by half is known as its *half-life*. An equation to find the fraction r of a substance remaining after t half-lives is $r = 2^{-t}$. What fraction of the substance remains after 4 half-lives? After how many half-lives does $\frac{1}{64}$ of the original amount remain? *Explain.*

38. **PHYSICS** Pressure is measured in *pascals*. This unit can be expressed as $\text{kg} \cdot \text{m}^{-1} \cdot \text{s}^{-2}$. Write the unit without negative exponents.

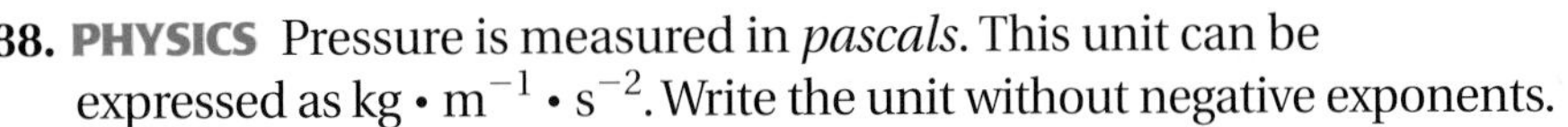

MEASUREMENT In Exercises 39–42, use the table. It shows the number of meters in some metric measures written as powers of ten.

Unit	*Meter*
decimeter	10^{-1}
centimeter	10^{-2}
nanometer	10^{-9}
picometer	10^{-12}
attometer	10^{-18}
yoctometer	10^{-24}

39. How many picometers are in a decimeter?

40. How many yoctometers are in a picometer?

41. How many nanometers are in a decimeter?

42. How many attometers are in a centimeter?

43. ★ **MULTIPLE CHOICE** What is the area of a rectangle with a length of 2^3 meters and a width of 4^{-2} meters?

Ⓐ $\frac{1}{2}\text{ m}^2$ Ⓑ 2 m^2 Ⓒ 4 m^2 Ⓓ 128 m^2

44. **MULTIPLE REPRESENTATIONS** The expanded form of 389.602 is

$$3 \times 100 + 8 \times 10 + 9 \times 1 + 6 \times 0.1 + 2 \times 0.001.$$

Write this expanded form using positive or zero powers of 10 and then using positive, negative, or zero powers of 10.

45. **CHALLENGE** Use the product of powers property to show why $a^0 = 1$, when a is a nonzero number.

MIXED REVIEW

Get-Ready
Prepare for Lesson 4.8 in Exs. 46–48

Write the number in expanded form. *(p. 759)*

46. 32,501.5

47. 8055.93

48. 163.427

Evaluate the expression. *(p. 19)*

49. $(4 \times 3)^2 + 13$

50. $405 \div (14 - 11)^4$

51. $96 \div 2^5 \times 6$

52. ★ **MULTIPLE CHOICE** Simplify the expression $b^3 \cdot b^2$. *(p. 202)*

Ⓐ $5b$ Ⓑ b^5 Ⓒ $6b$ Ⓓ b^6

4.8 Scientific Notation

Before You multiplied numbers by powers of 10.
Now You'll read and write numbers using scientific notation.
Why? So you can express small measurements, as bubbles in Example 2.

KEY VOCABULARY
- **scientific notation,** *p. 212*

One way to write very small numbers like the thickness of a soap bubble or very large numbers like the number of stars in the galaxy is to use powers of ten. This can be done by writing numbers using *scientific notation.*

KEY CONCEPT *For Your Notebook*

Using Scientific Notation

A number is written in **scientific notation** if it has the form $c \times 10^n$ where $c \geq 1$, $c < 10$, and n is an integer.

Standard form	Product form	Scientific notation
325,000	$3.25 \times 100{,}000$	3.25×10^5
0.0005	5×0.0001	5×10^{-4}

EXAMPLE 1 Writing Numbers in Scientific Notation

POWERS OF 10
$10^5 = 100{,}000$
$10^4 = 10{,}000$
$10^3 = 1000$
$10^2 = 100$
$10^1 = 10$
$10^0 = 1$
$10^{-1} = 0.1$
$10^{-2} = 0.01$
$10^{-3} = 0.001$
$10^{-4} = 0.0001$
$10^{-5} = 0.00001$

Stars There are over 300,000,000,000 stars in the Andromeda Galaxy. Write the number of stars in scientific notation.

SOLUTION

Standard form	Product form	Scientific notation
300,000,000,000	$3 \times 100{,}000{,}000{,}000$	3×10^{11}
Move decimal point 11 places to the left.		Exponent is 11.

▸ **Answer** The number in scientific notation is 3×10^{11}.

✓ **GUIDED PRACTICE** for Example 1

Write the number in scientific notation.

1. 4000 **2.** 7,300,000 **3.** 63,000,000,000

4. 230,000 **5.** 2,420,000 **6.** 105

EXAMPLE 2 Standardized Test Practice

Bubbles The thickness of a soap bubble is about 0.000004 meter. What is the thickness of a soap bubble written in scientific notation?

Ⓐ 4×10^{-7} m Ⓑ 4×10^{-6} m

Ⓒ 4×10^{-5} m Ⓓ 40×10^{7} m

ELIMINATE CHOICES
A correct answer must be in the form $c \times 10^n$ where the greatest place value for c is the ones place. Choice D is not in this form, so it can be eliminated.

SOLUTION

Standard form	Product form	Scientific notation
0.000004	4×0.000001	4×10^{-6}
Move decimal point 6 places to the right.		Exponent is −6.

▶ **Answer** The thickness of the bubble is 4×10^{-6} meter.
The correct answer is B. Ⓐ Ⓑ Ⓒ Ⓓ

GUIDED PRACTICE for Example 2

Write the number in scientific notation.

7. 0.00475 **8.** 0.00000526 **9.** 0.0000000082

10. 0.0237 **11.** 0.000097 **12.** 0.0003141

Standard Form A number in scientific notation can be written in standard form by using the exponent. Move the decimal point the appropriate number of places left or right, depending on the sign of the exponent.

EXAMPLE 3 Writing Numbers in Standard Form

	Scientific notation	Product form	Standard form
a.	7.2×10^{5}	$7.2 \times 100{,}000$	720,000
	Exponent is 5.		Move decimal point 5 places to the right.
b.	4.65×10^{-7}	4.65×0.0000001	0.000000465
	Exponent is −7.		Move decimal point 7 places to the left.

GUIDED PRACTICE for Example 3

Write the number in standard form.

13. 3.5×10^{3} **14.** 2.48×10^{6} **15.** 5.1×10^{-4} **16.** 9.16×10^{-2}

Products in Scientific Notation You can use the product of powers property to multiply two numbers written in scientific notation.

EXAMPLE 4 Multiplying Numbers in Scientific Notation

Find the product $(4.5 \times 10^3) \times (6.3 \times 10^7)$.

$(4.5 \times 10^3) \times (6.3 \times 10^7)$

$= 4.5 \times 6.3 \times 10^3 \times 10^7$	Commutative property of multiplication
$= (4.5 \times 6.3) \times (10^3 \times 10^7)$	Associative property of multiplication
$= 28.35 \times 10^{10}$	Product of powers property
$= 2.835 \times 10^1 \times 10^{10}$	Write 28.35 in scientific notation.
$= 2.835 \times 10^{11}$	Product of powers property

AVOID ERRORS
Make sure the product is written in proper scientific notation. The number 28.35×10^{10} is not written in scientific notation because $28.35 \geq 10$.

✓ GUIDED PRACTICE for Example 4

Write the product in scientific notation.

17. $(1.25 \times 10^6) \times (7.6 \times 10^{12})$

18. $(8 \times 10^5) \times (5.65 \times 10^4)$

4.8 EXERCISES

HOMEWORK KEY
★ = **STANDARDIZED TEST PRACTICE** Exs. 13, 46, 49, 51, 52, and 73
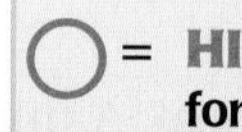
= **HINTS AND HOMEWORK HELP** for Exs. 5, 7, 15, 17, 23, 47 at classzone.com

SKILL PRACTICE

VOCABULARY Tell whether the number is expressed in scientific notation. *Explain* why or why not.

1. 9.32×10^5

2. 56.8×10^2

3. 7×10^{-4}

SCIENTIFIC NOTATION Write the number in scientific notation.

SEE EXAMPLES 1 AND 2 on pp. 212–213 for Exs. 4–13

4. 7900

5. 0.468

6. 0.0000671

7. 89,200,000,000

8. 8,100,000,000

9. 2,130,000

10. 0.0312

11. 0.000000415

12. 0.0000000342

13. ★ **MULTIPLE CHOICE** What is 0.000000765 written in scientific notation?

Ⓐ 7.65×10^{-9} Ⓑ 76.5×10^{-8} Ⓒ 7.65×10^{-7} Ⓓ 7.65×10^{-6}

STANDARD FORM Write the number in standard form.

SEE EXAMPLE 3 on p. 213 for Exs. 14–22

14. 5.72×10^{-3}

15. 4.35×10^6

16. 9.62×10^7

17. 8.71×10^{-2}

18. 6.35×10^{-6}

19. 1.76×10^{-9}

20. 4.13×10^9

21. 2.83×10^{12}

22. 3.61×10^7

SEE EXAMPLE 4 on p. 214 for Exs. 23–31

MULTIPLYING **Write the product in scientific notation.**

23. $(3 \times 10^3) \times (2 \times 10^5)$

24. $(2 \times 10^{-6}) \times (4 \times 10^{-4})$

25. $(1.5 \times 10^{-2}) \times (3.9 \times 10^{-5})$

26. $(3.6 \times 10^8) \times (2.4 \times 10^5)$

27. $(7.8 \times 10^6) \times (8.4 \times 10^7)$

28. $(7.6 \times 10^{-8}) \times (4.8 \times 10^{-6})$

29. $(2.6 \times 10^7) \times (4.1 \times 10^{-3})$

30. $(5.4 \times 10^5) \times (3.6 \times 10^{-9})$

31. **ERROR ANALYSIS** Describe and correct the error made in writing the product in scientific notation.

$$(3 \times 10^2) \times (6.2 \times 10^3) = (3 \times 6.2) \times (10^2 \times 10^3) = 18.6 \times 10^6$$

COMPARING **Copy and complete the statement with <, >, or =.**

32. 6.92×10^{11} _?_ 6.92×10^{12}

33. 1.06×10^6 _?_ 9.98×10^5

34. 3.67×10^{-3} _?_ 3.76×10^{-4}

35. 3.4×10^{-20} _?_ 4.1×10^{-21}

DIVIDING **Find the quotient. Write your answer in scientific notation.**

36. $\frac{4.08 \times 10^6}{3.4 \times 10^2}$

37. $\frac{2.765 \times 10^{21}}{7.9 \times 10^9}$

38. $\frac{5.46 \times 10^{28}}{6.5 \times 10^{24}}$

39. $\frac{2.015 \times 10^7}{6.2 \times 10^3}$

40. **ORDERING** Order the numbers from least to greatest.

3.75×10^8 37,500,000 3.57×10^9 5.37×10^7

CHALLENGE **Find the sum or difference. Write your answer in scientific notation.**

41. $(3.2 \times 10^5) + (8.1 \times 10^3)$

42. $(5 \times 10^{-1}) + (9.8 \times 10^{-3})$

43. $(4.1 \times 10^8) - (7.7 \times 10^6)$

44. $(6.4 \times 10^4) - (5.9 \times 10^{-2})$

PROBLEM SOLVING

45. **GUIDED PROBLEM SOLVING** The mass of Earth is about 1.3×10^{25} pounds. The mass of Jupiter is about 4.2×10^{27} pounds. About how many times Earth's mass is Jupiter's mass?

   a. Write the quotient of 4.2 and 1.3 as a decimal rounded to the nearest tenth.
   b. Write the quotient of 10^{27} and 10^{25}.
   c. Write the product of the quotients from parts (a) and (b) in scientific notation.

SEE EXAMPLE 1 on p. 212 for Exs. 46–47

46. ★ **MULTIPLE CHOICE** In 2000, there were approximately 281,000,000 people in the United States. Which of the following is *not* another way of expressing the number 281,000,000?

   (A) 28.1 million   (B) 0.281 billion   (C) 28.1×10^7 (D) 2.81×10^8

47. **WELL WATER** In the United States, 15,000,000 households use private wells for their water supply. Write this number in scientific notation.

SEE EXAMPLE 3 on p. 213 for Ex. 48

48. **STATE PARKS** The United States has a total of 1.2916×10^7 acres of land reserved for state parks. Write this number in standard form.

49. ★ **SHORT RESPONSE** The masses of an oxygen atom and a hydrogen atom are shown below. Write these numbers in standard form. Which atom has a greater mass? Approximately how many times greater? *Explain.*

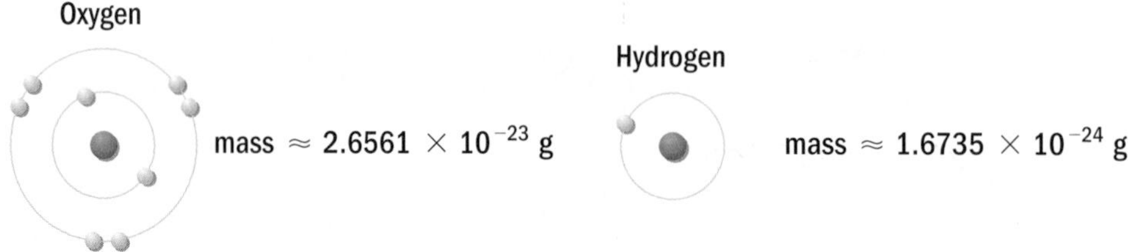

50. **SCIENCE** The radius of a proton is about 1.2 Fermis. One *Fermi* is equal to 10^{-15} meter. How many centimeters is the radius of a proton? Write your answer in scientific notation.

51. ★ **SHORT RESPONSE** A space probe travels about 1.5×10^6 kilometers per day to its destination 21 million kilometers away. After traveling 9 million kilometers, about how many days of travel remain? *Explain.*

52. ★ **WRITING** *Explain* how to compare numbers written in scientific notation.

READING *IN* MATH **Read the information below for Exercises 53–56.**

U.S. Currency Facts The United States Bureau of Engraving and Printing is responsible for printing new money. In 2004, the Bureau printed about 23.9 million bills daily for a face value of about \$351 million. More than half of these were \$1 and \$5 bills. About 11.4 million were \$1 bills and about 1.72 million were \$5 bills. The average life of a bill depends on its denomination. A \$1 bill lasts an average of about 22 months, while a \$100 bill lasts an average of 8.5 years.

53. **Calculate** About how many \$1 bills were printed in one week during 2004? one year? Write your answers in scientific notation.

54. **Calculate** About how many \$5 bills were printed in one week during 2004? one year? Write your answers in scientific notation.

55. **Compare** What is the total value of the number of \$5 bills that were printed each day? each week? each year? Write your answers in standard form.

56. **Compare** What is greater, the value of the \$5 bills printed in 2004 or the value of the \$1 bills? How much greater? Write your answer in standard form.

57. **CHALLENGE** Light travels approximately 1.86×10^5 miles in 1 second. About how far does light travel in one year? Write your answer in scientific notation.

58. **CHALLENGE** It takes about 8.3 minutes for sunlight to reach the Earth. Find the approximate distance, in miles, from the Earth to the sun. Use the speed of light given in Exercise 57. Write your answer in standard form.

MIXED REVIEW

Prepare for Lesson 5.1 in Exs. 59–62

Copy and complete the statement with <, >, or =, by using the LCD. *(p. 198)*

59. $\frac{11}{32} \ \underline{?} \ \frac{3}{8}$ 60. $\frac{254}{48} \ \underline{?} \ 5\frac{7}{24}$ 61. $\frac{5}{12} \ \underline{?} \ \frac{13}{36}$ 62. $2\frac{1}{6} \ \underline{?} \ \frac{79}{36}$

Write the fraction in simplest form. *(p. 187)*

63. $-\frac{9a^4}{15a}$ 64. $\frac{8x^2}{2x^5}$ 65. $\frac{6n}{9mn}$ 66. $\frac{10xy^5}{5x^2y^4}$

Evaluate the expression.

67. $-8 + 12 + (-16) + 18$ *(p. 63)* 68. $34 - (-43) - (3 - 6)$ *(p. 68)*

Solve the equation. *(p. 117)*

69. $6 + x = 15$ 70. $-4 + x = -7$ 71. $x - \frac{1}{3} = 2$ 72. $\frac{9}{10} = x + \frac{4}{5}$

73. ★ **MULTIPLE CHOICE** What amount of time has elapsed from 10:46 A.M. to 3:13 P.M.? *(p. 778)*

Ⓐ 4 hours and 27 minutes Ⓑ 4 hours and 33 minutes

Ⓒ 5 hours and 27 minutes Ⓓ 7 hours and 33 minutes

QUIZ *for Lessons 4.5–4.8*

Copy and complete the statement with <, >, or =. *(p. 198)*

1. $\frac{2}{5} \ \underline{?} \ \frac{6}{15}$ 2. $\frac{5}{6} \ \underline{?} \ \frac{4}{9}$ 3. $\frac{99}{15} \ \underline{?} \ 6\frac{5}{9}$ 4. $4\frac{35}{40} \ \underline{?} \ 4\frac{21}{24}$

Order the numbers from least to greatest. *(p. 198)*

5. $\frac{2}{3}, \frac{5}{6}, \frac{1}{2}, \frac{5}{12}$ 6. $\frac{3}{5}, \frac{7}{10}, \frac{3}{4}, \frac{7}{8}$ 7. $1\frac{4}{7}, 1\frac{5}{14}, \frac{5}{4}, 1\frac{5}{8}$ 8. $4\frac{8}{9}, 4\frac{17}{18}, \frac{65}{14}, 4\frac{6}{7}$

Multiply or divide. Write your answer as a power using only positive exponents.

9. $b^2 \cdot b^4$ *(p. 202)* 10. $c^5 \cdot c^{-2}$ *(p. 208)* 11. $\frac{a^7}{a^2}$ *(p. 202)* 12. $\frac{n^{-2}}{n^3}$ *(p. 208)*

13. **POPCORN** People in the United States eat approximately 1,120,000,000 pounds of popcorn a year. Write this number in scientific notation. *(p. 212)*

GOAL
Use a calculator to perform operations on numbers written in scientific notation.

4.8 Using Scientific Notation

EXAMPLE **The Sun is about 1.5×10^8 kilometers from Earth, and Proxima Centauri is about 2.5×10^5 times farther from Earth than the Sun. How far is Proxima Centauri from Earth?**

SOLUTION

To find how far Proxima Centauri is from Earth, multiply the distance between the Sun and Earth by 2.5×10^5.

Keystrokes	Display
1.5 [EE] 8 [×] 2.5 [EE] 5 [=]	3.75 ×10[13]

The [EE] key on a calculator means "times 10 raised to the power of."

Answer Proxima Centauri is approximately 3.75×10^{13} kilometers from Earth.

PRACTICE **Use a calculator to evaluate the expression. Write your answer in scientific notation.**

1. $(3.19 \times 10^7) \times (8.5 \times 10^6)$
2. $(6.7 \times 10^{-3}) \times (1.12 \times 10^{15})$
3. $(3.3 \times 10^{-3}) \times (4.8 \times 10^{-9})$
4. $(7.1 \times 10^{-9}) \times (2.05 \times 10^6)$
5. $\frac{1.681 \times 10^{10}}{2.05 \times 10^3}$
6. $\frac{1.44 \times 10^{-15}}{1.2 \times 10}$
7. $\frac{8.241 \times 10^{-11}}{2.05 \times 10^{-4}}$
8. $\frac{6.25 \times 10^{-8}}{1.25 \times 10^{-12}}$
9. $\frac{1.26 \times 10^9}{2.8 \times 10^2}$
10. $\frac{2.64 \times 10^{-8}}{2.2 \times 10^{-13}}$
11. $\frac{2.59 \times 10^{-6}}{1.85 \times 10^3}$
12. $\frac{3 \times 10^{16}}{3.75 \times 10^{-16}}$
13. **WATER** About 110 billion gallons of water flow through Lake Erie each day. How many gallons of water flow through Lake Erie in a week? in a year? Write your answers in scientific notation.
14. **BIOLOGY** The nucleus of a human cell is about 7×10^{-6} meter in diameter. A ribosome, another part of a cell, is about 3×10^{-8} meter in diameter. Approximately how many times larger is a nucleus than a ribosome?

Lessons 4.5–4.8

1. **MULTI-STEP PROBLEM** The table shows the approximate land areas in square kilometers of several countries.

Country	*Area (km^2)*
Antarctica	14,000,000
Canada	10×10^6
Egypt	1,000,000
India	0.33×10^7
Russia	1.7×10^7
United States	9,600,000

   a. Write the area of each country in scientific notation.

   b. Which country has the greatest land area?

   c. Which country has the least land area?

   d. How many times greater is the land area of the country in part (b) than the land area of the country in part (c)? *Explain* how you found your answer.

2. **MULTI-STEP PROBLEM** The table shows the numbers of shots you made and the number you attempted in five basketball games.

Game	1	2	3	4	5
Shots made	10	9	6	15	9
Attempts	22	12	18	25	18

   a. For each game, write the fraction of your shots that you made. Give your answers in simplest form.

   b. In which game did you make the greatest fraction of your shots?

   c. In which game did you make the least fraction of your shots?

   d. Can you conclude that your accuracy improved over time? *Justify* your reasoning.

3. **OPEN-ENDED** Give an example of something whose measure is best expressed in scientific notation using a negative power of 10.

4. **SHORT RESPONSE** A light-year is equal to 9.5×10^{12} kilometers. The Andromeda galaxy is approximately 2.3 million light-years away. How far is this in kilometers? Write your answer in scientific notation. *Explain* your reasoning.

5. **SHORT RESPONSE** In 1997, German teddy bear specialist Hanne Schramm made one of the smallest teddy bears in the world. It measures 0.47 inch, or about 12 millimeters long. A nanometer is 10^{-6} millimeter. How many nanometers long is the bear? *Explain* your reasoning.

6. **GRIDDED ANSWER** You have a wallet sized photo that is about 6.3×10^{-2} meters wide. How many centimeters wide is it? Write your answer in standard form.

7. **EXTENDED RESPONSE** The formula for the volume of a cube is given by $V = s^3$, where s is the side length. The side lengths of three cubes are listed below.

   Cube A: $s = 2$ meters

   Cube B: $s = 2^2$ meters

   Cube C: $s = 2^3$ meters

   a. Find the volume of each cube. Write your answer as a power.

   b. How many times greater is the volume of cube B than cube A? the volume of cube C than cube A?

   c. Without making any calculations, *predict* how many times greater the volume of a cube with a side length of 2^4 meters is than the volume of cube A. *Explain.*

4 CHAPTER REVIEW

@HomeTutor
classzone.com
Vocabulary Practice

REVIEW KEY VOCABULARY

- prime number, *p. 177*
- composite number, *p. 177*
- prime factorization, *p. 177*
- factor tree, *p. 177*
- monomial, *p. 178*
- common factor, *p. 181*
- greatest common factor (GCF), *p. 181*
- relatively prime, *p. 182*
- simplest form, *p. 187*
- equivalent fractions, *p. 187*
- multiple, *p. 192*
- common multiple, *p. 192*
- least common multiple (LCM), *p. 192*
- least common denominator (LCD), *p. 198*
- scientific notation, *p. 212*

VOCABULARY EXERCISES

1. Describe the difference between the *greatest common factor* and the *least common multiple* of two numbers.
2. Give three examples of prime numbers greater than 20.
3. Give three examples of monomials.
4. Describe what it means for two numbers to be relatively prime.

Copy and complete the statement.

5. A fraction is in __?__ if its numerator and denominator have 1 as their GCF.
6. A(n) __?__ is a whole number that has positive factors other than 1 and itself.
7. Two fractions are __?__ if they represent the same number.

REVIEW EXAMPLES AND EXERCISES

4.1 Factors and Prime Factorization

pp. 176–180

EXAMPLE

Write the prime factorization of 504.

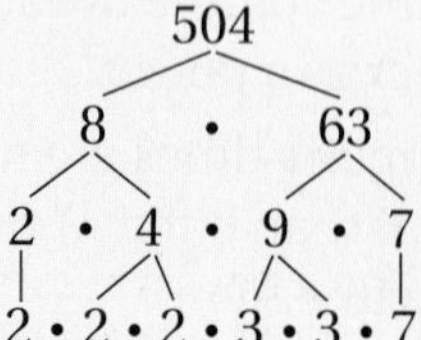

$504 = 2 \cdot 2 \cdot 2 \cdot 3 \cdot 3 \cdot 7$, or $2^3 \cdot 3^2 \cdot 7$

▶ **Answer** The prime factorization of 504 is $2^3 \cdot 3^2 \cdot 7$.

EXERCISES

Tell whether the number is *prime* or *composite*.

SEE EXAMPLES 2, 3, AND 4 on pp. 177–178 for Exs. 8–20

8. 24 **9.** 91 **10.** 53 **11.** 197

Write the prime factorization of the number.

12. 40 **13.** 7 **14.** 85 **15.** 120

Factor the monomial.

16. $19a^2b$ **17.** $28xy^3$ **18.** $56u^2v^2$ **19.** $80p^4q^3$

20. Planting Trees A conservation group wants to plant 48 trees in a rectangular arrangement so that each row has the same number of trees. How many trees can be planted in each row? List all possibilities.

4.2 Greatest Common Factor

pp. 181–185

EXAMPLE

Find the GCF of 36 and 60.

Begin by writing the prime factorization of each number. Look for the common prime factors.

$36 = 2 \times 2 \times 3 \times 3$ $\qquad 60 = 2 \times 2 \times 3 \times 5$

The common prime factors are 2, 2, and 3. The GCF of 36 and 60 is the product of these factors. $2 \cdot 2 \cdot 3 = 12$.

▶ **Answer** The GCF of 36 and 60 is 12.

EXERCISES

Find the GCF of the numbers or monomials.

SEE EXAMPLES 1, 2, 3, AND 4 on pp. 181–183 for Exs. 21–33

21. 48, 80 **22.** 60, 100 **23.** $14a^3, 21a$ **24.** $20y^4, 60y^5$

25. 20, 40, 90 **26.** 48, 60, 165 **27.** $2x, x^2, x^3$ **28.** $54s^4t^4, 164st^3$

Determine whether the numbers are relatively prime.

29. 11, 15 **30.** 92, 115 **31.** 72, 176 **32.** 30, 91

33. Food Baskets Your class is making Thanksgiving baskets for a food bank. You have 60 cans of cranberry sauce, 120 cans of fruit, 90 cans of corn, and 60 boxes of muffin mix. You want every basket to be the same with no leftover items. What is the greatest number of baskets you can assemble? What will each basket contain?

4.3 Simplifying Fractions

pp. 187–191

EXAMPLE

Write $\frac{48}{72}$ in simplest form.

Write the prime factorization of each number.

$48 = 2 \cdot 2 \cdot 2 \cdot 2 \cdot 3$
$72 = 2 \cdot 2 \cdot 2 \cdot 3 \cdot 3$

The GCF of 48 and 72 is $2 \cdot 2 \cdot 2 \cdot 3 = 24$.

$\frac{48}{72} = \frac{48 \div 24}{72 \div 24}$ **Divide numerator and denominator by GCF.**

$= \frac{2}{3}$ **Simplify.**

EXERCISES

SEE EXAMPLES 1 AND 4 on pp. 187, 189 for Exs. 34–37

Write the fraction in simplest form.

34. $\frac{15}{45}$ **35.** $\frac{12}{80}$ **36.** $\frac{9ab}{27a}$ **37.** $\frac{18n^3}{54n}$

4.4 Least Common Multiple

pp. 192–196

EXAMPLE

Find the LCM of 20 and 48.

STEP 1 **Write** the prime factorization of each number and circle the greatest power of each prime factor.

$20 = 2^2 \cdot \textcircled{5}$ $48 = \textcircled{2^4} \cdot \textcircled{3}$

STEP 2 **Find** the product of the circled numbers.

$2^4 \cdot 3 \cdot 5 = 240$

▶ **Answer** The LCM of 20 and 48 is 240.

EXERCISES

Find the LCM of the numbers or monomials.

SEE EXAMPLES 1 AND 3 on pp. 192–193 for Exs. 38–42

38. 28, 42 **39.** 54, 90 **40.** $10cd$, $25c^2$ **41.** $9n^3$, $12n^2$

42. Fitness Yolanda has a yoga class every 4 days and a pilates class every 3 days. If she has both classes today, in how many days will both classes be on the same day again?

4.5 Comparing Fractions and Mixed Numbers

pp. 198–201

EXAMPLE

Compare $\frac{11}{18}$ and $\frac{3}{4}$.

The LCM of 18 and 4 is 36, so the least common denominator is 36. Write each fraction using the LCD.

$$\frac{11}{18} = \frac{11 \cdot 2}{18 \cdot 2} = \frac{22}{36} \qquad \frac{3}{4} = \frac{3 \cdot 9}{4 \cdot 9} = \frac{27}{36}$$

▸ **Answer** Because $\frac{22}{36} < \frac{27}{36}$, you can write $\frac{11}{18} < \frac{3}{4}$.

EXERCISES

SEE EXAMPLES 1, 2, AND 3 on pp. 198–199 for Exs. 43–51

Copy and complete the statement with <, >, or =.

43. $\frac{79}{16}$? $\frac{35}{8}$
44. $6\frac{2}{3}$? $\frac{81}{12}$
45. $\frac{161}{9}$? $17\frac{8}{9}$
46. $\frac{223}{15}$? $14\frac{4}{5}$

Order the numbers from least to greatest.

47. $\frac{7}{11}, \frac{2}{3}, \frac{5}{8}$
48. $9\frac{1}{2}, \frac{29}{3}, \frac{37}{4}$
49. $5\frac{7}{8}, \frac{53}{9}, \frac{17}{3}$
50. $\frac{25}{6}, \frac{49}{12}, 4\frac{1}{10}$

51. **Gardening** Joe picked $4\frac{7}{8}$ cups of green beans and Sarah picked $\frac{29}{6}$ cups. Who picked more beans? How many cups more?

4.6 Rules of Exponents

pp. 202–207

EXAMPLE

Multiply or divide. Write your answer as a power.

a. $x^7 \cdot x^8 = x^{7+8}$

$= x^{15}$

b. $\frac{a^6}{a^3} = a^{6-3}$

$= a^3$

EXERCISES

SEE EXAMPLES 1, 2, 3, AND 4 on pp. 203–204 for Exs. 52–63

Simplify the expression. Write your answer as a power.

52. $n^4 \cdot n^9$
53. $9^6 \cdot 9^3$
54. $5^4 \cdot 5^7$
55. $a^{12} \cdot a^{11}$
56. $\frac{x^7}{x^5}$
57. $\frac{5^{10}}{5^7}$
58. $\frac{11^9}{11^3}$
59. $\frac{b^{15}}{b^8}$
60. $\frac{x^5 \cdot x^4}{x^8}$
61. $\frac{y^{20}}{y^3 \cdot y^9}$
62. $\frac{2^5 \cdot x^7}{2^3 \cdot x}$
63. $\frac{y^6 \cdot x^{12}}{y^4 \cdot x^9}$

4.7 Negative and Zero Exponents

pp. 208–211

EXAMPLE

Write $x^{-4} \cdot x^{-3}$ using only positive exponents.

$$x^{-4} \cdot x^{-3} = x^{-4+(-3)}$$
$$= x^{-7}$$
$$= \frac{1}{x^7}$$

EXERCISES

Simplify. Write the expression using only positive exponents.

SEE EXAMPLES 2 AND 3 on p. 209 for Exs. 64–71

64. $12a^{-5} \cdot a^0$ **65.** $n^7 \cdot n^{-10}$ **66.** $\frac{m^{-6}}{m^5}$ **67.** $\frac{18c^{-9}}{6c^4}$

68. $b^5 \cdot b^2$ **69.** $\frac{9z^{-4}}{6z^{-2}}$ **70.** $\frac{8y^5}{12y^{-11}}$ **71.** $5x^3 \cdot 4x^{-3}$

4.8 Scientific Notation

pp. 212–217

EXAMPLE

Write the number in scientific notation.

a. $980{,}000{,}000 = 9.8 \times 100{,}000{,}000$
$= 9.8 \times 10^8$

b. $0.000012 = 1.2 \times 0.00001$
$= 1.2 \times 10^{-5}$

EXERCISES

Write the number in scientific notation.

SEE EXAMPLES 1, 2, 3, AND 4 on pp. 212–214 for Exs. 72–82

72. 34,600,000,000 **73.** 0.0000009 **74.** 0.000000000502

Write the number in standard form.

75. 2.36×10^8 **76.** 0.015×10^5 **77.** 9.4×10^{-3}

Write the product in scientific notation.

78. $(3 \times 10^{16}) \times (5 \times 10^{-5})$ **79.** $(6.2 \times 10^{-4}) \times (2.6 \times 10^{12})$

80. $(1.08 \times 10^7) \times (2.09 \times 10^{-2})$ **81.** $(7.63 \times 10^{11}) \times (4.8 \times 10^{-3})$

82. Niagara Falls In tourist season, the water at Niagara Falls flows at a rate of 100,000 cubic feet per second during the day. How fast does it flow per minute? per hour? Write your answers in scientific notation.

4 CHAPTER TEST

@HomeTutor
classzone.com
Chapter Test Practice

Write the prime factorization of the number.

1. 49 **2.** 68 **3.** 95 **4.** 112

Find the greatest common factor of the numbers or monomials.

5. 36, 84 **6.** 45, 117 **7.** $2z^3, 3z^2$ **8.** $14r^2, 42r$

Find the least common multiple of the numbers or monomials.

9. 4, 16, 32 **10.** 18, 24, 36 **11.** $5x^2y, 21xy^3$ **12.** $54pq^2, 63p^3q^3$

Copy and complete the statement with <, >, or =.

13. $\frac{11}{12} \underline{?} \frac{41}{48}$ **14.** $4\frac{3}{6} \underline{?} \frac{9}{2}$ **15.** $8\frac{7}{16} \underline{?} \frac{17}{2}$ **16.** $\frac{35}{7} \underline{?} 5\frac{1}{7}$

Simplify the expression. Write your answer using only positive exponents.

17. $m^8 \cdot m^3$ **18.** $6^2 \cdot 6^6 \cdot 6^0$ **19.** $\frac{n^{16}}{n^{10}}$ **20.** $\frac{p^4 \cdot p^6}{p^2 \cdot p^7}$

21. $5x^{-3}$ **22.** $c^{-1} \cdot c^{-7}$ **23.** $\frac{-4u^{-9}}{u^3}$ **24.** $\frac{16a^2b^5}{8a^4b}$

Write the number in scientific notation.

25. 200,400 **26.** 0.000005126 **27.** 42,000

Write the number in standard form.

28. 7.72×10^6 **29.** 1.46×10^{-6} **30.** 8.22×10^{-4}

Write the product in scientific notation.

31. $(6 \times 10^5) \times (5 \times 10^7)$ **32.** $(8.1 \times 10^4) \times (9.2 \times 10^8)$

33. $(4.2 \times 10^{-5}) \times (6 \times 10^{-2})$ **34.** $(3.8 \times 10^{-4}) \times (2.9 \times 10^7)$

35. CAKE Three identical round layer cakes are served at a party. Each cake is cut into a different number of equal-sized slices. After the guests leave, $\frac{1}{8}$ of the yellow cake, $\frac{3}{16}$ of the chocolate cake, and $\frac{1}{6}$ of the carrot cake remain. Which type of cake has the least amount left over? Which has the most? *Explain* your reasoning.

36. SCIENCE Scientists have created a microfabric using molded plastic. Its narrowest links are $\frac{1}{1{,}000{,}000}$ meter across. Write this fraction as a power of ten.

37. ENVIRONMENT In the United States, approximately 120,000 aluminum cans are recycled each minute. Write this number in scientific notation.

38. BIRTH WEIGHT The western harvest mouse weighs approximately 1.5×10^{-3} kilograms at birth. Write this number in standard form.

CONTEXT-BASED MULTIPLE CHOICE QUESTIONS

Some of the information you need to solve a context-based multiple choice question may appear in a table, a diagram, or a graph.

PROBLEM 1

Four friends planted flower bulbs at the same time. The table shows the amount each person's plant grew in the first week. Whose plant grew the most?

Plant Growth (inches)			
Mark	**Julie**	**Brett**	**Sabrina**
$1\frac{3}{8}$	$\frac{7}{6}$	$\frac{17}{12}$	$1\frac{1}{4}$

Ⓐ Mark's Ⓑ Julie's Ⓒ Brett's Ⓓ Sabrina's

Plan

STEP 1 Read the problem carefully. Decide how you can use the given information to solve the problem.

INTERPRET THE TABLE The table shows the amount each plant grew. These amounts can be rewritten as improper fractions so they can be ordered. The greatest fraction indicates the correct answer.

Solution

STEP 2 Rewrite as improper fractions.

The least common denominator of 8, 6, 12, and 4 is 24. Using the LCD, write the numbers as improper fractions.

Mark: $1\frac{3}{8} = \frac{11}{8} = \frac{11 \times 3}{8 \times 3} = \frac{33}{24}$

Julie: $\frac{7}{6} = \frac{7 \times 4}{6 \times 4} = \frac{28}{24}$

Brett: $\frac{17}{12} = \frac{17 \times 2}{12 \times 2} = \frac{34}{24}$

Sabrina: $1\frac{1}{4} = \frac{5}{4} = \frac{5 \times 6}{4 \times 6} = \frac{30}{24}$

STEP 3 Compare and order the numbers from least to greatest.

Compare the numerators: $28 < 30 < 33 < 34$. So, $\frac{28}{24} < \frac{30}{24} < \frac{33}{24} < \frac{34}{24}$.

The numbers from least to greatest are $\frac{7}{6}$, $1\frac{1}{4}$, $1\frac{3}{8}$, and $\frac{17}{12}$.

Brett's plant grew $\frac{17}{12}$ inches, which was the greatest amount of growth. The correct answer is C. Ⓐ Ⓑ Ⓒ Ⓓ

PROBLEM 2

The graph shows the results of a survey that asked students what their favorite vegetable was. What fraction of the students said they liked corn best?

Ⓐ $\frac{1}{3}$ Ⓑ $\frac{3}{8}$

Ⓒ $\frac{3}{5}$ Ⓓ $\frac{5}{8}$

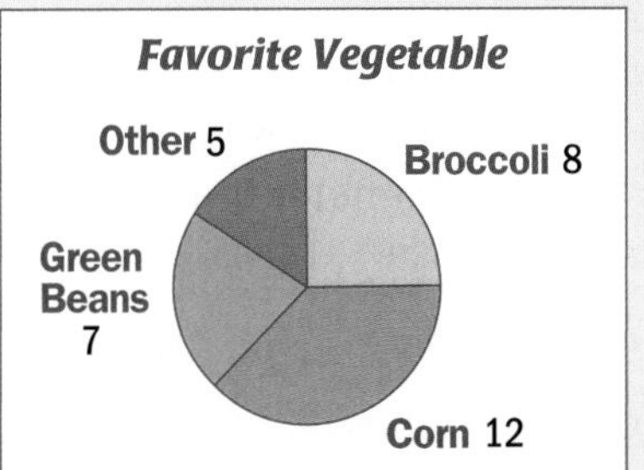

PLAN

STEP 1 Read the problem carefully and make a plan.

INTERPRET THE GRAPH The graph shows how many students said that corn was their favorite vegetable and how many students answered the survey. Find the fraction of students who liked corn best.

SOLUTION

STEP 2 Find number of students.

The number of students who said that corn was their favorite vegetable was 12. The total number of students surveyed is 8 + 12 + 7 + 5 = 32.

Write the fraction of students who liked corn best. Then simplify.

STEP 3 Write the fraction.

$$\frac{\text{Number of students who answered corn}}{\text{Number of students}} = \frac{12}{32} = \frac{3 \cdot \overset{1}{\cancel{4}}}{8 \cdot \underset{1}{\cancel{4}}} = \frac{3}{8}$$

The fraction of students who said they liked corn best was $\frac{3}{8}$.
The correct answer is B. Ⓐ Ⓑ Ⓒ Ⓓ

PRACTICE

The table shows the total calories and the amount of calories from protein contained in four types of energy bar.

	Bar A	*Bar B*	*Bar C*	*Bar D*
Total calories	170	210	250	260
Protein calories	40	60	65	60

1. What fraction of total calories is from protein in bar B?

   Ⓐ $\frac{2}{9}$ Ⓑ $\frac{2}{7}$ Ⓒ $\frac{2}{5}$ Ⓓ $\frac{5}{7}$

2. Which bar contains the greatest fraction of calories from protein?

   Ⓐ bar A Ⓑ bar B Ⓒ bar C Ⓓ bar D

4 ★ Standardized TEST PRACTICE

MULTIPLE CHOICE

1. You are making a rectangular arrangement of 80 square photos. Each photo has a length of 6 inches. What is the least possible perimeter that an arrangement can have?

   (A) 18 inches (B) 36 inches
   (C) 108 inches (D) 216 inches

2. Three scout troops are each divided into groups. Each group has exactly 4 scouts in it. Every scout is in a small group consisting of members from the same troop. How many total scouts could be in each of the three troops?

   (A) 12, 21, 27 (B) 36, 40, 60
   (C) 6, 18, 24 (D) 10, 40, 80

3. The thickness of a golden dollar coin is 2×10^{-3} meters. The thickness of a nickel is 1.95×10^{-3} meters. How many golden dollar coins do you need to stack so that the height of the stack is the same as the height of a stack of 3.6×10^2 nickels?

   (A) 18 coins (B) 351 coins
   (C) 360 coins (D) 702 coins

4. The graph shows the results of a survey in which students were asked their favorite pizza topping. What fraction of the students surveyed named pepperoni as their favorite?

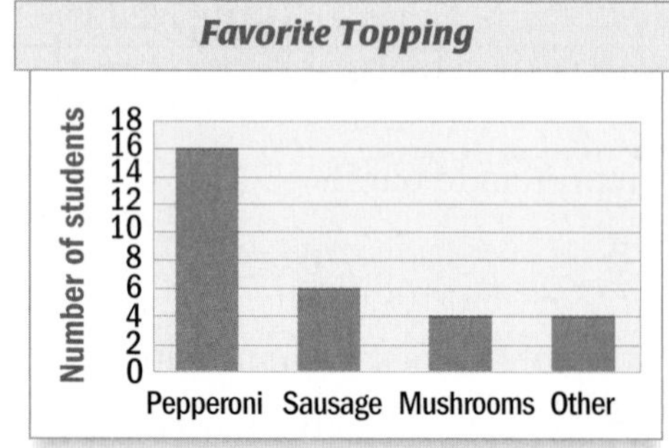

   (A) $\frac{8}{7}$ (B) $\frac{8}{13}$ (C) $\frac{8}{15}$ (D) $\frac{3}{15}$

5. The width of a rectangle is x inches. The perimeter of the rectangle is $10x$ inches. Which expression represents the following: $\frac{\text{perimeter of rectangle}}{\text{area of rectangle}}$?

   (A) $\frac{5x^{-1}}{2}$ in.$^{-1}$ (B) $\frac{5x}{2}$ in.$^{-1}$
   (C) $\frac{2x^{-1}}{5}$ in. (D) $\frac{2x}{5}$ in.

6. The director of a coed volleyball league is placing 120 girls and 150 boys on teams. Each team is to have an equal number of players and the same number of girls. The director creates as many teams as possible. How many girls are on each team?

   (A) 3 (B) 4 (C) 5 (D) 6

7. The table shows the number of hits a player had in a given number of at bats. Which player had the greatest fraction of hits?

   (A) Alexis
   (B) Jim
   (C) Eric
   (D) Brad

Player	Hits	At bats
Alexis	42	150
Jim	51	170
Eric	34	136
Brad	44	160

8. George sold bottles of water for 45 cents each. With the money he earned, he bought several snow cones for 60 cents each. He had no change after buying the snow cones. What is the least number of bottles he could have sold?

   (A) 2 (B) 3 (C) 4 (D) 5

9. Suppose a microorganism has a length of 5^{-7} meter. If 625 microorganisms of this length are arranged in a line, what is the length of the line?

   (A) 5^{-28} meter (B) 5^{-11} meter
   (C) 5^{-3} meter (D) 5^{11} meters

GRIDDED ANSWER

10. A florist has 240 yellow roses and 160 red roses. The florist wants to make identical bouquets consisting of yellow roses and red roses with no roses left over. What is the greatest number of bouquets that the florist can make?

11. Two toy cars begin at the starting line of a circular track at the same time. Car A goes around the track every 20 seconds. Car B goes around the track every 8 seconds. In how many seconds will the two cars first reach the starting line at the same time?

12. Rachel has two rolls of streamers to decorate the school gym for a dance. One roll is 45 feet long, and the other roll is 75 feet long. She wants to cut the streamers into strips of equal length and have no leftover materials. What is the longest each strip can be, in feet?

SHORT RESPONSE

13. Vincent has a math test every 14 school days and an English test every 8 school days. Vincent had both tests today. In how many school days will both tests occur on the same day again? There are approximately 180 school days in a year. What is the greatest number of days both tests will fall on the same day? *Explain.*

14. Train A leaves the station every 12 minutes. Train B leaves every 15 minutes. A bus leaves every 8 minutes. How often do two trains and a bus depart at the same time? *Explain.*

15. The mass of a proton is about 1.67×10^{-27} kilograms. The mass of an electron is about 9.11×10^{-31} kilograms. Which has a greater mass? Approximately how many times greater? Round your answer to the nearest hundredth.

EXTENDED RESPONSE

16. A hole at a miniature golf course has 3 doors that swing open on different schedules. You see the 3 doors open at the same time. After 4 seconds, the red door opens again. Two seconds after that, the blue door opens. The red door opens after 2 more seconds. One second later, the yellow door opens.

a. How often does each door open?

b. Which occurs first, the *blue and red* doors opening at the same time or the *blue and yellow* doors opening at the same time? *Explain* your answer.

c. How often do all 3 doors open at the same time? *Explain* your answer.

17. Although fractions are often compared using the LCD, any common denominator will work. Consider the fractions $\frac{17}{24}$ and $\frac{41}{60}$.

a. Rewrite the fractions so that the common denominator is the product of the denominators. Tell which fraction is greater and why.

b. What did you do to the numerators to rewrite the fractions in part (a)? Write a general rule for comparing two fractions without calculating a new denominator. Give an example and *justify* your results.

c. What are some advantages and disadvantages of using your rule for comparing fractions instead of rewriting the fractions using the LCD?

5 Rational Number Operations

Before

In previous chapters you've . . .

- Performed operations on integers
- Interpreted tables and graphs

Now

In Chapter 5 you'll study . . .

- 5.1 Common denominators
- 5.2 Different denominators
- 5.3 Multiplying fractions
- 5.4 Dividing fractions
- 5.5 Fractions and decimals
- 5.6 Adding and subtracting
- 5.7 Multiplying and dividing
- 5.8 Mean, median, mode

Why?

So you can solve real-world problems about . . .

- sledding, p. 241
- rafting, p. 265
- deep sea jellies, p. 272

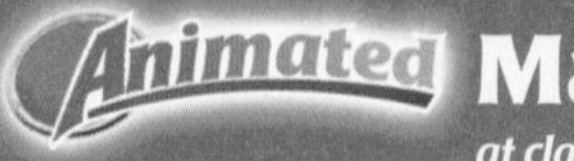

Math

at classzone.com

- Fractions with Different Denominators, p. 240
- Penalty Shot, p. 249
- Mean, Median, and Mode, p. 275

Get-Ready Games

Review Prerequisite Skills by playing *Scale the Cliff* and *Tangled Fractions.*

Scale the Cliff

$\frac{7}{32}$	$\frac{1}{3}$	$\frac{2}{7}$	$\frac{3}{11}$
$\frac{7}{17}$	$\frac{4}{9}$	$\frac{4}{15}$	$\frac{11}{25}$
$\frac{6}{11}$	$\frac{13}{21}$	$\frac{4}{7}$	$\frac{3}{8}$
$\frac{1}{2}$	$\frac{5}{8}$	$\frac{7}{11}$	$\frac{9}{14}$
$\frac{3}{4}$	$\frac{5}{6}$	$\frac{3}{5}$	$\frac{5}{7}$
	$\frac{2}{3}$		

Skill Focus: Comparing fractions

Find the handholds you can use to scale the cliff.

- Start at $\frac{2}{3}$ and move up, selecting a handhold in each row.
- The value of each handhold must be less than the value of the handhold below it.

Skill Focus: Identifying equivalent fractions

Susan is going rock climbing. Help her figure out what equipment she is missing.

- In each column, find a fraction equivalent to the top one to decode the name of the equipment Susan is missing.

Stop and Think

1. **CRITICAL THINKING** **A student thinks that a fraction cannot be smaller than another fraction if the first fraction's denominator is greater than the second fraction's denominator. *Explain* why the student is wrong.**
2. **WRITING** **Explain how to tell whether fractions with different denominators are equivalent.**

5 Getting Ready

Review Prerequisite Skills

REVIEW WORDS
- **like terms,** *p. 89*
- **simplest form,** *p. 187*
- **least common denominator (LCD),** *p. 198*
- **improper fraction,** *p. 762*
- **mixed number,** *p. 762*

VOCABULARY CHECK

Copy and complete using a review word from the list at the left.

1. If 1 is the greatest common factor of the numerator and the denominator, then the fraction is in __?__.
2. A number like $3\frac{4}{7}$, whose value is the sum of a whole number and a fraction, is a(n) __?__.
3. A fraction whose numerator is greater than or equal to its denominator is a(n) __?__.

SKILL CHECK

Find the product or quotient. ***(pp. 73, 77)***

4. $-125 \cdot 2$ **5.** $-4 \cdot (-23)$ **6.** $20 \cdot (-6)$ **7.** $-8 \cdot (-7)$

8. $-39 \div 3$ **9.** $-136 \div (-17)$ **10.** $64 \div (-16)$ **11.** $-27 \div (-9)$

Write the fraction in simplest form. ***(p. 187)***

12. $\frac{4}{12}$ **13.** $\frac{-35}{50}$ **14.** $\frac{24}{52}$ **15.** $\frac{14}{49}$

16. $\frac{-34}{51}$ **17.** $\frac{26}{65}$ **18.** $\frac{56}{72}$ **19.** $\frac{-16}{96}$

20. You bought a sweater for \$15.65 and a pair of jeans for \$23.95. What was the total cost of your purchase? ***(p. 764)***

@HomeTutor Prerequisite skills practice at classzone.com

Notetaking Skills Writing Helpful Hints

In each chapter you will learn a new notetaking skill. In Chapter 5 you will apply the strategy of writing helpful hints to Example 1 on p. 233.

In your notebook, write down any hints your teacher or your textbook gives you for solving problems.

Equivalent Fractions

Write equivalent fractions by multiplying by a fraction that is equal to 1.

$$\frac{3}{5} \times \frac{4}{4} = \frac{12}{20} \qquad \frac{3}{5} \times \frac{9}{9} = \frac{27}{45} \qquad \frac{3}{5} \times \frac{100}{100} = \frac{300}{500}$$

A fraction has many equivalent forms.

You can rename a mixed number as an equivalent improper fraction.

$$3\frac{5}{6} = \frac{3 \cdot 6 + 5}{6} = \frac{23}{6}$$

5.1 Fractions with Common Denominators

Before You added and subtracted whole numbers and integers.
Now You'll add and subtract fractions with common denominators.
Why? So you can interpret survey results, as in Ex. 44.

KEY VOCABULARY
- **order of operations,** *p. 8*
- **like terms,** *p. 89*
- **numerator,** *p. 762*
- **denominator,** *p. 762*

You may have used a model, such as the one below, to add or subtract fractions with common denominators.

$$\frac{2}{5} + \frac{1}{5} = \frac{3}{5}$$

The model illustrates the following rules for adding and subtracting fractions.

KEY CONCEPT *For Your Notebook*

Adding and Subtracting Fractions

Words To add fractions or subtract fractions with a common denominator, write the sum or difference of the numerators over the denominator.

Numbers $\frac{3}{9} + \frac{5}{9} = \frac{8}{9}$

$\frac{3}{5} - \frac{2}{5} = \frac{1}{5}$

Algebra $\frac{a}{c} + \frac{b}{c} = \frac{a+b}{c}$ $(c \neq 0)$

$\frac{a}{c} - \frac{b}{c} = \frac{a-b}{c}$ $(c \neq 0)$

To add or subtract negative fractions or mixed numbers, apply the rules you learned for integers in Chapter 2. Interpret negative signs as follows.

$$-\frac{11}{13} = \frac{-11}{13} \text{ or } \frac{11}{-13} \quad \text{and} \quad -5\frac{6}{7} = -5 - \frac{6}{7} \text{ or } -5 + \frac{-6}{7}$$

EXAMPLE 1 Fractions and Mixed Numbers

TAKE NOTES
You may wish to copy Example 1 and the helpful hint above about negative fractions into your notebook.

a. $-\frac{11}{13} + \frac{8}{13} = \frac{-11+8}{13}$

$= -\frac{3}{13}$

b. $-5\frac{6}{7} + 3\frac{2}{7} = -5 - \frac{6}{7} + 3 + \frac{2}{7}$

$= -5 + 3 - \frac{6}{7} + \frac{2}{7}$

$= -2\frac{4}{7}$

EXAMPLE 2 Simplifying Fractions with Variables

a. $-\frac{a}{9}+\frac{7a}{9}=\frac{-a+7a}{9}$ **Write sum over common denominator.**

$=\frac{6a}{9}$ **Combine like terms.**

$=\frac{\overset{2}{\cancel{6}}a}{\underset{3}{\cancel{9}}}$ **Divide out common factor.**

$=\frac{2a}{3}$ **Simplify.**

b. $\frac{6x}{11y}-\frac{10x}{11y}=\frac{6x-10x}{11y}$ **Write difference over common denominator.**

$=\frac{-4x}{11y}$, or $-\frac{4x}{11y}$ **Combine like terms.**

VOCABULARY

Recall that *like terms* are terms that have identical variable parts raised to the same power.

✓ GUIDED PRACTICE for Examples 1 and 2

Find the sum or difference. Then simplify if possible.

1. $\frac{1}{12}+\frac{5}{12}$ **2.** $\frac{3}{8}-2\frac{1}{8}$ **3.** $-\frac{t}{3}-\frac{2t}{3}$ **4.** $\frac{y}{8a}+\frac{-5y}{8a}$

EXAMPLE 3 Solving an Equation with Mixed Numbers

Biology A corn snake that is $14\frac{3}{4}$ inches long grows g inches to a length of $27\frac{1}{4}$ inches. How much does it grow?

SOLUTION

To find the amount of growth, subtract the original length from the current length.

$g=27\frac{1}{4}-14\frac{3}{4}$ **Original equation.**

$=26\frac{5}{4}-14\frac{3}{4}$ **Rename $27\frac{1}{4}$ so its fraction part is greater than $\frac{3}{4}$.**

$=\left(26+\frac{5}{4}\right)-\left(14+\frac{3}{4}\right)$ **Write mixed numbers in expanded form.**

$=26+\frac{5}{4}-14-\frac{3}{4}$ **Distribute the subtraction.**

$=(26-14)+\left(\frac{5}{4}-\frac{3}{4}\right)$ **Group whole numbers and fractions.**

$=12+\frac{2}{4}$ **Subtract whole numbers and fractions.**

$=12\frac{1}{2}$ **Simplify and write as a mixed number.**

▶ **Answer** The snake grows $12\frac{1}{2}$ inches.

AVOID ERRORS

When you subtract mixed numbers, compare their fraction parts. If the first fraction part is less, rename the mixed number before you subtract.

Order of Operations The rules for adding and subtracting fractions can be applied to evaluate longer expressions. Remember to always use the order of operations.

EXAMPLE 4 Evaluating Longer Expressions

a. $\frac{2}{11} - \frac{5}{11} + \frac{9}{11} = \frac{2 - 5 + 9}{11}$ **Write 2 − 5 + 9 over common denominator.**

$= \frac{6}{11}$ **Evaluate numerator from left to right.**

b. $3\frac{6}{7} - 2\frac{3}{7} + 4\frac{5}{7} = (3 - 2 + 4) + \left(\frac{6}{7} - \frac{3}{7} + \frac{5}{7}\right)$ **Group whole numbers and fractions.**

$= 5\frac{8}{7}$ **Evaluate inside parentheses.**

$= 6\frac{1}{7}$ **Rename.**

ANOTHER WAY

You can also write the mixed numbers as improper fractions and then evaluate: $\frac{27}{7} - \frac{17}{7} + \frac{33}{7} = \frac{43}{7}$, or $6\frac{1}{7}$.

✓ GUIDED PRACTICE for Examples 3 and 4

5. **Gardening** A plant that is $5\frac{7}{8}$ inches high grows x inches to a height of $8\frac{3}{8}$ inches. Write and solve an equation to find the amount of growth.

Evaluate. Then simplify if possible.

6. $\frac{3}{4} + \frac{7}{4} + \frac{5}{4}$
7. $\frac{15}{8} - \frac{7}{8} + \frac{3}{8}$
8. $2\frac{1}{3} - \frac{2}{3} + 3\frac{2}{3}$

5.1 EXERCISES

HOMEWORK KEY

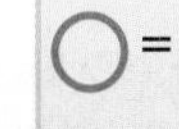

★ = **STANDARDIZED TEST PRACTICE** Exs. 42, 44, 46, 47, and 61

○ = **HINTS AND HOMEWORK HELP** for Exs. 9, 11, 19, 23, 43 at classzone.com

SKILL PRACTICE

1. **VOCABULARY** Copy and complete: In the fraction $\frac{4}{9}$, 9 is the __?__ and 4 is the __?__.

FRACTION OPERATIONS **Find the sum or difference. Then simplify if possible.**

SEE EXAMPLE 1 on p. 233 for Exs. 2–9

2. $\frac{5}{18} + \frac{7}{18}$
3. $\frac{5}{21} + \frac{2}{21}$
4. $\frac{3}{10} - \frac{7}{10}$
5. $\frac{7}{18} - \frac{5}{18}$
6. $-4\frac{2}{7} - 4\frac{2}{7}$
7. $-4\frac{9}{14} + 3\frac{5}{14}$
8. $2\frac{7}{9} + \frac{8}{9}$
9. $-7\frac{3}{5} - \frac{4}{5}$

SIMPLIFYING EXPRESSIONS **Simplify the expression.**

SEE EXAMPLE 2 on p. 234 for Exs. 10–17

10. $\frac{h}{13} + \frac{6h}{13}$
11. $-\frac{8n}{21} + \frac{5n}{21}$
12. $\frac{-8p}{9} - \frac{-p}{9}$
13. $\frac{12}{a} + \frac{3}{a}$
14. $\frac{4x}{5y} - \frac{9x}{5y}$
15. $\frac{9a}{20b} - \frac{7a}{20b}$
16. $-\frac{5q}{18p} - \frac{13q}{18p}$
17. $\frac{5a}{2b} - \frac{a}{2b}$

EVALUATING EXPRESSIONS **Evaluate the expression.**

SEE EXAMPLES 1 AND 4 on pp. 233, 235 for Exs. 18–27

18. $7\frac{1}{3} - 3\frac{2}{3}$ **(19.)** $19\frac{1}{4} - 17\frac{3}{4}$ **20.** $1\frac{4}{15} + \left(-\frac{11}{15}\right)$

21. $\frac{13}{18} + \frac{5}{18} + \frac{11}{18}$ **22.** $-\frac{4}{5} - \frac{1}{5} - \frac{2}{5}$ **(23.)** $4\frac{5}{12} - \left(1\frac{11}{12} - \frac{7}{12}\right)$

24. $-5\frac{4}{15} - \left(3\frac{7}{15} + \frac{8}{15}\right)$ **25.** $-\frac{3}{16} - 2\frac{1}{16} - \frac{15}{16}$ **26.** $1\frac{3}{8} + \frac{5}{8} - 1\frac{7}{8}$

27. **ERROR ANALYSIS** Describe and correct the error made in subtracting the fractions.

$$2\frac{4}{9} - 1\frac{1}{9} = (2 - 1) + \left(\frac{4}{9} + \frac{1}{9}\right) = 1\frac{5}{9}$$

ALGEBRA **Solve the equation.**

28. $x + \frac{5}{8} = 0$ **29.** $\frac{7}{17} + k = \frac{9}{17}$ **30.** $z - \frac{9}{15} = \frac{11}{15}$

31. $m - \frac{6}{9} = \frac{2}{9}$ **32.** $j + \frac{2}{13} + \frac{5}{13} = \frac{8}{13}$ **33.** $\frac{1}{7} + a + \frac{3}{7} = \frac{4}{7}$

34. $\frac{7}{16} + b - \frac{2}{16} = \frac{5}{16}$ **35.** $\frac{10}{11} - y = \frac{2}{11}$ **36.** $\frac{3}{19} - c = 0$

37. **EXAMPLES AND NONEXAMPLES** Give an example of a pair of mixed numbers whose sum is a mixed number. Then give an example of a pair of mixed numbers whose sum is *not* a mixed number.

CHALLENGE **Solve the equation.**

38. $\frac{a}{10} + \frac{2a}{10} = -\frac{9}{10}$ **39.** $\frac{-3b}{15} + \frac{7b}{15} = \frac{8}{15}$ **40.** $\frac{5}{4c} - \frac{13}{4c} = -\frac{1}{3}$

PROBLEM SOLVING

SEE EXAMPLE 3 on p. 234 for Exs. 41–43

41. **KNITTING** You find a mistake after knitting $21\frac{3}{8}$ inches of a scarf. You have to pull out $2\frac{5}{8}$ inches of the scarf. How many inches of the scarf are left?

42. ★ **MULTIPLE CHOICE** You are fencing a rectangular plot of land. The plot and its dimensions are shown. How many feet of fencing do you need in total?

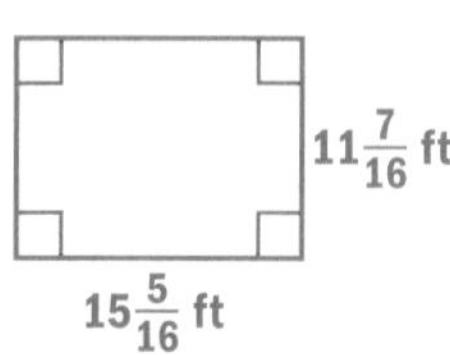

Ⓐ $26\frac{3}{4}$ feet Ⓑ $52\frac{1}{2}$ feet

Ⓒ $53\frac{1}{4}$ feet Ⓓ $53\frac{1}{2}$ feet

(43.) **EUROS** A 2-euro coin is $25\frac{3}{4}$ millimeters wide. A 1-euro coin is $23\frac{1}{4}$ millimeters wide. How much wider is a 2-euro coin than a 1-euro coin?

44. ★ **WRITING** One hundred people were asked to name their favorite pet. The results are shown in the circle graph at the right.

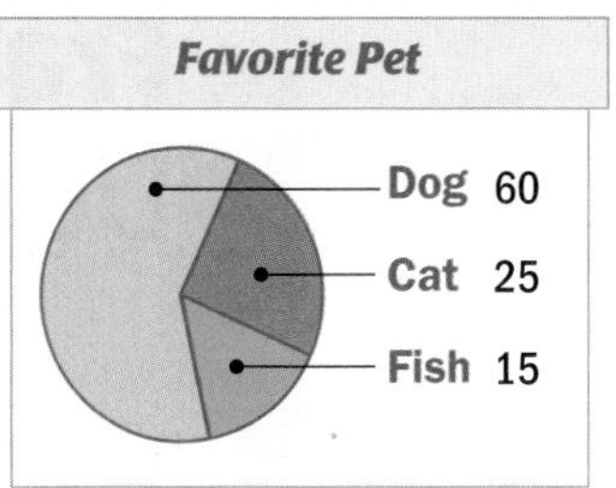

Your friend says that if you make each number the numerator in a fraction with a denominator of 100, the sum of these fractions must be 1. Is your friend correct? *Explain.*

45. **LONG JUMP RECORD** You want to match your school's long jump record of 17 feet $8\frac{1}{4}$ inches. Your best long jump so far is 15 feet $11\frac{3}{4}$ inches. How much farther do you need to jump to match the school record?

46. ★ **SHORT RESPONSE** You did volunteer work for $6\frac{1}{6}$ hours the first week of the month, $8\frac{5}{6}$ hours the second week, and $5\frac{1}{6}$ hours the third week. Your volunteer group gives awards to those who volunteer at least 25 hours per month. How many hours do you have to volunteer the last week of the month to win the award? *Explain* your reasoning.

47. ★ **SHORT RESPONSE** Some cars in a race were allowed to reduce the height of their rear spoilers by one fourth of an inch to reduce drag and increase speed. After the change, one car's spoiler was $6\frac{1}{4}$ inches tall.

a. How tall was the spoiler before the change in height? *Justify* your answer.

b. What fraction of the original height was removed? *Explain* how you found your answer.

48. **CHALLENGE** Bill is 1 foot $3\frac{1}{4}$ inches taller than Hollie. Hollie is $6\frac{1}{8}$ inches taller than Chris. Amanda is $4\frac{7}{8}$ inches shorter than Chris. Amanda is 4 feet $2\frac{1}{4}$ inches tall. How tall is each person in feet and inches?

MIXED REVIEW

Prepare for Lesson 5.2 in Exs. 49–56

Find the least common multiple of the numbers. *(p. 192)*

49. 15, 35 50. 19, 76 51. 37, 50 52. 27, 81

Find the least common denominator of the fractions. *(p. 198)*

53. $\frac{2}{3}, \frac{4}{9}$ 54. $\frac{1}{5}, \frac{9}{20}$ 55. $\frac{3}{8}, \frac{7}{12}$ 56. $\frac{1}{6}, \frac{4}{15}$

Write the number in scientific notation. *(p. 212)*

57. 2800 58. 0.0116 59. 362,000,000 60. 0.0000099

61. ★ **MULTIPLE CHOICE** What is the sum of -7 and -35? *(p. 63)*

Ⓐ -42 Ⓑ -28 Ⓒ 28 Ⓓ 42

5.2 Fractions with Different Denominators

Before	You added and subtracted with common denominators.
Now	You'll add and subtract with different denominators.
Why?	So you can find length, as of a wooden board in Example 3.

KEY VOCABULARY

- **least common denominator (LCD),** *p. 198*

Carpentry A board is $36\frac{5}{8}$ inches long. You cut off a piece $12\frac{3}{4}$ inches long. The saw blade destroys an additional $\frac{1}{16}$ inch of wood which is equal to its width. What is the length of the remaining piece of wood? You will solve this problem in Example 3 on page 239 by adding and subtracting mixed numbers and fractions with different denominators.

To add or subtract fractions with different denominators, first rewrite the fractions so the denominators are the same. Choose a denominator that is the least common multiple of denominators in the problem.

EXAMPLE 1 Adding and Subtracting Fractions

REVIEW LCD

Need help rewriting fractions with common denominators? See p. 198.

a. $\frac{7}{8} + \frac{-2}{5} = \frac{35}{40} + \frac{-16}{40}$ **Rewrite fractions using LCD of 40.**

$= \frac{35 + (-16)}{40}$ **Write sum over LCD.**

$= \frac{19}{40}$ **Evaluate numerator.**

b. $\frac{3}{10} - \frac{5}{6} = \frac{9}{30} - \frac{25}{30}$ **Rewrite fractions using LCD of 30.**

$= \frac{9 - 25}{30}$ **Write difference over LCD.**

$= \frac{-16}{30}$ **Evaluate numerator.**

$= -\frac{8}{15}$ **Simplify.**

✓ GUIDED PRACTICE for Example 1

Find the sum or difference. Then simplify if possible.

1. $\frac{1}{3} + \frac{3}{8}$ **2.** $\frac{3}{4} - \frac{9}{10}$ **3.** $\frac{5}{12} + \frac{-7}{9}$

4. $\frac{2}{8} + \frac{7}{16}$ **5.** $\frac{1}{6} - \frac{11}{15}$ **6.** $\frac{-4}{33} - \frac{1}{11}$

EXAMPLE 2 Simplifying Variable Expressions

Simplify the expression.

a. $\frac{2x}{5} - \frac{x}{6} = \frac{12x}{30} - \frac{5x}{30}$ **Rewrite fractions using LCD of 30.**

$= \frac{12x - 5x}{30}$ **Write difference over LCD.**

$= \frac{7x}{30}$ **Combine like terms.**

AVOID ERRORS

Notice in part (b) that $\frac{40 + 7y}{8y} \neq \frac{47y}{8y}$, because 40 and $7y$ are *not* like terms. The expression is already in simplest form.

b. $\frac{5}{y} + \frac{7}{8} = \left(\frac{5}{y} \cdot \frac{8}{8}\right) + \left(\frac{7}{8} \cdot \frac{y}{y}\right)$ **Multiply $\frac{5}{y}$ by $\frac{8}{8}$ and $\frac{7}{8}$ by $\frac{y}{y}$ for LCD of 8y.**

$= \frac{40}{8y} + \frac{7y}{8y}$ **Multiply inside parentheses.**

$= \frac{40 + 7y}{8y}$ **Write sum over LCD.**

EXAMPLE 3 Modeling with Mixed Numbers

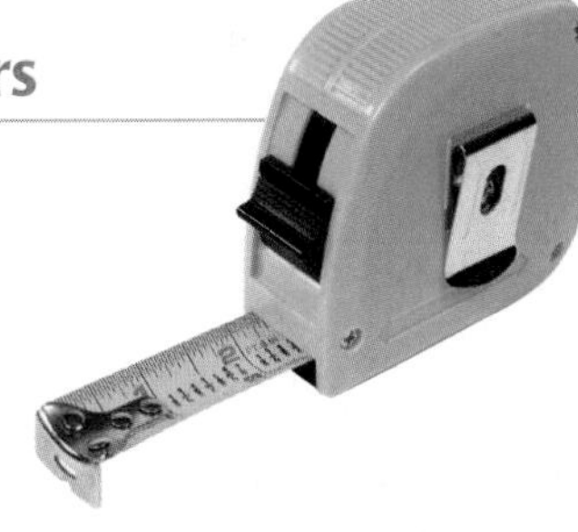

To find the length of the remaining piece of wood described on page 238, first write a verbal model.

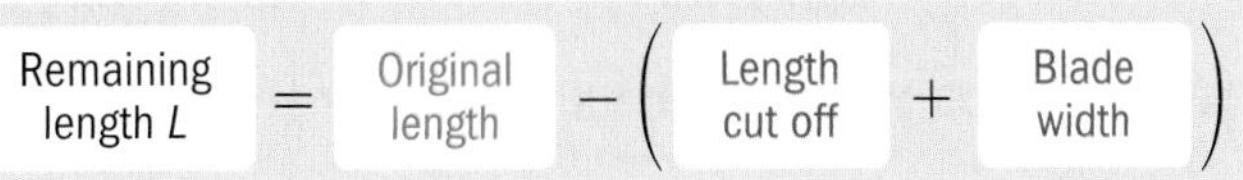

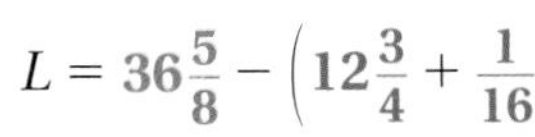

$L = 36\frac{5}{8} - \left(12\frac{3}{4} + \frac{1}{16}\right)$ **Write an algebraic model.**

$= 36\frac{10}{16} - \left(12\frac{12}{16} + \frac{1}{16}\right)$ **Rewrite fractions using LCD of 16.**

$= 36\frac{10}{16} - 12\frac{13}{16}$ **Add inside parentheses.**

$= 35\frac{26}{16} - 12\frac{13}{16}$ **Rename $36\frac{10}{16}$ as $35\frac{26}{16}$.**

$= (35 - 12) + \left(\frac{26}{16} - \frac{13}{16}\right)$ **Group whole numbers and fractions.**

$= 23\frac{13}{16}$ **Subtract whole numbers and fractions.**

▸ **Answer** The remaining piece of wood is $23\frac{13}{16}$ inches long.

CHECK REASONABLENESS

You can check that the sum or difference of mixed numbers is reasonable by rounding each number to the nearest whole number. In Example 3, $36\frac{5}{8} - \left(12\frac{3}{4} + \frac{1}{16}\right) \approx 37 - 13 = 24$.

✓ GUIDED PRACTICE for Examples 2 and 3

7. Find the sum and difference of $\frac{2}{5}$ and $\frac{2}{z}$.

8. **What If?** In Example 3 suppose you cut $4\frac{5}{6}$ inches off the original piece of wood. What is the length of the remaining piece of wood?

5.2 EXERCISES

HOMEWORK KEY

★ = **STANDARDIZED TEST PRACTICE** Exs. 22, 38, 39, 42, 43, 45, and 60

○ = **HINTS AND HOMEWORK HELP** for Exs. 7, 9, 15, 21, 41 at classzone.com

SKILL PRACTICE

1. **VOCABULARY** Copy and complete: To add fractions with different denominators, rewrite the fractions using the _?_ of the fractions.

SEE EXAMPLE 1 on p. 238 for Exs. 2–7, 22

ADDING AND SUBTRACTING FRACTIONS **Find the sum or difference. Simplify if possible.**

2. $\frac{1}{2} + \frac{1}{3}$
3. $\frac{7}{8} - \frac{1}{4}$
4. $\frac{1}{8} - \frac{5}{32}$
5. $\frac{5}{9} + \frac{1}{6}$

SEE EXAMPLE 3 on p. 239 for Exs. 8–13

6. $-\frac{7}{12} + \frac{4}{15}$
7. $\frac{-3}{8} + \frac{-9}{20}$
8. $4\frac{5}{8} - 2\frac{2}{3}$
9. $5\frac{1}{2} - \frac{7}{10}$
10. $7\frac{4}{5} + 5\frac{3}{7}$
11. $12\frac{5}{18} - \frac{3}{4}$
12. $12 - 16\frac{3}{7}$
13. $-7\frac{3}{11} - (-8)$

SIMPLIFYING VARIABLE EXPRESSIONS **Simplify the expression.**

SEE EXAMPLE 2 on p. 239 for Exs. 14–21

14. $-\frac{7y}{12} + \frac{4y}{15}$
15. $\frac{-3w}{8} + \frac{-9w}{20}$
16. $\frac{2x}{7} - \frac{x}{2}$
17. $\frac{9s}{4} - \frac{7s}{5}$
18. $\frac{4}{x} + \frac{1}{9}$
19. $\frac{16}{25n} - \frac{9}{10n}$
20. $\frac{16}{25n} + \frac{9}{10n}$
21. $\frac{18}{7a} + \frac{11}{21}$
22. ★ **MULTIPLE CHOICE** What is the value of $\frac{5}{6} + \frac{1}{9} - \frac{2}{3}$?

   (A) $\frac{1}{6}$ (B) $\frac{2}{9}$ (C) $\frac{5}{18}$ (D) $\frac{1}{3}$

CHOOSE A METHOD **Use *estimation, mental math,* or *pencil and paper* to tell whether the statement is *true* or *false*. Identify your choice of method.**

23. $\frac{1}{4} - \frac{6}{7} + \frac{3}{14} = -\frac{11}{28}$
24. $\frac{3}{4} + 2\frac{1}{2} - \frac{1}{4} = 3$
25. $\frac{4}{9} + \frac{7}{8} + \frac{1}{24} = \frac{7}{8}$
26. $3\frac{4}{9} - 1\frac{1}{2} - \frac{1}{3} = 2\frac{5}{18}$
27. $1\frac{1}{3} - \frac{2}{9} - \frac{5}{6} = \frac{7}{18}$
28. $10\frac{7}{8} - 3\frac{1}{10} = 5\frac{31}{40}$

ALGEBRA **Solve the equation.**

29. $z + 3\frac{4}{7} - 5\frac{2}{5} = 1\frac{1}{2}$
30. $2\frac{3}{5} + w - 4\frac{1}{3} = 7\frac{8}{15}$
31. $6\frac{3}{8} + 2\frac{5}{12} - x = 4\frac{3}{4}$
32. $7\frac{7}{8} - 6\frac{5}{9} - y = \frac{1}{6}$

Animated Math at classzone.com

CHALLENGE ***Describe*** **the pattern. Then write the next three fractions in the pattern.**

33. $1\frac{7}{10}, 2, 2\frac{3}{10}, 2\frac{3}{5}, \ldots$
34. $5\frac{3}{4}, 4\frac{5}{8}, 3\frac{1}{2}, 2\frac{3}{8}, \ldots$
35. $\frac{11}{12}, \frac{19}{24}, \frac{2}{3}, \frac{13}{24}, \ldots$

PROBLEM SOLVING

SEE EXAMPLE 3 on p. 239 for Exs. 36–41

36. **GUIDED PROBLEM SOLVING** You are building a stone wall 13 feet long. You build $4\frac{1}{3}$ feet of wall on Monday and $5\frac{3}{4}$ feet on Tuesday. How much wall do you have left to build?
    a. Write a verbal model to describe the problem.
    b. Substitute the given values into the model.
    c. Solve the equation to find the length left to build.

37. **OLYMPIC SLEDDING** What is the difference in the lengths of the skeleton sleds below?

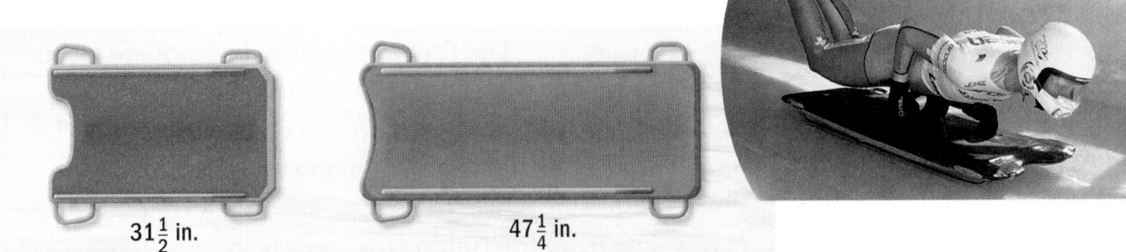

38. ★ **MULTIPLE CHOICE** A board $2\frac{1}{4}$ inches thick is placed on top of a board $\frac{5}{6}$ inch thick. What is the combined thickness of the boards?

    Ⓐ $1\frac{5}{12}$ in. Ⓑ $2\frac{1}{12}$ in. Ⓒ $2\frac{3}{5}$ in. Ⓓ $3\frac{1}{12}$ in.

39. ★ **SHORT RESPONSE** You bike $1\frac{5}{8}$ miles from school to the store, $\frac{1}{2}$ mile more to the post office, and then $2\frac{3}{4}$ miles home. *Explain* how to estimate the total distance traveled. Is it more or less than 5 miles?

40. **POLE VAULT** The gold medal winning men's pole vault at the 2004 Athens Summer Olympics was $5\frac{19}{20}$ meters. The world record, set in 1994, is $6\frac{7}{50}$ meters. How much higher is the world record than the gold medal winning vault at the 2004 Summer Olympics?

41. **TREE REMOVAL** A dead tree is being cut down in three parts. The lengths of the first and second cuts are shown at the right. Write and solve an equation to find how many feet of the tree remain to be cut down.

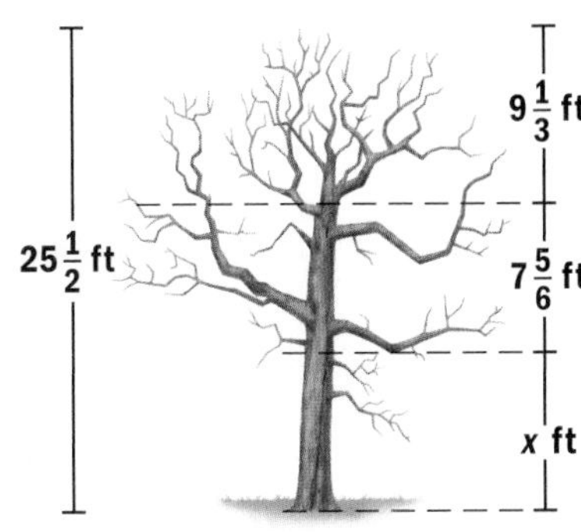

42. ★ **WRITING** *Describe* two strategies to evaluate the sum of two mixed numbers. In one strategy, use improper fractions. *Explain* when it might be better to use one strategy and when it might be better to use the other strategy.

43. ★ **OPEN-ENDED MATH** Write an addition or subtraction expression containing three fractions, with different denominators, that you can easily evaluate using mental math. *Explain* why you think it is appropriate.

44. MULTI-STEP PROBLEM The table shows the results of an annual softball throwing contest. The player with the greatest combined distance wins.

a. Who won the contest?

b. What was the difference between the winner's combined distance and the 3rd place player's combined distance?

c. What distance would the 2nd place player need on his or her 3rd throw to *tie* the winner's combined distance? *Explain* how you found your answer.

	Distance Thrown (feet)		
	1st throw	**2nd throw**	**3rd throw**
Curtis	$51\frac{1}{3}$	$85\frac{1}{2}$	$80\frac{1}{4}$
Shanee	$102\frac{1}{2}$	$54\frac{2}{3}$	$57\frac{3}{4}$
Dave	$71\frac{1}{3}$	$72\frac{3}{4}$	$67\frac{1}{6}$

45. ★ SHORT RESPONSE The fractions in the diagram are fractions of the total distance around Earth on the equator.

a. What fraction of the equator do you cover if you travel east from the Galápagos Islands to Singapore?

b. Is traveling from the Galápagos Islands to Singapore a shorter trip if you travel *east* or *west*? *Explain.*

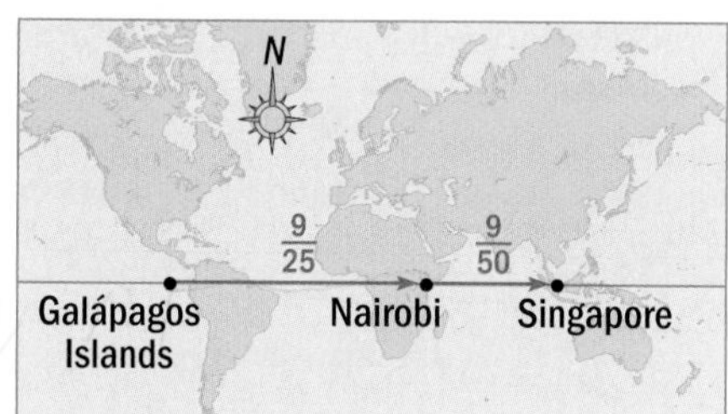

46. CLOCKS You put a cake in the oven to bake and notice that the hour hand on the oven's clock is broken. At the same time, you hear a radio announcer mention that it is 3:17 P.M. The minute hand on the clock makes $\frac{5}{8}$ revolution before you check the cake. The minute hand makes another $\frac{13}{24}$ revolution before you take the baked cake out of the oven. What time is it when the cake is done?

47. xy **CHALLENGE** Write the expression $\frac{a}{b} + \frac{c}{d}$ $(b, d \neq 0)$ as a single fraction.

MIXED REVIEW

Prepare for Lesson 5.3 in Exs. 48–55

Find the product. *(p. 73)*

48. $-9(7)$ **49.** $0(-5)$ **50.** $7(-3)(13)$ **51.** $-9(-7)(-2)$

Find the sum. *(p. 233)*

52. $\frac{3}{5} + \frac{3}{5}$ **53.** $\frac{1}{4} + \frac{1}{4} + \frac{1}{4}$ **54.** $2\frac{1}{3} + 2\frac{1}{3}$ **55.** $\frac{3}{8} + \frac{3}{8} + \frac{3}{8}$

Copy and complete the statement with <, >, or =. *(p. 198)*

56. $\frac{1}{7} \underline{?} \frac{1}{8}$ **57.** $\frac{3}{8} \underline{?} \frac{4}{9}$ **58.** $\frac{5}{12} \underline{?} \frac{7}{16}$ **59.** $\frac{7}{10} \underline{?} \frac{18}{25}$

60. ★ MULTIPLE CHOICE What is the greatest common factor of 284 and 426? *(p. 181)*

Ⓐ 2 Ⓑ 71 Ⓒ 142 Ⓓ 852

5.3 Multiplying Fractions

Utah

Before You added and subtracted fractions and mixed numbers.

Now You'll multiply fractions and mixed numbers.

Why? So you can find area, as of a postcard in Example 2.

KEY VOCABULARY

- **numerator,** *p. 762*
- **denominator,** *p. 762*

You can use the model at the right or the rule below to find the product of two fractions such as $\frac{5}{8}$ and $\frac{3}{4}$. When a product involves negative fractions, you can apply the rules for multiplying integers that you learned in Lesson 2.4.

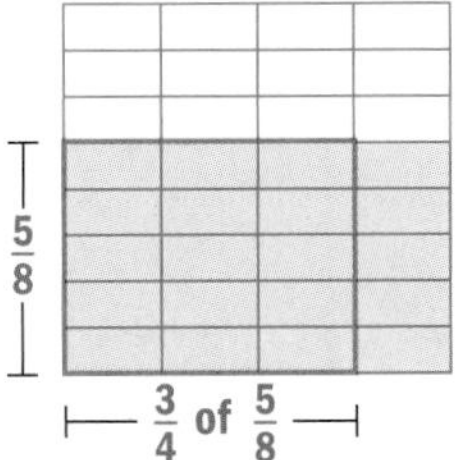

KEY CONCEPT *For Your Notebook*

Multiplying Fractions

Words The product of two or more fractions is equal to the product of the numerators divided by the product of the denominators.

Numbers $\frac{3}{4} \cdot \frac{5}{8} = \frac{3 \cdot 5}{4 \cdot 8} = \frac{15}{32}$

Algebra $\frac{a}{b} \cdot \frac{c}{d} = \frac{a \cdot c}{b \cdot d}\ (b, d \neq 0)$

EXAMPLE 1 Multiplying Fractions

REVIEW MULTIPLICATION

Remember that the product of two numbers with the same sign is positive. The product of two numbers with different signs is negative.

a. $-\frac{2}{5} \cdot \left(-\frac{2}{3}\right) = \frac{-2 \cdot (-2)}{5 \cdot 3}$ **Use rule for multiplying fractions.**

$= \frac{4}{15}$ **Evaluate numerator and denominator.**

b. $-\frac{3}{10} \cdot \frac{5}{6} = \frac{-3 \cdot 5}{10 \cdot 6}$ **Use rule for multiplying fractions.**

$= \frac{\overset{-1}{\cancel{-3}} \cdot \overset{1}{\cancel{5}}}{\underset{2}{\cancel{10}} \cdot \underset{2}{\cancel{6}}}$ **Divide out common factors.**

$= -\frac{1}{4}$ **Multiply.**

✓ **GUIDED PRACTICE** for Example 1

Find the product. Simplify if possible.

1. $-\frac{5}{12} \cdot \frac{9}{10}$ **2.** $\frac{-5}{6} \cdot \frac{-7}{9}$ **3.** $\frac{1}{6} \cdot \frac{12}{17}$ **4.** $\frac{7}{12} \cdot -15$

Mixed Numbers To multiply mixed numbers, first write them as improper fractions.

EXAMPLE 2 Multiplying Mixed Numbers

Postcards A postcard is $5\frac{1}{2}$ inches long and $3\frac{3}{4}$ inches wide. Find the area of the postcard.

SOLUTION

Area = length • width	**Write formula for area of a rectangle.**
$= 5\frac{1}{2} \cdot 3\frac{3}{4}$	**Substitute values.**
$= \frac{11}{2} \cdot \frac{15}{4}$	**Write as improper fractions.**
$= \frac{11 \cdot 15}{2 \cdot 4}$	**Use rule for multiplying fractions.**
$= \frac{165}{8}$, or $20\frac{5}{8}$	**Multiply.**

▸ **Answer** The area of the postcard is $20\frac{5}{8}$ square inches.

EXAMPLE 3 Evaluating a Variable Expression

Evaluate x^2y when $x = -\frac{4}{5}$ and $y = \frac{2}{3}$.

$x^2y = \left(-\frac{4}{5}\right)^2 \cdot \frac{2}{3}$	**Substitute $-\frac{4}{5}$ for x and $\frac{2}{3}$ for y.**
$= \left(-\frac{4}{5}\right) \cdot \left(-\frac{4}{5}\right) \cdot \frac{2}{3}$	**Write $-\frac{4}{5}$ as a factor 2 times.**
$= \frac{-4 \cdot (-4) \cdot 2}{5 \cdot 5 \cdot 3}$	**Use rule for multiplying fractions.**
$= \frac{32}{75}$	**Multiply.**

✓ GUIDED PRACTICE for Examples 2 and 3

AVOID ERRORS

Be careful when you write a negative mixed number as an improper fraction.

$-1\frac{5}{6} = \frac{-1 \cdot 6 + (-5)}{6}$

Find the product. Simplify if possible.

5. $1\frac{2}{5} \cdot 3\frac{1}{2}$ **6.** $5\frac{1}{2} \cdot \left(-1\frac{5}{6}\right)$ **7.** $-5\frac{3}{4} \cdot 2\frac{3}{5}$ **8.** $-2\frac{1}{3} \cdot \left(-\frac{3}{4}\right)$

Evaluate the expression when $x = -\frac{3}{4}$ and $y = \frac{5}{6}$. Simplify if possible.

9. $\frac{2}{3}x$ **10.** $2y$ **11.** xy **12.** xy^2

5.3 EXERCISES

HOMEWORK KEY

★ = **STANDARDIZED TEST PRACTICE** Exs. 22, 36, 38, and 45

◯ = **HINTS AND HOMEWORK HELP** for Exs. 3, 9, 11, 17, 33 at classzone.com

SKILL PRACTICE

1. **VOCABULARY** Copy and complete: The product of two or more fractions is equal to the product of the fractions' _?_ divided by the product of the fractions' _?_.

SEE EXAMPLE 1 on p. 243 for Exs. 2–9

MULTIPLYING FRACTIONS **Find the product. Simplify if possible.**

2. $\frac{5}{8} \cdot \frac{7}{16}$
3. $-\frac{9}{4} \cdot \frac{5}{6}$
4. $\frac{7}{11} \cdot \frac{1}{6}$
5. $\frac{4}{5} \cdot \frac{3}{10}$
6. $-\frac{3}{4} \cdot \left(-\frac{2}{9}\right)$
7. $-\frac{5}{6} \cdot \frac{5}{12}$
8. $-4 \cdot \frac{3}{5}$
9. $12 \cdot \frac{3}{8}$

SEE EXAMPLE 2 on p. 244 for Exs. 10–14

10. $-4 \cdot 2\frac{9}{16}$
11. $6\frac{3}{16} \cdot \left(-3\frac{1}{5}\right)$
12. $-9\frac{2}{7} \cdot 1\frac{2}{5}$
13. $5\frac{2}{3} \cdot (-6)$

14. **ERROR ANALYSIS** Alexia wants to multiply $2\frac{2}{3}$ by $3\frac{3}{4}$. She says she will multiply 2 by 3 and $\frac{2}{3}$ by $\frac{3}{4}$ and then add the results. Describe and correct the error in Alexia's method for multiplying the mixed numbers.

SEE EXAMPLE 3 on p. 244 for Exs. 15–18

ALGEBRA **Evaluate the expression when $a = \frac{5}{8}$, $b = -\frac{7}{6}$, and $c = -1\frac{1}{2}$.**

15. ac
16. bc
17. ab^2
18. $16c^3$

GEOMETRY **Find the area of the figure.**

19.

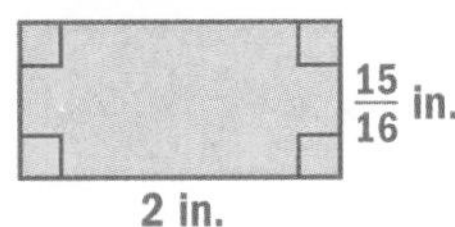

20.

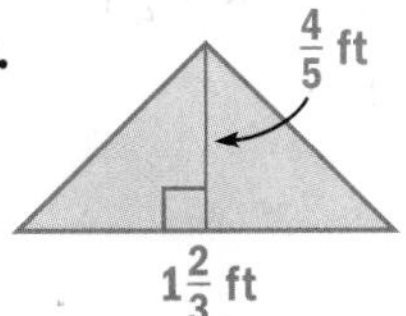

21.

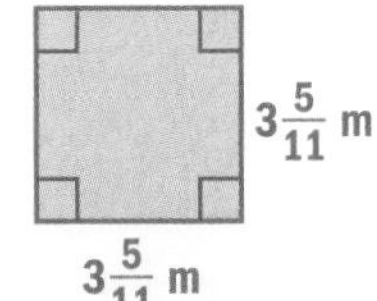

22. ★ **MULTIPLE CHOICE** Let n represent the position number in the pattern below. Which expression can be used to find any number in the pattern?

$$\frac{1}{3}, \frac{2}{3}, 1, 1\frac{1}{3}, 1\frac{2}{3}, \ldots$$

Ⓐ $\frac{1}{3}n$ Ⓑ $\frac{2}{3}n$ Ⓒ $2n$ Ⓓ $3n$

EVALUATING EXPRESSIONS **Evaluate the expression.**

23. $\frac{2}{5} \cdot 1\frac{1}{5} \cdot \left(-4\frac{7}{12}\right)$
24. $-\frac{7}{8} + 5\frac{1}{2} \cdot \frac{11}{15}$
25. $\frac{5}{2} \cdot \left(\frac{8}{9} - \frac{5}{12}\right)$
26. $5 - \left(\frac{1}{3} + \frac{1}{6}\right)^2$
27. $4 - \left(\frac{3}{4} + \frac{7}{8}\right)$
28. $\frac{2}{3}\left(\frac{3}{5} - \frac{7}{12}\right)$
29. $\frac{-7}{16} + 8\frac{1}{3} \cdot \frac{3}{5}$
30. $\frac{2}{9}\left(-2\frac{1}{5}\right)\left(3\frac{3}{10}\right)$

CHALLENGE **List the expressions in the order of their values from least to greatest when $a = 2\frac{3}{4}$, $b = \frac{2}{3}$, and $c = 3$.**

31. $2bc, bc^2, a^2b, a + bc$
32. $-b^2 + 2ac, -a + 5c, a^2bc$

PROBLEM SOLVING

SEE EXAMPLE 1 on p. 243 for Exs. 33–35

33. **MOON CRATERS** The depth of a simple impact crater on the moon is about $\frac{1}{5}$ of its width. One simple impact crater, Moltke Crater, is 7 kilometers wide. About how deep is Moltke Crater?

34. **SNACK MIX** A serving of a snack mix is $\frac{7}{8}$ cup. You need to take 15 servings to your friend's party. How many cups of snack mix should you take? *Explain* how you can use estimation to check your answer.

35. **COMPUTERS** One of the first computers, the ENIAC, took $\frac{1}{5000}$ second to perform one operation. How long did it take to perform 11,000 operations?

36. ★ **SHORT RESPONSE** You run 1 mile in 8 minutes at a constant speed. How far do you run in 1 minute? Write an equation to represent how far you can run in m minutes. *Explain* how you can use your equation to find how far you can run in 11 minutes.

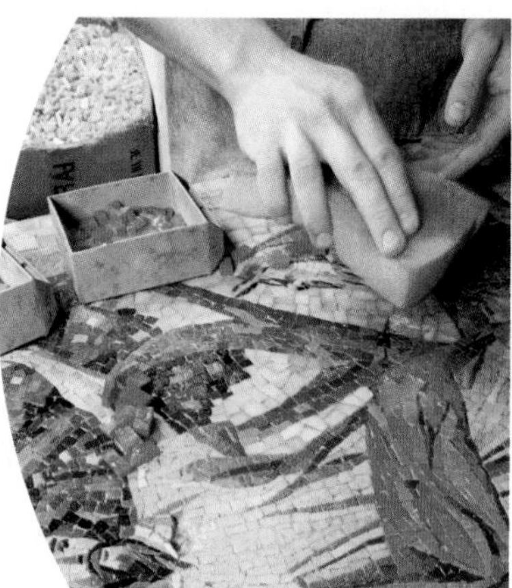

37. **MOSAICS** You have mosaic tiles that measure $1\frac{2}{5}$ inch by $1\frac{2}{5}$ inch. How many square feet will 1000 mosaic tiles cover? Write your answer in simplest form.

38. ★ **MULTIPLE CHOICE** A poster measures $8\frac{1}{2}$ inches by 11 inches. You enlarge it by increasing each dimension by a factor of $1\frac{1}{2}$. What is the area of the new poster?

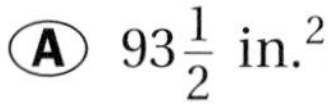

Ⓐ $93\frac{1}{2}$ in.^{2} Ⓑ $140\frac{1}{4}$ in.^{2}

Ⓒ $210\frac{3}{8}$ in.^{2} Ⓓ $280\frac{1}{2}$ in.^{2}

39. **CHALLENGE** To present a petition to the student council, $\frac{1}{8}$ of the student/teacher population of 1200 must sign the petition. Also, $\frac{1}{25}$ of the signatures must be from teachers. A petition currently has 150 signatures of which $\frac{73}{75}$ are student signatures. Can this petition be presented? *Explain.*

MIXED REVIEW

Get-Ready

Prepare for Lesson 5.4 in Exs. 40–43

Find the quotient. *(p. 77)*

40. $\frac{48}{-4}$ 41. $\frac{-24}{8}$ 42. $\frac{0}{-6}$ 43. $\frac{-32}{-2}$

44. Find the product and the quotient of 5^3 and 5^2. *(p. 202)*

45. ★ **MULTIPLE CHOICE** What is the value of $-2\frac{4}{9} + \frac{5}{21}$? *(p. 238)*

Ⓐ $-2\frac{13}{63}$ Ⓑ $-1\frac{20}{63}$ Ⓒ $-\frac{17}{30}$ Ⓓ $2\frac{43}{63}$

5.4 Dividing Fractions

Before You added, subtracted, and multiplied fractions.
Now You'll divide fractions.
Why? So you can calculate weight, as in pounds of chicken feed in Ex. 57.

KEY VOCABULARY
- **reciprocal,** *p. 247*
- **multiplicative inverse,** *p. 247*

ACTIVITY

You can use models to divide fractions.

STEP 1 The model shows that $\frac{3}{4}$ is a part of 6 eight times, so $6 \div \frac{3}{4} = 8$.

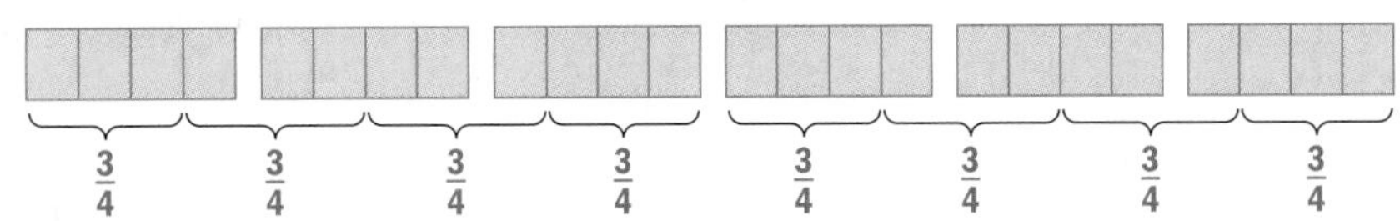

STEP 2 Calculate $6 \cdot \frac{4}{3}$. Compare the values of $6 \div \frac{3}{4}$ and $6 \cdot \frac{4}{3}$.

STEP 3 Use the model below to evaluate $4 \div \frac{2}{5}$.

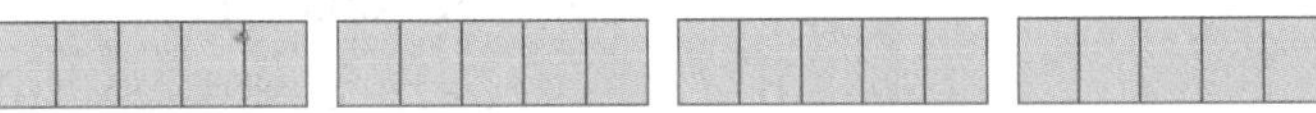

STEP 4 Calculate $4 \cdot \frac{5}{2}$. Compare the values of $4 \div \frac{2}{5}$ and $4 \cdot \frac{5}{2}$.

STEP 5 What fraction can you multiply by 5 to evaluate $5 \div \frac{2}{3}$?

Reciprocals As the activity suggests, dividing a number by a fraction and multiplying the number by the fraction's *reciprocal* give the same result. Two nonzero numbers are **reciprocals** if their product is 1.

Reciprocals, like $\frac{3}{7}$ and $\frac{7}{3}$, are also called **multiplicative inverses**.

KEY CONCEPT *For Your Notebook*

Dividing Fractions

Words To divide by a fraction, multiply by its reciprocal.

Numbers $\frac{3}{10} \div \frac{4}{7} = \frac{3}{10} \cdot \frac{7}{4} = \frac{21}{40}$

Algebra $\frac{a}{b} \div \frac{c}{d} = \frac{a}{b} \cdot \frac{d}{c} \quad (b, c, d \neq 0)$

EXAMPLE 1 Dividing a Fraction by a Fraction

VOCABULARY
Notice in part (b) that the reciprocal of a negative number is also a negative number.

a. $\frac{5}{6} \div \frac{10}{21} = \frac{5}{6} \cdot \frac{21}{10}$

$= \frac{\overset{1}{\cancel{5}} \cdot \overset{7}{\cancel{21}}}{\underset{2}{\cancel{6}} \cdot \underset{2}{\cancel{10}}}$

$= \frac{7}{4}$, or $1\frac{3}{4}$

b. $\frac{9}{14} \div \frac{-2}{7} = \frac{9}{14} \cdot \frac{7}{-2}$

$= \frac{9 \cdot \overset{1}{\cancel{7}}}{\underset{2}{\cancel{14}} \cdot (-2)}$

$= \frac{9}{-4}$, or $-2\frac{1}{4}$

EXAMPLE 2 Dividing a Fraction by a Whole Number

$\frac{6}{13} \div 3 = \frac{6}{13} \cdot \frac{1}{3}$ — $3 \cdot \frac{1}{3} = 1$, so the reciprocal of 3 is $\frac{1}{3}$.

$= \frac{\overset{2}{\cancel{6}} \cdot 1}{13 \cdot \underset{1}{\cancel{3}}}$ — Multiply fractions. Divide out common factor.

$= \frac{2}{13}$ — Multiply.

✓ GUIDED PRACTICE for Examples 1 and 2

Find the quotient. Simplify if possible.

1. $\frac{5}{8} \div \left(-\frac{7}{10}\right)$ **2.** $\frac{2}{15} \div 8$ **3.** $-\frac{3}{4} \div \frac{-7}{12}$ **4.** $\frac{6}{7} \div 2$

EXAMPLE 3 Dividing Mixed Numbers

$6\frac{1}{3} \div \left(-2\frac{5}{6}\right) = \frac{19}{3} \div \left(-\frac{17}{6}\right)$ — Write $6\frac{1}{3}$ and $-2\frac{5}{6}$ as improper fractions.

$= \frac{19}{3} \cdot \left(-\frac{6}{17}\right)$ — Multiply by $-\frac{6}{17}$, the reciprocal of $-\frac{17}{6}$.

$= \frac{19 \cdot \overset{-2}{\cancel{(-6)}}}{\underset{1}{\cancel{3}} \cdot 17}$ — Multiply. Divide out common factor.

$= -\frac{38}{17}$, or $-2\frac{4}{17}$ — Multiply.

Check Use estimation to check your answer. Replace the divisor and dividend with compatible whole numbers. Because $6 \div (-3) = -2$, you know that $-2\frac{4}{17}$ is a reasonable answer.

✓ GUIDED PRACTICE for Example 3

Find the quotient. Simplify if possible.

5. $6\frac{2}{7} \div 4$ **6.** $-12\frac{1}{4} \div 7$ **7.** $10 \div 3\frac{1}{3}$ **8.** $-15\frac{3}{4} \div \left(-2\frac{5}{8}\right)$

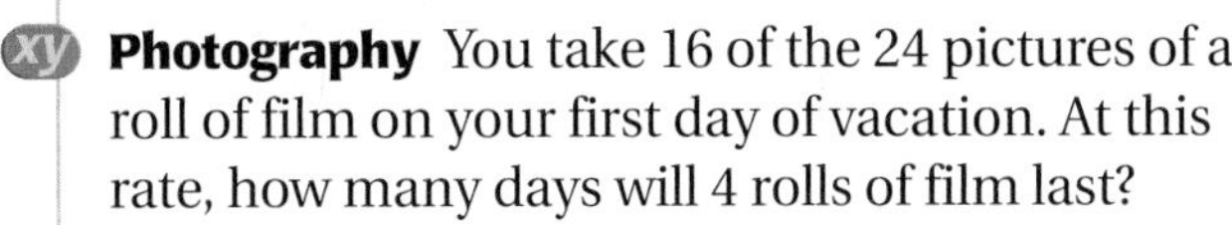

EXAMPLE 4 Solving an Equation with a Fraction

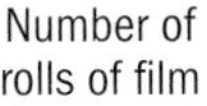

Photography You take 16 of the 24 pictures of a roll of film on your first day of vacation. At this rate, how many days will 4 rolls of film last?

SOLUTION

Write a verbal model to describe the problem. Let d represent the number of days.

Number of rolls of film	=	Fraction of pictures taken each day	•	Number of days

$4 = \frac{16}{24}d$ **Write an algebraic model.**

$4 \cdot \frac{24}{16} = \frac{24}{16} \cdot \frac{16}{24}d$ **The multiplicative inverse of $\frac{16}{24}$ is $\frac{24}{16}$.**

$\frac{\overset{1}{\cancel{4}}}{1} \cdot \frac{24}{\underset{4}{\cancel{16}}} = 1 \cdot d$ **Divide out common factor.**

$6 = d$ **Simplify.**

▶ **Answer** Four rolls of film will last 6 days.

at classzone.com

VOCABULARY

The product of a number and its multiplicative inverse is 1. You can use this fact to solve equations. This property is called the *inverse property of multiplication.*

✓ **GUIDED PRACTICE** for Example 4

9. **What If?** In Example 4, suppose you take 20 of the 24 pictures on the first day. At this rate, how many days will 5 rolls of film last?

5.4 EXERCISES

HOMEWORK KEY

★ = **STANDARDIZED TEST PRACTICE** Exs. 36, 58, 59, 60, 61, 63, and 73

◯ = **HINTS AND HOMEWORK HELP** for Exs. 9, 11, 29, 53, 57 at classzone.com

SKILL PRACTICE

1. **VOCABULARY** What is the multiplicative inverse of a number?

2. **VOCABULARY** Write the reciprocal of each of the numbers: $\frac{1}{2}, \frac{4}{7}, -8, 1\frac{1}{2}$.

DIVIDING FRACTIONS Find the quotient. Simplify if possible.

SEE EXAMPLES 1 AND 2 on p. 248 for Exs. 3–14

3. $\frac{3}{4} \div \frac{1}{8}$
4. $\frac{11}{12} \div \frac{11}{16}$
5. $\frac{5}{6} \div \left(-\frac{1}{3}\right)$
6. $-\frac{7}{10} \div \frac{4}{5}$
7. $\frac{4}{9} \div \frac{4}{7}$
8. $-\frac{3}{8} \div \frac{7}{12}$
9. $\frac{9}{14} \div \left(-\frac{3}{26}\right)$
10. $-\frac{21}{22} \div \frac{-7}{11}$
11. $-\frac{5}{6} \div (-2)$
12. $\frac{2}{3} \div 3$
13. $\frac{3}{5} \div (-4)$
14. $-\frac{8}{5} \div 12$

SEE EXAMPLES 1 AND 2
on p. 248
for Exs. 15–23

15. **ERROR ANALYSIS** Describe and correct the error made in dividing the fractions.

$$\times \quad -\frac{3}{10} \div \left(-\frac{4}{5}\right) = \frac{\overset{-2}{\cancel{-10}}}{3} \cdot \frac{-4}{\underset{1}{\cancel{5}}} = \frac{8}{3}, \text{ or } 2\frac{2}{3}$$

MENTAL MATH Use mental math to find the quotient.

16. $\frac{1}{2} \div 3$
17. $4 \div \frac{1}{2}$
18. $1 \div \frac{4}{7}$
19. $\frac{2}{3} \div \frac{3}{2}$
20. $9 \div \frac{1}{3}$
21. $\frac{5}{6} \div \frac{6}{5}$
22. $6 \div \frac{2}{3}$
23. $10 \div \frac{1}{10}$

DIVIDING MIXED NUMBERS Find the quotient. Simplify if possible.

SEE EXAMPLE 3
on p. 248
for Exs. 24–35

24. $5\frac{1}{4} \div 2\frac{1}{3}$
25. $12\frac{1}{7} \div 5\frac{5}{6}$
26. $7\frac{7}{8} \div \left(-2\frac{1}{4}\right)$
27. $-22\frac{2}{3} \div 3\frac{1}{5}$
28. $(-8) \div -9\frac{3}{5}$
29. $8\frac{4}{13} \div 6\frac{3}{4}$
30. $1\frac{5}{7} \div (-6)$
31. $15 \div 4\frac{1}{6}$
32. $2 \div 1\frac{1}{3}$
33. $6\frac{4}{7} \div (-4)$
34. $13\frac{1}{6} \div \frac{2}{5}$
35. $-9\frac{5}{6} \div 1\frac{2}{3}$

SEE EXAMPLE 4
on p. 249
for Ex. 36

36. ★ **MULTIPLE CHOICE** By what do you multiply each side to solve the equation $\frac{5}{6}a = -15$?

(A) $\frac{5}{6}$ (B) $\frac{6}{5}$ (C) $\frac{-1}{15}$ (D) -15

INTERPRETING MODELS Write and evaluate the division expression illustrated by the model.

37. 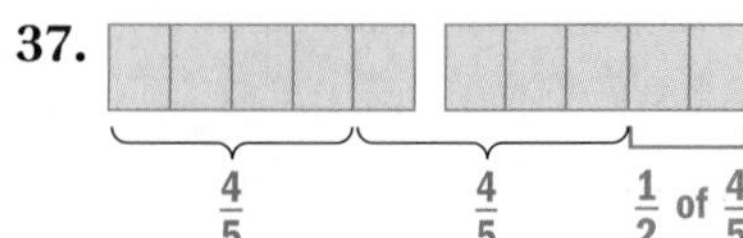

38. 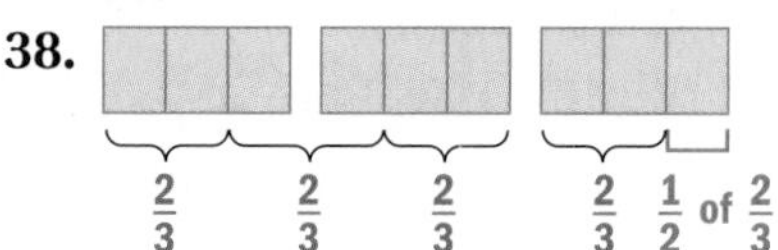

DRAWING MODELS Draw a model to show how to divide the fractions.

39. $3 \div \frac{1}{2}$
40. $2 \div \frac{2}{3}$
41. $5 \div \frac{2}{5}$
42. $4 \div \frac{3}{4}$

xy **ALGEBRA Solve the equation.**

SEE EXAMPLE 4
on p. 249
for Ex. 43–50

43. $\frac{3}{4}a = 15$
44. $\frac{7}{10}b = 28$
45. $-\frac{9}{17}r = 3$
46. $-11 = -9\frac{1}{6}h$
47. $\frac{-8}{11}k = -48$
48. $\frac{2}{5}m = -18$
49. $42 = -5\frac{1}{4}p$
50. $9 = \frac{-9}{10}t$

51. **REASONING** Juan says, "To divide a fraction by another fraction, rewrite the fractions with common denominators. Then use the formula $\frac{a}{c} \div \frac{b}{c} = \frac{a}{b}$." Does Juan's method work? *Explain* your reasoning.

52. **CHALLENGE** Find the quotient. Then go back and divide the numerators across and divide the denominators across in the original problem. Make and prove a generalization based on the results.

a. $\frac{10}{21} \div \frac{2}{3}$
b. $\frac{9}{20} \div \frac{3}{4}$
c. $\frac{15}{16} \div \frac{5}{8}$
d. $\frac{24}{25} \div \frac{4}{5}$

PROBLEM SOLVING

CHOOSE AN OPERATION In Exercises 53–57, tell which operation you would use to solve the problem and why. Then solve the problem.

53. **SERVING SIZES** How many hamburgers can you make from 5 pounds of hamburger if you use $\frac{1}{4}$ pound of meat per hamburger?

54. **CD PLAYER** Your CD player runs for about $6\frac{1}{2}$ hours on new batteries. The average length of the CDs in your collection is about $\frac{5}{6}$ hour. How many CDs can you expect to listen to using one new set of batteries?

55. **TRIPLE JUMP** Jasmine did the triple jump in gym class. What total distance did she cover?

56. **BOOKSHELVES** You have 4 bookshelves, each $2\frac{1}{3}$ feet wide. How many feet of wall space will all 4 take up if they are placed end to end?

57. **FARMING** You have 6 chickens and each chicken eats about 85 pounds of feed per year. How many pounds of feed will they eat in $1\frac{1}{2}$ years?

58. ★ **EXTENDED RESPONSE** Haley has a summer job at which she normally works $7\frac{1}{2}$ hours a day, 3 days per week. She plans to work for 7 weeks.

    a. Haley earns $180 per week. How much does she earn per hour?

    b. How much will Haley earn weekly if she works an extra 3 hour shift?

    c. How many extra 3 hour shifts does Haley need to work in order to earn a total of $1356 for the summer? *Explain* how you found your answer.

59. ★ **WRITING** *Explain* how to find the reciprocal of a positive fraction and the reciprocal of a negative fraction.

60. ★ **MULTIPLE CHOICE** Use the formula $C = (F - 32) \div \frac{9}{5}$. What is 77°F in degrees Celsius?

    (A) 20°C (B) 25°C (C) 30°C (D) 81°C

61. ★ **SHORT RESPONSE** You are creating a board game. You want to cut square game pieces that measure $1\frac{1}{4}$ inches on each side from a piece of paper that measures $8\frac{1}{2}$ inches by 11 inches. How many game pieces can you cut from the paper? How many square inches of paper are left over? *Explain* how you found your answer.

62. **ENROLLMENT** Two fifths of the students in your school, which is 270 students, are taking an art class. How many students are in your school? *Explain* how you got your answer.

63. ★ **OPEN-ENDED MATH** *Describe* a real-world situation that can be modeled by the equation $\frac{1}{2}\left(\frac{4}{9}x\right) = 28$. Then solve the equation.

64. **CHALLENGE** Students were asked whether they preferred watching fall, winter, or spring school sports. Then they were asked to choose their favorite sport from their preferred season. One third of the students chose fall sports. Of those students, two sevenths chose soccer. One half of the students chose spring sports. Of those students, three fifths chose baseball. The number of students who chose baseball was how many times the number who chose soccer?

MIXED REVIEW

Get-Ready

Prepare for Lesson 5.5 in Exs. 65–68

Copy and complete the statement with <, >, or =. *(p. 198)*

65. $3\frac{1}{2} \underline{?} \frac{11}{4}$ 66. $\frac{21}{4} \underline{?} 5\frac{1}{4}$ 67. $2\frac{2}{5} \underline{?} \frac{8}{3}$ 68. $\frac{44}{3} \underline{?} 14\frac{5}{12}$

Simplify the variable expression. *(p. 187)*

69. $\frac{9x^2}{27x}$ 70. $\frac{24y^4}{15y^2}$ 71. $\frac{14x^3y}{18xy^3}$ 72. $\frac{54yz^2}{81xz^2}$

73. ★ **MULTIPLE CHOICE** What is the product of $6\frac{1}{2}$ and $3\frac{3}{4}$? *(p. 243)*

Ⓐ $9\frac{3}{8}$ Ⓑ $18\frac{3}{8}$ Ⓒ $19\frac{1}{4}$ Ⓓ $24\frac{3}{8}$

QUIZ *for Lessons 5.1–5.4*

Evaluate the expression. *(pp. 233, 238)*

1. $1\frac{5}{8} - \frac{7}{8}$ 2. $-\frac{4}{9} + 3\frac{5}{9}$ 3. $\frac{x}{12} + \frac{5x}{12}$ 4. $\frac{4}{9} - \frac{8}{9} + \frac{5}{9}$

5. $\frac{2}{3} + \frac{9}{6}$ 6. $\frac{6y}{21} - \frac{2y}{7}$ 7. $-5\frac{3}{4} - 2\frac{1}{3}$ 8. $\frac{3}{10} + 4\frac{2}{5} - 1\frac{1}{2}$

9. **RECIPE** A recipe uses $4\frac{2}{3}$ cups of flour. Another recipe uses $4\frac{1}{4}$ cups. You have 9 cups of flour. Can you make both recipes? *Explain.* *(p. 238)*

Find the product or quotient. *(pp. 243, 247)*

10. $\frac{7}{12} \cdot \frac{8}{21}$ 11. $-\frac{11}{12} \cdot \left(-\frac{3}{10}\right)$ 12. $-\frac{14}{5} \cdot 2\frac{6}{7}$ 13. $1\frac{1}{8} \cdot (-3)$

14. $\frac{1}{2} \div \frac{5}{6}$ 15. $\frac{4}{9} \div 8$ 16. $-\frac{4}{5} \div \frac{3}{2}$ 17. $-1\frac{3}{4} \div \left(-\frac{7}{12}\right)$

18. **BIOLOGY** An average human hair grows about $\frac{1}{2}$ inch per month. How much does a human hair grow in $3\frac{1}{2}$ months? *(p. 243)*

Technology **ACTIVITY** *Use after Lesson 5.4*

GOAL
Use a fraction calculator to evaluate expressions with fractions.

5.4 Operations with Fractions

You can use a calculator to evaluate expressions with fractions. First, set your calculator to display the answers as fractions or mixed numbers in simplest form.

Press 2nd [FracMode]. Select *A⌴b/c* and press = to set the calculator to mixed number mode.

Press 2nd [FracMode]. Select *Auto* and press = to set the calculator to automatically simplify fractions.

EXPLORE **Use a calculator to evaluate the expression.**

		Keystrokes	Display	Answer
a.	$\frac{2}{3} - 4\frac{6}{7}$	2 / 3 − 4 UNIT 6 / 7 =	−4⌴4/21	$-4\frac{4}{21}$
b.	$-\frac{5}{17} \cdot \left(-\frac{8}{35}\right)$	(−) 5 / 17 × (−) 8 / 35 =	8/119	$\frac{8}{119}$
c.	$\frac{3}{10} \div \left(-1\frac{4}{5}\right)$	3 / 10 ÷ (−) 1 UNIT 4 / 5 =	−1/6	$-\frac{1}{6}$

PRACTICE **Use a calculator to evaluate the expression.**

1. $\frac{5}{11} + \frac{2}{5}$

2. $3\frac{1}{4} + \left(-\frac{6}{7}\right)$

3. $7\frac{1}{2} - 6\frac{5}{6}$

4. $\frac{2}{5} - \frac{2}{3}$

5. $\frac{7}{9} \cdot 1\frac{1}{3}$

6. $\frac{2}{5} \cdot \left(-\frac{3}{4}\right)$

7. $\frac{4}{7} \cdot \frac{1}{2}$

8. $2\frac{2}{3} \cdot \left(-\frac{1}{4}\right)$

9. $9\frac{4}{5} \div \frac{7}{8}$

10. $-10\frac{2}{13} \div \left(-3\frac{1}{3}\right)$

11. $1\frac{7}{9} \div \frac{1}{3}$

12. $\frac{5}{8} \div \left(-\frac{1}{7}\right)$

13. **PAPER DRIVE** A community center's members are having a newspaper drive. Their goal is to collect 1000 pounds of newspaper to be recycled. They have already collected $625\frac{3}{8}$ pounds. How many more pounds do they need to reach their goal?

14. **CAR CARE** Rosa's car needs $4\frac{1}{4}$ quarts of oil to run properly. She notices her car has only $\frac{3}{4}$ of the amount of oil that it needs. How much oil should she add for her car to run properly?

MIXED REVIEW *of Problem Solving*

Lessons 5.1–5.4

1. **EXTENDED RESPONSE** Bill and T.J. are going backpacking. The recommended weight of a backpack should not exceed $\frac{1}{5}$ of the carrier's bodyweight. Bill packs $8\frac{1}{2}$ pounds of food and $13\frac{1}{2}$ pounds of equipment into an empty $2\frac{1}{4}$ pound backpack.
   - **a.** Bill weighs 100 pounds. What is the maximum recommended weight for Bill's backpack?
   - **b.** How much more does Bill's backpack weigh than is recommended?
   - **c.** T.J. weighs 130 pounds and carries a 23 pound backpack. Should he carry Bill's extra weight? *Explain.*

2. **SHORT RESPONSE** You buy a roll of ribbon 20 yards long to make gift bows. Each bow uses $1\frac{1}{2}$ yards of ribbon and each gift gets one bow. You decorate 5 gifts. How many bows can you make with the ribbon you have left? *Explain* your reasoning.

3. **SHORT RESPONSE** A recipe for making rolls calls for $5\frac{2}{3}$ cups of flour. Each batch of the recipe makes $3\frac{1}{2}$ dozen rolls. How many dozen rolls can you make with 17 cups of flour? *Explain.*

4. **SHORT RESPONSE** You divide the number of hours in a feature length film by a fraction that is between zero and one. Will the result be *less than, equal to,* or *greater than* the original number of hours? *Explain.*

5. **MULTI-STEP PROBLEM** Anna takes $\frac{1}{6}$ of the 24 beads in a bowl. Then John takes 2 beads. Lena takes $\frac{1}{9}$ of what Anna and John left. Dawn takes $\frac{1}{4}$ of what Lena left, and then Jamal takes 5 beads.
   - **a.** How many beads did each person take?
   - **b.** What fraction of the original beads is left in the bowl?

6. **OPEN-ENDED** Find a fraction and a mixed number whose sum is greater than 1, whose product is less than 1, and whose difference is less than $\frac{1}{2}$.

7. **GRIDDED ANSWER** Two sevenths of the students in your school, or 400 students, have a part-time job. How many students in your school do *not* have a part-time job?

8. **EXTENDED RESPONSE** A fitness trail is broken into five segments, as shown below. You run the first segment of the trail, and walk the next. You continue to alternate between running and walking until you finish the trail.

   - **a.** Find the length of the entire fitness trail.
   - **b.** What fraction of the fitness trail do you run?
   - **c.** You run at a constant rate of 8 miles per hour and walk at a constant rate of 4 miles per hour. Can you complete the fitness trail in less than an hour? *Explain* your reasoning.

5.5 Fractions and Decimals

Before You divided whole numbers.

Now You'll write fractions as decimals and decimals as fractions.

Why? So you can compare lengths, as with caterpillars in Ex. 57.

KEY VOCABULARY

- **rational number,** *p. 255*
- **terminating decimal,** *p. 255*
- **repeating decimal,** *p. 255*

A **rational number** is a number that can be written as a quotient $\frac{a}{b}$, where a and b are integers and $b \neq 0$. The diagram below shows how rational numbers, integers, and whole numbers are related.

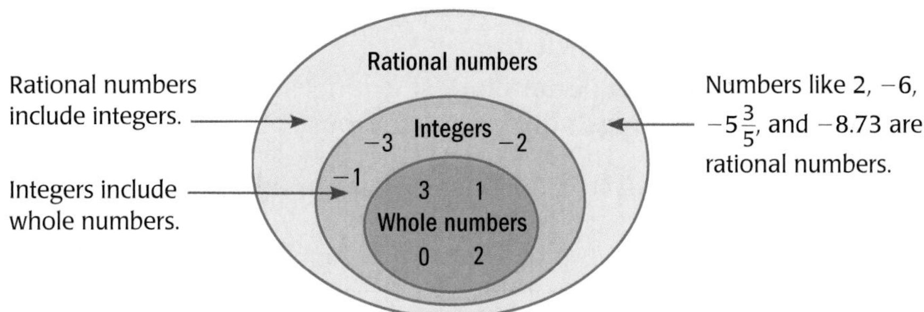
Rational numbers include integers.
Integers include whole numbers.
Rational numbers
Integers
−3
−2
−1
3
1
Whole numbers
0
2
Numbers like 2, −6, $-5\frac{3}{5}$, and −8.73 are rational numbers.

To write any rational number $\frac{a}{b}$ as a decimal, divide a by b. If the quotient has a remainder of zero, the result is a **terminating decimal**. If the quotient has a digit or group of digits that repeats without end, the result is a **repeating decimal**.

EXAMPLE 1 Writing Fractions as Decimals

Write the fraction as a decimal.

a. $\frac{5}{11} \longrightarrow 11\overline{)5.0000\ldots}$

$$\begin{array}{r} 0.4545\ldots \\ 11\overline{)5.0000\ldots} \\ \underline{4\,4} \\ 60 \\ \underline{55} \\ 50 \\ \underline{44} \\ 60 \\ \underline{55} \end{array}$$

← Repeating decimal

▶ **Answer** $\frac{5}{11} = 0.4545\ldots = 0.\overline{45}$

b. $\frac{7}{20} \longrightarrow 20\overline{)7.00}$

$$\begin{array}{r} 0.35 \\ 20\overline{)7.00} \\ \underline{6\,0} \\ 1\,00 \\ \underline{1\,00} \\ 0 \end{array}$$

← Terminating decimal

▶ **Answer** $\frac{7}{20} = 0.35$

WRITE REPEATING DECIMALS

You can use an ellipsis or an overbar to show that one or more digits repeat.

$0.333\ldots = 0.\overline{3}$

GUIDED PRACTICE for Example 1

1. Write $\frac{8}{25}$ as a decimal.

2. Write $\frac{1}{6}$ as a decimal.

EXAMPLE 2 Ordering Rational Numbers

Indigo bunting

Biology The table lists the mean lengths of five species of finches. Order the finch species from shortest to longest.

Finch species	House Finch	Indigo Bunting	Lazuli Bunting	Painted Bunting	Purple Finch
Length (inches)	$5\frac{5}{8}$	5.5	$5\frac{7}{16}$	5.25	$5\frac{3}{4}$

SOLUTION

Write all of the lengths as decimals. The **ones** digits are all the same, so order according to the **tenths** digits.

$5\frac{5}{8} = \mathbf{5.625}$ **5.5** $5\frac{7}{16} = \mathbf{5.4375}$ **5.25** $5\frac{3}{4} = \mathbf{5.75}$

KNOW COMMON CONVERSIONS
With practice, you'll recognize common equivalent fractions and decimals. For a table of these pairs, see page 820.

▶ **Answer** From shortest to longest the species are Painted Bunting, Lazuli Bunting, Indigo Bunting, House Finch, and Purple Finch.

Check Graph the finches' lengths on a number line.

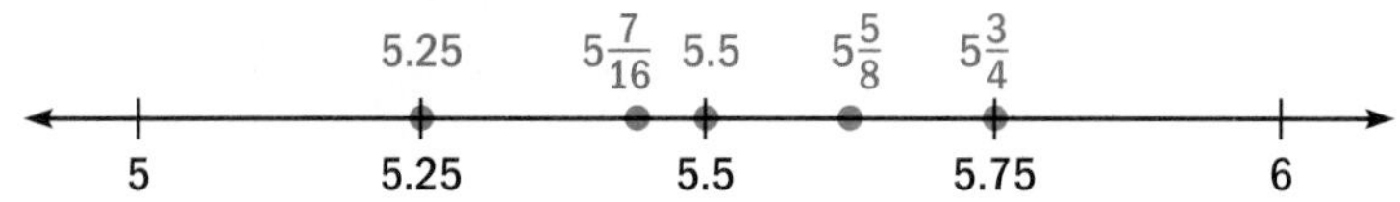

These lengths, from left to right, correspond to the answer.

✓ GUIDED PRACTICE for Example 2

Order the numbers from least to greatest.

3. $0.51, \frac{3}{5}, \frac{11}{20}, \frac{2}{3}, 0.62$

4. $-1\frac{1}{8}, -1\frac{3}{7}, -1.1, -1.43, -1\frac{4}{15}$

Terminating Decimals To write a terminating decimal as a fraction or mixed number, use the place value of the decimal's last digit as the denominator. For example, write 0.37 as $\frac{37}{100}$ because 7 is in the hundredths' place.

EXAMPLE 3 Writing Terminating Decimals as Fractions

REVIEW PLACE VALUE
Need help with place value? See the Skills Review Handbook, p. 759.

Write the decimal as a fraction or mixed number in simplest form.

a. $0.4 = \frac{4}{10}$ ← **4 is in the tenths' place.**

$= \frac{2}{5}$ **Simplify.**

b. $-1.905 = -1\frac{905}{1000}$ ← **5 is in the thousandths' place.**

$= -1\frac{\overset{181}{\cancel{905}}}{\underset{200}{\cancel{1000}}}$

$= -1\frac{181}{200}$ **Simplify.**

Repeating Decimals To write a repeating decimal as a fraction or mixed number, let the decimal equal x. Then form an equivalent equation by multiplying both sides of the equation by 10^n, where n is the number of repeating digits. Then subtract the equations.

EXAMPLE 4 Writing Repeating Decimals as Fractions

TAKE NOTES
You may wish to copy examples into your notebook that show writing repeating decimals as fractions. Include examples with one, two, and three repeating digits.

STEP 1 **Write** $0.\overline{48}$ as a fraction by first letting $x = 0.\overline{48}$ or $0.484848\ldots$.

STEP 2 **Multiply** by 10^2, or 100, because the number has 2 repeating digits. You get $100x = 48.\overline{48}$, or $48.484848\ldots$.

STEP 3 **Subtract** x from $100x$.

$$\begin{array}{r} 100x = 48.484848\ldots \\ -\quad x = 0.484848\ldots \\ \hline 99x = 48.000000\ldots \end{array}$$

STEP 4 **Solve** for x and simplify. $x = \frac{48}{99} = \frac{16}{33}$

▸ **Answer** The decimal $0.\overline{48}$ is equivalent to the fraction $\frac{16}{33}$.

✓ GUIDED PRACTICE for Examples 3 and 4

Write the decimal as a fraction or mixed number.

5. 0.62 **6.** −2.45 **7.** $-0.\overline{7}$ **8.** $0.\overline{36}$

5.5 EXERCISES

HOMEWORK KEY
★ = **STANDARDIZED TEST PRACTICE** Exs. 55, 58, 61, 62, and 69

○ = **HINTS AND HOMEWORK HELP** for Exs. 13, 15, 27, 35, 55 at classzone.com

SKILL PRACTICE

VOCABULARY **Tell whether the number is included in each of the following number sets: *rational number, integer, whole number.***

1. 0 **2.** 0.55 **3.** −14 **4.** $0.\overline{3}$

FRACTIONS AS DECIMALS **Write the fraction or mixed number as a decimal.**

SEE EXAMPLE 1 on p. 255 for Exs. 5–17

5. $\frac{3}{4}$ **6.** $-\frac{1}{9}$ **7.** $-\frac{12}{25}$ **8.** $\frac{7}{12}$

9. $-\frac{4}{25}$ **10.** $\frac{27}{50}$ **11.** $3\frac{11}{16}$ **12.** $-4\frac{33}{80}$

13. $-\frac{14}{33}$ **14.** $\frac{27}{44}$ **15.** $6\frac{8}{15}$ **16.** $-14\frac{7}{11}$

17. ERROR ANALYSIS Describe and correct the error made in writing the mixed number as a decimal.

✗ $2\frac{3}{10} = 2.03$

SEE EXAMPLE 2 on p. 256 for Exs. 18–28

COMPARING NUMBERS Complete the statement using <, >, or =.

18. $1.1 \underline{?} 1.09$ **19.** $-4.29 \underline{?} -4.3$ **20.** $-\frac{7}{15} \underline{?} -\frac{3}{8}$ **21.** $-\frac{11}{20} \underline{?} -\frac{5}{9}$

22. $\frac{11}{18} \underline{?} 0.6\overline{1}$ **23.** $0.857 \underline{?} \frac{6}{7}$ **24.** $-0.71 \underline{?} -\frac{17}{24}$ **25.** $-\frac{23}{30} \underline{?} -0.7\overline{6}$

ORDERING NUMBERS Order the numbers from least to greatest.

26. $7\frac{4}{5}, 7\frac{2}{3}, 7.6, 7.71, 7\frac{8}{21}$ **(27.)** $0.1, \frac{5}{6}, \frac{3}{10}, -\frac{2}{7}, -0.4$ **28.** $9\frac{3}{4}, 9.74, 9\frac{5}{7}, 9.72, 9\frac{9}{13}$

SEE EXAMPLES 3 AND 4 on pp. 256–257 for Exs. 29–44

DECIMALS AS FRACTIONS Write the decimal as a fraction or mixed number.

29. 0.6 **30.** -6.4 **31.** 0.48 **32.** -2.79

33. 0.365 **34.** 7.253 **(35.)** -5.0032 **36.** -0.0012

37. $0.\overline{8}$ **38.** $0.\overline{53}$ **39.** $0.\overline{21}$ **40.** $0.\overline{6}$

41. $0.\overline{635}$ **42.** $-0.\overline{187}$ **43.** $-0.1\overline{5}$ **44.** $4.0\overline{25}$

ORDERING EXPRESSIONS Order the values from greatest to least.

45. $1.21, \left(\frac{1}{3}\right)^3, 3^{-2}, 1.\overline{21}$ **46.** $2.411, \frac{13}{5}, 2\frac{2}{5}, 2.4\overline{1}$ **47.** $\left(\frac{1}{5}\right)^2, 0.\overline{4}, \frac{3}{7}, 4^{-2}$

48. $-3.\overline{4}, -3.4\overline{2}, \left(\frac{1}{3}\right)^{-1}, -3\frac{2}{5}$ **49.** $2^{-4}, \frac{-1}{15}, -0.\overline{6}, 0.66$ **50.** $\left(\frac{2}{3}\right)^{-2}, -2.2, -2.\overline{25}, \frac{-9}{4}$

51. REASONING In the following expressions, $x > 0$. Order the expressions from least to greatest. *Explain* your reasoning.

$$x, \frac{x}{5}, \frac{x}{3}, \frac{x}{7}, \frac{x}{8}, \frac{x}{6}, \frac{x}{2}, \frac{x}{4}$$

CHALLENGE Solve the equation.

52. $\frac{y}{15} = 2.\overline{45}$ **53.** $\frac{x}{12} = 0.41\overline{6}$ **54.** $\frac{z}{20} = 0.\overline{27}$

PROBLEM SOLVING

SEE EXAMPLE 1 on p. 255 for Exs. 55–56

(55.) ★ **MULTIPLE CHOICE** In a class, $\frac{22}{25}$ of the students are right-handed. What is another way to express this number?

Ⓐ 0.22 Ⓑ 0.25 Ⓒ 0.47 Ⓓ 0.88

56. STOCK LISTINGS The New York Stock Exchange once used fractions to list the values of its stocks. It switched to decimals in 2001. Write the following stock prices as decimals rounded to the nearest cent.

$$\$5\frac{1}{4}, \$44\frac{1}{2}, \$53\frac{3}{8}, \$17\frac{7}{16}$$

SEE EXAMPLES 1 AND 2 on pp. 255–256 for Ex. 57

57. CATERPILLARS Write the following lengths of caterpillars in order from shortest to longest. Express the lengths as decimals, in inches. (*Hint:* Convert from feet to inches first.)

$$1\frac{7}{8} \text{ inches}, \frac{3}{20} \text{ foot}, 2\frac{1}{9} \text{ inches}, \frac{7}{40} \text{ foot}$$

58. ★ **WRITING** Lake Superior has a surface area of about 32,000 square miles. Approximately what fraction of the 182,000 square miles of U.S. water surface area is this? Write this fraction as a decimal. *Explain* how you can use estimation to check that the answer is reasonable.

Lake Superior

59. **NUMBER SENSE** Is the number 0.1010010001 . . . a rational number? *Explain.*

60. **LOOK FOR A PATTERN** Write the fractions $\frac{1}{11}$, $\frac{2}{11}$, and $\frac{3}{11}$ as decimals. *Predict* the decimal forms of $\frac{4}{11}$ and $\frac{5}{11}$ using your results. Check your predictions.

61. ★ **EXTENDED RESPONSE** The table below lists the fraction of 1200 students in a survey that named each breakfast food as their favorite.

Breakfast food	bagels	bacon	eggs	cereal	pancakes
Fraction of students	$\frac{1}{8}$	$\frac{1}{12}$	$\frac{3}{16}$	$\frac{1}{4}$	$\frac{3}{25}$

a. Write each fraction as a decimal and order the foods from most popular to least popular.

b. How many more students picked the most popular food than the least popular food? *Explain* how you found your answer.

c. How many of the 1200 students did not choose any of the foods listed?

62. ★ **OPEN-ENDED MATH** Find a rational number between $-\frac{1}{64}$ and $-\frac{1}{63}$. Write your answer as a decimal and as a fraction.

63. **CHALLENGE** At the end of a race, all of the runners' times are posted as decimals rounded to the nearest thousandth of an hour. Kim finished the race in 1 hour, 22 minutes, and 34 seconds. What was Kim's posted time? If no two runners finished at the same time, how many runners could have the same *posted* time as Kim? *Explain.*

MIXED REVIEW

Prepare for Lesson 5.6 in Exs. 64–67

Estimate the sum or difference. ***(p. 766)***

64. 129 + 42   65. 457 + 304   66. 91 − 28   67. 217 − 188

CHOOSE A STRATEGY Use a strategy from the list to solve the following problem. *Explain* your choice.

68. You are racing with Al, Sue, and Kim. In how many orders can you and your friends finish the race?

Problem Solving Strategies
- Draw a Diagram *(p. 787)*
- Guess, Check, and Revise *(p. 788)*
- Make a List *(p. 790)*

69. ★ **MULTIPLE CHOICE** Solve $4x = 24$ using mental math. ***(p. 26)***

(A) 6   (B) 8   (C) 20   (D) 96

5.6 Adding and Subtracting Decimals

Before	You added and subtracted fractions.
Now	You'll add and subtract decimals.
Why?	So you can compare spending, as in Example 1.

KEY VOCABULARY
- **front-end estimation,** *p. 261*

You can use a vertical format to add or subtract decimals. Begin by lining up the decimal points. Then add or subtract as with whole numbers. Be sure to include the decimal point in your answer.

EXAMPLE 1 Adding and Subtracting Decimals

Dancing The table shows the amounts of money (in billions of dollars) that people in the United States spent on dance studios, schools, and halls. How much was spent in 1995 and 1996? How much more was spent in 1998 than in 1997?

Money Spent on Dancing

Year	Dollars (billions)
1994	0.906
1995	0.947
1996	1.046
1997	1.08
1998	1.138

SOLUTION

a. To find how many billions of dollars were spent in 1995 and 1996, add the values from the table for 1995 and 1996.

$$\begin{array}{r} \overset{1}{0.947} \\ +1.046 \\ \hline 1.993 \end{array}$$

▶ **Answer** In 1995 and 1996, \$1.993 billion was spent.

b. To find how much more was spent in 1998 than in 1997, subtract the value for 1997 from the value for 1998.

$$\begin{array}{r} 1.138 \\ -1.080 \\ \hline 0.058 \end{array}$$

Use a zero as a placeholder.

▶ **Answer** In 1998, \$0.058 billion more was spent than in 1997.

ADD AND SUBTRACT INTEGERS
Need help adding and subtracting integers? See Lessons 2.2 and 2.3.

In Chapter 2, you learned rules for adding and subtracting positive and negative integers. You can apply the same rules to adding and subtracting positive and negative decimals.

✓ GUIDED PRACTICE for Example 1

Find the sum or difference.

1. $-12.5 + (-4.55)$ **2.** $8.93 + 0.367$ **3.** $7.624 + (-0.05)$

4. $8.91 - 2.745$ **5.** $-5.3 - 11.49$ **6.** $5.376 - (-0.8)$

EXAMPLE 2 Solving Equations with Decimals

a. $y - 1.537 = 6.48$ — Original equation

$y - 1.537 + 1.537 = 6.48 + 1.537$ — Add 1.537 to each side.

$y = 8.017$ — Simplify.

b. $x + (-0.34) = 4.27$ — Original equation

$x + (-0.34) + 0.34 = 4.27 + 0.34$ — Add 0.34 to each side.

$x = 4.61$ — Simplify.

Estimating You can estimate sums using **front-end estimation**. Add the front-end digits to get a low estimate. Then use the remaining digits to adjust the sum to a closer estimate.

EXAMPLE 3 Using Front-End Estimation

Theater You want to estimate the cost of supplies for a play. Is the cost of the items shown (excluding tax) more or less than your $50 budget?

Play supplies	*Cost*
cowboy hat	$18.97
cotton fabric	$9.49
rope	$3.49
safety pins	$2.19
picnic basket	$16.77

SOLUTION

Use front-end estimation.

STEP 1 **Add** the front-end digits: the dollars.

$18.97
$9.49
$3.49
$2.19
$16.77
$48

STEP 2 **Estimate** the sum of the remaining digits: the cents.

$18.97 → $1
$9.49 and $3.49 → $1
$2.19 and $16.77 → $1
$3

STEP 3 **Add** the results.

$48
+ $3
$51

Answer The cost of the items is more than your $50 budget.

GUIDED PRACTICE for Examples 2 and 3

Solve the equation.

7. $x + 1.38 = 2.55$ **8.** $z - 5.3 = 16.29$ **9.** $y - (-0.83) = 0.48$

10. Use front-end estimation to estimate the sum $1.95 + $7.49 + $3.50.

EXAMPLE 4 Standardized Test Practice

Temperature The Kelvin scale for temperature is used by chemists. The formula $K = C + 273.15$ is used to convert from degrees Celsius to kelvins, where C is the degrees Celsius and K is kelvins. The average human body temperature is 37° C. What is this temperature in kelvins?

Ⓐ −97 K Ⓑ 236.15 K Ⓒ 273.52 K Ⓓ 310.15 K

SOLUTION

To find the temperature in kelvins, substitute the Celsius temperature into the equation.

$K = C + 273.15$ **Original equation**

$K = 37 + 273.15$ **Substitute 37 for C.**

$K = 310.15$ **Add.**

▸ **Answer** The temperature in kelvins is 310.15 K.
The correct answer is D. Ⓐ Ⓑ Ⓒ Ⓓ

GUIDED PRACTICE for Example 4

11. What is 29°C in kelvins?

12. What is 324.15 K in degrees Celsius?

5.6 EXERCISES

HOMEWORK KEY

★ = **STANDARDIZED TEST PRACTICE** Exs. 18, 46, 47, 48, and 60

○ = **HINTS AND HOMEWORK HELP** for Exs. 9, 13, 25, 29, 45 at classzone.com

SKILL PRACTICE

1. **VOCABULARY** Copy and complete: You can get a low estimate of 13.56 + 11.42 + 25.94 by adding the front-end digits _?_, _?_, and _?_.

EVALUATING EXPRESSIONS **Find the sum or difference.**

SEE EXAMPLE 1 on p. 260 for Exs. 2–18

2. $30.193 + 7.91$
3. $2.507 + 0.586$
4. $-6.08 + 2.661$
5. $-0.37 + (-1.8)$
6. $6.8 + (-1.812)$
7. $-12.09 + 1.20$
8. $3.28 + (-4.91)$
9. 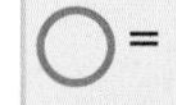 $1.46 + (-1.564)$
10. $1.57 - 9.28$
11. $68.79 - 9.18$
12. $15.7 - (-6.4)$
13. $-0.99 - 0.304$
14. $25.885 - 6.9$
15. $29.1 - (-3.05)$
16. $-4.22 - 0.807$

17. **ERROR ANALYSIS** Describe and correct the error made in the solution.

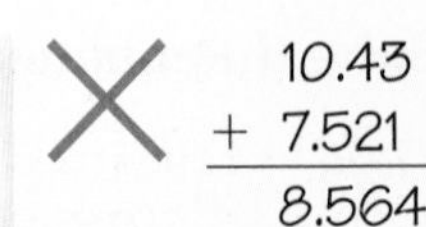

18. ★ **MULTIPLE CHOICE** An item costs \$9.87 plus sales tax of \$.49. What is the total cost of the item?

(A) \$8.38 (B) \$9.36 (C) \$9.38 (D) \$10.36

ALGEBRA Solve the equation.

SEE EXAMPLE 2 on p. 261 for Exs. 19–27

19. $x + 2.9 = 5.3$
20. $y - 4.15 = -4.26$
21. $z - (-7.7) = 13.31$
22. $y + 1.5 = 37$
23. $-2.8 + x = 4.51$
24. $10.4 = 12.46 + z$
25. $7.81 = 7.98 + y$
26. $z + (-3.19) = 5.83$
27. $x - 0.013 = -6.36$

SEE EXAMPLE 3 on p. 261 for Exs. 28–31

ESTIMATING SUMS Use front-end estimation to estimate the sum.

28. $2.32 + 6.69 + 8.50 + 4.46$
29. $10.23 + 6.98 + 9.05 + 5.80$
30. $5.62 + 4.89 + 3.44 + 9.98$
31. $23.70 + 16.12 + 5.96 + 14.18$

ALGEBRA Evaluate the expression when $a = 6.28$ and $b = -0.35$. Write your answer as a decimal.

32. $a - \frac{5}{2}$
33. $\frac{3}{8} + a$
34. $b - \frac{3}{4}$
35. $\frac{9}{20} + b$

GEOMETRY Find the perimeter of the figure.

36.

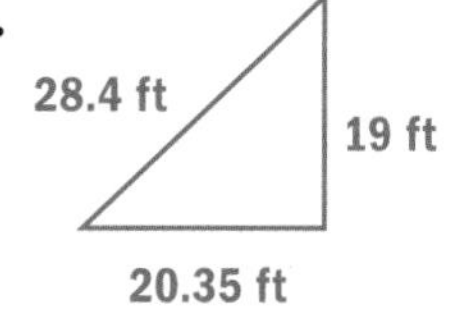

37.

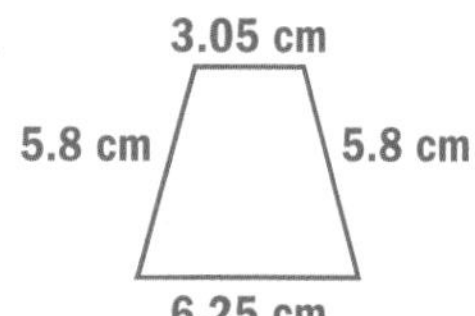

38.

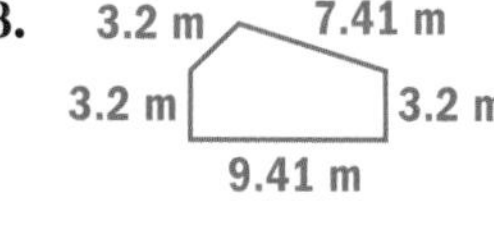

39. **GEOMETRY** Plot the following points in a coordinate plane. Then connect the points to form a rectangle and find its perimeter.

$A(1.25, 3.5)$, $B(4.25, 3.5)$, $C(4.25, 6.75)$, $D(1.25, 6.75)$

CHALLENGE Find the sum.

40. $0.\overline{67} + 0.\overline{6}$
41. $5.\overline{345} + 0.\overline{87}$
42. $1.\overline{7} + 1.\overline{876621}$
43. $3.\overline{19} + 7.\overline{91}$

PROBLEM SOLVING

44. **TRACK** You run 400 meters in 58.01 seconds. What is the difference of your time and the school record of 55.49 seconds?

45. **SHOT PUT** The world record for men's shot put is 23.12 meters. The Olympic record is 22.47 meters. The gold medal winning throw at the 2004 Summer Olympics was 21.16 meters.
    a. How much longer was the world record throw than the gold medal winning throw at the 2004 Olympics?
    b. How much longer is the Olympic record throw than the gold medal winning throw at the 2004 Olympics?

SEE EXAMPLE 4 on p. 262 for Ex. 46

46. ★ **MULTIPLE CHOICE** The formula $K = (F - 32)\frac{5}{9} + 273.15$ converts degrees Fahrenheit to kelvins. The boiling point of water is 212° F. What is this temperature in kelvins?

Ⓐ 390.93 K Ⓑ 373.15 K Ⓒ 273.15 K Ⓓ 100 K

47. ★ **SHORT RESPONSE** A city had 4.52 inches of rain in April, 5.23 inches of rain in May, and 3.41 inches of rain in June. During this three-month period, did the city have more than 12 inches of rain? *Explain* why an estimate is sufficient to answer the question.

48. ★ **WRITING** What do you know about the sum of two positive decimals that are less than 1? What do you *not* know about this sum? *Explain.*

49. **MULTI-STEP PROBLEM** Use the January bank record below. The beginning balance was $83.47.

a. Estimate the balance at the end of the month.

b. Find the exact balance.

c. After the next transaction, the new balance is $101.25. Was the transaction a deposit or withdrawal? How much was the deposit or withdrawal?

Date	Transaction	Deposit	Withdrawal
1/02	deposit	$50	
1/10	groceries		$75.35
1/16	bookstore		$12.95
1/22	deposit	$112.81	
1/29	movie rentals		$13.08
1/31	computer game		$21.98

50. **CHEMISTRY** One *mole* of hydrogen atoms has a mass of 1.0079 grams. One mole of oxygen atoms has a mass of 15.9994 grams. A mole of water is made up of 2 moles of hydrogen and 1 mole of oxygen. What is the mass of a mole of water?

51. **CHALLENGE**

a. Copy and complete the table.

b. Use the results of your table. What is another name for $0.\overline{9}$?

Fraction pair	$\frac{1}{3}, \frac{2}{3}$	$\frac{1}{6}, \frac{5}{6}$	$\frac{4}{9}, \frac{5}{9}$	$\frac{3}{11}, \frac{8}{11}$
Decimal pair	?	?	?	?
Fraction sum	?	?	?	?
Decimal sum	?	?	?	?

MIXED REVIEW

Prepare for Lesson 5.7 in Exs. 52–55

Find the product or quotient. Simplify if possible. *(pp. 243, 247)*

52. $-\frac{8}{9} \cdot \left(\frac{-5}{7}\right)$

53. $-5\frac{3}{7} \cdot \frac{21}{22}$

54. $-5 \div \left(\frac{-2}{3}\right)$

55. $6\frac{5}{12} \div 2\frac{3}{4}$

Simplify. Write the expression using only positive exponents. *(p. 208)*

56. -12^0

57. $3^{-2} \cdot 3^5$

58. $\frac{b^{-4}}{b^{10}}$

59. $\frac{32m^{-8}}{8m^2}$

60. ★ **MULTIPLE CHOICE** What is 1810 written in scientific notation? *(p. 212)*

Ⓐ 1.81×10^2 Ⓑ 1.81×10^3 Ⓒ 18.1×10^2 Ⓓ 0.181×10^4

5.7 Multiplying and Dividing Decimals

Before	You multiplied and divided integers and fractions.
Now	You'll multiply and divide decimals.
Why?	So you can find distance traveled, as in Example 1.

KEY VOCABULARY
- **leading digit,** *p. 265*

Rafting You travel downstream in a raft at a rate of about 4.3 miles per hour. How far will you travel in 2.5 hours? To answer this question, you need to multiply decimals.

KEY CONCEPT *For Your Notebook*

Multiplying Decimals

Words Multiply decimals as you do whole numbers. Then place the decimal point. The number of decimal places in the product is the total number of decimal places in the factors.

Numbers 2.25 × 8.9 = 20.025
2 places, 1 place, 3 places

EXAMPLE 1 Multiplying Decimals

To find how far you travel in the rafting problem above, substitute the given values into the distance formula: distance = rate • time.

$d = rt$

$= \mathbf{4.3 \cdot 2.5}$

$= 10.75$

$$\begin{array}{rl} 4.3 & \text{1 decimal place} \\ \times\ 2.5 & +\ \text{1 decimal place} \\ \hline 215 & \\ 86\ & \\ \hline 10.75 & \text{2 decimal places} \end{array}$$

▶ **Answer** You will travel about 10.75 miles.

Check A number's **leading digit** is its leftmost nonzero digit. To check for reasonableness, round each factor to its leading digit and multiply.

4.3 • 2.5 **Round factors to leading digit.** ➜ 4 • 3 = 12

GUIDED PRACTICE for Example 1

Find the product. Check that the answer is reasonable.

1. −7.39 • 2.1 **2.** 19.62 • 5.07 **3.** 1.13 • 0.04 **4.** −0.85 • (−8)

KEY CONCEPT — For Your Notebook

Dividing Decimals

Words When you divide by a decimal, multiply both the divisor and the dividend by the power of ten that will make the divisor an integer. Then divide.

Numbers $2.75\overline{)15.125}$ **Multiply by 100.** → $\begin{array}{r} 5.5 \\ 2.75\overline{)1512.5} \end{array}$

EXAMPLE 2 Dividing Decimals

To find the quotient 60.102 ÷ 6.3, multiply the divisor and dividend by 10. Move the decimal points 1 place to the right.

$6.3\overline{)60.102}$ **Move decimal points.** → $6.3\overline{)601.02}$

$\begin{array}{r} 9.54 \\ 63\overline{)601.02} \end{array}$ Then divide.

AVOID ERRORS
When checking your work, remember to use the *original* divisor, *not* the divisor you used after moving the decimal points.

Check To check that the quotient is reasonable, round the quotient and the divisor to the leading digit. Then multiply and compare to the dividend.

$9.54 \cdot 6.3$ **Round.** → $10 \cdot 6 = 60 \approx 60.102$

Animated Math at classzone.com

EXAMPLE 3 Using Zeros as Placeholders

To find some quotients, you may need to use zeros as placeholders.

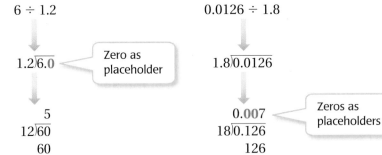

Placeholder in Dividend

$6 \div 1.2$

↓

$1.2\overline{)6.0}$ Zero as placeholder

↓

$\begin{array}{r} 5 \\ 12\overline{)60} \\ \underline{60} \\ 0 \end{array}$

Placeholder in Quotient

$0.0126 \div 1.8$

↓

$1.8\overline{)0.0126}$

↓

$\begin{array}{r} 0.007 \\ 18\overline{)0.126} \\ \underline{126} \\ 0 \end{array}$ Zeros as placeholders

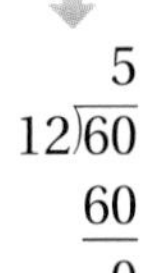

GUIDED PRACTICE for Examples 2 and 3

REVIEW DIVISION
Need help dividing negative numbers? See p. 77.

Find the quotient. Check that the answer is reasonable.

5. 1.6 ÷ 0.04
6. 0.632 ÷ 0.79
7. −13 ÷ (−0.65)
8. −4.365 ÷ (−4.5)
9. 0.3744 ÷ 1.56
10. −0.0108 ÷ 2.7

5.7 EXERCISES

HOMEWORK KEY

★ = **STANDARDIZED TEST PRACTICE** Exs. 26, 48, 49, 50, and 66

○ = **HINTS AND HOMEWORK HELP** for Exs. 3, 9, 19, 21, 47 at classzone.com

SKILL PRACTICE

1. **VOCABULARY** Copy and complete: In 0.0745, the digit "_?_" is the leading digit.

2. **VOCABULARY** Copy and complete the division problem. Use *quotient, dividend,* and *divisor* as labels.

$$\begin{array}{r} 0.8 \leftarrow \underline{?} \\ \underline{?} \rightarrow 9\overline{)7.2} \leftarrow \underline{?} \end{array}$$

MULTIPLYING AND DIVIDING DECIMALS **Find the product or quotient. Check that the answer is reasonable.**

SEE EXAMPLES 1, 2, AND 3 on pp. 265–266 for Exs. 3–24

3. $7.8 \cdot 2.6$
4. $3.75 \cdot (-0.4)$
5. $-8.2 \cdot 0.7$
6. $0.5 \div 1.25$
7. $25 \cdot 0.2$
8. $2.4 \cdot 0.3$
9. $13.2 \div 1.1$
10. $13.65 \cdot 1.1$
11. $4.8 \div 1.2$
12. $4.9 \div 0.07$
13. $-8 \div (-3.2)$
14. $5 \div (-0.1)$
15. $5.41 \cdot 0.35$
16. $4.844 \div 0.56$
17. $-0.57 \div 0.38$
18. $-2.687 \cdot (-9)$
19. $-37.41 \div 4.3$
20. $0.098 \cdot -0.55$
21. $6.025 \cdot 48.2$
22. $1.11 \div 0.925$

ERROR ANALYSIS **In Exercises 23 and 24, describe and correct the error made in evaluating the product or quotient.**

23.

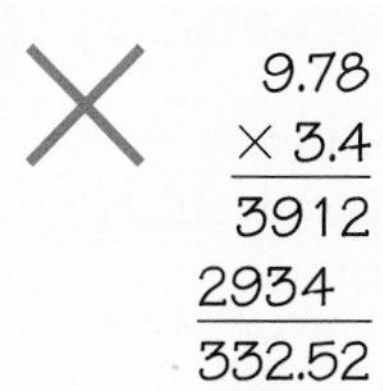

24.

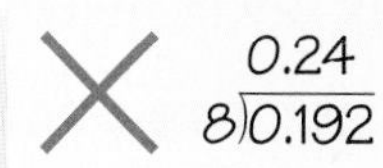

25. **WHICH ONE DOESN'T BELONG?** Which expression is *not* equivalent to the other expressions?

A. $3.5 \cdot 0.2$ **B.** $0.35 \cdot 2$ **C.** $3.5 \div 5$ **D.** $35 \div 0.5$

26. ★ **MULTIPLE CHOICE** The quotient of −0.67 and 0.42 is _?_.

Ⓐ more than 1 Ⓑ between 0 and 1 Ⓒ between 0 and −1 Ⓓ less than −1

ALGEBRA **Solve the equation.**

27. $9 = \frac{a}{-0.9}$
28. $\frac{c}{4.5} = 0.16$
29. $-2.8 = \frac{p}{6.2}$
30. $-5t = 0.085$
31. $1.2w = 0.321$
32. $-8.2y = -3.3$
33. $0.13z = -0.0544$
34. $\frac{g}{-7.2} = -0.022$
35. $-25.2z = 15.0012$

ESTIMATING QUOTIENTS **Estimate each quotient. Then copy and complete the statement using < or >.**

36. $105.4 \div 29.8$ _?_ $20.4 \div 5.1$
37. $3.8 \div (-2.1)$ _?_ $-1.8 \div 6.4$

EVALUATING EXPRESSIONS **Evaluate the expression.**

38. $3.4^3 + 5.1 \div 1.7 - 4.89$

39. $6.2 \cdot (18.77 - 6.27) + 9.1^2$

NUMBER SENSE ***Describe*** **the pattern. Then write the next two numbers.**

40. 125, 100, 80, 64, . . .

41. 1, −0.5, 0.25, −0.125, . . .

CHALLENGE **You can write the expression $\frac{1.6}{2.4}$ in rational form by multiplying by $\frac{10}{10}$, a form of 1, to get $\frac{16}{24} = \frac{2}{3}$. Write the expression as a fraction in rational form $\frac{a}{b}$, where a and b are integers, and then in simplest form. Tell by what form of 1 you multiplied.**

42. $\frac{0.5}{2}$

43. $\frac{1.75}{3.5}$

44. $\frac{0.75}{2.25}$

45. $\frac{4.8}{12}$

PROBLEM SOLVING

SEE EXAMPLE 1 on p. 265 for Ex. 46

46. GUIDED PROBLEM SOLVING A mother rhinoceros weighs 3600 pounds. Her baby weighs 0.038 of her weight. How much does the baby weigh? *Explain* why your answer is reasonable.

a. Write a verbal model to describe the problem.

b. Substitute the given values and solve.

c. Check that the answer is reasonable. Show your work.

47. LOOK FOR A PATTERN Copy and complete the table by multiplying each number in the left column by the number at the top of each other column. *Describe* the pattern.

x	1	0.1	0.01	0.001	0.0001
87	87	8.7	?	?	?
356	356	?	?	?	?
1200	?	?	?	?	?

SEE EXAMPLE 2 on p. 266 for Ex. 48

48. ★ MULTIPLE CHOICE You are buying balloons that cost \$.89 per package, including tax. You have \$14.75 to spend. How many packages of balloons can you buy?

Ⓐ 13.13 Ⓑ 16 Ⓒ 16.57 Ⓓ 17

SEE EXAMPLE 3 on p. 266 for Ex. 49

49. ★ WRITING *Explain* how 4.6 divided by 0.23 is related to 460 divided by 23. Are the quotients equal? *Explain* why or why not.

50. ★ SHORT RESPONSE You have \$75 to spend on daffodil bulbs.

a. Boxes of bulbs cost \$19.95 per box, including tax. How many boxes can you buy? Estimate to check that your answer is reasonable.

b. Individual bulbs cost \$1.20 each. How many bulbs can you buy with the money left over from purchasing the boxes of bulbs? *Explain.*

51. **REASONING** How many decimal places does 1.3^1 have? 1.3^2? 1.3^3? 1.3^7? *Explain* your reasoning.

52. **LAVA FLOWS** A lava flow is a stream of molten rock that pours from an erupting vent of a volcano. A lava flow travels 15.5 miles down a steep slope in 2.5 hours. Find the average rate at which the flow travels. Write your answer in miles per hour. *Explain* why your answer is reasonable.

53. **AIR TRAVEL** A plane travels from Boston to London in 6.25 hours, a distance of about 3285 miles. The return trip takes 7.5 hours. How many miles per hour faster is the faster speed than the slower speed? How many times as fast?

54. **POSTAL RATES** The table shows rates to mail a first class letter at one time. How much did it cost to mail a first class letter weighing 3.5 ounces?

First ounce or fraction of ounce	$.37
Each additional ounce or fraction	$.23

55. **POOLS** A rectangular deck surrounds a swimming pool on all four sides. The deck has the dimensions shown. What is the area of the water?

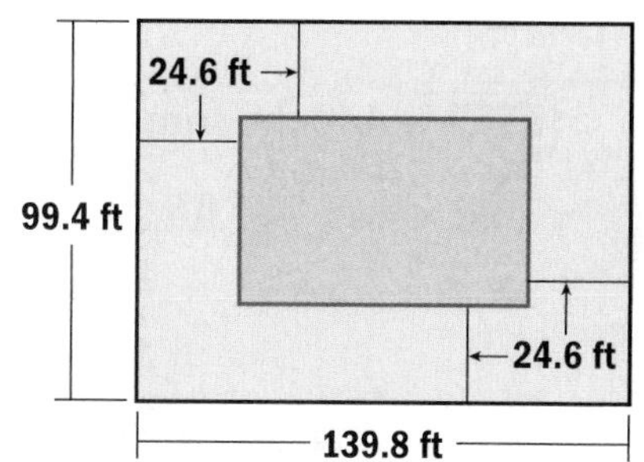

56. **CHALLENGE** One micrometer is equal to 0.001 millimeter. A bacterium is 4 micrometers wide. How many times would you have to magnify it for the bacterium to appear 1 millimeter wide?

57. **CHALLENGE** One inch is equal to 2.54 centimeters. The volume of a cube is 8 cubic inches. What is the volume of the cube in cubic centimeters? Round your answer to the nearest tenth.

MIXED REVIEW

Prepare for Lesson 5.8 in Exs. 58–61

Order the numbers from least to greatest. *(p. 255)*

58. $2.32, \frac{9}{4}, 2.5, 2\frac{3}{10}, 2, \frac{11}{5}$

59. $-5, -\frac{26}{5}, -5.1, -5.25, -4\frac{9}{10}$

60. $-\frac{9}{20}, -0.46, -\frac{3}{8}, -\frac{5}{12}, -0.4$

61. $\frac{15}{8}, 1.85, 1\frac{6}{7}, 1.79, \frac{11}{6}$

Write the number in standard form. *(p. 212)*

62. 6.89×10^9

63. 1.3×10^{-12}

64. 7.405×10^{-6}

65. 3.48×10^6

66. ★ **SHORT RESPONSE** A banana bread recipe uses 3 bananas and $\frac{1}{4}$ cup of butter. You need to make a smaller recipe because you have only 2 bananas. How much butter will you need? *Explain* your reasoning. *(p. 243)*

INVESTIGATION
Use before Lesson 5.8

GOAL
Collect and analyze data.

MATERIALS
• number cubes

5.8 Collecting and Analyzing Data

You can collect data and find a number that represents the data. The *median* is the middle value when the values are written in order. The *mode* is the value that occurs most often.

EXPLORE 1 **Collect data by rolling two number cubes to explore how often each sum occurs.**

STEP 1 **Roll** a pair of number cubes eleven times and record the results.

$3 + 2 = 5$ $4 + 4 = 8$ $6 + 6 = 12$ $1 + 2 = 3$ $1 + 6 = 7$ $2 + 1 = 3$

$5 + 3 = 8$ $4 + 1 = 5$ $1 + 5 = 6$ $2 + 6 = 8$ $2 + 2 = 4$

STEP 2 **Add** the sums together. Divide by the number of rolls to find the mean.

$$\frac{5 + 8 + 12 + 3 + 7 + 3 + 8 + 5 + 6 + 8 + 4}{11} = \frac{69}{11} \approx 6.3$$

STEP 3 **Order** the sums. Find the median and the mode.

3, 3, 4, 5, 5, 6, 7, 8, 8, 8, 12

middle number (6) most frequent number (8, 8, 8)

The median is 6, and the mode is 8.

STEP 4 **Compare** your results with the results of other groups. Which sum occurs most often?

PRACTICE **Find the mean, median, and mode of the data.**

1. 4.2, 6.1, 3.8, 4.1, 10.2, 9.6, 6.1, 7.3, 2.1, 2.4, 9.8

2. 105, 121, 42, 78, 77, 63, 108, 32, 33, 121, 64

3. $2\frac{1}{2}, 7\frac{3}{4}, 9\frac{1}{4}, 7\frac{1}{2}, 4\frac{3}{8}, 7\frac{3}{4}, 3\frac{7}{8}$

4. 56.4, 25.1, 24.3, 56.4, 48.7, 59.2, 37.9

EXPLORE 2 Collect data about the number of letters in the last name of each student in your class.

STEP 1 **Find** the shortest and longest names so you can make a frequency table.

Cho = 3
Fitzpatrick = 11

STEP 2 **Count** the number of letters in each name. Make a tally mark for each name.

Number of Letters

3	4	5	6	7	8	9	10	11
II	III	𝍸	𝍸	𝍸 I	II	I		I

$\begin{array}{r}3\\ \times 2\\ \hline\end{array}$ $\begin{array}{r}4\\ \times 3\\ \hline\end{array}$ $\begin{array}{r}5\\ \times 5\\ \hline\end{array}$ $\begin{array}{r}6\\ \times 5\\ \hline\end{array}$ $\begin{array}{r}7\\ \times 6\\ \hline\end{array}$ $\begin{array}{r}8\\ \times 2\\ \hline\end{array}$

$6 + 12 + 25 + 30 + 42 + 16 + 9 + 0 + 11 = 151$

STEP 3 **Find** the mean number of letters in the last names.

You can multiply to count the number of letters for each column. Then add the column totals.

Divide by the number of students. The mean is $151 \div 25 \approx 6$.

STEP 4 **Find** the most frequent name length. This is the mode.

Number of Letters

3	4	5	6	7	8	9	10	11
II	III	𝍸	𝍸	𝍸 I	II	I		I

The mode is 7.

STEP 5 **Decide** whether you can use the mean to describe the average length of a last name in your class. Then decide whether you can use the mode. *Explain* your choices.

PRACTICE

5. A new student whose last name has 16 letters joins your class. If you add "16" to your data, how does this affect the mean and the mode? *Explain.*

DRAW CONCLUSIONS

6. **WRITING** You are designing a form to collect data. Students will write their last names in a row of small boxes, one letter per box. How many boxes do you think the form should provide? *Explain.*

5.8 Mean, Median, and Mode

Before You used tables and graphs to analyze data sets.
Now You'll describe data sets using mean, median, mode, and range.
Why? So you can describe data, such as the location of jellyfish in Example 1.

KEY VOCABULARY
- **mean,** *p. 78*
- **median,** *p. 272*
- **mode,** *p. 272*
- **range,** *p. 273*

Three averages can be used to describe a data set. In Lesson 2.5, you learned how to find the *mean* of a data set. Investigation 5.8, on pages 270–271, explores the *median* and the *mode* of a data set. In this lesson, you will use these averages to describe data sets. You will also learn how to choose which average best represents a data set.

KEY CONCEPT *For Your Notebook*

Averages

The **mean** of a data set is the sum of the values divided by the number of values.

The **median** of a data set is the middle value when the values are written in numerical order. If a data set has an even number of values, the median is the mean of the two middle values.

The **mode** of a data set is the value that occurs most often. A data set can have no mode, one mode, or more than one mode.

EXAMPLE 1 Finding a Mean

Biology A marine biologist records the following locations of 6 deep sea jellyfish in relation to the ocean surface: −2278 feet, −1875 feet, −3210 feet, −2755 feet, −2407 feet, and −2901 feet. What is the mean location of the deep sea jellies?

$$\textbf{Mean} = \frac{-2278 + (-1875) + (-3210) + (-2755) + (-2407) + (-2901)}{6}$$

$$= \frac{-15{,}426}{6} = -2571$$

▸ **Answer** The mean location in relation to the ocean surface is −2571 feet.

GUIDED PRACTICE for Example 1

Find the mean of the data.

1. −3° C, 44° C, −11° C, 9° C, −21° C

2. $12\frac{1}{2}$ in., $14\frac{3}{4}$ in., $20\frac{1}{2}$ in., $16\frac{3}{4}$ in.

Range The **range** of a data set is the difference of the greatest value and the least value. The range measures how spread out the data are. An *outlier* is a value in a data set that is much greater or much less than the other values.

EXAMPLE 2 Finding Median, Mode, and Range

Find the median, mode(s), and range of the prices.

\$7.20, \$13.25, \$14.94, \$16.56, \$18.74, \$19.99, \$19.99, \$29.49

AVOID ERRORS
If the data are not ordered, you need to order the data to find the median.

Median: The data set has an even number of prices, so the median is the mean of the two middle values, \$16.56 and \$18.74.

$$\text{Median} = \frac{\$16.56 + \$18.74}{2} = \frac{\$35.30}{2} = \$17.65$$

Mode: The price that occurs most often is \$19.99. This is the mode.

Range: Find the difference of the greatest and the least values.

$$\text{Range} = \$29.49 - \$7.20 = \$22.29$$

EXAMPLE 3 Standardized Test Practice

Taste Test Ten people try a new cereal and rate it on a scale of 1 to 20. The ratings are shown below. Which averages best represent the data?

1, 1, 2, 2, 2, 2, 3, 3, 4, 20

Ⓐ mean and median Ⓑ mode and median

Ⓒ mean and mode Ⓓ mean, median, and mode

ELIMINATE CHOICES
By inspection, you can see that the mode is 2 and does represent the data well. So, Choice A, that does not include the mode, can be eliminated.

SOLUTION

Mean $= \frac{40}{10} = 4$

Median $= \frac{2 + 2}{2} = \frac{4}{2} = 2$

Mode: 2

▶ **Answer** Because 20 is an outlier, the mean is greater than all but two ratings. It does not represent the data well. The mode and median best represent the data. The correct answer is B. Ⓐ Ⓑ Ⓒ Ⓓ

GUIDED PRACTICE for Examples 2 and 3

Find the median, mode(s), and range of the data.

3. 14, 13, 20, 24, 15, 10, 22, 17, 18

4. 9, 7, 4, 9, 4, 10, 5, 14, 9, 4

5. What If? In Example 3, suppose another group tries the new cereal. Their ratings are: 1, 1, 1, 2, 3, 4, 4, 9, 10, 10. Which average or averages best represent the data?

5.8 EXERCISES

HOMEWORK KEY

★ = **STANDARDIZED TEST PRACTICE** Exs. 14, 33, 34, 36, 40, 45, and 57

○ = **HINTS AND HOMEWORK HELP** for Exs. 5, 11, 31, 35 at classzone.com

SKILL PRACTICE

VOCABULARY In Exercises 1–3, use the data set 6, 12, 4, 15, 10, 6, 2, and 9. Copy and complete the statement using *mean, median, mode,* or *range*.

1. The _?_ is 8.
2. The _?_ is 6.
3. The _?_ is 13.

FINDING AVERAGES AND RANGE Find the mean, median, mode(s), and range of the data.

SEE EXAMPLES 1 AND 2 on pp. 272–273 for Exs. 4–14

4. Weekly hits at a Web site: 115, 157, 289, 185, 164, 225, 185, 208
5. Distances: 16 km, 23 km, 11 km, 6 km, 15 km, 23 km, 17 km, 16 km
6. Depths of fish: −71 in., −56 in., −62 in., −44 in., −56 in., −47 in.
7. Golf scores relative to par: −2, 0, 3, 1, 0, −1, 2, −2, −3, 0, 4, 1
8. Elevations: 127 ft, −8 ft, 436 ft, 508 ft, −23 ft, 47 ft
9. Daily calories: 2000, 1872, 2112, 2255, 2080, 1795, 1977
10. Shoe lengths: $10\frac{3}{4}$ in., $9\frac{1}{2}$ in., $8\frac{7}{8}$ in., $10\frac{1}{2}$ in., $8\frac{3}{8}$ in., $10\frac{1}{2}$ in.
11. Temperatures (°F): 20°, −11°, 72°, −1°, 9°, 51°, 17°, −5°
12. Pages in a book: 156, 212, 538, 77, 388, 419, 212
13. **ERROR ANALYSIS** Describe and correct the error made in the solution.

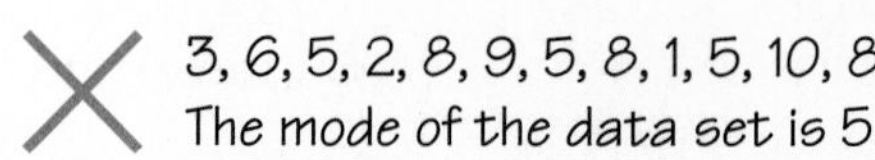

3, 6, 5, 2, 8, 9, 5, 8, 1, 5, 10, 8
The mode of the data set is 5.

14. ★ **MULTIPLE CHOICE** Which has the same value as the median of the following data set: 45, 56, 50, 43, 56, 64, 36?

    (A) mean (B) mode (C) range (D) none

CHOOSING AN AVERAGE Tell which average(s) best represent(s) the data.

SEE EXAMPLE 3 on p. 273 for Exs. 15–18

15. 23, 20, 30, 22, 24, 23, 24
16. 94, 47, 34, 45, 48, 38
17. 25, 58, 88, 74, 21, 20, 72, 22, 24
18. 124, 152, 108, 159, 116, 142, 175, 167, 119, 127, 112

EXAMINING OUTLIERS Find the mean, median, mode(s), and range of the data with and without the number(s) in red. *Describe* the effect of the red data value(s) on the averages and on the range.

19. 19, 16, 23, 35, 28, 20, 16, 36, 98, 13, 26, 29, 31
20. 58, 67, 94, 85, 78, 76, 6, 99, 100, 88, 76, 2, 82, 81, 94, 98

ALGEBRA Find the unknown number in the data set. Then find the mean, median, mode, and range, if not given.

21. 63, 52, 49, b, 68, 75 (greatest value), 57, range = 31

22. 17 (least value), 96, 54, 48, d, 27, range = 81

23. 6, 8, 14, 9, 3, c, 12, 5, median = 7.5

24. 11, z, 30, 42, 7, 39, 22, median = 28

25. 32, 18, 16, a, 23, 41, mean = 28

Animated Math at classzone.com

26. **ALGEBRA** Find the mean of $3b$, $5b$, b, $6b$, $-6b$, and $-2b$.

CHALLENGE Find a data set of five numbers with the given characteristics.

27. Mean: 11
Median: 12
Mode: 17
Range: 13

28. Mean: 16
Median: 15
Mode: 15
Range: 22

29. Mean: 5
Median: 1
Mode: −4
Range: 26

PROBLEM SOLVING

SEE EXAMPLE 1 on p. 272 for Ex. 30

30. **GUIDED PROBLEM SOLVING** Shana is training to run in a 5K race. Her practice times (in minutes and seconds) are 22:45, 21:56, 21:03, 20:33, and 20:28. Find her mean practice time.

a. Change Shana's practice times to seconds.

b. Find the sum of the practice times. Divide by the number of times.

c. Convert your answer to part (b) to minutes and seconds.

SEE EXAMPLES 1, 2, AND 3 on pp. 272–273 for Ex. 31

31. **BASEBALL** The attendance for the 2001 World Series is shown in the table below. Find the mean, median, and mode(s) of the data. Which average do you think best represents the attendance data? *Explain.*

Game	1	2	3	4	5	6	7
Attendance	49,646	49,646	55,820	55,863	56,018	49,707	49,589

32. **BASKETBALL** In basketball practice, the numbers of free throws made out of 20 shots are listed below. Find the mean, median, mode, and range of each set of data. Who is the more consistent player? *Justify* your reasoning.

Kendra: 8, 10, 9, 9, 10, 12, 10, 11

Jade: 8, 5, 9, 12, 13, 10, 7, 11

33. ★ **WRITING** You are researching the average salaries for several careers. Would you rather know the mean, median, or mode(s) of the salaries for each career? *Explain* your reasoning.

SEE EXAMPLE 3
on p. 273
for Ex. 34

34. ★ **MULTIPLE CHOICE** The scores on a 20-point quiz in math class are 8, 9, 11, 12, 14, 14, 15, 16, 17, 17, 18, and 20. Which averages best represent the data?

(A) mean and median (B) mode and median

(C) mean and mode (D) mean, median, and mode

35. **ICEBERGS** An iceberg's depth can be 3 to 9 times its height above the water surface. The image below shows the distances, in meters, below the water surface that six icebergs reach. What is the mean distance below the water surface these icebergs reach?

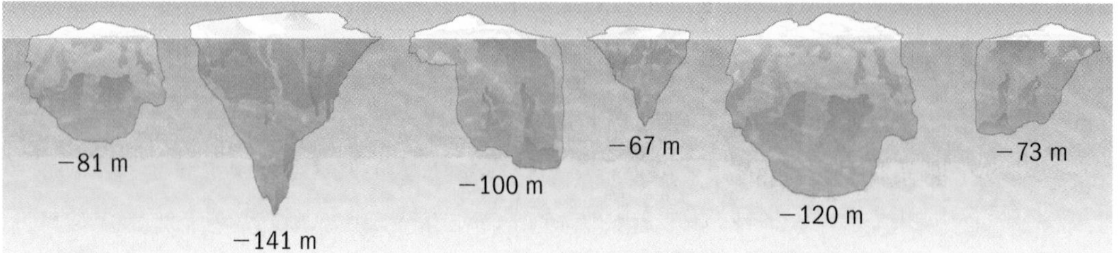

36. ★ **OPEN-ENDED MATH** Write an example of a data set whose mode is greater than its mean.

37. **COMPARE AND CONTRAST** Jerry and Roberta both find the mean of $-2a$, a, $3a$, $6a$, and $9a$ when $a = 2.5$, as shown below. *Describe* each method. How are they similar? How are they different?

Jerry

$-2a = -5 \quad a = 2.5 \quad 3a = 7.5$

$6a = 15 \quad 9a = 22.5$

$\frac{-5 + 2.5 + 7.5 + 15 + 22.5}{5} = \frac{42.5}{5}$

$= 8.5$

Roberta

$\frac{-2a + a + 3a + 6a + 9a}{5} = \frac{17a}{5}$

$= \frac{17 \cdot 2.5}{5}$

$= 8.5$

38. **BOWLING** You are bowling three games. In the first two games, you score 125 and 113 points. How many points do you need in the third game to have a mean score of 126 points?

39. **STREAMS** You want to know if you can wade across a local stream. The average depth of the stream is reported to be 2 feet. What information might be concealed when depth is reported as an average?

40. ★ **SHORT RESPONSE** Find the outlier in the data set: 318, 390, 592, 388, 375, 350, 410, 395. Find the mean, median, and mode of the data set with the outlier and without the outlier. Which average is most affected by the outlier? *Explain.*

READING *IN* MATH **Read the information below for Exercises 41–43.**

Gymnastics At Ramsey High's last gymnastics meet, the Rams overran the competition once again. They were lead by their top scorers on the rings. The scores for this event from each of the 6 judges are shown below. The final score for each gymnast is calculated by dropping the highest and lowest scores and taking the mean of the remaining 4 scores.

	Judge 1	*Judge 2*	*Judge 3*	*Judge 4*	*Judge 5*	*Judge 6*
Isaac	9.600	9.600	9.600	9.650	9.800	9.650
Carl	9.800	9.800	9.700	9.700	9.700	9.800
Kurt	9.550	9.400	9.800	9.750	9.800	9.600

41. **Calculate** Find the final score for each gymnast. Who was awarded first, second, and third places on the rings?

42. **Investigate** Find the mean score for each gymnast that includes all 6 judges' scores. If these averages were used as the final scores, would the top three gymnasts be the same? *Explain.*

43. **Interpret** *Explain* why it may be more fair to rank the gymnasts according to a final score that omits the highest and lowest scores.

44. **TELEVISION SURVEY** Ten people rate a television show on a scale from 1 to 10. The ratings are 1, 7, 7, 8, 8, 8, 8, 8, 9, and 9.
   a. Find the mean, median, and mode of the data with and without the outlier.
   b. *Describe* the effect on the averages.

45. ★ **EXTENDED RESPONSE** The table shows attendance at 6 school dances.
   a. Make a bar graph of the data.
   b. Find the mean and median attendance.
   c. The student council wants to find the total amount of money collected for admission to the dances. Would the bar graph, the mean, or the median be most useful? *Explain.*
   d. What other information is also needed to find how much money was collected?

Dance	*Number of students*
Fall	97
Winter Ball	88
Valentine's Day	133
Spring Fling	210
End of Year	198

46. **CHALLENGE** The table below shows the numbers of points you scored during the first 14 basketball games of a 15-game season. By halftime of the final game, you score 7 points. How many points do you need to score in the second half to have a mean of 10 points per game?

Game	1	2	3	4	5	6	7	8	9	10	11	12	13	14
Points	15	8	7	10	12	4	20	13	7	7	5	3	10	14

MIXED REVIEW

Get-Ready

Prepare for Lesson 6.1 in Exs. 47–52

Solve the equation. *(p. 129)*

47. $3x - 28 = -37$ **48.** $-8 + 2x = -24$ **49.** $-7x + 14 = 84$

50. $\frac{x}{5} - 10 = -10$ **51.** $2 - \frac{x}{6} = -11$ **52.** $-\frac{x}{4} + 12 = 16$

Find the product. *(p. 73)*

53. $-3(13)$ **54.** $-40(-5)$ **55.** $4(-11)$ **56.** $-19(0)$

57. ★ **MULTIPLE CHOICE** What is the value of $(-3)^{-4}$? *(p. 208)*

Ⓐ -81 Ⓑ $-\frac{1}{81}$ Ⓒ $\frac{1}{81}$ Ⓓ 81

QUIZ *for Lessons 5.5–5.8*

Write the fraction as a decimal or the decimal as a fraction. *(p. 255)*

1. 4.25 **2.** $\frac{4}{9}$ **3.** 0.58 **4.** $0.\overline{2}$

Find the sum or difference. *(p. 260)*

5. $-2.301 + 8.4$ **6.** $15.25 + 9.636$ **7.** $14.65 - 3.608$ **8.** $3.02 - (-0.225)$

Find the product or quotient. *(p. 265)*

9. $-15.3 \cdot 0.48$ **10.** $3.88 \cdot 0.9$ **11.** $0.162 \div 2.7$ **12.** $2.07 \div 0.225$

13. RACING A racing camel can travel at a speed of 11.75 miles per hour. How far does it travel in 0.02 hour at this speed? *(p. 265)*

14. TORNADOES The table shows the numbers of tornadoes in the United States from 1998–2004. Find the mean, median, mode(s), and range of the data. *(p. 272)*

Year	1998	1999	2000	2001	2002	2003	2004
Tornadoes	1424	1342	1071	805	941	1376	1819

Brain Game

The Prize is Right!

You are a contestant on a television game show. To win a trip you must find the prices of the five items in a shopping cart. The game show host gives you four hints about the prices.

- The mean of the prices is \$1.68
- The mode of the prices is \$1.50
- The median of the prices is \$1.65
- One item costs \$.10 more than the median.

List the prices of the items in the cart in order from least to greatest.

MIXED REVIEW *of Problem Solving*

Lessons 5.5–5.8

1. **MULTI-STEP PROBLEM** Rebecca's long distance plan charges \$.10 per minute before 7:00 P.M. and \$.05 per minute after 7:00 P.M. Rebecca makes a long distance call at 6:39 P.M. and talks for 18 minutes.

   a. Find the cost of the phone call.

   b. At 7:15 P.M. Rebecca makes another long distance call. She talks for the same amount of time as she did before. Find the cost of the second phone call.

   c. What is the price difference between Rebecca's two calls?

2. **GRIDDED ANSWER** A rectangular garden has a length of 3.2 meters and an area of 8.96 square meters. What is the perimeter of the garden, in meters?

3. **SHORT RESPONSE** You spend the following minutes instant messaging at different times: 18, 15, 7, 10, 32, 28, 17, 21, 94. Find the mean, median, and mode(s) of the session lengths. Which of these averages is most representative of the session lengths? *Explain.*

4. **MULTI-STEP PROBLEM** The table below shows the fraction of 800 people in a survey that named their favorite type of movie. Only the top three are shown.

Movie type	Comedy	Drama	Action
Fraction of students	$\frac{2}{5}$	$\frac{1}{8}$	$\frac{5}{16}$

   a. Write each fraction as a decimal.

   b. How many more people picked the most popular movie type than the third most popular movie type?

   c. How many of the 800 people did not choose any of the movie types shown?

5. **OPEN-ENDED** Find a set of 6 whole numbers with a mean of 8, a median of 9, and a mode of 10. *Explain* how you chose your numbers.

6. **GRIDDED ANSWER** Grapes cost \$1.30 per pound. You buy 2.3 pounds for yourself and 1.5 pounds for your friend. How much, in dollars, do you spend on grapes?

7. **EXTENDED RESPONSE** Numbered streets and lettered streets in a city meet at right angles. Each block is 0.2 mile long. A taxi costs \$2.50 for the first fifth of a mile and \$.40 for each additional fifth of a mile.

   a. How many miles is the shortest trip from Fourth and A to Third and D?

   b. How much would it cost to make that trip in a taxi?

   c. The taxi waits at Third and D for 8 minutes at a cost of \$.27 per minute and then continues on by the shortest route to First and B. What is the total cost for the trip? *Explain.*

8. **SHORT RESPONSE** Find the decimal form of $\frac{2}{9}$. *Explain* how you can use the result to find the decimal forms of $\frac{2}{90}$, $\frac{2}{900}$, and so on, without actually dividing.

9. **SHORT RESPONSE** Rectangle *A* has a length of 9.3 feet and a width of 7.5 feet. Rectangle *B* has a length of 27.9 feet and a width of 22.5 feet. How many times greater is the perimeter of rectangle *B* than the perimeter of rectangle *A*? How many times greater is the area of rectangle *B* than the area of rectangle *A*? *Explain.*

5 CHAPTER REVIEW

@HomeTutor
classzone.com
Vocabulary Practice

REVIEW KEY VOCABULARY

- reciprocal, *p. 247*
- multiplicative inverse, *p. 247*
- rational number, *p. 255*
- terminating decimal, *p. 255*
- repeating decimal, *p. 255*
- front-end estimation, *p. 261*
- leading digit, *p. 265*
- mean, median, mode, *p. 272*
- range, *p. 273*

VOCABULARY EXERCISES

Copy and complete the statement.

1. The fractions $\frac{3}{5}$ and $\frac{5}{3}$ are _?_ or _?_ because their product is 1.

2. If the remainder of the quotient $\frac{a}{b}$ is 0, then the decimal form of $\frac{a}{b}$ is a _?_.

3. You can use _?_ when you do not need to find an exact sum of a group of decimals.

4. A value that occurs most often in a data set is a _?_.

5. A number that can be written as $\frac{a}{b}$, where a and b are integers and $b \neq 0$, is a _?_.

REVIEW EXAMPLES AND EXERCISES

5.1 Fractions with Common Denominators

pp. 233–237

EXAMPLE

Find the sum.

$$\frac{2}{9} + 3\frac{4}{9} = 3 + \left(\frac{2}{9} + \frac{4}{9}\right) \quad \textbf{Group fractions.}$$

$$= 3\frac{6}{9} \quad \textbf{Add fractions.}$$

$$= 3\frac{2}{3} \quad \textbf{Simplify.}$$

EXERCISES

Find the sum or difference.

SEE EXAMPLES 1 AND 2 on pp. 233–234 for Exs. 6–13

6. $\frac{8}{9} + \frac{4}{9}$ **7.** $3\frac{5}{8} - 1\frac{7}{8}$ **8.** $\frac{3}{10} - \frac{7}{10} - \frac{9}{10}$ **9.** $\frac{4}{7} + \frac{2}{7} + \frac{6}{7}$

10. $\frac{6n}{18} - \frac{2n}{18}$ **11.** $-\frac{4n}{6} + \frac{3n}{6}$ **12.** $\frac{8n}{11} + \frac{4n}{11}$ **13.** $-\frac{7n}{9} - \frac{5n}{9}$

5.2 Fractions with Different Denominators

pp. 238–242

EXAMPLE

Find the difference.

$2\frac{9}{14} - \frac{6}{7} = 2\frac{9}{14} - \frac{12}{14}$ Rewrite fractions using LCD of 14.

$= 1\frac{23}{14} - \frac{12}{14}$ Rename $2\frac{9}{14}$ as $1\frac{23}{14}$.

$= 1 + \left(\frac{23}{14} - \frac{12}{14}\right)$ Group fractions.

$= 1\frac{11}{14}$ Subtract inside parentheses.

EXERCISES

SEE EXAMPLES 1, 2, AND 3 on pp. 238–239 for Exs. 14–22

Find the sum.

14. $\frac{3}{5} + \frac{2}{3}$ **15.** $\frac{3}{5} + \frac{1}{4}$ **16.** $6\frac{2}{7} + \left(-7\frac{1}{8}\right)$ **17.** $\frac{5v}{3} + \frac{4v}{5}$

Find the difference.

18. $\frac{8}{9} - \frac{2}{5}$ **19.** $\frac{7}{12} - \left(-\frac{5}{8}\right)$ **20.** $3\frac{1}{3} - 1\frac{1}{4}$ **21.** $\frac{8x}{17} - \frac{x}{2}$

22. Robots It took Central High's robot team $107\frac{1}{3}$ hours of labor to build their robot. East High built their robot in $111\frac{5}{6}$ hours. How much longer did East High School take to build their robot?

5.3 Multiplying Fractions

pp. 243–246

EXAMPLE

Find the product.

$3\frac{3}{5} \cdot \frac{4}{9} = \frac{18}{5} \cdot \frac{4}{9}$ Write $3\frac{3}{5}$ as an improper fraction.

$= \frac{18 \cdot 4}{5 \cdot 9}$ Use rule for multiplying fractions.

$= \frac{\overset{2}{\cancel{18}} \cdot 4}{5 \cdot \underset{1}{\cancel{9}}}$ Divide out common factor.

$= \frac{8}{5}$, or $1\frac{3}{5}$ Multiply and write as a mixed number.

EXERCISES

Find the product.

SEE EXAMPLES 1 AND 2 on pp. 243–244 for Exs. 23–30

23. $-\frac{5}{8} \cdot \frac{2}{5}$ **24.** $-\frac{9}{5} \cdot \left(-\frac{11}{15}\right)$ **25.** $-\frac{1}{3} \cdot \frac{2}{7}$ **26.** $\frac{3}{8} \cdot \left(-\frac{12}{13}\right)$

27. $8\frac{2}{3} \cdot (-3)$ **28.** $-7\frac{4}{9} \cdot \left(-\frac{1}{4}\right)$ **29.** $-6\frac{3}{7} \cdot 2\frac{1}{2}$ **30.** $4 \cdot \left(-3\frac{5}{12}\right)$

5.4 Dividing Fractions

pp. 247–252

EXAMPLE

Find the quotient.

$\frac{1}{3} \div \frac{5}{6} = \frac{1}{3} \cdot \frac{6}{5}$ $\frac{5}{6} \cdot \frac{6}{5} = 1$, so the reciprocal of $\frac{5}{6}$ is $\frac{6}{5}$.

$= \frac{1 \cdot \overset{2}{\cancel{6}}}{\underset{1}{\cancel{3}} \cdot 5}$ Divide out common factor.

$= \frac{2}{5}$ Multiply.

EXAMPLE

Find the quotient.

$2\frac{1}{5} \div 2\frac{3}{4} = \frac{11}{5} \div \frac{11}{4}$ Write $2\frac{1}{5}$ and $2\frac{3}{4}$ as improper fractions.

$= \frac{11}{5} \cdot \frac{4}{11}$ $\frac{11}{4} \cdot \frac{4}{11} = 1$, so the reciprocal of $\frac{11}{4}$ is $\frac{4}{11}$.

$= \frac{\overset{1}{\cancel{11}} \cdot 4}{5 \cdot \underset{1}{\cancel{11}}}$ Divide out common factor.

$= \frac{4}{5}$ Multiply.

EXERCISES

Find the quotient.

SEE EXAMPLES 1, 2, AND 3 on p. 248 for Exs. 31–39

31. $\frac{13}{18} \div \frac{5}{6}$ **32.** $\frac{7}{22} \div \frac{1}{11}$ **33.** $\frac{2}{3} \div \left(-\frac{1}{6}\right)$ **34.** $-\frac{4}{5} \div \left(-\frac{1}{2}\right)$

35. $2\frac{3}{4} \div 1\frac{1}{3}$ **36.** $\frac{9}{21} \div 5$ **37.** $5\frac{8}{11} \div \left(-\frac{3}{4}\right)$ **38.** $12\frac{1}{2} \div 4\frac{1}{6}$

39. Relay You participate in a $12\frac{1}{2}$ mile relay run for charity. Your team has 8 people and each person runs the same distance. How many miles does each person run?

5.5 Fractions and Decimals

pp. 255–259

EXAMPLE

Write $\frac{2}{5}$ as a decimal.

$$\frac{2}{5} = 5\overline{)2.0} = 0.4$$

$$\begin{array}{r} 0.4 \\ 5\overline{)2.0} \\ 2\,0 \\ \hline 0 \end{array}$$

EXAMPLE

Write $2.\overline{8}$ as a fraction.

Let $x = 2.\overline{8}$ or 2.888. . . .

The number has 1 repeating digit, so multiply by 10. Let $10x = 28.\overline{8}$ or 28.888. . . .

Subtract the two equations.

$$\begin{array}{rl} 10x = & 28.888\ldots \\ -\quad x = & 2.888\ldots \\ \hline 9x = & 26.000\ldots \end{array}$$

Then solve for x. $x = \frac{26}{9}$, or $2\frac{8}{9}$.

EXERCISES

Write the fraction as a decimal or the decimal as a fraction or mixed number.

SEE EXAMPLES 1, 3, AND 4 on pp. 255–257 for Exs. 40–47

40. $\frac{3}{5}$ **41.** $-\frac{7}{8}$ **42.** $-0.\overline{23}$ **43.** 3.45

44. $\frac{2}{9}$ **45.** $2.\overline{65}$ **46.** 0.16 **47.** $-\frac{3}{11}$

5.6 Adding and Subtracting Decimals

pp. 260–264

EXAMPLE

a. Find the sum of 14.02 and 9.81.

$$\begin{array}{r} 14.02 \\ +\ 9.81 \\ \hline 23.83 \end{array}$$

b. Find the difference of 20.5 and 3.764.

$$\begin{array}{r} 20.500 \\ -\ 3.764 \\ \hline 16.736 \end{array}$$

Use zeros as placeholders.

EXERCISES

Find the sum or difference.

SEE EXAMPLE 1 on p. 260 for Exs. 48–55

48. 1.2 + 0.67 **49.** 33.2 + 9.398 **50.** 3.16 − 1.845 **51.** 90.3 − (−7.81)

52. 5.2 + 20.68 **53.** 0.103 + 0.7 **54.** 9.6 − 3.555 **55.** −4.23 − 8.093

5.7 Multiplying and Dividing Decimals

pp. 265–269

EXAMPLE

a. Find the product of 14.75 and 1.3.

$$\begin{array}{rl} 14.75 & \textbf{2 decimal places} \\ \times \quad 1.3 & \textbf{+ 1 decimal place} \\ \hline 4425 & \\ 1475 & \\ \hline 19.175 & \textbf{3 decimal places} \end{array}$$

b. Find the quotient of 21.726 and 4.26.

$$4.26\overline{)21.726} \qquad \begin{array}{r} 5.1 \\ 426\overline{)2172.6} \end{array}$$

EXERCISES

Find the product or quotient.

SEE EXAMPLES 1, 2, AND 3 on pp. 265–266 for Exs. 56–60

56. $6.24 \cdot 0.375$ **57.** $3.348 \cdot 0.9$ **58.** $66.96 \div (-2.7)$ **59.** $18.91 \div 9.455$

60. Cats A tiger at a zoo has a mass of 144.9 kilograms. This is 40.25 times the mass of a house cat. What is the mass of a house cat?

5.8 Mean, Median, and Mode

pp. 272–278

EXAMPLE

Find the mean, median, mode(s), and range of the following ordered set of data.

4, 5, 6, 6, 7, 9, 11, 12

$$\text{Mean} = \frac{4+5+6+6+7+9+11+12}{8} = \frac{60}{8} = 7.5$$

$$\text{Median} = \frac{6+7}{2} = \frac{13}{2} = \frac{6}{5}$$

$$\text{Mode} = 6$$

$$\text{Range} = 12 - 4 = 8$$

EXERCISES

Find the mean, median, mode(s), and range of the data set.

SEE EXAMPLES 1 AND 2 on pp. 272–273 for Exs. 61–64

61. Temperatures (°C): −7, −1, 0, 8, 4, 2, −7, 2

62. Length of jumps (meters): 14.6, 19.2, 11, 16.5, 12, 11, 10.9

63. Length of bike trails (km): 7, 8.3, 17.1, 4.8, 3.9, 7, 4.8, 13.1

64. Thickness of books (inches): 2.4, 1, 3.7, 1.4, 1.3, 2.5, 2, 2.5

5 CHAPTER TEST

@HomeTutor
classzone.com
Chapter Test Practice

Find the sum or difference.

1. $4\frac{5}{11} - 2\frac{6}{11}$

2. $\frac{9}{16} - \left(-\frac{11}{16}\right)$

3. $-\frac{5}{6} + \frac{1}{8}$

4. $\frac{3}{7} + \left(-\frac{8}{21}\right) + \frac{2}{3}$

Find the product or quotient.

5. $\frac{2}{9} \cdot (-4)$

6. $\frac{5}{2} \cdot \frac{4}{15}$

7. $3\frac{1}{2} \div 2$

8. $7\frac{3}{4} \div 2\frac{7}{12}$

Write the fraction as a decimal or the decimal as a fraction.

9. $\frac{7}{20}$

10. $\frac{3}{40}$

11. 0.0082

12. $0.\overline{4}$

Find the sum, difference, product, or quotient.

13. $6.2 - 5.984$

14. $2.608 + 12.93$

15. $0.7992 \div 0.333$

16. $-34.69 \cdot 12.7$

17. $3.64 + 14.2$

18. $0.123 \cdot 4.53$

19. $15.68 - 4.94$

20. $3.7611 \div 0.597$

21. xy **ALGEBRA** Evaluate $0.2x$ and $\frac{x}{0.2}$ when $x = -4.1, 0.06,$ and 1.8.

22. **HOMEWORK** Yesterday you spent $3\frac{1}{4}$ hours on homework. Today you will spend $1\frac{4}{5}$ hours. How many more hours did you spend yesterday? How many minutes is this?

23. **BOOK CLUB** You are reading a novel for your book club. You can read one chapter in $\frac{5}{12}$ hour. How many chapters can you read in $3\frac{3}{4}$ hours?

BAGELS **In Exercises 24 and 25, use the table. It shows the approximate supermarket sales of three types of bagels (in billions of dollars) in 2003.**

24. How much greater were the sales for frozen bagels than the sales for refrigerated bagels?

25. What is the total amount of sales of all three types of bagels?

Bagels	*Sales (billions)*
Frozen	$.086
Refrigerated	$.077
Fresh	$.43

26. **ENERGY BILL** A gas supplier charges 64.5 cents per therm of gas used. How much does it cost for 116 therms of gas?

27. **STUDYING** Last week, twelve students spent the following hours studying. Find the mean, median, mode(s), and range of the data.

2, 5, 3, 7, 10, 9, 8, 7, 6, 7, 6, 2

28. **THEME PARKS** The mean number per week of theme park visitors over a four week period was 15,271. The numbers of visitors in each of the first three weeks were 15,514, 17,328, and 13,697. How many people visited the park in the fourth week?

Scoring Rubric

Full Credit
- solution is complete and correct

Partial Credit
- solution is complete but errors are made, *or*
- solution is without error, but incomplete

No Credit
- no solution is given, *or*
- solution makes no sense

SHORT RESPONSE QUESTIONS

PROBLEM

You have \$20 to spend on pretzels for a party. Pretzels cost \$2.49 per box, including tax. How many boxes can you buy? How much money do you have left over? *Justify* your answers.

Below are sample solutions to the problem. Read each solution and the comments in blue to see why the sample represents full credit, partial credit, or no credit.

SAMPLE 1: Full Credit Solution

Reasoning is key to choosing the correct operations.

Find how many boxes of pretzels you can buy by dividing the amount of money you have by the cost of each box.

$$2.49\overline{)20.00} \longrightarrow 249\overline{)2000}$$

The calculations are correct.

$$\begin{array}{r} 8.0 \\ 249\overline{)2000.00} \\ \underline{1992} \\ 8\,0 \end{array}$$

You can buy 8 boxes of pretzels.

The question is answered correctly.

Eight boxes of pretzels cost 8(\$2.49) = \$19.92. You have \$20, so the amount of money that you have left is \$20 − \$19.92 = \$.08.

SAMPLE 2: Partial Credit Solution

The initial reasoning and calculations are correct.

Find how many boxes of pretzels you can buy by dividing the amount of money you have by the cost of each box.

$$2.49\overline{)20.00} \longrightarrow 249\overline{)2000}$$

$$\begin{array}{r} 8.0 \\ 249\overline{)2000.00} \\ \underline{1992} \\ 8\,0 \end{array}$$

You can buy 8 boxes of pretzels.

8(\$2.49) = \$19.92

The final question was not answered correctly.

You will spend \$19.92.

STATE TEST PRACTICE
classzone.com

The problem does not call for an estimated answer.

The answer is incorrect.

SAMPLE 3: Partial Credit Solution

You can buy about 8 boxes.

Each box is about \$2.50, so you will not have any money left.

The answer is incorrect.

SAMPLE 4: No Credit Solution

You can buy 7 boxes of pretzels and will have \$2.57 left.

PRACTICE Apply the Scoring Rubric

Score the solution to the problem below as *full credit, partial credit,* or *no credit*. *Explain* your reasoning.

PROBLEM Four sevenths of people surveyed, or 336 people, said they prefer spring to fall. How many people were surveyed? *Justify* your answer.

1. Let p be the number of people that were surveyed. Solve the following equation to find the number of people surveyed.

$$\frac{4}{7}p = 336$$

$$\frac{7}{4} \cdot \frac{4}{7}p = 336 \cdot \frac{7}{4}$$

$$p = \frac{\overset{84}{\cancel{336}}}{1} \cdot \frac{7}{\underset{1}{\cancel{4}}}$$

$$p = 588$$

There were 588 people surveyed.

2. Let p be the number of people that were surveyed. Solve the following equation to find the number of people surveyed.

$$p = \frac{4}{7}(336)$$

$$p = \frac{4}{\underset{1}{\cancel{7}}} \cdot \frac{\overset{48}{\cancel{336}}}{1}$$

$$p = 192$$

There were 192 people surveyed.

5 ★ Standardized TEST PRACTICE

SHORT RESPONSE

1. Kwame has a discount card at a grocery store. His discounts this week are \$.90 per pound on 4 pounds of grapes, \$.45 per pound on 8 pounds of apples, \$1.35 per pound on 5 pounds of chicken, and \$2.40 per pound on 2 pounds of coffee. He gives the cashier \$100 and receives \$46.30 in change. How much change would Kwame receive *without* the discounts? *Explain* how you found your answer.

2. The Winter Dance committee has the idea of using paper snowflakes to completely cover the school cafeteria ceiling, which is a square with 75 feet on a side. The committee can buy packages of 50 snowflakes for \$1.89. The decorating budget for the dance is \$250 and 9 snowflakes cover one 3-foot by 18-inch acoustical ceiling tile. Will the committee's idea work? *Explain.*

3. A recipe for pizza dough uses $1\frac{3}{4}$ cups of flour. You want to make 8 batches of dough for a fundraiser pizza dinner. You have $14\frac{1}{2}$ cups of flour. Do you have enough flour? *Explain* your reasoning.

4. You have a rectangular patio and your friend has a square patio. The dimensions of each patio are shown below. Whose patio has a greater area? *Explain.*

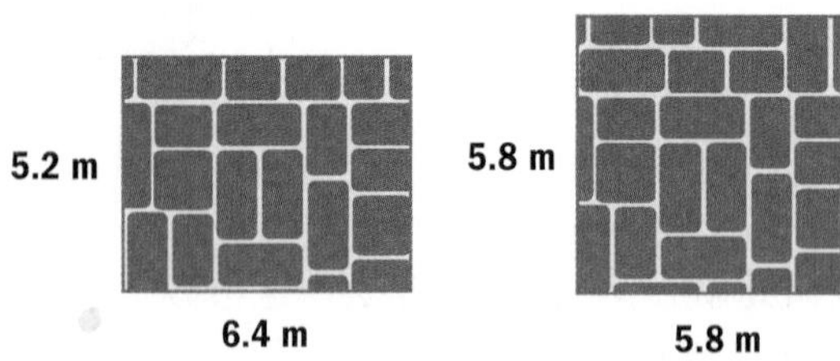

5. Last season, the school softball team played $\frac{3}{4}$ of their games at night and $\frac{1}{4}$ of their games during the day. The team won $\frac{4}{5}$ of their night games and $\frac{1}{2}$ of their day games. What fraction of the season did the team win? *Explain.*

6. A baseball coach counts the number of home runs that each player hits in a season. The table shows the current totals.

Player	Number of home runs
Carmine	5
Lia	1
Rose	4
Anthony	2
Malik	0
Damita	5
Paul	4
Mickey	4
Farah	?

The mean number of home runs hit by the players is 3. How many players hit more home runs than the median? *Explain* how you found your answer.

7. A small city park is a rectangle 50.25 feet by 72.14 feet. Residents want to plant a square garden in the park that is 324 square yards. Is this possible? *Justify* your reasoning.

8. What is $\frac{1}{2} \cdot \frac{2}{3} \cdot \frac{3}{4} \cdot \ldots \cdot \frac{14}{15}$ written in simplest form? *Explain* how you found your answer.

9. You have $3\frac{3}{5}$ bags of dried fruit that you would like to share with your class of 20 students. Do you have enough dried fruit to give each student $\frac{1}{5}$ of a bag? If so, what fraction of a bag will you have left? If not, what fraction of a bag should you give to each student without leaving any left over? *Explain* your reasoning.

10. You received test scores of 90, 91, 83, 90, 80, 97, 90, and 100. Find the mean, median, and mode of the scores. Which average(s) best represents the scores? *Explain* your reasoning.

MULTIPLE CHOICE

11. Find the product of $-1\frac{1}{2}$ and $\frac{9}{20}$.

Ⓐ $-1\frac{9}{20}$ Ⓑ $-1\frac{1}{20}$

Ⓒ $-\frac{27}{40}$ Ⓓ $-\frac{3}{10}$

12. A pepper grinder holds 1.8 ounces of peppercorns. You buy one pound of peppercorns. How many times can you fill the pepper grinder?

Ⓐ 5 times Ⓑ 8 times

Ⓒ 9 times Ⓓ 12 times

13. Which fraction is greater than 0.34?

Ⓐ $\frac{5}{16}$ Ⓑ $\frac{1}{3}$

Ⓒ $\frac{55}{162}$ Ⓓ $\frac{8}{23}$

GRIDDED ANSWER

14. You bike a mile in $3\frac{1}{3}$ minutes. How many miles can you bike in an hour?

15. You use 0.75 meter of wire to hold together bunches of flowers. How many bunches can you make with 15 meters of wire?

16. Some students were surveyed about how many clocks they have at home. Their answers were: 2, 4, 10, 5, 7, 12, 8, 4. What is the median number of clocks?

17. How many times must you run around a $\frac{1}{4}$ mile track to run $3\frac{1}{2}$ miles?

18. A middle school, of grades 6, 7, and 8, enrolls 940 students. The school reports that $\frac{3}{10}$ of the students are in grade 6 and $\frac{7}{20}$ of the students are in grade 7. How many students are in grade 8?

EXTENDED RESPONSE

19. Aretha is looking for a whole oat breakfast cereal. One cereal's label says a one cup serving is 54 grams, of which 12 grams are sugars and 6 grams are fiber. Another cereal's label says a one cup serving is 30 grams, of which 5 grams are sugars and 4 grams are fiber.

a. *Explain* how Aretha can compare the sugar and fiber content of the cereals using the sugar and fiber per serving, and using the sugar and fiber per gram. Show your work.

b. Which way do you think makes more sense from a nutritional standpoint? *Explain* your reasoning.

20. Mr. Fay has given his students 20 homework assignments. The table shows the number of homework assignments that each student has completed so far. Find the mean and median number of assignments completed.

Ana	Bill	Dan	Dom	Erin	Jack	Kyle	Iyo	Mike	Ron	Tira
17	16	19	20	17	18	17	15	16	19	20

Tonya was left off of Mr. Fay's list by mistake. What is the minimum number of assignments Tonya must complete for the median of the group to be 17.5? for the mean of the group to be 17.5? *Explain* your answers.

6 Multi-Step Equations and Inequalities

Before

In previous chapters you've . . .

- Solved equations by using one or two steps
- Solved one-step inequalities

Now

In Chapter 6 you'll study . . .

- 6.1 Multi-step equations
- 6.2 Collecting like terms
- 6.3 Fractions and decimals
- 6.4 Circumference
- 6.5 Multi-step inequalities
- 6.6 Problem solving

Why?

So you can solve real-world problems about . . .

- fundraising, p. 297
- drumming, p. 300
- bowling, p. 319

Math
at classzone.com

- Solving Multi-Step Equations, p. 295
- Solving Inequalities, p. 318
- Problem Solving and Inequalities, p. 325

Get-Ready Games

Review Prerequisite Skills by playing *Treasure Hunt.*

Skill Focus: Solving one- and two-step equations

TREASURE HUNT

MATERIALS

- 1 number cube
- 1 Treasure Hunt board
- 20 red markers
- 20 yellow markers

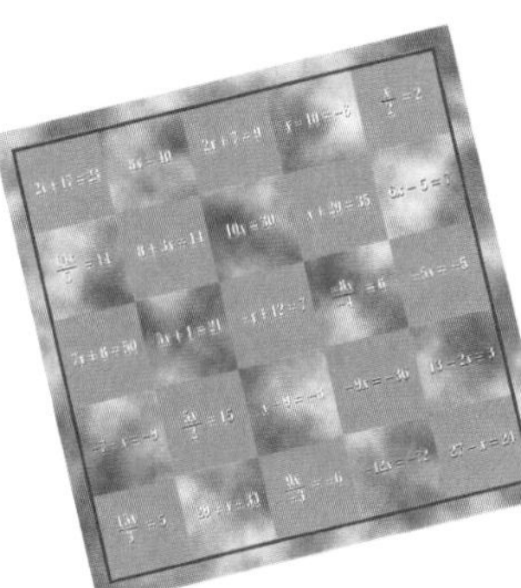

HOW TO PLAY Each player gets 20 markers of the same color. On your turn, follow the steps on the next page. You can challenge the other player when you believe they have covered an incorrect space.

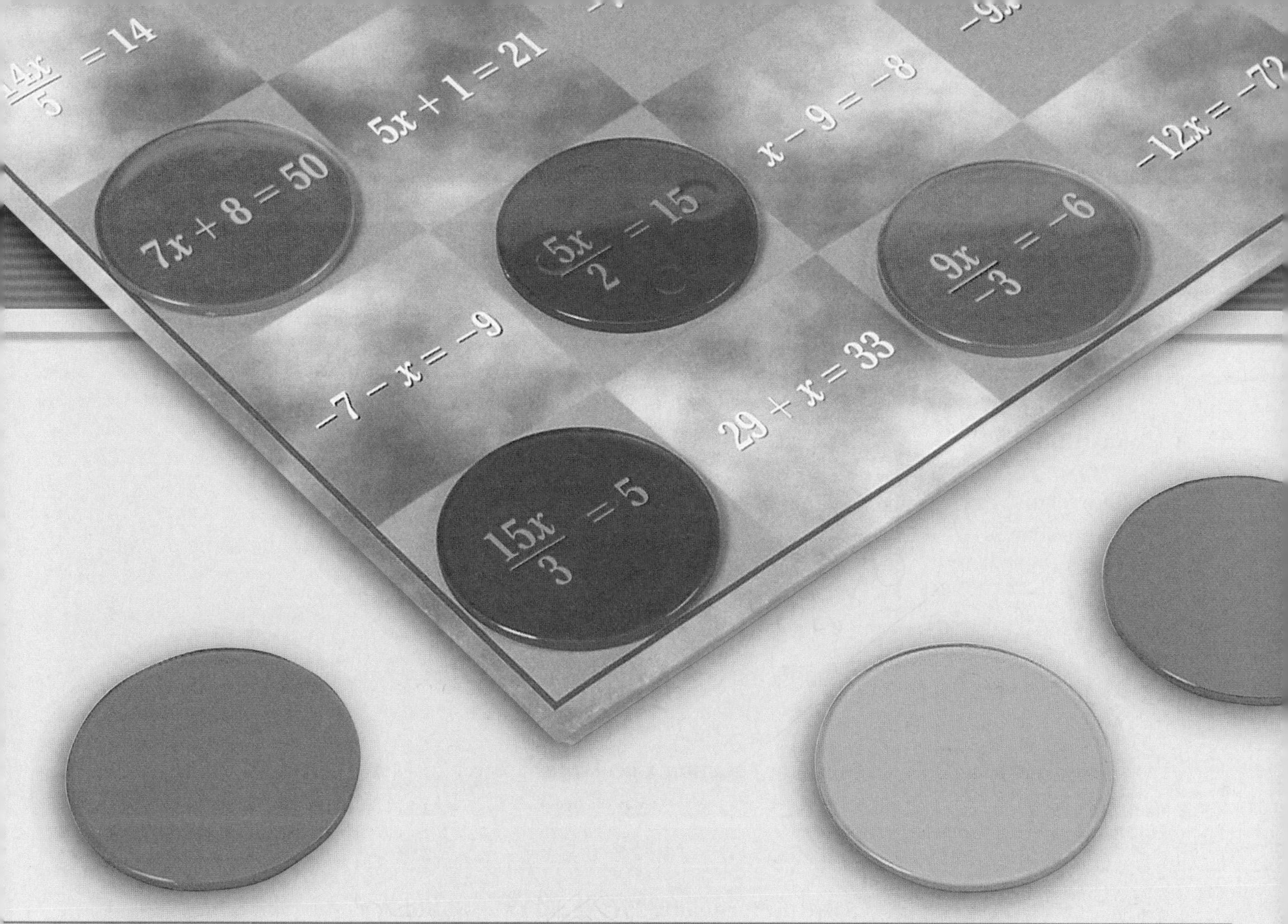

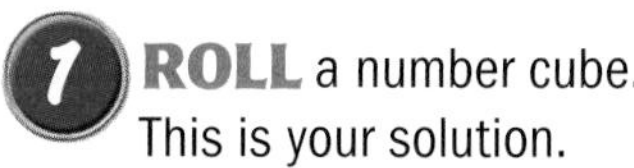

ROLL a number cube. This is your solution.

COVER an equation that has your solution with a marker. If there are no equations that have your solution, you cannot place a marker and it is the next player's turn. Each space you cover is a piece of treasure.

CHECK that you cover a correct space for your roll. If you cover an incorrect space, then you must remove your marker and it is the next player's turn.

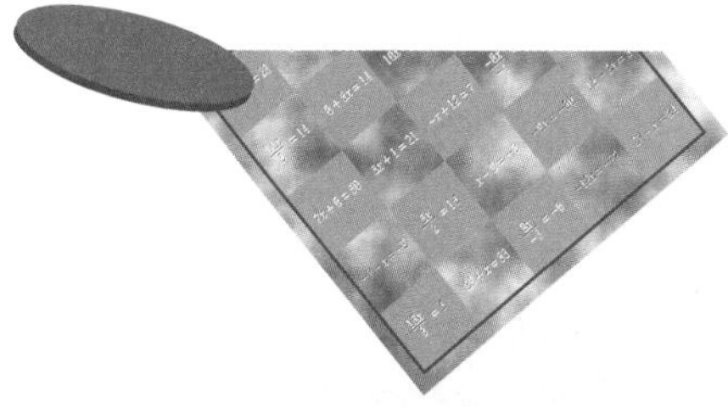

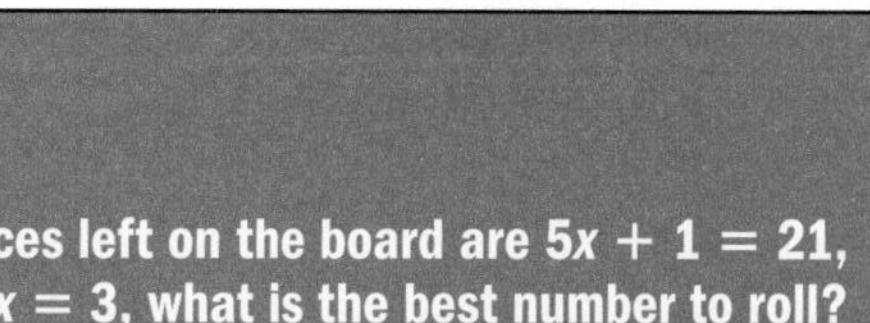

HOW TO WIN Be the player with the most spaces covered (the most treasure collected) when all spaces on the board are covered.

Stop and Think

1. **WRITING** If the only spaces left on the board are $5x + 1 = 21$, $-7 - x = -9$, and $11 - 2x = 3$, what is the best number to roll? What is the second best number to roll? *Explain.*
2. **CRITICAL THINKING** How many spaces on the board have a solution of 5? *Explain* how you found your answer.

6 Getting Ready

Review Prerequisite Skills

REVIEW WORDS
- **perimeter,** *p. 32*
- **distributive property,** *p. 88*
- **like terms,** *p. 89*
- **inequality,** *p. 148*
- **reciprocal,** *p. 247*

VOCABULARY CHECK

Copy and complete using a review word from the list at the left.

1. The __?__ of a figure is the sum of its side lengths.
2. The four __?__ symbols are <, >, ≤, and ≥.
3. To divide by a fraction, you multiply by its __?__.
4. Terms that have identical variable parts raised to the same power are __?__.

SKILL CHECK

Simplify the expression by combining like terms. *(p. 88)*

5. $3 - 2x + 4$
6. $4x + 5 + x - 1$
7. $-2(3x + 1) - 2$
8. $5(x - 4) - x$

Solve the equation. Check your answer. *(p. 129)*

9. $2x - 1 = 3$
10. $-3x - 2 = 7$
11. $4 - x = 12$
12. $13 = 2x + 3$
13. $-5x + 6 = -9$
14. $8 - x = -3$
15. $17 = 4x + 1$
16. $3x - 5 = 10$

Solve the inequality. Then graph its solution. *(pp. 148, 154)*

17. $x + 5 < 18$
18. $x - 4 \geq -6$
19. $17 + x > 19$
20. $-4 + x \leq -9$
21. $5x \geq 30$
22. $-6x \leq 54$
23. $\frac{4}{5}x > 20$
24. $\frac{2}{3}x \leq 12$

@HomeTutor Prerequisite skills practice at classzone.com

Notetaking Skills Recording the Process

In each chapter you will learn a new notetaking skill. In Chapter 6 you will apply the strategy of recording the process to Example 1 on p. 303.

Copy examples your teacher explains during class. Be sure to record each step of the solution to help you remember the process.

Solving Two-Step Equations

$-2x - 3 = 11$	Original equation
$-2x - 3 + 3 = 11 + 3$	Add 3 to each side.
$-2x = 14$	Simplify.
$\frac{-2x}{-2} = \frac{14}{-2}$	Divide each side by −2.
$x = -7$	Simplify.

Call attention to important steps in examples.

6.1 Solving Multi-Step Equations

Before You solved equations by using one or two steps.

Now You'll solve equations by using two or more steps.

Why? So you can plan science experiments, as in Example 1.

KEY VOCABULARY
- **distributive property,** *p. 88*
- **like terms,** *p. 89*

Science For a science fair, you perform an experiment to see how the number of Venus flytrap seeds planted in a cup affects plant growth. In each cup, you plant either 5 seeds or 10 seeds. You want to use an equal number of cups for each seed amount. You have 75 seeds. How many cups do you need? You can use an equation to solve this problem.

Before using inverse operations to solve an equation, check to see if you can simplify one or both sides of the equation by combining like terms.

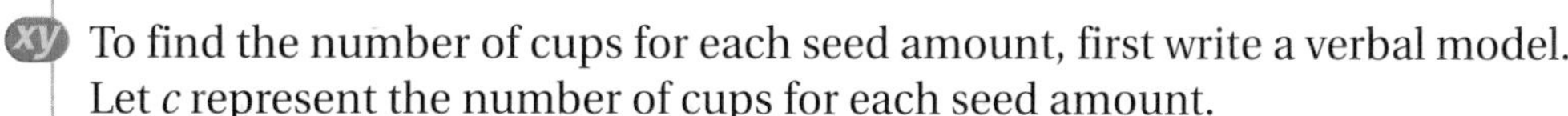

EXAMPLE 1 Writing and Solving a Multi-Step Equation

To find the number of cups for each seed amount, first write a verbal model. Let c represent the number of cups for each seed amount.

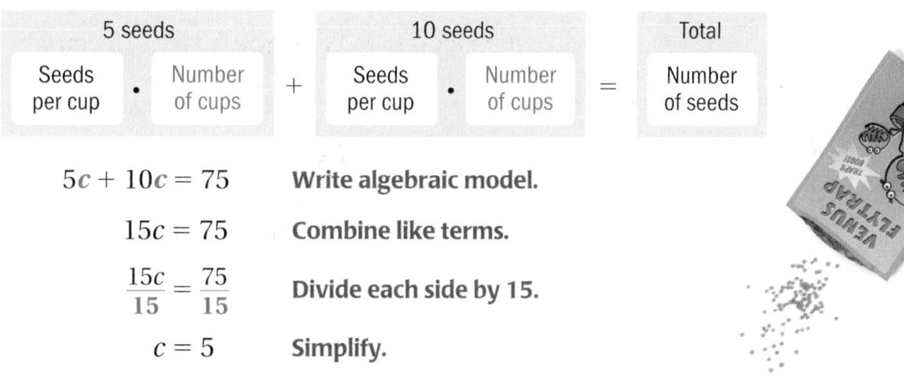

$5c + 10c = 75$ **Write algebraic model.**

$15c = 75$ **Combine like terms.**

$\frac{15c}{15} = \frac{75}{15}$ **Divide each side by 15.**

$c = 5$ **Simplify.**

▶ **Answer** You can plant five cups with 5 seeds and five cups with 10 seeds.

Check Substitute 5 for c in the original equation.

$5(5) + 10(5) \stackrel{?}{=} 75$

$25 + 50 \stackrel{?}{=} 75$

$75 = 75$ ✓

✓ GUIDED PRACTICE for Example 1

1. **Flowers** A pack of petunia seeds costs \$3 and a pack of balloon flower seeds costs \$4. You buy the same number of packs of each type of flower and pay \$42. How many packs of each do you buy?

EXAMPLE 2 Combining Like Terms

$3x + 12 - 4x = 20$	Original equation
$-x + 12 = 20$	Combine like terms.
$-x + 12 - 12 = 20 - 12$	Subtract 12 from each side.
$-x = 8$	Simplify.
$\frac{-x}{-1} = \frac{8}{-1}$	Divide each side by −1.
$x = -8$	Simplify.

Grouping Symbols When an equation involves parentheses, as in Example 3 below, you can use the distributive property before you combine like terms. When an equation involves a fraction, as in Example 4 on page 295, you can multiply each side of the equation by the same number to *clear* the fraction. This will allow you to write an equivalent equation without a fraction.

EXAMPLE 3 Using the Distributive Property

AVOID ERRORS

When distributing a negative number, remember to distribute the negative sign to *each* term inside the parentheses. For help with the distributive property, see p. 88.

$6n - 2(n + 1) = 26$	Original equation
$6n - 2n - 2 = 26$	Distributive property
$4n - 2 = 26$	Combine like terms.
$4n - 2 + 2 = 26 + 2$	Add 2 to each side.
$4n = 28$	Simplify.
$\frac{4n}{4} = \frac{28}{4}$	Divide each side by 4.
$n = 7$	Simplify.

Check Substitute 7 for n in the original equation.

$$6(7) - 2(7 + 1) \stackrel{?}{=} 26$$

$$6(7) - 2(8) \stackrel{?}{=} 26$$

$$42 - 16 \stackrel{?}{=} 26$$

$$26 = 26 \checkmark$$

GUIDED PRACTICE for Examples 2 and 3

Solve the equation. Then check the solution.

2. $-6 = 11w - 5w$

3. $4p + 10 + p = 25$

4. $-8r - 2 + 7r = -9$

5. $3(x - 9) = -39$

6. $z + 4(6 - z) = 21$

7. $8 = -7(y + 1) + 2y$

EXAMPLE 4 Standardized Test Practice

Volunteering Soup kitchen volunteers form 3 groups containing x volunteers each. Then 10 more volunteers arrive. The volunteers regroup into 4 groups containing 7 members each. The equation $\frac{3x + 10}{4} = 7$ models this situation, where x represents the original group size. What could you do first to produce a simpler, equivalent equation?

Ⓐ Divide by 3. Ⓑ Multiply by 4. Ⓒ Multiply by 2. Ⓓ Subtract 10.

ELIMINATE CHOICES
It's simplest to "undo" division before doing any inverse operations in the numerator. So, choices A and D can be eliminated.

SOLUTION

$\frac{3x + 10}{4} = 7$	**Original equation**
$\frac{3x + 10}{4} \cdot 4 = 7 \cdot 4$	**Multiply each side by 4.**
$3x + 10 = 28$	**Simplify.**
$3x = 18$	**Subtract 10 from each side.**
$x = 6$	**Divide each side by 3.**

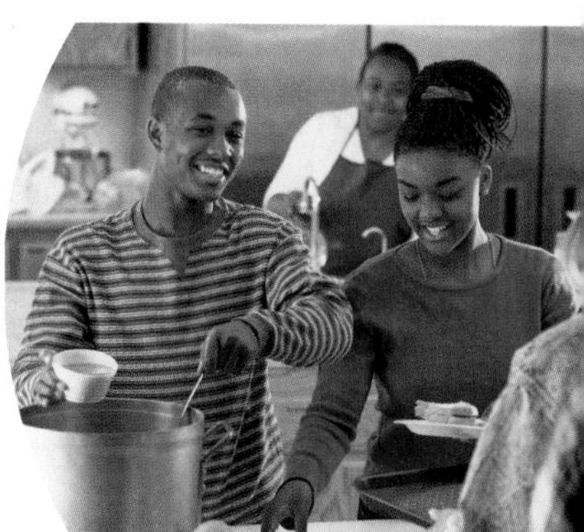

▶ **Answer** The first step is to multiply each side by 4.
The correct answer is B. Ⓐ Ⓑ Ⓒ Ⓓ

Animated Math at classzone.com

GUIDED PRACTICE for Example 4

Solve the equation. Then check the solution.

8. $\frac{2y + 4}{5} = 6$ **9.** $\frac{3x - 1}{8} = 4$ **10.** $\frac{9 - z}{8} = 3$

6.1 EXERCISES

HOMEWORK KEY
★ = **STANDARDIZED TEST PRACTICE** Exs. 16, 38, 39, 40, and 48
○ = **HINTS AND HOMEWORK HELP** for Exs. 5, 13, 23, 37 at classzone.com

SKILL PRACTICE

1. **VOCABULARY** Identify the like terms in the expression $5x + 6 - 2 - 9x$.

2. **VOCABULARY** Rewrite $3(x + 4)$ using the distributive property.

SOLVING EQUATIONS Solve the equation. Then check the solution.

SEE EXAMPLES 1, 2, AND 3 on pp. 293–294 for Exs. 3–14

3. $8b + 2b = 10$
4. $-n + 8n = 35$
5. $7y - 3y - 8 = -32$
6. $4x - 7 - 7x = -1$
7. $-2z + 6z - 9 = 15$
8. $-22 + 3k + 6 = -28$
9. $5(w - 7) = -15$
10. $-2(m + 7) = -22$
11. $5(3 - 2n) + 5n = 65$
12. $m + 3(m - 4) = 16$
13. $-4 = -1 - 3(2p + 3)$
14. $2z - 4(9 - 3z) = 62$

SEE EXAMPLES 2 AND 3 on p. 294 for Exs. 15–16

15. ERROR ANALYSIS Describe and correct the error made in solving the equation.

$$\begin{aligned} 3x - 2(x - 4) &= 5 \\ 3x - 2x - 8 &= 5 \\ x - 8 &= 5 \\ x &= 13 \end{aligned}$$

16. ★ MULTIPLE CHOICE What is the value of v in the equation $3 + 8v - 9v = 21$?

Ⓐ -24 Ⓑ -18 Ⓒ 18 Ⓓ 24

CLEARING FRACTIONS Solve the equation by first clearing fractions.

SEE EXAMPLE 4 on p. 295 for Exs. 17–24

17. $\frac{6k + 2}{4} = 2$ **18.** $\frac{2b + 8}{5} = -12$ **19.** $\frac{-c - 5}{8} = 4$ **20.** $\frac{-g + 4}{7} = 6$

21. $\frac{5 - 2d}{7} = 7$ **22.** $\frac{9 - 3h}{5} = -6$ **23.** $\frac{5a - 2}{3} = -9$ **24.** $\frac{4m - 16}{12} = -3$

SOLVING EQUATIONS Solve the equation. Then check the solution.

25. $5y + 8 - 2y + 9y = -16$

26. $8k - 7k - 16 - 3k = -21$

27. $7(t + 4) - 3(1 + t) = -19$

28. $-(6 - c) + 3(2c - 7) = 1$

29. $9z + 5(8 + z) - 6(2z - 7) = 40$

30. $4a + 7(2a - 5) - 5(3a + 1) = 50$

GEOMETRY Write an equation for the area of the triangle. Then solve for x.

31.

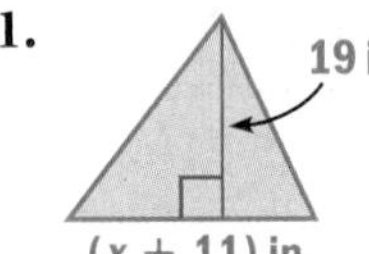

Area = 228 in.^{2}

32.

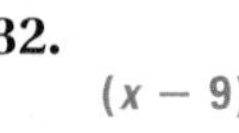

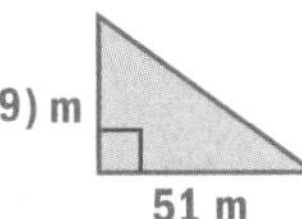

Area = 918 m^2

33. GEOMETRY Find the values of x and y so that the rectangle and the triangle have the same perimeter. What is the perimeter?

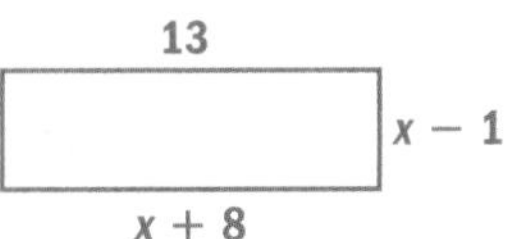

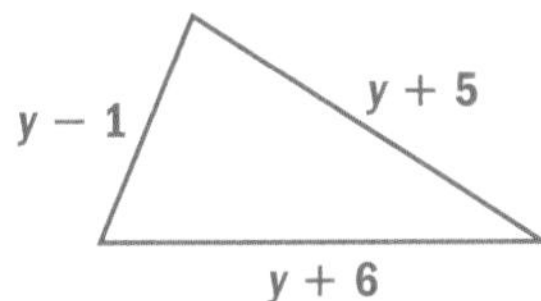

34. CHALLENGE The sum of 5 consecutive integers divided by 4 is 60. What are the integers?

PROBLEM SOLVING

SEE EXAMPLES 1 AND 3 on pp. 293–294 for Ex. 35

35. GUIDED PROBLEM SOLVING Tickets to the county fair cost \$8 each. Seventy people bought their tickets in advance and the rest bought them at the gate. The revenue from ticket sales is \$2560. How many people bought their tickets at the gate?

a. Use the verbal model to write an equation to find the number of tickets bought at the gate.

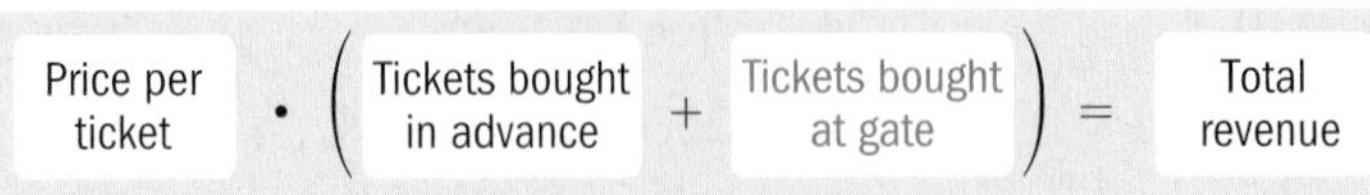

b. Solve the equation. Then check the solution.

SEE EXAMPLE 1
on p. 293
for Ex. 36

36. **FUNDRAISER** Student council members raised money selling T-shirts. Shirt sales numbers were: Maria, 13; Kevin, 9; and Emma, 10. The total raised was \$352. Write and solve an equation to find the price of one T-shirt.

37. **MEASUREMENT** The perimeter of the rectangle is $4(x - 8)$ millimeters. Use a ruler to measure the perimeter of the rectangle. Then find the value of x.

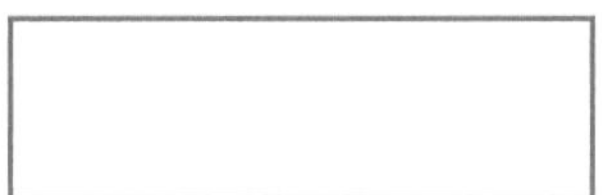

38. ★ **MULTIPLE CHOICE** You charge x dollars per hour for painting and $(x + 5)$ dollars per hour for hanging wallpaper. In one week you earn \$1020 painting for 12 hours and hanging wallpaper for 15 hours. Which equation represents this situation?

Ⓐ $12x + 15(x + 5) = 1020$ Ⓑ $x + (x + 5) + 12 + 15 = 1020$

Ⓒ $15x + 12(x + 5) = 1020$ Ⓓ $27(x + x + 5) = 1020$

39. ★ **WRITING** You volunteered at a senior citizens' center for 9 hours last month and 14 hours this month. *Describe* how you would use a division equation to find the number of hours you need to volunteer next month if you want your monthly mean to be 10 hours.

40. ★ **SHORT RESPONSE** Sara has \$26 to spend at a yard sale. She decides to buy a \$5 teapot and as many pairs of teacups and saucers as she can afford, plus one spare teacup. The teacups are \$2 each and the saucers are \$1 each. How many pairs can she buy? Can she also afford a \$.50 teaspoon? *Explain.*

41. **SAVING PLAN** You are saving to buy a mountain bike that costs \$235. You already have \$25. Each week, you earn \$15 babysitting and \$25 as a cashier, but you spend \$10 on lunches. Write and solve an equation to find in how many weeks you will have enough money saved.

42. **REASONING** Use the distributive property to solve the equation $3(x + 2) - 3 = 9$. Is it possible to solve this equation without distributing a 3? *Explain* your reasoning.

43. **CHALLENGE** Write an equation that has a solution of -2 and fits this description: The final step in solving the equation is dividing both sides by -18. Before that, 12 is added to both sides. The first step is distributing -3.

MIXED REVIEW

Get-Ready

Prepare for Lesson 6.2 in Exs. 44–45

Find the perimeter of a rectangle with the given dimensions. ***(p. 32)***

44. length = 15 cm, width = 7 cm   45. length = 14 ft, width = 21 ft

Copy and complete the statement with <, >, or =. ***(p. 212)***

46. 1.54×10^{-5} ? 1.54×10^{-6} 47. 3.75×10^{4} ? 5.7×10^{4}

48. ★ **MULTIPLE CHOICE** What is the median of the data set 101, 100, 101, 105, 112, and 105? ***(p. 272)***

Ⓐ 101   Ⓑ 103   Ⓒ 104   Ⓓ 105

6.2 Solving Equations with Variables on Both Sides

Before You solved equations that had variables on one side.

Now You'll solve equations that have variables on both sides.

Why? So you can compare costs, as for drum lessons in Example 4.

KEY VOCABULARY
- **perimeter,** *p. 32*
- **distributive property,** *p. 88*
- **like terms,** *p. 89*

ACTIVITY

Use algebra tiles to model and solve an equation.

STEP 1
Represent the equation $2x + 3 = x + 5$ using algebra tiles.

STEP 2
Remove one x-tile and three 1-tiles from each side.

STEP 3
Interpret the remaining tiles. The solution is 2.

Use algebra tiles to solve the equation.

1. $2x + 7 = 3x + 2$
2. $4x - 1 = x - 7$
3. $5x - 2 = 3x + 6$

Collecting like Terms To solve an equation with variables on both sides, as in the activity above, collect like terms on the same side.

EXAMPLE 1 Collecting Like Terms

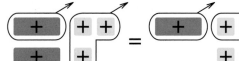

$x + 2 = 3x$	Original equation
$x + 2 - x = 3x - x$	Subtract x from each side.
$2 = 2x$	
$\frac{2}{2} = \frac{2x}{2}$	Divide both sides by 2.
$1 = x$	

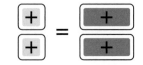

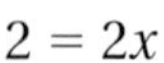 at classzone.com

EXAMPLE 2 Solve a Multi-Step Problem

Each side of the triangle has the same length. What is the perimeter of the triangle?

$5x + 9$ $7x + 5$

SOLUTION

$5x + 9 = 7x + 5$	**Write an equation.**
$5x + 9 - 5x = 7x + 5 - 5x$	**Subtract 5x from each side.**
$9 = 2x + 5$	**Simplify.**
$9 - 5 = 2x + 5 - 5$	**Subtract 5 from each side.**
$4 = 2x$	**Simplify.**
$\frac{4}{2} = \frac{2x}{2}$	**Divide each side by 2.**
$2 = x$	**Simplify.**

ANOTHER WAY

You can also begin by subtracting 5 from each side, and then subtracting 5x from each side.

$5x + 9 = 7x + 5$
$5x + 4 = 7x$
$4 = 2x$
$2 = x$

Because $5x + 9 = 5(2) + 9 = 19$, each side of the triangle is 19 units long. Since each side of the triangle has the same length, the perimeter is $3 \cdot 19$, or 57, units.

▶ **Answer** The perimeter of the triangle is 57 units.

Using the Distributive Property Sometimes you may have to use the distributive property to simplify one or both sides of an equation before you solve.

EXAMPLE 3 Using the Distributive Property

$21x = 3(2x + 30)$	**Original equation**
$21x = 6x + 90$	**Distributive property**
$21x - 6x = 6x + 90 - 6x$	**Subtract 6x from each side.**
$15x = 90$	**Simplify.**
$\frac{15x}{15} = \frac{90}{15}$	**Divide each side by 15.**
$x = 6$	**Simplify.**

✓ GUIDED PRACTICE for Examples 1, 2, and 3

Solve the equation.

1. $55 + 3x = 8x$ **2.** $9x = 12x - 9$ **3.** $-15x + 120 = 15x$

4. $4a + 5 = a + 11$ **5.** $3n + 7 = 2n - 1$ **6.** $-6c + 1 = -9c + 7$

7. $28 - 3s = 5s - 12$ **8.** $4(w - 9) = 7w + 18$ **9.** $2(y + 4) = -3y - 7$

EXAMPLE 4 Using a Verbal Model

Music You pay \$20 for a youth center membership. Drum lessons at the center cost \$8 each for members and \$12 each for nonmembers. You take two more lessons than your friend, a nonmember. For what number of lessons will your friend pay the same total amount as you?

SOLUTION

> ***READING***
> The problem is asking you to find the number of lessons for which the amount your friend pays for lessons equals the amount you pay *including* a membership fee.

Let n represent the number of lessons your friend takes.

Cost for friend				Cost for you				
Price per lesson	•	Number of lessons	=	Price per lesson	•	Number of lessons	+	Membership fee

$12n = 8(n + 2) + 20$	**Write algebraic model.**
$12n = 8n + 16 + 20$	**Distributive property**
$12n = 8n + 36$	**Simplify.**
$4n = 36$	**Subtract 8*n* from each side.**
$n = 9$	**Divide each side by 4.**

▶ **Answer** Your friend pays the same total amount as you for 9 lessons.

✓ GUIDED PRACTICE for Example 4

10. **What If?** In Example 4, suppose your friend takes 4 fewer lessons than you. For what number of lessons will your friend pay as much as you?

6.2 EXERCISES

HOMEWORK KEY
★ = **STANDARDIZED TEST PRACTICE** Exs. 14, 31, 32, 36, and 51

○ = **HINTS AND HOMEWORK HELP** for Exs. 3, 11, 15, 21, 33 at classzone.com

SKILL PRACTICE

1. **VOCABULARY** What is the perimeter of a figure?

SOLVING EQUATIONS Solve the equation.

> ***SEE EXAMPLES 1 AND 2*** on pp. 298–299 for Exs. 2–14

2. $7x = x + 18$
3. $7m = 4m + 21$
4. $30 - 2s = 4s$
5. $81 + 2k = 5k$
6. $13q - 48 = -3q$
7. $-11r = -4r + 56$
8. $5z - 43 = 2z + 80$
9. $16y - 43 = 4y + 65$
10. $8f + 11 = -7f - 19$
11. $-1 + 11a = 6 - 3a$
12. $9b - 10 = -b - 18$
13. $14s - 28 = 4s + 7$
14. ★ **MULTIPLE CHOICE** What is the value of x in $5x + 14 = 3x - 12$?

Ⓐ 1 Ⓑ -1 Ⓒ -13 Ⓓ -26

GEOMETRY **Find the perimeter. The triangles' sides are equal in length.**

SEE EXAMPLE 2 on p. 299 for Exs. 15–18

15. Rectangle with sides $2x - 3$, 7, 7, $3x - 10$

16.

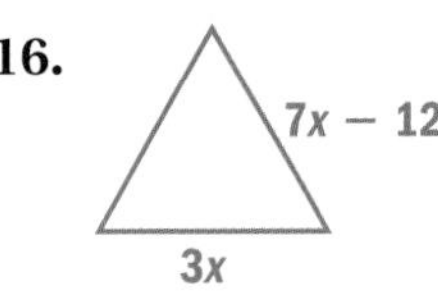

17. Triangle with sides $2x + 10$, $3x - 7$

18. ERROR ANALYSIS Describe and correct the error made in finding the perimeter P of the rectangle.

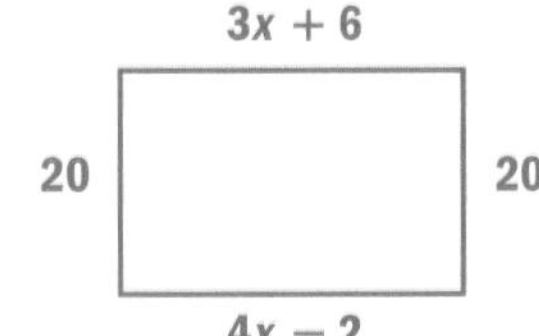

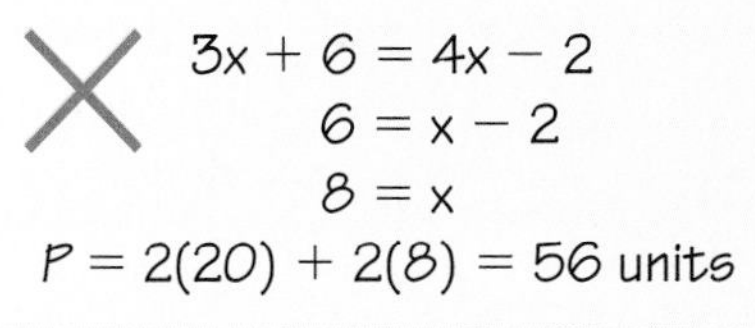

USING THE DISTRIBUTIVE PROPERTY **Solve the equation.**

SEE EXAMPLE 3 on p. 299 for Exs. 19–26

19. $3(t - 7) = 6t$

20. $-3h = 9(2 - 3h)$

21. $3(j + 4) = -2j + j$

22. $5(t + 7) = 2(2t + 7)$

23. $2(c + 6) = 5(c + 12)$

24. $6(s - 4) = 3(s + 9)$

25. $-2.5(2g + 6) = 3g - 6g$

26. $2(p + 2) = 1.8p - 2 - 0.2(p + 5)$

REASONING **Use the rectangle at the right to decide whether the statement is *true* or *false*. *Justify* your reasoning.**

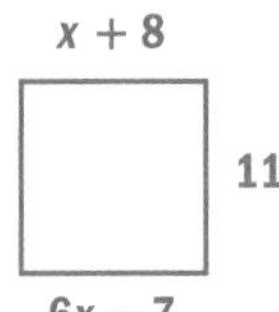

27. The rectangle is a square.

28. The area of the rectangle is 33 square units.

29. WHICH ONE DOESN'T BELONG? Which of the following triangles *cannot* have all three sides equal in length? (*Note:* Figures may not be to scale.)

A.

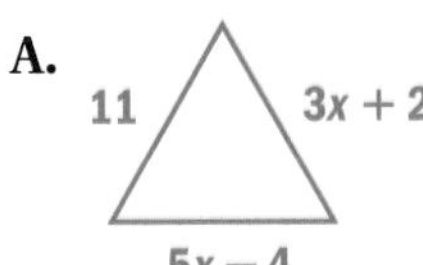

B. Triangle with sides 23, $3x - 1$, $2x + 7$

C.

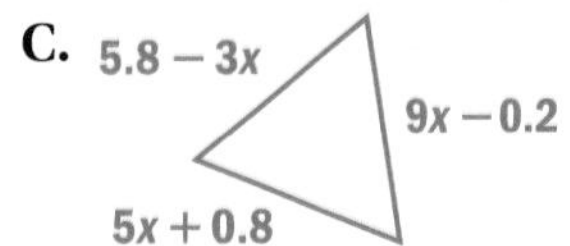

D. Triangle with sides $9x - 1$, $5x + 3$, $2x + 6$

30. CHALLENGE Try to solve the equation $2(5x + 1) = -7x + 2 + 17x$. What do you notice? *Explain* what this tells you about the number of solutions of the equation.

PROBLEM SOLVING

SEE EXAMPLE 4 on p. 300 for Ex. 31

31. ★ **MULTIPLE CHOICE** One phone card charges \$.018 per minute with a \$.25 weekly fee. Another card charges \$.029 per minute with no weekly fee. You need a card for 4 weeks. Which equation could you use to find the number of minutes for which both cards cost the same?

Ⓐ $0.018x = 0.029x + 4(0.25)$ Ⓑ $0.018x + 4(0.25) = 0.029x$

Ⓒ $0.018x = 0.029x$ Ⓓ $0.018x + 0.25 = 0.029x$

32. ★ **WRITING** Your friend says that when you solve an equation with the same variable on both sides, you must always begin by collecting the variable terms on the same side. Do you agree? *Explain* why or why not.

SEE EXAMPLE 4 on p. 300 for Ex. 33

33. **CONCERT TICKETS** Tickets to a concert cost \$30 for fan club members and \$35 for nonmembers. Fan club membership is \$25 per person. Write and solve an equation to find the number of tickets for which a member and a nonmember pay the same amount.

34. **ASSEMBLY LINE** Nia and Joseph are making fruit bowls. Joseph cuts the fruit and Nia distributes the fruit into the bowls. Joseph had already cut 72 pieces of fruit when Nia started. Joseph continues to cut fruit at the same rate. How many minutes will it take for Nia to catch up to Joseph?

Joseph cuts 3 pieces of fruit per minute.
Nia distributes 9 pieces of fruit per minute.

35. **DECORATIONS** You are decorating for a school dance. Balloons cost \$8 per dozen but cost more if bought singly. You have the exact amount of money for either 7 dozen and 5 single balloons or 75 single balloons. What is the cost of a single balloon? How much money do you have? *Explain.*

36. ★ **SHORT RESPONSE** David has \$26 and saves \$8 each week. Emily has \$56 and saves \$4 each week. How many weeks will it take for David and Emily to have the same amount of money? Will David ever have twice the amount of money that Emily has? *Justify* your answer.

37. **CHALLENGE** The sum of two numbers is 30. Three times one number is 6 more than 4 times the other number. What are the two numbers?

38. (xy) **CHALLENGE** Let a, b, c, and d be any numbers. What must be true about the relationship between a and c and the relationship between b and d for the equation $ax + b = cx + d$ to have *no* solution?

MIXED REVIEW

Get-Ready

Prepare for Lesson 6.3 in Exs. 39–44

Find the least common denominator of the fractions. *(p. 198)*

39. $\frac{1}{2}, \frac{2}{3}, \frac{5}{6}$ 40. $\frac{2}{9}, \frac{3}{4}, \frac{11}{12}$ 41. $\frac{4}{5}, \frac{1}{2}, \frac{3}{70}$

Find the sum or difference. *(p. 260)*

42. $7.31 + 2.248$ 43. $10.26 - 3.72$ 44. $16.508 + 4.53$

Solve the equation. *(p. 293)*

45. $3b - 5b = -14$ 46. $5c + 24 - 3c = 2$ 47. $4(x - 7) = 4$

48. $3(2z - 3) = 75$ 49. $7x - 2(x - 11) = -23$ 50. $\frac{y + 3}{5} = 10$

51. ★ **MULTIPLE CHOICE** What is the solution of $55 - 2x = -43$? *(p. 129)*

Ⓐ -49 Ⓑ -6 Ⓒ 6 Ⓓ 49

6.3 Solving Equations Involving Fractions and Decimals

Before	You solved equations involving whole numbers.
Now	You'll solve equations with fractions and decimals.
Why?	So you can compare heights, as with coral in Example 1.

KEY VOCABULARY

- **least common denominator (LCD),** *p. 198*

You may have noticed that equations sometimes have coefficients and constant terms that are not integers. In this lesson, you will solve multi-step equations that have fractions and decimals.

EXAMPLE 1 Solving an Equation Involving Decimals

Environment A colony of coral is 0.17 meter high and is growing at a rate of 0.025 meter per year. Another colony is 0.11 meter high and is growing at a rate of 0.041 meter per year. In how many years will the colonies be the same height?

SOLUTION

First write a verbal model. Let n represent the number of years.

Colony 1							Colony 2				
Height	+	Growth rate	•	Years	=	Height	+	Growth rate	•	Years

$0.17 + 0.025n = 0.11 + 0.041n$	**Write algebraic model.**
$0.17 = 0.11 + 0.016n$	**Subtract 0.025*n* from each side.**
$0.06 = 0.016n$	**Subtract 0.11 from each side.**
$\frac{0.06}{\mathbf{0.016}} = \frac{0.016n}{\mathbf{0.016}}$	**Divide each side by 0.016.**
$3.75 = n$	**Simplify.**

TAKE NOTES
Some of the steps in Example 1 are not shown. Identify these steps and include them in your notes.

▶ **Answer** The colonies will be the same height in 3.75 years.

✓ **GUIDED PRACTICE** for Example 1

1. **Snowboarding** You and a friend are buying snowboarding gear. You buy a pair of goggles that costs \$39.95 and 4 tubes of wax. Your friend buys a helmet that costs \$54.95 and 2 tubes of wax. You each spend the same amount. Write and solve an equation to find the price of one tube of wax.

Clearing Decimals The multiplication property of equality allows you to multiply each side of an equation by the same number. You can use this property to clear decimals from an equation. Multiply each side of the equation by a power of ten that makes all coefficients and constants integers.

EXAMPLE 2 Solving an Equation Involving Decimals

$1.4x - 1.8 + 2.35x = 0.21$	**Original equation**
$(1.4x - 1.8 + 2.35x)100 = (0.21)100$	**Multiply each side by 100 to clear decimals.**
$140x - 180 + 235x = 21$	**Simplify.**
$375x - 180 = 21$	**Combine like terms.**
$375x = 201$	**Add 180 to each side.**
$\frac{375x}{375} = \frac{201}{375}$	**Divide each side by 375.**
$x = 0.536$	**Simplify.**

Clearing Fractions When you solve an equation with fractions, you can multiply each side by the LCD to clear the fractions.

EXAMPLE 3 Solving an Equation Involving Fractions

$\frac{3}{10}x = -\frac{1}{6}x + \frac{7}{10}$	**Original equation**
$\left(\frac{3}{10}x\right)30 = \left(-\frac{1}{6}x + \frac{7}{10}\right)30$	**Multiply each side by the LCD, 30.**
$\left(\frac{3}{10}x\right)30 = \left(-\frac{1}{6}x\right)30 + \left(\frac{7}{10}\right)30$	**Distributive property**
$\frac{3 \cdot \overset{3}{\cancel{30}}}{\underset{1}{\cancel{10}}}x = -\frac{1 \cdot \overset{5}{\cancel{30}}}{\underset{1}{\cancel{6}}}x + \frac{7 \cdot \overset{3}{\cancel{30}}}{\underset{1}{\cancel{10}}}$	**Divide out common factors.**
$9x = -5x + 21$	**Simplify.**
$14x = 21$	**Add 5x to each side.**
$x = \frac{21}{14} = \frac{3}{2}$, or $1\frac{1}{2}$	**Divide each side by 14. Simplify.**

AVOID ERRORS
When multiplying both sides of an equation by the same number, be sure to multiply *each* term by that number.

GUIDED PRACTICE for Examples 2 and 3

Solve the equation.

2. $-1.7k + 6.7k = 13.1$ **3.** $1.2n - 0.24 = 0.7n$ **4.** $8.3 - 8y = 1.2y + 6$

5. $\frac{4}{5}x + 3 = -\frac{7}{10}$ **6.** $2s - 1\frac{1}{4}s = \frac{1}{3}$ **7.** $\frac{5}{6}v + \frac{5}{8} = \frac{3}{8}v$

6.3 EXERCISES

HOMEWORK KEY

★ = **STANDARDIZED TEST PRACTICE** Exs. 20, 29, 34, 37, 39, 40, 42, and 54

○ = **HINTS AND HOMEWORK HELP** for Exs. 5, 11, 17, 35 at classzone.com

SKILL PRACTICE

VOCABULARY **Copy and complete the statement.**

1. Twenty-four is the _?_ of $\frac{1}{4}$, $\frac{5}{6}$, and $\frac{3}{8}$.

2. The process of multiplying both sides of the equation $2.4 + 0.2x = 5$ by 10 is used to _?_ decimals.

SOLVING EQUATIONS **Solve the equation.**

SEE EXAMPLES 1 AND 2 on pp. 303–304 for Exs. 3–10, 19

3. $1.5a - 1.2 = 1.8a$
4. $5.85b = 8.68 + 3.68b$
5. $0.5c + 3.49 - 2c = 4$
6. $r + 8.2 + 0.4r = -8.6$
7. $1.5s - 1.2 - s = 0.5$
8. $5.3 + u = 3.2u - 2.7$
9. $4.93 - 9.20v = 0.66v$
10. $7.6a + 9.6 = 1.2a$

SEE EXAMPLE 3 on p. 304 for Exs. 11–18

11. $\frac{3}{8}m + \frac{7}{8} = 2m$
12. $\frac{3}{4} - \frac{1}{2}b = -3b$
13. $-\frac{4}{15}n + \frac{2}{3} = \frac{2}{5}n$
14. $p - \frac{4}{9}p = -\frac{7}{9}$
15. $-\frac{1}{5}p + \frac{3}{4}p = 11$
16. $\frac{1}{6}x + \frac{2}{3}x = 1$
17. $\frac{3}{10} - w = \frac{4}{5} - \frac{3}{5}w$
18. $\frac{7}{4}z - \frac{1}{6} = \frac{17}{6} + \frac{3}{4}z$

19. **ERROR ANALYSIS** Describe and correct the error made in the solution.

$$1.5x + 0.25 = 1.6x$$
$$15x + 25 = 16x$$
$$25 = x$$

20. ★ **MULTIPLE CHOICE** By what do you multiply each side of the equation $3.75x - \frac{1}{2} = 1.125 - \frac{9}{4}x$ to clear all fractions and decimals?

Ⓐ 2 Ⓑ 4 Ⓒ 8 Ⓓ 100

CLEARING DECIMALS AND FRACTIONS **Tell what number you multiply each side of the equation by to clear the decimals and fractions. Then solve.**

21. $-4.42x + 0.9 = -9.070 - 0.432x$
22. $0.025(x + 4) = 1.2415$
23. $6\frac{4}{5}n - \frac{8}{9} = \frac{7}{15}n$
24. $\frac{3}{8} + \frac{9}{20}m = \frac{23}{20} + \frac{7}{8}m$
25. $5\frac{3}{10} - 0.2x = \frac{1}{5}x + 0.8$
26. $1.25(x - 9) = \frac{13}{4}$
27. $\frac{1}{2}x - 3 + 0.625x = 5$
28. $2.25 - 3z = 0.375 - \frac{3}{4}z$

29. ★ **OPEN-ENDED MATH** Write three equivalent equations for $\frac{5}{6}x - \frac{1}{2} = 3$.

CHALLENGE Solve the equation. Then check the solution.

30. $\frac{7}{2a} - \frac{5}{4} = \frac{1}{a}$

31. $\frac{3}{4x} = \frac{1}{2x} - \frac{7}{12}$

32. $1.8 - \frac{3}{8y} = \frac{9}{10y} - 6$

33. $3\frac{4}{9} - \frac{2}{3c} = 6\left(\frac{1}{c} + 3\right)$

PROBLEM SOLVING

SEE EXAMPLES 1 AND 2 on pp. 303–304 for Exs. 34–36

34. ★ **MULTIPLE CHOICE** At a basketball game, you buy 10 raffle tickets. Your friend buys a T-shirt for \$13.50 and 1 raffle ticket. If you each spend the same amount, which equation can you use to find the cost x of one ticket?

Ⓐ $11x = 13.5$ Ⓑ $13.5 = 10x + x$

Ⓒ $10x + 13.5 = x$ Ⓓ $10x = 13.5 + x$

35. **DELI PRICES** At the deli, Swiss cheese costs \$3.96 per pound and turkey costs \$4.76 per pound. You buy the same amount of each and spend \$13.08. Write and solve an equation to find how many pounds of each you buy.

36. **PICNIC** Rosa and Arlene are shopping for a neighborhood picnic. Rosa buys paper plates and cups for \$19.10 and 5 pints of potato salad. Arlene buys watermelons for \$15.55 and 6 pints of potato salad. They each spend the same total amount and each pint of potato salad costs the same amount. Write and solve an equation to find the cost of one pint of potato salad.

37. ★ **OPEN-ENDED MATH** Write a real-world problem that can be solved using the equation $2.1r + 0.4r = 127.5$. The units for r should be miles per hour and the units for the constant term should be miles. What does the solution represent?

SEE EXAMPLE 3 on p. 304 for Ex. 38

38. **SEWING SUPPLIES** You buy a clothes pattern for \$7 at a fabric store. You also buy $\frac{3}{4}$ yard of red fabric, $2\frac{1}{2}$ yards of purple fabric, and $\frac{7}{8}$ yard of blue fabric. The total cost is \$23.50. All three fabrics cost the same per yard.

a. Write and solve an equation to find the price per yard.

b. How much do you spend on each fabric? *Explain.*

39. ★ **WRITING** Suppose you multiply each side of an equation containing fractions by a common multiple of the denominators that is the product of all the denominators. Will you still get the correct answer? *Describe* advantages and disadvantages of this method.

40. ★ **SHORT RESPONSE** Use the equation $6.95x - 2.13 = 1.8x + 3.07$.

a. **Solve** Solve the equation.

b. **Estimate** *Describe* a way to estimate the solution. Then estimate the solution. *Explain* how this estimation method might be useful.

41. **GEOMETRY** You mow $\frac{1}{3}$ of the lawn, and your sister mows $\frac{2}{5}$ of the lawn. What is the area of the entire lawn? What is the length of the section left to mow?

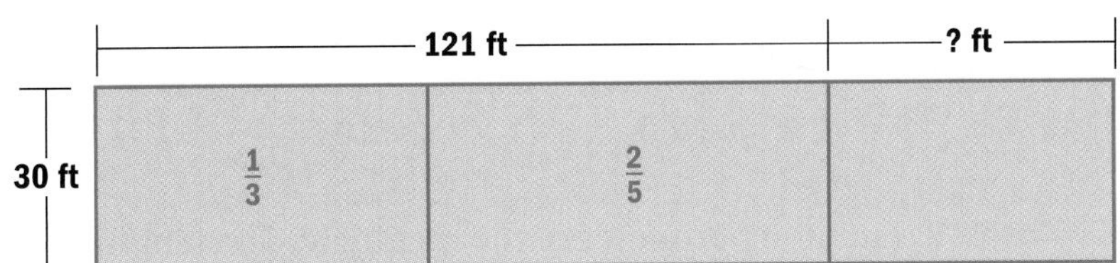

42. ★ **EXTENDED RESPONSE** You deposit half of your money in the bank. You spend half of the remaining amount on a movie ticket, and you spend another four dollars on popcorn. You have five dollars left.

a. Write an equation to model this situation.

b. How much money did you start with?

c. *Describe* another method for solving the problem that does not involve writing and solving an equation.

d. *Compare* the methods. How are they alike? How are they different?

43. **CHALLENGE** The mean rainfall in Honolulu, Hawaii, from January through the end of May was 3.756 inches. The mean rainfall from January through the end of June was 2.872 inches more than the amount of rain that fell in June. How many inches of rain fell in June? Round your answer to the nearest hundredth.

44. **CHALLENGE** The length of a rectangle is $2\frac{2}{3}$ times the width. The perimeter of the rectangle is $2\frac{1}{2}$ units less than 3 times the length. Find the width and the area of the rectangle.

MIXED REVIEW

Get-Ready

Prepare for Lesson 6.4 in Exs. 45–50

Find the unknown value in the formula $A = \frac{1}{2}bh$. *(p. 142)*

45. $b = \frac{1}{2}, h = 4$

46. $A = 15, b = \frac{5}{6}$

47. $A = 22, h = 2.5$

48. $A = 9, b = 4.5$

49. $A = 2.1, h = 6$

50. $b = 3.25, h = 8$

Solve the equation. *(p. 298)*

51. $6n + 12 = 2n$

52. $16 - 3s = 2s - 14$

53. $-3(w - 7) = 5w + 3$

54. ★ **MULTIPLE CHOICE** Which expression is equivalent to $9(8 + x)$? *(p. 88)*

Ⓐ $72x$ Ⓑ $72 + x$ Ⓒ $8 + 9x$ Ⓓ $72 + 9x$

QUIZ for Lessons 6.1–6.3

Solve the equation.

1. $2(x + 16) = 46$ *(p. 293)*
2. $79 = 10x - 23 + 7x$ *(p. 293)*
3. $-108 - 9x = -16(x + 5)$ *(p. 298)*
4. $12n = 17 - 22n$ *(p. 298)*
5. $\frac{x + 8}{3} = -4$ *(p. 293)*
6. $\frac{2x - 1}{5} = 7$ *(p. 293)*
7. $27.2m + 15.7 = -85.94 + 0.8m$ *(p. 303)*
8. $14.6p + 34.25 = 11.8p + 45.45$ *(p. 303)*
9. $\frac{1}{2}v + \frac{11}{12} - \frac{5}{4}v = -\frac{5}{12}$ *(p. 303)*
10. $2\frac{5}{6} - \frac{1}{3}w = w + \frac{1}{6}$ *(p. 303)*
11. **GEOMETRY** Find the perimeter of the rectangle. The length and width are measured in feet. *(p. 298)*

4y − 12

2x − 3 | 7x − 18

y + 3

12. **COLOR PRINTER** You have \$445 to buy a printer. You find one that costs \$235. It uses a black ink cartridge that costs \$30 and a color ink cartridge that costs \$40. You buy the same number of each type of cartridge.
    a. Write and solve an equation to determine how many pairs of ink cartridges you can buy for the printer. *(p. 293)*
    b. How much money will you spend on color ink cartridges?

Brain Game

City Solutions

Solve the equations. Then fill in each blank with the variable that corresponds to the solution. When you are finished, the letters will spell out the name of a city found in 19 states.

?	?	?	?	?	?	?	?	?
−5	4	6	−1	2	5	−4	−2	1

1. $2g - 7 - 3g = -12$
2. $4n + 1 = 9n - 4$
3. $1.6o + 13 = 5 - 2.4o$
4. $12 = -2r - 12 + 8r$
5. $\frac{9}{16}l - \frac{9}{8} = \frac{3}{8}l$
6. $a - 2(a + 1) = 3$
7. $\frac{9}{10}n + \frac{1}{5} = \frac{7}{10}n + \frac{3}{5}$
8. $i + 4 - 7i = 10$
9. $7 - 2.65t = -4.4t$

Lessons 6.1–6.3

1. **MULTI-STEP PROBLEM** You buy 5 ringtones and a \$9.99 cover for your cell phone. Your friend Kaylee buys 3 ringtones and a \$15.97 flashing antenna top for her phone. You each spend the same amount of money.
   a. Write a verbal model for the situation.
   b. Use the verbal model to write and solve an equation to find the cost c per ringtone.
   c. How much does Kaylee pay altogether?

2. **MULTI-STEP PROBLEM** Over the next 10 years, a bald cypress tree will grow at a rate of about 30 inches per year and a bur oak tree will grow at a rate of about 10 inches per year. The bald cypress is 15 feet tall and the bur oak is 22 feet tall.
   a. How many years will it take for the trees to be the same height? What is that height, in feet?
   b. How many more years, from the time that the trees are the same height, will it take for the bald cypress tree to be 5 feet taller than the bur oak tree?

3. **SHORT RESPONSE** Jené is planting a garden in a corner of her yard. The yard is bordered by a fence on the outer edges. She has a 9 foot log to form one edge of the garden. Jené has enough seeds to cover 138 square feet. Write and solve an equation to find how long the other log must be so that the garden covers 138 square feet. How many feet of fence border the garden? *Explain.*

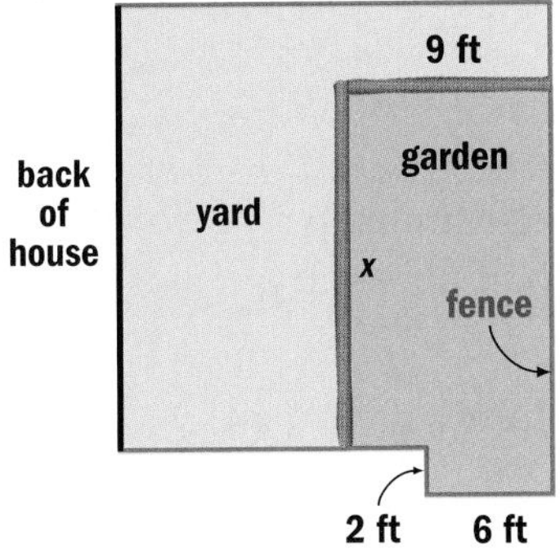

4. **GRIDDED ANSWER** Each side of the triangle has the same length. How many units is the perimeter of the triangle?

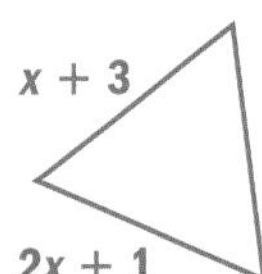

5. **OPEN-ENDED** Write a real-world problem that can be modeled by an equation that has variables on both sides, involves fractions or decimals, and requires multiple steps to solve. Then solve the equation, showing all steps.

6. **SHORT RESPONSE** You drove $\frac{1}{3}$ of the distance on a road trip, and your friend Al drove $\frac{1}{2}$ of the distance. The two of you drove a total of 900 miles, and your friend Rita drove the remaining distance. How far did Rita drive? Who drove the farthest? *Explain.*

7. **EXTENDED RESPONSE** You buy n shirts for \$8 per shirt. Every shirt after the second shirt is \$3 off the original price. You spend \$36.
   a. Write a verbal model for the situation.
   b. Use the verbal model to write and solve an equation. How many shirts do you buy?
   c. What is the mean cost per shirt? *Explain* how you found your answer.

INVESTIGATION

Use before Lesson 6.4

GOAL

Find the relationship between diameter and circumference.

MATERIALS

- metric tape measure or ruler
- string
- paper and pencil

6.4 Diameter and Circumference

In this Investigation, you will explore the relationship between the diameter and circumference of a circle.

The *diameter* is the distance across a circle through the center.

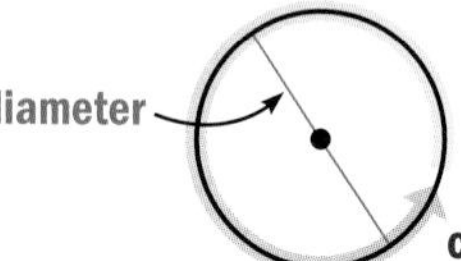

The ***circumference*** is the distance around a circle.

EXPLORE 1 **Find the diameter and circumference of circular objects.**

STEP 1 **Measure** the diameter and circumference of several circular objects. If necessary, wrap a string around the object and measure the length of the string with a ruler.

STEP 2 **Record** the measurements in a table like the one below.

Object	*Diameter*	*Circumference*	$\frac{\text{Circumference}}{\text{Diameter}}$
water bottle	65 mm	206 mm	?
tuna can	84 mm	264 mm	?
clock	174 mm	549 mm	?
quarter	24 mm	74 mm	?
mug	82 mm	261 mm	?

PRACTICE

1. Find the quotient of the circumference and the diameter for each object you measured. Round to the nearest hundredth, if necessary. Record the quotients in another column of the table.
2. What do you notice about the numbers in the new column of your table?

EXPLORE 2 Write a circumference formula.

STEP 1 **Find** the mean of the quotients $\frac{\text{circumference}}{\text{diameter}}$ in your table. How does your mean compare with the means found by the other students in your class?

STEP 2 **Find** the mean of the quotients $\frac{\text{circumference}}{\text{diameter}}$ collected by your whole class.

STEP 3 **Use** the result in Step 2 to write a formula for the circumference C of a circle in terms of the diameter d.

PRACTICE **Use the formula you wrote in Step 3 above to calculate the circumference of the circle given its diameter *d*.**

3. $d = 64$ mm

4. $d = 140$ mm

5. $d = 36$ cm

6. $d = 20$ cm

7. $d = 4$ in.

8. $d = 1.25$ in.

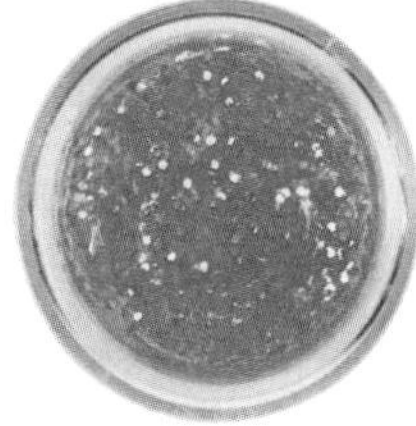

DRAW CONCLUSIONS

9. WRITING A FORMULA Write a formula for the diameter d of a circle in terms of the circumference C.

6.4 Solving Equations Involving Circumference

Before	You solved equations involving fractions and decimals.
Now	You'll solve equations involving the circumference of a circle.
Why?	So you can find a diameter, as of a Ferris wheel in Example 3.

KEY VOCABULARY
- **circle,** *p. 312*
- **center,** *p. 312*
- **radius,** *p. 312*
- **diameter,** *p. 312*
- **circumference,** *p. 312*
- **pi** (π), *p. 312*

A **circle** is the set of all points in a plane that are the same distance from a fixed point called the **center**. The distance from the center to any point on the circle is the **radius**. The **diameter** is the distance across the circle through the center, or twice the radius.

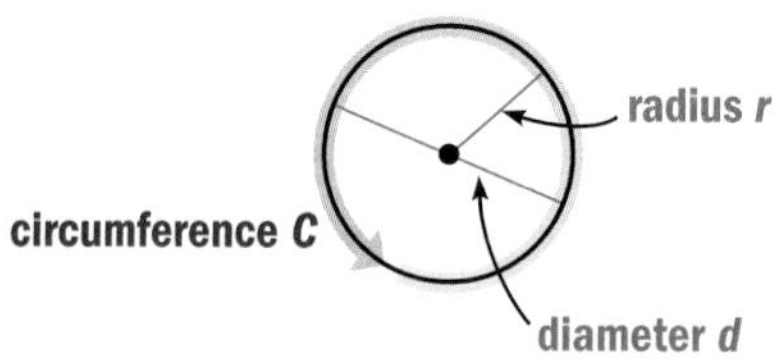

VOCABULARY
Even though π is a Greek letter, remember that π is *not* a variable. It has a specific value.

The **circumference** of a circle is the distance around the circle. For every circle, the quotient of its circumference and its diameter is the same: about 3.14159. This constant is represented by the Greek letter **pi**, π. You can approximate π using 3.14, $\frac{22}{7}$, or the π key on a calculator.

KEY CONCEPT *For Your Notebook*

Circumference of a Circle

Words The circumference of a circle is the product of π and the diameter.

Algebra $C = \pi d$ or $C = 2\pi r$

$d = 2r$

EXAMPLE 1 Using Radius to Find Circumference

Find the circumference of a circle with a radius of 11 meters.

SOLUTION

$C = 2\pi r$	**Circumference formula**
$\approx 2(3.14)(11)$	**Substitute 3.14 for π and 11 for r.**
$= 69.08$	**Multiply.**

▸ **Answer** The circumference is about 69.08 meters.

Check Estimate: $2(3.14)(11) \approx 2(3)(11) = 66$, so 69.08 is reasonable.

EXAMPLE 2 Using Diameter to Find Circumference

Find the circumference of the circle.

21 ft

SOLUTION

The measure shown is a diameter, so use the circumference formula that involves the diameter.

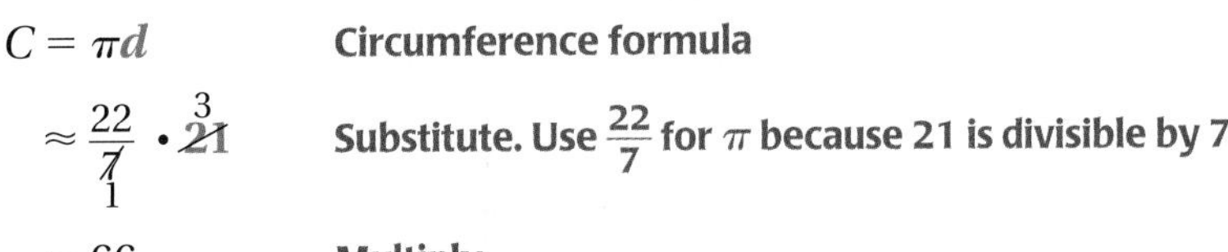

$C = \pi d$	**Circumference formula**
$\approx \frac{22}{7} \cdot 21$	**Substitute. Use $\frac{22}{7}$ for π because 21 is divisible by 7.**
$= 66$	**Multiply.**

▶ **Answer** The circumference is about 66 feet.

SUBSTITUTE FOR π
When considering whether to use $\frac{22}{7}$ for π, look for numbers that are divisible by 22 or 7.

★ EXAMPLE 3 Standardized Test Practice

Ferris Wheel A Ferris wheel has a circumference of about 423.9 feet. What is the diameter of the Ferris wheel? Use 3.14 for π.

Ⓐ 13.5 feet Ⓑ 67.5 feet Ⓒ 135 feet Ⓓ 1350 feet

ELIMINATE CHOICES
The diameter of a circle cannot be greater than the circumference of the circle. So, choice D can be eliminated.

SOLUTION

You are asked to find the diameter, so use the circumference formula that involves diameter.

$C = \pi d$	**Circumference formula**
$423.9 \approx 3.14d$	**Substitute 423.9 for C and 3.14 for π.**
$\frac{423.9}{3.14} = \frac{3.14d}{3.14}$	**Divide each side by 3.14.**
$135 = d$	**Simplify.**

▶ **Answer** The diameter is about 135 feet.
The correct answer is C. Ⓐ Ⓑ Ⓒ Ⓓ

✓ GUIDED PRACTICE for Examples 1, 2, and 3

Find the circumference of the circle. Use 3.14 or $\frac{22}{7}$ for π. Explain your choice of π.

1.

2.
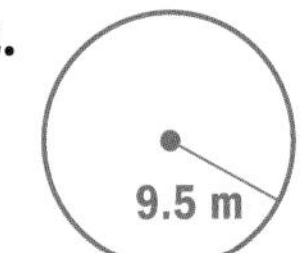

3.
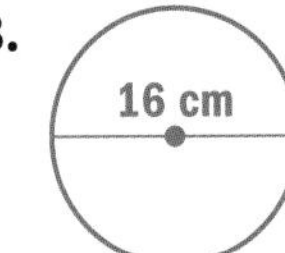

4. diameter = 32 in.

5. diameter = 140 ft

6. radius = 1.5 km

7. What If? In Example 3, suppose the circumference of the Ferris wheel is 462 feet. What is the diameter of the Ferris wheel?

EXAMPLE 4 Using Circumference to Find the Radius

A pottery wheel has a circumference of 44 inches. Find the radius.

SOLUTION

$C = 2\pi r$	Circumference formula
$44 \approx 2\left(\frac{22}{7}\right)r$	Use $\frac{22}{7}$ for π.
$44 = \frac{44}{7}r$	Simplify.
$\overset{1}{\cancel{44}} \cdot \frac{7}{\underset{1}{\cancel{44}}} = \frac{44}{7}r \cdot \frac{7}{44}$	Multiply each side by $\frac{7}{44}$, the reciprocal of $\frac{44}{7}$.
$7 = r$	Simplify.

REVIEW RECIPROCALS
Need help with reciprocals? See p. 247.

▸ **Answer** The radius is about 7 inches.

GUIDED PRACTICE for Example 4

8. **What If?** In Example 4, suppose the pottery wheel has a circumference of 38 inches. Find the radius to the nearest hundredth. Explain your choice of π.

6.4 EXERCISES

HOMEWORK KEY

★ = **STANDARDIZED TEST PRACTICE** Exs. 22, 40, 41, 43, 44, 46, and 55

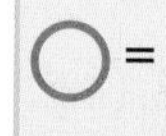 = **HINTS AND HOMEWORK HELP** for Exs. 7, 11, 15, 19, 39 at classzone.com

SKILL PRACTICE

1. **VOCABULARY** Draw and label a circle with a radius and a diameter.

2. **VOCABULARY** Copy and complete: The distance around a circle is its __?__.

FINDING CIRCUMFERENCE Find the circumference of a circle with the given radius or diameter. Use 3.14 or $\frac{22}{7}$ for π. *Explain* your choice.

SEE EXAMPLES 1 AND 2
on pp. 312–313 for Exs. 3–12

3. $r = 10$ mm
4. $r = 3\frac{1}{2}$ ft
5. $d = 100$ cm
6. $r = 21$ ft
7. $d = 14$ in.
8. $d = 20$ mi
9. $d = 63$ mm
10. $d = 56$ m
11. $r = 42$ ft

12. **ERROR ANALYSIS** Describe and correct the error made in finding the circumference of the circle.

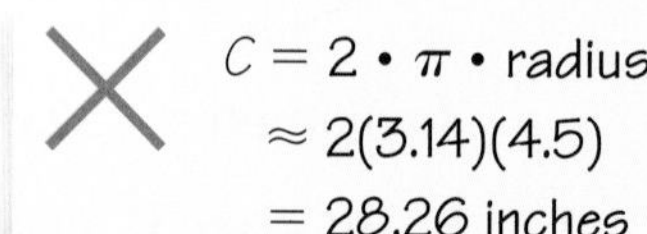

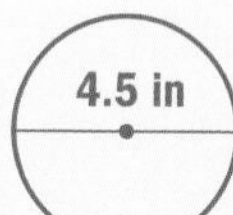

FINDING RADIUS OR DIAMETER **Find the radius or diameter of the circle with the given circumference. Use 3.14 or $\frac{22}{7}$ for π.**

SEE EXAMPLES 3 AND 4 on pp. 313–314 for Exs. 13–22

13. $C = 66$ in., $d = \underline{\ ?\ }$ **14.** $C = 3.14$ m, $r = \underline{\ ?\ }$ **15.** $C = 33$ km, $d = \underline{\ ?\ }$

16. $C = 628$ cm, $r = \underline{\ ?\ }$ **17.** $C = 9.42$ cm, $r = \underline{\ ?\ }$ **18.** $C = 330$ yd, $d = \underline{\ ?\ }$

19. $C = 157$ yd, $r = \underline{\ ?\ }$ **20.** $C = 235.5$ cm, $d = \underline{\ ?\ }$ **21.** $C = 44$ m, $r = \underline{\ ?\ }$

22. ★ **MULTIPLE CHOICE** Which circle has a circumference of 50.24 feet? Use 3.14 for π.

Ⓐ 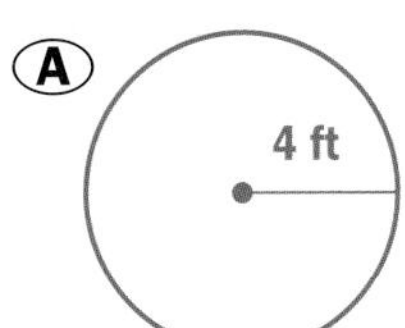

Ⓑ 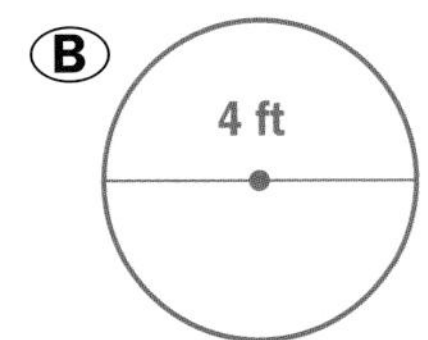

Ⓒ 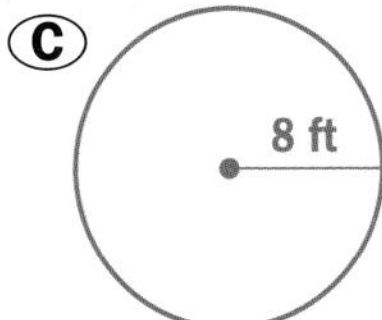

Ⓓ 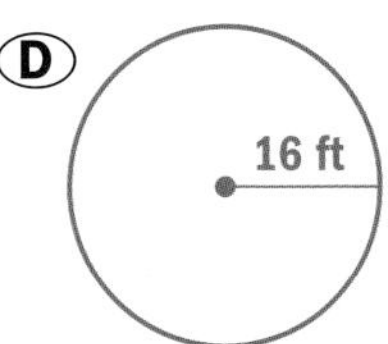

MEASUREMENT **Use a ruler to measure the unknown dimension. Then find the circumference of the circle. Use 3.14 for π. Estimate to check.**

SEE EXAMPLES 1 AND 2 on pp. 312–313 for Exs. 23–25

23.

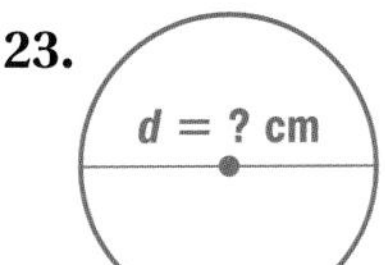

24.

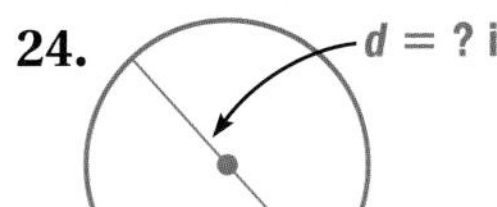

25.

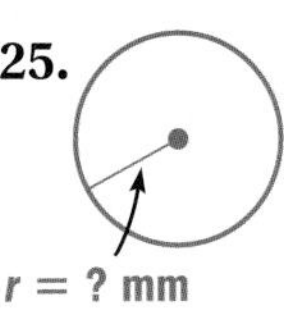

PERIMETER **Find the perimeter of the figure. Use 3.14 for π.**

26.

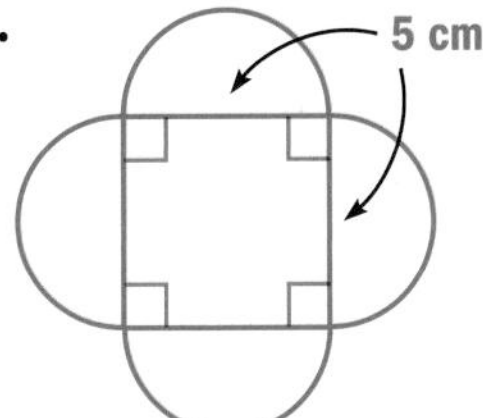

27.

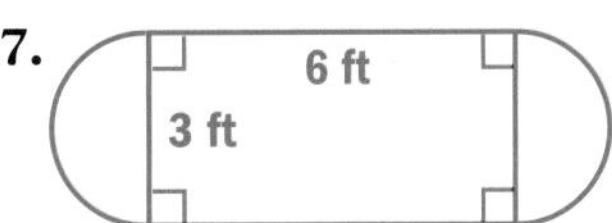

28.

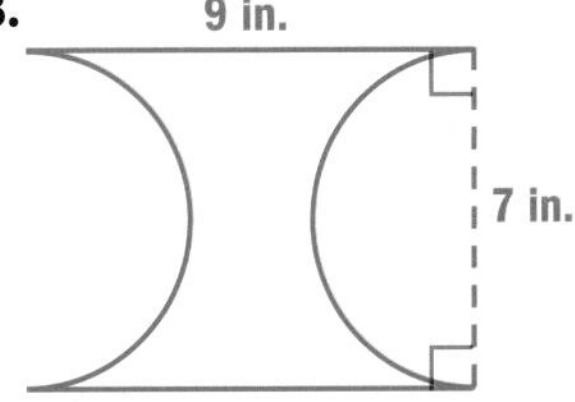

ALGEBRA **In Chapter 1 you learned three ways to write the distance formula. Copy and complete each statement by using the properties of equality to rewrite the circumference formula. *Justify* each step.**

REWRITE FORMULAS Need help rewriting formulas? See p. 32.

29. If $C = \pi d$, then $\pi = \underline{\ ?\ }$. **30.** If $C = \pi d$, then $d = \underline{\ ?\ }$.

31. If $C = 2\pi r$, then $r = \underline{\ ?\ }$. **32.** If $C = 2\pi r$, then $\pi = \underline{\ ?\ }$.

CHALLENGE **Two circles are *concentric* if they share a center, as in the diagrams below. The circumference of the outer circle is given. Find the value of x. Use 3.14 for π. (All measures are in meters.)**

33. $C = 75.36$ m

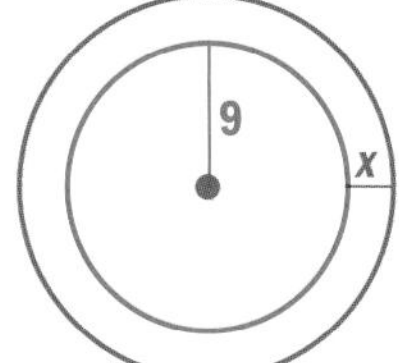

34. $C = 109.9$ m

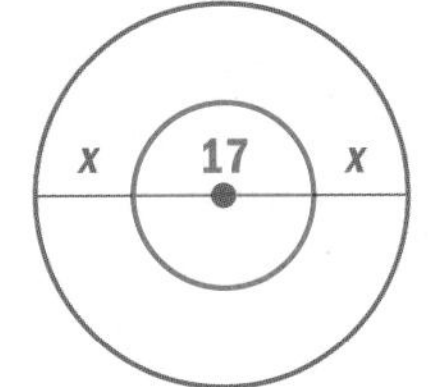

35. $C = 94.2$ m

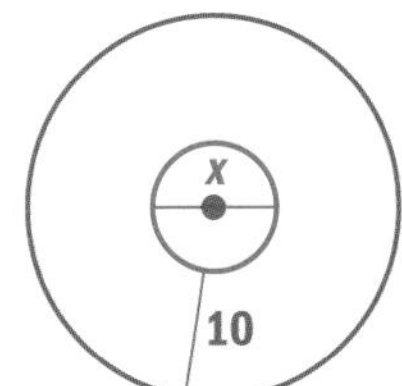

PROBLEM SOLVING

SEE EXAMPLES 1 AND 2 on pp. 312–313 for Exs. 36–37

36. **ARCHITECTURE** The diameter of the U.S. Capitol Building's dome is 96 feet at its widest point. Find its circumference. Use 3.14 for π.

37. **GEARS** One circular gear has a radius of 3.5 inches. It meshes with another gear that has a radius 3 times as great. What is the circumference of each gear? How do the circumferences compare? Use $\frac{22}{7}$ for π.

SEE EXAMPLES 3 AND 4 on pp. 313–314 for Exs. 38–39, 42

38. **CHECKING REASONABLENESS** The circumference of a circular fountain is 35.5 feet. A friend says that the diameter of the fountain is approximately 12 feet. Is this approximation reasonable? *Explain.*

39. **ESTIMATION** The Great Clock of Westminster rings the bell known as "Big Ben" in London, England. The circumference of the clock face is about 72 feet 3 inches. Estimate the diameter of the clock face.

40. ★ **WRITING** Look up *circumnavigate* in the dictionary. *Describe* how the definition is similar to the definition of *circumference.*

41. ★ **OPEN-ENDED MATH** Find a circular object in your house. Measure the diameter of the object. Then calculate the circumference.

42. **FASHION** To measure the leg opening of a pair of flared jeans, you flatten them out and measure the width. The width is 12 inches, which is half the circumference. What is the diameter of the leg opening? Use 3.14 for π. Round your answer to the nearest hundredth.

43. ★ **MULTIPLE CHOICE** A basketball hoop has a circumference of about 56.5 inches. A basketball has a circumference of about 28.5 inches. What is the approximate difference between the diameter of the hoop and the diameter of the basketball? Use 3.14 for π.

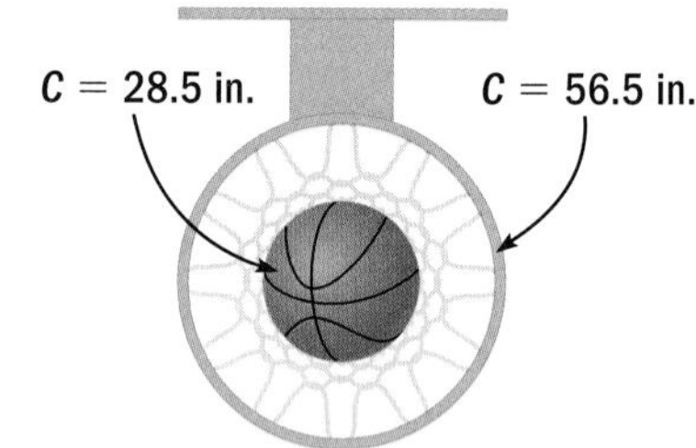

Ⓐ 4.5 in. Ⓑ 9 in.

Ⓒ 18 in. Ⓓ 27 in.

44. ★ **SHORT RESPONSE** Find the circumferences of circles with radii 1, 2, 4, 8, and 16 meters. Leave your answers in terms of π. *Compare* the circumferences. What happens to the circumference of a circle as its radius doubles? What do you think happens as the radius triples? *Explain* your reasoning.

45. **REASONING** The circumference of the larger circle is approximately 37.7 centimeters. Between what two whole numbers of centimeters is the perimeter of the square? Which of these numbers do you think the perimeter of the square is closer to? *Explain.*

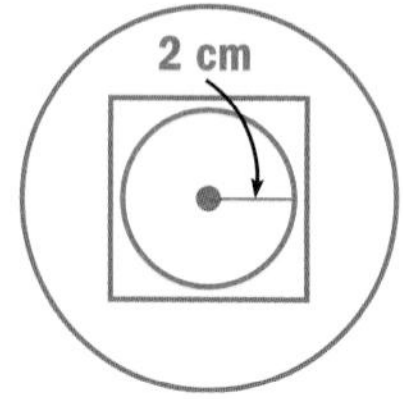

46. ★ **EXTENDED RESPONSE** Adventurer Mike Horn traveled around the world as close to the equator as possible without using any motorized transportation.

a. **Calculate** The radius of Earth is about 3963 miles. Approximate its circumference. Use 3.14 for π.

b. **Compare** Mike Horn actually traveled a total of 29,000 miles. About how much farther did Mike Horn travel than if he had followed the equator exactly?

c. **Analyze** To the nearest mile, find what the radius of Earth would be if its circumference were 29,000 miles. Use 3.14 for π. *Compare* this radius to the actual radius.

d. **Draw Conclusions** Why do you think the circumference of Earth is different from the distance Mike Horn traveled?

47. **CHALLENGE** A single rotation of a car's wheel is shown below. How many rotations will the wheel make if the car travels 6 miles? Round your answer to the nearest whole number.

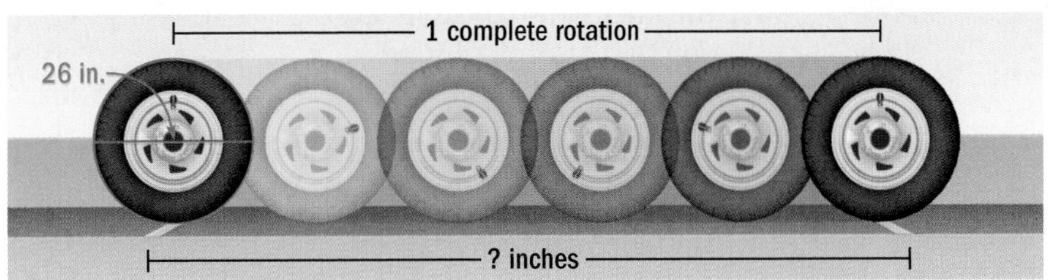

48. **CHALLENGE** Each circle below is divided into equal sections. The radius of each circle is 5 units. Write your answers in terms of π.

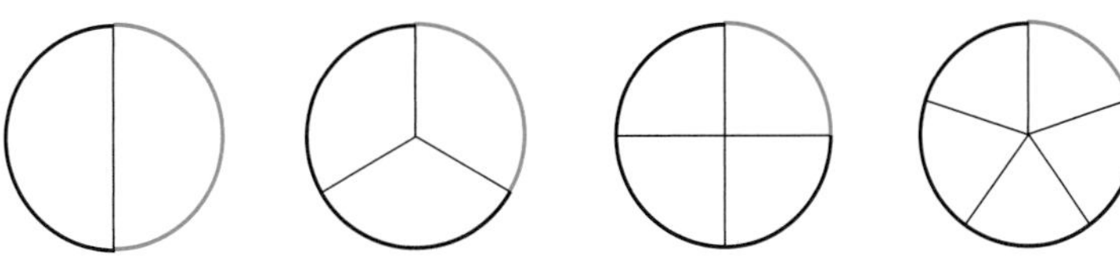

a. Find the length of the blue portion of each circle.

b. Write a formula for the length of the blue portion of the nth circle.

c. Find the length of the blue portion of the 11th circle.

MIXED REVIEW

Prepare for Lesson 6.5 in Exs. 49–51

Solve the inequality.

49. $-15 + x \leq 8$ ***(p. 148)***

50. $r + 11 > 6$ ***(p. 148)***

51. $-4a \geq -8$ ***(p. 154)***

Plot the point in a coordinate plane. ***(p. 94)***

52. $A(6, -10)$

53. $B(-4, 4)$

54. $C(-2, -6)$

55. ★ **WRITING** *Explain* how to find the product $(5 \times 10^9) \times (4 \times 10^{15})$ without using a calculator. ***(p. 212)***

6.5 Solving Multi-Step Inequalities

Before You solved multi-step equations and one-step inequalities.
Now You'll use two or more steps to solve inequalities.
Why? So you can analyze event fundraising, as in Ex. 33.

KEY VOCABULARY
- **distributive property,** *p. 88*
- **like terms,** *p. 89*
- **inequality,** *p. 148*

ACTIVITY

Use a table to solve the inequality $x + 4 \geq 3x$.

STEP 1 **Copy** and complete the table.

x	$x + 4$	$3x$	*Is $x + 4 \geq 3x$?*
−1	3	−3	Yes
0	?	?	?
1	?	?	?
2	?	?	?
3	?	?	?
4	?	?	?

STEP 2 **Find** the values of x that make the inequality true. What do you think is the solution of the inequality? *Explain* your reasoning.

STEP 3 **Make** a similar table to find the solution of $4x + 3 > 9x - 7$.

How is this solution different from the solution in Step 2?

STEP 4 **Determine** if the inequalities above are true when you substitute a number less than −1 for x. *Explain.*

In Lessons 6.1 through 6.3, you solved multi-step equations algebraically. You can use many of the same steps to solve multi-step inequalities.

EXAMPLE 1 Solving and Graphing a Two-Step Inequality

$10 + 4y < 18$ **Original inequality**

$10 + 4y - 10 < 18 - 10$ **Subtract 10 from each side.**

$4y < 8$ **Simplify.**

$\frac{4y}{4} < \frac{8}{4}$ **Divide each side by 4.**

$y < 2$ **Simplify.**

Number line: 0 1 2 3 4 5 — **Use an open circle and draw the arrow to the left.**

Animated Math at classzone.com

CHECK SOLUTIONS
To check your solution, try three values for the variable in the original inequality. In Example 1, choose a value less than 2, a value greater than 2, and 2.

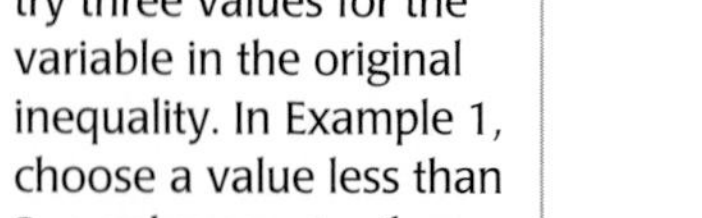

EXAMPLE 2 Combining Like Terms

$3x - 8 < -x + 4$	**Original inequality**
$3x - 8 - 3x < -x + 4 - 3x$	**Subtract 3x from each side.**
$-8 < -4x + 4$	**Combine like terms.**
$-8 - 4 < -4x + 4 - 4$	**Subtract 4 from each side.**
$-12 < -4x$	**Simplify.**
$\frac{-12}{-4} > \frac{-4x}{-4}$	**Divide each side by −4 and reverse the inequality symbol.**
$3 > x$	**Simplify.**

AVOID ERRORS

Remember to reverse the inequality symbol when multiplying or dividing both sides of an inequality by a negative number. For help, see p. 154.

EXAMPLE 3 Writing and Solving a Multi-Step Inequality

Charity Bowling You are organizing a bowling night for charity. Each ticket costs \$10 and includes shoe rental. Shoe rental costs you \$5 per pair, and door prizes cost you \$50. What are the possible numbers of people who need to attend for you to make a profit of at least \$200?

SOLUTION

To find the amount you can raise, subtract the total costs from the total ticket sales. Let x represent the number of people.

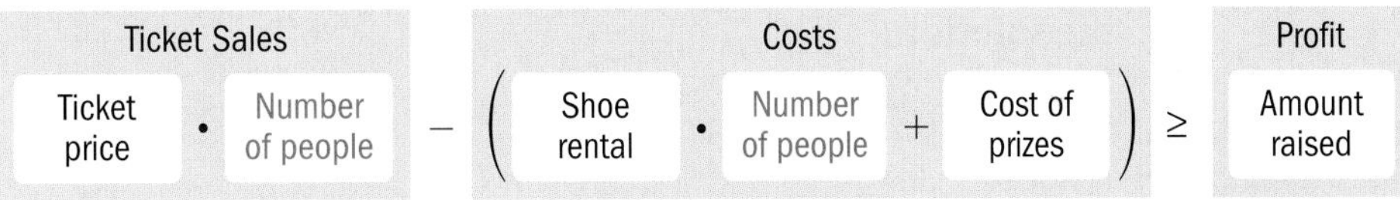

$10x - (5x + 50) \geq 200$	**Write an inequality.**
$10x - 5x - 50 \geq 200$	**Distributive property**
$5x - 50 \geq 200$	**Combine like terms.**
$5x \geq 250$	**Add 50 to each side.**
$x \geq 50$	**Divide each side by 5.**

▸ **Answer** At least 50 people need to attend the bowling night.

✓ GUIDED PRACTICE for Examples 1, 2, and 3

Solve the inequality. Then graph the solution.

1. $-7z + 15 \geq 57$ **2.** $11n + 36 < 3n - 4$ **3.** $9(y - 2) > -16$

4. What If? In Example 3, suppose that each ticket also includes a \$1 beverage. How many people need to attend for you to make a profit of at least \$200?

6.5 EXERCISES

HOMEWORK KEY

★ = **STANDARDIZED TEST PRACTICE**
Exs. 18, 34, 36, 37, 38, and 49

○ = **HINTS AND HOMEWORK HELP**
for Exs. 3, 11, 15, 35 at classzone.com

SKILL PRACTICE

1. **VOCABULARY** Write the meanings of the symbols <, >, ≤ and ≥.

2. **VOCABULARY** Copy and complete: When you solve an inequality, you reverse the inequality symbol when multiplying or dividing by a _?_ number.

SOLVING INEQUALITIES Solve the inequality. Then graph the solution.

SEE EXAMPLES 1 AND 2 on pp. 318–319 for Exs. 3–19

3. $4a + 7 \geq 11$
4. $16 < 3b + 22$
5. $7 - 2p \geq -5$
6. $-3y + 2 < -16$
7. $-2w + 6 < 2$
8. $26s \leq 3s + 69$
9. $12c + 12 > 48c$
10. $5x - 14 \leq 2x + 7$
11. $5 - 4z > 17 - z$
12. $10 \geq 5(3 + t)$
13. $2(5 + n) \leq 6$
14. $-3(d + 2) < -3$
15. $10a > -5(a + 6)$
16. $2(5x - 4) \leq 8(x + 1)$
17. $4(6k - 4) \geq 7k - (2k - 3)$

18. ★ **MULTIPLE CHOICE** Solve the inequality $-3b + 9 - 11b < 65$.

Ⓐ $b < -4$　Ⓑ $b > -4$　Ⓒ $b < 4$　Ⓓ $b > 4$

19. **ERROR ANALYSIS** Describe and correct the error made in the solution.

$9 - 2x \leq 3$
$-2x \leq -6$
$\frac{-2x}{-2} \leq \frac{-6}{-2}$
$x \leq 3$　✗

CLEARING RATIONALS Tell what number you should multiply each side of the inequality by to clear the decimals and fractions. Then solve.

20. $\frac{2}{3}x + \frac{4}{3} - \frac{3}{4}x < -\frac{3}{4}$
21. $\frac{2}{3}y + 18 \geq 5 - \frac{4}{7}y$
22. $\frac{1}{2}k - 6 \geq -\frac{1}{6}k$
23. $\frac{1}{3}m - \frac{1}{2}m > -4$
24. $3.7z \leq 33.32 - 3.1z$
25. $-0.6y - 3.79 + 5.2y < 19.67$
26. $0.05a + 9.367 - 1.65a \leq 4.183$
27. $2.3x - 52.46 \leq -0.9(x - 117)$

28. **EXAMPLES AND NONEXAMPLES** You want to create circles that have a circumference that is less than 5 units plus twice the radius. Write an inequality that represents the situation. Use 3.14 for π. Solve the inequality and use the solution to give two examples and two nonexamples of radii for the circles.

REVIEW COMPOUND INEQUALITIES Need help with compound inequalities? See p. 151.

GRAPHING INEQUALITIES Solve and graph the compound inequality.

29. $-13 < 3x - 4 < 8$
30. $9 < -x + 6 \leq 17$
31. $2 \leq 2(x + 4) < 20$

32. **CHALLENGE** Solve $|a| \geq 2$. Then graph the solution.

PROBLEM SOLVING

SEE EXAMPLE 3 on p. 319 for Exs. 33–35

33. GUIDED PROBLEM SOLVING You agree to raise at least \$2500 for charity to enter the Boston Marathon. You've already raised \$925 by asking people to pledge \$25 each. How many more \$25 pledges do you need?

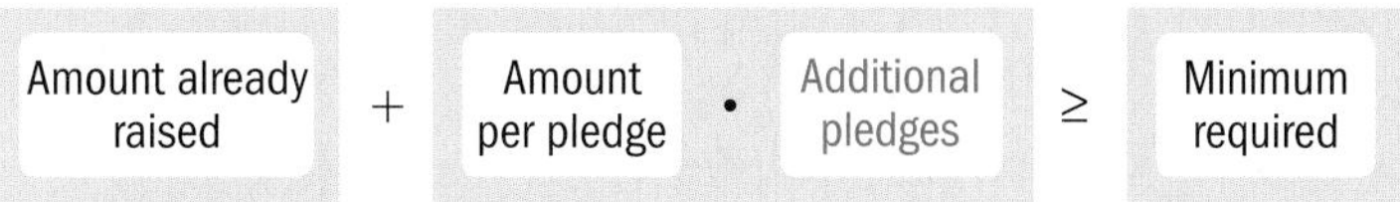

a. Use the verbal model to write an inequality for the number p of additional pledges that will satisfy the donation requirement.

b. Solve the inequality. *Interpret* the solution.

34. ★ MULTIPLE CHOICE While at camp, you call your parents from a pay phone. The first minute costs you \$.25 and each additional minute costs \$.10. You have \$1.65 in change. Solve the inequality $0.25 + 0.10m \leq 1.65$ to find the number of additional minutes m you can talk.

Ⓐ less than 14 Ⓑ no more than 14 Ⓒ at most 19 Ⓓ fewer than 19

35. VIDEO GAMES You are approaching the high score of 18,550 on a video game in which you have to catch discs for 150 points each. Your current score is 16,000. Use the verbal model to write and solve an inequality to find how many more discs you need to catch to have a new high score. *Interpret* the solution.

36. ★ WRITING How is solving a multi-step inequality similar to solving a multi-step equation? How is it different?

37. ★ SHORT RESPONSE Jade works in a clothing store and earns \$350 per week, plus \$.20 for every dollar of clothing she sells. Solve the inequality $350 + 0.2x \geq 500$ to find how much she has to sell in one week to earn at least \$500. *Explain* what the solution means in this situation. How would the solution change if she earns only \$.15 for every dollar? *Explain.*

38. ★ EXTENDED RESPONSE It costs a magazine publisher \$1.20 to produce each magazine. Overhead costs, such as salaries and office space, are \$25,000 per month. The publisher sells the magazine for \$3.95.

a. *Explain* what the verbal model represents in this situation.

b. Write and solve an inequality. *Interpret* the solution.

c. If the magazine publisher cuts costs to \$1.10 per magazine and \$24,000 in overhead, what effect will this have? *Explain.*

READING IN MATH **Read the information below for Exercises 39–41.**

Clouds Clouds form when the air is cooled to its dew point or when the air reaches saturation. The three basic cloud types stem from Latin words that are related to their heights above the ground. *Cirro* is the prefix given to high level clouds that have bases at or above 20,000 feet above the ground. *Alto* is the prefix given to mid-level clouds. *Strato* is the prefix given to low-level clouds that can cover the entire sky like a blanket.

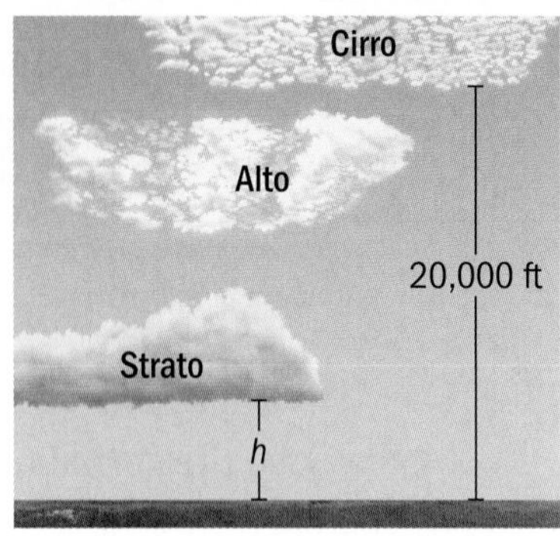

39. **Solve** The minimum base height of a *Cirro* cloud is more than 3500 feet above 2.75 times the base height h of a *Strato* cloud. Solve the inequality $20{,}000 > 2.75h + 3500$. What does this solution say about the base height of a *Strato* cloud?

40. **Apply** A cloud base forms at 6300 feet. How would you classify this cloud? *Explain* your reasoning.

41. **Interpret** *Describe* the range of base heights for the cloud type in Exercise 40.

NUMBER SENSE In Exercises 42–44, use the information below. Tell why the given solution *cannot* be correct.

You and your sisters have \$25 to spend at a baseball game. You buy 3 ice creams for \$4 each, and then use the rest for drinks that cost \$3 each. You write and solve an inequality to find the number of drinks d you can afford.

42. $d < 120$

43. $d \leq 0$

44. $d \geq 4$

45. **CHALLENGE** Solve the inequality $ax + b < c$ to find the value of x in terms of a, b, and c. *Justify* each step.

MIXED REVIEW

Prepare for Lesson 6.6 in Exs. 46–47

Write the phrase as a variable expression using x. *(p. 13)*

46. the quotient of 13 and a number

47. a number decreased by 480

CHOOSE A STRATEGY Use a strategy from the list to solve the following problem. *Explain* your choice of strategy.

Problem Solving Strategies
- Draw a Diagram *(p. 787)*
- Guess, Check, and Revise *(p. 788)*
- Make a List *(p. 790)*

48. You are making a sandwich. You can use white or wheat bread and you can use turkey, ham, or roast beef. Finally, you can have mustard, mayonnaise, or neither. How many different sandwiches can you make?

49. ★ **MULTIPLE CHOICE** What is the solution of $3.3c - 2.1 = 7.8$? *(p. 303)*

Ⓐ -3 Ⓑ $1.\overline{72}$ Ⓒ 3 Ⓓ 30

GOAL
Use a spreadsheet and truth functions to solve inequalities.

6.5 Solving Inequalities

EXAMPLE **Use spreadsheet software to solve $3x + 2 < 2x - 6$.**

SOLUTION

STEP 1 **Enter** the integers -10 to 10 in column A. Column A contains possible solutions of the inequality.

STEP 2 **Type** the formula "=3*A2 + 2" in cell B2. Use the fill down feature. Column B contains calculated values of the left side of the inequality.

B2	= 3*A2 + 2			
	A	**B**	**C**	**D**
1	x-values	3x + 2		
2	–10	–28		
3	–9	–25		
4	–8	–22		
5	–7	–19		

STEP 3 **Type** the formula "=2*A2 − 6" in cell C2. Use the fill down feature. Column C contains values of the right side of the inequality.

STEP 4 **Type** the *truth function* "=B2 < C2" in cell D2. Use the fill down feature. Column D tells whether the inequality is true or false for the x-value in that row.

C4	= 2*A2 – 6			
	A	**B**	**C**	**D**
1	x-values	3x + 2	2x – 6	B < C?
2	–10	–28	–26	True
3	–9	–25	–24	True
4	–8	–22	–22	False
5	–7	–19	–20	False

A *truth function* compares values and returns *True* or *False*.

▸ **Answer** The solution is all numbers less than -8.

PRACTICE **Use spreadsheet software to solve the inequality.**

1. $13 - 3y > -2y$

2. $7 - 2s < s - 2$

3. $2n - 10 \geq 12n$

4. $p + 16 \leq -3p$

5. $-2t + 9 > -5t$

6. $x - 3 < 5x + 1$

7. **SHOPPING** Dani has at most \$10 to buy school supplies. A notebook costs \$1.50, a pencil costs \$.25, and a pen costs \$.95. She needs two notebooks, three pens, and some pencils. What are the possible numbers of pencils she can buy?

6.6 Problem Solving and Inequalities

Before You solved multi-step inequalities.
Now You'll write and solve multi-step inequalities.
Why? So you can solve real world problems, as in Example 1.

KEY VOCABULARY
- **inequality,** *p. 148*

Season Tickets Individual tickets for a college hockey game cost \$8 each plus a one-time transaction fee of \$5. You can buy a season ticket for \$99. How many games would you have to attend so that buying a season ticket is a better value than buying individual tickets?

EXAMPLE 1 Writing and Solving an Inequality

To solve the problem above, write and solve an inequality. Let x represent the number of games.

$8x + 5 > 99$ **Write an inequality.**

$8x > 94$ **Subtract 5 from each side.**

$x > 11.75$ **Divide each side by 8.**

▸ **Answer** It doesn't make sense to attend 11.75 games. So, you would have to attend 12 or more games to make buying a season ticket the better value.

Check Try three values for x. Use 11.75, and one value on either side of it.

When $x = 10$
$8(10) + 5 = 80 + 5 < 99$
not a solution

When $x = 11.75$
$8(11.75) + 5 = 94 + 5 = 99$
not a solution

When $x = 15$
$8(15) + 5 = 120 + 5 > 99$
a solution

ANOTHER WAY

You can use guess-and-check to solve the problem.

Games	Cost
10	85
11	93
12	101

Writing Inequalities The following common sentences indicate the four types of inequalities.

$a < b$	$a > b$
a is less than *b*. *a* is fewer than *b*.	*a* is greater than *b*. *a* is more than *b*.
$a \leq b$	$a \geq b$
a is less than or equal to *b*. *a* is at most *b*. *a* is no more than *b*.	*a* is greater than or equal to *b*. *a* is at least *b*. *a* is no less than *b*.

EXAMPLE 2 Translating Verbal Sentences

Write the sentence as an inequality.

a. Six times the difference of a number and 3 is more than 24.

b. Nine more than 4 times a number is at least 30 plus 11 times the number.

c. Three times a number divided by 4 is no more than 5 plus twice the number.

READING
The phrase "a more than b" means $b + a$, or $a + b$, while "a is more than b" means $a > b$.

SOLUTION

First decide which inequality symbol to use. Then substitute numbers, variables, and operation symbols.

a. The phrase "is more than" means >.

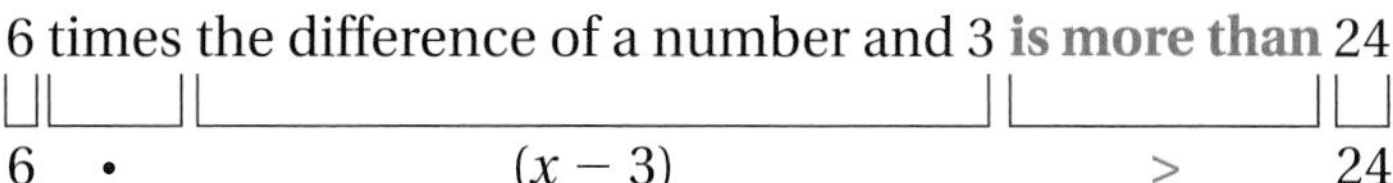

6 times the difference of a number and 3 is more than 24.
6 • (x − 3) > 24

▸ **Answer** The inequality is $6(x - 3) > 24$.

b. The phrase "is at least" means ≥.

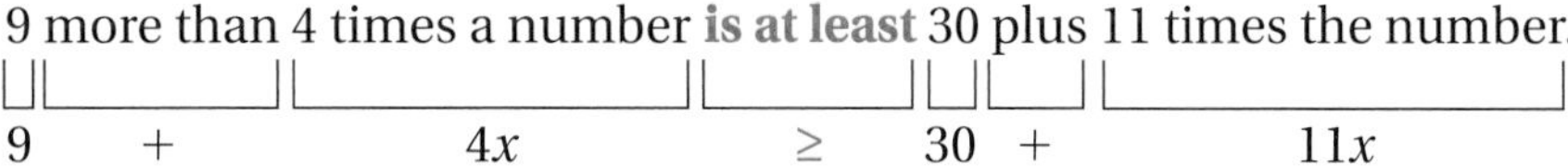

▸ **Answer** The inequality is $9 + 4x \geq 30 + 11x$.

c. The phrase "is no more than" means ≤.

▸ **Answer** The inequality is $\frac{3x}{4} \leq 5 + 2x$.

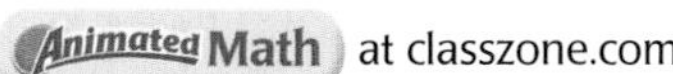

GUIDED PRACTICE for Examples 1 and 2

1. **Basketball** Individual tickets for a college basketball game cost $12 each plus a one-time transaction fee of $8. A season ticket costs $125. How many games would you have to attend so that buying a season ticket is a better value than buying individual tickets?

Write the sentence as an inequality. Let x represent the unknown number.

2. The difference of a number and 4 is less than 10 more than 3 times the number.

3. Six times the sum of a number and 8 is no more than 12 less than twice the number.

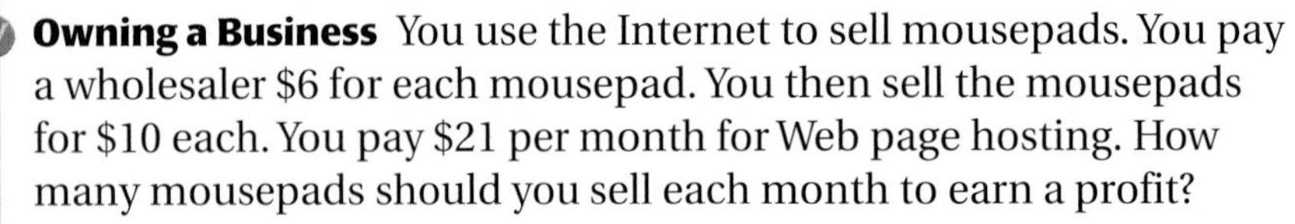

EXAMPLE 3 Writing and Solving an Inequality

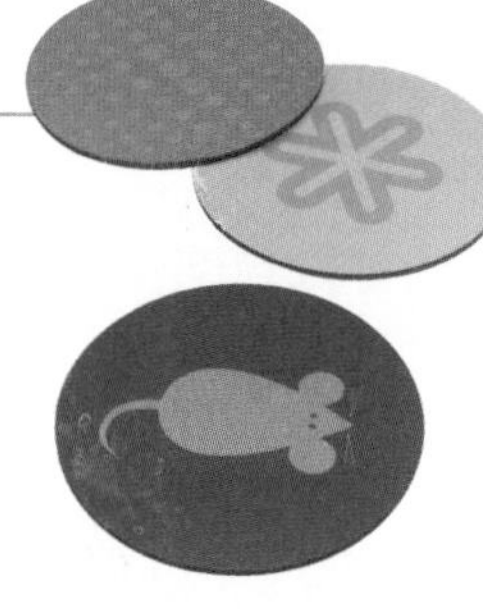

Owning a Business You use the Internet to sell mousepads. You pay a wholesaler $6 for each mousepad. You then sell the mousepads for $10 each. You pay $21 per month for Web page hosting. How many mousepads should you sell each month to earn a profit?

SOLUTION

To earn a profit, your revenue must be greater than your expenses.

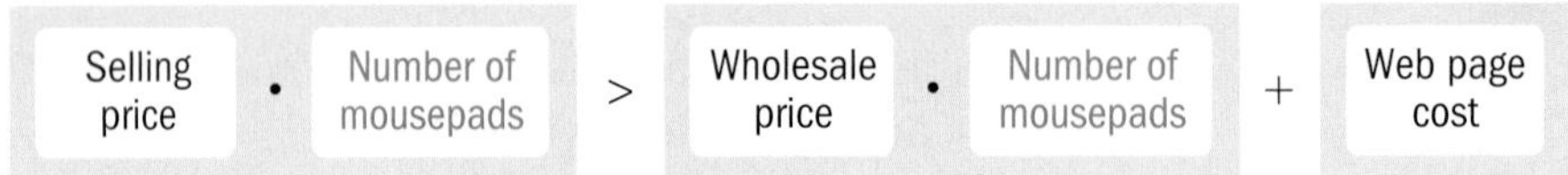

$10x > 6x + 21$ **Write an inequality.**

$4x > 21$ **Subtract 6x from each side.**

$x > 5.25$ **Divide each side by 4.**

▶ **Answer** You cannot sell part of a mousepad. So, you should sell at least 6 mousepads per month to earn a profit.

✓ GUIDED PRACTICE for Example 3

4. **Nutrition** A membership at a nutrition store costs $20 per year. You can buy vitamins for $18 a bottle without a membership, and $15 a bottle with a membership. How many bottles of vitamins do you need to buy each year to make a membership worthwhile?

6.6 EXERCISES

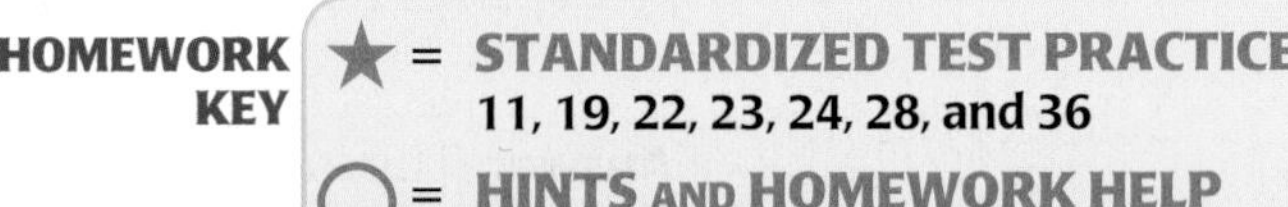

HOMEWORK KEY

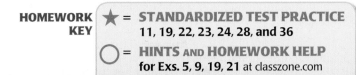

★ = **STANDARDIZED TEST PRACTICE** 11, 19, 22, 23, 24, 28, and 36

○ = **HINTS AND HOMEWORK HELP** for Exs. 5, 9, 19, 21 at classzone.com

SKILL PRACTICE

VOCABULARY Tell whether the sentence can be translated as an inequality. *Explain* your reasoning.

1. A number is at least 5.
2. A number plus 5 is 9.
3. Eight more than a number is equal to 6.
4. Four times a number is less than 28.

TRANSLATING VERBAL SENTENCES Write the sentence as an inequality. Let x represent the unknown number. Then solve the inequality.

SEE EXAMPLE 2 on p. 325 for Exs. 5–10

5. A number plus 2 is at most 6.
6. Nine is less than a number plus 1.
7. Six less than a number is more than 14.
8. Eight times a number is at least 40.
9. Twelve more than a number is less than 4.
10. Seven is more than a number minus 5.

SEE EXAMPLE 2 on p. 325 for Exs. 11–12

11. ★ **MULTIPLE CHOICE** Match the verbal sentence with the inequality: The sum of 4 times a number and 2 is fewer than 18.

Ⓐ $4(x + 2) < 18$ Ⓑ $4x + 2 < 18$ Ⓒ $2x - 4 > 18$ Ⓓ $2(x - 4) \leq 18$

12. **ERROR ANALYSIS** Describe and correct the error made in translating the verbal sentence. Then solve the inequality.

Three times the sum of a number and 5 is at least 26.

✗
$$3(x + 5) \leq 26$$
$$3x + 15 \leq 26$$
$$3x \leq 11$$
$$x \leq 3\frac{2}{3}$$

NUMBER SENSE **Tell whether it makes sense for the variable in red to have a value that is *not* a whole number. *Explain* your reasoning.**

13. Entrance fee + Ride ticket price • Number of ride tickets ≤ \$20

14. Cost per pound of ham • Pounds of ham + Cost of a loaf of bread ≤ \$15

15. Number of hot dogs • Cost per hot dog + Cost of a ticket ≤ \$30

CHALLENGE **Write the sentence as a compound inequality. Then solve.**

16. Eight times the sum of a number and 3 is at least −16 and less than 72.

17. 12 is less than the difference of 6 times a number and 4, which is at most 26.

PROBLEM SOLVING

SEE EXAMPLES 1 AND 3 on p. 324 for Exs. 18–19

18. **MULTIPLE REPRESENTATIONS** You have at most \$200 to spend on a health club membership. The initial fee to join is \$50. There is a monthly fee of \$32.

a. Write a verbal model for the total cost of a health club membership.

b. Write and solve an inequality to find the number of months you can be a member without spending more than \$200.

c. Graph the solution and check that the answer makes sense. *Explain* what the solution means in the situation.

19. ★ **MULTIPLE CHOICE** You are making craft items to sell for \$2 each. The materials cost you \$55. You want to make a profit of at least \$100. Which inequality can you use to find the number of items you need to sell?

Ⓐ $2x - 55 \leq 100$ Ⓑ $2x - 55 \geq 100$ Ⓒ $2x + 55 \geq 100$ Ⓓ $2x + 55 \leq 100$

SEE EXAMPLES 1 AND 3 on p. 324 for Exs. 20–21

20. BUYING CDs Each CD you order online costs \$12. Shipping charges are \$4. You have at most \$50 to spend. Copy and complete the verbal model. Write and solve an inequality to find how many CDs you can buy.

Cost of CD	•	Number of CDs	+	Shipping charges	$\underline{?}$	Money you have

21. TEEN CLUB A teen club has weekly dances. You can become a member of the club for \$30 a year and pay only \$4 to attend each dance. Otherwise, each dance costs \$6. Write and solve an inequality to find how many dances you have to attend so that becoming a member will cost less than paying the nonmember rate.

22. ★ WRITING *Explain* the difference between *3 less than a number* and *3 is less than a number*. Include examples.

23. ★ OPEN-ENDED MATH *Describe* a real-world problem that can be solved using the inequality $5 + 8x \le 31$. Solve the inequality and explain what the solution means in the situation.

24. ★ SHORT RESPONSE School will be cancelled if there are at least 6 inches of snow at 6 A.M. At 7 P.M. the night before, 2 inches of snow has covered the ground. Snow is predicted to continue falling at a rate of 0.5 inch per hour. Write an inequality to represent the situation. At what time will there be at least 6 inches of snow? Will school be held the next day? *Explain.*

25. BOWLING Your scores on the last 3 bowling games are 90, 92, and 115. Write and solve an inequality to find the score you need in the next game to have a mean score of at least 100.

26. SUMMER JOB You earn \$6.50 an hour working at the snack bar at a community pool. You earn time and a half for any hours you work over 30 hours. Write and solve an inequality to find how many hours over 30 you must work to make more than \$273 in a week.

27. EXPRESS MAIL A package sent via express mail must be no more than 108 inches in total length and girth. You want to wrap as many boxes together as possible to send as one package. Each box is the same size. Write and solve an inequality to find how many boxes you could wrap as one package if they are arranged as shown.

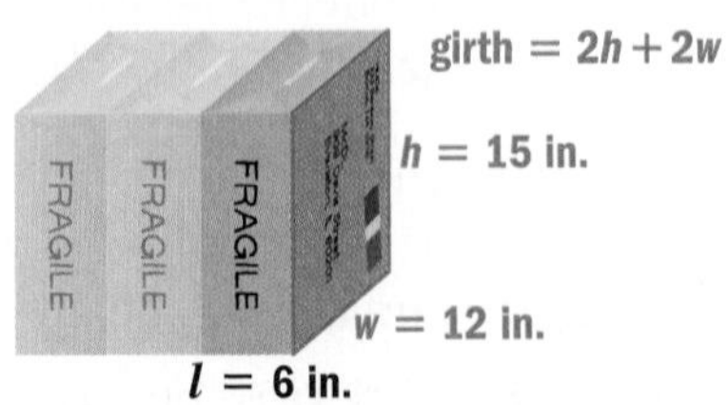

28. ★ **EXTENDED RESPONSE** Town Taxi charges \$2.00 plus \$.40 for every $\frac{1}{5}$ mile. City Cab charges \$2.50 plus \$.15 for every $\frac{1}{10}$ mile.

a. **Interpret** Write algebraic expressions for the total cost of a ride with Town Taxi and the total cost of a ride with City Cab.

b. **Compare** Your friends decide that Town Taxi is the better deal, because Town Taxi charges only \$2 initially and City Cab charges \$2.50. Is your friends' reasoning valid? *Explain.*

c. **Analyze** For what distances is the total cost for City Cab less than the total cost for Town Taxi? *Explain* your reasoning.

29. **CHALLENGE** The sum of two consecutive odd integers is no more than 232 and no less than 216. Use inequalities to find all possible pairs of consecutive odd integers. *Justify* your answer.

MIXED REVIEW

Get-Ready

Prepare for Lesson 7.1 in Exs. 30–32

Write the fraction in simplest form. ***(p. 187)***

30. $\frac{15}{18}$ 31. $\frac{-7}{42}$ 32. $\frac{24}{-168}$

Solve the inequality. ***(p. 318)***

33. $6a - 15 \le 27$ 34. $-9 < 5 - 7k$ 35. $2p + 24 > 10p$

36. ★ **MULTIPLE CHOICE** The area of a rectangle is 42 square meters. One side is 7 meters long. What is the perimeter of the rectangle? ***(p. 32)***

Ⓐ 6 meters Ⓑ 13 meters Ⓒ 26 meters Ⓓ 294 meters

QUIZ *for Lessons 6.4–6.6*

Find the unknown measurement, where r = radius, d = diameter, and C = circumference. Use 3.14 or $\frac{22}{7}$ for π. Round to the nearest hundredth if necessary. ***(p. 312)***

1. $d = 28$ in., $C = \underline{\ ?\ }$ 2. $C = 132$ ft, $d = \underline{\ ?\ }$ 3. $C = 150$ cm, $r = \underline{\ ?\ }$

Solve the inequality. ***(p. 318)***

4. $-8a - 10 > 14$ 5. $3z \le 35 - 2z$ 6. $5b \ge 2(b + 2.25)$

Write the sentence as an inequality. Then solve. ***(p. 324)***

7. Two less than 6 times a number is at least 40.

8. Five times the sum of 4 and a number is greater than 10.

9. **VIDEO GAMES** Your current score in a video game is 33,600 points. At the end of each level you earn 2500 points for catching objects and 1700 points for overcoming the obstacles. How many more levels must you go through to beat your high score of 54,000? ***(p. 324)***

Lessons 6.4–6.6

1. **MULTI-STEP PROBLEM** A penny-farthing bicycle has a front wheel diameter of 50 inches and a rear wheel diameter of 17 inches.

   a. What is the circumference of each wheel? Use 3.14 for π.

   b. About how many rotations will the rear wheel take during one rotation of the front wheel? *Explain* your reasoning.

   c. About how many rotations will it take each wheel to travel 2000 feet?

2. **SHORT RESPONSE** The diagram shows the approximate measures of a track. Find the perimeter to the nearest hundredth. Use 3.14 for π. *Explain* your steps.

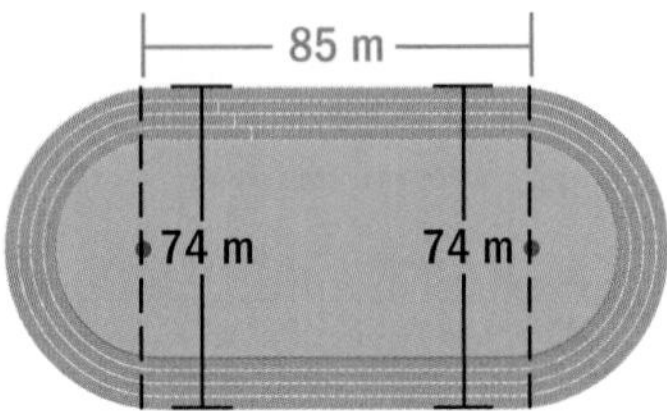

3. **GRIDDED ANSWER** A pretzel shop sells large pretzels for \$2.50 each and pretzel bites for \$.50 each. One weekend, the pretzel shop sells 130 large pretzels. What is the minimum number of pretzel bites the shop needs to sell to make a total of at least \$668?

4. **OPEN-ENDED** Write a real-world problem that can be modeled by an inequality with decimal coefficients and variables on both sides. Solve the inequality and explain what the solution means in the situation.

5. **SHORT RESPONSE** Each ride on the subway costs \$1.25. If you buy a monthly pass for \$47, you can ride as often as you want. Write and solve an inequality to find the number of times you need to ride the subway so that buying a pass costs less than paying for each ride. *Explain* what the solution means in this situation.

6. **SHORT RESPONSE** The largest doll in a set of nesting dolls has a circumference of 24 centimeters. The radius of each doll inside is 0.7 times the radius of the doll that encloses it. To the nearest tenth of a centimeter, what is the radius of the fifth doll? *Explain* your reasoning. Use 3.14 for π.

7. **EXTENDED RESPONSE** Isaac makes chairs in a small shop for which he pays \$760 per month in rent. The materials cost \$70 per chair, and he sells the chairs for \$380 each. Isaac's other monthly expenses total \$720.

   a. Write and solve an inequality to find how many chairs Isaac must sell monthly to make a profit.

   b. Isaac hires an apprentice to do all the chair making for one month. Isaac pays the apprentice \$155 per chair. Write and solve an inequality to find how many of the apprentice's chairs Isaac must sell that month to make a profit.

   c. Suppose in one month Isaac sells 8 chairs, 5 of which are made by the apprentice. Will Isaac make a profit? *Explain*.

6 CHAPTER REVIEW

@HomeTutor
classzone.com
Vocabulary Practice

REVIEW KEY VOCABULARY

- circle, *p. 312*
- center, *p. 312*
- radius, *p. 312*
- diameter, *p. 312*
- circumference, *p. 312*
- pi (π), *p. 312*

VOCABULARY EXERCISES

1. The set of all points in a plane that are the same distance from a fixed point called the center is a __?__.

2. You can approximate __?__ with the decimal 3.14 or the fraction $\frac{22}{7}$.

Matching Match the word with the correct definition.

3. diameter
4. circumference
5. radius

A. the distance around a circle
B. the distance across a circle through the center
C. the distance from the center to any point on the circle

REVIEW EXAMPLES AND EXERCISES

6.1 Solving Multi-Step Equations

pp. 293–297

EXAMPLE

Solve the equation.

a. $5x + 8 - 4x = 17$ **Original equation**

$x + 8 = 17$ **Combine like terms.**

$x = 9$ **Subtract 8 from each side.**

b. $4(x - 4) = -12$ **Original equation**

$4x - 16 = -12$ **Distributive property**

$4x = 4$ **Add 16 to both sides.**

$x = 1$ **Divide each side by 4.**

EXERCISES

Solve the equation.

SEE EXAMPLES 2, 3, AND 4 on pp. 294–295 for Exs. 6–11

6. $6a + 8 - 14a = 96$
7. $18 + 4(p - 9) = 6$
8. $4(12 + z) - z = -192$
9. $12 + 5(b - 7) = 2$
10. $\frac{a + 4}{3} = 10$
11. $\frac{-5c - 12}{4} = 2$

6.2 Solving Equations with Variables on Both Sides *pp. 298–302*

EXAMPLE

$4(x - 8) = -x + 4 + 7x$	**Original equation**
$4x - 32 = 6x + 4$	**Use the distributive property and combine like terms.**
$-32 = 2x + 4$	**Subtract 4x from each side.**
$-36 = 2x$	**Subtract 4 from each side.**
$-18 = x$	**Divide each side by 2.**

EXERCISES

Solve the equation.

SEE EXAMPLES 2 AND 3 on p. 299 for Exs. 12–18

12. $-7b + 10 = -11 - 4b$ **13.** $5(m - 9) = -27 - 4m$ **14.** $6(t - 5) = 2(t + 5)$

15. $3(11 + c) = 19 + c$ **16.** $2q + 17 = 19q - 51$ **17.** $2 - (a - 4) = -2(a - 1)$

18. Rowing At the Rolling River Regatta, fifty more than twice the number of women's rowing teams is equal to eighty-seven less than three times the number of women's rowing teams. Write and solve an equation to find the number of women's rowing teams at the regatta.

6.3 Solving Equations Involving Fractions and Decimals *pp. 303–307*

EXAMPLE

Solve the equation.

a. $\frac{1}{4}y = \frac{1}{6}y - 5 + \frac{1}{2}y$	**Original equation**
$3y = 2y - 60 + 6y$	**Multiply each side by the LCD, 12.**
$3y = 8y - 60$	**Combine like terms.**
$-5y = -60$	**Subtract 8y from each side.**
$y = 12$	**Divide each side by −5.**
b. $-7 + 0.03x = 0.31x$	**Original equation**
$-700 + 3x = 31x$	**Multiply each side by 100.**
$-700 = 28x$	**Subtract 3x from each side.**
$-25 = x$	**Divide each side by 28.**

EXERCISES

Solve the equation.

SEE EXAMPLES 1, 2, AND 3 on pp. 303–304 for Exs. 19–25

19. $-3.5a - 11.4 + 9.9a = 3$

20. $\frac{11}{16}n - 3 + \frac{1}{4}n = \frac{7}{4}$

21. $5s + 3\frac{1}{8} = \frac{5}{24} - 2s$

22. $\frac{2}{3}b + \frac{4}{5} = \frac{1}{6}b + 2\frac{3}{10}$

23. $16.7m - 167.2 = 60.8 + 2.45m$

24. $-8 + 4.6r = 4r - 2.6$

25. Recycling When you buy a can of seltzer water, you pay for the seltzer water and a \$.05 recycling deposit. You pay \$4.56 for a 12-pack of seltzer water. How much did each can of seltzer water cost before the deposit?

6.4 Solving Equations Involving Circumference *pp. 312–317*

EXAMPLE

Find the unknown measurement, where r = radius, d = diameter, and C = circumference. Use 3.14 or $\frac{22}{7}$ for π.

a. $C = \underline{\ ?\ }$, $d = 30.5$ cm

$C = \pi d$

$\approx (3.14)(30.5)$

$= 95.77$ cm

b. $C = 47\frac{2}{3}$ in., $r = \underline{\ ?\ }$

$C = 2\pi r$

$\frac{143}{3} \approx 2\left(\frac{22}{7}\right)r$

$r = \frac{143}{3} \cdot \frac{7}{44} = 7\frac{7}{12}$ in.

EXERCISES

Find the unknown radius, r, diameter, d, or circumference, C. Use 3.14 or $\frac{22}{7}$ for π. Round to the nearest hundredth if necessary.

SEE EXAMPLES 1, 2, 3, AND 4 on pp. 312–314 for Exs. 26–35

26. $C = \underline{\ ?\ }$

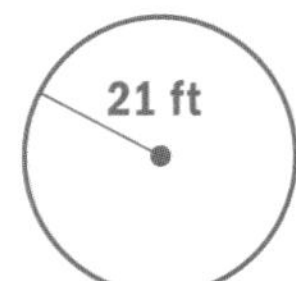

27. $C = 62.8$ mm

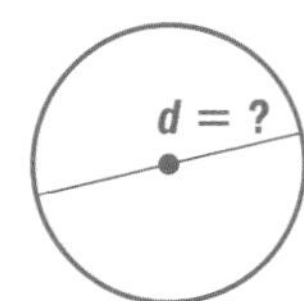

28. $C = 12$ in.

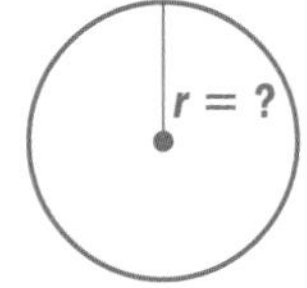

29. $C = 66$ ft, $d = \underline{\ ?\ }$

30. $C = 100.48$ cm, $r = \underline{\ ?\ }$

31. $C = \underline{\ ?\ }$, $d = 1$ mi

32. $C = \underline{\ ?\ }$, $r = 7$ in.

33. $C = 440$ m, $d = \underline{\ ?\ }$

34. $C = 176$ cm, $r = \underline{\ ?\ }$

35. Architecture The Minnesota State Capitol has one of the largest unsupported marble domes in the world, with a diameter of 89 feet at its widest point. Find its circumference. Use 3.14 for π.

6.5 Solving Multi-Step Inequalities

pp. 318–322

EXAMPLE

$-5(x + 9) \geq 30$	**Original inequality**
$-5x - 45 \geq 30$	**Distributive property**
$-5x \geq 75$	**Add 45 to each side.**
$x \leq -15$	**Divide each side by −5 and reverse the inequality symbol.**

EXERCISES

SEE EXAMPLES 1 AND 2 on pp. 318–319 for Exs. 36–38

Solve the inequality.

36. $-5 < 3x + 16$ **37.** $m + 4(5 - m) > -7$ **38.** $6 - (g - 7) \leq 6 - 8g$

6.6 Problem Solving and Inequalities

pp. 324–329

EXAMPLE

You and 3 friends plan to use a \$50 gift certificate to pay for dinner. You order an appetizer to share that costs \$6. What is the most each of you can spend so the total cost of the meal is no more than \$50?

Number of people • Cost per person + Price of appetizer ≤ Amount of gift certificate

$4x + 6 \leq 50$	**Write an inequality.**
$4x \leq 44$	**Subtract 6 from each side.**
$x \leq 11$	**Divide each side by 4.**

▶ **Answer** The most that each of you can spend is \$11.

EXERCISES

Write the sentence as an inequality. Then solve the inequality.

SEE EXAMPLES 1 AND 2 on pp. 324–325 for Exs. 39–41

39. Fourteen minus three times a number is at most eleven.

40. Seven times the difference of fifteen and a number is at least fifty-six.

41. Fundraiser The school chorus is selling \$2 raffle tickets to raise money for a trip. The chorus already has \$116 saved. How many tickets does the chorus need to sell in order to have at least \$250 to help pay for the trip?

6 CHAPTER TEST

@HomeTutor
classzone.com
Chapter Test Practice

Solve the equation.

1. $-3z + 17 + 12z = 11$

2. $m - 6(m + 10) = 50$

3. $7(12 - r) = -84$

4. $3b + 4 = b - 4$

5. $-25 - a = 2a + 20$

6. $3(2x - 11) = 3(x + 10)$

7. $\frac{3x - 5}{10} = 7$

8. $\frac{-3r + 54}{5} = 2r + 3$

9. $\frac{3}{5}w = 5w + \frac{22}{25}$

Find the unknown measurement, where r = radius, d = diameter, and C = circumference. Use 3.14 or $\frac{22}{7}$ for π.

10. $C =$ __?__, $d = 12.3$ mm

11. $C = 22$ in., $r =$ __?__

12. $C = 9.42$ ft, $d =$ __?__

Solve the inequality.

13. $6n + 19 \leq 7$

14. $10 - 3x > 25$

15. $9c - 8 \geq 3c + 16$

16. $3(k + 3) > k - 1$

17. $8y + 3y + 36 \leq 124$

18. $w - 4(w + 5) < -8$

Write the sentence as an inequality. Then solve the inequality.

19. Nine added to the product of 11 and a number is at most 4.

20. Two times a number, minus 13, is less than the number plus 8.

21. Seven times the difference of 12 and a number is at least 14.

22. **SHOPPING** You bought a new shirt for $15.95 and 5 pairs of socks. Your friend bought 10 pairs of socks and spent $4.20 less than you. How much did each pair of socks cost?

23. **NEWSPAPERS** In 1999 there were 1647 daily and 7471 weekly newspapers published in the United States, as well as x other kinds of newspapers. The total number of newspapers was 700 greater than seven times the number of other kinds of newpapers. How many newspapers were published in 1999 that were not daily or weekly?

24. **TETHERBALL** A tetherball pole is 10 feet high. The tetherball is attached to the top of the pole with a string so that the ball hangs 2 feet above the ground. The diameter of the ball is 8.4 inches. How long is the string attached to the tetherball? What is the circumference of the longest path that point P could make through the air around the pole? Use 3.14 for π. Round your answer to the nearest tenth of a foot.

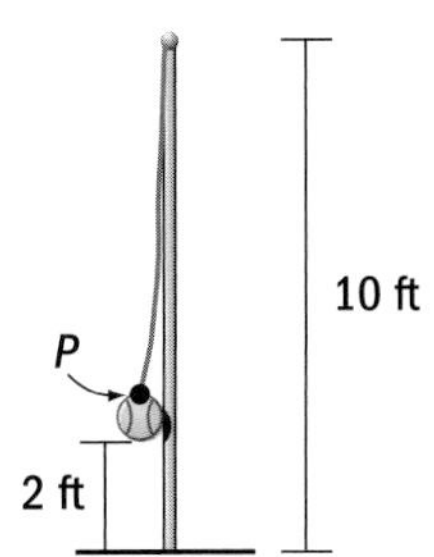

25. **SNACK MIX** You are buying 2.2 pounds of peanuts that cost $4.50 per pound and sesame sticks that cost $1.70 per pound. You can't spend more than $15. What are the possible numbers of pounds of sesame sticks you can buy?

6 ★ Standardized TEST PREPARATION

Scoring Rubric

Full Credit
- solution is complete and correct

Partial Credit
- solution is complete but errors are made, *or*
- solution is without error, but incomplete

No Credit
- no solution is given, *or*
- solution makes no sense

EXTENDED RESPONSE QUESTIONS

PROBLEM

Bowling The costs of bowling at two alleys are given in the table.

a. Write expressions for the total cost of bowling at each alley.

b. Find the number of games you must bowl at each alley for the total costs to be equal.

Bowling alley	*Cost per game*	*Shoe rental*
A	\$2.00	\$3.50
B	\$2.50	\$2.00

c. For what number of games is the total cost at alley A less than the total cost at alley B? *Explain* your reasoning.

Below are sample solutions to the problem. Read each solution and the comments in blue to see why the sample represents full credit, partial credit, or no credit.

SAMPLE 1: Full Credit Solution

The steps are clearly stated and reflect correct mathematical reasoning.

An expression for the total cost of g games at bowling alley A is $2g + 3.5$. An expression for the total cost of g games at bowling alley B is $2.5g + 2$. Set the expressions equal to each other to find the number of games for which the total costs are equal.

$$2g + 3.5 = 2.5g + 2$$
$$3.5 = 0.5g + 2$$
$$1.5 = 0.5g$$
$$3 = g$$

The answer is correct.

The total cost to bowl at each alley is the same for 3 games.

To find the number of games for which the total cost at alley A would be less, solve an inequality.

$$2g + 3.5 < 2.5g + 2$$
$$3.5 < 0.5g + 2$$
$$1.5 < 0.5g$$
$$3 < g$$

The answer is correct.

The solution $3 < g$ means the number of games is greater than 3. Because it does not make sense to bowl part of a game, you need to bowl at least 4 games for total cost at alley A to be less.

SAMPLE 2: Partial Credit Solution

Without explanation, the reasoning behind this step is unclear.

$$2g + 3.5 = 2.5g + 2$$
$$3.5 = 0.5g + 2$$
$$1.5 = 0.5g$$
$$3 = g$$

The answer to this part is correct.

The total cost to bowl at each alley is the same for 3 games.

Write the equation above as an inequality to find the number of games for which the total cost at bowling alley A is less.

$$2g + 3.5 < 2.5g + 2$$
$$3.5 < 0.5g + 2$$
$$1.5 < 0.5g$$
$$3 < g$$

The answer to this part is incorrect.

It costs less to bowl at bowling alley A when you want to bowl 3 or more games.

SAMPLE 3: No Credit Solution

The equation and the answer are incorrect.

An equation for the number of games for which the total cost at each alley is the same is $2g + 2.5 = 3.5g + 2$. The total costs to bowl at each alley are never the same. Bowling alley A is always less.

PRACTICE Apply the Scoring Rubric

A student's solution to the problem on the previous page is given below. Score the solution as *full credit, partial credit,* or *no credit. Explain* your reasoning. If you choose partial credit or no credit, explain how you would change the solution so that it earns a score of full credit.

1. An expression for the total cost of g games is $2g + 3.5$ at bowling alley A and is $2.5g + 2$ at bowling alley B. Make a table to find the number of games for which the total cost to bowl at each alley is the same.

Games	1	2	3	4	5	6
Bowling alley A	\$5.50	\$7.50	\$9.50	\$11.50	\$13.50	\$15.50
Bowling alley B	\$4.50	\$7.00	\$9.50	\$12.00	\$14.50	\$17.00

The total cost to bowl at each alley is the same for 3 games. It costs less to bowl at bowling alley A when you bowl 4 or more games.

6 ★ Standardized TEST PRACTICE

EXTENDED RESPONSE

1. Tran rides his bike at a speed of 9 miles per hour. Rick rides at a speed of 8 miles per hour.
   a. How many hours and minutes will it take for Rick to ride 12 miles?
   b. Tran starts riding a half hour later than Rick and follows the same route. How far will Tran ride when Rick reaches 12 miles?
   c. Suppose Tran and Rick continue riding. Will Tran ever catch up to Rick? If so, how much longer will it take? *Explain* your reasoning.

2. A pizza store owner's cost of ingredients to make each pizza is $2.25. Overhead costs, such as salaries and store space, are $5,000 per month. The store sells each pizza for $7.95.

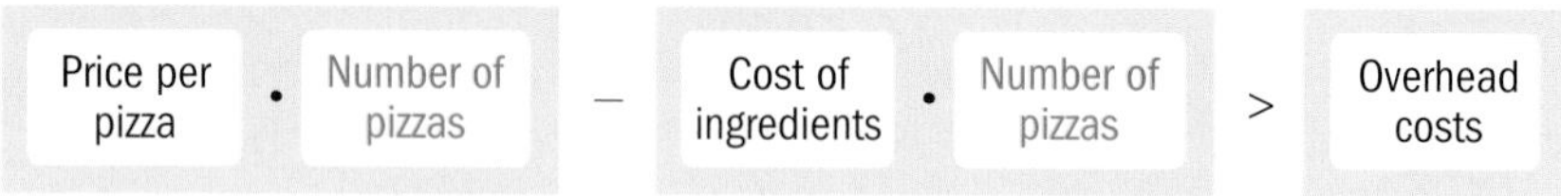

   a. *Describe* what this verbal model represents for the pizza store.
   b. Use the verbal model to write and solve an inequality.
   c. *Explain* what the solution means in this situation.

3. You deposit two thirds of your money in the bank. You spend half of the remaining amount on an amusement park ticket, and you spend another fifteen dollars on a shirt. You have seven dollars left.
   a. Write an equation to model this situation.
   b. How much money did you start with?
   c. *Describe* another method for solving the problem that does not involve writing and solving an equation.
   d. *Compare* the methods. How are they alike? How are they different?

4. You buy shorts for $12 per pair. Every pair of shorts after the third pair is $2 off the original price. You spend $56.
   a. Write a verbal model for the situation.
   b. Use the verbal model to write and solve an equation. How many pairs of shorts do you buy?
   c. What is the mean cost per pair of shorts? *Explain* how you found your answer.

5. You are using ribbon to trim the edges of circular tables for a picnic. Each table has a diameter of 2 meters.
   a. Find the circumference of one table. Use 3.14 for π.
   b. You have 40 meters of ribbon. How many tables can you fully trim? *Explain* how you found your answer.
   c. There are 10 tables. How much more ribbon do you need to fully trim all the tables? Round your answer to the nearest meter.

MULTIPLE CHOICE

6. A farmer uses 38 feet of fencing to make a circular animal pen. What is the best estimate of the pen's diameter?

Ⓐ 6 ft Ⓑ 6.3 ft

Ⓒ 12.1 ft Ⓓ 12.6 ft

7. A parking garage charges \$3 for the first 3 hours and \$2 for each hour *after* 3 hours. How many hours is a car parked if the total charge is \$15?

Ⓐ 5 hours Ⓑ 6 hours

Ⓒ 7.5 hours Ⓓ 9 hours

8. Which of the following numbers would *not* clear the decimals when you multiply both sides of the equation $6.02x + 5.1 = 0.7 + 22$?

Ⓐ 10 Ⓑ 100

Ⓒ 1000 Ⓓ 10,000

GRIDDED ANSWER

9. A pre-paid phone card for calls from the United States to India charges \$.10 per minute. It has a connection fee of \$.50 per call and a weekly fee of \$.75. Rajev bought a \$20 card, which he used up in 4 weeks. He made 9 calls. How many minutes did Rajev use?

10. All three sides of the triangle have equal length. How many units is the perimeter?

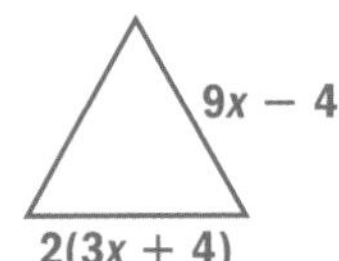

11. A circular pool has a radius of 20 feet. A circular deck surrounding the entire pool is 4 feet wide. What is the circumference of the deck? Round your answer to the nearest foot.

SHORT RESPONSE

12. John has a pile of quarters. Justin has five more than twice as many quarters as John. Jason has three times as many quarters as John. Justin and Jason have the same number of quarters. How much money does John have, in dollars and cents? *Explain* how you found your answer.

13. Michelle needs at least \$75 for a school trip. She has \$22 already and she makes \$5 per hour babysitting. Write and solve an inequality to find how many hours Michelle needs to babysit to have enough money for her trip. *Explain* how you found your answer.

14. Trish parks in front of a parking meter at 2:15 P.M. She plans to leave her car there until after 6:00 P.M. when there is no longer a charge for the meter. The meter takes only quarters, and each quarter pays for 30 minutes of parking. Can Trish pay the full charge with the 7 quarters she has? If not, how many more quarters does she need? *Explain* your reasoning.

15. A car salesperson earns \$300 per week plus \$.02 for every dollar of car sales. Write and solve an inequality to find how many dollars in car sales the car salesperson has to make in one week to earn at least \$1500. *Explain* what the solution means in this situation.

7 Ratio, Proportion, and Percent

Before

In previous chapters you've . . .

- Found equivalent fractions
- Rewritten fractions and decimals

Now

In Chapter 7 you'll study . . .

- 7.1 Rates and ratios
- 7.2 Proportions
- 7.3 Percent problems
- 7.4 Rewriting percents
- 7.5 Percent of change
- 7.6 Percent applications
- 7.7 The percent equation
- 7.8 Simple probability

Why?

So you can solve real-world problems about . . .

- lightning, p. 344
- crocodiles, p. 357
- guitars, p. 370
- beaches, p. 375

at *classzone.com*

- Rates, p. 344
- Percent Applications, p. 379
- Simple Probability, p. 383

Get-Ready Games

Review Prerequisite Skills by playing *Video Maze* and *Find the Path.*

Video Maze
START
72 ÷ x = 8
x − 6 = 9
21 + x = 24
21 ÷ x = 3
x + 7 = 11
x ÷ 4 = 3
x − 1 = 3
7x = 7
8x = 24
x + 10 = 14
2 + x = 21
9 − x = 8
15 − x = 12
5x = 35
x + 14 = 18
64 ÷ x = 8
x ÷ 6 = 5
x − 9 = 17
3x = 27
x + 8 = 19
33 ÷ x = 3
11x = 55
10 − x = 6
2x = 14
5 + x = 13
42 ÷ x = 7
6x = 24
14 − x = 8
FINISH

Skill Focus: Solving equations

Find a path through the maze from start to finish.

- Then find the sum of all the solutions of the equations to find your total number of points.
- Which path has the least number of points?

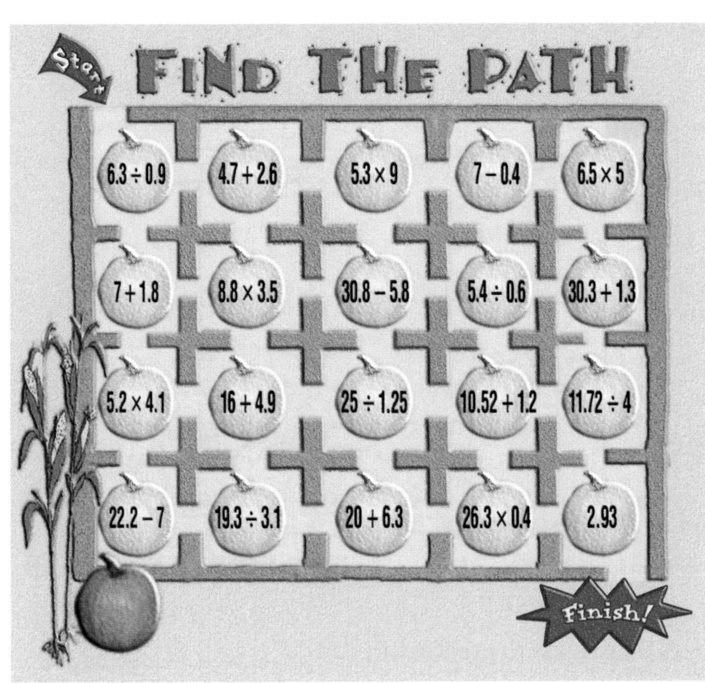

Skill Focus: Performing operations on decimals

Find your way from start to finish in the maze above.

- Evaluate each expression. Then move to the nearest expression that begins with the number that is the value of the previous expression.
- For example, if you start from 5.3 + 4.2 and your choices are 1.4 + 7.2 and 9.5 − 8, you would move to 9.5 − 8 because 5.3 + 4.2 = 9.5.

Stop and Think

1. **WRITING** A student says that a decimal divided by a decimal is never a whole number. *Explain* the error in the student's reasoning.
2. **CRITICAL THINKING** How many different paths are there through the *Video Maze* that do not cover the same ground more than once?

7 Getting Ready

Review Prerequisite Skills

REVIEW WORDS

- **data,** *p. 3*
- **equation,** *p. 26*
- **formula,** *p. 32*
- **simplest form,** *p. 187*
- **equivalent fractions,** *p. 187*

VOCABULARY CHECK

Copy and complete using a review word from the list at the left.

1. The fraction $\frac{1}{2}$ is in __?__, but $\frac{2}{4}$ is not.
2. The fractions $\frac{2}{3}$ and $\frac{4}{6}$ are __?__.
3. A mathematical sentence that shows two expressions have the same value is called a(n) __?__.

SKILL CHECK

Solve the equation. ***(p. 122)***

4. $\frac{x}{7} = 3$
5. $\frac{x}{-2} = 4$
6. $-9x = 108$
7. $8x = 56$
8. You have 15 pairs of socks in your drawer, including exactly 6 pairs of black socks. What fraction of your socks are black? ***(p. 187)***

Write the fraction in simplest form. ***(p. 187)***

9. $\frac{15}{75}$
10. $\frac{12}{60}$
11. $\frac{9ab}{36a}$
12. $\frac{18n^3}{36n}$

Order the numbers from least to greatest. ***(p. 255)***

13. $0, -0.25, \frac{1}{3}, \frac{12}{9}, -1.11, \frac{9}{8}$
14. $1.28, -\frac{7}{8}, \frac{1}{12}, \frac{10}{3}, -0.02, 0.34$

@HomeTutor Prerequisite skills practice at classzone.com

Notetaking Skills

Taking Notes in Class

In each chapter you will learn a new notetaking skill. In Chapter 7 you will apply the strategy of taking notes in class to topics such as Example 3 on p. 355.

As you participate in class, be sure to ask questions about things you don't understand. Write the answers in your notes.

Writing Decimals as Fractions

$0.007 = \frac{7}{1000}$ 0.007 has 3 decimal places.
1000 has 3 zeros.

$0.13 = \frac{13}{100}$ 0.13 has 2 decimal places.
100 has 2 zeros.

Number of decimal places equals number of zeros!

7.1 Ratios and Rates

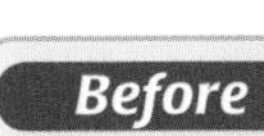

Before	You found equivalent fractions.
Now	You'll find ratios and unit rates.
Why?	So you can compare speeds, as in Ex. 46.

KEY VOCABULARY

- **ratio,** *p. 343*
- **equivalent ratios,** *p. 343*
- **rate,** *p. 344*
- **unit rate,** *p. 344*

ACTIVITY

You can compare side lengths and perimeters of squares.

STEP 1 **Copy** and complete the table using the squares shown. Write the fractions in simplest form.

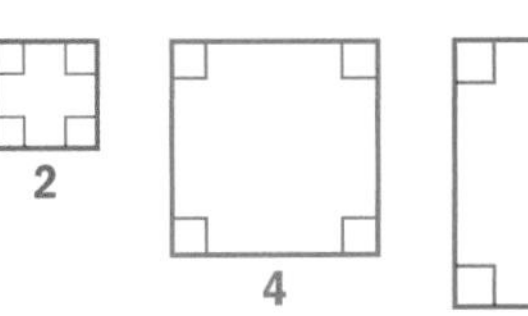

STEP 2 **Describe** what you notice about the fractions in the table.

Side length	2	4	5
Perimeter	?	?	?
$\frac{\text{Side length}}{\text{Perimeter}}$	?	?	?

STEP 3 **Describe** the relationship between the side length and the perimeter of a square with side length *s*.

READING
All three ways of writing a ratio of two numbers are read in the same manner. So $\frac{9}{5}$, 9 : 5, and 9 to 5 are all read "the ratio of nine to five."

In the activity, you used a *ratio* to compare the side length of a square to its perimeter. A **ratio** uses division to compare two numbers. You can write the ratio of a to b ($b \neq 0$) in the following three ways.

$\frac{a}{b}$ $\qquad$ $a : b$ $\qquad$ a to b

Ratios that have the same value are called **equivalent ratios**. For example: 9 : 5, 18 : 10, and 3 : $1\frac{2}{3}$ are all equivalent ratios.

EXAMPLE 1 Writing a Ratio

Skiing A ski resort has 15 easy, 25 intermediate, 7 difficult, and 11 expert-only trails. Write the ratio "intermediate trails : easy trails" in three ways.

$$\frac{\text{intermediate trails}}{\text{easy trails}} = \frac{25}{15} = \frac{5}{3}$$ **Write as a fraction and simplify.**

▶ **Answer** The ratio can be written as $\frac{5}{3}$, 5 : 3, or 5 to 3.

Rates A **rate** is a ratio of two quantities that have different units. Two rates are equivalent if they have the same value.

EXAMPLE 2 Finding an Equivalent Rate

Weather Lightning strikes about 100 times per second around the world. About how many times does lightning strike per minute around the world?

SOLUTION

CONVERT UNITS
Need help with converting units? See p. 815.

Because 60 seconds = 1 minute, $\frac{60 \text{ sec}}{1 \text{ min}}$ is equivalent to 1.

$\frac{100 \text{ times}}{1 \text{ sec}} = \frac{100 \text{ times}}{1 \cancel{\text{sec}}} \cdot \frac{60 \cancel{\text{sec}}}{1 \text{ min}}$ **Multiply by a fraction that is equivalent to 1.**

$= \frac{6000 \text{ times}}{1 \text{ min}}$ **Simplify.**

▶ **Answer** Lightning strikes about 6000 times per minute around the world.

Unit Rates A **unit rate** is a rate that has a denominator of 1 unit. To write a unit rate, find an equivalent rate with a denominator of 1 unit.

EXAMPLE 3 Finding a Unit Rate

WRITE EQUIVALENT FRACTIONS
Need help with equivalent fractions? See p. 187.

Write −24 feet per 5 seconds as a unit rate.

$\frac{-24 \text{ ft}}{5 \text{ sec}} = -\frac{24 \div 5}{5 \div 5}$ **Divide numerator and denominator by 5 to get a denominator of 1 unit.**

$= \frac{-4.8}{1}$ **Simplify.**

▶ **Answer** The unit rate is −4.8 feet per second.

Animated Math at classzone.com

Check Round −4.8 feet per second to −5 feet per second. The product $-5 \cdot 5 = -25$, which is about −24, so the answer is reasonable.

✓ GUIDED PRACTICE for Examples 1, 2, and 3

Use the information in Example 1 to write the ratio in three ways.

1. expert-only trails : easy trails
2. easy trails : difficult trails
3. **Pumping Water** A water pump moves 2 gallons of water per second. How many gallons of water are pumped per minute? Write your answer as a rate.

Write the rate as a unit rate.

4. $\frac{114 \text{ points}}{6 \text{ games}}$
5. $\frac{365 \text{ people}}{5 \text{ months}}$
6. $\frac{329 \text{ miles}}{10 \text{ gallons}}$
7. $\frac{-49 \text{ m}}{14 \text{ sec}}$

7.1 EXERCISES

HOMEWORK KEY

★ = **STANDARDIZED TEST PRACTICE** Exs. 28, 41, 42, 45, 46, and 53

○ = **HINTS AND HOMEWORK HELP** for Exs. 5, 7, 13, 19, 43 at classzone.com

SKILL PRACTICE

1. **VOCABULARY** What is the difference between a ratio and a rate?

2. **VOCABULARY** Copy and complete: "Three gallons to $4.50" and "five gallons to $7.50" are equivalent __?__.

WRITING AND SIMPLIFYING RATIOS **Write the ratio as a fraction in simplest form and two other ways.**

SEE EXAMPLE 1 on p. 343 for Exs. 3–10

3. $\frac{33}{22}$ 4. $\frac{20}{25}$ 5. $\frac{27}{42}$ 6. $\frac{-12}{4}$

7. 51 to 17 8. 26 : 39 9. 28 : 6 10. 35 to 49

MEASUREMENT **Write the equivalent rate.**

SEE EXAMPLE 2 on p. 344 for Exs. 11–18

11. $\frac{60 \text{ mi}}{\text{h}} = \frac{? \text{ mi}}{\text{min}}$ 12. $\frac{32 \text{ oz}}{\text{serving}} = \frac{? \text{ lb}}{\text{serving}}$ 13. $\frac{105 \text{ min}}{\text{game}} = \frac{? \text{ h}}{\text{game}}$ 14. $\frac{\$1.44}{\text{ft}} = \frac{\$?}{\text{yd}}$

15. $\frac{50 \text{ ft}}{\text{sec}} = \frac{? \text{ ft}}{\text{min}}$ 16. $\frac{87 \text{ cents}}{30 \text{ in.}} = \frac{? \text{ cents}}{\text{ft}}$ 17. $\frac{15 \text{ min}}{\text{quarter}} = \frac{? \text{ hr}}{\text{quarter}}$ 18. $\frac{20 \text{ mi}}{\text{h}} = \frac{? \text{ ft}}{\text{h}}$

UNIT RATES **Write the rate as a unit rate. Check for reasonableness.**

SEE EXAMPLE 3 on p. 344 for Exs. 19–26

19. $\frac{24 \text{ adults}}{6 \text{ cars}}$ 20. $\frac{80 \text{ mi}}{4 \text{ h}}$ 21. $\frac{18 \text{ degrees}}{6 \text{ min}}$ 22. $\frac{610 \text{ rotations}}{5 \text{ min}}$

23. $\frac{50 \text{ oz}}{5 \text{ servings}}$ 24. $\frac{-75 \text{ ft}}{20 \text{ sec}}$ 25. $\frac{-34 \text{ m}}{8 \text{ sec}}$ 26. $\frac{3 \text{ lb}}{\$2}$

27. **ERROR ANALYSIS** Your friend multiplied $\frac{14 \text{ times}}{\text{day}}$ by $\frac{1 \text{ week}}{7 \text{ days}}$ to get $\frac{2 \text{ times}}{\text{week}}$ as an equivalent ratio. Describe and correct the error that your friend made in writing the equivalent rate.

28. ★ **MULTIPLE CHOICE** Which rate is equivalent to 232 miles per 4 hours?

(A) $\frac{58 \text{ mi}}{4 \text{ h}}$ (B) $\frac{174 \text{ mi}}{3 \text{ h}}$ (C) $\frac{229 \text{ mi}}{1 \text{ h}}$ (D) $\frac{116 \text{ mi}}{1 \text{ h}}$

COMPARING RATIOS **Tell whether the ratios are equivalent.**

29. 3 to 12 and 2 to 6 30. 6 : 18 and 10 : 30 31. 15 : 35 and 18 : 42

xy ALGEBRA **Find a value of the variable that makes the ratios equivalent.**

32. $\frac{x}{8} = \frac{4}{16}$ 33. $\frac{9}{c} = \frac{27}{30}$ 34. $\frac{6}{10} = \frac{15}{n}$ 35. $\frac{2}{12} = \frac{z}{18}$

36. $\frac{8}{x} = \frac{x}{18}$ 37. $\frac{16}{y} = \frac{y}{4}$ 38. $\frac{3}{a} = \frac{a}{27}$ 39. $\frac{t}{2} = \frac{18}{t}$

40. **CHALLENGE** Write all pairs of equivalent ratios that use the numbers 6, 9, 10, and 15 exactly once.

PROBLEM SOLVING

SEE EXAMPLE 1 on p. 343 for Ex. 41

41. ★ **WRITING** The aspect ratio of a TV screen is the ratio of its length to its width. The aspect ratio of a *standard* TV screen is 4 : 3. The aspect ratio of a *wide screen* TV in the United States is 16 : 9. *Describe* how to tell whether a TV has a standard or wide screen, given its length and width.

SEE EXAMPLE 2 on p. 344 for Exs. 42–43

42. ★ **OPEN-ENDED MATH** About 1 of every 10 people is left-handed. How many people in your math class would you predict are left-handed? *Explain.*

43. **CLOCKS** A clock chimes 4 times each hour. How many times does it chime in a week?

SEE EXAMPLE 3 on p. 344 for Ex. 44

44. **WAGES** You are paid \$47.25 for 7 hours. How much are you paid per hour?

45. ★ **MULTIPLE CHOICE** The table shows the costs of oranges at four grocery stores. Which grocery store prices its oranges using a constant unit rate?

Amount	Cost of Oranges at Four Stores			
	A	B	C	D
10-lb bag	\$11.70	\$11.70	\$12.00	\$12.00
20-lb bag	\$22.90	\$23.40	\$24.00	\$22.00
30-lb bag	\$33.60	\$35.10	\$35.00	\$32.00

Ⓐ Store A Ⓑ Store B

Ⓒ Store C Ⓓ Store D

46. ★ **SHORT RESPONSE** At top speed, a greyhound, a roadrunner, and a cheetah can achieve the following distances in the given length of time. Which animal is the fastest? Which animal is the slowest? *Explain* your reasoning.

47. **CHALLENGE** Elliot and Colin both bring pretzels to school for a snack. The ratio of the number of pretzels Elliot brings to the number of pretzels Colin brings is 5 to 1. Elliot gives four pretzels to Colin, so the ratio is 3 to 1. How many pretzels does Elliot now have? *Explain.*

MIXED REVIEW

Prepare for Lesson 7.2 in Exs. 48–51

Solve the equation. Check your solution. *(p. 122)*

48. $3c = 18$ 49. $9x = -81$ 50. $\frac{v}{4} = -2$ 51. $\frac{n}{10} = 8$

52. Solve the inequality $10y + 4 < 24$ and graph the solution. *(p. 318)*

53. ★ **MULTIPLE CHOICE** What is the radius of a circle with a circumference of 39.25 feet? Use 3.14 for π. *(p. 312)*

Ⓐ 6.25 ft Ⓑ 12.5 ft Ⓒ 19.625 ft Ⓓ 39.25 ft

INVESTIGATION

Use before Lesson 7.2

GOAL
Make scale drawings.

MATERIALS
- ruler
- colored pencils
- grid paper
- magazine

7.2 Making a Scale Drawing

A *scale drawing* of an object preserves ratios of lengths but is either smaller or larger than the original object.

EXPLORE **Make an enlarged drawing of the picture.**

STEP 1 **Draw** a grid on the original picture. Use unit squares that are smaller than the unit squares on your grid paper.

STEP 2 **Draw** a rectangle on your grid paper that is the same number of units long and wide as the picture you want to enlarge.

STEP 3 **Copy** the image that appears in a corner of the original onto your grid paper at the corresponding corner. Continue copying the image one block at a time until you have drawn the entire picture.

STEP 4 **Measure** the width of the copy and of the original. The *scale* of the drawing is the ratio of corresponding measurements of the copy to the measurements of the original. What is the scale of your drawing?

PRACTICE

1. Cut out a picture from a magazine and create an enlarged scale drawing of it as described in Steps 1–3 above. Measure the original picture and the enlarged drawing to determine the scale.

DRAW CONCLUSIONS

2. **REASONING** Is the ratio of the area of a unit square in the copy to the area of a unit square in the original the same as the ratio of their sides? *Explain* using data from the scale drawing that you made.

3. **WRITING** *Explain* what would happen if different scales were used in the same drawing.

7.2 Writing and Solving Proportions

Before You wrote ratios.

Now You'll write and solve proportions.

Why? So you can find proportional amounts, as in Example 1.

KEY VOCABULARY
- **proportion,** *p. 348*
- **cross products,** *p. 349*
- **scale model,** *p. 350*
- **scale,** *p. 350*

A **proportion** is an equation that states that two ratios are equivalent. The proportion below is read "*a* is to *b* as *c* is to *d*."

$$\frac{a}{b} = \frac{c}{d}, b \neq 0, d \neq 0$$

EXAMPLE 1 Writing and Solving a Proportion

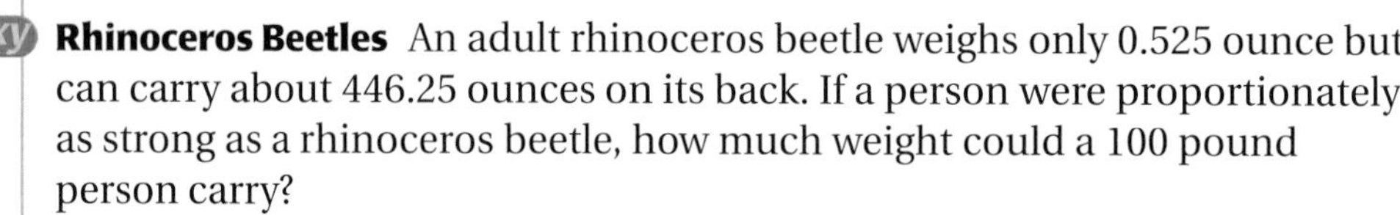

Rhinoceros Beetles An adult rhinoceros beetle weighs only 0.525 ounce but can carry about 446.25 ounces on its back. If a person were proportionately as strong as a rhinoceros beetle, how much weight could a 100 pound person carry?

SOLUTION

	Beetle	*Person*
Carries	446.25 oz	*x* lb
Weighs	0.525 oz	100 lb

Use a table to set up a proportion.

$\frac{446.25}{0.525} = \frac{x}{100}$ Write a proportion $\frac{\text{ounces}}{\text{ounces}} = \frac{\text{pounds}}{\text{pounds}}$.

$\frac{446.25}{0.525} \cdot 100 = \frac{x}{100} \cdot 100$ Multiply each side by 100.

$85{,}000 = x$ Simplify.

▶ **Answer** If human strength were proportional to that of a rhinoceros beetle, a 100 pound person could carry 85,000 pounds.

ANOTHER WAY
You can also use the following proportion in Example 1:

$$\frac{x}{446.25} = \frac{100}{0.525}$$

✓ GUIDED PRACTICE for Example 1

1. **What If?** Some ants weigh only 0.0001 ounce but can carry about 0.005 ounce. If a person were proportionately as strong as one of these ants, how much weight could a 100 pound person carry?

Solve the proportion.

2. $\frac{n}{12} = \frac{3}{4}$ 3. $\frac{50}{20} = \frac{z}{16}$ 4. $\frac{25}{3} = \frac{t}{51}$

VOCABULARY

The phrase *cross products* comes from the "X" shape formed by the diagonal numbers in the proportion.

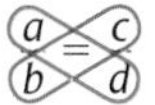

Cross Products The proportion $\frac{a}{b} = \frac{c}{d}$ has **cross products** ad and bc.

$$\frac{a}{b} \times \frac{c}{d} \qquad a \cdot d \qquad b \cdot c$$

You can use cross products to solve a proportion. You can also use cross products to check whether two ratios form a proportion.

KEY CONCEPT — *For Your Notebook*

Cross Products Property

Words The cross products of a proportion are equal.

Numbers Because $\frac{3}{4} = \frac{9}{12}$, you know that $3 \cdot 12 = 4 \cdot 9$.

Algebra If $\frac{a}{b} = \frac{c}{d}$, where b and d are nonzero numbers, then $ad = bc$.

EXAMPLE 2 Using the Cross Products Property

$\frac{6.8}{15.4} = \frac{40.8}{m}$	Write original proportion.
$6.8m = 15.4(40.8)$	Cross products property
$6.8m = 628.32$	Multiply.
$\frac{6.8m}{6.8} = \frac{628.32}{6.8}$	Divide each side by 6.8.
$m = 92.4$	Simplify.

Check You can check your solution by finding the cross products of the proportion. If the cross products are equal, the solution is correct.

$\frac{6.8}{15.4} \stackrel{?}{=} \frac{40.8}{92.4}$	Substitute 92.4 for m.
$6.8(92.4) \stackrel{?}{=} 15.4(40.8)$	Multiply.
$628.32 = 628.32$ ✓	

Animated Math at classzone.com

✓ GUIDED PRACTICE for Example 2

Solve the proportion. Then check your solution.

5. $\frac{6}{c} = \frac{54}{99}$

6. $\frac{n}{14} = \frac{63}{84}$

7. $\frac{2.1}{0.9} = \frac{27.3}{y}$

8. $\frac{16.2}{67.4} = \frac{x}{134.8}$

9. $\frac{8}{a} = \frac{0.4}{0.62}$

10. $\frac{b}{1.8} = \frac{49.6}{14.4}$

Scale The dimensions of a **scale model** are proportional to the dimensions of the actual object. The relationship between the model's dimensions and the actual object's dimensions is called the **scale**. A scale can be written as a ratio with or without units. For example, the scale 1 in. : 3 ft can also be written as 1 : 36.

EXAMPLE 3 Standardized Test Practice

Sculpture Strawberry Point, Iowa, has a strawberry sculpture that is 15 feet tall. If the scale of this model is 10 feet to 1 inch, how tall was the actual strawberry?

Ⓐ 1.5 inches Ⓑ 15 inches Ⓒ 1.5 feet Ⓓ 15 feet

ELIMINATE CHOICES
According to the scale, the actual strawberry should be smaller than the sculpture. So, you can eliminate choice D.

SOLUTION

$$\text{Scale} = \frac{\text{Height of strawberry model}}{\text{Height of actual strawberry}}$$

$\frac{10 \text{ ft}}{1 \text{ in.}} = \frac{15 \text{ ft}}{h \text{ in.}}$ **Write a proportion.**

$10h = 15$ **Cross products property**

$h = 1.5$ **Divide each side by 10.**

▶ **Answer** The height of the actual strawberry was 1.5 inches. The correct answer is A. Ⓐ Ⓑ Ⓒ Ⓓ

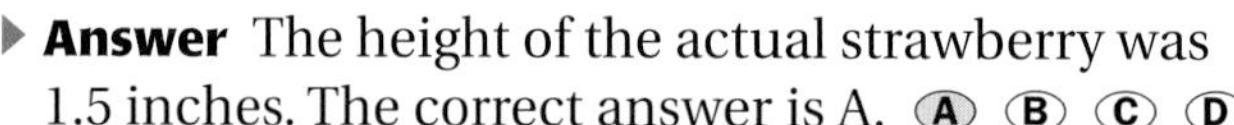

✓ GUIDED PRACTICE for Example 3

11. **What If?** Suppose the scale of the model in Example 3 is 25 feet to 3 inches. How tall was the actual strawberry?

7.2 EXERCISES

HOMEWORK KEY
★ = **STANDARDIZED TEST PRACTICE** Exs. 7, 42, 44, 45, 46, and 61
○ = **HINTS AND HOMEWORK HELP** for Exs. 5, 9, 15, 21, 39 at classzone.com

SKILL PRACTICE

1. **VOCABULARY** *Describe* how to use cross products to solve a proportion.

2. **VOCABULARY** Copy and complete: The relationship between a model's dimensions and the actual object's dimensions is given by the _?_.

SEE EXAMPLE 1 on p. 348 for Exs. 3–6

SOLVING PROPORTIONS **Solve the proportion. Then check your solution.**

3. $\frac{1}{2} = \frac{x}{6}$ 4. $\frac{c}{10} = \frac{3}{5}$ 5. $\frac{h}{4} = \frac{45}{20}$ 6. $\frac{3}{8} = \frac{x}{32}$

SEE EXAMPLE 1 on p. 348 for Ex. 7

7. ★ **MULTIPLE CHOICE** What is the solution of the proportion $\frac{12}{15} = \frac{x}{25}$?

(A) 7.2 (B) 20 (C) 22 (D) 31.25

CHECKING PROPORTIONS Tell whether the ratios form a proportion.

SEE EXAMPLE 2 on p. 349 for Exs. 8–24

8. $\frac{3}{4} \stackrel{?}{=} \frac{6}{8}$
9. $\frac{1}{2} \stackrel{?}{=} \frac{2}{5}$
10. $\frac{14}{21} \stackrel{?}{=} \frac{26}{39}$
11. $\frac{15}{45} \stackrel{?}{=} \frac{45}{135}$

USING CROSS PRODUCTS Solve the proportion.

12. $\frac{2}{3} = \frac{4}{z}$
13. $\frac{6}{a} = \frac{3}{1}$
14. $\frac{39}{13} = \frac{9}{d}$
15. $\frac{68}{12} = \frac{51}{p}$
16. $\frac{17}{12} = \frac{k}{36}$
17. $\frac{2}{5} = \frac{c}{20}$
18. $\frac{7.2}{m} = \frac{2.4}{1.8}$
19. $\frac{256}{9.6} = \frac{1.6}{g}$
20. $\frac{67.2}{g} = \frac{16.8}{3.3}$
21. $\frac{t}{29.4} = \frac{5.5}{4.2}$
22. $\frac{f}{5.4} = \frac{483}{18.9}$
23. $\frac{712}{8.8} = \frac{x}{18.7}$

24. **ERROR ANALYSIS** Describe and correct the error made in solving the proportion.

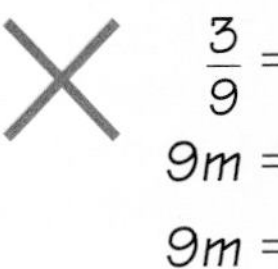
$\frac{3}{9} = \frac{12}{m}$
$9m = 3 \cdot 12$
$9m = 36$
$m = 4$

SCALE MODELS You use a scale of 3 inches to 50 feet to make scale models of buildings. A building's actual height is given. Find the model's height.

SEE EXAMPLE 3 on p. 350 for Exs. 25–28

25. $h = 100$ ft
26. $h = 240$ ft
27. $h = 316$ ft
28. $h = 545$ ft

In Exercises 29–34, find the value of x. Use this example to help you.

EXTENSION Solving Multi-Step Proportions

$\frac{30}{2+x} = \frac{6}{7}$	Write original proportion.
$30 \cdot 7 = (2 + x) \cdot 6$	Cross products property
$210 = 12 + 6x$	Multiply and use distributive property.
$33 = x$	Solve the two-step equation for x.

29. $\frac{2}{x+2} = \frac{18}{27}$
30. $\frac{x-2}{8} = \frac{30}{40}$
31. $\frac{9}{5} = \frac{36}{x-3}$
32. $\frac{5}{x} = \frac{7}{x+4}$
33. $\frac{x}{5} = \frac{3x-4}{7}$
34. $\frac{3-5x}{4} = \frac{x+5}{9}$

MULTIPLE VARIABLES Find the value of each variable. Check your solution.

35. $\frac{4}{x-5} = \frac{3}{2x} = \frac{y}{21}$
36. $\frac{7}{b-36} = \frac{a}{72} = \frac{28}{b}$
37. $\frac{8}{p-10} = \frac{16}{p-5} = \frac{n+8}{p}$

38. **CHALLENGE** If $\frac{a}{b} = \frac{c}{d}$, where a, b, c, and d are nonzero numbers, is it true that $\frac{a}{c} = \frac{b}{d}$? Is it true that $\frac{d}{a} = \frac{c}{b}$? *Justify* your answers using algebraic properties or *counterexamples* (examples of when the statement is false).

PROBLEM SOLVING

SEE EXAMPLE 1 on p. 348 for Exs. 39–41

39. **CARS** A car moving at a constant speed travels 88 feet in 2 seconds. Use a proportion to find how many feet it travels in one minute.

40. **EARNINGS** You earn $54 mowing 3 lawns. You charge the same amount for each lawn. How much do you earn for mowing 5 lawns?

41. **MENTAL MATH** Ten pounds of organic pasta cost $16. *Explain* how to use equivalent fractions and mental math to find the cost of 5 pounds of pasta.

SEE EXAMPLE 3 on p. 350 for Exs. 42–44

42. ★ **SHORT RESPONSE** The Transamerica Building in San Francisco is 853 feet tall and is 145 feet wide at its widest point. You want to make a drawing of the building that has a scale of 1 in. : 80 ft. Will your drawing fit on a regular $8\frac{1}{2} \times 11$ sheet of paper? *Explain* your reasoning.

43. **MULTIPLE REPRESENTATIONS** You want to sketch three views of a car using a scale of 1 inch to 40 inches. The actual car is 215 inches long, 76 inches wide, and 54 inches high.
    a. **Calculate** Calculate the length, width, and height of the car for your drawing.
    b. **Draw Views** Draw rectangles for a front, side, and overhead view of the car with the dimensions you found in part (a). Then sketch the views.

44. ★ **MULTIPLE CHOICE** The scale on a map is $\frac{1}{4}$ inch : 20 miles. The distance from Montgomery, Alabama, to Atlanta, Georgia, is about 2 inches on the map. About how far is it from Montgomery to Atlanta?

(A) 20 miles (B) 80 miles (C) 160 miles (D) 200 miles

45. ★ **WRITING** The wingspan and length of a space shuttle orbiter model are shown. What additional pieces of information could be used to find the scale of the model? *Explain.*

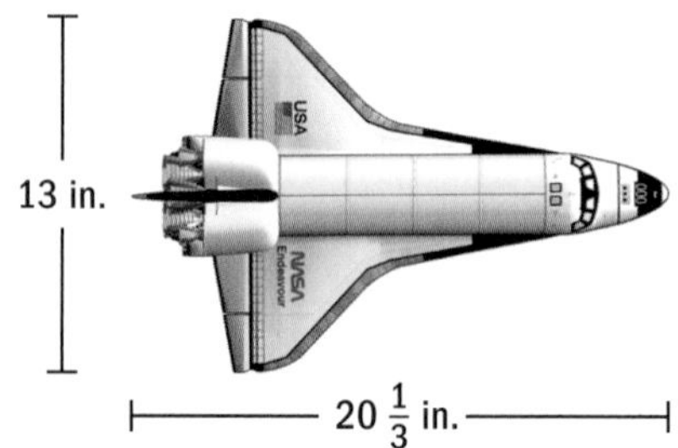

46. ★ **EXTENDED RESPONSE** To produce one pound of honey, the bees from a hive fly over 55,000 miles and visit about 2 million flowers.
    a. Estimate how many flowers are visited to make 10 ounces of honey.
    b. Estimate how many miles the bees fly to make 10 ounces of honey.
    c. Estimate the mean number of flowers visited per mile traveled. *Explain* your reasoning.

READING *IN* MATH **Read the information below for Exercises 47–49.**

The Green Park The Green Park in London, England, was given its name in 1746 and opened to the public in 1826. Once stocked with deer and used as hunting grounds, the park is presently a place used by tourists and Londoners for exercising, picnicking, and relaxing. The park is roughly the shape of a triangle, as shown in the map at the right, whose longest side is about 2600 feet long.

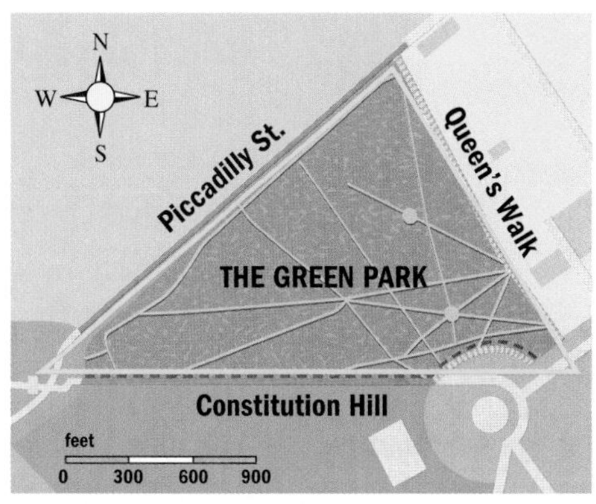

47. **Find a Scale** Use a ruler to find the scale of the map in centimeters to feet.

48. **Estimation** Estimate the dimensions of the triangular shaped park. Use the dimensions to estimate the perimeter and area of the park.

49. **Calculate** A type of grass seed costs about $.36 for every square yard. About how much would it cost to cover all of The Green Park with this grass seed?

50. **SOCCER** Your school's soccer team had a record of 4 wins and 6 losses after losing its last game. To make the playoffs, your team needs to win 75% of all of its games. If your team wins the rest of its games, at least how many games *must be* left in the schedule for your team to make the playoffs?

51. **CHALLENGE** A 5-inch by 8-inch photo needs to be proportionally increased in size to fit a space whose width is 5 inches less than its length. Find the perimeter and area of the enlarged photo.

MIXED REVIEW

Prepare for Lesson 7.3 in Exs. 52–57

Evaluate the expression. *(p. 768)*

52. $\frac{13}{104} \times 100$

53. $\frac{16}{80} \times 100$

54. $\frac{37}{100} \times 82$

55. $\frac{15}{100} \times 68$

56. $\frac{105}{28} \times 100$

57. $\frac{291}{97} \times 100$

Write the rate as a unit rate. *(p. 343)*

58. $\frac{\text{42 people}}{\text{14 taxis}}$

59. $\frac{\text{258 miles}}{\text{6 hours}}$

60. $\frac{\text{36 dogs}}{\text{18 households}}$

61. ★ **MULTIPLE CHOICE** Which inequality corresponds to this sentence: Four less than nine times a number is at most 95? *(p. 324)*

Ⓐ $4 - 9x \leq 95$

Ⓑ $9x - 4 < 95$

Ⓒ $9x - 4 \leq 95$

Ⓓ $9x - 4 \geq 95$

7.3 Solving Percent Problems

Before	You solved proportions.
Now	You'll solve percent problems using proportions.
Why?	So you can use data to find percents, as in Example 1.

KEY VOCABULARY
- **percent,** *p. 354*

The word *percent* means "per hundred." A **percent** is a ratio whose denominator is 100. The symbol for percent is %.

KEY CONCEPT *For Your Notebook*

Solving Percent Problems

To represent "a is p percent of b," use the proportion

$$\frac{a}{b} = \frac{p}{100}$$

where a is part of the base b and $p\%$, or $\frac{p}{100}$, is the percent.

EXAMPLE 1 Finding a Percent

Environment A service club is planting seedlings as part of an erosion prevention project. Out of 240 newly planted seedlings, 15 are laurel sumac. What percent of the seedlings are laurel sumac?

SOLUTION

To find the percent of seedlings that are laurel sumac, use a percent proportion.

$\frac{a}{b} = \frac{p}{100}$ **Write a percent proportion.**

$\frac{15}{240} = \frac{p}{100}$ **Substitute 15 for *a* and 240 for *b*.**

$\frac{15}{240} \cdot 100 = \frac{p}{100} \cdot 100$ **Multiply each side by 100.**

$6.25 = p$ **Simplify.**

Answer 6.25% of the seedlings are laurel sumac.

LOOK BACK
Need help with multiplying a fraction by a whole number? See p. 243.

GUIDED PRACTICE for Example 1

Use a percent proportion.

1. 63 is what percent of 75?
2. 84 is what percent of 70?

EXAMPLE 2 Finding Part of a Base

School Newspaper Your school newspaper's budget this year is 160% of last year's budget, which was \$2125. What is this year's budget?

SOLUTION

ANOTHER WAY
You can also solve these proportions by using cross products.

$\frac{a}{b} = \frac{p}{100}$	Write a percent proportion.
$\frac{a}{2125} = \frac{160}{100}$	Substitute 2125 for b and 160 for p.
$\frac{a}{2125} \cdot 2125 = \frac{160}{100} \cdot 2125$	Multiply each side by 2125.
$a = 3400$	Simplify.

▶ **Answer** This year's budget is \$3400.

EXAMPLE 3 Finding a Base

24 is 0.8% of what number?

TAKE NOTES
In your notes, you may want to include each step needed to solve a percent proportion.

$\frac{a}{b} = \frac{p}{100}$	Write a percent proportion.
$\frac{24}{b} = \frac{0.8}{100}$	Substitute 24 for a and 0.8 for p.
$24 \cdot 100 = b \cdot 0.8$	Cross products property
$3000 = b$	Divide each side by 0.8 and simplify.

▶ **Answer** 24 is 0.8% of 3000.

CONCEPT SUMMARY *For Your Notebook*

Percent Problems

Question	Method	Proportion
a is what percent of b?	Solve for p.	$\frac{a}{b} = \frac{p}{100}$
What number is p% of b?	Solve for a.	$\frac{a}{b} = \frac{p}{100}$
a is p% of what number?	Solve for b.	$\frac{a}{b} = \frac{p}{100}$

✓ GUIDED PRACTICE for Examples 2 and 3

Use a percent proportion.

3. What number is 16% of 75?

4. What number is 35% of 92?

5. 260 is 325% of what number?

6. What number is 0.5% of 65?

7.3 EXERCISES

HOMEWORK KEY

★ = **STANDARDIZED TEST PRACTICE** Exs. 17, 19, 32, 34, 36, 39, and 56

○ = **HINTS AND HOMEWORK HELP** for Exs. 3, 7, 9, 13, 33 at classzone.com

SKILL PRACTICE

1. **VOCABULARY** Copy and complete: Another way to say "25 songs out of 100" is to say "25 _?_ of the songs."

2. **VOCABULARY** In the sentence "30 is 75% of 40," which number is the base?

USING PROPORTIONS **Write a proportion to represent the percent problem. Then solve the proportion to answer the question.**

SEE EXAMPLES 1, 2, AND 3 on pp. 354–355 for Exs. 3–17

3. 209 is 38% of what number?
4. 6 is what percent of 75?
5. 5 is what percent of 125?
6. 481 is 52% of what number?
7. What number is 45% of 245?
8. What number is 30% of 120?

USING PROPORTIONS **Use a percent proportion to answer the question.**

9. 756 is what percent of 840?
10. 39 is what percent of 50?
11. 918 is 170% of what number?
12. 111 is what percent of 740?
13. 567 is what percent of 420?
14. What number is 520% of 150?
15. What number is 0.36% of 700?
16. 179.2 is 32% of what number?

17. ★ **MULTIPLE CHOICE** How much is 20% of $90?

 Ⓐ $18 Ⓑ $20 Ⓒ $70 Ⓓ $72

18. **ERROR ANALYSIS** Describe and correct the error made in answering the following question: *What percent of 60 is 12*?

$$\frac{a}{b} = \frac{p}{100}$$

$$\frac{60}{12} = \frac{p}{100}$$

$500 = p$

500% of 60 is 12.

19. ★ **OPEN-ENDED MATH** Write three percent problems in which you find the percent, three in which you find the part, and three in which you find the base.

NUMBER SENSE **Copy and complete the statement using <, >, or =.**

20. 30% of 120 _?_ 120% of 30
21. 20% of 80 _?_ 40% of 50
22. 15% of 140 _?_ 75% of 24
23. 25% of 80 _?_ 125% of 12
24. 150% of 30 _?_ 75% of 48
25. 10% of 400 _?_ 25% of 160

ALGEBRA **Solve the percent problem in terms of y.**

26. What number is 50% of $8y$?
27. $3y$ is 60% of what number?

CHALLENGE **Find the unknown number.**

28. 85% of 20% of what number is 34?
29. 115% of 25% of what number is 46?

PROBLEM SOLVING

SEE EXAMPLES 1, 2, AND 3 on pp. 354–355 for Exs. 30–35

30. **GUIDED PROBLEM SOLVING** You ask 356 people if they enjoy drawing. Of these people, 89 say they do like to draw. What percent of the people surveyed like to draw?

    a. Write a percent proportion.

    b. Substitute the known values for the variables.

    c. Solve the proportion.

31. **MARATHON** Of the 23,513 people who entered the Honolulu Marathon one year, 19,236 finished. What percent of the runners finished? Round your answer to the nearest tenth of a percent.

32. ★ **MULTIPLE CHOICE** A bag of 150 stickers contains 28% blue, 26% red, 34% green, and 12% yellow stickers. Which proportion can be used to find g, the number of green stickers in the bag?

    Ⓐ $\frac{g}{100} = \frac{34}{150}$ Ⓑ $\frac{34}{100} = \frac{g}{150}$ Ⓒ $\frac{100}{150} = \frac{g}{34}$ Ⓓ $\frac{34}{100} = \frac{150}{g}$

33. **WATER** A child's body weight is approximately 75% water. About how many pounds of a 60 pound child's weight is water?

34. ★ **SHORT RESPONSE** You read that 560 of the 875 students at your school belong to a school club. Write and solve a proportion to find the percent of students who belong to a club. *Explain* how you could use equivalent fractions and estimation to check your answer.

35. **REPTILES** The largest crocodiles alive today are 24 feet in length. Recently, researchers found bones of an ancient crocodile. It was 167% as long as today's longest crocodiles. How much longer was the ancient crocodile than today's longest crocodile? *Round* to the nearest foot.

36. ★ **WRITING** *Explain* how you might find 10% of 400 without writing a proportion.

37. **NUMBER SENSE** One day, 32 of 80 people wore a red shirt to school. What percent of the 80 people did *not* wear a red shirt to school?

38. **QUIZ SCORES** You earned 32 points on a quiz. Your score was 80%. What was the maximum number of points on the quiz? How many more points would you have needed to earn a score of 90%? *Explain.*

39. ★ **OPEN-ENDED MATH** *Describe* a real-world situation where a percent greater than 100% can be used.

40. **DINOSAURS** You buy a scale model of a Dilophosaurus for your brother. The scale of the model is 1 inch to 3 feet 4 inches. To the nearest percent, what percent of the actual height is the model's height?

41. **MULTI-STEP PROBLEM** Mary Anne and Josefina are mowing the lawn of their neighbor's town house to make extra money. Use the diagram below to answer the questions.

a. How many square feet has each mowed so far?

b. Who has mowed the greatest percent of her section so far?

c. Mary Anne finishes her section while Josefina takes a break to get them both some water and helps Josefina by mowing 5% of the unmowed portion of the back lawn. Josefina mows the rest. How many square feet does Josefina mow? What percent of the entire lawn does she mow?

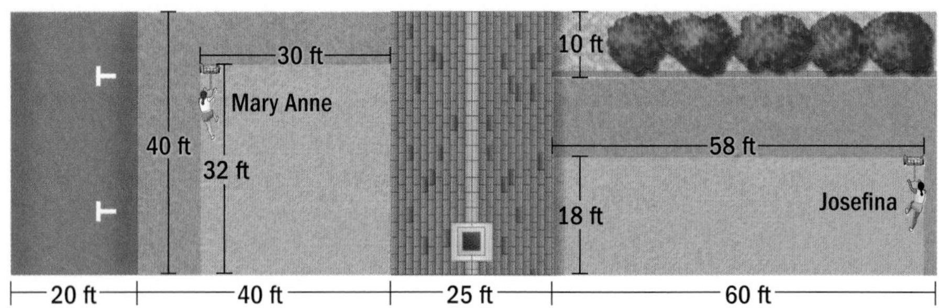

42. **CHALLENGE** You use a photocopier to reduce an 8 inch by 10 inch photograph. When you press the reduction button, it reduces both the length and width by the percent selected. What is the new area if you reduce the photograph to 64% of its original size and then reduce the result to 78% of its size? What is the new area if you reduce to 78% first and then to 64%? *Compare* the two values.

43. **CHALLENGE** A worker gets a raise so that his pay is now 120% of what it was. Then the employer offers the worker the option of working less time but making only 80% of the new pay rate. Would choosing this option enable the worker to make *more, less,* or *the same amount* as before the raise? *Explain.*

MIXED REVIEW

Prepare for Lesson 7.4 in Exs. 44–47

Write two fractions that are equivalent to the given fractions. *(p. 187)*

44. $\frac{48}{72}$ **45.** $\frac{21}{28}$ **46.** $\frac{18}{54}$ **47.** $\frac{75}{125}$

Write the decimal as a fraction or mixed number. *(p. 255)*

48. 1.86 **49.** 8.714 **50.** 0.624 **51.** 3.28

Find the product or quotient. *(p. 265)*

52. 0.023×8.45 **53.** 47.1×0.96 **54.** $11.48 \div 8.2$ **55.** $17.92 \div 6.4$

56. ★ **MULTIPLE CHOICE** You and a friend have a total of $30 to go to a baseball game. A ticket costs $10 and hot dogs cost $2 each. What is the greatest number of hot dogs that you and your friend can buy? *(p. 293)*

Ⓐ 5 Ⓑ 10 Ⓒ 15 Ⓓ 20

7.4 Fractions, Decimals, and Percents

Before You wrote fractions as decimals and decimals as fractions.

Now You'll rewrite fractions, decimals, and percents.

Why? So you can express survey data as percents, as in Example 4.

KEY VOCABULARY
- **circle graph,** *p. 360*

The diagram below shows several ways to represent 20% using concepts from Lessons 4.3, 5.5, and 7.3.

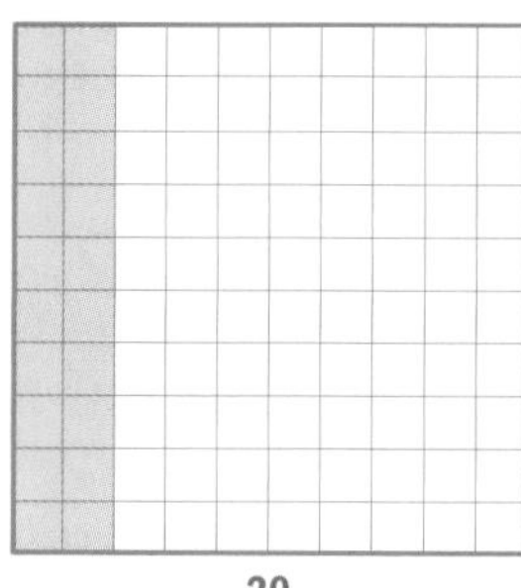

$20\% = \frac{20}{100} = 0.20$

$20\% = \frac{20}{100} = \frac{20 \div 20}{100 \div 20} = \frac{1}{5}$

Percents and Decimals To write a percent as a decimal, you can divide by 100, because $p\% = \frac{p}{100} = p \div 100$. Recall that dividing by 100 is the same as moving the decimal point two places to the left.

EXAMPLE 1 Writing a Percent as a Decimal

AVOID ERRORS
Add a zero on the left if necessary to move the decimal point two places to the left.

a. $65\% = 65 \div 100 = .65 = 0.65$

b. $250\% = 250 \div 100 = 2.50 = 2.5$

c. $0.3\% = 0.3 \div 100 = .003 = 0.003$

To write a decimal as a percent, reverse the process in Example 1 and multiply by 100. Note that multiplying by 100 is the same as moving the decimal point two places to the left.

EXAMPLE 2 Writing a Decimal as a Percent

AVOID ERRORS
Add a zero on the right if necessary to move the decimal point two places to the right.

a. $0.95 = (0.95 \times 100)\% = 095. = 95\%$

b. $2.7 = (2.7 \times 100)\% = 270. = 270\%$

c. $0.004 = (0.004 \times 100)\% = 000.4 = 0.4\%$

Percents and Fractions Since percent means per 100, to write $p\%$ as a fraction, use p as the numerator and 100 as the denominator. Then simplify.

EXAMPLE 3 Writing a Percent as a Fraction

COMMON EQUIVALENTS
For a list of common fraction, decimal, and percent equivalents, see p. 820

a. $25\% = \frac{25}{100} = \frac{25 \div 25}{100 \div 25} = \frac{1}{4}$

b. $325\% = \frac{325}{100} = \frac{325 \div 25}{100 \div 25} = \frac{13}{4} = 3\frac{1}{4}$

c. $0.2\% = \frac{0.2}{100} = \frac{0.2 \times 10}{100 \times 10} = \frac{2}{1000} = \frac{1}{500}$

Circle Graphs A **circle graph** represents data as parts of a circle, with each part labeled with its fraction or equivalent percent. Each item of data belongs in exactly one of the parts. So, the sum of the fractions equals 1, or the sum of the percents equals 100.

EXAMPLE 4 Writing a Fraction as a Percent

Survey The circle graph below shows the results of a survey of how 500 students prefer to spend their time.

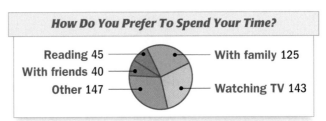

How Do You Prefer To Spend Your Time?

a. What percent of students prefer to spend time with friends?

$\frac{40}{500} = \frac{p}{100}$

$4000 = 500p$

$8 = p$

▶ **Answer** 8% of all of the students prefer to spend time with friends.

b. What percent of those who didn't answer "other" said "with friends"?

$\frac{40}{353} = \frac{p}{100}$

$4000 = 353p$

$11.33 \approx p$

▶ **Answer** About 11% of the selected group said "with friends."

ANOTHER WAY
You can also write fractions as percents by using equivalent fractions.
$\frac{40}{500} = \frac{8}{100} = 8\%$

✓ GUIDED PRACTICE for Examples 3 and 4

Write the percent as a decimal and as a fraction in simplest form.

1. 35% **2.** 140% **3.** 0.75% **4.** 12.12%

Write the decimal or fraction as a percent.

5. 0.9 **6.** 5.04 **7.** $\frac{1}{20}$ **8.** $\frac{3}{8}$

EXAMPLE 5 Ordering Fractions, Decimals, and Percents

Sleep Habits A survey of dog owners found the following portions represent the three most popular sleeping places for dogs: $\frac{9}{40}$ on owner's bed, 0.19 in a dog house, and 16.8% on the floor. Order these numbers from least to greatest.

STEP 1 **Write** the numbers as decimals with the same number of decimal places.

$\frac{9}{40} = 0.225$ $\quad$ $0.19 = 0.190$ $\quad$ $16.8\% = 0.168$

STEP 2 **Compare** the decimals: $0.168 < 0.190$ and $0.190 < 0.225$.

▶ **Answer** The numbers ordered from least to greatest are 16.8%, 0.19, and $\frac{9}{40}$.

Check Use a number line to order the decimals.

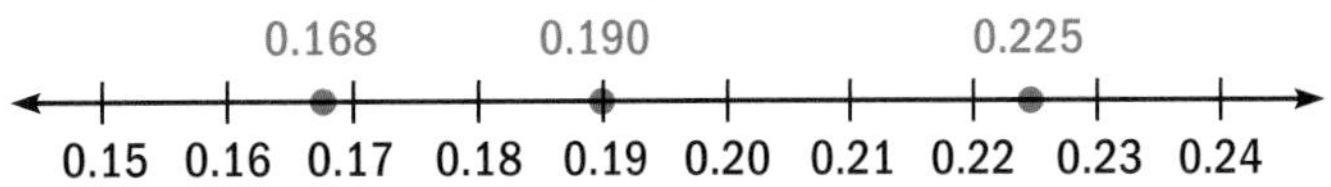

Animated Math at classzone.com

✓ GUIDED PRACTICE for Example 5

Order the numbers from least to greatest.

9. 41%, $\frac{9}{20}$, 0.389 $\quad$ **10.** $\frac{9}{10}$, 0.099, 95% $\quad$ **11.** 1.5, 145%, $\frac{7}{5}$

7.4 EXERCISES

HOMEWORK KEY

★ = **STANDARDIZED TEST PRACTICE** Exs. 58, 71, 74, 75, 76, and 83

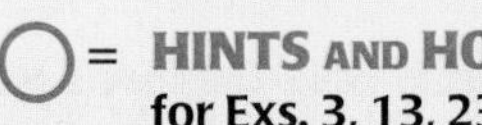

○ = **HINTS AND HOMEWORK HELP** for Exs. 3, 13, 23, 43, 67 at classzone.com

SKILL PRACTICE

1. VOCABULARY In a circle graph, what is the sum of the percents? What is the sum of the fractions?

SEE EXAMPLE 1 on p. 359 for Exs. 2–11

REWRITING PERCENTS Write the percent as a decimal.

2. 80% $\quad$ **3.** 12.5% $\quad$ **4.** 7.5% $\quad$ **5.** 110% $\quad$ **6.** 1.05%

7. 44.55% $\quad$ **8.** 0.4% $\quad$ **9.** 0.78% $\quad$ **10.** 187.09% $\quad$ **11.** 0.08%

SEE EXAMPLE 2 on p. 359 for Exs. 12–21

REWRITING DECIMALS Write the decimal as a percent.

12. 0.09 $\quad$ **13.** 1.27 $\quad$ **14.** 0.7 $\quad$ **15.** 2.1 $\quad$ **16.** 4

17. 0.51 $\quad$ **18.** 0.003 $\quad$ **19.** 0.057 $\quad$ **20.** 0.039 $\quad$ **21.** 0.004

SEE EXAMPLE 2
on p. 359
for Ex. 22

22. **ERROR ANALYSIS** Describe and correct the error made in writing 0.001 as a percent.

✗ $0.001 = \frac{1}{100} = 1\%$

REWRITING PERCENTS **Write the percent as a fraction.**

SEE EXAMPLE 3
on p. 360
for Exs. 23–32

23. 40% 24. 87% 25. 32.5% 26. 5% 27. 124%

28. 1% 29. 4.2% 30. 200.2% 31. 8.03% 32. 0.07%

REWRITING FRACTIONS **Write the fraction as a percent.**

SEE EXAMPLE 4
on p. 360
for Exs. 33–42

33. $\frac{5}{8}$ 34. $\frac{3}{2}$ 35. $\frac{1}{80}$ 36. $\frac{3}{20}$ 37. $\frac{31}{10}$

38. $\frac{4}{800}$ 39. $\frac{4}{50}$ 40. $\frac{117}{200}$ 41. $\frac{7}{16}$ 42. $\frac{11}{12}$

COMPARING **Copy and complete the statement using <, >, or =.**

SEE EXAMPLE 5
on p. 361
for Exs. 43–51

43. $\frac{1}{4}$? 26% 44. 450% ? $\frac{9}{2}$ 45. $\frac{13}{25}$? 0.5

46. 0.0825 ? $\frac{17}{200}$ 47. 27% ? $\frac{1}{5}$ 48. $\frac{7}{20}$? 35%

49. 4.5% ? 0.045 50. 3.83% ? 0.383 51. 101% ? 0.101

ORDERING NUMBERS **Order the numbers from least to greatest.**

52. 0.3, $\frac{9}{40}$, 22%, 0.228, $\frac{41}{125}$

53. 6.5%, $\frac{9}{50}$, 0.65, 66%, 0.5

54. $\frac{4}{7}$, 0.058, 58, 58%, 0.58%

55. 212%, 21.2, $\frac{21}{100}$, 0.212, $\frac{21}{10}$

56. $\frac{11}{15}$, 0.73, 7.3%, $\frac{75}{100}$, 0.73%

57. $\frac{12}{25}$, 480%, 0.484, 4.84, 4.8%

58. ★ **MULTIPLE CHOICE** Which numbers are in order from least to greatest?

Ⓐ 0.25, 2.5%, $\frac{2}{7}$ Ⓑ 2.5%, 0.25, $\frac{2}{7}$ Ⓒ 0.25, $\frac{2}{7}$, 2.5% Ⓓ 2.5%, $\frac{2}{7}$, 0.25

59. **WHICH ONE DOESN'T BELONG?** When written as a percent, which fraction is not like the others?

A. $\frac{9}{8}$ B. $\frac{5}{4}$ C. $\frac{7}{4}$ D. $\frac{31}{20}$

60. **ERROR ANALYSIS** A student says that because $\frac{1}{4}$ equals 25% and 5 is greater than 4, $\frac{1}{5}$ must be greater than 25%. Describe and correct the error in the student's reasoning.

COMPARING PERCENTS **Use graph paper to illustrate.**

61. 45% and 4.5% 62. $33\frac{1}{3}\%$ and $3\frac{1}{3}\%$ 63. 20% and 2% 64. 75% and 7.5%

65. **CHALLENGE** Is 50% of 30% of 120 the same as $\frac{3}{20}$ of 120? *Explain.*

PROBLEM SOLVING

LANGUAGES The circle graph shows the world languages that U.S. high school students studied in a recent year. Each fraction represents part of the total number of U.S. high school students who studied a world language.

SEE EXAMPLE 4 on p. 360 for Exs. 66–72

66. Which language was the most popular?

67. What percent of the students studied German?

68. What percent of the students studied French or German?

69. What percent of the students did *not* study Spanish?

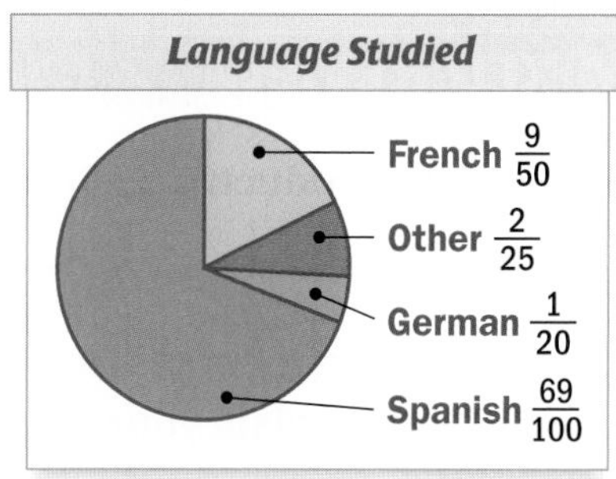

70. **SLEEPING** You survey 48 people and find that 18 of them sleep eight hours a night. What percent sleep eight hours a night?

71. ★ **SHORT RESPONSE** There are 25 cars in a parking lot. Nine of the cars are red. The rest of the cars are black or white.

a. What percent of cars in the lot are red? *not* red?

b. *Describe* two ways to determine the percent of cars that are *not* black given the number of white cars.

72. **REASONING** If a fraction is greater than 1, what do you know about the equivalent percent? *Explain.*

SEE EXAMPLE 5 on p. 361 for Ex. 73

73. **MULTIPLE REPRESENTATIONS** A survey asked fathers to name the five most indispensable products to fathers with a newborn. The results are as follows: $\frac{17}{20}$ said infant carrier/car seat, $\frac{1}{2}$ said pacifier, 0.7 said stroller, $\frac{19}{50}$ said baby monitor, and 79% said disposable diapers. Order the numbers from least to greatest. *Check* using a number line.

74. ★ **WRITING** The table shows the percents of people who buy various types of music. *Explain* why the data should *not* be represented in a circle graph. Then display the data in an appropriate way.

Music	Rock	Pop	Rap	R&B	Country
Percent	25.2%	8.9%	13.3%	10.6%	10.4%

75. ★ **OPEN-ENDED MATH** Sometimes a percent is greater than 100. For example, a store can sell 125% of the number of sweaters it sold last year. *Describe* a situation where a percent should not be greater than 100.

76. ★ **MULTIPLE CHOICE** A football field is 100 yards long, excluding the end zones. Approximately what percent of a mile is a football field's length?

Ⓐ 1.9% Ⓑ 5.7% Ⓒ 17.6% Ⓓ 52.8%

77. **CHALLENGE** You conduct a survey about laundry detergent. Brand A is preferred by $\frac{2}{15}$ of the people. Brand B is preferred by $\frac{5}{12}$ of the people. Of the remaining people, 80% prefer Brand C and the rest have no preference. What percent of all the people surveyed have no preference?

MIXED REVIEW

Prepare for Lesson 7.5 in Exs. 78–81

Find the product. ***(p. 265)***

78. 9×0.13 79. 0.41×11 80. 9×4.5 81. 1.98×6

CHOOSE A STRATEGY **Use a strategy from the list to solve the following problem. Explain your choice of strategy.**

82. You work for 4 hours. You spend \$5.75 of the money you earn on a movie ticket and \$2 on popcorn. Then your sister gives you \$3 she owes you. You now have \$19.25. How much were you paid per hour?

Problem Solving Strategies
- **Guess, Check, and Revise,** *(p. 788)*
- **Work Backward,** *(p. 789)*
- **Act It Out,** *(p. 795)*

83. ★ **MULTIPLE CHOICE** Which is not a solution to the inequality $10 + 4x < 31$? ***(p. 318)***

Ⓐ 3 Ⓑ 4 Ⓒ 5 Ⓓ 6

QUIZ *for Lessons 7.1–7.4*

SIMPLIFYING RATIOS **A box of animal crackers contains 6 gorillas, 5 bears, 4 camels, 2 monkeys, 2 sheep, and 1 lion. Write the ratio in simplest form.** ***(p. 343)***

1. gorillas to sheep 2. monkeys to camels 3. bears to lions

Solve the proportion. ***(p. 348)***

4. $\frac{a}{72} = \frac{5}{6}$ 5. $\frac{2}{3} = \frac{7}{x}$ 6. $\frac{18}{27} = \frac{y}{3}$

7. $\frac{6}{8} = \frac{b}{28}$ 8. $\frac{12}{c} = \frac{23}{92}$ 9. $\frac{z}{8} = \frac{95}{19}$

10. **CLOTHING SALES** You save 40% when buying a shirt that originally cost \$29. How much do you save? ***(p. 354)***

GARDENING **The circle graph shows the numbers of flowers that you planted in a flowerbed.** ***(p. 359)***

11. How many flowers did you plant?

12. What percent of the flowerbed is daffodils?

13. What two types of flowers combine to equal 70%?

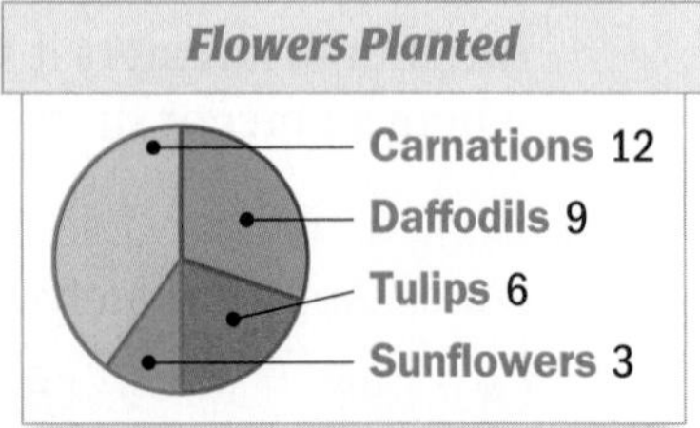

MIXED REVIEW *of Problem Solving*

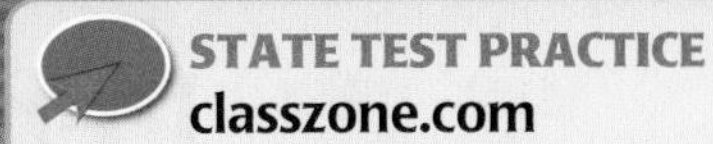

Lessons 7.1–7.4

1. **EXTENDED RESPONSE** In a 3 game basketball tournament, Alma made 1 out of 4 free throws in the first game. She made 2 out of 5 free throws in the second game. In the third game, she attempted 6 free throws.
   a. Alma finished the tournament making 60% of her free throws. Let x represent the number of free throws she made in all of the games. Write a percent proportion for the situation.
   b. Solve the proportion in part (a). Find how many free throws she made in the third game. Show your work.

2. **MULTI-STEP PROBLEM** You are using a photocopier to proportionally enlarge a design that measures 5 inches by 8 inches. You want the design to fit on an 8.5 inch by 11 inch sheet of paper with a 0.5 inch margin on all four sides.
   a. Find the maximum possible length of the enlarged design.
   b. What percent of the original length will the enlarged length be?
   c. What will be the width of the enlarged design?

3. **OPEN-ENDED** Write a ratio in three ways for the portion of days that you have been to school in the past 10 days.

4. **GRIDDED ANSWER** Water makes up about 95% of the weight of a watermelon. How many pounds of a 12 pound watermelon is *not* water?

5. **SHORT RESPONSE** Two cars are traveling at the rates of speed shown below.

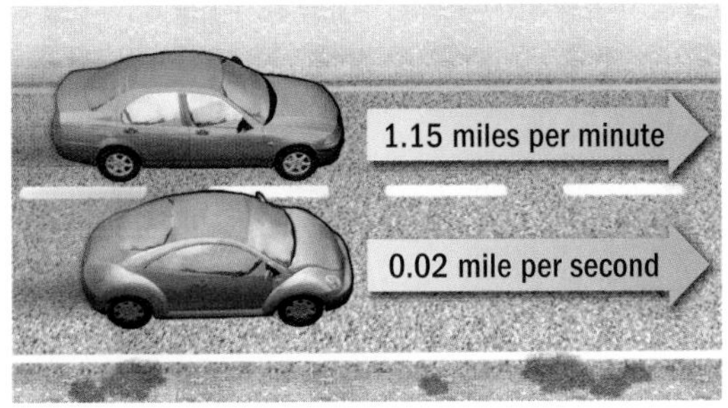

   a. Write the rates of speed in miles per hour and compare them. Show your work.
   b. Are all of the rates in this problem unit rates? *Explain.*

6. **MULTI-STEP PROBLEM** A survey was taken asking students their favorite day of the week. Of those who replied, 0.9% said Wednesday, $\frac{1}{4}$ said Friday, 60% said Saturday, and 0.1 said Sunday.
   a. Order the responses from the one chosen the most to the one chosen the least.
   b. What percent of the students chose the two most favored days of the week?
   c. What percent of the students surveyed were *not* included in the results listed? *Explain* how you found your answer.

7. **GRIDDED ANSWER** A photocopier was upgraded. The new machine outputs 223% more copies per minute than before. The original machine produced 10 copies per minute. How many copies per minute does the new machine produce?

8. **GRIDDED ANSWER** A scale model of the Chrysler Building in New York City has a scale of 1 in. : 200 ft. The height of the actual Chrysler Building is 1046 feet. The width of the model is 4.23 inches less than the height of the model. What is the width of the model in inches?

7.5 Percent of Change

Before	You solved problems with percents.
Now	You'll solve problems with percent of increase or decrease.
Why?	To find percent of change, as with tourism in Example 3.

KEY VOCABULARY
- **percent of change,** *p. 366*
- **percent of increase,** *p. 366*
- **percent of decrease,** *p. 366*

A **percent of change** shows how much a quantity has increased or decreased from the original amount. When the new amount is greater than the original amount, the percent of change is called a **percent of increase**. When the new amount is less than the original amount, it is called a **percent of decrease**.

KEY CONCEPT *For Your Notebook*

Percent of Change

Use the following equation to find the percent of change.

$$\text{Percent of change, } p\% = \frac{\text{Amount of increase or decrease}}{\text{Original amount}}$$

EXAMPLE 1 Finding a Percent of Decrease

Bears During the summer, a bear's heart rate is about 60 beats per minute, but it can drop to as low as 8 beats per minute during the winter. What is the percent of change in a bear's heart rate from the summer rate to the winter low rate?

SOLUTION

To find the percent of decrease, use the percent of change equation.

$p\% = \frac{60 - 8}{60}$ **Write amount of decrease and divide by original amount.**

$= \frac{52}{60}$ **Subtract.**

$= 0.8\overline{6}$ **Write fraction as a decimal.**

$\approx 86.67\%$ **Write decimal as a percent.**

REVIEW DECIMALS
Need help with repeating decimals? See p. 255.

▸ **Answer** The percent of decrease is about 86.7%.

EXAMPLE 2 Finding a Percent of Increase

School Enrollment A school had 825 students enrolled last year. This year, 870 students are enrolled. Find the percent of increase to the nearest tenth.

SOLUTION

AVOID ERRORS

Make sure you use the original amount, not the new amount, in the denominator when finding a percent of change.

$p\% = \frac{870 - 825}{825}$ **Write amount of decrease and divide by original amount.**

$= \frac{45}{825}$ **Subtract.**

$= 0.05\overline{45}$ **Write fraction as a decimal.**

$\approx 5.45\%$ **Write decimal as a percent.**

▸ **Answer** The percent of increase is about 5.5%.

Decimal Method A shortcut to finding a percent of a number is to write the percent as a decimal and then find the product of the decimal and the number. For example, 10% of 60 = 0.10(60) = 6.

EXAMPLE 3 Using Percent of Increase

National Parks From October to November one year, attendance at Everglades National Park increased about 27.4%. There were 59,084 visitors in October. To the nearest hundred, how many people visited in November?

SOLUTION

ANOTHER WAY

Using a proportion in Step 1 will give the same result as multiplying by a decimal.

$\frac{a}{60} = \frac{10}{100}$

$a = \frac{10}{100}(60)$

$a = 0.1(60)$

STEP 1 **Find** the increase.

Increase = 27.4% of 59,084

= 0.274(59,084) **Write 27.4% as a decimal.**

≈ 16,189 **Multiply.**

STEP 2 **Add** the increase to the original amount.

New Amount ≈ 59,084 + 16,189 = 75,273

▸ **Answer** About 75,300 people visited the park in November.

✓ GUIDED PRACTICE for Examples 1, 2, and 3

Tell whether the change is an *increase* or *decrease*. Then find the percent of change. Round to the nearest percent.

1. Original amount: 50
   New amount: 36
2. Original amount: 10
   New amount: 29.5
3. Original amount: 90
   New amount: 110
4. **What If?** In Example 3, suppose the attendance decreased by about 11%. Approximate, to the nearest thousand, the attendance in November.

7.5 EXERCISES

HOMEWORK KEY

★ = **STANDARDIZED TEST PRACTICE** Exs. 8, 27, 28, 29, 33, and 41

○ = **HINTS AND HOMEWORK HELP** for Exs. 3, 7, 9, 13, 27 at classzone.com

SKILL PRACTICE

1. **VOCABULARY** Copy and complete: When the original amount is less than the new amount, the percent of change is called a(n) _?_.

FINDING PERCENT OF CHANGE **Tell whether the change is an *increase* or *decrease*. Then find the percent of change. Round to the nearest percent.**

SEE EXAMPLES 1 AND 2 on pp. 366–367 for Exs. 2–8

2. 10 rabbits to 16 rabbits
3. 360 pounds to 352 pounds
4. $33,300 to $31,080
5. 12,200 voters to 13,908 voters
6. 50 minutes to 45 minutes
7. 350 meters to 420 meters
8. ★ **MULTIPLE CHOICE** An increase from 1 to 3 is what percent of increase?

   (A) 66.7% (B) 100% (C) 200% (D) 300%

FINDING NEW AMOUNTS **Find the new amount.**

SEE EXAMPLE 3 on p. 367 for Exs. 9–14

9. 1100 is increased by 4%.
10. 24,700 is decreased by 13%.
11. 8 is increased by 60%.
12. 65 is decreased by 30%.
13. 88,000 is decreased by 12.5%.
14. 26,000 is increased by 14.6%.
15. **ERROR ANALYSIS** Your friend says "Multiplying a number by 5 is a 500% increase." Describe and correct the error in your friend's reasoning.

ALGEBRA **Find the percent of increase or decrease.**

16. x to $4x$
17. $6b$ to $9b$
18. d to $5d$
19. $4h$ to $6h$
20. y to $\frac{3}{8}y$
21. $4.5a$ to $2.25a$
22. $5m$ to $4.5m$
23. z to $\frac{3}{4}z$
24. **CHALLENGE** A number increases by 50%, and then decreases by 50%. What is the percent of change from the original number to the final number?

PROBLEM SOLVING

SEE EXAMPLE 3 on p. 367 for Ex. 25

25. **GUIDED PROBLEM SOLVING** In 1975, there were 130,000 tennis courts in the United States. This number increased by 69% from 1975 to 1985. The number then increased by 9% from 1985 to 1995. How many tennis courts were in the United States in 1985 and in 1995?

   a. Find the number of tennis courts in 1985.

   b. Find the amount of the second increase.

   c. Find the number of tennis courts in 1995.

SEE EXAMPLE 3 on p. 367 for Ex. 26

26. **POPULATION** The population of the United States in 1993 was about 260,255,000. In 2003, it was about 291,049,000. Find the percent of increase to the nearest tenth of a percent.

27. ★ **MULTIPLE CHOICE** A camera is on sale for 10% off $170, and you have a coupon for an extra 10% off. How much will this camera cost?

(A) $136 (B) $137.70 (C) $153 (D) $168.30

28. ★ **SHORT RESPONSE** Oregon produces about 99% of the hazelnuts grown in the United States. Its record harvest was in 1997. In 2004 about how many tons of hazelnuts were produced in the United States? *Explain.*

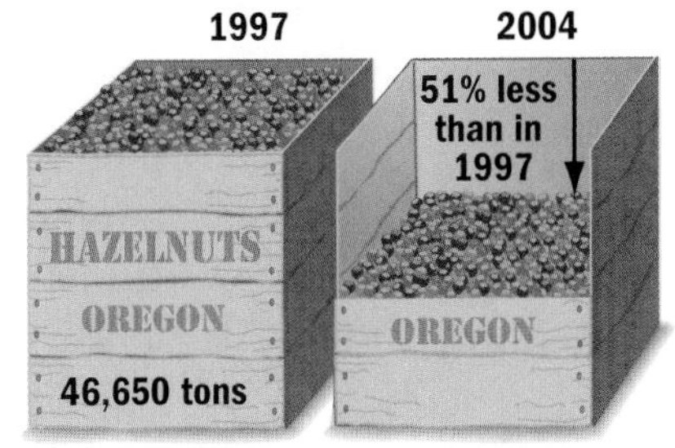

29. ★ **WRITING** A friend says that multiplying a number by $\frac{1}{4}$ is a 25% decrease. *Explain* why this is *not* true.

30. **NUMBER SENSE** Dividing a number by 5 is a decrease of what percent?

31. **ENLARGEMENT** You have a photograph that is 6 inches by 4 inches. You want to enlarge it so that these dimensions are increased by 50%. What will the new dimensions be? Will the increase in area be *greater than, less than,* or *equal to* 50%? *Explain.*

32. **GEOMETRY** The side lengths of the triangle at the right are increased by 100% to form a new triangle. What is the percent increase in area from the original triangle to the new triangle?

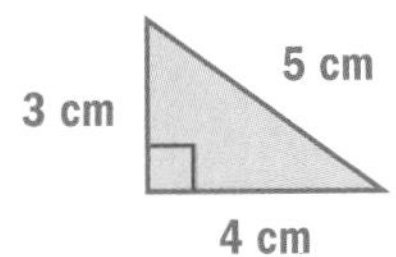

33. ★ **EXTENDED RESPONSE** The average time spent playing video games by a person in the United States was 60 hours in 2001. This time increased by about 11.7% from 2001 to 2002. At this rate, how many hours would you expect each person to spend playing video games in 2007? *Justify* your reasoning.

34. **CHALLENGE** From 1990 to 2000 the population of Houston, Texas, increased by about 9.3%. In 2000, the population was 1,953,631. At this growth rate, is 1,772,000 a reasonable estimate for the population of Houston in 1990? *Explain.*

MIXED REVIEW

Get-Ready

Prepare for Lesson 7.6 in Exs. 35–37

Find the product. *(p. 265)*

35. 4.412(0.36) 36. −6.7(0.8) 37. −0.91(0.35)

Solve the equation. *(p. 303)*

38. $14.2 + 1.4x = -5.4$ 39. $0.2s - 1.3 = 0.3$ 40. $1.14y - 2 = y + 1.64$

41. ★ **MULTIPLE CHOICE** What is the median of 7, 4, 7, 9, 3, and 6? *(p. 272)*

(A) 6 (B) 6.5 (C) 7 (D) 8

7.6 Percent Applications

Before You solved problems with percent of increase or decrease.

Now You'll solve percent application problems.

Why? So you can calculate sale prices, as in Example 1.

KEY VOCABULARY
- **markup,** *p. 370*
- **discount,** *p. 370*

A retail store buys items from manufacturers at wholesale prices. The store then sells the items to customers at retail prices. The increase in the wholesale price of an item is a **markup**. A decrease in the retail price of an item is a **discount**. You can find the retail price or sale price of an item using the equations below.

Retail price = Wholesale price + Markup

Sale price = Original price − Discount

EXAMPLE 1 Finding a Sale Price

Guitars You are shopping for a guitar and find one with an original price of \$160. The store is offering a 30% discount on all guitars. What is the sale price of the guitar?

SOLUTION

STEP 1 **Find** the amount of the discount.

Discount = 30% of \$160

= 0.3(160) **Write 30% as a decimal.**

= 48 **Multiply.**

STEP 2 **Subtract** the discount from the original price.

160 − 48 = 112

▸ **Answer** The sale price of the guitar is \$112.

CHECK FOR REASONABLENESS

Receiving a 30% discount is the same as paying 70% of the original price. So, you can find the sale price by multiplying its original price by 70%.

70% of $160 \approx$

$\frac{3}{4} \times 160 = 120$

The answer is reasonable.

✓ GUIDED PRACTICE for Example 1

Find the sale price. Check that your answer is reasonable.

1. Original price: \$25
   Percent discount: 10%
2. Original price: \$85.50
   Percent discount: 30%
3. Original price: \$14.20
   Percent discount: 20%
4. Original price: \$136.24
   Percent discount: 25%

EXAMPLE 2 Finding a Retail Price

Clothing A shirt has a wholesale price of \$16. The percent markup is 120%. What is the retail price?

SOLUTION

STEP 1 **Find** the amount of the markup.

Markup = 120% of \$16

= 1.2(16) **Write 120% as a decimal.**

= 19.2 **Multiply.**

STEP 2 **Add** the markup to the wholesale price.

$16 + 19.2 = 35.2$

▸ **Answer** The retail price of the shirt is \$35.20.

AVOID ERRORS
Remember that the markup must be added to the wholesale price to find the retail price.

Sales Tax and Tips Sales tax and tips are amounts that are added to the price of some purchases. Sales tax and tips are usually calculated using a percent of the purchase price.

EXAMPLE 3 Finding Sales Tax

CD Player A portable CD player costs \$48 before tax. The sales tax is 4.5%. What is the total cost?

SOLUTION

STEP 1 **Find** the amount of the sales tax.

4.5% of \$48 = 0.045(48) = 2.16

STEP 2 **Add** the sales tax to the price of the portable CD player.

$2.16 + 48 = 50.16$

▸ **Answer** The total cost of the CD player is \$50.16.

ANOTHER WAY
Paying 4.5% tax on an item is the same as paying 104.5% of the original price. So, in Example 3 you can find the total cost of the CD player as follows.

$1.045(48) = 50.16.$

✓ GUIDED PRACTICE for Examples 2 and 3

Find the retail price.

5. Wholesale price: \$64
Percent markup: 85%

6. Wholesale price: \$35
Percent markup: 110%

Find the total cost. Round to the nearest cent.

7. Price: \$8.90
Sales tax: 5%

8. Price: \$54.07
Sales tax: 7%

EXAMPLE 4 Solve a Multi-Step Problem

Restaurants Your food bill at a restaurant is $24. You leave a 20% tip. The sales tax is 6%. What is the total cost of the meal?

SOLUTION

AVOID ERRORS
The tip at a restaurant is generally based on the food bill only. Do not include the sales tax when finding a tip.

STEP 1 **Find** the amount of the tip.

20% of $24 = 0.20(24) = 4.8

STEP 2 **Find** the amount of the sales tax.

6% of $24 = 0.06(24) = 1.44

STEP 3 **Add** the food bill, tip, and sales tax.

24 + 4.8 + 1.44 = 30.24

▶ **Answer** The total cost of the meal is $30.24.

GUIDED PRACTICE for Example 4

9. **What If?** In Example 4 suppose that your bill is $35, the sales tax is 6%, and you leave a 15% tip. What is the total cost of the meal?

7.6 EXERCISES

HOMEWORK KEY

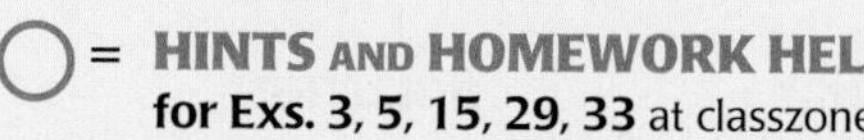

★ = **STANDARDIZED TEST PRACTICE** Exs. 9, 28, 29, 31, 37, and 54

○ = **HINTS AND HOMEWORK HELP** for Exs. 3, 5, 15, 29, 33 at classzone.com

SKILL PRACTICE

VOCABULARY **Copy and complete the statement.**

1. To find the retail price, add the _?_ to the wholesale price.
2. The sale price is the original price minus the _?_.

FINDING PRICES **Find the sale price or retail price. Round to the nearest cent. Check that your answer is reasonable.**

SEE EXAMPLES 1 AND 2 on pp. 370–371 for Exs. 3–9

3. Original price: $60
Percent discount: 15%

4. Original price: $28.50
Percent discount: 60%

5. Wholesale price: $25
Percent markup: 65%

6. Wholesale price: $14.50
Percent markup: 140%

7. Original price: $42
Percent discount: 30%

8. Wholesale price: $19
Percent markup: 110%

9. ★ **MULTIPLE CHOICE** What is the price of a $16.49 item marked up 130%?

Ⓐ $12.68　　Ⓑ $21.44　　Ⓒ $37.93　　Ⓓ $146.49

FINDING COSTS Find the total cost. Round to the nearest cent.

SEE EXAMPLES 3 AND 4 on pp. 371–372 for Exs. 10–15

10. Original price: $72
Sales tax: 6%

11. Original price: $58.40
Sales tax: 5.5%

12. Original price: $8.40
Sales tax: 7%

13. Original price: $258.20
Sales tax: 6.5%

14. Food bill: $28.50
Tip: 18%
Sales tax: 4.5%

15. Food bill: $18
Tip: 20%
Sales tax: 5%

16. **ERROR ANALYSIS** The original cost of an item is $28. It has a 5% discount and a 5% sales tax. A friend says that the item should cost $28 after the discount and sales tax. Describe and correct the error in your friend's reasoning.

PERCENT CHANGES Tell whether the price is a *discount* or *markup*, and find the percent of discount or markup. Then find the new price for a $96 item, with the same percent of change.

17. Old price: $32
New price: $24

18. Old price: $45
New price: $40.50

19. Old price: $19
New price: $33.25

20. Old price: $55
New price: $121

21. Old price: $12.50
New price: $22.50

22. Old price: $199.99
New price: $119.99

CHALLENGE Find the indicated value.

23. Original price: ?
Discount: 20%
Sales tax: 7.5%
Final price: $43

24. Original price: $150
Discount: ?
Sales tax: 5%
Final price: $126

25. Original price: $75
Discount: 18%
Sales tax: ?
Final price: $63.96

PROBLEM SOLVING

SEE EXAMPLES 3 AND 4 on pp. 371–372 for Exs. 26–29

26. **LAMP COSTS** A lamp costs $25.75. The sales tax is 4%. What is the total cost?

27. **RESTAURANT COSTS** Your food bill at a restaurant is $30. You leave a 20% tip. The sales tax is 6%. What is the total cost of the meal?

28. ★ **MULTIPLE CHOICE** A book costs $12.95 and is on sale for 15% off. The sales tax is 6%. What is the total cost of the book?

   (A) $11.01 (B) $11.67 (C) $11.78 (D) $13.73

29. ★ **MULTIPLE CHOICE** You and two friends eat at a restaurant and split the total bill evenly. The food bill is $20.88. Sales tax is 5%. You leave a 20% tip. How much should each person pay?

   (A) $6.96 (B) $7.31 (C) $8.35 (D) $8.70

30. **ESTIMATION** The original price of an item is $42 and the percent of discount is 25%. *Explain* how to estimate the sale price.

SEE EXAMPLE 4 on p. 372 for Ex. 31

31. ★ **SHORT RESPONSE** Find both the 15% and 20% tips for a food bill that totals \$24.20. *Explain* why people often leave a tip between 15% and 20% rather than leaving exactly 15% or 20%.

SEE EXAMPLES 1 AND 2 on pp. 370–371 for Exs. 32–33

32. **GASOLINE** Though gasoline prices may change quickly, the markup is usually \$.12 per gallon. What percent is that if the wholesale price is \$3 per gallon?

33. **CLOTHING** The wholesale price of a shirt is \$15. A store marks up the price by 75%. When the shirts don't sell, the store offers a 20% discount. What is the sale price of the shirts?

34. **TIPPING** You order a pizza to be delivered. The bill comes to \$12.60. You pay \$15 and tell the delivery person to keep the change. Is your tip *more* or *less* than 20%? *Explain.*

35. **DVD COSTS** A DVD has a regular price of \$26 and is on sale for \$16.90. What is the percent discount? How much would a \$59 DVD boxed set cost if it has the same discount?

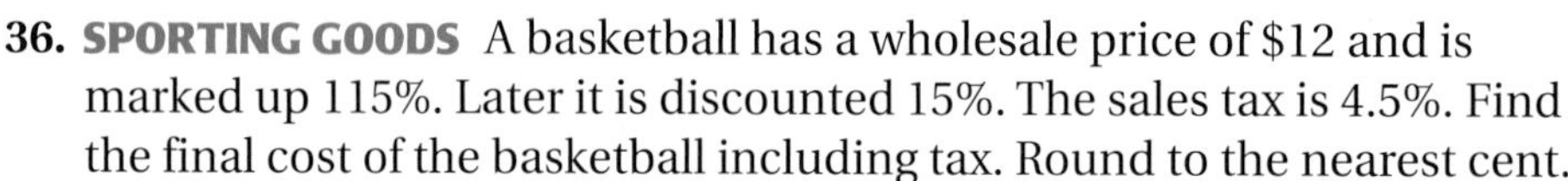

36. **SPORTING GOODS** A basketball has a wholesale price of \$12 and is marked up 115%. Later it is discounted 15%. The sales tax is 4.5%. Find the final cost of the basketball including tax. Round to the nearest cent.

37. ★ **WRITING** A store is having a sale offering a discount of 40% on all coats. One week later the store discounts the coats an extra 60%. Is the store giving away the coats for free? *Explain* your reasoning.

38. **ELECTRONICS** After a 125% markup and a 10% discount, the price of an MP3 player is \$30.78 before tax. What was the wholesale price?

39. **CHALLENGE** A total bill, including sales tax and tip, is \$33. The tax is 4% and the tip is 16% of the bill before tax. Find the cost before tax and tip.

MIXED REVIEW

Prepare for Lesson 7.7 in Exs. 40–47

Solve the equation. *(p. 122)*

40. $2.4b = 108$	41. $8.5y = 51$	42. $3.5x = 140$	43. $1.6d = 384$
44. $6.5a = 286$	45. $1.3k = 39$	46. $4.2m = 84$	47. $3.6n = 270$

Solve the equation. *(p. 298)*

48. $4a = a + 9$	49. $n - 2 = 2n - 9$	50. $j = 4(j - 12)$	51. $6k + 9 = 11k - 1$

Use a percent proportion. *(p. 354)*

52. What number is 35% of 80?

53. 308 is what percent of 440?

54. ★ **MULTIPLE CHOICE** What is the percent of increase from 45 to 75? *(p. 366)*

Ⓐ 40% Ⓑ 60% Ⓒ $66\frac{2}{3}\%$ Ⓓ $166\frac{2}{3}\%$

7.7 Using the Percent Equation

Before You solved percent problems using proportions.
Now You'll solve percent problems using the percent equation.
Why? So you can use percents to explain surveys of people's activities, as in Example 1.

KEY VOCABULARY
- **interest,** *p. 376*
- **principal,** *p. 376*
- **annual interest rate,** *p. 376*

In Lesson 7.3, you solved percent problems using the proportion $\frac{a}{b} = \frac{p}{100}$. If you multiply each side of this by b, you get the *percent equation* summarized below and used in this lesson.

KEY CONCEPT *For Your Notebook*

The Percent Equation

To represent the statement "a is p percent of b" use the equation:

$a = p\% \cdot b$ Part of the base = Percent • Base

EXAMPLE 1 Finding Part of a Base

ANOTHER WAY
You could also find the answer by solving the proportion:
$\frac{a}{2000} = \frac{26.7}{100}$

Beaches In a survey of 2000 people, 26.7% said that they visited a beach during the past year. How many people said they visited a beach during the past year?

SOLUTION

Use the percent equation.

$a = p\% \cdot b$ **Write percent equation.**

$= 26.7\% \cdot 2000$ **Substitute 26.7 for p and 2000 for b.**

$= 0.267 \cdot 2000$ **Write percent as a decimal.**

$= 534$ **Multiply.**

▸ **Answer** The number of people who said they visited a beach during the past year is 534.

Check Estimate $26.7 \approx 25$, and 25% of 2000 is 500. So the answer is reasonable.

GUIDED PRACTICE for Example 1

Use the percent equation.

1. Find 45% of 700.
2. Find 110% of 320.
3. Find 0.5% of 450.

EXAMPLE 2 Finding a Base

READING
To set up the percent equation correctly, make sure you read the problem carefully. Then think of a question that represents what you need to find out: "273 is 35% of what number?"

Student Council Marc received 273, or 35%, of the votes in the student council election. How many students voted in the election?

$a = p\% \cdot b$	**Write percent equation.**
$273 = 35\% \cdot b$	**Substitute 273 for *a* and 35 for *p*.**
$273 = 0.35 \cdot b$	**Write 35% as a decimal.**
$780 = b$	**Divide each side by 0.35.**

▶ **Answer** 780 students voted in the election.

VOCABULARY
When you borrow money from a bank, you pay interest on the amount you borrowed.

Simple Interest **Interest** is an amount paid for the use of money. **Principal** is the amount you borrow or deposit. When interest is paid only on the principal, it is called *simple interest.* The percent of the principal you pay or earn per year is the **annual interest rate**.

KEY CONCEPT — *For Your Notebook*

Simple Interest

Words To find simple interest I, find the product of the principal P, the *annual* interest rate r written as a decimal, and the time t in years.

Algebra $I = Prt$

EXAMPLE 3 Finding Simple Interest

CHECK FOR REASONABLENESS
The interest for 1 year is a little over 2% of $500, or $10. So the interest for a year and a half is a little over $15. The answer is reasonable.

Savings You deposit $500 in a savings account that pays a simple interest rate of 2.5% per year. How much interest will you earn after 18 months?

$I = Prt$	**Write formula for simple interest.**
$= (500)(0.025)(1.5)$	**Substitute values. 18 months = 1.5 years.**
$= 18.75$	**Multiply.**

▶ **Answer** You will earn $18.75 in interest.

Animated Math at classzone.com

✓ GUIDED PRACTICE for Examples 2 and 3

Solve using the percent equation.

4. 6.4 is 62.5% of what number?

5. 15 is what percent of 120?

6. What If? Suppose the simple interest rate in Example 3 is 3.5%. How much interest will you earn after 24 months?

7.7 EXERCISES

HOMEWORK KEY

★ = **STANDARDIZED TEST PRACTICE** Exs. 23, 31, 32, 35, 38, and 46

○ = **HINTS AND HOMEWORK HELP** for Exs. 3, 5, 13, 17, 33 at classzone.com

SKILL PRACTICE

1. **VOCABULARY** What do you call the amount earned or paid for the use of money?

2. **VOCABULARY** Copy and complete: To find simple interest, multiply the annual interest rate written as a decimal, the time in years, and the _?_.

PERCENT EQUATION **Solve using the percent equation.**

SEE EXAMPLES 1 AND 2 on pp. 375–376 for Exs. 3–15

3. What number is 46% of 900?
4. 205 is what percent of 250?
5. 132 is 24% of what number?
6. What number is 95% of 420?
7. What number is 120% of 55?
8. What number is 0.4% of 150?
9. 115 is 46% of what number?
10. 26 is 130% of what number?
11. 62.4 is 80% of what number?
12. 289.25 is 89% of what number?
13. 3 is what percent of 600?
14. 291.04 is what percent of 856?

15. **ERROR ANALYSIS** Describe and correct the error made in finding the solution.

   ✗ 54 is 60% of what number?
   $54 = 60 \cdot b$
   $0.9 = b$

INTEREST **Find the amount of simple interest earned. Check for reasonableness.**

SEE EXAMPLE 3 on p. 376 for Exs. 16–18

16. Principal: \$250
   Annual rate: 2%
   Time: 3 years

17. Principal : \$940
   Annual rate: 3.5%
   Time: 30 months

18. Principal : \$620
   Annual rate: 3%
   Time: 20 months

MENTAL MATH **Solve for the unknown amount.**

19. 60% of 60 = 90% of _?_
20. 20% of 70 = _?_% of 280
21. 0.5% of 140 = _?_% of 70
22. 160% of 25 = 80% of _?_

23. ★ **MULTIPLE CHOICE** You deposit \$450 into an account that earns simple interest at an annual rate of 4.5%. Which expression could be used to find the amount of money in the account after 2 years?

   (A) 450(0.045)(2)
   (B) 450(0.45)(2)
   (C) 450 + 450(0.045)(2)
   (D) 450 + 450(0.45)(2)

USING A FORMULA **Use the formula $I = Prt$ to find the unknown value.**

24. I = \$12.50
   P = \$500
   r = _?_
   t = 6 months

25. I = \$89.25
   P = \$850
   r = 5.25%
   t = _?_

26. I = \$260
   P = _?_
   r = 6.5%
   t = 4 years

27. I = \$320
   P = _?_
   r = 8%
   t = 2 years

28. **CHALLENGE** Using principal = \$10,000, rate = x%, and years = y, write an expression for interest. Suppose the interest rate doubles to $2x$%. What values of y result in the same interest as before? more interest than before? less interest than before?

PROBLEM SOLVING

SEE EXAMPLE 3 on p. 376 for Exs. 29, 33

29. **GUIDED PROBLEM SOLVING** A savings account pays a 3% simple annual interest rate. How much must you put in the savings account to earn \$100 in interest in 6 months?
    a. Write the simple interest formula.
    b. Substitute known values in the formula.
    c. Solve the equation for P. Round to the nearest cent.

SEE EXAMPLES 1 AND 2 on pp. 375–376 for Exs. 30–32

30. **WEATHER** In Charlotte, North Carolina, an average of 30.7% of the days of a year have precipitation. How many days in a year does Charlotte have precipitation? Round to the nearest day.

31. ★ **MULTIPLE CHOICE** You save \$63.60 when you purchase a jacket on sale. The jacket was discounted 30% off its regular price. What was the regular price of the jacket?

    (A) \$82.68 (B) \$90.86 (C) \$108.12 (D) \$212.00

32. ★ **SHORT RESPONSE** Vicki hears on the local news that 37.5% of the movie theaters in her city, or 6 theaters, offer discount tickets to students. Write and solve a percent equation to determine the number of theaters in Vicki's city. Then solve the problem using a proportion. *Compare* the methods.

33. **LOAN** You borrow \$1200 from a bank that charges 9.5% simple annual interest. After 15 months you pay back the loan. How much interest do you pay on the loan? What is the total amount that you pay the bank?

34. **MULTI-STEP PROBLEM** The area of the state of Texas is 171.1 million acres. Of this, 15.7% is cropland.
    a. How much of Texas is cropland? Round to the nearest hundred thousand acres.
    b. About 10,500 acres of the cropland in Texas are planted with peppers. What percent of cropland in Texas is planted with peppers? Round to the nearest hundredth of a percent.

35. ★ **WRITING** Are the solutions of $\frac{12}{b} = \frac{3}{100}$ and $12 = 3\% \cdot b$ the same or different? *Explain* your reasoning.

36. **SAVINGS** How much money must you deposit in a savings account that pays a 4% simple annual interest rate to earn \$50 in 60 months?

37. LOOK FOR A PATTERN Copy and complete the table by finding the percent of each number. *Describe* the relationship you see among the three results in each row. *Explain* how you could use this relationship to help you find a percent of a number.

	5%	10%	15%
22	?	2.2	?
50	?	?	?
76	?	?	?

38. ★ OPEN-ENDED MATH Give two different principals and simple interest rates for a bank account that pays \$39 in interest over a 3 year period.

CHALLENGE ***Compound interest*** **on a savings account is earned on both the principal and on any interest that has already been earned. Each time the interest is compounded, you multiply the amount currently in the account, including interest, by the interest rate for that time period.**

39. You deposit \$500 into an account that earns an annual interest rate of 4% compounded annually. How much will you have in your account after the third year? after the sixth year? Round your answers to the nearest cent.

40. You have the option to invest \$1000 in a 6 month certificate of deposit that earns 3.6% simple interest or in a savings account that pays a monthly interest rate of 0.22% compounded monthly. How long would you have to leave your money in the savings account to earn the same amount as by investing in the CD?

MIXED REVIEW

Get-Ready

Prepare for Lesson 7.8 in Exs. 41–44

Write the ratio as a fraction in simplest form and two other ways. *(p. 343)*

41. $\frac{6}{8}$ **42.** 33 to 55 **43.** 64 : 16 **44.** $\frac{7}{56}$

45. Solve and graph the inequality $-3x - 2 \leq 4 - x$. *(p. 324)*

46. ★ SHORT RESPONSE You have \$30 and you want to buy two DVDs. Each DVD costs \$15.95 and is on sale for 15% off. The sales tax is 6%. Do you have enough money? *Explain.* *(p. 370)*

Brain Game

Shrink Ray

Ray invents two zappers that shrink and enlarge things.

After shrinking almost everything in the house to **40%** of its original size, Ray's mother demands that he return things to normal. What percent setting should he use to zap objects back to their original size?

The next day Ray uses the zapper to enlarge things by **60%**. What percent setting should he use to get them back to their normal size?

Animated Math at classzone.com

GOAL
Use a calculator to compute compound interest.

7.7 Compound Interest

Compound interest is interest earned on both the principal and on any interest that has already been earned.

Mark deposits $2000 into an account that pays an annual interest rate of 3.5% compounded annually. He doesn't add or remove money from his account for 4 years. How much money will Mark have in 4 years?

SOLUTION

The balance of an account after a year can be found by multiplying the principal balance by the sum of 1 and the annual interest rate written as a decimal. Use the keystrokes below to find the amount of money in the account in 4 years. Round the answer only after the final 4th year, not after each year.

Keystrokes	Display	
2000 [=] [×] 1.035 [=]	2070	In 1 year
[=]	2142.45	In 2 years
[=]	2217.43575	In 3 years
[=]	2295.046001	In 4 years

▸ **Answer** Mark will have $2295.05 in his account in 4 years.

PRACTICE **Find the balance of the account earning compound interest.**

1. Principal: $7000
   Annual rate: 2%
   Time: 4 years

2. Principal: $7000
   Annual rate: 4%
   Time: 2 years

3. Principal: $1995
   Annual rate: 6.5%
   Time: 10 years

4. **COMPARE** You deposit $1500 into an account that pays an interest rate of 4% compounded annually. Your friend deposits $1500 into an account that pays a simple annual interest rate of 4%. Compare the balances of the two accounts after 5 years.

5. **COMPARE** You deposit $9000, into an account that pays an interest rate of 3.5% compounded annually. Your sister deposits $10,000 into an account that pays a simple annual interest rate of 2.5%. Compare balances of the two accounts after 10 years.

7.8 Simple Probability

Before You found ratios.
Now You'll find probabilities of events.
Why? So you can make predictions, as for picking shirt colors in Ex. 37.

KEY VOCABULARY
- **outcome,** *p. 381*
- **event,** *p. 381*
- **favorable outcome,** *p. 381*
- **probability of an event,** *p. 381*
- **theoretical probability,** *p. 381*
- **experimental probability,** *p. 382*

ACTIVITY

You can toss a coin to perform a probability experiment.

STEP 1 **Copy** and complete the table at the right by tossing a coin 20 times.

Number of heads	?
Number of tails	?

STEP 2 **Use** the data to write each ratio below. Then compare the ratios.

a. $\frac{\text{Number of heads}}{\text{Total number of coin tosses}}$ **b.** $\frac{\text{Number of tails}}{\text{Total number of coin tosses}}$

STEP 3 **Combine** your results with those of the other students in your class. Compare the class ratios with your own ratios.

In the activity, you performed an experiment. The possible results of an experiment are **outcomes**. An **event** is a collection of outcomes. Once you specify an event, the outcomes for that event are called **favorable outcomes**. The **probability of an event** is the likelihood that the event will occur.

Probabilities can range from 0 to 1. The closer the probability of an event is to 1, the more likely it is that the event will occur.

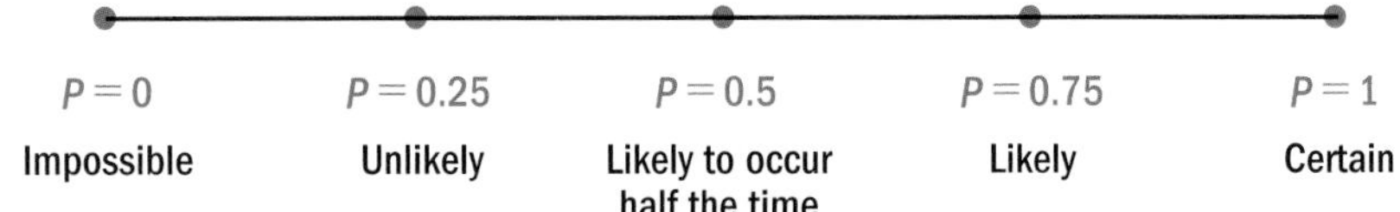

$P = 0$ Impossible; $P = 0.25$ Unlikely; $P = 0.5$ Likely to occur half the time; $P = 0.75$ Likely; $P = 1$ Certain

KEY CONCEPT *For Your Notebook*

Probability of an Event

The **theoretical probability** of an event when all outcomes are equally likely is:

$$P(\text{event}) = \frac{\text{Number of favorable outcomes}}{\text{Number of possible outcomes}}$$

EXAMPLE 1 Using Theoretical Probability

Coin Toss Predict the number of times a coin will land heads up in 50 coin tosses. There are two equally likely outcomes when you toss the coin, heads or tails.

$$P(\text{heads}) = \frac{\text{Number of favorable outcomes}}{\text{Number of possible outcomes}} = \frac{1}{2}$$

READING
The notation "P(event)" is read "the probability of an event."

▶ **Answer** You can predict that $\frac{1}{2}$, or 25, of the tosses will land heads up.

Experimental Probability An **experimental probability** is based on the results of a sample or experiment. Experimental probability is the ratio of number of favorable outcomes to the total number of times the experiment was performed. This ratio is sometimes called *relative frequency*.

EXAMPLE 2 Finding Experimental Probability

You roll a number cube 100 times. Your results are given in the table below. Find the experimental probability of rolling a 6.

Number	1	2	3	4	5	6
Rolls	17	15	20	16	14	18

$$P(\text{rolling a 6}) = \frac{18}{100}$$

18 ← Number of favorable outcomes
100 ← Total number of rolls

$$= 0.18 = 18\%$$

WRITE PROBABILITIES
A probability can be expressed as a fraction, as a decimal, or as a percent.

▶ **Answer** The experimental probability of rolling a 6 is 18%.

★ EXAMPLE 3 Standardized Test Practice

Quality Control A company manufactures buttons. A quality control inspector finds 2 defective buttons in a batch of 300 buttons. About how many buttons would you expect to be defective in a shipment of 20,000 buttons?

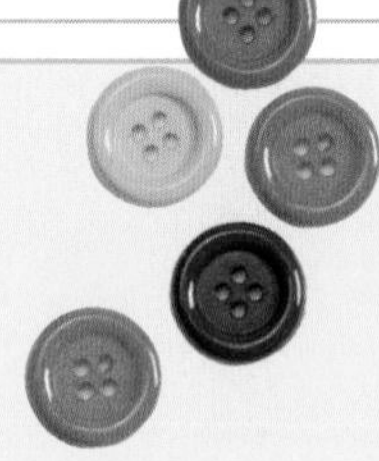

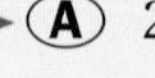

Ⓐ 2 Ⓑ 67 Ⓒ 133 Ⓓ 300

ELIMINATE CHOICES
Because about 2 buttons are defective in every batch of 300, the number of defective buttons in a shipment of 20,000 must be well over 2. So, you can eliminate choice A.

SOLUTION

STEP 1 **Find** the experimental probability of a button being defective. $P(\text{defective}) = \frac{2}{300} = \frac{1}{150}$

STEP 2 **Multiply** the probability by the total number of buttons in the shipment and round to the nearest whole number. $\frac{1}{150} \times 20{,}000 \approx 133$

▶ **Answer** You could expect about 133 buttons in a shipment of 20,000 to be defective. The correct answer is C. Ⓐ Ⓑ Ⓒ Ⓓ

✓ GUIDED PRACTICE for Examples 1, 2, and 3

1. **Number Cube** Use the information given in Example 2. What is the experimental probability of rolling a number greater than 3? What is the theoretical probability of this event?

2. **What If?** Use the information in Example 3. About how many buttons would you expect to be defective in a shipment of 25,000 buttons?

7.8 EXERCISES

HOMEWORK KEY
★ = **STANDARDIZED TEST PRACTICE** Exs. 19, 30, 32, 34, 36, 37, 38, and 46
○ = **HINTS AND HOMEWORK HELP** for Exs. 5, 9, 11, 15, 29 at classzone.com

SKILL PRACTICE

1. **VOCABULARY** Copy and complete: The favorable outcomes for rolling an even number on a number cube are _?_.

2. **VOCABULARY** Describe the difference between experimental and theoretical probability.

THEORETICAL PROBABILITY You randomly draw a tile from a bag that contains 10 A-tiles, 7 E-tiles, 6 I-tiles, 5 O-tiles, and 2 U-tiles. Find the theoretical probability of the event. Write as a fraction in simplest form.

SEE EXAMPLE 1 on p. 382 for Exs. 3–8

3. You draw an A.
4. You draw an I.
5. You draw an I or an O.
6. You draw an E or a U.
7. You draw a Z.
8. You draw a vowel.

EXPERIMENTAL PROBABILITY You roll a number cube 250 times. Your results are shown in the table. Find the experimental probability of the event.

SEE EXAMPLE 2 on p. 382 for Exs. 9–13

9. You roll a 4.
10. You roll a 2.
11. You roll a number greater than 3.
12. You roll an odd number.
13. You roll a number divisible by 1.

Number	Outcomes	Number	Outcomes
1	40	4	50
2	42	5	35
3	48	6	35

Animated Math at classzone.com

USING EXPERIMENTAL PROBABILITY You randomly draw a marble from a bag of 120 marbles. You record its color and replace it. Use the results to estimate the number of marbles in the bag that are the given color.

SEE EXAMPLE 3 on p. 382 for Exs. 14–17

14. Yellow
15. Green
16. Red
17. Blue

Red	Yellow	Green
7	3	5

Animated Math at classzone.com

18. **ERROR ANALYSIS** A student spins a two-color spinner a number of times. The pointer lands on red 7 times and on blue 13 times. Describe and correct the error made in the solution.

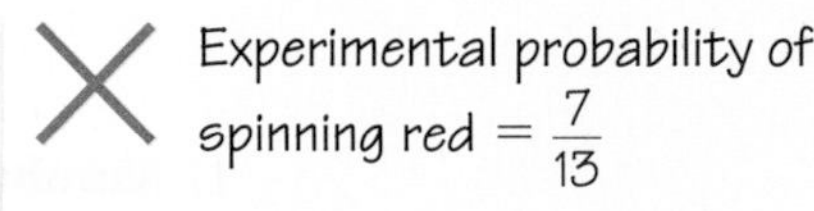

19. ★ **MULTIPLE CHOICE** What is the probability of getting a multiple of 3 when rolling a number cube?

Ⓐ $\frac{3}{10}$ Ⓑ $\frac{1}{3}$ Ⓒ $\frac{1}{2}$ Ⓓ $\frac{2}{3}$

FINDING PROBABILITY In Exercises 20–23, find the probability of the event.

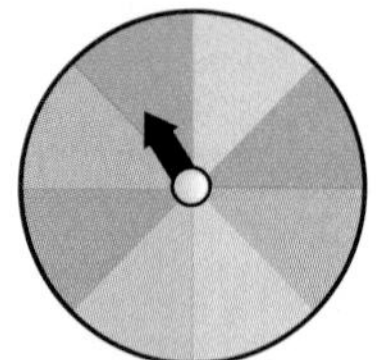

20. *Not* rolling a 2 on a number cube
21. *Not* rolling a number less than 3 on a number cube
22. *Not* spinning blue on the spinner shown
23. *Not* spinning blue, red, or yellow on the spinner shown

24. **REASONING** Refer to the spinner above. Is spinning green *impossible, unlikely, likely,* or *certain*? *Explain* your reasoning.

25. **CHALLENGE** You toss two coins at the same time. How likely are you to get two tails? *Justify* your answer.

26. **CHALLENGE** You roll two number cubes. What is the probability that the sum of the numbers is a multiple of 5? *Explain* your reasoning.

PROBLEM SOLVING

SEE EXAMPLE 1 on p. 382 for Exs. 27–28

27. **MULTIPLE REPRESENTATIONS** You randomly pick one sock from a drawer that has 4 white socks, 12 black socks, and 8 brown socks.
   a. **Draw a Picture** Draw a picture that represents those probabilities.
   b. **Write** Write the probabilities of picking each color sock.

28. **REASONING** You have 15 coins in your pocket: 4 quarters, 3 pennies, 5 dimes, and 3 nickels. *Explain* why theoretical probability wouldn't be a good way to predict which coin you pull out of your pocket?

SEE EXAMPLES 2 AND 3 on p. 382 for Exs. 29–31

29. **SURVEYS** In a survey of 896 people, 409 said that their second toes are longer than their big toes. What is the probability to the nearest percent that a randomly chosen person from the survey has a longer second toe?

30. ★ **MULTIPLE CHOICE** In a group of 40 people, 24 prefer dogs to cats. One person is selected at random from the group. What is the probability that the person will prefer dogs to cats?

Ⓐ 0.24 Ⓑ 0.4 Ⓒ 0.6 Ⓓ 0.67

31. **BOARD GAMES** You are playing a board game that uses a spinner like the one shown to determine how many spaces to move. Predict the number of times you would move exactly 5 spaces in 50 spins.

32. ★ **SHORT RESPONSE** Sharon and Erica are softball players. Out of 20 times at bat, Sharon got 7 hits. Out of 35 times at bat, Erica got 10 hits. Who do you think is more likely to get a hit her next time at bat? *Explain.*

33. **PERFORM AN EXPERIMENT** Write each of the letters of your last name on a slip of paper and perform an experiment.

    a. Place the slips into a bag and then randomly draw one slip. Record the result and replace it. Repeat this process 19 more times.

    b. What is the experimental probability of drawing the first letter of your name? *Predict* the number of times you would draw the first letter of your name out of 100 draws.

34. ★ **OPEN-ENDED MATH** *Describe* a real-life event that is certain to occur and a real-life event that cannot occur. *Explain.*

35. **LEFT-HANDEDNESS** The circle graphs below show the likelihood of each handedness for a child based on the handedness of its parents. Out of 500 pairs of parents with one child, how many of the children would you expect to be left-handed if both parents are right-handed? If only the mom is left-handed? How many of the children would you expect to be right-handed if both parents are left-handed? If only the dad is left-handed?

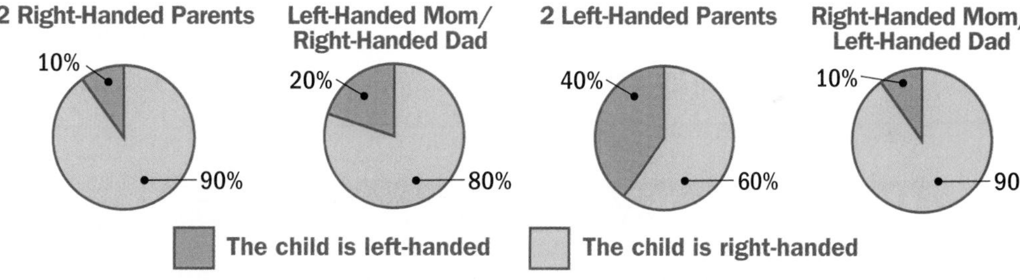

36. ★ **EXTENDED RESPONSE** Use a coin to complete the following.

    a. **Calculate** Using theoretical probability, predict the number of times a coin would land heads up in 20 tosses.

    b. **Experiment** Flip a coin 20 times and record the outcomes in a table.

    c. **Compare** Were the results from part (a) and part (b) the same?

    d. **Extend** Repeat parts (b) and (c) two more times. What does this tell you about theoretical and experimental probabilities?

37. ★ **OPEN-ENDED MATH** A clothing store surveys 100 girls ages 12 to 16 about the color of T-shirt they prefer. The results are given in the table at the right. The store uses this data to order more T-shirts. What conclusion(s) can you make about the numbers and colors of T-shirts that should be ordered?

T-Shirt Colors

Color	***Number***
blue	15
pink	40
purple	35
orange	10

38. ★ **WRITING** Vernon rolled a number cube 24 times and got a 6 once. He thinks that his chances of getting a 6 on his next roll are high. Is his reasoning correct? *Explain* why or why not.

39. **CHOOSING NAMES** There are exactly 20 girls and 20 boys in your gym class. The teacher writes each name on a slip of paper and places the slips in a hat. You randomly draw one slip, replace it, choose another, and record the genders of the names you drew. You repeat this 100 times. Predict the number of times you would draw two boys' names. *Explain.*

40. **CHALLENGE** You and a friend are playing a game where you take turns rolling a number cube. You gain 2 points for rolling a prime number, and your friend gains 2 points for rolling a composite number. Does this game favor you or your friend? A game is fair if each player has an equal chance of winning. *Describe* how you can change the game to make it fair.

MIXED REVIEW

Prepare for Lesson 8.1 in Exs. 41–44

Solve the equation. Then check the solution.

41. $10 + 9y = -8 + 3y$ *(p. 298)*

42. $3f + 6 = 6f - 18$ *(p. 298)*

43. $7(t + 4) + 2(t - 5) = 90$ *(p. 293)*

44. $8 - c + 5(c - 1) = 180$ *(p. 293)*

45. **SIMPLE INTEREST** You put \$750 in an account at a simple annual rate of 2.7%. Find the interest you will earn after 30 months. *(p. 375)*

46. ★ **MULTIPLE CHOICE** Which inequality can be used to represent the following: 338 more than 5 times a number x is more than 453? *(p. 324)*

(A) $338 + 5x < 453$

(B) $338 + 5x > 453$

(C) $453 + 5x > 338$

(D) $453 + 5x < 338$

QUIZ *for Lessons 7.5–7.8*

Tell if the change is an *increase* or *decrease*. Then find the percent of change. *(p. 366)*

1. Original amount: \$120
   New amount: \$138

2. Original amount: 260 miles
   New amount: 169 miles

3. **RETAIL** A shirt has a \$20 wholesale price and is marked up 50%. The sales tax is 5%. What is the total cost of the shirt? *(p. 370)*

Solve using the percent equation. *(p. 375)*

4. 75 is 125% of what number?

5. 552.5 is what percent of 85,000?

6. **KOALAS** Koalas absorb only about 25% of the fiber they eat. How much fiber is absorbed by a koala that eats 10.5 ounces of fiber per day? *(p. 375)*

You spin the spinner at the right 40 times. Predict how many times the spinner lands on the specified color. *(p. 381)*

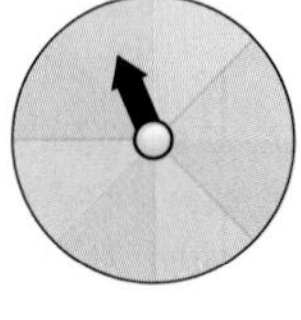

7. Red

8. Blue

9. Yellow

10. White

Lessons 7.5–7.8

1. **MULTI-STEP PROBLEM** At a clothing store, all sweaters are the same price. You pick out a sweater and a pair of pants. When you get to the cashier, you find that all sweaters are on sale for 40% off the original price and your bill is $40.40. So, you add two more sweaters to your purchase, bringing the bill to $81.20.
   a. How much does one sweater cost after the discount? How much do all three sweaters cost?
   b. How much does the pair of pants cost?
   c. What percent of the final bill is the cost of the pants? Round to the nearest percent.

2. **GRIDDED ANSWER** A grocery store places a 25% markup on a bottle of olive oil for which it paid $8. The store later discounts the price so that a customer can buy the bottle at the store's cost. By exactly what percent must the store discount the oil?

3. **GRIDDED ANSWER** Find the probability of *not* spinning yellow on the spinner. Write your answer as a fraction in simplest form.

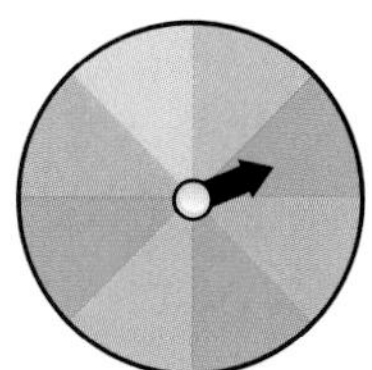

4. **GRIDDED ANSWER** You have 5 blue marbles, 2 red marbles, and 3 yellow marbles. You choose one marble at random. What is the probability that you will choose a red marble? Write your answer as a decimal.

5. **SHORT RESPONSE** At a diner, Jay and Gia pay for their $22.20 meal with a $20 bill and a $10 bill. The change they are given consists of a $5 bill, two $1 bills, and some coins. Can Jay and Gia leave a tip that is between 15% and 20% of the bill using only the change they are given, without having to ask that the $5 bill be exchanged for ones? *Explain.*

6. **EXTENDED RESPONSE** Angie can pick one of the three plans shown in the table to increase her compensation at her job. She works an average of 160 hours per month, gets paid $10.50 per hour, and pays $210 per month for medical insurance. Which plan offers Angie the greatest percent monthly increase in her total compensation? What is this increase? *Describe* how you found your answer.

Plan A	Increase hourly rate to $11.50
Plan B	Increase hourly rate by 10%
Plan C	Company pays insurance

7. **SHORT RESPONSE** Arthur grows water plants as a treat for his turtle. Properly fed, the plants can grow 50% in mass each week. Arthur plans to feed 50% of the plant mass to the turtle at the end of each week, letting the plants grow for a week in between feedings. Using a model, explain what will happen to the amount of food available to the turtle using Arthur's plan.

8. **OPEN-ENDED** Mark deposits $300 in a savings account that pays a simple interest rate of 2.3% per year. He doesn't add or remove money from his account. Find the total amount of money in the account after three different lengths of time.

9. **OPEN-ENDED** *Describe* three events involving a number cube that each have a probability of one-half.

7 CHAPTER REVIEW

@HomeTutor
classzone.com
Vocabulary Practice

REVIEW KEY VOCABULARY

- ratio, *p. 343*
- equivalent ratios, *p. 343*
- rate, unit rate, *p. 344*
- proportion, *p. 348*
- cross products, *p. 349*
- scale model, *p. 350*
- scale, *p. 350*
- percent, *p. 354*
- circle graph, *p. 360*
- percent of change, *p. 366*
- percent of increase, *p. 366*
- percent of decrease, *p. 366*
- markup, discount, *p. 370*
- interest, *p. 376*
- principal, *p. 376*
- annual interest rate, *p. 376*
- outcome, event, *p. 381*
- favorable outcome, *p. 381*
- probability of an event, *p. 381*
- theoretical probability, *p. 381*
- experimental probability, *p. 382*

VOCABULARY EXERCISES

Copy and complete the statement.

1. If you write $\frac{180 \text{ miles}}{3 \text{ hours}}$ as $\frac{60 \text{ miles}}{1 \text{ hour}}$, you have written the rate as a(n) _?_.
2. A ratio whose denominator is 100 is a _?_.
3. The theoretical probability of an event is the ratio of the number of _?_ to the number of _?_ when all outcomes are equally likely.
4. The increase in the wholesale price of an item is a _?_.
5. A decrease in the price of an item is a _?_.

Match the definition with the correct word at the right.

6. the amount of money that you borrow or deposit
7. the amount paid for the use of money
8. the percent of the principal that you pay or earn each year

A. annual interest rate
B. interest
C. principal

REVIEW EXAMPLES AND EXERCISES

7.1 Ratios and Rates *pp. 343–346*

EXAMPLE

Write 282 miles per 6 hours as a unit rate.

$$\frac{282 \text{ miles}}{6 \text{ hours}} = \frac{282 \div 6}{6 \div 6}$$ **Divide numerator and denominator by 6.**

$$= \frac{47}{1}$$ **Simplify.**

▸ **Answer** The unit rate is 47 miles per hour.

EXERCISES

Write the ratio of shaded to unshaded squares in simplest form.

SEE EXAMPLES 1, 2, AND 3 on pp. 343–344 for Exs. 9–19

9. 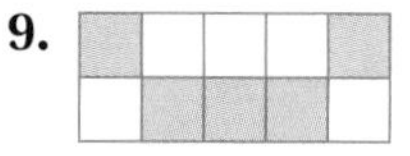

10. 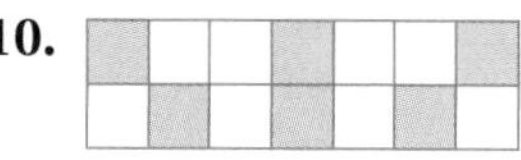

Write the rate as a unit rate.

11. $\frac{\text{30 feet}}{\text{4 seconds}}$ **12.** $\frac{\$3.36}{\text{2 gallons}}$ **13.** $\frac{\text{72 people}}{\text{4 groups}}$ **14.** $\frac{\text{90 miles}}{\text{4 hours}}$

15. $\frac{\text{28 feet}}{\text{2 seconds}}$ **16.** $\frac{\text{48 points}}{\text{4 quarters}}$ **17.** $\frac{\text{356 kilometers}}{\text{8 hours}}$ **18.** $\frac{\$17.25}{\text{5 pounds}}$

19. Running Emily runs 1600 meters in 5 minutes 30 seconds, and Megan runs 800 meters in 2 minutes 40 seconds. Who has the faster average speed?

7.2 Writing and Solving Proportions

pp. 348–353

EXAMPLE

Solve the proportion.

$\frac{7.2}{9.4} = \frac{36}{x}$	**Write original proportion.**
$7.2 \cdot x = 9.4 \cdot 36$	**Cross products property**
$7.2x = 338.4$	**Multiply.**
$\frac{7.2x}{7.2} = \frac{338.4}{7.2}$	**Divide each side by 7.2.**
$x = 47$	**Simplify.**

EXERCISES

Solve the proportion.

SEE EXAMPLES 2 AND 3 on pp. 349–350 for Exs. 20–26

20. $\frac{5}{13} = \frac{18}{c}$ **21.** $\frac{48}{54} = \frac{x}{6}$ **22.** $\frac{n}{12} = \frac{7}{8}$ **23.** $\frac{25}{b+1} = \frac{5}{2}$

24. Maps A map has a scale of 1 inch : 10 miles. The actual distance between two cities is 105 miles. Write and solve a proportion to find the distance between the cities on the map.

25. Earnings You earn $12 walking 3 dogs. You charge the same amount for each dog. How much do you earn for walking 5 dogs?

26. Reading You can read 51 pages in 45 minutes. How many pages can you read in an hour?

7.3 Solving Percent Problems

pp. 354–358

EXAMPLE

36 is 15% of what number?

$\frac{a}{b} = \frac{p}{100}$ Write a percent proportion.

$\frac{36}{b} = \frac{15}{100}$ Substitute 36 for *a* and 15 for *p*.

$36 \cdot 100 = 15b$ Cross products property

$240 = b$ Divide each side by 15.

EXERCISES

Use a percent proportion.

SEE EXAMPLES 1 AND 2 on pp. 354–355 for Exs. 27–29

27. 72 is what percent of 1200?

28. What number is 95% of 26?

29. **Surveys** You ask 270 people if they read for fun. Of these people, 146 say they do. What percent of the people surveyed like to read for fun?

7.4 Fractions, Decimals, and Percents

pp. 359–364

EXAMPLE

Write 28% as a decimal and as a fraction.

$28\% = 28\% = 0.28$ Remove % sign. Move decimal point two places to the left.

$28\% = \frac{28}{100} = \frac{7}{25}$ Write as a fraction and simplify.

▸ **Answer** 28% can be written as 0.28 and as $\frac{7}{25}$.

EXERCISES

Write the percent as a decimal and as a fraction.

SEE EXAMPLES 1, 2, 3, AND 4 on pp. 359–360 for Exs. 30–38

30. 74%

31. 3.8%

32. 16.8%

33. 130%

Write the fraction or decimal as a percent.

34. $\frac{3}{5}$

35. $\frac{5}{2}$

36. 0.02

37. 18.6

38. **Food Surveys** You survey 72 people and find that 18 of them like pork chops. What percent like pork chops?

7.5 Percent of Change

pp. 366–369

EXAMPLE

Plant Growth Find the percent of increase in height of a plant 60 inches tall that grows to 84 inches.

$p\% = \frac{84 - 60}{60}$ **Write amount of increase and divide by original amount.**

$= \frac{24}{60}$ **Subtract.**

$= 0.4$ **Write fraction as a decimal.**

$= 40\%$ **Write decimal as a percent.**

▶ **Answer** The percent of increase in height is 40%.

EXERCISES

Find the percent of increase or decrease. Round to the nearest percent.

SEE EXAMPLES 1 AND 2 on pp. 366–367 for Exs. 39–41

39. original amount: 50; new amount: 35

40. original amount: 90; new amount: 220

41. Weight A moving van's load changes from 800 pounds to 984 pounds after picking up an appliance. Find the percent of increase.

7.6 Percent Applications

pp. 370–374

EXAMPLE

Sale Price A pair of shoes has an original price of \$40. What is the sale price after a 15% discount?

$40 \times 0.15 = 6$ **Multiply to find discount.**

$40 - 6 = 34$ **Subtract discount from original price.**

▶ **Answer** The sale price of the shoes is \$34.

EXERCISES

Find the sale price or retail price.

SEE EXAMPLES 1, 2, AND 3 on pp. 370–371 for Exs. 42–44

42. wholesale price: \$30; percent markup: 70%

43. original price: \$72; percent discount: 18%

44. Restaurant Costs Your meal at a restaurant costs \$14.99. Sales tax is 3%. You leave a 15% tip. How much did you spend?

7.7 Using the Percent Equation

pp. 375–379

EXAMPLE

What number is 26% of 300?

$a = p\% \cdot b$	**Write percent equation.**
$a = 26\% \cdot 300$	**Substitute 26 for *p* and 300 for *b*.**
$a = 0.26(300)$	**Write percent as a decimal.**
$a = 78$	**Multiply.**

EXERCISES

SEE EXAMPLES 1, 2, AND 3 on pp. 375–376 for Exs. 45–48

Solve using the percent equation.

45. 72 is 75% of what number?

46. What number is 34% of 856?

Find the amount of simple interest earned in 3 years.

47. principal: \$460; annual rate: 3.5%

48. principal: \$1540; annual rate: 2.75%

7.8 Simple Probability

pp. 381–386

EXAMPLE

Probability Rosa tosses the box 250 times and 28 tosses resulted in a 1. Find the experimental probability of the box landing on 1.

Use the results to find the experimental probability.

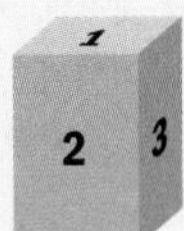

$$P(1) = \frac{28}{250} \begin{array}{l}\leftarrow \text{Number of favorable outcomes} \\ \leftarrow \text{Total number of tosses}\end{array}$$

$$= \frac{14}{125} = 0.112 = 11.2\%$$

EXERCISES

SEE EXAMPLES 1 AND 2 on p. 382 for Exs. 49–52

49. Marbles You randomly draw a marble out of a bag that contains 8 red, 5 yellow, and 4 blue marbles. Find the probability of drawing each color.

Experimental Probability You roll a number cube 200 times. Your results are shown in the table. Find the experimental probability of the event.

Number	1	2	3	4	5	6
Outcomes	35	28	46	27	30	34

50. You roll a 5.

51. You roll a number less than 5.

52. You roll a number divisible by 3.

7 CHAPTER TEST

@HomeTutor
classzone.com
Chapter Test Practice

Write the ratio of shaded to unshaded squares in simplest form.

1. 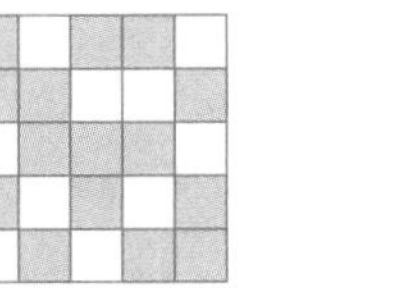

2. 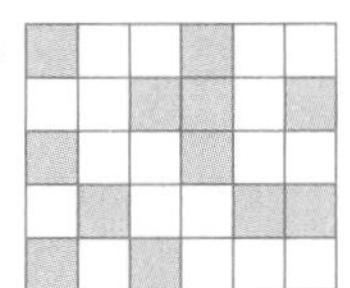

3. 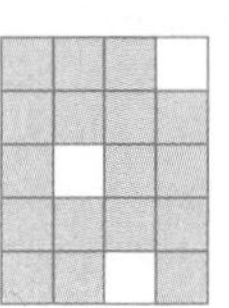

4. 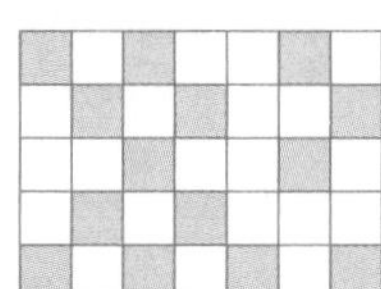

Write the rate as a unit rate.

5. $\frac{156 \text{ miles}}{3 \text{ hours}}$

6. $\frac{18 \text{ servings}}{6 \text{ people}}$

7. $\frac{448 \text{ cycles}}{5 \text{ days}}$

8. $\frac{525 \text{ meters}}{21 \text{ seconds}}$

Solve the proportion.

9. $\frac{12}{16} = \frac{18}{a}$

10. $\frac{15}{6} = \frac{d}{4}$

11. $\frac{9}{n} = \frac{21}{14}$

12. $\frac{t-3}{12} = \frac{11}{6}$

Find the missing number.

13. What number is 320% of 120?

14. What number is 0.5% of 700?

15. 19 is what percent of 50?

16. 192 is what percent of 32?

17. 27 is 8% of what number?

18. 5.1 is 30% of what number?

Write the percent as a decimal and as a fraction.

19. 0.7%

20. 419%

21. 8%

22. 7.8%

Find the percent of change. Tell whether it is an increase or decrease.

23. Original amount: 40
New amount: 36

24. Original amount: 225
New amount: 324

25. Original amount: 258
New amount: 6.45

A box contains 9 tiles that together spell the word "TENNESSEE." You draw at random one tile from the box. Find the probability of the event.

26. Drawing an E

27. Drawing an S

28. MAPS The road distance from Miami, Florida, to Columbia, South Carolina, on a map is about 6.7 centimeters. The scale is 1 cm : 150 km. What is the actual distance from Miami to Columbia?

29. SURVEY In a survey, 34%, or 102 people, said they enjoy canoeing. How many people were surveyed?

30. FOOD Your food bill at a restaurant totals $26. There is a 6.5% sales tax and you leave a 16% tip. What is the total cost of the meal?

31. RECYCLING The average person in the United States generates about 4.5 pounds of waste per day. About 30% of this waste is recycled. About how many pounds of waste are recycled per person per week?

MULTIPLE CHOICE QUESTIONS

If you have difficulty solving a multiple choice problem directly, you may be able to use another approach to eliminate incorrect answer choices and obtain the correct answer.

PROBLEM 1

A scale model of a rectangular garden is 15 inches long and 5 inches wide. The actual garden is 36 feet long. How wide is the actual garden?

Ⓐ 2.4 inches Ⓑ 7.2 feet Ⓒ 12 feet Ⓓ 108 feet

METHOD 1

SOLVE DIRECTLY Find the scale. Then use the scale to find the width of the garden.

STEP 1 **Find** the scale by dividing the model length of the garden by the actual length.

$$\text{scale} = \frac{\text{length of model garden}}{\text{length of actual garden}}$$

$$= \frac{15 \text{ inches}}{36 \text{ feet}}$$

$$= \frac{1 \text{ inch}}{2.4 \text{ feet}}$$

The scale of the model is 1 inch to 2.4 feet.

STEP 2 **Find** the width of the garden using the scale.

$$\text{scale} = \frac{\text{width of model garden}}{\text{width of actual garden}}$$

$$\frac{1 \text{ inch}}{2.4 \text{ feet}} = \frac{5 \text{ inches}}{x \text{ feet}}$$

$$x = 12$$

The actual length of the garden is 12 feet.
The correct answer is C. Ⓐ Ⓑ Ⓒ Ⓓ

METHOD 2

ELIMINATE CHOICES In some multiple choice questions, you can identify answer choices that can be eliminated.

Choice A: Because the length of the actual garden is greater than the length of the model, the width of the actual garden is also greater than the width of the model. So, you can eliminate choice A. ✗

You can see that the length of the model is 3 times the width of the model. So, the actual length should also be 3 times the actual width. Use this to determine which of the remaining choices is the correct answer.

Write an equation comparing the length and the width and then substitute the remaining choices into the equation.

$$\text{width} \times 3 = \text{length}$$

Choice B: $7.2 \times 3 = 21.6 \text{ ft} \neq 36 \text{ ft}$ ✗

Choice C: $12 \times 3 = 36 \text{ ft} = 36 \text{ ft}$ ✓

The correct answer is C. Ⓐ Ⓑ Ⓒ Ⓓ

PROBLEM 2

Eric deposits $500 in a savings account that pays a simple interest rate of 3% per year. How much money will he have in his account after 42 months?

Ⓐ $52.50   Ⓑ $515   Ⓒ $552.50   Ⓓ $1130

METHOD 1

SOLVE DIRECTLY Use the formula for simple interest to find the interest earned. Then add the interest to the principal to find the balance of the account.

STEP 1 **Find** the simple interest. For the formula, time is in years. So, write 42 months as 3.5 years.

$I = Prt$

$= (500)(0.03)(3.5)$

$= \$52.50$

Eric will earn $52.50 in interest.

STEP 2 **Add** the interest to principal.

$\text{Balance} = \text{Principal} + \text{Interest}$

$= 500 + 52.50$

$= 552.50$

After 42 months, Eric will have $552.50 in his account.

The correct answer is C. Ⓐ Ⓑ Ⓒ Ⓓ

METHOD 2

ELIMINATE CHOICES In some multiple choice questions, you can identify answer choices that can be eliminated.

Choice A: Because Eric is earning interest on his account, he will have more money in his account after 42 months than he has now. So, you can eliminate choice A. ✗

You can work backwards to determine which of the remaining choices is correct. Find how much interest is added for each choice.

Choice B: $515 - 500 = 15$

Choice C: $552.50 - 500 = 52.50$

Choice D: $1130 - 500 = 630$

Then substitute the amounts into the simple interest formula to see if they make a true statement.

When $I = 15$:	When $I = 52.50$:
$15 = 500(0.03)(3.5)$	$52.50 = 500(0.03)(3.5)$
$15 = 52.50$ ✗	$52.50 = 52.50$ ✓

The correct answer is C. Ⓐ Ⓑ Ⓒ Ⓓ

PRACTICE

Explain why you can eliminate the highlighted answer choice.

1. A magazine subscription has a regular price of $24.50. You pay $14.70 for your subscription. What is the percent discount?

   Ⓐ 40%   Ⓑ 60%   Ⓒ 66.7%   ✗ Ⓓ **166.7%**

2. What is the total cost of a television priced at $86.90 with 7% sales tax?

   ✗ Ⓐ **$66.88**   Ⓑ $80.82   Ⓒ $89.99   Ⓓ $92.98

7 ★ Standardized TEST PRACTICE

MULTIPLE CHOICE

1. A softball team keeps 15 metal bats and 9 wooden bats in the equipment bag. A player chooses her bat at random. What is the probability that the bat is made of wood?

   (A) $\frac{3}{8}$ (B) $\frac{8}{15}$

   (C) $\frac{3}{5}$ (D) $\frac{5}{8}$

2. A crowd of 280 people grows to a crowd of 315 people. What is the percent of increase?

   (A) $11.\overline{1}\%$ (B) 12.5%

   (C) 35% (D) $88.\overline{8}\%$

3. An item with a wholesale price of $8.40 is marked up 60%. What is the retail price?

   (A) $3.36 (B) $5.04

   (C) $13.44 (D) $14.40

4. You and your friend are leaving a tip after eating dinner. The cost of the dinner is $15.35. You want to leave *about* an 18% tip. How much should you leave as a tip?

   (A) $1.25 (B) $2.75

   (C) $3.25 (D) $18.00

5. The cost of a concert ticket increased by 4%. The new cost is $31.20. What was the cost before the increase?

   (A) $29.95 (B) $30.00

   (C) $32.45 (D) $32.50

6. Lucia has 5 quarters for every 7 nickels in her purse. Lucia has 35 quarters. She wants to know how many nickels she has. Which proportion can Lucia use?

   (A) $\frac{n}{35} = \frac{5}{7}$ (B) $\frac{35}{n} = \frac{7}{5}$

   (C) $\frac{5}{n} = \frac{7}{35}$ (D) $\frac{35}{n} = \frac{5}{7}$

7. Lauren types 1040 words in 15 minutes. What is Lauren's typing speed in words per minute?

   (A) $69.\overline{3}$ (B) 156

   (C) 260 (D) 4160

8. Joan invested $100 in an account that pays 5% simple annual interest. What is the account balance after 5 years, in dollars?

   (A) $25 (B) $105

   (C) $125 (D) $350

9. Which choice shows $\frac{10 \text{ feet}}{4 \text{ seconds}}$ correctly written as a unit rate?

   (A) $\frac{5 \text{ feet}}{2 \text{ seconds}}$ (B) $\frac{5 \text{ feet}}{\text{second}}$

   (C) $\frac{2.5 \text{ feet}}{\text{second}}$ (D) $\frac{2 \text{ feet}}{5 \text{ seconds}}$

10. A scale model of a school building is 11 inches long and 3 inches high. The actual building is 231 feet long. How tall is the actual building?

    (A) 21 feet (B) 33 feet

    (C) 63 feet (D) 99 feet

11. Houses on your block include all of the numbers from 31 through 50. You choose a house at random. What is the probability that the house you choose has a 4 in its number?

    (A) $\frac{1}{10}$ (B) $\frac{2}{19}$

    (C) $\frac{11}{20}$ (D) $\frac{11}{19}$

12. You randomly draw a marble from a bag of 3 red, 8 yellow, and 13 blue marbles. What is the probability that the marble is yellow?

    (A) $\frac{13}{24}$ (B) $\frac{1}{2}$

    (C) $\frac{1}{3}$ (D) $\frac{1}{8}$

GRIDDED ANSWER

13. What is the least whole number by which you can multiply each side of the equation below to clear the fractions and decimals?

$$\frac{1}{2}x - 0.5 + 3x = \frac{1}{4}x + 0.05$$

14. A bowl contains 5 yellow marbles, 4 green marbles, 3 blue marbles, and 2 red marbles. Kim picks one marble at random. What is the probability that Kim's marble is *not* green?

15. You draw a marble at random 24 times from a bag of red, blue, green, and yellow marbles. Each time you record its color and place it back in the bag of 75 marbles. The results are shown in the table below. How many blue marbles do you predict are in the bag?

Red	*Blue*	*Green*	*Yellow*
7	6	5	6

SHORT RESPONSE

16. Joanne is using a map to plan her trip. Measure the distance, in inches, between the two cities on the map. Then use the scale on the map to estimate the actual distance in miles. *Explain* whether your answer is likely to be greater than or less than the driving distance.

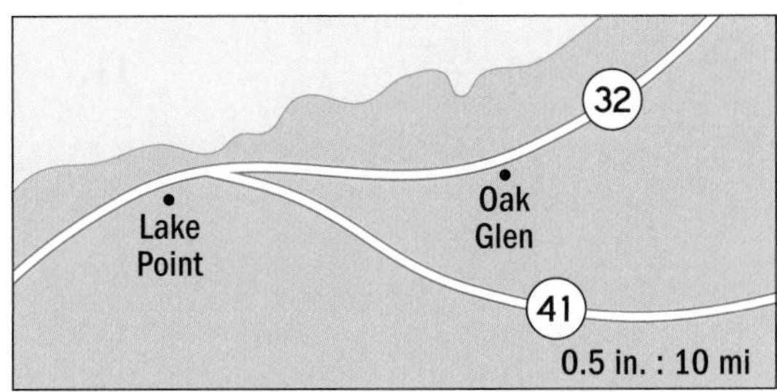

17. Amber is shopping for a new watch. The first watch she finds is on sale for 10% off the original price of \$35.95. The second watch she finds is on sale for 20% off the original price of \$38.25. There is an 8% sales tax on both watches. Which watch costs less? *Explain.*

EXTENDED RESPONSE

18. The graph shows the results of a poll in which 504 people would choose to be a zookeeper if they had to take an animal career.

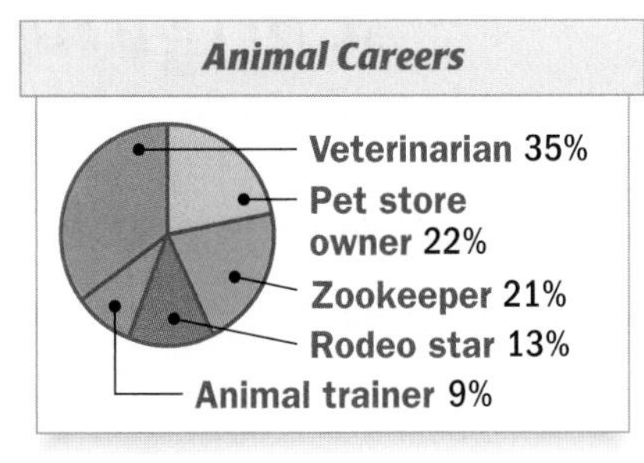

a. Find the total number of people who participated in the poll.

b. How many people chose a rodeo star?

c. How many people chose either a veterinarian or a rodeo star?

d. *Explain* how the percents might change if the poll asked only 54 people.

19. Cindy wants to use a 20% discount coupon to buy a coat that originally cost \$78. She also wants to use a 10% discount coupon to buy a sweater that originally cost \$36. To find the total cost of the items after the discounts, Cindy found the sum of their original prices and subtracted 30% of the total. *Explain* the mistake that Cindy made. Then show how to find the correct total cost before sales tax. Then find the cost if sales tax on clothing is 4%.

7 CUMULATIVE REVIEW Chapters 1–7

Evaluate the expression.

1. $66 - 11 \times 5$ *(p. 8)*
2. $8 \div (3.5 + 0.5)$ *(p. 8)*
3. $17 + (3 \times 4)^2$ *(p. 19)*
4. $8 \times 6 \div 2^4$ *(p. 19)*
5. $(-3 + 11) + 5$ *(p. 83)*
6. $(14 - 8) - 13$ *(p. 83)*
7. $-3(8 + 6)$ *(p. 88)*
8. $-5(-3 - 7)$ *(p. 88)*
9. $(-5 \cdot 8) \cdot 4$ *(p. 88)*

Write the fraction in simplest form. *(p. 187)*

10. $\frac{104}{39}$
11. $-\frac{32}{102}$
12. $-\frac{9abc}{12a}$
13. $\frac{21bcd}{7bc}$

Write the equivalent rate. *(p. 343)*

14. $\frac{\$5.97}{\text{yd}} = \frac{\$?}{\text{ft}}$
15. $\frac{30 \text{ mi}}{\text{h}} = \frac{? \text{ mi}}{\text{min}}$
16. $\frac{4 \text{ oz}}{\text{serving}} = \frac{? \text{ lb}}{\text{serving}}$
17. $\frac{180 \text{ ft}}{\text{sec}} = \frac{? \text{ ft}}{\text{min}}$

Simplify. Write the expression using only positive exponents. *(p. 208)*

18. $7x^{-4}$
19. $a^{-6} \cdot a^4$
20. $\frac{8w^{-6}}{24w^2}$
21. $\frac{16r^{-2}}{4r^3}$

Find the sum, difference, product, or quotient.

22. $-55 + (-43)$ *(p. 63)*
23. $0 + (-144)$ *(p. 63)*
24. $-21 - 33$ *(p. 68)*
25. $-17 - (-67)$ *(p. 68)*
26. $-5(-16)$ *(p. 73)*
27. $3(-8)(10)$ *(p. 73)*
28. $\frac{-51}{-17}$ *(p. 77)*
29. $\frac{0}{-25}$ *(p. 77)*
30. $-9\frac{3}{4} + 4\frac{2}{3}$ *(p. 233)*
31. $-\frac{19x}{25} - \frac{11x}{25}$ *(p. 233)*
32. $\frac{3}{c} - \frac{7}{2c}$ *(p. 238)*
33. $\frac{9}{21} \cdot \frac{7}{5}$ *(p. 243)*
34. $12\frac{1}{2} \cdot \frac{6}{25}$ *(p. 243)*
35. $\frac{13}{18} \div \frac{5}{6}$ *(p. 247)*
36. $5\frac{8}{11} \div \left(-\frac{3}{4}\right)$ *(p. 247)*
37. $16.7 \cdot (-3.2)$ *(p. 265)*
38. $43.4 \cdot 0.13$ *(p. 265)*
39. $3.434 \div 8.08$ *(p. 265)*

Solve the equation or inequality.

40. $8 = b - (-6)$ *(p. 117)*
41. $9y = -63$ *(p. 122)*
42. $2c - 5 = 17$ *(p. 129)*
43. $d + 3.4 \le 9.1$ *(p. 148)*
44. $\frac{1}{3}x > -2$ *(p. 154)*
45. $7 - 2y \le 11$ *(p. 154)*
46. $x = 5(2x + 3)$ *(p. 298)*
47. $6 - \frac{2}{5}a > 2$ *(p. 318)*
48. $2(3k + 1) \le 5k - 30$ *(p. 318)*

Write the decimal or fraction as a percent. *(p. 359)*

49. 0.43
50. 0.003
51. $\frac{3}{10}$
52. $\frac{29}{20}$

Find the probability of the event. *(p. 381)*

53. A vowel is randomly chosen from the letters A, B, C, D, E, and F.
54. A number less than 4 is randomly drawn from the numbers 1, 2, 3, and 4.

55. **CLOTHES** A sweater costs $45 and a pair of jeans cost $35.You buy 3 sweaters and 2 pairs of jeans on a sale day where sweaters are $10 off and jeans are $5 off. Write an expression for the cost of the clothes, and evaluate it. *(p. 13)*

56. **STOCK MARKET** Your uncle owns 25 shares of stock A, 45 shares of stock B, and 60 shares of stock C. In one day, the price per share changed by +$.56 for stock A, −$1.80 for stock B, and −$.50 for stock C. Find the total change in value of your uncle's stocks. *(p. 73)*

57. **SAVING** You have $80 today. You save $40 a week. How many weeks will it take to save enough to buy a camera that costs $320? How many weeks will it take if you save $35 a week? *(p. 154)*

58. **FOUNTAIN** A fountain in an amusement park has special-effect devices called *shooters*. They shoot columns of water at different time intervals. One shooter goes off every 8 seconds while another goes off every 12 seconds. How long after the fountain is turned on will both shooters go off at the same time? *(p. 192)*

BIRTH WEIGHTS In Exercises 59 and 60, use the table. It shows approximate weights, in pounds, of several newborn animals. *(p. 260)*

Newborn Animal	*Birth Weight (lb)*
Hippopotamus	66
Giant panda	0.25
Giraffe	150
Polar bear	1.32
Gentoo penguin	0.29

59. How much more does the hippopotamus weigh than the gentoo penguin?

60. How much more does the polar bear weigh than the giant panda?

61. **ICEBERGS** When an iceberg broke free from Antarctica in May of 2002, it was about 34.5 miles long and 11.5 miles wide. About how much area did the iceberg cover? *(p. 265)*

62. **SCHOOL FUNDRAISER** You are selling magazine subscriptions for a school fundraiser. If you sell at least 75 subscriptions in 2 weeks you win a prize. You sold 26 subscriptions in one week. The next week, what is the mean number of subscriptions you have to sell per day to sell 75 total? *(p. 324)*

CLASS PROJECTS In Exercises 63–65, use the circle graph. It shows the results of a survey of 300 students who were asked what they would choose for a final project. *(p. 359)*

Final Project

63. What percent of students chose an oral report?

64. What fraction of students chose a visual project? Write the fraction in simplest form.

65. Which final project was chosen by 21% of the students?

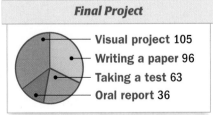

8 Polygons and Transformations

Before

In previous chapters you've . . .

- Solved equations
- Plotted points in a coordinate plane

Now

In Chapter 8 you'll study . . .

- 8.1 Angle pairs
- 8.2 Classifying triangles
- 8.3 Quadrilaterals
- 8.4 Polygons
- 8.5 Congruent polygons
- 8.6 Reflections and symmetry
- 8.7 Translations and rotations
- 8.8 Similarity and Dilations

Why?

So you can solve real-world problems about . . .

- rugs, p. 404
- referees, p. 413
- origami, p. 443

Math

at classzone.com

- Playing Golf with Angles, p. 413
- Polygons and Angles, p. 421
- Transformations and Symmetry, p. 442

Get-Ready Games

Review Prerequisite Skills by playing *Find the Flags.*

Skill Focus: Plotting points on a coordinate plane

FIND THE FLAGS

MATERIALS

- 2 sheets of grid paper for each player
- Pencils

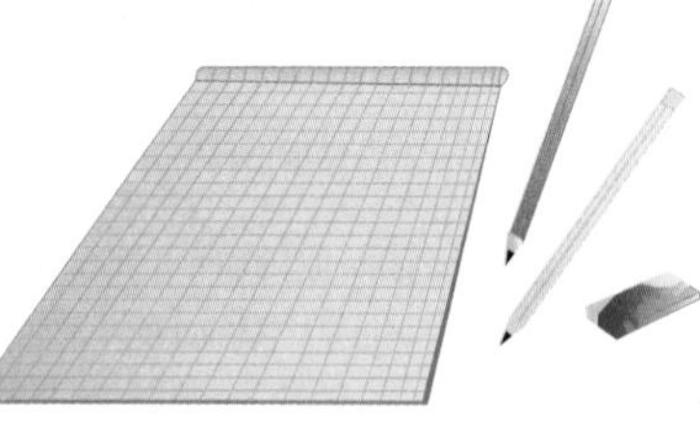

HOW TO PLAY Each player draws a coordinate graph on both sheets of grid paper. Each player draws squares along the grid lines passing through the points (7, 0), (0, −7), (−7, 0), and (0, 7). A player secretly marks 4 flags on one graph. A flag is three consecutive points with integer coordinates, either horizontally or vertically. Flags cannot touch the outside borders. On each turn, a player should follow the steps on the next page.

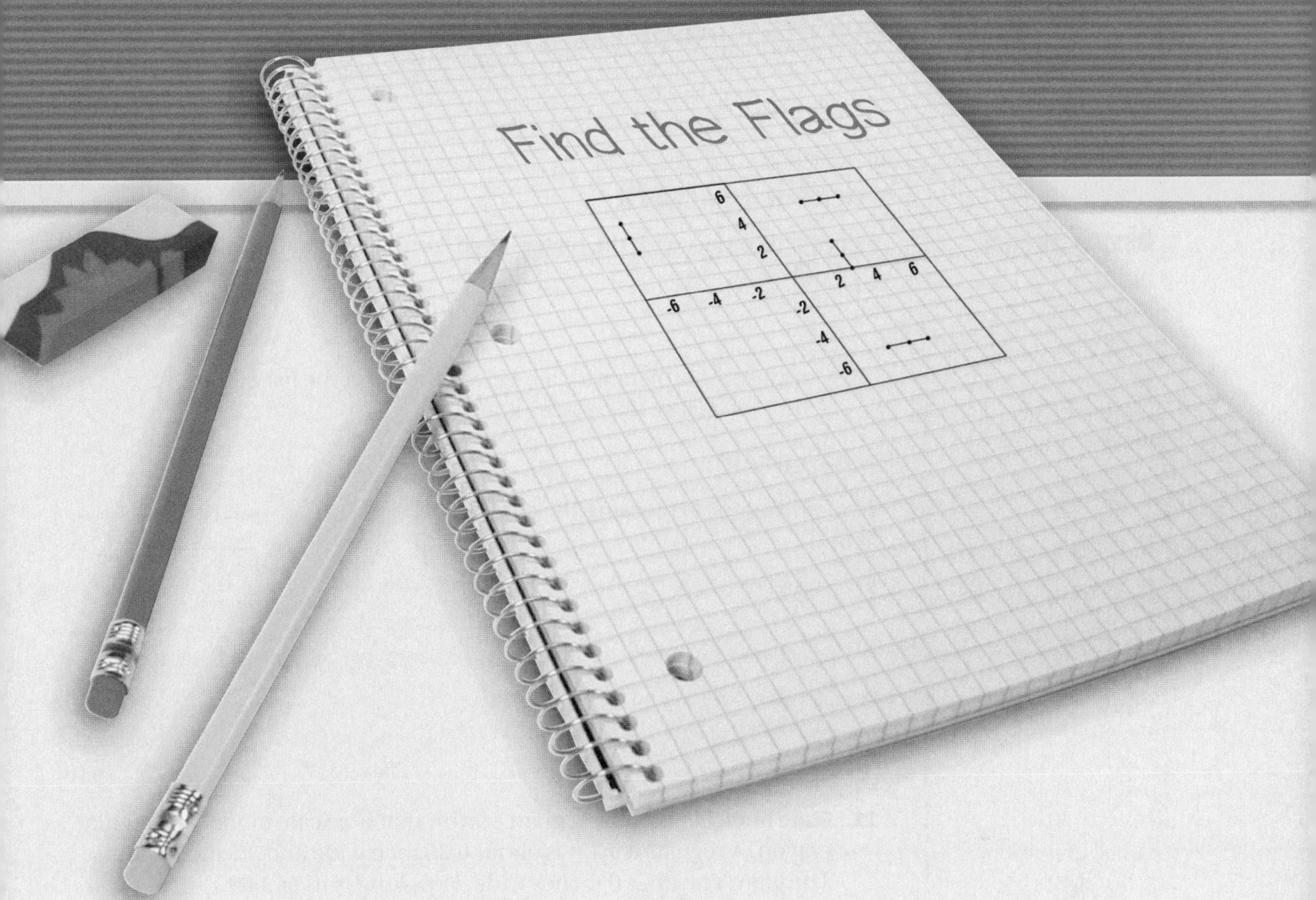

Find the Flags

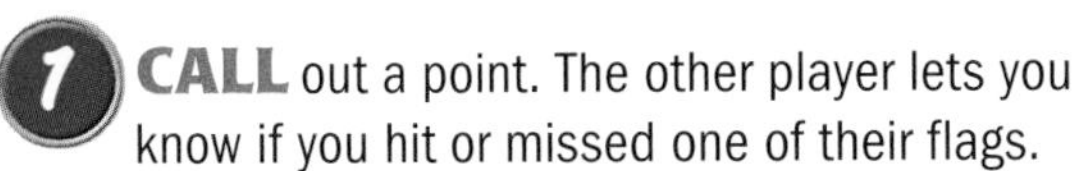

CALL out a point. The other player lets you know if you hit or missed one of their flags.

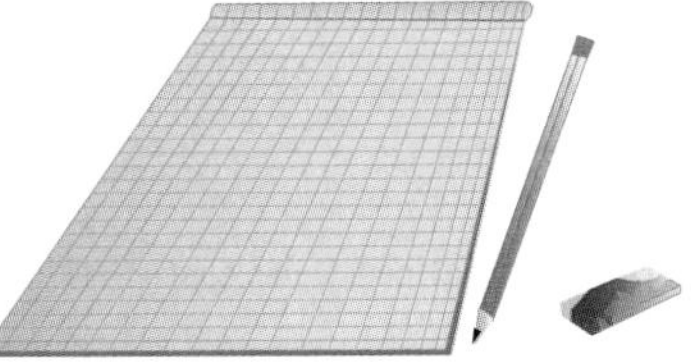

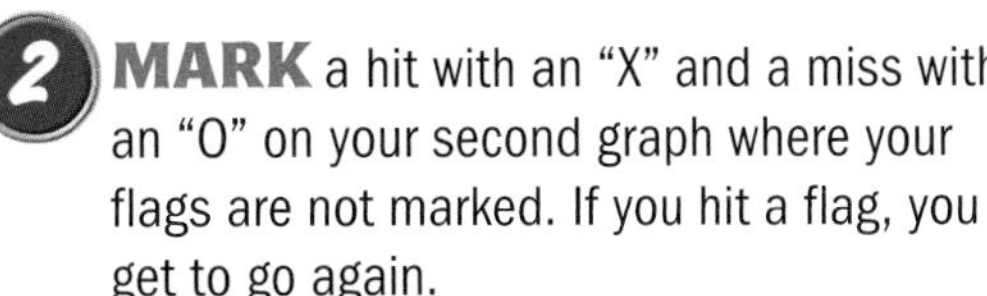

MARK a hit with an "X" and a miss with an "O" on your second graph where your flags are not marked. If you hit a flag, you get to go again.

X O

HOW TO WIN Be the first player to hit all the points in the other player's flags.

Stop and Think

1. **WRITING** How did you decide where to put your flags? Did it work? *Explain.* What strategy did you use when trying to find the other player's flags? Did it work? *Explain.*
2. **CRITICAL THINKING** How many points are there (not including any on the border) in each graph? *Explain* how you got your answer.

8 Getting Ready

Review Prerequisite Skills

REVIEW WORDS

- **point,** *p. 773*
- **line,** *p. 773*
- **ray,** *p. 773*
- **plane,** *p. 773*
- **angle,** *p. 774*
- **vertex,** *p. 774*
- **degree,** *p. 776*

VOCABULARY CHECK

Identify the object with the review word from the list at the left. ***(p. 773)***

1. **2.** **3.**

4. Copy and complete with a review word from the list at the left: A unit for measuring angles is a(n) __?__.

SKILL CHECK

Use a protractor to measure the angle. ***(p. 776)***

5.

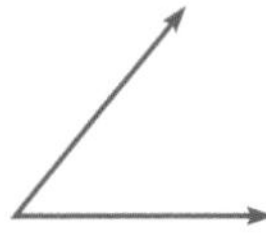

6.

7.

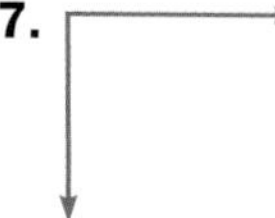

8.

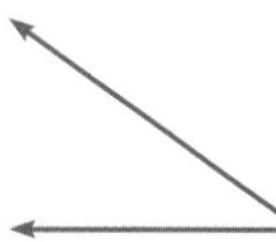

9.

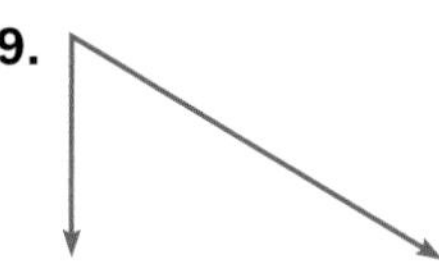

10.

11. Scale Models You have a giant crayon that is a scale model of a regular crayon. A regular crayon is about 0.25 inch wide and 3.5 inches long. The giant crayon is 6 inches wide. How long is it? ***(p. 348)***

@HomeTutor Prerequisite skills practice at classzone.com

Notetaking Skills Making a Concept Map

In each chapter you will learn a new notetaking skill. In Chapter 8, you can apply the strategy of making a concept map to Example 1 on page 416.

You will often learn new concepts that are related to each other. It is helpful to organize these concepts in your notes with a map or chart.

A rectangle is a figure with four sides. Its opposite sides have the same length, and its angles are right angles.

A square is a rectangle with sides that have the same length.

8.1 Angle Pairs

Before You solved equations to find the value of a variable.

Now You'll solve equations to find angle measures.

Why? So you can find angle measures in objects, such as skis as in Ex. 28.

KEY VOCABULARY
- **straight angle, right angle,** *p. 403*
- **supplementary, complementary,** *p. 403*
- **vertical angles,** *p. 404*
- **perpendicular lines,** *p. 404*
- **parallel lines,** *p. 405*

A **straight angle** measures 180°. A **right angle** measures 90°. The mark ⌉ tells you that an angle is a right angle.

Straight angle **Right angle**

Two angles are **supplementary** if the sum of their measures is 180°. Two angles are **complementary** if the sum of their measures is 90°. You can write "the measure of angle 1" as $m\angle 1$.

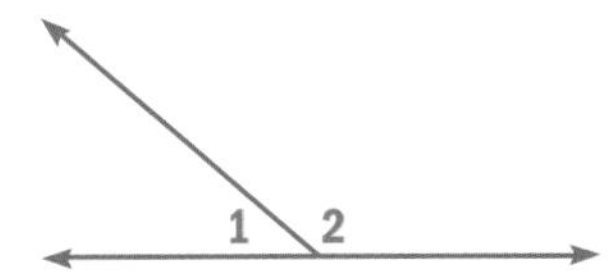

$\angle 1$ and $\angle 2$ are supplementary.
$m\angle 1 + m\angle 2 = 180°$

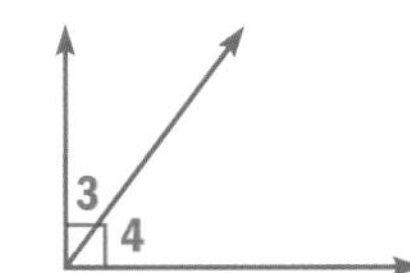

$\angle 3$ and $\angle 4$ are complementary.
$m\angle 3 + m\angle 4 = 90°$

EXAMPLE 1 Finding an Angle Measure

$\angle 1$ and $\angle 2$ are complementary, and $m\angle 2 = 32°$. Find $m\angle 1$.

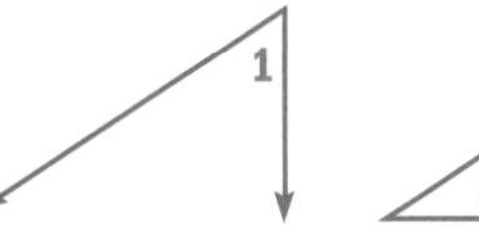

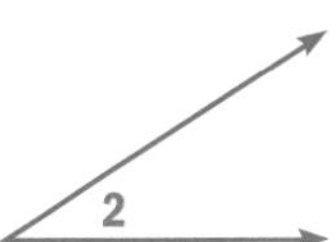

SOLUTION

$m\angle 1 + m\angle 2 = 90°$ **Definition of complementary angles**

$m\angle 1 + 32° = 90°$ **Substitute 32° for $m\angle 2$.**

$m\angle 1 = 58°$ **Subtract 32° from each side.**

Animated Math at classzone.com

✓ GUIDED PRACTICE for Example 1

Tell whether $\angle 1$ and $\angle 2$ are *complementary*, *supplementary*, or *neither*.

1. $m\angle 1 = 79°$
$m\angle 2 = 101°$

2. $m\angle 1 = 64°$
$m\angle 2 = 36°$

3. $m\angle 1 = 52°$
$m\angle 2 = 38°$

4. $m\angle 1 = 44°$
$m\angle 2 = 46°$

5. $m\angle 1 = 53°$
$m\angle 2 = 47°$

6. $m\angle 1 = 95°$
$m\angle 2 = 85°$

Vertical Angles When two lines intersect at a point, they form two pairs of angles that do not share a side. These pairs are called **vertical angles**, and they always have the same measure.

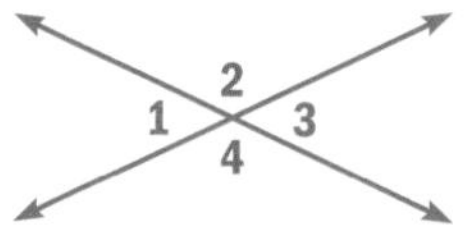

$\angle 1$ and $\angle 3$ are vertical angles.
$m\angle 1 = m\angle 3$

$\angle 2$ and $\angle 4$ are vertical angles.
$m\angle 2 = m\angle 4$

EXAMPLE 2 Solve a Multi-Step Problem

Textiles Find the angle measures indicated in the rug design if $m\angle 1 = 122°$.

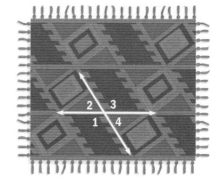

SOLUTION

It is given that $m\angle 1 = 122°$.

STEP 1 $\angle 1$ and $\angle 3$ are vertical angles. Their measures are equal, so $m\angle 3 = 122°$.

STEP 2 $\angle 1$ and $\angle 2$ are supplementary.

$m\angle 1 + m\angle 2 = 180°$	**Definition of supplementary angles**
$122° + m\angle 2 = 180°$	**Substitute 122° for $m\angle 1$.**
$m\angle 2 = 58°$	**Subtract 122° from each side.**

STEP 3 $\angle 2$ and $\angle 4$ are vertical angles. Their measures are equal, so $m\angle 4 = 58°$.

▶ **Answer** $m\angle 1 = m\angle 3 = 122°$, $m\angle 2 = m\angle 4 = 58°$

✓ GUIDED PRACTICE for Example 2

Find the measures of the numbered angles.

7.

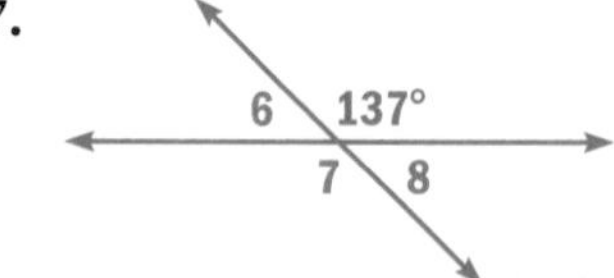

8.

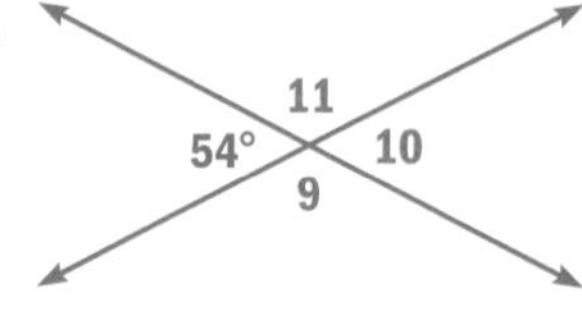

Lines in a Plane Using vertical and supplementary angles, you can see that when two lines intersect to form one right angle, they form four right angles. Two lines that intersect at a right angle are called **perpendicular lines**.

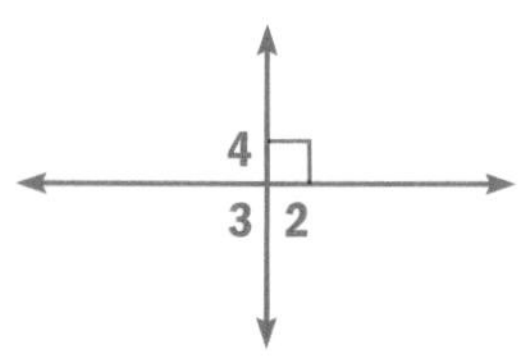

Two lines in the same plane that do not intersect are called **parallel lines**. When a line intersects two parallel lines, several pairs of angles that are formed have equal measures.

KEY CONCEPT — *For Your Notebook*

Angles and Parallel Lines

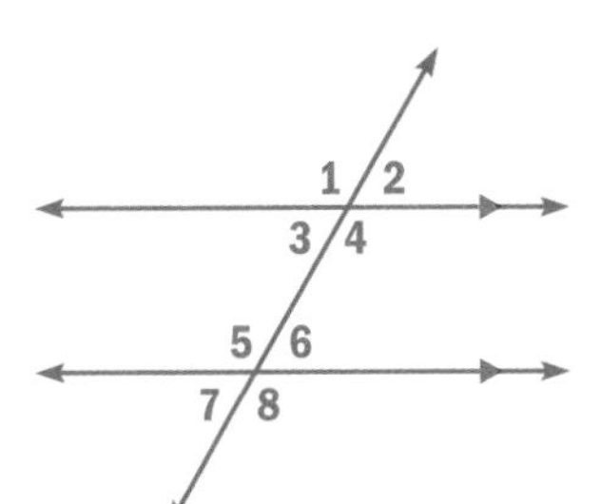

Corresponding Angles

$m\angle 1 = m\angle 5$ $\quad$ $m\angle 2 = m\angle 6$

$m\angle 3 = m\angle 7$ $\quad$ $m\angle 4 = m\angle 8$

Alternate Interior Angles

$m\angle 3 = m\angle 6$ $\quad$ $m\angle 4 = m\angle 5$

Alternate Exterior Angles

$m\angle 1 = m\angle 8$ $\quad$ $m\angle 2 = m\angle 7$

READING The red arrows on the lines indicate that the lines in the diagram are parallel.

EXAMPLE 3 Using Parallel Lines

Use the diagram to find the angle measure.

a. $m\angle 1$

b. $m\angle 2$

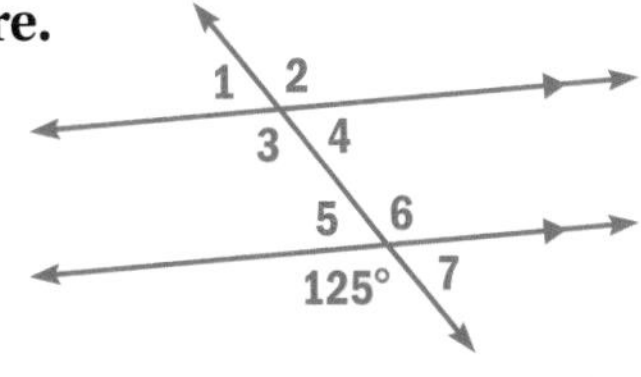

SOLUTION

a. $\angle 1$ and $\angle 5$ are corresponding angles, so they have equal measures. You can find $m\angle 5$ because it is the supplement of the given angle.

$m\angle 5 + 125° = 180°$ $\quad$ **Definition of supplementary angles**

$m\angle 5 = 55°$ $\quad$ **Subtract 125° from each side.**

▶ **Answer** $m\angle 1 = 55°$

b. $\angle 2$ and the given angle are alternate exterior angles, so they have equal measures.

▶ **Answer** $m\angle 2 = 125°$

ANOTHER WAY You could also find $m\angle 1$ by finding the $m\angle 7$, its alternate exterior angle.

✓ GUIDED PRACTICE for Example 3

Find the angle measure.

9. $m\angle 2$ $\quad$ **10.** $m\angle 3$

11. $m\angle 4$ $\quad$ **12.** $m\angle 1$

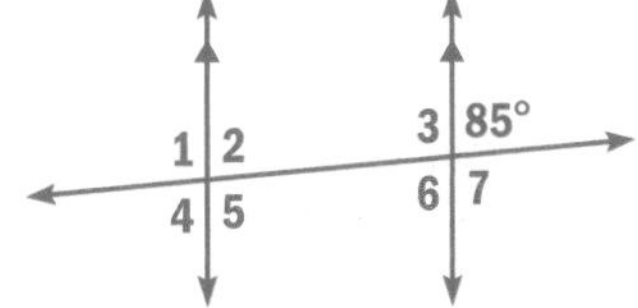

8.1 EXERCISES

HOMEWORK KEY

★ = **STANDARDIZED TEST PRACTICE** Exs. 9, 31, 33, 34, 36, and 48

○ = **HINTS AND HOMEWORK HELP** for Exs. 3, 5, 9, 11, 29 at classzone.com

SKILL PRACTICE

VOCABULARY **Copy and complete the statement.**

1. The sum of the measures of two _?_ angles is 180°.
2. Two lines that intersect to form a right angle are called _?_.

CLASSIFYING ANGLES **Tell whether the angles are *complementary*, *supplementary*, or *neither*.**

SEE EXAMPLE 1 on p. 403 for Exs. 3–9

3. $m\angle 1 = 62°$, $m\angle 2 = 118°$
4. $m\angle 1 = 51°$, $m\angle 2 = 39°$

FINDING ANGLE MEASURES **Find the angle measure.**

5. $\angle 1$ and $\angle 2$ are complementary, and $m\angle 1 = 56°$. Find $m\angle 2$.
6. $\angle 3$ and $\angle 4$ are supplementary, and $m\angle 4 = 71°$. Find $m\angle 3$.
7. $\angle 5$ and $\angle 6$ are supplementary, and $m\angle 5 = 22°$. Find $m\angle 6$.
8. $\angle 7$ and $\angle 8$ are complementary, and $m\angle 8 = 84°$. Find $m\angle 7$.
9. ★ **MULTIPLE CHOICE** Which angles are complementary?

   (A) $\angle 1$ and $\angle 2$ (B) $\angle 2$ and $\angle 3$

   (C) $\angle 3$ and $\angle 4$ (D) $\angle 4$ and $\angle 1$

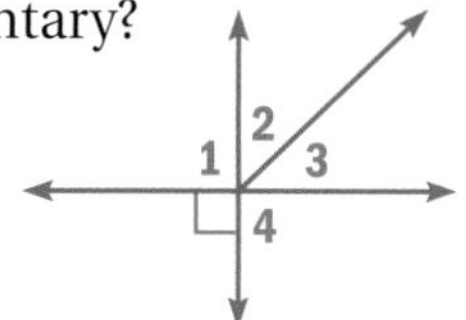

ANGLE PAIRS **Find the measures of the numbered angles.**

SEE EXAMPLES 2 AND 3 on pp. 404–405 for Exs. 10–14

10.

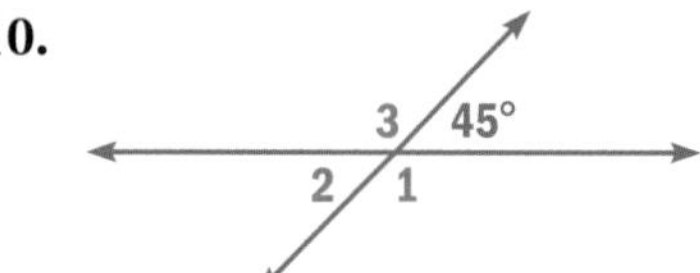

11. 2, 80°, 1, 3

12.

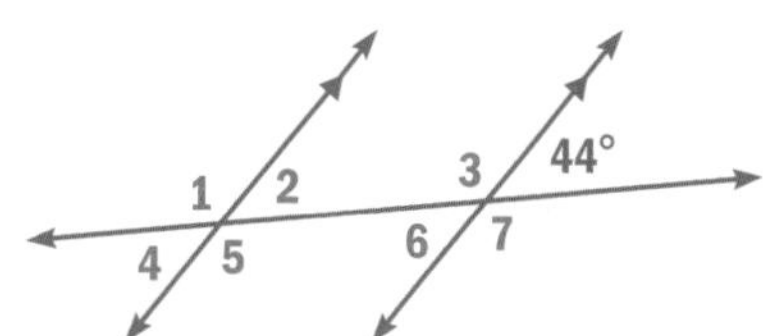

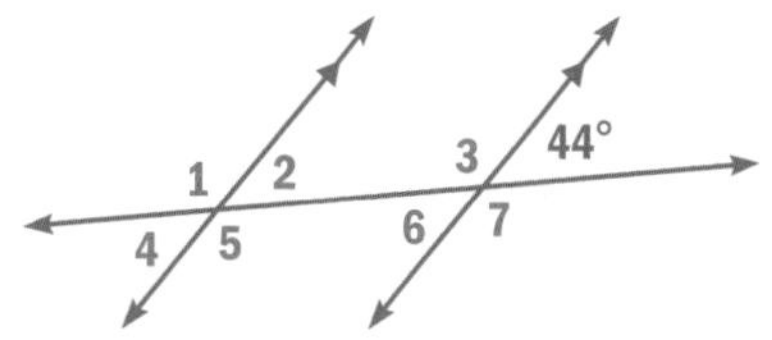

13. 1, 2, 3, 4, 5, 6, 7, 8, 106°, 9, 10, 11

14. **ERROR ANALYSIS** Describe and correct the error made in the statement.

> ✗ $m\angle 2 = 68°$ because the measures of vertical angles add up to 180°
>
> 112°, 1, 3, 2

15. **WHICH ONE DOESN'T BELONG?** Which of the angle pairs doesn't belong?

   A. $m\angle 1 = 21°$, $m\angle 2 = 69°$ **B.** $m\angle 3 = 12°$, $m\angle 4 = 68°$

   C. $m\angle 5 = 79°$, $m\angle 6 = 11°$ **D.** $m\angle 7 = 45°$, $m\angle 8 = 45°$

PARALLEL LINES In Exercises 16–19, use the figure at the right. Find the measure of the angle. Tell which types of angle pairs you used.

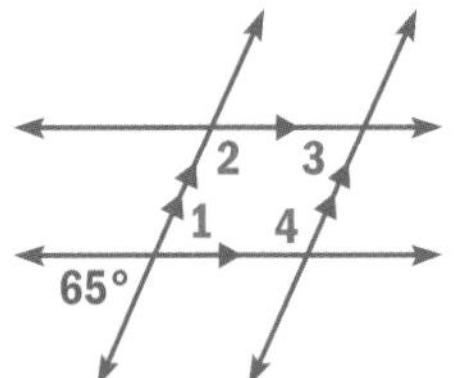

16. $m\angle 1$

17. $m\angle 2$

18. $m\angle 3$

19. $m\angle 4$

20. **GEOMETRY** A four sided figure is formed by the intersecting lines in the diagram above. *Describe* the angle relationships in this figure, based on your answers to Exercises 16–19.

REASONING Copy and complete each sentence with *always*, *sometimes*, or *never*. *Explain* your reasoning.

21. Two angles are __?__ supplementary.

22. Vertical angles __?__ have different measures.

23. Perpendicular lines __?__ form four right angles.

xy ALGEBRA Find the value of the variable and the angle measures.

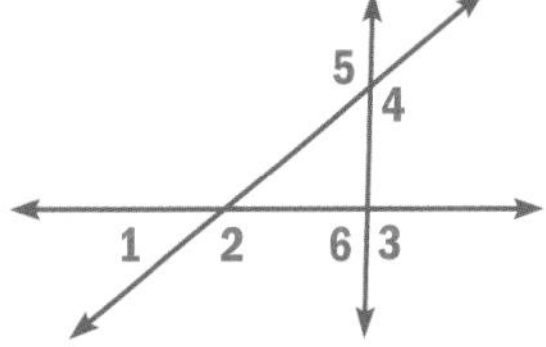

24. $m\angle 1 = (5x + 15)^\circ$ and $m\angle 2 = 28x^\circ$

25. $m\angle 6 = (100 - 10y)^\circ$ and $m\angle 3 = 45y^\circ$

26. $m\angle 4 = (7n + 39)^\circ$ and $m\angle 5 = (11n - 13)^\circ$

27. **CHALLENGE** $\angle B$ and $\angle C$ are supplementary. The measure of $\angle C$ is four times the measure of $\angle B$. Find $m\angle B$.

PROBLEM SOLVING

28. **SKIS** One of the angle measures formed by the skis in the diagram at the right is 60°. What are the measures of the other 3 angles?

29. **PARALLEL LINES** A line intersects three parallel lines. How many pairs of vertical angles are formed? *Explain* your answer and include an example.

30. **STATIONERY** A student designed the stationery border shown at the right. *Explain* how to find $m\angle 2$ if $m\angle 1 = 135^\circ$.

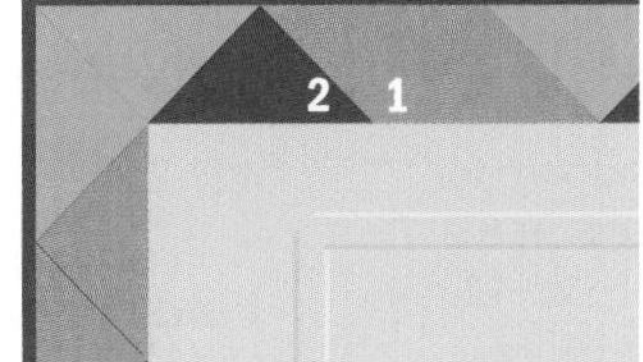

31. ★ **OPEN-ENDED MATH** Draw a pair of complementary angles and a pair of supplementary angles. Then draw a pair of angles that are neither complementary nor supplementary.

32. **ESTIMATION** Estimate the measure of the angle. Then approximate the measure of the complement of the angle.

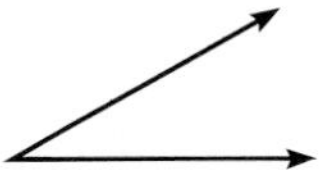

33. ★ **MULTIPLE CHOICE** In the diagram of the parking lot, $m\angle 1 = 120°$. What is $m\angle 1 + m\angle 3$?

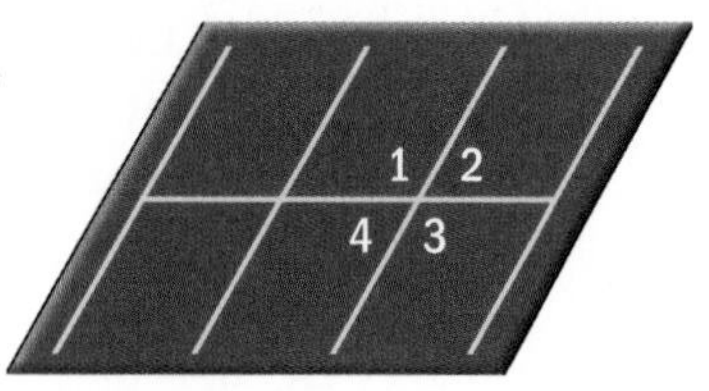

Ⓐ 90° Ⓑ 120°

Ⓒ 240° Ⓓ 225°

34. ★ **SHORT RESPONSE** Two complementary angles have the same measure. *Explain* how you can find the measure of each angle.

35. **INTERSECTING PATHS** Two bicycle paths intersect to form a 75° angle. Sketch the intersection and find the measure of each angle formed.

36. ★ **OPEN-ENDED MATH** *Describe* three real-world situations involving perpendicular lines.

37. **ARCHITECTURE** The upright supports shown at the right are parallel. What are $m\angle 1$, $m\angle 2$, and $m\angle 3$? *Explain.*

38. **GEOMETRY** Draw two parallel lines m and n. Then draw two more parallel lines that are perpendicular to line m. How many right angles are formed? *Explain* how you know they are right angles.

39. **GEOMETRY** Draw two parallel lines. Then draw a line that intersects the two parallel lines at a 60° angle. How many 60° angles are formed?

40. **ORIENTATION** A man walks with traffic toward the intersection of two perpendicular streets. He looks directly in front of him at the corner across the street. Then he turns 45° counterclockwise and looks at the northeast corner of the intersection. Using directions, describe the corner he is standing on.

41. **CHALLENGE** Use the diagram to find the unknown angle measure between Mulberry Street and Walnut Street.

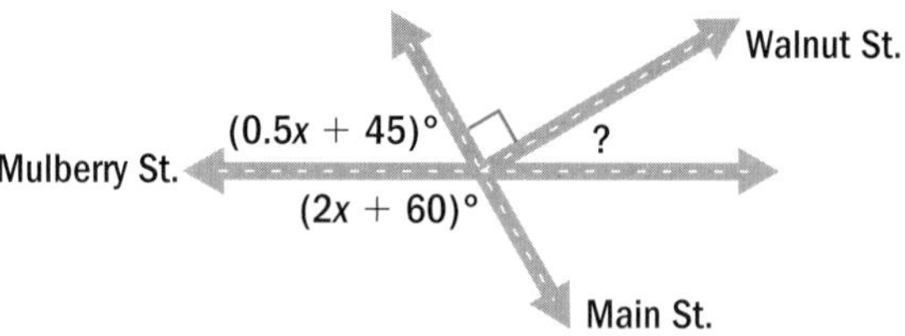

MIXED REVIEW

Get-Ready

Prepare for Lesson 8.2 in Exs. 42–44

Solve the equation. *(p. 293)*

42. $2x + 7x = 90$ 43. $10x - 7x + 120 = 360$ 44. $x + 3x + 45 = 180$

Find the area of the triangle with the given base and height. *(p. 142)*

45. $b = 3$ in., $h = 2$ in. 46. $b = 9$ cm, $h = 4$ cm 47. $b = 13$ ft, $h = 5$ ft

48. ★ **MULTIPLE CHOICE** Which choice shows 53.72% written as a decimal? *(p. 359)*

Ⓐ 5372 Ⓑ 53.72 Ⓒ 5.372 Ⓓ 0.5372

Constructions

GOAL Copy an angle and construct perpendicular lines and parallel lines.

You can *construct* geometric figures using special tools. A *compass* is used to draw parts of circles called *arcs.* A *straightedge* is used to draw straight lines.

EXAMPLE 1 Copying an Angle

STEP 1 **Draw** an angle. Label its vertex A. Then draw a ray with endpoint X.

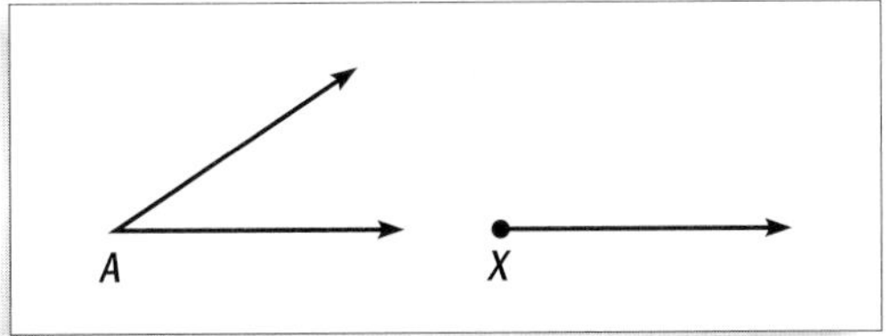

USE A COMPASS
Need help using a compass? See p. 777.

STEP 2 **Draw** an arc with center A. Label B and C on $\angle A$. Use the same compass setting to draw an arc with center X. Label point Y.

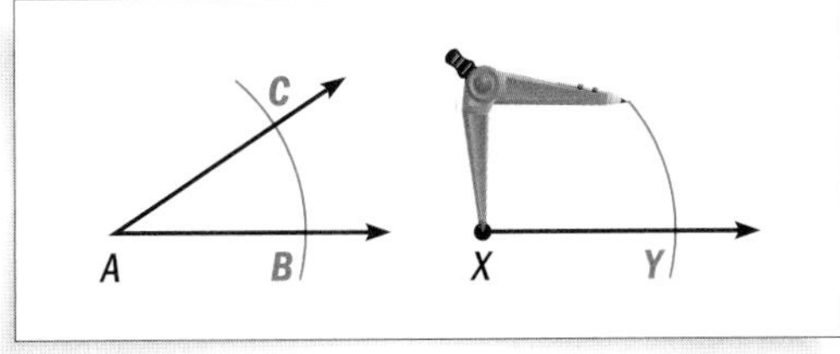

STEP 3 **Draw** an arc with center B that passes through C. Use the same compass setting to draw an arc with center Y. Label point Z.

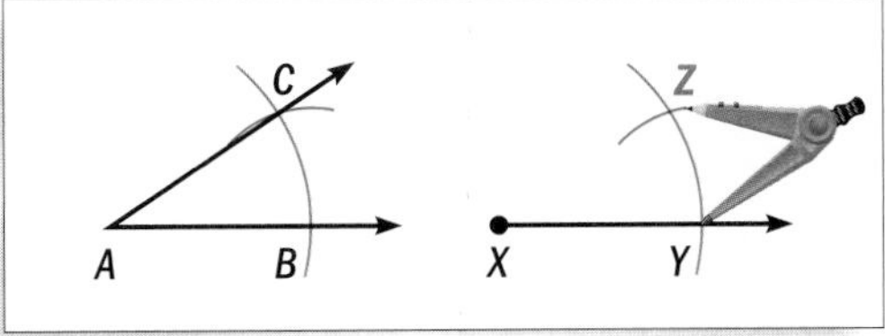

STEP 4 **Use** a straightedge to draw a ray with endpoint X through Z.

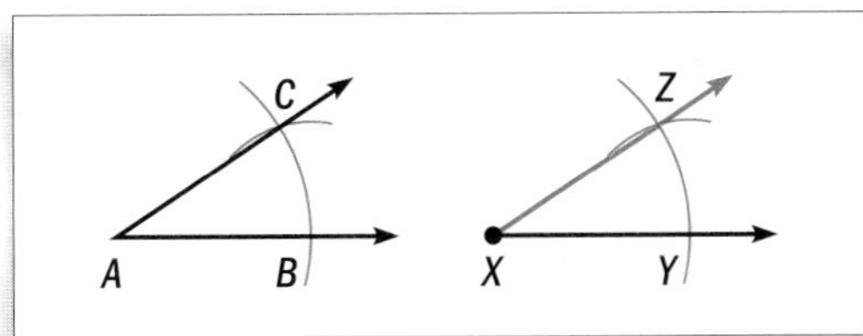

Check Use a protractor to check that $m\angle A = m\angle X$.

EXAMPLE 2 Constructing a Perpendicular Line

STEP 1 **Draw** a line and a point P not on the line. Draw an arc with center P that intersects the line twice. Label A and B. Using the same compass setting, draw arcs with centers A and B.

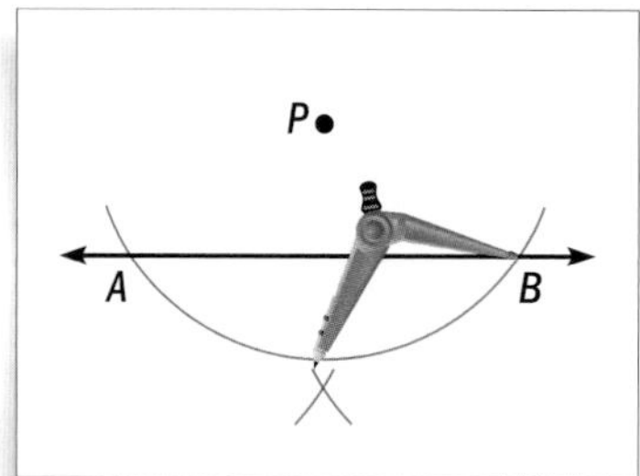

STEP 2 **Label** point Q where the last two arcs intersect. Draw a line through P and Q. Lines PQ and AB are perpendicular.

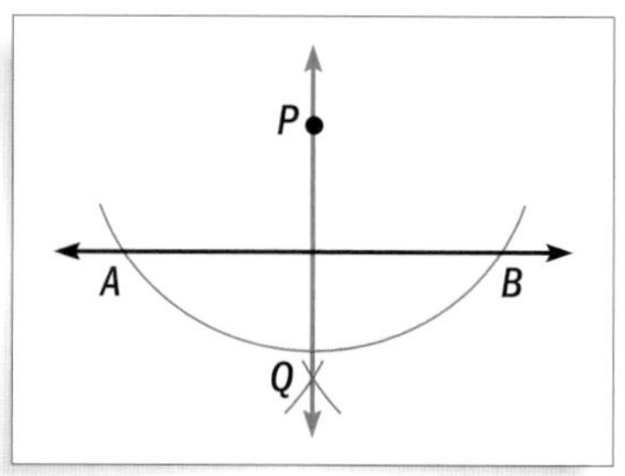

EXAMPLE 3 Constructing a Parallel Line

ANOTHER WAY

In Step 1, you can make line *PQ* intersect line *AB* at any angle. Step 2 will still make a line parallel to line *AB*.

STEP 1 **Follow** the steps in Example 2 to construct perpendicular lines. Label $\angle 1$.

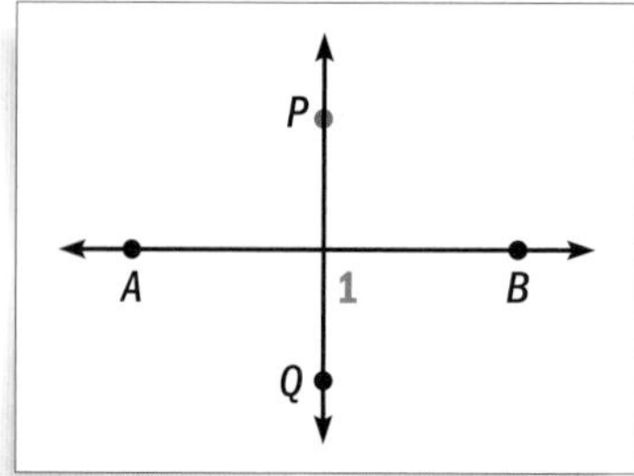

STEP 2 **Follow** the steps in Example 1 to copy $\angle 1$ at point P as shown.

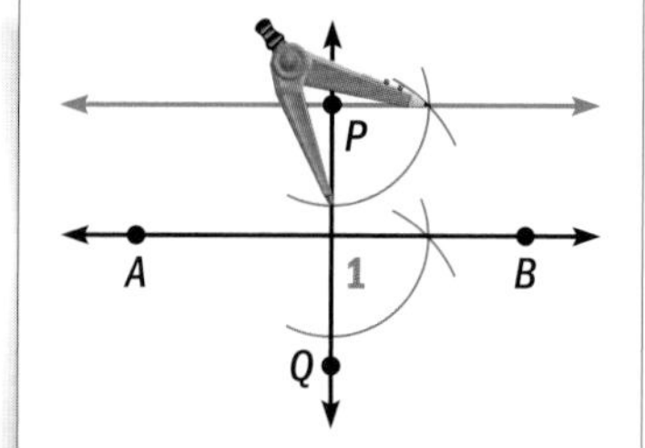

EXERCISES

In Exercises 1–4, use a protractor to draw an angle with the given measure. Then use a compass and straightedge to copy the angle.

1. $45°$ **2.** $120°$ **3.** $135°$ **4.** $60°$

CONSTRUCTIONS **Use a compass and straightedge to construct the figure.**

5. Three parallel lines **6.** Right triangle **7.** Rectangle

8. **POINT ON A LINE** Example 2 can be adjusted so you can make perpendicular lines when P is on a line. Draw a line and label point P on it. In Step 2, to find Q, open your compass wider than it was in Step 1. Draw line PQ, which is perpendicular to the given line.

8.2 Angles and Triangles

Before	You identified pairs of angles.
Now	You'll classify angles and triangles.
Why?	So you can classify triangles in architecture, as in Ex. 32.

KEY VOCABULARY

- **acute, right, obtuse angle,** *p. 411*
- **acute, right, obtuse triangle,** *p. 411*
- **equilateral, isosceles, scalene triangle,** *p. 411*

An angle can be classified by its measure.

Acute angle

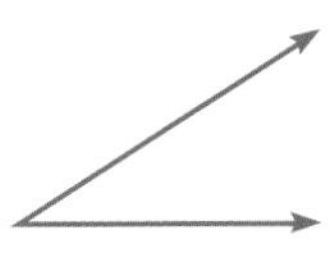

Measure is less than 90°.

Right angle

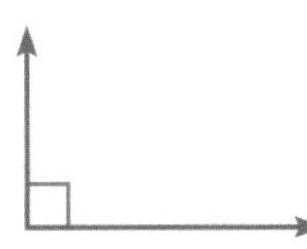

Measure is exactly 90°.

Obtuse angle

Measure is greater than 90° and less than 180°.

KEY CONCEPT — *For Your Notebook*

Classifying Triangles

By Angles

An **acute triangle** has three acute angles.

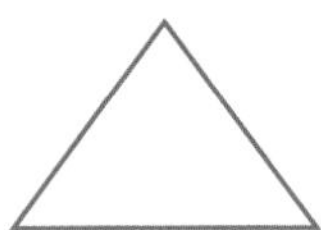

A **right triangle** has one right angle.

An **obtuse triangle** has one obtuse angle.

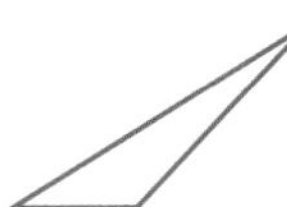

By Sides

An **equilateral triangle** has three sides of equal length.

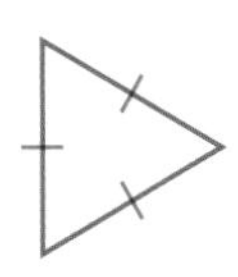

An **isosceles triangle** has at least two sides of equal length.

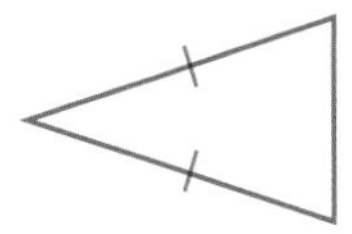

A **scalene triangle** has no sides of equal length.

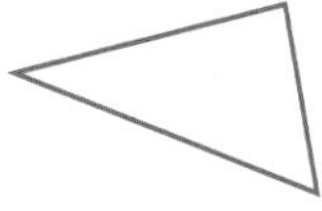

A geometric figure can be named using the vertices of each of its angles. Use either a clockwise or counterclockwise order such as $\triangle ACB$ or $\triangle DEF$.

Tick marks in a drawing show that side lengths are equal. Arc marks show that angle measures are equal.

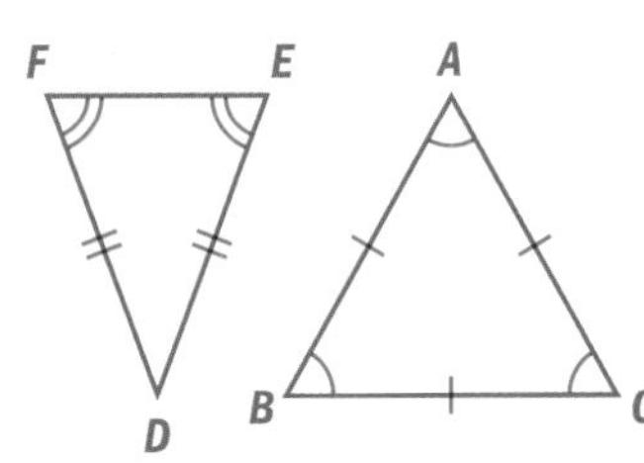

EXAMPLE 1 Classifying a Triangle

a. Classify $\triangle XYZ$ by its angles.

b. Classify $\triangle XYZ$ by its side lengths.

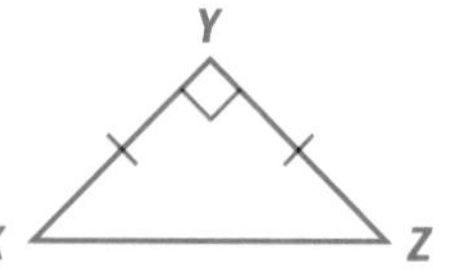

RIGHT TRIANGLES
Right triangles with two congruent sides can be called *isosceles right triangles.*

SOLUTION

a. The triangle has a right angle at Y. So, it is a right triangle.

b. The triangle has two sides of equal length. So, it is an isosceles triangle.

Angles in a Triangle From the diagram below you can see that the sum of the angle measures in the triangle is 180°. This is true for any triangle.

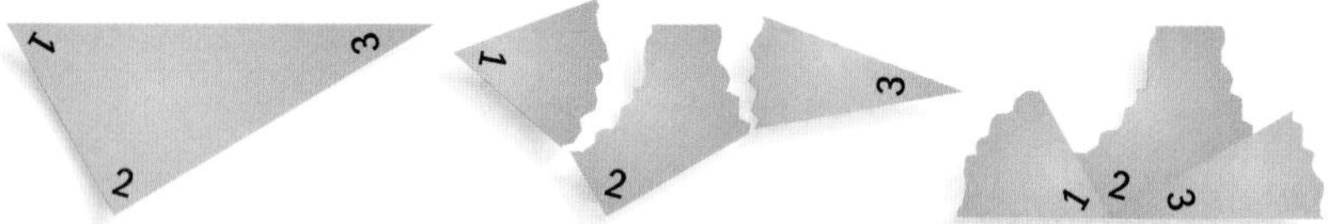

EXAMPLE 2 Finding an Unknown Angle Measure

Find the value of x. Then classify the triangle by its angles.

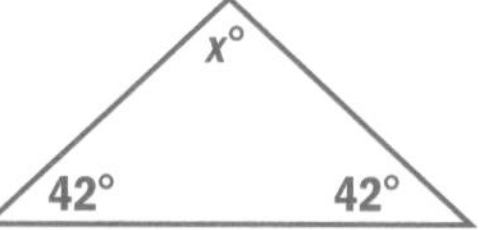

SOLUTION

The sum of the angle measures of a triangle is 180°.

$x° + 42° + 42° = 180°$	**Write an equation.**
$x + 84 = 180$	**Add.**
$x + 84 - 84 = 180 - 84$	**Subtract 84 from each side.**
$x = 96$	**Simplify.**

▶ **Answer** The value of x is 96. The triangle has one obtuse angle, so it is an obtuse triangle.

GUIDED PRACTICE for Examples 1 and 2

Classify the triangle by its side lengths.

1. 7 cm, 9 cm, 7 cm **2.** 11 ft, 11 ft, 11 ft **3.** 4 in., 5 in., 6 in.

4. 6 ft, 6 ft, 6 ft **5.** 10 mm, 10 mm, 8 mm **6.** 2 cm, 8 cm, 7 cm

7. Find the value of x. Then classify the triangle by its angles.

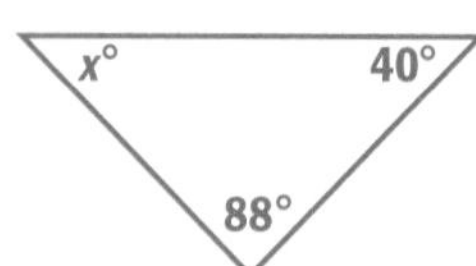

8.2 EXERCISES

HOMEWORK KEY

★ = **STANDARDIZED TEST PRACTICE**
Exs. 16, 30, 33, 34, and 44

○ = **HINTS AND HOMEWORK HELP**
for Exs. 5, 7, 11, 13, 29 at classzone.com

SKILL PRACTICE

VOCABULARY Copy and complete the statement.

1. A(n) _?_ triangle has no sides of equal length.

2. A(n) _?_ triangle has at least two sides of equal length.

VOCABULARY The referee is making calls during a hockey game. Classify the angle made by his arms as *acute, obtuse,* or *right.*

3. Cross checking

4. Roughing

5. Delayed calling of penalty

Animated Math at classzone.com

CLASSIFYING BY SIDES Classify the triangle by its side lengths.

SEE EXAMPLE 1 on p. 412 for Exs. 6–12

6. 4 in., 2 in., 3 in.

7.

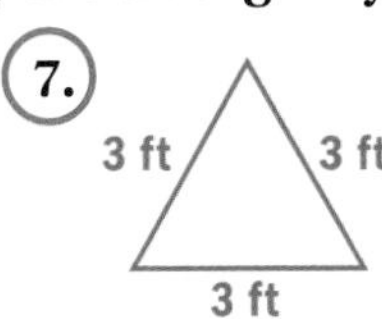

8.

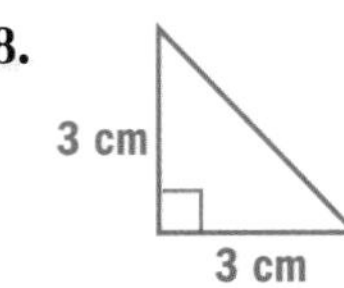

9.

10.

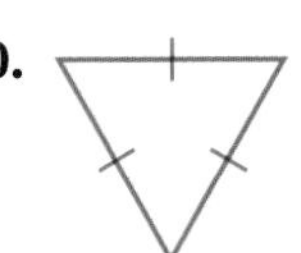

11.

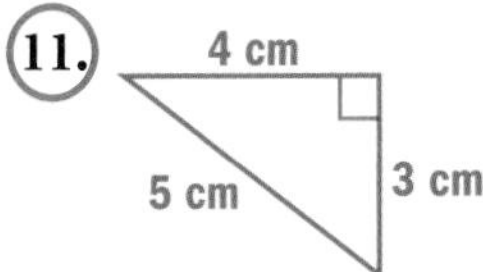

12. **ERROR ANALYSIS** Describe and correct the error made in the statement.

The triangle has an acute angle, so it is an acute triangle.

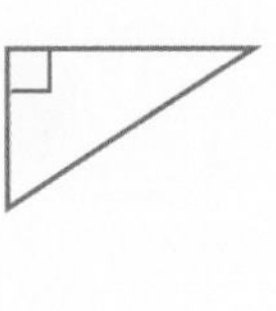

CLASSIFYING BY ANGLES Find the value of *x*. Classify the triangle by its angles.

SEE EXAMPLES 1 AND 2 on p. 412 for Exs. 13–15

13.

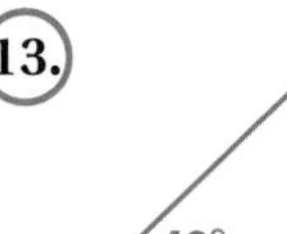

14.

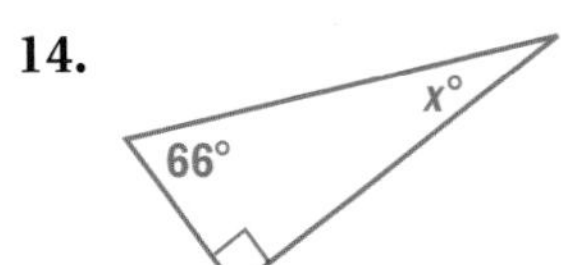

15.

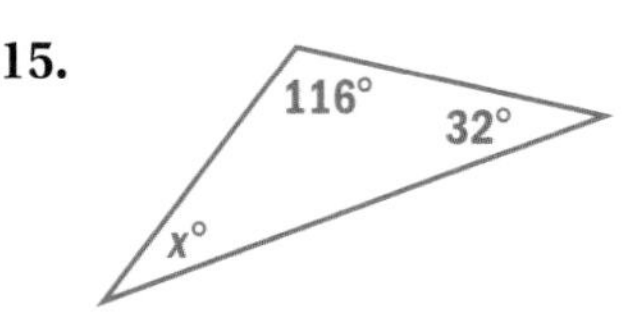

SEE EXAMPLE 2 on p. 412 for Ex. 16–19

16. ★ **MULTIPLE CHOICE** The angles of a triangle measure 110°, 40°, and x°. What is the value of x?

Ⓐ 30 Ⓑ 40 Ⓒ 50 Ⓓ 210

REASONING Can the angles of a triangle have the given measures? *Explain* your reasoning.

17. 43°, 48°, 90° **18.** 1.5°, 0.5°, 178° **19.** 21.3°, 56.7°, 102°

ISOSCELES TRIANGLES In an isosceles triangle, the angles opposite the sides with the same length have the same measure. Find the measure of the unknown angles of the triangle and classify it by its angles.

20.

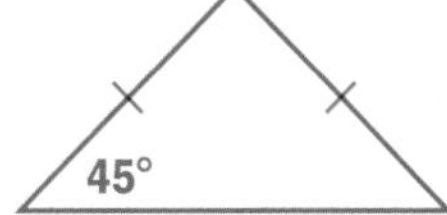

21.

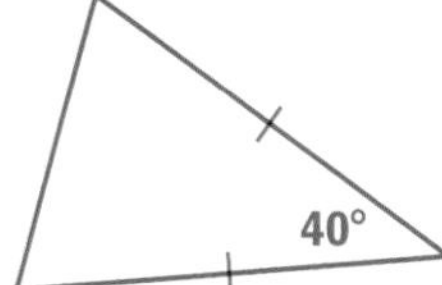

22.

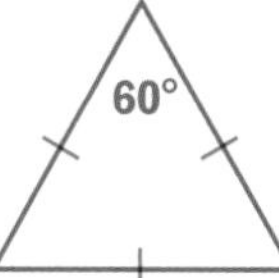

ALGEBRA Find the measure of each angle of the triangle.

23.

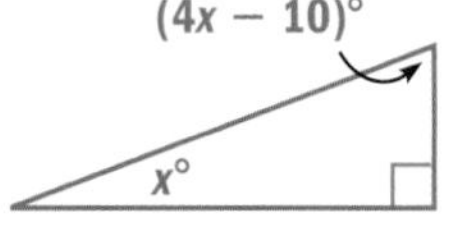

24.

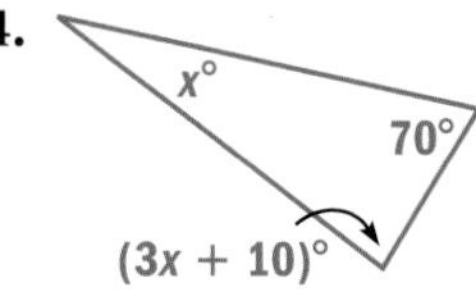

25.

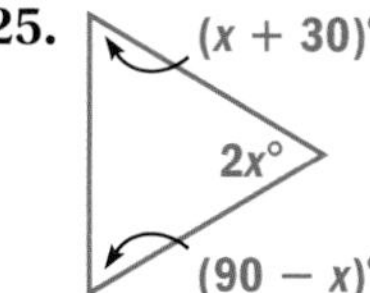

26. **USING PARALLEL LINES** Find the measures of the numbered angles.

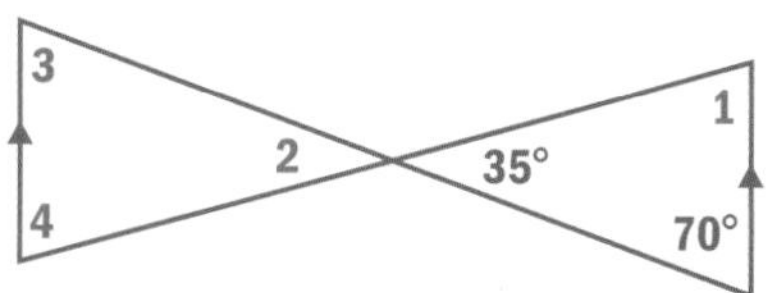

27. **CHALLENGE** Name all ten of the triangles in the figure and classify each triangle by its angles. Are there any triangles in the figure that are isosceles? If so, *explain* your reasoning and name the isosceles triangles.

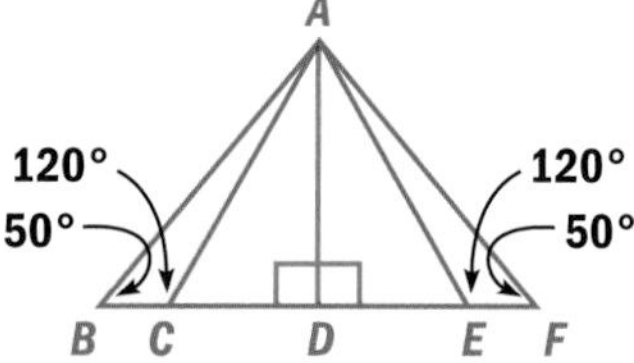

PROBLEM SOLVING

28. **ARCHITECTURE** The two side edges of the gable in the illustration at the right have the same length. What kind of triangle is formed? *Explain.*

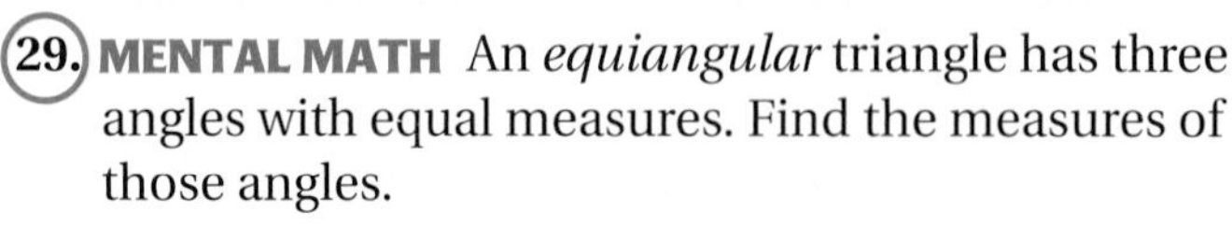

29. **MENTAL MATH** An *equiangular* triangle has three angles with equal measures. Find the measures of those angles.

30. ★ **WRITING** Can a right triangle be equilateral? *Explain* your reasoning.

31. **REASONING** Can two angles of a triangle be supplementary? *Explain.*

32. **TELESCOPE** The McMath-Pierce Solar Telescope is located at the Kitt Peak National Observatory near Tucson, Arizona. The telescope has a 100 foot tall tower and a 200 foot shaft that slants to the ground. Classify the triangle formed by the telescope and the ground by its sides and by its angles.

33. ★ **MULTIPLE CHOICE** The following statements about $\triangle ABC$ are true: $m\angle C$ is greater than $m\angle B$, $m\angle B$ is greater than $m\angle A$, and $m\angle A$ is greater than 40°. What are the angle measures of $\triangle ABC$?

Ⓐ $m\angle A = 48°$, $m\angle B = 78°$, $m\angle C = 54°$

Ⓑ $m\angle A = 36°$, $m\angle B = 54°$, $m\angle C = 90°$

Ⓒ $m\angle A = 60°$, $m\angle B = 60°$, $m\angle C = 60°$

Ⓓ $m\angle A = 48°$, $m\angle B = 54°$, $m\angle C = 78°$

34. ★ **SHORT RESPONSE** Try to draw each triangle whose side lengths are given at the right. Which triangles are possible to draw? *Explain* why the other triangle(s) cannot be drawn.

$\triangle ABC$	9 cm, 8 cm, 4 cm
$\triangle DEF$	9 cm, 6 cm, 4 cm
$\triangle GHI$	9 cm, 2 cm, 4 cm

REFLEX ANGLES An angle whose measure is greater than 180°, but less than 360°, is called a *reflex angle*. Two reflex angles are shown at the right. In Exercises 35–37, find the value of *x* and classify the angle.

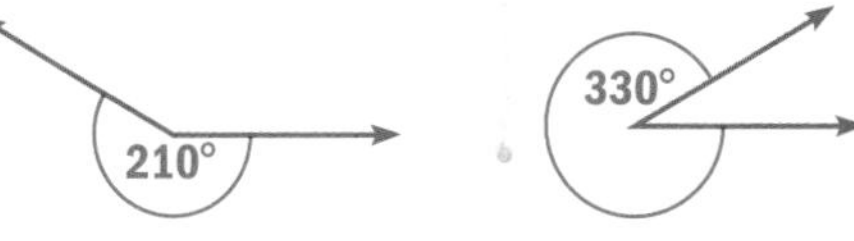

35.

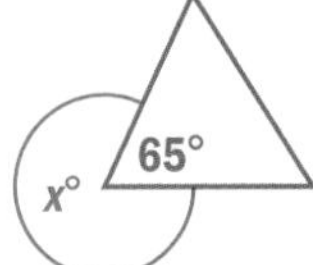

36.

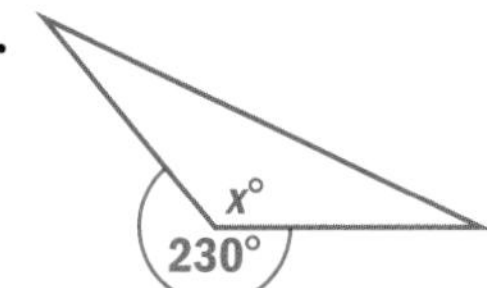

37.

38. **CHALLENGE** List all sets of three whole numbers that total 10 units, such as 3, 3, and 4. Which of these sets could be lengths of the sides of a triangle? How is the longest side in each of these sets related to the other two sides?

MIXED REVIEW

Prepare for Lesson 8.3 in Exs. 39–42

Find the unknown dimension of the rectangle. *(p. 32)*

39. Perimeter = 124 cm, $l = 48$ cm, $w =$ __?__

40. Area = 105 in.^{2}, $w = 7$ in., $l =$ __?__

41. Area = 216 m^2, $l = 24$ m, $w =$ __?__

42. Perimeter = 144 ft, $w = 16$ ft, $l =$ __?__

43. **GEOGRAPHY** Earth's surface is 29.2% land. The total surface area is 510,072,000 square kilometers. Find the total land area. *(p. 354)*

44. ★ **MULTIPLE CHOICE** A backpack is on sale for 20% off of \$20. The sales tax is 4%. What is the total cost of the backpack? *(p. 370)*

Ⓐ \$15.36 Ⓑ \$16.00 Ⓒ \$16.64 Ⓓ \$20.80

8.3 Quadrilaterals

Before	You classified angles and triangles.
Now	You'll classify quadrilaterals.
Why?	So you can find angles of quadrilaterals, as in a compass rose in Ex. 28.

KEY VOCABULARY
- **quadrilateral,** *p. 416*
- **trapezoid,** *p. 416*
- **parallelogram,** *p. 416*
- **rhombus,** *p. 416*

A **quadrilateral** is a closed figure with four sides that are line segments. The figures below are special types of quadrilaterals.

Special Quadrilaterals	*Diagram*
Trapezoid A **trapezoid** is a quadrilateral with exactly 1 pair of parallel sides.	
Parallelogram A **parallelogram** is a quadrilateral with two pairs of parallel sides.	
Rhombus A **rhombus** is a parallelogram with 4 sides of equal length.	
Rectangle A *rectangle* is a parallelogram with 4 right angles.	
Square A *square* is a parallelogram with 4 sides of equal length and 4 right angles.	

EXAMPLE 1 Classifying a Quadrilateral

TAKE NOTES
You can organize the definitions of quadrilaterals in your notebook using a concept map.

Classify the quadrilateral.

a. 5 cm, 5 cm, 5 cm, 5 cm

The quadrilateral is a parallelogram with 4 sides of equal length. So, it is a rhombus.

b.

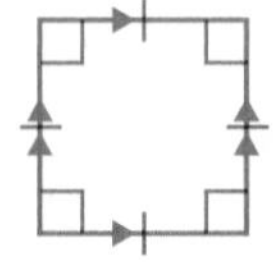

The quadrilateral is a parallelogram with 4 sides of equal length and 4 right angles. So, it is a square.

Angles in a Quadrilateral A *diagonal* is a segment that joins two vertices of a quadrilateral but is not a side. You can use a diagonal of a quadrilateral to show that the sum of the angle measures in a quadrilateral is 360°.

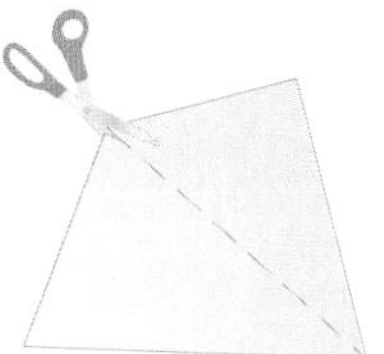

Cut a quadrilateral along a diagonal to form two triangles.

The sum of the angle measures in each triangle is 180°.

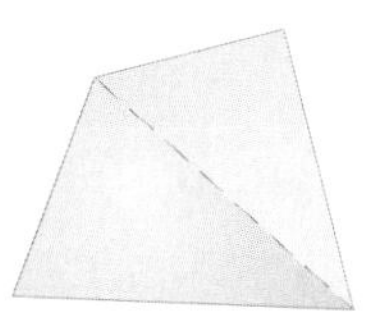

The sum of the angle measures in a quadrilateral is 180° + 180° = 360°.

EXAMPLE 2 Finding an Unknown Angle Measure

Find the value of x.

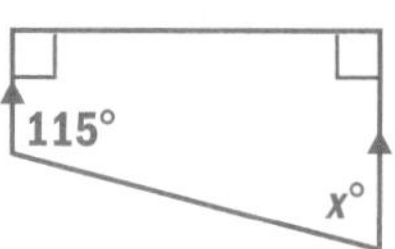

SOLUTION

$x° + 51° + 129° + 129° = 360°$ — The sum of the angle measures is 360°.

$x + 309 = 360$ — Add.

$x = 51$ — Subtract 309 from each side.

✓ GUIDED PRACTICE for Examples 1 and 2

Use the figure at the right.

1. Classify the quadrilateral.
2. Find the value of x.

8.3 EXERCISES

HOMEWORK KEY

★ = **STANDARDIZED TEST PRACTICE** Exs. 16, 29, 30, and 38

◯ = **HINTS AND HOMEWORK HELP** for Exs. 3, 7, 9, 13, 27 at classzone.com

SKILL PRACTICE

VOCABULARY Copy and complete the statement.

1. A quadrilateral with exactly 1 pair of parallel sides is a __?__.
2. A parallelogram with 4 right angles is a __?__.

CLASSIFYING QUADRILATERALS Classify the quadrilateral.

SEE EXAMPLE 1 on p. 416 for Exs. 3–5

3.

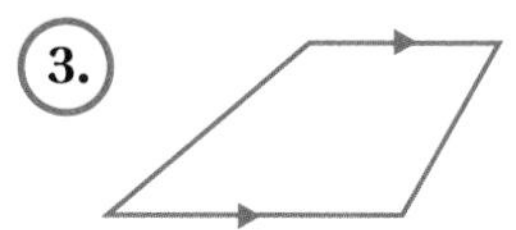

4.

5.

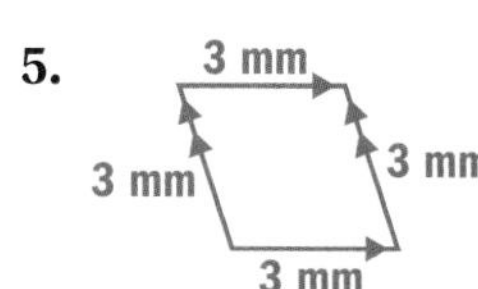

MEASUREMENT **Measure the side lengths. Then classify the quadrilateral.**

SEE EXAMPLE 1 on p. 416 for Exs. 6–8

6.

7. 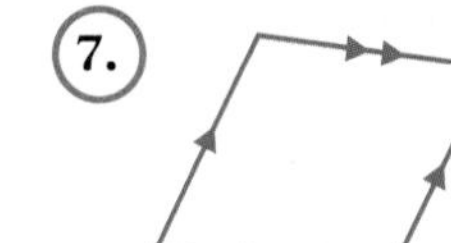

8. 

ALGEBRA **Find the values of x and y.**

SEE EXAMPLE 2 on p. 417 for Exs. 9–14

9. 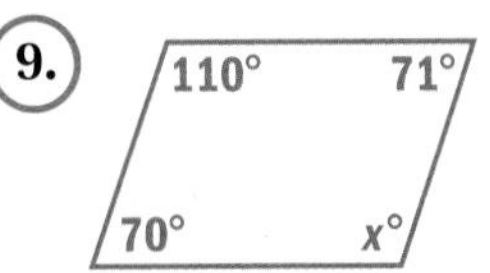

10.

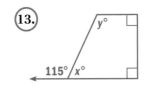

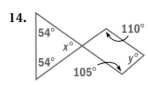

11.

12. 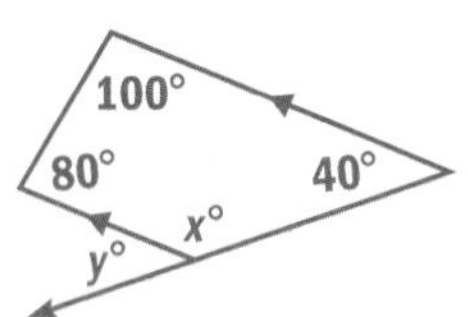

13.

14.

15. **ERROR ANALYSIS** Describe and correct the error made in listing the diagonals of parallelogram $ABCD$.

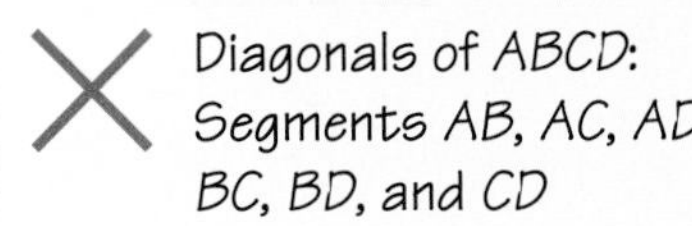
Diagonals of ABCD:
Segments AB, AC, AD,
BC, BD, and CD

16. ★ **MULTIPLE CHOICE** Classify the fourth angle of a quadrilateral that has three acute angles.

Ⓐ Acute Ⓑ Right Ⓒ Obtuse Ⓓ Straight

ALGEBRA **Find the value of x and the unknown angle measures.**

17. 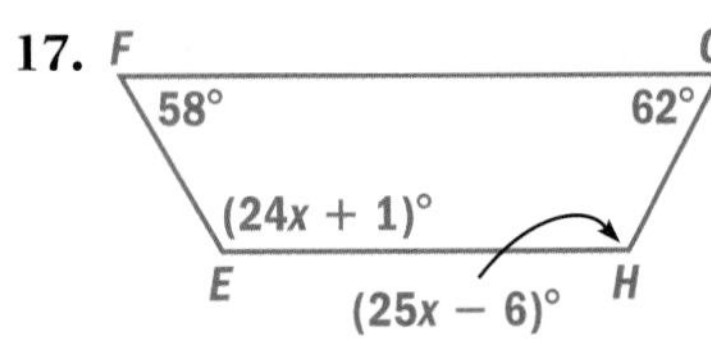

18. 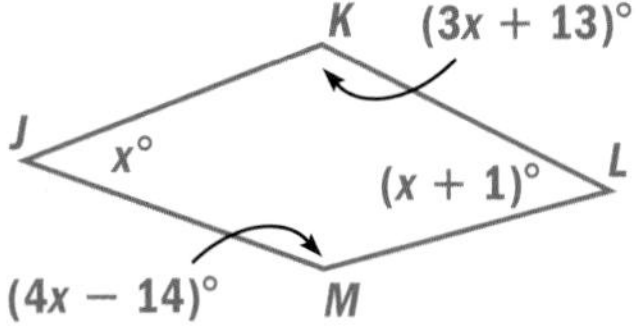

REASONING **Tell whether the statement is *always, sometimes,* or *never* true. *Justify* your reasoning.**

19. A rhombus is a parallelogram.

20. A rectangle is a square.

21. A square is a parallelogram.

22. A triangle is a quadrilateral.

23. A trapezoid is a parallelogram.

24. A quadrilateral is a rectangle.

Animated Math at classzone.com

25. **CHALLENGE** Find the values of x, y, and z in the diagram. *Explain* your reasoning.

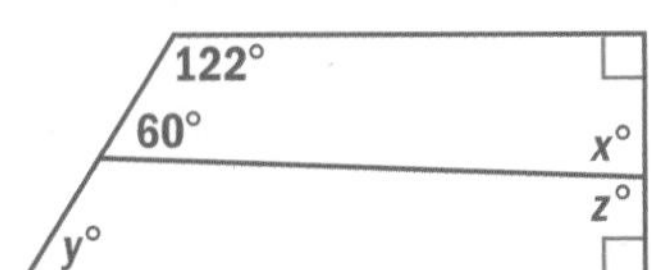

PROBLEM SOLVING

SEE EXAMPLE 1 on p. 416 for Ex. 26

26. DESIGN Classify the quadrilaterals of each color in the design below.

27. REASONING How many different diagonals can be drawn in any quadrilateral? *Justify* your answer by sketching each quadrilateral discussed on page 416 and all of its diagonals.

SEE EXAMPLE 2 on p. 417 for Ex. 28

28. COMPASS ROSE A compass rose is a figure used on a map to show direction. The compass rose shown includes four red rhombuses. Find the value of x and the unknown angle measures.

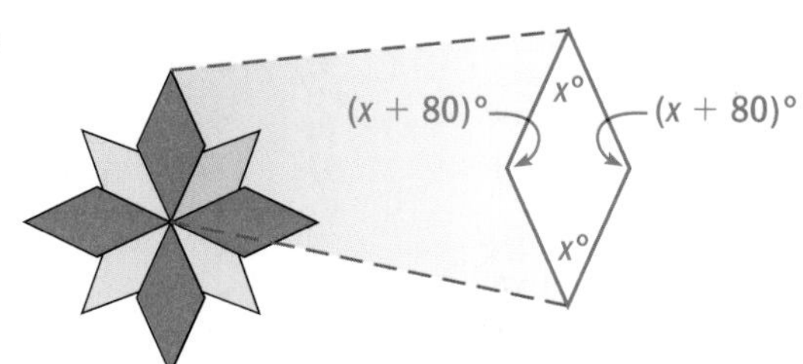

29. ★ SHORT RESPONSE Two equilateral triangles share a common side. Which quadrilateral does the figure form? *Explain.*

30. ★ WRITING What is the greatest number of obtuse angles that a quadrilateral can have? *Explain* your reasoning.

31. REASONING Is it possible for a quadrilateral to have three 60° angles? *Explain* why or why not.

32. CHALLENGE Use the figure at the right.

a. A trapezoid is divided into four quadrilaterals, as shown. Classify the quadrilaterals. Then find the measure of each labeled angle. *Explain* your reasoning.

b. *Describe* the relationship between opposite angles in a parallelogram and between consecutive angles. *Justify* your reasoning.

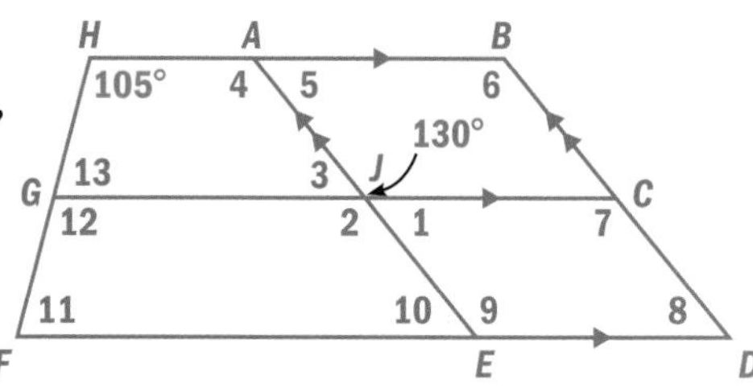

MIXED REVIEW

Get-Ready

Prepare for Lesson 8.4 in Exs. 33–36

A triangle has two angles with the given measures. Find the measure of the third angle. ***(p. 411)***

33. 17°, 92° **34.** 26°, 34° **35.** 61°, 68° **36.** 72°, 81°

37. What number is 430% of 130? ***(p. 375)***

38. ★ MULTIPLE CHOICE What is the measure of an angle complementary to a 40° angle? ***(p. 403)***

Ⓐ 40° Ⓑ 50° Ⓒ 60° Ⓓ 140°

8.4 Polygons and Angles

Before You found angle measures in triangles and quadrilaterals.
Now You'll find angle measures in polygons.
Why? So you can classify polygons in nature, as in Ex. 27.

KEY VOCABULARY
- **polygon,** *p. 420*
- **regular polygon,** *p. 420*
- **pentagon,** *p. 420*
- **hexagon,** *p. 420*
- **heptagon,** *p. 420*
- **octagon,** *p. 420*

ACTIVITY

You can use triangles to find the sum of the angle measures in other figures.

STEP 1 **Copy** the table. Divide each figure into triangles by drawing all the diagonal lines that begin at the point marked.

STEP 2 **Use** your drawings to complete the table.

Shape	*Quadrilateral*	*Pentagon*	*Hexagon*	*Heptagon*	*Octagon*
Number of Sides	4	?	?	?	?
Number of Diagonal Lines	1	?	?	?	?
Number of Triangles Formed	2	?	?	?	?
Sum of Angle Measures	360°	?	?	?	?

STEP 3 **Use** your results to complete a column for a 10-sided figure.

Polygons A **polygon** is a closed figure whose sides are line segments that intersect only at their endpoints. In a **regular polygon**, all the angles have the same measure and all the sides have the same length. Polygons can be identified by the number of their sides as shown in the table in the Activity.

READING
You can use "*n*-gon," where *n* is the number of sides, to identify a polygon if you haven't learned its name. A 13-gon is a 13-sided polygon.

Polygons

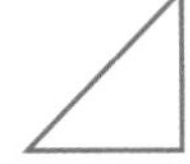

Regular polygons

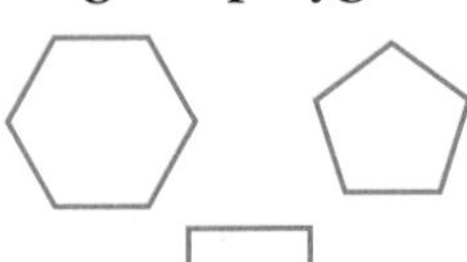

Not polygons

EXAMPLE 1 Identifying Figures

Is the bottom of the box a *polygon*, a *regular polygon*, or *not a polygon*? Explain.

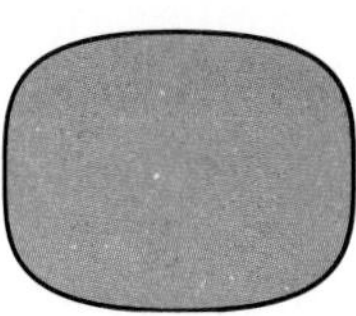

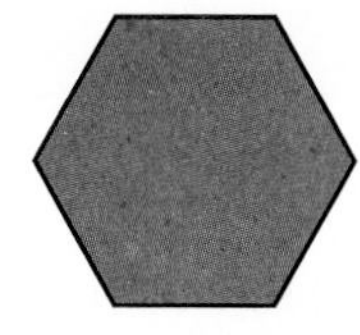

a. It is not a polygon. The bottom edge does not have line segments.

b. It is a regular polygon. Its angles have equal measures, and its sides have equal lengths.

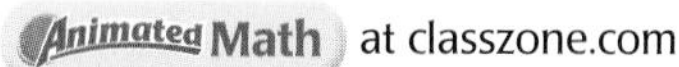

Animated Math at classzone.com

Angles In the activity on page 420, you used triangles to find the sum of the angle measures in polygons. In a regular polygon, the measure of one angle is the sum of the angle measures divided by the number of sides.

KEY CONCEPT *For Your Notebook*

Angle Measures in a Polygon

Sum of angle measures in an n-gon: $(n - 2) \cdot 180°$

Measure of one angle in a *regular* n-gon: $\dfrac{(n - 2) \cdot 180°}{n}$

EXAMPLE 2 Finding an Angle Measure

Find the measure of one angle in a regular octagon.

A regular octagon has 8 sides, so $n = 8$.

$$\frac{(n-2) \cdot 180°}{n} = \frac{(8-2) \cdot 180°}{8}$$ **Substitute 8 for *n*.**

$$= \frac{1080°}{8}$$ **Simplify numerator.**

$$= 135°$$ **Divide.**

▶ **Answer** The measure of one angle in a regular octagon is 135°.

✓ **GUIDED PRACTICE** for Examples 1 and 2

1. Find the sum of the angle measures in a 9-gon.
2. Find the measure of one angle in a regular heptagon. Round to the nearest tenth of a degree.

8.4 EXERCISES

HOMEWORK KEY

★ = **STANDARDIZED TEST PRACTICE**
Exs. 14, 28, 30, 31, 32, and 49

○ = **HINTS AND HOMEWORK HELP**
for Exs. 3, 7, 13, 25 at classzone.com

SKILL PRACTICE

VOCABULARY Copy and complete the statement.

1. A __?__ is a closed figure with sides that are line segments that intersect only at their endpoints.

2. A __?__ is a closed figure with sides that are line segments of equal length meeting only at their endpoints, and with all angles of equal measure.

SEE EXAMPLE 1 on p. 421 for Exs. 3–5

CLASSIFYING FIGURES Tell whether the figure is a *polygon*, a *regular polygon*, or *not a polygon*.

3. 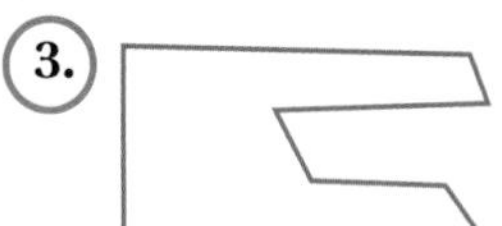

4. 

5. 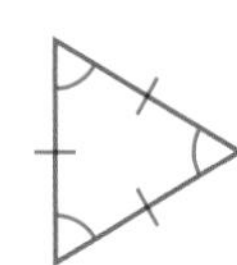

SEE EXAMPLE 2 on p. 421 for Exs. 6–14

FINDING ANGLE MEASURES Find the sum of the angle measures in the polygon.

6. 12-gon
7. 16-gon
8. 11-gon
9. 20-gon

10. **ERROR ANALYSIS** Describe and correct the error made in finding the sum of the angle measures of a hexagon.

> Sum of angle measures = 6 • 180° = 1080° ✗

FINDING AN ANGLE MEASURE Find the measure of one angle in the polygon. Round to the nearest degree if necessary.

11. Regular 10-gon
12. Regular 14-gon
13. Regular 15-gon

14. ★ **MULTIPLE CHOICE** Four angles in a pentagon measure 90°, 85°, 120°, and 130°. What is the measure of the fifth angle?

Ⓐ 105° Ⓑ 115° Ⓒ 120° Ⓓ 165°

ALGEBRA Find the value of x and the unknown angle measures.

15. 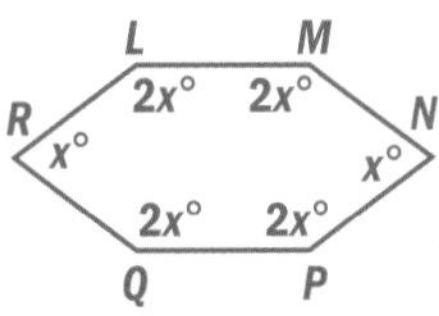

16. 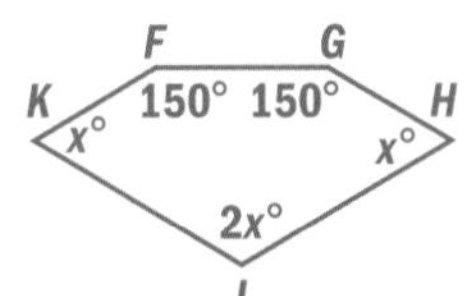

17. 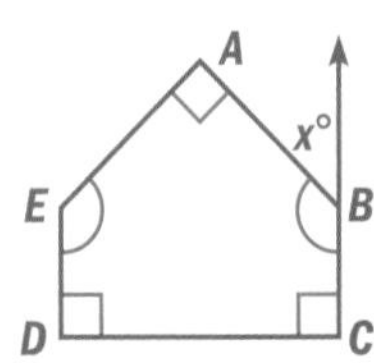

18. **WHICH ONE DOESN'T BELONG?** Which of the following is not a regular polygon?

A. 107° 107° 107°

B. 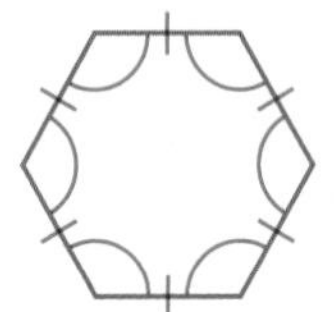

C. 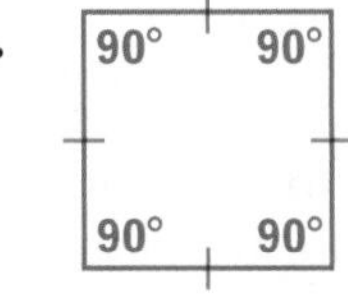

D. 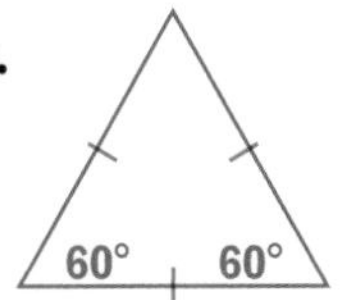

IDENTIFYING POLYGONS Find the type of n-gon whose angle measures have the given sum.

19. 1980° **20.** 2520° **21.** 2880° **22.** 3600°

23. CHALLENGE The measures of the angles of a regular polygon are whole numbers. What is the greatest number of sides that the polygon can have? *Explain.*

PROBLEM SOLVING

SWIMMING POOL DESIGNS Tell whether the swimming pool design is a polygon. *Justify* your reasoning.

24. 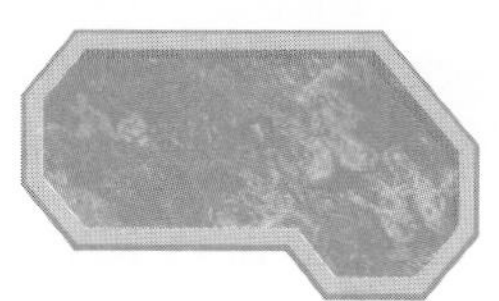

25. 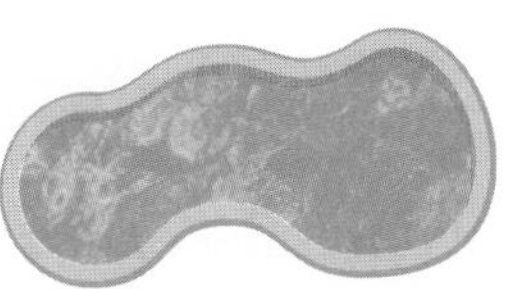

26. 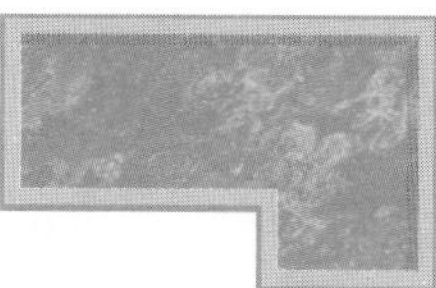

27. GEOLOGY Classify the polygons shown in the photograph of the rock formation in Yellowstone National Park at the top of page 420.

28. ★ MULTIPLE CHOICE A table has 7 sides of equal length and 7 angles of equal measure. What is the measure of one angle of the table?

(A) 25.7° (B) 128.6° (C) 210.0° (D) 252.0°

29. MAKE A MODEL You want to cut a 10-gon out of a piece of paper. You are told to first draw a pentagon on the paper and cut it out. *Explain* how you can cut your pentagon to create a 10-gon. Then follow your procedure to create a 10-gon.

30. ★ OPEN-ENDED MATH Sketch a polygon that is not regular, but has sides of equal length.

31. ★ SHORT RESPONSE Is a figure eight a polygon? Give two reasons to justify your answer.

32. ★ EXTENDED RESPONSE The angles marked with letters in the figures below are called *exterior angles.*

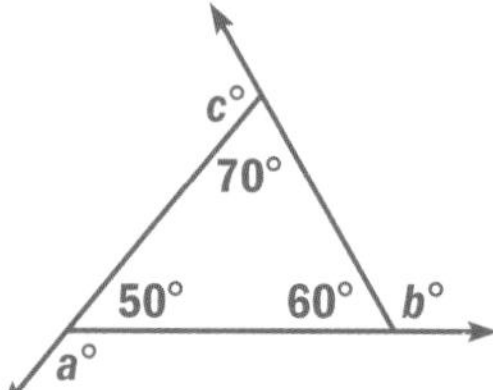

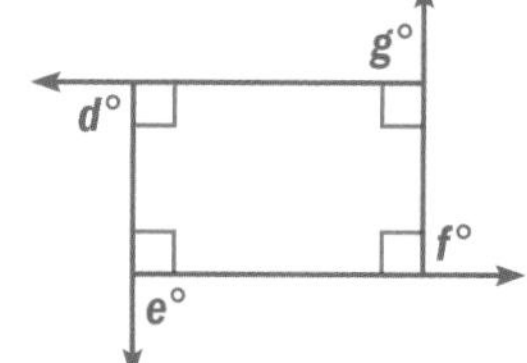

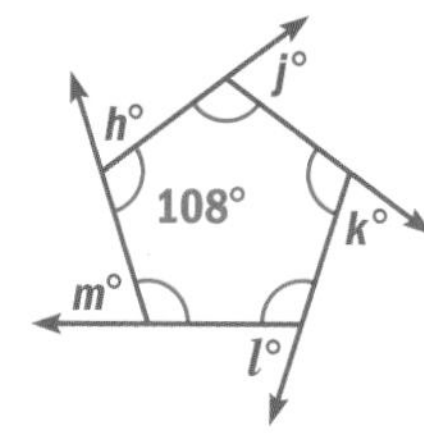

a. **Evaluate** Find the measures of the exterior angles of each polygon.

b. **Calculate** Find the sum of the exterior angle measures for each polygon.

c. **Patterns** Describe a pattern in the sums you found in part (b).

33. **MAKE A CONJECTURE** Draw all diagonals of a quadrilateral, a pentagon, and a hexagon. Write the numbers of diagonals as a pattern. *Predict* the next number in the pattern. Draw a heptagon and check your predictions.

34. **BASES** You want to design a new base marker for a new type of baseball game. Is it possible to make a base marker that is a regular polygon with each angle having a measure of 135°? of 145°? *Explain.*

35. **CHALLENGE** In a regular polygon, the measure of each exterior angle, as described in Exercise 32, is 25% of the measure of each interior angle. Name this polygon.

36. **CHALLENGE** The sum of a polygon's angle measures is 15 times the measure of the exterior angle of a regular pentagon. Identify the polygon.

MIXED REVIEW

Get-Ready
Prepare for Lesson 8.5 in Exs. 37–40

The measures of three angles of a quadrilateral are given. Find the measure of the fourth angle. *(p. 416)*

37. 90°, 90°, and 90° 38. 87°, 93°, and 87° 39. 39°, 141°, and 13° 40. 90°, 80°, and 90°

Write the percent as a fraction or mixed number in simplest form. *(p. 359)*

41. 98% 42. 141.3% 43. 0.14% 44. 7.6%

45. 0.45% 46. 18.2% 47. 0.98% 48. 156%

49. ★ **MULTIPLE CHOICE** The wholesale price of a pair of shoes is \$12.50. The retail price of the shoes is \$25.70. What is the percent markup? *(p. 370)*

(A) 48.6% (B) 51.4% (C) 105.6% (D) 205.6%

QUIZ *for Lessons 8.1–8.4*

Tell whether the angles are *complementary, supplementary,* or *neither.* *(p. 403)*

1. $m\angle 1 = 32°, m\angle 2 = 148°$ 2. $m\angle 3 = 59°, m\angle 4 = 41°$ 3. $m\angle 5 = 12°, m\angle 6 = 78°$

4. $m\angle 7 = 116°, m\angle 8 = 64°$ 5. $m\angle A = 73°, m\angle B = 117°$ 6. $m\angle C = 48°, m\angle D = 42°$

Can the angles in a triangle have the measures given? *Explain* why or why not. If so, classify the triangle. *(p. 411)*

7. 23°, 57°, 95° 8. 64.6°, 77.3°, 38.1° 9. 155°, 24.9°, 0.1°

Find the value of *x*.

10. 

(p. 416)

11. 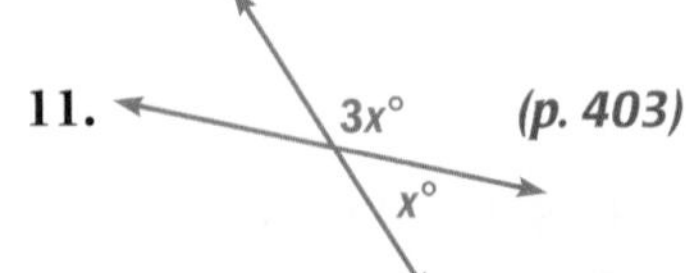

(p. 403)

12. 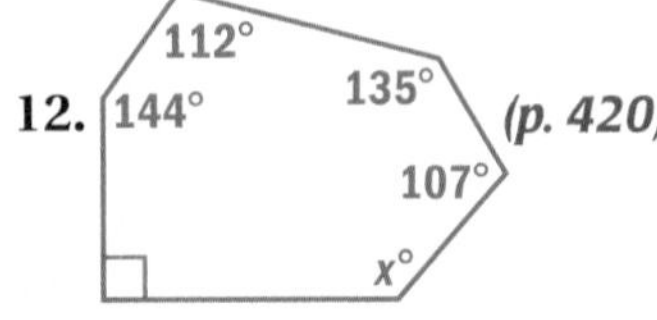

(p. 420)

13. Classify the figures in Exercises 10 and 12. *(pp. 416, 420)*

MIXED REVIEW of Problem Solving

Lessons 8.1–8.4

1. **MULTI-STEP PROBLEM** Use the figure to answer the questions.

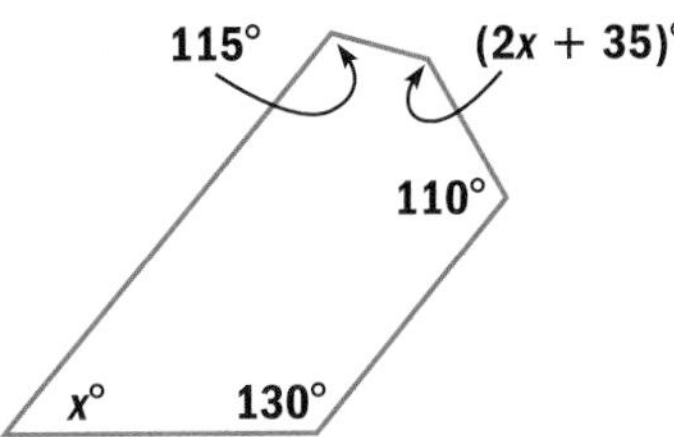

   a. Identify the polygon.
   b. Find the sum of the angle measures in the polygon.
   c. Find the unknown angle measures.
   d. Is the polygon regular? Why or why not?

2. **GRIDDED ANSWER** A regular octagon is divided into two polygons by drawing a segment connecting the midpoints of two opposite sides. In each polygon, what is the sum of the angle measures in degrees?

3. **SHORT RESPONSE** The flag of the Bahamas is shown below.

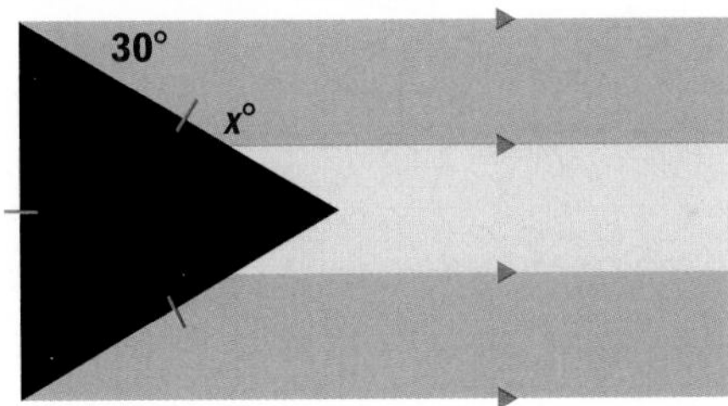

   a. Classify the black, blue, and yellow polygons.
   b. *Describe* two ways to find the value of x.

4. **SHORT RESPONSE** Find the value of x. *Explain* your method.

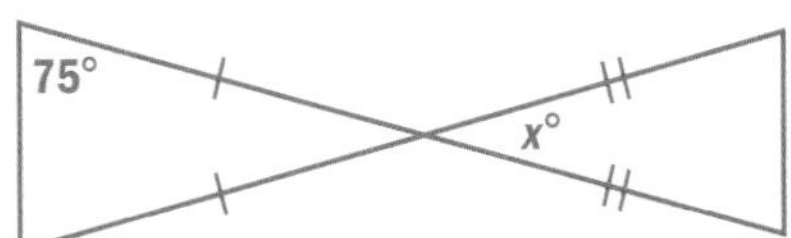

5. **OPEN-ENDED** Draw a polygon that has two sets of parallel sides but is *not* a parallelogram.

6. **OPEN-ENDED** Write one sentence about a rhombus that is always true and one sentence about a rhombus that is sometimes true.

7. **EXTENDED RESPONSE** A pair of scissors forms four angles.

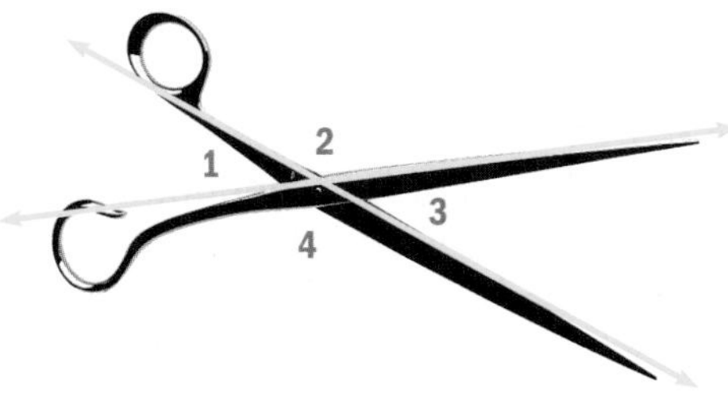

   a. List two pairs of supplementary angles and two pairs of vertical angles.
   b. Find $m\angle 3$ if $m\angle 1$ is 20°.
   c. Find $m\angle 4$ if $m\angle 3$ is 30°.
   d. What happens to each of the angles as you close the handles of the scissors? *Explain.*

8. **GRIDDED ANSWER** Vida is driving south on Kendell Road when she makes a 35° left turn. After a while, she turns left onto Linden Road, which runs parallel to Kendell Road. What is the measure, in degrees, of Vida's left turn?

9. **GRIDDED ANSWER** The arrow in the highway sign below is composed of an isosceles triangle and a rectangle. Find the sum, in degrees, of the measures of the angles of the polygon formed by these two shapes.

INVESTIGATION

Use before Lesson 8.5

GOAL
Copy a triangle.

MATERIALS
- compass
- straightedge
- protractor

8.5 Copying a Triangle

You can use a compass and a straightedge to copy a triangle.

EXPLORE **Use a compass and straightedge to copy a triangle.**

STEP 1 **Draw** a triangle with vertices *A*, *B*, and *C*. Draw a ray with endpoint *P*. Draw an arc with center *A* through point *C*. Use the same compass setting to draw an arc with center *P*. Label point *Q*.

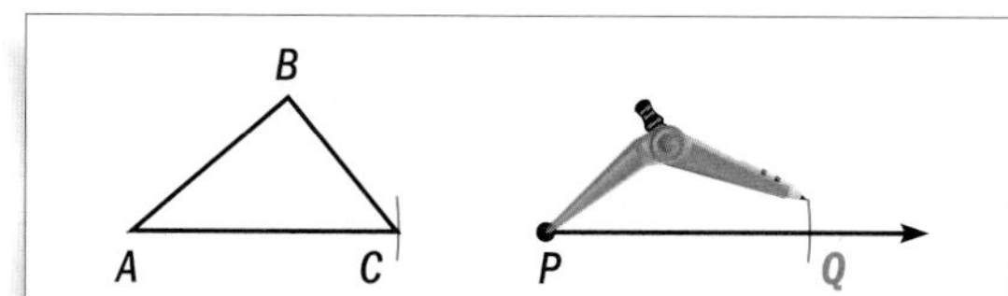

STEP 2 **Draw** an arc with center *C* through point *B*. Use the same compass setting to draw an arc with center *Q*.

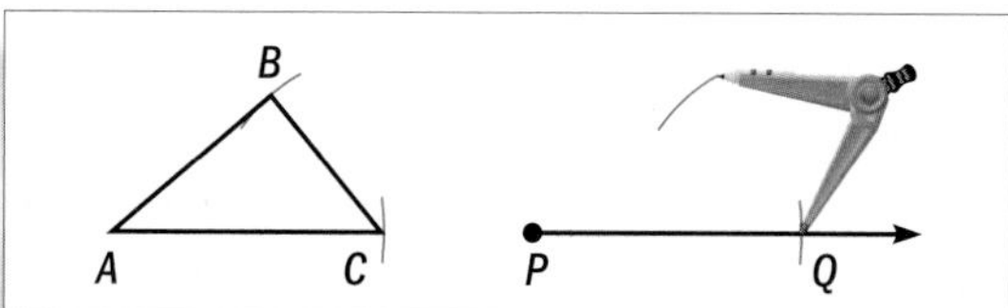

STEP 3 **Draw** an arc with center *A* through point *B*. Use the same compass setting to draw an arc with center *P*. Label point *R*. Connect *P* and *R*. Connect *R* and *Q*.

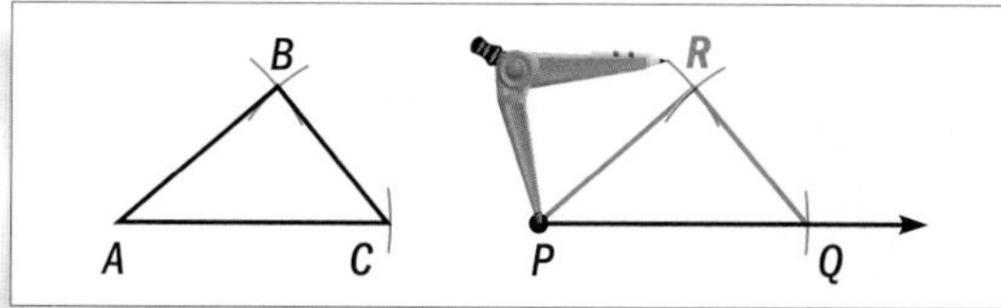

PRACTICE **Draw a triangle that fits the description. Then use a compass and straightedge to copy the triangle.**

1. acute

2. obtuse

3. right

DRAW CONCLUSIONS

4. REASONING Measure the angles of each triangle you drew in Exercises 1–3. Then measure the angles of the triangles you copied. What do you notice? *Explain.*

5. WRITING Suppose you use a compass and straightedge to copy a triangle. What angle measures of the new triangle are identical to the original triangle?

8.5 Congruent Polygons

Before You identified polygons.
Now You'll identify and name congruent polygons.
Why? So you can identify congruent triangles, as in Example 3.

KEY VOCABULARY
- **congruent segments,** *p. 427*
- **congruent angles,** *p. 427*
- **corresponding parts,** *p. 427*

Congruent segments have equal lengths. **Congruent angles** have equal measures. The symbol $\cong$ means "is congruent to."

Congruent polygons have the same shape and size. Polygons are congruent if their *corresponding* angles and sides are congruent. **Corresponding parts** are in the same position in different figures. To name congruent polygons, list their corresponding vertices in the same order. In the diagram $\triangle KLM \cong \triangle PQR$.

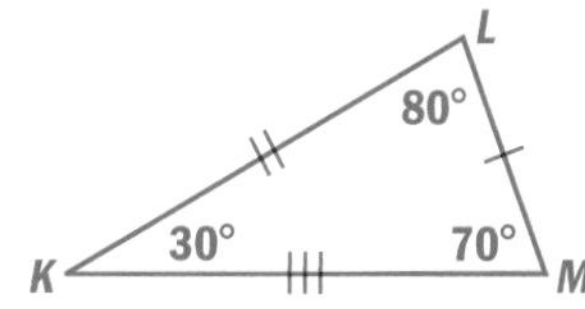

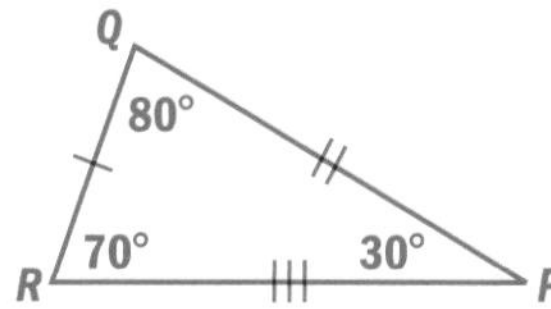

READING
Two letters with a line over them refer to a *line segment*. For example, $\overline{PR}$ is read "segment *PR*" and means "the side with endpoints *P* and *R*."

Corresponding angles are congruent.

$\angle K \cong \angle P$ $\qquad \angle L \cong \angle Q$ $\qquad \angle M \cong \angle R$

Corresponding sides are congruent.

$\overline{LM} \cong \overline{QR}$ $\qquad \overline{KL} \cong \overline{PQ}$ $\qquad \overline{KM} \cong \overline{PR}$

EXAMPLE 1 Name Corresponding Parts

Picture Frames In the frame below, quadrilateral $ABCD \cong$ quadrilateral $JKLM$. Name all pairs of corresponding angles and sides.

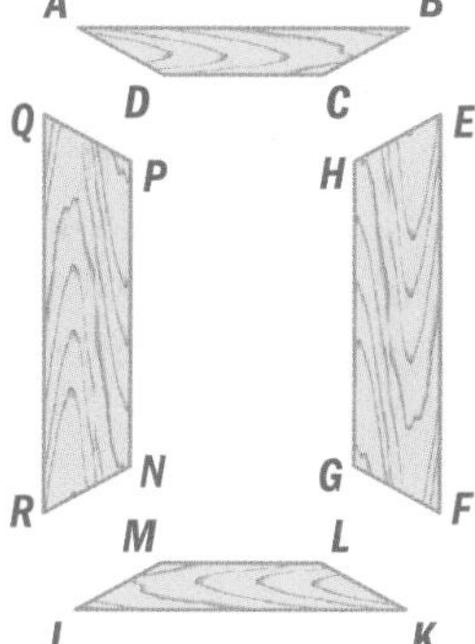

SOLUTION

Corresponding angles are congruent.

$\angle A, \angle J$ $\qquad \angle B, \angle K$

$\angle C, \angle L$ $\qquad \angle D, \angle M$

Corresponding sides are congruent.

$\overline{AB}, \overline{JK}$ $\qquad \overline{BC}, \overline{KL}$

$\overline{CD}, \overline{LM}$ $\qquad \overline{AD}, \overline{JM}$

GUIDED PRACTICE for Example 1

1. In Example 1, quadrilateral $EFGH \cong$ quadrilateral $QRNP$. Name all pairs of corresponding angles and sides.

EXAMPLE 2 Using Congruent Polygons

 **$\triangle JKL \cong \triangle TSR$. Find $m\angle S$.**

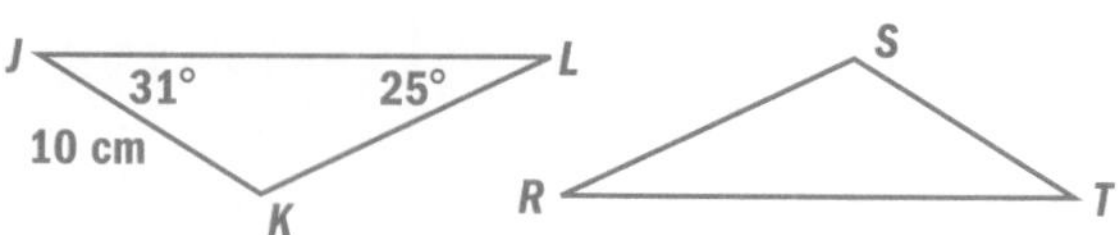

SOLUTION

Corresponding angles are congruent.

$\angle K$ and $\angle S$ are corresponding angles, so they have the same measure. Find $m\angle K$.

$31° + m\angle K + 25° = 180°$	**Sum of angle measures is 180°.**
$m\angle K + 56° = 180°$	**Add.**
$m\angle K + 56 - 56 = 180 - 56$	**Subtract 56 from each side.**
$m\angle K = 124°$	**Simplify.**

▸ **Answer** Because $m\angle K = m\angle S$, $m\angle S = 124°$.

Congruent Triangles You can use the special rules below in the chart to tell whether triangles are congruent.

READING
The angle between two sides is sometimes called the *included* angle. The side between two angles is sometimes called the *included* side.

Determining Whether Triangles Are Congruent

Side-Side-Side (SSS)

If three sides of one triangle are congruent to three sides of another triangle, then the triangles are congruent.

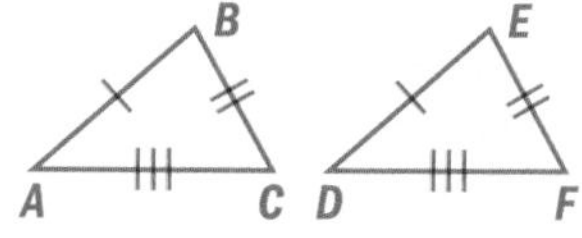

$\triangle ABC \cong \triangle DEF$

Side-Angle-Side (SAS)

If two sides and the angle between them in one triangle are congruent to two sides and the angle between them in another triangle, then the triangles are congruent.

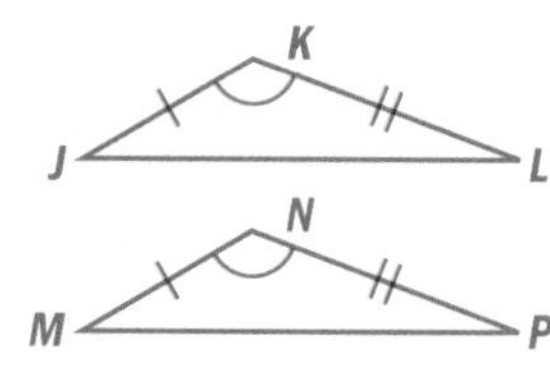

$\triangle JKL \cong \triangle MNP$

Angle-Side-Angle (ASA)

If two angles and the side between them in one triangle are congruent to two angles and the side between them in another triangle, then the triangles are congruent.

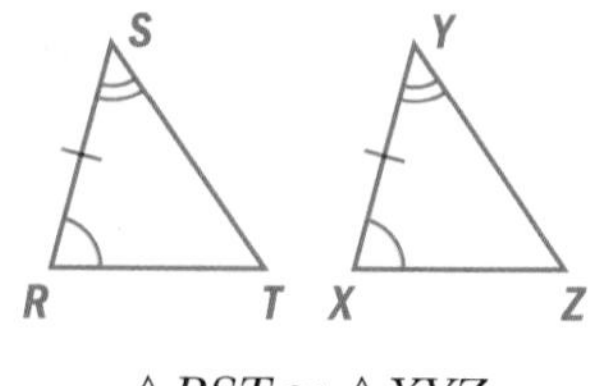

$\triangle RST \cong \triangle XYZ$

 **GUIDED PRACTICE** for Example 2

Find the value using the triangles in Example 2.

2. length of $\overline{ST}$ **3.** $m\angle T$ **4.** $m\angle R$

EXAMPLE 3 Identifying Congruent Triangles

Bridges Name the congruent triangles formed by the bridge cables. Explain how you know they are congruent.

SOLUTION

Identify congruent corresponding parts.

$\overline{CB} \cong \overline{CD}$	**Sides are congruent.**
$\overline{AC} \cong \overline{AC}$	**Side is congruent to itself.**
$\angle ACB \cong \angle ACD$	**Right angles are congruent.**

▶ **Answer** $\triangle ACB \cong \triangle ACD$ by Side-Angle-Side.

✓ GUIDED PRACTICE for Example 3

Determine whether the triangles are congruent.

5.

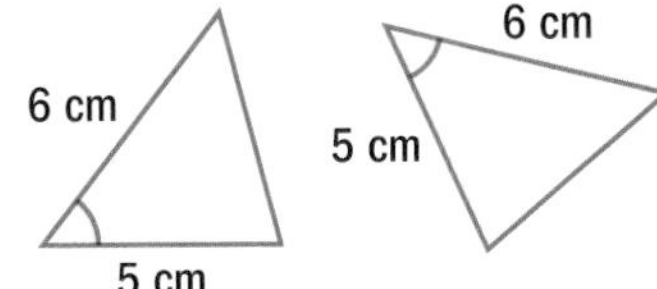

6.

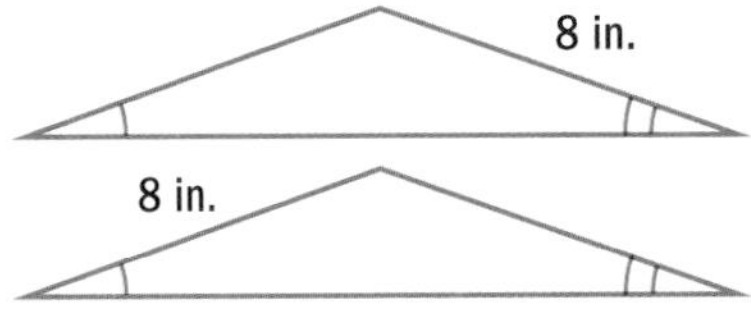

8.5 EXERCISES

HOMEWORK KEY

★ = **STANDARDIZED TEST PRACTICE** Exs. 13, 22, 24, 25, 26, and 41

○ = **HINTS AND HOMEWORK HELP** for Exs. 3, 5, 7, 11, 19 at classzone.com

SKILL PRACTICE

VOCABULARY Copy and complete the statement.

1. Two angles with the same measure are _?_.
2. Sides and angles that are in the same position in different figures are called _?_.

USING CONGRUENT POLYGONS In the diagram, quadrilateral *KLMN* ≅ quadrilateral *SPQR*.

SEE EXAMPLES 1 AND 2 on pp. 427–428 for Exs. 3–6

3. Name four pairs of congruent angles.
4. Find $m\angle S$.
5. Find the length of $\overline{NK}$.
6. Find $m\angle R$.

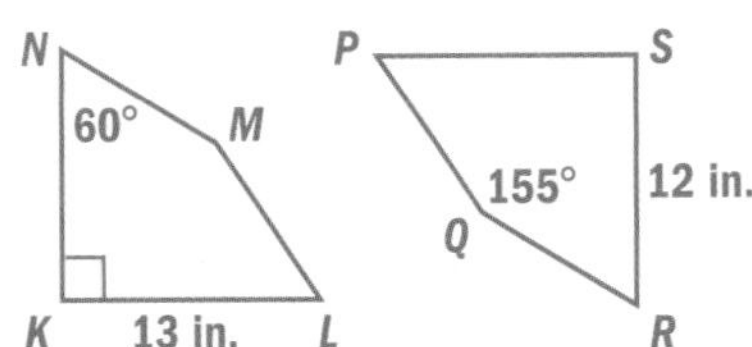

MEASUREMENT Quadrilateral $ABEF \cong$ quadrilateral $DGHC$. Find the unknown measure.

SEE EXAMPLE 2 on p. 428 for Exs. 7–10

7. $m\angle C$

8. length of $\overline{AF}$

9. $m\angle A$

10. length of $\overline{HC}$

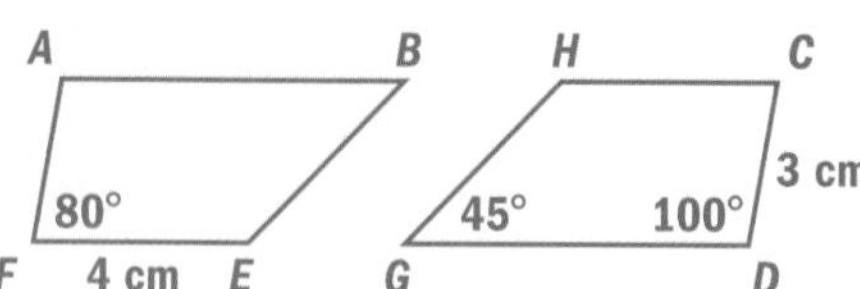

SEE EXAMPLE 3 on p. 429 for Exs. 11–12

11. **IDENTIFYING CONGRUENT TRIANGLES** Name all the congruent triangles shown. *Justify* your answers.

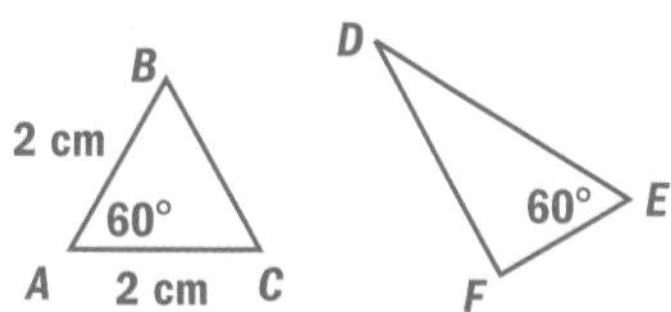

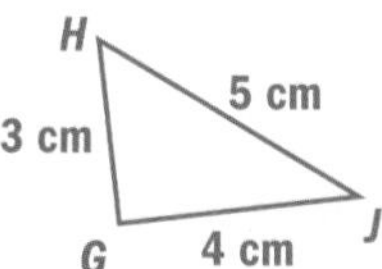

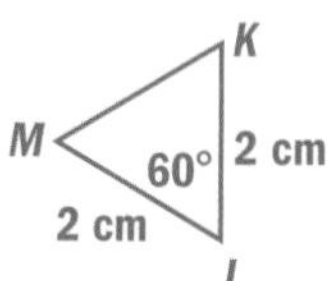

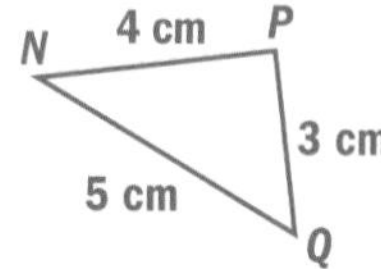

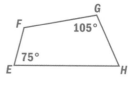

12. **ERROR ANALYSIS** Describe and correct the error made in the solution.

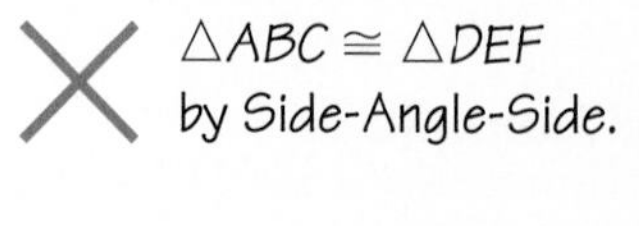

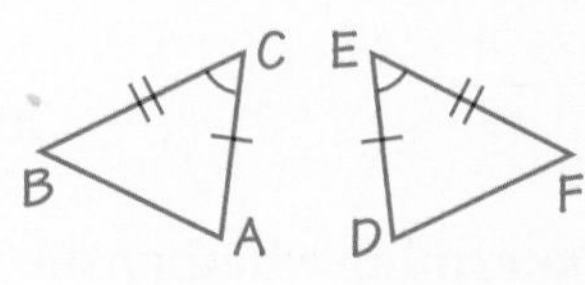

13. ★ **MULTIPLE CHOICE** Polygon $ABCD \cong$ polygon $EFGH$. Find the value of x.

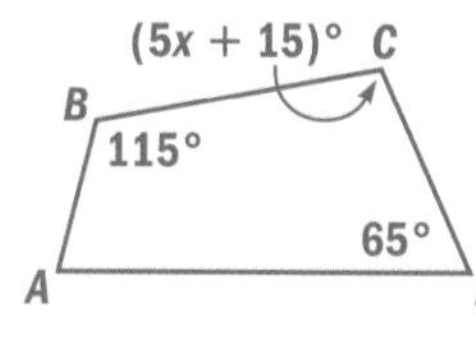

F, G, 105°, 75°, E, H

Ⓐ 10 Ⓑ 12 Ⓒ 18 Ⓓ 20

REASONING *Explain* how you know the triangles are congruent. Then write an equation and solve for x.

14.

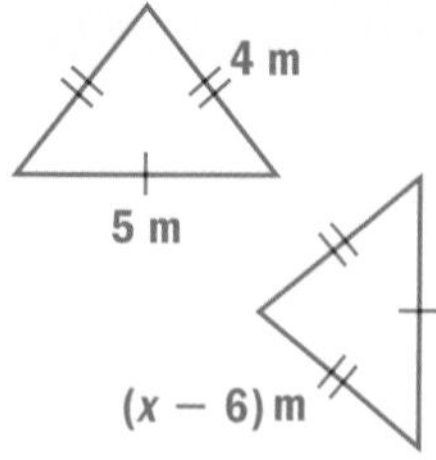

15.

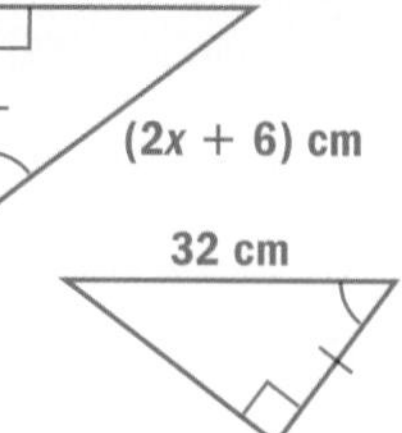

16.

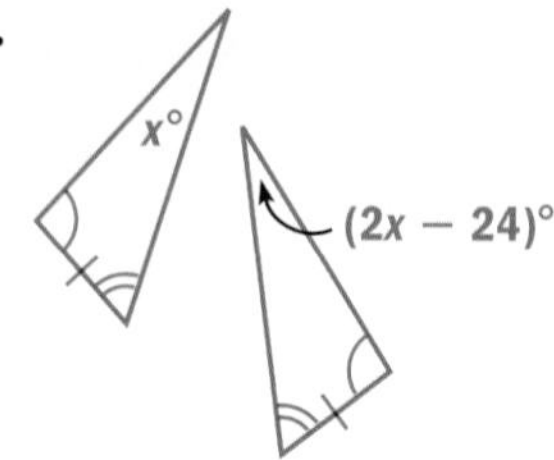

17. **EXAMPLE AND NONEXAMPLES** Sketch two polygons whose corresponding angles are congruent but whose corresponding sides are *not* congruent. Sketch two polygons whose corresponding sides are congruent but whose corresponding angles are *not* congruent.

18. **CHALLENGE** Is it true that if any two sides and an angle of one triangle are congruent to any two sides and an angle of another triangle, then the triangles are congruent? *Justify* your answer with a sketch of two such triangles.

PROBLEM SOLVING

19. SOCCER FIELD In 1994, Michigan State University covered the floor of the Silverdome with natural grass for the World Cup Tournament. The pieces of sod were in the shape of regular hexagons. *Explain* how you know the regular hexagons were congruent.

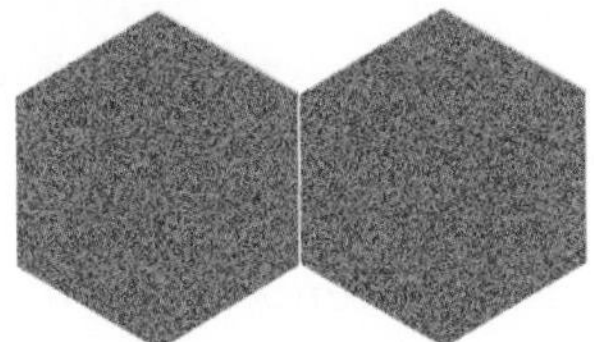

KITES *Explain* **how you know the red triangles in the kites are congruent.**

SEE EXAMPLE 3 on p. 429 for Exs. 20–21

20.

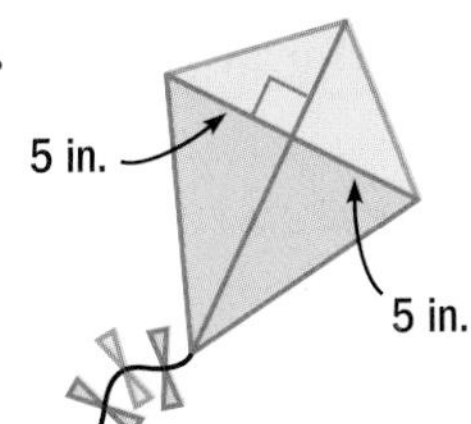

21.

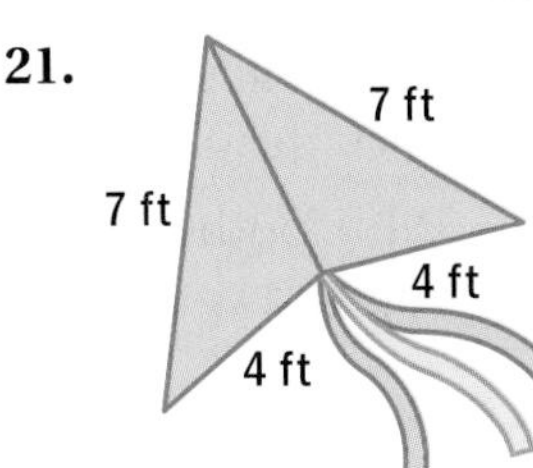

22. ★ WRITING *Explain* how equality and congruence are similar. *Explain* how equality and congruence are different.

23. CLOTHING Two back pockets on a pair of jeans are congruent. Find $m\angle 1$.

24. ★ SHORT RESPONSE What is the fewest pairs of corresponding parts that have to be congruent to establish that two triangles are congruent? Once you know that the triangles are congruent, how many pairs of corresponding parts do you know are congruent? *Explain.*

25. ★ MULTIPLE CHOICE *ABCDE* is a regular pentagon. Which statement is not true?

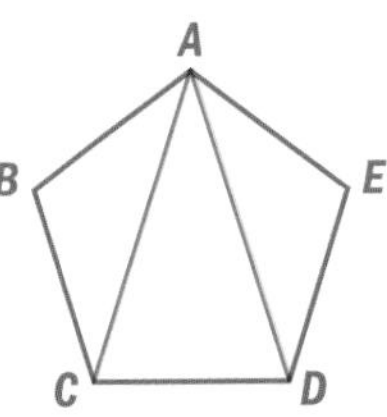

Ⓐ $\overline{AC} \cong \overline{AD}$ Ⓑ $\overline{CB} \cong \overline{AD}$

Ⓒ $\overline{AB} \cong \overline{DC}$ Ⓓ $\angle BAE \cong \angle AED$

26. ★ WRITING Use the regular pentagon in Exercise 25. *Explain* how you can show that $\triangle ACD$ is isosceles.

27. REASONING In $\triangle ABC$ and $\triangle XYZ$, $\overline{AB} \cong \overline{XY}$, $\overline{BC} \cong \overline{YZ}$, and $m\angle C = m\angle Z$. Can you conclude that another pair of congruent angles is present? *Explain* your reasoning.

28. DIAGONALS Draw a rectangle and mark the congruent sides and right angles. Then draw a diagonal. *Explain* how you know that the two triangles formed are congruent.

29. **POD SHELTERS** The triangles in the pod shelter shown are isosceles triangles. Two sides of each triangle are 7 feet long. What other information do you need to know to show that these triangles are congruent?

30. **DRAW A DIAGRAM** Sketch regular hexagon *LMNOPQ* and mark the congruent sides and angles. Draw three different diagonals from vertex *L* of the hexagon.
    a. Which triangle is congruent to $\triangle LMN$?
    b. Name all the corresponding congruent parts in the two triangles in part (a).
    c. Which other two triangles do you now know are congruent? Which rule did you use?

31. **CHALLENGE** You are standing beside a stream at *A*. You walk off the distance shown to *C*. Your friend walks the same distance on the opposite bank from the tree to *D*. What corresponding parts of the two triangles are congruent? Are the triangles congruent? *Justify* your reasoning.

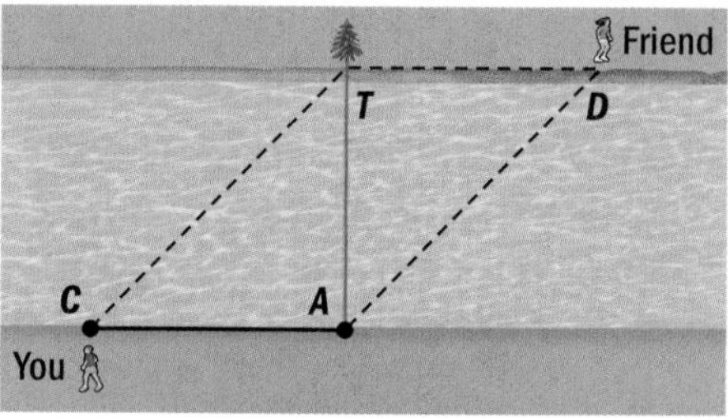

MIXED REVIEW

Get-Ready

Prepare for Lesson 8.6 in Exs. 32–35

Plot the point in a coordinate plane. ***(p. 94)***

32. $A(-9, 6)$
33. $B(-3, -5)$
34. $C(0, -4)$
35. $D(4, -1)$

36. If you pick a whole number at random from 1 to 100, what is the probability that the number is a multiple of 5? ***(p. 381)***

37. Find 1.25% of 400. ***(p. 375)***

38. Find 65% of 91. ***(p. 375)***

Find the value of *x*.

39. (Quadrilateral with angles 109°, $x°$, 72°, 76°) ***(p. 416)***

40. (Pentagon with angles 101°, $x°$, 101°, and two right angles) ***(p. 420)***

41. ★ **MULTIPLE CHOICE** What is the measure of one angle in a regular 18-gon? ***(p. 420)***

Ⓐ 200° Ⓑ 180° Ⓒ 160° Ⓓ 140°

8.6 Reflections and Symmetry

Before You plotted points in a coordinate plane.

Now You'll reflect figures and identify lines of symmetry.

Why? So you can find reflections, as in Example 2.

KEY VOCABULARY

- **reflection,** *p. 433*
- **transformation,** *p. 433*
- **image,** *p. 433*
- **line symmetry,** *p. 435*

The photo above illustrates a *reflection*. A **reflection** creates a mirror image of each point of a figure.

A reflection is a type of **transformation**, an operation that changes a figure into another figure. The new figure created is called the **image**.

EXAMPLE 1 Identifying a Reflection

Tell whether the red figure is a reflection of the blue figure.

a.

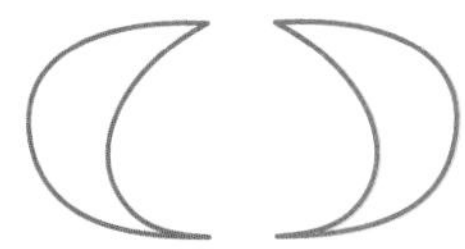

The figure is a reflection.

b.

The figure is *not* a reflection.

EXAMPLE 2 Reflecting in the y-Axis

Quadrilateral $ABCD$ is reflected in the y-axis. Write the coordinates of each vertex of quadrilateral $ABCD$ and its image, quadrilateral $A'B'C'D'$.

SOLUTION

READING You can describe reflections of figures in a coordinate plane using coordinate notation. The notation $A \rightarrow A'$ is read "A goes to A prime."

Original		Image
$A(-1, 1)$	$\rightarrow$	$A'(1, 1)$
$B(-3, 1)$	$\rightarrow$	$B'(3, 1)$
$C(-4, 3)$	$\rightarrow$	$C'(4, 3)$
$D(-2, 4)$	$\rightarrow$	$D'(2, 4)$

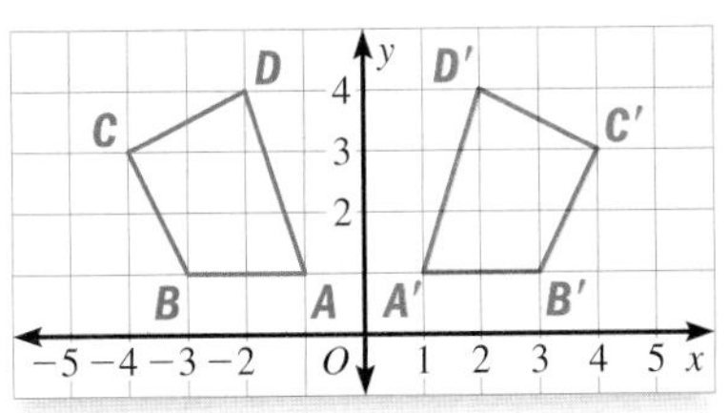

✓ GUIDED PRACTICE for Examples 1 and 2

1. Tell whether the red arrow is a reflection of the blue arrow.

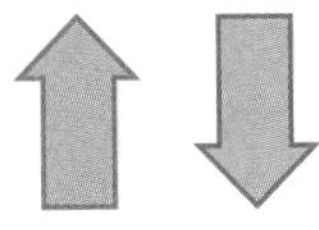

2. Graph the triangle with vertices $J(0, 1)$, $K(0, 4)$, and $L(5, 2)$. Reflect the triangle in the y-axis.

When you reflect a figure in a line, the line is called the **line of reflection**. You may have noticed in Example 2 that when the line of reflection is the y-axis, the x-coordinate of each point is multiplied by -1.

KEY CONCEPT *For Your Notebook*

Reflections in the x-axis

Words To reflect a point in the x-axis, multiply its y-coordinate by -1.

Numbers $P(2, -3) \rightarrow P'(2, 3)$ **Algebra** $(x, y) \rightarrow (x, -y)$

Reflections in the y-axis

Words To reflect a point in the y-axis, multiply its x-coordinate by -1.

Numbers $P(2, -3) \rightarrow P'(-2, 3)$ **Algebra** $(x, y) \rightarrow (-x, y)$

EXAMPLE 3 Standardized Test Practice

Reflect $\triangle PQR$ in the x-axis. What are the coordinates of the vertices of $\triangle P'Q'R'$?

Ⓐ $(-1, 3), (-4, 4), (-5, 2)$

Ⓑ $(1, 3), (4, 4), (5, 2)$

Ⓒ $(1, -3), (4, -4), (5, -2)$

Ⓓ $(-1, -3), (-4, -4), (-5, -2)$

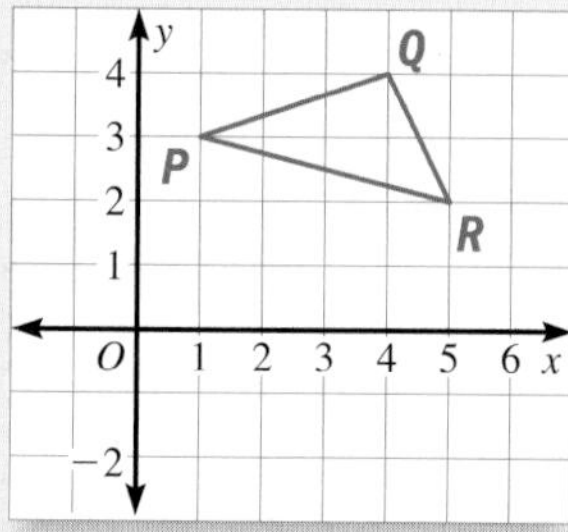

ELIMINATE CHOICES
When you reflect a point in the x-axis, you multiply the y-coordinate by -1. So, you can eliminate choices A and B.

SOLUTION

Multiply each y-coordinate by -1.

Original		Image
(x, y)	$\rightarrow$	$(x, -y)$
$P(1, 3)$	$\rightarrow$	$P'(1, -3)$
$Q(4, 4)$	$\rightarrow$	$Q'(4, -4)$
$R(5, 2)$	$\rightarrow$	$R'(5, -2)$

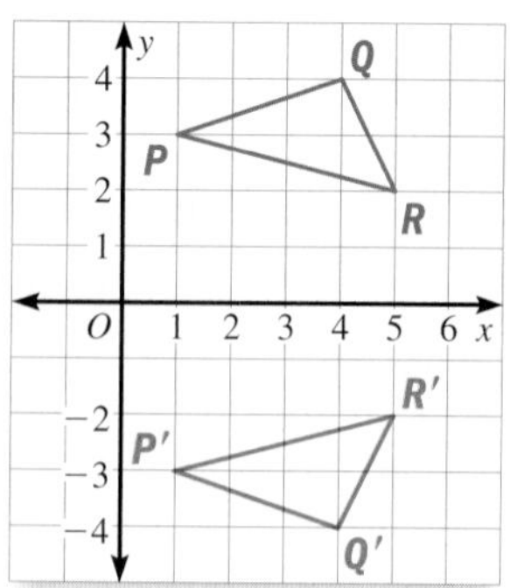

▶ **Answer** The coordinates of the vertices of $\triangle P'Q'R'$ are $(1, -3), (4, -4), (5, -2)$. The correct answer is C. Ⓐ Ⓑ Ⓒ Ⓓ

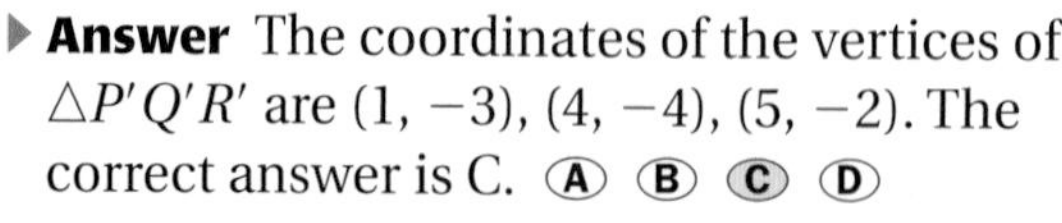

✓ **GUIDED PRACTICE** for Example 3

3. Graph the figure with vertices $S(-3, 2)$, $T(-1, 4)$, $U(-4, 5)$, and $V(-5, 3)$. Reflect the figure in the x-axis. Label the coordinates of the vertices of $S'T'U'V'$.

Symmetry A figure has **line symmetry** if one half of the figure is a mirror image of the other half. A *line of symmetry* divides the figure into two congruent parts that are mirror images of each other.

EXAMPLE 4 Identifying Lines of Symmetry

AVOID ERRORS
Symmetry is a property of points and lines, but not of color. For example, regardless of the colorings in parts (a) and (b), the figures would still be symmetric.

How many lines of symmetry does the picture have?

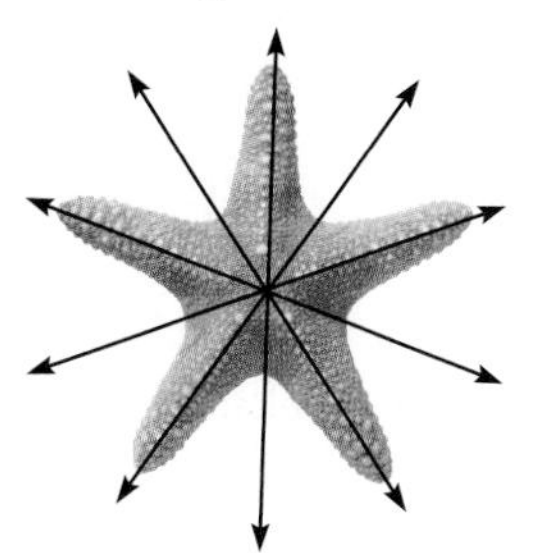

a. one line of symmetry **b.** five lines of symmetry **c.** no lines of symmetry

Animated Math at classzone.com

✓ GUIDED PRACTICE for Example 4

4. How many lines of symmetry does a square have? a rhombus?

8.6 EXERCISES

HOMEWORK KEY
★ = STANDARDIZED TEST PRACTICE Exs. 10, 11, 25, 26, 27, 28, 30, and 40
○ = HINTS AND HOMEWORK HELP for Exs. 3, 7, 13, 25 at classzone.com

SKILL PRACTICE

VOCABULARY **Copy and complete the statement.**

1. A(n) _?_ creates a mirror image of the original figure.
2. A(n) _?_ is an operation that changes a figure into another figure.

SEE EXAMPLE 1 on p. 433 for Exs. 3–5

REFLECTIONS **Tell whether the red figure is a reflection of the blue figure.**

3. 4.  5.

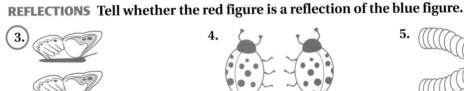

DRAWING REFLECTIONS **Graph the polygon and its reflection in the given axis.**

SEE EXAMPLES 2 AND 3 on pp. 433–434 for Exs. 6–8

6. $A(3, 6)$, $B(6, 3)$, $C(5, 0)$, $D(1, 1)$; x-axis
7. $Q(-1, 3)$, $R(-3, 6)$, $S(-6, 4)$, $T(-6, 0)$; x-axis
8. $B(2, -1)$, $C(5, 0)$, $D(7, -2)$, $E(0, -6)$; y-axis

SEE EXAMPLES 2 AND 3
on pp. 433–434
for Exs. 9–10

9. **ERROR ANALYSIS** Describe and correct the error made in finding the coordinates of the vertices of the image of $\triangle ABC$ after a reflection in the x-axis.

Original:	Image:
$A(4, 5)$	$A'(-4, 5)$
$B(2, 0)$	$B'(-2, 0)$
$C(6, 2)$	$C'(-6, 2)$

10. ★ **MULTIPLE CHOICE** Which figure is a reflected image of figure D?

Ⓐ Figure A　Ⓑ Figure B
Ⓒ Figure C　Ⓓ None

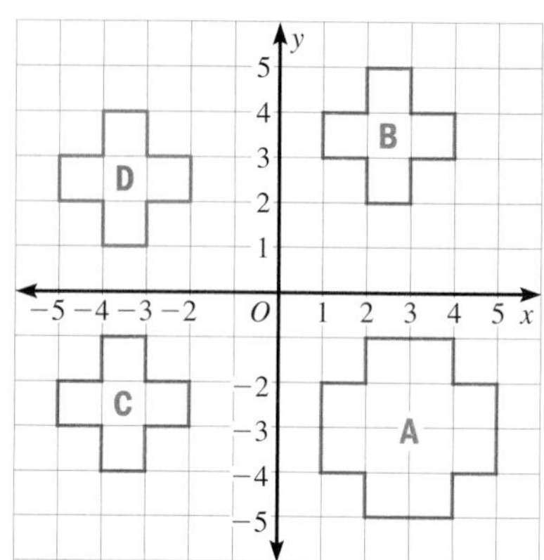

SEE EXAMPLE 4
on p. 435
for Exs. 11–14

11. ★ **MULTIPLE CHOICE** How many lines of symmetry does figure A have?

Ⓐ 0　Ⓑ 1
Ⓒ 2　Ⓓ 4

LINE SYMMETRY How many lines of symmetry does the figure have?

12. 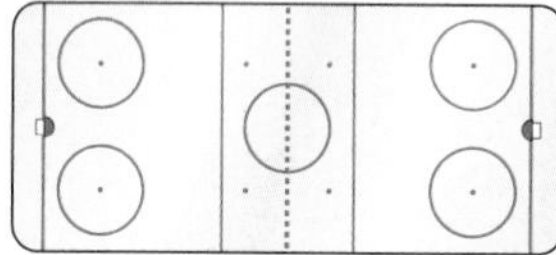

13. 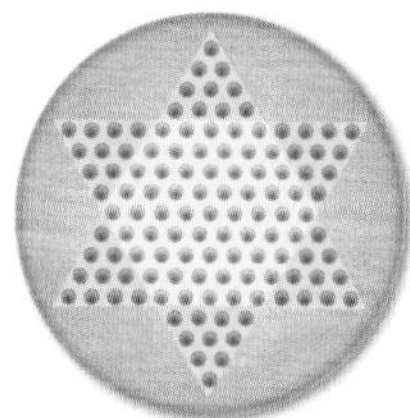

14. 

REASONING Draw and classify the described polygon. Draw the lines of symmetry, if any. Is there more than one possible polygon? If so, name the polygon(s).

15. Triangle with no lines of of symmetry

16. Triangle with exactly three lines of symmetry

17. Quadrilateral with exactly two lines of symmetry

18. Quadrilateral with only one line of symmetry

REFLECTIONS In a coordinate plane you can reflect a figure in a line other than the x- or y-axis. In the diagram below, quadrilateral $ABCD$ is reflected in the red line. In Exercises 19–22, copy the coordinate plane including the red line. Then graph the polygon and its reflection in the red line.

19. $R(0, 0)$, $S(1, 3)$, $T(2, 0)$

20. $X(-2, 3)$, $Y(1, -2)$, $Z(-2, -3)$

21. $E(-3, 2)$, $F(1, 2)$, $G(1, -1)$, $H(-3, -1)$

22. $J(-4, 5)$, $K(-1, 5)$, $L(-1, 1)$, $M(-4, 1)$

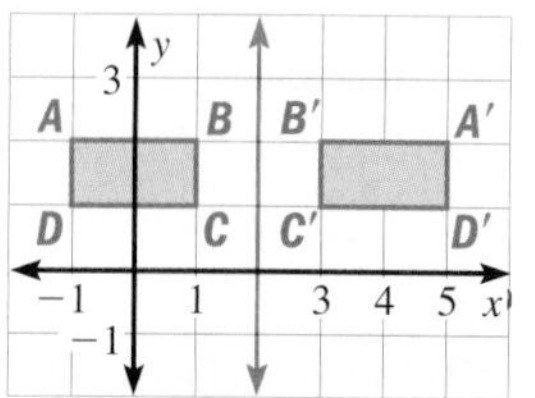

23. **CHALLENGE** Which of the 26 capital letters in the English alphabet have no line of symmetry? one line of symmetry? two lines of symmetry? or more than two lines of symmetry?

PROBLEM SOLVING

SEE EXAMPLES 2 AND 3 on pp. 433–434 for Exs. 24, 27–28

24. MAKE A MODEL Write your name at the top of a piece of tracing paper. Fold the paper and trace your name to create a reflection. Unfold the paper to see your name and its reflection.

Sara Jeanne

25. ★ **WRITING** *Explain* how to determine whether two figures are reflections of one another in the y-axis.

26. ★ **MULTIPLE CHOICE** $\triangle RST$ is reflected in the x-axis to form $\triangle R'S'T'$. The coordinates of point R are $(-4, 3)$. What are the coordinates of R'?

Ⓐ $(4, 3)$ Ⓑ $(4, -3)$ Ⓒ $(-4, 3)$ Ⓓ $(-4, -3)$

SEE EXAMPLE 4 on p. 435 for Exs. 27–28

27. ★ **SHORT RESPONSE** Part of a pattern is shown at the right. Using grid paper, copy and transform the pattern so that it has exactly one line of symmetry. Draw the line of symmetry. *Compare* your drawing with your classmates' drawings. Is there more than one possible pattern?

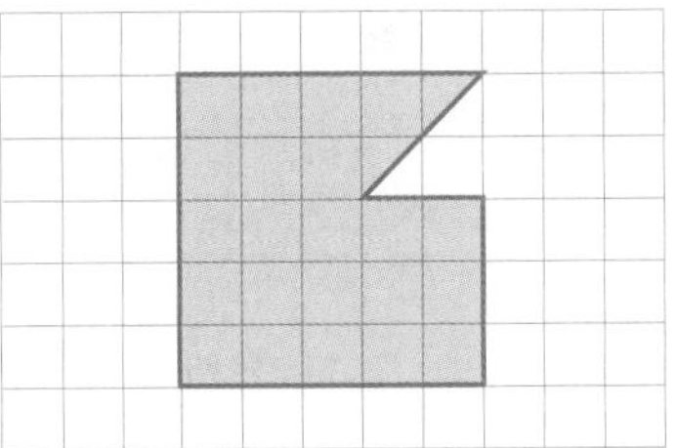

28. ★ **EXTENDED RESPONSE** Use the table below.

Sides	3	4	5	6	8
Regular Polygon		?	?	?	?
Lines of Symmetry	?	?	?	?	?

a. **Sketch** Copy the table and sketch a regular polygon with the given number of sides in each column. Draw all the lines of symmetry.

b. **Evaluate** Count the lines of symmetry. Complete the table.

c. **Look for a Pattern** How is the number of sides related to the number of lines of symmetry?

29. **MULTIPLE REPRESENTATIONS** Telephone companies want to place a telephone pole near the street, giving the shortest distance between house A and house B. This is accomplished by reflecting house A in the line of the street, then drawing a line that contains the image of house A and house B. The point where this line and the street meet is where the telephone pole will be placed. Draw this scenario. Give another real world situation where this reasoning can be used.

30. ★ **OPEN-ENDED MATH** The words WOW and HI have line symmetry. Write two more words that have line symmetry.

31. **GEOMETRY** Graph the polygon with vertices $S(-6, 0)$, $T(0, 6)$, $V(6, 0)$, $W(2, -4)$, and $X(-2, -4)$. Reflect the polygon in the x-axis and graph its image in the same coordinate plane. Does the figure have more than one line of symmetry? *Explain.*

32. **MULTI-STEP PROBLEM** The vertices of polygon $ABCDEF$ are $A(0, 0)$, $B(0, 2)$, $C(2, 2)$, $D(2, 6)$, $E(4, 6)$, and $F(4,0)$.
    - **a.** Draw polygon $ABCDEF$ in a coordinate plane. Classify the polygon.
    - **b.** In the same coordinate plane used in part (a), reflect polygon $ABCDEF$ in the y-axis. Next, reflect the image of polygon $ABCDEF$ in the x-axis. Then reflect the second image of polygon $ABCDEF$ in the y-axis.
    - **c.** *Describe* the figure formed by polygon $ABCDEF$ and its 3 images. Is this figure a polygon?

33. **CHALLENGE** The vertices of two triangles are given below. Using graph paper, graph both triangles in the same coordinate plane. Fold the graph paper once so that $\triangle ABC$ coincides with $\triangle EFG$. Are the triangles congruent? *Describe* the fold line. How are the coordinates related?

    $\triangle ABC$: $A(2, 1)$, $B(8, 1)$, $C(7, 3)$ $\qquad$ $\triangle EFG$: $E(1, 2)$, $F(1, 8)$, $G(3, 7)$

34. **CHALLENGE** A polygon has vertices $A(1, -2)$, $B(5, -1)$, $C(8, -4)$, $D(7, -7)$, and $E(4, -8)$. Reflect the polygon in the x-axis and find the coordinates of the vertices of its image. Then reflect the image in the y-axis. Is the third polygon a reflection of the original polygon? *Explain.*

MIXED REVIEW

Prepare for Lesson 8.7 in Exs. 35–37

Plot and label the point when $x = -2$ and $y = 3$. *(p. 94)*

35. $(x + 1, y + 2)$ 36. $(x - 2, y + 8)$ 37. $(x - 3, y - 3)$

Find the number. *(p. 375)*

38. What is 0.8% of 500? 39. 756 is what percent of 270?

40. ★ **MULTIPLE CHOICE** What is the sum of the angle measures in a polygon with nine sides? *(p. 420)*

    Ⓐ 140° Ⓑ 1260° Ⓒ 1620° Ⓓ 2520°

Brain Game

Deep Reflections

Use a mirror to read this quotation from William Shakespeare.

8.7 Translations and Rotations

Before You reflected figures in a coordinate plane.
Now You'll translate or rotate figures in a coordinate plane.
Why? So you can describe transformations, as in Ex. 19.

KEY VOCABULARY
- **translation,** *p. 439*
- **rotation,** *p. 440*

ACTIVITY

You can see how moving a triangle changes its vertices.

STEP 1 **Graph** an image of A by moving it 7 units to the right and 2 units up. Plot the new vertex and label it A'.

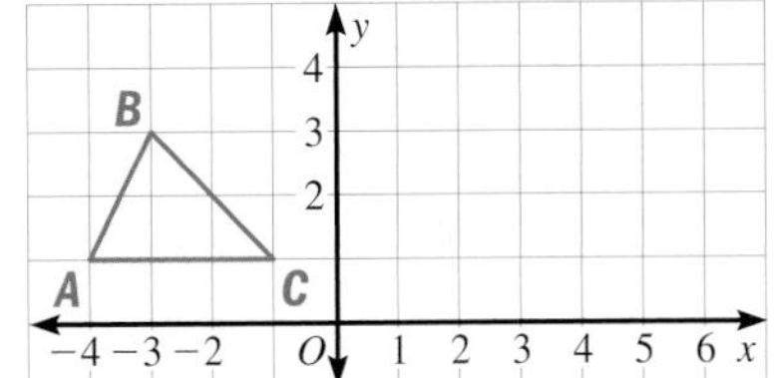

STEP 2 **Repeat** Step 1 with B and C. Then connect the vertices to form $\triangle A'B'C'$.

STEP 3 **Compare** the coordinates of A, B, and C to those of A', B', and C'.

Translations In the activity, you transformed $\triangle ABC$ by *sliding* it. A **translation** is a transformation that moves each point of a figure the same distance in the same direction. The image is congruent to the original figure.

To translate a figure in a coordinate plane, you change the coordinates of its points by using the guidelines below, assuming a and b are positive.

Slide to the right a units
$x \rightarrow x + a$

Slide up b units
$y \rightarrow y + b$

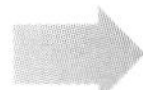

Slide to the left a units
$x \rightarrow x - a$

Slide down b units
$y \rightarrow y - b$

EXAMPLE 1 Using Coordinate Notation

Describe the translation from the blue figure to the red figure.

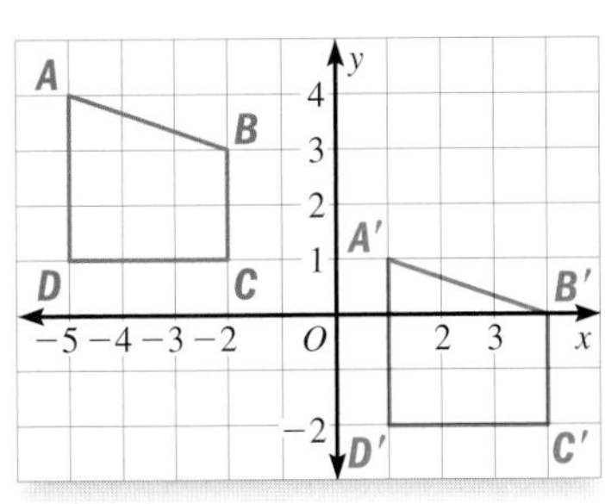

SOLUTION

Each point moves 6 units to the right and 3 units down. The translation is

$$(x, y) \rightarrow (x + 6, y - 3)$$

✓ GUIDED PRACTICE for Example 1

1. *Describe* the translation from the blue figure to the red figure.

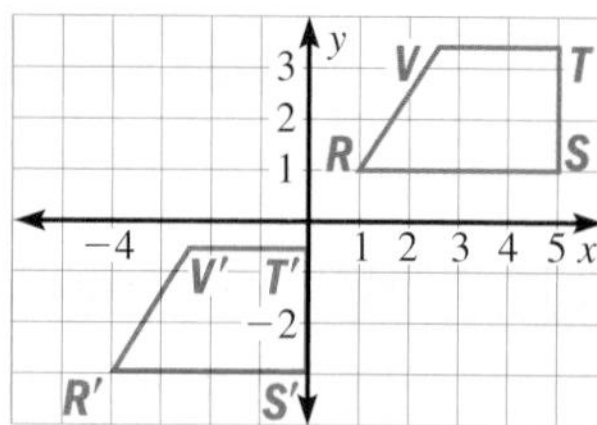

VOCABULARY

The angle through which a figure is rotated is called the *angle of rotation*. The common point at the rotation's center is called the *center of rotation*.

Rotations A **rotation** is a transformation that turns each point of a figure the same number of degrees around a common point. In this lesson, figures in a coordinate plane will always be rotated around the origin.

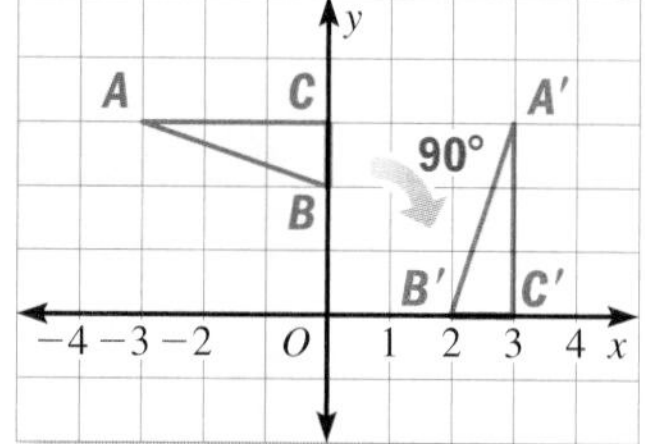

KEY CONCEPT — For Your Notebook

90° Clockwise Rotation

Words To rotate a point P 90° *clockwise*, switch the coordinates, then multiply the new y-coordinate by -1.

Numbers $P(6, 2) \rightarrow P'(2, -6)$ **Algebra** $P(x, y) \rightarrow P'(y, -x)$

90° Counterclockwise Rotation

Words To rotate a point P 90° *counterclockwise*, switch the coordinates, then multiply the new x-coordinate by -1.

Numbers $P(5, 3) \rightarrow P'(-3, 5)$ **Algebra** $P(x, y) \rightarrow P'(-y, x)$

EXAMPLE 2 Rotating 90° Clockwise

READING

Clockwise is the direction the hands on a clock turn. Counterclockwise is the opposite direction.

Rotate quadrilateral *FGHJ* 90° clockwise.

SOLUTION

Original		Image
(x, y)	$\rightarrow$	$(y, -x)$
$F(2, 2)$	$\rightarrow$	$F'(2, -2)$
$G(2, 4)$	$\rightarrow$	$G'(4, -2)$
$H(4, 4)$	$\rightarrow$	$H'(4, -4)$
$J(5, 2)$	$\rightarrow$	$J'(2, -5)$

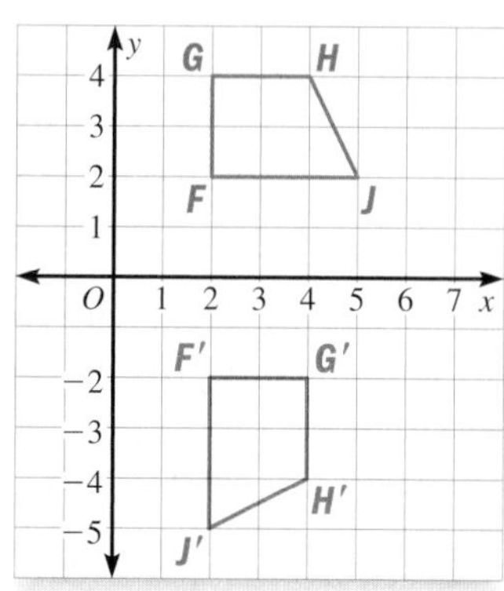

The graph shows $FGHJ$ and $F'G'H'J'$.

KEY CONCEPT *For Your Notebook*

180° Rotations

Words To rotate a point 180°, multiply its coordinates by -1.

Numbers $P(4, 1) \rightarrow P'(-4, -1)$ **Algebra** $P(x, y) \rightarrow P'(-x, -y)$

EXAMPLE 3 Rotating 180°

Rotate $\triangle ABC$ 180°.

SOLUTION

Original		**Image**
(x, y)	$\rightarrow$	$(-x, -y)$
$A(-6, 0)$	$\rightarrow$	$A'(6, 0)$
$B(-5, 2)$	$\rightarrow$	$B'(5, -2)$
$C(-1, 3)$	$\rightarrow$	$C'(1, -3)$

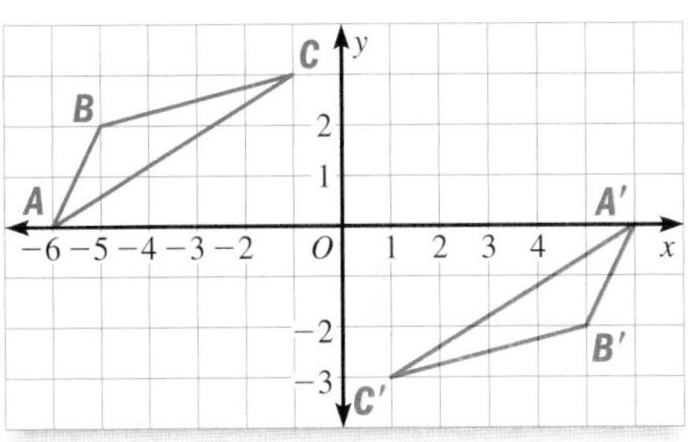

The graph shows $\triangle ABC$ and $\triangle A'B'C'$.

✓ **GUIDED PRACTICE for Examples 2 and 3**

Graph $A(1, 1)$, $B(3, 1)$, $C(3, 3)$, and $D(1, 4)$. Find its image after the given rotation.

2. 90° clockwise **3.** 90° counterclockwise **4.** 180°

8.7 EXERCISES

HOMEWORK KEY

★ = **STANDARDIZED TEST PRACTICE** Exs. 26, 30, 31, 32, and 41

○ = **HINTS AND HOMEWORK HELP** for Exs. 5, 7, 11, 13, 23 at classzone.com

SKILL PRACTICE

VOCABULARY Identify the transformation shown in the graph.

1.

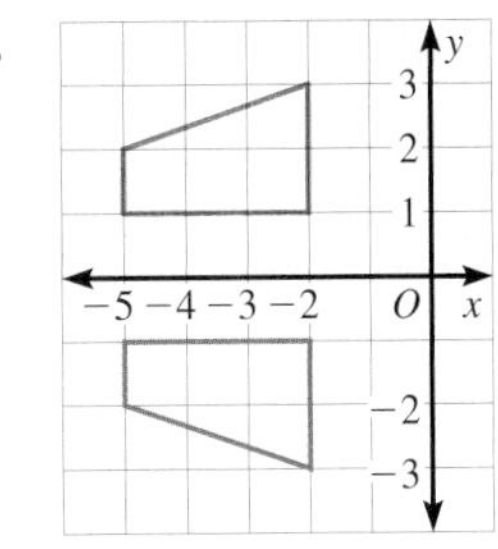

2.

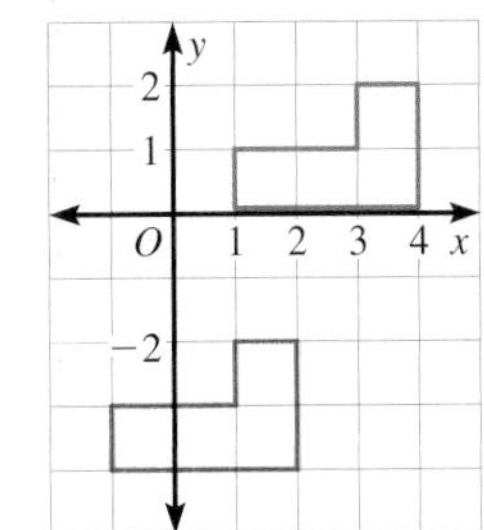

3.

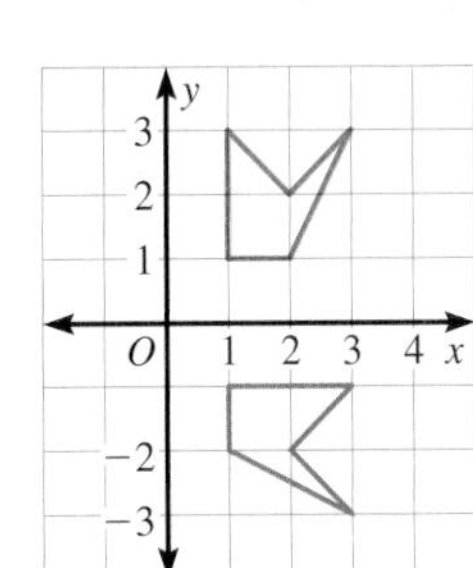

USING COORDINATE NOTATION Use coordinate notation to describe the translation from the blue figure to the red figure.

SEE EXAMPLE 1 on p. 439 for Exs. 4–7, 13

4. 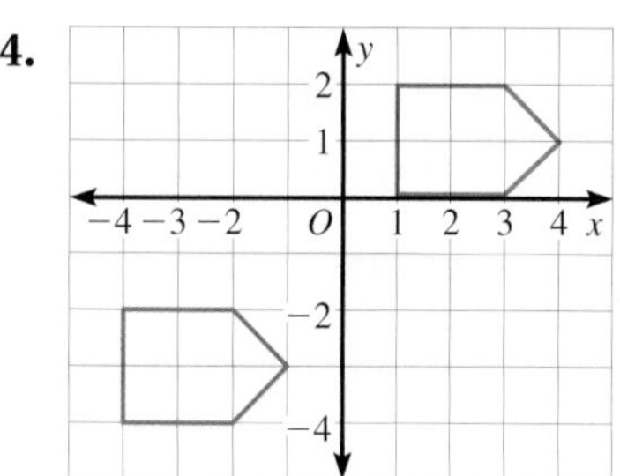

5. 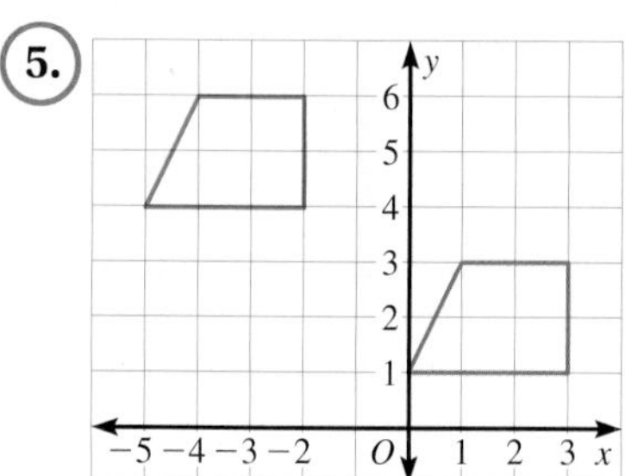

TRANSLATING TRIANGLES Find the coordinates of the vertices of the triangle's image after the translation. Then graph the triangle's image.

6. $\triangle PQR$: $P(0, -1)$, $Q(3, -1)$, $R(5, -3)$; translation: $(x, y) \rightarrow (x - 5, y + 1)$

7. $\triangle LMN$: $L(4, 2)$, $M(0, 3)$, $N(1, 1)$; translation: $(x, y) \rightarrow (x + 1, y - 6)$

SEE EXAMPLE 2 on p. 440 for Exs. 8–12

8. **ERROR ANALYSIS** $\triangle JKL$ has vertices $J(-4, -3)$, $K(-2, 0)$, and $L(1, 2)$. Describe and correct the error made in finding the coordinates of the vertices of its image when it is rotated 90° clockwise.

> X
> $(x, y) \rightarrow (-y, x)$
> $J(-4, -3) \rightarrow J'(3, -4)$
> $K(-2, 0) \rightarrow K'(0, -2)$
> $L(1, 2) \rightarrow L'(-2, 1)$
> The vertices are $(3, -4)$, $(0, -2)$, and $(-2, 1)$.

9. **MULTI-STEP PROBLEM** Rotate $\triangle RST$ 90° counterclockwise.
   a. Graph $\triangle RST$ with vertices $R(-2, -1)$, $S(-5, -2)$, and $T(-4, 2)$.
   b. Find the coordinates of the vertices of the triangle's image.
   c. Graph $\triangle R'S'T'$, the image of $\triangle RST$ after the rotation.

10. **ROTATING A TRIANGLE** Use the triangle described in Exercise 9. Find the coordinates of the vertices of the image after a 180° rotation and after a clockwise rotation of 90°. Graph each image.

TRANSFORMATIONS In Exercises 11–16, graph $\triangle LMN$ with vertices $L(2, 0)$, $M(2, 3)$, and $N(6, 0)$. Then graph its image after the transformation.

11. Rotate 180°.

12. Rotate 90° counterclockwise.

13. Translate using $(x, y) \rightarrow (x - 3, y - 4)$.

14. Rotate 180°. Then translate using $(x, y) \rightarrow (x + 1, y + 1)$.

15. Translate using $(x, y) \rightarrow (x + 3, y)$. Then rotate 180°.

Animated Math at classzone.com

16. **TRANSFORMATIONS** Graph quadrilateral $ABCD$ with vertices $A(-4, 2)$, $B(-2, 0)$, $C(-2, -2)$, and $D(0, 2)$.
   a. Graph $A'B'C'D'$ by reflecting $ABCD$ in the x-axis.
   b. Graph $A''B''C''D''$ by translating $A'B'C'D'$ 4 units to the right.
   c. Graph $A'''B'''C'''D'''$ by rotating $A''B''C''D''$ 180°.

17. **MULTIPLE METHODS** *Describe* one translation, one reflection, and one rotation that make the red square the image of the blue square. Then find 3 combinations of transformations that make the red square the image of the blue square.

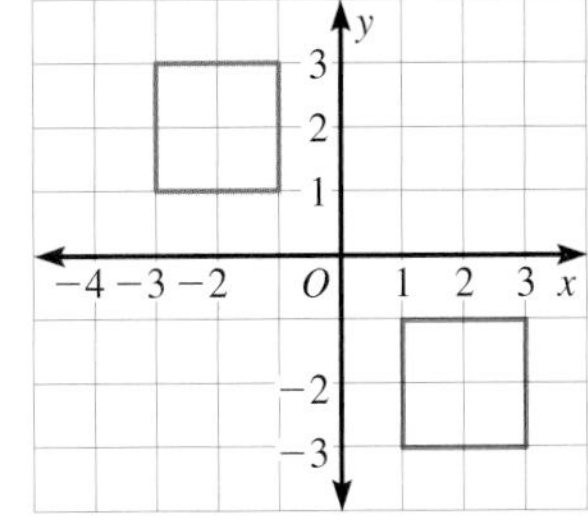

18. **CHALLENGE** Use the coordinate notation for a 180° rotation and 90° rotation clockwise. Show that combining these two gives the coordinate notation for rotating a figure 90° counterclockwise.

PROBLEM SOLVING

19. **ORIGAMI** *Describe* all possible rotations that will produce an image identical in shape to the given figure.

TRANSFORMATIONS Name the type of transformation modeled by the action.

20. Riding down an escalator
21. Making a handprint in clay
22. Opening a combination lock
23. Going down a water slide
24. Looking in a mirror
25. Riding a carousel

26. ★ **WRITING** Point A in Quadrant II is rotated 180°. Find the quadrant in which point A' lies. Point B in Quadrant IV is rotated 90° clockwise. Find the quadrant in which point B' lies. *Explain* your reasoning.

READING IN MATH **Read the information below for Exercises 28–30.**

Kaleidoscopes A figure has *rotational symmetry* if a turn of 180° or less about a point produces an image that fits exactly on the original figure. Kaleidoscopes use mirrors to create images with rotational symmetry. The number of repeats in a pattern depends on the angle measure of the mirrors.

27. **Interpret** Tell whether each image has rotational symmetry. If so, describe the least angle of rotation that produces each image.

28. **Predict** If you turned each image upside down, would it appear the same? *Explain.*

29. **Analyze** Can a figure have rotational symmetry without having line symmetry? *Explain.*

30. ★ **MULTIPLE CHOICE** The figures below follow a pattern.

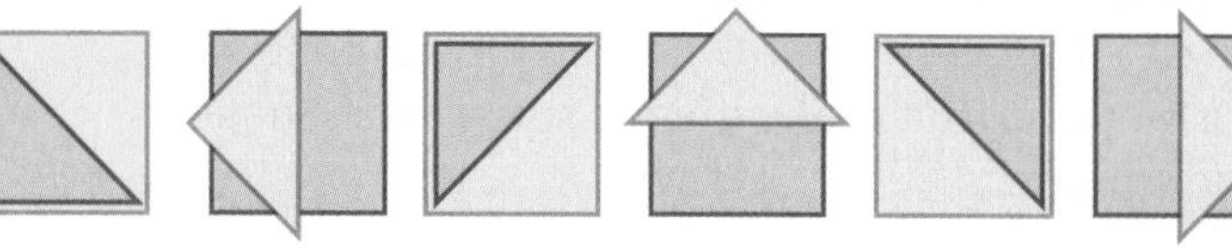

Figure 1 Figure 2 Figure 3 Figure 4 Figure 5 Figure 6 ...

Which figure shows a 90° clockwise rotation of Figure 10 in the pattern?

Ⓐ 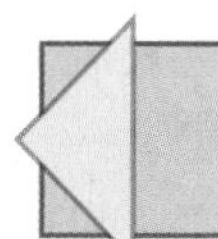

Ⓑ 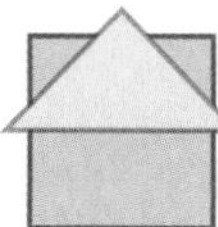

Ⓒ 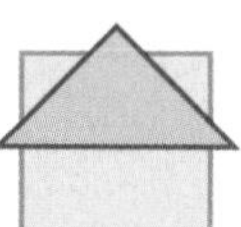

Ⓓ 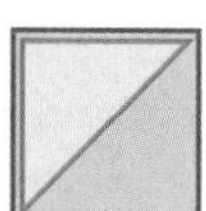

31. ★ **OPEN-ENDED MATH** Draw a polygon that appears the same when rotated clockwise or counterclockwise by angles of 45°, 90°, and 180°.

32. ★ **EXTENDED RESPONSE** Rotate the figure at the right 90° clockwise. Reflect the image in the y-axis. Graph the final image. Complete the rule for the combination of transformations you performed. *Explain* your reasoning.

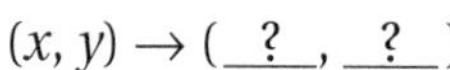

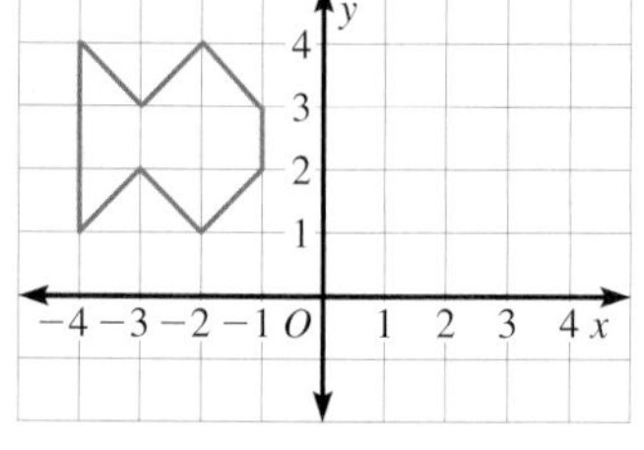

33. **CHALLENGE** A line l passes through Quadrants I and III at a 45° angle to both axes. It is the line of reflection $(x, y) \rightarrow (y, x)$. Draw any $\triangle ABC$ and reflect it in line l. Then reflect the image in the y-axis. Which single transformation of $\triangle ABC$ will form the second image? *Justify* your answer.

34. **CHALLENGE** The figure at the right is the image of a triangle rotated 90° clockwise and reflected in the y-axis. Graph the original figure.

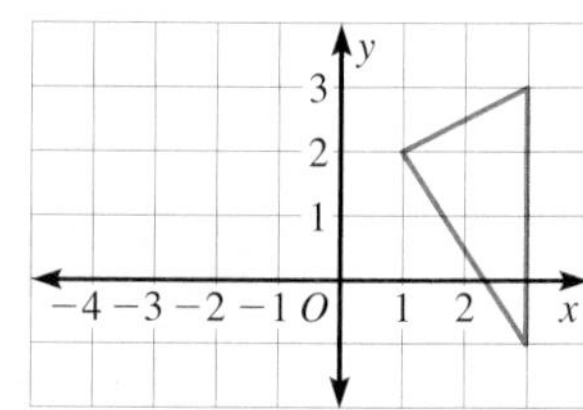

MIXED REVIEW

Get-Ready

Prepare for Lesson 8.8 in Exs. 35–37

Solve the proportion. *(p. 348)*

35. $\frac{a}{25} = \frac{24}{200}$

36. $\frac{32}{9} = \frac{c}{108}$

37. $\frac{7}{60} = \frac{154}{d}$

Find the value of x. Classify the triangle by its angles. *(p. 411)*

38. 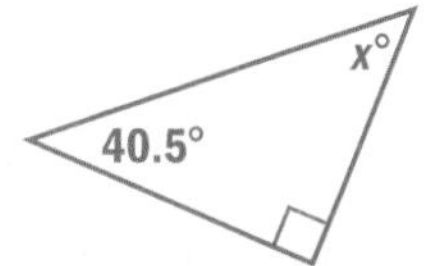

39. 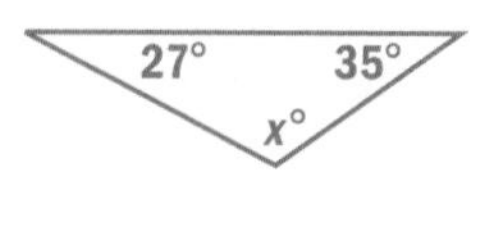

40. 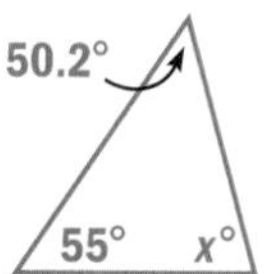

41. ★ **MULTIPLE CHOICE** What is the mean of the following data set: 39, 45, 43, 28, 45, 48, 39, and 45? *(p. 272)*

Ⓐ 41.5 Ⓑ 43 Ⓒ 44 Ⓓ 45

Tessellations

GOAL Decide if a shape tessellates. Create tessellations.

KEY VOCABULARY
- **tessellation,** *p. 445*

You can use reflections, rotations, and translations to create a *tessellation,* like the one shown here. A **tessellation** is a repeating pattern of figures that covers a plane with no gaps or overlaps. If a figure can be used to create a tessellation, you say the figure *tessellates.*

EXAMPLE 1 Identifying Tessellating Polygons

Tell whether the polygon tessellates.

a.

Yes, you can create a tessellation by translating a rectangle.

b. 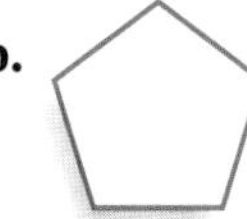

No, regular pentagons will not cover the plane without gaps or overlaps.

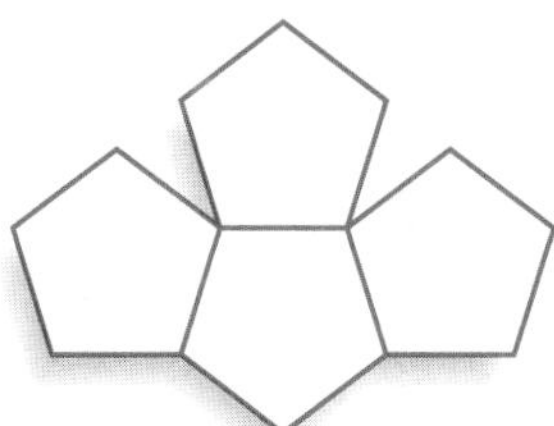

You can create a tessellation by altering a polygon that tessellates.

EXAMPLE 2 Creating a Tessellation

Alter a parallelogram to create a tessellation.

SOLUTION

STEP 1
Cut a triangle from the parallelogram.

STEP 2
Slide the triangle to the opposite side.

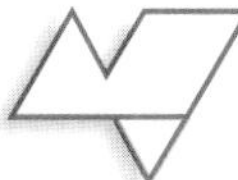

STEP 3
Translate the figure to create a tessellation.

EXAMPLE 3 Creating a Tessellation

Create a tessellation by altering an equilateral triangle.

STEP 1
Cut a piece from the triangle.

STEP 2
Slide the piece to another side.

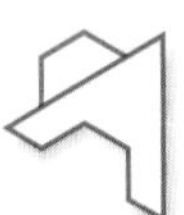

STEP 3
Reflect the figure, then translate the pair.

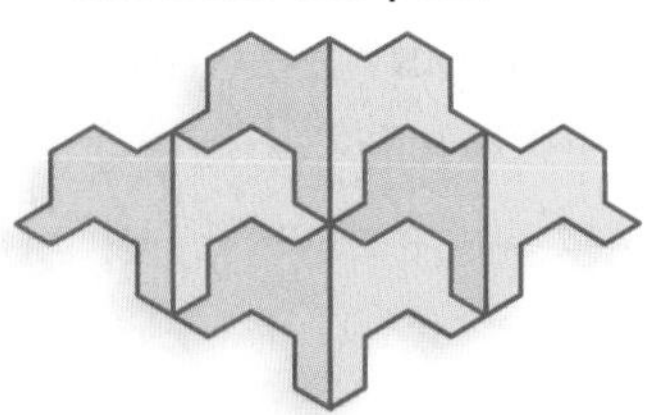

EXERCISES

Tell whether the figure tessellates.

1. 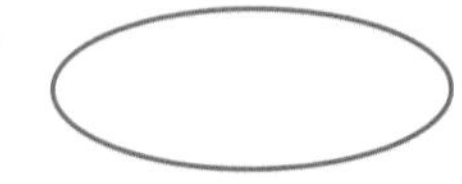

2. 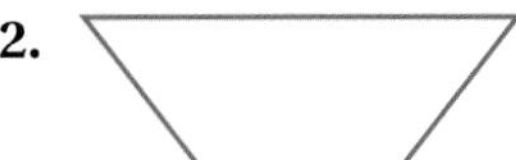

3. 

4. *Explain* how you can transform the blue shape to create the tessellation.

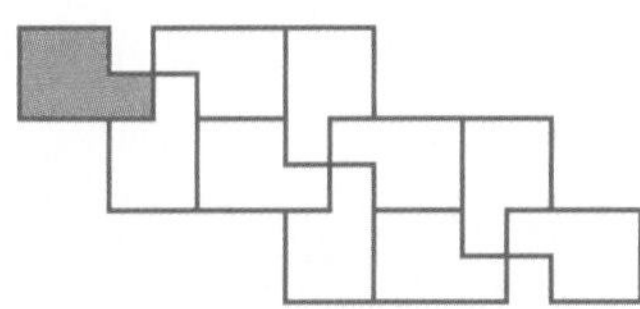

5. Copy and continue the pattern.

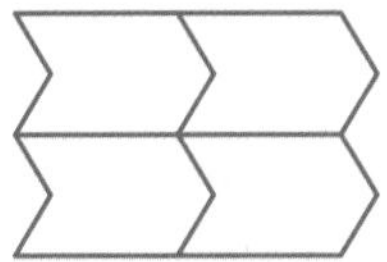

Copy the polygon and use it to create a tessellation. Describe how the polygon was transformed in your tessellation.

6. 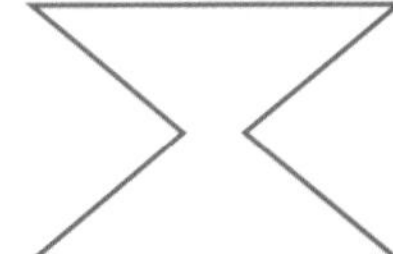

7. 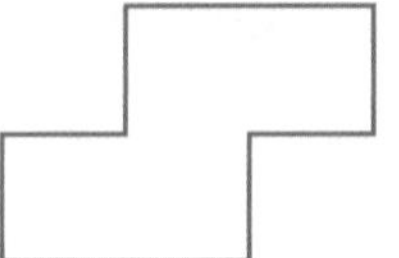

8. 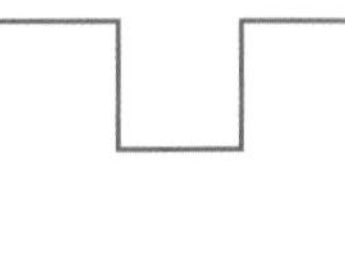

9. Create two different tessellations using the shape at the right.

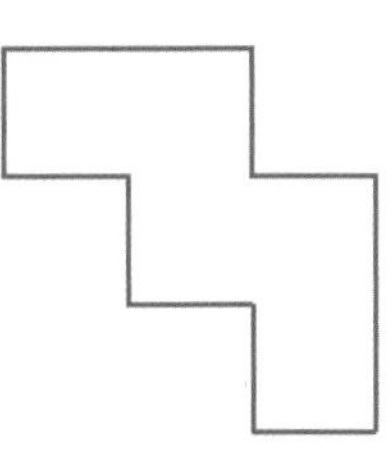

10. Create a tessellation by altering a rectangle.

11. Create a tessellation by altering a parallelogram that is not a rectangle.

8.8 Similarity and Dilations

Before	You used congruent polygons to find missing measures.
Now	You'll use similar polygons to find missing measures.
Why?	So you can compare real-world shapes, as in Example 1.

KEY VOCABULARY
- **similar polygons,** *p. 447*
- **dilation,** *p. 449*
- **scale factor,** *p. 449*

Similar polygons have the same shape, but they can be different sizes. The symbol ~ means "is similar to." When you name similar polygons, list their corresponding vertices in the same order.

KEY CONCEPT — *For Your Notebook*

Similar Polygons

$\triangle ABC \sim \triangle XYZ$

Corresponding angles are congruent.

$\angle A \cong \angle X \quad \angle B \cong \angle Y \quad \angle C \cong \angle Z$

Corresponding side lengths are proportional.

$\frac{AB}{XY} = \frac{BC}{YZ} \quad \frac{BC}{YZ} = \frac{AC}{XZ} \quad \frac{AC}{XZ} = \frac{AB}{XY}$

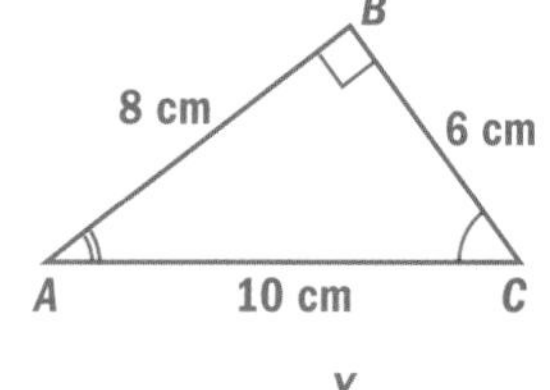

EXAMPLE 1 Identifying Similar Polygons

Tell whether the television screens are similar.

STEP 1 **Decide** whether corresponding angles are congruent. Each angle measures 90°.

$\angle A \cong \angle E \qquad \angle B \cong \angle F$

$\angle C \cong \angle G \qquad \angle D \cong \angle H$

STEP 2 **Decide** whether corresponding side lengths are proportional.

$$\frac{30 \text{ inches}}{18 \text{ inches}} \stackrel{?}{=} \frac{40 \text{ inches}}{24 \text{ inches}}$$

$$\frac{5 \cdot \cancel{6}}{3 \cdot \cancel{6}} \stackrel{?}{=} \frac{5 \cdot \cancel{8}}{3 \cdot \cancel{8}}$$

$$\frac{5}{3} = \frac{5}{3}$$

A 40 in. B, 30 in., E D C, 18 in., H G, 24 in.

REVIEW PROPORTIONS
For help with proportions, see p. 348.

▶ **Answer** Yes, quadrilateral *ABCD* ~ quadrilateral *EFGH*.

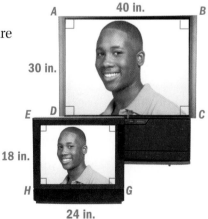

✓ GUIDED PRACTICE for Example 1

1. Measure the rectangles. Tell which rectangles are similar.

A B C D E

EXAMPLE 2 Standardized Test Practice

In the diagram, $\triangle KLM \sim \triangle NPQ$. What is the length of $\overline{KL}$?

Ⓐ 6 m Ⓑ 12 m

Ⓒ 24 m Ⓓ 26 m

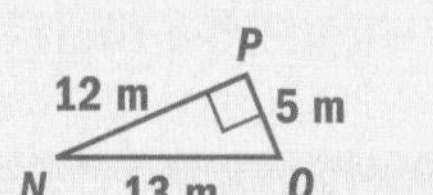

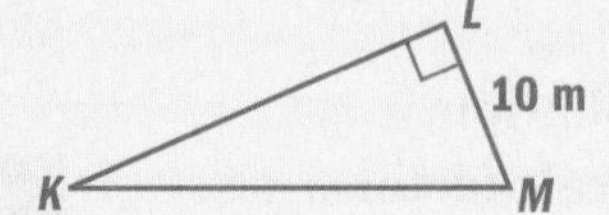

ELIMINATE CHOICES

Because $\triangle KLM$ is larger than $\triangle NPQ$, you know that the length of $\overline{KL}$ is greater than 12 m. So, you can eliminate choices A and B.

SOLUTION

Corresponding side lengths are proportional.

VOCABULARY

KL represents the length of $\overline{KL}$.

$\frac{KL}{NP} = \frac{LM}{PQ}$ **Write a proportion.**

$\frac{KL}{12\text{ m}} = \frac{10\text{ m}}{5\text{ m}}$ **Substitute given values.**

$KL = 24$ **Solve the proportion.**

▶ **Answer** The length of $\overline{KL}$ is 24 meters. The correct answer is C. Ⓐ Ⓑ Ⓒ Ⓓ

EXAMPLE 3 Using Indirect Measurement

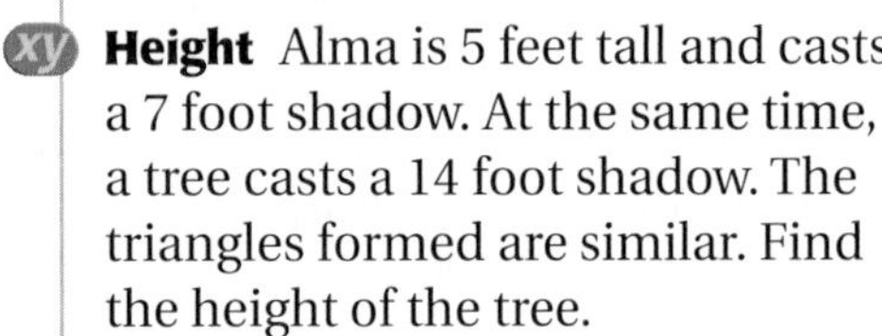

Height Alma is 5 feet tall and casts a 7 foot shadow. At the same time, a tree casts a 14 foot shadow. The triangles formed are similar. Find the height of the tree.

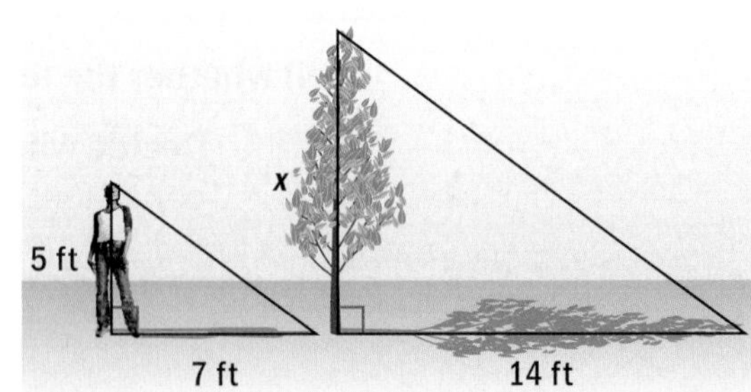

SOLUTION

You can use a proportion to find the height of the tree.

$\frac{\text{Tree's height}}{\text{Alma's height}} = \frac{\text{Length of tree's shadow}}{\text{Length of Alma's shadow}}$ **Write a proportion.**

$\frac{x\text{ feet}}{5\text{ feet}} = \frac{14\text{ feet}}{7\text{ feet}}$ **Substitute given values.**

$x = 10$ **Solve the proportion.**

▶ **Answer** The tree is 10 feet tall.

Dilations A **dilation** stretches or shrinks a figure. The image created by a dilation is similar to the original figure. The **scale factor** of a dilation is the ratio of a side length after the dilation to the corresponding side length before the dilation. In this lesson, the center of a dilation will always be the origin.

KEY CONCEPT *For Your Notebook*

Dilations

Words To dilate a polygon, multiply the coordinates of each vertex by the scale factor k.

Numbers $P(4, 1) \rightarrow P'(8, 2)$ **Algebra** $P(x, y) \rightarrow P'(kx, ky)$

EXAMPLE 4 Dilating a Polygon

Quadrilateral *ABCD* has vertices $A(-1, -1)$, $B(0, 1)$, $C(2, 2)$, and $D(3, 0)$. Dilate using a scale factor of 3.

SOLUTION

Graph the quadrilateral. Find the coordinates of the vertices of the image.

Original		Image
(x, y)	$\rightarrow$	$(3x, 3y)$
$A(-1, -1)$	$\rightarrow$	$A'(-3, -3)$
$B(0, 1)$	$\rightarrow$	$B'(0, 3)$
$C(2, 2)$	$\rightarrow$	$C'(6, 6)$
$D(3, 0)$	$\rightarrow$	$D'(9, 0)$

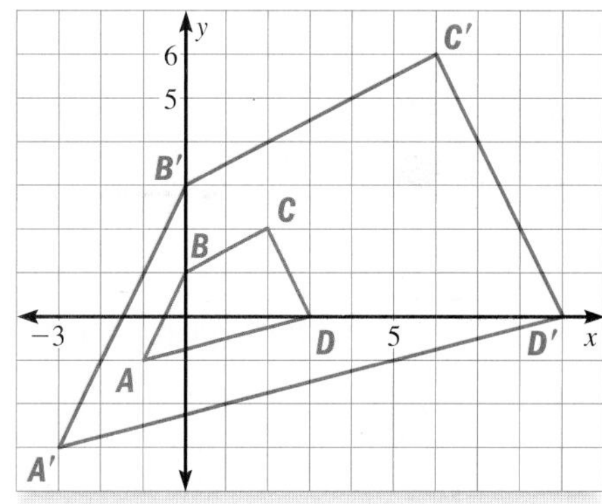

Graph the image of the quadrilateral.

SCALE FACTOR
A scale factor greater than 1 results in an enlargement of the original figure. A scale factor between 0 and 1 results in a reduction of the original figure.

GUIDED PRACTICE for Examples 2, 3, and 4

2. At the right, $ABCD \sim FGHJ$. Find the value of x.

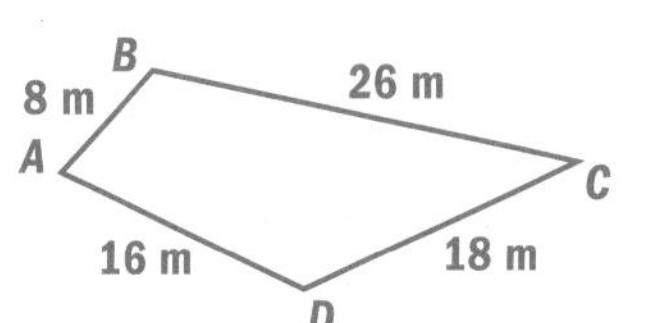

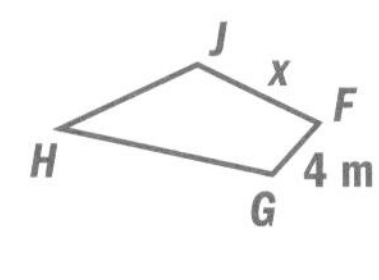

3. **What If?** Suppose the tree in Example 3 casts a shadow of 18 feet, a 6 foot tall person casts a 9 foot shadow, and the triangles are similar. Find the height of the tree. Check your answer for reasonableness.

4. Graph $\triangle RST$ with vertices $R(1, 1)$, $S(3, 2)$, and $T(2, 3)$. Then graph its image after a dilation using a scale factor of 2; a scale factor of $\frac{1}{3}$.

8.8 EXERCISES

HOMEWORK KEY

★ = **STANDARDIZED TEST PRACTICE** Exs. 18, 27, 29, 32, and 44

◯ = **HINTS AND HOMEWORK HELP** for Exs. 5, 9, 11, 15, 27 at classzone.com

SKILL PRACTICE

VOCABULARY **Copy and complete the statement.**

1. The __?__ of a dilation is the ratio of corresponding side lengths.

2. A polygon and its image after dilation are always __?__.

IDENTIFYING SIMILAR POLYGONS **Tell whether the polygons are similar. *Justify* your reasoning.**

SEE EXAMPLE 1 on p. 447 for Exs. 3–6

3.

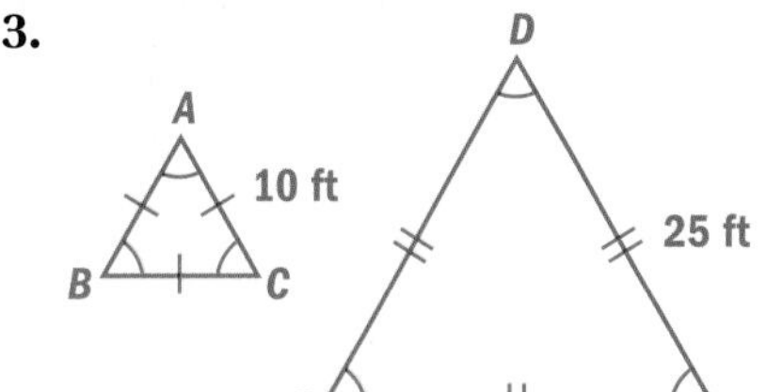

4.

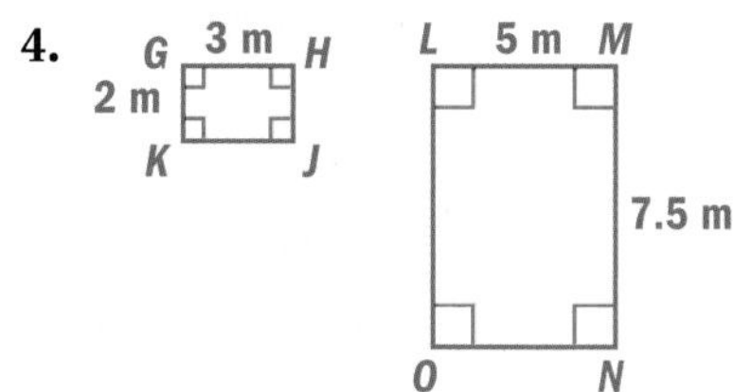

5.

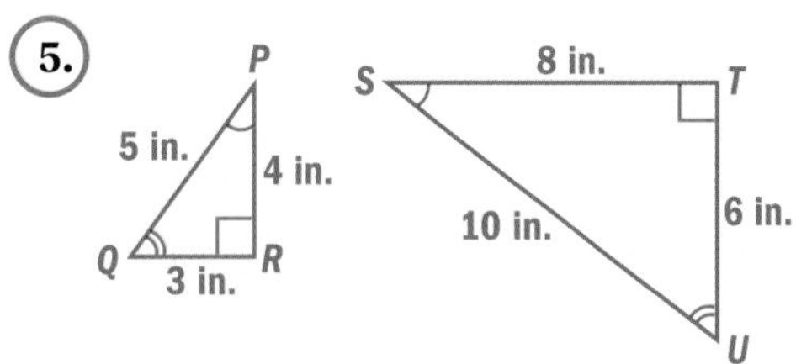

6.

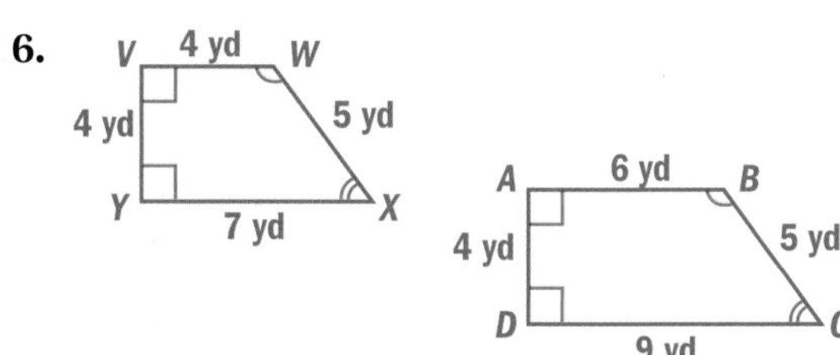

USING SIMILAR POLYGONS **Use the similar polygons to find the value of *x*.**

SEE EXAMPLE 2 on p. 448 for Exs. 7–10

7. $\triangle ABC \sim \triangle DEF$

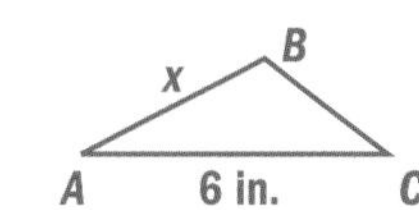

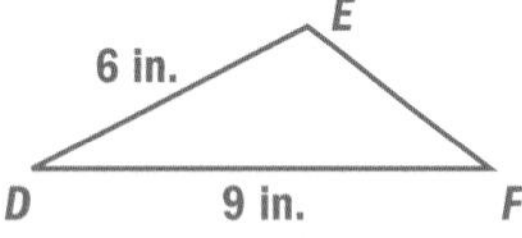

8. $\triangle GHJ \sim \triangle KHM$

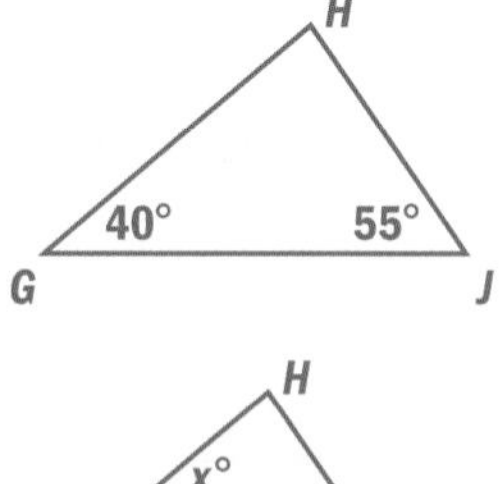

9. $CDFG \sim HJLK$.

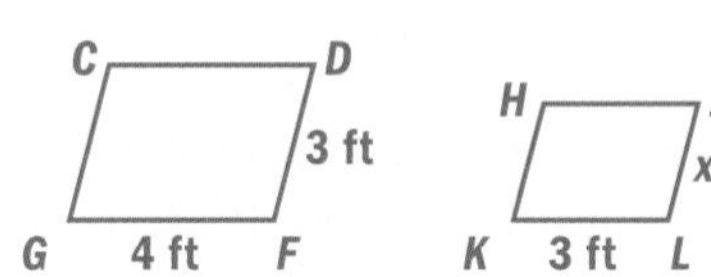

10. $MNPQ \sim RSTV$.

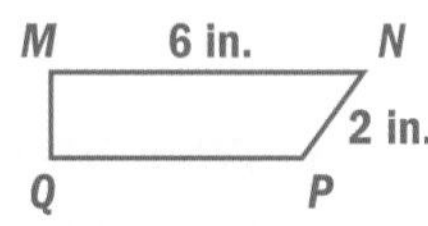

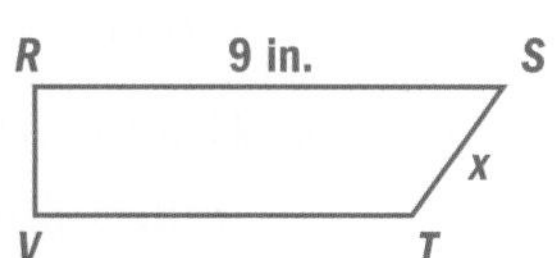

GRAPHING DILATIONS Graph the polygon with the given vertices. Then graph its image after dilation using a scale factor k.

SEE EXAMPLE 4 on p. 449 for Exs. 11–17

11. $W(2, 2), X(0, 4), Y(4, 6), Z(6, 0); k = 3$

12. $B(0, -2), C(4, 2), D(-, 6), E(-2, 6), F(-4, 2); k = \frac{1}{2}$

13. $R(8, 8), S(-4, 4), T(-4, -4); k = \frac{3}{4}$

14. $L(2, -2), M(4, 2), N(-3, 2), P(-1, -2); k = 4$

15. $G(-2, -6), H(-8, -8), J(-6, -2), K(0, 0); k = 1.5$

16. $K(24, 6), L(8, 10), M(8, 0), N(0, 18), P(20, 22); k = 1.75$

17. **ERROR ANALYSIS** A student is asked to graph the image of polygon *ABCD* after a dilation using a scale factor of 3. Describe and correct the student's error.

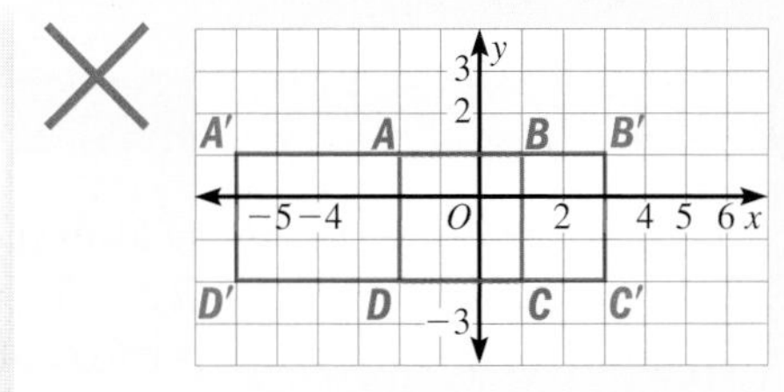

18. ★ **MULTIPLE CHOICE** $\triangle ABC \sim \triangle DEF$ by a scale factor of $\frac{1}{2}$. How does the area of $\triangle DEF$ compare to the area of $\triangle ABC$?

(A) 4 times as great (B) 2 times as great (C) $\frac{1}{2}$ as great (D) $\frac{1}{4}$ as great

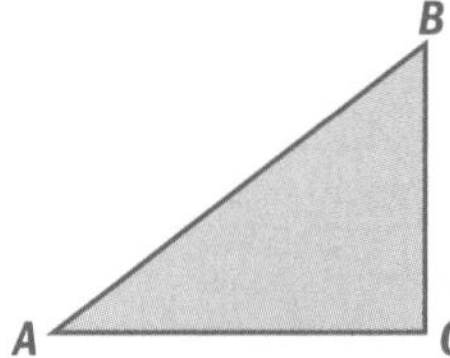

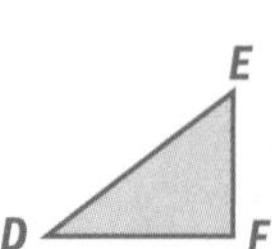

DILATIONS Graph the similar figures and find the scale factor.

19. $\triangle ABC$: $A(4, 6), B(8, 8), C(12, 4)$
$\triangle DEF$: $D(2, 3), E(4, 4), F(6, 2)$

20. *GHIJ*: $G(1, 4), H(6, 4), I(6, 1), J(1, 1)$
KLMN: $K(3, 12), L(18, 12), M(18, 3), N(3, 3)$

21. *PQRS*: $P(4, 8), Q(8, 8), R(8, 2), S(4, 2)$
TUVW: $T(8, 14), U(16, 14), V(16, 2), W(8, 2)$

22. **NAMING SIMILAR POLYGONS** Name two similar polygons in the diagram. Find the scale factor.

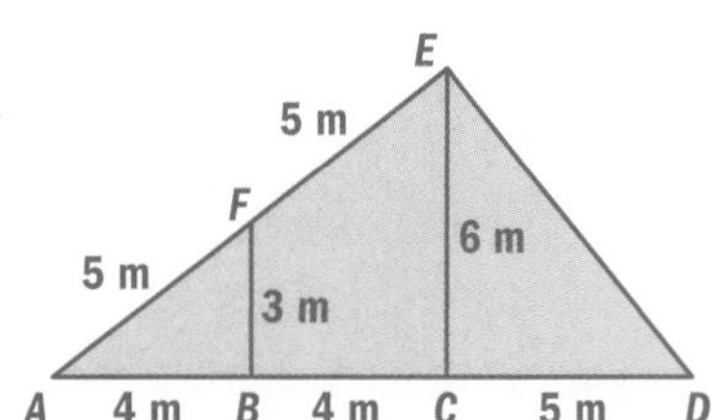

23. **USING SIMILAR POLYGONS** Pentagon *ABCDE* ~ pentagon *FGHJK*. Find the values of *x* and *y*.

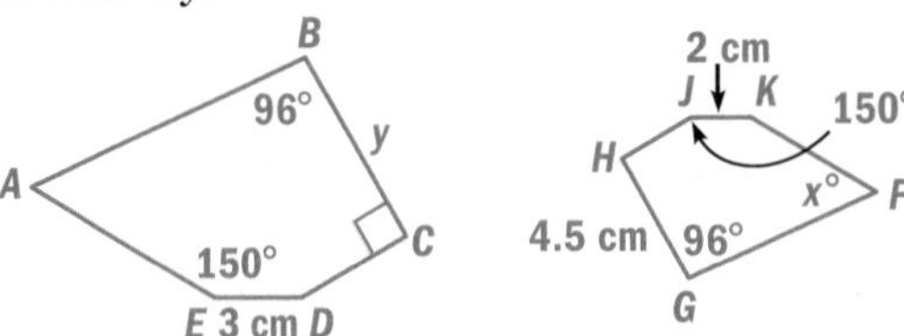

24. **CHALLENGE** Hexagon *ABCDEF* is similar to hexagon *PQRSTU*. Find the values of *x* and *y*.

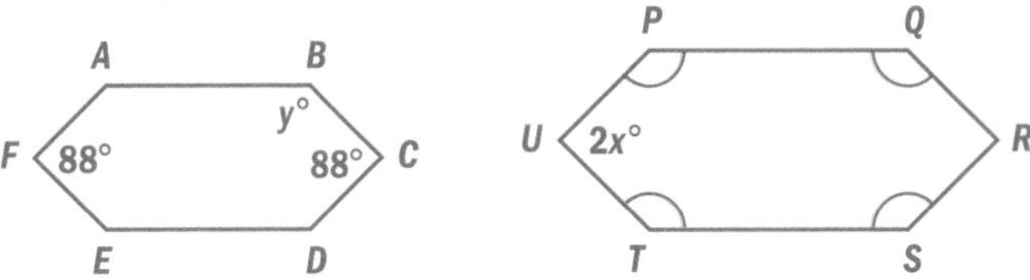

PROBLEM SOLVING

25. **SCALE FACTOR** *EFGH* is the image of *ABCD* after a dilation. The vertices of *ABCD* and *EFGH* are $A(-1, 2)$, $B(3, 2)$, $C(3, -1)$, $D(-1, -1)$, $E(-4, 8)$, $F(12, 8)$, $G(12, -4)$, and $H(-4, -4)$. What is the scale factor? What is the perimeter of *ABCD*? How is the ratio of the perimeter related to the scale factor?

26. **BOOKSHELF** A friend buys the bookshelf shown below for her bedroom. The assembly instructions include the diagram shown below. Is the diagram drawn to scale? *Justify* your reasoning.

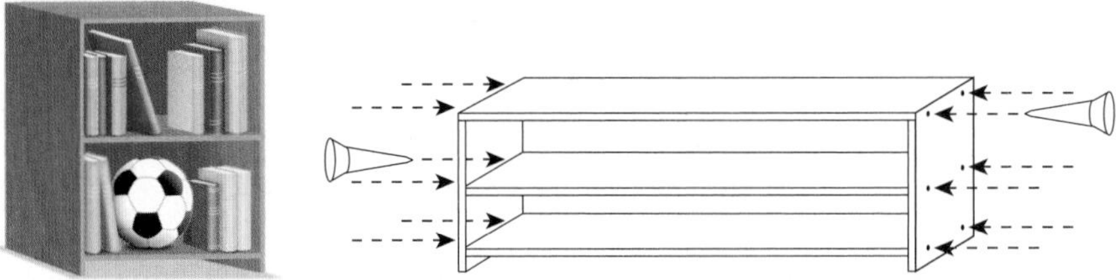

27. ★ **MULTIPLE CHOICE** Jenny is 5 feet tall and casts a 3 foot shadow. At the same time, a flagpole casts a 15 foot shadow. What is the height of the flagpole?

(A) 9 feet (B) 15 feet (C) 17 feet (D) 25 feet

28. **ESTIMATION** Rectangle *ABCD* is similar to rectangle *EFGH*. A friend says that *EF* is about 8 meters. Is this estimate reasonable? *Explain.*

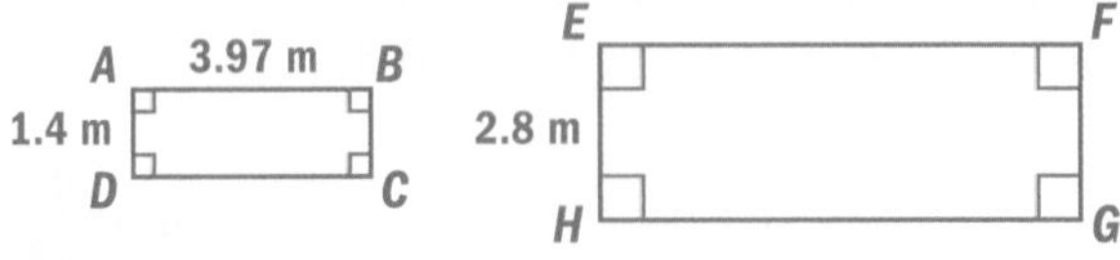

29. ★ **SHORT RESPONSE** If two triangles are congruent, are they also similar? *Explain.*

SEE EXAMPLE 3 on p. 448 for Ex. 30

30. INDIRECT MEASUREMENT Castle Fantastica on Camps Bay Beach in Cape Town, South Africa is one of the tallest sandcastles ever built. Its sculptors used over 400,000 pounds of sand. Suppose the sandcastle casts a shadow 140 feet long at the same time that your 5.5 feet tall friend casts a shadow 28 feet long. How tall is the sandcastle? Check for reasonableness.

31. REASONING A polygon is dilated by a scale factor of 1. Will the image be *larger than, smaller than,* or *identical to* the original polygon? *Explain.*

32. ★ WRITING *Explain* why all squares are similar, but not all rectangles are similar.

33. AREA The area of $ABCD$ is 80 square inches. $ABCD \sim WXYZ$. *Explain* how to find the area of $WXYZ$.

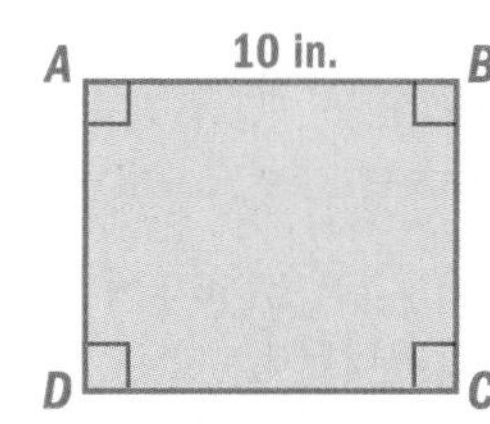

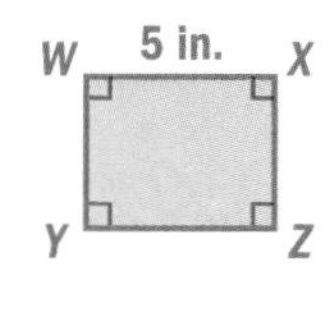

34. PERIMETER $\triangle RST$ is similar to $\triangle VWX$ where $RS = 10$ feet and $VW = 30$ feet. *Describe* the perimeter of $\triangle VWX$.

35. PHOTOGRAPHY The dimensions of a negative made from 35 mm film are 24 mm by 36 mm. If a 100 mm by 150 mm print is made from this negative, what is the scale factor?

36. CHALLENGE Show that $\triangle LMQ$ is similar to $\triangle ONQ$. *Justify* your reasoning.

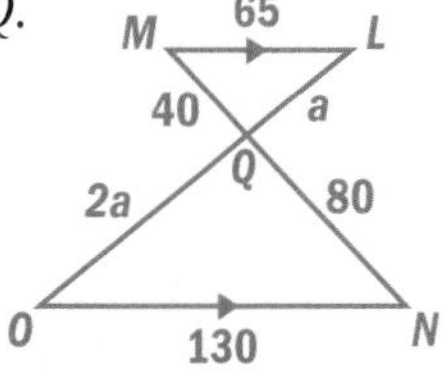

37. CHALLENGE A golden rectangle is one whose length and width are in a ratio of about 8 to 5. The golden spiral is formed by drawing arcs centered at the corner of each square. These rectangles and spirals are often found in nature, art, and architecture. Measure the dimensions of the rectangles below in millimeters. Name all the golden rectangles. Are they similar? *Explain.*

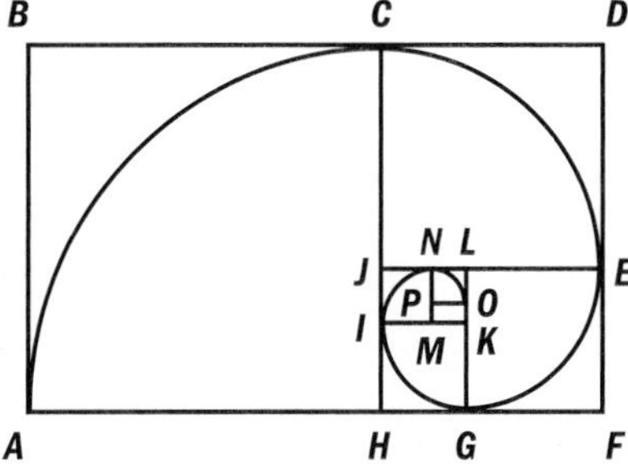

38. **CHALLENGE** Polygon *ABCD* is similar to polygon *RSTU*. The area of *ABCD* is 51 square centimeters. Find the area of *RSTU*. *Explain* your method.

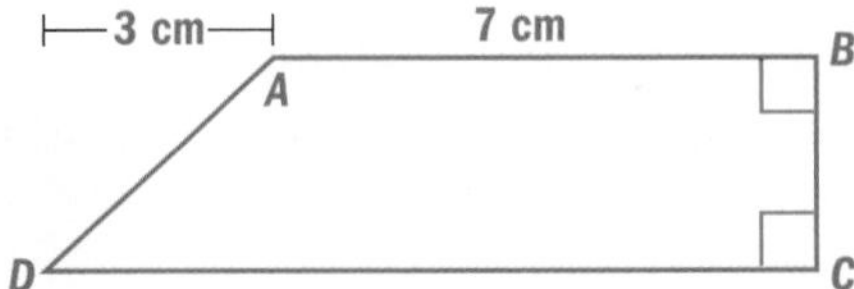

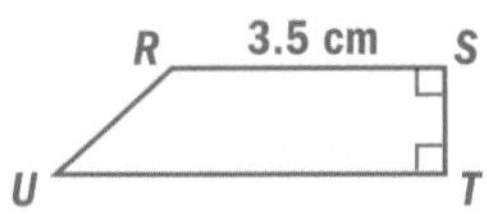

MIXED REVIEW

Get-Ready

Prepare for Lesson 9.1 in Exs. 39–42

Evaluate the power. ***(p. 19)***

39. 5^3 **40.** 2^4 **41.** 0^2 **42.** 1^9

CHOOSE A STRATEGY **Use a strategy from the list to solve the following problem. *Explain* your choice of strategy.**

43. An ice cream stand offers vanilla, chocolate, mint chip, cookie crumble, and strawberry ice cream. Write all the possible two scoop cones you can order. How many possibilities are there?

Problem Solving Strategies
- Draw a Diagram *(p. 787)*
- Make a List *(p. 790)*
- Look for a Pattern *(p. 791)*

44. ★ **MULTIPLE CHOICE** Triangle *ABC* has vertices at *A*(1, 4), *B*(3, 3), and *C*(1, 1). Which of the following are the vertices of the image of △*ABC* after a reflection in the *x*-axis? ***(p. 433)***

Ⓐ *A*′(−1, 4) *B*′(−3, 3) *C*′(−1, 1)
Ⓑ *A*′(1, −4) *B*′(3, −3) *C*′(1, −1)
Ⓒ *A*′(−3, 4) *B*′(−1, 3) *C*′(−3, 1)
Ⓓ *A*′(1, −1) *B*′(3, −2) *C*′(1, −4)

QUIZ for Lessons 8.5–8.8

Find the value of *x*.

1. △*ABC* ≅ △*DEF* ***(p. 427)***

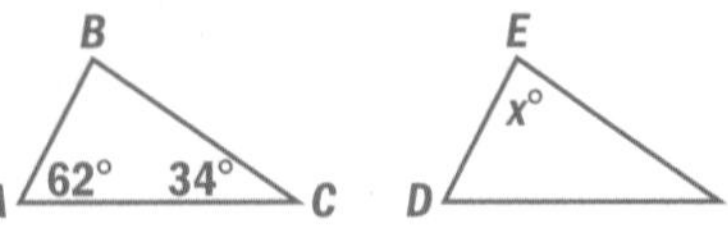

2. *PQRS* ~ *WXYZ* ***(p. 447)***

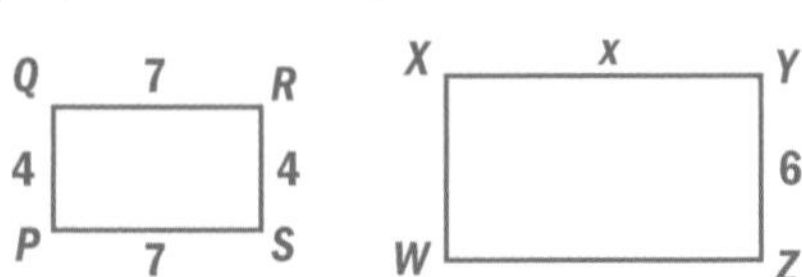

Name the type of transformation modeled by the action. ***(pp. 433, 439)***

3. Sledding downhill

4. Leaving fingerprints

5. Spinning in place

6. Opening a drawer

7. Graph △*ABC* with vertices *A*(1, 1), *B*(2, 3), and *C*(3, 0). Dilate the triangle using a scale factor of 4. Translate 2 units to the right and 3 units down, then reflect the triangle over the *y*-axis. ***(p. 447)***

MIXED REVIEW *of Problem Solving*

Lessons 8.5–8.8

1. **MULTI-STEP PROBLEM** You are designing a model car that is a replica of a full-sized car. The scale factor of the model to the full-sized car is $\frac{1}{24}$.

   a. The license plate on the model car is $\frac{1}{4}$ inch high and $\frac{1}{2}$ inch wide. What are the dimensions of the license plate on the full-sized car?

   b. Find the perimeter of the license plate on the model car.

   c. Show two methods to find the perimeter of the license plate on the full-sized car.

   d. You design a second model car that is $\frac{1}{4}$ the size of the first model you designed. Use three methods to find the perimeter of the license plate on the second model car.

2. **OPEN-ENDED** Translate $\triangle ABC$ using a rule of your choice. *Describe* the rules you used and give the coordinates of the vertices of the image of $\triangle ABC$.

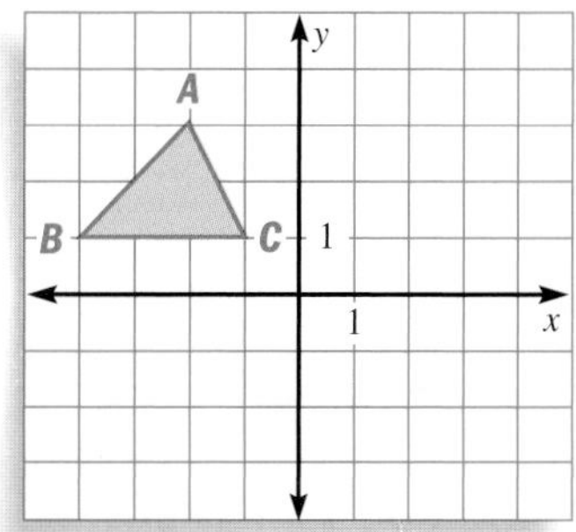

3. **GRIDDED ANSWER** Karen wants to find the height of a tree that is 75 feet away from a pole that is 25 feet tall. When she stands 15 feet from the pole, she can see the top of the tree and the top of the pole line up in her line of sight. Her eyes are 5 feet from the ground. How tall is the tree?

4. **SHORT RESPONSE** A non-square rhombus is divided into two triangles by a diagonal. Tell whether the two triangles formed are congruent. *Justify* your reasoning. Does it matter whether the diagonal is drawn between the corners that are closer together or between the corners that are farther apart? *Explain.*

5. **EXTENDED RESPONSE** Refer to Figure *A* and Figure *B* shown below.

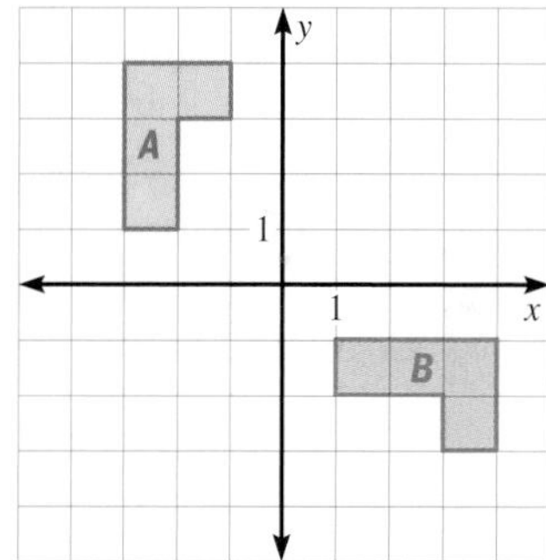

   a. *Describe* how to transform Figure *A* to Figure *B* using a translation followed by a rotation about the origin.

   b. *Describe* how to transform Figure *A* to Figure *B* using a rotation about the origin followed by a translation.

   c. Figure *A* can be transformed to Figure *B* using only one rotation if the common center of rotation were a point other than the origin. In which quadrant would this point lie? *Explain.*

8 CHAPTER REVIEW

@HomeTutor
classzone.com
Vocabulary Practice

REVIEW KEY VOCABULARY

- straight angle, *p. 403*
- right angle, *p. 403*
- supplementary, *p. 403*
- complementary, *p. 403*
- vertical angles, *p. 404*
- perpendicular lines, *p. 404*
- parallel lines, *p. 405*
- acute, obtuse angle, *p. 411*
- acute, right, obtuse triangle, *p. 411*
- equilateral, isosceles, scalene triangle, *p. 411*
- quadrilateral, trapezoid, *p. 416*
- parallelogram, rhombus, *p. 416*
- polygon, pentagon, *p. 420*
- regular polygon, *p. 420*
- hexagon, heptagon, *p. 420*
- octagon, *p. 420*
- congruent segments, *p. 427*
- congruent angles, *p. 427*
- corresponding parts, *p. 427*
- reflection, *p. 433*
- transformation, *p. 433*
- image, *p. 433*
- line symmetry, *p. 435*
- translation, *p. 439*
- rotation, *p. 440*
- similar polygons, *p. 447*
- dilation, *p. 449*
- scale factor, *p. 449*

VOCABULARY EXERCISES

Match each word with the correct definition.

1. Transformation

2. Reflection

3. Translation

4. Dilation

A. A transformation that stretches or shrinks a figure

B. A transformation that slides a figure

C. A transformation that creates a mirror image of a figure

D. An operation that changes one figure into another figure

Copy and complete the statement.

5. Two angles whose measures have a sum of 90° are __?__ angles.

6. Two lines on the same plane that never intersect are __?__.

7. A(n) __?__ is a polygon with seven sides.

8. A figure has __?__ if one half of the figure is a mirror image of the other half.

REVIEW EXAMPLES AND EXERCISES

8.1 Angle Pairs *pp. 403–408*

EXAMPLE

The measure of $\angle 1$ is 115°. Find the measure of $\angle 2$.

$m\angle 1 + m\angle 2 = 180°$ **Definition of supplementary angles**

$115° + m\angle 2 = 180°$ **Substitute 115° for $m\angle 1$.**

$m\angle 2 = 65°$ **Subtract 115° from each side.**

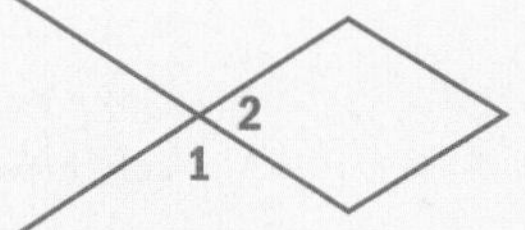

EXERCISES

Find the measure of $\angle 1$.

SEE EXAMPLES 1, 2, AND 3 on pp. 403–405 for Exs. 9–12

9. 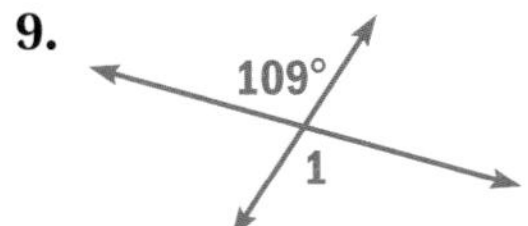

10. 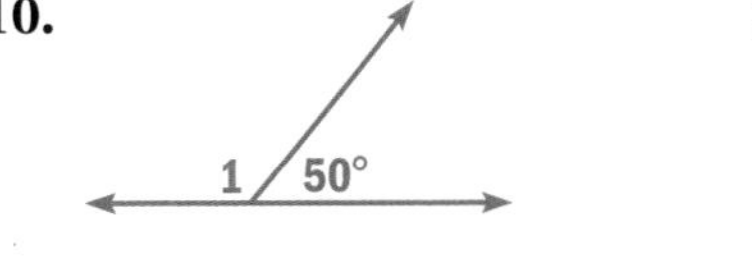

11. 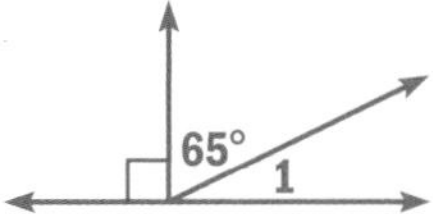

12. Find the measures of $\angle 1$, $\angle 2$, $\angle 3$, $\angle 4$, and $\angle 5$. *Justify* your reasoning.

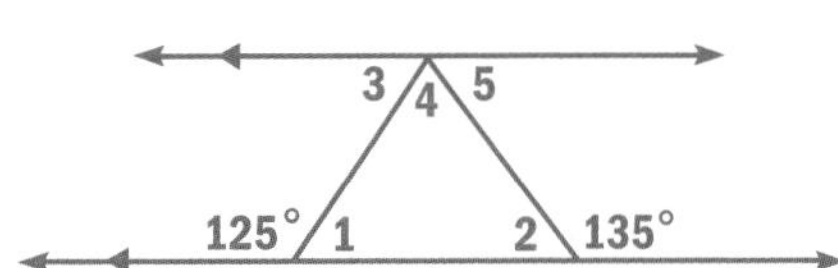

8.2 Angles and Triangles

pp. 411–415

EXAMPLE

Find the value of x.

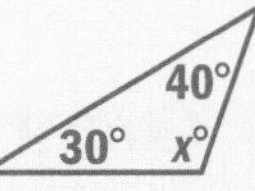

$x° + 30° + 40° = 180°$	**Sum of angle measures is 180°.**
$x + 70 = 180$	**Add.**
$x = 110$	**Subtract 70 from each side.**

EXERCISES

SEE EXAMPLE 2 on p. 412 for Exs. 13–15

The measures of two angles of a triangle are given. Find the value of x. Then classify the triangle by its angles.

13. 90°, 64°, $x°$

14. 17°, 55°, $x°$

15. 40°, 52°, $x°$

8.3 Quadrilaterals

pp. 416–419

EXAMPLE

Classify the quadrilateral.

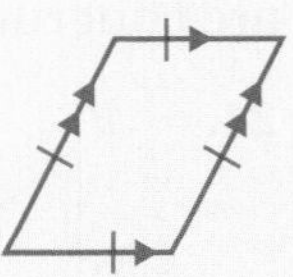

The figure is a parallelogram with 4 sides of equal length. So, it is a rhombus.

EXERCISES

SEE EXAMPLES 1 AND 2 on pp. 416–417 for Exs. 16–18

Classify the quadrilateral and find the value of x.

16. 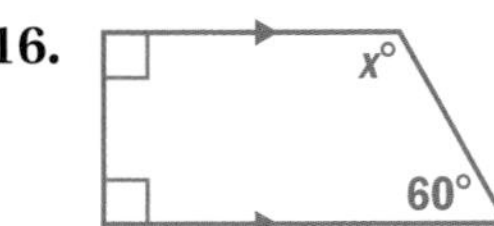

17. 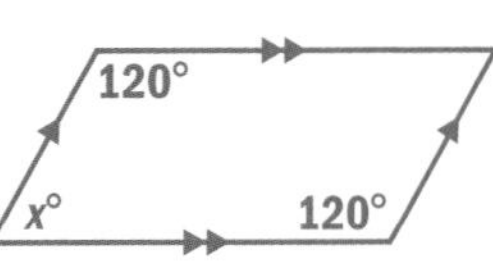

18. 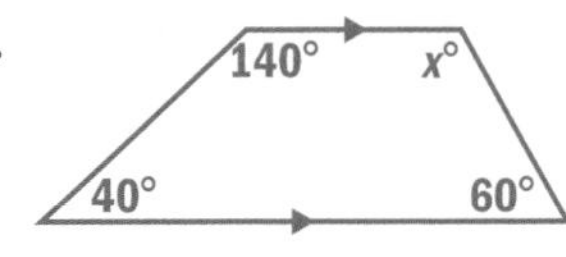

8.4 Polygons and Angles

pp. 420–424

EXAMPLE

Find the measure of $\angle A$ in regular pentagon *ABCDE*.

$m\angle A = \frac{(n-2) \cdot 180°}{n}$ **Formula for measure of one angle in regular polygon**

$= \frac{(5-2) \cdot 180°}{5}$ **Substitute 5 for *n*.**

$= 108°$ **Simplify.**

EXERCISES

SEE EXAMPLE 2 on p. 421 for Exs. 19–20

19. Find the measure of one angle in a regular 12-gon.

20. Find the sum of the angle measures in a hexagon.

8.5 Congruent Polygons

pp. 427–432

EXAMPLE

Name the congruent triangles. *Explain* how you know that they are congruent.

$\angle M \cong \angle R$ **Angles are congruent.**

$\overline{LM} \cong \overline{SR}$ **Sides are congruent.**

$\angle L \cong \angle S$ **Angles are congruent.**

$\triangle LMN \cong \triangle SRT$ by Angle-Side-Angle.

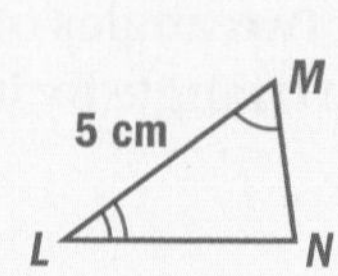

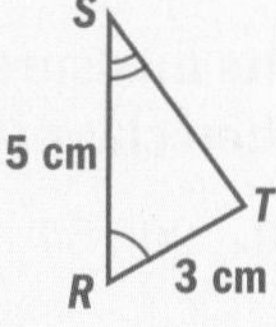

EXERCISES

Name the congruent triangles. *Explain* how you know they are congruent.

SEE EXAMPLE 3 on p. 429 for Exs. 21–24

21.

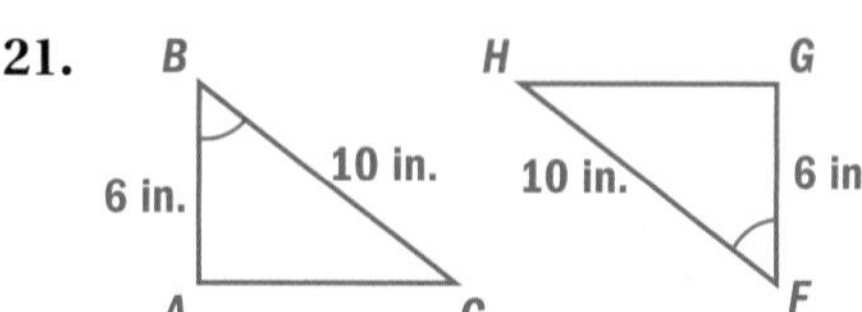

22.

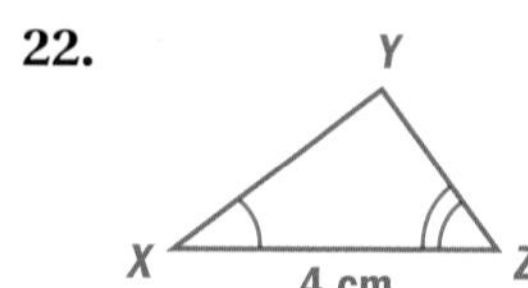

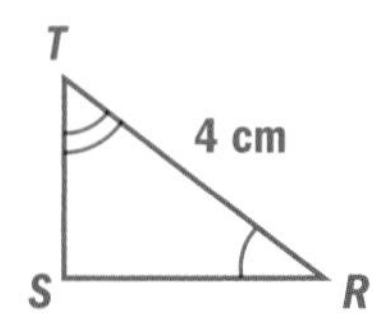

23. L M N R Q P

24.

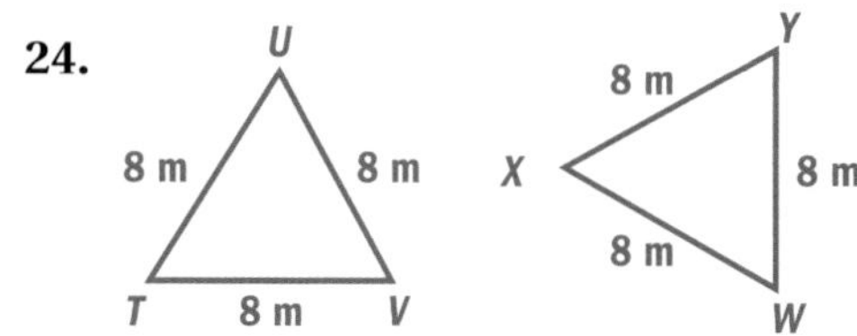

8.6 Reflections and Symmetry

pp. 433–438

EXAMPLE 1

Graph $\triangle ABC$ with vertices $A(1, 3)$, $B(4, 3)$, and $C(3, 1)$. Then graph its reflection in the x-axis.

Original		Image
(x, y)	$\rightarrow$	$(x, -y)$
$A(1, 3)$	$\rightarrow$	$A'(1, -3)$
$B(4, 3)$	$\rightarrow$	$B'(4, -3)$
$C(3, 1)$	$\rightarrow$	$C'(3, -1)$

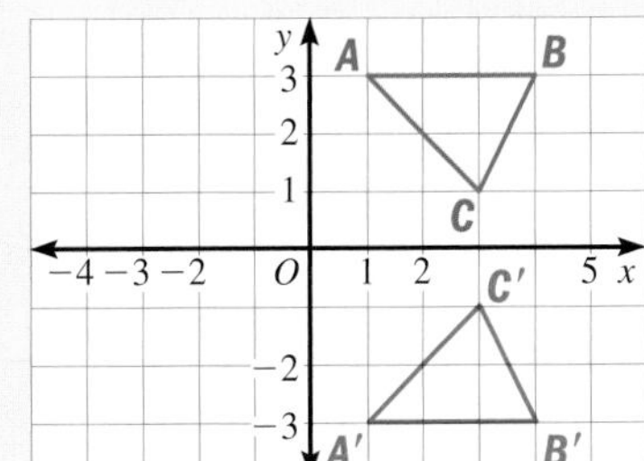

SEE EXAMPLE 2 on p. 433 for Ex. 25

EXERCISES

25. Graph the reflection of $\triangle ABC$ shown above in the y-axis.

EXAMPLE 2

How many lines of symmetry does the butterfly have?

The butterfly has one line of symmetry.

EXERCISES

How many lines of symmetry does the figure have?

SEE EXAMPLE 4 on p. 435 for Exs. 26–28

26. 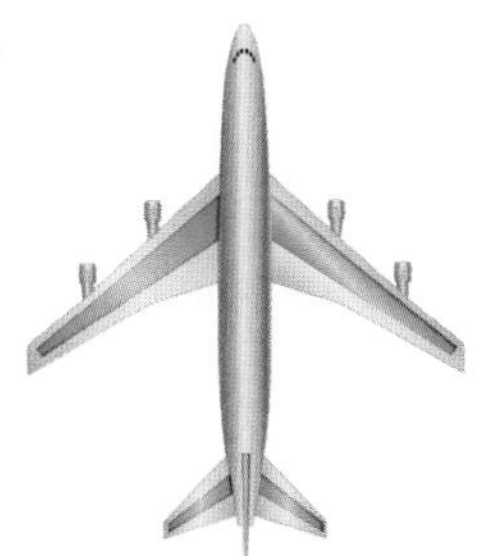

27. 

28. 

8.7 Translations and Rotations

pp. 439–444

EXAMPLE

Graph $\triangle KLM$ with vertices $K(3, 1)$, $L(1, 4)$, and $M(3, 3)$. Then rotate it 90° counterclockwise, and graph the image.

Original		**Image**
(x, y)	$\rightarrow$	$(-y, x)$
$K(3, 1)$	$\rightarrow$	$K'(-1, 3)$
$L(1, 4)$	$\rightarrow$	$L'(-4, 1)$
$M(3, 3)$	$\rightarrow$	$M'(-3, 3)$

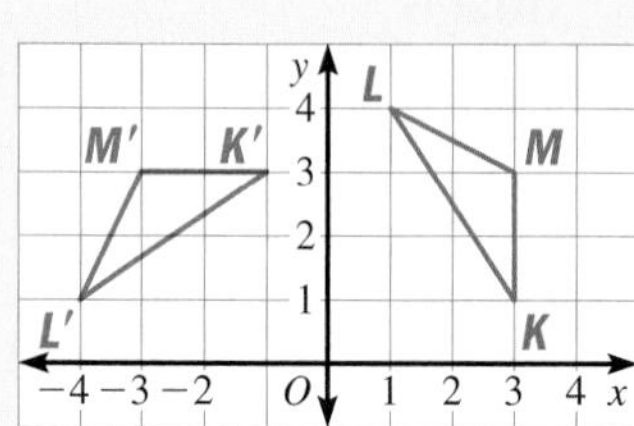

EXERCISES

SEE EXAMPLES 1 AND 3 on pp. 439, 441 for Exs. 29–30

Use $\triangle KLM$ in the Example above.

29. Translate $\triangle KLM$ using $(x, y) \rightarrow (x - 2, y + 1)$.

30. Rotate $\triangle KLM$ 180° and graph its image.

8.8 Similarity and Dilations

pp. 447–454

EXAMPLE

Polygons *ABCD* and *FGHJ* are similar. Find the length of $\overline{BC}$.

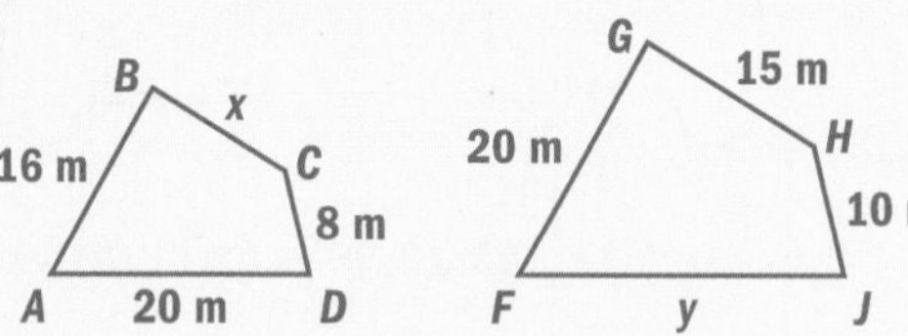

$\frac{AB}{FG} = \frac{BC}{GH}$ **Write a proportion.**

$\frac{16}{20} = \frac{x}{15}$ **Substitute.**

$x = 12$ **Solve for *x*.**

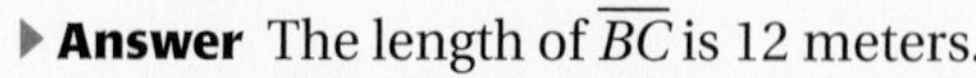

▸ **Answer** The length of $\overline{BC}$ is 12 meters.

EXERCISES

SEE EXAMPLES 2 AND 3 on p. 448 for Exs. 31–32

31. Building Heights A 20 foot flagpole stands beside a building. The flagpole casts a shadow that is 25 feet long. At the same time, the building casts a shadow that is 60 feet long. How tall is the building?

32. Rectangle *JKLM* is the image of rectangle *PQRS* after a dilation. *PQRS* has a length of 40 centimeters and a width of 10 centimeters. *JKLM* has a perimeter of 20 centimeters. Find the scale factor, then find the length and width of *JKLM*.

8 CHAPTER TEST

@HomeTutor
classzone.com
Chapter Test Practice

Find the measures of the numbered angles.

1. 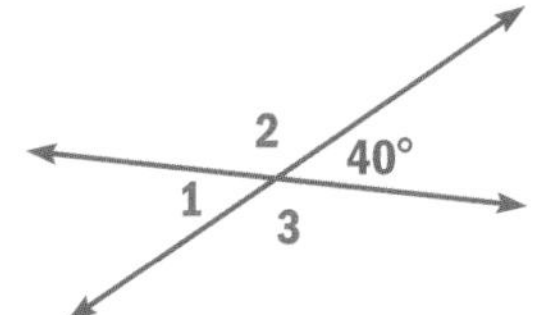

2. 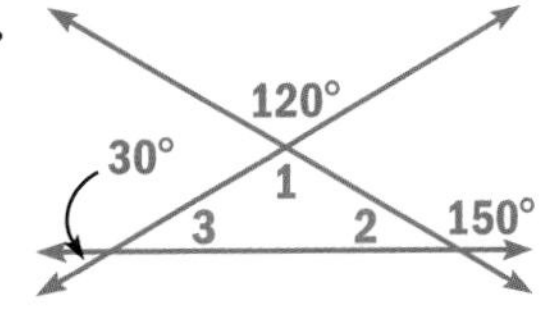

3. 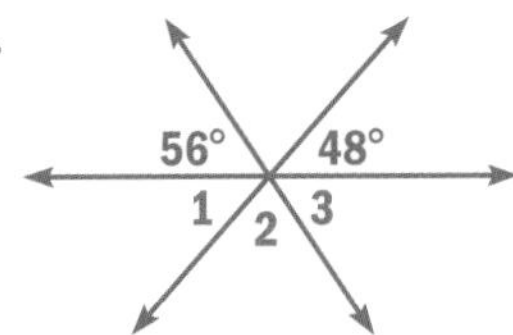

Find the measure of the numbered angle.

4. 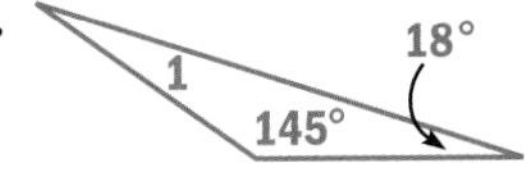

5. 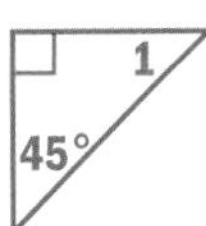

6. 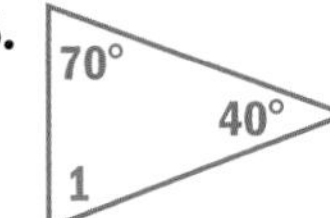

Classify the quadrilateral.

7. 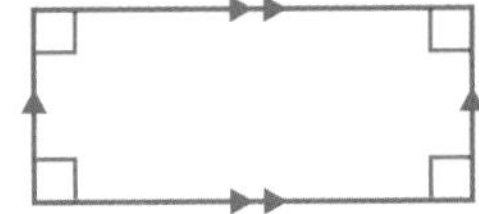

8. 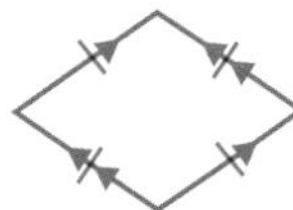

9. 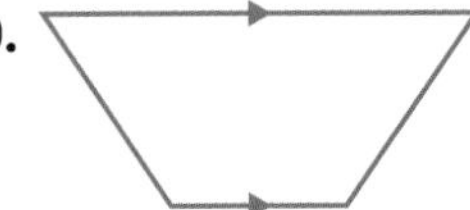

Find the measure of one angle in the polygon.

10. Square

11. Regular octagon

12. Regular 9-gon

13. **ALGEBRA** Write and solve an equation to find the value of x.

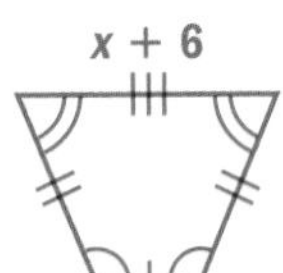

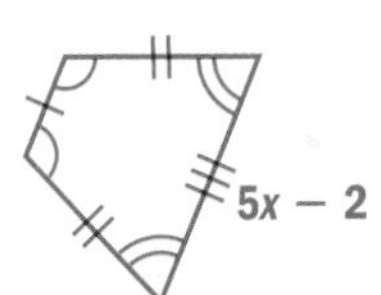

Graph the figure and its image after the given transformation.

14. Rotate 180°.

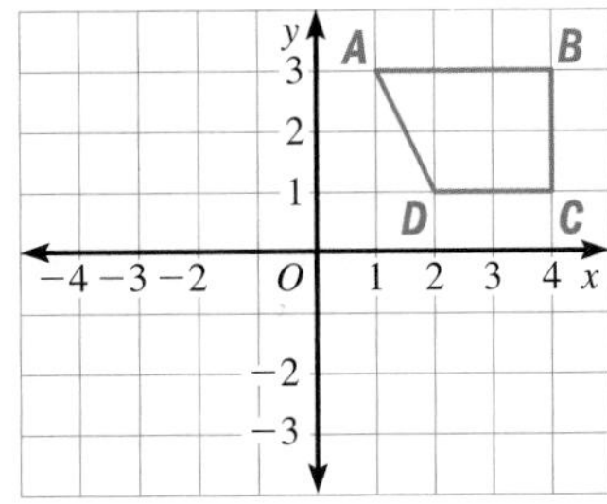

15. Translate using $(x, y) \to (x - 5, y + 3)$.

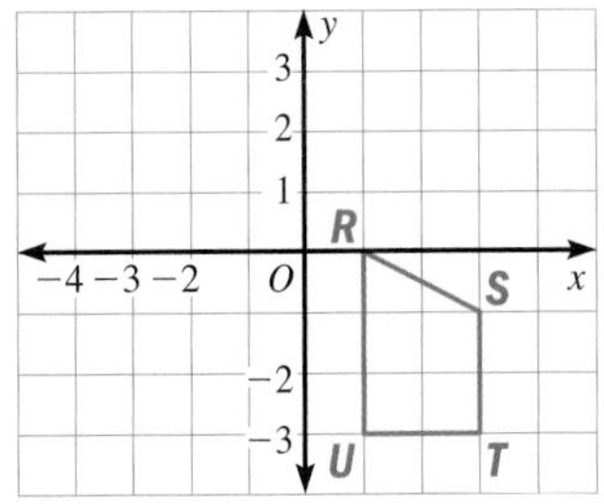

16. **SHADOWS** Joe is 72 inches tall and has a 108 inch shadow. At the same time, Martha has a 96 inch shadow. How tall is Martha?

17. The lengths of the sides of a triangle are 5 centimeters, 12 centimeters, and 15 centimeters. The shortest side of a similar triangle has a length of 12.5 centimeters. Find the lengths of the other two sides. What is the perimeter of each triangle? What is the scale factor?

CONTEXT-BASED MULTIPLE CHOICE QUESTIONS

Some of the information you need to solve a context-based multiple choice question may appear in a table, a diagram, or a graph.

PROBLEM 1

Which graph shows the image of $\triangle LMN$ after a 90° clockwise rotation followed by a translation using $(x, y) \rightarrow (x + 1, y + 3)$?

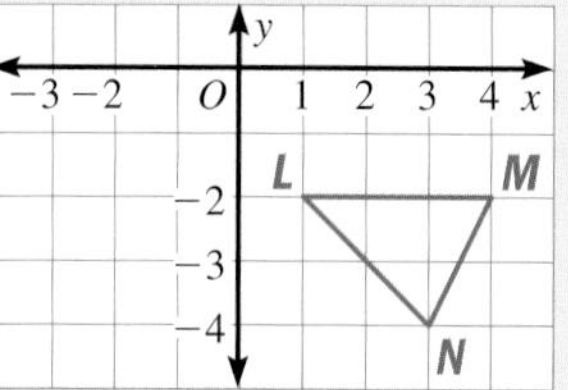

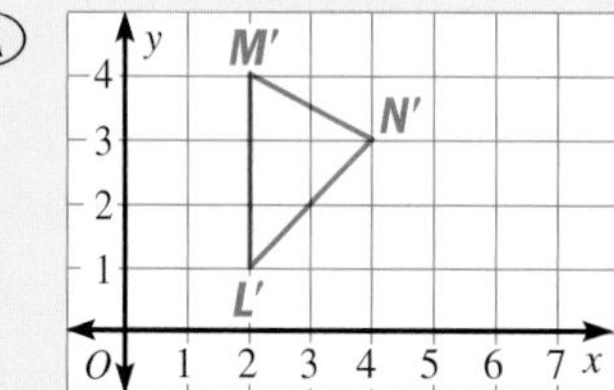

(B)

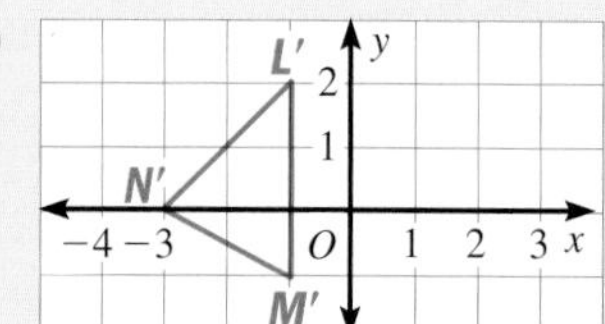

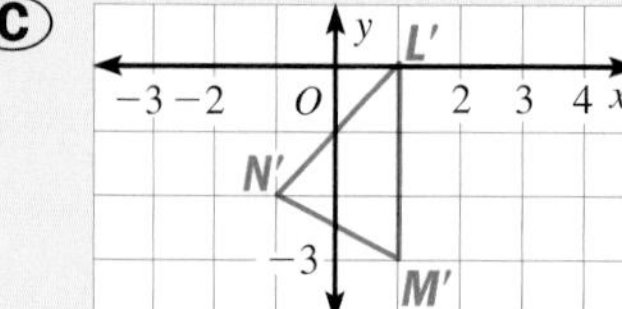

(D)

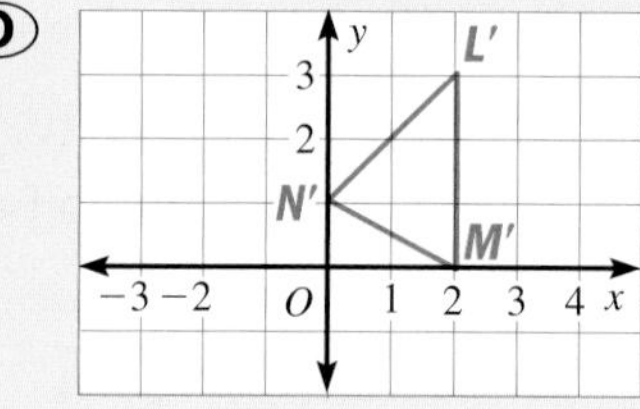

Plan

STEP 1 Read the problem carefully and make a plan.

INTERPRET THE GRAPH List the vertices of $\triangle LMN$. Then rotate and translate each vertex. To rotate a point 90° clockwise, switch the coordinates, then multiply the new y-coordinate by -1. To translate a point, add 1 to the x-coordinate and add 3 to the y-coordinate.

Solution

STEP 2 List the vertices of $\triangle LMN$. Then rotate and translate each vertex.

The vertices of $\triangle LMN$ are $L(1, -2)$, $M(4, -2)$, and $N(3, -4)$.

Original vertex	Rotated Image	Translated Image
$L(1, -2)$	$L'(-2, -1)$	$L''(-1, 2)$
$M(4, -2)$	$M'(-2, -4)$	$M''(-1, -1)$
$N(3, -4)$	$N'(-4, -3)$	$N''(-3, 0)$

STEP 3 Determine which graph shows the correct image of $\triangle LMN$.

The vertices of the image of $\triangle LMN$ are $L''(-1, 2)$, $M''(-1, -1)$, and $N''(-3, 0)$.

The correct answer is B. (A) (B) (C) (D)

PROBLEM 2

In the diagram at the right, $\triangle ABC \sim \triangle DEF$. The area of $\triangle ABC$ is 24 square feet. What is the area of $\triangle DEF$?

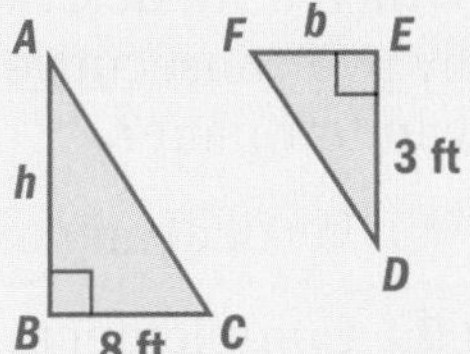

Ⓐ 4 square feet Ⓑ 6 square feet

Ⓒ 12 square feet Ⓓ 24 square feet

STEP 1
Read the problem carefully. Decide how you can use the given information to solve the problem.

Plan

INTERPRET THE DIAGRAM The base of $\triangle ABC$ and the height of $\triangle DEF$ are given. Because the two triangles are similar, you know that their corresponding sides are proportional. Find the height of $\triangle ABC$ and then write and solve a proportion to find the base of $\triangle DEF$.

Solution

STEP 2
Find the height of $\triangle ABC$.

Find the height of $\triangle ABC$ using the area of $\triangle ABC$.

$A = \frac{1}{2}bh$ $\qquad 24 = \frac{1}{2}(8)(h)$, so $h = 6$

STEP 3
Write and solve a proportion.

Write a proportion to solve for b:

$\frac{AB}{DE} = \frac{BC}{b}$ $\qquad \frac{6}{3} = \frac{8}{b}$, so $b = 4$.

STEP 4
Find the area of $\triangle DEF$.

Use b to find the area of $\triangle DEF$.

$A = \frac{1}{2}bh$ $\qquad A = \frac{1}{2}(4)(3) = 6$

The correct answer is B. Ⓐ Ⓑ Ⓒ Ⓓ

PRACTICE

In Exercises 1–3, use the diagram at the right.

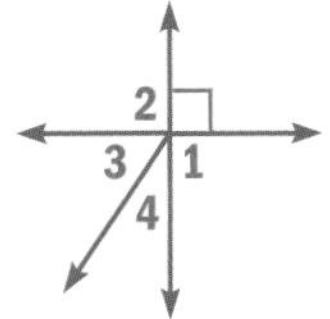

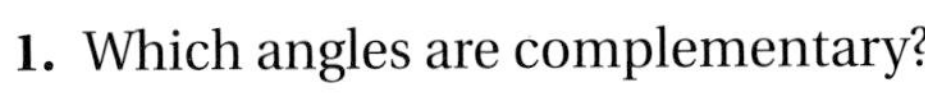

1. Which angles are complementary?

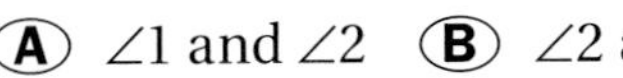

Ⓐ $\angle 1$ and $\angle 2$ Ⓑ $\angle 2$ and $\angle 3$
Ⓒ $\angle 3$ and $\angle 4$ Ⓓ $\angle 1$ and $\angle 4$

2. Which angles are vertical angles?

Ⓐ $\angle 1$ and $\angle 2$ Ⓑ $\angle 2$ and $\angle 4$ Ⓒ $\angle 3$ and $\angle 1$ Ⓓ $\angle 1$ and $\angle 4$

3. What kind of angle is $\angle 1$?

Ⓐ Acute Ⓑ Obtuse Ⓒ Right Ⓓ Straight

MULTIPLE CHOICE

1. Which term describes the figure formed by two consecutive sides of a rectangular window pane?

   Ⓐ Vertical angles

   Ⓑ Complementary angle

   Ⓒ Acute angle

   Ⓓ Perpendicular lines

2. What is the value of $x + z$ in the figure below?

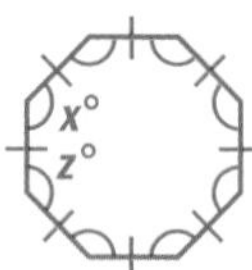

   Ⓐ 90 Ⓑ 180

   Ⓒ 270 Ⓓ 360

3. How many lines of symmetry does the figure have?

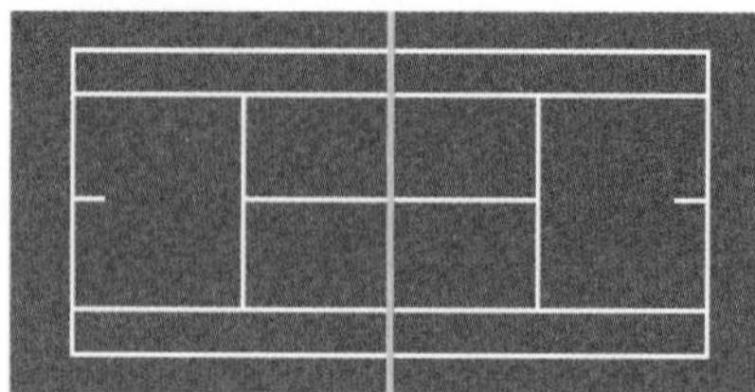

   Ⓐ 1 Ⓑ 2

   Ⓒ 3 Ⓓ 4

4. $\angle A$ is supplementary to $\angle B$, and $\angle B$ is supplementary to $\angle C$. If $m\angle A = 118°$, what is $m\angle C$?

   Ⓐ 28° Ⓑ 34°

   Ⓒ 62° Ⓓ 118°

5. Which transformation makes the red figure the image of the blue figure?

   Ⓐ Reflection in x-axis

   Ⓑ 90° clockwise rotation

   Ⓒ $(x, y) \rightarrow (x + 3, y + 2)$

   Ⓓ $(x, y) \rightarrow (x - 3, y - 2)$

6. Which of the following statements is *not* true about x and y in the figure below?

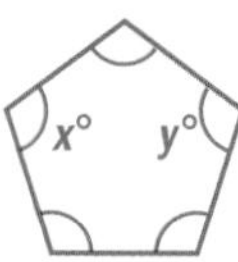

   Ⓐ $x = y$ Ⓑ $x + y = 144$

   Ⓒ $x + y = 216$ Ⓓ $2x + y = 324$

7. What is the sum of the angle measures in a 9-gon?

   Ⓐ 1260° Ⓑ 1620°

   Ⓒ 2520° Ⓓ 3240°

8. How many lines of symmetry does the figure at the right have?

   Ⓐ 0 Ⓑ 1 Ⓒ 2 Ⓓ 4

9. In the diagrams, the red figure is the image of the blue figure. Which diagram shows a reflection followed by a rotation of 180°?

   Ⓐ A ∀ Ⓑ B ᗺ

   Ⓒ C Ɔ Ⓓ D D

10. Which statement is *always* true?

    Ⓐ Supplementary angles are congruent.

    Ⓑ Complementary angles are congruent.

    Ⓒ Acute angles are congruent.

    Ⓓ Vertical angles are congruent.

11. Find the sum of the measure of one angle in a regular 12-gon and the measure of one angle in a regular octagon.

    Ⓐ 75° Ⓑ 150° Ⓒ 200° Ⓓ 285°

GRIDDED ANSWER

12. What is the value of x?

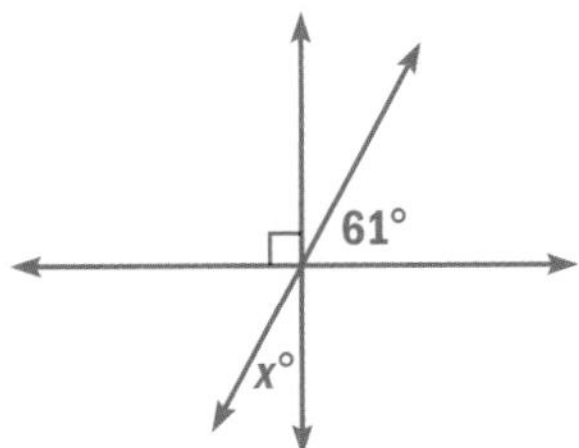

13. In the diagram below, $\triangle ABD \sim \triangle BCD$. What is the length of $\overline{AB}$?

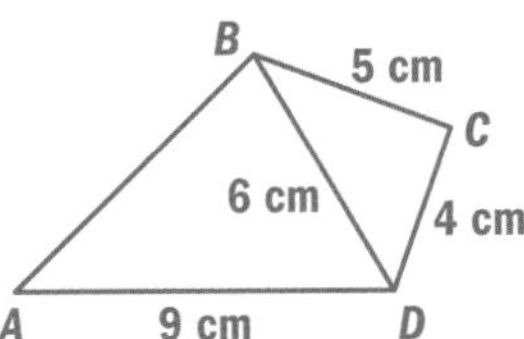

14. In the triangle below, find $m\angle C$.

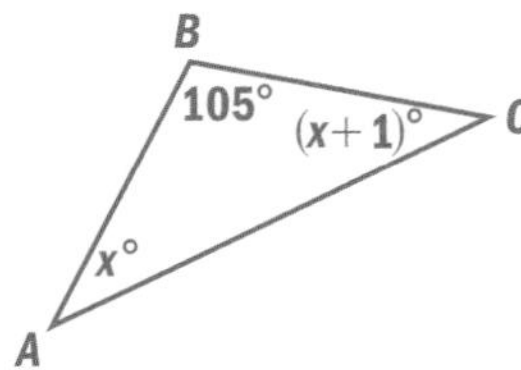

SHORT RESPONSE

15. Find the value of x in the diagram below. *Explain* how you found your answer.

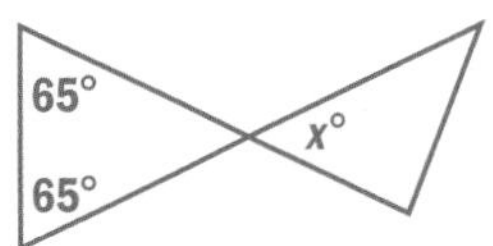

16. *Explain* how you know that $\triangle ABC \sim \triangle PQR$.

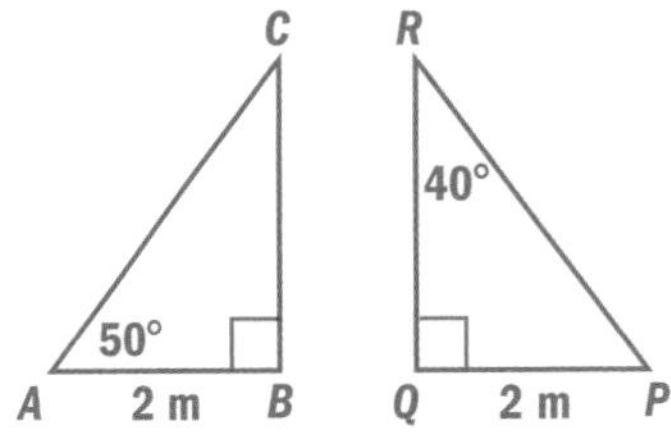

17. Graph $\triangle RST$ with vertices $R(1, 3)$, $S(3, 0)$, and $T(1, 0)$. Graph $\triangle BAC$ with vertices $A(-3, 0)$, $B(-1, 3)$, and $C(-1, 0)$. Use two methods to show that the triangles are congruent.

EXTENDED RESPONSE

18. You reduce a 16 inch by 24 inch photo to $\frac{1}{4}$ its original dimensions.

- **a.** What are the dimensions of the photo after it is reduced?
- **b.** Each page of a photo album holds two 3 inch by 5 inch photos. Will the reduced photo fit in the album? *Explain.*
- **c.** A matte is placed around the reduced photo, as shown. The area of the matte is 11 square inches, and the length of the matte is 7 inches. Find the height of the matte.

19. Quadrilateral $ABCD$ has vertices $A(-2, 0)$, $B(-2, 4)$, $C(-6, 8)$, and $D(-12, 6)$.

- **a.** Dilate $ABCD$ using a scale factor of 2.
- **b.** Dilate the quadrilateral from part (a) by a scale factor of $\frac{1}{4}$.
- **c.** What is the scale factor for a single dilation that changes $ABCD$ to the final quadrilateral in part (b)? *Explain* how you found your answer.

9 Real Numbers and Right Triangles

Before

In previous chapters you've . . .

- Found the square of a number
- Investigated rational numbers

Now

In Chapter 9 you'll study . . .

- 9.1 Square roots
- 9.2 Real numbers
- 9.3 The Pythagorean theorem
- 9.4 Pythagorean triples
- 9.5 Special right triangles
- 9.6 Trigonometric ratios

Why?

So you can solve real-world problems about . . .

- fire towers, p. 474
- parasailing, p. 483
- softball, p. 493
- totem poles, p. 504

at classzone.com

- Rational Numbers, p. 475
- The Pythagorean Theorem, p. 483
- Special Right Triangles, p. 495

Get-Ready Games

Review Prerequisite Skills by playing *Spin Your Wheels and Ramp Match.*

Skill Focus: Evaluating powers

Spin the wheels until all three red lines connect equal values.

- You can turn the wheels one click at a time. Each click moves a wheel one space clockwise.
- How many clicks do you need to turn the left wheel?
- How many clicks do you need to turn the right wheel?

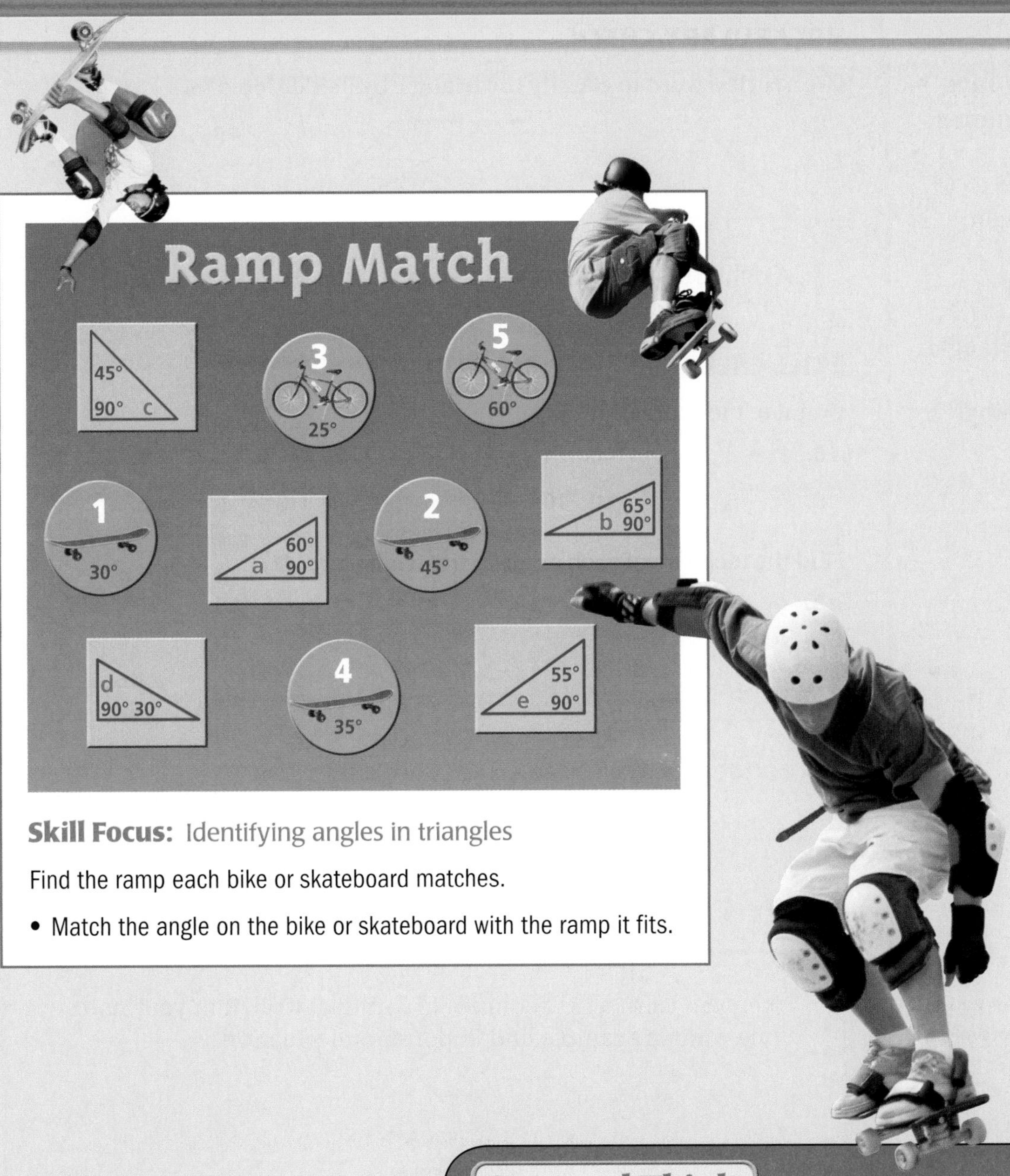

Skill Focus: Identifying angles in triangles

Find the ramp each bike or skateboard matches.

- Match the angle on the bike or skateboard with the ramp it fits.

Stop and Think

1. **CRITICAL THINKING** How can you write 4^4 as a power of 2? *Explain.*
2. **WRITING** *Explain* why a triangular ramp that has angles of 90°, 40°, and 55° cannot exist.

9 Getting Ready

Review Prerequisite Skills

REVIEW WORDS

- **rational number,** *p. 255*
- **right angle,** *p. 403*
- **right triangle,** *p. 411*
- **equilateral triangle,** *p. 411*
- **isosceles triangle,** *p. 411*
- **scalene triangle,** *p. 411*

VOCABULARY CHECK

Use a review word to classify the triangle by its side lengths.

1. 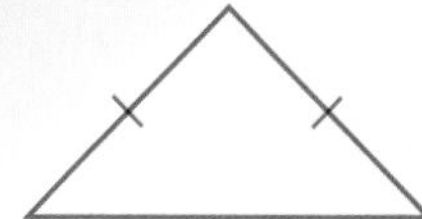

2. 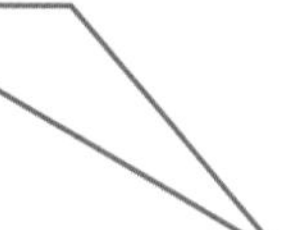

3. 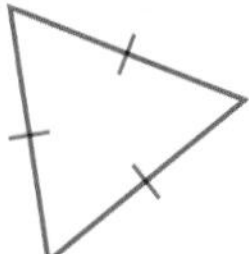

4. A right triangle, when classified by its side lengths, may *not* be a(n) __?__ triangle.

SKILL CHECK

Evaluate the expression. ***(p. 19)***

5. $4^2 + 3^2$ **6.** $14^2 - 5^2$ **7.** $27^2 - 3^2$ **8.** $2^2 + 6^2$

9. $6^2 - 3^2$ **10.** $10^2 - 5^2$ **11.** $5^2 + 6^2$ **12.** $7^2 + 3^2$

Find the measure of each angle in the triangle. ***(p. 411)***

13. 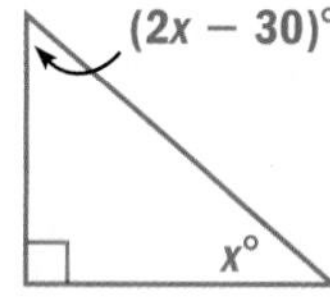

14. 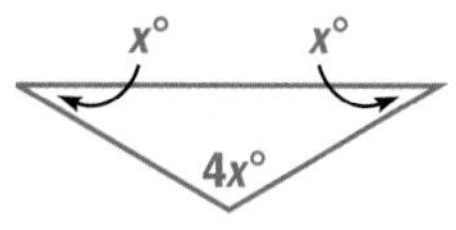

15. 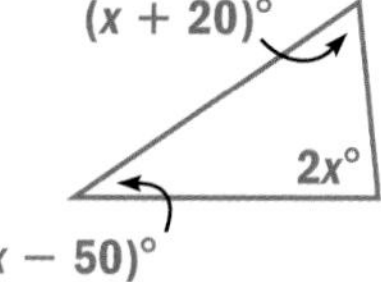

@HomeTutor Prerequisite skills practice at classzone.com

Notetaking Skills Illustrating with Examples

In each chapter you will learn a new notetaking skill. In Chapter 9 you will illustrate new concepts with examples, as in Example 1 on p. 482.

When you learn a new concept or formula, write it in your notes along with an example and important information.

Right triangle

1 right angle (90°)
Sum of measures of other 2 angles is 90°.

Can be isosceles or scalene. Never equilateral.

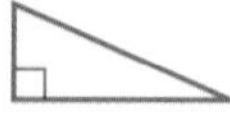

9.1 Square Roots

Before	You found squares of numbers.
Now	You'll find and approximate square roots of numbers.
Why?	So you can find side lengths, as in Ex. 54.

KEY VOCABULARY
- **square root,** *p. 469*
- **radical expression,** *p. 469*
- **perfect square,** *p. 470*

ACTIVITY

You can find the side length of a square if you know its area.

STEP 1 **Copy** and complete the table using the diagram.

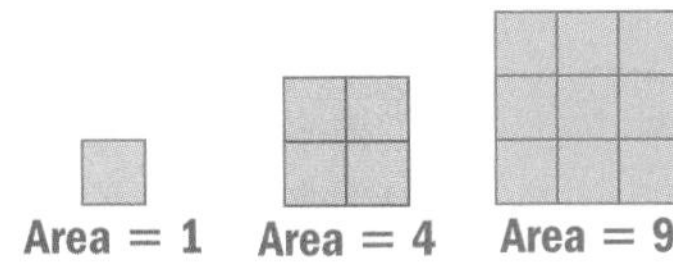

Area of square (square units)	1	4	9	16	25	36
Side length (units)	1	2	3	?	?	?

STEP 2 **Find** the length of each side of a square with an area of 49 square units, 64 square units, 100 square units, and 400 square units.

STEP 3 **Describe** the length of a side of a square that has an area between 81 and 100 square units.

The numbers 5 and -5 are the *square roots* of 25 because $5^2 = 25$ and $(-5)^2 = 25$. If $m^2 = n$, then m is a **square root** of n. Every positive number has a positive square root and a negative square root. Zero has one square root, which is zero.

The symbol $\sqrt{\ }$ is called a *radical sign.* It is used to represent the positive square root. The symbol $-\sqrt{\ }$ represents the negative square root. A **radical expression** is an expression that involves a radical sign.

$\sqrt{25} = 5$ **positive square root**

$-\sqrt{25} = -5$ **negative square root**

EXAMPLE 1 Evaluating Square Roots

a. $\sqrt{36} = 6$ because $6^2 = 36$.

b. $-\sqrt{64} = -8$ because $(-8)^2 = 64$.

c. $\sqrt{\frac{4}{25}} = \frac{2}{5}$ because $\left(\frac{2}{5}\right)^2 = \frac{4}{25}$

d. $\sqrt{0.81} = 0.9$ because $(0.9)^2 = 0.81$.

Perfect Squares A **perfect square** is any number that has integer square roots, such as 1, 4, 9, and 16. You can approximate the square roots of a number that is not a perfect square using a number line or a calculator.

★ EXAMPLE 2 Standardized Test Practice

Round $\sqrt{95}$ to the nearest whole number.

Ⓐ 8 Ⓑ 9 Ⓒ 10 Ⓓ 11

ELIMINATE CHOICES
You know that 95 is between 81 (or 9^2) and 100 (or 10^2), so $\sqrt{95}$ is between 9 and 10. Choices A and D can be eliminated.

SOLUTION

You can use a number line to approximate $\sqrt{95}$ to the nearest whole number. Because $\sqrt{95}$ is between 9 and 10, you need to decide whether $\sqrt{95}$ is closer to 9 or 10. Find 9.5^2. You can calculate that $9.5^2 = 90.25$ and $(\sqrt{95})^2 = 95$.

$\sqrt{81}$ $\sqrt{90.25}$ $\sqrt{95}$ $\sqrt{100}$

9 9.5 10

$9^2 = 81$ $9.5^2 = 90.25$ $10^2 = 100$

As shown on the number line, $\sqrt{95}$ is between $\sqrt{90.25}$ and $\sqrt{100}$, so it has a value between 9.5 and 10. Therefore, $\sqrt{95}$ is closer to 10 than it is to 9.

▶ **Answer** To the nearest whole number, $\sqrt{95} \approx 10$.
The correct answer is C. Ⓐ Ⓑ Ⓒ Ⓓ

✓ GUIDED PRACTICE for Examples 1 and 2

USE A TABLE
You may want to use the Table of Square Roots on p. 819.

Find or approximate the square root to the nearest integer.

1. $\sqrt{4}$ **2.** $\sqrt{0}$ **3.** $-\sqrt{36}$ **4.** $-\sqrt{81}$

5. $\sqrt{23}$ **6.** $\sqrt{41}$ **7.** $\sqrt{\frac{25}{81}}$ **8.** $\sqrt{0.36}$

EXAMPLE 3 Using a Calculator

Evaluate the square root. Round to the nearest tenth, if necessary.

a. $-\sqrt{56.25}$ **b.** $\sqrt{8}$ **c.** $-\sqrt{1256}$

SOLUTION

	Keystrokes	Display	Answer
a.	(−) 2nd [√] **56.25** =	**−7.5**	**−7.5**
b.	2nd [√] **8** =	**2.828427125**	**2.8**
c.	(−) 2nd [√] **1256** =	**−35.44009029**	**−35.4**

EXAMPLE 4 Using a Square Root Equation

Amusement Parks On an amusement park ride, riders stand against a circular wall that spins. At a certain speed, the floor drops out and the force of the rotation keeps the riders pinned to the wall.

The model $s = 4.95\sqrt{r}$ gives the speed needed to keep riders pinned to the wall. In the model, s is the speed in meters per second and r is the radius of the ride in meters. Find the speed necessary to keep riders pinned to the wall of a ride that has a radius of 2.61 meters.

SOLUTION

$s = 4.95\sqrt{r}$	**Write equation for speed of the ride.**
$= 4.95\sqrt{2.61}$	**Substitute 2.61 for *r*.**
$\approx 4.95(1.62)$	**Approximate the square root using a calculator.**
$= 8.019$	**Multiply.**

▶ **Answer** The speed should be about 8 meters per second.

EXAMPLE 5 Solving Equations Using Square Roots

READING
The symbol $\pm$ is read "plus or minus." The statement $x = \pm 8$ means that 8 and -8 are the solutions of $x^2 = 64$.

a.

$x^2 = 64$	**Original equation**
$x = \pm\sqrt{64}$	**Definition of square root**
$x = \pm 8$	**Evaluate square roots.**

▶ **Answer** The solutions are 8 and -8.

b.

$z^2 + 14 = 20$	**Original equation**
$z^2 + 14 - 14 = 20 - 14$	**Subtract 14 from each side.**
$z^2 = 6$	**Simplify.**
$z = \pm\sqrt{6}$	**Definition of square root**
$z \approx \pm 2.4$	**Approximate square roots.**

▶ **Answer** The solutions are about 2.4 and -2.4.

✓ GUIDED PRACTICE for Examples 3, 4, and 5

Use a calculator to evaluate. Round to the nearest tenth.

9. $\sqrt{236}$ **10.** $\sqrt{11}$ **11.** $-\sqrt{20.96}$ **12.** $-\sqrt{3590}$

Solve the equation. Check your solutions.

13. $t^2 = 36$ **14.** $k^2 = 121$ **15.** $y^2 - 15 = 10$ **16.** $x^2 + 7 = 16$

9.1 EXERCISES

HOMEWORK KEY

★ = **STANDARDIZED TEST PRACTICE** Exs. 20, 55, 56, 60, and 70

○ = **HINTS AND HOMEWORK HELP** for Exs. 5, 13, 17, 57 at classzone.com

SKILL PRACTICE

1. **VOCABULARY** Copy and complete: A number b is a square root of c if _?_.

2. **VOCABULARY** *Explain* why the number 121 is a perfect square.

SEE EXAMPLE 1 on p. 469 for Exs. 3–7

EVALUATING SQUARE ROOTS Find the square root.

3. $-\sqrt{1}$ 4. $\sqrt{100}$ 5. $\sqrt{144}$ 6. $-\sqrt{16}$

7. **ERROR ANALYSIS** Describe and correct the error made in finding the square root of $-\sqrt{49}$.

✗ $-\sqrt{49} = 7$

APPROXIMATING SQUARE ROOTS Approximate the square root to the nearest whole number.

SEE EXAMPLE 2 on p. 470 for Exs. 8–15

8. $\sqrt{33}$ 9. $\sqrt{14}$ 10. $\sqrt{117}$ 11. $\sqrt{52}$

12. $\sqrt{74}$ 13. $\sqrt{22}$ 14. $\sqrt{48}$ 15. $\sqrt{123}$

SEE EXAMPLE 3 on p. 470 for Exs. 16–20

USING A CALCULATOR Use a calculator to approximate the square root. Round to the nearest tenth if necessary.

16. $-\sqrt{34.6}$ 17. $\sqrt{43.56}$ 18. $\sqrt{2440}$ 19. $-\sqrt{6204}$

20. ★ **MULTIPLE CHOICE** Which square root is closest to 13?

(A) $\sqrt{165}$ (B) $\sqrt{175}$ (C) $\sqrt{185}$ (D) $\sqrt{193}$

SOLVING EQUATIONS Solve the equation. Round to the nearest hundredth if necessary. Check your solution(s).

SEE EXAMPLE 5 on p. 471 for Exs. 21–35

21. $x^2 = 0$ 22. $b^2 = 49$ 23. $y^2 = 81$

24. $z^2 - 169 = 0$ 25. $y^2 + 7 = 56$ 26. $a^2 + 12 = 48$

27. $n^2 - 27 = 94$ 28. $y^2 - 31 = 36$ 29. $62 + z^2 = 198$

30. $c^2 - 0.35 = 1.65$ 31. $58 + m^2 = 253$ 32. $k^2 - 0.17 = 0.64$

33. $m^2 + 0.38 = 1.82$ 34. $p^2 + 0.06 = 1.27$ 35. $s^2 - 0.52 = 1.44$

REASONING Complete the statement with *always, sometimes,* or *never*.

36. Square roots are _?_ whole numbers.

37. Square roots of perfect squares are _?_ integers.

38. A number _?_ has more than two square roots.

ALGEBRA Evaluate the expression $\sqrt{a^2 - b^2}$ for the given values.

39. $a = 5, b = 5$ 40. $a = 10, b = 8$ 41. $a = 15, b = 12$

RATIONAL SQUARE ROOTS **Find the square root.**

42. $-\sqrt{\frac{1}{4}}$ **43.** $\sqrt{\frac{16}{25}}$ **44.** $-\sqrt{\frac{81}{100}}$ **45.** $\sqrt{\frac{144}{169}}$

46. $\sqrt{1.44}$ **47.** $\sqrt{1.96}$ **48.** $-\sqrt{0.25}$ **49.** $\sqrt{11.56}$

CHALLENGE **Simplify the expression. Round to the nearest hundredth if necessary.**

50. $\sqrt{\sqrt{625}}$ **51.** $-\sqrt{\sqrt{1296}}$ **52.** $-\sqrt{\sqrt{\sqrt{256}}}$ **53.** $\sqrt{\sqrt{\sqrt{4096}}}$

PROBLEM SOLVING

SEE EXAMPLES 1 AND 3 on pp. 469–470 for Exs. 54, 55

54. **GUIDED PROBLEM SOLVING** You have a square piece of fabric for the front of a square pillow. The fabric has an area of 729 square inches. You use all the fabric. What is the length of one side of the pillow?

a. Write an equation using the formula for the area of a square.

b. Use the definition of square root to solve the equation.

c. Evaluate the positive square root.

55. ★ **MULTIPLE CHOICE** You want to put a fence around a square plot of land that has an area of 6250 square yards. What is the length of a side, to the nearest tenth of a yard?

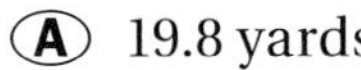

Ⓐ 19.8 yards Ⓑ 79.0 yards

Ⓒ 79.1 yards Ⓓ 625.0 yards

56. ★ **SHORT RESPONSE** *Explain* how to find the perimeter of a square given its area. To the nearest yard, what is the perimeter of the square plot of land in Exercise 55?

57. **HOME DECORATING** A tablecloth measures 50 inches by 50 inches. Will it cover a square table with an area of 21.5 square feet? *Explain.*

58. **EXAMPLES AND NONEXAMPLES** Give three examples of numbers whose square roots are not rational numbers. Give three examples of numbers whose square roots are rational. Include at least one non-integer in each list.

59. **ROADWAYS** A road is 330 feet long. The region where the road intersects the other roads is shaded darker in the diagram. The area of each intersection is 576 square feet. Find the length w in the diagram. Then find the area of the entire roadway, including both intersections.

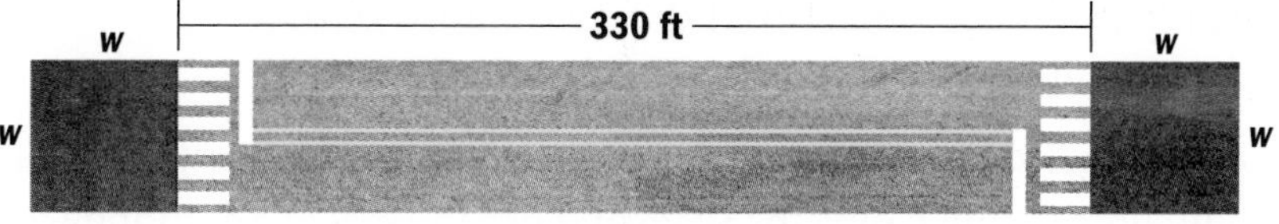

60. ★ **WRITING** Your friend tells you that $\sqrt{5}$ is a rational number because you can write it as $\frac{\sqrt{5}}{1}$. Do you agree or disagree? *Explain.*

READING IN MATH **Read the information below for Exercises 61–63.**

Fire Towers New Hampshire lookout towers were built in the early 1900s to spot forest fires. Mount Cardigan, which has a view of the 6288 foot tall Mount Washington, was built in 1924. Many towers were constructed over the next few decades. Sixteen towers are still in operation. Ideally, the distance d in miles that a person can see from a tower is given by the formula $d = \sqrt{1.5h}$, where h is the height in feet above the surrounding land.

SEE EXAMPLE 4 on p. 472 for Exs. 61–63

61. **Calculate** A ranger standing at Mount Cardigan is about 3100 feet above the surrounding land. How far can the ranger ideally see?

62. **Reasoning** A person standing in the fire tower of Mount Monadnock, which is no longer in use, could see 104 miles to Mount Washington. Mount Monadnock is about 3100 feet above the surrounding land. *Explain* how it is possible to see farther than the formula suggests.

63. **Elevation** A ranger at Mount Prospect tower can see about 57.6 miles. At about what height above the surrounding land is the ranger?

64. **LOOK FOR A PATTERN** Find the positive square roots of 0.36, 0.0036, 0.000036, and 0.00000036. What pattern do you notice? Using the pattern, predict the positive square root of 0.0000000036.

65. **CHALLENGE** In Example 2, you learned how to approximate the value of a square root to the nearest whole number without using a calculator. *Explain* how to approximate the value of a square root to the nearest tenth if you do not have a calculator.

MIXED REVIEW

Prepare for Lesson 9.2 in Exs. 66–68

Order the numbers from least to greatest. ***(p. 359)***

66. 12.4%, $\frac{1}{8}$, 0.1

67. 0.85, 8.5%, $\frac{5}{8}$

68. $\frac{3}{4}$, 74%, 0.7

CHOOSE A STRATEGY **Use a strategy from the list to solve the following problem. *Explain* your choice of strategy.**

Problem Solving Strategies
- Make a Model *(p. 786)*
- Draw a Diagram *(p. 787)*
- Look for a Pattern *(p. 791)*

69. In how many different ways can a row of three postage stamps be torn from a 4 by 3 sheet of stamps so that the three stamps are still attached to one another?

70. ★ **MULTIPLE CHOICE** Nikki is at a carnival and has \$6. She would like to buy some cotton candy for \$2.25 and use the rest of her money to go on the rides. Each ride costs \$.75. How many rides can she go on? ***(p. 134)***

Ⓐ 3   Ⓑ 4   Ⓒ 5   Ⓓ 6

9.2 Rational and Irrational Numbers

Before	You investigated rational numbers.
Now	You'll work with irrational numbers.
Why?	So you can analyze effects of weather, as in Example 4.

KEY VOCABULARY
- **irrational number,** p. 475
- **real number,** p. 475

Recall that a *rational number* is a number that can be written as a quotient $\frac{a}{b}$, where a and b are integers and $b \neq 0$. An **irrational number** is a number that cannot be written as a quotient of two integers. If n is a positive integer and is not a perfect square, then $\sqrt{n}$ and $-\sqrt{n}$ are irrational numbers.

Together, rational numbers and irrational numbers make up the set of **real numbers**. The Venn diagram shows the relationships among numbers in the real number system.

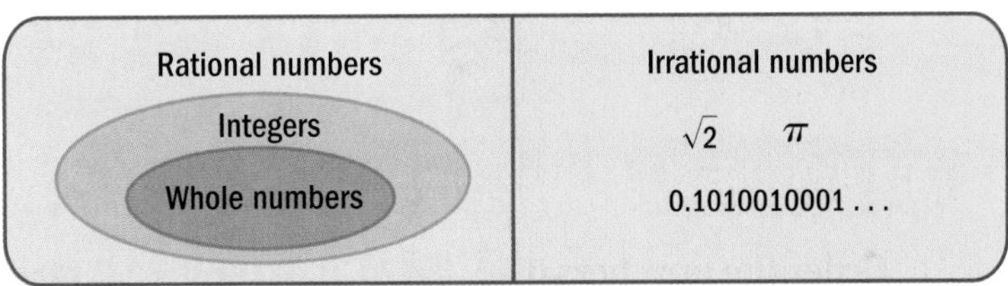

The decimal form of a rational number is either terminating or repeating. The decimal form of an irrational number neither terminates nor repeats.

EXAMPLE 1 Classifying Real Numbers

REWRITE NUMBERS
Need help writing a rational number as a decimal? See p. 255.

Number	Type	Decimal Form	Type of Decimal
a. $\frac{3}{4}$	Rational	$\frac{3}{4} = 0.75$	Terminating
b. $\frac{1}{11}$	Rational	$\frac{1}{11} = 0.0909\ldots = 0.\overline{09}$	Repeating
c. $\sqrt{3}$	Irrational	$\sqrt{3} = 1.7320508\ldots$	Nonterminating and nonrepeating

Animated Math at classzone.com

✓ GUIDED PRACTICE for Example 1

Tell whether the number is *rational* or *irrational*. *Explain* your reasoning.

1. $\frac{5}{8}$ **2.** $\sqrt{7}$ **3.** $\sqrt{25}$ **4.** $\frac{2}{9}$

EXAMPLE 2 Comparing Real Numbers

Graph $\sqrt{\frac{1}{2}}$ and $\frac{1}{2}$ on a number line. Then copy and complete the statement $\sqrt{\frac{1}{2}}$? $\frac{1}{2}$ with <, >, or =.

SOLUTION

> **AVOID ERRORS**
> A radical sign acts as a grouping symbol. So, you must evaluate the expression under the radical sign before finding its square root.

Use a calculator to approximate the square root. Graph the decimal forms of the numbers on a number line and compare.

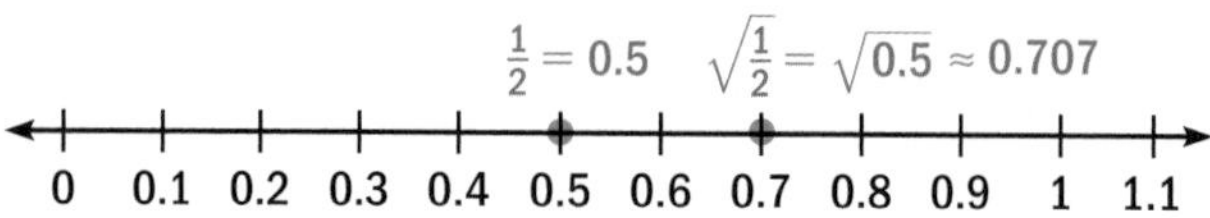

▸ **Answer** Because $\frac{1}{2}$ is to the left of $\sqrt{\frac{1}{2}}$, $\sqrt{\frac{1}{2}} > \frac{1}{2}$.

✓ GUIDED PRACTICE for Example 2

Copy and complete the statement with <, >, or =.

5. 4 ? $\sqrt{8}$

6. $\frac{4}{5}$? $\sqrt{\frac{4}{5}}$

7. $\frac{1}{4}$? $\sqrt{\frac{1}{4}}$

8. $\sqrt{7}$? 3

EXAMPLE 3 Ordering Real Numbers

Order the numbers $0.4\overline{7}$, $0.\overline{474}$, $0.\overline{47}$, and $\sqrt{0.23}$ from least to greatest.

SOLUTION

STEP 1 **Write** each decimal out to six decimal places.

$0.4\overline{7} = 0.477777\ldots$

$0.\overline{474} = 0.474474\ldots$

$0.\overline{47} = 0.474747\ldots$

$\sqrt{0.23} = 0.479583\ldots$

Notice that the first two digits after the decimal point are the same for each number.

Use the second pair of digits to order the decimals.

STEP 2 **Write** the decimals in order:

$0.474474\ldots$, $0.474747\ldots$, $0.477777\ldots$, and $0.479583\ldots$

▸ **Answer** From least to greatest, the order is $0.\overline{474}$, $0.\overline{47}$, $0.4\overline{7}$, and $\sqrt{0.23}$.

Animated Math at classzone.com

✓ GUIDED PRACTICE for Example 3

9. Order the decimals $0.\overline{52}$, $0.\overline{525}$, $0.52\overline{5}$, and $\sqrt{0.276}$ from least to greatest.

10. Order the decimals 1.7, $\sqrt{1.7}$, $1.\overline{89}$, and $1.\overline{3}$ from least to greatest.

EXAMPLE 4 Using an Irrational Number

Waves For large ocean waves, the wind speed s in knots and the height of the waves h in feet are related by the equation $s = \sqrt{\frac{h}{0.019}}$. If the waves are about 9.5 feet tall, what must the wind speed be? (1 knot is equivalent to 1.15 miles per hour.)

SOLUTION

$s = \sqrt{\frac{h}{0.019}}$ **Write original equation.**

$= \sqrt{\frac{9.5}{0.019}}$ **Substitute 9.5 for *h*.**

$= \sqrt{500}$ **Divide.**

≈ 22.4 **Approximate square root.**

▶ **Answer** The wind speed is about 22 knots.

GUIDED PRACTICE for Example 4

11. **What If?** In Example 4, suppose the waves grow to about 15 feet tall. What is the wind speed rounded to the nearest knot?

9.2 EXERCISES

HOMEWORK KEY
★ = **STANDARDIZED TEST PRACTICE** Exs. 31, 33, 63, 65, 66, 70, and 90
○ = **HINTS AND HOMEWORK HELP** for Exs. 5, 9, 13, 27, 67 at classzone.com

SKILL PRACTICE

VOCABULARY Copy and complete the statement.

1. Numbers that cannot be written as a quotient of two integers are _?_.
2. Together, rational and irrational numbers make up the set of _?_.

CLASSIFYING REAL NUMBERS Tell whether the number is *rational* or *irrational*. *Explain* your reasoning.

SEE EXAMPLE 1 on p. 475 for Exs. 3–15

3. 0.682
4. 0.12345 . . .
5. $0.\overline{2}$
6. 0.30311
7. $\sqrt{36}$
8. $\sqrt{62}$
9. $\sqrt{5}$
10. $\sqrt{144}$
11. $\frac{9}{46}$
12. $\sqrt{\frac{25}{49}}$
13. $\sqrt{\frac{100}{81}}$
14. $\frac{22}{31}$
15. **WHICH ONE DOESN'T BELONG?** Tell which number does not belong. *Justify* your reasoning.

A. $\sqrt{\frac{1}{4}}$ B. $\sqrt{\frac{1}{3}}$ C. $\sqrt{\frac{2}{5}}$ D. $\sqrt{\frac{5}{6}}$

COMPARING REAL NUMBERS Graph the pair of numbers on a number line. Then copy and complete the statement with <, >, or =.

SEE EXAMPLE 2 on p. 476 for Exs. 16–31

16. $\frac{5}{6} \underline{?} \sqrt{\frac{5}{6}}$

17. $\sqrt{0.9} \underline{?} 0.9$

18. $\sqrt{2.25} \underline{?} \frac{3.5}{2.4}$

19. $\sqrt{4.6} \underline{?} 2.5$

20. $2.6 \underline{?} \sqrt{6.7}$

21. $\sqrt{\frac{8}{11}} \underline{?} \frac{9}{10}$

CHOOSE A METHOD Copy and complete with <, >, or =. Tell whether you used *mental math, estimation,* or a *calculator.*

22. $0.81 \underline{?} \sqrt{0.81}$

23. $5 \underline{?} \sqrt{10}$

24. $\sqrt{\frac{64}{121}} \underline{?} \frac{8}{11}$

25. $\sqrt{\frac{16}{3}} \underline{?} 5$

26. $\sqrt{21} \underline{?} 7$

27. $-5 \underline{?} -\sqrt{25}$

28. $\sqrt{9.9} \underline{?} 3.3$

29. $1.3 \underline{?} \sqrt{1.7}$

30. $-0.4 \underline{?} -\sqrt{1.6}$

31. ★ **MULTIPLE CHOICE** Which statement is *not* true?

Ⓐ $\sqrt{12} < 4$ Ⓑ $8 > \sqrt{16}$ Ⓒ $\sqrt{169} = 13$ Ⓓ $\sqrt{30} < 5$

SEE EXAMPLE 3 on p. 476 for Exs. 32–41

32. **GRAPHING REAL NUMBERS** Graph the numbers $-\sqrt{9}$, 8.69, $\sqrt{45}$, and $\frac{141}{25}$ on a number line. Then order the numbers from least to greatest.

33. ★ **MULTIPLE CHOICE** Which of the following shows the numbers in order from least to greatest?

Ⓐ $\sqrt{2}, \sqrt{5}, 1, 2, 3$ Ⓑ $1, \sqrt{2}, \sqrt{5}, 2, 3$

Ⓒ $1, \sqrt{2}, 2, \sqrt{5}, 3$ Ⓓ $1, \sqrt{2}, 2, 3, \sqrt{5}$

ORDERING REAL NUMBERS Order the numbers from least to greatest.

34. $0.1\overline{3}, 0.\overline{131}, 0.\overline{13}, 0.133$

35. $0.\overline{26}, 0.266, 0.2\overline{6}, 0.\overline{262}$

36. $\sqrt{0.68}, 0.4\overline{5}, 0.455, 0.\overline{45}$

37. $0.3\overline{9}, \sqrt{0.17}, 0.\overline{39}, 0.399$

38. $1.5, \sqrt{8}, -4, -3.75$

39. $\sqrt{81}, 10.3, \sqrt{220}, -9$

40. $-\sqrt{12}, -\sqrt{\frac{1}{4}}, -3.5, -\frac{3}{4}$

41. $1.02, \sqrt{2.5}, \sqrt{1.25}, \frac{2}{5}$

42. **ERROR ANALYSIS** A student says $\sqrt{64}$ is irrational because of the radical symbol. What is incorrect with this reasoning?

xy ALGEBRA Evaluate when $a = 2$, $b = 4$, and $c = 9$. Classify the result as *rational* or *irrational*. Round to the nearest tenth, if necessary.

43. $\sqrt{b + c}$

44. $\sqrt{c^2 - (a + b)}$

45. $\sqrt{a^2 - b + c}$

46. $\sqrt{bc + b + c}$

47. $\sqrt{c^2 - b^2 + 1}$

48. $\sqrt{ab + bc - a^2}$

CLASSIFYING REAL NUMBERS Classify the value of the expression as *rational, irrational,* or *cannot be determined* when $\sqrt{x}$ is irrational and n is an integer. *Explain* your reasoning.

49. $\sqrt{x} + n$

50. $\sqrt{x} + \sqrt{x}$

51. $n\sqrt{x}$

52. **REASONING** Is $\sqrt{-4}$ a rational number? *Explain* your reasoning.

REASONING **Evaluate the expressions when $a = 4, b = 3, c = 9$, and $d = 5$. Then tell whether the expressions are *always, sometimes,* or *never* equal if a, b, c, and d are real numbers greater than zero. *Explain* your reasoning.**

53. $\sqrt{a + c}, \sqrt{a} + \sqrt{c}$

54. $\sqrt{a^2}, (\sqrt{a})^2$

55. $\sqrt{ac}, \sqrt{a} \cdot \sqrt{c}$

56. $\sqrt{a^2 + b^2}, \sqrt{a^2} + \sqrt{b^2}$

57. $\sqrt{d^2 - a^2}, \sqrt{d^2} - \sqrt{a^2}$

58. $\sqrt{\frac{a}{c}}, \frac{\sqrt{a}}{\sqrt{c}}$

REASONING **Determine whether the expression is *always, sometimes,* or *never* irrational for whole number values of x.**

59. $\sqrt{x + 3}$

60. $\sqrt{x^2}$

61. $\sqrt{x} \div 4$

62. CHALLENGE Describe the values of x for which $\sqrt{x^2} = -x$. Give an example to support your answer.

PROBLEM SOLVING

SEE EXAMPLE 1 on p. 475 for Exs. 63–64

63. ★ MULTIPLE CHOICE The area of a square judo mat is 400 square feet. What is *not* true about the perimeter?

Ⓐ It is rational. Ⓑ It is irrational.

Ⓒ It is an integer. Ⓓ It is a real number.

64. FLOOR DIMENSIONS The floor of a square room has an area of 212 square feet. Are the dimensions of the room *rational* or *irrational*?

65. ★ OPEN-ENDED MATH Give an example of a rational number and an irrational number between 8 and 9.

66. ★ WRITING Your aunt offers you a square piece of carpet that has an area of 110 square feet. You want to use the carpet in a bedroom that measures 10.5 feet by 11.2 feet. Will the carpet fit in the room? *Explain.*

67. DECORATING You are decorating your room. You have a square stencil that covers an area of 20.25 square inches. The wall you are decorating is $7\frac{1}{2}$ feet high. How many stencils fit between the floor and the ceiling?

68. MULTIPLE REPRESENTATIONS Use the numbers in the list below.

$$-0.122333\ldots, \sqrt{7.9}, \frac{3\sqrt{7}}{6}, \frac{\sqrt{3 + 22}}{4}, \frac{\sqrt{9}}{1}, -\frac{\sqrt{144}}{2}$$

a. Decimals Write each number as a decimal. If needed, round to the nearest tenth.

b. Diagram Draw a Venn diagram showing rational and irrational numbers. Place the numbers from the list above in your diagram.

c. Detailed Diagram Draw a Venn diagram showing real numbers, rational numbers, integers, irrational numbers, and positive and negative numbers. Place the numbers from the list above in your diagram.

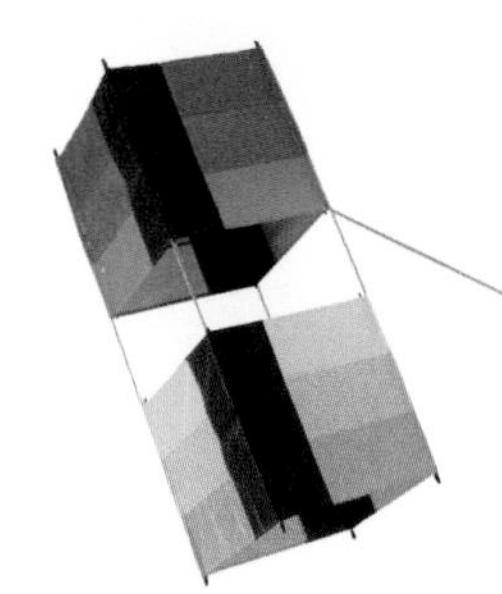

69. **BOX KITES** To find the minimum wind speed required to fly a box kite, use the formula $m = 5\sqrt{\frac{w}{A}}$, where m is minimum speed in miles per hour, w is weight in ounces, and A is the area in square feet of the surface used to lift the kite. A box kite weighs 19.6 ounces and its surface area is 11.71 square feet. The wind is blowing at 6 miles per hour. Can you fly your kite? *Explain* your reasoning.

SEE EXAMPLE 4 on p. 477 for Ex. 70

70. ★ **EXTENDED RESPONSE** The radius of a circle is given by the formula $r = \sqrt{\frac{A}{\pi}}$, where A is the area of the circle.
   a. Find the radius of a circle to the nearest tenth when the area is 6 square feet.
   b. Find the radius and diameter of the circle when the area is 9π square feet.
   c. *Describe* the type of number the area needs to be for the radius to be an integer.

71. **REASONING** Your friend gets a result of 2.645751311 on a calculator and says that it has to be an irrational number. Is your friend right? *Explain* your reasoning.

72. **GEOMETRY** The figure is composed of one large square and four smaller congruent squares. The area of the shaded region is 45 square centimeters. Is the side length of the large square *rational* or *irrational*? *Explain* your reasoning.

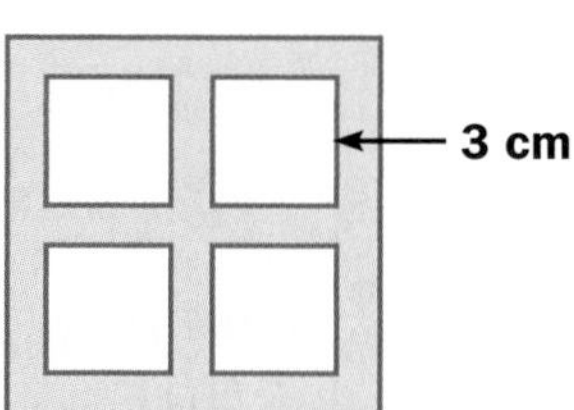

73. **CHALLENGE** Find three rational numbers and three irrational numbers between $\frac{2}{3}$ and $\frac{3}{4}$. Can you write all of the rational numbers that are between these two numbers? *Explain* your reasoning.

MIXED REVIEW

Prepare for Lesson 9.3 in Exs. 74–81

Evaluate the expression when $a = 4$, $b = 3$, and $c = 2$. *(p. 13)*

74. $a^2 + b^2$
75. $a^2 - b^2$
76. $c + a^2$
77. $b^2 - b$
78. $a^2 + c$
79. $c^2 - b$
80. $b^2 - a + c$
81. $a^2 - b^2 + c^2$

Simplify. Write the expression using only positive exponents.

82. $5a^2 \cdot 6a^9$ *(p. 202)*
83. $d^8 \cdot 4d^5$ *(p. 202)*
84. $\frac{c^5 \cdot c^3}{c^4}$ *(p. 208)*
85. $\frac{-8n^8}{12n^{12}}$ *(p. 208)*
86. $\frac{10m^7}{5m^3}$ *(p. 208)*
87. $p^5 \cdot p^5$ *(p. 202)*
88. $\frac{16r}{r^4}$ *(p. 208)*
89. $\frac{36s^{12}}{12s^{36}}$ *(p. 208)*

90. ★ **WRITING** You draw a regular hexagon with side lengths of 2 centimeters on an overhead projector transparency. When it is projected, the hexagon is enlarged by a scale factor of 15. *Explain* how to find the perimeter of the image. *(p. 447)*

INVESTIGATION

Use before Lesson 9.3

GOAL
Use graph paper to relate the side lengths of a right triangle.

MATERIALS
- graph paper
- pen or pencil

9.3 Modeling the Pythagorean Theorem

You can use graph paper to find the length of a right triangle's *hypotenuse*, which is the side opposite the right angle.

EXPLORE **Find the length of the hypotenuse of a right triangle with side lengths of three units and four units.**

STEP 1 **Draw** the right triangle on graph paper. The sides of the triangle that form the right angle are called *legs*. For each leg, draw a square that has a leg as one side. What is the sum of the areas of these two squares?

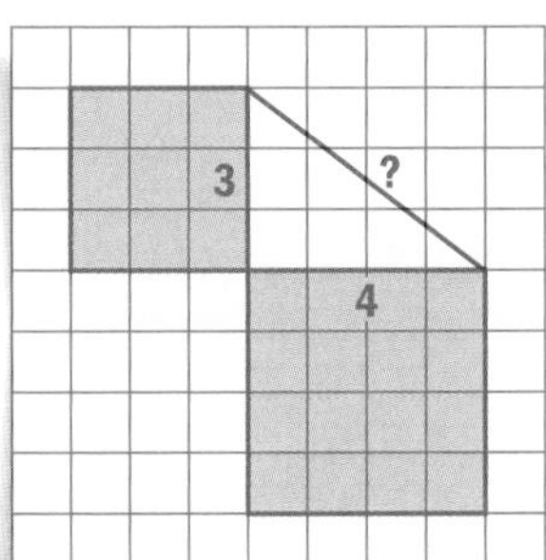

STEP 2 **Measure** the hypotenuse using graph paper. If you draw a square with the hypotenuse as one side, what is its area?

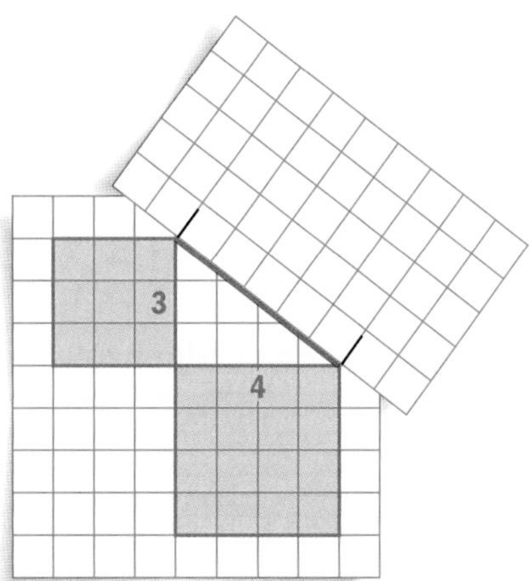

STEP 3 **Compare** the sum of the areas you found in Step 1 to the area you found in Step 2. What do you notice?

PRACTICE **Repeat Steps 1–3 for right triangles with legs of the given lengths.**

1. 5, 12

2. 6, 8

3. 8, 15

DRAW CONCLUSIONS

4. REASONING Let the lengths of the legs of a right triangle be a and b, and the length of the hypotenuse be c. Write a conjecture about the relationship between the lengths of the legs and the length of the hypotenuse.

9.3 The Pythagorean Theorem

Before You used formulas to solve problems.

Now You'll use the Pythagorean Theorem to solve problems.

Why? So you can find distances, as in Example 2.

KEY VOCABULARY

- **leg,** *p. 482*
- **hypotenuse,** *p. 482*
- **Pythagorean Theorem,** *p. 482*
- **converse,** *p. 483*

In a right triangle, the sides that form the right angle are called **legs**. The side opposite the right angle, which is always the longest side, is the **hypotenuse**. As you may have observed in the Investigation on page 481, the lengths of the legs and the hypotenuse are related by the **Pythagorean Theorem**.

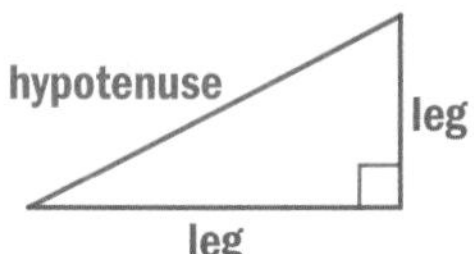

KEY CONCEPT *For Your Notebook*

Pythagorean Theorem

Words For any right triangle, the sum of the squares of the lengths of the legs equals the square of the length of the hypotenuse.

$a = 3$, $b = 4$, $c = 5$

Algebra $a^2 + b^2 = c^2$ **Numbers** $3^2 + 4^2 = 5^2$

EXAMPLE 1 Finding the Length of a Hypotenuse

TAKE NOTES

Be sure to write the Pythagorean Theorem and a few examples in your notebook.

Find the length of the hypotenuse of a right triangle with a 15 inch leg and a 20 inch leg.

$a^2 + b^2 = c^2$ **Pythagorean Theorem**

$15^2 + 20^2 = c^2$ **Substitute 15 for *a* and 20 for *b*.**

$225 + 400 = c^2$ **Evaluate powers.**

$625 = c^2$ **Add.**

$\sqrt{625} = c$ **Take positive square root of each side.**

$25 = c$ **Evaluate square root.**

▶ **Answer** The length of the hypotenuse is 25 inches.

GUIDED PRACTICE **for Example 1**

1. Find the length of the hypotenuse of a right triangle with a 28 inch leg and a 45 inch leg.

Interpreting Results In application problems, you usually need to take only the positive square root. For example, length, speed, and height are positive, so a negative square root would not give a reasonable answer.

EXAMPLE 2 Standardized Test Practice

Parasailing You are parasailing as shown in the diagram at the right. After getting airborne and reaching cruising speed, your position is 200 feet behind the boat. To the nearest foot, how high are you above the water?

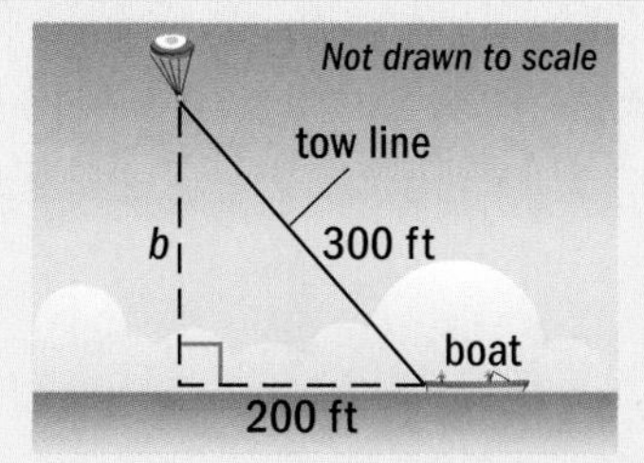

Ⓐ −224 ft Ⓑ 224 ft

Ⓒ 301 ft Ⓓ 361 ft

ELIMINATE CHOICES
Height is positive, so choice A can be eliminated.

SOLUTION

$a^2 + b^2 = c^2$	**Pythagorean Theorem**
$200^2 + b^2 = 300^2$	**Substitute 200 for *a* and 300 for *c*.**
$40{,}000 + b^2 = 90{,}000$	**Evaluate powers.**
$b^2 = 50{,}000$	**Subtract 40,000 from each side.**
$b = \sqrt{50{,}000}$	**Take positive square root of each side.**
$b \approx 223.6$	**Approximate square root.**

▶ **Answer** You are about 224 feet above the water.
The correct answer is B. Ⓐ Ⓑ Ⓒ Ⓓ

at classzone.com

GUIDED PRACTICE for Example 2

Find the unknown length. Round to the nearest tenth, if necessary.

2. c, $a = 7.5$ in., $b = 18$ in.

3. a, $b = 8$ m, $c = 16$ m

4. b, $c = 15$ ft, $a = 9$ ft

Converse of the Pythagorean Theorem The Pythagorean Theorem can be written as an if-then statement with two parts.

Theorem If **a triangle is a right triangle**, then $a^2 + b^2 = c^2$.

When you reverse the parts of an if-then statement, the new statement is called the **converse** of the statement.

Converse If $a^2 + b^2 = c^2$, then **the triangle is a right triangle**.

The converse of a *true* statement may or may not be true. The converse of the Pythagorean Theorem is true. You can use the converse of the Pythagorean Theorem to decide whether a triangle is a right triangle.

EXAMPLE 3 Identifying Right Triangles

Use the converse of the Pythagorean Theorem to determine whether a triangle with the given side lengths is a right triangle.

a. $a = 6, b = 8, c = 10$

$a^2 + b^2 \stackrel{?}{=} c^2$

$6^2 + 8^2 \stackrel{?}{=} 10^2$

$36 + 64 \stackrel{?}{=} 100$

$100 = 100$ ✓

▶ **Answer** A right triangle

b. $a = 10, b = 12, c = 16$

$a^2 + b^2 \stackrel{?}{=} c^2$

$10^2 + 12^2 \stackrel{?}{=} 16^2$

$100 + 144 \stackrel{?}{=} 256$

$244 \neq 256$ ✗

▶ **Answer** Not a right triangle

GUIDED PRACTICE for Example 3

5. Is a triangle with side lengths 14, 17, and 23 a right triangle? *Explain.*

9.3 EXERCISES

HOMEWORK KEY

★ = **STANDARDIZED TEST PRACTICE** Exs. 6, 31, 32, 34, 35, and 44

= **HINTS AND HOMEWORK HELP** for Exs. 3, 9, 13, 33 at classzone.com

SKILL PRACTICE

VOCABULARY **Copy and complete the statement.**

1. In a right triangle, the side opposite the right angle is called the __?__.

2. The theorem that relates the lengths of the legs to the length of the hypotenuse of a right triangle is the __?__.

FINDING THE HYPOTENUSE **Find the length of the hypotenuse.**

SEE EXAMPLE 1 on p. 482 for Exs. 3–6

3.

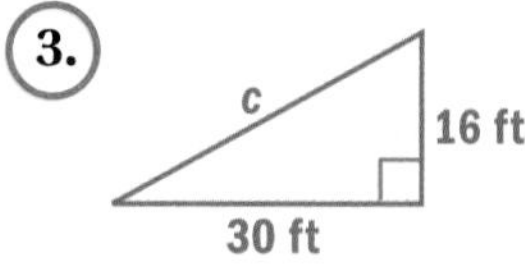

4.

24 in.
18 in.
c

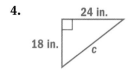

5.

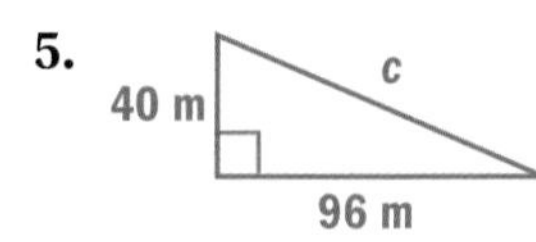

6. ★ **MULTIPLE CHOICE** The legs of a right triangle have lengths of 24 inches and 32 inches. What is the length of the hypotenuse?

Ⓐ 20 inches Ⓑ 40 inches Ⓒ 48 inches Ⓓ 56 inches

FINDING LEGS **Find the length of the unknown leg. Round to the nearest tenth if necessary.**

SEE EXAMPLE 2 on p. 483 for Exs. 7–10

7.

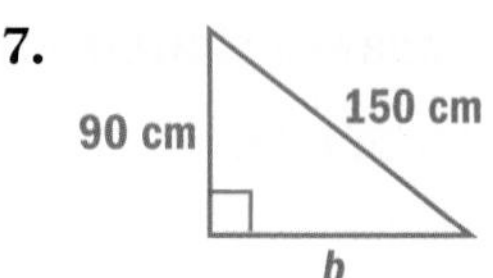

8.

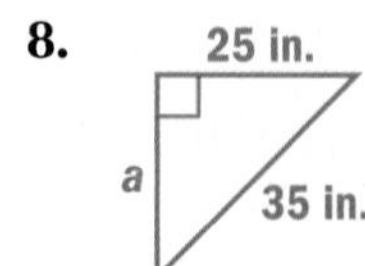

9.

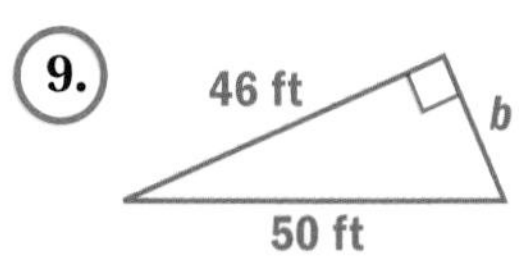

10. **ERROR ANALYSIS** Describe and correct the error made in finding the length of the third side of the right triangle. Round to the nearest tenth of a foot.

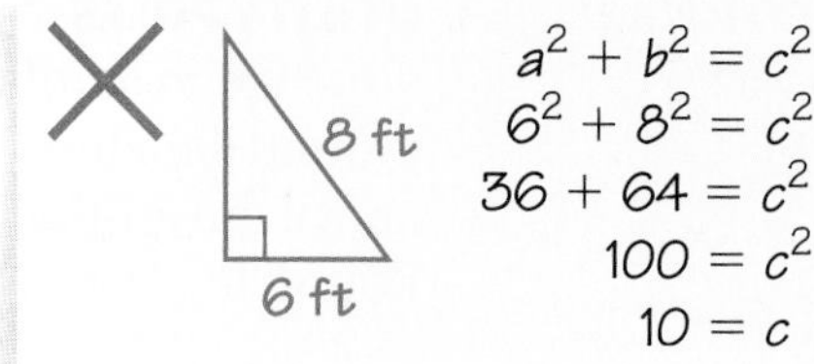

CLASSIFYING TRIANGLES Determine whether the given triangle side lengths form a right triangle.

SEE EXAMPLE 3 on p. 484 for Exs. 11–16

11. 4 m, 5 m, 7 m
12. 50 in., 64 in., 80 in.
13. 85 ft, 204 ft, 221 ft
14. 1.2 mi, 1.6 mi, 2 mi
15. 6.5 cm, 15.6 cm, 16.9 cm
16. 28.8 m, 8.4 m, 31 m

FINDING UNKNOWN LENGTHS Let *a* and *b* represent the lengths of the legs of a right triangle, and let *c* represent the length of the hypotenuse. Find the unknown length.

17. $a = 1.5$, $b =$ __?__, $c = 2.5$
18. $a =$ __?__, $b = 123$, $c = 139.4$
19. $a = 2.8$, $b = 4.5$, $c =$ __?__
20. $a = 4.5$, $b =$ __?__, $c = 7.5$
21. $a =$ __?__, $b = 2$, $c = \sqrt{13}$
22. $a = \sqrt{8}$, $b = 1$, $c =$ __?__
23. $a =$ __?__, $b = 37.5$, $c = 42.5$
24. $a = 2.5$, $b = 6$, $c =$ __?__
25. $a = 2$, $b = \sqrt{21}$, $c =$ __?__
26. $a = \sqrt{6}$, $b =$ __?__, $c = \sqrt{15}$

27. **REASONING** An isosceles right triangle has a hypotenuse length of 6 feet. Find the length of each leg. Round to the nearest hundredth foot.

28. **ALGEBRA** A rectangle is x feet by $3x$ feet. The length of a diagonal is $\sqrt{5}$ feet. Find the dimensions of the rectangle to the nearest hundredth of a foot.

29. **CHALLENGE** Find the length of segment AB in the rectangular prism shown.

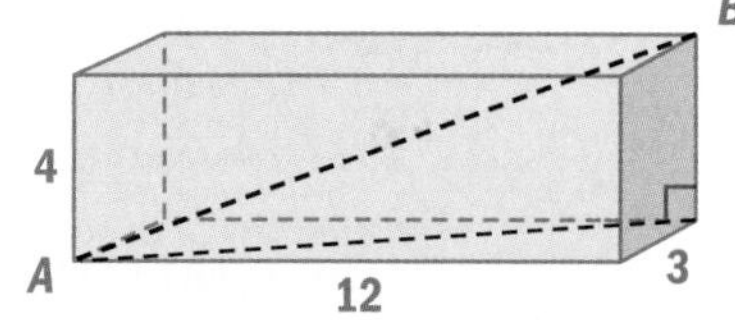

PROBLEM SOLVING

SEE EXAMPLE 1 on p. 482 for Ex. 30

30. **VOLLEYBALL NET** You are setting up a volleyball net using two 8 foot poles to hold up the net. You are going to attach each pole to a stake in the ground using a piece of rope. Each stake should be 4 feet from the pole. Assume that the ropes are stretched tight. How long should each rope be? Round to the nearest tenth of a foot.

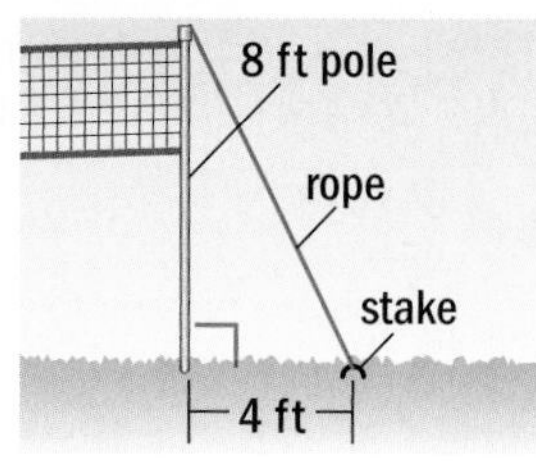

31. ★ **WRITING** *Explain* the difference between the Pythagorean Theorem and the converse of the Pythagorean Theorem. Give an example to show how each is used.

SEE EXAMPLE 2 on p. 483 for Ex. 32

32. ★ **MULTIPLE CHOICE** A 13 foot ladder is leaning against a building. The bottom of the ladder is 5 feet from the building. How high up does the ladder meet the wall?

Ⓐ 12 feet Ⓑ 13.9 feet Ⓒ 14 feet Ⓓ 18 feet

SEE EXAMPLE 2 on p. 483 for Ex. 33

33. **UTILITY POLES** A wire with a length of 23.8 meters is attached to a utility pole. The wire is anchored to the ground 9 meters from the base of the pole. How high above the ground is the wire attached to the utility pole? Round to the nearest tenth of a meter.

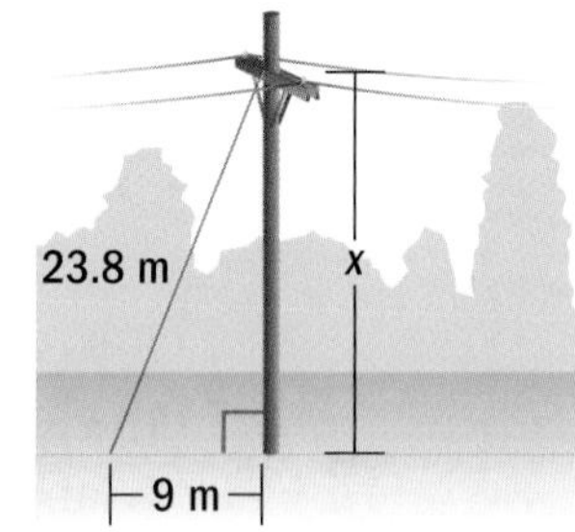

34. ★ **OPEN-ENDED MATH** Write a true if-then statement whose converse is also true. Then write a true if-then statement whose converse is false.

35. ★ **SHORT RESPONSE** A rectangular window is similar to the shape of the wall in which it is located. The wall is 20 feet wide with a diagonal of 25 feet. The window is $3\frac{1}{3}$ feet wide. Find the height of the window using two different methods: (a) by first finding the height of the wall, and (b) by first finding the diagonal of the window. *Explain* your methods.

36. **DRAW A DIAGRAM** Eric is hiking from his campsite to a creek. He walks 3.5 miles directly south, 4 miles directly east, and then 1.5 miles directly south.

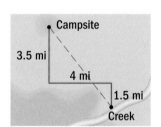

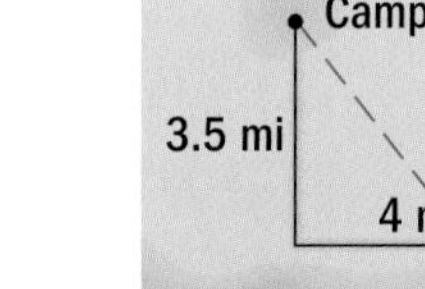

a. Draw and label a triangle you can use to find the distance between the campsite and the creek.

b. Find the distance from the campsite to the creek.

c. Assume that the ground is flat. How much shorter is it to walk in a straight line than it is to take Eric's route?

37. **CHALLENGE** Draw several different obtuse triangles and measure the lengths of the sides. Let a and b represent the lengths of the two shorter sides and let c represent the length of the longest side. Make a conjecture about the relationship between the lengths of the sides of obtuse triangles.

38. **CHALLENGE** Two sides of a quadrilateral are each 5 inches long. The other two sides are each a inches long. One diagonal is $\sqrt{a^2 + 25}$ inches long. Can the quadrilateral be a rectangle? *Explain* your reasoning.

MIXED REVIEW

Prepare for Lesson 9.4 in Exs. 39–42

Solve the equation. Check your solutions. ***(p. 469)***

39. $x^2 = 49$ **40.** $a^2 + 12 = 15$ **41.** $y^2 - 11 = 0$ **42.** $z^2 - 2 = 79$

43. Graph $\triangle LMN$ with vertices $L(1, 5)$, $M(4, 2)$, and $N(0, 0)$. Then graph its image after a dilation by the scale factor 3. ***(p. 447)***

44. ★ **MULTIPLE CHOICE** In the figure, $ABCD \sim WXYZ$. Find $m\angle D$. ***(p. 447)***

Ⓐ 58° Ⓑ 64°

Ⓒ 115° Ⓓ 123°

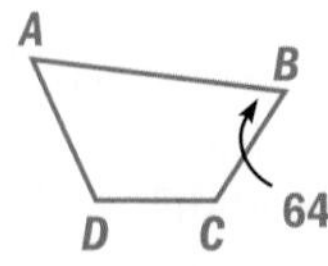

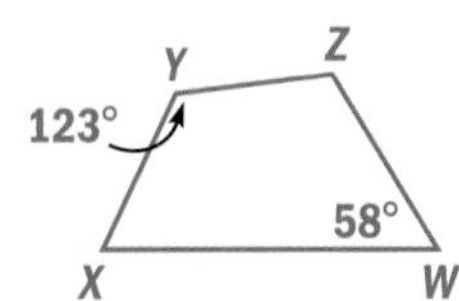

9.4 Using the Pythagorean Theorem

Before You found the side lengths of right triangles.

Now You'll solve real-world problems using the Pythagorean Theorem.

Why? So you can find distances indirectly, as in Example 1.

KEY VOCABULARY

- **Pythagorean triple,** *p. 488*

Boating You and your friend live on different sides of a lake. To ride your bicycle to your friend's house, you travel 0.5 mile directly east, and then 1.2 miles directly south. How far is it to your friend's house by boat?

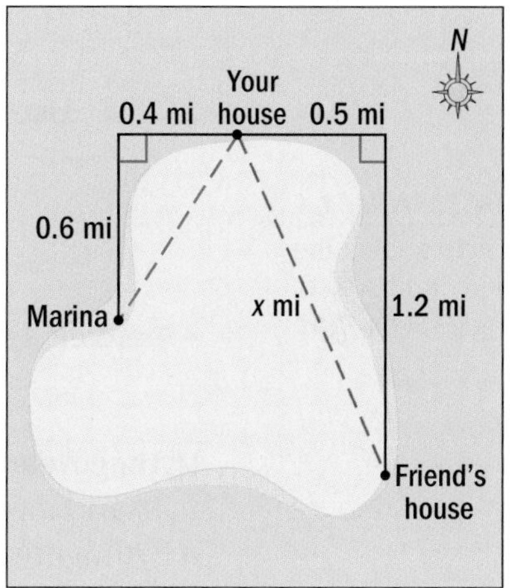

One way to find the distance from your house to your friend's house by boat is to measure the distance *indirectly*. Because the bicycle and boat paths form a right triangle, you can do this using the Pythagorean Theorem.

EXAMPLE 1 Using Indirect Measurement

To answer the question above, let a and b represent the lengths of the legs (bicycle paths) of the right triangle connecting your house and your friend's house. Let x represent the length of the hypotenuse (boat path).

$a^2 + b^2 = x^2$	Pythagorean Theorem
$0.5^2 + 1.2^2 = x^2$	Substitute 0.5 for a and 1.2 for b.
$0.25 + 1.44 = x^2$	Evaluate powers.
$1.69 = x^2$	Add.
$1.3 = x$	Take positive square root of each side.

ANOTHER WAY

Because a and b are both legs, you can also substitute 1.2 for a and 0.5 for b. The result will be the same.

▶ **Answer** It is 1.3 miles to your friend's house by boat.

✓ GUIDED PRACTICE for Example 1

1. **What If?** What if your friend's house is 0.5 mile east and 0.9 mile south. How far is your friend's house from your house? Round your answer to the nearest tenth of a mile.

2. **Marina** Use the map in Example 1. How far is it to the marina from your house by boat? Round your answer to the nearest tenth of a mile.

EXAMPLE 2 Finding Perimeter and Area

Find the perimeter and area of the triangle.

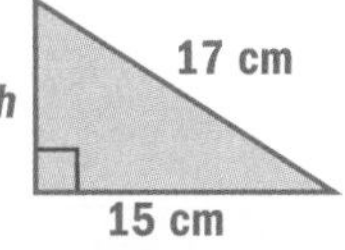

SOLUTION

STEP 1 **Find** the height of the triangle.

$h^2 + 15^2 = 17^2$ Pythagorean Theorem

$h^2 + 225 = 289$ Evaluate powers.

$h^2 = 64$ Subtract 225 from each side.

$h = 8$ Take positive square root of each side.

STEP 2 **Use** the height to find the perimeter and area.

Perimeter $= 8 + 15 + 17 = 40$

Area $= \frac{1}{2}(15)(8) = 60$

▸ **Answer** The perimeter is 40 cm and the area is 60 cm^2.

REVIEW FORMULAS
Need help finding the perimeter and area of a triangle? See p. 142.

Pythagorean Triples A **Pythagorean triple** is a set of three positive integers a, b, and c such that $a^2 + b^2 = c^2$. For example, the integers 3, 4, and 5 form a Pythagorean triple because $3^2 + 4^2 = 5^2$.

EXAMPLE 3 Identifying a Pythagorean Triple

Use the converse of the Pythagorean Theorem to determine whether the side lengths of the triangle form a Pythagorean triple.

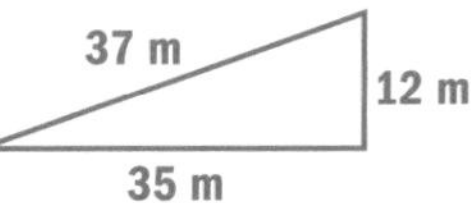

$a^2 + b^2 = c^2$ Definition of Pythagorean triple

$12^2 + 35^2 \stackrel{?}{=} 37^2$ Substitute 12 for *a*, 35 for *b*, and 37 for *c*.

$144 + 1225 \stackrel{?}{=} 1369$ Evaluate powers.

$1369 = 1369$ Add.

▸ **Answer** Because $12^2 + 35^2 = 37^2$ and the side lengths are integers, the side lengths form a Pythagorean triple.

AVOID ERRORS
Even though a drawing of a triangle may appear to have a right angle, you should confirm this using the converse of the Pythagorean Theorem.

✓ GUIDED PRACTICE for Examples 2 and 3

3. Find the perimeter and area of a right triangle that has a hypotenuse of length 74 feet and a leg of length 70 feet.

4. Determine whether the side lengths of the triangle form a Pythagorean triple.

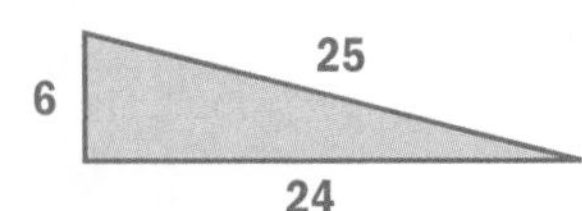

9.4 EXERCISES

HOMEWORK KEY

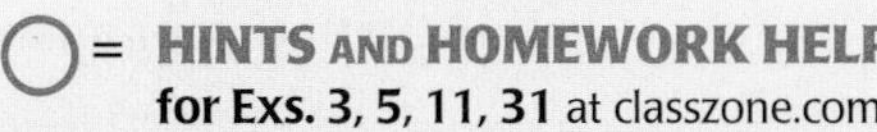

★ = STANDARDIZED TEST PRACTICE Exs. 10, 33, 34, and 42

◯ = HINTS AND HOMEWORK HELP for Exs. 3, 5, 11, 31 at classzone.com

SKILL PRACTICE

1. **VOCABULARY** Copy and complete: The integers 5, 12, and 13 form a ___?___ because $5^2 + 12^2 = 13^2$.

FINDING PERIMETER AND AREA **Let a and b represent the lengths of the legs of a right triangle, and let c represent the length of the hypotenuse. Find the unknown length. Then find the perimeter and area.**

SEE EXAMPLE 2 on p. 488 for Exs. 2–9

2. $a = 12$ cm, $b = 16$ cm, $c =$ ___?___
3. $a = 20$ ft, $b =$ ___?___, $c = 25$ ft
4. $a =$ ___?___, $b = 4.2$ km, $c = 5.8$ km
5. $a = 4.8$ in., $b = 3.6$ in., $c =$ ___?___
6. $a = 60$ yd, $b =$ ___?___, $c = 601.5$ yd
7. $a =$ ___?___, $b = 117$ m, $c = 125$ m
8. $a = 1.1$ cm, $b = 6$ cm, $c =$ ___?___
9. $a = 15$ yd, $b =$ ___?___, $c = 25$ yd

10. ★ **MULTIPLE CHOICE** What is the perimeter of a right triangle whose leg lengths are 3.6 inches and 7.7 inches?

Ⓐ 8.5 in. Ⓑ 18.1 in. Ⓒ 19.8 in. Ⓓ 27.72 in.^{2}

11. **ERROR ANALYSIS** Describe and correct the error made in finding the area of the triangle below.

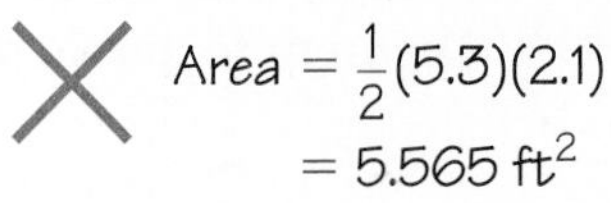

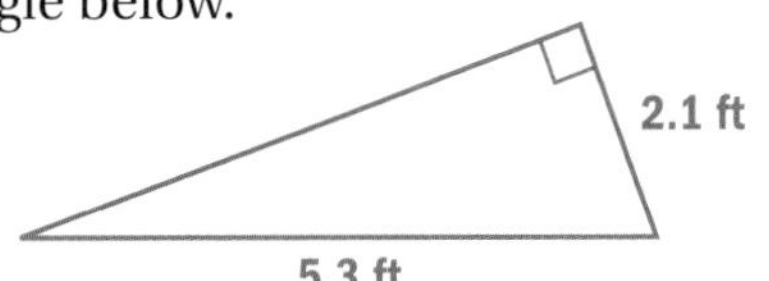

SEE EXAMPLE 3 on p. 488 for Exs. 12–15

IDENTIFYING PYTHAGOREAN TRIPLES **Determine whether the numbers form a Pythagorean triple.**

12. 9, 36, 41
13. 55, 48, 73
14. 39, 80, 89
15. 45, 96, 104

USING AREA **Find the perimeter of the right triangle given the length of one leg and the area.**

16. $a = 6$ m, Area $= 24$ m^2
17. $a = 8.8$ mi, Area $= 46.2$ mi^2
18. $a = 84$ cm, Area $= 546$ cm^2

USING PERIMETER **An isosceles triangle has perimeter P, in yards. Exactly one side has length c yards. Find the lengths of the other two sides. Then determine whether the triangle is an isosceles right triangle.**

19. $c = \sqrt{50}$, $P = 10 + \sqrt{50}$
20. $c = 4$, $P = 4 + \sqrt{32}$
21. $c = \sqrt{13}$, $P = 5 + \sqrt{13}$

22. **REASONING** The numbers 5, 12, and 13 form a Pythagorean triple. If each number is multiplied by the same positive integer, do the new numbers form a Pythagorean triple? *Justify* your reasoning.

23. **ALGEBRA** Write an equation for the perimeter of an isosceles right triangle in terms of its leg length a. Evaluate the equation for $a = 9$. Round your answer to the nearest tenth.

In Exercises 24–29, find the distance between the points. Round your answer to the nearest tenth if necessary.

EXTENSION **Finding the Distance Between Two Points**

The distance d between two points (s, t) and (u, v) is given by the formula $d = \sqrt{(u - s)^2 + (v - t)^2}$. Find the distance between (2, 3) and (8, 11).

$d = \sqrt{(u - s)^2 + (v - t)^2}$ **Distance formula**

$= \sqrt{(8 - 2)^2 + (11 - 3)^2}$ **Substitute values.**

$= \sqrt{36 + 64}$ **Simplify.**

$= 10$ **Evaluate square root.**

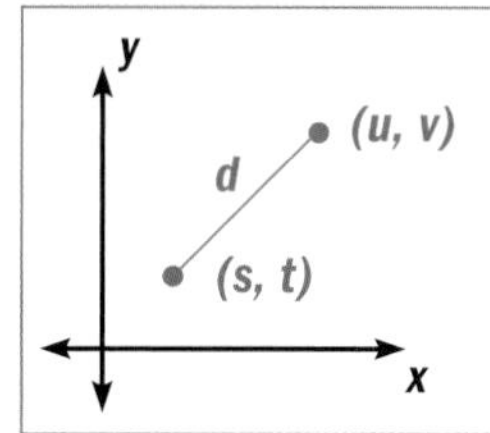

24. (0, −12), (5, 0)
25. (−2, 4), (5, −6)
26. (1, 6), (3, 4)
27. (−4, 7), (3, 3)
28. (6, −3), (−5, −1)
29. (−2, 0), (1, 9)

30. **CHALLENGE** Copy the diagram above in the Extension to form a right triangle with the given segment as the hypotenuse. Use the Pythagorean Theorem to derive the distance formula used above.

PROBLEM SOLVING

SEE EXAMPLE 1 on p. 487 for Exs. 31–33

31. **GUIDED PROBLEM SOLVING** A rectangular swimming pool has a length of 41 feet and a width of 11 feet. Tina swims the diagonal distance across the pool. About how far does she swim?

a. Draw a diagram.

b. Label the known distances.

c. Use the Pythagorean Theorem to find the unknown length. Round your answer to the nearest tenth of a foot.

32. **LANDMARKS** You are standing 500 feet from the Washington Monument. Using a range finder on the ground, you measure the distance from your location to the top of the monument to be 747 feet. Find the height of the Washington Monument to the nearest foot.

33. ★ **WRITING** In what situations might it be easier to use indirect measurement than direct measurement? When might direct measurement be the better method? Give examples to justify your reasoning.

34. ★ **MULTIPLE CHOICE** You are making a bookshelf, as shown. What is the value of x, rounded to the nearest inch?

Ⓐ 18 in. Ⓑ 25 in. Ⓒ 43 in. Ⓓ 63 in.

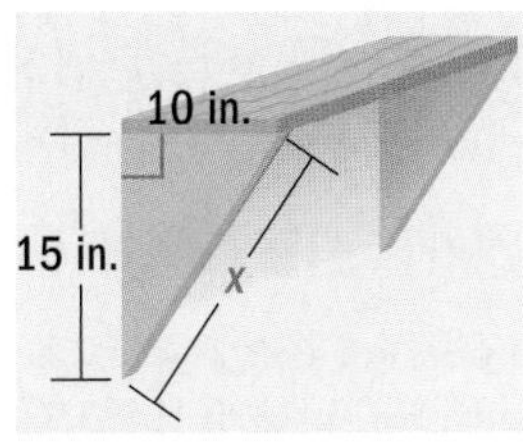

35. ◆ **MULTIPLE REPRESENTATIONS** Right triangle ABC has side lengths of 3 inches, 4 inches, and 5 inches. Triangle DEF has double the side lengths of triangle ABC. Triangle TUV has triple the side lengths of triangle ABC.
    a. **Make a Table** Make a table of the side lengths, perimeters, and areas of the three triangles. Compare the results.
    b. **Draw a Diagram** Use a ruler to draw the three triangles. *Describe* how to use the diagrams to compare the perimeters and areas of the triangles.

36. **CHALLENGE** Find the area of the shaded region given $\triangle ABC \sim \triangle ADE$, $AB = 10$ ft, $AC = 6$ ft, and $DE = 16$ ft.

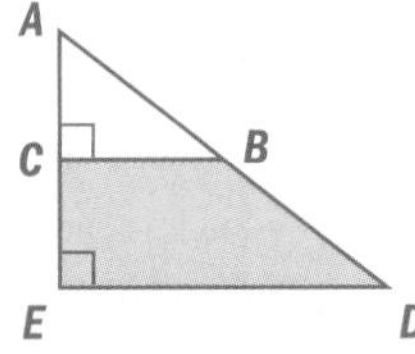

MIXED REVIEW

Get-Ready
Prepare for Lesson 9.5 in Exs. 37–40

The measure of one angle of a right triangle is given. Find the measure of the remaining acute angle in the triangle. *(p. 411)*

37. $60°$ 38. $45°$ 39. $15°$ 40. $81°$

41. Graph the polygon with vertices $A(-3, 3)$, $B(-3, 6)$, $C(-5, 3)$, and $D(-6, 1)$. Then graph its image after a reflection across the y-axis. *(p. 433)*

42. ★ **MULTIPLE CHOICE** Which number is equivalent to $-\sqrt{625}$? *(p. 469)*

Ⓐ -25 Ⓑ -15 Ⓒ 15 Ⓓ 25

QUIZ *for Lessons 9.1–9.4*

Use a calculator to approximate the square root. Round to the nearest tenth. *(p. 469)*

1. $\sqrt{50}$ 2. $\sqrt{18}$ 3. $-\sqrt{160}$ 4. $\sqrt{462}$

Solve the equation. Check your solutions. *(p. 469)*

5. $x^2 = 400$ 6. $b^2 - 11 = -2$ 7. $m^2 + 140 = 284$

8. Find the length of the hypotenuse of a right triangle with leg lengths of 12 meters and 16 meters. *(p. 482)*

9. Find the perimeter and area of a right triangle that has a hypotenuse of length 41 feet and one leg of length 9 feet. *(p. 487)*

Determine whether the numbers form a Pythagorean triple. *(p. 482)*

10. 5, 12, 15 11. 60, 91, 109 12. 11, 40, 41

MIXED REVIEW *of Problem Solving*

Lessons 9.1–9.4

1. **MULTI-STEP PROBLEM** You are making a quilt using a design based on the pattern shown below called the Wheel of Theodorus. This pattern is a spiral design using right triangles.

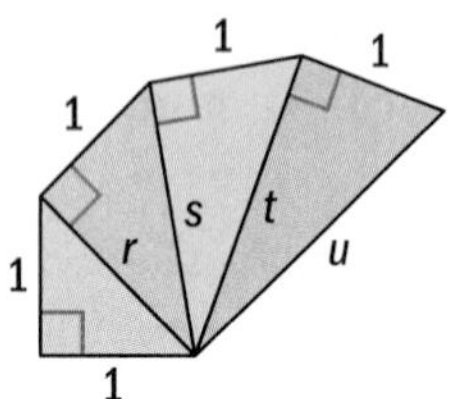

   a. Use the Pythagorean Theorem to find the exact values of r, s, t, and u, in this order.

   b. Find the perimeter and area of the portion of the design shown.

2. **MULTI-STEP PROBLEM** A support wire is stretched tightly from the top of a 7 meter utility pole to the ground. The distance from the base of the pole to the point where the wire meets the ground is 7.5 meters.

   a. Draw a diagram of the situation.

   b. Find the length of the wire to the nearest tenth of a meter without using a calculator. *Explain* your reasoning.

   c. Is the length of the wire a *rational* or *irrational* number? *Explain.*

3. **GRIDDED ANSWER** You are standing 200 feet from the base of the Space Needle in Seattle, Washington. Your friend is on the observation deck platform, 520 feet above the ground. To the nearest tenth of a foot, how much greater is the distance between you and your friend than the height of the observation deck?

4. **EXTENDED RESPONSE** A 3 foot tall banner will be hung in a hotel ballroom. Jacob is standing 36 feet away from the wall where the banner will hang. A tool was used to measure a distance of 45 feet from Jacob's eye level (6 feet) to the top of the banner. How far above the floor will the bottom of the banner hang? *Explain.*

5. **OPEN-ENDED** The number 0.010010001 . . . is irrational because no set of digits ever repeats. Find an irrational number between 0.43 and 0.44. *Explain* why your answer is an irrational number.

6. **SHORT RESPONSE** You are moving into a new house. The doorway is 78 inches high and 36 inches wide. Can a round table top with a radius of 41 inches fit through the doorway? *Explain* your reasoning.

7. **GRIDDED ANSWER** Find the area of the kite. Round to the nearest square inch.

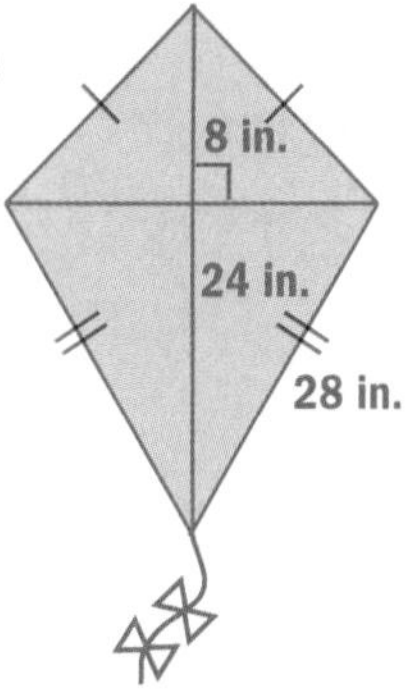

8. **EXTENDED RESPONSE** Martha is purchasing a rug for her den. Her den is 12 feet long and 9 feet wide.

   a. Will a square rug with an area of 100 square feet fit in Martha's den? Why or why not?

   b. How will the diameter of a circular rug with an area of 100 square feet compare with the dimensions of the square rug in part (a)? Will such a rug fit in Martha's den? *Explain* your reasoning.

   c. Will a rectangular rug with an area of 100 square feet fit in Martha's den? If so, give one possible set of dimensions. If not, *explain* why not.

9.5 Special Right Triangles

Before You solved real-life problems using the Pythagorean Theorem.
Now You'll use special right triangles to solve real-life problems.
Why? So you can find distances in sports, as in Example 1.

KEY VOCABULARY
- **equilateral triangle, isosceles triangle, right triangle, scalene triangle,** *p. 411*
- **leg,** *p. 482*
- **hypotenuse,** *p. 482*

To find unknown side lengths of some right triangles, you can use special side length relationships. You can think of a 45°-45°-90° as half of a square and use the Pythagorean Theorem to get the result below.

KEY CONCEPT *For Your Notebook*

45°-45°-90° Triangle

Words In a 45°-45°-90° isosceles triangle, the length of the hypotenuse is the product of the length of a leg and $\sqrt{2}$.

Algebra hypotenuse = leg • $\sqrt{2}$

$= x\sqrt{2}$

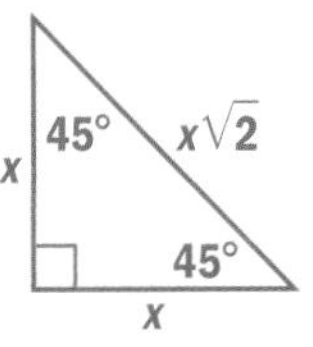

EXAMPLE 1 Using a 45°-45°-90° Triangle

Softball The infield of a softball field is a square with a side length of 60 feet. A catcher throws the ball from home plate to second base. How far does the catcher have to throw the ball?

SOLUTION

To find the distance, use the rule for a 45°-45°-90° triangle.

hypotenuse = **leg** • $\sqrt{2}$

$= \mathbf{60} \cdot \sqrt{2}$

$\approx 60(1.414)$

$= 84.84$

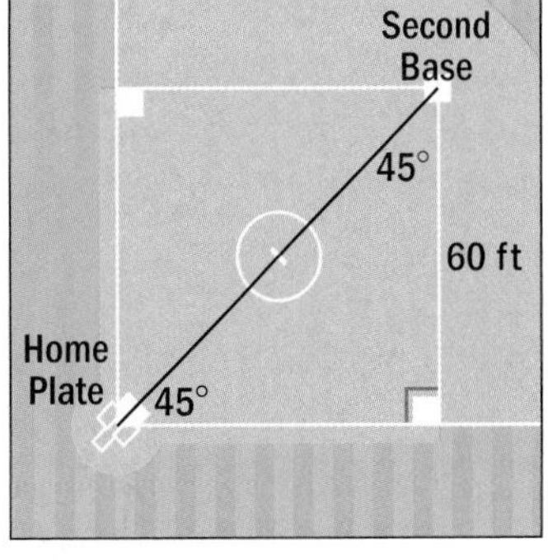

▶ **Answer** A catcher has to throw the ball about 85 feet.

ANOTHER WAY
You can use the Pythagorean Theorem to find the hypotenuse.

$a^2 + b^2 = c^2$

$60^2 + 60^2 = c^2$

$7200 = c^2$

$84.84 \approx c$

✓ **GUIDED PRACTICE** for Example 1

1. **City Parks** A city park is shaped like a square with a side length of 150 feet. What is the distance diagonally across the park?

30°-60°-90° Triangles You can think of a 30°-60°-90° triangle as half of an equilateral triangle and use the Pythagorean Theorem to get the result below. To give the triangle's *exact dimensions*, you may leave your answers as a radical expression.

KEY CONCEPT *For Your Notebook*

30°-60°-90° Triangle

Words In a 30°-60°-90° triangle, the hypotenuse is twice as long as the shorter leg. The length of the longer leg is the product of the length of the shorter leg and $\sqrt{3}$.

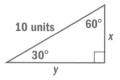

Algebra

$$\text{hypotenuse} = 2 \cdot \text{shorter leg} = 2x$$

$$\text{longer leg} = \text{shorter leg} \cdot \sqrt{3} = x\sqrt{3}$$

Diagram

30°, 2x, $x\sqrt{3}$, 60°, x

EXAMPLE 2 Using a 30°-60°-90° Triangle

Find the value of each variable in the triangle. Give the exact answer.

10 units, 60°, x, 30°, y

You need to find the length of the shorter leg first in order to find the length of the longer leg.

STEP 1 **Find** the length of the shorter leg.

$\text{hypotenuse} = 2 \cdot \text{shorter leg}$ **Rule for 30°-60°-90° triangle**

$10 = 2 \cdot x$ **Substitute.**

$5 = x$ **Divide each side by 2.**

STEP 2 **Find** the length of the longer leg.

$\text{longer leg} = \text{shorter leg} \cdot \sqrt{3}$ **Rule for 30°-60°-90° triangle**

$y = 5\sqrt{3}$ **Substitute.**

▶ **Answer** The shorter leg is 5 units long. The longer leg is $5\sqrt{3}$ units long.

CHECK ANSWERS
You can use the Pythagorean Theorem to check the solutions in Example 2.

✓ **GUIDED PRACTICE** for Example 2

Find the value of each variable. Give the exact answer.

2. 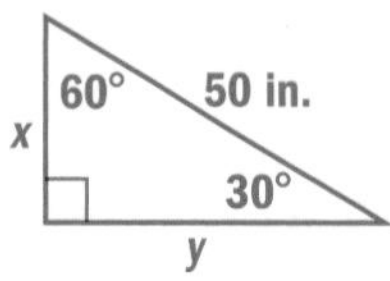

3. 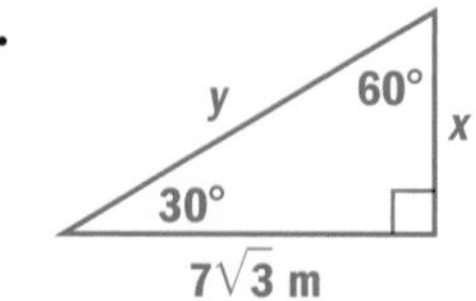

4. 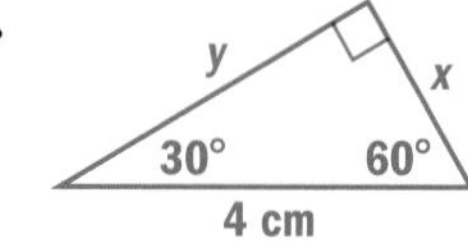

EXAMPLE 3 Using a Special Right Triangle

MULTIPLY SQUARE ROOTS

You may need to multiply square roots to find a side length. You can use the following relationship:

$\sqrt{a} \cdot \sqrt{b} = \sqrt{a \cdot b}$.

For example, $\sqrt{2} \cdot \sqrt{3} = \sqrt{2 \cdot 3} = \sqrt{6}$.

Water Ski Show The pyramid ski show is a common attraction at water parks. Find the horizontal distance from the pyramid to the boat.

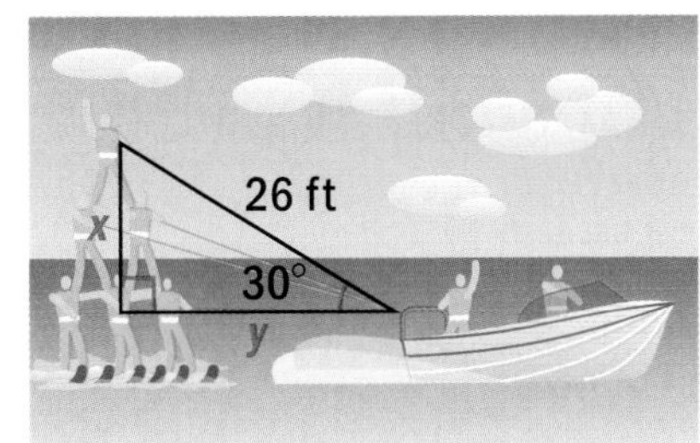

STEP 1 **Find** the length of the shorter leg.

$$\text{hypotenuse} = 2 \cdot \text{shorter leg}$$
$$26 = 2 \cdot x$$
$$13 = x$$

STEP 2 **Find** the length of the longer leg.

$$\text{longer leg} = \text{shorter leg} \cdot \sqrt{3}$$
$$y = 13 \cdot \sqrt{3}$$
$$\approx 22.52$$

▸ **Answer** The horizontal distance is about 23 feet.

at classzone.com

GUIDED PRACTICE for Example 3

5. **What If?** In Example 3, suppose that the horizontal distance from the pyramid to the boat is $15\sqrt{3}$ feet. What is the distance from the top of the pyramid to the boat?

9.5 EXERCISES

HOMEWORK KEY

★ = **STANDARDIZED TEST PRACTICE** Exs. 16, 22, 25, 28, 29, and 37

○ = **HINTS AND HOMEWORK HELP** for Exs. 3, 5, 11, 23 at classzone.com

SKILL PRACTICE

1. **VOCABULARY** Copy and complete: A 45°-45°-90° triangle is a(n) __?__ triangle.

2. **VOCABULARY** *Explain* how the length of the hypotenuse in a 45°-45°-90° triangle is related to the length of a leg.

45°-45°-90° TRIANGLES **Find the value of the variable. Give the exact answer.**

SEE EXAMPLE 1 on p. 493 for Exs. 3–8

3. 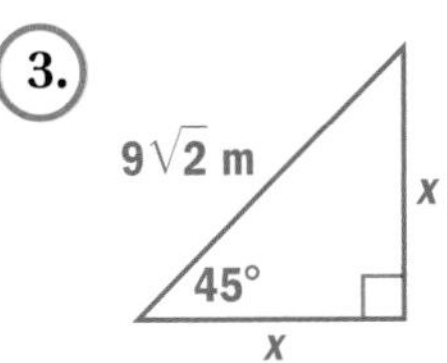

4. 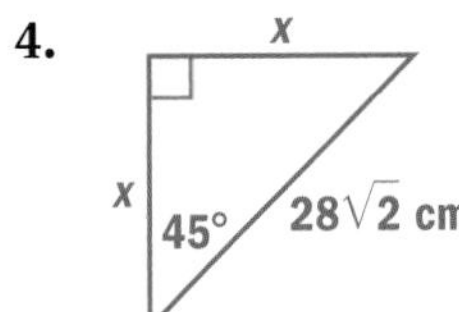

5. 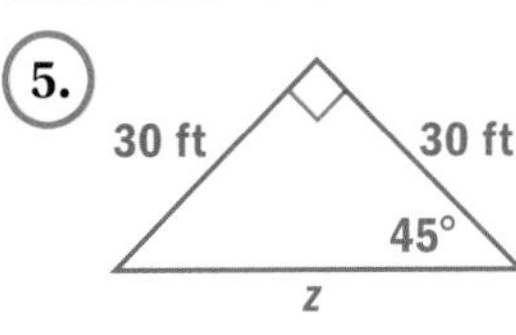

6. 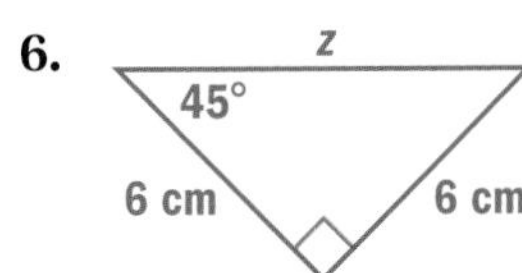

7. 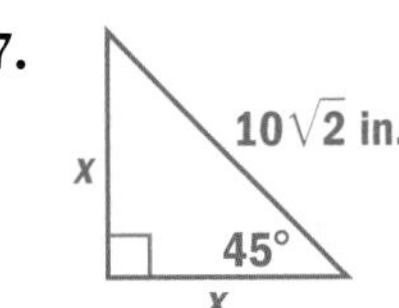

8. 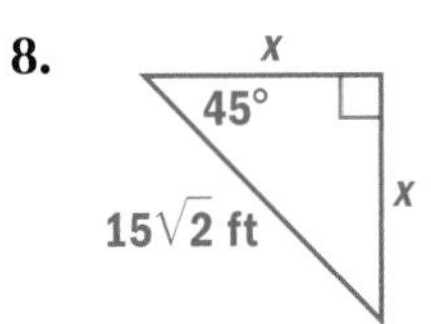

SEE EXAMPLE 1
on p. 493
for Ex. 9

9. **ERROR ANALYSIS** Bailey calculated the length of the hypotenuse of an isosceles right triangle with a leg length of 8 inches. Describe and correct the error.

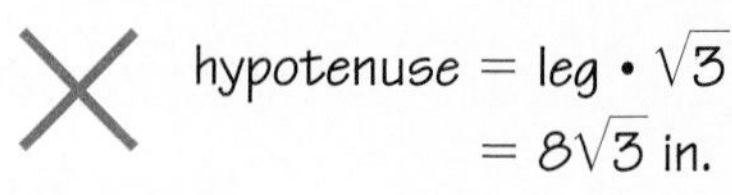

30°-60°-90° TRIANGLES **Find the exact value of each variable.**

SEE EXAMPLE 2
on p. 494
for Exs. 10–16

10. 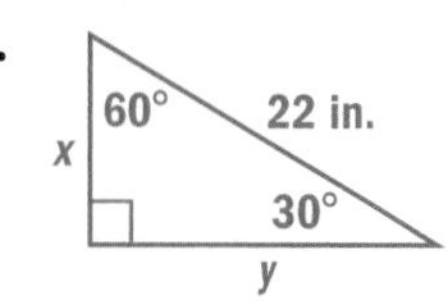

11. 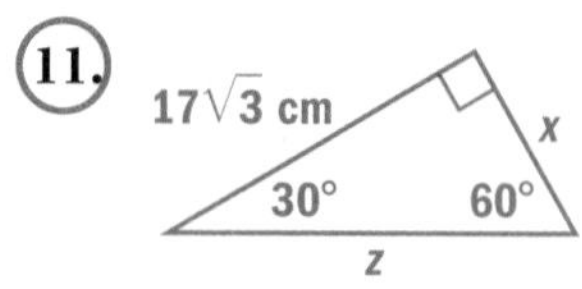

12. 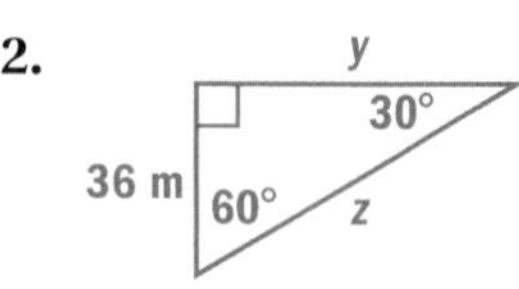

13. 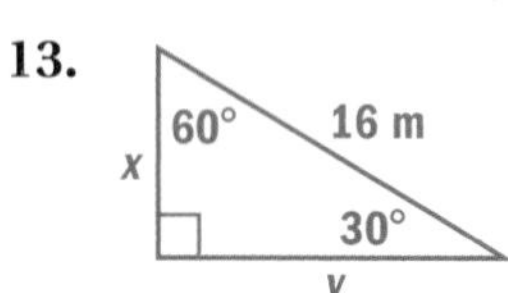

14. 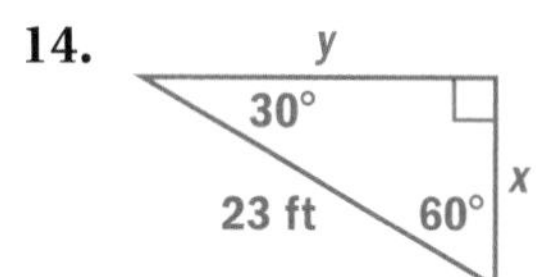

15. 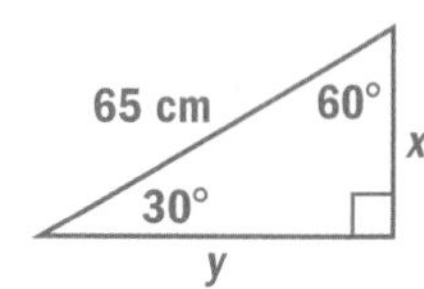

16. ★ **MULTIPLE CHOICE** The hypotenuse of a 30°-60°-90° triangle has a length of $10\sqrt{3}$ feet. What is the length of the shorter leg?

(A) $20\sqrt{3}$ feet (B) 10 feet (C) $5\sqrt{3}$ feet (D) 5 feet

PERIMETER **Find the perimeter of the figure. Round to the nearest unit.**

17. 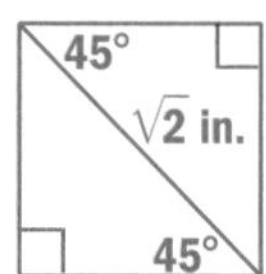

18. 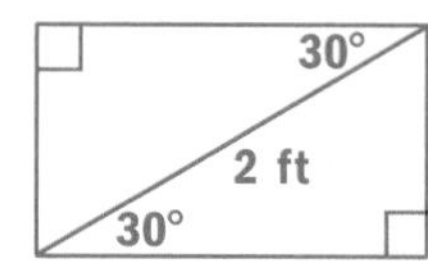

19. 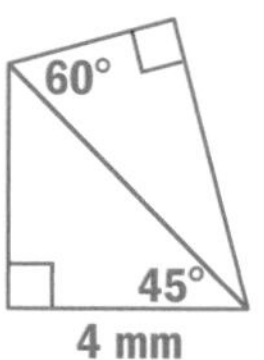

20. **AREA** In the diagram at the right, $\triangle ABC \sim \triangle XYZ$. Find all unknown side lengths of the triangles. What is the area of $\triangle XYZ$? Give exact answers.

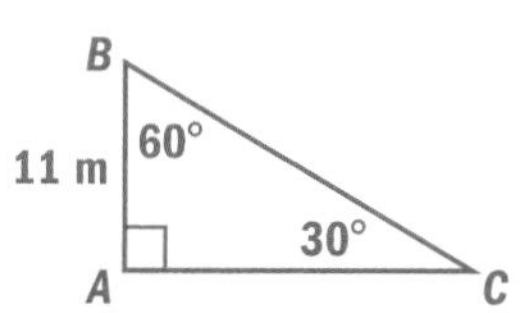

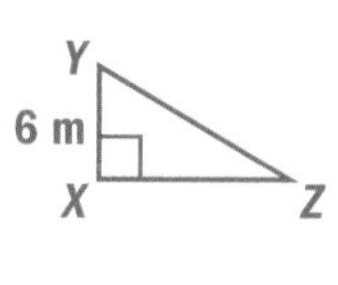

21. **CHALLENGE** Find the lengths *AD*, *DC*, *BD*, and *BC* in $\triangle ABC$. Name each 30°-60°-90° triangle in the diagram. Find and compare the areas of each 30°-60°-90° triangle.

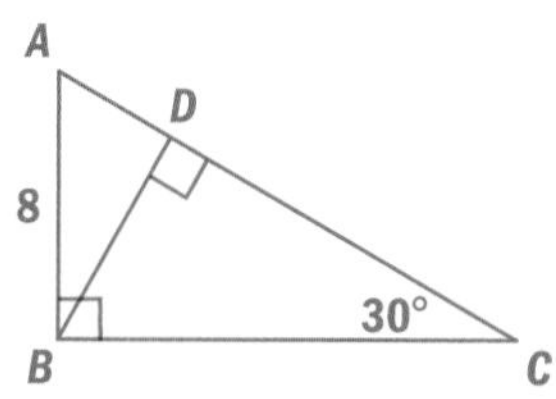

PROBLEM SOLVING

SEE EXAMPLE 3
on p. 495
for Exs. 22–23

22. ★ **MULTIPLE CHOICE** A flag is folded into the shape of a 45°-45°-90° triangle with a hypotenuse length of 20 inches. What is the approximate value of *x*?

(A) 10 inches (B) 11.5 inches

(C) 14.1 inches (D) 28.3 inches

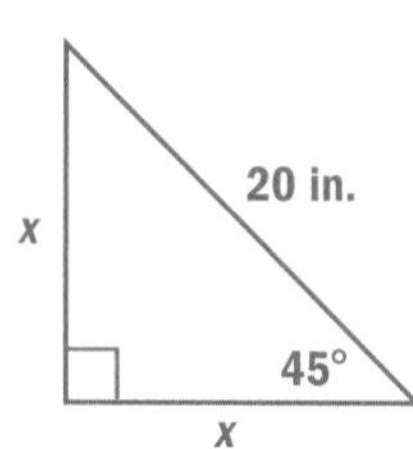

23. **ESCALATOR** An escalator going down to the main floor of a subway station is 230 feet long and makes a 30° angle with the main floor. How many feet below the main floor is the subway station?

24. **REASONING** Is it possible to have an equilateral right triangle? *Explain* your reasoning.

25. ★ **OPEN-ENDED MATH** Use a protractor to draw a 30°-60° -90° triangle. Use a ruler to measure one of the sides. Then use the 30°-60°-90° rules to find the lengths of the other two sides. Measure to check your calculations.

26. **QUILTING** Find the perimeters of the five squares within the diagram of the Snail's Trail quilt pattern at the right. The triangles are all 45°-45°-90° triangles. Round your answers to the nearest inch if necessary.

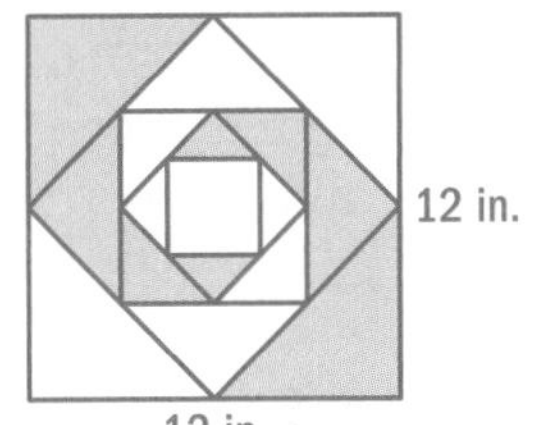

27. **TRIANGLES** Find the perimeters of the four large right triangles in the quilt pattern at the right. Then find the sum of the perimeters. Give exact answers.

28. ★ **SHORT RESPONSE** A 45°-45°-90° triangle is drawn inside of a 30°-60°-90° triangle, as shown. Write a variable expression for the area of the shaded region. *Explain* how you found your answer.

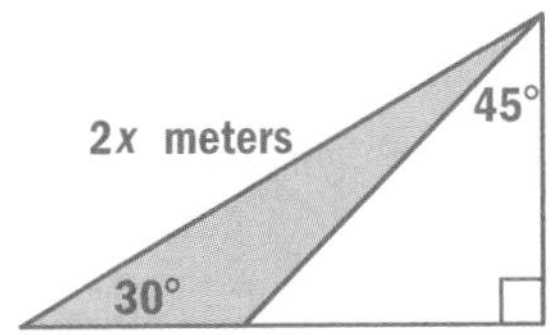

29. ★ **WRITING** Use the Pythagorean Theorem to verify the 30°-60°-90° rule. Give an example.

30. **CHALLENGE** A regular hexagon can be divided into 6 equilateral triangles as shown. Find the perimeter and area of the hexagon.

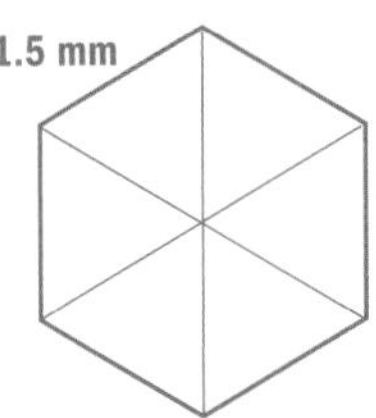

MIXED REVIEW

Prepare for Lesson 9.6 in Exs. 31–33

Solve the equation. *(p. 122)*

31. $0.45 = \frac{x}{20}$

32. $0.217 = \frac{x}{50}$

33. $0.4001 = \frac{x}{13}$

Write the rate as a unit rate. *(p. 343)*

34. $\frac{\text{28 people}}{\text{4 teams}}$

35. $\frac{\text{60 meters}}{\text{20 seconds}}$

36. $\frac{\text{488 rotations}}{\text{8 minutes}}$

37. ★ **MULTIPLE CHOICE** Evaluate $a^2 + 5b$ when $a = -8$ and $b = -2$. *(p. 73)*

(A) −74 (B) −54 (C) 54 (D) 74

GOAL
Find the sine and cosine ratios of right triangles.

MATERIALS
- metric ruler
- protractor

9.6 Exploring Trigonometric Ratios

You can use a protractor and metric ruler to find the ratios of the length of each leg of a right triangle to the length of the hypotenuse.

EXPLORE **Find ratios of side lengths of similar right triangles.**

STEP 1 **Draw** a 40° angle. Mark tick marks every 5 centimeters along one side.

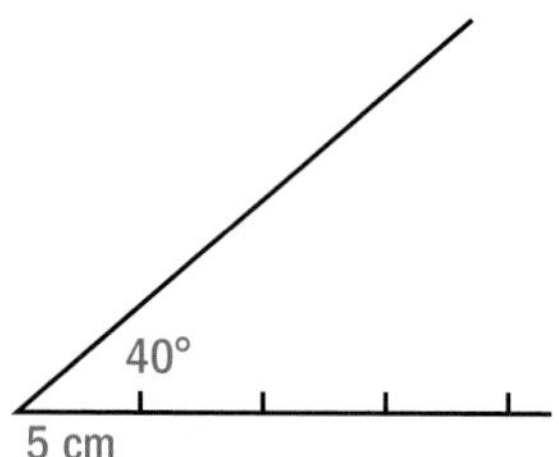

STEP 2 **Draw** perpendicular line segments from four of the tick marks to intersect with the other side of the angle.

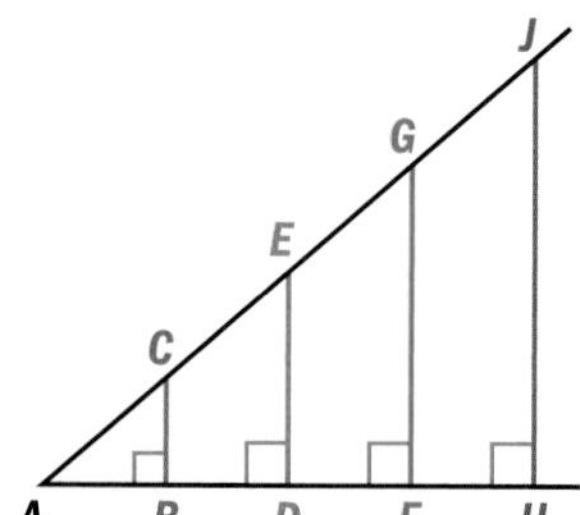

STEP 3 **Identify** the four similar triangles in your drawing. Measure the legs of each triangle in your drawing to the nearest tenth of a centimeter. Then copy and complete the table. Round your answers to the nearest hundredth.

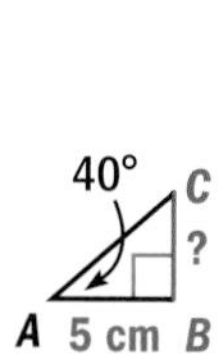

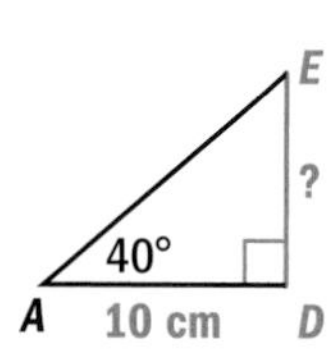

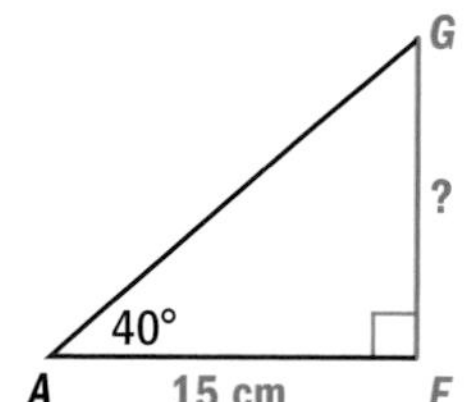

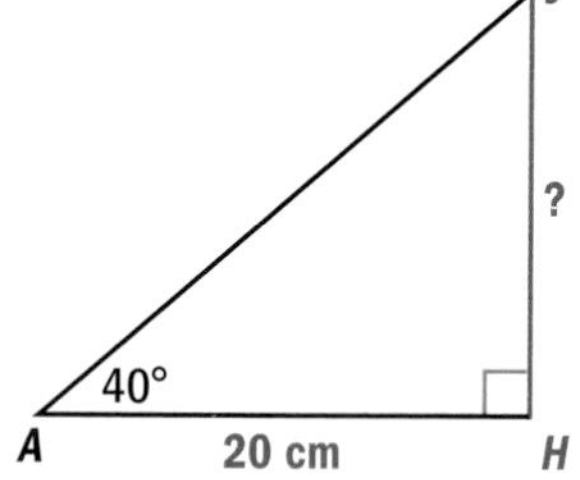

Triangle	Leg 1	Leg 2	Hypotenuse	$\frac{\text{Leg 1}}{\text{Hypotenuse}}$	$\frac{\text{Leg 2}}{\text{Hypotenuse}}$
$\triangle ABC$	5 cm	?	?	?	?
$\triangle ADE$	10 cm	?	?	?	?
$\triangle AFG$	15 cm	?	?	?	?
$\triangle AHJ$	20 cm	?	?	?	?

STEP 4 **Describe** the pattern in the ratios $\frac{\text{Leg 1}}{\text{Hypotenuse}}$ in your table.

STEP 5 **Describe** the pattern in the ratios $\frac{\text{Leg 2}}{\text{Hypotenuse}}$ in your table.

STEP 6 **Repeat** Steps 1–5 using a 70° angle. Based on your results, do the ratios depend on the lengths of the right triangles' sides or on the measures of their angles?

The ratios $\frac{\text{Leg 1}}{\text{Hypotenuse}}$ and $\frac{\text{Leg 2}}{\text{Hypotenuse}}$ have special names. They are called the *sine* and *cosine* ratios and can be defined as follows:

$$\sin A = \frac{\text{length of leg opposite } \angle A}{\text{length of hypotenuse}} \qquad \cos A = \frac{\text{length of leg adjacent } \angle A}{\text{length of hypotenuse}}$$

PRACTICE

Find the sine and cosine ratios for $\angle A$ and $\angle B$.

1. 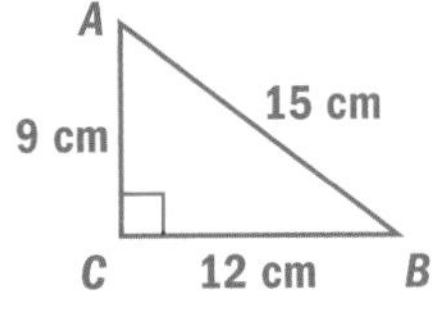

2. 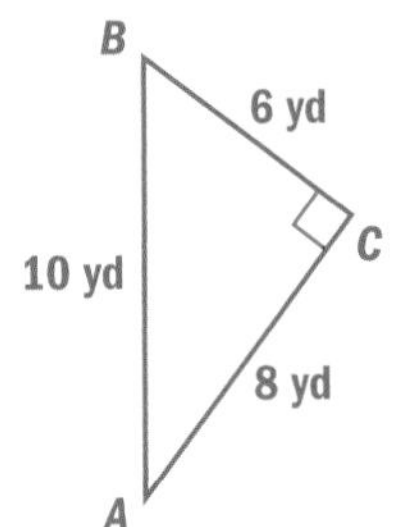

3. 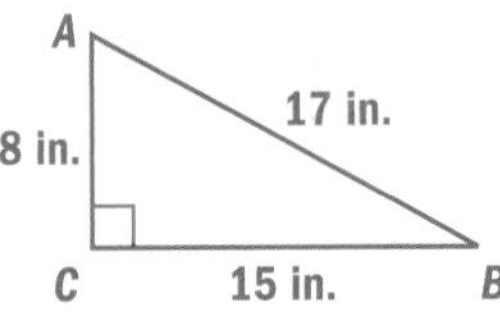

4. 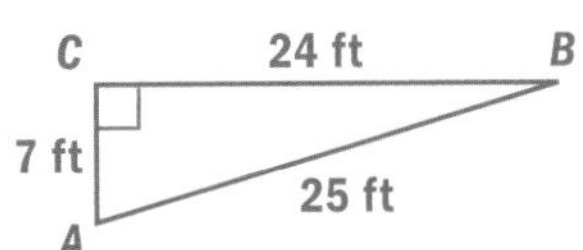

5. 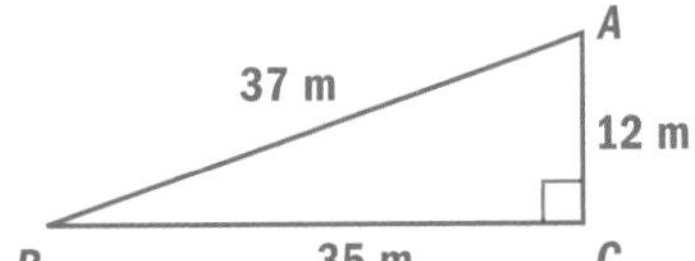

6. 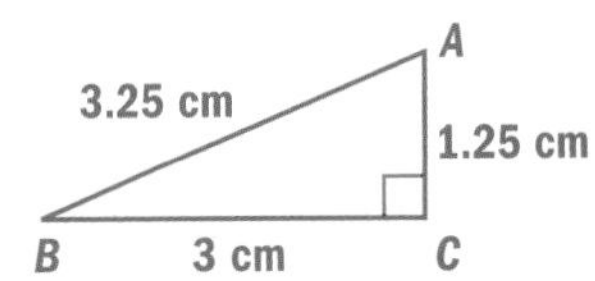

DRAW CONCLUSIONS

7. **REASONING** Measure $\angle A$ in each triangle in Exercises 1–6. Write the measures in order from least to greatest. Make a table that shows $m\angle A$, $\sin A$, and $\cos A$. Then copy and complete the following two statements using *increases* or *decreases*.

   a. As $m\angle A$ increases from 0° to 90°, the value of $\sin A$ __?__.

   b. As $m\angle A$ increases from 0° to 90°, the value of $\cos A$ __?__.

9.6 Using Trigonometric Ratios

Before	You found the side lengths of special right triangles.
Now	You'll use trigonometric ratios to find the side lengths.
Why?	So you can use angles to find heights, as in Example 5.

KEY VOCABULARY

- **trigonometric ratio,** *p. 500*
- **sine,** *p. 500*
- **cosine,** *p. 500*
- **tangent,** *p. 500*

Water Slide A water slide makes an angle of about 18° with the ground. The slide extends horizontally about 64.2 meters. What is the height of the slide? You will find out how to solve this problem in Example 5.

You can find the height of the water slide using a *trigonometric ratio*. A **trigonometric ratio** is a ratio of the lengths of two sides of a right triangle. The three basic trigonometric ratios are **sine**, **cosine**, and **tangent**. These are abbreviated as sin, cos, and tan.

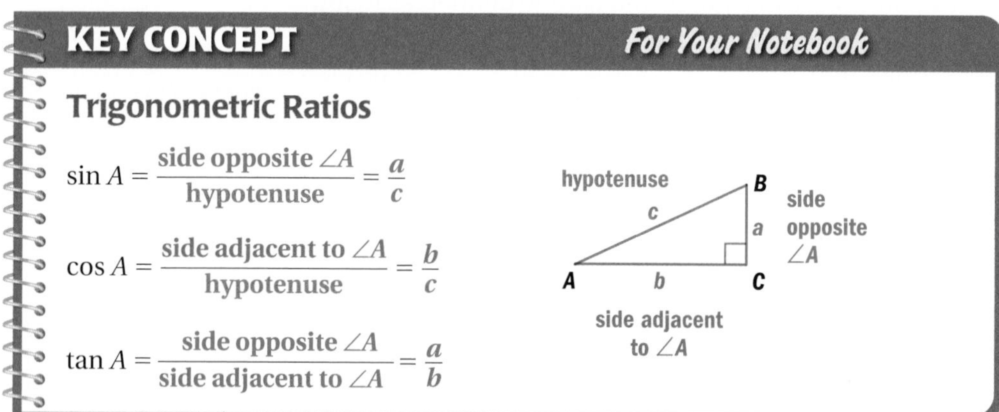

KEY CONCEPT *For Your Notebook*

Trigonometric Ratios

$$\sin A = \frac{\text{side opposite } \angle A}{\text{hypotenuse}} = \frac{a}{c}$$

$$\cos A = \frac{\text{side adjacent to } \angle A}{\text{hypotenuse}} = \frac{b}{c}$$

$$\tan A = \frac{\text{side opposite } \angle A}{\text{side adjacent to } \angle A} = \frac{a}{b}$$

EXAMPLE 1 Finding Trigonometric Ratios

DETERMINE SIDES
Determining the opposite and adjacent sides depends on the angle being used. For $\angle Q$, the length of the opposite side is 12 feet, and the length of the adjacent side is 5 feet.

For $\triangle PQR$, write the sine, cosine, and tangent ratios for $\angle P$.

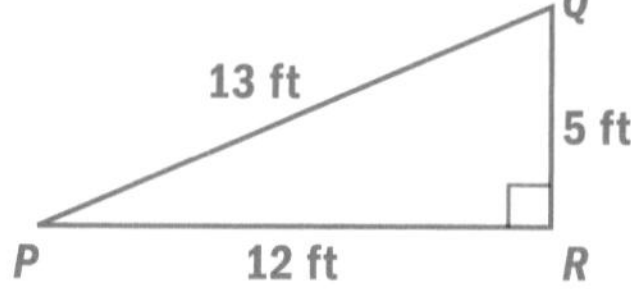

SOLUTION

For $\angle P$, the length of the opposite side is 5 feet, and the length of the adjacent side is 12 feet. The length of the hypotenuse is 13 feet.

$$\sin P = \frac{\text{opposite}}{\text{hypotenuse}} = \frac{5}{13}$$

$$\cos P = \frac{\text{adjacent}}{\text{hypotenuse}} = \frac{12}{13}$$

$$\tan P = \frac{\text{opposite}}{\text{adjacent}} = \frac{5}{12}$$

EXAMPLE 2 Using a Calculator

AVOID ERRORS

When using a calculator to find trigonometric ratios of angles measured in degrees, be sure the calculator is in *degree mode*. You can test this by checking that tan 45° = 1.

Use a calculator to find sine, cosine, and tangent of 30°.

	Keystrokes	Display	Answer
a.	2nd TRIG = 30 = 2nd	0.5	$\sin 30° = 0.5$
b.	2nd TRIG ▶ ▶ = 30 = 2nd	0.8660254	$\cos 30° \approx 0.8660$
c.	2nd TRIG ◀ ◀ = 30 = 2nd	0.5773503	$\tan 30° \approx 0.5774$

✓ GUIDED PRACTICE for Examples 1 and 2

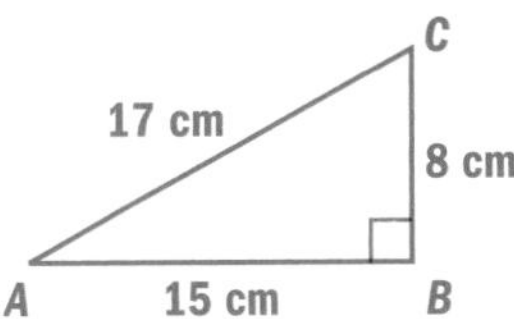

1. For $\triangle ABC$, write the sine, cosine, and tangent ratios for $\angle A$ and $\angle C$. Which ratio has a value greater than 1?
2. Draw a 45°-45°-90° triangle. Label the legs 2 ft and the hypotenuse appropriately. Write the sine, cosine, and tangent ratios for one of the 45° angles. Does it make a difference which 45° angle you choose? *Explain.*

Use a calculator to approximate the expression. Round your answer to four decimal places.

3. cos 70°
4. tan 50°
5. sin 25°
6. tan 7°

EXAMPLE 3 Using a Cosine Ratio

Find the value of x in the triangle.

The length of the hypotenuse is 8 inches. The unknown side is adjacent to the given angle. Use the cosine of $\angle K$.

$\cos K = \frac{\text{adjacent}}{\text{hypotenuse}}$ **Definition of cosine**

$\cos 55° = \frac{x}{8}$ **Substitute.**

$8 \cdot \cos 55° = 8 \cdot \frac{x}{8}$ **Multiply each side by 8.**

$4.5886 \approx x$ **Use a calculator.**

▶ **Answer** The value of x is about 4.59 inches.

✓ GUIDED PRACTICE for Example 3

7. Find the value of x in the triangle. Round your answer to the nearest hundredth of a foot.

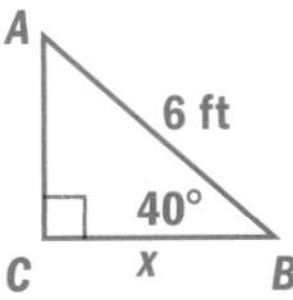

EXAMPLE 4 Using a Sine Ratio

Ski Jump A ski jump is 380 feet long and makes a 27.6° angle with the ground. Find the height x of the ski jump.

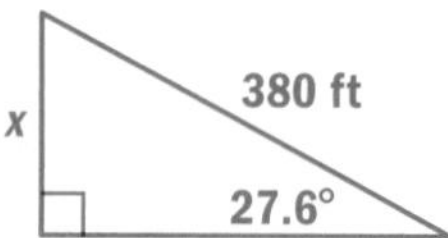

SOLUTION

The unknown side is opposite the given angle. Use the sine ratio.

$$\sin 27.6° = \frac{\text{opposite}}{\text{hypotenuse}}$$ **Definition of sine**

$$\sin 27.6° = \frac{x}{380}$$ **Substitute.**

$$380 \cdot \sin 27.6° = 380 \cdot \frac{x}{380}$$ **Multiply each side by 380.**

$$176.05 \approx x$$ **Use a calculator.**

▶ **Answer** The ski jump is about 176 feet high.

EXAMPLE 5 Using a Tangent Ratio

Water Slide Find the height h of the water slide described on page 500.

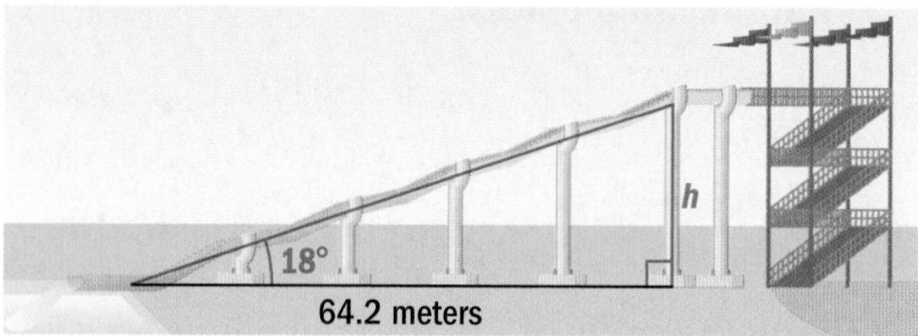

SOLUTION

Use the tangent ratio.

$$\tan 18° = \frac{\text{opposite}}{\text{adjacent}}$$ **Definition of tangent**

$$\tan 18° = \frac{h}{64.2}$$ **Substitute.**

$$64.2 \cdot \tan 18° = 64.2 \cdot \frac{h}{64.2}$$ **Multiply each side by 64.2.**

$$20.85984 \approx h$$ **Use a calculator.**

▶ **Answer** The height of the water slide is about 20.9 meters.

✓ GUIDED PRACTICE for Examples 4 and 5

8. **What If?** In Example 4, what is the height x if the angle measure is 31°?

9. **What If?** In Example 5, what is the height h if the angle measure is 16°?

9.6 EXERCISES

HOMEWORK KEY

★ = **STANDARDIZED TEST PRACTICE** Exs. 7, 15, 32, 34, 35, 36, and 50

○ = **HINTS AND HOMEWORK HELP** for Exs. 5, 9, 13, 31 at classzone.com

SKILL PRACTICE

VOCABULARY **Match the term with the correct trigonometric ratio.**

1. sine
2. cosine
3. tangent

A. $\frac{\text{adjacent}}{\text{hypotenuse}}$ B. $\frac{\text{opposite}}{\text{hypotenuse}}$ C. $\frac{\text{opposite}}{\text{adjacent}}$

SEE EXAMPLE 1 on p. 500 for Exs. 4–7

FINDING TRIGONOMETRIC RATIOS **In $\triangle PQR$, write the sine, cosine, and tangent ratios for $\angle P$ and $\angle R$.**

4. 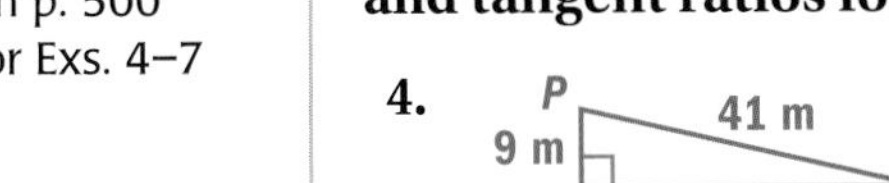

5. 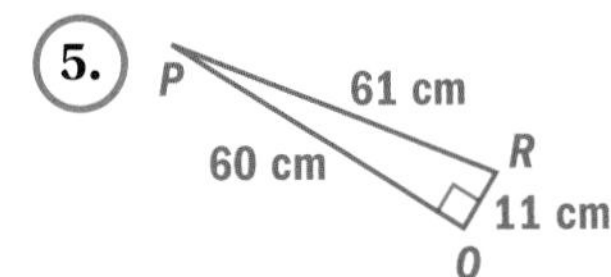

6. 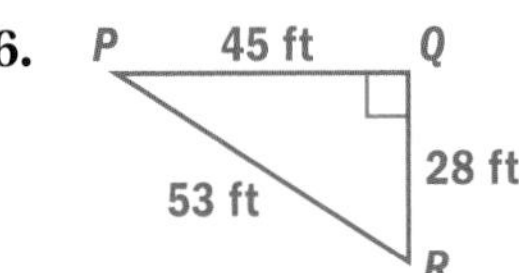

7. ★ **MULTIPLE CHOICE** What is the cosine of $\angle E$?

Ⓐ $\frac{5}{13}$ Ⓑ $\frac{12}{13}$ Ⓒ $\frac{13}{5}$ Ⓓ 13

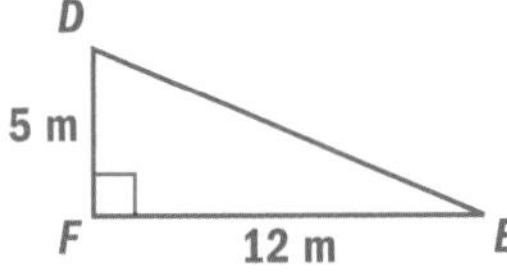

SEE EXAMPLE 2 on p. 501 for Exs. 8–11

USING A CALCULATOR **Use a calculator to approximate the given expression. Round your answer to four decimal places.**

8. $\tan 51°$
9. $\sin 80°$
10. $\sin 36°$
11. $\cos 76°$

SEE EXAMPLES 3, 4, AND 5 on pp. 501–502 for Exs. 12–16

USING TRIGONOMETRIC RATIOS **Find the value of x. Round your answer to the nearest thousandth.**

12. 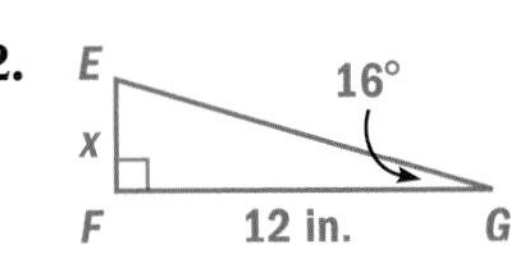

13. 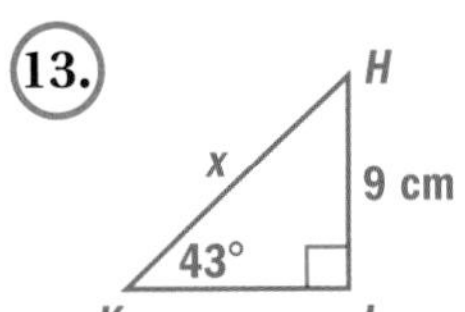

14. 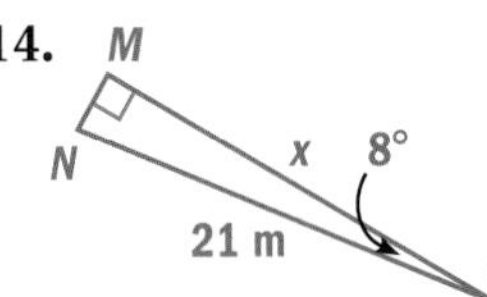

15. ★ **MULTIPLE CHOICE** What is the approximate length of side $\overline{AC}$?

Ⓐ 7 ft Ⓑ 10 ft Ⓒ $7\sqrt{3}$ ft Ⓓ 14 ft

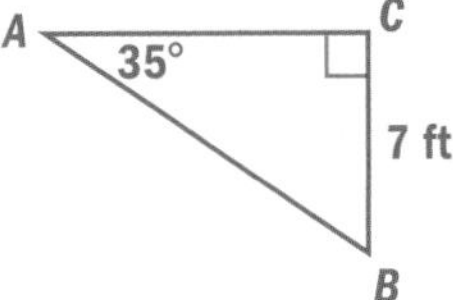

16. **ERROR ANALYSIS** Describe and correct the error made in finding the length of side LK.

✗ $\tan 25° = \frac{x}{15}$

so $x \approx 7$ cm

L
15 cm
x
25°
J
13 cm
K

FINDING PERIMETER **Find the perimeter of the triangle. Round your answer to the nearest tenth.**

17. 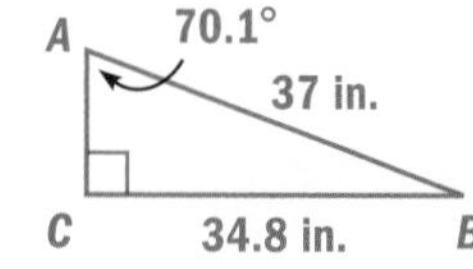

18. 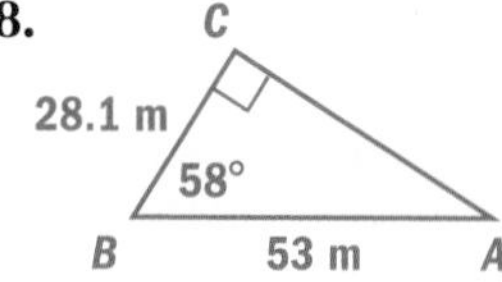

19. 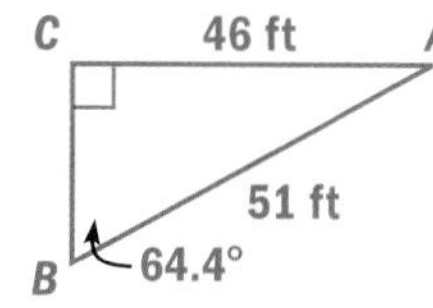

20. **ALGEBRA** Write the trigonometric ratios for $\angle A$ and $\angle B$ in $\triangle ABC$ in terms of x.

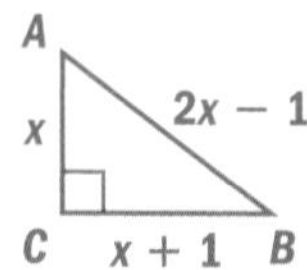

FINDING ANGLES AND SIDE LENGTHS **Find the measure of the unknown angle and sides. Then use the side lengths to write three trigonometric ratios for $\angle C$.**

21. 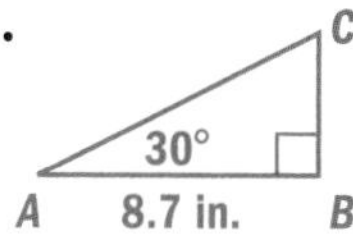

22. 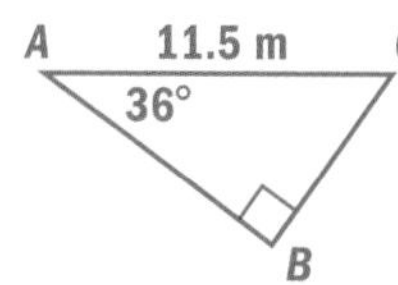

23. 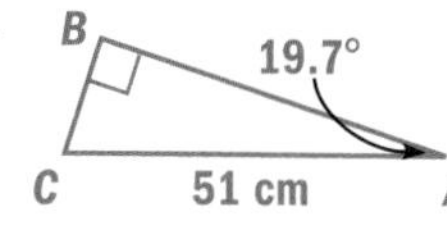

24. **REASONING** Use the definitions of the trigonometric ratios to show $\frac{\sin A}{\cos A} = \tan A$.

CHALLENGE **Given $\triangle ABC$ with $\angle C = 90°$, tell whether the statement is *always, sometimes,* or *never* true. *Explain* your reasoning.**

25. $\sin A = \sin B$

26. $\sin A = \cos B$

27. $\sin A = \tan A$

28. $\sin A = \cos A$

PROBLEM SOLVING

SEE EXAMPLES 3, 4, AND 5 on pp. 501–502 for Exs. 29, 31

29. **GUIDED PROBLEM SOLVING** You stand 50 feet from a totem pole that is perpendicular to the ground. The angle from the point where you stand to the top of the totem pole is 42°. How tall is the totem pole?

a. Draw a diagram and identify the sides of the triangle.

b. Write an equation using a trigonometric ratio.

c. Solve the equation. Round your answer to the nearest foot.

30. **DRAW A DIAGRAM** A piece of sheet metal is in the shape of right triangle ABC where $\tan A = \frac{15}{8}$ and $\cos B = \frac{15}{17}$. Sketch a triangle to represent the sheet metal and label each side with the appropriate length.

31. **PET SUPPLIES** You are constructing a scratching post and platform for your cat as shown at the right. Find the length x of the scratching post to the nearest tenth of a foot.

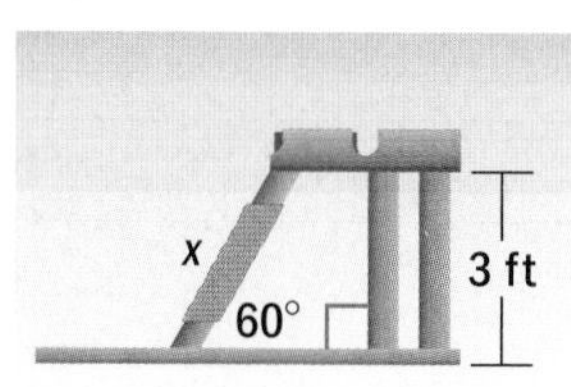

32. ★ **WRITING** *Explain* how to find the sine, cosine, and tangent ratios of an acute angle of a right triangle.

33. **MULTI-STEP PROBLEM** Some whales have been known to dive as deep as 3000 meters in search of their favorite food.

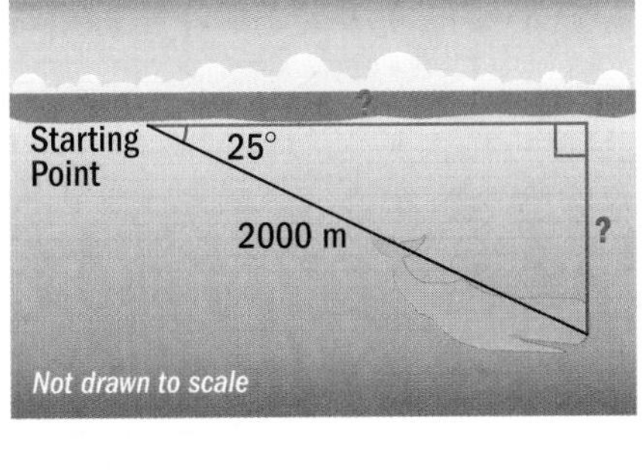

a. The whale shown finds food after swimming 2000 meters. About how far is the whale's starting point from the point on the water's surface directly above its food?

b. To the nearest meter, at what depth did the whale find its food?

c. Did this whale dive more or less than half of the deepest known dive?

34. ★ **MULTIPLE CHOICE** What is the approximate area of the boat sail?

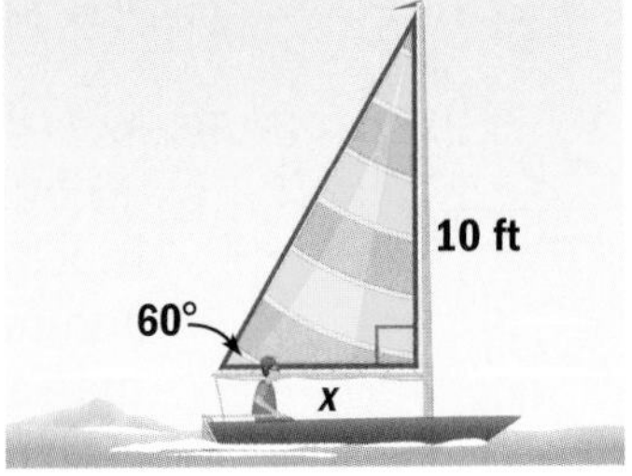

Ⓐ 5.77 ft^2 Ⓑ 17.32 ft^2

Ⓒ 28.87 ft^2 Ⓓ 57.74 ft^2

35. ★ **OPEN-ENDED MATH** Describe a real-world situation that can be modeled by $\sin 10° = \frac{x}{20}$.

36. ★ **EXTENDED RESPONSE** A tethered hot air balloon is released from point B and rises straight upward. You are standing at point A, which is 30 meters from point B.

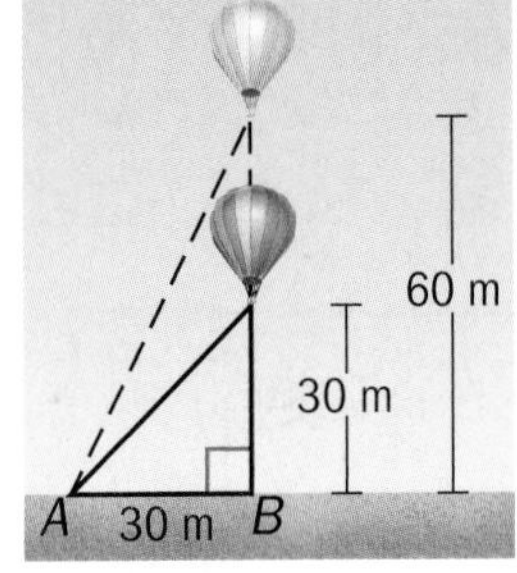

a. Write the tangent ratio for each height of the balloon shown in the diagram.

b. Would you expect the value of tan A to *increase* or *decrease* as the balloon rises to 60 meters? *Explain* your reasoning.

c. As the balloon lands, it travels straight downward. How does $m\angle A$ change? Does cos A *increase* or *decrease*? *Explain* your reasoning.

37. **REASONING** Jared is standing about 400 feet from an office building and about the same distance from an apartment complex. The apartment complex is half the height of the office building. To see the top of the office building, Jared looks up about 60° from horizontal. Will the angle Jared looks up from horizontal to see the top of the apartment complex be half the previous angle measure? *Explain* your reasoning.

REASONING Is there a value of x which makes the equation true? *Explain* your reasoning.

38. $\sin x° > 1$ 39. $\tan x° > 1$ 40. $\sin x° = 1$ 41. $\cos x° = 1$

42. **CHALLENGE** Find the area of an isosceles triangle that has two 50° angles and two sides of length 6 meters.

43. **CHALLENGE** An airplane is at an altitude of 33,000 feet when the pilot starts the descent to the airport. The pilot wants the plane to descend at an angle of 3°. How many miles away from the airport must the descent begin? Round your answer to the nearest mile.

MIXED REVIEW

Get-Ready

Prepare for Lesson 10.1 in Exs. 44–46

Find the area of the figure.

44. 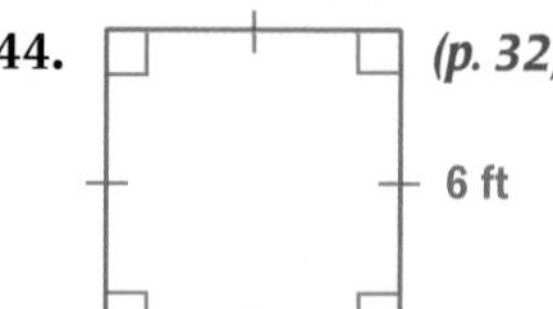

45. 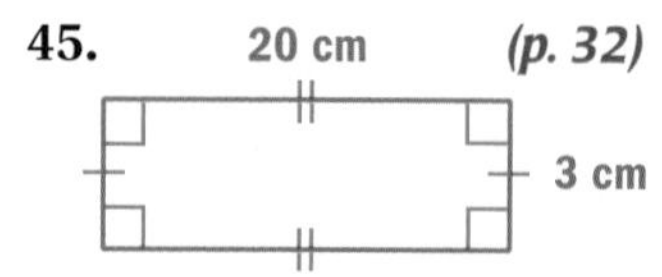

46. 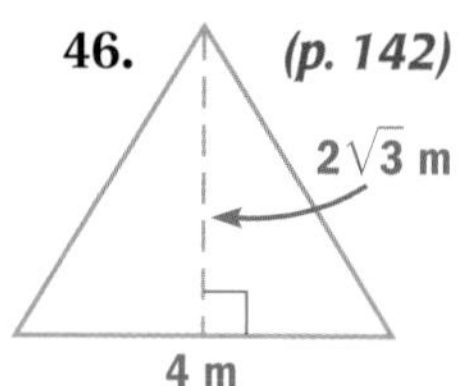

Use the formula $d = rt$ to find the rate. Include the unit. *(p. 32)*

47. $d = 145$ mi, $t = 40$ h

48. $d = 78$ m, $t = 20$ sec

49. $d = 768$ km, $t = 15$ sec

50. ★ **SHORT RESPONSE** You can deposit $1350 into either of two savings accounts that pay a simple annual interest rate of 2.5% or 4%. How much interest will you earn in 15 months in each account? How many additional months will it take to earn more in interest at the lesser rate than at the higher rate for 15 months? *(p. 375)*

QUIZ *for Lessons 9.5–9.6*

Find the value of each variable. Give exact answers. *(p. 493)*

1.

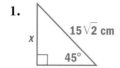

x
15√2 cm
45°
x

2. 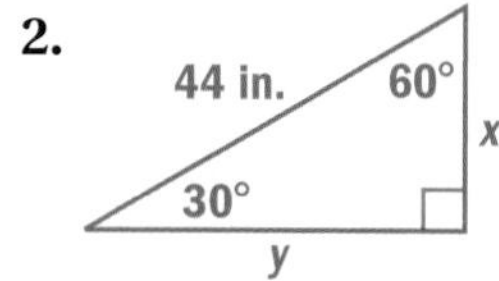

3. 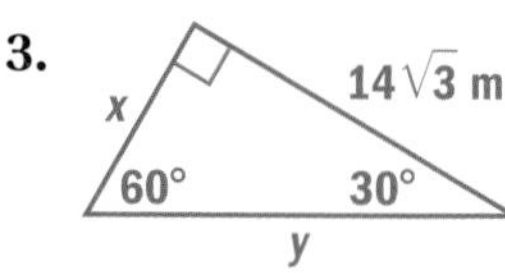

In $\triangle ABC$, write the sine, cosine, and tangent ratios for $\angle A$ and $\angle B$. *(p. 500)*

4. 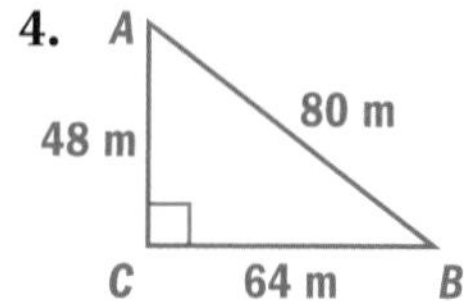

5. 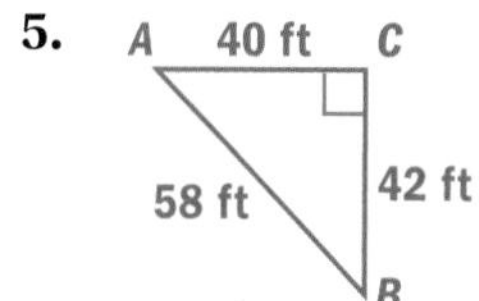

6. 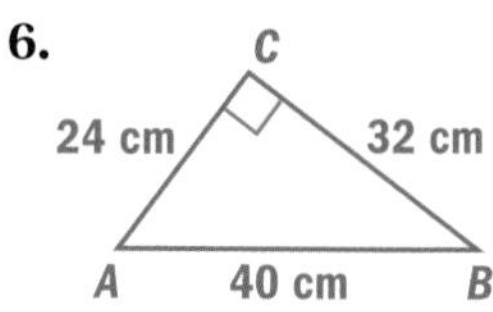

7. AVIATION A plane flies 1° off course for 2000 miles. To the nearest tenth of a mile, how far will the plane be from its course? *(p. 500)*

Brain Game

A Real Winner

Replace each expression with the letter of its decimal approximation to find the name of a person who won the Nobel Prize in both physics and chemistry.

cos 15° sin 52° cos 85° sin 60° cos 45°

tan 30° tan 12° sin 5° cos 30° sin 45°

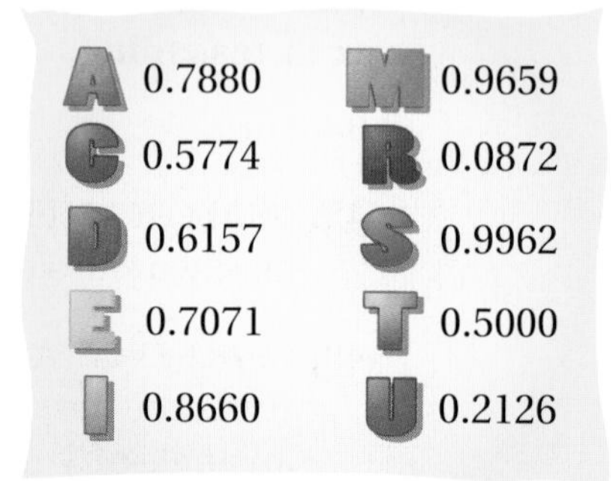

A	0.7880	M	0.9659
C	0.5774	R	0.0872
D	0.6157	S	0.9962
E	0.7071	T	0.5000
I	0.8660	U	0.2126

GOAL
Use a calculator to find an angle measure using the inverse of a trigonometric ratio.

9.6 Finding an Angle Measure

You can use the *inverse* of a trigonometric ratio to find the measure of an angle in a right triangle. For example, you can use the inverse tangent feature of your calculator to solve the following problem. The inverse tangent formula is:

$$\text{If } \tan x^\circ = \frac{a}{b}, \text{ then } x^\circ = \tan^{-1}\left(\frac{a}{b}\right).$$

Read this as "the angle whose tangent is $\frac{a}{b}$."

EXPLORE **In the 1870s, a cable car system was built in San Francisco. A section of California Street has a vertical height of 76 feet and a horizontal length of 420 feet. Find the angle of the hill, $x°$.**

x°
76 ft
420 ft

Solution To find the angle, use inverse tangent.

$\tan x^\circ = \frac{\text{opposite}}{\text{adjacent}}$	**Definition of tangent**
$\tan x^\circ = \frac{76}{420}$	**Substitute.**
$x^\circ = \tan^{-1}\left(\frac{76}{420}\right)$	**Definition of inverse tangent**
$x \approx 10.3$	**Use your calculator to approximate.**

Press the 2nd key and then press the TRIG key. Highlight the inverse tangent feature and then press =. Enter the ratio and press = again.

▸ **Answer** The angle of the hill is about 10°.

PRACTICE **Use a calculator to approximate the expression. Round to the nearest tenth of a degree.**

1. $\tan^{-1}(0.25)$
2. $\tan^{-1}(0.14)$
3. $\tan^{-1}(0.92)$
4. $\tan^{-1}(1.05)$
5. $\tan^{-1}(24.65)$
6. $\tan^{-1}(64.25)$

DRAW CONCLUSIONS

7. **REASONING** Given $\tan^{-1}(0.18)$ and $\tan^{-1}(32.46)$, which one would you expect to represent the larger angle? Why?

8. **OPEN-ENDED** Write a positive ratio and its reciprocal in fraction form. Find the inverse tangent of each ratio. How are the two angles related?

MIXED REVIEW of Problem Solving

Lessons 9.5–9.6

1. **MULTI-STEP PROBLEM** A wallpaper designer draws triangle A as a 45°-45°-90° triangle. Triangle B has the hypotenuse of Triangle A as one leg, and the other leg has length 1.

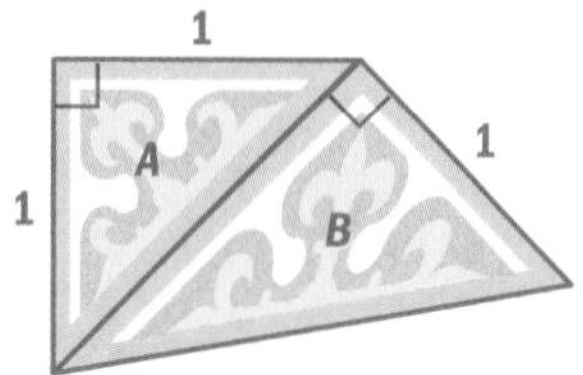

   a. Copy and continue the pattern by drawing three more right triangles. In each, one leg has a length of 1, and the other leg is the hypotenuse of the previous triangle.

   b. *Describe* your observations about the dimensions of the triangles. Find the exact lengths of each hypotenuse.

2. **MULTI-STEP PROBLEM** A roller coaster climbs 300 feet above ground on a 45° inclined track and descends sharply as shown in the diagram.

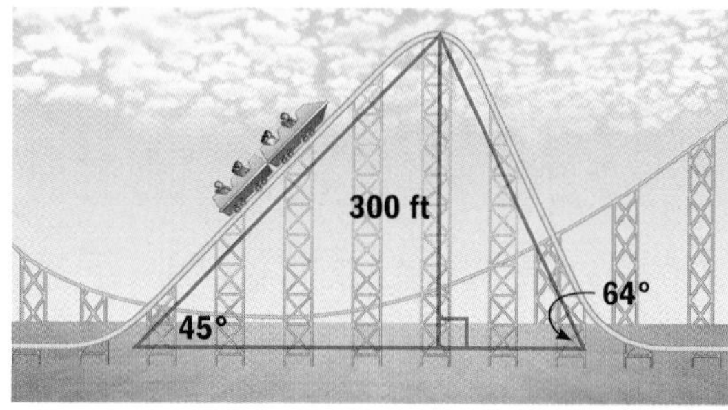

   a. Approximate the length of the track to the nearest foot through the ascent and descent.

   b. Approximate the horizontal length traveled to the nearest foot.

3. **GRIDDED ANSWER** An architect draws a square with the hypotenuse of a 30°-60°-90° triangle as one side. The square has an area of 0.09 square yards. What is the length of the shorter leg of the triangle to the nearest hundredth of a yard?

4. **GRIDDED ANSWER** You are constructing a skateboard ramp like the one shown in the diagram below. Find x, the height of the top edge of the ramp. Round your answer to the nearest tenth of a foot.

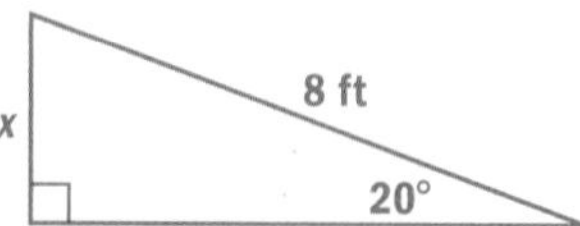

5. **SHORT RESPONSE** The directions for doing abdominal crunches say "*Legs bent; arms back, supporting head and neck; chin up. Lift shoulders and back about 30° off the floor.*" Alice read these directions and wondered how high, in inches, she should lift her shoulders. Alice's shoulder-to-hip length is 28 inches. How high should she lift her shoulders to do this exercise correctly? *Explain.*

6. **OPEN-ENDED** Draw a triangle and label the measures of two sides and one angle so that you can use either the sine or tangent ratio to find the unknown side length. Then use both methods to find the length and compare their results.

7. **EXTENDED RESPONSE** Kirsten and Madison are both on a city sidewalk looking up at their friend Jan in a restaurant at the top of a skyscraper, 500 feet above the ground. The angle of elevation is 45° for Kirsten and 30° for Madison.

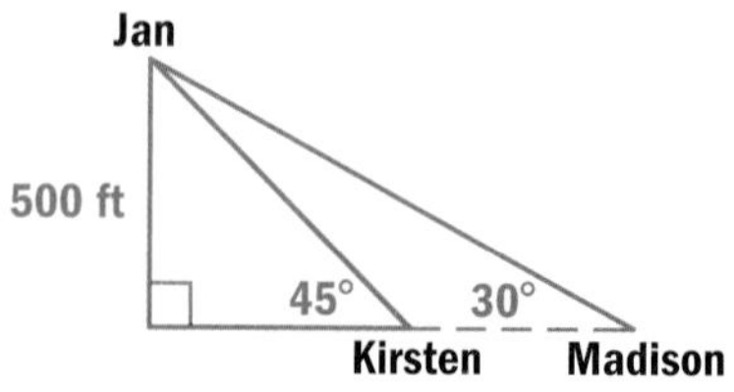

   a. How far is Kirsten from Jan?

   b. How far is Madison from Jan?

   c. How far is Kirsten from Madison?

9 CHAPTER REVIEW

@HomeTutor
classzone.com
Vocabulary Practice

REVIEW KEY VOCABULARY

- square root, *p. 469*
- radical expression, *p. 469*
- perfect square, *p. 470*
- irrational number, *p. 475*
- real number, *p. 475*
- leg, *p. 482*
- hypotenuse, *p. 482*
- Pythagorean Theorem, *p. 482*
- converse, *p. 483*
- Pythagorean triple, *p. 488*
- trigonometric ratio, *p. 500*
- sine, *p. 500*
- cosine, *p. 500*
- tangent, *p. 500*

VOCABULARY EXERCISES

1. Describe the difference between a rational number and an irrational number.
2. Give three examples of rational numbers and three examples of irrational numbers.
3. Describe how the lengths of the legs and the length of the hypotenuse of a right triangle are related.
4. Give three examples of a perfect square and its roots. Write a product equation for each as proof.

Copy and complete the statement.

5. A(n) __?__ is any number that has an integer as its square root.
6. In a right triangle, the side opposite the right angle is the __?__.
7. In a 30°-60°-90° triangle, the __?__ leg is opposite the 30° angle.
8. Sine, cosine, and tangent are __?__ ratios.
9. Reversing the parts of an if-then statement produces a(n) __?__ statement.

REVIEW EXAMPLES AND EXERCISES

9.1 Square Roots

pp. 469–474

EXAMPLE

Solve the equation $x^2 - 18 = 4$.

$x^2 - 18 = 4$	**Original equation**
$x^2 = 22$	**Add 18 to each side.**
$x = \pm\sqrt{22}$	**Definition of square root**
$x \approx \pm 4.69$	**Approximate square root.**

EXERCISES

Use a calculator to approximate the square root. Round to the nearest tenth, if necessary.

SEE EXAMPLES 1, 3, 4, AND 5 on pp. 470–471 for Exs. 10–27

10. $\sqrt{94.09}$ **11.** $-\sqrt{784}$ **12.** $-\sqrt{2125}$ **13.** $\sqrt{941}$

14. $\sqrt{63.42}$ **15.** $-\sqrt{1200}$ **16.** $\sqrt{861}$ **17.** $-\sqrt{306.12}$

Solve the equation using mental math.

18. $a^2 = 169$ **19.** $b^2 - 20 = 101$ **20.** $c^2 + 25 = 89$ **21.** $15 + x^2 = 51$

22. $y^2 - 12 = 13$ **23.** $40 + z^2 = 56$ **24.** $v^2 + 36 = 85$ **25.** $214 - w^2 = 60$

26. Architecture The area of the square base of a building is 2025 square feet. Write and solve a square root equation for the length of one side of the base.

27. Distance Ken is 2 miles east and n miles north of Central Square. The distance d from the square is given by the formula $d = \sqrt{2^2 + n^2}$. To the nearest tenth mile, how far away from Central Square is Ken if $n = 5$?

9.2 Rational and Irrational Numbers

pp. 475–480

EXAMPLE

Graph the numbers $\sqrt{7}$ and 3 on a number line. Then complete the statement $\sqrt{7}$? 3 with <, >, or =.

Use a calculator to approximate the square root. Then graph the numbers on a number line and compare.

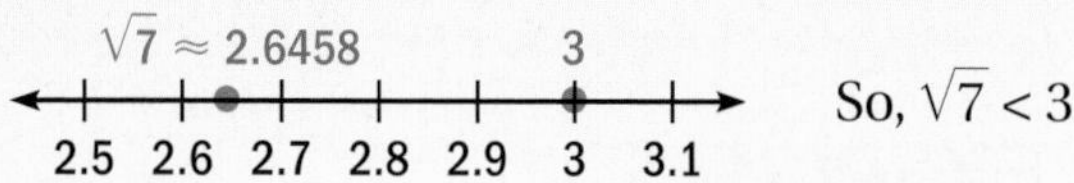

So, $\sqrt{7} < 3$.

EXERCISES

Tell whether the number is *rational* or *irrational*. *Explain* your reasoning.

SEE EXAMPLES 1 AND 2 on pp. 475–476 for Exs. 28–39

28. $\sqrt{100}$ **29.** $0.\overline{6}$ **30.** $\frac{16}{25}$ **31.** $\sqrt{6}$

32. $\frac{1}{3}$ **33.** $\sqrt{\frac{27}{3}}$ **34.** $5.\overline{8}$ **35.** $\sqrt{44}$

Graph the pair of numbers on a number line. Then complete the statement with <, >, or =.

36. $\sqrt{31}$? 4 **37.** 7 ? $\sqrt{59}$ **38.** -9 ? $-\sqrt{81}$ **39.** $\sqrt{48}$? 6.3

9.3 The Pythagorean Theorem

pp. 482–486

EXAMPLE

Find the unknown length.

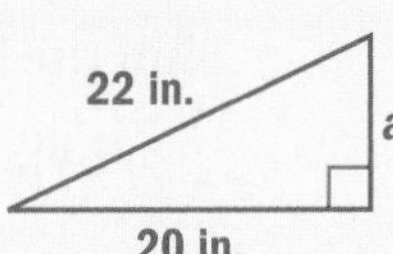

$a^2 + b^2 = c^2$	Pythagorean Theorem
$a^2 + 20^2 = 22^2$	Substitute 20 for b and 22 for c.
$a^2 = 84$	Simplify.
$a \approx 9.2$ in.	Take positive square root of each side.

EXERCISES

The lengths of the legs of a right triangle are a and b, and c is the length of the hypotenuse. Find the unknown length.

SEE EXAMPLE 1 on p. 482 for Exs. 40–45

40. $a = 2.4$, $b = 0.7$, $c =$ __?__ **41.** $b = 24$, $c = 40$, $a =$ __?__ **42.** $a = 8$, $c = 17$, $b =$ __?__

Determine whether the given triangle side lengths form a right triangle.

43. 12, 35, 37 **44.** 15, 48, 50 **45.** 10, 24, 26

9.4 Using the Pythagorean Theorem

pp. 487–491

EXAMPLE

Find the perimeter and area of the triangle.

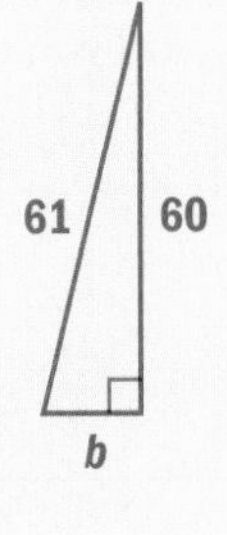

$a^2 + b^2 = c^2$

$60^2 + b^2 = 61^2$

$b^2 = 121$

$b = 11$

Perimeter $= a + b + c$

$= 60 + 11 + 61 = 132$ units

Area $= \frac{1}{2}ab = \frac{1}{2} \times 60 \times 11$

$= 330$ square units

EXERCISES

The lengths of the legs of a right triangle are a and b, and c is the length of the hypotenuse. Find the unknown length, the perimeter, and area.

SEE EXAMPLE 2 on p. 488 for Exs. 46–50

46. $a = 21$ in., $b = 50.4$ in., $c =$ __?__ in. **47.** $a =$ __?__ cm, $b = 63$ cm, $c = 225$ cm

48. $a = 12$ m, $b =$ __?__ m, $c = 25.5$ m **49.** $a = 44$ ft, $b = 33$ ft, $c =$ __?__ ft

50. National Parks A tree in Sequoia National Park in California is about 250 feet tall. You are standing 50 feet away. To the nearest foot, how far away is the top of the tree?

9.5 Special Right Triangles

pp. 493–497

EXAMPLE

Find the length of the hypotenuse. Give the exact answer.

$$\text{hypotenuse} = \text{leg} \cdot \sqrt{2} \qquad \textbf{Rule for 45°-45°-90° triangle}$$

$$= 26\sqrt{2} \qquad \textbf{Substitute.}$$

▸ **Answer** The length of the hypotenuse is $26\sqrt{2}$ feet.

EXERCISES

Find the value of each variable. Give the exact answer.

SEE EXAMPLES 1 AND 2 on pp. 493–494 for Exs. 51–54

51.

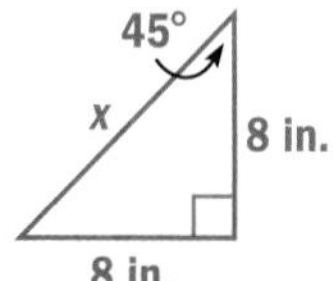

52.

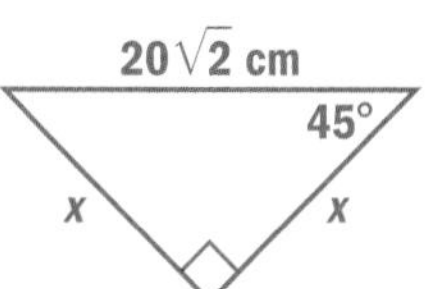

53.

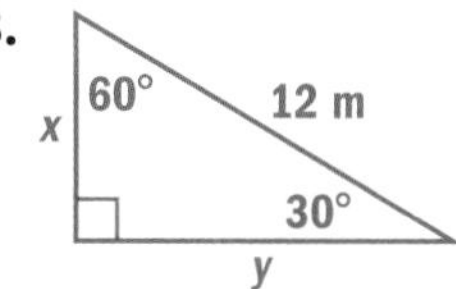

54. Pyramid Four sides of a pyramid are congruent equilateral triangles. The side lengths of the triangles are 6 inches. Find the area of one triangle.

9.6 Using Trigonometric Ratios

pp. 500–505

EXAMPLE

In $\triangle ABC$, write the sine, cosine, and tangent ratios for $\angle A$.

$$\sin A = \frac{\text{opposite}}{\text{hypotenuse}} = \frac{12}{37}$$

$$\cos A = \frac{\text{adjacent}}{\text{hypotenuse}} = \frac{35}{37}$$

$$\tan A = \frac{\text{opposite}}{\text{adjacent}} = \frac{12}{35}$$

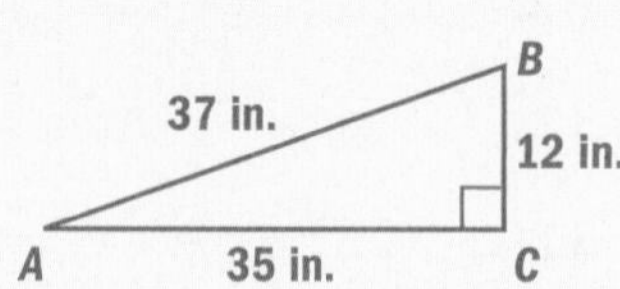

EXERCISES

In $\triangle ABC$, write the sine, cosine, and tangent ratios for $\angle A$ and $\angle B$. Simplify if necessary.

SEE EXAMPLE 1 on p. 500 for Exs. 55–57

55.

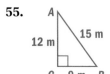

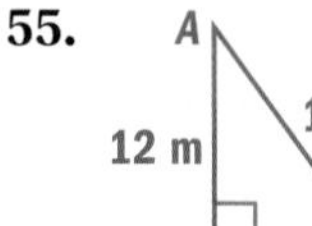

56.

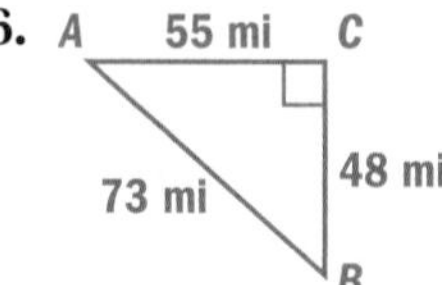

57.

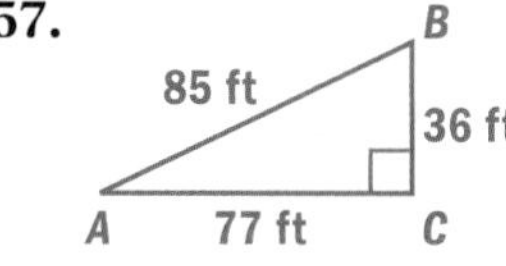

9 CHAPTER TEST

@HomeTutor
classzone.com
Chapter Test Practice

Solve the equation.

1. $x^2 = 49$
2. $m^2 + 41 = 162$
3. $n^2 - 63 = 162$
4. $a^2 + 88 = 232$

Tell whether the number is *rational* or *irrational*. *Explain* your reasoning.

5. $\sqrt{16}$
6. $\frac{23}{24}$
7. $\sqrt{39}$
8. $\sqrt{\frac{1}{4}}$

Graph each pair of numbers on a number line. Then copy and complete the statement with <, >, or =.

9. $\sqrt{9}$? 3
10. -11 ? $-\sqrt{11}$
11. $\sqrt{12}$? 4

Find the length of the unknown side of the right triangle. Round to the nearest tenth, if necessary. Then find the area and perimeter.

12. 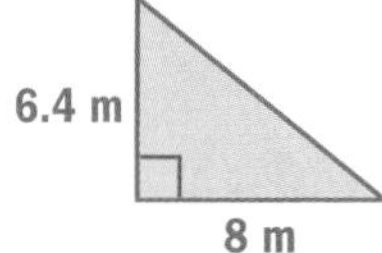

13. 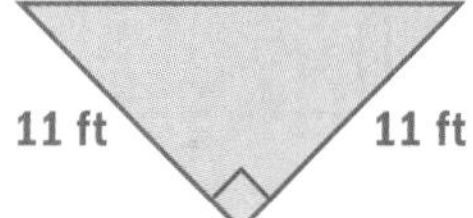

14. 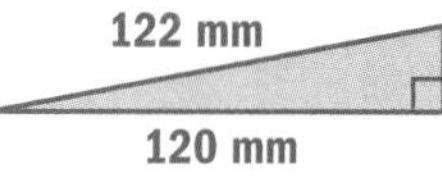

Determine whether the given side lengths can form a right triangle.

15. 15, 24, 25
16. 28, 96, 100
17. 3.6, 5.8, 5.9
18. 22.5, 30, 37.5

Find the value of the unknown variables. Give the exact answer.

19. 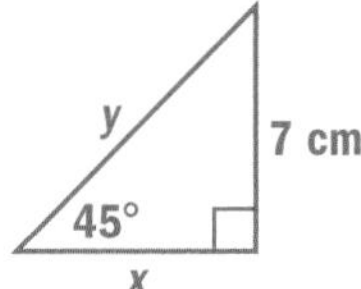

20. 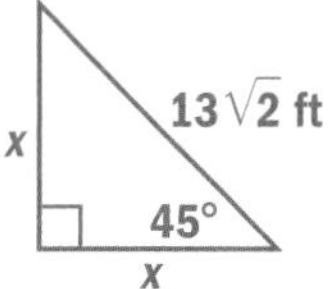

21. 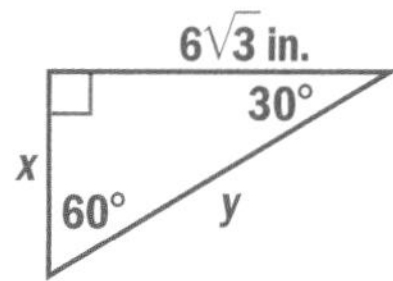

22. **ZOOLOGY** A study of animal motion determined that the maximum walking speed s, in feet per second, that an animal can walk is $s = 5.66\sqrt{l}$, where l is the animal's leg length, in feet. What is the maximum walking speed for an ostrich with a leg length of 4 feet?

23. **INCLINE** In the 1870s, a motorized incline was built in Pittsburgh, PA, to climb the steep hill known as Mt. Washington. The track of the incline is 793 feet long and makes a 30° angle with the ground, as shown at the right. Find the height of the boarding platform at the top of the incline.

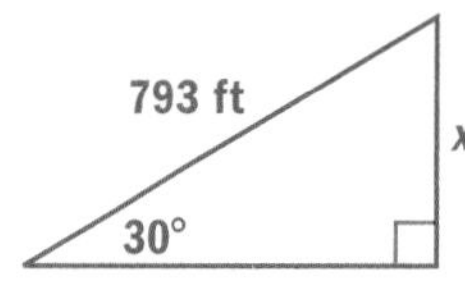

Scoring Rubric

Full Credit
- solution is complete and correct

Partial Credit
- solution is complete but errors are made, *or*
- solution is without error, but incomplete

No Credit
- no solution is given, *or*
- solution makes no sense

SHORT RESPONSE QUESTIONS

PROBLEM

Martha walks along the length and width of a park. Jim walks diagonally as shown. They start walking at the same time. Jim walks at a speed of 200 feet per minute. How fast does Martha need to walk to finish at the same time as Jim?

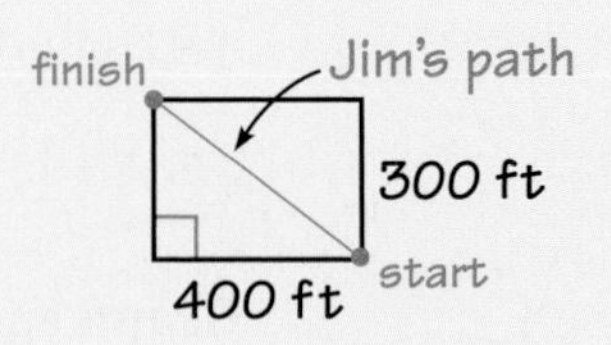

Below are sample solutions to the problem. Read each solution and the comments in blue to see why the sample represents full credit, partial credit, or no credit.

SAMPLE 1: Full Credit Solution

This step is essential to solve the problem. →

Use the Pythagorean Theorem, $a^2 + b^2 = c^2$, to find the length of Jim's path.

$300^2 + 400^2 = c^2$ **Substitute for *a* and *b*.**

$250{,}000 = c^2$ **Simplify.**

$500 = c$ **Evaluate positive square root.**

The calculations for both distances are correct. →

Jim walks 500 feet. Martha walks along the length and width of the rectangle, so the length of her path is $300 + 400 = 700$ feet.

Jim's speed is given. Use $d = rt$ to find the time it takes Jim to reach the finish. Then use the time and $d = rt$ again to find Martha's speed r.

Jim: $500 = 200t$ Martha: $700 = 2.5r$

$t = 2.5$ min $r = 280$ ft/min

The problem is answered correctly. →

Martha needs to walk at 280 feet per minute to finish at the same time.

SAMPLE 2: Partial Credit Solution

This step is essential to solve the problem. →

Use the Pythagorean Theorem to find the length of Jim's path.

$300^2 + 400^2 = c^2$ **Substitute for *a* and *b*.**

$250{,}000 = c^2$ **Simplify.**

$500 = c$ **Evaluate positive square root.**

The calculations for both distances are correct. →

Jim walks 500 feet. Martha walks along the length and width of the rectangle, so the length of her path is $300 + 400 = 700$ feet.

The answer is incorrect. →

Use $d = rt$ to find Martha's speed: $700 = 200t$; $t = 3.5$ feet per minute.

SAMPLE 3: Partial Credit Solution

This step is essential to solve the problem. → Use the Pythagorean Theorem to find the length of Jim's path.

$300^2 + b^2 = 400^2$ **Substitute for *a* and *c*.**

The substitutions are incorrect. → $b \approx 265$ **Evaluate positive square root.**

The work is incomplete and the answer is incorrect. → Jim walked a 265 foot path. Martha's path is 700 feet to get to the same point as Jim. So, she must walk $700 - 265 = 435$ feet per minute.

SAMPLE 4: No Credit Solution

No work is shown, and the answer is incorrect. → Jim's path is $400\sqrt{2}$ feet and Martha's path is 700 feet. When Jim finishes his walk, Martha is $700 - 400\sqrt{2} \approx 134$ feet from Jim.

PRACTICE Apply the Scoring Rubric

Score the solution to the problem below as full credit, partial credit, or no credit. *Explain* your reasoning.

PROBLEM When Brett's arms are extended upwards, he can reach a height of 7 feet above his feet. Can Brett reach the top of the chimney shown when he is standing on the roof near the chimney as shown? *Explain.*

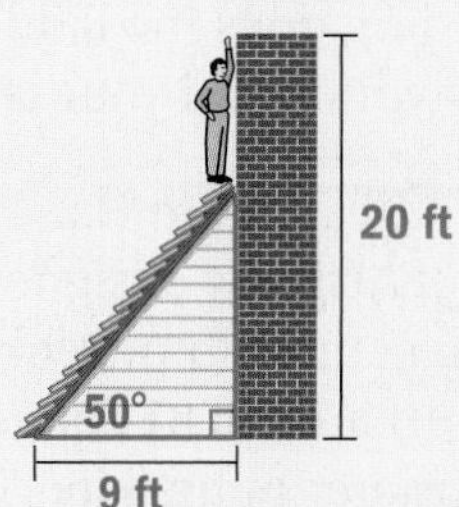

1. Use the tangent ratio to find how far up the roof meets the chimney.

$\tan 50° = \frac{\text{opposite}}{\text{adjacent}}$ **Definition of tangent**

$\tan 50° = \frac{h}{9}$ **Substitute.**

$1.1918 \approx \frac{h}{9}$ **Use a calculator to approximate tan 50°.**

$10.7 \approx h$ **Simplify.**

The roof meets the chimney about 10.7 feet up and Brett can extend his arms 7 feet above his feet, so he can reach about 17.7 feet up the chimney. The chimney is 20 feet high, so Brett cannot reach the top.

2. Because $9 \cos 50° \approx 5.8$, Brett cannot reach the top of the building.

9 ★ Standardized TEST PRACTICE

SHORT RESPONSE

1. Ben has a rectangular garden as shown below. He wants to plant a row of marigolds along the diagonal of the garden. He has enough marigolds to plant a 15 foot long row. Does Ben have enough marigolds to plant along the diagonal of the garden? *Explain.*

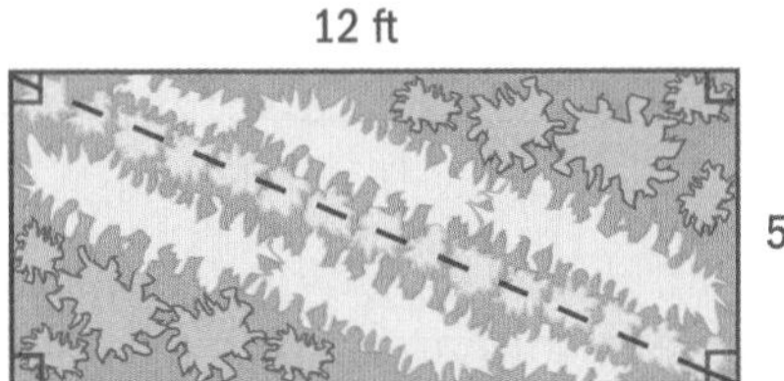

2. Your town purchases a new fire truck with a 100 foot extension ladder. About how close can the fire truck come to a building when the ladder is fully extended at an angle of 60°? The ladder extends from the top of the truck, 8 feet up. About how high up the building does the ladder reach? *Explain* how you found your answers.

3. In 1891, Captain Dansey of the British Royal Artillery designed a square kite for rescuing shipwreck victims. The kite has an area of 81 square feet. What is the perimeter of the kite? *Explain* how you found your answer.

4. A boarding ramp extends down from a dock to a ship, as shown below. The angle of the ramp to the dock changes with the tide. At high tide, the 10 foot ramp meets the dock at an angle of 78°. At low tide, it meets the dock at an angle of 72°. About how much does the water level rise from low tide to high tide? *Explain* how you found your answer.

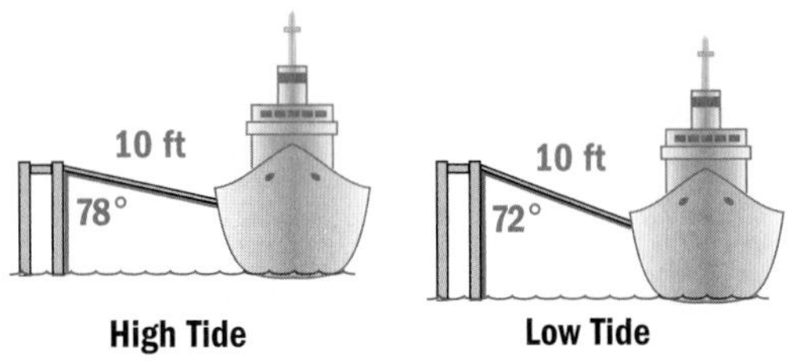

5. Can a circle with an irrational radius have a rational area? *Justify* your reasoning using examples.

6. Julie designs a wheelchair ramp that reaches a door 2 feet above the ground. The ramp makes an angle of 4.76° with the ground. What is the length of the ramp's base to the nearest foot? Draw a diagram and explain your steps.

7. Jeff is flying a kite. He holds the end of the kite string 3 feet above the ground, and the length of the string is 35 feet. He is standing 28 feet from the base of a tree when the wind changes and the kite gets stuck in the tree. If he can reach up 22 feet using a pole, can he reach the kite? *Explain.*

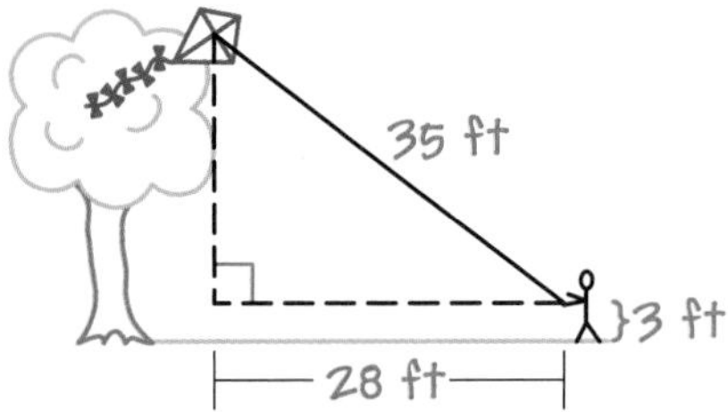

8. You stand some distance from a 26 foot tall flagpole. The angle from the point where you stand to the top of the flagpole is 60°. You move in a straight line away from the flagpole so that angle from the point where you now stand to the top of the flagpole is 45°. How far do you move? Round your answer to the nearest whole number. *Explain* how you found your answer.

9. For safety reasons, ideally ladders should be used so that the horizontal distance from the base of the ladder to a building is one quarter of the length of the ladder. An 11 foot ladder leans against a building. The top of the ladder rests 10 feet up the wall. Is the bottom of the ladder *too close* or *too far* from the wall? by how much? *Explain* your reasoning.

MULTIPLE CHOICE

10. What are the values of a in the equation $a^2 - 81 = 115$?

Ⓐ ± 5.8 Ⓑ ± 9

Ⓒ ± 10.7 Ⓓ ± 14

11. Which set of numbers is *not* a Pythagorean triple?

Ⓐ 5, 12, 13 Ⓑ 9, 40, 41

Ⓒ 8, 15, 17 Ⓓ 6, 24, 25

12. In $\triangle ABC$, what is $\tan A$?

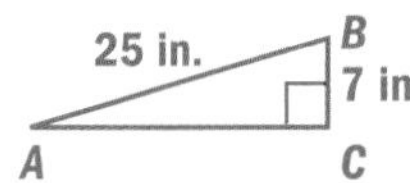

Ⓐ $\frac{7}{24}$ Ⓑ $\frac{7}{25}$

Ⓒ $\frac{24}{25}$ Ⓓ $\frac{24}{7}$

GRIDDED ANSWER

13. A right triangle has leg lengths of 27 inches and 36 inches. In a similar right triangle, the longer leg has a length of 108 inches. How many inches long is the hypotenuse of the larger triangle?

14. The size of a television screen is given by the length of the diagonal of the screen. What size (in inches) is a television screen that is 28 inches wide and 21 inches high?

15. A square dinner napkin is folded corner to corner to create a right triangle. The longest edge of the folded napkin is $11\sqrt{2}$ inches long. What is the area of the napkin, in square inches, in its original form?

EXTENDED RESPONSE

16. A jet takes off at an angle of 15° with the ground. The jet's speed is 300 feet per second.

a. If the jet continues at the same speed and the same angle of elevation, how far does the jet travel in 10 seconds?

b. Find the height of the jet 10 seconds after take off. *Explain* how you found your answer.

c. *Describe* two ways to find the horizontal distance the jet travels in the 10 seconds.

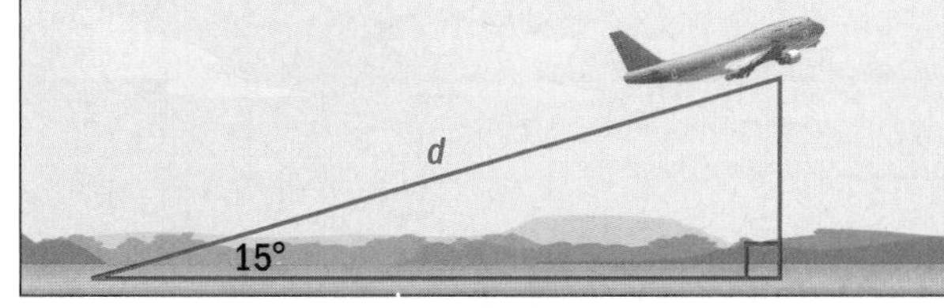

17. The diagram shows the path of a ski lift and the path of the mountain a skier skis down from the lift. The lift ride is 4810 feet.

a. How high h is the mountain? Round to the nearest foot.

b. The skier traveled 2000 feet down the mountain. Use part (a) to find the horizontal distance traveled while skiing. Round to the nearest foot.

c. Did the skier travel more than a mile horizontally from beginning to end? *Explain* how you found your answer.

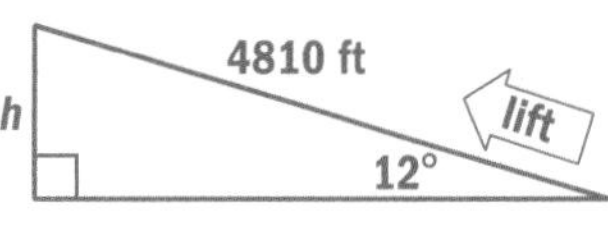

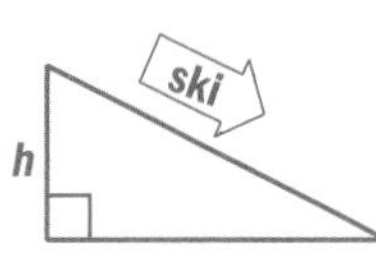

10 Measurement, Area, and Volume

Before

In previous chapters you've . . .

- Found the areas of rectangles
- Identified and sketched polygons

Now

In Chapter 10 you'll study . . .

- 10.1 Areas of quadrilaterals
- 10.2 Areas of circles
- 10.3 Solid figures
- 10.4 Surface areas
- 10.5 More surface areas
- 10.6 Volumes
- 10.7 More volumes

Why?

So you can solve real-world problems about . . .

- architecture, p. 522
- hockey, p. 528
- recycling, p. 556
- swimming pools, p. 559

Math *at classzone.com*

- Areas of Parallelograms and Trapezoids, p. 522
- Classifying Solids, p. 535
- Volume of a Prism, p. 554

Get-Ready Games

Review Prerequisite Skills by playing *Measure Match.*

Skill Focus: Finding the perimeter, area, or circumference of squares, rectangles, triangles, and circles

MEASURE MATCH

MATERIALS

- 15 Picture Cards

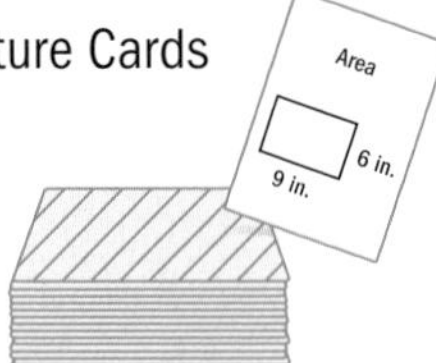

- 15 Measure Cards

HOW TO PLAY Place all cards face down and mix them up. On your turn follow the steps on the next page.

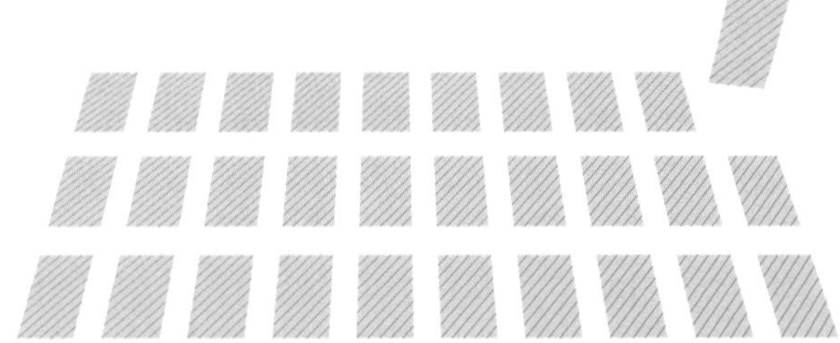

1 TURN over two cards.

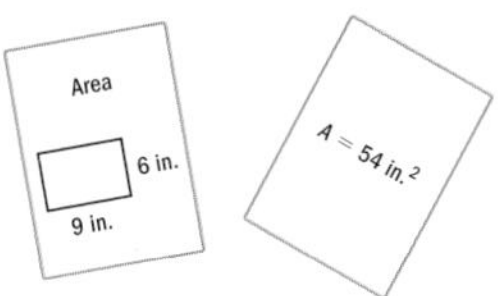

2 DECIDE whether the two cards match. Cards match when you turn over a Picture Card and a Measure Card that describes the picture. If the cards match, you may keep them. Otherwise, turn them back over.

3 REMEMBER where the cards are so you can find matching pairs on future turns.

HOW TO WIN

Be the player with the most cards once all the cards have been matched.

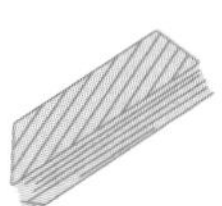

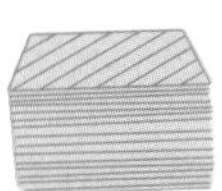

Stop and Think

1. **WRITING** **If the Measure Cards did not have *A*, *P*, or *C* on them, would you still be able to tell what was being measured? *Explain.***
2. **EXTENSION** **Design six new cards for *Measure Match.* Three should be Picture Cards and three should be Measure Cards. Make sure each Picture Card matches a Measure Card.**

10 Getting Ready

Review Prerequisite Skills

REVIEW WORDS

- **area,** *p. 32*
- **base,** *p. 142*
- **height,** *p. 142*
- **circle,** *p. 312*
- **radius,** *p. 312*
- **pi** (π), *p. 312*
- **trapezoid,** *p. 416*
- **parallelogram,** *p. 416*
- **rhombus,** *p. 416*

VOCABULARY CHECK

Classify the figure using a review word from the list at the left.

1. quadrilateral *ABCD*

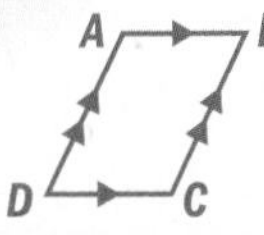

2. $\overline{PQ}$

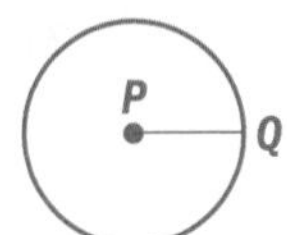

3. quadrilateral *JKLM*

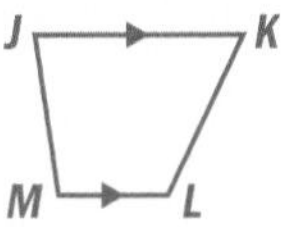

SKILL CHECK

Find the area of the shaded region. ***(p. 142)***

4.

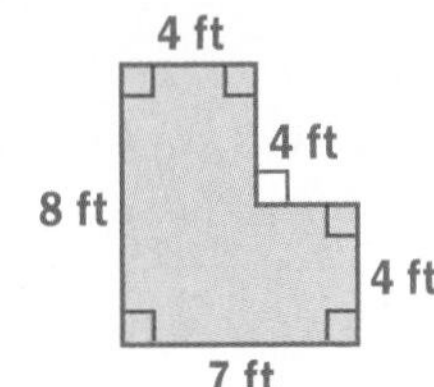

5.

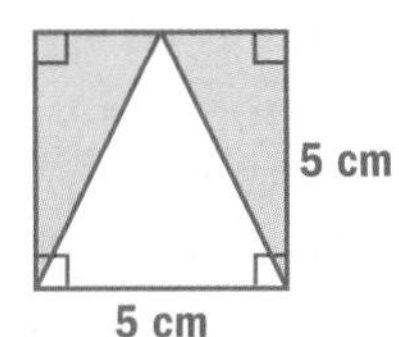

6.

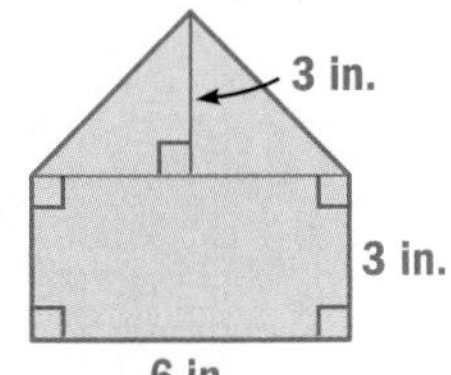

@HomeTutor Prerequisite skills practice at classzone.com

Notetaking Skills Using a Concept Grid

In each chapter you will learn a new notetaking skill. In Chapter 10 you will apply the strategy of using a concept grid to circles in Example 1 on p. 527.

You can use a *concept grid* to organize what you know about a topic.

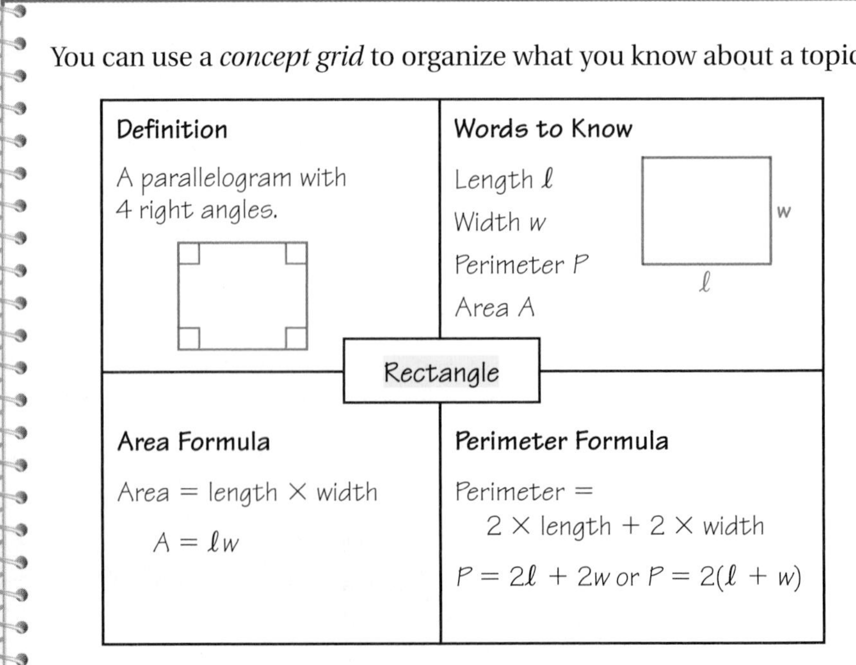

Definition
A parallelogram with 4 right angles.
Words to Know
Length ℓ
Width w
Perimeter P
Area A
w
ℓ
Rectangle
Area Formula
Area = length × width
A = ℓw
Perimeter Formula
Perimeter = 2 × length + 2 × width
P = 2ℓ + 2w or P = 2(ℓ + w)

10.1 Areas of Parallelograms and Trapezoids

Before	You found the areas of triangles and rectangles.
Now	You'll find the areas of parallelograms and trapezoids.
Why?	So you can find areas of surfaces, such as golf greens in Ex. 38.

KEY VOCABULARY

- **base of a parallelogram,** *p. 521*
- **height of a parallelogram,** *p. 521*
- **bases of a trapezoid,** *p. 522*
- **height of a trapezoid,** *p. 522*

The **base of a parallelogram** is the length of any one of its sides. The perpendicular distance between the base and the opposite side is the **height of a parallelogram**. The diagram below shows how to change a parallelogram into a rectangle with the same base, height, and area.

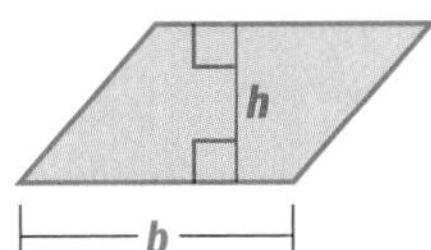

Start with any parallelogram.

Cut the parallelogram to form a right triangle and a trapezoid.

Move the triangle to form a rectangle.

The area of the rectangle is the product of the base and the height, so the formula for the area of the parallelogram is $A = bh$.

KEY CONCEPT *For Your Notebook*

Area of a Parallelogram

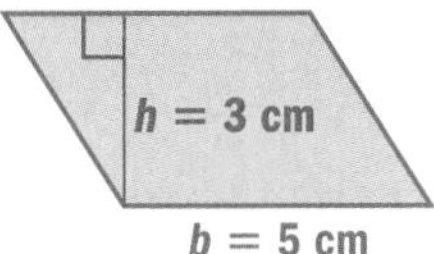

Words The area of a parallelogram is the product of the base and the height.

Algebra $A = bh$

Numbers $A = 5 \cdot 3 = 15 \text{ cm}^2$

EXAMPLE 1 Finding the Area of a Parallelogram

Find the area of the parallelogram.

10 in.

8 in.

SOLUTION

$A = bh$ **Write formula for area.**

$= 8 \cdot 10$ **Substitute 8 for *b* and 10 for *h*.**

$= 80$ **Multiply.**

▶ **Answer** The parallelogram has an area of 80 square inches.

READING

The bases of a trapezoid are labeled b_1 and b_2. You read these labels as "*b* sub one" and "*b* sub two." Need more help with trapezoids? See p. 416

Trapezoids The **bases of a trapezoid** are its two parallel sides. The perpendicular distance between the bases is the **height of a trapezoid**. The diagram below shows how two congruent trapezoids with height h and bases b_1 and b_2 can form a parallelogram with height h and base $b_1 + b_2$.

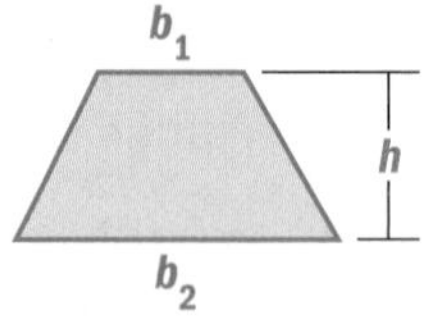

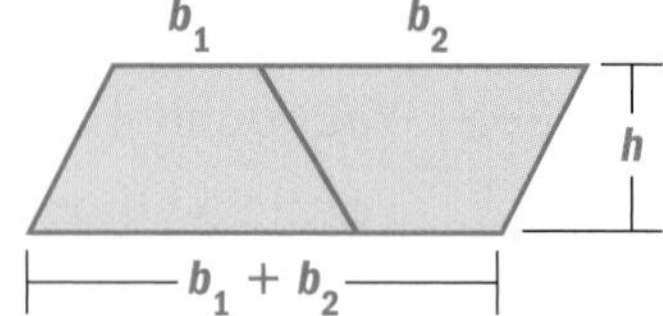

The area of the parallelogram is $(b_1 + b_2)h$, so the area of each trapezoid is $\frac{1}{2}(b_1 + b_2)h$.

KEY CONCEPT — *For Your Notebook*

Area of a Trapezoid

$b_1 = 4$ m

$h = 3$ m

$b_2 = 8$ m

Words The area of a trapezoid is one half the product of the sum of the bases and the height.

Algebra $A = \frac{1}{2}(b_1 + b_2)h$ **Numbers** $A = \frac{1}{2}(4 + 8)3 = 18 \text{ m}^2$

EXAMPLE 2 Finding the Area of a Trapezoid

Architecture The Winslow House in River Forest, Illinois, was designed by Frank Lloyd Wright. The front part of the roof is a trapezoid, as shown. What is its area?

SOLUTION

$A = \frac{1}{2}(b_1 + b_2)h$ **Write formula for area of a trapezoid.**

$= \frac{1}{2}(31 + 77)25$ **Substitute values for b_1, b_2, and h.**

$= 1350$ **Multiply.**

▶ **Answer** The front of the roof has an area of 1350 square feet.

at classzone.com

GUIDED PRACTICE for Examples 1 and 2

Sketch the quadrilateral and find its area.

1. A parallelogram with a base of 20 meters and a height of 9 meters
2. A trapezoid with bases of 14 feet and 17 feet and a height of 6 feet

 **EXAMPLE 3** Standardized Test Practice

Geometry The dimensions of trapezoid *ABCD* are shown below. A similar trapezoid can be produced by doubling the dimension of the trapezoid. How does the area change when the dimensions are doubled?

Ⓐ The area is cut in half.

Ⓑ The area is doubled.

Ⓒ The area is tripled.

Ⓓ The area is quadrupled.

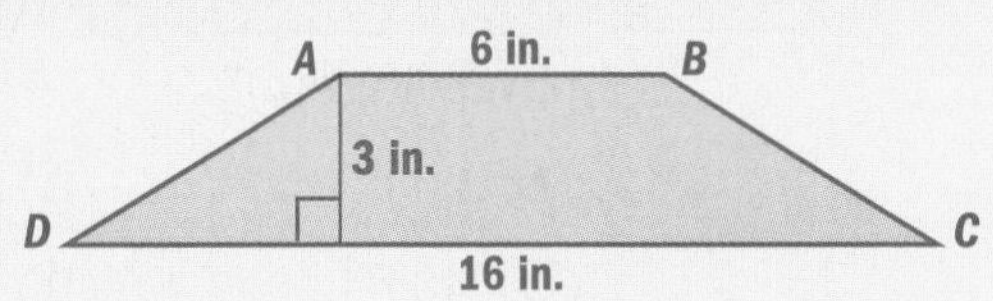

ELIMINATE CHOICES
Because doubling the side lengths of trapezoid *ABCD* increases its size, its area will also increase. You can eliminate choice A.

SOLUTION

STEP 1 **Find** the area of trapezoid *ABCD* and the enlarged trapezoid.

$A = \frac{1}{2}(b_1 + b_2)h$ $\qquad$ $A = \frac{1}{2}(b_1 + b_2)(h)$

$= \frac{1}{2}(6 + 16)3$ $\qquad$ $= \frac{1}{2}(2 \cdot 6 + 2 \cdot 16)(2 \cdot 3)$

$= 33 \text{ in.}^2$ $\qquad$ $= 132 \text{ in.}^2$

STEP 2 **Compare** the areas: $\frac{132 \text{ in.}^2}{33 \text{ in.}^2} = 4.$

▸ **Answer** When the side lengths of trapezoid *ABCD* are doubled, the area becomes 4 times the original area. The correct answer is D. Ⓐ Ⓑ Ⓒ Ⓓ

 **GUIDED PRACTICE** for Example 3

3. **What If?** Suppose the side lengths of trapezoid *ABCD* in Example 3 are tripled. How does the area change?

10.1 EXERCISES

HOMEWORK KEY
★ = **STANDARDIZED TEST PRACTICE** Exs. 8, 37, 40, 42, 43, and 52
○ = **HINTS AND HOMEWORK HELP** for Exs. 5, 9, 15, 19, 39 at classzone.com

SKILL PRACTICE

VOCABULARY **Write the area formula for the polygon.**

1. parallelogram
2. triangle
3. trapezoid

FINDING AREA **Find the area of the parallelogram.**

SEE EXAMPLE 1 on p. 521 for Exs. 4–6

4. 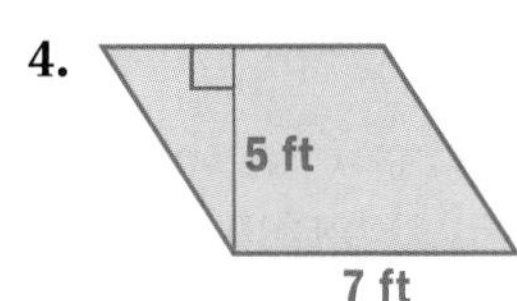

5. 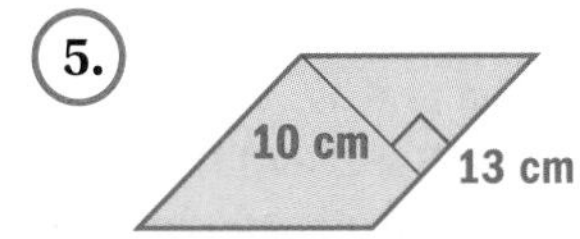

6. 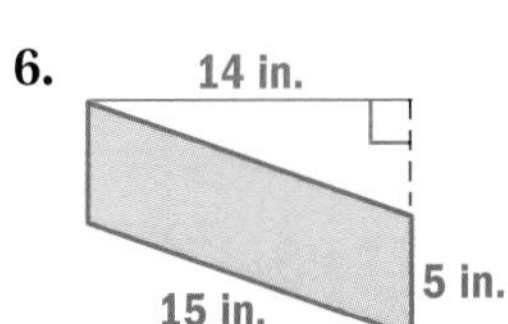

SEE EXAMPLE 1 on p. 521 for Exs. 7–14

7. **ERROR ANALYSIS** Describe and correct the error made in finding the area of a parallelogram.

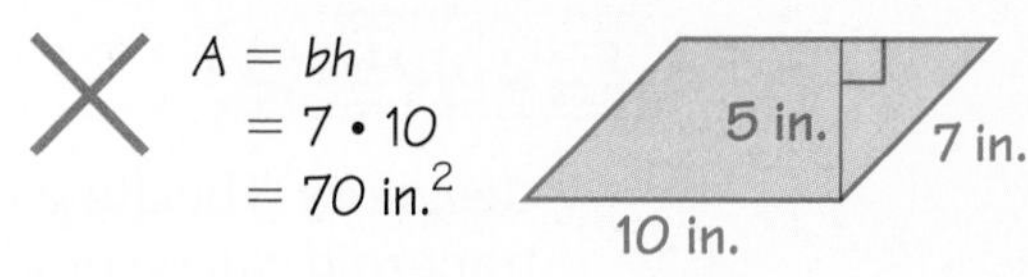

8. ★ **MULTIPLE CHOICE** What is the area of the parallelogram?

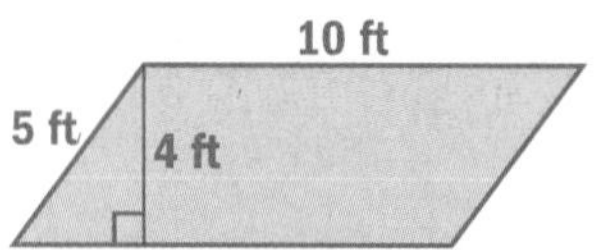

Ⓐ 20 ft^2 Ⓑ 25 ft^2 Ⓒ 40 ft^2 Ⓓ 50 ft^2

SKETCHING PARALLELOGRAMS **Sketch a parallelogram with base b units and height h units. Then find its area.**

9. $b = 12, h = 8$
10. $b = 9, h = 14$
11. $b = 10, h = 22$
12. $b = 2, h = 1.5$
13. $b = 3.2, h = 5$
14. $b = 12, h = 18$

FINDING AREA **Find the area of the trapezoid.**

SEE EXAMPLE 2 on p. 522 for Exs. 15–21

15.

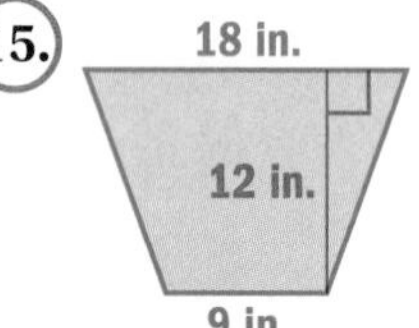

16. 13 yd, 5 yd, 10 yd, 12 yd

17.

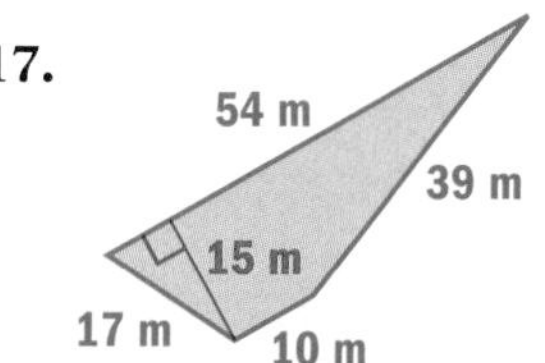

SKETCHING TRAPEZOIDS **Sketch a trapezoid with bases b_1 units and b_2 units and height h units. Then find its area.**

18. $b_1 = 13, b_2 = 7, h = 6$
19. $b_1 = 8, b_2 = 16, h = 11$
20. $b_1 = 5.5, b_2 = 2.5, h = 3$
21. $b_1 = 16.2, b_2 = 10, h = 4$

COMPARING AREAS **Quadrilateral *EFGH* is similar to quadrilateral *ABCD*. Find and compare the areas of the quadrilaterals.**

SEE EXAMPLE 3 on p. 523 for Exs. 22–23

22.

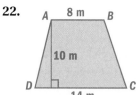

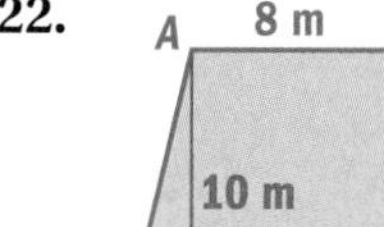

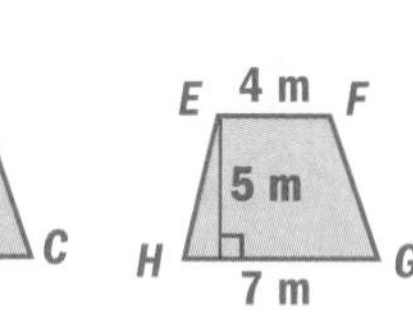

23.

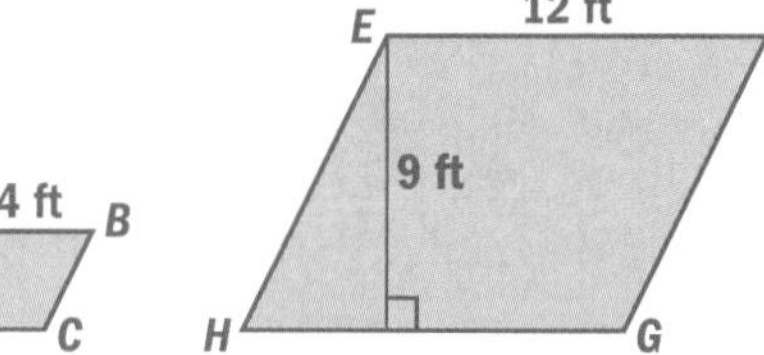

FINDING AREA **Find the area of the polygon.**

24.

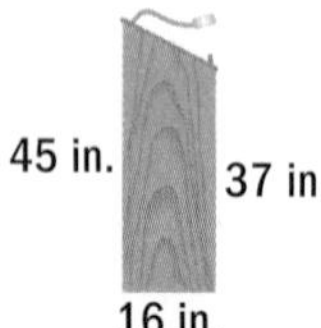

25.

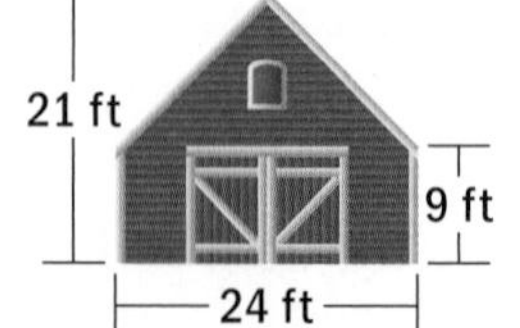

26.

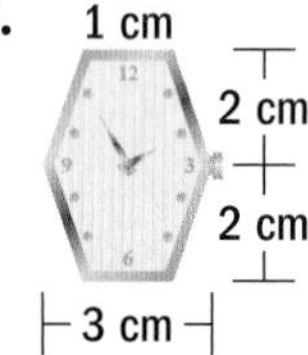

GRAPHING **Plot the points in a coordinate plane and connect them to form a parallelogram. Then find the area of the parallelogram.**

27. $(-3, -1), (0, 4), (6, 4), (3, -1)$
28. $(8, 0), (11, -5), (-2, -5), (-5, 0)$

ALGEBRA Write and solve an equation to find the unknown dimension of the quadrilateral.

29. parallelogram: $A = 84\text{ cm}^2$, $b = \underline{\ ?\ }$, $h = 12\text{ cm}$

30. parallelogram: $A = 105\text{ m}^2$, $b = 15\text{ m}$, $h = \underline{\ ?\ }$

31. trapezoid: $A = 100\text{ in.}^2$, $b_1 = 10\text{ in.}$, $b_2 = 15\text{ in.}$, $h = \underline{\ ?\ }$

32. trapezoid: $A = 78\text{ ft}^2$, $b_1 = 12\text{ ft}$, $b_2 = \underline{\ ?\ }$, $h = 6\text{ ft}$

FINDING AREA Find the area of the parallelogram or trapezoid.

33. 18 in. 15 in. 27 in.

34.

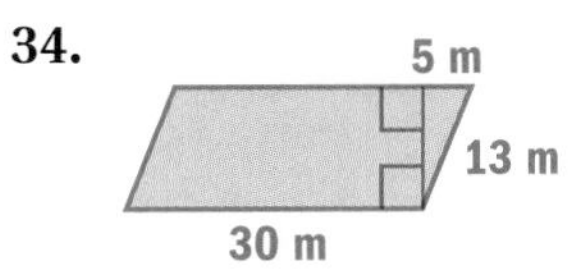

35.

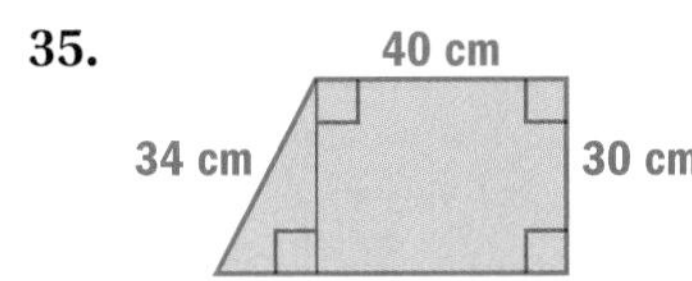

36. **CHALLENGE** The area of the trapezoid is 225 square inches. Find the values of x and y. Round to the nearest tenth if necessary.

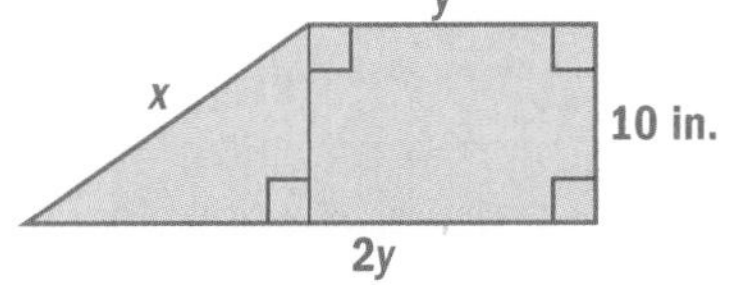

PROBLEM SOLVING

SEE EXAMPLES 1 AND 2 on pp. 521–522 for Exs. 37–39

37. ★ **MULTIPLE CHOICE** The front of an audio speaker is the shape of a trapezoid. Its top edge is 14 inches wide, its bottom edge is 16 inches wide, and its height is 23 inches. What is the area of the front of the speaker?

(A) 173 in.^2 (B) 345 in.^2 (C) 368 in.^2 (D) 5152 in.^2

38. **GUIDED PROBLEM SOLVING** You are designing a putting green for a miniature golf course, as shown. What is the area of the green?

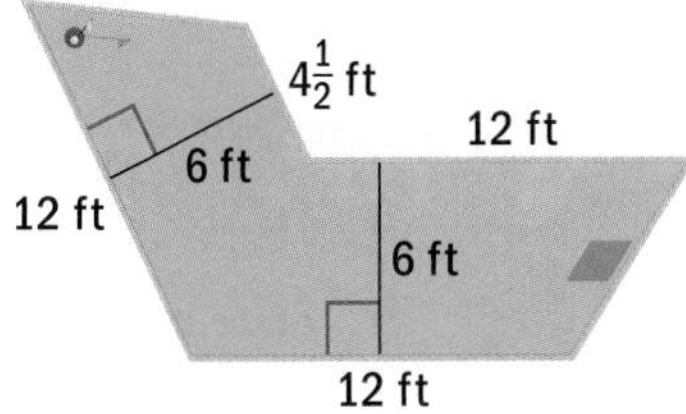

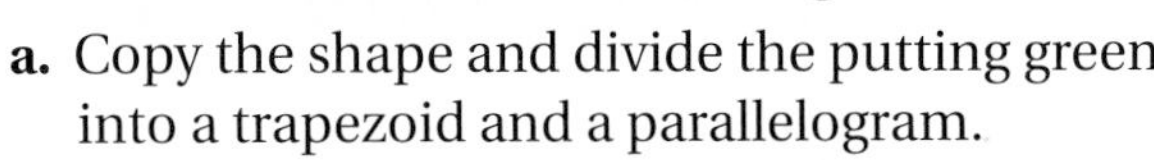

a. Copy the shape and divide the putting green into a trapezoid and a parallelogram.

b. Find the area of each quadrilateral.

c. Add the two areas to find the total area.

39. **FURNITURE** Alice is making an end table with a top surface in the shape of a trapezoid. If the parallel sides have lengths 18 inches and 24 inches, and the perpendicular distance between them is 15 inches, how many square inches of tile does Alice need for the table top?

40. ★ **OPEN-ENDED MATH** Sketch a trapezoid and a parallelogram, each with an area of 54 square feet. Label the dimensions needed to find each area.

41. **MEASUREMENT** Use a metric ruler to measure the dimensions of the parallelogram in millimeters. Then find the area.

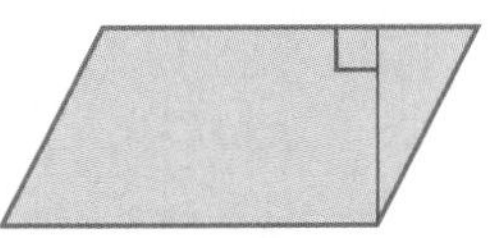

42. ★ **WRITING** What do you think an isosceles trapezoid is? *Explain* your reasoning. Include a drawing with your answer.

SEE EXAMPLE 3 on p. 523 for Ex. 43

43. ★ **EXTENDED RESPONSE** Use the parallelogram shown.

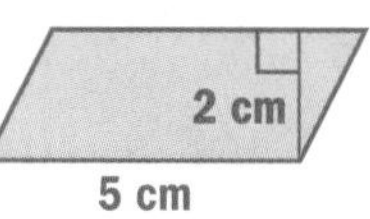

a. **Calculate** Find the area of the parallelogram.

b. **Compare** What happens to the area when the dimensions of the parallelogram are doubled? tripled?

c. **Predict** Suppose you multiply each dimension of a parallelogram by a positive number k. Write a formula for the area of the new parallelogram. Test your formula for several values of k. How does this formula compare with the original formula? How will the areas compare?

d. **Compare** Suppose you multiply each dimension of a trapezoid by a positive number k. Write a formula for the area of the new trapezoid. Test your formula for several values of k. How does this formula compare with the original formula? How will the areas compare?

ESTIMATION Use the given scale and the formula for the area of a trapezoid or a parallelogram to estimate the area of the state.

44. Nevada

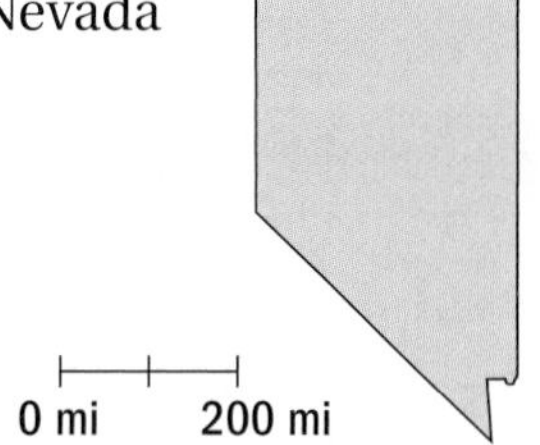

45. Tennessee

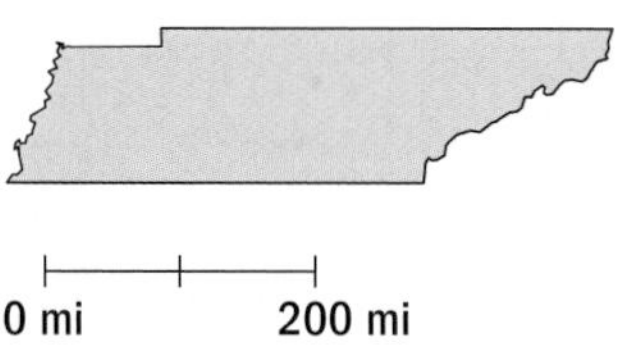

46. **CHALLENGE** The floor of a gazebo is in the shape of a regular hexagon with sides that are each 6 feet long. Find the area of the floor to the nearest tenth of a square foot.

MIXED REVIEW

Get-Ready Prepare for Lesson 10.2 in Exs. 47–49

Find the circumference of the circle. Use 3.14 for π. ***(p. 312)***

47.

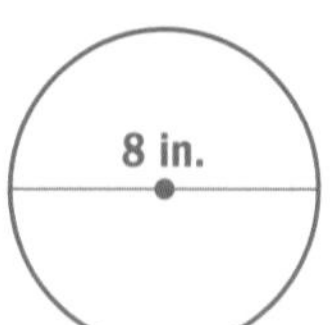

48.

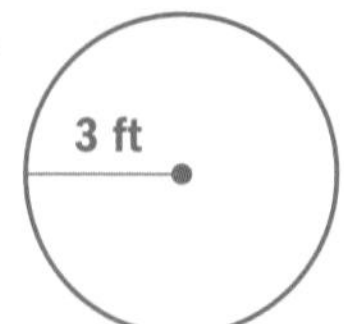

49.

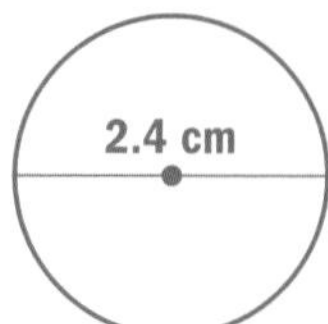

50. In $\triangle PQR$, find the length of $\overline{QR}$. ***(p. 482)***

51. In $\triangle PQR$, write the sine, cosine, and tangent ratios for $\angle P$ and $\angle R$. ***(p. 500)***

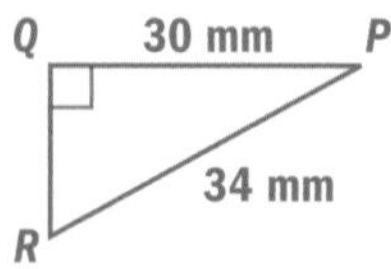

52. ★ **MULTIPLE CHOICE** Which of the following numbers is irrational? ***(p. 475)***

Ⓐ $\frac{3}{11}$ Ⓑ 2.78 Ⓒ $5.\overline{06}$ Ⓓ $\sqrt{26}$

10.2 Areas of Circles

Before You found the areas of parallelograms and trapezoids.

Now You'll find the areas of circles.

Why? So you can find areas of regions, as in a hockey rink in Example 3.

KEY VOCABULARY

- **area,** *p. 32*
- **circle, radius, diameter, circumference,** *p. 312*
- **pi (π),** *p. 312*

ACTIVITY

You can use a model to find a formula for the area of a circle.

STEP 1 **Draw** a circle and cut it into 8 congruent sections. Arrange the sections of the circle to resemble a parallelogram, as shown. How are the base and height of the "parallelogram" related to the circumference and the radius of the circle?

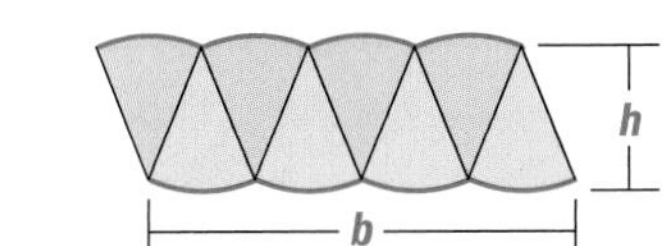

STEP 2 **Write** a formula for the area of the circle in terms of r. Use your results from Step 1 and the formulas for the area of a parallelogram and the circumference of a circle.

KEY CONCEPT — *For Your Notebook*

Area of a Circle

Words The area of a circle is the product of π and the square of the radius.

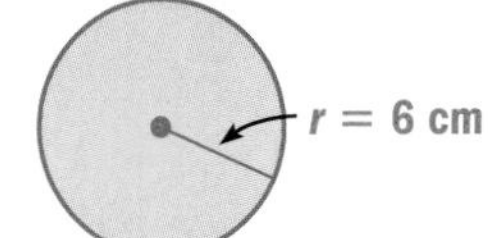

Algebra $A = \pi r^2$ **Numbers** $A = \pi(6)^2 = 36\pi \text{ cm}^2$

EXAMPLE 1 Finding the Area of a Circle

TAKE NOTES

To help organize information about circles in your notebook, make a concept grid. Be sure to include approximations for π, as shown on p. 312.

Find the area of a circle with a diameter of 10 inches.

$A = \pi r^2$ **Write formula for area.**

$\approx 3.14(5)^2$ **Substitute 3.14 for π and 5 for r.**

$= 78.5$ **Evaluate using a calculator.**

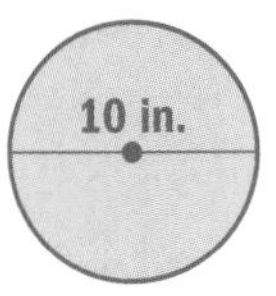

▸ **Answer** The area is about 78.5 square inches.

Animated Math at classzone.com

EXAMPLE 2 Finding the Radius of a Circle

Find the radius of a circle that has an area of 530.66 square feet.

SOLUTION

$A = \pi r^2$	Write formula for area of a circle.
$530.66 \approx (3.14)r^2$	Substitute 530.66 for *A* and 3.14 for π.
$169 \approx r^2$	Divide each side by 3.14.
$\sqrt{169} \approx r$	Take positive square root of each side.
$13 \approx r$	Evaluate square root.

▶ **Answer** The radius of the circle is about 13 feet.

AVOID ERRORS

Make sure you use the correct units when writing your answer. Linear units should be used to describe the radius of a circle.

GUIDED PRACTICE for Examples 1 and 2

Find the unknown area or radius of the circle. Use 3.14 for π.

1. $r = 7$ ft, $A =$ __?__
2. $d = 3$ km, $A =$ __?__
3. $A = 628\text{ cm}^2$, $r =$ __?__

EXAMPLE 3 Solve a Multi-Step Problem

Hockey Find the combined area of the two face-off circles of the ice hockey rink shown.

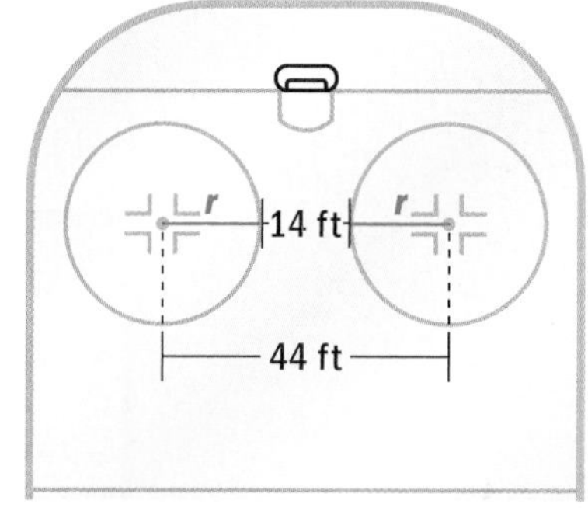

SOLUTION

STEP 1 **Find** the radius. The distance between the centers is 44 feet and the gap between the circles is 14 feet. So,

$r + 14 + r = 44$ and $r = 15$.

STEP 2 **Calculate** the area. Use the formula for the area of a circle.

$A = 2\pi r^2$	Area of two circles
$\approx 2(3.14)(15)^2$	Substitute 3.14 for π and 15 for *r*.
$= 1413$	Evaluate using a calculator.

▶ **Answer** The area of the circles is about 1413 square feet.

at classzone.com

CHECK REASONABLENESS

Estimate to check your answer.

$2\pi(15)^2 \approx 2(3)(225)$
≈ 1350

GUIDED PRACTICE for Example 3

Find the area of the shaded region. Use 3.14 for π.

4. 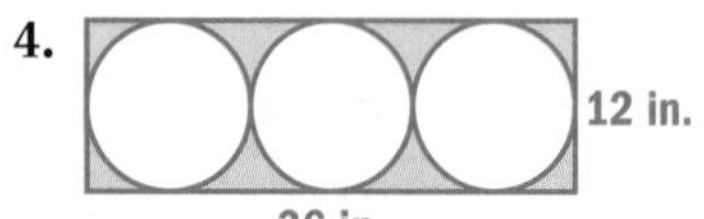

5. 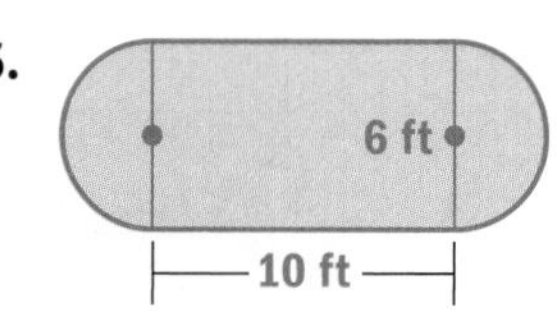

10.2 EXERCISES

HOMEWORK KEY

★ = **STANDARDIZED TEST PRACTICE**
Exs. 28, 38, 40, 44, and 52

○ = **HINTS AND HOMEWORK HELP**
for Exs. 3, 11, 13, 17, 37 at classzone.com

SKILL PRACTICE

VOCABULARY **Copy and complete the statement.**

1. The area of a circle is the product of π and the square of the __?__.

2. The circumference of a circle is the product of π and the __?__.

USING DRAWINGS **Find the area of the circle. Use 3.14 for π.**

SEE EXAMPLE 1 on p. 527 for Exs. 3–15

3.

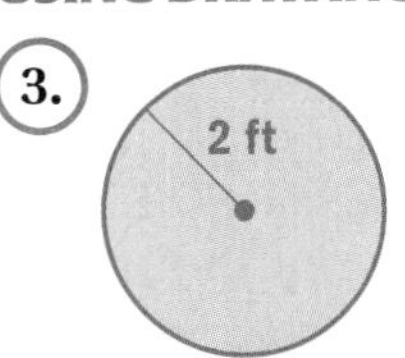

4.

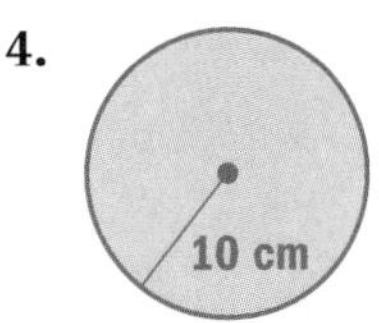

5.

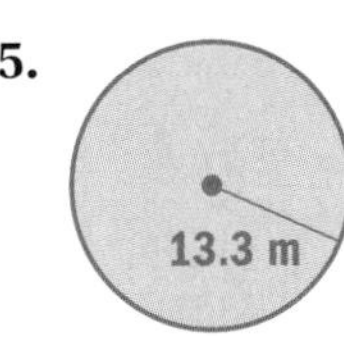

6.

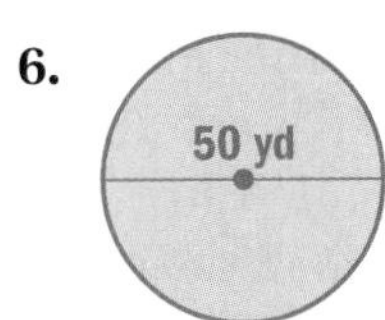

7.

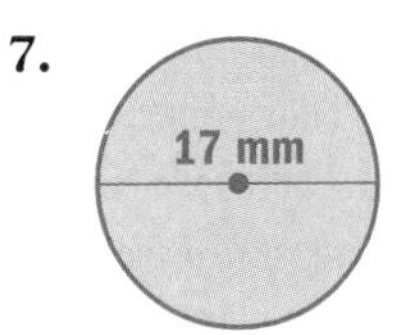

8.

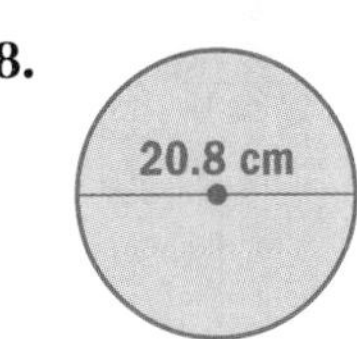

9. ERROR ANALYSIS Describe and correct the error made in finding the area of the circle.

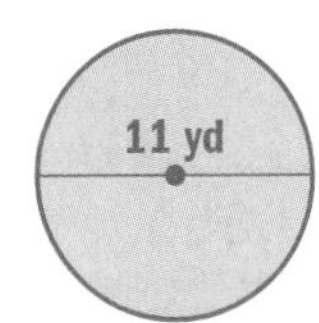

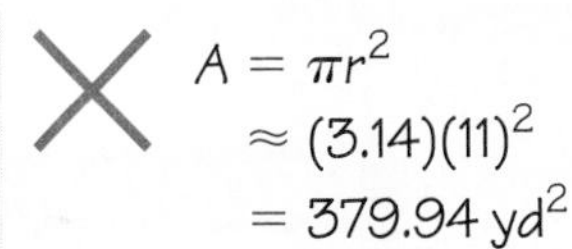

FINDING AREA **Find the area of the circle with the given radius or diameter. Use 3.14 for π. Estimate to check your answer.**

10. $r = 9$ cm
11. $r = 17$ ft
12. $r = 30.4$ m
13. $d = 28$ mm
14. $d = 6$ yd
15. $d = 40.2$ in.

FINDING THE RADIUS **Find the radius of the circle with the given area A. Use 3.14 for π.**

SEE EXAMPLE 2 on p. 528 for Exs. 16–24

16. $A = 28.26\ \text{ft}^2$
17. $A = 3.14\ \text{m}^2$
18. $A = 200.96\ \text{yd}^2$
19. $A = 113.04\ \text{in.}^2$
20. $A = 12.56\ \text{mm}^2$
21. $A = 254.34\ \text{cm}^2$
22. $A = 907.46\ \text{mi}^2$
23. $A = 4069.44\ \text{cm}^2$
24. $A = 1808.64\ \text{ft}^2$

ALGEBRA **Find the area of the circle with the given circumference C. Use 3.14 for π.**

25. $C = 18.84$ ft
26. $C = 81.64$ m
27. $C = 37.68$ cm

28. ★ **MULTIPLE CHOICE** What is the approximate area of a circle with a circumference of 50.24 millimeters? Use 3.14 for π.

Ⓐ 8 mm Ⓑ 16 mm Ⓒ 200.96 mm^2 Ⓓ 803.84 mm^2

29. MEASUREMENT Use a ruler to measure the radius of the circle in millimeters. Then find the area of the circle. Use 3.14 for π.

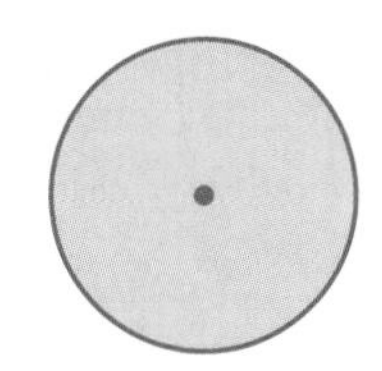

30. MENTAL MATH The area of a circle is 25π square feet. What is the radius?

SEE EXAMPLE 3 on p. 528 for Exs. 31–34

31. AREA Find the area of the shaded region. Use $\frac{22}{7}$ for π.

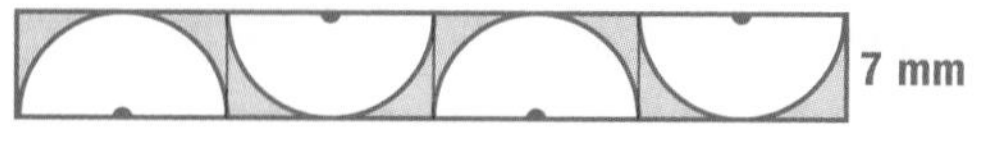

FINDING AREA **Find the area of the shaded region. Use 3.14 for π.**

32.

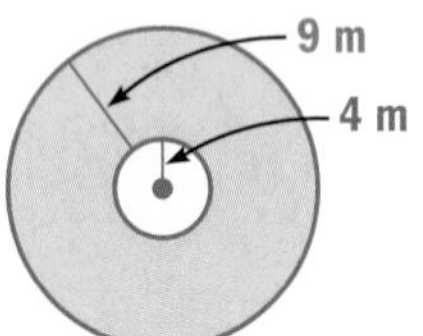

33.

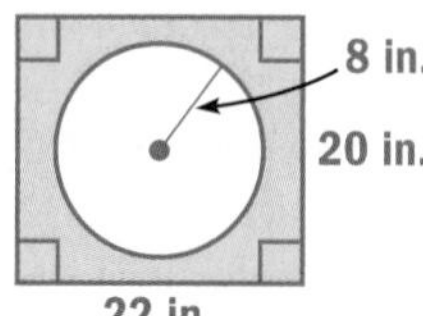

34.

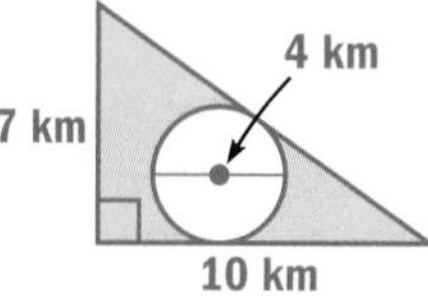

35. xy **REASONING** A circle has a circumference of c units and an area of a square units. What is the radius of the circle if $c = a$? *Explain.*

36. CHALLENGE The circles in the pattern shown share the same center, and every other circle is shaded. The radii of the circles, going from the innermost to the outermost, are $1, \sqrt{2}, \sqrt{3}, 2, \sqrt{5}, \sqrt{6}$, and so on. Assume the pattern continues to n circles, where n is even. Write a formula for the area of the shaded region.

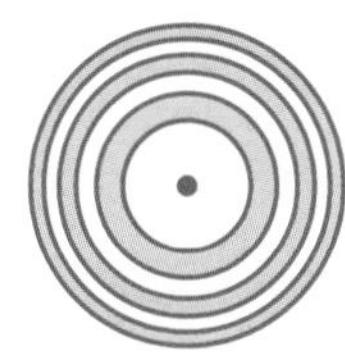

PROBLEM SOLVING

SEE EXAMPLE 1 on p. 527 for Exs. 37–38

(37.) SPRINKLERS You are using a rotating sprinkler to water your yard. The sprinkler rotates in a complete circle. It sprays water at most 12 feet. Find the area of the yard that is watered. Use 3.14 for π.

38. ★ MULTIPLE CHOICE A circular swimming pool has a diameter of 18 feet. To the nearest square foot, what is the smallest amount of material needed to cover the surface of the pool? Use 3.14 for π.

Ⓐ 57 ft^2 Ⓑ 113 ft^2

Ⓒ 254 ft^2 Ⓓ 1017 ft^2

SEE EXAMPLE 3 on p. 528 for Exs. 39–40

39. TENNIS CENTER The roof of the New South Wales Tennis Center in Sydney, Australia, can be approximated by a circle. A level of seats is covered by the ring-shaped roof shown in the photo, whose outer diameter is about 100 meters and inner diameter is about 65 meters. What is the area covered by the roof? Use 3.14 for π.

40. ★ WRITING The rectangle intersecting the circle passes through the center of the circle. *Explain* how to find the area of the shaded region.

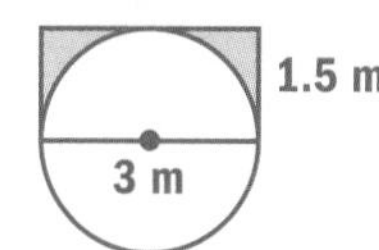

READING *IN* MATH **Read the information below for Exercises 41–43.**

Energy Savings The type of windows in a home affects heating costs. Double-paned windows will reduce the amount of heat lost during the winter. They cost about $1.50 more per square foot than single-paned windows. Low-emissivity windows have an invisible coating on the glass that reflects heat. They cost about $3.00 more per square foot than double-paned windows.

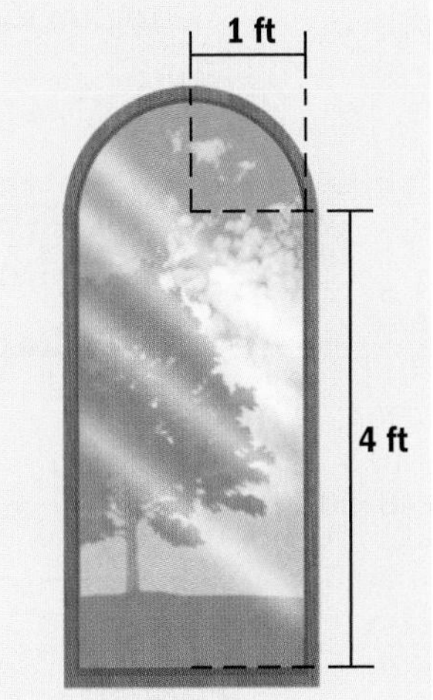

41. **Calculate** You want to install the window shown. Find its area to the nearest square foot. Use the area to calculate the additional cost of installing a double-paned window instead of a single-paned window.

42. **Calculate** Find the additional cost of installing a double-paned window with the low-emissivity coating instead of a single-paned window.

43. **Analyze** Double-paned windows offer an annual energy savings of $.60 per square foot. Low-emissivity windows save an additional $.50 per square foot annually. After how many years is the extra cost of the double-paned low-emissivity window offset by the energy savings?

44. ★ **SHORT RESPONSE** Copy and complete the table. Leave your answers in terms of π. What happens to the area of a circle when the radius is multiplied by a positive number k? *Justify* your reasoning.

Radius r	*Area of a circle with radius r*	*Area of a circle with radius $2r$*	*Area of a circle with radius $3r$*	*Area of a circle with radius $4r$*
2 in.	4π in.^{2}	?	?	?
3 in.	?	?	?	?
5 in.	?	?	?	?

45. **MULTI-STEP PROBLEM** You are using a disk sander to sand a porch that has an area of 11,520 square inches. One disk for the sander has a diameter of 7 inches. Another disk has a diameter of 10 inches.

    a. You can sand a section of the porch with an area equal to that of five disks in one minute. Find the area that you can sand in one minute with each size disk. Use 3.14 for π.

    b. About how much time would you save by sanding the entire porch with the larger disk? Round your answer to the nearest minute.

46. **ESTIMATION** The diameter of the circle in the diagram is 20 centimeters. Find the area of each square to the nearest tenth and use the areas to estimate the area of the circle. Then calculate the area of the circle and compare it to your estimate. Use 3.14 for π.

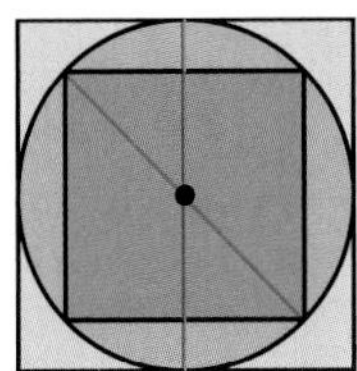

47. **CHALLENGE** You cut a circle of radius r out of a square piece of paper as shown. You want the area of the shaded region to be $(4 - \pi)$ square inches. Find the value of r.

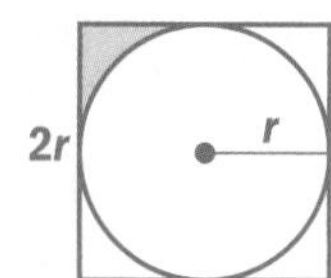

MIXED REVIEW

Get-Ready

Prepare for Lesson 10.3 in Exs. 48–50

Classify the quadrilateral. *(p. 416)*

48. 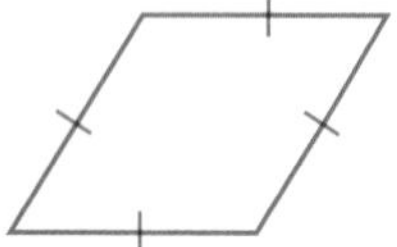

49. 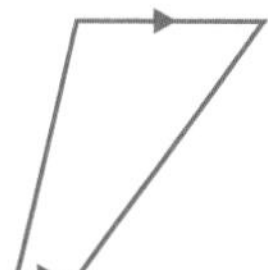

50. 

CHOOSE A STRATEGY Use a strategy from the list to solve the following problem. *Explain* your choice of strategy.

51. For each quarter you put in a parking meter you can park your car for 15 minutes. You know you'll be away from your car for up to an hour and 40 minutes. You have a \$10 roll of quarters. How many quarters will you have after you put the necessary amount in the meter?

Problem Solving Strategies
- Work Backward *(p. 789)*
- Make a Table *(p. 790)*
- Act It Out *(p. 795)*

52. ★ **MULTIPLE CHOICE** Which side lengths a, b, and c form a right triangle? *(p. 482)*

(A) $a = 0.5, b = 0.9, c = 1.06$ (B) $a = 3, b = 4, c = 6$

(C) $a = 3.6, b = 4.8, c = 6$ (D) $a = 1.2, b = 3.4, c = 3.7$

Brain Game

What's the Score?

The center circle of the target has a radius of 3 inches and each ring is 3 inches wide. Find the area of each region in terms of π. Then use the formula below to find the score for each region. Round to the nearest whole number.

$$score = \frac{225\pi}{area}$$

For example, the yellow region has an area of $\pi(3)^2$, or 9π square inches. The score in the yellow region is

$$\frac{225\pi}{area} = \frac{225\pi}{9\pi} = 25.$$

Who has a higher score, Greg or Jamie?

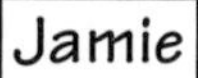

Greg 

Jamie 

Technology **ACTIVITY** *Use after Lesson 10.2*

GOAL
Use a spreadsheet to find how the radius of a circle changes when its area changes.

10.2 Comparing Radii of Circles

EXPLORE **How does the radius of a circle change when its area is multiplied by 4?**

STEP 1 **Create** a spreadsheet with an original circle area in cell A1 and the multiplier 4 in cell A2. Enter formulas for the Area column that refer to these cells, as shown.

Comparing Radii

	A	B	C
1	1	Original circle area	
2	4	Multiplier	
3			
4	Area	Radius	Ratio
5	=A1	=SQRT(A5/PI())	
6	=A5*A2	=SQRT(A6/PI())	=B6/B5

STEP 2 **Enter** formulas for the Radius column, as shown. The radius of a circle with area A is given by $\sqrt{\frac{A}{\pi}}$.

STEP 3 **Compare** the radii of the two circles by dividing the second radius by the first radius. Enter a formula for this quotient in the Ratio column.

STEP 4 **Change** the value of the original circle area in cell A1 several times. What do you notice about the ratio of the radii?

	A	B	C
1	1	Original circle area	
2	4	Multiplier	
3			
4	Area	Radius	Ratio
5	1	0.564190	
6	4	1.128379	2

	A	B	C
1	5	Original circle area	
2	4	Multiplier	
3			
4	Area	Radius	Ratio
5	5	1.261566	
6	20	2.523133	2

	A	B	C
1	15	Original circle area	
2	4	Multiplier	
3			
4	Area	Radius	Ratio
5	15	2.185097	
6	60	4.370194	2

▸ **Answer** When the area of a circle is multiplied by 4, the radius is multiplied by 2.

PRACTICE **Find how the radius of a circle changes when its area is multiplied by the given number.**

1. 9 **2.** 16 **3.** 25 **4.** 36

DRAW CONCLUSIONS

5. REASONING How does the radius of a circle change when its area is doubled? tripled? *Explain.*

6. ANALYZE *Explain* why $r = \sqrt{\frac{A}{\pi}}$ is the formula for the radius of a circle with area A.

10.3 Three-Dimensional Figures

Before	You classified and sketched polygons.
Now	You'll classify and sketch solids.
Why?	So you can classify solids that form structures, as in Exs. 14–16.

KEY VOCABULARY

- **solid, polyhedron, face,** *p. 534*
- **prism,** *p. 534*
- **pyramid,** *p. 534*
- **cylinder,** *p. 534*
- **cone,** *p. 534*
- **sphere,** *p. 534*
- **edge, vertex,** *p. 534*

A **solid** is a three-dimensional figure that encloses a part of space. A **polyhedron** is a solid that is enclosed by polygons. A polyhedron has only flat surfaces. The polygons that form a polyhedron are called **faces**.

Classifying Solids

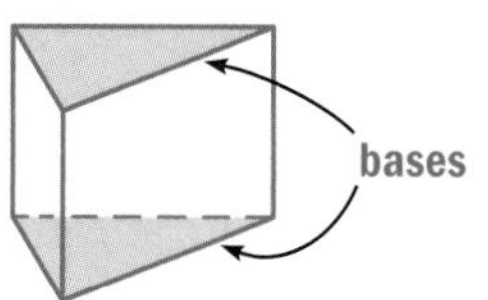

A **prism** is a polyhedron. Prisms have two congruent bases that lie in parallel planes. The other faces are rectangles. A *cube* is a prism with six square faces.

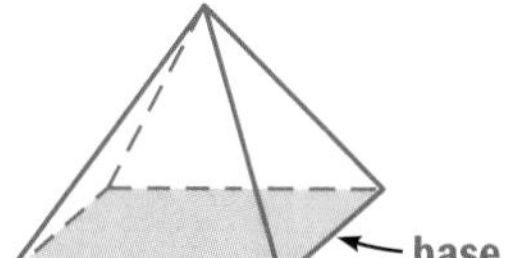

A **pyramid** is a polyhedron. Pyramids have one base. The other faces are triangles.

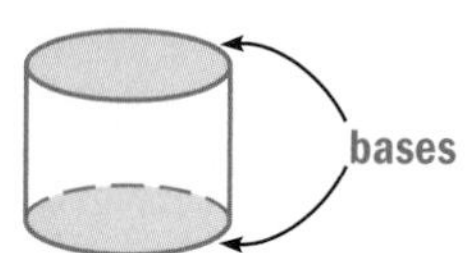

A **cylinder** is a solid with two congruent circular bases that lie in parallel planes.

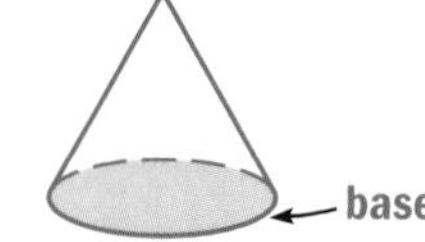

A **cone** is a solid with one circular base.

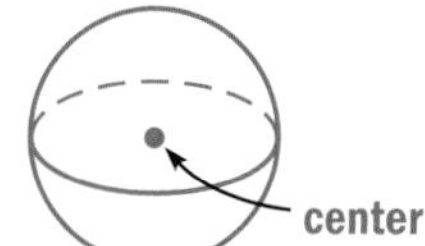

A **sphere** is a solid formed by all points in space that are the same distance from a fixed point called the center.

EXAMPLE 1 Classifying Solids

Classify the solid. Tell whether it is a polyhedron.

The solid has two congruent circular bases that lie in parallel planes, so it is a cylinder. It is not a polyhedron, because circles are not polygons.

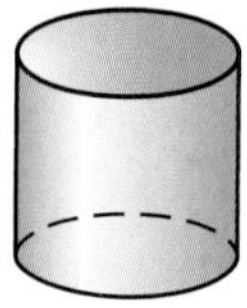

at classzone.com

Edges and Vertices The segments where faces of a polyhedron meet are called **edges**. A **vertex** is a point where three or more edges meet. The plural of vertex is *vertices*.

EXAMPLE 2 Counting Faces, Edges, and Vertices

Classify the solid. Then count the number of faces, edges, and vertices.

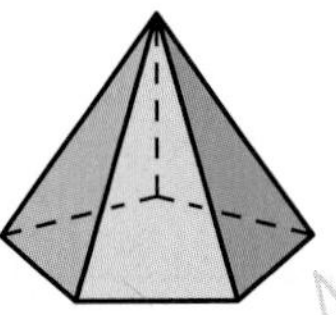

SOLUTION

The solid is a pentagonal pyramid.

Remember to include the base when counting faces.

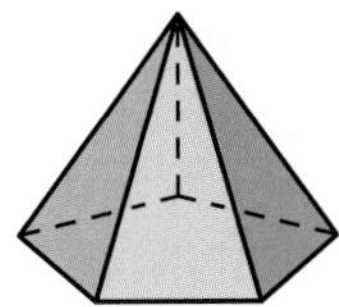
6 faces

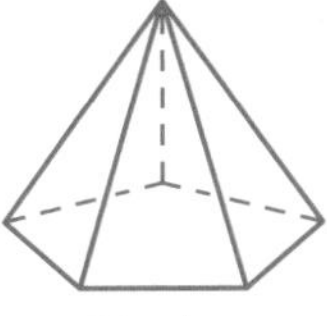
10 edges

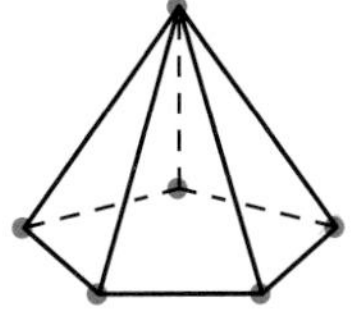
6 vertices

at classzone.com

VOCABULARY

You can name a prism or pyramid using the shape of its base. For example, in Example 2 the base is a pentagon, so the solid is called a *pentagonal pyramid*.

EXAMPLE 3 Sketching a Solid

Show two ways to represent a triangular prism.

METHOD 1 Sketch the solid.

STEP 1 **Sketch** two congruent bases.

STEP 2 **Connect** the vertices.

STEP 3 **Make** any hidden lines dashed.

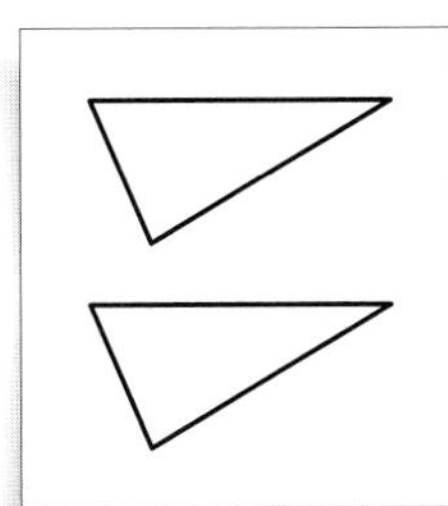

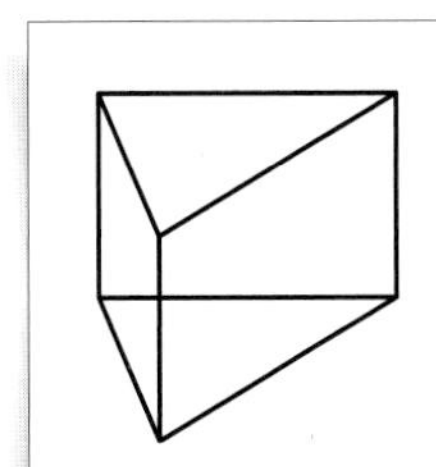

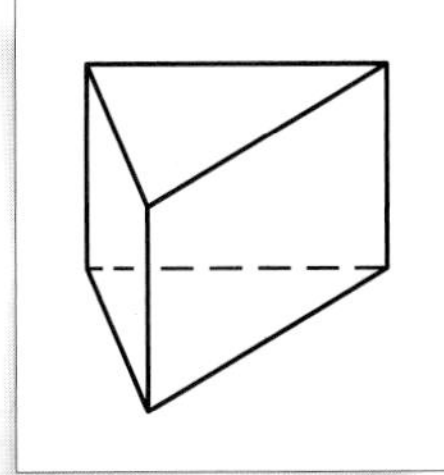

ANOTHER WAY

You can draw other views of the triangular prism in Example 3 by using a different perspective.

METHOD 2 Sketch the top, front, and side views of the solid.

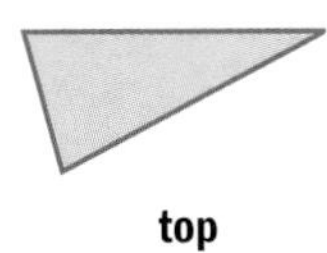
top

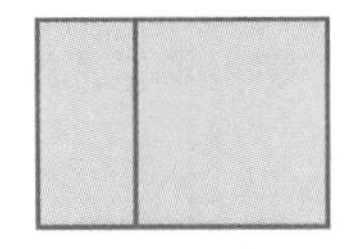
front

side

Animated Math at classzone.com

GUIDED PRACTICE for Examples 1, 2, and 3

Classify the solid. Then tell whether it is a polyhedron.

1. 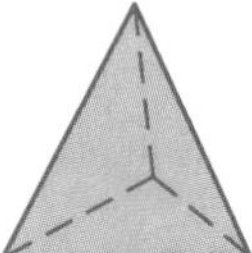

2. 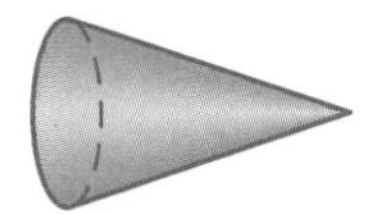

3. 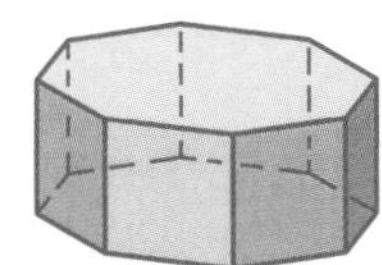

4. Show two ways to represent a rectangular pyramid. Then count the number of faces, edges, and vertices.

10.3 EXERCISES

HOMEWORK KEY

★ = **STANDARDIZED TEST PRACTICE**
Exs. 17, 25, 26, 27, and 35

○ = **HINTS AND HOMEWORK HELP**
for Exs. 5, 7, 9, 11, 25 at classzone.com

SKILL PRACTICE

VOCABULARY Match the description with the solid.

1. two rectangular bases
2. three rectangular faces
3. four triangular faces

A. triangular prism
B. rectangular pyramid
C. rectangular prism

CLASSIFYING SOLIDS Classify the solid. Then tell whether it is a polyhedron.

SEE EXAMPLE 1 on p. 534 for Exs. 4–6

4. 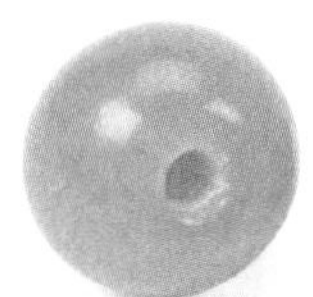

5. 

6. 

COUNTING FACES, EDGES, AND VERTICES Classify the solid. Then count the number of faces, edges, and vertices.

SEE EXAMPLES 2 AND 3 on p. 535 for Exs. 7–13

7. 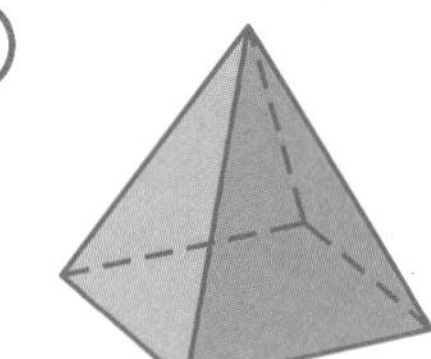

8. 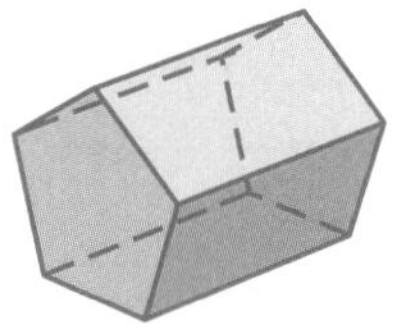

9. 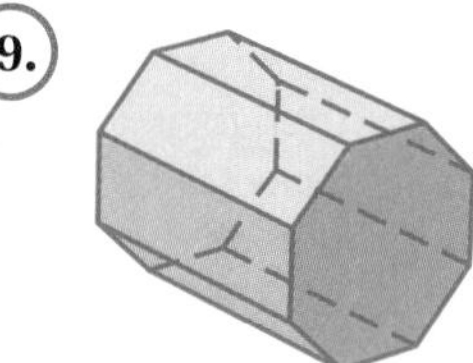

10. **ERROR ANALYSIS** A student says that because a hexagon has 6 sides, a hexagonal pyramid has 6 edges. What is wrong with this statement?

SKETCHING SOLIDS Show two ways to represent the solid.

11. rectangular prism
12. hexagonal prism
13. cylinder

CLASSIFYING SOLIDS Classify the solids that form the structure.

14. 

15. 

16. 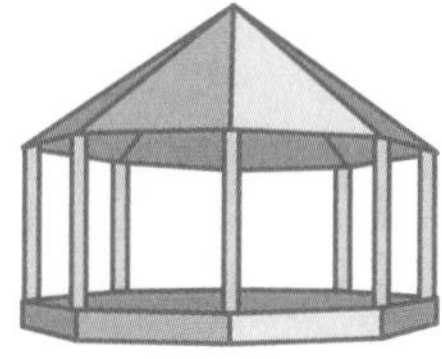

17. ★ **MULTIPLE CHOICE** What is the name of the solid with the given views?

(A) triangle
(B) triangular prism
(C) triangular pyramid
(D) rectangular pyramid

top

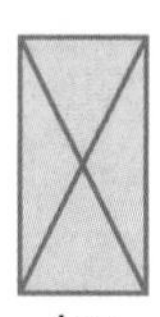

front

side

SKETCHING SOLIDS **Sketch the solid with the given views.**

18.

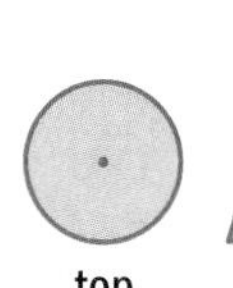

top

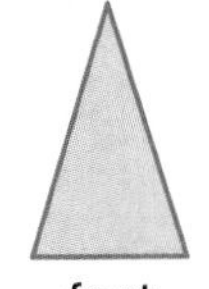

front

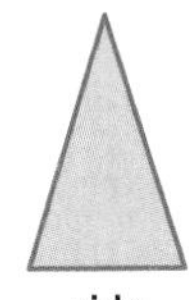

side

19.

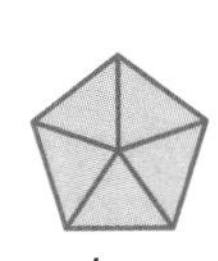

top

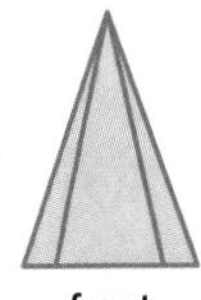

front

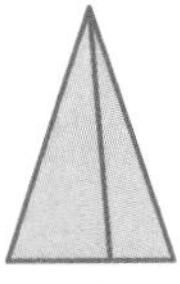

side

CHALLENGE **Classify the quadrilateral outlined in green, formed by the intersection of a cube and a plane.**

20.

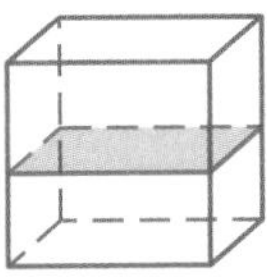

21.

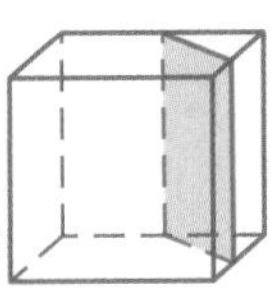

22.

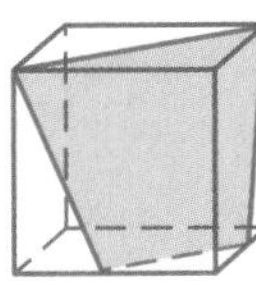

23. **CHALLENGE** Sketch a cube and a plane whose intersection is (a) a triangle and (b) a hexagon.

PROBLEM SOLVING

24. **GUIDED PROBLEM SOLVING** Sketch a square pyramid.

a. Sketch a parallelogram for the square base.

b. Draw a dot centered above the parallelogram.

c. Connect the vertices of the parallelogram to the dot. Make any hidden lines dashed.

SEE EXAMPLE 1 on p. 534 for Exs. 25–27

25. ★ **MULTIPLE CHOICE** Which of the following solids is a polyhedron?

Ⓐ 

Ⓑ 

Ⓒ 

Ⓓ 

26. ★ **WRITING** *Explain* how a pyramid and a prism with congruent bases are alike and how they are different.

27. ★ **OPEN-ENDED MATH** Give an example of a cylinder, a cone, and a square prism that you find in your classroom or at home.

28. **LOOK FOR A PATTERN** Copy and complete the table. Use the pattern to write a formula that gives the number of edges of a polyhedron in terms of the number of faces and vertices. This is called *Euler's Formula.*

Figure	*Number of faces F*	*Number of vertices V*	*Number of edges E*	*F + V*
pentagonal pyramid	6	6	10	12
rectangular pyramid	?	?	?	?
triangular prism	?	?	?	?
rectangular prism	?	?	?	?

29. **CHALLENGE** The polyhedron shown is a cube. Find the length AB in terms of s.

30. **CHALLENGE** Describe how you could divide a cube into congruent square pyramids.

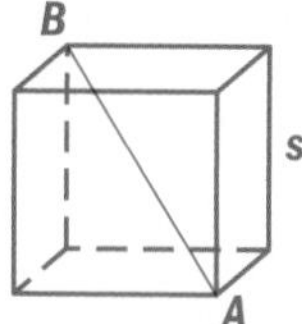

MIXED REVIEW

Get-Ready

Prepare for Lesson 10.4 in Exs. 31–33

Find the area of the triangle. *(p. 134)*

31.

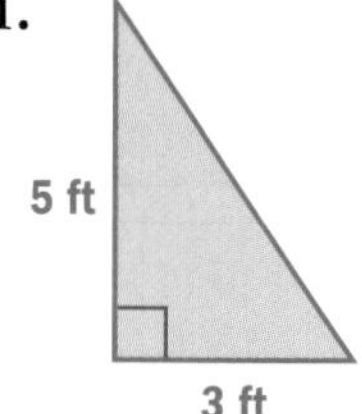

32.

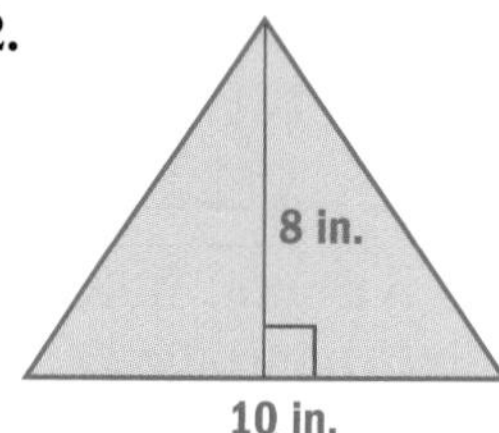

33.

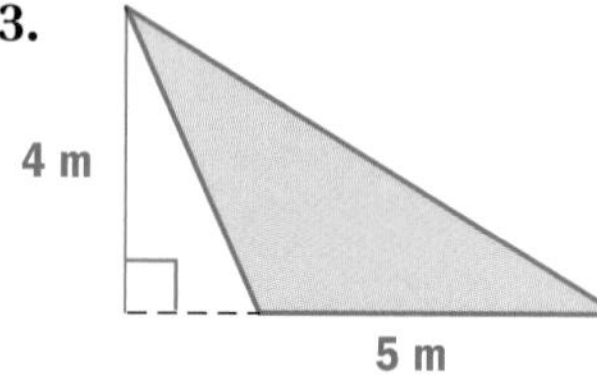

34. Find the area of a circle whose diameter is 21 inches. Use $\frac{22}{7}$ for π. *(p. 527)*

35. ★ **MULTIPLE CHOICE** In $\triangle ABC$, what is $\sin A$? *(p. 500)*

Ⓐ $\frac{8}{17}$ Ⓑ $\frac{8}{15}$

Ⓒ $\frac{15}{17}$ Ⓓ $\frac{15}{8}$

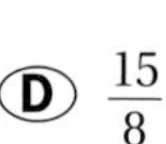

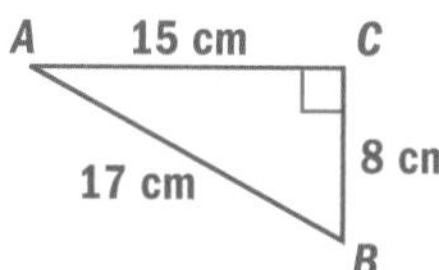

QUIZ *for Lessons 10.1–10.3*

Find the area of the parallelogram or trapezoid. *(p. 521)*

1.

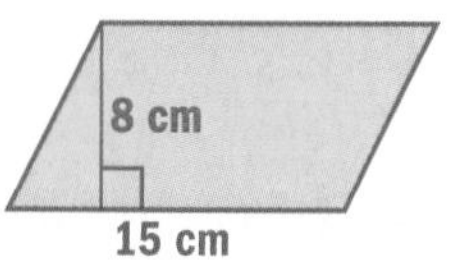

2.

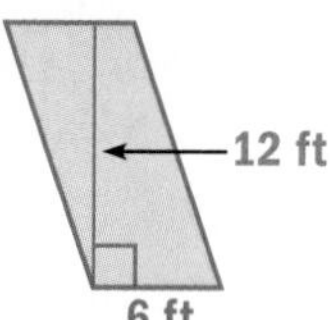

3.

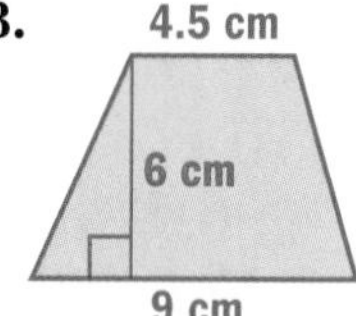

4. A trapezoid has a height of 8 feet. The lengths of the bases are 10 feet and 14 feet. Find the area of the trapezoid. *(p. 521)*

5. Find the area of a circle with diameter 22 feet. Use 3.14 for π. *(p. 527)*

Find the radius of the circle with the given area. Use 3.14 for π. *(p. 527)*

6. $A = 254.34 \text{ ft}^2$

7. $A = 452.16 \text{ cm}^2$

8. $A = 78.5 \text{ m}^2$

9. The triangular faces of the solid are all congruent. Classify the solid in as many ways as possible. Then tell whether it is a polyhedron. *(p. 534)*

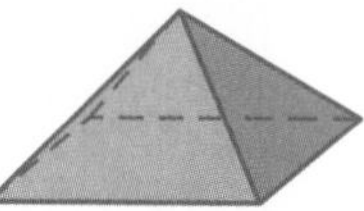

10. Show two ways to represent a triangular pyramid. Then count the number of faces, edges, and vertices. *(p. 534)*

Sketching Solids

GOAL Draw views of solids and make isometric drawings.

KEY VOCABULARY
- **isometric drawing,** *p. 539*

In Lesson 10.3, you drew the top, front, and side views of common solids. In the following examples, you will see how to draw the top, front, and side views of more complicated solids.

EXAMPLE 1 Drawing Views of a Solid

Draw the top, front, and side views of the solid.

SOLUTION

top

front

side

The interior lines represent edges of faces.

Isometric Drawings An **isometric drawing** is another way to make a two-dimensional drawing of a three-dimensional figure. It is created using a grid of dots and a set of three axes that intersect to form 1208 angles. Use the dots to guide your drawing and give depth to the figure.

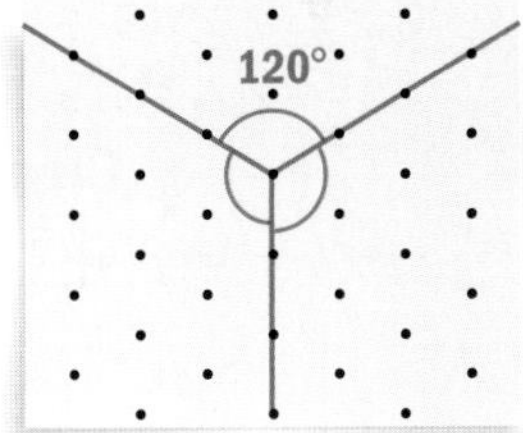

EXAMPLE 2 Creating an Isometric Drawing

Create an isometric drawing of the solid from Example 1.

SOLUTION

The isometric drawing is shown at the right. Each vertical edge of the solid is represented by a vertical line segment.

Add depth to the drawing by shading the top, front, and sides differently.

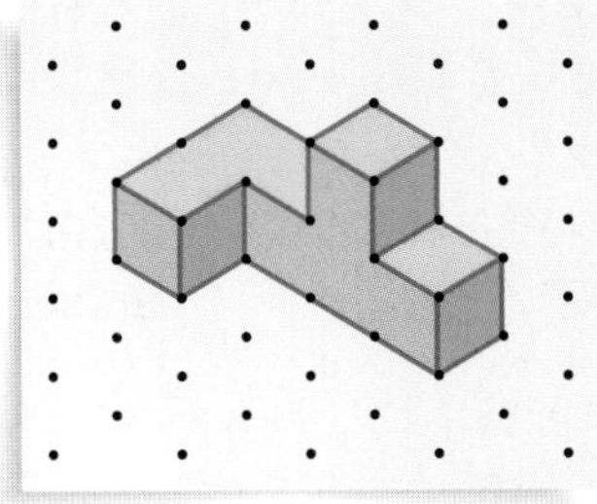

EXAMPLE 3 Interpreting an Isometric Drawing

Draw the top, front, and side views of the solid.

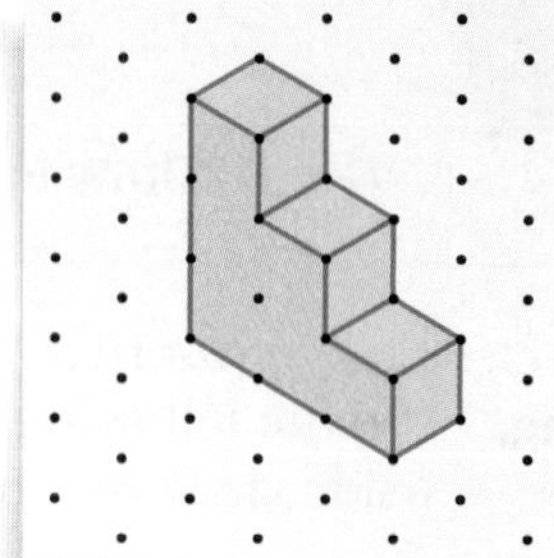

SOLUTION

You can arrange the views in the following way.

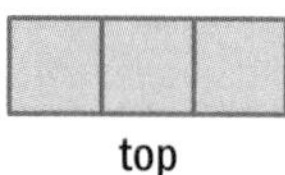

top

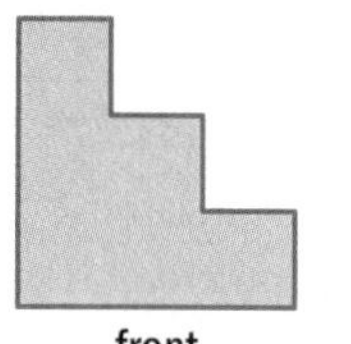

front side

EXERCISES

Draw the top, front, and side views of the solid.

1. 

2. 

3. 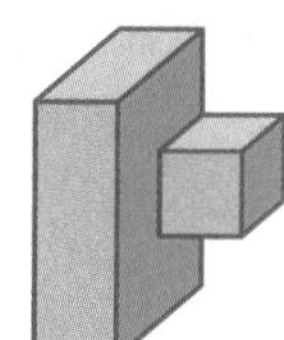

Create an isometric drawing of the solid.

4. 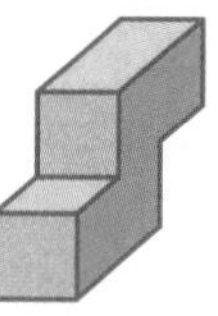

5. 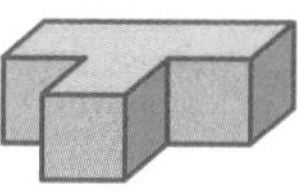

6. 

Draw the top, front, and side views of the solid. Assume no cubes, except those needed to support the visible ones, are hidden from view.

7. 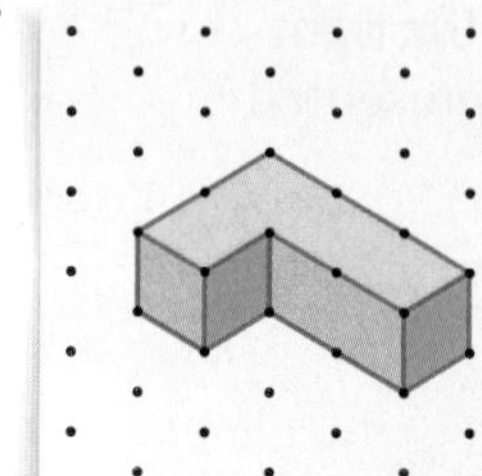

8. 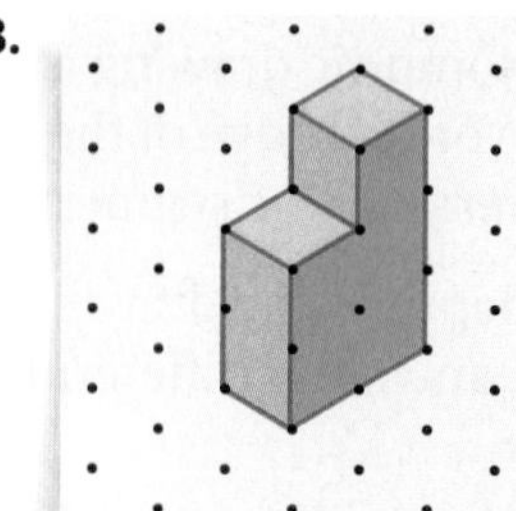

9. 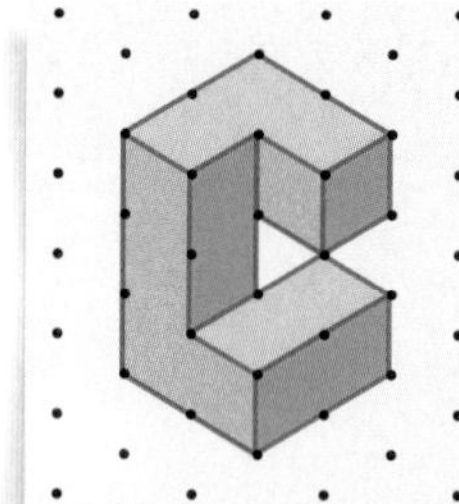

Lessons 10.1–10.3

1. **SHORT RESPONSE** A rectangular house is built on a lot that is shaped like a trapezoid. The house is completely surrounded by a grass-covered lawn. The house is 55 feet long and 35 feet wide. The lot has base lengths of 75 feet and 125 feet, and a height of 65 feet.
   a. Draw and label a diagram of the lot, including the house.
   b. Find the area of the lot covered by grass.
   c. Does the position of the house on the lot affect the area covered by grass? Why or why not?

2. **MULTI-STEP PROBLEM** You are watering two areas of your yard with rotating sprinklers. One sprinkler rotates in a complete circle and sprays water up to 10 feet. The other sprinkler rotates only half of a circle and sprays water up to 15 feet.
   a. Find the area that is watered by each sprinkler. Use 3.14 for π.
   b. Which sprinkler covers a greater area of the yard? About how much more area does the sprinkler cover? Round your answer to the nearest whole square foot.

3. **GRIDDED ANSWER** The total area of the four congruent parking spaces below is 72 square meters. How long is each line dividing the spaces, in meters?

4. **SHORT RESPONSE** The dimensions of two polygons are given below. For what values of b_2 is the area of the trapezoid greater than the area of the parallelogram? *Explain.*

   Parallelogram: $b = 20$ m, $h = 30$ m

   Trapezoid: $b_1 = 10$ m, $b_2 =$ __?__ m, $h = 30$ m

5. **GRIDDED ANSWER** A candle has the shape of a pentagonal prism. How many faces does it have?

6. **OPEN-ENDED** Sketch a polyhedron that has two congruent bases. Then sketch another solid that is not a polyhedron but still has two congruent bases. Classify each solid.

7. **EXTENDED RESPONSE** The diagram below shows the dimensions of a circular pool and an attached deck. You want to protect the deck by covering it with two coats of a waterproof sealant. One half-gallon can of sealant covers 150 square feet and costs $4.50.

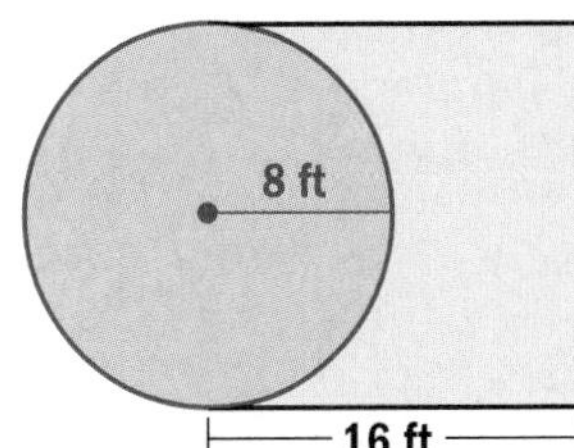

   a. Find the total area of the deck. *Explain* how you found your answer.
   b. How many cans of sealant should you buy? *Explain* your reasoning.
   c. How much should you expect to pay for enough sealant to complete the project? Assume the sales tax is 6%.

8. **SHORT RESPONSE** Sketch and classify a solid that has a total of 5 faces: three rectangular faces and two triangular faces. Is there more than one possible type of solid? *Explain.*

9. **SHORT RESPONSE** The crystal below is a composite of several solids. Identify the solids that make up the crystal. Then sketch its top, front, and side views.

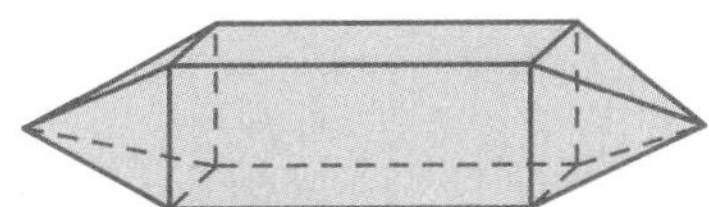

10.4 Surface Areas of Prisms and Cylinders

Before You classified prisms and cylinders.
Now You'll find the surface areas of prisms and cylinders.
Why? So you can find areas of objects, as the mailbox in Ex. 33.

KEY VOCABULARY
- **net,** *p. 542*
- **surface area,** *p. 542*

One way to represent a solid is to use a *net*. A **net** is a two-dimensional pattern that forms a solid when it is folded.

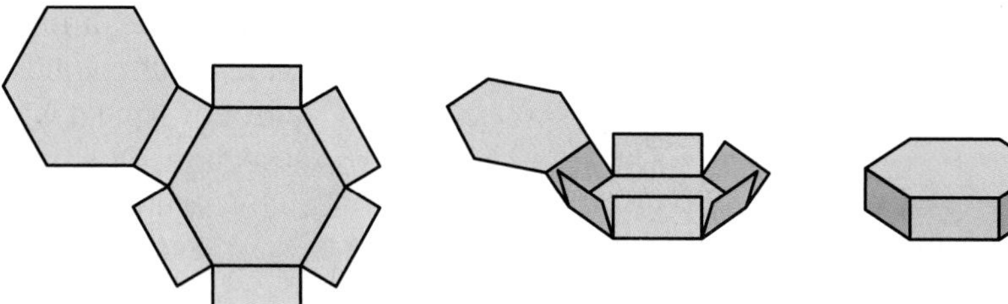

Each polygon of the net represents one face of the solid. For a given solid, several arrangements of these polygons are usually possible.

EXAMPLE 1 Drawing a Net

Draw a net of the triangular prism.

SOLUTION

METHOD 1
Draw one base with a rectangle adjacent to each side. Draw the other base adjacent to one of the rectangles.

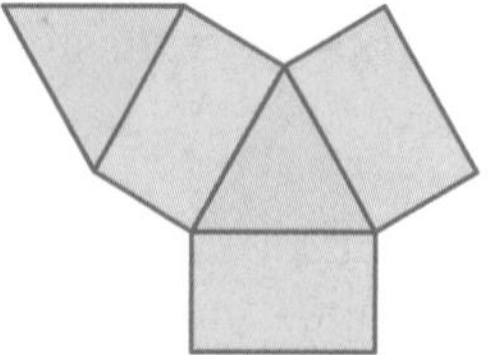

METHOD 2
For the rectangular faces, draw adjacent rectangles. Draw the bases on opposite sides of one rectangle.

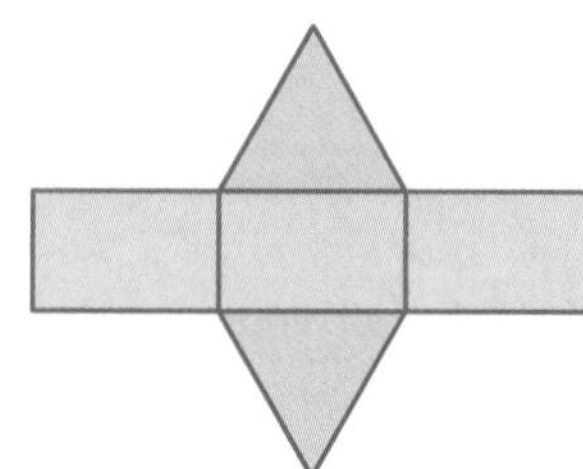

Surface Area The **surface area** of a polyhedron is the sum of the areas of its faces. To find the surface area of the triangular prism above, find the sum of the areas of the two triangular faces and the three rectangular faces.

EXAMPLE 2 Using a Net to Find Surface Area

Storage Chest You are painting a storage chest with the given dimensions. Find the surface area to be painted.

ANOTHER WAY

Any pair of parallel faces in a rectangular prism can be considered the bases of the solid. Another way to draw a net for the storage chest is:

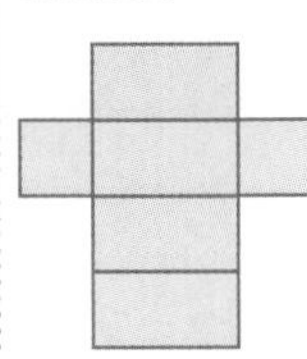

SOLUTION

Draw a net of the chest.

The area of each square face is 15 in. • 15 in. = **225 in.^{2}**

The area of each rectangular face is 30 in. • 15 in. = **450 in.^{2}**

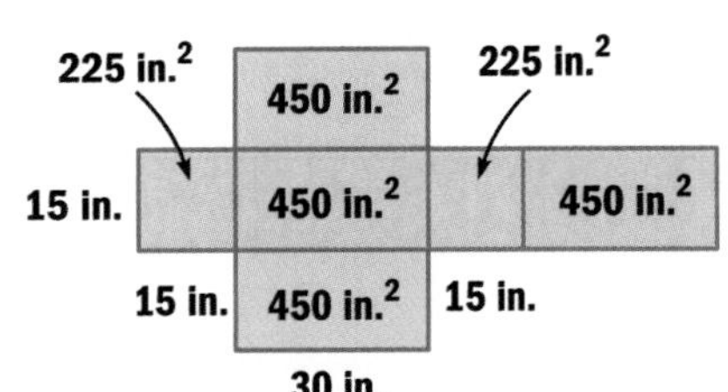

There are two square faces and four rectangular faces, so the surface area is 2 • **225 in.^{2}** + 4 • **450 in.^{2}** = 2250 in.^{2}

▸ **Answer** The surface area of the storage chest is 2250 square inches.

Notice that in Example 2 the four blue faces form a large rectangle that has length equal to the perimeter of the red base.

KEY CONCEPT — *For Your Notebook*

Surface Area of a Prism

Words The surface area of a prism is the sum of twice the area of a base B and the product of the base's perimeter P and the height h.

P B B h

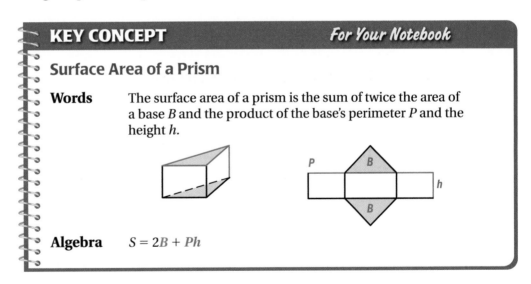

Algebra $S = 2B + Ph$

EXAMPLE 3 Using a Formula to Find Surface Area

Find the surface area of the triangular prism.

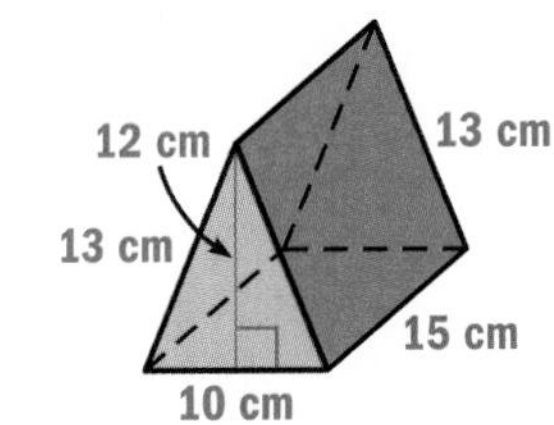

$$S = 2B + Ph$$

$$= 2\left(\frac{1}{2} \cdot 10 \cdot 12\right) + (13 + 13 + 10)15$$

$$= 660$$

▸ **Answer** The surface area of the prism is 660 square centimeters.

CHECK FOR REASONABLENESS

Round each length to its leading digit. Then, $S \approx 2\left(\frac{1}{2}\right)(10^2) + 30 \cdot 20 = 100 + 600 = 700 \text{ cm}^2$.

Cylinders The net of a cylinder has two circles for the bases. The curved surface of the cylinder becomes a rectangle in the net. The width of the rectangle is the height of the cylinder, and the length of the rectangle is the circumference of the base.

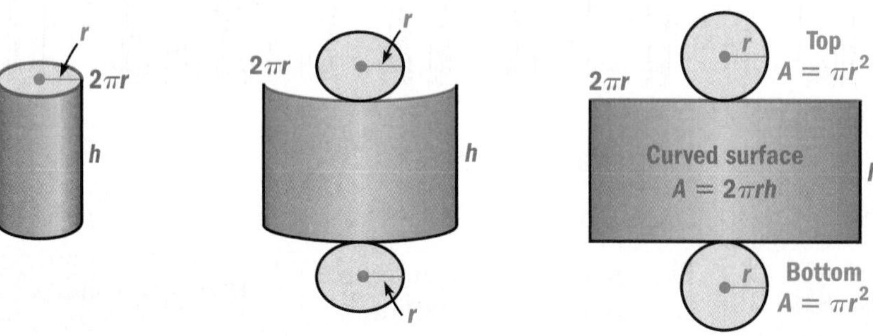

KEY CONCEPT *For Your Notebook*

Surface Area of a Cylinder

Words The surface area of a cylinder is the sum of twice the area of a base B and the product of the base's circumference C and the height h.

Algebra $S = 2B + Ch = 2\pi r^2 + 2\pi rh$

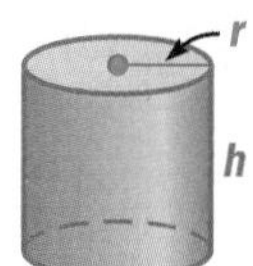

EXAMPLE 4 Finding the Surface Area of a Cylinder

Packaging Find the surface area of the can of sloppy joe sauce.

SOLUTION

The radius is one half the diameter, so $r = 4$ cm.

$S = 2\pi r^2 + 2\pi rh$	**Write formula for surface area.**
$= 2\pi(4)^2 + 2\pi(4)(10.7)$	**Substitute 4 for *r* and 10.7 for *h*.**
≈ 369.45	**Evaluate using a calculator.**

▸ **Answer** The surface area of the can is about 369 square centimeters.

USE A CALCULATOR

You can use the π key on your calculator instead of 3.14 when evaluating formulas.

✓ **GUIDED PRACTICE** for Examples 1, 2, 3, and 4

Draw a net of the solid. Then find the surface area. Round to the nearest tenth. Check your answer for reasonableness.

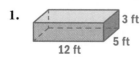

1. 3 ft, 5 ft, 12 ft

2. 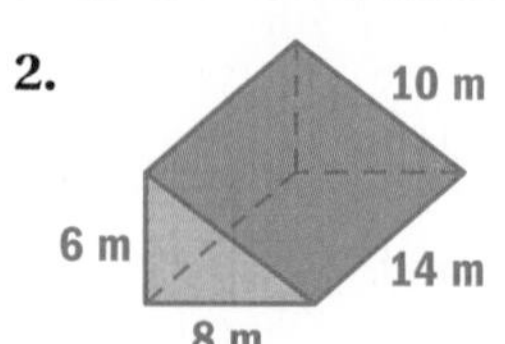

3. 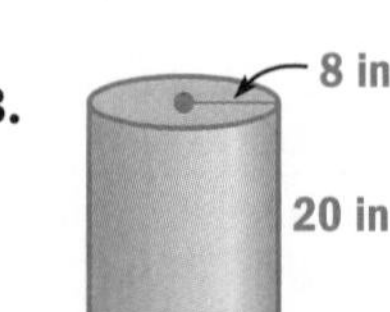

Lateral Surface Area The *lateral surface area* of a three-dimensional figure is the surface area of the figure excluding the area of its bases.

EXAMPLE 5 Standardized Test Practice

Storage Container A net for a cylindrical paint can is shown at the right. Approximate the lateral surface area of the container.

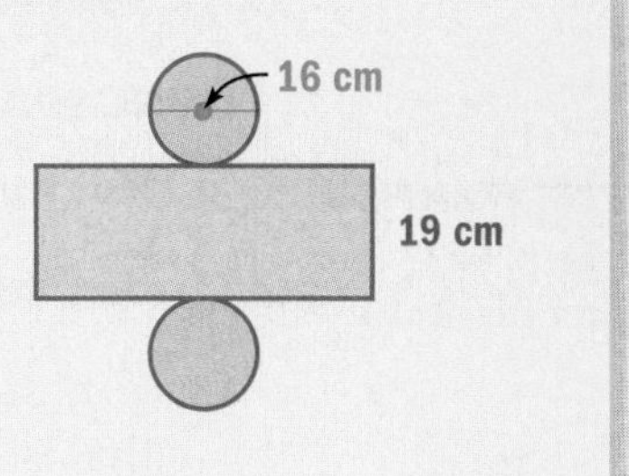

Ⓐ 304 cm^2 Ⓑ 478 cm^2

Ⓒ 955 cm^2 Ⓓ 3820 cm^2

ELIMINATE CHOICES
Use estimation. The height of the rectangle is about 20 cm and its length is about $3 \cdot 16 \approx 50$ cm. The area is about 1000 cm^2. You can eliminate choices A, B, and D using mental math.

SOLUTION

The lateral surface area of a cylinder is equal to the area of its curved surface. This surface becomes a rectangle in the net of the cylinder, with length equal to the circumference of the base.

Lateral surface area $= 2\pi rh$ **Multiply circumference and height.**

$= 2\pi(8)(19)$ **Substitute 8 for *r* and 19 for *h*.**

≈ 955.04 **Evaluate using a calculator.**

▶ **Answer** The lateral surface area of the container is about 955 cm^2. The correct answer is C. Ⓐ Ⓑ Ⓒ Ⓓ

GUIDED PRACTICE for Example 5

4. **What If?** Suppose the radius of the cylinder in Example 5 is 5 inches and the height is 10 inches. Approximate the lateral surface area.

10.4 EXERCISES

HOMEWORK KEY
★ = STANDARDIZED TEST PRACTICE Exs. 13, 28, 30, 31, 34, and 45
○ = HINTS AND HOMEWORK HELP for Exs. 3, 7, 9, 15, 29 at classzone.com

SKILL PRACTICE

1. **VOCABULARY** In your own words, explain what surface area is.

2. **VOCABULARY** Copy and complete: The net of a cylinder is made up of two __?__ and one __?__.

DRAWING NETS Draw a net of the prism.

SEE EXAMPLE 1 on p. 542 for Exs. 3–5

3. 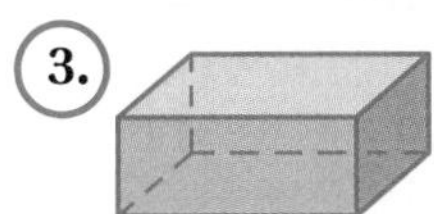

4.  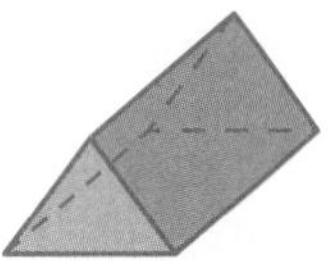

5. 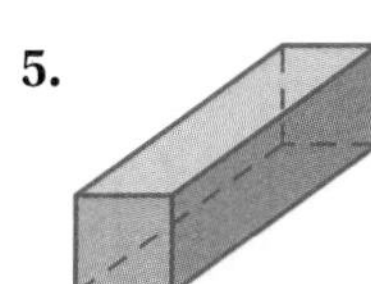

USING NETS **Draw a net. Then use the net to find the surface area.**

SEE EXAMPLE 2 on p. 543 for Exs. 6–8

6. 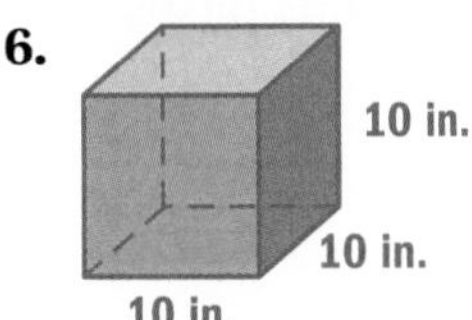

7. 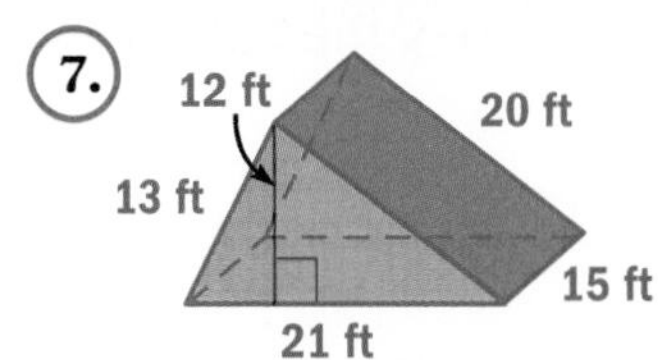

8. 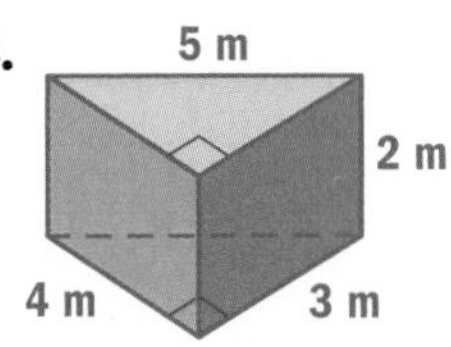

USING FORMULAS **Find the surface area of the prism given *B*, *P*, and *h*.**

SEE EXAMPLE 3 on p. 543 for Exs. 9–13

9. $B = 4 \text{ in.}^2$, $P = 8$ in., $h = 5$ in.

10. $B = 20 \text{ cm}^2$, $P = 12$ cm, $h = 3$ cm

11. $B = 45 \text{ yd}^2$, $P = 30$ yd, $h = 2.8$ yd

12. $B = 19.3 \text{ m}^2$, $P = 16$ m, $h = 0.5$ m

13. ★ **MULTIPLE CHOICE** What is the surface area of a rectangular prism that is 3 feet long, 2 feet wide, and 9 feet high?

Ⓐ 14 ft^2 Ⓑ 54 ft^2 Ⓒ 61 ft^2 Ⓓ 102 ft^2

SURFACE AREA OF CYLINDERS **Draw a net. Then use the net to find the surface area of the cylinder. Round to the nearest tenth.**

SEE EXAMPLE 4 on p. 544 for Exs. 14–16

14. 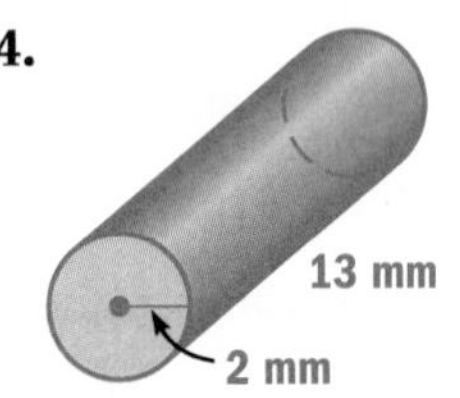

15. 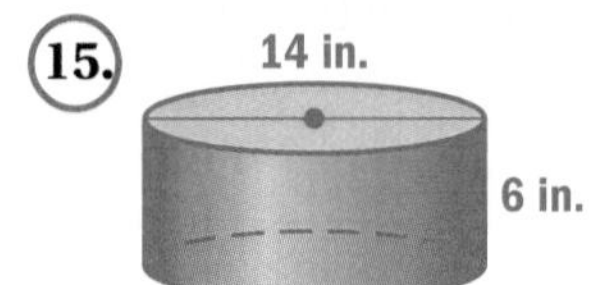

16. 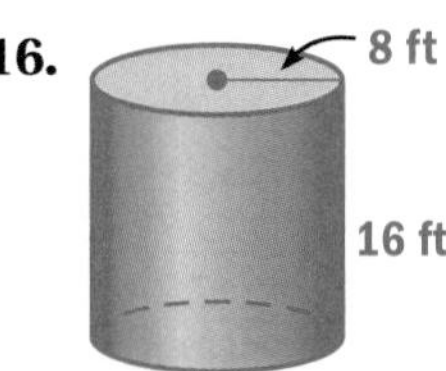

SKETCHING CYLINDERS **Sketch a cylinder with radius *r* and height *h*. Then find its surface area and lateral surface area. Round to the nearest tenth.**

SEE EXAMPLE 5 on p. 545 for Exs. 17–19

17. $r = 6$ m, $h = 2$ m

18. $r = 1$ ft, $h = 7$ ft

19. $r = 10$ cm, $h = 20$ cm

20. **INTERPRETING NETS** Find the area of the net shown. Will the net form a closed figure when folded? If not, copy and complete the net so it will form a closed figure.

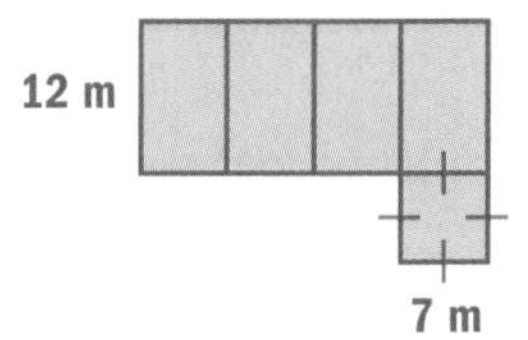

LATERAL SURFACE AREA **Find the lateral surface area of the prism given *B*, *P*, and *h*. Check that your answer is reasonable.**

21. $B = 56 \text{ ft}^2$, $P = 30$ ft, $h = 5$ ft

22. $B = 27 \text{ in.}^2$, $P = 24$ in., $h = 12$ in.

23. $B = 42 \text{ cm}^2$, $P = 34$ cm, $h = 6$ cm

24. $B = 24 \text{ m}^2$, $P = 20$ m, $h = 7$ m

25. **ERROR ANALYSIS** Describe and correct the error made in finding the lateral surface area of the cylinder.

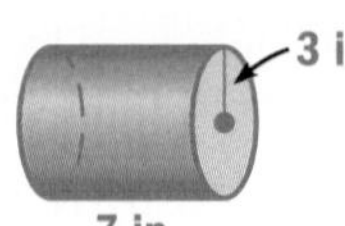

$$S = 2\pi r^2 + 2\pi rh$$
$$= 2\pi(3)^2 + 2\pi(3)(7)$$
$$\approx 188.5 \text{ in.}^2$$

26. **CHALLENGE** Draw a net of the triangular prism shown whose edge lengths are all 1 foot. *Explain* how to find the height of the triangular bases. Then find its surface area and lateral surface area. Round to the nearest tenth.

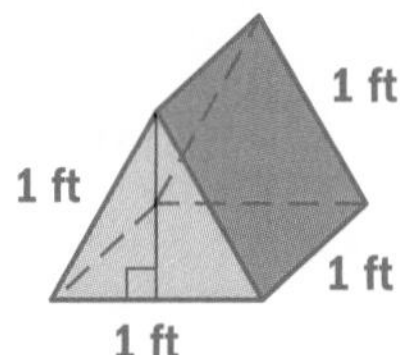

27. **CHALLENGE** The height of a cylinder is 2 feet. Its lateral surface area is $4\pi^2$ square feet. What is its radius?

PROBLEM SOLVING

28. ★ **OPEN-ENDED MATH** Draw a net of a cylindrical object at home or at school. Find the surface area of the object.

SEE EXAMPLE 4 on p. 544 for Ex. 29

29. **CRYSTAL BRIDGE** At the Myriad Botanical Gardens in Oklahoma City, a tropical conservatory bridges a small lake. The Crystal Bridge is a cylinder 224 feet long and 70 feet in diameter. Find the surface area of the Crystal Bridge, including bases. Round to the nearest tenth.

SEE EXAMPLE 3 on p. 543 for Ex. 30

30. ★ **MULTIPLE CHOICE** A cubic package has side lengths of 2 feet. What is the least amount of wrapping paper needed to wrap the package?

   (A) 8 ft^2 (B) 16 ft^2 (C) 24 ft^2 (D) 48 ft^2

31. ★ **SHORT RESPONSE** You are dipping pieces of bread into fondue. The fondue coats the outside of the bread. Some of the pieces of bread are 1 inch cubes. Others are cylinders that are 1 inch high and 1 inch in diameter. Which uses more fondue? *Explain.*

BREAK INTO PARTS **Draw a net of the solid with the correct proportions. Then find the surface area. Round to the nearest tenth if necessary.**

32.

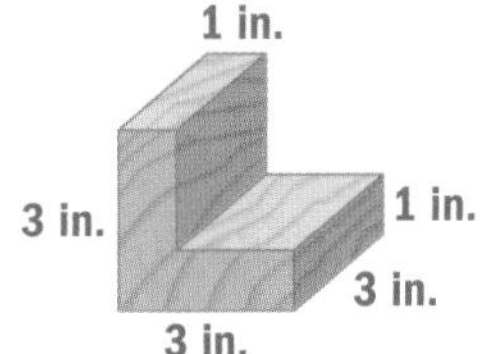

33.

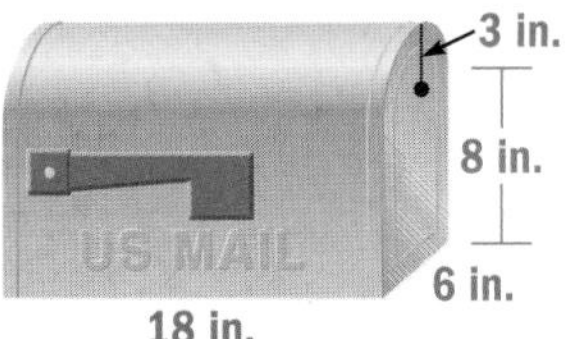

34. ★ **WRITING** *Explain* why you can multiply the perimeter of the base times the height to find the lateral surface area of a prism.

35. *xy* **ALGEBRA** Each edge of a cube has length s. Write and simplify an expression for the surface area of a cube in terms of s.

36. **CHALLENGE** Does doubling the height of a prism or cylinder result in a doubling of the surface area? of the lateral surface area? *Explain.*

MIXED REVIEW

Prepare for Lesson 10.5 in Exs. 37–40

Find the area of a circle with the given radius or diameter. Use 3.14 for π. *(p. 527)*

37. $r = 13$ in. 38. $r = 50$ cm 39. $d = 36$ ft 40. $d = 24$ m

Use a calculator to approximate the value to four decimal places. *(p. 500)*

41. sin 78° 42. tan 23° 43. cos 14° 44. sin 66°

45. ★ **MULTIPLE CHOICE** What is the area of a parallelogram with a base of 16 feet and a height of 11 feet? *(p. 521)*

   (A) 54 ft^2 (B) 88 ft^2 (C) 176 ft^2 (D) 352 ft^2

10.5 Surface Areas of Pyramids and Cones

Before You found the surface areas of prisms and cylinders.
Now You'll find the surface areas of pyramids and cones.
Why? So you can find the surface area of buildings, as the pyramid in Ex. 33.

KEY VOCABULARY
- **slant height,** *p. 548*

The height h of a pyramid is the perpendicular distance between the vertex and the base.

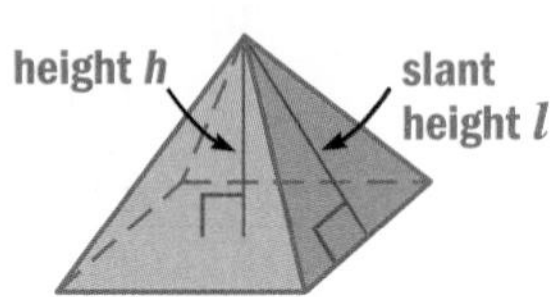

The **slant height** l of a regular pyramid is the height of a *lateral* face, that is, any face that is not the base.

TAKE NOTES
All the pyramids in this lesson are regular. For a regular pyramid, the slant height is the same on any face that is not the base.

The net for a regular pyramid has a regular polygon as the base and congruent isosceles triangles on each side of the base.

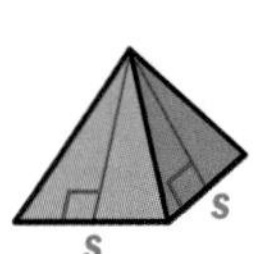

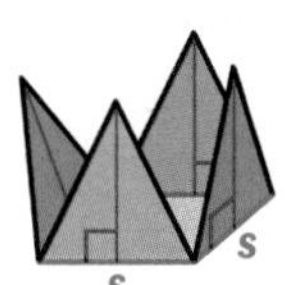

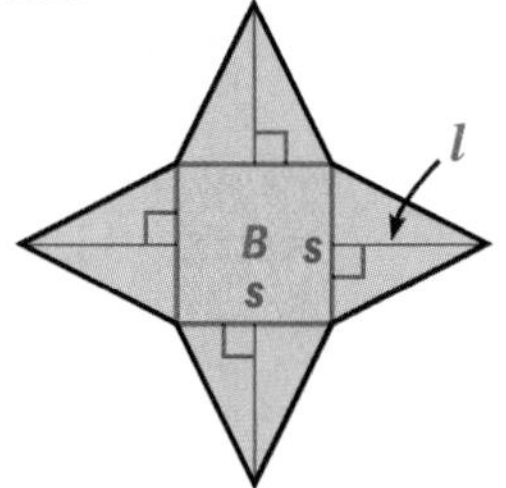

You can use the net of a pyramid to find the surface area of the pyramid.

		Base area		Area of lateral faces		
Surface area	=	Area of base	+	Number of triangles	×	Area of each triangle
	=	B	+	4	×	$\left(\frac{1}{2}sl\right)$
	=	$B + \frac{1}{2}(4s)l$				
	=	$B + \frac{1}{2}Pl$				

The product of the number of triangles and the side length of the base is the perimeter of the base.

KEY CONCEPT *For Your Notebook*

Surface Area of a Pyramid

Words The surface area of a regular pyramid is the sum of the area of the base B and one half the product of the base perimeter P and the slant height l.

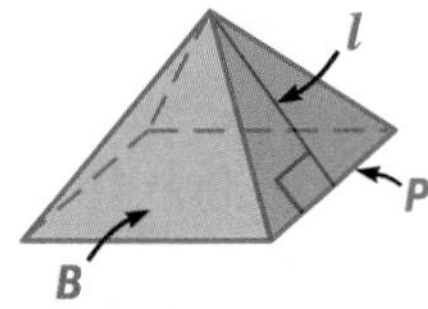

Algebra  $S = B + \frac{1}{2}Pl$

EXAMPLE 1 Finding the Surface Area of a Pyramid

Find the surface area of the regular pyramid. Round to the nearest tenth.

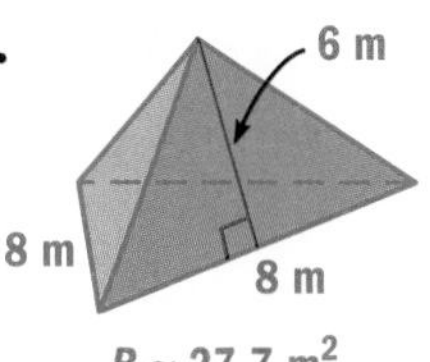

SOLUTION

STEP 1 **Find** the perimeter of the base.

$P = 8 + 8 + 8 = 24$

AVOID ERRORS
Remember to include the area of the base since the question does not ask for lateral surface area.

STEP 2 **Substitute** into the formula for surface area.

$S = B + \frac{1}{2}Pl$ — Write formula for surface area of a pyramid.

$\approx 27.7 + \frac{1}{2}(24)(6)$ — Substitute 27.7 for *B*, 24 for *P*, and 6 for *l*.

$= 99.7$ — Simplify.

▶ **Answer** The surface area is about 99.7 square meters.

✓ GUIDED PRACTICE for Example 1

Draw a net. Use it to find the surface area. Round to the nearest tenth.

1.

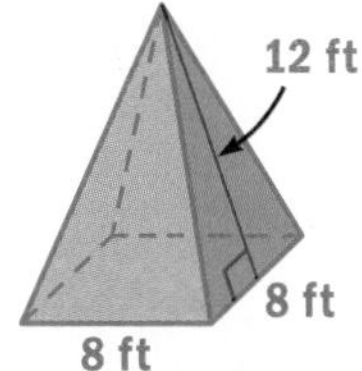

2.

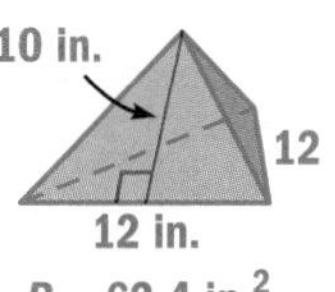

3.

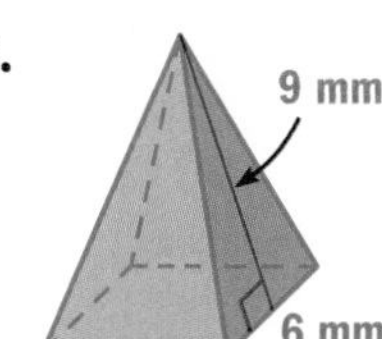

4. Find the lateral surface area of a square pyramid with a base side length of 12.5 centimeters and a slant height of 8.4 centimeters.

Cones You can use the net of a cone to find its surface area. The curved surface of a cone is a section of a circle with radius *l*, the slant height of the cone.

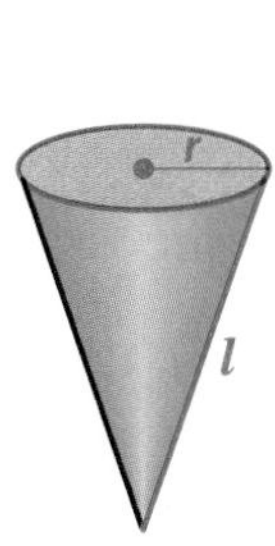

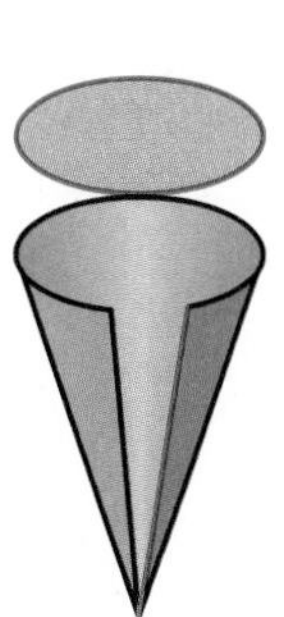

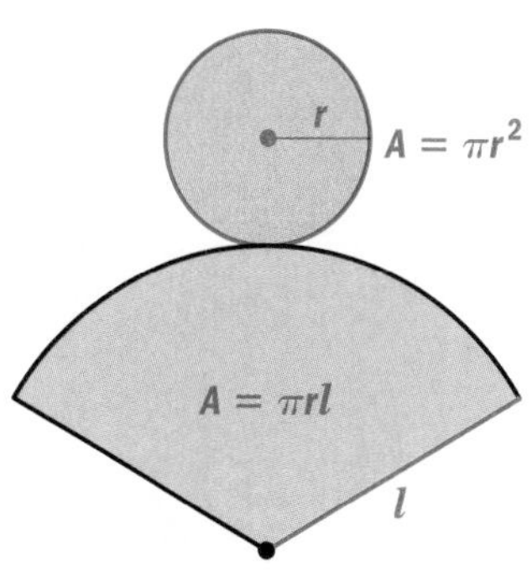

The area of the curved, lateral surface, called the *lateral surface area* of the cone, is $A = \pi rl$, where r is the radius of the base of the cone.

KEY CONCEPT — *For Your Notebook*

Surface Area of a Cone

Words The surface area of a cone is the sum of the area of the circular base with radius r and the product of pi, the radius r of the base, and the slant height l.

Algebra $S = \pi r^2 + \pi rl$

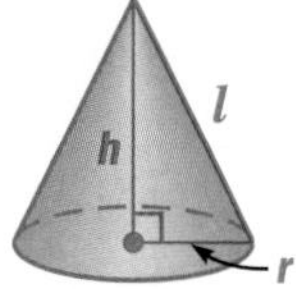

EXAMPLE 2 Finding the Surface Area of a Cone

Find the surface area of a cone with radius 4 m and slant height 9 m.

$S = \pi r^2 + \pi rl$	**Write formula for surface area of a cone.**
$= \pi(4)^2 + \pi(4)(9)$	**Substitute 4 for r and 9 for l.**
≈ 163.4	**Evaluate using a calculator.**

 **Answer** The surface area is about 163.4 square meters.

✓ GUIDED PRACTICE for Example 2

5. Find the surface area and lateral surface area of a cone with radius 6 meters and slant height 12 meters. Round to the nearest tenth.

10.5 EXERCISES

HOMEWORK KEY

★ = **STANDARDIZED TEST PRACTICE** Exs. 8, 24, 25, 33, and 38

○ = **HINTS AND HOMEWORK HELP** for Exs. 3, 5, 9, 11, 23 at classzone.com

SKILL PRACTICE

1. **VOCABULARY** Draw a square pyramid. Label h, l, and B.

NETS AND SURFACE AREA Sketch a net of the solid. Then find the surface area. Round to the nearest tenth if necessary.

SEE EXAMPLE 1 on p. 549 for Exs. 2–4

2. 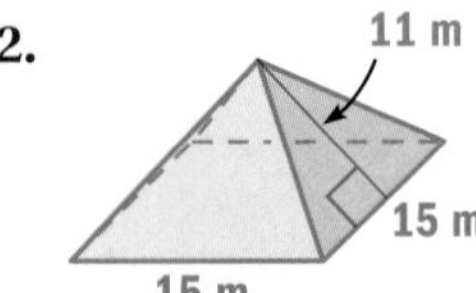

3. 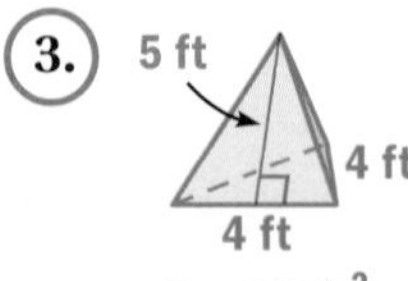

4. 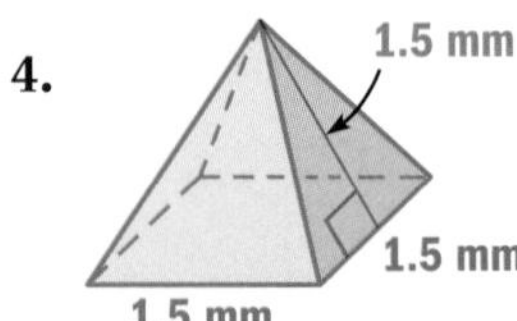

SEE EXAMPLE 2 on p. 550 for Exs. 5–7

5. 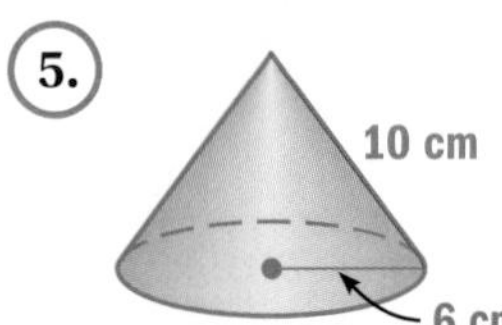

6. 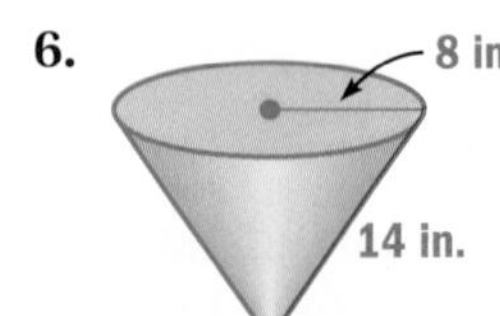

7. 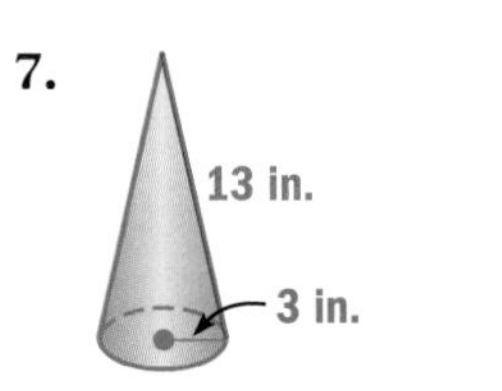

SEE EXAMPLES 1 AND 2 on pp. 549–550 for Exs. 8–13

8. ★ **MULTIPLE CHOICE** What is the surface area of a square pyramid with a base side length of 7 meters and a slant height of 5 meters?

Ⓐ 70 m^2 Ⓑ 95 m^2 Ⓒ 119 m^2 Ⓓ 150.5 m^2

FINDING SURFACE AREA Find the surface area of the square pyramid with base side length *s* and slant height *l*, or of the cone with radius *r* and slant height *l*. Round to the nearest tenth if necessary.

9. $s = 5$ cm, $l = 4.2$ cm
10. $s = 15$ yd, $l = 10$ yd
11. $r = 12$ m, $l = 6.5$ m
12. $r = 4$ mm, $l = 5.5$ mm

13. **ERROR ANALYSIS** Describe and correct the error made in finding the surface area of the solid.

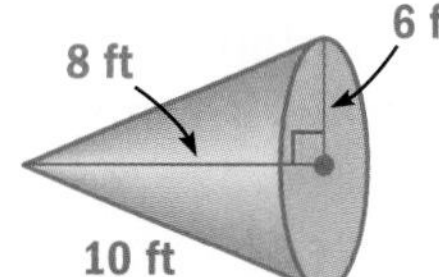

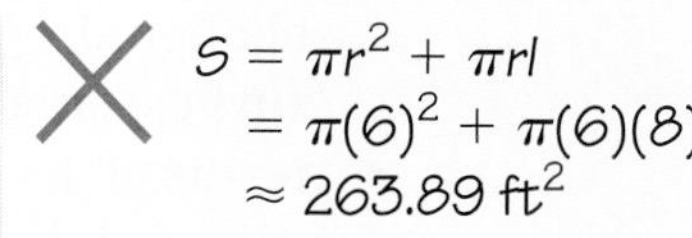

REASONING *Explain* how to find the slant height of the solid. Then find it and calculate the surface area. Round to the nearest tenth if necessary.

14.

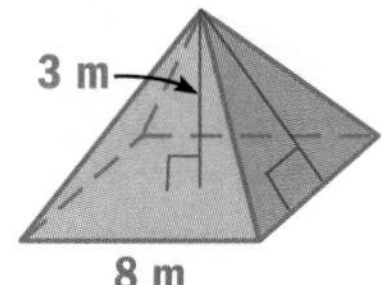

15.

16.

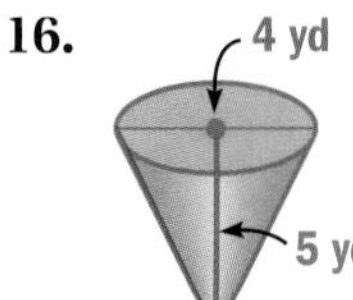

SPHERES The surface area *S* of a sphere is $S = 4\pi r^2$ where *r* is the radius of the sphere. Find the surface area of the sphere. Round to the nearest tenth.

17.

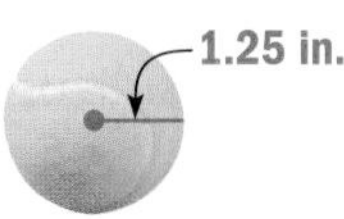

18.

19.

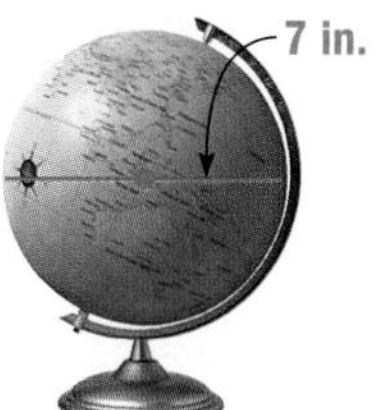

CHALLENGE The surface area *S*, base side length *b*, and slant height *l* of a square pyramid are given. Find the value of *x*.

20. $S = 555 \text{ m}^2$, $b = 15$ m, $l = (2x + 1)$ m
21. $S = 460 \text{ cm}^2$, $b = 10$ cm, $l = (3x - 3)$ cm
22. $S = 125.6 \text{ in.}^2$, $b = 5$ in., $l = (x + 2)$ in.

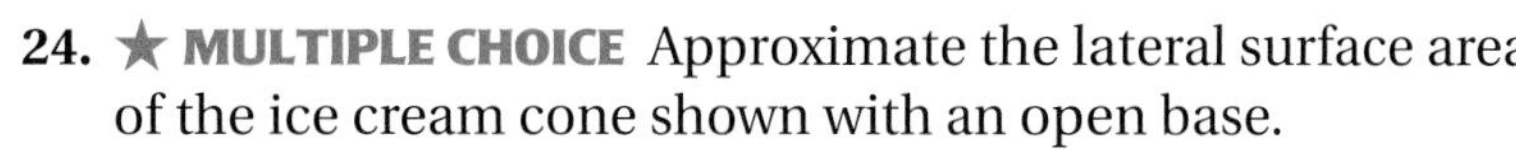

PROBLEM SOLVING

SEE EXAMPLES 1 AND 2 on pp. 549–550 for Exs. 23–24

23. **SET DESIGN** Your school needs a square pyramid with a base for a play. Each side of the base will have a length of 10 feet. The slant height will be 15 feet. How many square feet of material are needed to build this pyramid?

24. ★ **MULTIPLE CHOICE** Approximate the lateral surface area of the ice cream cone shown with an open base.

Ⓐ 13.4 in.^2 Ⓑ 16.5 in.^2

Ⓒ 26.7 in.^2 Ⓓ 39.3 in.^2

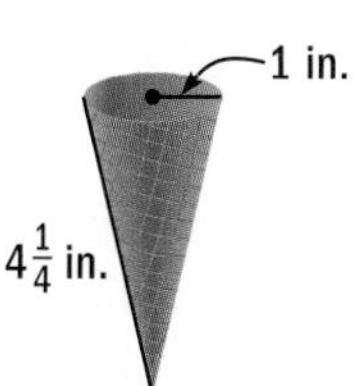

25. ★ **WRITING** *Describe* the difference between the *slant height* and the *height* of a pyramid and of a cone.

SEE EXAMPLE 2 on p. 550 for Exs. 26–30

26. **MULTI-STEP PROBLEM** Pablo makes a paper cone with no base. It has a radius of 4 inches and a slant height of 7 inches.
    a. What is the surface area of Pablo's cone? Round to the nearest tenth.
    b. Monica makes a larger cone that has a radius and slant height that are twice the lengths of those on Pablo's cone. *Compare* the surface area of Monica's cone to that of Pablo's cone.

ICICLES Icicles are shaped like cones. As they melt, icicles change size but stay similar in shape. Find the lateral surface area of an icicle with the given dimensions in terms of π.

27. $r = 1$ in., $l = 6$ in.

28. $r = 2$ in., $l = 12$ in.

29. $r = 3$ in., $l = 18$ in.

30. $r = 4$ in., $l = 24$ in.

31. **LOOK FOR A PATTERN** *Describe* the pattern developed in Exercises 27–30. Then predict the surface area of an icicle with a radius of 5 inches and a slant height of 30 inches.

32. **NUMBER SENSE** Predict which solid has a greater surface area: a *square pyramid* with a slant height of 12 units and a base side length of 10 units or a *cone* with a slant height of 12 units and a diameter of 10 units. *Explain* your reasoning. Then check your answer.

33. ★ **SHORT RESPONSE** The Rainforest Pyramid in Galveston Island, Texas, is a square pyramid with a height of 100 feet. Each side of its base measures 200 feet. *Explain* how to find the slant height. Then find the slant height and the lateral surface area of the pyramid.

34. **CHALLENGE** Find the surface area of the regular hexagonal pyramid shown. In the diagram of its base, all the triangles are equilateral and congruent. *Explain* how you found your answer.

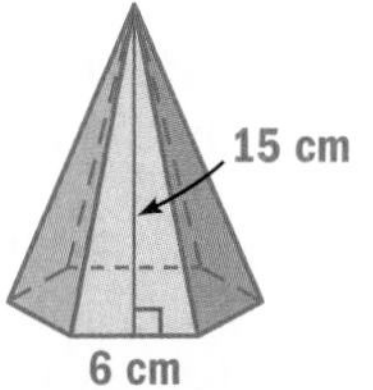

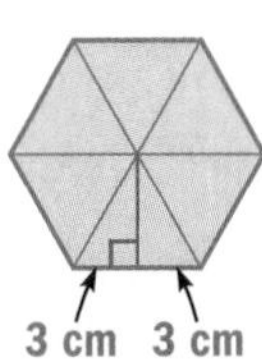

MIXED REVIEW

Get-Ready

Prepare for Lesson 10.6 in Exs. 35–37

Find the surface area of the solid. Round to the nearest tenth. *(p. 542)*

35.

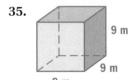

36.
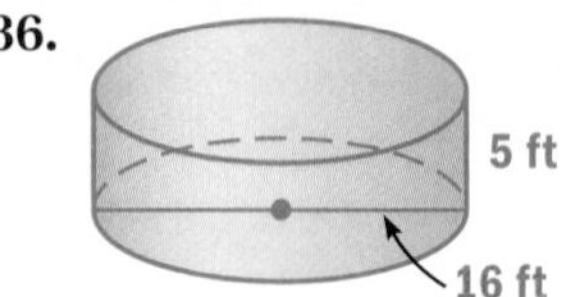

37.
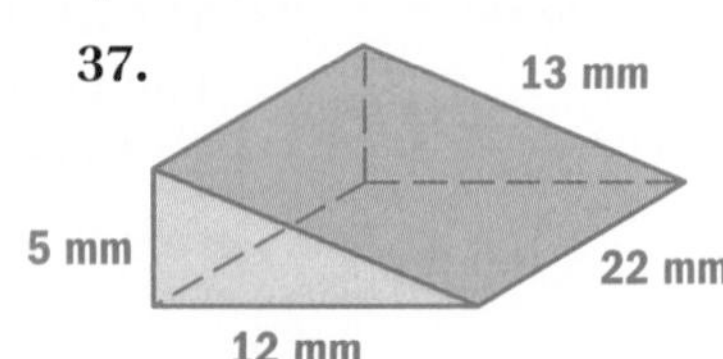

38. ★ **SHORT RESPONSE** Sketch and classify a solid that has a total of 5 faces: one rectangular face and four triangular faces. Is there more than one possible type of solid? *Explain.* *(p. 534)*

INVESTIGATION

Use before Lesson 10.6

GOAL
Find the volume of a rectangular prism.

MATERIALS
• sugar cubes

10.6 Exploring Volume

The *volume* of a solid is a measure of how much space it occupies. Volume is measured in cubic units. One cubic unit is the amount of space occupied by a cube that measures one unit on each side. This cube is called the *unit cube.*

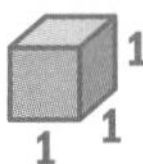

EXPLORE **Find the volume of the rectangular prism.**

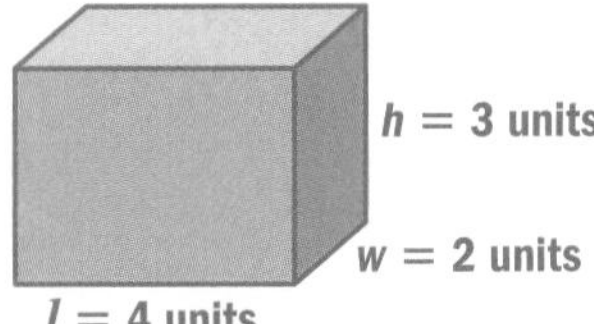

To find the volume of the prism shown, first build the prism using sugar cubes to represent unit cubes. Then count the number of cubes you used.

STEP 1

It takes 2 rows of 4 cubes, or 8 cubes, to make the bottom of the prism.

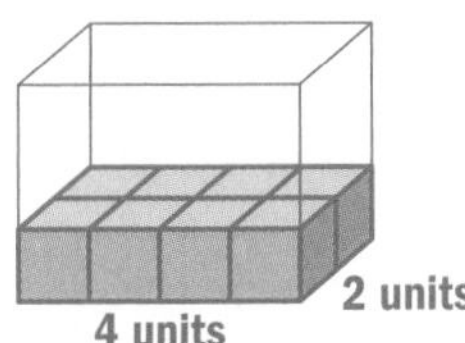

STEP 2

It takes 3 layers of 8 cubes, or 24 cubes, to make the prism the right height.

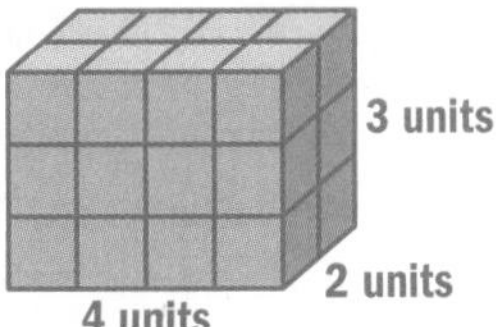

STEP 3 Because each cube is 1 cubic unit, the prism's volume is 24 cubic units.

PRACTICE **Use cubes to model the volume of rectangular prisms.**

1. Copy and complete the table to find the volume of the rectangular prism with the given dimensions.

Dimensions of the prism	*Cubes to cover the bottom of the prism*	*Layers of cubes to make the prism*	*Volume of the prism*
$4 \times 2 \times 3$	8	3	24
$6 \times 1 \times 2$	?	?	?
$7 \times 5 \times 3$	?	?	?
$4 \times 2 \times 8$	?	?	?

DRAW CONCLUSIONS

2. **REASONING** Write a formula for the area B of the base of a rectangular prism. Then write a formula for the volume of the prism.

10.6 Volumes of Prisms and Cylinders

Before	You found the surface areas of prisms and cylinders.
Now	You'll find the volumes of prisms and cylinders.
Why?	So you can compare capacities, as in Example 3.

KEY VOCABULARY

- **volume,** *p. 554*

Recycling Residents of a community can choose between two recycling bins. Which recycling bin holds more? You will find the answer in Example 3 by comparing the *volumes* of the containers.

The **volume** of a solid is a measure of the amount of space it occupies. Volume is measured in *cubic units*. One cubic unit is the amount of space occupied by a cube that measures one unit on each side.

KEY CONCEPT — *For Your Notebook*

Volume of a Prism

Words The volume of a prism is the product of the area of the base B and the height h.

h

B

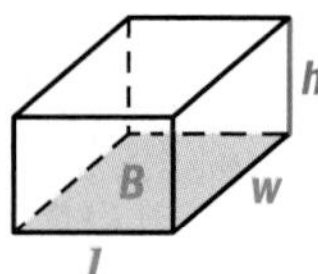

Algebra $V = Bh$

EXAMPLE 1 Finding Volumes of Prisms

Find the volume of the prism.

a.

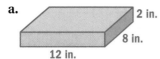

2 in.

8 in.

12 in.

Base is a rectangle with area lw.

$V = Bh$

$= lwh$

$= 12(8)(2)$

$= 192$

▶ **Answer** The volume is 192 cubic inches.

b.

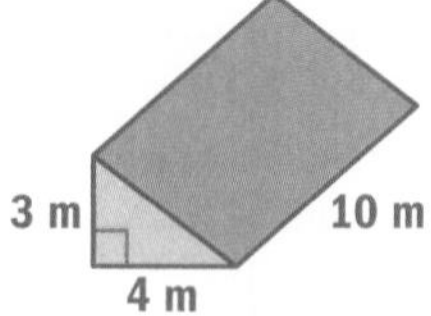

Base is a triangle with area $\frac{1}{2}bh$.

$V = Bh$

$= \frac{1}{2}(4)(3)(10)$

$= 60$

▶ **Answer** The volume is 60 cubic meters.

AVOID ERRORS

When you find the volume of a triangular prism, be careful not to confuse the height of the prism with the height of the triangular base. In part (b) of Example 1, $h = 10$.

Animated Math at classzone.com

Volumes of Cylinders As you discovered in the Investigation on p. 553, the volume of a prism can be calculated by finding the number of square units in the base and multiplying by the height. The formula for the volume of a cylinder is similar to the formula for the volume of a prism.

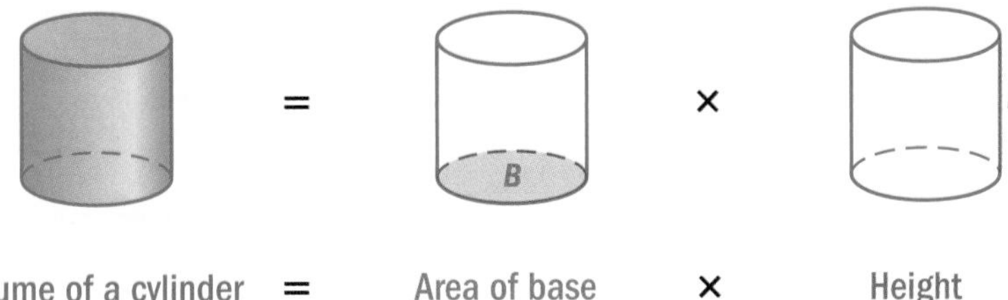

REVIEW CYLINDERS
Remember, the base of the cylinder is a circle. So its area is πr^2.

Volume of a cylinder = Area of base × Height

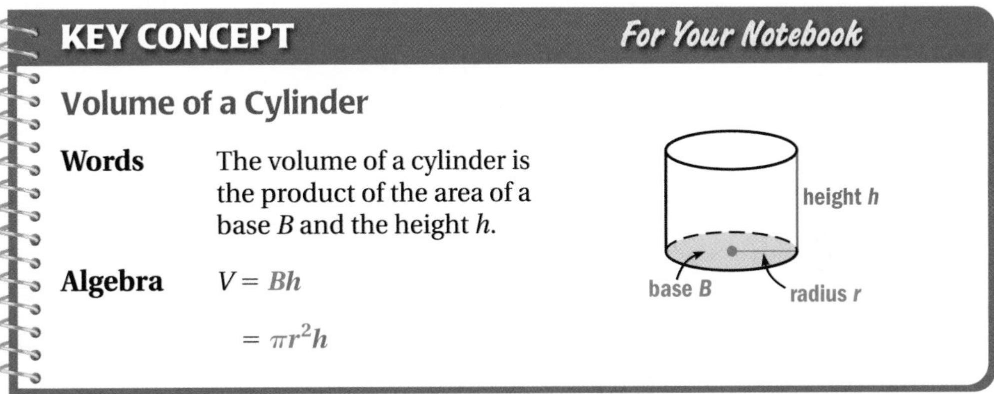

KEY CONCEPT *For Your Notebook*

Volume of a Cylinder

Words The volume of a cylinder is the product of the area of a base B and the height h.

Algebra $V = Bh$

$= \pi r^2 h$

EXAMPLE 2 Finding the Volume of a Cylinder

Find the volume of the cylinder.

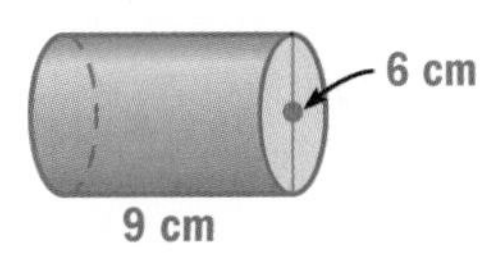

SOLUTION

The radius is one half the diameter, so $r = 3$ cm.

$V = Bh$	**Write formula for volume.**
$= \pi r^2 h$	**Write formula for volume of a cylinder.**
$= \pi(3)^2(9)$	**Substitute 3 for *r* and 9 for *h*.**
$= 81\pi$	**Simplify.**
≈ 254.469	**Evaluate using a calculator.**

▶ **Answer** The volume is about 254 cubic centimeters.

✓ **GUIDED PRACTICE** for Examples 1 and 2

Find the volume of the solid. Round to the nearest tenth if necessary.

1.
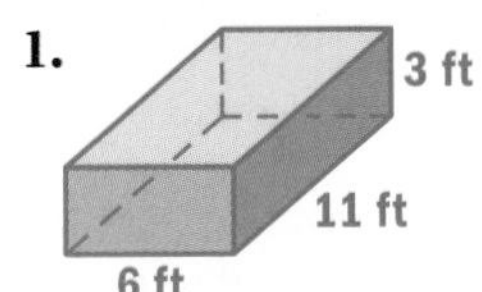

2.
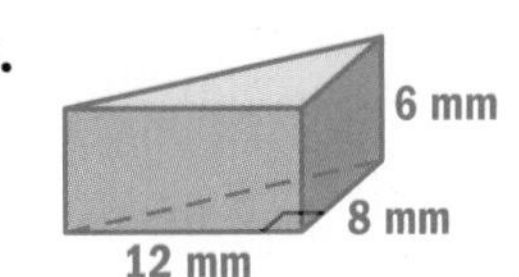

3.
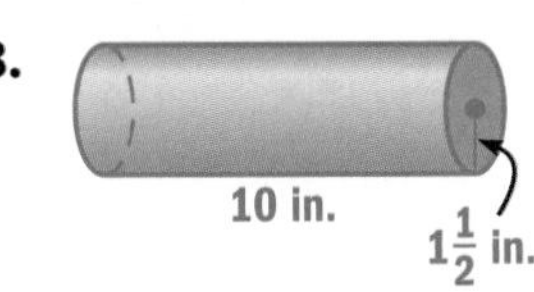

EXAMPLE 3 Comparing Capacities

Recycling To decide which recycling bin shown on page 554 can hold more, find the volume of each bin.

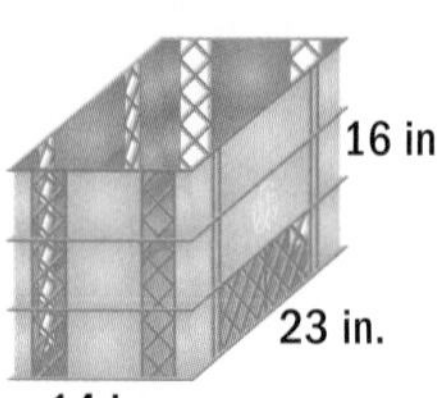

9 in.

23 in.

READING
When the abbreviation for a unit of measure has an exponent of 3, you read the 3 as "cubic."
ft^3 means "cubic feet"
m^3 means "cubic meters"

$V = Bh$
$= lwh$
$= 23(14)(16)$
$= 5152 \text{ in.}^3$

$V = Bh$
$= \pi r^2 h$
$= \pi(9)^2(23)$
$\approx 5852.8 \text{ in.}^3$

▶**Answer** The cylindrical recycling bin holds more.

Similar Solids As with polygons, two solids are similar if they have the same shape but not necessarily the same size. The corresponding linear measures of similar solids are proportional.

EXAMPLE 4 Standardized Test Practice

The dimensions of a prism are shown below. A *similar prism* can be produced by multiplying each dimension by the same factor. What happens to the volume when the dimensions are doubled?

ELIMINATE CHOICES
Because doubling the linear dimensions of the prism will increase its size, its volume will also increase. You can eliminate choice A.

Ⓐ The volume is cut in half.

Ⓑ The volume is multiplied by 2.

Ⓒ The volume is multiplied by 4.

Ⓓ The volume is multiplied by 8.

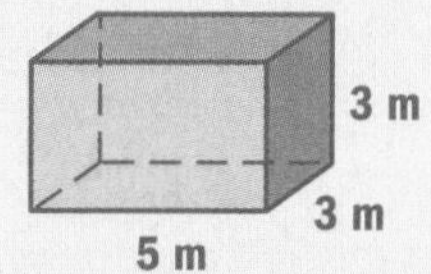

SOLUTION

STEP 1 **Find** the volume of the original prism.

$V = Bh$
$= (5 \cdot 3)(3)$
$= 45 \text{ m}^3$

STEP 2 **Find** the volume of the similar prism

$V = Bh$
$= [(5 \cdot 2) \cdot (3 \cdot 2)](3 \cdot 2)$
$= 360 \text{ m}^3$

STEP 3 **Compare** the volumes: $\frac{360 \text{ m}^3}{45 \text{ m}^3} = 8$.

▶**Answer** When the dimensions are doubled, the volume is multiplied by 8. The correct answer is D. Ⓐ Ⓑ Ⓒ Ⓓ

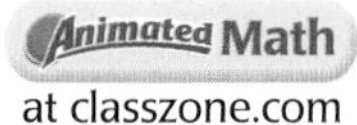

at classzone.com

✓ GUIDED PRACTICE for Examples 3 and 4

4. Which solid has the greater volume? *Explain* your answer.

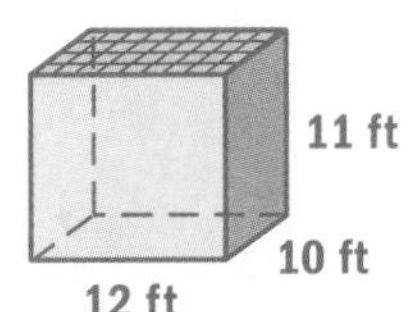

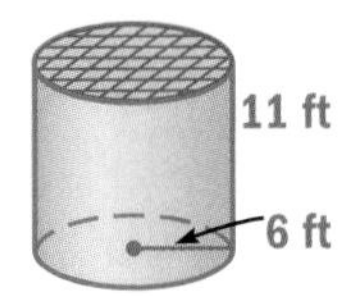

5. **What If?** Suppose the dimensions of the original prism in Example 4 were tripled. What would happen to its volume?

10.6 EXERCISES

HOMEWORK KEY

★ = **STANDARDIZED TEST PRACTICE** Exs. 26, 32, 34, 36, 37, and 44

○ = **HINTS AND HOMEWORK HELP** for Exs. 3, 7, 15, 17, 33 at classzone.com

SKILL PRACTICE

1. **VOCABULARY** *Explain* the difference between surface area and volume.

2. **VOCABULARY** Copy and complete: The volume of a prism or cylinder is the area of the _?_ times the _?_.

PRISMS **Find the volume of the rectangular prism with length l, width w, and height h.**

SEE EXAMPLE 1 on p. 554 for Exs. 3–6

3. $l = 6$ m, $w = 2$ m, $h = 11$ m
4. $l = 7$ in., $w = 7$ in., $h = 7$ in.
5. $l = 3.8$ cm, $w = 3$ cm, $h = 1.2$ cm
6. $l = 16$ ft, $w = 3$ ft, $h = 2\frac{1}{2}$ ft

VOLUMES OF CYLINDERS **Find the volume of the cylinder with radius r and height h. Round to the nearest tenth.**

SEE EXAMPLE 2 on p. 555 for Exs. 7–12

7. $r = 4$ ft, $h = 11$ ft
8. $r = 3$ cm, $h = 9$ cm
9. $r = 1.2$ m, $h = 4.5$ m
10. $r = 6.4$ in., $h = 12$ in.
11. $r = 7$ m, $h = 15$ m
12. $r = 8.3$ yd, $h = 1.6$ yd

FINDING VOLUMES **Find the volume of the solid. Round to the nearest tenth.**

SEE EXAMPLES 1 AND 2 on pp. 554–555 for Exs. 13–19

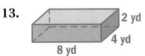

13. 2 yd, 4 yd, 8 yd

14. 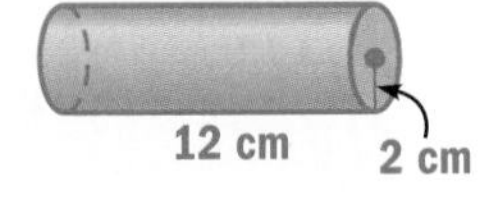

15. 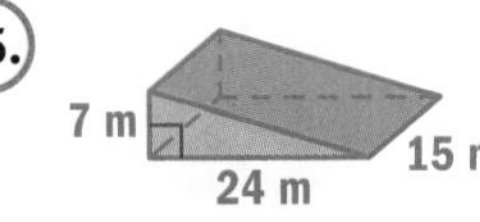

16. 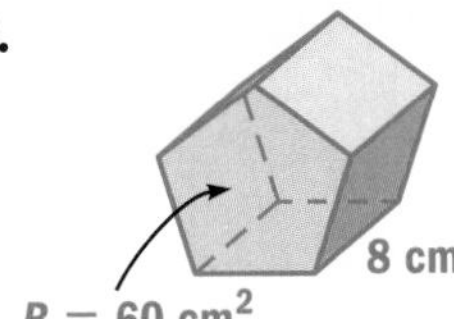

17. 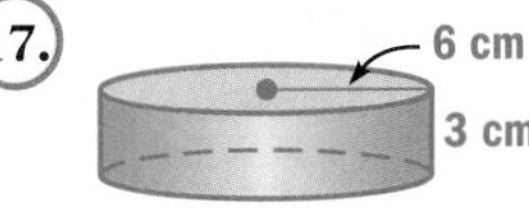

18. 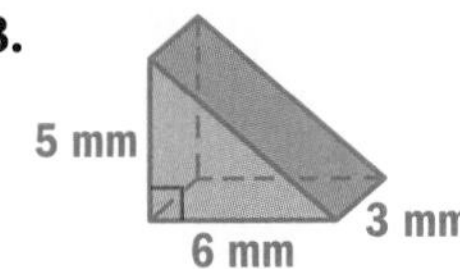

19. **ERROR ANALYSIS** Describe and correct the error in finding the volume of the cylinder.

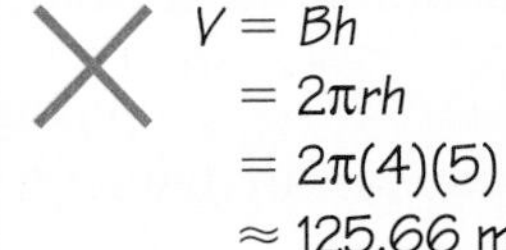

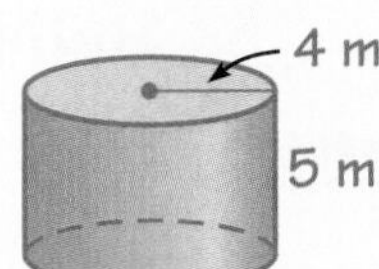

FINDING VOLUME **Find the volume of the solid. Round to the nearest tenth. Give your answer in the smaller units.**

20.

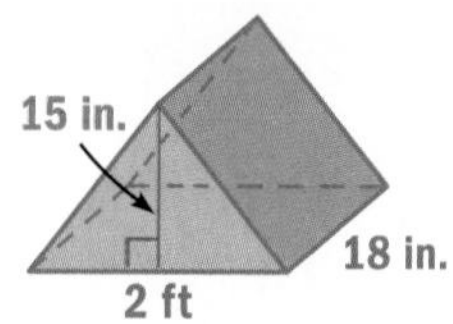

21.

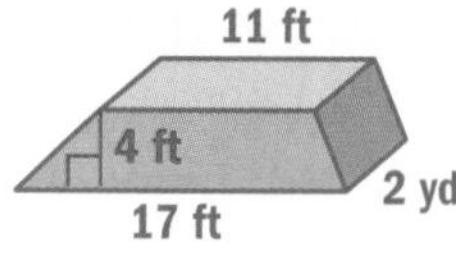

22.

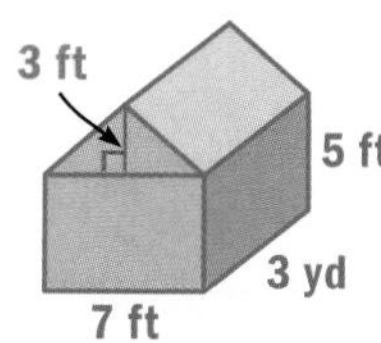

SIMILAR SOLIDS **Solid A is similar to solid B. Find the unknown height. Then find the volumes of the solids. How are they related?**

SEE EXAMPLE 4 on p. 556 for Exs. 23–25

23. Solid A Solid B

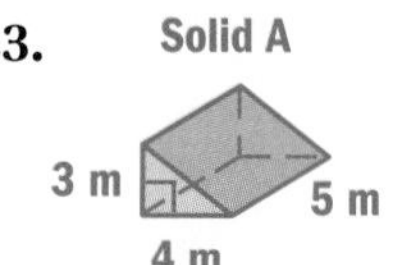

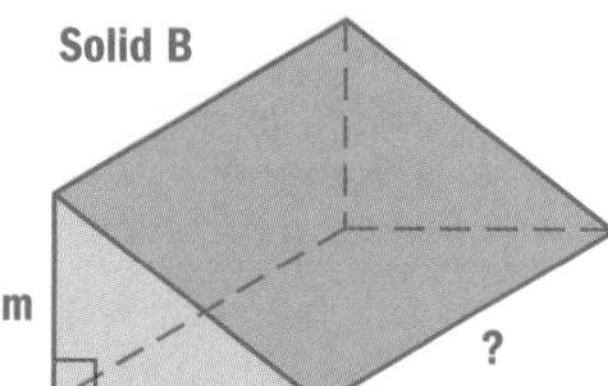

24. Solid A Solid B

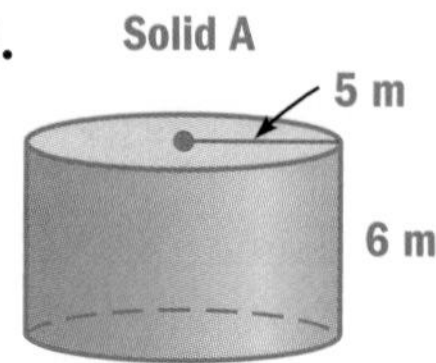

2.5 m

?

25. **NUMBER SENSE** Which has a greater effect on the volume of a cylinder: *doubling the height* or *doubling the radius*? Which has a greater effect on the volume of a rectangular prism that is longer than it is wide: *doubling the length* or *doubling the width*? *Explain.*

26. ★ **MULTIPLE CHOICE** The volume of a solid is 6 cubic yards. What is the volume of the solid in cubic feet?

Ⓐ 2 ft^3 Ⓑ 18 ft^3 Ⓒ 54 ft^3 Ⓓ 162 ft^3

CHALLENGE **Find the volume. Round to the nearest tenth if necessary.**

27.

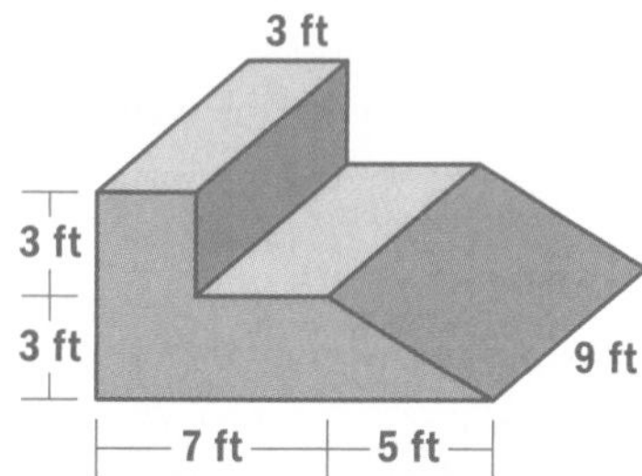

28.

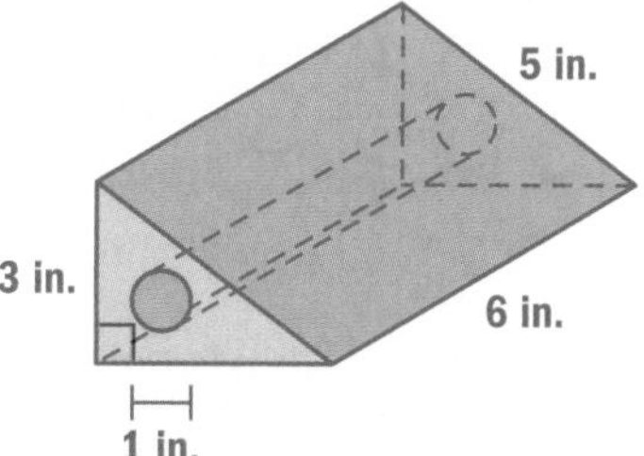

PROBLEM SOLVING

REASONING **In Exercises 29–31, tell whether you would need to calculate *surface area* or *volume* to find the quantity.**

29. The amount of wrapping paper needed to wrap a gift

30. The amount of cereal that will fit in a box

31. The amount of water needed to fill a watering can

SEE EXAMPLE 2 on p. 555 for Ex. 32

32. ★ **MULTIPLE CHOICE** A paint can is a cylinder 19 centimeters tall and 16 centimeters in diameter. What is the volume of the paint can?

Ⓐ 955 cm^3 Ⓑ 3820 cm^3 Ⓒ 4536 cm^3 Ⓓ $15{,}281 \text{ cm}^3$

SEE EXAMPLE 3 on p. 556 for Exs. 33–35

33. **SWIMMING POOLS** A rectangular in-ground pool is 40 feet long, 16 feet wide, and 4 feet deep. A cylindrical above-ground pool is 6 feet deep and has a radius of 12 feet. Which pool holds more water? About how much more? *Explain.*

34. ★ **SHORT RESPONSE** Find the volume of each eraser to the nearest tenth. How many pencil-top erasers would you use in the time it takes you to completely use the larger eraser? *Explain* your answer.

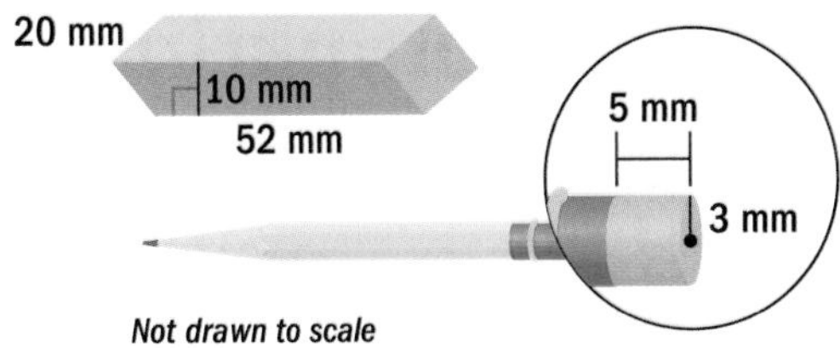

35. **SALT SHAKERS** You buy a cylindrical box of salt that has a diameter of 4 inches and a height of 6 inches. Your salt shaker is a rectangular prism that is $1\frac{1}{2}$ inches by $1\frac{1}{2}$ inches by 3 inches. Estimate how many times the salt in the box can fill the salt shaker.

36. ★ **WRITING** Two prisms have different surface areas. Can they have the same volume? *Explain.*

37. ★ **EXTENDED RESPONSE** Use the cylinder at the right.

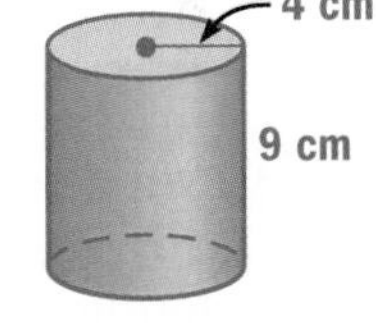

a. What is the effect of tripling the radius on the surface area and volume of the cylinder?

b. What is the effect of tripling the height on the surface area and volume of the cylinder?

c. What is the effect of tripling *both* the height and the radius on the surface area and volume of the cylinder?

38. **CHALLENGE** Find the surface area S and volume V of the cube at the right. Give the dimensions of another prism with a square base such that the ratio of the surface area to S is equal to the ratio of the volume to V.

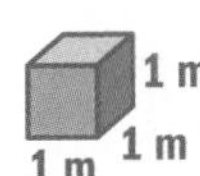

MIXED REVIEW

Get-Ready Prepare for Lesson 10.7 in Exs. 39–41

Find the surface area of the solid to the nearest tenth. *(p. 548)*

39.

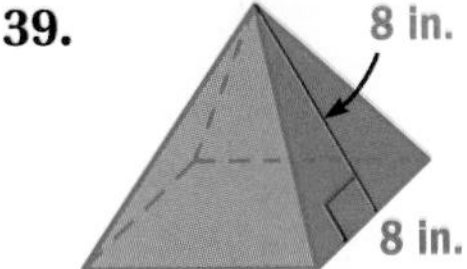

40.

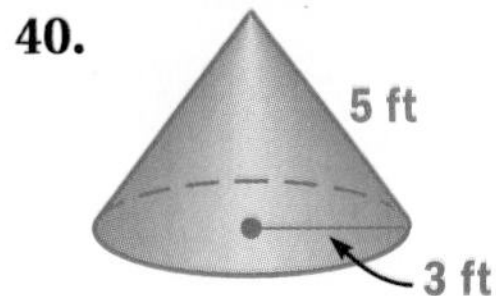

41.

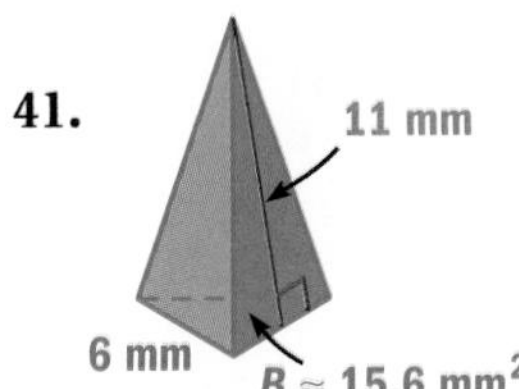

Let a and b represent the lengths of the legs of a right triangle and let c represent the length of the hypotenuse. Find the unknown length. *(p. 482)*

42. $a = 15, b = ?, c = 39$

43. $a = 16, b = 63, c = ?$

44. ★ **MULTIPLE CHOICE** The diameter of a nickel is about 2 centimeters. What is the approximate area of one side of the coin? Use 3.14 for π. *(p. 527)*

Ⓐ 3.14 cm^2 Ⓑ 12.56 cm^2 Ⓒ 25.12 cm^2 Ⓓ 50.24 cm^2

INVESTIGATION

Use before Lesson 10.7

GOAL

Compare the volumes of a prism and a pyramid.

MATERIALS

- tape
- scissors
- metric ruler
- thin cardboard
- popcorn kernels
- protractor

10.7 Comparing Volumes

Compare the volume of a pyramid to the volume of a prism.

EXPLORE Compare pyramids and prisms.

STEP 1 **Draw** the nets shown on cardboard. Then cut out the nets and use tape to make an open square prism and an open square pyramid.

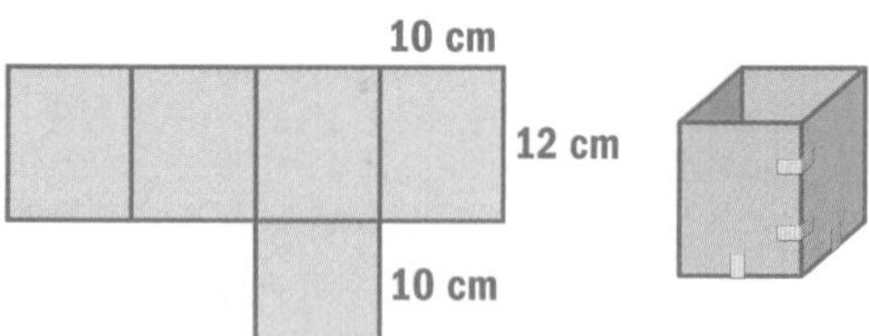

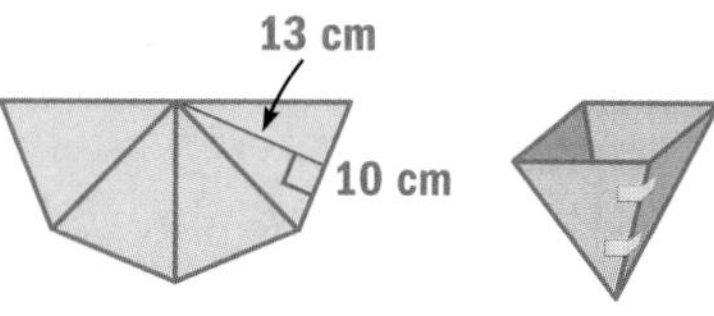

STEP 2 **Compare** the height of the prism to the height of the pyramid. Then compare the base of the prism to the base of the pyramid. What do you notice?

STEP 3 **Fill** the pyramid with popcorn kernels and pour the contents into the prism. Repeat until the prism is full. How many times did you have to empty the pyramid into the prism? Use this number to write the ratio of the volume of the pyramid to the volume of the prism.

PRACTICE Use the formula for the volume of a rectangular prism and the ratio found in the activity to find the volume of the square pyramid.

1. 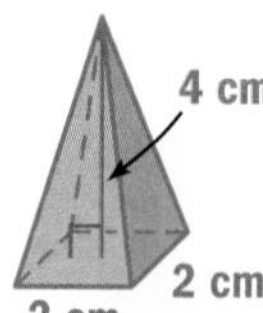

2. 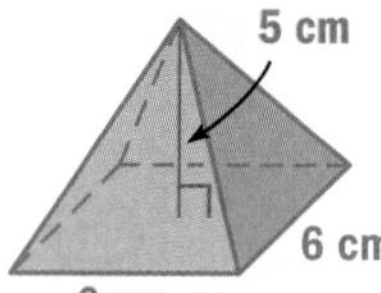

3. 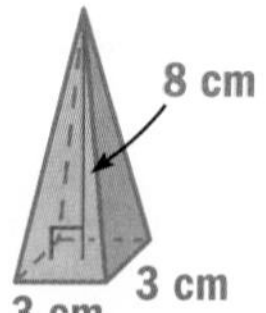

DRAW CONCLUSIONS

4. **MAKE A MODEL** Draw the nets shown on cardboard. Use the nets to make an open cylinder and an open cone. Repeat steps 2 and 3 above using the cylinder and cone.

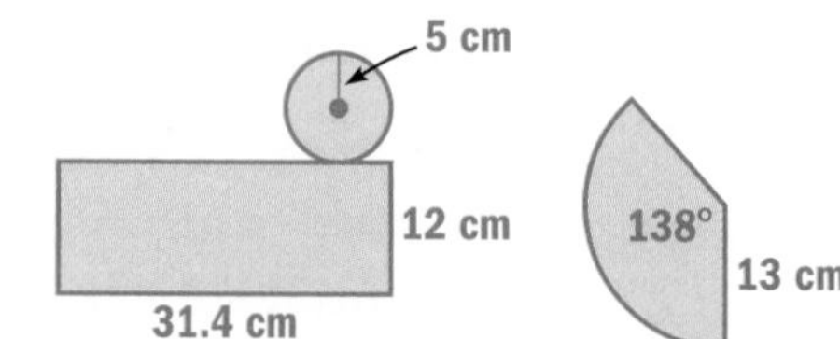

10.7 Volumes of Pyramids and Cones

Before You found the volumes of prisms and cylinders.

Now You'll find the volumes of pyramids and cones.

Why? So you can find the volume of structures, as in Example 3.

KEY VOCABULARY

- **pyramid,** *p. 534*
- **cone,** *p. 534*
- **volume,** *p. 554*

The volumes of a pyramid and a prism with the same base area and the same height are related. As you may have discovered in the Investigation on p. 560, the volume of the pyramid is exactly one third the volume of the prism.

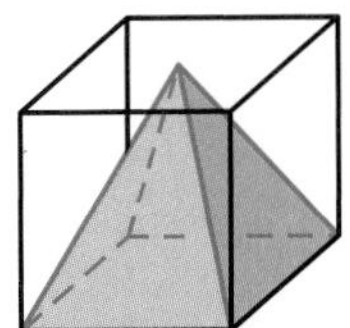

KEY CONCEPT *For Your Notebook*

Volume of a Pyramid

Words The volume V of a pyramid is one third the product of the area of the base B and the height h.

Algebra $V = \frac{1}{3}Bh$

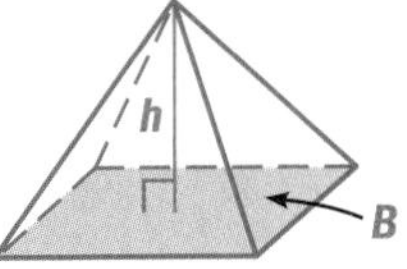

EXAMPLE 1 Finding the Volume of a Pyramid

Find the volume of the square pyramid.

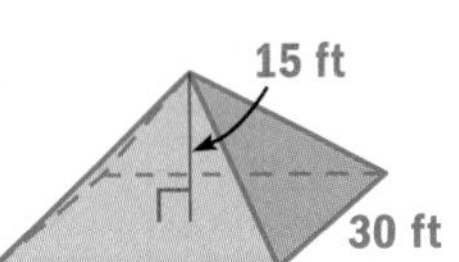

SOLUTION

CONNECT THE MODEL AND THE FORMULA
Because the base is a square, $B = s^2$.

$V = \frac{1}{3}Bh$ Write formula for volume of a pyramid.

$= \frac{1}{3}(30^2)(15)$ Substitute 30^2 for b and 15 for h.

$= 4500$ Evaluate using a calculator.

▶ **Answer** The pyramid has a volume of 4500 cubic feet.

✓ **GUIDED PRACTICE** for Example 1

Find the volume of the square pyramid with base side length s and height h.

1. $s = 4$ cm, $h = 5$ cm **2.** $s = 6$ in., $h = 15$ in. **3.** $s = 8$ mm, $h = 27$ mm

4. $s = 3$ yd, $h = 3$ yd **5.** $s = 7$ m, $h = 9$ m **6.** $s = 12$ ft, $h = 21$ ft

Notice that the volume formula for pyramids does not require that the pyramid be regular, unlike the surface area formula.

EXAMPLE 2 Finding the Volume of a Pyramid

Find the volume of the pyramid.

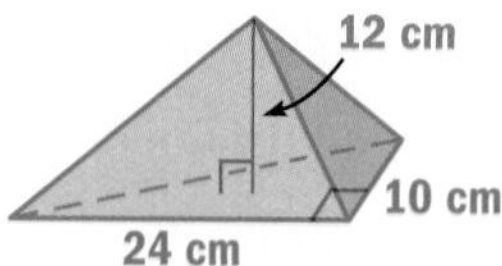

SOLUTION

$V = \frac{1}{3}Bh$ — **Write formula for volume of a pyramid.**

$= \frac{1}{3}\left(\frac{1}{2} \cdot 24 \cdot 10\right)(12)$ — **The base is a triangle, so $B = \frac{1}{2}bh$.**

$= 480$ — **Multiply.**

▸ **Answer** The pyramid has a volume of 480 cubic centimeters.

✓ GUIDED PRACTICE for Example 2

Find the volume of the pyramid given the area of the base *B* and the height *h*.

7. $B = 8 \text{ cm}^2, h = 4 \text{ cm}$
8. $B = 81 \text{ in.}^2, h = 12 \text{ in.}$
9. $B = 21 \text{ yd}^2, h = 5 \text{ yd}$

Find the area of the base and volume of the pyramid.

10. 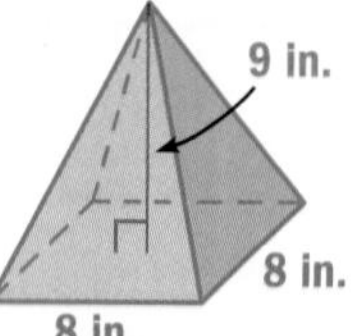

11. 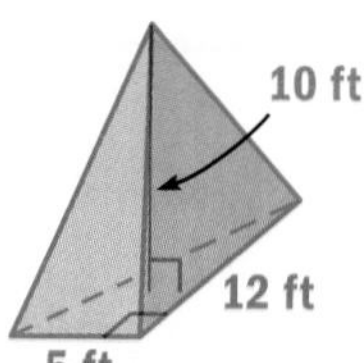

12. 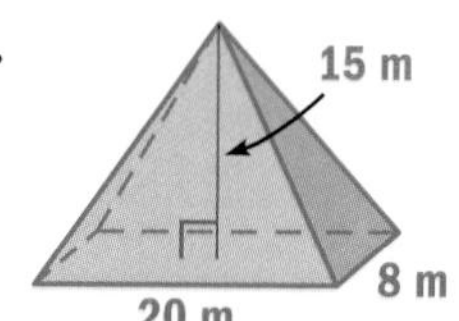

Volumes of Cones The volume of a cone is related to the volume of a cylinder in the same way the volumes of a pyramid and a prism are related. That is, the volume of a cone is one third the volume of a cylinder with the same base and height.

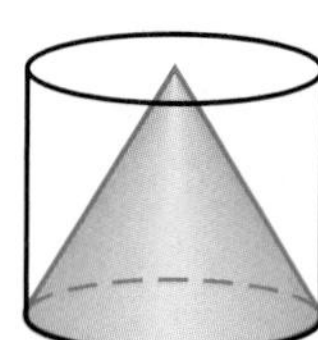

KEY CONCEPT *For Your Notebook*

Volume of a Cone

Words The volume of a cone *V* is one third the product of the area of the base *B* and the height *h*.

Algebra $V = \frac{1}{3}Bh = \frac{1}{3}\pi r^2 h$

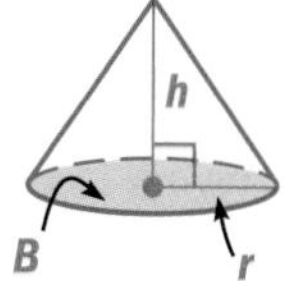

EXAMPLE 3 Finding the Volume of a Cone

Native Americans Many Native American tribes built tepees that were similar to a cone in shape. A tepee has a height of 12 feet and a base diameter of 12 feet. Approximate the volume of the tepee.

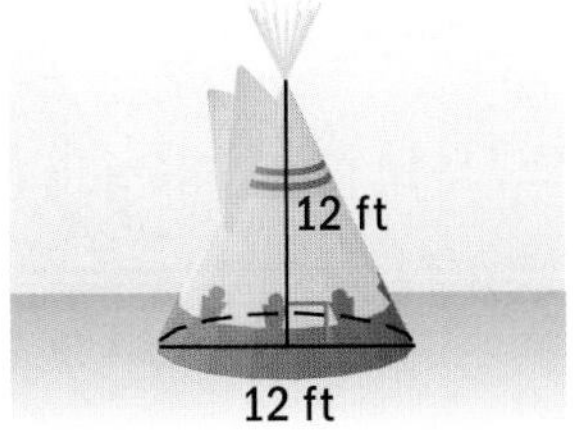

SOLUTION

The radius is one half the diameter, so $r = 6$ ft.

$V = \frac{1}{3}\pi r^2 h$	**Write formula for volume of a cone.**
$= \frac{1}{3}\pi(6)^2(12)$	**Substitute 6 for *r* and 12 for *h*.**
$= 144\pi$	**Simplify.**
≈ 452.389	**Evaluate using a calculator.**

▶ **Answer** The tepee has a volume of about 452 cubic feet.

Check Because $\frac{1}{3}\pi \approx 1$, $V \approx 36 \cdot 12 \approx 40 \cdot 10 = 400$ ft^3. The answer is reasonable.

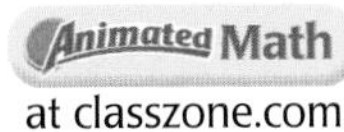

at classzone.com

GUIDED PRACTICE for Example 3

Find the volume of the cone with radius *r* and height *h*.

13. $r = 24$ m, $h = 18$ m **14.** $r = 4$ in., $h = 16$ in. **15.** $r = 15$ ft, $h = 28$ ft

10.7 EXERCISES

HOMEWORK KEY

★ = **STANDARDIZED TEST PRACTICE** Exs. 17, 39, 41, and 52

○ = **HINTS AND HOMEWORK HELP** for Exs. 5, 9, 15, 19, 39 at classzone.com

SKILL PRACTICE

VOCABULARY **Match each solid with the *best* formula for its volume.**

1. prism **2.** cylinder **3.** pyramid **4.** cone

A. $V = \frac{1}{3}Bh$ **B.** $V = \pi r^2 h$ **C.** $V = \frac{1}{3}\pi r^2 h$ **D.** $V = Bh$

VOLUME OF A PYRAMID **Find the volume of the pyramid given the area of the base *B* and the height *h*.**

SEE EXAMPLES 1 AND 2 on pp. 561–562 for Exs. 5–10

5. $B = 9$ in.^{2}, $h = 4$ in. **6.** $B = 12$ ft^2, $h = 15$ ft **7.** $B = 1.5$ m^2, $h = 0.6$ m

VOLUME OF A SQUARE PYRAMID **Find the volume of the square pyramid with base side length *s* and height *h*.**

8. $s = 15$ m, $h = 4$ m **9.** $s = 12$ yd, $h = 3$ yd **10.** $s = 6$ in., $h = \frac{1}{2}$ in.

VOLUME OF A SOLID **Find the volume of the solid. Round to the nearest tenth if necessary. Check that your answer is reasonable.**

SEE EXAMPLE 2 on p. 562 for Exs. 11–13

11.

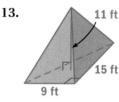

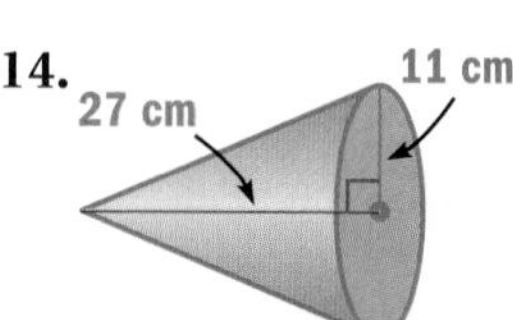

12.

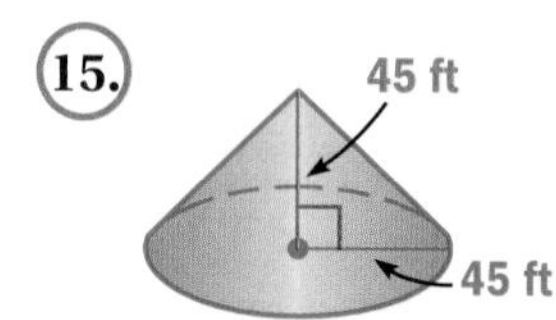

13.

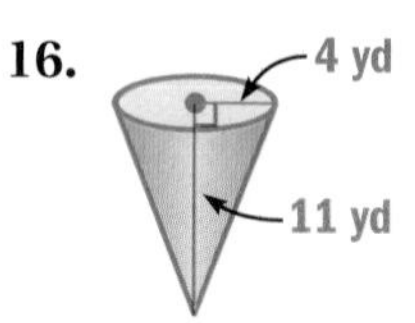

SEE EXAMPLE 3 on p. 563 for Exs. 14–23

14. 27 cm, 11 cm

15. 45 ft, 45 ft

16. 4 yd, 11 yd

17. ★ **MULTIPLE CHOICE** What is the volume of the cone?

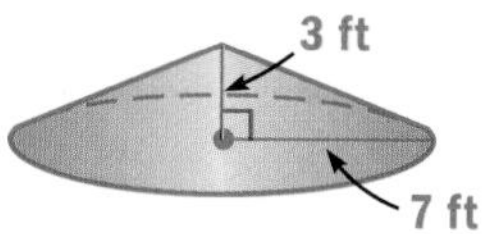

Ⓐ 10π ft^3 Ⓑ 21π ft^3

Ⓒ 49π ft^3 Ⓓ 147π ft^3

VOLUME OF A CONE **Find the volume of the cone with the given dimensions. If two units of measure are used, give your answer in the smaller units. Round to the nearest tenth.**

18. $r = 3$ in., $h = 7$ in. **19.** $r = 11$ ft, $h = 4$ ft **20.** $d = 1.2$ m, $h = 4.5$ m

21. $r = 83$ cm, $h = 2.8$ m **22.** $d = 5$ m, $h = 492$ cm **23.** $d = 3$ ft, $h = 10$ yd

VOLUME OF A PYRAMID **Find the area of the base and volume of the pyramid with the given height *h* and base shown.**

24. $h = 1.8$ cm

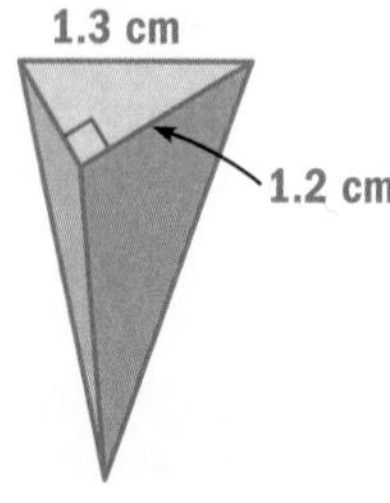

25. $h = 8$ m

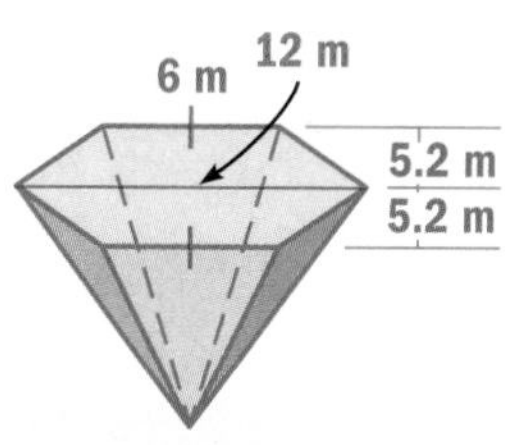

26. $h = 18$ in.

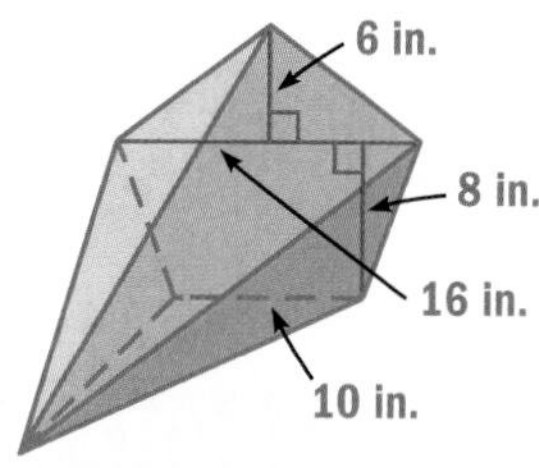

ALGEBRA **Find the unknown dimension using the given information.**

27. Square pyramid
volume = 156 yd^3
base side length = 6 yd
height = ?

28. Cone
volume = 216π ft^3
height = 8 ft
radius = ?

29. Right triangular pyramid
volume = 28 in.^{3}
legs = 3 in., 4 in.
height = ?

FINDING VOLUME **Find the volume of the solid. Round to the nearest tenth.**

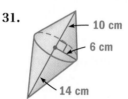

30. 15 ft, 20 ft, 20 ft, 20 ft

31. 10 cm, 6 cm, 14 cm

32.

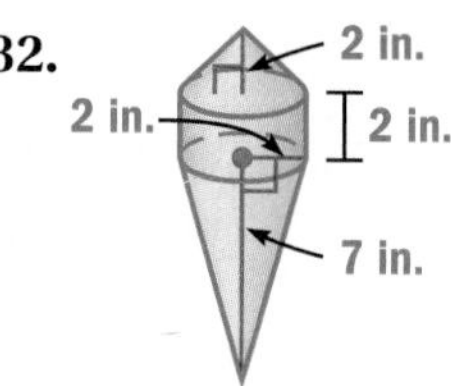

33. **ERROR ANALYSIS** Harry says that when you double the dimensions of a square pyramid, you double the volume. *Describe* and correct his error.

ALGEBRA Write a formula for the volume of the solid.

34. 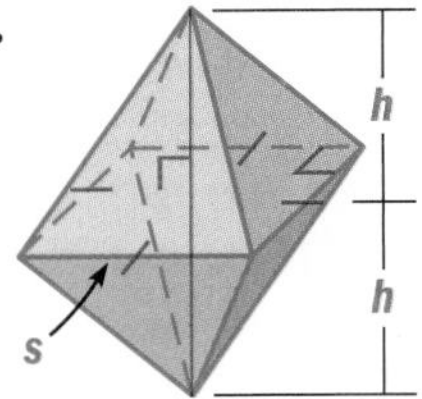

35. 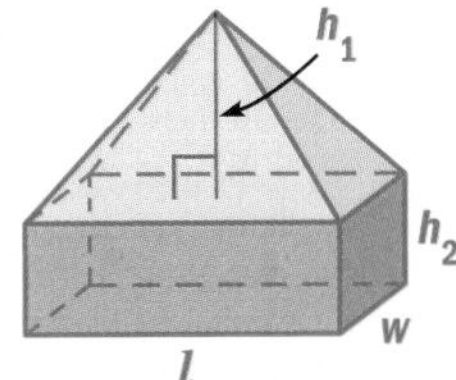

36. 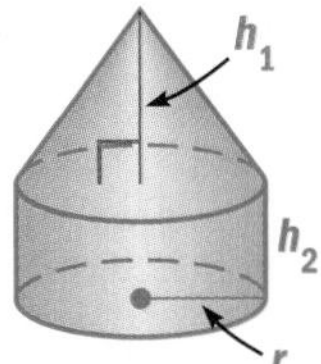

37. **CHALLENGE** Find the volume of a regular hexagonal pyramid with a height of 6 meters and a base side length of 4 meters. Round to the nearest tenth.

PROBLEM SOLVING

SEE EXAMPLE 3 on p. 563 for Ex. 38

38. **SPOTLIGHT** The light from a spotlight extends out in a cone shape from the bulb. The light of the beam extends 24 feet before it hits the floor under the spotlight and creates a circle with a radius of 10 feet. What is the volume of the space directly lit by the spotlight? Round to the nearest tenth.

39. ★ **MULTIPLE CHOICE** Each of four wooden models has a height of 6 inches. Which has the greatest volume?

(A) a square pyramid with base side length 8 in.

(B) a rectangular pyramid with base side lengths 8 in. and 6 in.

(C) a cylinder with diameter 8 in.

(D) a cone with diameter 8 in.

40. **REASONING** Which would change the volume of a cone more: *doubling the height* or *doubling the radius*? *Explain* your reasoning.

41. ★ **SHORT RESPONSE** A rectangular prism-shaped hole 10 feet by 12 feet by 8 feet is dug into the ground. Which is the taller solid that can be formed with the excavated dirt: a *square pyramid* with a base side length of 10 feet or a *cone* with a radius of 5 feet? *Explain* your reasoning.

42. **HISTORY** Early civilizations in the Andes Mountains in Peru used cone-shaped bricks to build homes. Find the volume of a brick with a diameter of 8.3 centimeters and a slant height of 10.1 centimeters. How much space would 27 of these bricks occupy?

43. **MULTI-STEP PROBLEM** A diagram of an hourglass is shown.

a. Find the volume of the cone-shaped pile of sand.

b. If this is an accurate hourglass, at what rate does the sand fall through the opening? Give your answer in cubic inches per minute.

c. The sand in the hourglass falls into a conical shape with a 3 to 2 ratio between the radius and the height. How many minutes have passed when the pile of sand is about 2 inches tall?

44. **CHALLENGE** A cone-shaped cup has a height of 11 centimeters and a radius of 4 centimeters. You pour water into the cup until it is 2 centimeters from the top. Sketch the cone. How many fluid ounces of water are in the cup? Round to the nearest tenth. (*Hint:* Use similar triangles and the fact that $1 \text{ cm}^3 \approx 0.0338$ fl oz.)

MIXED REVIEW

Prepare for Lesson 11.1 in Exs. 45–48

Evaluate the expression when $x = 6$. *(p. 19)*

45. $5x - 4^2$

46. $3x + 9^2$

47. $2x^2 + 14$

48. $7x^2 - 23$

Show two ways to represent the solid. *(p. 534)*

49. hexagonal prism

50. square pyramid

51. **TEMPERATURE** The table shows the average high temperatures in Alexandria, Egypt, during the months of April through September. Make a bar graph of the data. *(p. 783)*

Month	April	May	June	July	August	September
Temperature	75°F	79°F	83°F	84°F	86°F	84°F

52. ★ **MULTIPLE CHOICE** What is the volume of a cylinder with a radius of 5 inches and a height of 14 inches? *(p. 554)*

Ⓐ 70π in.^{3} Ⓑ 116.67π in.^{3} Ⓒ 350π in.^{3} Ⓓ 980π in.^{3}

QUIZ for Lessons 10.4–10.7

Find the surface area of the solid. Round to the nearest tenth.

1. 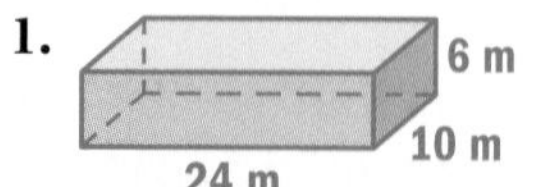

(p. 542)

2. 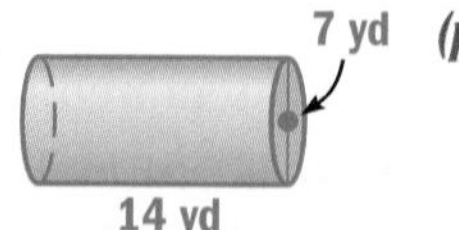

(p. 542)

3. 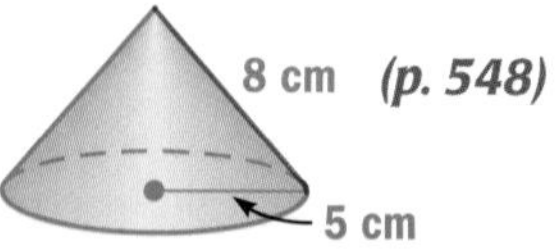

(p. 548)

Find the volume of the solid. Round to the nearest tenth.

4. 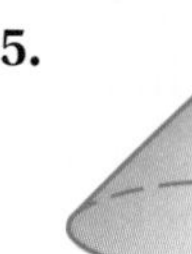

(p. 554)

5. 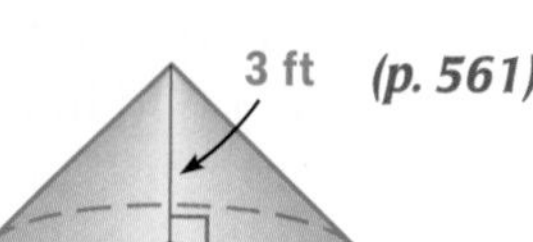

(p. 561)

6. 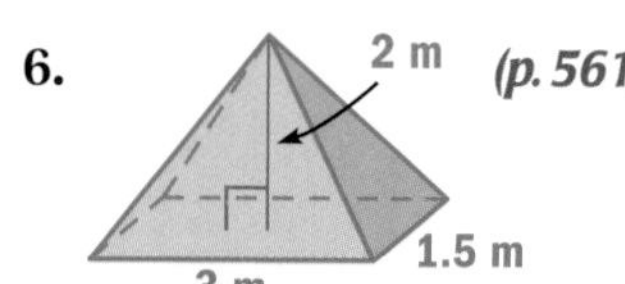

(p. 561)

7. **ACCESS RAMPS** How many cubic feet of cement are needed to make the access ramp shown? *(p. 554)*

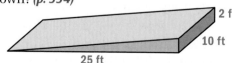

2 ft
10 ft
25 ft

Volume of a Sphere

GOAL Find the volumes of spheres.

KEY VOCABULARY
- **sphere,** *p. 534*
- **volume,** *p. 554*

From Lesson 10.3, you know that a sphere is a solid formed by all points in space that are the same distance from a fixed point (the center). You can find the volume of a sphere using the following formula.

KEY CONCEPT *For Your Notebook*

Volume of a Sphere

Words The volume V of a sphere is four thirds the product of π and the cube of the radius r.

Algebra $V = \frac{4}{3}\pi r^3$

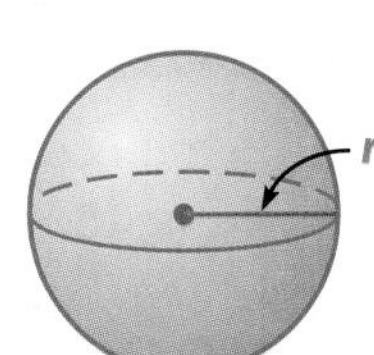

EXAMPLE Finding the Volume of a Sphere

Find the volume of a sphere with a radius of 5 inches.

$V = \frac{4}{3}\pi r^3$ Write formula for volume of a sphere.

$= \frac{4}{3}\pi(5)^3$ Substitute 5 for r.

≈ 523.6 Evaluate using a calculator.

▶ **Answer** The volume of the sphere is about 523.6 cubic inches.

EXERCISES

Find the volume of the sphere. Round to the nearest tenth.

1.
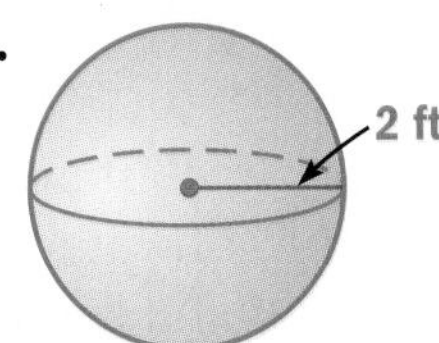

2.
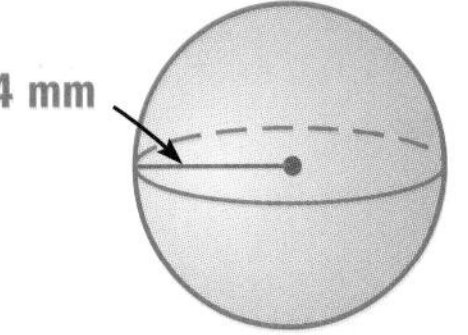

3.
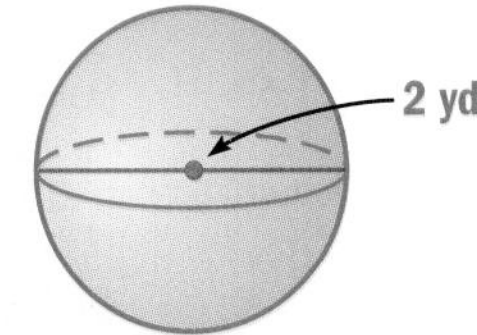

4. radius = 9 in.

5. diameter = 12 m

6. diameter = 16 km

7. Reasoning What is the volume of each figure at the right? Write a word equation that relates the three volumes.

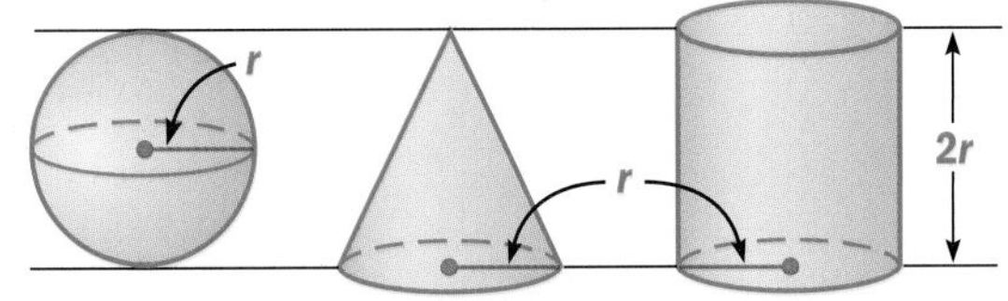

MIXED REVIEW *of Problem Solving*

Lessons 10.4–10.7

1. **MULTI-STEP PROBLEM** A company is making two types of covered aluminum containers. One is a cylinder with a height of 1.25 feet and a diameter of 1 foot. The other is a rectangular prism with a length of 0.75 foot, a width of 0.75 foot, and a height of 1 foot. Aluminum costs \$.02 per square foot.
   a. How much will the aluminum cost to produce each type of container? Round to the nearest cent.
   b. Which container has a greater capacity?
   c. Which container has a lower cost per cubic foot of capacity? *Explain.*

2. **SHORT RESPONSE** A pool service is treating algae in a rectangular pool that is 40 feet long, 20 feet wide, and 4 feet deep using sodium hypochlorite. The company uses 10 parts of sodium hypochlorite per million parts of water. Given that 1 cubic foot of water contains about 7.5 gallons, about how many gallons of sodium hypochlorite are needed? *Explain* your steps.

3. **GRIDDED ANSWER** Leon weighs a log of firewood that is one foot long and one foot in diameter. He finds that it weighs 36 pounds. He estimates that after being split, the wood will take up four thirds as much space as it does before being split. A cord of split firewood is 128 cubic feet. His truck has a capacity of 1200 pounds. How many trips must he make to deliver a cord of split firewood?

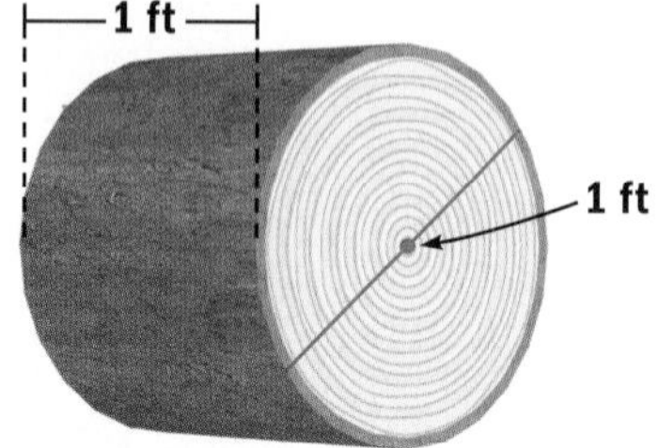

4. **OPEN-ENDED** Draw a pyramid and a cone with whole number dimensions. Find their volumes. Then draw similar solids whose dimensions are 1.5 times as large as the original solids and find their volumes. Compare the volumes of the similar solids.

5. **EXTENDED RESPONSE** Lee is wrapping a gift in a box 8 inches long, 4 inches wide, and 2 inches high.
   a. Draw a net of the box. What is the least amount of wrapping paper needed to cover the package?
   b. Lee wants to tie a ribbon around the length of the box. She leaves 10 extra inches to tie it. How long is the ribbon?
   c. An identical gift box is placed on top of the one above and the two are wrapped together. Does it take twice as much paper to wrap the gifts? *Explain.*

6. **MULTI-STEP PROBLEM** You are filling cone shaped paper cups with water. A small cup has a radius of 1.2 inches and is 3 inches high. A large cup has a radius of 1.5 inches and is 3.5 inches high.
   a. What is the capacity of the small cup?
   b. What is the capacity of the large cup?
   c. A larger container holds about 41 cubic inches of water. How many small cups can you fill from a full large container? How many large cups can be completely filled by a full large container? *Explain.*

10 CHAPTER REVIEW

@HomeTutor
classzone.com
Vocabulary Practice

REVIEW KEY VOCABULARY

- base of a parallelogram, *p. 521*
- height of a parallelogram, *p. 521*
- bases of a trapezoid, *p. 522*
- height of a trapezoid, *p. 522*
- solid, polyhedron, *p. 534*
- face, *p. 534*
- prism, *p. 534*
- pyramid, *p. 534*
- cylinder, *p. 534*
- cone, *p. 534*
- sphere, *p. 534*
- edge, vertex, *p. 534*
- net, *p. 542*
- surface area, *p. 543*
- slant height, *p. 548*
- volume, *p. 554*

VOCABULARY EXERCISES

Match the figure with its name.

1. 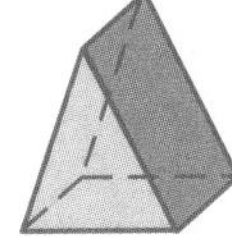

2. 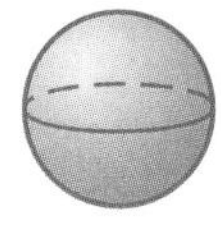

3. 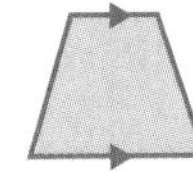

4. 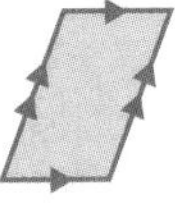

A. parallelogram **B.** prism **C.** sphere **D.** trapezoid

REVIEW EXAMPLES AND EXERCISES

10.1 Areas of Parallelograms and Trapezoids *pp. 521–526*

EXAMPLE

Find the area of the trapezoid.

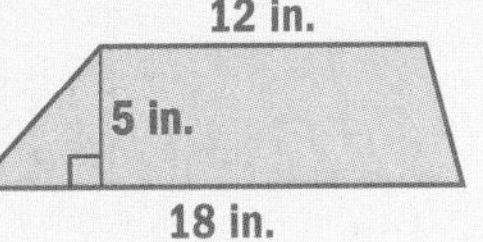

$A = \frac{1}{2}(b_1 + b_2)h$ **Formula for area of a trapezoid**

$= \frac{1}{2}(12 + 18)(5) = 75$ **Substitute and evaluate.**

The area of the trapezoid is 75 square inches.

EXERCISES

SEE EXAMPLES 1, 2, AND 3 on pp. 521–523 for Exs. 5–7

5. Find the area of a trapezoid with bases of 6 yards and 9 yards and a height of 8 yards.

6. Find the area of a parallelogram with a base of 20 feet and a height of 8 feet.

7. A parallelogram has a base of 36 centimeters and a height of 21 centimeters. A similar parallelogram has dimensions one third of the original dimensions. Find and compare the areas of the parallelograms.

10.2 Areas of Circles

pp. 527–532

EXAMPLE

Find the area of the circle. Use 3.14 for π.

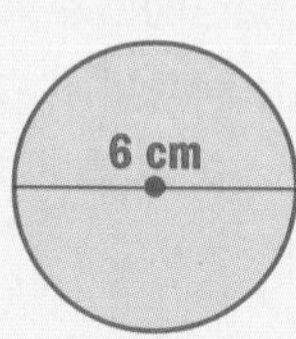

$A = \pi r^2$ — Formula for area of a circle

$\approx 3.14(3)^2$ — Substitute.

$= 28.26$ — Evaluate.

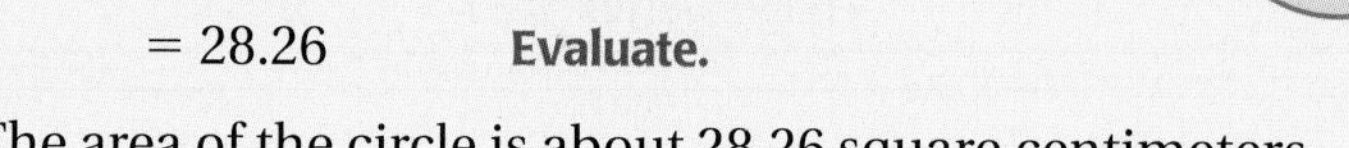

The area of the circle is about 28.26 square centimeters.

EXERCISES

Find the area of the circle with the given radius or diameter. Use 3.14 for π.

SEE EXAMPLES 1 AND 2 on pp. 527–528 for Exs. 8–13

8. $r = 2.5$ mm **9.** $r = 3.7$ mi **10.** $d = 7$ km

Find the radius of the circle with the given area. Use 3.14 for π.

11. $A = 1808.64$ in.^{2} **12.** $A = 50.24$ mm^2 **13.** $A = 254.34$ yd^2

10.3 Three-Dimensional Figures

pp. 534–538

EXAMPLE

Classify the solid. Then count the number of faces, edges, and vertices.

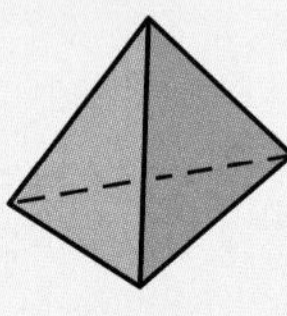
4 faces

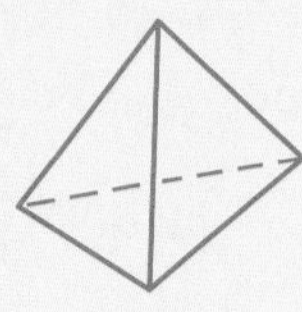
6 edges

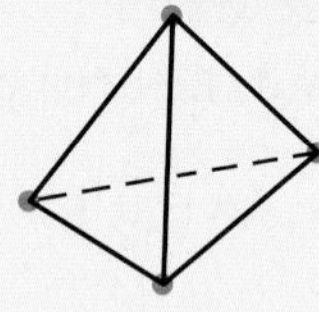
4 vertices

The solid has 4 triangular faces, so it is a triangular pyramid. It is a polyhedron.

EXERCISES

Classify the solid. Then tell whether it is a polyhedron.

SEE EXAMPLES 1 AND 2 on pp. 534–535 for Exs. 14–17

14. 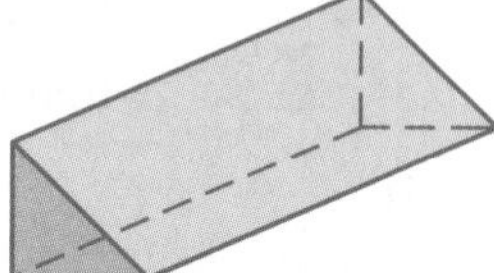

15. 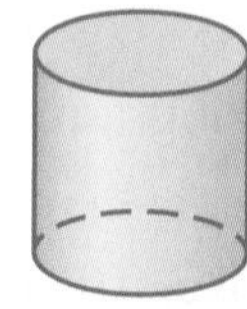

16. 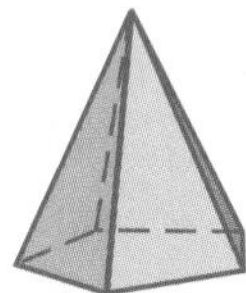

17. Count the number of faces, edges, and vertices in the figure in Exercise 14.

10.4 Surface Areas of Prisms and Cylinders

pp. 542–547

EXAMPLE

Find the surface area of the cylinder.

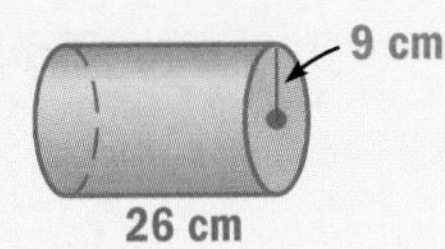

$S = 2\pi r^2 + 2\pi rh$	**Formula for surface area of a cylinder**
$= 2\pi(9)^2 + 2\pi(9)(26)$	**Substitute.**
≈ 1979.203	**Evaluate using a calculator.**

The surface area of the cylinder is about 1979 square centimeters.

EXERCISES

SEE EXAMPLES 2, 3, AND 4 on pp. 543–544 for Exs. 18–20

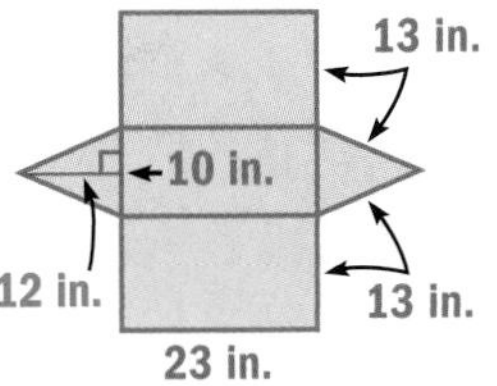

18. Find the surface area of the net. Identify the solid it forms.

Find the surface area of the solid. Round to the nearest tenth.

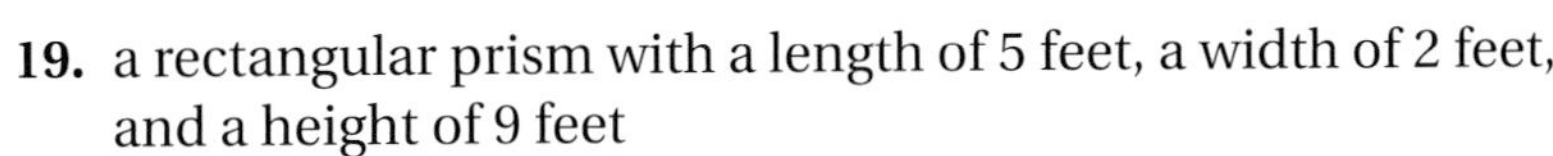

19. a rectangular prism with a length of 5 feet, a width of 2 feet, and a height of 9 feet

20. a cylinder with a radius of 5 meters and a height of 10 meters

10.5 Surface Areas of Pyramids and Cones

pp. 548–552

EXAMPLE

Find the surface area of the square pyramid.

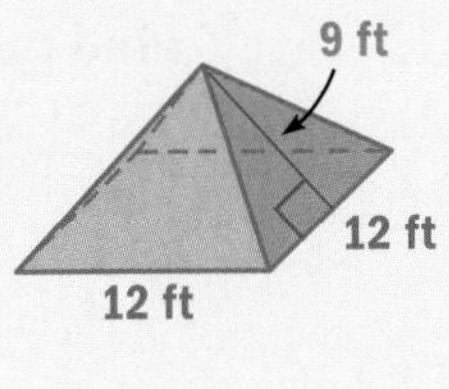

$S = B + \frac{1}{2}Pl$	**Formula for surface area of a pyramid**
$= 12^2 + \frac{1}{2}(4 \cdot 12)(9)$	**Substitute.**
$= 360$	**Evaluate.**

The surface area of the pyramid is 360 square feet.

EXERCISES

SEE EXAMPLES 1 AND 2 on pp. 549–550 for Exs. 21–23

Find the surface area of the solid. Round to the nearest tenth.

21. a square pyramid with a base area of 49 square meters and a slant height of 4 meters

22. a cone with a diameter of 20 feet and a slant height of 15 feet

23. Gifts You are wrapping a square pyramid puzzle. The base side lengths are 4 inches and the slant height is 5 inches. How much wrapping paper do you need?

10.6 Volumes of Prisms and Cylinders

pp. 554–559

EXAMPLE

Find the volume of the prism.

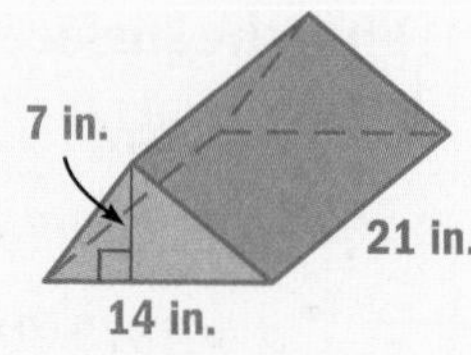

$V = Bh$ **Formula for volume of a prism**

$= \frac{1}{2}(7 \cdot 14)(21)$ **Substitute.**

$= 1029$ **Evaluate.**

The volume of the prism is 1029 cubic inches.

EXERCISES

Find the volume of the solid. Round to the nearest tenth if necessary.

SEE EXAMPLES 1 AND 2 on pp. 554–555 for Exs. 24–26

24. 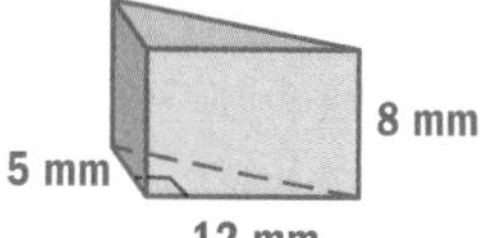

25. 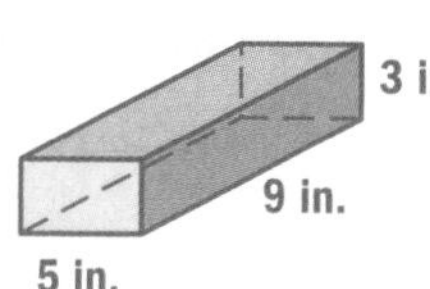

26. 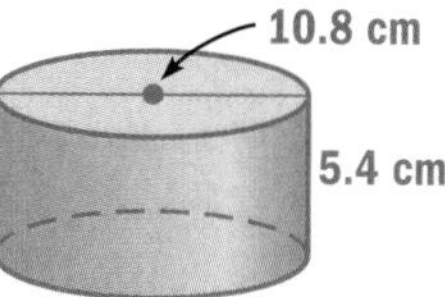

10.7 Volumes of Pyramids and Cones

pp. 561–566

EXAMPLE

Find the volume of the cone.

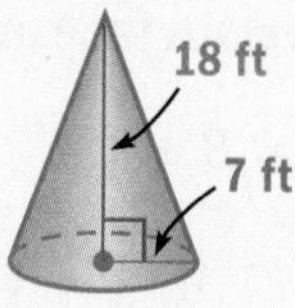

$V = \frac{1}{3}\pi r^2 h$ **Formula for volume of a cone**

$= \frac{1}{3}\pi(7)^2(18)$ **Substitute.**

≈ 923.628 **Evaluate using a calculator.**

The volume of the cone is about 924 cubic feet.

EXERCISES

Find the volume of the solid. Round to the nearest tenth.

SEE EXAMPLES 1, 2, AND 3 on pp. 561–563 for Exs. 27–29

27. a rectangular pyramid with base side lengths of 6 centimeters and 9 centimeters and a height of 7 centimeters

28. a cone with a radius of 4 inches and a height of 8 inches

29. **Candles** You have 12 cubic inches of candle wax. You have a mold for a square pyramid candle that has a base side length of 3 inches and a height of 5 inches. Do you have enough wax to make this candle? *Explain.*

10 CHAPTER TEST

@HomeTutor
classzone.com
Chapter Test Practice

Find the area of the parallelogram or trapezoid.

1. 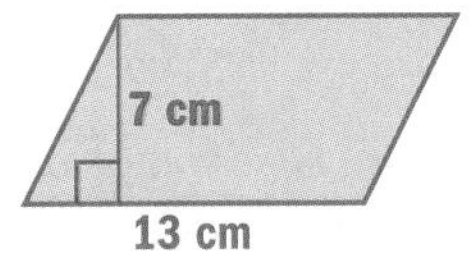

2. 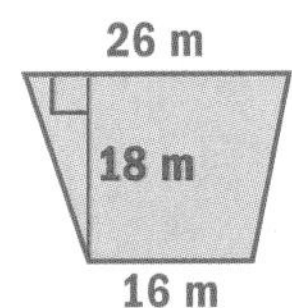

3. 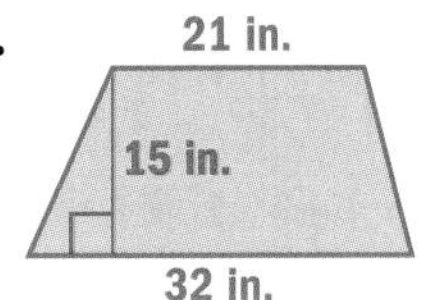

Find the area of the circle given its radius or diameter. Use 3.14 for π.

4. $r = 4$ ft
5. $d = 14$ yd
6. $r = 9$ mm

Determine the radius of the circle given its area. Use 3.14 for π.

7. $A = 3.7994\text{ ft}^2$
8. $A = 0.785\text{ m}^2$
9. $A = 94.985\text{ yd}^2$

Classify the solid. Then tell whether it is a polyhedron.

10. 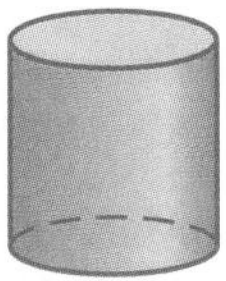

11. 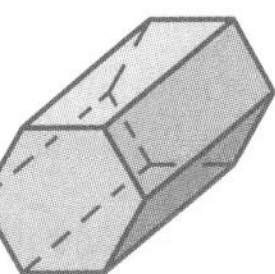

12. 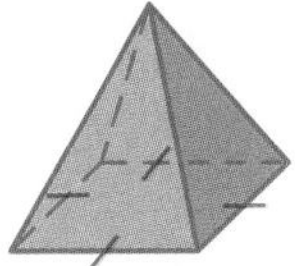

13. Count the number of faces, edges, and vertices in the figure in Exercise 11.

Find the surface area of the solid. Round to the nearest tenth if necessary.

14. 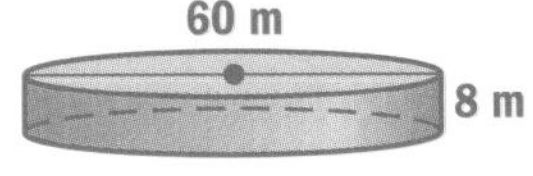

15. 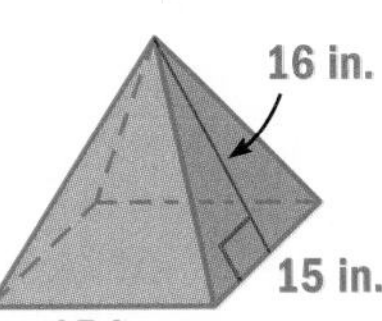

16. 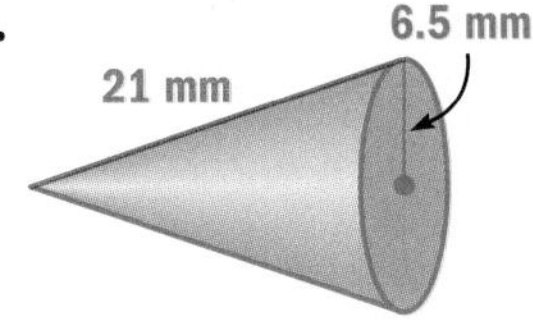

Find the volume of the solid. Round to the nearest tenth if necessary.

17. 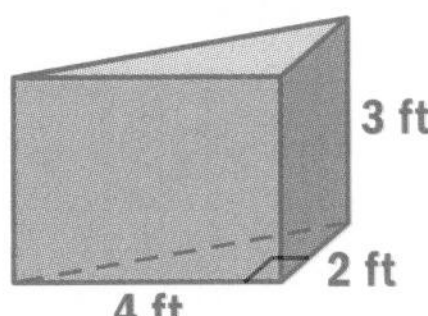

18. 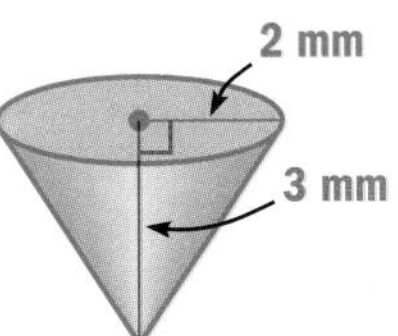

19. 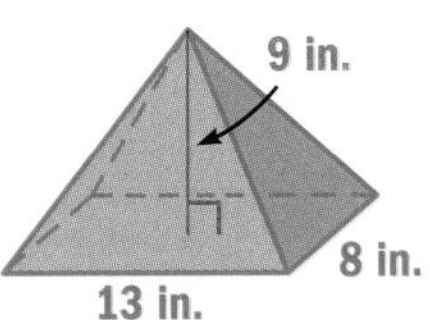

20. **PAINTING** You plan to paint the 4 walls and ceiling of a rectangular room. The dimensions of the floor are 15 feet by 12 feet. The height of the room is 8 feet. A can of paint covers 400 square feet. How many cans of paint will you need to buy?

21. **FOOD PREPARATION** A stick of pepperoni is a cylinder, with a radius of 2 centimeters and a length of 12 centimeters. If a slice of pepperoni is 2 cubic centimeters, how many whole slices can be cut from the stick?

Scoring Rubric

Full Credit
- solution is complete and correct

Partial Credit
- solution is complete but errors are made, *or*
- solution is without error, but incomplete

No Credit
- no solution is given, *or*
- solution makes no sense

EXTENDED RESPONSE QUESTIONS

PROBLEM

A movie theater serves a small size of popcorn in a conical container and a large size of popcorn in a cylindrical container, as shown. Find the volume of each container. Then determine which container is the better buy. *Explain* your reasoning.

Below are sample solutions to the problem. Read each solution and the comments in blue to see why the sample represents full credit, partial credit, or no credit.

SAMPLE 1: Full Credit Solution

The steps are clearly stated.

Find the volume of each container of popcorn.

Volume of small container

$V = \frac{1}{3}\pi r^2 h$

$\approx \frac{1}{3}(3.14)(3)^2(6)$

$= 56.52 \text{ in.}^3$

Volume of large container

$V = \pi r^2 h$

$\approx (3.14)(2.5)^2(6)$

$= 117.75 \text{ in.}^3$

Find the cost per cubic inch for each container.

The calculations are correct.

Small container: $\frac{\$2.00}{56.52 \text{ in.}^3} \approx \frac{\$.035}{\text{in.}^3}$

Large container: $\frac{\$4.00}{117.75 \text{ in.}^3} \approx \frac{\$.034}{\text{in.}^3}$

The answer is correct and the explanation is clear.

Popcorn in the small container costs about $.04 per cubic inch. Popcorn in the large container costs about $.03 per cubic inch. The large container of popcorn is the better buy.

SAMPLE 2: Partial Credit Solution

The calculations are correct.

Volume of the small container: $V \approx \frac{1}{3}(3.14)(3)^2(6) = 56.52 \text{ in.}^3$

Volume of the large container: $V \approx (3.14)(2.5)^2(6) = 117.75 \text{ in.}^3$

Then find the ratio of volume to cost for each container.

Small container: $\frac{56.52 \text{ in.}^3}{\$2.00} = \frac{56.52 \text{ in.}^3 \div 2}{\$2.00 \div 2} = \frac{28.26 \text{ in.}^3}{\$1.00}$

Large container: $\frac{117.75 \text{ in.}^3}{\$4.00} = \frac{117.75 \text{ in.}^3 \div 4}{\$4.00 \div 4} = \frac{29.44 \text{ in.}^3}{\$1.00}$

The answer is incorrect because the unit rates were misinterpreted. The greater number indicates more popcorn for $1.

Because $28.26 < 29.44$, the small container is the better buy.

SAMPLE 3: No Credit Solution

The volumes are calculated incorrectly. The solution given does not address the problem stated.

Small container: $V \approx \frac{1}{3}(3.14)(3)(2)(6) = 37.68 \text{ in.}^3$

Large container: $V \approx (3.14)(2.5)(2)(6) = 94.2 \text{ in.}^3$

The small container costs less.

PRACTICE Apply the Scoring Rubric

A student's solution to the problem on the previous page is shown below. Score the solution as *full credit, partial credit,* or *no credit. Explain* your reasoning. If you choose *partial credit* or *no credit,* explain how you would change the solution so that it earns a score of full credit.

1. Volume of the small container:

$V = \pi r^2 + \pi r l$

$\approx (3.14)(3)^2 + (3.14)(3)(6)$

$= 84.78 \text{ in.}^3$

Volume of the large container:

$V = 2\pi r^2 + 2\pi r h$

$\approx 2(3.14)(3)^2 + 2(3.14)(3)(6)$

$= 169.56 \text{ in.}^3$

Then find the unit price for each container.

Small container: $\frac{\$2.00}{84.76 \text{ in.}^3} = \frac{2 \div 84.76}{84.76 \div 84.76} \approx \frac{\$.024}{\text{in.}^3}$

Large container: $\frac{\$4.00}{169.56 \text{ in.}^3} = \frac{4 \div 169.56}{169.56 \div 169.56} \approx \frac{\$.024}{\text{in.}^3}$

The popcorn containers give the same amount of popcorn for your money.

EXTENDED RESPONSE

1. Plot and connect the points $A(4, 3)$, $B(8, 3)$, $C(6, 1)$, and $D(2, 1)$ in a coordinate plane. Classify the figure in as many ways as possible. What is the area of the figure? *Explain* how you found your answer. What happens to the area of the figure when its side lengths are doubled? *Justify* your reasoning.

2. A high school running track surrounds a grass field, as shown.

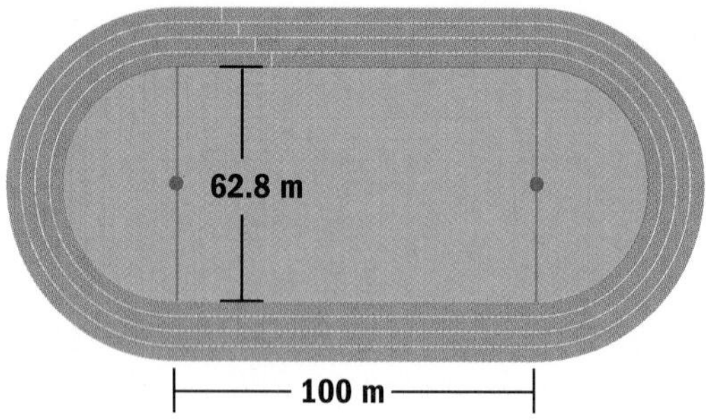

   a. *Explain* how to find the area of the grass field enclosed by the track.

   b. Write and simplify an expression to find the area of the grass field.

   c. You water the field at a rate of about $1\frac{1}{4}$ gallons per square meter. Approximate how much water you will use to water the field.

3. The Giant Ocean Tank at the New England Aquarium is a cylinder that is 23 feet deep and 40 feet in diameter.

   a. Find the area of the curved wall of the tank. Round your answer to the nearest tenth.

   b. Find the volume of the tank. Round your answer to the nearest tenth.

   c. Use the fact that $1\text{ ft}^3 \approx 7.48$ gal to find the capacity of the tank in gallons. Round your answer to the nearest tenth.

4. A company is making two types of plastic storage containers. One is a cylinder with a height of 8 inches and a diameter of 6 inches. The other is a rectangular prism with a length of 12 inches, a width of 6 inches, and a height of 4 inches. Which container has the greater capacity? *Explain.* The outer surface, except the top and bottom, of each container must be covered with labels. Which container requires more material for labels? *Explain* your reasoning.

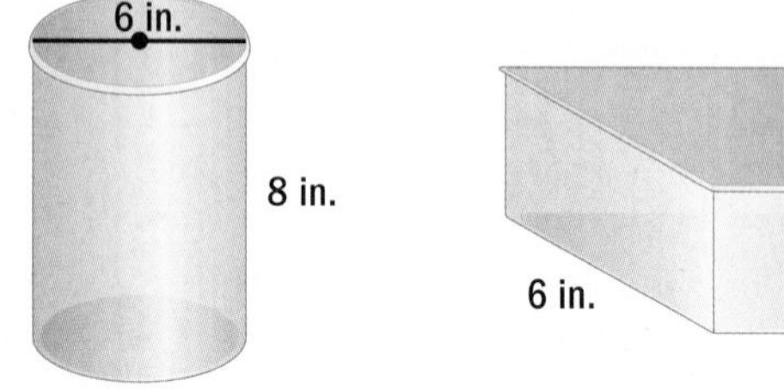

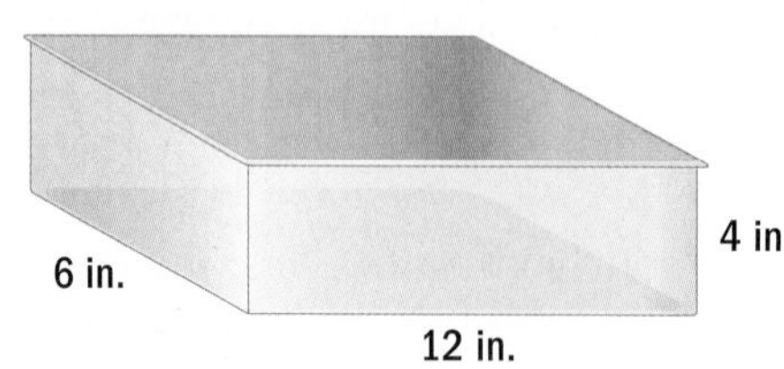

MULTIPLE CHOICE

5. Ali plants a flower garden in a circle around a tree as shown. The circle formed by the outer edge of the garden has twice the radius of the circle formed by the inner edge. What is the area of the flower garden?

Ⓐ 12.56 ft^2

Ⓑ 25.12 ft^2

Ⓒ 37.68 ft^2

Ⓓ 50.24 ft^2

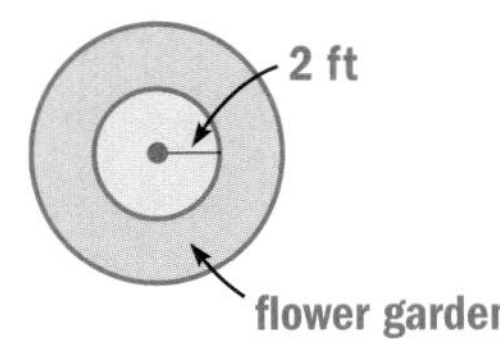

6. Which of the following statements is true about the prisms?

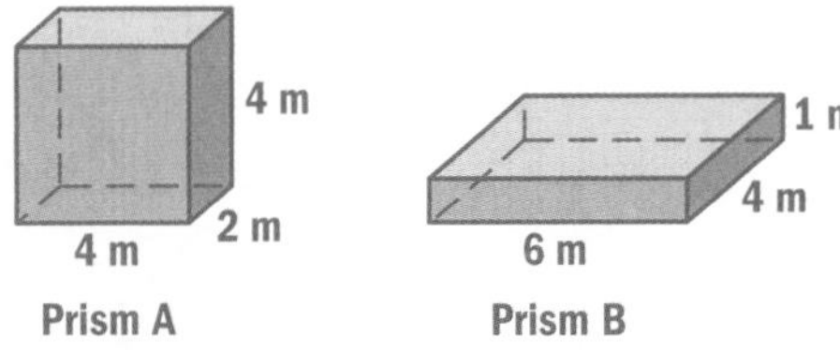

Ⓐ Prism A has a greater surface area than Prism B.

Ⓑ Prism B has a greater surface area than Prism A.

Ⓒ Prism A and Prism B have equal surface areas.

Ⓓ Prism A and Prism B have equal volumes.

GRIDDED ANSWER

7. What is the volume, in cubic yards, of a rectangular crate that has a length of 10 yards, a width of 3.5 yards, and a height of 5 yards?

8. What is the surface area, in square meters, of the square pyramid?

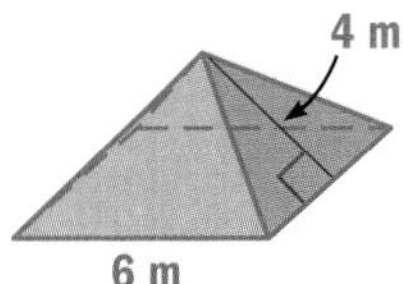

9. What is the approximate surface area of a cylindrical container with a radius of 2 inches and a height of 5.5 inches not including the top? Use 3.14 for π. Round your answer to the nearest tenth of a square inch.

10. What is the volume, in cubic feet, of the solid below? Use 3.14 for π. Round your answer to the nearest cubic foot.

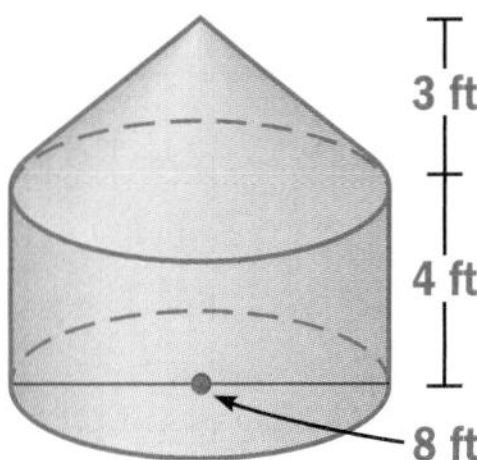

SHORT RESPONSE

11. Classify the solids shown at the right in as many ways as possible. Then count the number of faces, edges, and vertices in each solid.

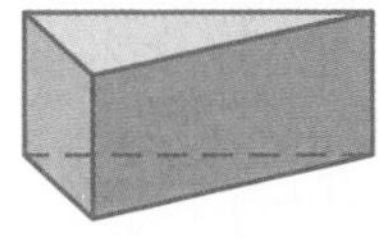

12. A radio station broadcasts to a circular region with an area of 182 square miles. Can a radio receive the broadcast signal if it is 8 miles away from the radio station? 6 miles away from the radio station? *Explain* your reasoning.

13. The Inuit people of the Arctic use blocks of snow to build igloos in the shape of a half sphere as shown. Each block is about 8 inches thick. Approximate the area of the igloo's floor to the nearest square foot. How tall is the highest point of the igloo? *Explain* your answers.

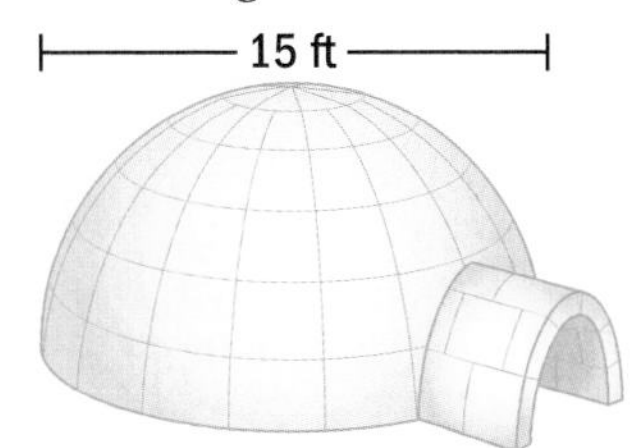

10 CUMULATIVE REVIEW Chapters 1–10

Evaluate the expression when $a = 3, b = -15, c = 15, x = 7,$ and $y = 5$. *(pp. 13, 77)*

1. $3x + 2$ **2.** $30 - 2x$ **3.** $2c - y$ **4.** $8a - 3c$

5. $\frac{y + x}{x - y}$ **6.** $\frac{6b}{2c}$ **7.** $\frac{c}{-5a}$ **8.** $\frac{b^2}{a^2}$

Write the prime factorization of the number. *(p. 176)*

9. 54 **10.** 70 **11.** 150 **12.** 184

Use a percent proportion. *(p. 354)*

13. What number is 500% of 16? **14.** 200.2 is 65% of what number?

15. 44 is what percent of 80? **16.** 1.7 is what percent of 340?

Classify the polygon.

17. 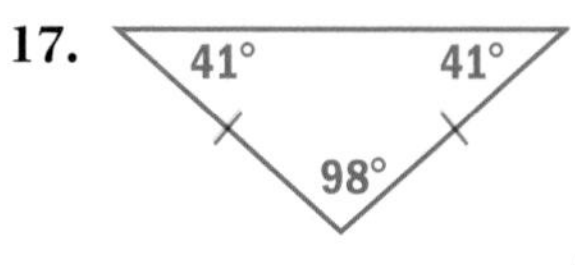

(p. 411)

18. 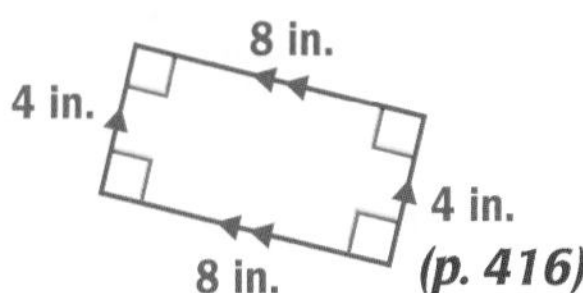

(p. 416)

19. 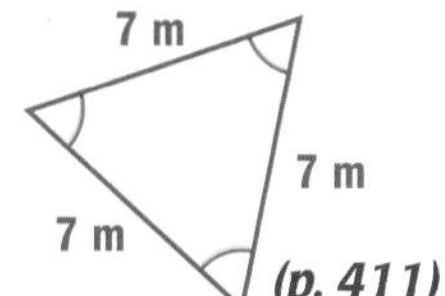

(p. 411)

Solve the equation or inequality. *(pp. 129, 318, 469)*

20. $\frac{d}{5} + 13 = -10$ **21.** $17 = \frac{x}{12} - 31$ **22.** $-21 - \frac{t}{3} = -6$

23. $\frac{2}{3}h - 3 \geq 1$ **24.** $\frac{1}{2}x + 4 \leq 7$ **25.** $-\frac{3}{4}x - 10 \geq 8$

26. $m^2 = 196$ **27.** $a^2 - 1296 = 0$ **28.** $c^2 - 28 = 36$

Find the area of the figure.

29. *(p. 142)* 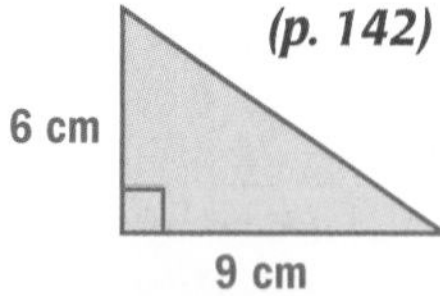

30. *(p. 521)* 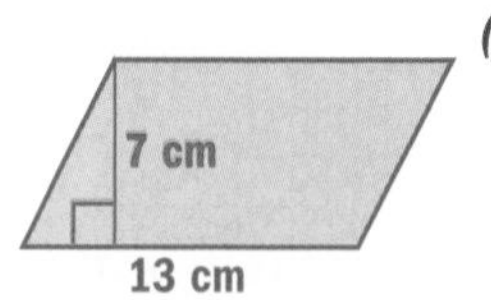

31. *(p. 142)* 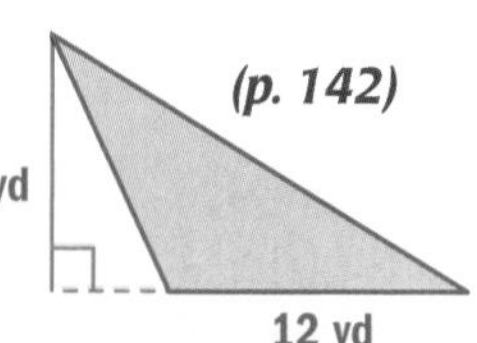

32. *(p. 521)* 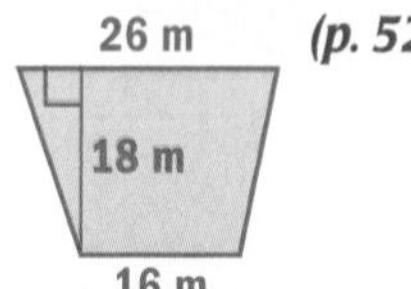

33. *(p. 527)* 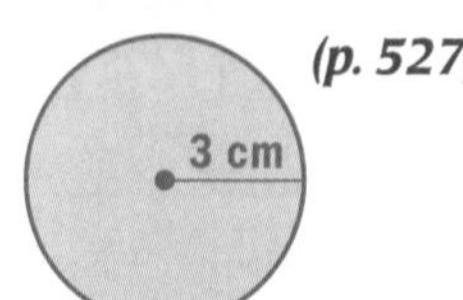

34. *(p. 527)* 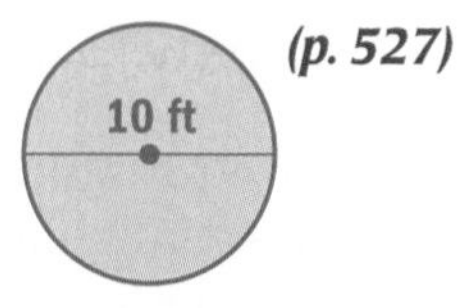

Find the volume of the figure. Round to the nearest tenth if necessary.

35. *(p. 554)* 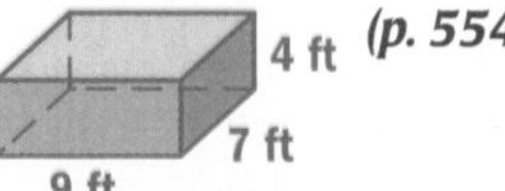

36. *(p. 554)* 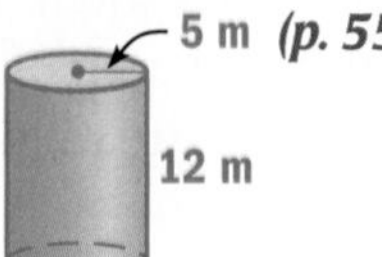

37. *(p. 561)* 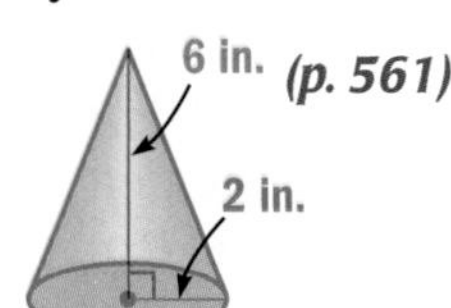

38. **WEATHER** The data show the daily high temperature in degrees Fahrenheit for two weeks.

67, 76, 78, 62, 58, 64, 70, 74, 78, 69, 68, 76, 67, 62

Make a histogram of the data. *Explain* your choice of intervals. *(p. 3)*

39. **CLASSROOM** A classroom is 25 feet by 40 feet and has seating for 28 students. Each student has a desk and chair that take up 9 square feet. There also is one large table that takes up 20 square feet. How many square feet of walking space does the classroom have? *(p. 142)*

40. **CALORIES** One serving of rice pilaf has 220 calories, including 35 calories from fat. One serving of soup has 70 calories, including 15 calories from fat. Write the calories from fat as a fraction of the total calories for each food. Which food has a greater fraction of calories from fat? *(p. 198)*

41. **COINS** A quarter's width is about $\frac{15}{16}$ inch. A dime's width is about $\frac{11}{16}$ inch. How many inches wider is a quarter? *(p. 233)*

42. **INTEREST** You invest $300 at a simple annual interest rate of 3.5% for one year. How much would you need to invest at a 2% simple annual interest rate to earn the same amount of interest that year? *(p. 375)*

43. **HIKING** Two hiking trails meet at a 24° angle. Sketch the intersection and label the measure of each angle formed. *(p. 403)*

44. **HOME PLATE** A rulebook specifies the shape of home plate as shown. Find the value of x. Round to the nearest whole number. *(p. 487)*

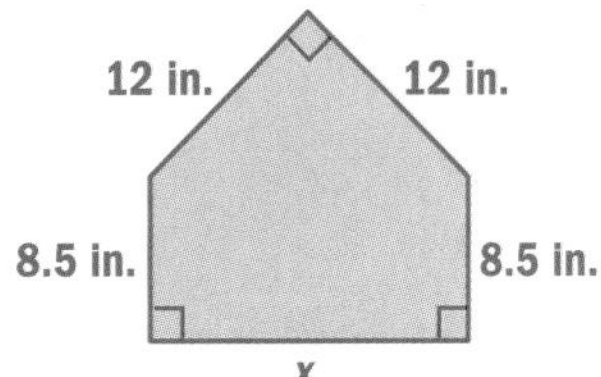

45. **SKATEBOARD RAMP** You are constructing a skateboard ramp as shown in the diagram. Find the lengths of the legs of the triangle that supports the ramp. Round your answers to the nearest tenth of a foot. *(p. 500)*

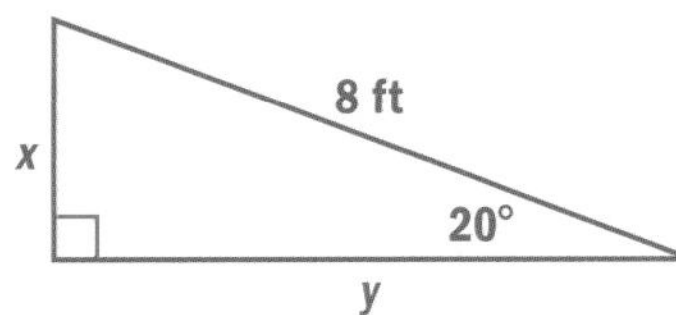

46. **CONTAINERS** A cylinder with a radius of 6 centimeters and a height of 7 centimeters has about the same volume as a rectangular prism with a length of 9 centimeters, a width of 8 centimeters, and a height of 11 centimeters. Which container uses less material to hold the same amount? About how much less material? Round to the nearest tenth. *(pp. 542, 554)*

11 Linear Equations and Graphs

Before

In previous chapters you've . . .

- Translated verbal sentences into mathematical statements
- Solved one-variable equations

Now

In Chapter 11 you'll study . . .

- 11.1 Relations and functions
- 11.2 Scatter plots
- 11.3 Two-variable equations
- 11.4 Linear equation graphs
- 11.5 Using intercepts
- 11.6 Slope
- 11.7 Slope-intercept form
- 11.8 Linear inequality graphs

Why?

So you can solve real-world problems about . . .

- gray whales, p. 587
- elevators, p. 597
- hiking, p. 623

Math
at classzone.com

- Relations and Functions, p. 586
- Slope, p. 612
- Slope-Intercept Form, p. 623

Get-Ready Games

Review Prerequisite Skills by playing *Sidewalk Scramble* and *Plot the Picture.*

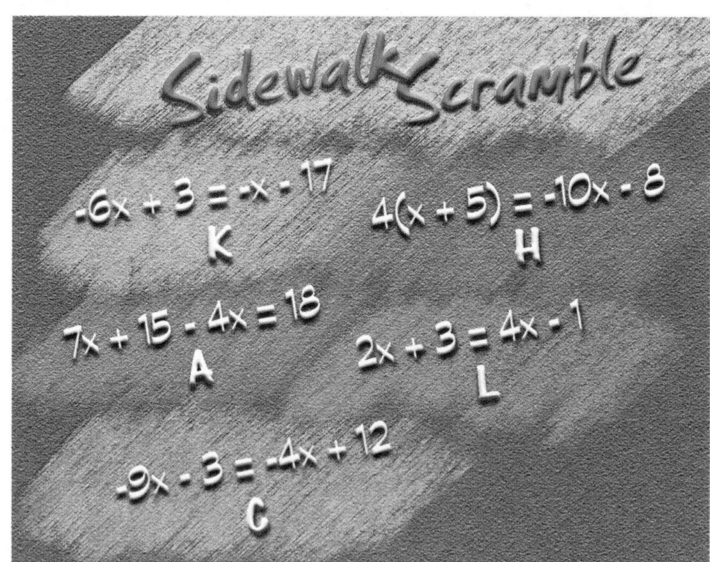

Skill Focus: Solving equations in one variable

Solve the scramble to spell a word associated with sidewalk art.

- Find the solution of each equation.
- Order the equations so that the one with the least solution is first and the one with the greatest solution is last. This will unscramble the letters.

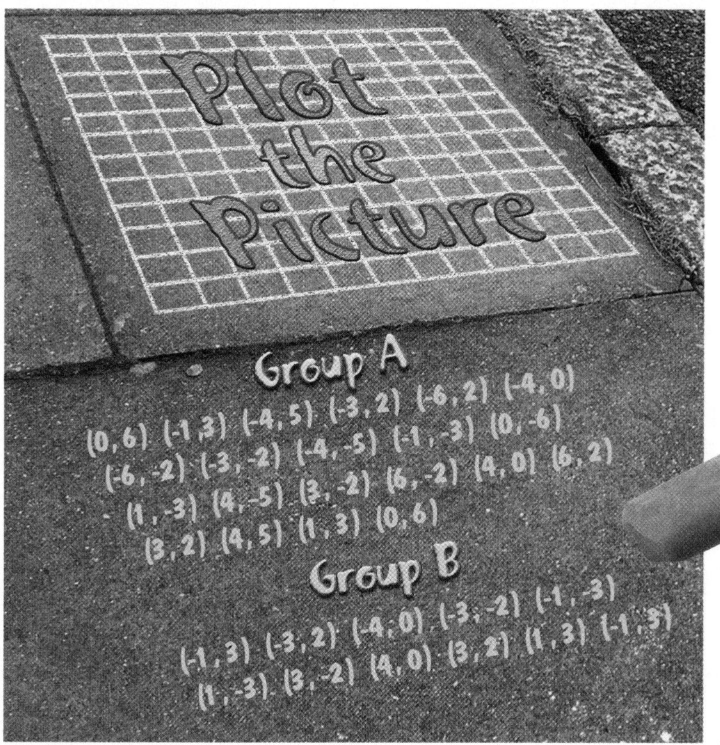

Plot the Picture
Group A
(0,6) (-1,3) (-4,5) (-3,2) (-6,2) (-4,0)
(-6,-2) (-3,-2) (-4,-5) (-1,-3) (0,-6)
(1,-3) (4,-5) (3,-2) (6,-2) (4,0) (6,2)
(3,2) (4,5) (1,3) (0,6)
Group B
(-1,3) (-3,2) (-4,0) (-3,-2) (-1,-3)
(1,-3) (3,-2) (4,0) (3,2) (1,3) (-1,3)

Skill Focus: Plotting points on a coordinate grid

Create a piece of sidewalk art.

- Plot the points listed in Group A on a coordinate grid. Connect each point with a line to the point that follows it.
- Now find and connect the points in Group B in order.

Stop and Think

1. **WRITING** A student says that in *Sidewalk Scramble* the first step in solving the equation $-6x + 3 = -x - 17$ is to subtract x from both sides. *Explain* why the student is wrong.
2. **EXTENSION** Design your own piece of sidewalk art. Write directions for making your sidewalk art using points on a coordinate grid.

11 Getting Ready

Review Prerequisite Skills

REVIEW WORDS

- **coordinate plane,** *p. 94*
- ***x*-axis,** *p. 94*
- ***y*-axis,** *p. 94*
- **origin,** *p. 94*
- **quadrant,** *p. 94*
- **ordered pair,** *p. 94*
- **inequality,** *p. 148*
- **ratio,** *p. 343*

VOCABULARY CHECK

1. Draw a coordinate plane and label the x-axis, y-axis, origin, and Quadrant III.

2. In the inequality $x \geq 8$, what does the symbol $\geq$ mean?

3. Describe the meaning of the numbers in the ordered pair $(-3, 2)$.

SKILL CHECK

4. Write the ordered pair for each labeled point in the coordinate plane at the right. *(p. 94)*

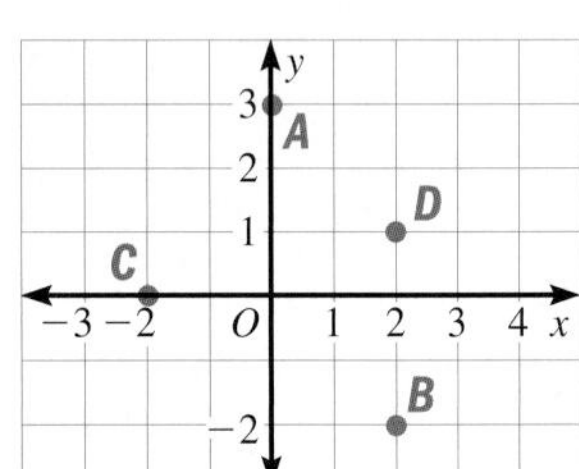

Plot the point in a coordinate plane. *(p. 94)*

5. $(0, 4)$ **6.** $(-2, 3)$

7. $(5, -4)$ **8.** $(-2, -3)$

Solve the equation. *(p. 129)*

9. $3 = 9x - 24$ **10.** $7 - 8x = 3$ **11.** $6x + 9 = -45$

12. $\frac{x}{4} - 1 = 6$ **13.** $15 - x = -22$ **14.** $-9 = \frac{x}{2} + 4$

Solve the inequality. *(p. 318)*

15. $3x - 4 \leq 5$ **16.** $-4x - 3 \geq 12$ **17.** $6 + 2x < 2$

@HomeTutor Prerequisite skills practice at classzone.com

Notetaking Skills Write Down Your Questions

In each chapter you will learn a new notetaking skill. In Chapter 11 you will apply the strategy of writing questions about homework to exercises on pp. 590–592.

If you don't know how to solve a homework problem, make a note in your notebook. Leave room to write the answer to your question.

What is the distance from A to C?

I can't use the grid to count along a diagonal, so how do I solve this?

Use the Pythagorean Theorem. $AB = 3$, $BC = 4$, and $\triangle ABC$ is a right triangle, so $AC = 5$.

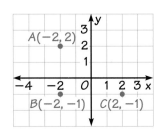

A(−2, 2)
B(−2, −1)
C(2, −1)

11.1 Relations and Functions

Before	You translated verbal sentences into algebraic models.
Now	You'll use tables to represent functions.
Why?	So you can write real-world function rules, as for feeding whales in Ex. 23.

KEY VOCABULARY
- **relation,** *p. 583*
- **input,** *p. 583*
- **output,** *p. 583*
- **function,** *p. 583*
- **domain,** *p. 584*
- **range,** *p. 584*

A **relation** is a set of ordered pairs that relates an **input** to an **output**. A relation can be written as a set of ordered pairs or by using an *input-output table.*

(Input, Output)
(2, 5)
(4, 7)
(−1, 15)
(0, 0)

Input	Output
2	5
4	7
−1	15
0	0

A relation is a **function** if for each input there is exactly one output. In a function, you can say that the output is a *function of* the input.

EXAMPLE 1 Identifying Functions

AVOID ERRORS
In a function, two different inputs can have the same output, but each input must have *exactly one* output.

Tell whether the relation is a function. *Explain* your answer.

a. (0, 2), (1, 4), (2, 6), (3, 8)

▶ **Answer** The relation is a function. Each input has exactly one output.

b.

Input	9	9	25	25
Output	3	−3	5	−5

▶ **Answer** The relation is a *not* a function. The inputs 9 and 25 both have two outputs.

Animated Math at classzone.com

GUIDED PRACTICE for Example 1

Tell whether the relation is a function. *Explain* your answer.

1. (−2, 4), (2, 4), (4, 2), (−2, −4)

2. (3, −2), (6, 1), (−3, 5), (4, 1)

3.

Input	−4	0	4	8
Output	8	0	8	32

Domain and Range The **domain** of a function is the set of all possible input values. The **range** of a function is the set of all possible output values. A *function rule* assigns each number in the domain to exactly one number in the range.

EXAMPLE 2 Evaluating a Function

Fundraising Your soccer team is selling glow sticks to raise money. The team paid \$50 for a case of 48 glow sticks and sells each glow stick for \$3. How many glow sticks does the team need to sell to start earning a profit? Use the function rule $P = 3g - 50$, where P is the profit in dollars and g is the number of glow sticks your team sells.

SOLUTION

READING

The domain and range of a function can be represented using *set notation.* In Example 2, the domain is $\{0, 1, 2, \ldots, 48\}$ and the range is $\{-50, -47, \ldots, 94\}$.

Make a table to determine how many glow sticks your soccer team needs to sell to start earning a profit.

Input g	*Function*	*Output P*
0	$P = 3(0) - 50$	−50
10	$P = 3(10) - 50$	−20
16	$P = 3(16) - 50$	−2
17	$P = 3(17) - 50$	1

There are 48 glow sticks, so the domain is 0, 1, 2, 3, . . ., 48. The range is −50, −47, −44, −41, . . ., 94.

▸ **Answer** Your soccer team needs to sell 17 glow sticks.

EXAMPLE 3 Writing a Function Rule

Write a function rule that relates *x* and *y*.

Input x	−4	−2	0	2	4
Output y	1	3	5	7	9

(Inputs: +2, +2, +2, +2; Outputs: +2, +2, +2, +2)

SOLUTION

To write a function rule, try to find an equation of the form $y = ax + b$. You can look at differences in the function to find the values of a and b.

STEP 1 The value of a is $\frac{\text{change in output}}{\text{change in input}}$.

$a = \frac{2}{2} = 1$, so $y = 1x + b$.

STEP 2 To find b, substitute an input-output pair for x and y.

Let $(x, y) = (0, 5)$. $5 = 1(0) + b$, so $b = 5$.

▸ **Answer** A function rule that relates x and y is $y = x + 5$.

Check Substitute a different input-output pair in the function rule to check.

$3 \stackrel{?}{=} -2 + 5$ **Substitute (−2, 3) in function rule.**

$3 = 3$ ✓

Sequences A *sequence* is an ordered list of numbers. It is a special type of function whose domain includes only positive integers such as 1, 2, 3, and so on. Each sequence is made up of n numbers, or *terms*, and the value of each term is A. In an *arithmetic sequence*, the difference between consecutive terms is constant. Its function rule has the form $A = an + b$.

EXAMPLE 4 Standardized Test Practice

Which function rule relates n and A in the arithmetic sequence: 1, 4, 7, 10, . . .?

Ⓐ $A = n + 3$ Ⓑ $A = 3n$ Ⓒ $A = 3n - 2$ Ⓓ $A = -3n + 4$

ELIMINATE CHOICES
The terms of the sequence are increasing in value. So, the ratio of the change in output to the change in input must be positive. You can eliminate choice D.

SOLUTION

Find an equation of the form $A = an + b$.

	+1	+1	+1		
Position	1	2	3	4	n
Value of term	1	4	7	10	A
	+3	+3	+3		

STEP 1 The value of a is $\frac{\text{change in output}}{\text{change in input.}}$

$a = \frac{3}{1} = 3$, so $A = 3n + b$.

STEP 2 To find b, substitute an input-output pair for n and A.

Let $(n, A) = (2, 4)$ $\quad 4 = 3(2) + b$, so $b = -2$.

▶ **Answer** A function rule that relates n and A is $A = 3n - 2$.
The correct answer is C. Ⓐ Ⓑ Ⓒ Ⓓ

✓ GUIDED PRACTICE for Examples 2, 3, and 4

4. **What If?** In Example 2, suppose each glow stick sells for $4. How many glow sticks would the team need to sell to start earning a profit?

5. Write a function rule that relates x and y in the table at the right.

Input x	1	2	3	4
Output y	−7	−6	−5	−4

11.1 EXERCISES

HOMEWORK KEY

★ = **STANDARDIZED TEST PRACTICE** Exs. 12, 24, 25, 26, and 36

○ = **HINTS AND HOMEWORK HELP** for Exs. 7, 9, 13, 21 at classzone.com

SKILL PRACTICE

1. **VOCABULARY** Copy and complete: For a function, the set of all possible input values is its __?__ and the set of all possible output values is its __?__.

SEE EXAMPLE 1 on p. 583 for Exs. 2–5

IDENTIFYING FUNCTIONS **Tell whether the relation is a function. *Explain.***

2. (4, 5), (2, −3), (4, 9), (−2, −3)
3. (−3, 7), (3, 7), (7, 3), (−7, −3)
4. (2, 3), (1, −6), (5, 3), (−1, −6)
5. (−8, 10), (9, 2), (2, 11), (−8, −4)

SEE EXAMPLE 1 on p. 583 for Exs. 6–7

IDENTIFYING FUNCTIONS **Tell whether the relation is a function. *Explain.***

6.

Input	−3	−2	0	2
Output	9	4	0	4

7.

Input	4	4	2	5
Output	2	−2	5	−5

SEE EXAMPLE 2 on p. 584 for Exs. 8–11

EVALUATING FUNCTIONS **Make an input-output table for the function rule. Use the domain −2, −1, 0, 1, and 2. Identify the range.**

8. $y = x - 1$ **9.** $y = -\frac{1}{4}x$ **10.** $y = 5x$ **11.** $y = x^2$

SEE EXAMPLE 3 on p. 584 for Exs. 12–16

12. ★ **MULTIPLE CHOICE** Which function rule relates x and y for the set of ordered pairs (3, 1), (6, 2), (9, 3)?

Ⓐ $y = \frac{1}{3}x$ Ⓑ $y = 3x$ Ⓒ $y = x - 2$ Ⓓ $y = x - 6$

WRITING FUNCTION RULES **Write a function rule that relates x and y.**

13.

Input x	−1	0	1	2
Output y	5	6	7	8

14.

Input x	0	1	2	3
Output y	0	−5	−10	−15

15.

Input x	1	2	3	4
Output y	1	4	7	10

16.

Input x	0	1	2	3
Output y	2	1.5	1	0.5

Animated Math at classzone.com

SEE EXAMPLE 4 on p. 585 for Exs. 17–18

ARITHMETIC SEQUENCES **Write a function rule that relates n and A in the arithmetic sequence.**

17. 3, 7, 11, 15, . . . **18.** 7, 10, 13, 16, . . .

19. **ERROR ANALYSIS** A student says that in order to write a function rule that relates input x to output y, the change in output must be the same as the change in input. Create an input-output table and write the related function rule to show that this statement is incorrect.

20. **CHALLENGE** Find the missing terms and write a function rule that relates n and A in the arithmetic sequence: $-\frac{1}{6}, \underline{?}, \frac{1}{2}, \underline{?}, \frac{7}{6}$.

PROBLEM SOLVING

SEE EXAMPLE 2 on p. 584 for Ex. 21

21. **RECYCLING** Stanley receives \$.40 per pound of aluminum cans he recycles. A function rule for this situation is $E = 0.40p$, where E is the amount he earns in dollars and p is the number of pounds of cans. Make an input-output table to find the number of pounds of cans Stanley needs to recycle to earn \$6.

22. **TICKETS** Ashley buys movie tickets that are all the same price. Is the total cost a function of the number of tickets? *Explain.*

SEE EXAMPLE 3 on p. 584 for Ex. 23

23. **WHALES** A gray whale calf is nursed back to health with milk-based formula. The table shows the total gallons of formula consumed over the course of f feedings. Use the table to write a function rule. Then use your function rule to find how much the whale consumes in 7 feedings.

Feedings (f)	*Gallons consumed (g)*
1	2
2	4
3	6
4	8

24. ★ **SHORT RESPONSE** Your friend says that the set of ordered pairs $(-9, 81)$, $(-4, 16)$, $(0, 0)$, $(4, 16)$, and $(-9, -81)$ is a function. Is your friend correct? If not, what is your friend's likely mistake? *Explain.*

25. ★ **WRITING** *Explain* why the output a is *not* a function of the input b in the equation $a = \pm\sqrt{b}$.

26. ★ **OPEN-ENDED MATH** *Describe* a real-world relation that is a function. *Describe* a real-world relation that is *not* a function.

27. **CHALLENGE** On a road trip, you stop every 90 minutes for a total of 4 stops. The speed you travel between stops is shown below. Assume the car travels at a constant speed between stops.

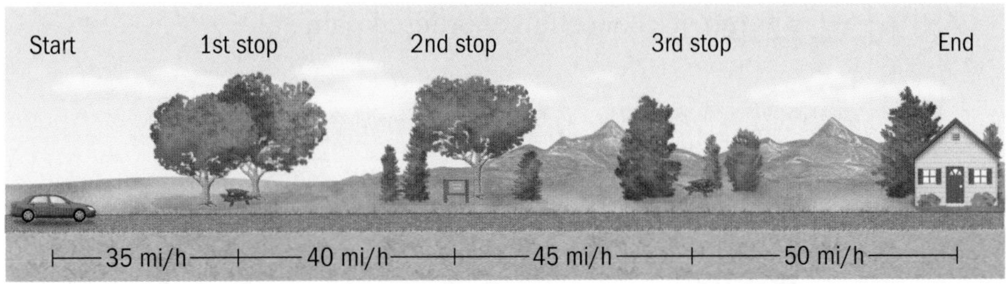

a. Write a function rule that relates the speed x, in miles per hour, to the distance y, in miles, traveled between stops.

b. How long, in hours and minutes, would it take to complete the entire trip at 60 miles per hour with no stops?

MIXED REVIEW

Get-Ready

Prepare for Lesson 11.2 in Exs. 28–31

Plot the point in a coordinate plane. *(p. 94)*

28. $(3, 2)$ 29. $(1, -4)$ 30. $(-5, -2)$ 31. $(-3, 0)$

Write the fraction in simplest form. *(p. 187)*

32. $\frac{-2x^3y}{xy}$ 33. $\frac{5xy^2z}{5xy}$ 34. $\frac{2x^3y}{-3xyz}$ 35. $\frac{-8^2z^2}{16x^2yz}$

36. ★ **MULTIPLE CHOICE** Which of the following is equal to -10? *(p. 57)*

Ⓐ $-|-10|$ Ⓑ $-(-10)$ Ⓒ $|10|$ Ⓓ $|-10|$

11.2 Scatter Plots

Before You found a function rule given a table of values.
Now You'll make and interpret scatter plots.
Why? So you can compare data, such as quantity and cost of cereal in Example 2.

KEY VOCABULARY
- **scatter plot,** *p. 588*

NASA NASA's Crawler Transporter is a large vehicle that moves the space shuttle and its launch platform to the launch pad. The crawler uses about 126 gallons of fuel to travel 1 mile.

The table below shows the amount of fuel, in gallons, that is used to travel different numbers of miles. How can you present this information using a graph?

Distance (miles)	1	2	3	4	5	6
Fuel used (gallons)	126	252	378	504	630	756

You can represent the information using a *scatter plot.* A **scatter plot** is a graph of a collection of ordered pairs.

EXAMPLE 1 Making a Scatter Plot

Make a scatter plot of the data given above.

SOLUTION

STEP 1 **Plot** the ordered pairs from the table.

(1, 126), (2, 252), (3, 378),

(4, 504), (5, 630), (6, 756)

STEP 2 **Label** the horizontal and vertical axes.

Put *Distance (mi)* on the horizontal axis and *Fuel used (gal)* on the vertical axis.

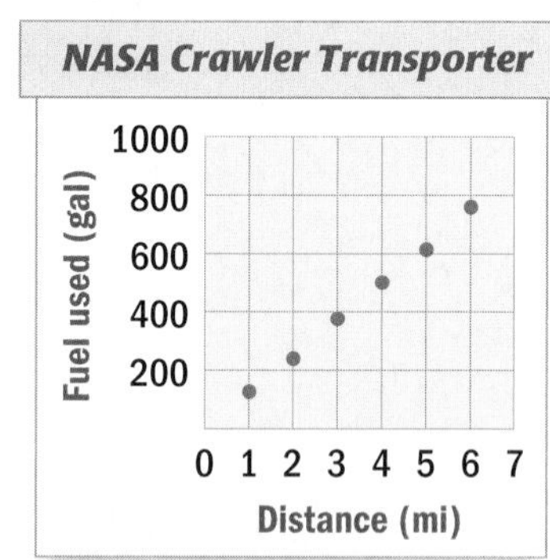

✓ GUIDED PRACTICE for Example 1

Make a scatter plot of the data.

1.

c	−2	−1	0	1
d	−5	−4	−3	−2

2.

x	0	3	6	9
y	−2	−4	−6	−8

Interpreting Scatter Plots Scatter plots show what kind of relationship exists between two sets of data.

Positive relationship

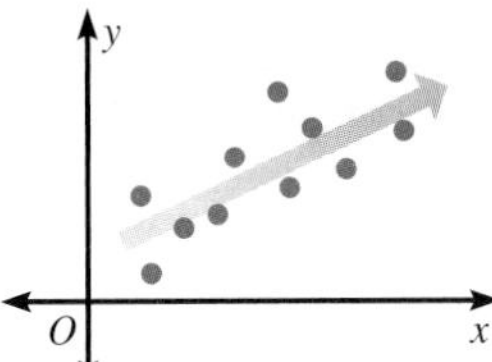

The y-coordinates tend to increase as the x-coordinates increase.

Negative relationship

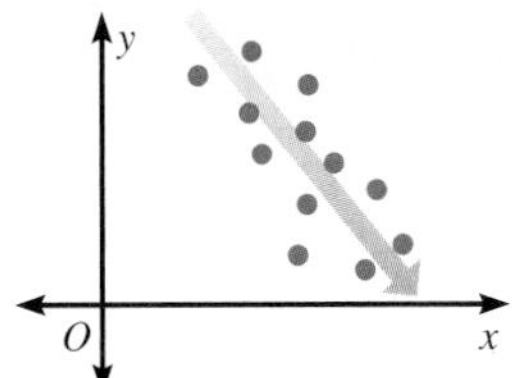

The y-coordinates tend to decrease as the x-coordinates increase.

No relationship

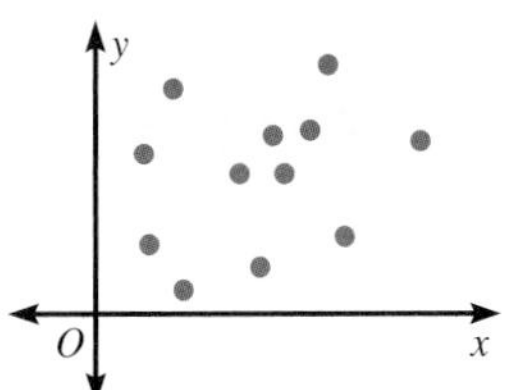

No obvious pattern exists between the coordinates.

EXAMPLE 2 Interpreting a Scatter Plot

Unit Cost The table shows the cost per ounce y of breakfast cereal when you buy x ounces. Make a scatter plot of the data. Predict whether the cost per ounce for a 22 ounce box of cereal will be *more than* or *less than* \$.22. *Explain.*

Number of ounces x	9.6	11.4	18.2	18.3	24	25.5
Cost per ounce y	\$.44	\$.33	\$.25	\$.22	\$.17	\$.16

SOLUTION

STEP 1 **Make** a scatter plot of the data from the table.

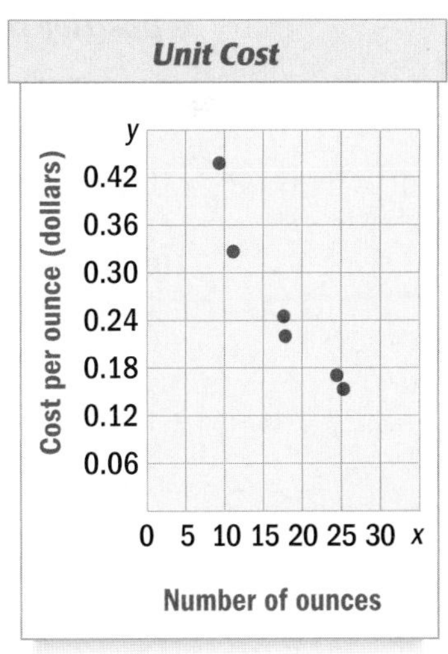

STEP 2 **Describe** the relationship between the variables. The y-coordinates decrease as the x-coordinates increase. So, the quantities have a *negative relationship.*

▶ **Answer** The cost per ounce of a 22 ounce box of cereal will be less than \$.22. The quantities have a negative relationship and a 22 ounce box weighs more than an 18.3 ounce box.

✓ GUIDED PRACTICE for Example 2

Make a scatter plot of the data. Tell whether x and y have a *positive relationship*, a *negative relationship*, or *no relationship*.

3.

x	0	1	2	3	4
y	3	6	12	15	20

4.

x	5	10	15	20	25
y	24	18	25	15	22

11.2 EXERCISES

HOMEWORK KEY

★ = **STANDARDIZED TEST PRACTICE** Exs. 14, 19, 20, 21, 23, and 34

○ = **HINTS AND HOMEWORK HELP** for Exs. 3, 7, 9, 19 at classzone.com

SKILL PRACTICE

1. **VOCABULARY** What type of graph is a collection of ordered pairs?

2. **VOCABULARY** In what type of relationship do both coordinates increase?

MAKING SCATTER PLOTS Make a scatter plot of the data.

SEE EXAMPLE 1 on p. 588 for Exs. 3–4

3.

x	1	2	3	4	5
y	5	3	−5	7	−1

4.

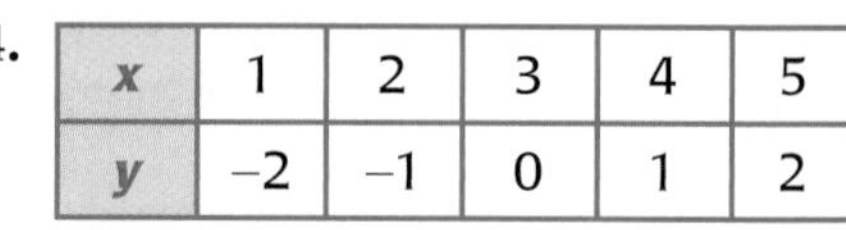

x	1	2	3	4	5
y	−2	−1	0	1	2

IDENTIFYING RELATIONSHIPS Tell whether x and y have a *positive relationship*, a *negative relationship*, or *no relationship*.

SEE EXAMPLE 2 on p. 589 for Exs. 5–9

5.

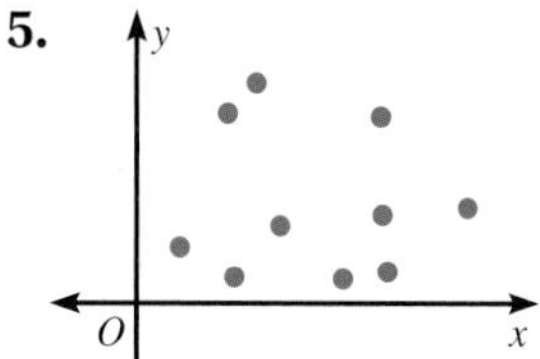

6.

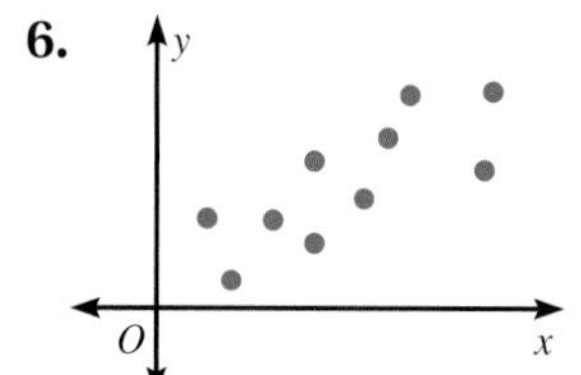

7.

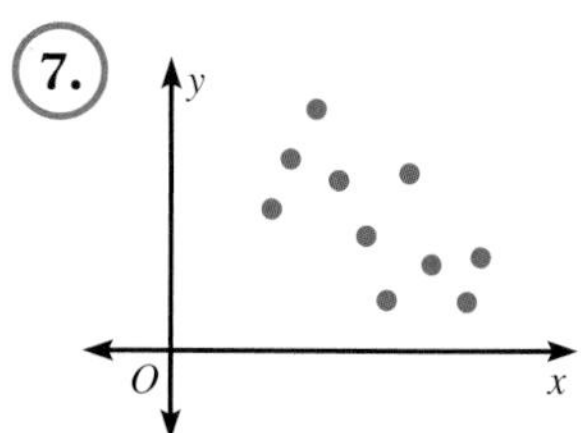

INTERPRETING Make a scatter plot of the data. Tell whether x and y have a *positive relationship*, a *negative relationship*, or *no relationship*.

8.

x	1	2	3	4	5
y	5	6	15	18	26

9.

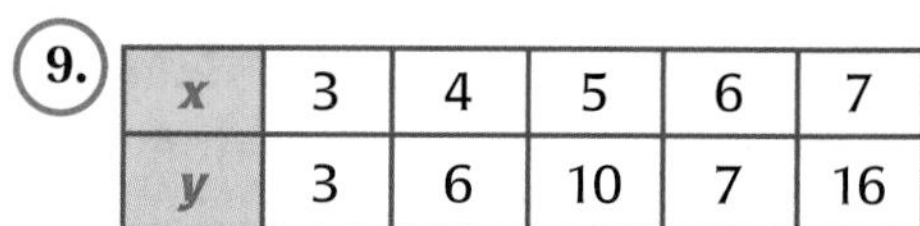

x	3	4	5	6	7
y	3	6	10	7	16

10. **ERROR ANALYSIS** Describe and correct the error made in determining the relationship between the variables.

x	−4	−3	−2	−1	0	1
y	3	2	0	4	2	3

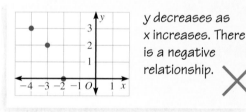

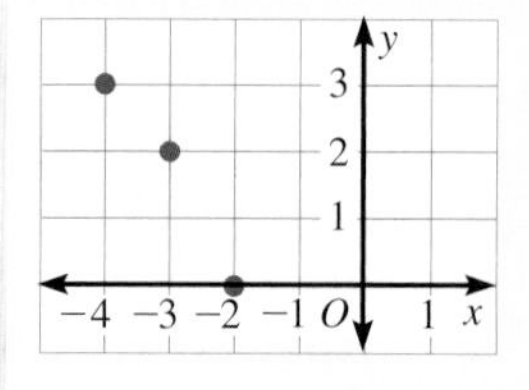

y decreases as x increases. There is a negative relationship. ✗

REASONING Predict the type of relationship the data have. *Explain.*

11. The height of a student in 8th grade and a test score of the student

12. The size of a pizza and the price of a pizza

13. The amount of money you pay and the amount you still owe

TAKE NOTES As you work on the exercises, write down any questions you want to ask your teacher.

14. ★ **MULTIPLE CHOICE** The variables m and n have a positive relationship. What conclusion can you make?

Ⓐ m is a function of n.

Ⓑ n is a function of m.

Ⓒ n increases as m increases.

Ⓓ n increases as m decreases.

15. **CHALLENGE** Make an input-output table for $y = (-1)^x$. Use the domain 0, 1, 2, 3, 4, 5, and 6. Then make a scatter plot of the data. What do you think the value of y will be when $x = 500$? *Explain* your reasoning.

In Exercises 16 and 17, use a scatter plot to estimate the value of the output when the input is 6.

EXTENSION Drawing Trend Lines

Basketball The table relates the height of a basketball player and the average number of rebounds per game. Use a scatter plot to estimate the number of rebounds that a 78 inch tall player makes.

Height (inches)	76	77	79	80	83	84
Average rebounds per game	4.2	4	5.2	5.4	6.8	10

SOLUTION

Plot the data as shown. There appears to be a positive relationship. Use a ruler to draw a line showing the trend in the data.

The line appears to pass through (78, 4.8). You can estimate that a 78 inch tall player averages about 4.8 rebounds per game.

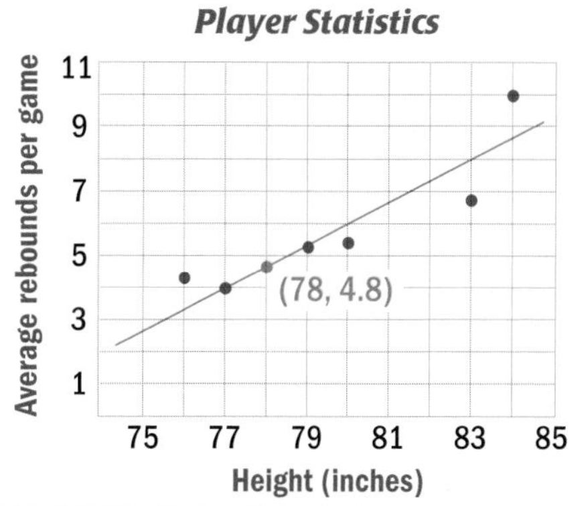

16.

Year	1	9	15	19	32
Mean winter temp. (°F)	21	25	24	28	30

17.

Week	1	3	4	5	7
Amount owed ($)	30	25	20	16	5

PROBLEM SOLVING

SEE EXAMPLE 2 on p. 589 for Ex. 18

18. **GUIDED PROBLEM SOLVING** The table shows the number of cookbooks sold at a bookstore in the first 6 years. Make a prediction about the number of cookbooks that will be sold in year 9.

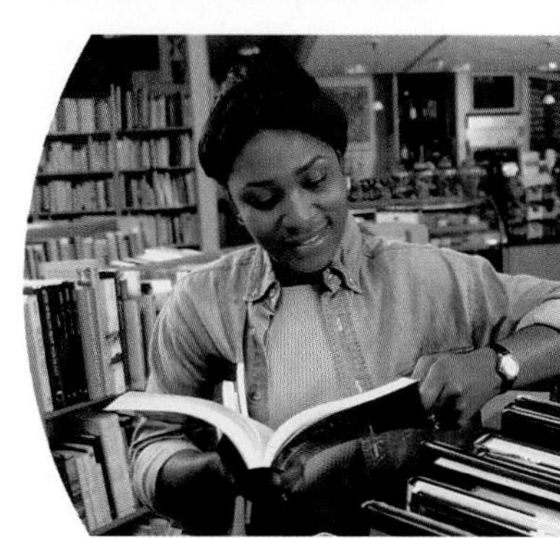

Year x	1	2	3	4	5	6
Books y	450	650	700	800	1100	1250

a. Make a scatter plot of the data.

b. Tell whether x and y have a *positive relationship*, a *negative relationship*, or *no relationship*.

c. In year 9, would you expect to sell *more than* or *fewer than* 1250 books?

19. ★ **OPEN-ENDED MATH** *Describe* a real-world set of data that have a positive relationship at one time of the year and a negative relationship at a different time of the year.

SEE EXAMPLE 2 on p. 589 for Exs. 20–21

20. ★ **SHORT RESPONSE** Make a scatter plot of the data at the right. *Describe* the relationship between the time spent studying for a test and the test score. *Predict* what will happen as study time continues to increase.

Study time (hours)	Test score (percent)
1	70
2	80
3	85

21. ★ **MULTIPLE CHOICE** A scatter plot of the amount of bottled water sold each month from August through December shows a negative relationship. Which conclusion is valid based on the plot?

Ⓐ the most water is sold in July
Ⓑ as months pass, less water is sold
Ⓒ the most water is sold in December
Ⓓ as months pass, more water is sold

22. **REASONING** A table relates the time after which a vehicle starts traveling and its distance from point A. A scatter plot of the data shows a negative relationship. Is the vehicle traveling *toward* or *away from* point A? *Explain* your reasoning.

23. ★ **WRITING** A newspaper claims there is a strong relationship between the weather on the day of an election and voter turnout. What do you think the newspaper means? Could the newspaper use a scatter plot to support its claim? If so, what would the labels on each axis be? *Explain.*

24. **GEOMETRY** Make a table showing the lengths and widths of four different rectangles with perimeters of 16 inches. Make a scatter plot of the data. Estimate the width of a rectangle when the length is 5.5 inches. *Explain* how you made your estimate.

25. **CHALLENGE** For the top eight teams during the regular season of the National Football League in 2004, there was a positive relationship between the average margin of victory (points scored − points allowed) and the number of wins. There was *no* relationship between points scored and number of wins. *Explain* how this is possible.

MIXED REVIEW

Prepare for Lesson 11.3 in Exs. 26–29

Solve the equation. Check your answer. *(p. 129)*

26. $2y - 3 = 7$ **27.** $9 - 3x = 6$ **28.** $5 = 12 + \frac{z}{4}$ **29.** $-5w + 11 = -34$

Make an input-output table for the function. Use the domain −2, −1, 0, 1, and 2. Identify the range. *(p. 583)*

30. $y = 0.7x$ **31.** $y = 3x + 4$ **32.** $y = 0.4x - 1$ **33.** $y = -2x + 1$

34. ★ **MULTIPLE CHOICE** What is the area of a 6 meter high trapezoid with bases 14 meters and 16 meters? *(p. 521)*

Ⓐ 84 m^2 Ⓑ 90 m^2 Ⓒ 96 m^2 Ⓓ 180 m^2

11.3 Equations in Two Variables

Before You found solutions of equations in one variable.

Now You'll find solutions of equations in two variables.

Why? So you can find costs, such as rental costs in Example 1.

KEY VOCABULARY
- **solution of an equation in two variables,** *p. 593*

A **solution of an equation in two variables** is an ordered pair whose values make the equation true. For example, (2, 3) is a solution of $x + y = 5$ because $2 + 3 = 5$.

EXAMPLE 1 Standardized Test Practice

In-line Skates At a sports store, it costs \$7 per hour to rent in-line skates plus \$10 for the safety equipment. The total cost can be modeled by the equation $C = 10 + 7h$, where C is the total cost in dollars and h is the number of hours skated. Which table shows some possible total costs for renting in-line skates and safety equipment?

ELIMINATE CHOICES
You know that a one hour rental will cost \$7 plus \$10, or \$17. So, you can eliminate choices A and B.

Ⓐ

Hours h	1	2	3	4
Cost C	\$7	\$14	\$21	\$28

Ⓑ

Hours h	1	2	3	4
Cost C	\$7	\$17	\$27	\$37

Ⓒ

Hours h	1	2	3	4
Cost C	\$17	\$24	\$31	\$38

Ⓓ

Hours h	1	2	3	4
Cost C	\$17	\$34	\$51	\$68

SOLUTION

Substitute several values of h into the equation $C = 10 + 7h$ and solve for C. Then identify the table that contains the solutions.

h-value	Substitute for h.	Evaluate.	Solution (h, C)
$h = 1$	$C = 10 + 7(1)$	$C = 17$	(1, 17)
$h = 2$	$C = 10 + 7(2)$	$C = 24$	(2, 24)
$h = 3$	$C = 10 + 7(3)$	$C = 31$	(3, 31)
$h = 4$	$C = 10 + 7(4)$	$C = 38$	(4, 38)

▶ **Answer** The correct answer is C. Ⓐ Ⓑ Ⓒ Ⓓ

GUIDED PRACTICE for Example 1

1. **What If?** In Example 1, suppose the store rounds your time to the nearest half hour. How long can you skate if you have \$35?

EXAMPLE 2 Checking Solutions

Tell whether (7, −6) is a solution of $x + 3y = 14$.

$x + 3y = 14$	Write original equation.
$7 + 3(-6) \stackrel{?}{=} 14$	Substitute 7 for *x* and −6 for *y*.
$7 + (-18) \stackrel{?}{=} 14$	Simplify.
$-11 \neq 14$ ✗	Solution does not check.

▸ **Answer** The ordered pair (7, −6) is *not* a solution of $x + 3y = 14$.

Function Form When you are finding solutions of an equation, it can be helpful to rewrite the equation in *function form*. To write an equation in function form, solve for *y*.

Function form	Not function form
$y = -2x + 15$	$2x + y = 15$

EXAMPLE 3 Finding Solutions of an Equation

Write the equation $4x + y = 15$ in function form. Then list four solutions.

SOLUTION

STEP 1 **Rewrite** the equation in function form.

$4x + y = 15$	Write original equation.
$y = 15 - 4x$	Subtract 4*x* from each side.

STEP 2 **Choose** several values to substitute for *x*. Then solve for *y*.

x-value	Substitute for *x*.	Evaluate.	Solution
$x = -1$	$y = 15 - 4(-1)$	$y = 19$	(−1, 19)
$x = 0$	$y = 15 - 4(0)$	$y = 15$	(0, 15)
$x = 1$	$y = 15 - 4(1)$	$y = 11$	(1, 11)
$x = 2$	$y = 15 - 4(2)$	$y = 7$	(2, 7)

▸ **Answer** Four solutions are (−1, 19), (0, 15), (1, 11), and (2, 7).

SUBSTITUTE FOR X

Generally, an equation involving two variables has an infinite number of solutions. When finding solutions, you can choose any *x*-value that is in the domain.

✓ GUIDED PRACTICE for Examples 2 and 3

Tell whether the ordered pair is a solution of the equation.

2. $y = 3x - 7$; (6, 5)

3. $-2x - 4y = 12$; (−4, −1)

List four solutions of the equation.

4. $y = -2x + 6$

5. $3x + y = 4$

11.3 EXERCISES

HOMEWORK KEY

★ = **STANDARDIZED TEST PRACTICE** Exs. 13, 44, 45, 47, and 58

○ = **HINTS AND HOMEWORK HELP** for Exs. 5, 7, 15, 21, 43 at classzone.com

SKILL PRACTICE

VOCABULARY **Copy and complete the statement.**

1. A(n) _?_ of an equation in two variables is an ordered pair.

2. When an equation is solved for y, the equation is in _?_ form.

CALCULATING *Y*-VALUES **Copy and complete the table for the equation.**

SEE EXAMPLE 1 on p. 593 for Exs. 3–5

3. $y = x + 8$

4. $y = 4 - 3x$

5. $y = -20 + x$

x	-5	0	5	10
y	?	?	?	?

CHECKING SOLUTIONS **Tell whether the ordered pair is a solution of the equation.**

SEE EXAMPLE 2 on p. 594 for Exs. 6–13

6. $y = 4x + 2$; (2, 10) **7.** $2x + y = 5$; (7, 5) **8.** $y = 6 - x$; $(-3, 3)$

9. $x + 8y = 2$; $(10, -1)$ **10.** $y = 6x + 7$; (2, 21) **11.** $3x - y = 26$; $(6, -8)$

12. ERROR ANALYSIS Describe and correct the error made in deciding whether $(-5, 4)$ is a solution of $2x + 3y = -7$.

$$2x + 3y = -7$$
$$2(4) + 3(-5) \stackrel{?}{=} -7$$
$$8 + (-15) \stackrel{?}{=} -7$$
$$-7 = -7 \checkmark$$

So, $(-5, 4)$ is a solution.

13. ★ **MULTIPLE CHOICE** Which ordered pair is a solution of $y = -3x + 11$?

Ⓐ $(-2, 17)$ Ⓑ $(0, -11)$ Ⓒ $(2, 3)$ Ⓓ $(-1, -14)$

FINDING SOLUTIONS **List four solutions of the equation.**

SEE EXAMPLE 3 on p. 594 for Exs. 14–31

14. $y = -2x + 5$ **15.** $y = -51 - 6x$ **16.** $16x + 24 = y$

17. $-5x + 3 = y$ **18.** $y = \frac{1}{2}x - 1$ **19.** $y = \frac{1}{3}x - 5$

SOLVING FOR *Y* **Write the equation in function form. Then list four solutions of the equation.**

20. $x + y = 8$ **21.** $42 = 4x + y$ **22.** $33 = -3x + y$

23. $5x + y = 10$ **24.** $12 = 3x + y$ **25.** $19 = -2x + y$

26. $4y = 8x + 12$ **27.** $5y + 15x = 10$ **28.** $-32 = 4x - 12y$

29. $8y = 16x - 10$ **30.** $-6y + 3x = 9$ **31.** $42 - 7y = 15x$

32. EXAMPLES AND NONEXAMPLES Give two ordered pairs that are solutions of the equation $-24 = 6x - y$ and two ordered pairs that are *not* solutions of the equation.

33. **ESTIMATION** Estimate the values of $9x$ and $8y$ for the ordered pair $\left(\frac{7}{3}, \frac{5}{8}\right)$. *Explain* why the ordered pair cannot be a solution of $9x + 8y = 16$.

WRITING EQUATIONS Write an equation for the values in the table. Then list four solutions with x-values greater than 100.

34.

x	−1	0	1	2
y	2	4	6	8

35.

x	0	2	4	6
y	2	3	4	5

36.

x	−1	0	1	2
y	−8	−5	−2	1

37.

x	0	4	8	12
y	6	7	8	9

CHALLENGE Find the ordered pair that is a solution of both equations.

38. $y = -2x + 3$
$y = 0.5x - 2$

39. $y = 6x - 10$
$y = -3x + 26$

40. $x + 2y = 4$
$x + y = -2$

41. $-x - 4y = 4$
$x - 2y = 14$

PROBLEM SOLVING

SEE EXAMPLE 1 on p. 593 for Exs. 42–44

42. **LOAN** Your friend agrees to lend you \$15 to buy a model rocket. You promise to pay your friend \$2.50 each week until you have paid back the full \$15. Use the equation $P = 15 - 2.5n$, where P is the number of dollars that you have left to pay and n is the number of weeks. Find the number of weeks it takes to pay back your friend.

43. **SKATEBOARD WHEELS** Your skateboard club decides to replace each club member's wheels for a competition. A set of four wheels sells for \$24 plus a \$14 shipping and handling cost.

a. Use the equation $C = 24n + 14$, where C is the total cost in dollars and n is the number of sets of wheels ordered. What is the total cost of 4 sets of wheels?

b. The total cost of your club's order is \$182. How many sets of wheels are purchased?

c. Suppose your club doubles the order. Will the total cost be \$364 (\$182 × 2)? *Explain.*

44. ★ **MULTIPLE CHOICE** You pay \$25 to join the summer movie club at your local theater. Each movie you see costs only \$3. You can model this situation with the equation $C = 25 + 3m$, where C is the total cost in dollars and m is the number of movies you see. You have \$60 to spend on the movie club. What is the greatest number of movies you can see?

(A) 10 movies (B) 11 movies (C) 28 movies (D) 205 movies

45. ★ **WRITING** *Explain* why it can be helpful to rewrite equations in function form when finding solutions of an equation.

46. **GLASS ELEVATOR** A glass elevator is at a height of 1200 feet. It is descending at a rate of 1000 feet per minute.

    a. Use the equation $h = 1200 - 1000m$, where h is the height of the elevator in feet and m is the time in minutes. What is the height of the elevator after 1 minute?

    b. How long, in minutes and seconds, will it take the elevator to reach a height of 0 feet?

47. ★ **SHORT RESPONSE** You want to buy x bottles of water and y bottles of sports drink. Each bottle of water costs \$1 and each bottle of sports drink costs \$2. You have \$9. Write an equation in two variables to model the total cost. Can you buy 3 bottles of sports drink and 4 bottles of water? *Explain.*

48. **REASONING** In Example 3 on page 594, you solved the equation for y before substituting the x-values. Will you get the same solutions if you substitute the x-values before solving for y? *Justify* your reasoning.

49. **CARNIVAL** You have 2 hours to spend at a carnival where you plan to go on rides and play games. You know that each ride takes about 10 minutes, including the wait in line. Write an equation in two variables to model this situation, where x is the number of rides and y is the number of minutes spent playing games. You plan to go on 8 rides. How long can you play games?

50. (xy) **ALGEBRA** Write the equation $ax + by = c$ in function form.

51. **CHALLENGE** As part of a class project, you simulate a dog walking-and-feeding service. In week one, you charge \$2 per walk and \$4 per meal. In week two, you charge \$4 per walk and \$2 per meal. In week three, you charge \$4 per walk and \$4 per meal. You collect \$38, \$40, and \$52 respectively for the three weeks. Each week had the same combination of walks and meals. Find the numbers of walks and meals per week.

MIXED REVIEW

Get-Ready

Prepare for Lesson 11.4 in Exs. 52–55

Identify the quadrant or axis where the given point is located. *(p. 94)*

52. $(-3, 8)$ 53. $(0, -10)$ 54. $(4, -1)$ 55. $(6, 0)$

56. Graph a triangle with vertices $A(1, 2)$, $B(2, 6)$, and $C(4, 1)$. Reflect the triangle in the x-axis. *(p. 433)*

57. Graph a triangle with vertices $R(-5, 8)$, $S(-3, 0)$, and $T(0, 4)$. Reflect the triangle in the y-axis. *(p. 433)*

58. ★ **MULTIPLE CHOICE** What is the approximate area of a circle whose diameter is 25 inches? Use 3.14 for π. *(p. 527)*

    (A) 78.5 in. (B) 78.5 in.^{2} (C) 490.6 in. (D) 490.6 in.^{2}

11.4 Graphs of Linear Equations

Before	You found solutions of equations in two variables.
Now	You'll learn to sketch the graph of a linear equation.
Why?	So you can recognize linear patterns, as in Ex. 42.

KEY VOCABULARY

- **linear equation,** *p. 598*

ACTIVITY

You can graph a function by plotting ordered pairs from a table.

STEP 1 **Copy** and complete the table of values using the equation $y = 3x + 2$.

x	−4	−2	0	2	4
y	−10	?	?	?	?

STEP 2 **Plot** each ordered pair (x, y) from the table in a coordinate plane like the one shown.

$(-4, -10), (-2, ?), (0, ?), (2, ?), (4, ?)$.

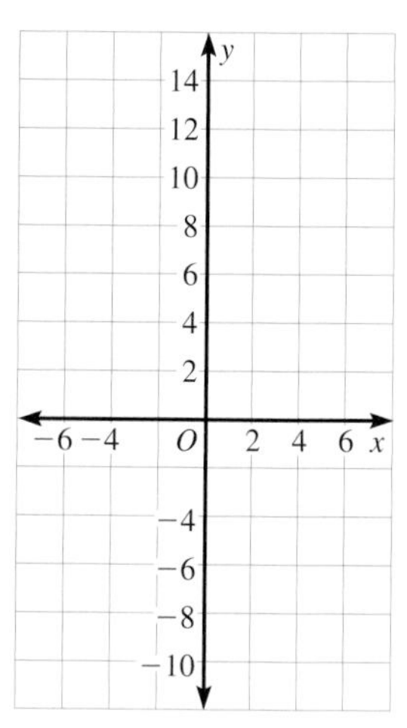

STEP 3 **Connect** the points. What pattern do you notice?

STEP 4 **Find** several more solutions of $y = 3x + 2$. Locate each solution in your coordinate plane. What do you notice?

STEP 5 **Make** a conjecture about the graph of all solutions of $y = 3x + 2$.

Linear Equations In the activity, you graphed solutions of a *linear equation*. A **linear equation** in two variables has the two variables in separate terms with each variable occurring only to the first power. The graph is a line.

Linear equations	**Not linear equations**
$y = x - 1$	$24 = rt$
$3p + 5q = 16$	$a^2 + b^2 = c^2$
$s = 0.2t$	

The equation $24 = rt$ is not linear because it has two variables in the same term. The equation $a^2 + b^2 = c^2$ is not linear because the variables are squared.

EXAMPLE 1 Graphing a Linear Equation

Graph $y = \frac{1}{2}x + 1$.

STEP 1 **Choose** several values to substitute for x. Then evaluate to find y and make a table of values.

x	−4	−2	0	2	4
y	−1	0	1	2	3

STEP 2 **List** the solutions as ordered pairs.
(−4, −1), (−2, 0), (0, 1), (2, 2), (4, 3)

STEP 3 **Plot** the ordered pairs and draw a line through them. The line is the graph of $y = \frac{1}{2}x + 1$.

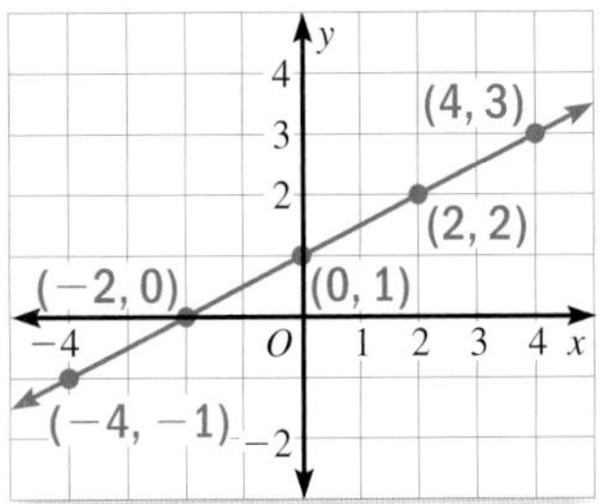

Animated Math at classzone.com

READING GRAPHS
The arrowheads on the graph in Example 1 indicate that the line extends forever in both directions.

EXAMPLE 2 Using the Graph of a Linear Equation

Growth Rate Sue's hair is 3 inches long and grows $\frac{1}{2}$ inch per month. The length l, in inches, of her hair can be modeled by the equation $l = \frac{1}{2}m + 3$, where m is the time in months. Use a graph to estimate how long it will take Sue to grow her hair to a length of $5\frac{1}{2}$ inches.

SOLUTION

Make a table of values and plot each solution. Draw a ray through the points. Then locate the point on the ray where $l = 5\frac{1}{2}$.

m	0	1	2	3
l	3	$3\frac{1}{2}$	4	$4\frac{1}{2}$

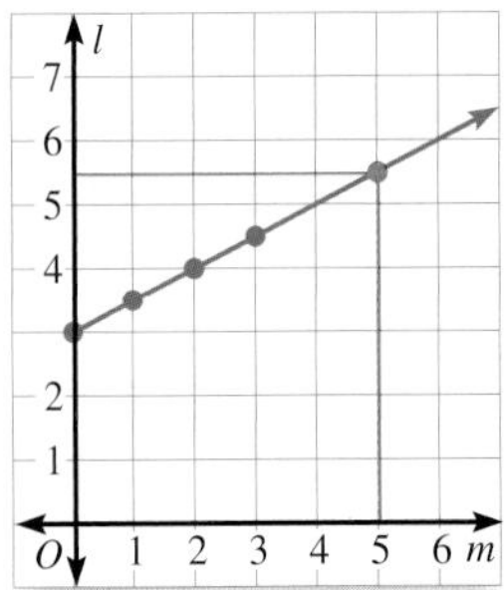

▶ **Answer** The graph shows that it will take about 5 months for Sue to grow her hair to a length of $5\frac{1}{2}$ inches.

AVOID ERRORS
In real-world contexts, be sure to choose domain values that make sense in real-world situations. In Example 2, the domain should include only positive numbers.

✓ GUIDED PRACTICE for Examples 1 and 2

Graph the linear equation.

1. $y = x + 4$
2. $y = x + 6$
3. $y = \frac{1}{2}x - 7$
4. $y = -2x - 3$

5. **What If?** In Example 2, suppose Sue's hair is 4 inches long. The length l, in inches, of her hair can be modeled by the equation $l = \frac{1}{2}m + 4$, where m is the time in months. Use a graph to estimate how long it will take Sue to grow her hair to a length of $5\frac{1}{2}$ inches.

Vertical and Horizontal Lines Some linear equations have only one variable. The graphs of these equations are vertical or horizontal lines.

KEY CONCEPT *For Your Notebook*

Vertical and Horizontal Lines

The graph of $x = a$ is the vertical line passing through $(a, 0)$.

The graph of $y = b$ is the horizontal line passing through $(0, b)$.

EXAMPLE 3 Graphing Vertical and Horizontal Lines

AVOID ERRORS

The graph of a linear equation may not be a function. A vertical line does *not* represent a function, because one input has infinitely many outputs. A horizontal line *does* represent a function.

a. The graph of $x = -2$ is the vertical line through $(-2, 0)$.

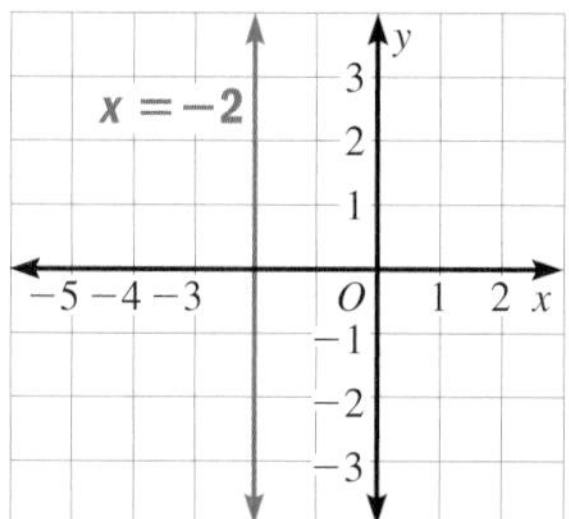

For all values of y, the x-value is -2.

b. The graph of $y = 4$ is the horizontal line through $(0, 4)$.

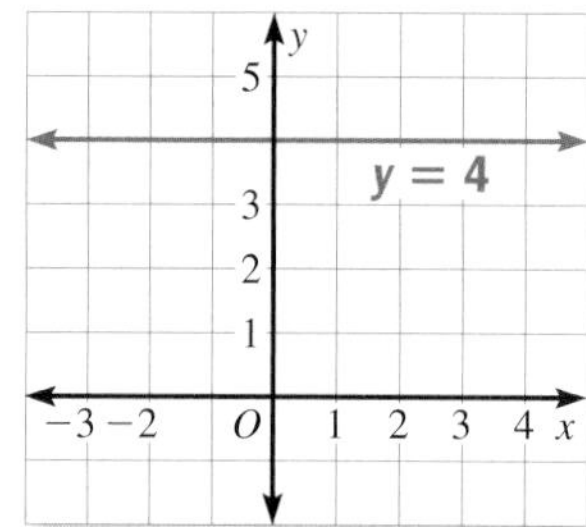

For all values of x, the y-value is 4.

✓ **GUIDED PRACTICE** for Example 3

6. Graph $y = -3$.

7. Graph $x = 1$.

11.4 EXERCISES

HOMEWORK KEY

★ = **STANDARDIZED TEST PRACTICE** Exs. 6, 42, 43, and 56

○ = **HINTS AND HOMEWORK HELP** for Exs. 3, 13, 15, 17, 41 at classzone.com

SKILL PRACTICE

1. VOCABULARY Copy and complete: The graph of the solutions of a linear equation is a(n) _?_.

VOCABULARY Tell whether the equation is a linear equation.

2. $3x + y = 8$

3. $2y - 5x = 10$

4. $9x^2 = y + 4$

5. $y = -4$

SEE EXAMPLE 1 on p. 599 for Ex. 6

6. ★ **MULTIPLE CHOICE** Which equation's graph includes the point $(0, 0)$?

Ⓐ $y = \frac{1}{2}x + 6$ Ⓑ $2x + 3y = 6$ Ⓒ $y = \frac{1}{2}x$ Ⓓ $2x = 6 - 3y$

GRAPHING WITH TWO VARIABLES **Graph the linear equation.**

SEE EXAMPLE 1 on p. 599 for Exs. 7–15

7. $y = x + 9$
8. $y = x - 14$
9. $y = x - 17$
10. $y = -2x + 1$
11. $y = -4x + 8$
12. $y = 8x$
13. $y = -3x$
14. $y = \frac{1}{2}x + 5$
15. $y = -\frac{1}{4}x + 12$

GRAPHING WITH ONE VARIABLE **Graph the vertical or horizontal line.**

SEE EXAMPLE 3 on p. 600 for Exs. 16–22

16. $x = 2$
17. $y = 6$
18. $y = -9$
19. $y = -1.5$
20. $x = 1.5$
21. $x = 3.5$

22. **ERROR ANALYSIS** A student says that the equation of the line shown at the right is $y = 5$. Describe and correct the error made in the student's statement.

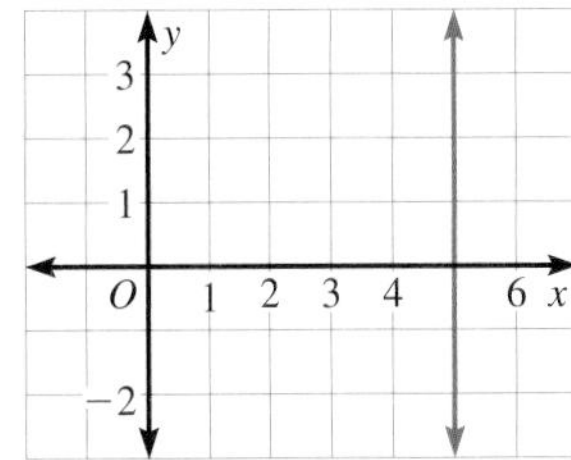

SOLVING FOR Y **Solve the linear equation for *y* and then graph.**

23. $16x - 4y = 8$
24. $9x + 3y = 18$
25. $10x = -2y$

WRITING EQUATIONS **Write the equation of the line.**

26. 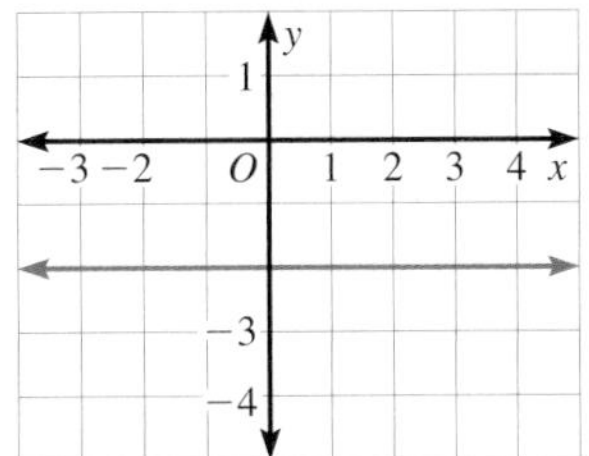

27. 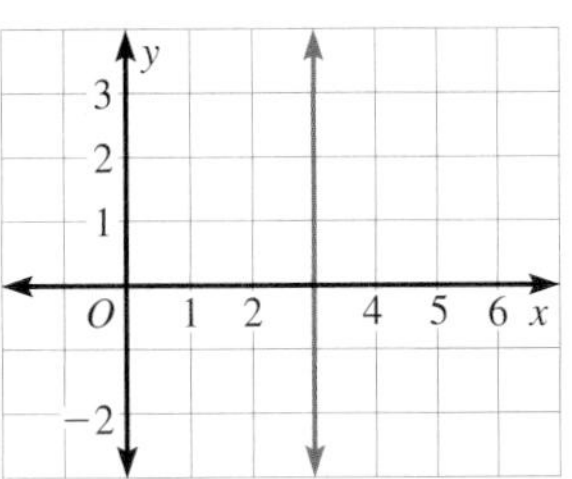

28. 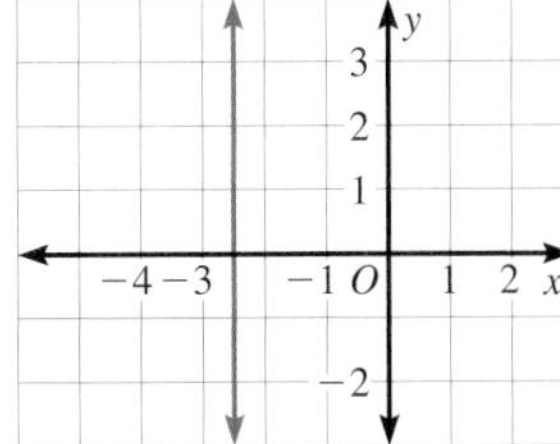

COMPARING GRAPHS **Graph the equations in Exercises 29–32 in the same coordinate plane. How are the graphs alike? How are they different?**

29. $y = x$
30. $y = x + 7$
31. $y = x - 5$
32. $y = x - 9$

COMPARING GRAPHS **Graph the equations in Exercises 33–36 in the same coordinate plane. How are the graphs alike? How are they different?**

33. $y = x$
34. $y = 3x$
35. $y = -x$
36. $y = -4x$

CHALLENGE **Write the equation of the line.**

37. 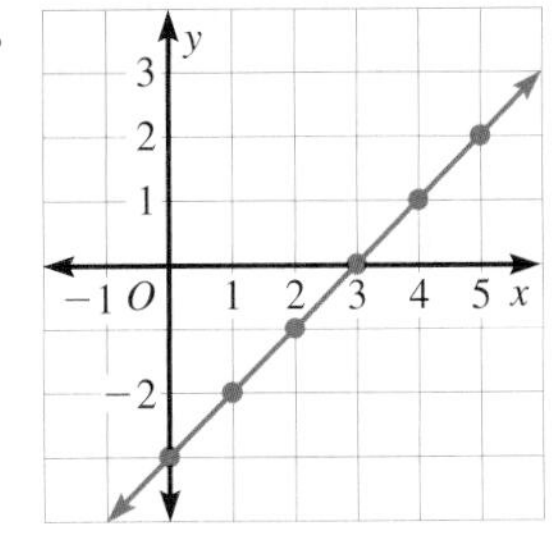

38. 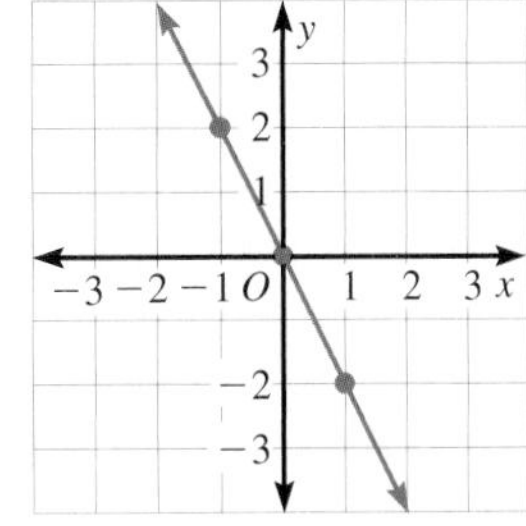

39. 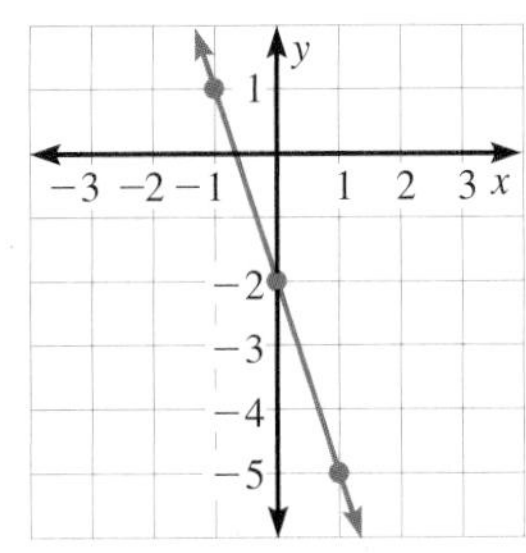

PROBLEM SOLVING

SEE EXAMPLE 2 on p. 599 for Exs. 40–41

40. PHOTOGRAPHY You need a digital camera for a photography class. The payment plan for the camera can be modeled by the equation $C = 10m + 50$, where C is the total cost, in dollars, and m is the number of months. Graph the equation and use your graph to estimate how much you pay in 12 months.

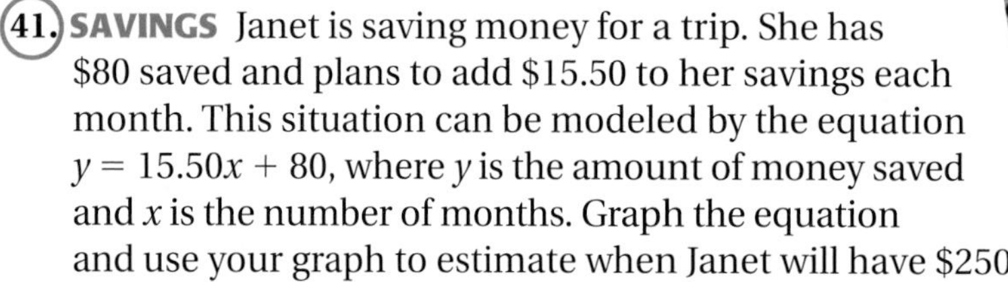

41. SAVINGS Janet is saving money for a trip. She has \$80 saved and plans to add \$15.50 to her savings each month. This situation can be modeled by the equation $y = 15.50x + 80$, where y is the amount of money saved and x is the number of months. Graph the equation and use your graph to estimate when Janet will have \$250.

42. ★ SHORT RESPONSE A deep-sea diver is 160 feet below the surface of the water. The diver is ascending at a rate of 20 feet every 4 minutes.

Time (minutes)	4	8	12	16
Depth (feet)	?	?	?	?

a. Copy and complete the table.

b. Is the relationship between depth and time linear? *Explain.*

43. ★ MULTIPLE CHOICE The total cost C of a cell phone plan with unlimited minutes m is \$40 a month. Which equation models this situation?

Ⓐ $C = 40$ Ⓑ $m = 40$ Ⓒ $C = 40m$ Ⓓ $m = 40C$

READING *IN* MATH **Read the information below for Exercises 44–46.**

Temperature Temperature can be measured in degrees Fahrenheit or degrees Celsius. On the Fahrenheit scale, the difference between the freezing point and boiling point of water is 180°. On the Celsius scale, the difference is 100°.

Because these differences represent the same change in temperature, every change of 9°F equals a change of 5°C. This ratio appears in fraction form in the formula for changing degrees Celsius to degrees Fahrenheit: $F = \frac{9}{5}C + 32$.

Common Temperatures	
Freezing point of water	32°F
Ideal room temperature	70°F
Normal body temperature	98.6°F
Boiling point of water	212°F

44. Graph Graph the equation that relates degrees Celsius to degrees Fahrenheit. Use $C = 0°, 10°, 20°, 30°$, and $40°$ in your table of values.

45. Interpret Use the Common Temperatures table and your graph. Approximate the normal body temperature in degrees Celsius.

46. Analyze Is 10°C *warmer* or *colder* than room temperature? *Explain* how you can use your graph to answer this question.

47. **MULTIPLE REPRESENTATIONS** Max teaches youth swimming lessons. He starts students with 1 minute of treading water and then adds 2 minutes each month.

a. **Write an Equation** Model this situation with an equation, where y is the total time spent treading water and x is the number of months.

b. **Draw a Graph** Graph the equation and estimate the number of months it will take for the students to tread water for 13 minutes.

c. **Evaluate Results** Use your equation from part (a) to confirm the estimate you made in part (b).

48. **REASONING** *Explain* how to find the equation of a line that is parallel to the x-axis and lies 8.6 units below it.

49. **CHALLENGE** Jared's age j is seven years more than his sister Karen's age k. Write and graph an equation in two variables to model this situation. *Explain* how to use your graph to find out how old they will be when Jared is twice as old as Karen.

MIXED REVIEW

Get-Ready

Prepare for Lesson 11.5 in Exs. 50–52

List three solutions of the equation. *(p. 593)*

50. $y = 3x + 2$ 51. $y = -6x - 5$ 52. $y = -2x + 4$

Find the area of the parallelogram with height h and base b. *(p. 521)*

53. $h = 10, b = 14$ 54. $h = 17, b = 23$ 55. $h = 32, b = 33$

56. ★ **MULTIPLE CHOICE** For which value of x is the set of ordered pairs $(x, 3), (2, 1), (4, 5), (1, 1)$ a function? *(p. 583)*

(A) 1 (B) 2 (C) 3 (D) 4

QUIZ for Lessons 11.1–11.4

1. Make an input-output table for $y = -\frac{1}{3}x$. Use the domain 0, 1, 2, and 3. Identify the range. *(p. 583)*

List three solutions of the equation. Then graph the equation. *(pp. 593, 598)*

2. $7y + x = 21$ 3. $-5x - 2y = -20$ 4. $-3x + 9y = -18$

Write a function rule that relates x and y. *(p. 583)*

5. $(-2, 0), (-1, 1), (0, 2), (1, 3), (2, 4)$ 6. $(-3, -5), (0, 1), (3, 7), (6, 13), (9, 19)$

7. **FUNDRAISING** An art club raised \$120 for supplies by selling pottery. Mugs cost \$4 and bowls cost \$2. Graph the equation $4x + 2y = 120$, where x is the number of mugs sold and y is the number of bowls sold. Is there a *positive relationship*, a *negative relationship*, or *no relationship* between number of mugs sold and number of bowls sold? *Explain*. *(pp. 588, 598)*

Technology **ACTIVITY** *Use after Lesson 11.4*

GOAL
Use a graphing calculator to graph linear functions.

11.4 Graphing Linear Functions

EXAMPLE **Use a calculator to graph $x - 2y = 6$.**

SOLUTION

STEP 1 **Rewrite** the equation so that it is in function form: $y = \frac{1}{2}x - 3$.

STEP 2 **Use** the following keystrokes on a graphing calculator to enter the function:

Keystrokes

  1  2 

 3

Display

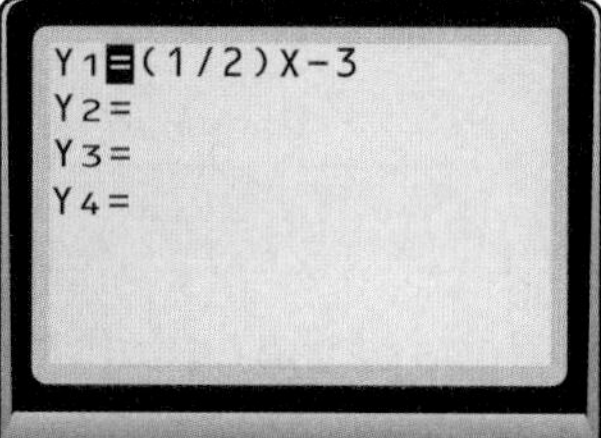

STEP 3 **Use** the WINDOW feature to set the viewing window for the graph. Then view the graph by pressing the GRAPH button.

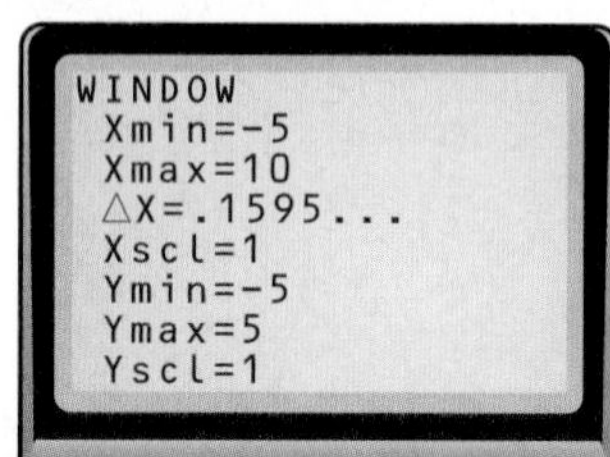

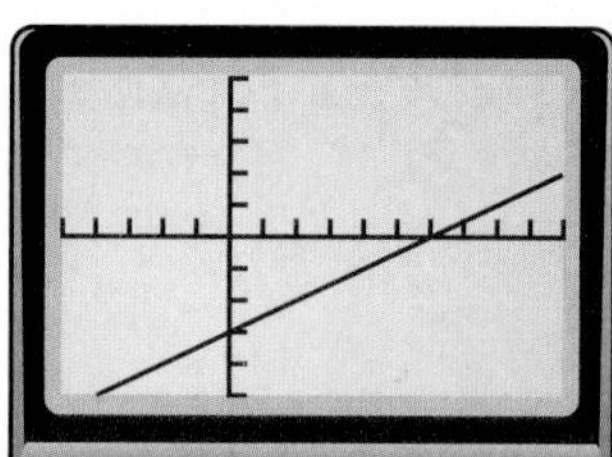

PRACTICE **Use a calculator to graph the equation.**

1. $y = 2x - 5$
2. $y = -x + 10$
3. $x - y = 11$
4. $x + y = 6$

Tell whether the viewing window is appropriate for the graph of the equation. If not, give an appropriate window.

5. $y = 4x + 5$

Xmin=-5
Xmax=5
△X=.1063...
Ymin=-5
Ymax=5

6. $y = 2x + 14$

Xmin=-5
Xmax=5
△X=.1063...
Ymin=-5
Ymax=5

MIXED REVIEW *of Problem Solving*

Lessons 11.1–11.4

1. **MULTI-STEP PROBLEM** A hot-air balloon is 5 feet off the ground and starts rising at a rate of 2 feet per second. The height h, in feet, of the balloon can be modeled by the equation $h = 5 + 2t$, where t is the time in seconds.
   a. Graph $h = 5 + 2t$.
   b. Use your graph to estimate how many seconds it will take for the balloon to be 8 feet off the ground.
   c. Double your answer to part (b). Will the balloon be twice as high off the ground (16 feet) in that many seconds? *Explain.*

2. **GRIDDED ANSWER** A \$45 model plane requires \$8 of new batteries each month. The total cost C, in dollars, is $C = 45 + 8m$, where m is the number of months. You receive a gift of \$25 to put toward the purchase and operation of a plane. How much more, in dollars, will you need to operate the plane in the first year?

3. **MULTI-STEP PROBLEM** The table below shows the number of miles you run in the first four weeks of training for a 10 mile race.

Week w	1	2	3	4
Distance d (miles)	3	3.5	4	4.5

   a. Write a function rule for this situation.
   b. How many miles will you run in week 9?
   c. In what week will you run 10 miles?

4. **OPEN-ENDED** *Describe* three real-world data relationships whose scatter plots you expect to show a positive relationship, a negative relationship, and no relationship. *Explain* your reasoning.

5. **EXTENDED RESPONSE** An electric clothes dryer costs \$300 and uses \$.43 worth of electricity per hour. Each load of laundry takes 1 hour to dry.
   a. Write an equation to model the total cost C, in dollars, of running the dryer for h hours.
   b. A laundromat charges \$2.50 per load to use a dryer. Does it cost *more, less,* or *about the same* to dry 200 loads of laundry at home? *Explain.*
   c. For about how many loads would the costs be the same? *Explain.*

6. **MULTI-STEP PROBLEM** A car moving at 8 feet per second begins increasing speed by 4 feet per second each second.
   a. Write an equation for the situation. Use S for the speed of the car, in feet per second, and t for the number of seconds.
   b. How many seconds will it take for the car to reach a speed of 60 miles per hour?

7. **SHORT RESPONSE** Casey and Krystal are each saving money to buy the DVD player shown. Casey already has \$36 saved. He will add \$2 every week to his fund. Krystal does not have any money saved. She will put \$5 in her fund every week until she can afford it.

   a. For each person, write an equation to model the total amount of money m, in dollars, saved after w weeks.
   b. Who can double the amount of money he or she has if the time is doubled? *Justify* your answer using the equations.
   c. Who will be able to purchase the DVD player first?

11.5 Using Intercepts

Before You graphed linear equations.
Now You'll find *x*- and *y*-intercepts of lines.
Why? So you can find options for exercising, as in Example 3.

KEY VOCABULARY
- ***x*-intercept,** *p. 606*
- ***y*-intercept,** *p. 606*

The ***x*-intercept** of a graph is the *x*-coordinate of the point where the graph crosses the *x*-axis. The graph of $2x + 3y = 12$ crosses the *x*-axis at (6, 0), so its *x*-intercept is 6.

The ***y*-intercept** of a graph is the *y*-coordinate of the point where the graph intersects the *y*-axis. The graph of $2x + 3y = 12$ crosses the *y*-axis at (0, 4), so its *y*-intercept is 4.

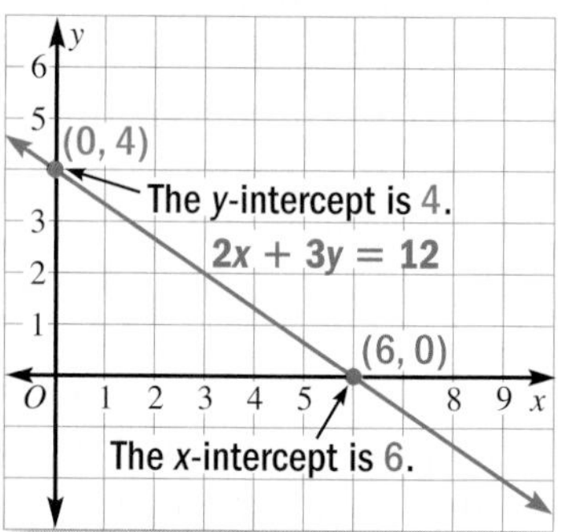

KEY CONCEPT *For Your Notebook*

Finding Intercepts

***x*-intercept** To find the *x*-intercept of a graph, substitute 0 for *y* into the equation of the line and solve for *x*.

***y*-intercept** To find the *y*-intercept of a graph, substitute 0 for *x* into the equation of the line and solve for *y*.

EXAMPLE 1 Finding Intercepts

Find the intercepts of the graph of $y = \frac{1}{2}x - 5$.

STEP 1 To find the *x*-intercept, let $y = 0$ and solve for *x*.

$$y = \frac{1}{2}x - 5$$
$$0 = \frac{1}{2}x - 5$$
$$5 = \frac{1}{2}x$$
$$10 = x$$

STEP 2 To find the *y*-intercept, let $x = 0$ and solve for *y*.

$$y = \frac{1}{2}x - 5$$
$$y = \frac{1}{2}(0) - 5$$
$$y = 0 - 5$$
$$y = -5$$

▸ **Answer** The *x*-intercept is 10 and the *y*-intercept is −5. The graph of the equation crosses the *x*-axis at (10, 0) and the *y*-axis at (0, −5).

Graphing Lines The intercepts indicate the points where a line intersects the x-axis and the y-axis. You can use these points to graph a line.

EXAMPLE 2 Using Intercepts to Graph a Line

Graph the line with an x-intercept of -3 and a y-intercept of 2.

The x-intercept is -3, so plot the point $(-3, 0)$. The y-intercept is 2, so plot the point $(0, 2)$. Then draw a line through the two points.

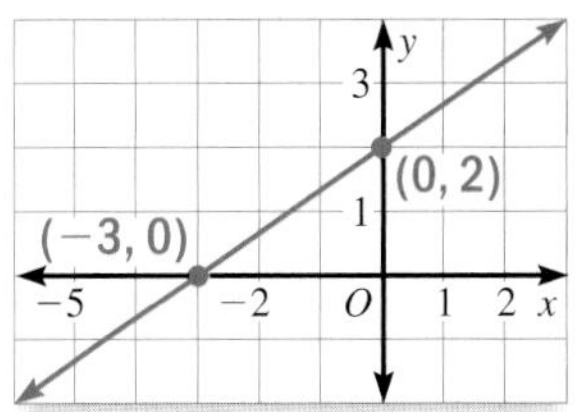

EXAMPLE 3 Using and Interpreting Intercepts

Fitness Deena runs and walks with her dog on a trail that is 8 miles long. She can run 4 miles per hour and walk 2 miles per hour. Graph the equation $4x + 2y = 8$, where x is the number of hours she runs and y is the number of hours she walks. What do the intercepts represent?

SOLUTION

STEP 1 Find the x-intercept.

$$4x + 2y = 8$$
$$4x + 2(0) = 8$$
$$4x = 8$$
$$x = 2$$

STEP 2 Find the y-intercept.

$$4x + 2y = 8$$
$$4(0) + 2y = 8$$
$$2y = 8$$
$$y = 4$$

STEP 3 The x-intercept is 2 and the y-intercept is 4. So the points $(2, 0)$ and $(0, 4)$ are on the graph. Plot these points and draw a line through them.

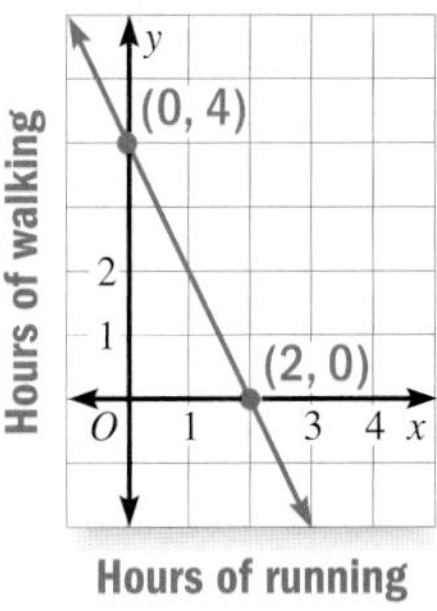

▶ **Answer** The x-intercept represents the number of hours it takes Deena to run the entire time. The y-intercept represents the number of hours it takes Deena to walk the entire time.

✓ GUIDED PRACTICE for Examples 1, 2, and 3

Find the intercepts of the graph of the equation. Then graph the line using the intercepts.

1. $y = 2x - 10$ **2.** $3x + y = -1$ **3.** $5x + 3y = 18$

4. What If? In Example 3, suppose Deena runs and walks with her dog on a trail that is 12 miles long. Graph the equation $4x + 2y = 12$, where x is the number of hours she runs and y is the number of hours she walks. How are the intercepts affected by the change in the trail length?

11.5 EXERCISES

HOMEWORK KEY

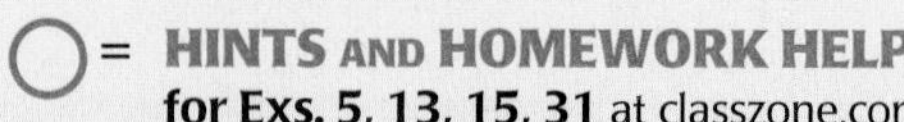

★ = STANDARDIZED TEST PRACTICE Exs. 9, 31, 32, 34, and 43

○ = HINTS AND HOMEWORK HELP for Exs. 5, 13, 15, 31 at classzone.com

SKILL PRACTICE

VOCABULARY **Identify the x-intercept and the y-intercept.**

1. 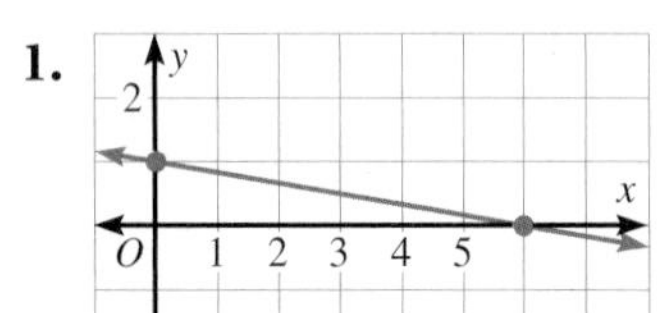

2. 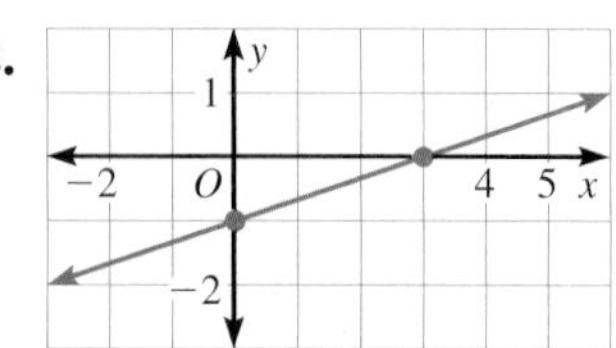

FINDING INTERCEPTS **Find the intercepts of the graph of the equation.**

SEE EXAMPLE 1 on p. 606 for Exs. 3–10

3. $y = 6x - 3$
4. $x + 4y = 12$
5. $5x - 2y = 10$
6. $x + 9y = 18$
7. $4x + 5y = 20$
8. $7x - 9y = -63$

9. ★ **MULTIPLE CHOICE** What is the y-intercept of the graph of $2x - y = 4$?

(A) -4 (B) -1 (C) 2 (D) 4

10. **ERROR ANALYSIS** Describe and correct the error made in finding the intercepts of the graph of $4x - 3y = 12$.

$4x - 3y = 12$
$4(0) - 3(0) \stackrel{?}{=} 12$
$0 \neq 12$ There are no intercepts. ✗

GRAPHING WITH INTERCEPTS **Graph the line that has the given intercepts.**

SEE EXAMPLE 2 on p. 607 for Exs. 11–13

11. x-intercept: 9, y-intercept: 4
12. x-intercept: -3, y-intercept: 1
13. x-intercept: 6, y-intercept: -10

FINDING INTERCEPTS TO GRAPH **Find the intercepts of the graph of the equation. Then graph the equation.**

SEE EXAMPLES 1 AND 2 on p. 607 for Exs. 14–19

14. $y = 5x - 15$
15. $y = -2x + 7$
16. $8x + 10y = 30$
17. $7.5x + 3y = 19.5$
18. $-\frac{3}{4}x + y = -\frac{1}{2}$
19. $-\frac{1}{6}x + \frac{1}{3}y = \frac{1}{3}$

COMPARING INTERCEPTS **Tell which intercept(s), if any, of the graphs of the two equations are equal.**

20. $x + 2y = 5$, $x - 2y = 5$
21. $3x - 2y = 6$, $-3x - 2y = 6$
22. $7x + 5y = 35$, $7x + 5y = -35$

FINDING INTERCEPTS **Find the intercepts of the graph of the equation.**

23. $y = 9$
24. $y = 14$
25. $x = 21$

CHALLENGE **Graph the line and its reflection in the given axis.** ***Describe*** **how the intercepts change due to the reflection.**

26. $-3x + y = 12$; x-axis
27. $-4x + 6y = 20$; x-axis
28. $3x - 8y = 32$; y-axis

PROBLEM SOLVING

SEE EXAMPLE 3 on p. 607 for Exs. 29–31

29. **GUIDED PROBLEM SOLVING** You have \$60 to spend. CDs are \$12 each and videos are \$10 each. The equation $12x + 10y = 60$ models this situation. Graph the equation and explain what the intercepts represent.

    a. Decide what x and y represent in the equation.

    b. Find the intercepts. Then graph the equation.

    c. *Explain* what the intercepts represent in this situation.

30. **PRIZES** You need to buy 12 prizes for a school contest. T-shirts come in packs of 4, and DVD gift certificates come in packs of 2. The number of packs you can buy of each item is represented by the equation $4x + 2y = 12$. What does the x-intercept tell you in this situation?

31. ★ **SHORT RESPONSE** You are riding the bus home from school. After x minutes, the number of miles from home y is given by $2x + 3y = 18$. Find the intercepts. Then graph the equation. *Explain* what the points along the graph and the intercepts represent.

32. ★ **WRITING** Do all graphs of linear equations have a y-intercept? *Explain* why or why not.

33. **REASONING** The x-intercept of a line is positive and the y-intercept is negative. Does the line slant *up* or *down* from left to right? Through which quadrant(s) does the line pass? *Explain* your reasoning.

34. ★ **SHORT RESPONSE** A bank offers a savings account at a 2% simple interest rate and a certificate of deposit at a 5% simple interest rate. The equation $0.02s + 0.05c = 100$ models ways to earn \$100 in interest in 1 year. What do the intercepts represent in this situation? *Describe* one way you can invest \$3500 and earn exactly \$100 interest.

35. **CHALLENGE** Find the intercepts of the graphs of $y = 0.5x$, $y = 3x$, and $y = 5x$. Using your results, write a conjecture about the intercepts and the graph of $y = kx$, where k is a nonzero number. *Justify* your reasoning.

MIXED REVIEW

Prepare for Lesson 11.6 in Exs. 36–39

Find the difference. *(p. 68)*

36. $7 - 16$ 37. $8 - (-15)$ 38. $-4 - 31$ 39. $-24 - (-18)$

Graph the equation using a table of values. *(p. 598)*

40. $y = x + 5$ 41. $y = 2x - 6$ 42. $y = -7x + 4$

43. ★ **MULTIPLE CHOICE** What is the value of $\frac{2ab^2}{6a^2}$ when $a = 4$ and $b = 6$? *(p. 187)*

    Ⓐ 2 Ⓑ 3 Ⓒ 4 Ⓓ 6

INVESTIGATION

Use before Lesson 11.6

GOAL
Understand slope as a measure of steepness.

MATERIALS
- pencil
- straightedge
- graph paper

11.6 Finding the Slope of a Line

You can describe the steepness of a line using its *slope*, or ratio of vertical change (rise) to horizontal change (run) between any two points on a line. You can find the slope using the formula $slope = \frac{rise}{run}$.

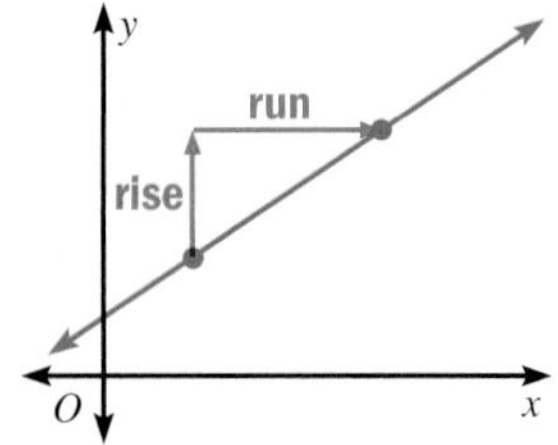

EXPLORE 1 **Find the slope of the line passing through the points (3, 3) and (7, 5).**

STEP 1 **Plot** the points (3, 3) and (7, 5) in a coordinate plane. Draw a line through the points.

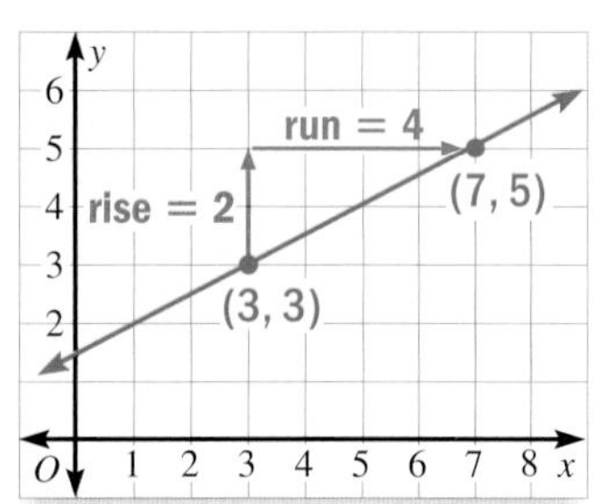

STEP 2 **Find** the rise. Then find the run. Substitute for rise and run in the formula for slope.

$$\text{slope} = \frac{\text{rise}}{\text{run}} = \frac{2}{4} = \frac{1}{2}$$

The slope of the line passing through the points (3, 3) and (7, 5) is $\frac{1}{2}$.

PRACTICE **Use the formula for slope.**

1. Find the slope of the line passing through the points (−1, 1) and (−3, 5). Follow the same steps as in Explore 1.

   - Plot the points (−1, 1) and (−3, 5) in a coordinate plane. Draw a line through the points.

   - Find the rise. Then find the run. Substitute for rise and run in the formula for slope.

2. Using the same points, (−1, 1) and (−3, 5), what operation can you perform on the y-coordinates to find the rise? What operation can you perform on the x-coordinates to find the run?

3. Find the slope of the line passing through the points (5, 6) and (−2, 3).

EXPLORE 2 Use two points to find the slope of a line.

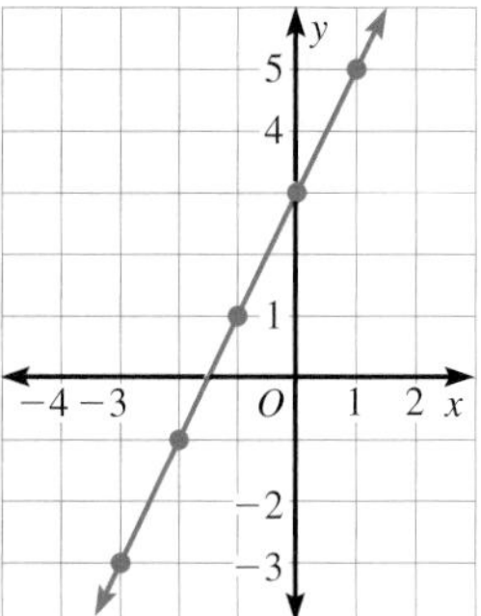

STEP 1 **Copy** the graph at the right.

STEP 2 **Choose** two points on the line. Find the rise and run. Calculate the slope.

STEP 3 **Choose** a different pair of points on the line. Find the rise and run. Calculate the slope.

STEP 4 **Describe** a pattern in your answers to Steps 2 and 3. Make a conjecture about the slope of a line.

PRACTICE Find the slope of the line passing through the points.

4. (1, 4), (4, 2)

5. (1, −3), (5, −2)

6. (−3, 4), (0, 6)

7. (7, 8), (−1, −5)

8. (−2, 6), (0, −3)

9. (−9, 3), (3, −9)

10. If a line slants down from left to right, what can you say about the rise and run?

11. If a line slants up from left to right, what can you say about the rise and run?

12. *Compare* a line that has a slope greater than 1 with a line that has a slope between 0 and 1.

Find the slope of the line.

13.

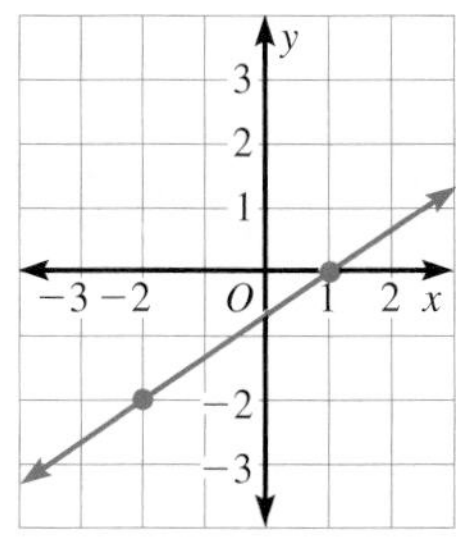

14.

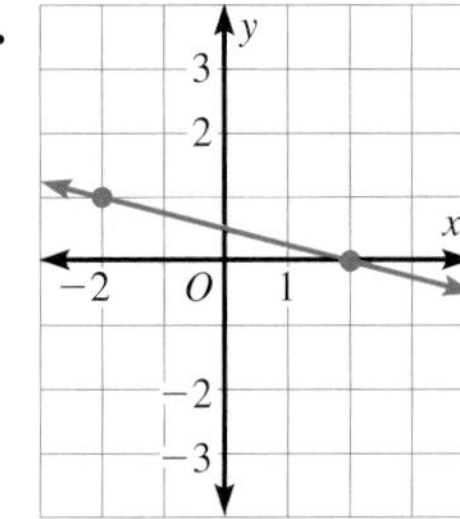

15.

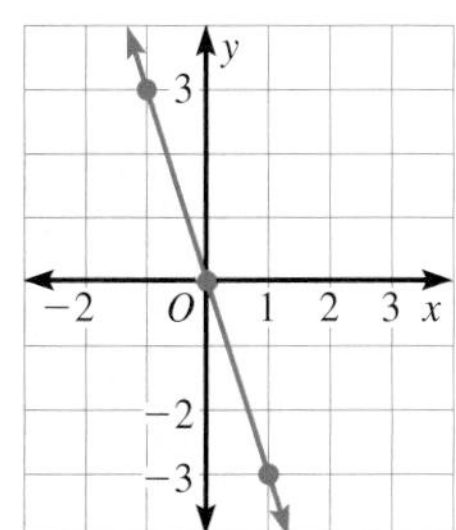

DRAW CONCLUSIONS

16. **REASONING** What is the slope of the line passing through the points (a, b) and (c, d)?

11.6 Slope

Before	You graphed linear equations.
Now	You'll find and interpret slopes of lines.
Why?	So you can describe steepness, as of a railway in Example 1.

KEY VOCABULARY
- **slope,** *p. 612*
- **rise,** *p. 612*
- **run,** *p. 612*

Cogwheel Railway The Mount Pilatus Railway in the Swiss Alps is the steepest cogwheel railway in the world. The track rises about 20 feet vertically for every 50 feet it runs horizontally. How can you describe the steepness of the track?

You can describe steepness using *slope*. The **slope** of a nonvertical line is the ratio of its vertical change, the **rise**, to its horizontal change, the **run**.

EXAMPLE 1 Finding Slope

The diagram shows the rise and the run of the Mount Pilatus Railway described above.

$$\text{slope} = \frac{\text{rise}}{\text{run}} = \frac{\overset{2}{\cancel{20}}\ \cancel{\text{ft}}}{\underset{5}{\cancel{50}}\ \cancel{\text{ft}}} = \frac{2}{5}$$

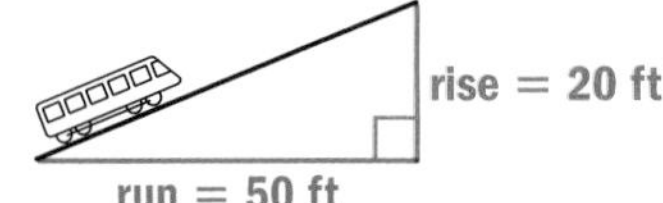

▶ **Answer** The track has a slope of $\frac{2}{5}$.

Animated Math at classzone.com

✓ GUIDED PRACTICE for Example 1

1. **Ramps** Using slope, describe the steepness of a ramp that rises 6 feet vertically for every 18 feet it reaches horizontally.

KEY CONCEPT *For Your Notebook*

Slope of a Line

The slope m of a nonvertical line passing through the points (x_1, y_1) and (x_2, y_2) is

$$m = \frac{\text{rise}}{\text{run}} = \frac{\text{change in } y}{\text{change in } x} = \frac{y_2 - y_1}{x_2 - x_1}$$

The slope of a line is the same no matter which two points on the line you choose to use in the formula.

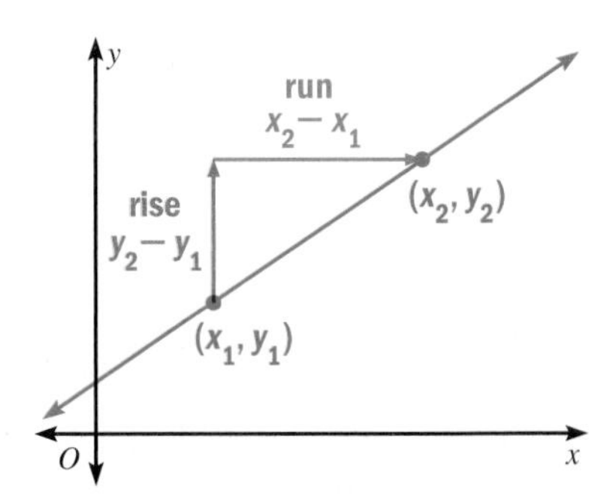

EXAMPLE 2 Positive and Negative Slope

Find the slope of the line.

a.

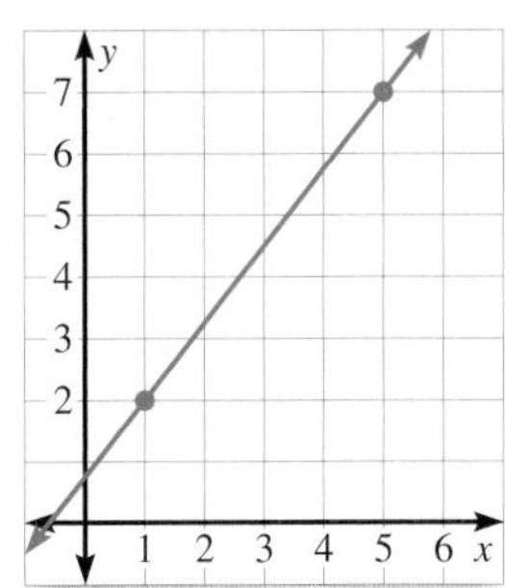

$$m = \frac{\text{rise}}{\text{run}} = \frac{y_2 - y_1}{x_2 - x_1}$$

$$= \frac{7 - 2}{5 - 1}$$

$$= \frac{5}{4}$$

b.

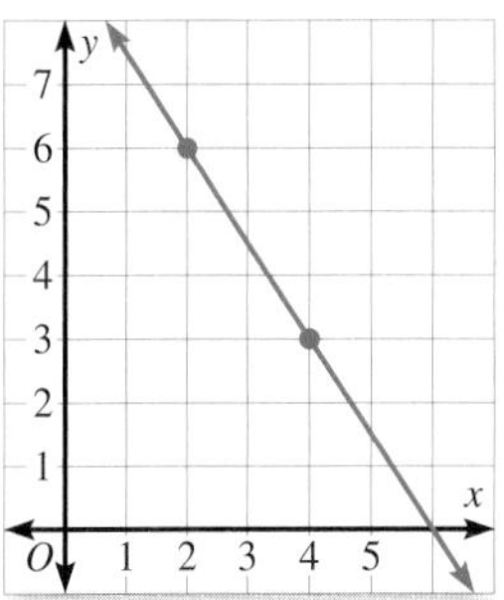

$$m = \frac{\text{rise}}{\text{run}} = \frac{y_2 - y_1}{x_2 - x_1}$$

$$= \frac{3 - 6}{4 - 2}$$

$$= \frac{-3}{2} \text{ or } -\frac{3}{2}$$

AVOID ERRORS

When finding the slope of a line, make sure that you are using the *x*- and *y*-coordinates in the same order.

EXAMPLE 3 Zero and Undefined Slope

Find the slope of the line.

a.

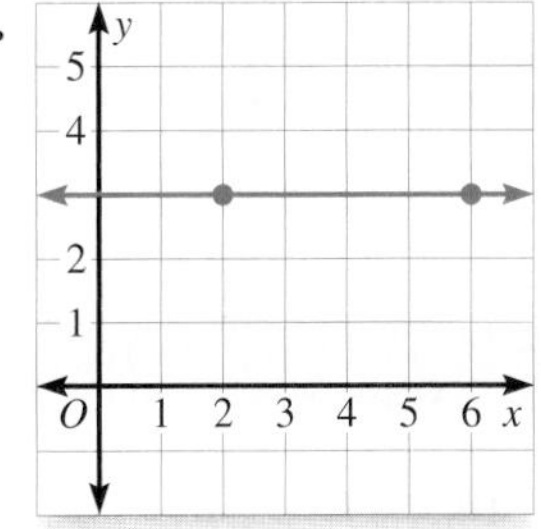

$$m = \frac{\text{rise}}{\text{run}} = \frac{y_2 - y_1}{x_2 - x_1}$$

$$= \frac{3 - 3}{6 - 2}$$

$$= \frac{0}{4}$$

$$= 0$$

b.

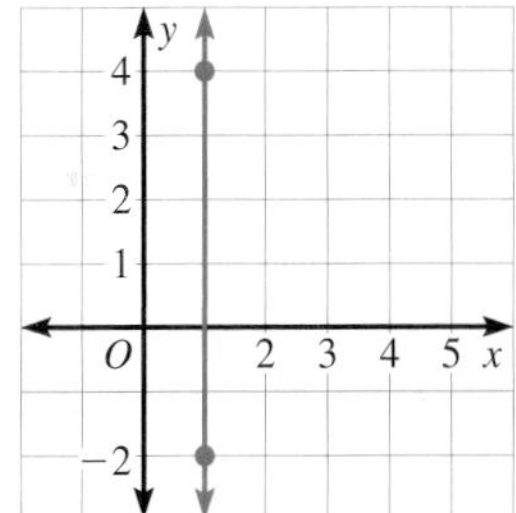

$$m = \frac{\text{rise}}{\text{run}} = \frac{y_2 - y_1}{x_2 - x_1}$$

$$= \frac{4 - (-2)}{1 - 1}$$

$$= \frac{6}{0}$$

The slope is undefined.

REVIEW RULES OF DIVISION

Remember that zero divided by any nonzero number is zero and that any number divided by zero is *undefined*.

✓ GUIDED PRACTICE for Examples 2 and 3

Find the slope of the line passing through the points.

2. (2, 1), (6, 4)

3. (0, 6), (10, 0)

4. (−3, −4), (5, 2)

5. (1, 5), (−3, 5)

6. (1, 6), (1, 2)

7. (−8, 3), (8, 3)

CONCEPT SUMMARY *For Your Notebook*

Slope of a Line

A line with *positive* slope rises from left to right.

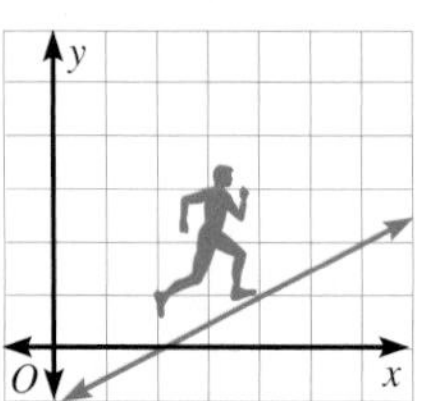

A line with *negative* slope falls from left to right.

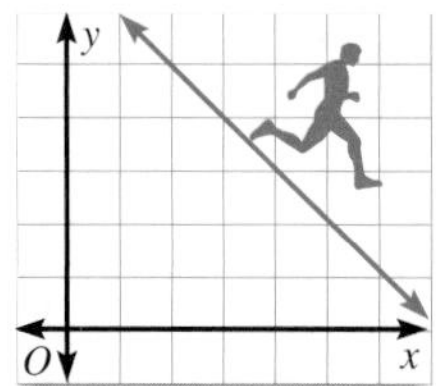

A line with *zero* slope is horizontal.

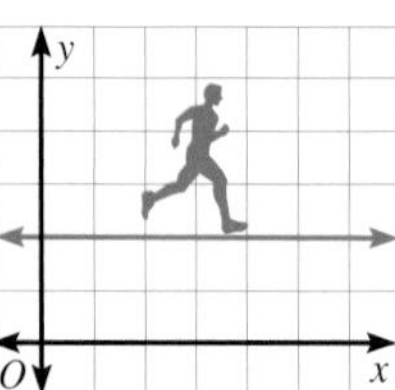

A line with *undefined* slope is vertical.

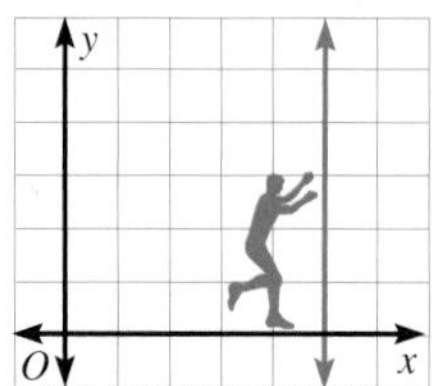

11.6 EXERCISES

HOMEWORK KEY

★ = **STANDARDIZED TEST PRACTICE** Exs. 27, 37, 39, 40, 41, 44, and 54

○ = **HINTS AND HOMEWORK HELP** for Exs. 5, 9, 11, 19, 35 at classzone.com

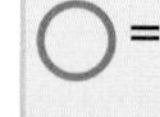

SKILL PRACTICE

VOCABULARY Copy and complete the statement.

1. Between two points, the change in the y-coordinate is called the _?_.
2. Between two points, the change in the x-coordinate is called the _?_.
3. The ratio of vertical change to horizontal change between any two points on a line is the _?_ of the line.

SLOPE FROM A GRAPH Write the coordinates of the two given points on the line. Then find the slope of the line.

SEE EXAMPLES 2 AND 3 on p. 613 for Exs. 4–6

4. 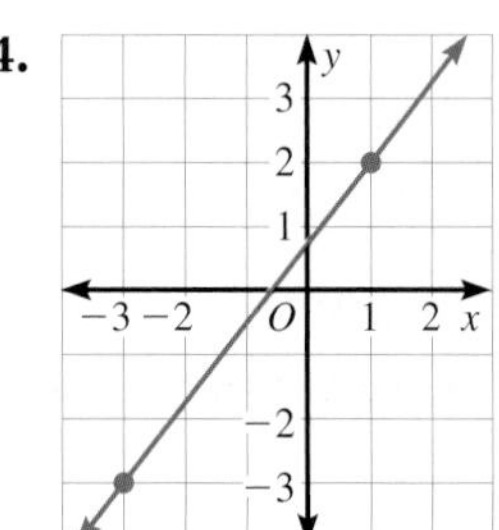

5. 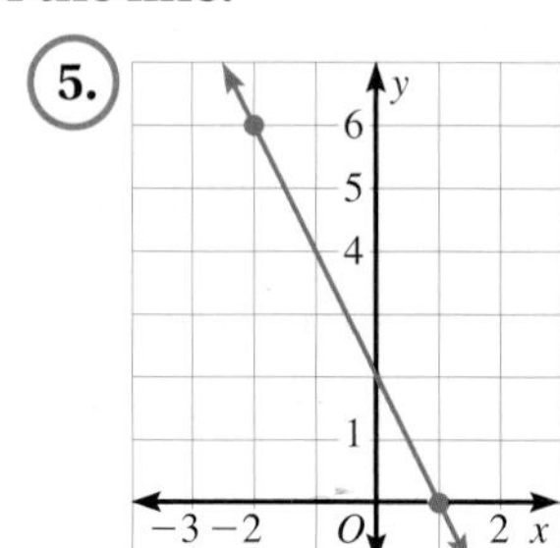

6. 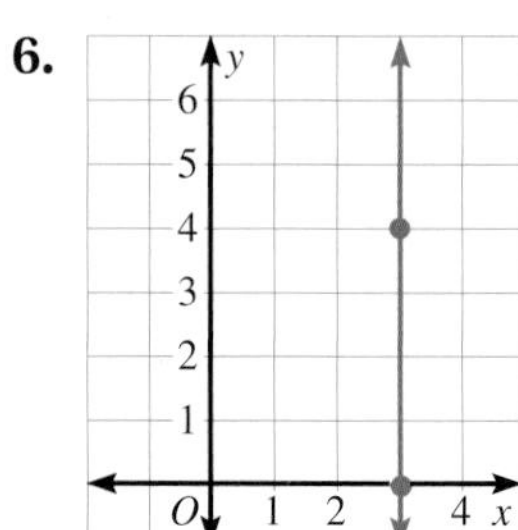

SEE EXAMPLES 2 AND 3
on p. 613 for Exs. 7–20

SLOPE FROM POINTS Find the slope of the line through the points.

7. $(-4, 8), (6, 6)$ **8.** $(1, 4), (1, -7)$ **9.** $(-5, 4), (3, 4)$

10. $(-2, -4), (4, 2)$ **11.** $(-3, 1), (-3, -2)$ **12.** $(5, 8), (0, 5)$

13. $(-6, -2), (6, -7)$ **14.** $(9, -8), (15, -8)$ **15.** $(12, 22), (-20, 19)$

16. ERROR ANALYSIS Describe and correct the error made in finding the slope of the line shown at the right.

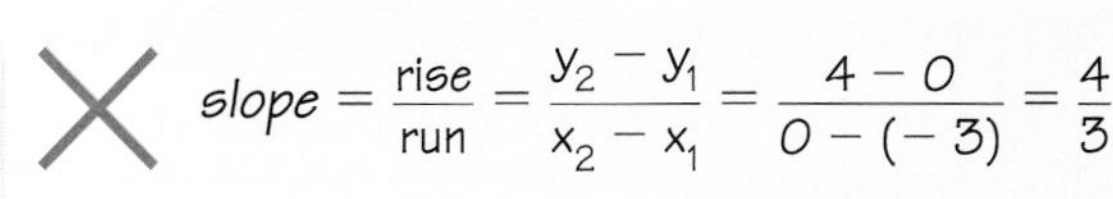

slope = rise/run = (y2 − y1)/(x2 − x1) = (4 − 0)/(0 − (−3)) = 4/3

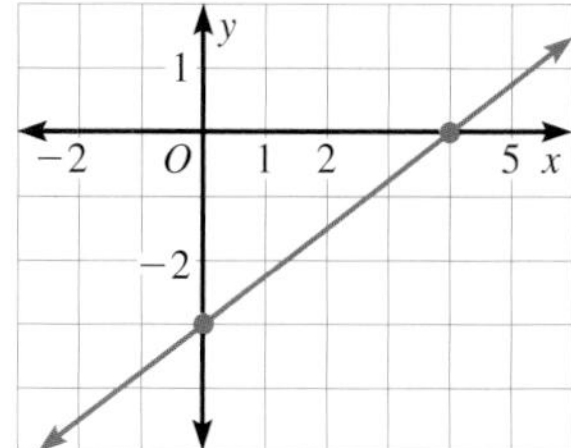

SKETCHING LINES Sketch a line with the given type of slope.

17. negative **18.** undefined **19.** positive **20.** zero

USING TRIANGLES The given points are vertices of a triangle. Plot and connect the points. Then find the slope of each side of the triangle.

21. $A(0, 0), B(0, 8), C(6, 0)$ **22.** $D(-3, 4), E(4, 1), F(-1, -7)$

23. $G(0, 6), H(4, 0), J(-4, 0)$ **24.** $K(-5, 1), L(-1, -4), M(-2, 4)$

COMPARING SLOPES The greater the absolute value of a line's slope, the *steeper* the line is. The lines *a* and *b* pass through the given points. Determine which line, *a* or *b*, is steeper.

25. line a: $\left(\frac{1}{2}, -\frac{3}{2}\right), (1, 0)$
line b: $(4, 10), \left(-\frac{1}{2}, 1\right)$

26. line a: $(2, -9), (-11, 3)$
line b: $\left(\frac{5}{8}, -\frac{1}{4}\right), \left(-\frac{5}{8}, 6\right)$

27. ★ MULTIPLE CHOICE A line passing through the point $(-7, -3)$ has a slope of 0. Which point is *not* on the line?

(A) $(-3, 3)$ (B) $(-145, -3)$ (C) $(756, -3)$ (D) $\left(\frac{2}{9}, -3\right)$

xy ALGEBRA Find the unknown value using the given slope and points on the line.

28. $m = \frac{7}{4}; (x, -7), (16, 0)$ **29.** $m = 0; (0, 7), (3, y)$

30. xy ALGEBRA A line contains the points (p, q) and $(p + 2, q + 2)$. Find the slope of the line.

31. GEOMETRY A triangle has vertices $R(a, b)$, $S(c, b)$, and $T(c, d)$. Classify the triangle by its angles. Write and simplify an expression for the slope of each side of the triangle.

xy CHALLENGE Find the unknown values using the given slope and points on the line.

32. $m = \frac{1}{2}; (-8, 4), (x, 2), (6, y)$ **33.** $m = -4; (2, y), (-1, 1), (x, -19)$

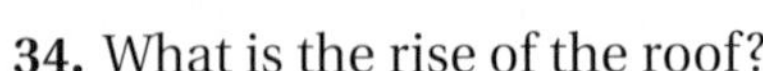

PROBLEM SOLVING

SEE EXAMPLE 1
on p. 612
for Exs. 34–38

BIRDHOUSE **Use the red line on the diagram of a birdhouse.**

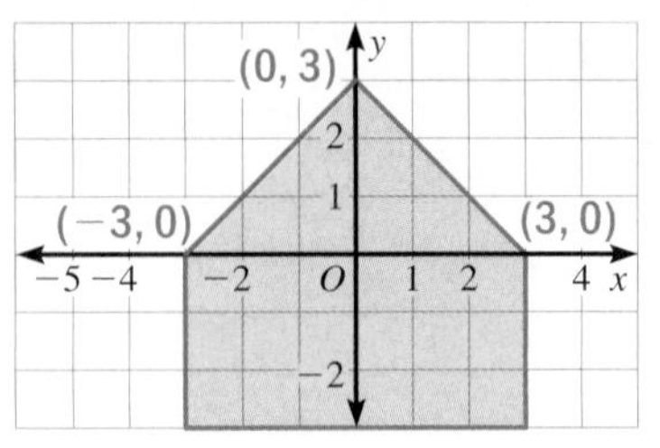

34. What is the rise of the roof?

35. What is the run of the roof?

36. What is the slope of the roof?

37. ★ **MULTIPLE CHOICE** A roof rises 6 feet over a horizontal distance of 14 feet. What is the slope of the roof?

Ⓐ -8　　Ⓑ $\frac{3}{7}$　　Ⓒ $\frac{7}{3}$　　Ⓓ 8

38. **TIDES** The images below show a floating dock at low and high tide. Find the slope of the ramp in both images. Is the ramp steeper at high tide or at low tide? *Explain.*

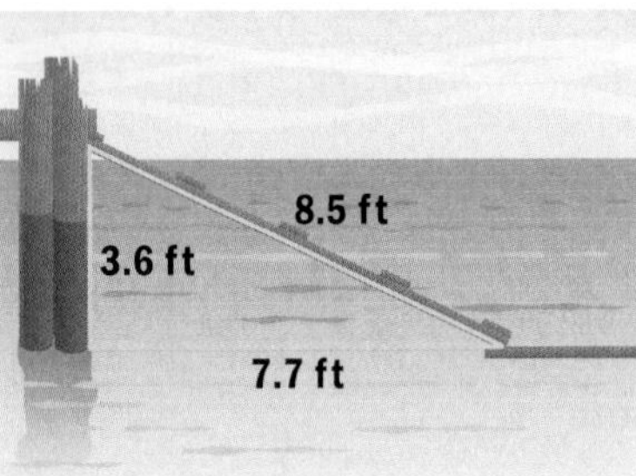

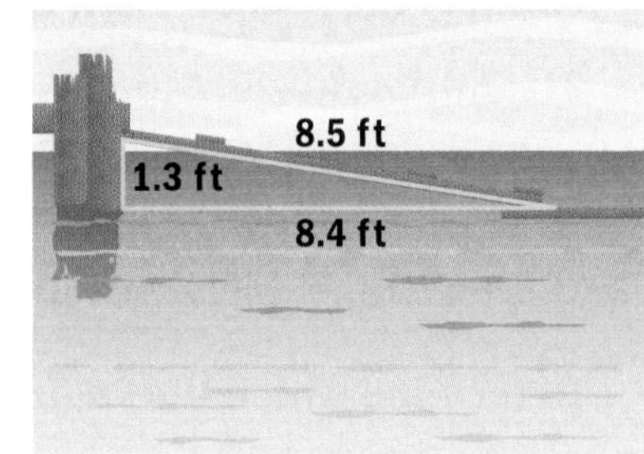

39. ★ **WRITING** One line passes through the points $M(1, 1)$ and $N(3, 4)$. Another line passes through the points $P(2, 5)$ and $Q(5, 8)$. Which line has a greater slope? *Explain* how you can tell by graphing the two lines. *Explain* how you can tell by calculating the slopes of the lines.

40. ★ **OPEN-ENDED MATH** Find the coordinates of the endpoints of a line segment that has a slope of $\frac{5}{7}$.

41. ★ **SHORT RESPONSE** You have selected two points on a line to find its slope. Does it matter which point is (x_1, y_1) and which point is (x_2, y_2)? *Justify* your reasoning using examples.

42. **SKIING** A ski slope has a starting altitude of 2800 meters and an ending altitude of 1886 meters. The horizontal length of the ski slope is about 3299 meters. Approximate its slope. Round to the nearest hundredth.

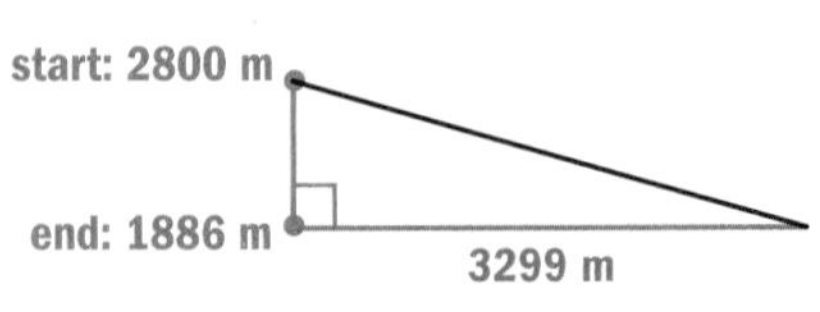

FIND VOLUME
Need help finding the volume of a cylinder? See p. 555.

43. **REASONING** You pour a solution into a cylindrical beaker that has a 30 mm radius. Find the volume of the solution when you fill the beaker to heights of 20 mm, 40 mm, 100 mm, and 120 mm. Graph the ordered pairs (height, volume). Choose two points and find the slope of the line passing through the points. Will the slope be the same if you choose two other points? *Justify* your reasoning.

44. ★ **EXTENDED RESPONSE** Most states' standards require that wheelchair ramps have a slope no greater than $\frac{1}{12}$.

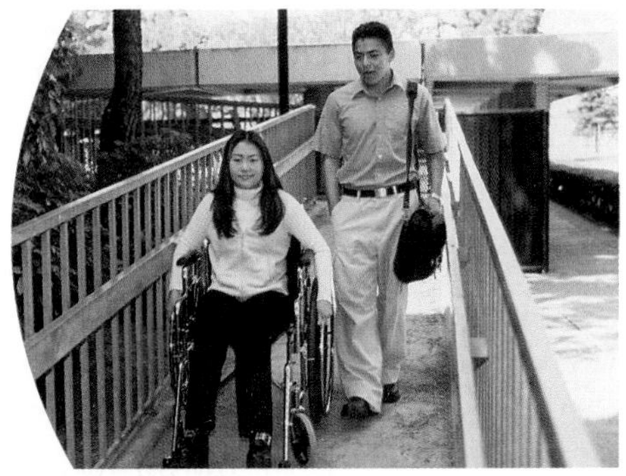

a. A ramp is designed to be 2 feet high and have a horizontal length of 45 feet. Does this ramp meet standards? *Explain.*

b. What is the minimum horizontal length a 2 foot high ramp can have to meet standards? *Explain.*

c. Handrails are generally required on ramps that have a slope greater than $\frac{1}{20}$. If a 2 foot high ramp is built with a horizontal length between the lengths in (a) and (b), will it need a handrail? *Justify* your reasoning.

45. **CHALLENGE** A car travels 1613 meters on a road with a 6.21% grade. Use the Pythagorean Theorem and slope to find the meaning of road grade. *Explain* your reasoning.

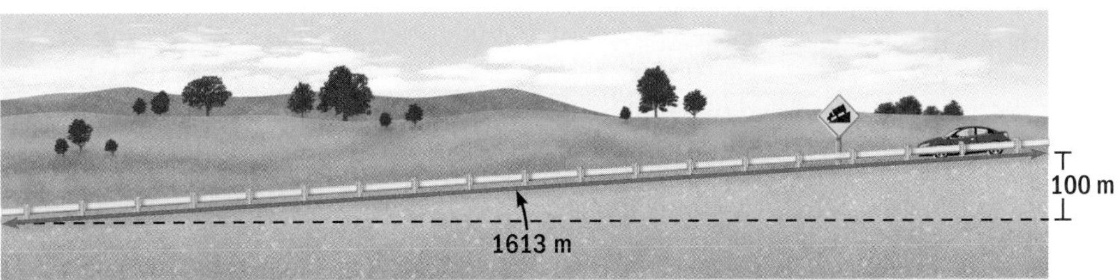

46. **CHALLENGE** A highway off-ramp takes cars from the top of a bridge to a road that is 16 feet beneath the bridge. The ramp is $\frac{3}{4}$ of a circle that has a radius of 200 feet. Find the slope of the ramp to the nearest thousandth.

MIXED REVIEW

Prepare for Lesson 11.7 in Exs. 47–52

Write the equation in function form. *(p. 593)*

47. $y - 5x = 12$

48. $-6 = 12y + 3x$

49. $9x - y = 15$

50. $4y = 2x - 2$

51. $6x - y = -1$

52. $3x + 10y = 20$

53. **SOFTBALL** The table shows the number of runs scored in each inning of a seven inning softball game. Make a scatter plot of the data. Tell whether the two quantities have a *positive relationship*, a *negative relationship*, or *no relationship*. *(p. 588)*

Inning	1	2	3	4	5	6	7
Runs	0	0	4	2	1	0	1

54. ★ **MULTIPLE CHOICE** What is the solution of $42 = \frac{t}{3} + 21$? *(p. 129)*

Ⓐ 7 Ⓑ 21 Ⓒ 42 Ⓓ 63

Direct and Inverse Variation

GOAL Identify direct and inverse variation in tables and equations.

KEY VOCABULARY
- **direct variation,** p. 618
- **inverse variation,** p. 619

Direct Variation Two variables x and y show **direct variation** if $y = kx$ for some nonzero number k. The direct variation equation can also be written in the form $\frac{y}{x} = k$. So, x and y show direct variation if the ratio of y to x is constant.

EXAMPLE 1 Identifying Direct Variation

Tell whether the equation represents direct variation.

a. $-2x + y = 0$

b. $-2x + y = 3$

SOLUTION

a. *METHOD 1*
Make a table of values and find the ratios of y to x.

x	1	2	3	4	5
y	2	4	6	8	10
Ratio $\frac{y}{x}$	2	2	2	2	2

The ratio is constant.

METHOD 2
Write the equation in function form.

$-2x + y = 0$

$y = 2x$

The equation can be written in the form $y = kx$, where $k = 2$.

▶ **Answer** The equation represents direct variation.

b. *METHOD 1*
Make a table of values and find the ratios of y to x.

x	1	2	3	4	5
y	5	7	9	11	13
Ratio $\frac{y}{x}$	5	$\frac{7}{2}$	3	$\frac{11}{4}$	$\frac{13}{5}$

The ratio is *not* constant.

METHOD 2
Write the equation in function form.

$-2x + y = 3$

$y = 2x + 3$

The equation *cannot* be written in the form $y = kx$.

▶ **Answer** The equation does *not* represent direct variation.

Direct Variation Graphs The graph shows the linear equations from Example 1. Both graphs have a slope of 2, but only the graph of the direct variation equation from part (a) of Example 1 passes through the origin. All direct variation equations $y = kx$ are lines, with slope $m = k$, that pass through the origin.

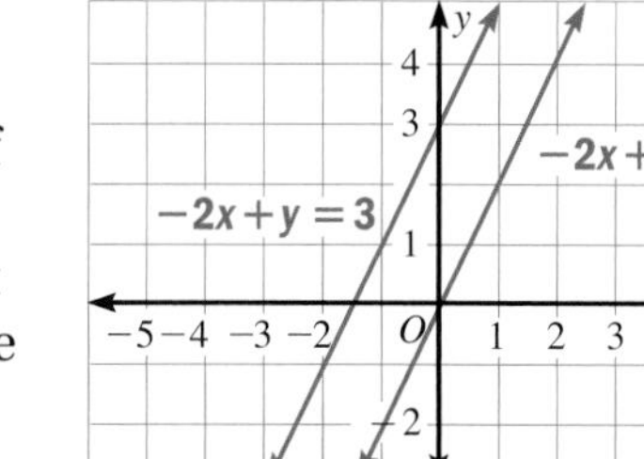

VOCABULARY
If two quantities show direct variation, they are said to be *directly proportional* to one another.

Inverse Variation Two variables x and y show **inverse variation** if $y = \frac{k}{x}$ for some nonzero number k. The inverse variation equation can be written in the form $xy = k$. So, x and y show inverse variation if the product xy is constant.

EXAMPLE 2 Identifying Inverse Variation

Tell whether the equation $y = \frac{4}{x}$ represents inverse variation.

SOLUTION

Make a table of values for the equation and find the products xy.

x	1	2	3	4	5
y	4	2	$1.\overline{3}$	1	0.8
xy	4	4	4	4	4

▶ **Answer** The products are equivalent, so the equation represents inverse variation.

VOCABULARY
If two quantities show indirect variation, they are said to be *inversely proportional* to one another.

Inverse Variation Graphs The graph shows the equation from Example 2. The graph is *not* a line. So, the ratio of the change in y to the change in x, or *rate of change*, is not constant as in direct variation.

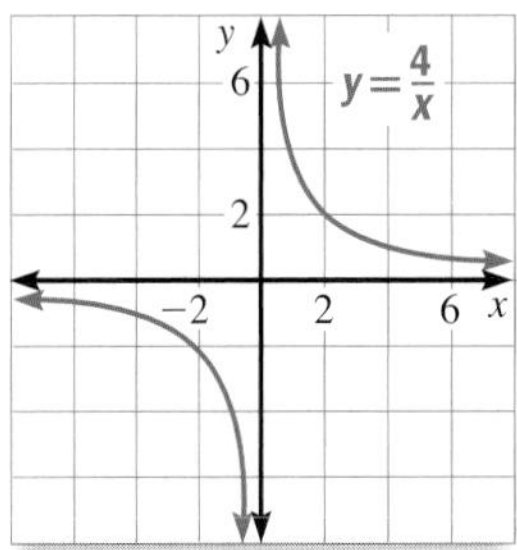

EXERCISES

Tell whether the table represents *direct variation, inverse variation,* or *neither*. *Justify* your answer.

1.

x	1	2	3	4
y	2	3	4	5

2.

x	1	2	3	4
y	3	6	9	12

3.

x	1	2	4	5
y	2	1	0.5	0.4

Tell whether the equation represents *direct variation, inverse variation,* or *neither*. *Justify* your answer.

4. $xy = 8$

5. $11x - 2.2y = 0$

6. $y + 5x = -3$

7. $y = -\frac{x}{3}$

8. $y = -\frac{3}{x}$

9. $y = -\frac{3}{x} + 1$

10. Raffle Anthony is selling \$4 raffle tickets. Write an equation representing the amount of money m, in dollars, that he will have by selling t tickets. Is the amount of money Anthony has *directly proportional* to the number of tickets he sells? *Justify* your answer.

11. What If? In Exercise 10, suppose Anthony already has \$20 when he begins selling raffle tickets. Is the total amount of money Anthony has *directly proportional* to the number of tickets he sells? *Justify* your answer.

INVESTIGATION

Use before Lesson 11.7

GOAL

Find how slope, y-intercept, and an equation are related.

MATERIALS

- pencil
- straightedge
- graph paper

11.7 Slope-Intercept Form

You can find the slope and y-intercept of a line by looking at its equation in *slope-intercept form.*

EXPLORE 1 **Use a graph to find the slope and y-intercept of $y = 4x + 3$.**

STEP 1 **Make** a table of values for the equation $y = 4x + 3$.

x	0	1	2
y	3	7	11

STEP 2 **Plot** the points and draw a line.

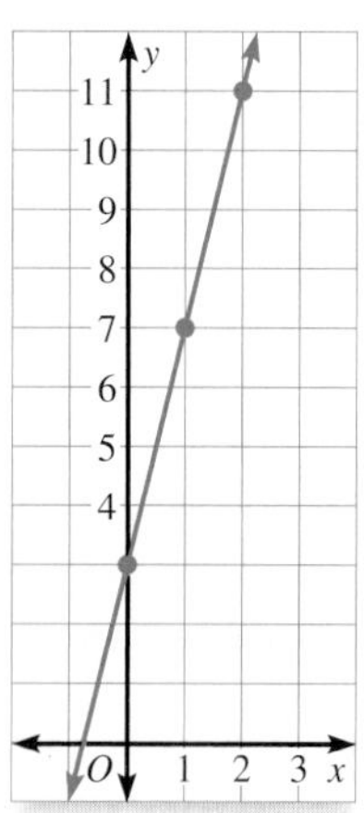

STEP 3 **Use** the graph to find the slope and y-intercept of $y = 4x + 3$.

slope $= \frac{4}{1} = 4$ y-intercept $= 3$

PRACTICE **In Exercises 1–3, use the table at the right.**

x	−1	0	1
y	?	?	?

1. Copy and complete the table of values for the equation $y = -2x - 1$.
2. Plot the points and draw a line.
3. Use the graph to find the slope and y-intercept.
4. Copy and complete the table below.

Equation	Slope	y-intercept
$y = 4x + 3$	?	?
$y = -2x - 1$	?	?

EXPLORE 2 Calculate the slope and y-intercept of $y = 3x + 5$.

STEP 1 **Make** a table of values for the equation $y = 3x + 5$.

x	1	2	3
y	8	11	14

STEP 2 **Calculate** the slope of the line using two points from the table.

$$m = \frac{y_2 - y_1}{x_2 - x_1} = \frac{11 - 8}{2 - 1} = 3$$

STEP 3 **Calculate** the y-intercept by substituting 0 for x.

$$y = 3x + 5 = 3(0) + 5 = 5$$

PRACTICE Graph the line using a table of values. Then use the graph to find the slope and y-intercept.

5. $y = 5x - 7$

6. $y = -3x + 2$

7. $y = -\frac{2}{3}x - 6$

8. $y = \frac{5}{4}x + 1$

Solve the equation for y. Make a table of values for the equation. Calculate the slope and y-intercept.

9. $y + 2 = \frac{1}{2}x$

10. $3y = -2x + 9$

11. $y + 4x = -5$

12. $6x - 2y = 10$

DRAW CONCLUSIONS

13. LOOK FOR A PATTERN

a. Include a row for $y = 3x + 5$ in your table from Exercise 4 on page 620.

b. Use your table to make a conjecture about how to use the equation of a line to find the slope and y-intercept of the line.

c. Does your conjecture in part (b) seem to be true for the equations in Exercises 5–12?

14. xy **ALGEBRA** What does m stand for in the equation $y = mx + b$? What does b stand for in the equation $y = mx + b$?

11.7 Slope-Intercept Form

Before You graphed equations using intercepts.
Now You'll write and graph equations in slope-intercept form.
Why? So you can predict values, such as mountain temperatures in Example 3.

KEY VOCABULARY
- **slope-intercept form,** *p. 622*

In Investigation 11.7 on pages 620–621, you may have observed that you can solve a linear equation for y to help you identify the slope and y-intercept, as summarized below.

KEY CONCEPT *For Your Notebook*

Slope-Intercept Form

Words The linear equation $y = mx + b$ is written in **slope-intercept form**. The slope is m. The y-intercept is b.

Algebra $y = mx + b$ **Numbers** $y = 3x + 2$

EXAMPLE 1 Identifying Slopes and y-intercepts

Find the slope and y-intercept of the graph of the equation.

a. $y = x - 3$ **b.** $-4x + 2y = 16$

SOLUTION

a. The equation $y = x - 3$ can be written as $y = 1x + (-3)$.

▸ **Answer** The line has a slope of 1 and a y-intercept of -3.

b. Write the equation $-4x + 2y = 16$ in slope-intercept form.

$-4x + 2y = 16$ **Write original equation.**

$2y = 4x + 16$ **Add 4x to each side.**

$y = 2x + 8$ **Divide each side by 2.**

▸ **Answer** The line has a slope of 2 and a y-intercept of 8.

AVOID ERRORS
When you rewrite the equation in part (b) of Example 1, be sure to divide *both* terms of $4x + 16$ by 2.

 **GUIDED PRACTICE for Example 1**

Find the slope and y-intercept of the graph of the equation.

1. $y = 6x + 1$ **2.** $y = \frac{1}{4}x$ **3.** $-2x + 3y = 6$

EXAMPLE 2 Graphing Using Slope-Intercept Form

Graph the equation $y = \frac{1}{2}x + 3$.

STEP 1 The y-intercept is 3, so plot the point (0, 3).

STEP 2 The slope is $\frac{1}{2}$, so plot a second point by moving up 1 unit and right 2 units.

STEP 3 Draw a line through the points.

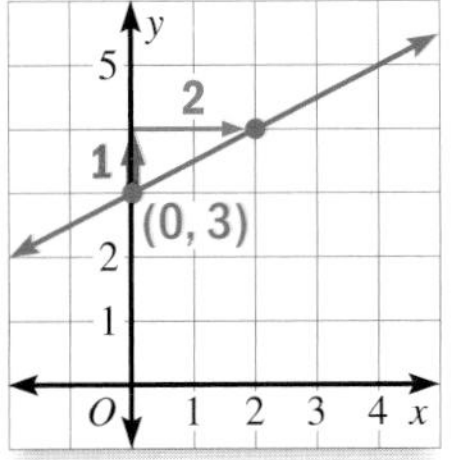

Animated Math at classzone.com

EXAMPLE 3 Writing a Function Rule

Hiking You are at the base of a trail on Mount Rainier in Washington. The temperature is 50.9°F. The temperature changes at a rate of −0.005°F per foot of elevation as you hike up. What is the temperature 1000 feet above the base?

SOLUTION

STEP 1 **Write** a verbal model.

Temperature = Rate of temperature change • Increase in elevation + Initial temperature

STEP 2 **Write** an algebraic model in slope-intercept form.

The temperature changes at a rate of −0.005°F per foot, so $m = -0.005$. The initial temperature is 50.9°F, so $b = 50.9$. Let y be the temperature and x be the change in elevation.

$y = mx + b$ **Write slope-intercept form.**

$y = \mathbf{-0.005}x + \mathbf{50.9}$ **Substitute −0.005 for m and 50.9 for b.**

STEP 3 **Find** the value of y when $x = 1000$.

$y = -0.005x + 50.9$ **Write the equation.**

$= -0.005(1000) + 50.9$ **Substitute 1000 for x.**

$= 45.9$ **Simplify.**

▶ **Answer** The temperature 1000 feet above the base is 45.9°F.

✓ GUIDED PRACTICE for Examples 2 and 3

Use the slope and y-intercept to graph the equation.

4. $y = 2x + 5$

5. $y = 7x$

6. $-x + y = 6$

7. **What If?** In Example 3, suppose the temperature at the base of the trail is 55.2°F. What is the temperature 2500 feet above the base?

11.7 EXERCISES

HOMEWORK KEY

★ = **STANDARDIZED TEST PRACTICE** Exs. 16, 39, 40, 41, 42, 44, 45, and 53

○ = **HINTS AND HOMEWORK HELP** for Exs. 3, 9, 19, 41 at classzone.com

SKILL PRACTICE

VOCABULARY **Copy and complete the statement.**

1. For the graph of the linear equation $y = -5x + 7$, -5 is the _?_.
2. The linear equation $y = mx + b$ is in _?_ form.

REWRITING EQUATIONS **Rewrite the equation in slope-intercept form.**

SEE EXAMPLE 1 on p. 622 for Exs. 3–16

3. $2x = y + 5$
4. $8x - 4y = 32$
5. $x - y = -2$
6. **WHICH ONE DOESN'T BELONG?** Which of the following equations does not belong? *Explain* your choice.

   A. $y = 3x - 1$ **B.** $y = -4x - 2$ **C.** $3x + y = 5$ **D.** $y = 2x - 9$

SLOPES AND Y-INTERCEPTS **Find the slope and y-intercept of the graph of the equation.**

7. $y = x + 3$
8. $y = 6 - x$
9. $1 = 2x - y$
10. $6x = 10 - y$
11. $y - 9 = -\frac{3}{4}x$
12. $\frac{2}{3}x - y = 3$
13. $2y - 6 = 0$
14. $y + 12x = 0$
15. $13x - 11y = 143$
16. ★ **MULTIPLE CHOICE** What is the slope of the graph of $3x + y = 4$?

   (A) -4 (B) -3 (C) 3 (D) 4

GRAPHING EQUATIONS **Use the slope and y-intercept to graph the equation.**

SEE EXAMPLE 2 on p. 623 for Exs. 17–23

17. $y = x - 8$
18. $y = -x + 7$
19. $y = 3$
20. $2x - 2y = 1$
21. $-2x + 3y = -12$
22. $y = \frac{1}{5}x$
23. **ERROR ANALYSIS** Describe and correct the error made by a student in graphing the equation $y = -2x - 1$ using the slope and y-intercept.

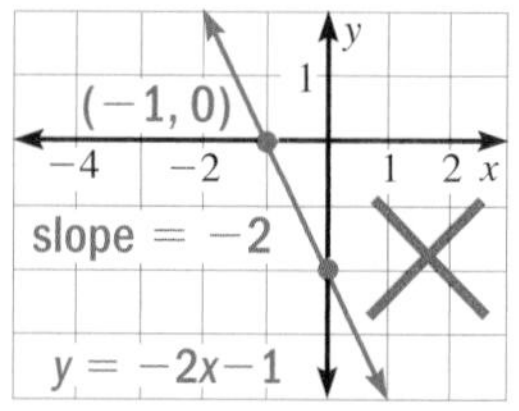

INTERPRETING GRAPHS **Write the equation of the line in slope-intercept form.**

24.
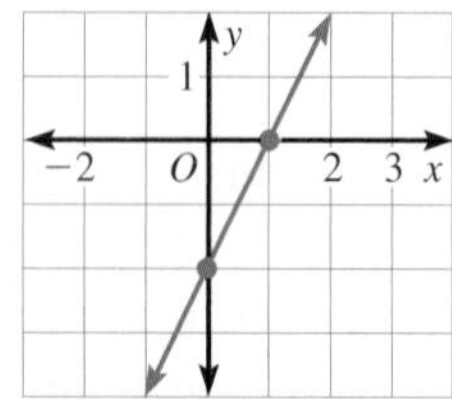

25.
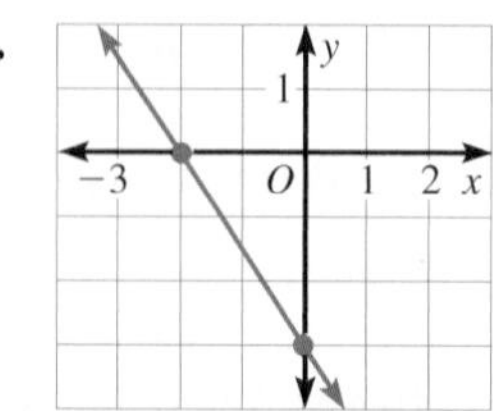

26.
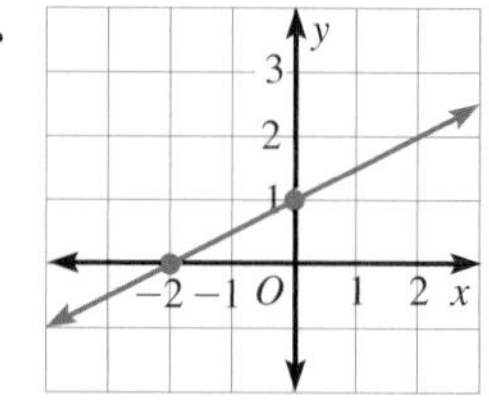

27. **NUMBER SENSE** Which equation has a steeper graph, $y = 3x - 1$ or $y = 2x - 1$? *Justify* your answer.

WRITING EQUATIONS **Use the point on the line and the slope of the line to find the y-intercept of the line. Then write the slope-intercept form of the equation of the line.**

28. $(1, 4)$; $m = 4$ **29.** $(3, -4)$; $m = 0$ **30.** $(9, 0)$; $m = \frac{1}{3}$

31. $(-2, 2)$; $m = -\frac{1}{2}$ **32.** $(-5, 6)$; $m = 0$ **33.** $\left(\frac{1}{2}, 6\right)$; $m = 2$

WRITING EQUATIONS FROM TWO POINTS **Write the equation of the line passing through the given points.**

34. $(-2, 9)$ and $(-4, -1)$ **35.** $(6, 10)$ and $(3, 12)$ **36.** $(-4, 4)$ and $(6, 7)$

37. xy **CHALLENGE** Find the slope and y-intercept of the graph of $ax + by + c = 0$, in terms of a, b, and c, where b is not equal to 0.

PROBLEM SOLVING

SEE EXAMPLE 3 on p. 623 for Exs. 38–40

38. **PARACHUTING** The graph shows the altitude y, in feet, of a parachutist x seconds after opening the parachute. Find the slope and y-intercept of the graph. Write the equation for the altitude in slope-intercept form. What do the slope and y-intercept represent in this situation?

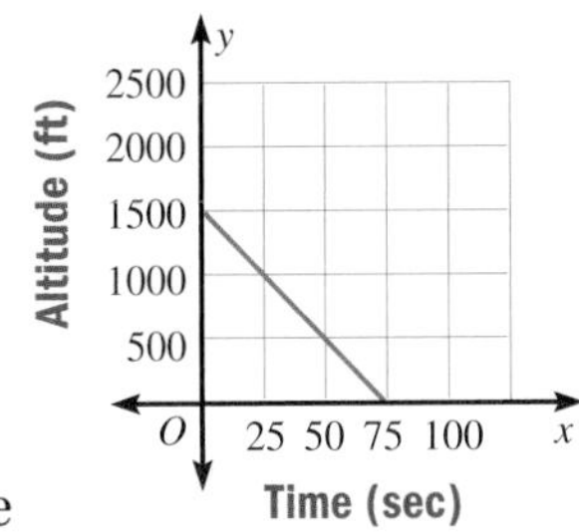

39. ★ **MULTIPLE CHOICE** You pay by the hour to rent a canoe. The cost for a ride back to the starting point is \$12. The total cost C, in dollars, of renting the canoe for h hours can be modeled by $C = 9h + 12$. How much does the rental cost per hour?

Ⓐ \$3 Ⓑ \$9 Ⓒ \$12 Ⓓ \$21

40. ★ **SHORT RESPONSE** The number of chirps per minute made by a cricket can be modeled by the equation $y = 4x - 156$, where y is the number of chirps per minute and x is the temperature in degrees Fahrenheit.

a. Graph the equation.

b. What does the x-intercept mean in this situation?

c. What does the y-intercept mean in this situation? Does it make sense? *Explain.*

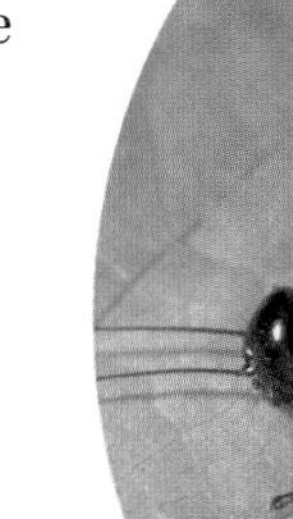

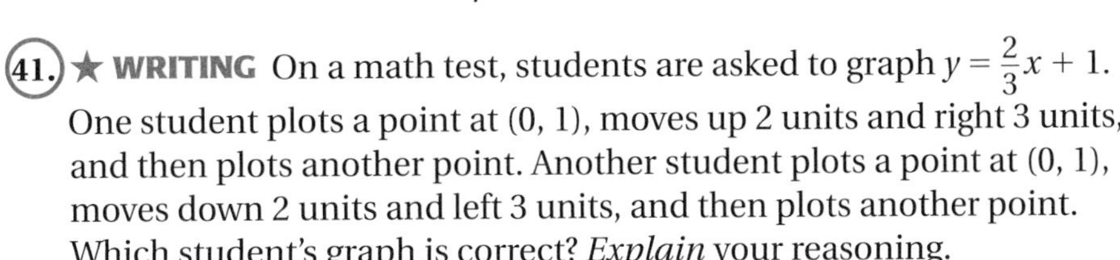

41. ★ **WRITING** On a math test, students are asked to graph $y = \frac{2}{3}x + 1$. One student plots a point at $(0, 1)$, moves up 2 units and right 3 units, and then plots another point. Another student plots a point at $(0, 1)$, moves down 2 units and left 3 units, and then plots another point. Which student's graph is correct? *Explain* your reasoning.

SEE EXAMPLE 3 on p. 623 for Ex. 42

42. MULTI-STEP PROBLEM You make and sell bracelets. You spend \$28 for supplies and sell the bracelets for \$3.50 each.

a. Write an equation to model your profit. Use P for profit and b for the number of bracelets sold.

b. Graph the equation.

c. How many bracelets do you need to exactly cover your expenses? to make a profit?

43. REASONING When two lines are perpendicular, and neither has a slope of zero, the product of their slopes is -1. What is the slope-intercept form of the equation of the line that is perpendicular to and has the same y-intercept as the graph of $y = 2x + 8$? *Justify* your answer.

44. ★ OPEN-ENDED MATH *Describe* a real-world situation that can be represented by the graph at the right. What do the x- and y-intercepts mean in the situation?

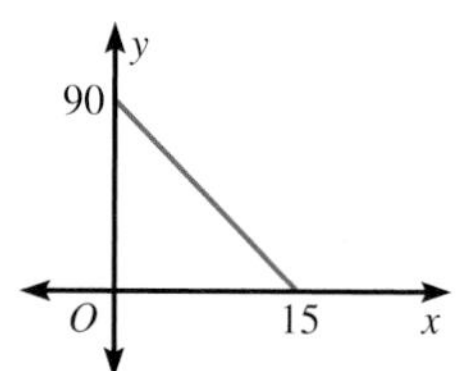

45. ★ EXTENDED RESPONSE Use the equations $4x - 6y = -18$ and $-2x + 3y = 15$.

a. Rewrite the equations in slope-intercept form. *Describe* any similarities.

b. Graph the equations on the same coordinate plane. *Describe* how the graphs relate to each other.

c. Use your answers from parts (a) and (b) to make a conjecture about how the graphs of $y = -2x - 8$ and $y = -2x - 1$ are related. *Explain* your reasoning.

46. GEOMETRY Find the area of the triangle formed by the x-axis, the y-axis, and the line $y = -2x + 6$.

47. CHALLENGE The line $y = 3x - 3$ forms one side of a rectangle. Write the equations of 3 lines that could form the other sides.

MIXED REVIEW

Prepare for Lesson 11.8 in Exs. 48–50

Solve the inequality. Then graph its solution on a number line. *(p. 318)*

48. $2y + 3 \le 11$ **49.** $-4x + 6 > 18$ **50.** $7x + 2 < 5x - 9$

Find the volume of the figure.

51. A cylinder with radius 3 inches and height 7 inches *(p. 554)*

52. A pyramid with base area 25 square feet and height 9 feet *(p. 561)*

53. ★ MULTIPLE CHOICE The length of the hypotenuse of a right triangle is 85 inches and the length of one leg is 68 inches. What is the length of the other leg? *(p. 482)*

Ⓐ 17 in. Ⓑ 51 in. Ⓒ 68 in. Ⓓ 153 in.

Systems of Equations

GOAL Solve systems of linear equations.

KEY VOCABULARY
- **system of linear equations,** *p. 627*
- **solution of a linear system,** *p. 627*

A **system of linear equations** in two variables is a set of two linear equations with the same variables. A **solution of a linear system** in two variables is an ordered pair that is a solution of each equation in the system.

In the system of equations below, (3, 2) is a solution.

System of equations	Check
$2x + 4y = 14$	$2(3) + 4(2) = 6 + 8 = 14$ ✓
$3x - 5y = -1$	$3(3) - 5(2) = 9 - 10 = -1$ ✓

If a system of linear equations has a solution, then the graphs of the equations intersect.

EXAMPLE 1 Solving Linear Systems by Graphing

Solve the linear system. **Equation 1** $x + y = 5$
Equation 2 $y = 2x - 1$

SOLUTION

STEP 1 **Write** each equation in slope-intercept form.

Equation 1	Equation 2
$x + y = 5$	$y = 2x - 1$
$y = -x + 5$	

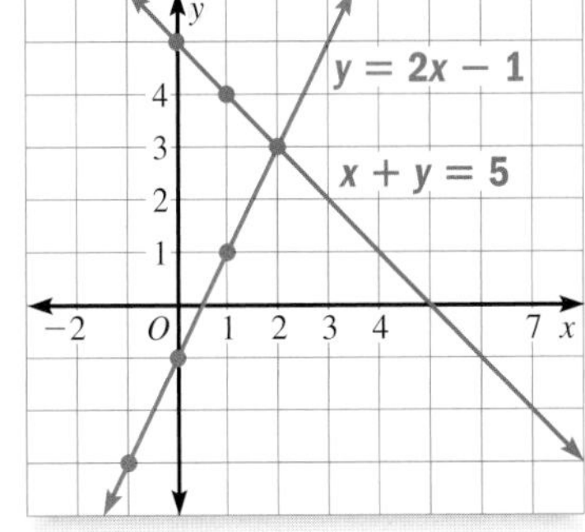

STEP 2 **Graph** both equations.

STEP 3 **Estimate** the point of intersection using the graph. It appears that the point of intersection is (2, 3).

STEP 4 **Check** whether (2, 3) is the solution by substituting 2 for x and 3 for y in each of the equations.

Equation 1	Equation 2
$x + y = 5$	$y = 2x - 1$
$2 + 3 \stackrel{?}{=} 5$	$3 \stackrel{?}{=} 2(2) - 1$
$5 = 5$ ✓	$3 = 3$ ✓

▶ **Answer** The solution is (2, 3).

EXAMPLE 2 Solving Linear Systems by Substitution

Solve the linear system. **Equation 1** $x + 4y = 4$

Equation 2 $x - y = -6$

SOLUTION

> ***SOLVE FOR A VARIABLE***
> When solving by substitution, solve for the variable that is easier to isolate. You will get the same solution whether you begin by solving for x or for y.

STEP 1 **Choose** an equation to solve for one of the variables.

$x - y = -6$ **Write Equation 2.**

$x = y - 6$ **Add y to each side.**

STEP 2 **Substitute** $y - 6$ for x in Equation 1. Then solve for y.

$x + 4y = 4$ **Write Equation 1.**

$(y - 6) + 4y = 4$ **Substitute $y - 6$ for x.**

$5y - 6 = 4$ **Combine like terms.**

$5y = 10$ **Add 6 to each side.**

$y = 2$ **Divide each side by 5.**

STEP 3 **Substitute** 2 for y in the original Equation 2 and solve for x.

$x - y = -6$ **Write Equation 2.**

$x - 2 = -6$ **Substitute 2 for y.**

$x = -4$ **Add 2 to each side.**

▶ **Answer** The solution is $(-4, 2)$.

EXERCISES

Solve the linear system by graphing. Then check the solution in both equations.

1. $y = -x + 3$
   $y = x + 1$

2. $x - y = 1$
   $5x - 4y = 0$

3. $y = 2x - 15$
   $x = -2y$

Solve the linear system by substitution.

4. $x = 4$
   $x + y = 2$

5. $x + y = 4$
   $4x + y = 1$

6. $2x - y = -2$
   $4x + y = 20$

7. Graph the linear system at the right. *Explain* why there is *no* solution. $x + y = 8$, $3x + 3y = 6$

8. **Trading Cards** You have 100 trading cards and your friend has 20. Every day you give your friend one card. Use the equations $c = 100 - d$ and $c = 20 + d$ to model this situation. Solve this system. *Explain* what the solution means in this situation.

11.8 Graphs of Linear Inequalities

Before	You graphed linear equations.
Now	You'll graph linear inequalities.
Why?	So you can compare choices, as for buying art supplies in Example 3.

KEY VOCABULARY
- **linear inequality,** *p. 629*
- **solution of a linear inequality,** *p. 629*
- **half-plane,** *p. 630*

ACTIVITY

You can use a graph to model linear inequalities.

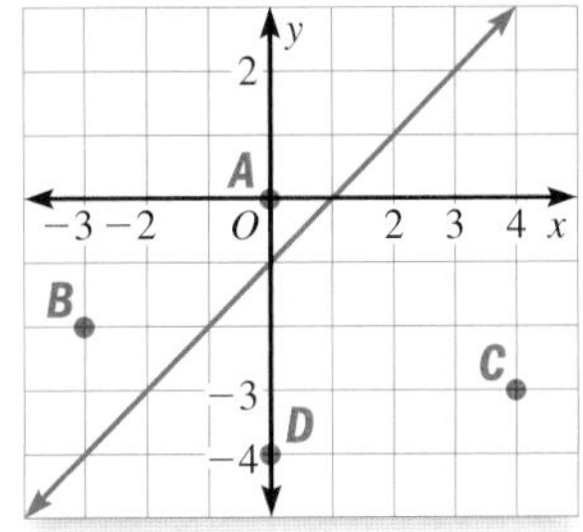

STEP 1 **Sketch** the graph of $y = x - 1$.

STEP 2 **Plot** and label the following points:

$A(0, 0), B(-3, -2), C(4, -3), D(0, -4)$

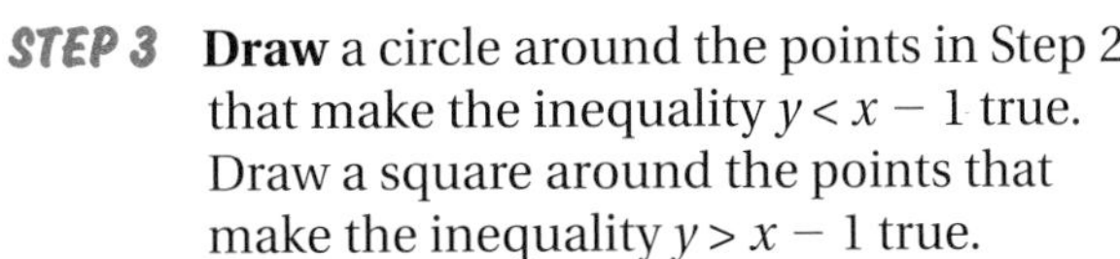

STEP 3 **Draw** a circle around the points in Step 2 that make the inequality $y < x - 1$ true. Draw a square around the points that make the inequality $y > x - 1$ true.

STEP 4 **Make** an observation about the solutions of $y < x - 1$ and the solutions of $y > x - 1$.

In the activity, you explored solutions of *linear inequalities*. Two examples of **linear inequalities** in two variables are $y \le 2x + 5$ and $2x + 5y < 7$. An ordered pair (x, y) is a **solution of a linear inequality** if the inequality is true when the values of x and y are substituted into the inequality.

EXAMPLE 1 Checking Solutions of a Linear Inequality

READING
The symbol $\not\le$ means *not less than or equal to.* It is equivalent to the symbol >, which means *greater than.*

Tell whether the ordered pair is a solution of $3x - 4y \le -8$.

	(x, y)	$3x - 4y$	$3x - 4y \overset{?}{\le} -8$	Conclusion
a.	$(0, 0)$	$3(0) - 4(0) = 0$	$0 \not\le -8$	(0, 0) is *not* a solution.
b.	$(-1, 4)$	$3(-1) - 4(4) = -19$	$-19 \le -8$	(−1, 4) is a solution.

✓ GUIDED PRACTICE for Example 1

Tell whether the ordered pair is a solution of $2x + 3y < 5$.

1. $(0, 0)$ **2.** $(-4, 2)$ **3.** $(5, -1)$ **4.** $(1, 1)$

:VOCABULARY
A line divides a coordinate plane into two half-planes.

Graphing Linear Inequalities The graph of a linear inequality in two variables is a **half-plane**. The shaded region includes all the solutions of the inequality.

A solid line indicates that points on the line *are* solutions of an inequality. A dashed line indicates that points on the line are *not* solutions.

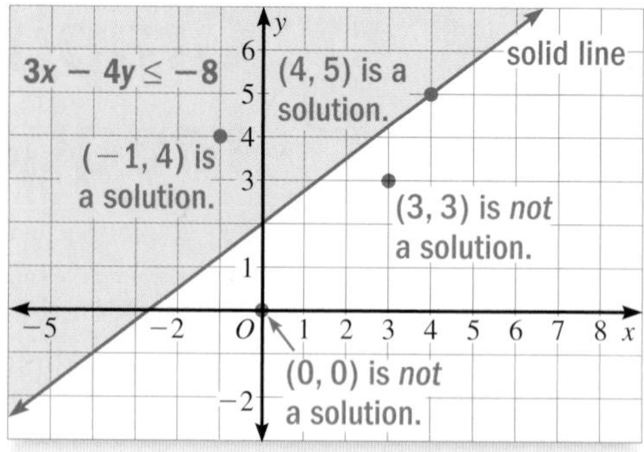

KEY CONCEPT — *For Your Notebook*

Graphing Linear Inequalities

1. Change the inequality symbol to "=". Graph the equation. Use a dashed line for < or >. Use a solid line for ≤ or ≥.
2. Test a point in one of the half-planes to check whether it is a solution of the inequality.
3. If the test point is a solution, shade the half-plane that contains the point. If the test point is not a solution, shade the other half-plane.

EXAMPLE 2 Graphing a Linear Inequality

Graph $y - 2x > 3$.

STEP 1 **Change** > to = and write the equation in slope-intercept form.

$y - 2x = 3$ **Replace > with = sign.**

$y = 2x + 3$ **Add $2x$ to each side.**

Graph the line that has a slope of 2 and a y-intercept of 3. Because the inequality is >, use a dashed line.

:ANOTHER WAY
Using (0, 0) is convenient because 0 is substituted for each variable. However, you can use any point *not* on the line as a test point.

STEP 2 **Use** (0, 0) as a test point. Substitute the point into the original inequality.

$y - 2x > 3$

$0 - 2(0) \overset{?}{>} 3$

$0 \not> 3$ **(0, 0) is not a solution.**

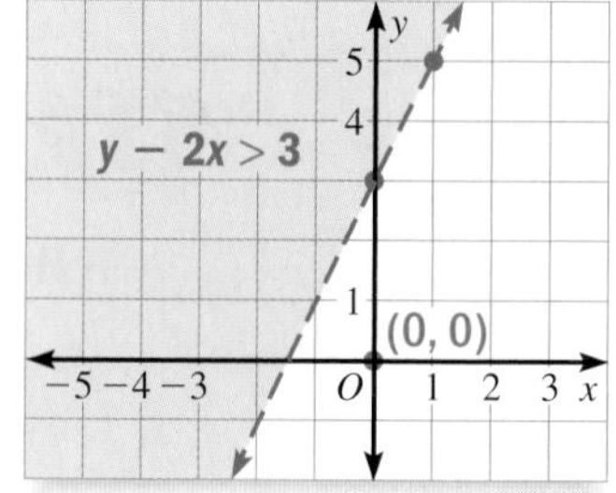

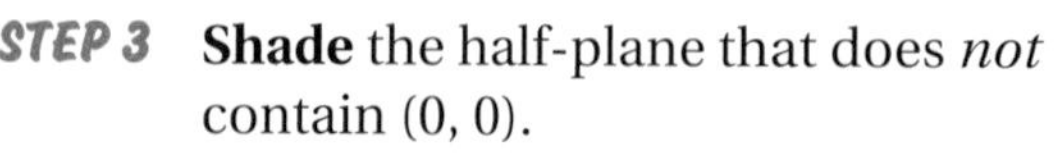

STEP 3 **Shade** the half-plane that does *not* contain (0, 0).

✓ GUIDED PRACTICE for Example 2

Graph the inequality.

5. $y < x + 1$ 6. $3x + y \geq 3$ 7. $x - 2y \geq -1$ 8. $y \geq -2$

EXAMPLE 3 Using the Graph of a Linear Inequality

Art Supplies You have at most \$40 to buy art supplies. Tubes of paint cost \$6 each and brushes cost \$4 each. This situation can be modeled by the inequality $6x + 4y \le 40$, where x represents the number of tubes of paint and y represents the number of brushes.

a. Graph the inequality.

b. How many tubes of paint and how many brushes can you buy with \$40?

SOLUTION

a. Change $\le$ to $=$ and write the equation in slope-intercept form: $y = -\frac{3}{2}x + 10$.

Graph the equation using a solid line.

Use (0, 0) as a test point: $6(0) + 4(0) \overset{?}{\le} 40$

$0 \le 40$ ✓

Shade the half-plane that contains (0, 0).

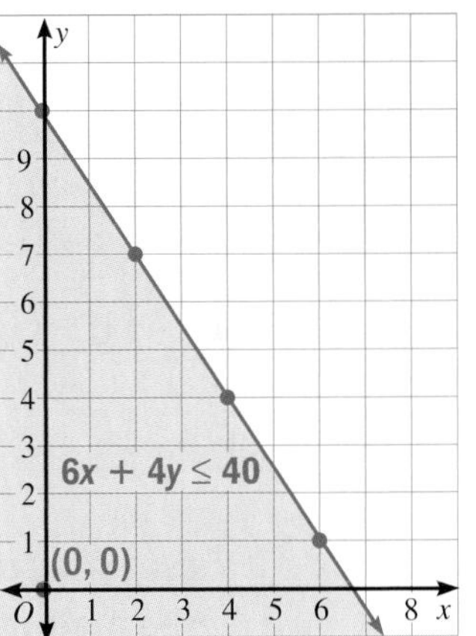

b. Many solutions are possible, such as (4, 4) and (2, 5). You could buy 4 tubes of paint and 4 brushes or 2 tubes of paint and 5 brushes.

INTERPRET A GRAPH
All the points in the shaded region and on the line are solutions of the inequality. However, negative and fractional solutions do not make sense in this situation.

✓ GUIDED PRACTICE for Example 3

9. **What If?** In Example 3, suppose you have at most \$36 to spend. Graph the inequality $6x + 4y \le 36$ and find two possible solutions.

11.8 EXERCISES

HOMEWORK KEY
★ = **STANDARDIZED TEST PRACTICE** Exs. 24, 36, 37, 38, 39, 40, and 48
◯ = **HINTS AND HOMEWORK HELP** for Exs. 3, 9, 17, 35 at classzone.com

SKILL PRACTICE

1. **VOCABULARY** Copy and complete: When graphing $y < 2x + 1$, the dashed line on the graph divides the coordinate plane into two _?_.

2. **VOCABULARY** Copy and complete: All the points in the shaded region of the graph of an inequality are _?_ of the inequality.

SEE EXAMPLE 1 on p. 629 for Exs. 3–6

CHECKING **Tell whether the ordered pair is a solution of the inequality.**

3. $5x + y \le 17$; (1, 2)
4. $3x + 7y < 20$; (−11, 2)
5. $9x + 12y > 26$; (3, −4)
6. $11x + 18y \ge 31$; (−6, −7)

SEE EXAMPLE 2
on p. 630
for Exs. 7–24

GRAPHING INEQUALITIES Graph the inequality.

7. $y > 14 - 4x$
8. $y < x + 5$
9. $3x - 4 \geq y$
10. $y + 3 \geq 4x$
11. $-96 \leq -3x$
12. $6y > 36$
13. $y \geq 3x - 7$
14. $y \leq 4x - 12$
15. $y < 7x + 19$
16. $4x - 13 > y$
17. $y > 9 - 2x$
18. $22 < 2x$
19. $-2y \geq 74$
20. $4x - 3y \geq 12$
21. $-2x - 4y > 8$
22. $6x + 3y \leq -12$

23. **ERROR ANALYSIS** Describe and correct the error made in graphing $y \leq 2x + 1$.

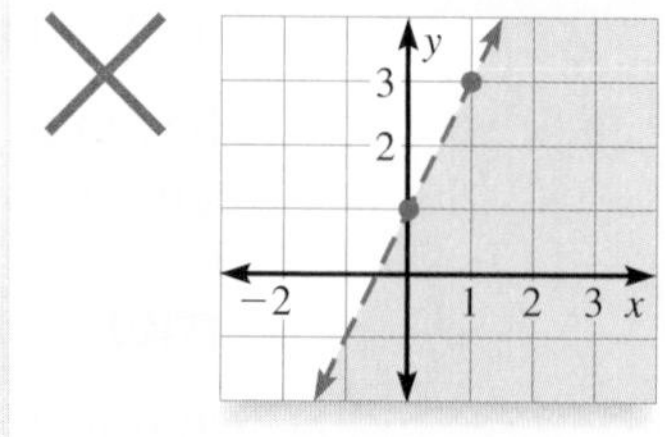

24. ★ **MULTIPLE CHOICE** Which inequality describes the graph?

Ⓐ $y \leq 2x + 200$ Ⓑ $y \geq 2x + 200$

Ⓒ $y \leq -2x + 200$ Ⓓ $y \geq -2x + 200$

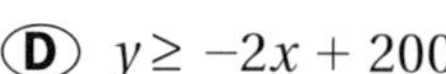

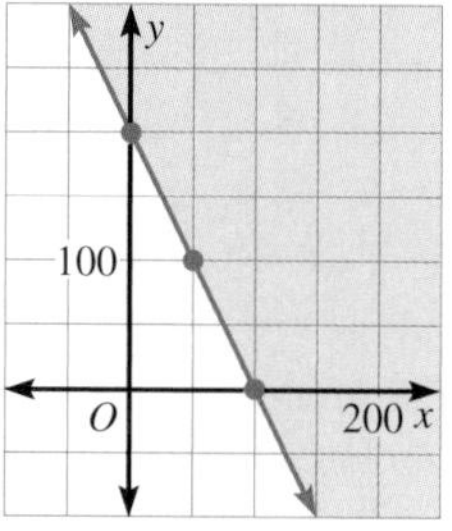

WRITING INEQUALITIES Write the sentence as an inequality. Then graph the inequality in a coordinate plane.

25. The sum of x and y is greater than 10.
26. y is no more than 15.
27. x is at least 20.
28. The difference of x and y is at most 15.
29. y is more than two times x.
30. x is no more than three times y.

ALGEBRA Let *a* be a nonzero whole number. Tell whether a point of the given form is *always, sometimes,* or *never* a solution of the inequality.

31. $y \leq 5x - a$; $(a, 2a)$
32. $3y > x + a$; $(a, a + 1)$
33. $10x > a - 2y$; $(-a, 5a)$

34. **CHALLENGE** Graph the shaded region bounded by $y < \frac{2}{3}x + 5$, $y > -\frac{1}{3}x - 7$, and $y < \frac{8}{3}x - 1$. Find two ordered pairs that are solutions of all three inequalities. *Justify* your answers.

PROBLEM SOLVING

SEE EXAMPLE 3
on p. 631
for Ex. 35

35. **TRAIL MIX** You are making a trail mix of peanuts and raisins. You have \$6.00 to spend. Peanuts cost \$2.00 per pound and raisins cost \$1.50 per pound. Graph the inequality $2x + 1.5y \leq 6$ to find two possible combinations of pounds of peanuts x and pounds of raisins y that you could buy for your trail mix.

36. ★ **WRITING** If you graph the inequalities $y < x + 3$ and $y > x + 3$, are there any points in the coordinate plane that are *not* solutions? *Explain* your reasoning.

SEE EXAMPLE 3 on p. 631 for Ex. 37

37. ★ **MULTIPLE CHOICE** Sonya can spend up to \$125 on decorations for a dance. A bag of balloons costs \$4 and a roll of streamers costs \$2. To find how much she can buy she uses the inequality $4x + 2y \le 125$, where x is the number of bags of balloons and y is the number of rolls of streamers. Which of the following is a solution of the inequality?

   Ⓐ (30, 6) Ⓑ (30, 4) Ⓒ (25, 15) Ⓓ (25, 12)

38. ★ **OPEN-ENDED MATH** Write an inequality whose graph is a half-plane shaded above a dashed line. Then write an inequality whose graph is a half-plane shaded below a solid line.

39. ★ **SHORT RESPONSE** Write an inequality whose graph is the half-plane that contains all the points that are *not* the solutions of the inequality $5x + y \ge 2$. *Explain* your method.

40. ★ **EXTENDED RESPONSE** Catherine is going on a canoe trip. She has to carry a backpack containing the meals and water she will need. Catherine can take no more than 10 pounds in her backpack. One bottle of water weighs 16 ounces and one meal weighs 10 ounces.

   a. Write an inequality to model the situation, where x is the number of water bottles and y is the number of meals.

   b. Graph the inequality. Use your graph to find the maximum number of water bottles she can carry when she packs 4 meals. *Explain* how you found your answer.

   c. Can she take 5 water bottles and 6 meals? *Explain* how your graph helps you answer this question.

41. **CHALLENGE** Lee sells 6 videos and 3 CDs at a yard sale and makes at most \$12. Vivian sells 4 videos and 2 CDs and makes at least \$10. Write an inequality to model each situation, where x is the price of a video and y is the price of a CD. Graph both inequalities in the same coordinate plane. Is it possible that Lee and Vivian charge the same prices? *Explain.*

MIXED REVIEW

Prepare for Lesson 12.1 in Exs. 42–43

Make a line plot of the data. ***(p. 782)***

42. 10, 9, 8, 8, 9, 7, 11, 10, 8, 9, 8

43. 1, 2, 2, 4, 1, 2, 3, 1, 4, 3, 3, 4

Write the decimal as a mixed number in simplest form. ***(p. 255)***

44. 1.34

45. 3.75

46. 8.125

47. 7.164

48. ★ **MULTIPLE CHOICE** What is the slope of the line that passes through $(-3, -4)$ and $(7, 8)$? ***(p. 612)***

   Ⓐ $-\frac{6}{5}$ Ⓑ $-\frac{5}{6}$ Ⓒ $\frac{5}{6}$ Ⓓ $\frac{6}{5}$

QUIZ for Lessons 11.5–11.8

Find the intercepts of the graph of the equation. *(p. 606)*

1. $y = 2x + 3$
2. $2y + x = 6$
3. $x = 3$

Find the slope of the line passing through the points. *(p. 612)*

4. $(3, 4), (5, 7)$
5. $(-1, -3), (0, 0)$
6. $(-5, 3), (4, 3)$

Find the slope and y-intercept of the graph of the equation. Then graph the equation. *(p. 622)*

7. $y = \frac{6}{5}x - 2$
8. $-5x - 5y = -20$
9. $y = -x$

Graph the inequality. Then list three solutions of the inequality. *(p. 629)*

10. $y > x - 3$
11. $x - 3y \leq -9$
12. $6x + 7y < -21$

13. **CAR WASH** Your club holds a car wash to raise money for a charity. In 180 minutes, the club members can wash x small vehicles and y large vehicles. The equation $10x + 15y = 180$ models this situation. Find the intercepts. Then graph the equation. What do the intercepts represent in this situation? *(p. 606)*

14. **LEMONADE STAND** Some children on your street are selling lemonade. They charge \$.50 for a small lemonade and \$1 for a large lemonade. Graph the inequality $0.5x + y \geq 20$ to find two possible combinations of small lemonades x and large lemonades y they could sell to make at least \$20. *(p. 629)*

Brain Game

Late Night Show

Each slope or y-intercept can be matched with exactly one lettered equation. Write the appropriate letters in the blanks to find what kind of show is being advertised.

?	?	?	?	?	?	?	?	?	?	?
$m = \frac{3}{2}$	$b = -6$	$m = -1$	$m = 3$	$b = 1$	$m = -4$	$b = 10$	$m = 1$	$b = -18$	$b = 2$	$m = -\frac{1}{3}$

E. $y = 2x + 1$ **L.** $2x - y = 6$ **P.** $4y = 6x - 20$ **S.** $2x + 4y = 12$

U. $y = \frac{1}{3}x + 2$ **N.** $2y = 6x - 14$ **A.** $2x + 2y = 20$ **O.** $y = 5x + 9$

T. $4x + y = 20$ **I.** $6x - y = 18$ **R.** $5x - 5y = 40$ **M.** $x + 3y = 18$

MIXED REVIEW of Problem Solving

Lessons 11.5–11.8

1. **SHORT RESPONSE** Dara spends 24 hours a month at ice skating lessons. In one month, she usually attends 12 individual lessons and 8 partner lessons. The number of hours Dara spends in lessons can be modeled by the equation $12x + 8y = 24$. Identify what the variables represent. Then find the intercepts and graph the equation. *Explain* what the intercepts mean in this situation.

2. **OPEN-ENDED** *Describe* a real-world situation that can be modeled by $4x + 3y = 9$.

3. **MULTI-STEP PROBLEM** Paul is buying food at a basketball game. He has at most $10 to buy boxes of popcorn and drinks.

   a. Write an inequality to model the situation, where x is the number of boxes of popcorn and y is the number of drinks.

   b. Graph the inequality.

   c. Use your graph to find the maximum number of boxes of popcorn he can buy when he buys 2 drinks.

   d. Can Paul buy 2 boxes of popcorn and 3 drinks? *Explain* how your graph helps you answer this question.

4. **GRIDDED ANSWER** A line passes through the points $(5, -1)$ and $(x, 3)$ and has an undefined slope. What is the value of x?

5. **SHORT RESPONSE** The inequality $3.75x + 2y \le 30$ describes the number of pounds of strawberries x, at $3.75 per pound, and the number of pounds of grapes y, at $2.00 per pound, that can be bought with $30. Is it possible to buy 14 pounds of fruit? If so, give the ordered pairs with whole number coordinates that meet this condition. *Justify* your answer.

6. **SHORT RESPONSE** The graph at the right represents all the points that are solutions to four inequalities. The equations used to graph the inequalities are

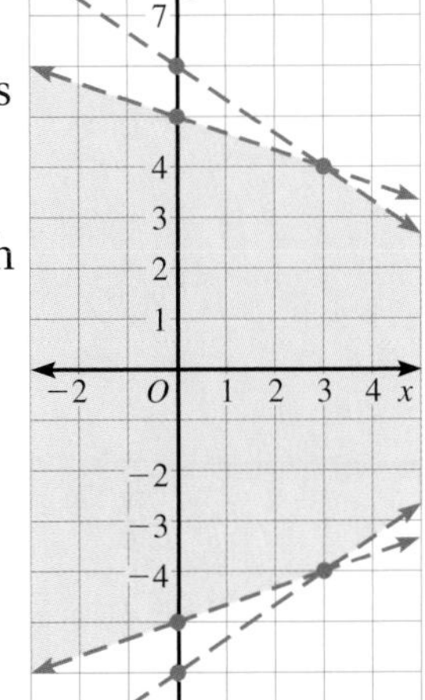

$y = -\frac{1}{3}x + 5$,

$y = \frac{1}{3}x - 5$,

$y = \frac{2}{3}x - 6$, and

$y = -\frac{2}{3}x + 6$.

What are the four inequalities? *Explain* your answers.

7. **EXTENDED RESPONSE** Yen buys sweet curry powder at $1.10 per ounce and hot curry powder at $1.30 per ounce. Yen wants a total of 10 ounces of curry powder.

   a. Write an equation for the total cost y of the curry powder if x represents the number of ounces of sweet curry powder.

   b. Write the equation in slope-intercept form and graph it. *Explain* how you chose a reasonable scale for your graph.

   c. *Describe* the meaning of the graph's slope, y-intercept, and the point on the graph where x equals 10.

11 CHAPTER REVIEW

@HomeTutor
classzone.com
Vocabulary Practice

REVIEW KEY VOCABULARY

- relation, *p. 583*
- input, *p. 583*
- output, *p. 583*
- function, *p. 583*
- domain, *p. 584*
- range, *p. 584*
- scatter plot, *p. 588*
- solution of an equation in two variables, *p. 593*
- linear equation, *p. 598*
- *x*-intercept, *p. 606*
- *y*-intercept, *p. 606*
- slope, *p. 612*
- rise, run, *p. 612*
- slope-intercept form, *p. 622*
- linear inequality, solution, *p. 629*
- half-plane, *p. 630*

VOCABULARY EXERCISES

1. A relation that has exactly one output for each input is a(n) __?__.
2. The graph of a linear inequality in two variables is a(n) __?__.
3. For a function, the set of all possible __?__ values is the domain, and the set of all possible __?__ values is the range.
4. The slope of a nonvertical line is the ratio of its __?__ to its __?__.
5. *Explain* how to find the *x*-intercept and the *y*-intercept of the graph of an equation.
6. *Describe* a real-world situation that can be represented by a linear equation. What does the slope of the line tell you about the situation?
7. Write the steps you would take to graph a linear inequality.

REVIEW EXAMPLES AND EXERCISES

11.1 Relations and Functions

pp. 583–587

EXAMPLE

Tell whether the relation is a function. If so, write a function rule that relates *x* and *y*.

a. (3, 2), (5, 3), (5, 5), (6, 7)

▸ **Answer** The relation is *not* a function because 5 has two outputs.

b.

Input x	−4	−3	−2	−1
Output y	4	3	2	1

▸ **Answer** The relation is a function because each input has exactly one output. Each *y* is the opposite of *x*, so the function rule is $y = -x$.

EXERCISES

Tell whether the relation is a function. If so, write a function rule that relates x and y.

SEE EXAMPLES 1 AND 3 on pp. 583–584 for Exs. 8–11

8. (0, 6), (2, 6), (4, 7), (0, 3), (2, 3)

9. (−5, 1), (−2, 4), (1, 7), (2, 8), (5, 11)

10.

Input x	Output y
−8	4
−2	1
4	−2
10	−5

11.

Input x	Output y
0	−8
1	−11
2	−14
3	−17

11.2 Scatter Plots

pp. 588–592

EXAMPLE

Make a scatter plot of the data. Then describe the relationship.

x	−1	0	1	2
y	−6	−5	−4	−3

To make a scatter plot, plot the ordered pairs from the table.

(−1, −6), (0, −5),
(1, −4), (2, −3)

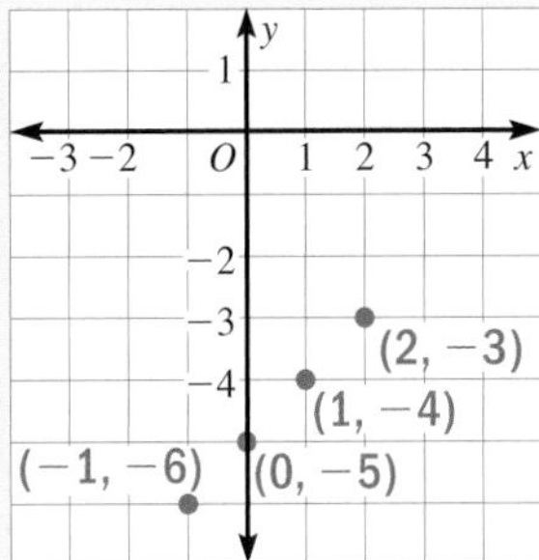

The y-coordinates increase as the x-coordinates increase. So, the quantities have a positive relationship.

EXERCISES

Make a scatter plot of the data. Then describe the relationship.

SEE EXAMPLES 1 AND 2 on pp. 588–589 for Exs. 12–14

12.

Muffins sold	12	24	36	48
Profit	\$6	\$12	\$18	\$24

13.

Speed (mi/h)	30	40	50	60
Time (h)	4	3	2.4	2

14.

Age	8	14	19	31
Bowling score	77	237	125	149

11.3 Equations in Two Variables

pp. 593–597

EXAMPLE

List three solutions of the equation $y = 2x + 3$.

x-value	Substitute for x.	Evaluate.	Solution
$x = -2$	$y = 2(-2) + 3$	$y = -1$	$(-2, -1)$
$x = 0$	$y = 2(0) + 3$	$y = 3$	$(0, 3)$
$x = 2$	$y = 2(2) + 3$	$y = 7$	$(2, 7)$

EXERCISES

SEE EXAMPLE 3 on p. 594 for Exs. 15–16

15. List three solutions of the equation $x + 4y = 16$.

16. Temperature The temperature is 81°F as Ella begins climbing a mountain. The temperature t in degrees Fahrenheit after climbing a feet is approximated by $t = 81 - 0.005a$. Ella can climb 800 feet per hour. What will the temperature be if Ella climbs for 4 hours?

11.4 Graphs of Linear Equations

pp. 598–603

EXAMPLE

Graph $y = 2x + 2$.

STEP 1 **Choose** several values to substitute for x. Then evaluate to find y and make a table of values.

x	−2	−1	0	1	2
y	−2	0	2	4	6

STEP 2 **List** the solutions as ordered pairs.
$(-2, -2), (-1, 0), (0, 2), (1, 4), (2, 6)$

STEP 3 **Plot** the ordered pairs and draw a line through them.

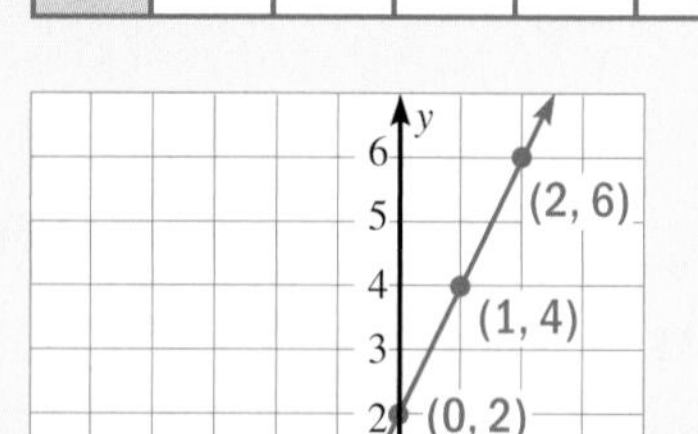

EXERCISES

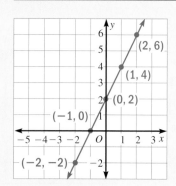

SEE EXAMPLES 1 AND 3 on pp. 599–600 for Exs. 17–19

Graph the linear equation.

17. $y = x + 2$

18. $3x + 2y = -2$

19. $y = 8$

11.5 Using Intercepts

pp. 606–609

EXAMPLE

Find the intercepts of the graph of $y = 5x + 20$.

To find the x-intercept, let $y = 0$ and solve for x.

$$y = 5x + 20$$
$$0 = 5x + 20$$
$$-20 = 5x$$
$$-4 = x$$

To find the y-intercept, let $x = 0$ and solve for y.

$$y = 5x + 20$$
$$y = 5(0) + 20$$
$$y = 0 + 20$$
$$y = 20$$

▶ **Answer** The x-intercept is -4 and the y-intercept is 20.

EXERCISES

SEE EXAMPLES 1 AND 3 on pp. 606–607 for Exs. 20–21

20. Find the intercepts of the graph of $-6x + 2y = 9$.

21. Taxes The approximate amount of taxes collected by the Internal Revenue Service from 1980 to 1990 can be modeled by $y = 57.1x + 488$, where y represents taxes, in billions of dollars, and x represents the number of years since 1980. What is the y-intercept of the graph of this equation? What does the y-intercept mean in this situation?

11.6 Slope

pp. 612–617

EXAMPLE

Find the slope of the line passing through (0, 3) and (4, 6).

$$m = \frac{\text{rise}}{\text{run}} = \frac{y_2 - y_1}{x_2 - x_1} = \frac{6 - 3}{4 - 0} = \frac{3}{4}$$

EXERCISES

Write the coordinates of two points on the line. Then find the slope of the line.

SEE EXAMPLES 2 AND 3 on p. 613 for Exs. 22–23

22.

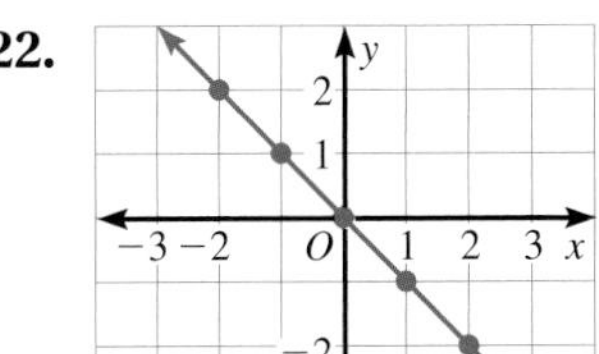

23.

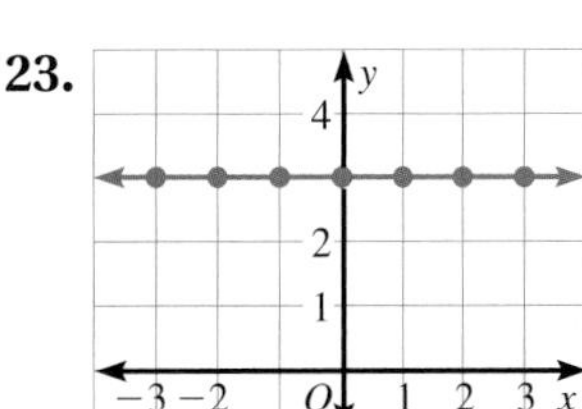

11.7 Slope-Intercept Form

pp. 622–626

EXAMPLE

Find the slope and y-intercept of the graph of $-9x + 3y = 21$.

Write the equation $-9x + 3y = 21$ in slope-intercept form.

$-9x + 3y = 21$ **Write original equation.**

$3y = 9x + 21$ **Add 9x to each side.**

$y = 3x + 7$ **Divide each side by 3.**

▶ **Answer** The line has a slope of 3 and a y-intercept of 7.

EXERCISES

SEE EXAMPLE 1 on p. 622 for Exs. 24–29

Find the slope and y-intercept of the graph of the equation.

24. $y = 6x - 1$ **25.** $y = -\frac{2}{3}x + 4$ **26.** $y = 8$

Rewrite the equation in slope-intercept form. Then find the slope and y-intercept of the graph of the equation.

27. $y - 4x = 10$ **28.** $2y + 6 = x$ **29.** $-3x - 7y = 21$

11.8 Graphs of Linear Inequalities

pp. 629–633

EXAMPLE

Graph $y > -2x + 4$.

The graph of $y = -2x + 4$ has a slope of -2 and a y-intercept of 4.

Because the inequality is $>$, use a dashed line.

Use (0, 0) as a test point:

$0 \overset{?}{>} -2(0) + 4$

$0 \not> 4$

Shade the half-plane that does *not* contain (0, 0).

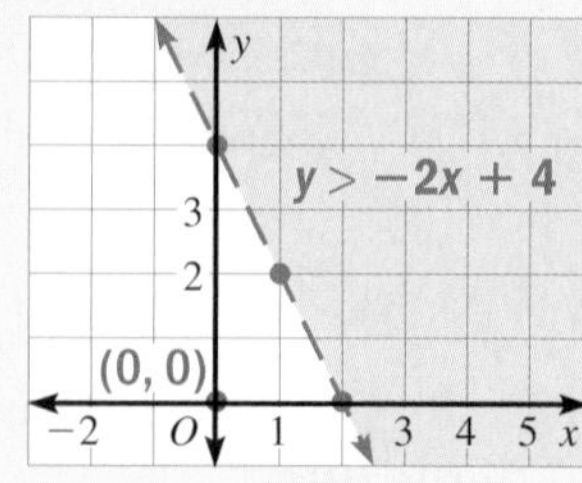

EXERCISES

SEE EXAMPLE 2 on p. 630 for Exs. 30–32

Graph the inequality.

30. $y < -\frac{3}{5}x - 3$ **31.** $3x - 7y \geq 21$ **32.** $4x + 8y \leq 32$

11 CHAPTER TEST

@HomeTutor classzone.com Chapter Test Practice

In Exercises 1 and 2, tell whether the relation is a function. If so, write a function rule that relates x and y.

1.

Input x	0	1	2	3
Output y	0	−0.25	−0.5	−0.75

2.

Input x	−2	−1	0	1
Output y	−9	−3	3	9

Tell whether the ordered pair is a solution of the equation $12x + 3y = 21$.

3. $(-1, 11)$ **4.** $(-4, -9)$ **5.** $(2, -15)$ **6.** $(6, -17)$

Find the slope and y-intercept of the graph of the equation. Then graph the equation.

7. $y = 6x - 3$ **8.** $-5x + y = 1$ **9.** $y = -\frac{1}{4}x$

Graph the inequality.

10. $3x + 6y \geq 12$ **11.** $7x - y \leq 49$ **12.** $8x - 15y > 30$

For Exercises 13–15, use the diagram of a seesaw.

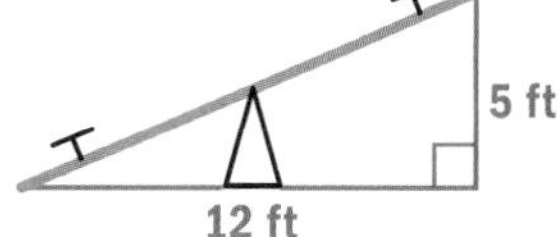

13. What is the run of the seesaw?

14. What is the rise of the seesaw?

15. What is the slope of the seesaw?

16. What type of relationship do you expect to find in a scatter plot when comparing the number of math problems assigned and the time spent doing the assignment?

17. YARD WORK You have a job raking leaves. You charge \$10 plus \$.50 for each bag you fill with leaves. The equation $y = 0.50x + 10$ models this situation, where x is the number of bags and y is the total amount, in dollars, you earn. Your friend tells you that you will make \$16 if you fill 8 bags. Is your friend correct? If not, find the amount you will make for filling 8 bags.

18. GASOLINE A scooter uses 1 gallon of gasoline per 60 miles. The equation $n = 60g$ models this relationship, where n is the number of miles driven and g is the number of gallons of gas used. Graph the equation and use the graph to estimate the number of miles traveled using 12 gallons of gasoline.

19. GIFT CARD Ken received a \$25 movie gift card. Matinee shows cost \$4 each and evening shows cost \$8 each. The inequality $4x + 8y \leq 25$ models this situation, where x is the number of matinees and y is the number of evening shows. Graph the inequality and use the graph to find the greatest number of evening shows Ken can see if he sees 3 matinees.

11 ★ Standardized TEST PREPARATION

MULTIPLE CHOICE QUESTIONS

If you have difficulty solving a multiple choice problem directly, you may be able to use another approach to eliminate incorrect answer choices and obtain the correct answer.

PROBLEM 1

Reading You have \$45 to spend at a bookstore. Books cost \$12 each and magazines cost \$3 each. The inequality $12x + 3y \le 45$ models this situation, where x represents the number of books and y represents the number of magazines. Which of the following combinations of books and magazines could *not* be purchased?

Ⓐ 2 books 3 magazines Ⓑ 2 books 4 magazines Ⓒ 3 books 3 magazines Ⓓ 3 books 4 magazines

METHOD 1

SOLVE DIRECTLY Check possible solutions (x, y) of the inequality by substituting x and y into the inequality.

(x, y)	$12x + 3y$	$12x + 3y \stackrel{?}{\le} 45$
(2, 3)	12(2) + 3(3)	$33 \le 45$ ✓
(2, 4)	12(2) + 3(4)	$36 \le 45$ ✓
(3, 3)	12(3) + 3(3)	$45 \le 45$ ✓
(3, 4)	12(3) + 3(4)	$48 \le 45$ ✗

The ordered pair (3, 4) is *not* a solution of the inequality. The combination of 3 books and 4 magazines could *not* be purchased.

The correct answer is D. Ⓐ Ⓑ Ⓒ Ⓓ

METHOD 2

ELIMINATE CHOICES In some cases, you can identify choices of a multiple choice question that can be eliminated.

Because you are looking for the combination of books and magazines that could *not* be purchased, the correct answer is the combination of books and magazines whose total cost *exceeds* the \$45 limit.

The number of books in choice A is the same as in choice B, but the number of magazines is less. The total cost of choice A will be less than the total cost of choice B. So, choice A can be eliminated.

The number of magazines in choice B is the same as in choice D, but the number of books is less. The total cost of choice B will be less than the total cost of choice D. So, choice B can be eliminated.

The number of books in choice C is the same as in choice D, but the number of magazines is less. The total cost of choice C will be less than the total cost of choice D. So, choice C can be eliminated.

The correct answer is D. Ⓐ Ⓑ Ⓒ Ⓓ

PROBLEM 2

A line with a slope of $\frac{5}{2}$ passes through $(-8, -3)$. What is the slope-intercept form of the equation of the line?

Ⓐ $y = -\frac{5}{2}x - 23$ Ⓑ $y = \frac{5}{2}x - 3$ Ⓒ $y = \frac{5}{2}x + 17$ Ⓓ $2y - 5x = 34$

METHOD 1

SOLVE DIRECTLY Find the y-intercept of the line, and then use slope-intercept form to write an equation for the line.

STEP 1 **Find** the y-intercept by substituting the slope and the coordinates of $(-8, -3)$ into the equation $y = mx + b$.

$$y = mx + b$$

$$-3 = \frac{5}{2}(-8) + b$$

$$-3 = -20 + b$$

$$17 = b$$

The y-intercept is 17.

STEP 2 **Use** the slope and y-intercept to write the equation.

$$y = mx + b$$

$$y = \frac{5}{2}x + 17$$

The correct answer is C. Ⓐ Ⓑ Ⓒ Ⓓ

METHOD 2

ELIMINATE CHOICES In some cases, you can identify choices of a multiple choice question that can be eliminated.

The slope of the line is $\frac{5}{2}$, but the slope of the line in choice A is $-\frac{5}{2}$. So, choice A can be eliminated.

You are looking for an equation in slope-intercept form. The equation in choice D is *not* written in slope-intercept form. So, choice D can be eliminated.

In choice B, the y-intercept of the line is -3. So, the line contains the point $(0, -3)$. If the line also contained the point $(-8, -3)$, it would be a horizontal line with a slope of 0. But, this is impossible because the slope of the line is $\frac{5}{2}$. So, choice B can be eliminated.

The correct answer is C. Ⓐ Ⓑ Ⓒ Ⓓ

PRACTICE

Explain why you can eliminate the highlighted answer choice.

1. What is the value of x if the line passing through $(-3, 5)$ and $(x, 8)$ has a slope of $\frac{1}{2}$?

   × **Ⓐ -9** Ⓑ -3 Ⓒ 3 Ⓓ 9

2. Which point is a solution of $7x - 2y \leq 5$?

   Ⓐ $(0, -3)$ Ⓑ $(0, 0)$ Ⓒ $(1, 0)$ × **Ⓓ $(3, -5)$**

11 ★ Standardized TEST PRACTICE

MULTIPLE CHOICE

1. The scatter plot below shows the average test score of each class on a recent English exam. Describe the relationship shown.

Average Test Scores

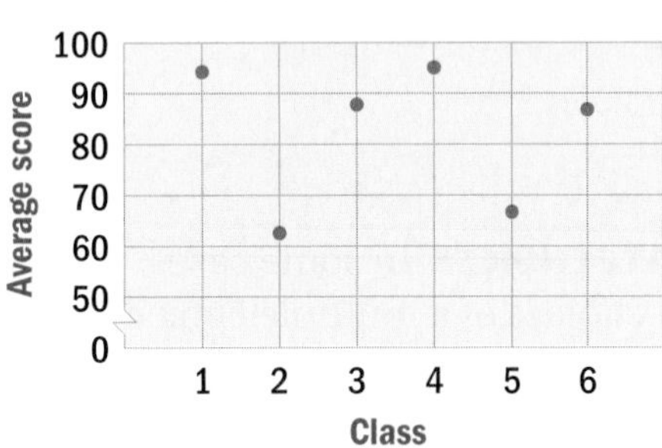

Ⓐ positive　Ⓑ negative

Ⓒ linear　Ⓓ none

2. What is the slope of the line?

Ⓐ $-\frac{3}{2}$

Ⓑ 0

Ⓒ 1

Ⓓ $\frac{3}{2}$

3. A line passes through the points (1, 2) and (2, y) and has a slope of 0. What is the value of y?

Ⓐ -1　Ⓑ 2

Ⓒ 3　Ⓓ 5

4. A 4 foot board is leaning against a wall so that it forms a right triangle with the wall and the floor. The board touches the wall 24 inches above the ground. What is the slope of the board as a decimal rounded to the nearest tenth?

Ⓐ 0.5　Ⓑ 0.6

Ⓒ 1.7　Ⓓ 2.0

5. Which equation is *not* linear?

Ⓐ $y = -2x + 4$　Ⓑ $3x + 4y = 8$

Ⓒ $y = x^3 - 8$　Ⓓ $4x = 8 - 2y$

6. Which equation is represented by the graph?

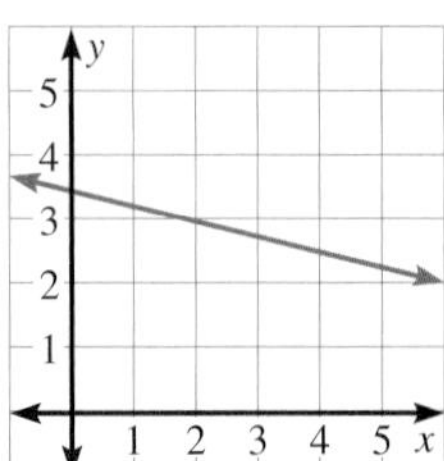

Ⓐ $y = \frac{1}{4}x + 3.5$　Ⓑ $y = -\frac{1}{4}x + 3.5$

Ⓒ $y = 4x + 3.5$　Ⓓ $y = -4x + 3.5$

7. You earn money to go to the movies by baby-sitting for x dollars an hour. One weekend, you baby-sit for 9 hours and see 3 movies. Each movie costs y dollars. You have $12 left at the end of the weekend. Which equation models this situation in *slope-intercept form*?

Ⓐ $-3y = -9x + 12$　Ⓑ $x = \frac{1}{3}y + \frac{4}{3}$

Ⓒ $y = 3x + 4$　Ⓓ $y = 3x - 4$

8. Which of the following relations is *not* a function?

Ⓐ (0, −3), (1, −1), (2, 1), (3, 3)

Ⓑ (−4, 0), (2, 1), (0, 2), (2, 3)

Ⓒ (0, 5), (2, 0), (4, −5), (−1, 3)

Ⓓ (6, 5), (0, −1), (3, 6), (−2, −1)

9. The total cost C, in dollars, of a horse rental can be modeled by $C = 10h + 15$, where h is the number of hours *after* the first hour. You have $50. What is the greatest *total* number of hours you can ride the horse?

Ⓐ 2 hours　Ⓑ 3 hours

Ⓒ 4 hours　Ⓓ 5 hours

GRIDDED ANSWER

10. What is the value of y in the table below when x is 7?

Input x	3	5	7	9
Output y	−4	−2	?	2

11. A line passes through the point $(-4, 29)$. The slope of the line is 0. What is the y-intercept of the line?

12. What is the slope of the graph of the function represented by the input-output table below?

Input x	2	4	6	8
Output y	5	9	13	17

SHORT RESPONSE

13. Your class needs to raise $120 selling hats and T-shirts. The equation $6x + 5y = 120$ models the situation, where x is the number of hats sold and y is the number of T-shirts sold. Find the x- and y-intercepts. *Explain* what the intercepts mean in this situation.

14. Graph the inequalities $x + y \leq 5$, $x \geq 0$, and $y \geq 0$. Find the area of the shaded region. *Explain* how you found your answer.

15. You pay $50 to rent a karaoke machine for a party. Food will cost $6 per person. Graph the equation $y = 6x + 50$, where x is the number of people and y is the total cost, in dollars. You want to spend no more than $100. Use your graph to find the maximum number of people you can invite. *Explain.*

EXTENDED RESPONSE

16. The table at the right shows the latitude L and average low temperature t in January for each of 5 U.S. cities.

a. Make a scatter plot of the data.

b. What type of relationship between latitude and average low temperature does the scatter plot show?

c. The latitude of Jacksonville is 30°N. Estimate its average low temperature in January. *Explain* your method of estimation.

City	*L*	*t*
Miami	26°N	63°F
Helena	47°N	10°F
Reno	40°N	22°F
Buffalo	43°N	18°F
Memphis	35°N	31°F

17. The table at the right shows the prices of circular cheese pizzas with different diameters (in inches). The cost, in dollars, of each topping is also shown.

a. The total cost p, in dollars, of a 12 inch pizza can be modeled by the equation $p = 0.75t + 6.25$, where t is the number of toppings. Make a table of values that shows the total cost of a 12 inch pizza with 1 to 6 toppings.

b. Graph the equation using your table from part (a).

c. Suppose you graphed the equations for the total cost of each size pizza listed in the table. Which graph would have the greatest slope? *Explain* your reasoning.

Diameter	*Price*	*Cost per topping*
10	4.25	0.50
12	6.25	0.75
14	7.75	0.75
16	8.75	1.00
18	9.75	1.25
24	13.00	1.75

12 Data Analysis and Probability

Before

In previous chapters you've . . .

- Found the median and range of a data set
- Found probabilities of events

Now

In Chapter 12 you'll study . . .

- 12.1 Stem-and-leaf plots
- 12.2 Box-and-whisker plots
- 12.3 Using data displays
- 12.4 Counting methods
- 12.5 Permutations
- 12.6 Combinations
- 12.7 Probability and odds
- 12.8 Probability of events

Why?

So you can solve real-world problems about . . .

- skateboards, p. 671
- poetry, p. 676
- archery, p. 689

at classzone.com

- Stem-and-Leaf Plots, p. 649
- Box-and-Whisker Plot, p. 654
- Finding Outcomes, p. 670

Get-Ready Games

Review Prerequisite Skills by playing *Galapagos Graphs.*

Skill Focus: Interpreting bar and circle graphs

GALAPAGOS GRAPHS

HOW TO PLAY

USE the data displays to answer each question. Record the letter for each correct answer.

About how many times larger is Santa Cruz than San Cristobal?

A. 2 **B.** 3 **C.** 4

What is the area of Isabela?

D. 1680 mi^2 **E.** 1771 mi^2 **F.** 1800 mi^2

What percent of the land vertebrate species in the Galapagos Islands are reptiles?

G. 10% **H.** 26% **I.** 30%

WRITE the letters of the correct answers to the questions in order. Find the number that corresponds to the letter. Put all three numbers together in the order of the answers. This will tell you the age of the oldest Galapagos tortoise on record.

A. 1 **B.** 2 **C.** 0 **D.** 9 **E.** 5

F. 2 **G.** 7 **H.** 2 **I.** 5

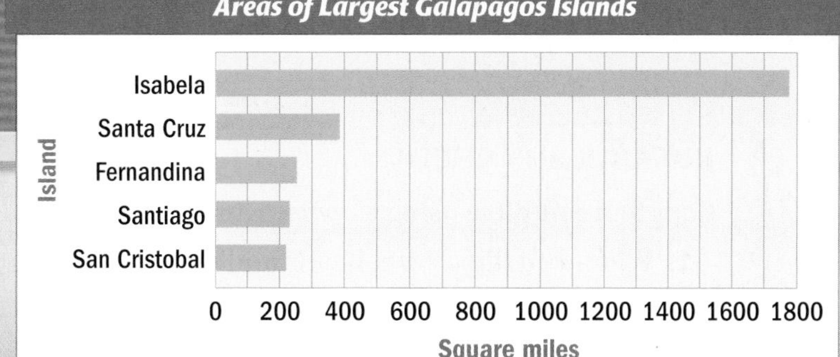

Great Frigatebird

Giant Galapagos Tortoise

Galapagos Sea Lion

Stop and Think

1. **WRITING** *Describe* one way the circle graph would change if you included the ocean life of the Galapagos Islands.
2. **CRITICAL THINKING** Is the area of Isabela greater than the total area of the next four largest islands? *Explain.*

12 Getting Ready

Review Prerequisite Skills

REVIEW WORDS

- **data,** *p. 3*
- **mean,** *p. 272*
- **median,** *p. 272*
- **range,** *p. 273*
- **outcome,** *p. 381*
- **probability of an event,** *p. 381*

VOCABULARY CHECK

Copy and complete using a review word from the list at the left.

1. When you flip a coin, heads and tails are the two possible __?__.
2. Find the sum of the values of a set of data and then divide by the number of data values to find the __?__ of the data.
3. The __?__ is a measure of how likely it is that the event will occur.

SKILL CHECK

Find the mean and the median of the data set. *(p. 272)*

4. 23, 27, 13, 24, 19, 21, 25, 25, 12
5. 0.2, 0.35, 1.33, 1.32, 0.05, 0.5

Find the probability of the event. *(p. 381)*

6. You roll a number cube and get a number greater than 4.
7. You randomly choose the letter A from a bag holding the eight lettered tiles that spell ARKANSAS.

@HomeTutor Prerequisite skills practice at classzone.com

Notetaking Skills — Contrasting Terms

In each chapter you will learn a new notetaking skill. In Chapter 12 you will apply the strategy of contrasting terms to Example 3 on p. 682.

When words have similar meanings, you should emphasize their differences in your notes.

Pairs of Angles

Complementary Angles: The sum of the angle measures is 90°.

Supplementary Angles: The sum of the angle measures is 180°.

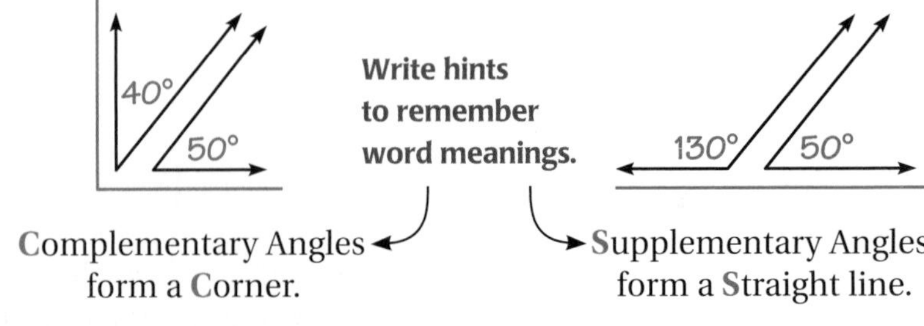
40°
50°
Write hints to remember word meanings.
130°
50°
Complementary Angles form a Corner.
Supplementary Angles form a Straight line.

In Lesson 12.6, you should note the difference between combinations and permutations.

12.1 Stem-and-Leaf Plots

Before	You organized data using bar graphs and histograms.
Now	You will make and interpret stem-and-leaf plots.
Why?	So you can organize sports data, as in Example 1.

KEY VOCABULARY
- **stem-and-leaf plot,** *p. 649*

Track Hurdlers entering the 200 meter hurdles at a track meet were ranked according to their qualifying times, in seconds, shown below.

28.6 29.2 28.1 27.5 29.8 28.7
30.2 29.3 28.3 28.9 29.9 28.4

How can the data be displayed to show the distribution of the times?

A **stem-and-leaf plot** is a data display that helps you see how data are distributed. A stem-and-leaf plot is useful for ordering large sets of data like the one above.

EXAMPLE 1 Making a Stem-and-Leaf Plot

STEP 1 **Identify** the stems. The times range from 27.5 seconds to 30.2 seconds. Let the **stems** be the digits in the tens' and ones' places. Then the **leaves** are the tenths' digits.

STEP 2 **Write** the stems first. Then record each time by writing its tenths' digit on the same line as its corresponding stem. Include a key that shows what the stems and leaves represent.

STEP 3 **Make** an ordered stem-and-leaf plot.

Unordered Plot

Stem	Leaves
27	5
28	6 1 7 3 9 4
29	2 8 3 9
30	2

Key: 27 | 5 = 27.5

Ordered Plot

Stem	Leaves
27	5
28	1 3 4 6 7 9
29	2 3 8 9
30	2

Key: 27 | 5 = 27.5

The leaves for each stem are listed in order from least to greatest.

READING
In a stem-and-leaf plot, a stem can be one or more digits. A leaf is usually a single digit.

Animated Math at classzone.com

✓ GUIDED PRACTICE for Example 1

1. Make an ordered stem-and-leaf plot of the video game prices: \$40, \$15, \$10, \$19, \$12, \$24, \$15, \$39, \$51, \$50, \$35, \$20, \$47, \$36, \$30, \$25, \$27, \$29, \$24, \$43, \$29.

EXAMPLE 2 Interpreting a Stem-and-Leaf Plot

AVOID ERRORS
Read the key carefully so you understand the data in a stem-and-leaf plot. In Example 2, 6 | 8 means 68, not 6.8.

Biology The stem-and-leaf plot at the right shows the lengths, in millimeters, of fish in a tank. Use the stem-and-leaf plot to describe the data. What interval includes the most lengths?

Stem	Leaves
4	9
5	7 7 9
6	1 2 4 4 7 8 8 9
7	6 8
8	4

Key: 6 | 8 = 68

SOLUTION

The longest fish is 84 millimeters and the shortest fish is 49 millimeters. So the range of lengths is 35 millimeters. Most of the lengths are in the 60–69 interval.

Double Stem-and-Leaf Plots A double stem-and-leaf plot can be used to compare two sets of data. You read to the left of the stems for one set of data and to the right for the other.

EXAMPLE 3 Making a Double Stem-and-Leaf Plot

Test Scores The data below show the test scores for Beth's class and Marisa's class. Overall, which class had the better test scores?

Beth's class: 95, 86, 79, 79, 58, 68, 90, 63, 71, 81, 82, 94, 64, 76, 77, 79, 83, 91, 83, 68, 74, 71

Marisa's class: 95, 73, 76, 84, 84, 89, 67, 82, 88, 86, 93, 97, 96, 84, 60, 75, 91, 87, 89, 86, 76, 93

SOLUTION

You can use a double stem-and-leaf plot to compare the test scores.

Beth's Class		Marisa's Class
8	5	
8 8 4 3	6	0 7
9 9 9 7 6 4 1 1	7	3 5 6 6
6 3 3 2 1	8	2 4 4 4 6 6 7 8 9 9
5 4 1 0	9	1 3 3 5 6 7

Key: 0 | 9 | 1 represents 90 and 91

▸ **Answer** Marisa's class had better scores, because her class had more scores in the eighties and nineties.

✓ GUIDED PRACTICE for Examples 2 and 3

2. Make an ordered double stem-and-leaf plot to compare the lengths, in minutes, of the last 15 phone calls made by two friends. In general, who made longer calls, Kenyon or Jason? *Justify* your reasoning.

Kenyon: 8, 12, 8, 17, 5, 28, 16, 23, 29, 14, 21, 34, 16, 28, 31
Jason: 31, 16, 24, 28, 7, 12, 5, 11, 5, 13, 14, 6, 11, 19, 24

12.1 EXERCISES

HOMEWORK KEY

★ = **STANDARDIZED TEST PRACTICE** Exs. 14, 15, 26, 28, 29, and 41

○ = **HINTS AND HOMEWORK HELP** for Exs. 5, 9, 11, 15, 27 at classzone.com

SKILL PRACTICE

1. **VOCABULARY** Copy and complete: The key for a stem-and-leaf plot says 7 | 4 = 74. In the plot, 7 is the _?_ and 4 is the _?_.

2. **VOCABULARY** Why is it important to include a key in a stem-and-leaf plot?

SEE EXAMPLE 1 on p. 649 for Exs. 3–13

STEMS AND LEAVES Write the number as it would appear in a stem-and-leaf plot. Identify the stem and the leaf.

3. 80
4. 117
5. 12.9
6. 4.6

STEM-AND-LEAF PLOTS Make an ordered stem-and-leaf plot of the data. Identify the interval that includes the most data values.

7. 45, 48, 65, 50, 67, 82, 74, 63, 52, 61, 84, 66, 40
8. 33, 12, 8, 14, 35, 9, 26, 37, 4, 6, 8, 20, 15, 32, 29
9. 108, 95, 89, 112, 109, 94, 103, 115, 105, 92
10. 461, 492, 439, 467, 501, 485, 475, 451, 510, 468, 494, 461
11. 20.2, 22.6, 18.3, 18.7, 22.5, 18.1, 18.6, 21.9, 18.4, 22.8
12. 5.1, 4.0, 5.3, 3.2, 5.7, 6.9, 5.3, 4.6, 5.2, 6.7, 4.9, 4.7, 5.5

13. **ERROR ANALYSIS** Describe and correct the error made in making a stem-and-leaf plot for the data set:

    115, 111, 108, 95, 91, 83

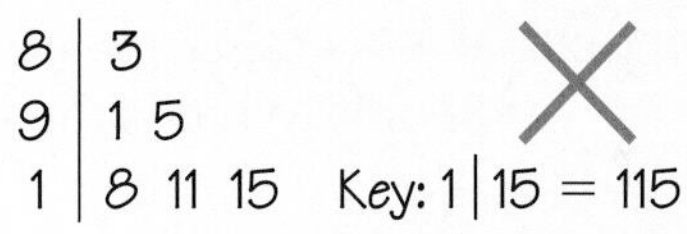

SEE EXAMPLE 2 on p. 650 for Exs. 14–15

14. ★ **MULTIPLE CHOICE** What is the range of the data in the stem-and-leaf plot?

Stem	Leaves
10	1 4
11	2 3 5 5 9
12	0 0
13	1 6 8 8

Key: 12 | 0 = 120

Ⓐ 3 Ⓑ 3.7 Ⓒ 7 Ⓓ 37

15. ★ **MULTIPLE CHOICE** Use the stem-and-leaf plot from Exercise 14. Which interval has the most data values?

Ⓐ 100–109 Ⓑ 110–119 Ⓒ 120–129 Ⓓ 130–139

DOUBLE STEM-AND-LEAF PLOTS Make an ordered double stem-and-leaf plot of the two sets of data.

SEE EXAMPLE 3 on p. 650 for Exs. 16–19

16. Set A: 16, 19, 8, 22, 18, 20, 32, 5
    Set B: 12, 8, 25, 42, 31, 15, 16, 9

17. Set C: 102, 98, 111, 70, 118, 92, 77
    Set D: 115, 88, 87, 102, 65, 95, 93

18. Set A: 24, 27, 28, 32, 58, 32, 32, 25
    Set B: 22, 31, 43, 22, 21, 55, 36, 29

19. Set C: 8.8, 9.8, 4.7, 6.3, 6.8, 8.0, 7.7
    Set D: 9.5, 6.8, 7.8, 10, 5.5, 9.1, 9.3

AVERAGES Find the mean, median, and mode(s) of the data.

20.

Stem	Leaves
5	0 0 1 6
6	5 9 9
7	1 1 2 4 4 4 8

Key: 5 | 3 = 53

21.

Stem	Leaves
0	1 1
1	4 5 9
2	0 0 5 8 8
3	0 9

Key: 1 | 4 = 1.4

CHALLENGE Make an ordered stem-and-leaf plot with data that have the given characteristics. The display should have at least 8 data values.

22. a range of 52 and a mode of 30

23. a mean of 10 and a median of 15

PROBLEM SOLVING

SEE EXAMPLES 1 AND 2 on pp. 649–650 for Ex. 24

24. **GUIDED PROBLEM SOLVING** The times, in minutes, it takes fifteen students to get ready for school are as follows: 25, 10, 25, 15, 30, 18, 35, 40, 28, 20, 28, 17, 12, 22, 32. Make an ordered stem-and-leaf plot of the data. What interval includes the most time values?

   a. Identify the highest and lowest data values.

   b. Make an ordered stem-and-leaf plot. Include a key.

   c. Use the plot to find where most of the times fall.

SEE EXAMPLE 2 on p. 650 for Exs. 25–28

25. **RESTAURANTS** The stem-and-leaf plot shows the average waiting times, in minutes, to be seated for fifteen restaurants. What are the shortest and longest waiting times? Which interval has the fewest number of waiting times?

Stem	Leaves
0	5 6 9
1	2 5 5
2	0 0 5 8
3	2 8
4	0 5 5

Key: 2 | 5 = 25

26. ★ **MULTIPLE CHOICE** The stem-and-leaf plot shows the ages of several people. What is the median age?

   (A) 25 (B) 30

   (C) 31 (D) 37

Stem	Leaves
1	3 7 9
2	0 1 4 5
3	7 9
4	0 1 2 2 2

Key: 4 | 1 = 41

ELECTRIC BILLS In Exercises 27 and 28, use the line graph. It shows the cost of a family's electric bills for each of 11 months.

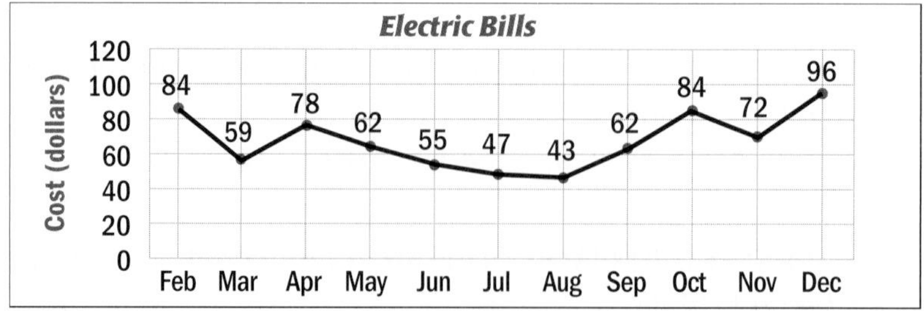

27. Make an ordered stem-and-leaf plot of the monthly costs. Find the median and the range of the data.

28. ★ **SHORT RESPONSE** Which display is more useful for finding the range? the median? *Explain.*

29. ★ **WRITING** Can you make a stem-and-leaf plot from a frequency table? *Explain* why or why not.

SEE EXAMPLE 3 on p. 650 for Ex. 30

30. **FOOTBALL** The total points that the Cleveland Browns scored in each game of a recent season are given below. Red numbers represent wins, and blue numbers represent losses. Make an ordered double stem-and-leaf plot of the data. *Describe* the relationship between points scored and the outcome of the game.

6 24 23 20 14 24 21 12
27 18 15 16 10 7 41 7

31. **MULTIPLE REPRESENTATIONS** The average monthly temperatures in degrees Fahrenheit (°F) for Los Angeles, California, are given below.

56.8, 57.6, 58.0, 60.1, 62.7, 65.7, 69.1, 70.5, 69.9, 66.8, 61.6, 56.9

a. **Display** Make an ordered stem-and-leaf plot of the data. What is the range?

b. **Convert** Convert the data to degrees Celsius (°C) using the formula $C = \frac{5}{9}(F - 32)$. Round to the nearest tenth of a degree.

c. **Compare** Make an ordered stem-and-leaf plot of the converted data. *Describe* how the plots are alike and how they are different.

32. **CHALLENGE** For an awards banquet, you are making a highlight video that can last no more than 15 minutes. Use the following lengths, in minutes, of the video segments you'd like to include.

2:30, 2:29, 2:14, 2:19, 1:49, 2:30, 2:57, 2:30, 2:01, 2:21, 1:53

Make an ordered stem-and-leaf plot of the data. *Explain* how you chose a key. What is the greatest and least number of segments that you can show without leaving time for another? *Justify* your reasoning.

MIXED REVIEW

Prepare for Lesson 12.2 in Exs. 33–34

Find the mean, median, mode(s), and range of the data. *(p. 272)*

33. 93, 84, 100, 95, 89, 78, 78, 85, 83, 95

34. −22, 14, 12, 6, −10, 14, 20, 16, −7, −5, 6, −2

Find the sum or difference.

35. $-17 + (-5)$ *(p. 63)*

36. $-28 + 19$ *(p. 63)*

37. $59 + (-34)$ *(p. 63)*

38. $18 - (-11)$ *(p. 68)*

39. $-48 - 7$ *(p. 68)*

40. $-74 - (-52)$ *(p. 68)*

41. ★ **MULTIPLE CHOICE** What is the slope of the graph of $7x + 4y = 24$? *(p. 622)*

Ⓐ $-\frac{7}{4}$ Ⓑ $-\frac{4}{7}$ Ⓒ 4 Ⓓ 6

12.2 Box-and-Whisker Plots

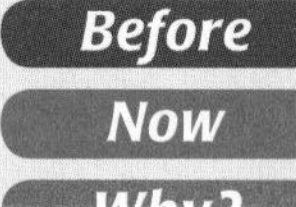

Before You found the median and range of a data set.

Now You will make and interpret box-and-whisker plots.

Why? So you can show data distribution, as in Example 1.

KEY VOCABULARY
- **box-and-whisker plot,** *p. 654*
- **lower quartile,** *p. 654*
- **upper quartile,** *p. 654*
- **lower extreme,** *p. 654*
- **upper extreme,** *p. 654*

Bridges The lengths, in meters, of the world's ten longest suspension bridges are listed below. How can you display these data to show how the lengths are distributed?

1280 1490 1991 1377 1298 1210 1624 1158 1385 1410

A **box-and-whisker plot** is a data display that organizes data values into four parts. Ordered data are divided into lower and upper halves by the median.

The **lower quartile** is the median of the lower half of the data set. The median of the upper half of the data set is the **upper quartile**.

The **lower extreme** is the least data value and the **upper extreme** is the greatest data value.

EXAMPLE 1 Making a Box-and-Whisker Plot

FIND QUARTILES

If a data set has an odd number of values, then the median is not included in either half of the data when finding the quartiles. For help with finding a median, see p. 272.

Display the bridge lengths above in a box-and-whisker plot.

STEP 1 **Order** the data to find the median, the quartiles, and the extremes.

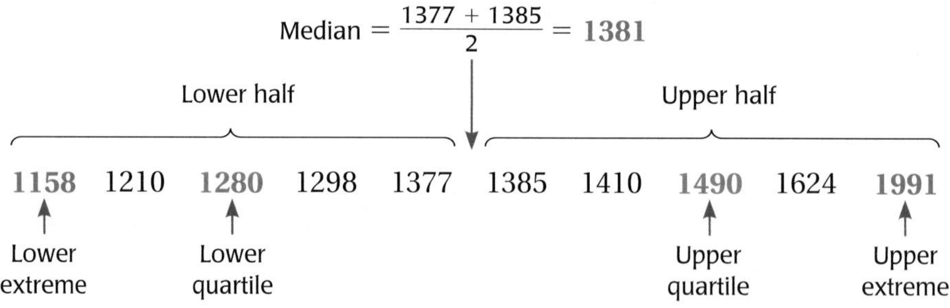

STEP 2 **Plot** these values below a number line.

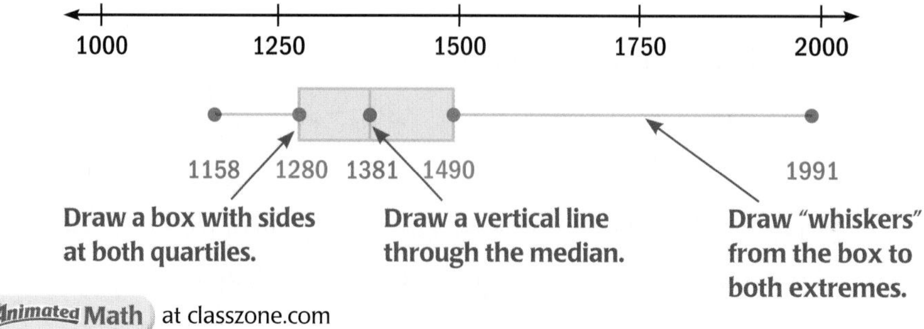

Animated Math at classzone.com

Interpreting a Box-and-Whisker Plot A box-and-whisker plot helps to show how varied, or spread out, the data are. The points divide the data into four parts. Each part represents about one quarter of the data. The *interquartile range* is the difference of the upper quartile and the lower quartile.

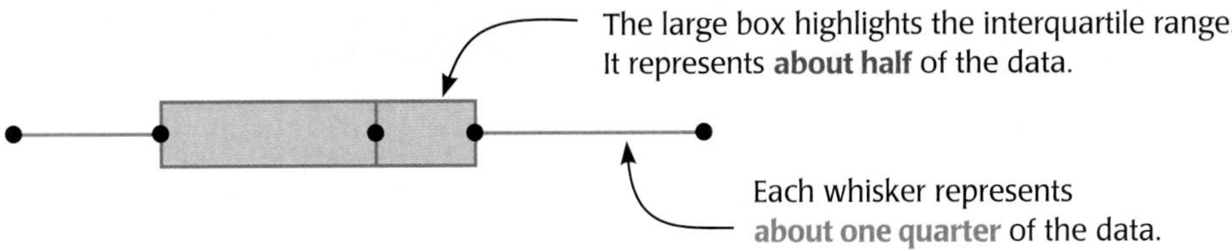

The large box highlights the interquartile range. It represents **about half** of the data.
Each whisker represents **about one quarter** of the data.

You can use box-and-whisker plots to compare two or more data sets.

EXAMPLE 2 Interpreting Box-and-Whisker Plots

Food Science You are testing whether a fertilizer helps tomato plants grow. You divide the plants into two equal groups, and give fertilizer to the plants in Group 2, but not to Group 1. The box-and-whisker plots show how much the plants grew, in centimeters, for each group of plants after two weeks.

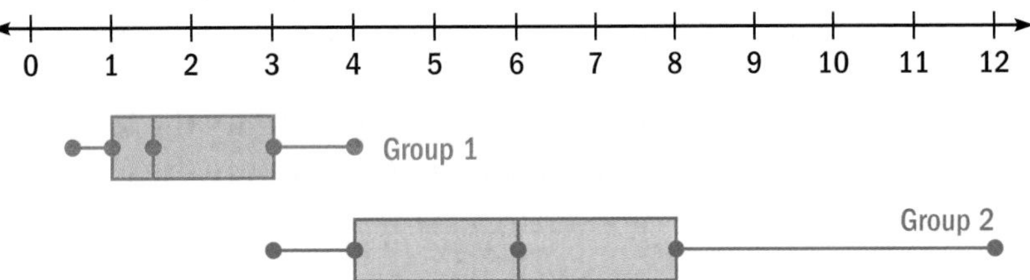

a. About what fraction of the unfertilized plants grew as much as any of the fertilized plants?

b. About what fraction of the fertilized plants grew 4 to 8 centimeters?

SOLUTION

a. The right whisker for Group 1 overlaps the left whisker for Group 2. So about one quarter of the unfertilized plants grew as much as any of the fertilized plants.

b. The large box in the plot for Group 2 ranges from 4 to 8, so about one half of the fertilized plants grew 4 to 8 centimeters.

✓ GUIDED PRACTICE for Examples 1 and 2

Exercising Over a period of ten days, Ming exercised for 34, 27, 26, 15, 24, 21, 30, 23, 24, and 35 minutes. Chantelle exercised for 26, 33, 36, 21, 41, 36, 29, 25, 34, and 35 minutes.

1. Make a box-and-whisker plot of the data for each person.

2. Who usually exercised longer? *Explain.*

3. About how often did each person exercise for 25–35 minutes?

12.2 EXERCISES

HOMEWORK KEY

★ = **STANDARDIZED TEST PRACTICE** Exs. 14, 20, 22, 26, 27, 28, and 36

○ = **HINTS AND HOMEWORK HELP** for Exs. 3, 9, 13, 23 at classzone.com

SKILL PRACTICE

VOCABULARY **Copy and complete the statement.**

1. The median of the lower half of a data set is the _?_.
2. The upper and lower _?_ of a data set are the greatest and least data values.

MAKING BOX-AND-WHISKER PLOTS **Make a box-and-whisker plot of the data.**

SEE EXAMPLE 1 on p. 654 for Exs. 3–7

3. $67, $53, $41, $33, $52, $28, $70, $56, $54, $48, $65, $72, $44, $59, $62
4. 327 ft, 419 ft, 9 ft, 299 ft, 111 ft, 0 ft, 254 ft, 126 ft, 192 ft, 284 ft
5. 26 m, 389 m, 878 m, 144 m, 515 m, 404 m, 423 m, 357 m, 421 m, 593 m
6. 92 cm, 106 cm, 84 cm, 120 cm, 12 cm, 256 cm, 396 cm, 1024 cm, 297 cm
7. **ERROR ANALYSIS** You are analyzing the data set 23, 25, 29, 31, 33, 35. Your friend says that because the greatest data value is 35, the upper quartile is 35. Describe and correct the error made by your friend.

SEE EXAMPLE 2 on p. 655 for Exs. 8–14

ESTIMATION **The box-and-whisker plot shows the lengths, in inches, of the jumps in a frog-jumping contest. Estimate the following values.**

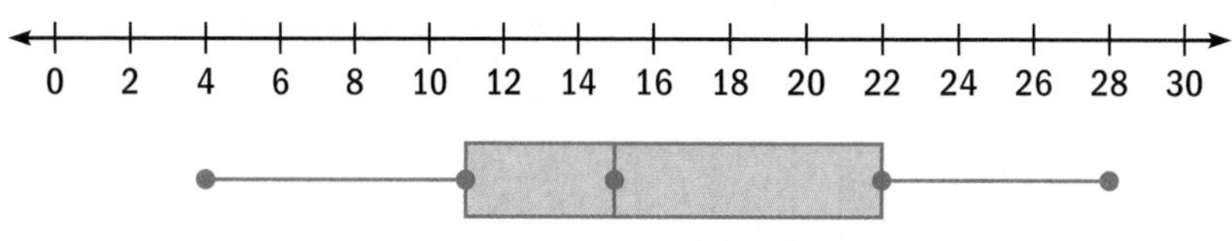

8. median
9. lower quartile
10. range
11. upper extreme

USING A BOX-AND-WHISKER PLOT **In Exercises 12–15, use the plot below.**

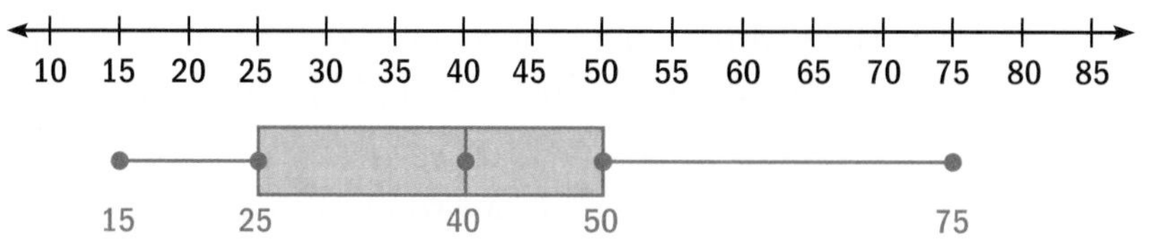

12. About what fraction of the data values are in the interval from 40 to 50?
13. Between what two values are the median and about half of the data located?
14. ★ **MULTIPLE CHOICE** About what percent of the data values are *not* in the range from 15 to 25?

    (A) 25% (B) 50% (C) 75% (D) 100%

15. **WHICH ONE DOESN'T BELONG?** Which number below must be a data value from which the box-and-whisker plot was made?

    A. 25 **B.** 40 **C.** 50 **D.** 75

REASONING **Tell whether the statement is *true* or *false*. *Justify* your reasoning.**

16. The interquartile range includes about half of the data.

17. There are more data values from the lower extreme to the lower quartile than there are from the median to the upper quartile.

18. The range of a data set is twice the interquartile range.

19. **CHALLENGE** Change one value in the data set below so that the median of the data becomes 13, the lower quartile becomes 7, and the upper quartile becomes 17. *Explain* your reasoning.

3, 4, 5, 7, 9, 11, 13, 15, 17, 18, 21

PROBLEM SOLVING

SEE EXAMPLE 1 on p. 654 for Exs. 20–21

20. ★ **MULTIPLE CHOICE** The data below are the weights, in pounds, of 10 giant pumpkins.

853, 811.5, 785, 1020, 826.5, 789, 838, 810, 731, 822.5

What is the upper quartile of the data?

Ⓐ 789 Ⓑ 810 Ⓒ 817 Ⓓ 838

21. **GUIDED PROBLEM SOLVING** You had the following scores while playing a math game: 306, 211, 235, 197, 351, 141, 227, 296, 159, 324, 280, and 267. Make a box-and-whisker plot of your scores.

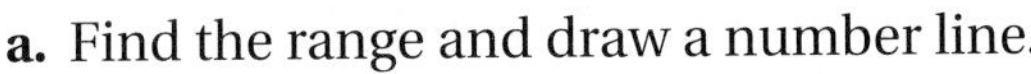

a. Find the range and draw a number line.

b. Find the median, quartiles, and extremes.

c. Draw the box-and-whisker plot.

22. ★ **SHORT RESPONSE** *Explain* how making a line plot or stem-and-leaf plot can help you to make a box-and-whisker plot. When would a line plot be a better choice?

SEE EXAMPLE 2 on p. 655 for Exs. 23–24

23. **BASKETBALL** The box-and-whisker plots show the points scored in several games for two players. What conclusions can you make about the players' performances? Which player is more consistent? *Explain.*

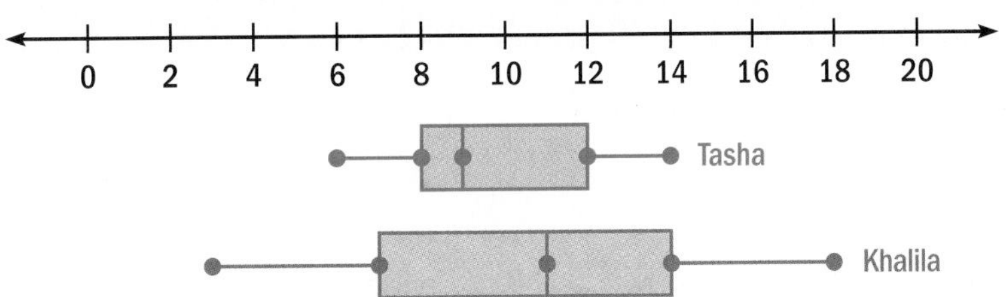

24. **CAMERA PRICES** The prices of several cameras are \$179.99, \$329.99, \$229.99, \$284.99, \$399.99, \$379.99, \$299.99, \$259.99, and \$259.99. Order the list of prices from least to greatest. Then make a box-and-whisker plot of the data. What conclusions can you make?

LAKE AREA Use the following areas, in square kilometers, of the world's ten largest lakes: 371,000, 82,100, 69,500, 64,500, 59,600, 57,800, 32,900, 31,500, 31,300, 28,900.

25. An *outlier* is a data value that is much less or much greater than all or most of the other values in a data set. Make a box-and-whisker plot of the data above. Which value is an outlier?

26. ★ **WRITING** Remove the outlier and then make another box-and-whisker plot. *Describe* how an outlier affects a box-and-whisker plot.

27. ★ **OPEN-ENDED MATH** Choose three exercises from Exercises 20–30 in this lesson. Count the number of words in each sentence. Record this data in a stem-and-leaf plot or a line plot. Repeat using a long newspaper article. Make a box-and-whisker plot comparing the two sets of data. What conclusions can you make?

28. ★ **EXTENDED RESPONSE** The masses, in grams, of 10 sample bolts from two factories are shown. The masses should be between 198.5 and 202 grams.

    Factory A: 199, 201, 200, 198.5, 200.5, 202, 201, 200.8, 200.9, 198.5
    Factory B: 201, 200.4, 203, 200.8, 201, 203.4, 200.6, 201, 200.9, 203.1

    a. Make box-and-whisker plots using the same number line to compare the samples.

    b. *Describe* how well each factory makes bolts within the desired mass range, based on the samples.

CHALLENGE For Exercises 29 and 30, use the circle graph. It displays the age groups of 16 people in a club.

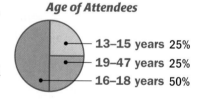

Age of Attendees

13–15 years	25%
19–47 years	25%
16–18 years	50%

29. Make two sets of data that could be represented by the circle graph. Make each set have different medians and quartiles. Then make box-and-whisker plots of each set.

30. In a friend's answer to Exercise 29, one data set has 13 ages ranging from 13 to 19. In the other, one age is 18 and four are greater than 40. *Explain* how the upper quartiles of these data sets vary.

MIXED REVIEW

Prepare for Lesson 12.3 in Exs. 31–34

Solve the proportion. *(p. 348)*

31. $\frac{x}{9} = \frac{5}{36}$ 32. $\frac{21}{9} = \frac{7}{a}$ 33. $\frac{10}{40} = \frac{b}{4}$ 34. $\frac{2}{c} = \frac{8}{20}$

35. Find the x-intercept, y-intercept, and slope of the graph of the equation $3x - 5y = 30$. Then graph the line. *(p. 606)*

36. ★ **MULTIPLE CHOICE** When the number 24 is plotted on a stem-and-leaf plot, the digit 4 is which of the following? *(p. 649)*

    Ⓐ the stem Ⓑ the leaf Ⓒ the quartile Ⓓ the median

12.3 Using Data Displays

Before You organized data using box-and-whisker plots.

Now You will organize data using circle graphs and line graphs.

Why? So you can analyze data, such as for insect species in Example 2.

KEY VOCABULARY

- **circle graph,** *p. 659*
- **line graph,** *p. 660*

Whistling Survey A survey asked, "How well can you whistle?" The results are shown in the *circle graph* below.

A **circle graph** represents data as sections of a circle. Each section can be labeled with its data value or with the data value's portion of the whole written as a fraction, decimal, or percent. Because the graph represents all the data, the sum of the portions must equal 1, or 100%.

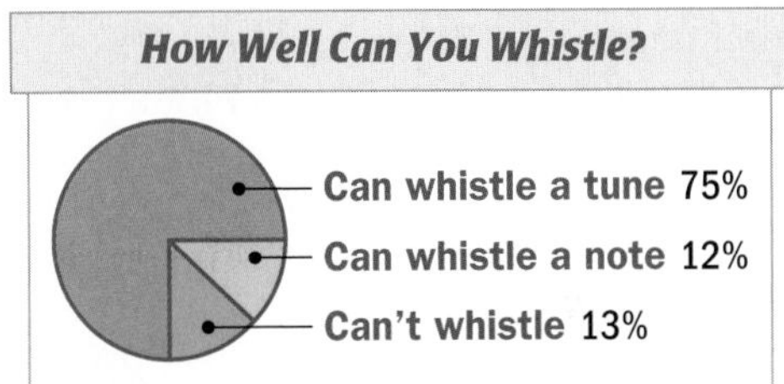

To make a circle graph, find the angle measure, to the nearest degree, that represents each data value's portion of the whole. The sum of all the angle measures must equal 360°, the number of degrees in a circle.

EXAMPLE 1 Making a Circle Graph

E-mail A survey asked, "How often do you check your e-mail?" Of the 100 people asked, 4 responded *less than weekly*, 23 responded *weekly*, and 73 responded *every day*. Display the data in a circle graph.

STEP 1 **Use** a proportion to find the number of degrees you should use to represent each response as a section of a circle graph.

Less than weekly	Weekly	Every day
$\frac{4}{100} = \frac{a}{360^\circ}$	$\frac{23}{100} = \frac{b}{360^\circ}$	$\frac{73}{100} = \frac{c}{360^\circ}$
$a = 14.4^\circ \approx$ **14°**	$b = 82.8^\circ \approx$ **83°**	$c = 262.8^\circ \approx$ **263°**

STEP 2 **Draw** a circle. Show its center.

STEP 3 **Use** a protractor to draw the first angle measure. Label the section.

STEP 4 **Draw** and label remaining sections. Include a title.

Check Your E-mail?

Less than weekly 4

Weekly 23

Every day 73

The graph shows that most people check their e-mail every day.

DRAW SECTIONS

In Example 1, you can draw the 14° and 83° angles first. Then the remaining section of the circle will have a measure of 263°.

Line Graphs A **line graph** uses line segments to connect data points. A line graph is often used to represent data that change over time.

EXAMPLE 2 Making a Line Graph

Environment The table shows the number of insect species on the United States endangered species list. Make a line graph of the data.

Year	1994	1996	1998	2000	2002	2004
Number	19	20	28	33	35	35

AVOID ERRORS
Make sure you choose the horizontal and vertical scales carefully so that the data are not distorted.

STEP 1 **Draw** and label the horizontal and vertical scales.

STEP 2 **Plot** a point for each data pair.

STEP 3 **Draw** line segments to connect the points. Include a title.

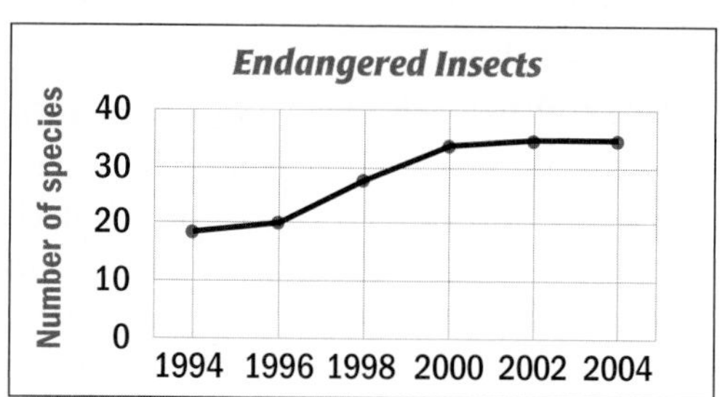

The graph shows an increase over time.

✓ GUIDED PRACTICE for Examples 1 and 2

Use the table of polling data.

1. Make a circle graph of the data for Week 1. What does the graph show?
2. Make a line graph of the data for Ben. What does the graph show?

Who Will You Vote For?			
Week	1	2	3
Ben	55%	50%	40%
Alice	45%	50%	60%

CONCEPT SUMMARY *For Your Notebook*

Using Appropriate Data Displays

Using appropriate data displays helps you analyze data.

- Use a *circle graph* to represent data as parts of a whole.
- Use a *line graph* to display data over time.
- Use a *stem-and-leaf plot* to order a data set.
- Use a *box-and-whisker plot* to show the data's distribution in quarters, using the median, quartiles, and extremes.
- Use a *bar graph* to display data in distinct categories.
- Use a *Venn diagram* to display data in overlapping categories.
- Use a *histogram* to compare the frequencies of data that are grouped in equal intervals.

TAKING NOTES
For each type of data display you study, include an example in your notebook along with a summary of the information that you can read from the display.

EXAMPLE 3 Choosing a Data Display

Choose an appropriate display for the data.

a. The table shows the results of a survey that asked students if they are going away during summer vacation.

Response	*Percent*
Yes	48%
No	37%
Don't know	15%

b. The table shows the results of a survey that asked students why they use the Internet.

Purpose	*Percent*
Research	62%
Shopping	34%
E-mail	45%
Browsing	18%

AVOID ERRORS
You can only display data with a circle graph if the categories don't overlap and the percents add up to 100%, as in part (a) of Example 3.

SOLUTION

a. The percents total 100%, so a circle graph is appropriate.

b. The percents total more than 100%. An appropriate display is a bar graph.

GUIDED PRACTICE for Example 3

3. **Surveys** Choose an appropriate display for the results of a survey asking "How often do you finish your homework before dinner?" The results were: *always*, 25%; *sometimes*, 45%; *never*, 30%. *Explain* your choice.

12.3 EXERCISES

HOMEWORK KEY
★ = STANDARDIZED TEST PRACTICE Exs. 15, 16, 25, 26, 30, and 38
◯ = HINTS AND HOMEWORK HELP for Exs. 3, 5, 7, 11, 25 at classzone.com

SKILL PRACTICE

1. **VOCABULARY** Copy and complete: Use a _?_ to display data as parts of a whole, and a _?_ to display changes in a quantity over time.

FINDING ANGLES **Find the angle measure in a circle graph for the given ratio.**

SEE EXAMPLE 1 on p. 659 for Exs. 2–8

2. 31%
3. $\frac{3}{8}$
4. 14%
5. 27 out of 60

MAKING CIRCLE GRAPHS **A survey asked 200 students "How often do you snack during the day?" Make a circle graph of the survey data.**

6.

Answer	*Students*
Never	20
Rarely	90
Sometimes	70
Often	20

7.

Answer	*Students*
Never	0
Rarely	50
Sometimes	120
Often	30

8.

Answer	*Students*
Never	40
Rarely	20
Sometimes	85
Often	55

MAKING LINE GRAPHS Make a line graph of the data.

SEE EXAMPLE 2 on p. 660 for Exs. 9–11

9.

Day	Mon	Tue	Wed	Thu	Fri
Distance (mi)	480	400	355	350	402

10.

Month	Jan	Feb	Mar	Apr	May	Jun
Sales	\$4500	\$4800	\$6250	\$5000	\$5400	\$7300

11.

Year	2000	2001	2002	2003	2004
Rainfall (in.)	8.5	6.8	2.4	2.4	8.2

SEE EXAMPLE 1 on p. 659 for Ex. 12

12. **ERROR ANALYSIS** A survey asked 75 students "Do you like the new lunch menu?" The responses were: *yes*, 50; *no*, 10; *undecided*, 15. Describe and correct the error made in finding the angle measures for a circle graph of the data.

✗ Yes = 50%, or 180°
No = 10%, or 36°
Undecided = 360 − (180 + 36)
= 144°

CHOOSING APPROPRIATE DISPLAYS Choose an appropriate display for the data. *Justify* your choice.

SEE EXAMPLE 3 on p. 661 for Exs. 13–19

13.

Response	Students
Yes	240
No	640
Not sure	120

14.

Week	Percent
1	50%
2	59%
3	53%

15. ★ **MULTIPLE CHOICE** You polled 30 students in your class about how much their families pay for Internet service. Twelve of the 30 pay more than \$25 per month. Which proportion could you use to find the number of degrees in the section of a circle graph that represents these results?

(A) $\frac{12}{30} = \frac{x}{360}$ (B) $\frac{12}{30} = \frac{360}{x}$ (C) $\frac{12}{25} = \frac{x}{30}$ (D) $\frac{12}{25} = \frac{30}{x}$

16. ★ **OPEN-ENDED MATH** *Write* a survey question that meets the condition. *Justify* your answer.

   a. The results can be displayed in a circle graph.

   b. The results cannot be displayed in a circle graph.

REASONING In Exercises 17–19, tell which type of display you would use for the data described. *Explain* your reasoning.

17. You record the temperature at noon every day for a month.

18. You record the temperature at five locations at a given time.

19. You record the high temperature every day for a month, and find how often the daily high temperature falls within each 10 degree temperature interval.

20. **CHALLENGE** *Describe* a set of data that could be displayed in three types of data displays. *Explain* how to display it in each.

PROBLEM SOLVING

SEE EXAMPLES 1 AND 2 on pp. 659–660 for Exs. 21–22

THEATER Use the table showing attendance at your school play.

Play Attendance	
Friday	130
Saturday (2:00 P.M.)	231
Saturday (8:00 P.M.)	291
Sunday	185

21. Make a circle graph to display each attendance number as a portion of the total attendance.

22. Tickets cost \$7 each. Make a line graph that shows how much money was collected from each performance.

NEW YORK CITY In Exercises 23 and 24, use the map. It shows the land area in square miles of each of the five boroughs of New York City.

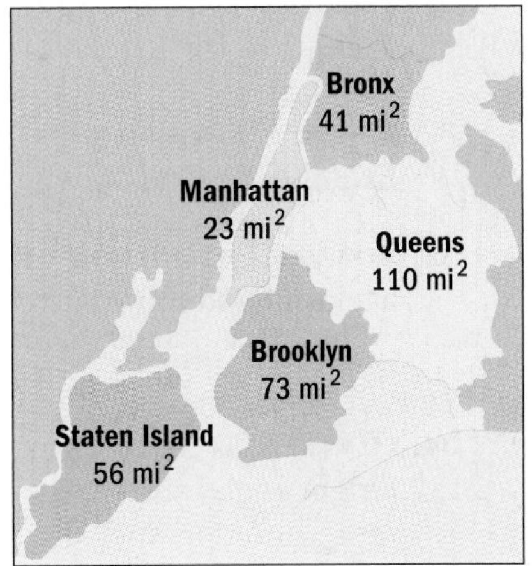

23. To the nearest whole percent, find the total area of New York City that each borough covers.

24. Represent the data using a circle graph. Then compare the areas of the boroughs.

25. ★ **SHORT RESPONSE** You ask 100 people a yes or no question. The possible answers are *yes*, *no*, and *no answer*. What types of displays would be appropriate for this type of data? *Explain* your reasoning.

26. ★ **MULTIPLE CHOICE** Use the whistling graph on page 659. Which is a reasonable estimate of the number of people out of 500 who will be unable to whistle?

(A) 375 (B) 65 (C) 60 (D) 13

TELEPHONE SALES Use the table showing the number, in thousands, of corded and cordless telephones sold to dealers from 1999 to 2004.

	1999	*2000*	*2001*	*2002*	*2003*	*2004*
Corded	34,486	29,670	24,957	23,813	21,918	20,051
Cordless	39,654	39,042	40,000	36,556	37,998	33,809

27. Make a double line graph showing these data. *Explain* how you chose the scale you used on the vertical axis.

28. Between which two consecutive years did the number of cordless telephones sold increase the most? Is this easier to tell from the *table* or the *graph*? *Justify* your answer.

29. What is the mean of the annual decreases in sales of corded telephones from 1999 to 2004?

30. ★ **WRITING** What can you conclude about the trends in sales of each type of telephone? *Justify* your answer using the graph.

READING *IN* MATH **Read the information below for Exercises 31–33.**

Football Barry Sanders was a running back for the Detroit Lions from 1989 to 1998. He was inducted into the Professional Football Hall of Fame in 2004. During his career, he rushed for a total of 15,269 yards and led the league in rushing yards four times. The table below shows his rushing attempts and average rushing yards per attempt.

Season	1989	1990	1991	1992	1993	1994	1995	1996	1997	1998
Attempts	280	255	342	312	243	331	314	307	335	343
Average Yards	5.25	5.10	4.53	4.33	4.59	5.69	4.78	5.06	6.13	4.35

31. **Calculate** Copy the table. Add a third row showing Sanders's *total* career rushing yards at the end of each season. Round to the nearest yard.

32. **Decide** Choose an appropriate display for the data calculated in Exercise 31. *Explain* why you chose the display.

33. **Analyze** *Explain* how you can use the display to determine if Sanders accumulated more rushing yards from 1989–1993 or 1994–1998.

34. **CHALLENGE** A circle graph has 4 sections formed using an obtuse angle, a right angle, and two acute angles. *Describe* two data sets that could be represented by such a graph.

MIXED REVIEW

Prepare for Lesson 12.4 in Exs. 35–37

You randomly draw a marble from a bag containing 12 blue marbles, 15 red marbles, and 5 green marbles. Find the probability of the event. *(p. 381)*

35. You draw red.
36. You draw blue.
37. You draw yellow.

38. ★ **SHORT RESPONSE** Make an ordered stem-and-leaf plot of the following data: 17, 10, 11, 15, 21, 34, 26, 16, 36, 24, 17, 37, 20, 18, 31, 39, 29, 28. Describe how to use the plot to find the median. *(p. 649)*

QUIZ *for Lessons 12.1–12.3*

1. **ATTENDANCE** Make an ordered double stem-and-leaf plot comparing the ballpark attendance data below for April and June. Then make a pair of box-and-whisker plots that compare the data. Use the displays to compare April attendance to June attendance. *(p. 649)*

   April: 1025, 1058, 1030, 997, 990, 1116, 1001, 995, 1122, 1099

   June: 1056, 1125, 1151, 1048, 1123, 1097, 1042, 1164, 1125, 1131

2. **FOOD** Consumption of peanuts per person in the United States was as follows: 1999, 6 lb; 2000, 5.8 lb; 2001, 5.9 lb; 2002, 5.8 lb; 2003, 6.3 lb. Make a circle graph or a line graph of the data. *Explain* your choice. *(p. 659)*

Technology **ACTIVITY** *Use after Lesson 12.3*

GOAL
Use a graphing calculator to create data displays.

12.3 Making Data Displays

EXAMPLE 1 **The table shows the cost, in dollars, of a phone call based on the length, in minutes, of the call. Make a scatter plot or a line graph using a calculator.**

Minutes	*Cost*
5	0.5
10	1
15	1.5
20	2
25	2.4
30	2.7

SOLUTION

STEP 1 **Enter** the data into two lists.

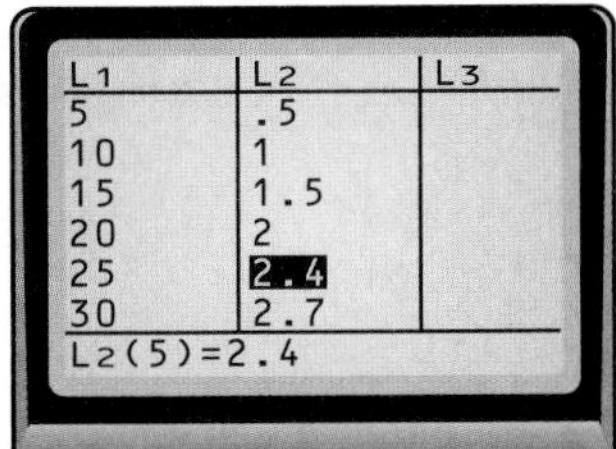

L1 L2 L3
5 .5
10 1
15 1.5
20 2
25 2.4
30 2.7
L2(5)=2.4

STEP 2 **Choose** maximums and minimums for the window.

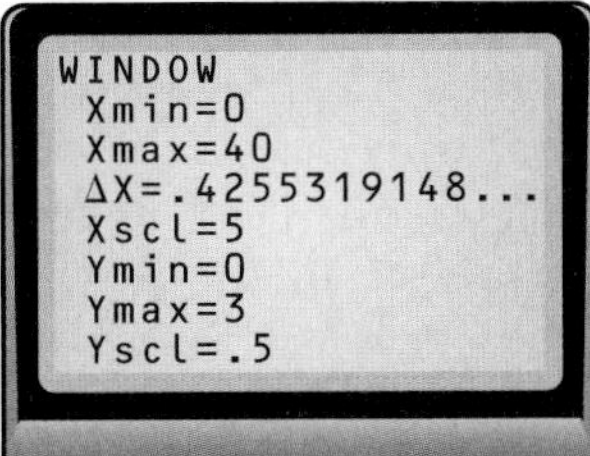

STEP 3 **Choose** a display from the PLOT menu and set the Xlist and Ylist.

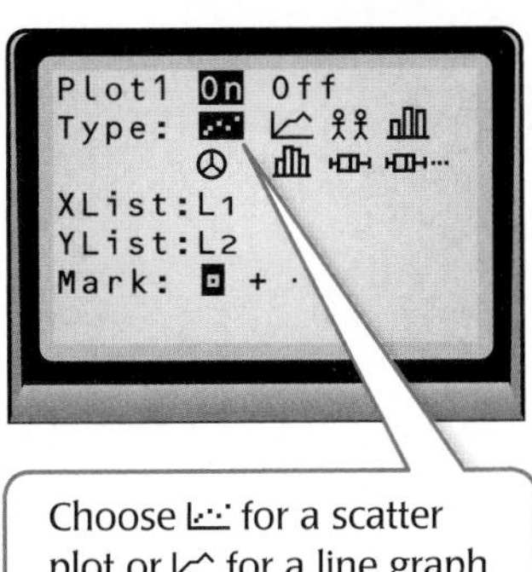

STEP 4 **Press** GRAPH to show the display you have chosen.

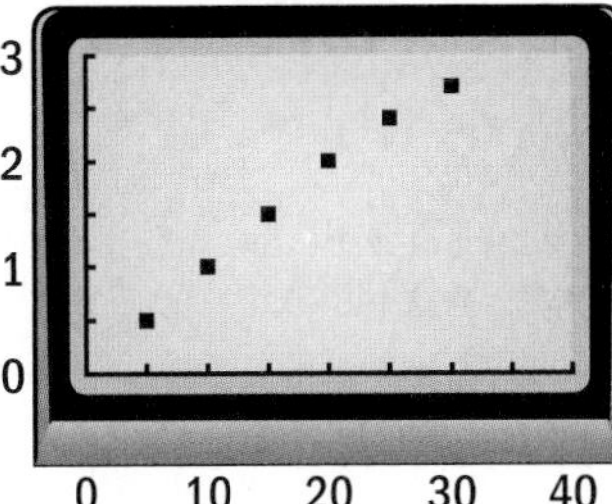

PRACTICE **Make a scatter plot and a line graph of the data.**

1.

Year	2000	2001	2002	2003	2004	2005
Rainfall (in.)	21.4	39.8	34.5	26.1	44.9	38.7

Continued on next page

EXAMPLE 2 **The table shows the number of people out of 200 surveyed who prefer each type of music. Use a graphing calculator to make a circle graph of the data.**

Favorite Music	
Pop	75
Rock	62
Country	43
Classical	20

SOLUTION

STEP 1 **Press** LIST. Then use the TEXT menu to name a list and its categories. Use quotation marks for the first item, so the calculator recognizes that the list is *categorical* (contains words).

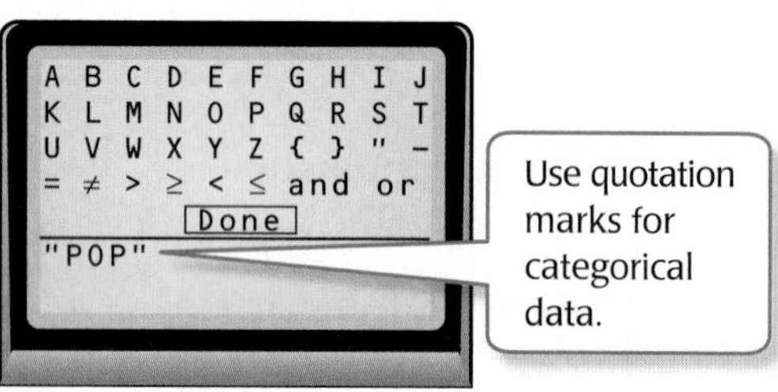

STEP 2 **Use** the PLOT menu to choose the two lists.

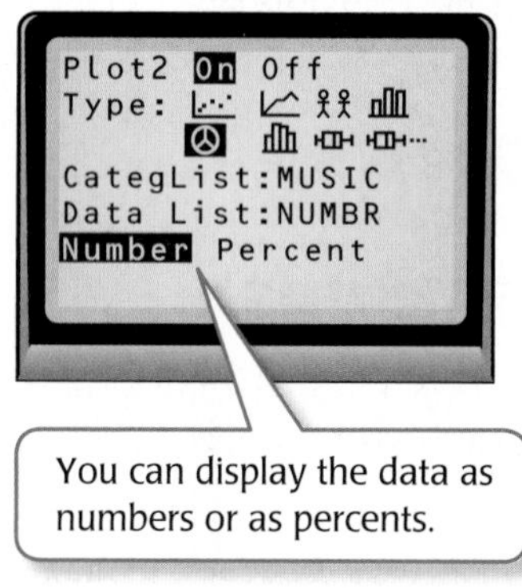

STEP 3 **Press** GRAPH to display the circle graph.

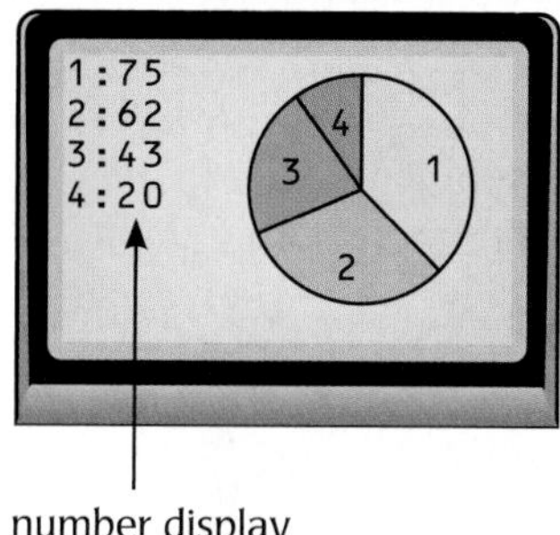

number display

PRACTICE **Make a circle graph of the survey data.**

2.

Did You Get Enough Sleep?	
Need more	541
Need less	167
Just right	282
Don't know	21

3.

The Last Movie I Saw I Watched . . .	
in a theater.	410
on television.	483
on a computer.	21

Misleading Graphs

GOAL Identify and analyze misleading graphs.

KEY VOCABULARY
- **bar graph,** *p. 3*
- **line graph,** *p. 660*

When you analyze a graph to make conclusions about the data, be aware that the display may be misleading.

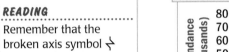

EXAMPLE 1 Identifying a Misleading Graph

Attendance Which of the bar graphs that show attendance at an annual rock festival from 2006 to 2010 could be misleading?

READING
Remember that the broken axis symbol indicates that some of the values in the axis have been left out.

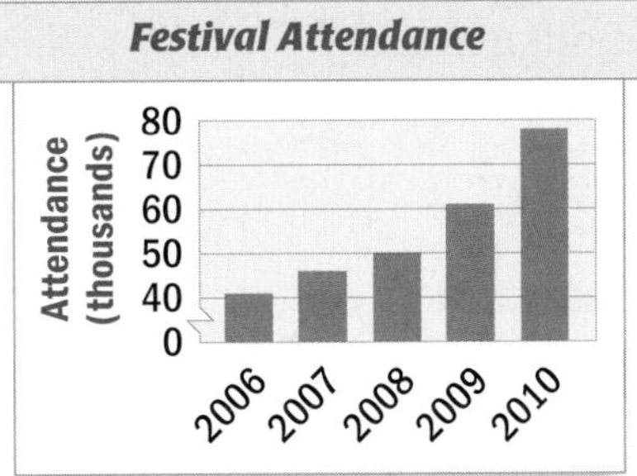

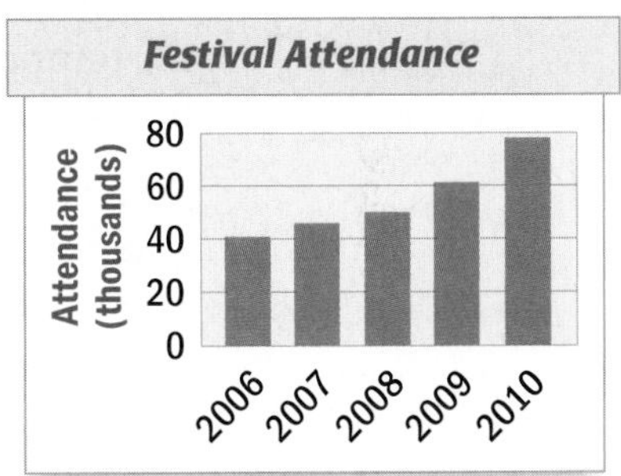

The first graph has a break in the vertical axis, so comparing the bars may lead to incorrect conclusions. It looks as if attendance in 2010 was three or four times as great as in 2006, but attendance only doubled during this time. The second graph is less likely to mislead.

EXAMPLE 2 Analyzing Misleading Graphs

Business The line graphs below display a company's profits and sales for each year from 2006 to 2010. What is misleading about each graph?

a.

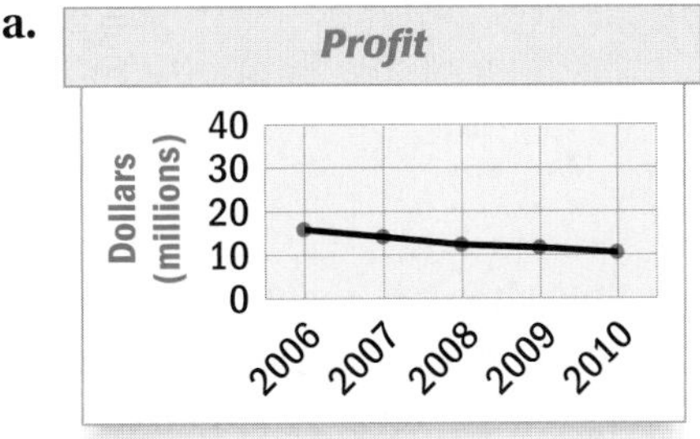

b.

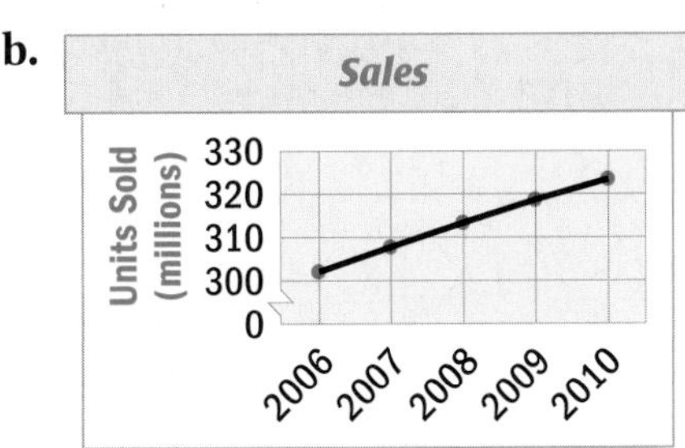

SOLUTION

a. The range on the vertical scale is greater than needed. The graph suggests that profits have decreased only slightly, when they have decreased by a third.

b. Because the vertical axis starts at 300, sales seem to have risen rapidly. An unbroken axis would show that sales have risen slowly, at less than 2% per year.

EXAMPLE 3 Misleading Comparisons

Resorts Compare the average monthly temperatures at two resorts.

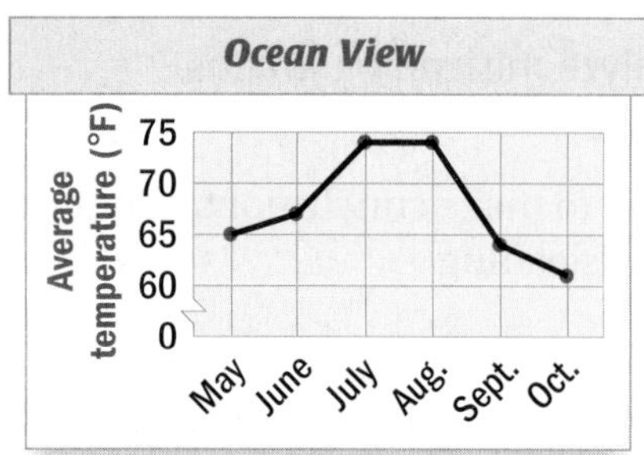

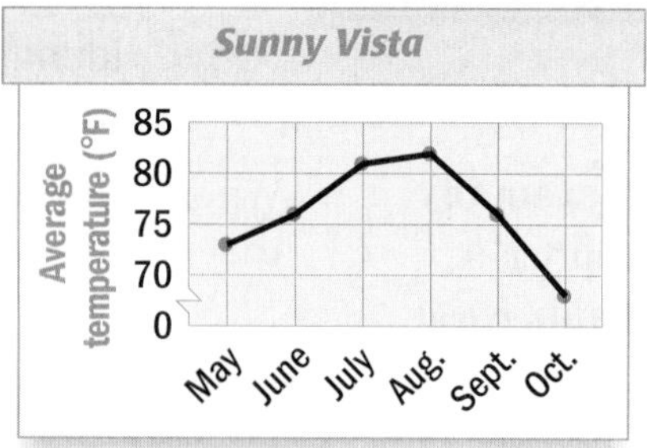

SOLUTION

At a glance, the displays suggest that the temperatures are about the same, but the vertical axes are different.

When data for both resorts are graphed together, it becomes clear that Sunny Vista has warmer temperatures.

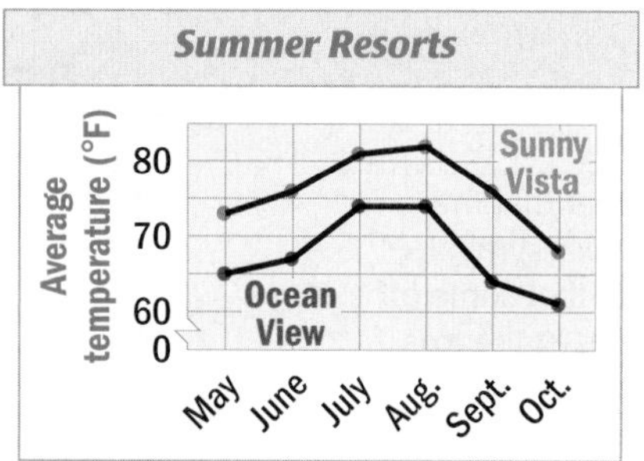

EXERCISES

Tell whether the data are represented clearly. If the graph is misleading, explain why. Then redraw the graph so that it is not misleading.

1.

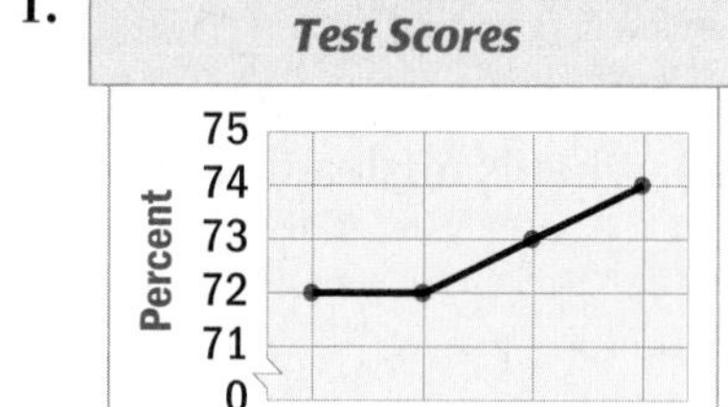

2.

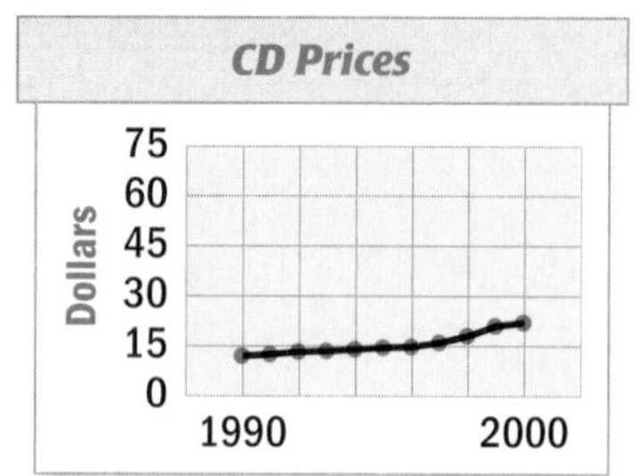

3. **Baseball** The table below shows a baseball pitcher's wins and losses per season. Make a graph that suggests a positive performance. Then make another graph that suggests a negative performance.

Year	2000	2001	2002	2003	2004
Wins	6	8	10	12	16
Losses	7	9	9	13	14

MIXED REVIEW *of Problem Solving*

Lessons 12.1–12.3

1. **MULTI-STEP PROBLEM** The stem-and-leaf plot shows the number of home runs for each player on a softball team.

Home Runs

Stem	Leaves
0	4 5 7 8
1	2 4 5 6 6 8
2	1 4 5

Key: 1|2 = 12

   a. What is the range of the data?

   b. What interval includes the most home runs?

   c. Create a box-and-whisker plot of the data.

2. **MULTI-STEP PROBLEM** The number of miles per gallon that 8 cars traveled on one tank of gas are 27, 23, 33, 38, 29, 42, 30, and 32.

   a. Make an ordered stem-and-leaf plot of the data.

   b. The number of miles per gallon that 8 trucks traveled on one tank of gas are 25, 16, 23, 28, 21, 20, 19, and 24. Use this data and the data from part (a) to make a double stem-and-leaf plot.

   c. Compare the miles per gallon for the cars and the trucks.

3. **SHORT RESPONSE** You asked 100 students whether they owned several common items. Your results were: *backpack,* 94%; *cell phone,* 68%; *baseball glove,* 43%. Would a circle graph be a good display for the data? *Explain* why or why not.

4. **SHORT RESPONSE** The box-and-whisker plot shows the prices of gasoline for several weeks in two cities. Compare the gasoline prices in these cities.

Gasoline Prices

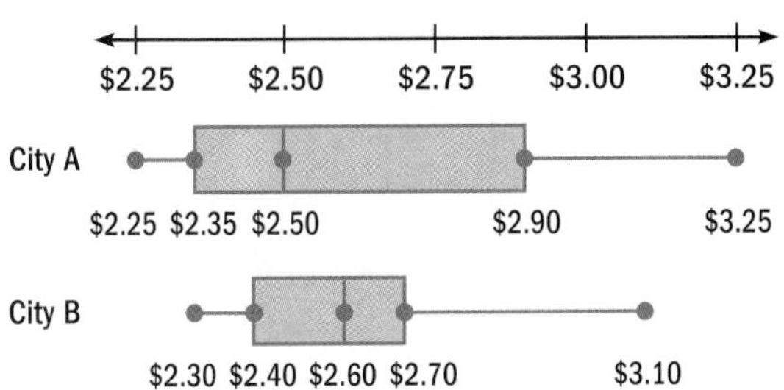

5. **SHORT RESPONSE** You have two sets of data. Each set consists of 15 camera prices. Both data sets have identical box-and-whisker plots. Does this mean that the sets of data are identical? *Explain.*

6. **OPEN-ENDED** Make a set of 17 data values representing people's ages. Make the data set have a lower extreme of 32, a range of 23, an upper quartile of 45, an interquartile range of 10, and a median of 41.

7. **EXTENDED RESPONSE** The numbers of minutes that you and a friend played a video game are given below. Red numbers represent your times, and blue numbers represent your friend's times.

   12, 10, 26, 22, 18, 17, 5, 20, 22, 18, 15, 8, 14, 19, 22, 23, 25, 8, 16, 20

   a. Use an appropriate display to represent the data.

   b. *Explain* your choice of display.

   c. Identify a type of display that is *not* a good choice for the data. *Explain* why it is not a good choice.

8. **GRIDDED ANSWER** Your class has 18 males and 30 females. You want to display this information in a circle graph. What angle, in degrees, should you use to represent the portion of your class that is male?

12.4 Counting Methods

Before You found theoretical and experimental probability.

Now You will use counting methods to count the number of choices.

Why? So you can count the number of skateboard designs, as in Example 2.

KEY VOCABULARY

- **tree diagram,** *p. 670*

ACTIVITY

You can count choices using an organized list.

You are choosing an outfit. You can choose a T-shirt (T), a button-down shirt (B), or a sweater (S) as a top, and jeans (J) or khakis (K) for pants.

 T-shirt (T)  button-down (B) 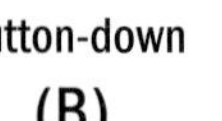  sweater (S) jeans (J)  khakis (K)

STEP 1 **Make** a list of all possible outfits. Use the letters to represent possible outfits. One possible outfit is TJ, which means a T-shirt and jeans.

STEP 2 **Add** dress pants (D) in addition to jeans and khakis as a choice for pants. How many outfits are possible now?

Animated Math at classzone.com

In the activity, you made lists to count the number of choices. Another way to count the number of choices is to use a **tree diagram**.

EXAMPLE 1 Making a Tree Diagram

You can make a tree diagram to count the number of possible outfits after adding a green polo shirt (P) following Step 2 of the activity above. Use branches to match each type of shirt with each type of pants.

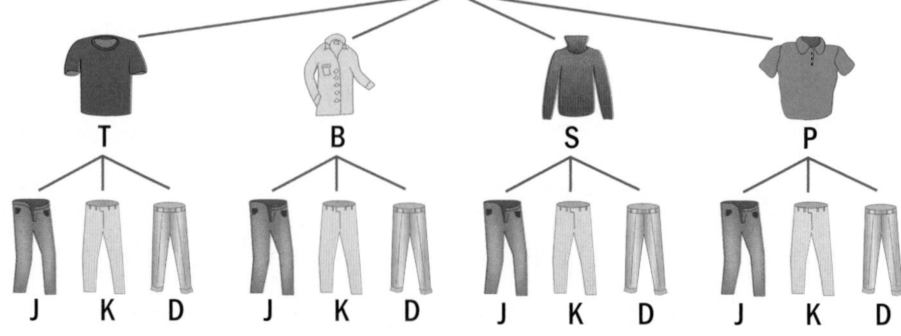

There are 12 different possible outfits.

Another way to count choices is to use the *counting principle.*

KEY CONCEPT *For Your Notebook*

The Counting Principle

If one event can occur in m ways, and for each of these a second event can occur in n ways, then the number of ways that the two events can occur together is $m \cdot n$.

This principle can be extended to three or more events.

EXAMPLE 2 Using the Counting Principle

Skateboards To build a skateboard, you can choose one deck and one type of wheel assembly from those shown. To count the number of different skateboards you can build, use the counting principle.

Decks

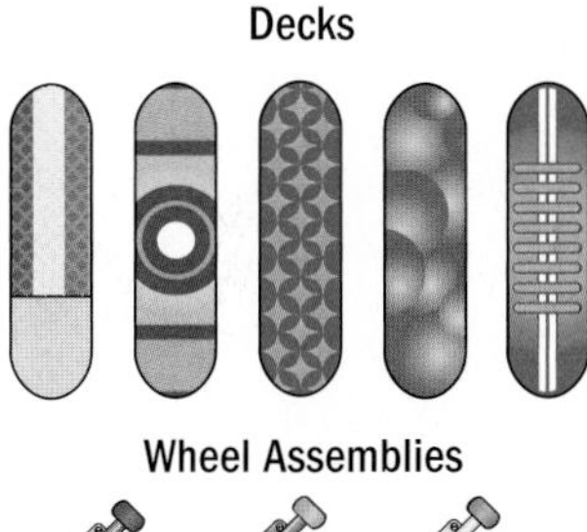

Wheel Assemblies

$$\underset{\textbf{decks}}{5} \cdot \underset{\textbf{wheel assemblies}}{3} = 15 \qquad \textbf{Counting principle}$$

▶**Answer** You can build 15 different skateboards.

EXAMPLE 3 Using the Counting Principle

Passwords You are choosing a password that starts with 3 letters and then has 2 digits. How many different passwords are possible?

SOLUTION

$$\underbrace{26 \cdot 26 \cdot 26}_{\text{letters}} \cdot \underbrace{10 \cdot 10}_{\text{digits}} = 1{,}757{,}600 \qquad \textbf{Counting principle}$$

▶**Answer** There are 1,757,600 different possible passwords.

✓ **GUIDED PRACTICE for Examples 1, 2, and 3**

1. **What If?** You decide to include socks as part of the outfit in Example 1. You can choose between red (R) and green (G). How many outfits are possible?

2. **Soccer Uniforms** Your soccer team's uniform choices include yellow and green shirts, white, black, and green shorts, and four colors of socks. How many different uniforms are possible?

3. **What If?** In Example 3, suppose that the passwords may *not* start with an A or use the letter Q. How many different passwords are possible? *Explain.*

EXAMPLE 4 Solve a Multi-Step Problem

Number Cubes You and three friends each roll a number cube. What is the probability that you each roll the same number?

STEP 1 **List** the favorable outcomes. There are 6:

1-1-1-1 2-2-2-2 3-3-3-3 4-4-4-4 5-5-5-5 6-6-6-6

STEP 2 **Find** the number of possible outcomes using the counting principle.

$$\underbrace{6 \cdot 6 \cdot 6 \cdot 6}_{\text{4 number cubes}} = 1296$$

STEP 3 **Find** the probability: $\frac{\text{Number of favorable outcomes}}{\text{Number of possible outcomes}} = \frac{6}{1296} = \frac{1}{216}$

REVIEW PROBABILITY
For help with probability, see p. 381.

▶ **Answer** The probability that you each roll the same number is $\frac{1}{216}$.

GUIDED PRACTICE for Example 4

4. **Coins** Six people each flip a coin. What is the probability of 6 heads?

12.4 EXERCISES

HOMEWORK KEY
★ = **STANDARDIZED TEST PRACTICE** Exs. 7, 17, 19, 21, 25, and 29
○ = **HINTS AND HOMEWORK HELP** for Exs. 3, 5, 7, 17 at classzone.com

SKILL PRACTICE

VOCABULARY **Copy and complete the statement.**

1. If one event can occur in m ways and for each of those a second event can occur in n ways, then the two events can occur together in _?_ ways.
2. The probability of an event when all outcomes are equally likely is the number of _?_ outcomes divided by the number of _?_ outcomes.

SOLVING TWO WAYS **Use the counting principle to find the number of choices that are possible. Then check your answer using a tree diagram.**

SEE EXAMPLES 1, 2, AND 3 on pp. 670–671 for Exs. 3–7

3. Choose apple, blueberry, lemon, or cherry pie with juice or tea.
4. Choose a small, medium, or large shirt in red, yellow, or blue.
5. Choose a hat or scarf in gray, white, or black.
6. Choose one of 5 essays and one of 2 extra credit questions.
7. ★ **MULTIPLE CHOICE** A license plate is composed of 3 letters followed by 4 digits. How many different license plates are possible?

Ⓐ 7 Ⓑ 12 Ⓒ 175,760,000 Ⓓ 456,976,000

8. **ERROR ANALYSIS** Describe and correct the error in solving the following problem: *A snack stand sells small and large drinks in 3 flavors. How many drink choices are available?*

$m = 2$
$n = 3$
$2 + 3 = 5$

PROBABILITY A website randomly generates a confirmation code after purchases. The code consists of 4 letters. Find the probability that the code fits the given description. Count only *a, e, i, o,* and *u* as vowels.

SEE EXAMPLE 4 on p. 672 for Exs. 9–12

9. starts with a consonant
10. contains only vowels
11. code is MNYR
12. uses the same letter in each spot

COUNTING OUTCOMES You have 4 U.S. coins, 8 foreign coins, and 3 U.S. currency bills at home. Find how many different outcomes are possible if the following are chosen at random.

13. 2 U.S. bills and 2 U.S. coins from your U.S. bills and coins
14. 2 U.S. coins and 3 foreign coins from your U.S. coins and foreign coins
15. **CHALLENGE** A password with 5 numbers has 10^5 possible choices, from 00000 to 99999. How does the number of possible passwords change if no password may use a digit more than once? *Explain.*

PROBLEM SOLVING

SEE EXAMPLES 1 AND 2 on pp. 670–671 for Exs. 16–18

16. **WEEKEND PLANS** You would like to go to the movies, a play, or the zoo. You can invite your cousin or your best friend. You can go on Friday or Saturday. Make a tree diagram to list all of the possibilities. Then use the counting principle to check your answer.
17. ★ **WRITING** You are interested in 5 CDs and 4 books. *Describe* how to find the number of different pairs of 1 CD and 1 book that you can buy.

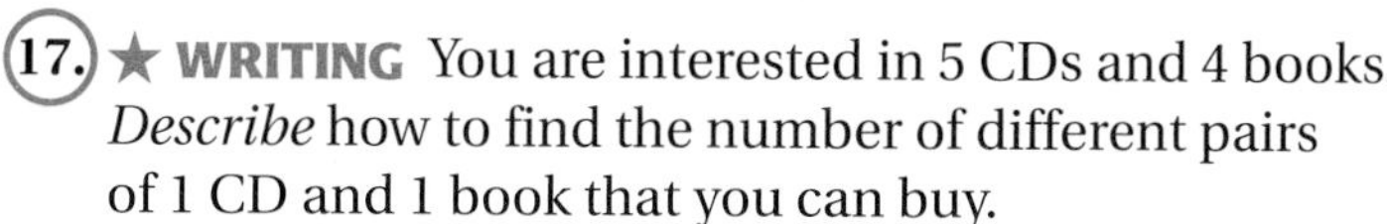

18. **CLASS ELECTION** The ballot shows the candidates in a class election. Make a tree diagram to find the number of different ways a president, treasurer, and secretary can be chosen. Use the counting principle to check your answer.

President	Treasurer	Secretary
☐ Amy	☐ Jessica	☐ Scott
☐ Hector	☐ Michael	☐ Nicole
	☐ Carson	☐ Thomas
		☐ Angela
		☐ Isabel

SEE EXAMPLE 4 on p. 672 for Exs. 19–20

19. ★ **MULTIPLE CHOICE** You and three friends each pick a movie at random from four choices. What is the probability that you all pick the same movie?

Ⓐ $\frac{1}{27}$ Ⓑ $\frac{1}{64}$ Ⓒ $\frac{1}{81}$ Ⓓ $\frac{1}{256}$

20. **STATES** You and Terry randomly choose the name of a state. What is the probability that you both choose a state whose name starts with a T? (Tennessee and Texas are the two states that start with the letter T.)

21. ★ **SHORT RESPONSE** You want a sandwich, a side order, and a drink from a lunch cart that offers 3 sandwiches, 2 side orders, and 5 drink choices. Draw two different tree diagrams that show how many lunches are possible. Do both tree diagrams yield the same result? *Explain.*

22. **REASONING** A restaurant has 36 possible meals that you can choose. A meal has a main course, a salad, and a dessert. The menu lists 6 main courses and 2 salads. How many desserts are available? *Explain.*

BRAILLE In Exercises 23 and 24, use the following information.

Braille uses arrangements of raised dots to form symbols that represent letters, numbers, and punctuation marks. Braille is read by touching the symbols. Each symbol is a cell of 6 dots arranged in 3 rows of 2. In the cell, certain dots are raised to make a particular symbol.

23. How many different Braille symbols are possible? How many symbols are possible with no raised dots? With 6 raised dots?

24. Is the number of symbols possible with one raised dot the same as with 5 raised dots? *Explain.*

25. ★ **EXTENDED RESPONSE** You are at a grocery store buying flavored water. You can choose lime, lemon, cherry, or orange. You can choose a 0.5 liter, 1 liter, or 2 liter bottle.

    a. **Draw** Make a tree diagram that shows all of the different bottles of flavored water that you can choose.

    b. **Calculate** How many different bottles can you choose from if 5 new flavors become available?

    c. **Challenge** The sign shows the prices for each bottle size. What are the different total prices that you could be charged for three bottles? What is the greatest total quantity of water you can buy if you have only $2.60?

Water Sale
0.5 liter – $0.59
1 liter – $0.69
2 liter – $0.99

MIXED REVIEW

Get-Ready
Prepare for Lesson 12.5 in Exs. 26–27

A bag contains 12 slips of paper numbered from 1 through 12. A slip of paper is chosen at random. Find the probability of the event. *(p. 381)*

26. Drawing a number greater than 4

27. Drawing a number that is divisible by 5

28. The ages, in years, of youth group members are 12, 9, 8, 16, 12, 13, 8, 10, 11, and 17. Make a box-and-whisker plot of the data. *(p. 654)*

29. ★ **MULTIPLE CHOICE** What is the slope of the line passing through the points $(-2, 3)$ and $(4, 6)$? *(p. 612)*

    Ⓐ -2 Ⓑ $-\frac{1}{2}$ Ⓒ $\frac{1}{2}$ Ⓓ 2

12.5 Permutations

Before You used the counting principle to count possibilities.
Now You will use permutations to count possibilities.
Why? So you can count color possibilities, as in Ex. 32.

KEY VOCABULARY
- **permutation,** *p. 675*
- **factorial,** *p. 675*

In some arrangements of groups, order is important. For example, the diagram shows the different ways that a group of three dogs could finish first, second, and third at a dog show.

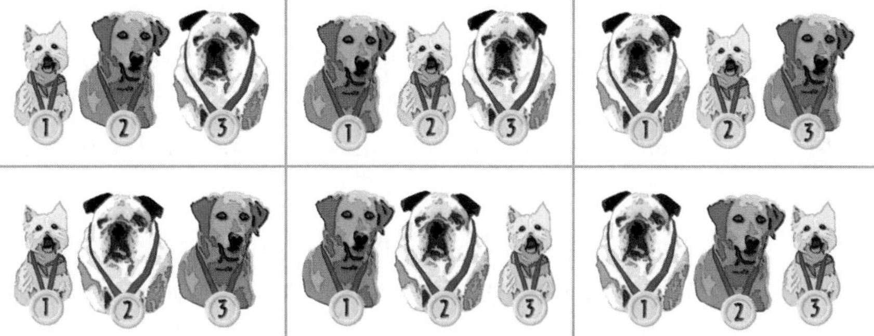

Each arrangement lists the same dogs, but the orders are different. Arrangements such as these are called *permutations.* A **permutation** is an arrangement in which order is important. You can use the counting principle to count permutations.

EXAMPLE 1 Counting Permutations

Music You have five CDs. You can use the counting principle to count the number of permutations of 5 CDs. This is the number of different orders in which you can listen to the CDs.

Choices for 1st CD		Choices for 2nd CD		Choices for 3rd CD		Choices for 4th CD		Choices for 5th CD	
5	•	4	•	3	•	2	•	1	= 120

▸**Answer** You can listen to the CDs in 120 different orders.

USE A FACTORIAL
You can use $n!$ to find the number of permutations of n objects, where n is a positive integer.

Factorials In Example 1, you evaluated $5 \cdot 4 \cdot 3 \cdot 2 \cdot 1$. You can write $5 \cdot 4 \cdot 3 \cdot 2 \cdot 1$ as $5!$, which is read "5 **factorial**."

Numbers $5! = 5 \cdot 4 \cdot 3 \cdot 2 \cdot 1$

Algebra $n! = n \cdot (n-1) \cdot (n-2) \cdot \ldots \cdot 1$

The value of 0! is defined to be 1.

EXAMPLE 2 Counting Permutations

Band Competition Twelve marching bands are entered in a competition. You can use the counting principle to count how many ways first, second, and third places can be awarded.

Choices for 1st place		Choices for 2nd place		Choices for 3rd place		
12	•	11	•	10	= 1320	**Counting principle**

▶ **Answer** There are 1320 ways to award the three places.

✓ GUIDED PRACTICE for Examples 1 and 2

1. Evaluate 3!.

2. Evaluate 6!.

3. Evaluate 1!.

4. Chris wants to see four movies that were released in the past month. In how many different orders can Chris watch the movies?

5. In how many ways can 7 runners finish in first, second, and third place?

Permutation Notation Example 2 shows how to find the number of permutations of 12 objects taken 3 at a time. This is written ${}_{12}P_3$.

KEY CONCEPT *For Your Notebook*

Permutations

Algebra The number of permutations of n objects taken r at a time can be written as ${}_nP_r$ and evaluated using $\frac{n!}{(n-r)!}$.

Numbers ${}_7P_3 = \frac{7!}{(7-3)!} = \frac{7!}{4!} = \frac{7 \cdot 6 \cdot 5 \cdot \cancel{4} \cdot \cancel{3} \cdot \cancel{2} \cdot \cancel{1}}{\cancel{4} \cdot \cancel{3} \cdot \cancel{2} \cdot \cancel{1}} = 7 \cdot 6 \cdot 5$

EXAMPLE 3 Evaluating a Permutation

Poetry Two students are chosen from a group of 6 to read the first and second poems at the school's poetry reading. To find how many different ways the students can be chosen, find ${}_6P_2$.

$${}_6P_2 = \frac{6!}{(6-2)!} = \frac{6!}{4!}$$ **Use permutation formula.**

$$= \frac{6 \cdot 5 \cdot \cancel{4} \cdot \cancel{3} \cdot \cancel{2} \cdot \cancel{1}}{\cancel{4} \cdot \cancel{3} \cdot \cancel{2} \cdot \cancel{1}}$$ **Divide out common factors.**

$$= 30$$ **Multiply.**

▶ **Answer** The students can be chosen in 30 ways.

ANOTHER WAY

In Example 3, you can also write 6! as 6 • 5 • 4! and divide out 4!.

$\frac{6 \cdot 5 \cdot 4!}{4!} = 6 \cdot 5.$

✓ **GUIDED PRACTICE** for Example 3

Find the number of permutations.

6. ${}_5P_3$ **7.** ${}_6P_6$ **8.** ${}_8P_7$ **9.** ${}_{100}P_2$

10. What If? Suppose 3 students are chosen from a group of 8 to read in Example 3. In how many different ways can the students be chosen?

12.5 EXERCISES

HOMEWORK KEY

★ = **STANDARDIZED TEST PRACTICE** Exs. 16, 31, 32, 34, 37, and 45

○ = **HINTS AND HOMEWORK HELP** for Exs. 5, 7, 13, 15, 33 at classzone.com

SKILL PRACTICE

VOCABULARY **Copy and complete the statement.**

1. The number of permutations of 15 objects taken 7 at a time is written _?_.
2. The product of all integers from 1 to a number n is written _?_.

SEE EXAMPLE 1 on p. 675 for Exs. 3–6

EVALUATING FACTORIALS **Evaluate the factorial.**

3. 2! **4.** 0! **5.** 7! **6.** 9!

SEE EXAMPLES 2 AND 3 on p. 676 for Exs. 7–15

EVALUATING PERMUTATIONS **Find the number of permutations.**

7. ${}_4P_2$ **8.** ${}_9P_6$ **9.** ${}_{10}P_7$ **10.** ${}_5P_5$

11. ${}_{12}P_6$ **12.** ${}_7P_4$ **13.** ${}_{15}P_5$ **14.** ${}_{20}P_3$

15. ERROR ANALYSIS Describe and correct the error made in evaluating ${}_5P_3$.

$${}_5P_3 = \frac{5!}{3!} = \frac{5 \cdot 4 \cdot \cancel{3} \cdot \cancel{2} \cdot \cancel{1}}{\cancel{3} \cdot \cancel{2} \cdot \cancel{1}} = 5 \cdot 4 = 20$$

SEE EXAMPLE 1 on p. 675 for Exs. 16–21

16. ★ MULTIPLE CHOICE You go to the cafeteria with five friends. Which expression can you use to find how many different ways you and your friends can stand in the lunch line?

Ⓐ ${}_6P_1$ Ⓑ ${}_6P_5$ Ⓒ ${}_5P_5$ Ⓓ ${}_6P_6$

FINDING PERMUTATIONS **Describe the permutation you need to evaluate to find the answer. Then solve the problem.**

17. How many different ways can you arrange the letters in the word HOLIDAY?
18. There are 8 students in the school play. How many different ways can 6 of the cast members be arranged in a row?
19. A deck of cards has 52 cards. How many different arrangements of 5 cards can be made from the deck?
20. You borrow 5 books. In how many different orders can you read the books?
21. The German Club has 24 members. In how many ways can the club select a president, vice president, secretary, and treasurer from its members?

COMPARING **Copy and complete the statement with <, >, or =.**

22. ${}_8P_5 \ \underline{?}\ {}_8P_1$

23. ${}_6P_2 \ \underline{?}\ {}_6P_4$

24. ${}_{10}P_{10} \ \underline{?}\ {}_9P_9$

25. ${}_5P_1 \ \underline{?}\ {}_8P_1$

26. ${}_7P_7 \ \underline{?}\ 7!$

27. ${}_4P_3 \ \underline{?}\ {}_6P_2$

28. **CHALLENGE** Why do you think that 0! = 1? *Explain.* (Hint: Try to write this statement as a permutation in words.)

PROBLEM SOLVING

SEE EXAMPLES 2 AND 3 on p. 676 for Exs. 29–30, 32–33, 35

29. **SUMMER CAMP** You are given a list of 10 activities you can do while camping. You are asked to pick your first, second, third, and fourth choices. How many different permutations are possible?

30. **SOFTBALL** Your softball team has 15 players. Find the number of different ways that the first, second, third, fourth, and fifth batters can be chosen.

31. ★ **SHORT RESPONSE** Your friend says that 11! = 11 • 10!. Is your friend correct? *Explain.*

32. ★ **MULTIPLE CHOICE** You are knitting a stocking hat, and you want it to have 4 different colored stripes of equal width. You have 6 colors of yarn. How many different hats can you knit?

Ⓐ 24 Ⓑ 30 Ⓒ 360 Ⓓ 720

33. **GARDENING** You are planning a garden with 3 rows. Each row will have one type of flower, and none of the rows will be the same. You can choose from the flowers below. Find the number of permutations.

Day Lily

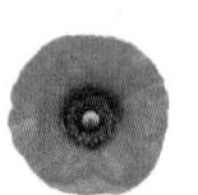
Poppy

Gladiolus

Daffodil

Rose

Sunflower

Tulip

SEE EXAMPLE 3 on p. 676 for Ex. 34

34. ★ **WRITING** In Example 1 on page 675, you found the number of permutations of 5 CDs taken how many at a time? *Explain.*

35. **PHONE CALLS** When you come back from vacation, you want to call Ed, Sue, Ty, and Nestor. You have time to make only two calls. Find the number of different ways in which you can call two friends. Then make an organized list to show all the different ways to make 2 calls.

36. **MULTI-STEP PROBLEM** There are 50 people entered in a drawing to win three door prizes. Only 1 prize will be awarded to each winner.

a. How many different ways can the winners be chosen?

b. Another prize is added to the drawing. How many different ways can four winners be chosen?

c. Compare the number of permutations in parts (a) and (b). *Explain* any differences.

37. ★ **EXTENDED RESPONSE** Your school team is 1 of 15 in a cheerleading competition.

a. Trophies are awarded for first, second, third, and fourth places. In how many different ways can the trophies be awarded?

b. Suppose the four teams that perform best are all given *excellence* medals instead of first, second, third, and fourth place trophies. In this case, are there more or fewer ways to give the awards than in part (a)? *Explain.*

FUNCTIONS In Exercises 38 and 39, consider the functions $_6P_r$, $_7P_r$, and $_8P_r$.

38. Make an input-output table for each of the 3 functions. The domain of each is $r = 1, 2, 3, \dots n$. The range consists of the values of $_6P_r$, $_7P_r$, and $_8P_r$. Describe any patterns that you see.

39. **CHALLENGE** Predict which of these expressions has the greatest value: $_{23}P_6$, $_{23}P_{12}$, $_{23}P_{18}$, $_{23}P_{23}$. *Justify* your reasoning using the patterns in your tables.

40. **CHALLENGE** For a science fair, 20 students submit a project. The top r projects can be awarded ribbons in $_{20}P_r$ ways. If one more project is awarded a ribbon, how many times greater is the number of permutations of ribbons awarded?

MIXED REVIEW

Get-Ready

Prepare for Lesson 12.6 in Exs. 41–43

Make a tree diagram to find the number of choices that are possible. Then check your answer using the counting principle. *(p. 670)*

41. Choose a car or truck with an MP3 player or a CD player.

42. Choose a red, green, blue, or gray ball with a black or silver racquet.

43. Choose a cake that is vanilla or chocolate, with white, yellow, or blue frosting, and with a balloon or flower design.

CHOOSE A STRATEGY Use a strategy from the list to solve the following problem. *Explain* your choice of strategy.

44. A rectangular room is 20 feet by 12 feet, with walls 7.5 feet high. A decorator charges $.40 per square foot to use paint and $.70 per square foot for wallpaper. Find the total cost to decorate the walls of the room with each material.

Problem Solving Strategies
- Draw a Diagram *(p. 787)*
- Make a Table *(p. 790)*
- Solve a Simpler Problem *(p. 793)*
- Act It Out *(p. 795)*

45. ★ **MULTIPLE CHOICE** What is the surface area of a cone that has a slant height of 24 inches and a diameter of 10 inches? ***(p. 548)***

Ⓐ 145π in.^{2} Ⓑ 200π in.^{2} Ⓒ 340π in.^{2} Ⓓ 800π in.^{2}

12.6 Combinations

Before	You used permutations to count possibilities.
Now	You will use combinations to count possibilities.
Why?	So you can count possible groups, as for a fair in Example 1.

KEY VOCABULARY

- **combination,** *p. 680*

In Lesson 12.5, you studied permutations, which are arrangements in which order is important. A **combination** is a group of items whose order is *not* important. For example, suppose you go to lunch with a friend. You choose milk, soup, and a salad. Your friend chooses soup, a salad, and milk. The order in which the items are chosen does not matter. You both have the same meal.

The two meals are the same.

EXAMPLE 1 Listing Combinations

County Fair You have 4 tickets to the county fair and can take 3 of your friends. You can choose from Abby (A), Brian (B), Chloe (C), and David (D). How many different choices of groups of friends do you have?

SOLUTION

List all possible arrangements of three friends. Then cross out any duplicate groupings that represent the same group of friends.

ANOTHER WAY

The answer makes sense because you can leave out Abby, Brian, Chloe, or David with each choice.

(ABC)	~~ACB~~	~~BAC~~	~~BCA~~	~~CAB~~	~~CBA~~
(ABD)	~~ADB~~	~~BAD~~	~~BDA~~	~~DAB~~	~~DBA~~
(ACD)	~~ADC~~	~~CAD~~	~~CDA~~	~~DAC~~	~~DCA~~
(BCD)	~~BDC~~	~~CBD~~	~~CDB~~	~~DBC~~	~~DCB~~

ABC, ACB, BAC, BCA, CAB, and CBA all represent the same group.

▸ **Answer** You have 4 different choices of groups to take to the fair.

✓ GUIDED PRACTICE for Example 1

1. **What If?** In Example 1, suppose you have only 3 tickets and can take 2 of your friends. Now how many different choices of groups do you have?

Combination Notation In Example 1, after you cross out the duplicate groupings, you are left with the number of combinations of 4 items chosen 3 at a time. Using combination notation, this is written ${}_4C_3$.

KEY CONCEPT *For Your Notebook*

Combination Notation

Words To find the number of combinations of n objects taken r at a time, divide the number of permutations of n objects taken r at a time by $r!$.

Algebra ${}_nC_r = \frac{{}_nP_r}{r!}$ **Numbers** ${}_9C_4 = \frac{{}_9P_4}{4!}$

EXAMPLE 2 Evaluating Combinations

Find the number of combinations.

a. ${}_8C_3$

b. ${}_9C_7$

SOLUTION

a. ${}_8C_3 = \frac{{}_8P_3}{3!}$ Combination formula

$= \frac{8 \cdot 7 \cdot 6}{3!}$ ${}_8P_3 = \frac{8!}{(8-3)!} = 8 \cdot 7 \cdot 6$

$= \frac{8 \cdot 7 \cdot \cancel{6}}{\cancel{3} \cdot \cancel{2} \cdot 1}$ Expand. $3! = 3 \cdot 2 \cdot 1$. Divide out common factors.

$= 56$ Simplify.

b. ${}_9C_7 = \frac{{}_9P_7}{7!}$ Combination formula

$= \frac{9 \cdot 8 \cdot 7 \cdot 6 \cdot 5 \cdot 4 \cdot 3}{7!}$ ${}_9P_7 = \frac{9!}{(9-7)!} = 9 \cdot 8 \cdot 7 \cdot 6 \cdot 5 \cdot 4 \cdot 3$

$= \frac{9 \cdot \overset{4}{\cancel{8}} \cdot \cancel{7} \cdot \cancel{6} \cdot \cancel{5} \cdot \cancel{4} \cdot \cancel{3}}{\cancel{7} \cdot \cancel{6} \cdot \cancel{5} \cdot \cancel{4} \cdot \cancel{3} \cdot \underset{1}{\cancel{2}} \cdot 1}$ Expand 7!. Divide out common factors.

$= 36$ Simplify.

GUIDED PRACTICE for Example 2

Find the number of combinations.

2. ${}_8C_8$ **3.** ${}_8C_7$ **4.** ${}_7C_2$ **5.** ${}_6C_1$

6. Bookstore You are shopping at a bookstore. You have enough money to buy 4 books. There are 7 books at the store that you want to read. How many combinations of books can be purchased?

EXAMPLE 3 Permutations and Combinations

VOCABULARY
Mutate means to change. For *permutations,* you count changes in the order of items. For *combinations,* objects *combined* in any order represent the same group.

Tell whether the possibilities can be counted using a *permutation* or *combination*. Then write an expression for the number of possibilities.

a. Swimming There are 8 swimmers in the 400 meter freestyle race. In how many ways can the swimmers finish first, second, and third?

b. Track Your track team has 6 runners available for the 4 person relay event. How many different 4 person teams can be chosen?

SOLUTION

a. Because the swimmers can finish first, second, or third, order is important. So the possibilities can be counted by evaluating ${}_8P_3$.

b. Order is not important in choosing the team members, so the possibilities can be counted by evaluating ${}_6C_4$.

GUIDED PRACTICE for Example 3

Tell whether the possibilities can be counted using a *permutation* or *combination*. Then write an expression for the number of possibilities.

7. **Pizza Toppings** A pizza shop offers 12 different pizza toppings. How many different 3-topping pizzas are possible?

8. **Student Council** There are 15 members on the student council. In how many ways can they elect a president and a vice president for the council?

12.6 EXERCISES

HOMEWORK KEY
★ = **STANDARDIZED TEST PRACTICE** Exs. 4, 31, 32, 33, and 46
○ = **HINTS AND HOMEWORK HELP** for Exs. 3, 7, 9, 15, 29 at classzone.com

SKILL PRACTICE

VOCABULARY Copy and complete the statement.

1. The expression ${}_9C_5$ represents the number of combinations of __?__ objects taken __?__ at a time.

2. To find the number of combinations of n objects taken r at a time, divide the number of __?__ of n objects taken r at a time by $r!$.

SEE EXAMPLE 1 on p. 680 for Ex. 3

3. **LISTING COMBINATIONS** For a test, you can choose any 2 essay questions to answer from the 5 questions asked. Make a list and cross out the duplicate choices to show how many different pairs of essay questions you could answer.

SEE EXAMPLE 2 on p. 681 for Ex. 4

4. ★ **MULTIPLE CHOICE** Which expression is equivalent to ${}_6C_3$?

Ⓐ $\frac{6!}{(6-3)!}$ Ⓑ $6 \cdot 5 \cdot 4$ Ⓒ $\frac{{}_6P_3}{6!}$ Ⓓ $\frac{6 \cdot 5 \cdot 4}{3!}$

SEE EXAMPLE 2 on p. 681 for Exs. 5–16

COMBINATIONS Find the number of combinations.

5. ${}_4C_1$ 6. ${}_4C_4$ 7. ${}_7C_6$ 8. ${}_5C_2$

9. ${}_8C_6$ 10. ${}_8C_1$ 11. ${}_{10}C_8$ 12. ${}_9C_5$

13. ${}_{11}C_3$ 14. ${}_{13}C_{11}$ 15. ${}_9C_2$ 16. ${}_{100}C_{99}$

17. **ERROR ANALYSIS** Your class is voting for the new school colors. You are asked to choose 2 colors from a list of 8 colors. *Describe* and correct the error made in counting the color pairs you can choose.

$$ {}_8P_2 = \frac{8!}{(8-2)!} = \frac{8 \cdot 7 \cdot 6 \cdot 5 \cdot 4 \cdot 3 \cdot 2 \cdot 1}{6 \cdot 5 \cdot 4 \cdot 3 \cdot 2 \cdot 1} = 56 \text{ color pairs} $$

COUNTING CHOICES Answer the question. Tell whether you used a *permutation* or *combination*.

SEE EXAMPLE 3 on p. 682 for Exs. 18–21

18. How many groups of 2 colors of balloons can you choose from 4 colors of balloons?

19. How many ways can you do your homework for 4 subjects?

20. How many ways can you play your 5 favorite songs?

21. How many groups of 3 vegetables can you choose from 5 vegetables to make vegetable soup?

22. **LOOK FOR A PATTERN** Copy and complete the table by finding the number of combinations. Then describe the pattern.

${}_7C_0$	${}_7C_1$	${}_7C_2$	${}_7C_3$	${}_7C_4$	${}_7C_5$	${}_7C_6$	${}_7C_7$
?	?	?	?	?	?	?	?

CHALLENGE Solve the inequality for *n* or *r*.

23. ${}_nC_3 \geq 20$ 24. ${}_nC_2 < 21$ 25. ${}_6C_r \leq 15$ 26. ${}_8C_r > 28$

PROBLEM SOLVING

SEE EXAMPLES 2 AND 3 on pp. 681–682 for Exs. 27–30

27. **ART** An art instructor must choose 2 art projects for students to complete from this list: clay, plaster, wood, wire, drawing, painting. How many combinations of 2 projects are possible?

28. **HOCKEY** Your hockey team is choosing 2 team captains from its 18 members. Find the number of combinations that are possible.

29. **DEBATING** A debate team has 5 members. Your debating club has 12 students. How many different teams can be chosen?

30. **GARDENING** You want to grow 4 different vegetables. You can choose from 9 types of vegetable seed. How many different groups of 4 types of seed can you choose?

31. ★ **MULTIPLE CHOICE** You are at a fair with 4 friends. All of you want to ride the roller coaster, but only 3 people can fit in the first car. How many different groups of 3 can you and your friends make?

Ⓐ 60 Ⓑ 15 Ⓒ 10 Ⓓ 4

32. ★ **SHORT RESPONSE** Is it possible to evaluate a combination such as ${}_3C_4$, ${}_2C_6$, or ${}_1C_{10}$? *Explain* why or why not.

33. ★ **WRITING** *Describe* the difference between a permutation and a combination using real-world examples.

34. **NUMBER SENSE** Tell whether the value of ${}_nP_r$ is *always, sometimes,* or *never* greater than the value of ${}_nC_r$. *Explain* your reasoning.

SEE EXAMPLES 2 AND 3 on pp. 681–682 for Ex. 35

35. **MULTI-STEP PROBLEM** You are coloring the map shown at the right. You want each state to be a different color.

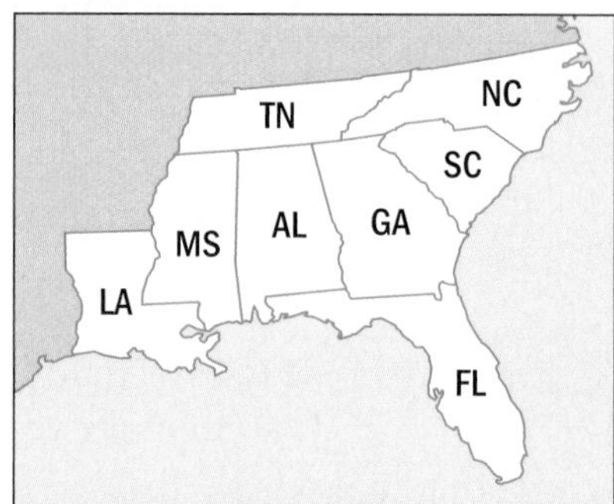

a. In how many ways can you color the map if you have 8 colors?

b. How many 8-color groups can you choose from 10 colors?

c. In how many ways can you color the map using 8 out of 10 colors? *Explain.*

36. **VIDEO GAMES** You want to borrow 4 out of 20 video games from a friend. How many different groups of four games can you choose? Suppose you are already sure about two of the game choices. How many different groups of four games can you choose? *Explain.*

37. **CHALLENGE** What is the value of ${}_nC_r$ when $r = n$? What is the value of ${}_nC_r$ when $n - r = 1$? *Explain.*

MIXED REVIEW

Prepare for Lesson 12.7 in Exs. 38–41

The spinner at the right has 6 equal sections. Find the probability of landing on the given color if you spin it once. ***(p. 381)***

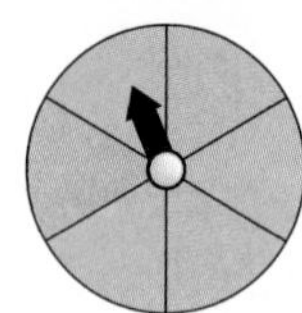

38. blue
39. red
40. green
41. white

Find the number of permutations. ***(p. 675)***

42. ${}_{10}P_5$
43. ${}_{11}P_4$
44. ${}_{18}P_3$
45. ${}_{21}P_2$

46. ★ **SHORT RESPONSE** The table shows the number of people, in millions, who attended symphony orchestra concerts in the United States each year from 1998 to 2002. Make a line graph of the data. *Describe* the trend. ***(p. 659)***

Year	1998	1999	2000	2001	2002
Attendees (millions)	32.2	30.8	31.7	31.5	30.3

12.7 Probability and Odds

Before	You found the probability of events.
Now	You will find the odds in favor of events.
Why?	So you can find odds in sports, as in Example 3.

KEY VOCABULARY

- **complementary events,** *p. 685*
- **unfavorable outcome,** *p. 686*
- **odds,** *p. 686*

ACTIVITY

Use the spinner at the right.

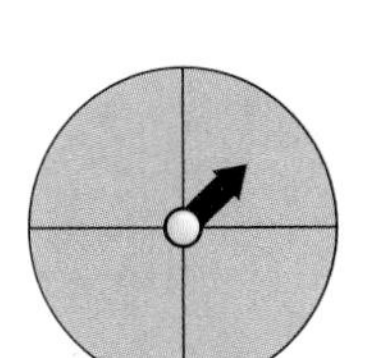

STEP 1 **Decide** whether it is more likely for the spinner to land on blue or red. *Explain* your reasoning.

STEP 2 **Find** each ratio. Use the ratios to compare the chance of landing on red to the chance of landing on blue.

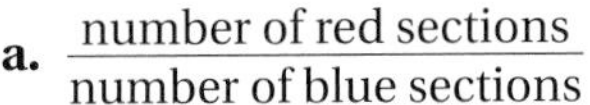

a. $\dfrac{\text{number of red sections}}{\text{number of blue sections}}$ **b.** $\dfrac{\text{number of blue sections}}{\text{number of red sections}}$

STEP 3 **Explain** how to find the probability of the spinner *not* landing on red.

In the activity, the spinner will land on either red or blue. Two events are **complementary** when one event or the other (but not both) must occur. The sum of the probabilities of complementary events is always 1.

When Events A and B are complementary, $P(\text{Event A}) = 1 - P(\text{Event B})$.

EXAMPLE 1 Finding Probabilities

USE PROBABILITY

The probability that Event A occurs and the probability that Event A does *not* occur have a sum of 1 because they are complementary events. For help with probability, see p. 381.

Gifts You and seven friends contribute money for a gift. Everyone's name is put in a hat. The person whose name is chosen at random picks the gift.

a. What is the probability that your name is chosen?

b. What is the probability that your name is *not* chosen?

SOLUTION

a. $P(\text{your name is chosen}) = \dfrac{\text{Number of favorable outcomes}}{\text{Number of possible outcomes}} = \dfrac{1}{8}$

b. $P(\text{your name is not chosen}) = 1 - P(\text{your name is chosen})$

$$= 1 - \frac{1}{8}$$

$$= \frac{7}{8}$$

Odds Once you specify the event for which you are finding the probability, outcomes for that event are called *favorable outcomes.* The other outcomes are **unfavorable outcomes**.

When all outcomes are equally likely, the **odds** in favor of an event are equal to the ratio of favorable outcomes to unfavorable outcomes.

$$\textbf{Odds in favor} = \frac{\textbf{Number of favorable outcomes}}{\textbf{Number of unfavorable outcomes}}$$

EXAMPLE 2 Finding Odds

Vacation Survey You do a survey asking your class to rank three vacation choices. Results for "the beach" are shown at the right. What are the odds in favor of a randomly chosen student from your class ranking a beach vacation first?

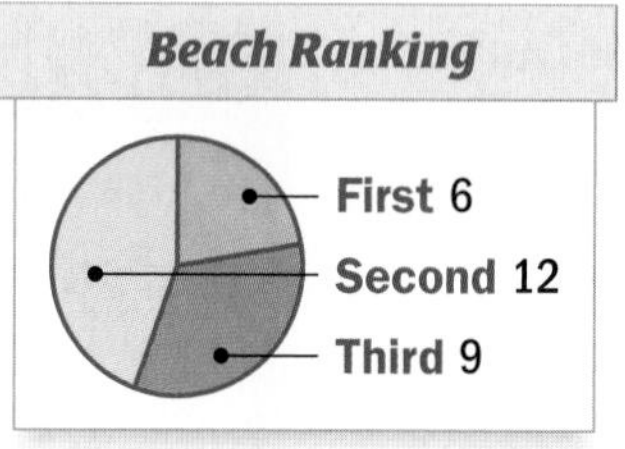

SOLUTION

READING
Odds are always read as a ratio. For example, $\frac{5}{2}$ is read "five to two," not "five halves."

The beach was ranked first by 6 students, so there are 6 favorable outcomes. It was ranked second by 12 students, and ranked third by 9 students, so there are $12 + 9 = 21$ unfavorable outcomes.

$$\text{Odds in favor} = \frac{\text{Number of favorable outcomes}}{\text{Number of unfavorable outcomes}}$$

$$= \frac{6}{21}$$

$$= \frac{2}{7}$$

▶ **Answer** The odds in favor of a randomly chosen student ranking a beach vacation first are 2 to 7.

✓ GUIDED PRACTICE for Examples 1 and 2

You are given the probability that event A will occur. Find the probability that event A will *not* occur.

1. $P(\text{A}) = \frac{3}{4}$ **2.** $P(\text{A}) = 0.45$ **3.** $P(\text{A}) = 32\%$ **4.** $P(\text{A}) = \frac{7}{10}$

5. The 11 letters in the word MISSISSIPPI are each written on pieces of paper and randomly chosen from a bag. What is the probability of drawing an S from the bag? What is the probability of *not* drawing an S?

You choose a card at random from a set of cards numbered 1 to 24. Find the odds in favor of the event.

6. You choose a 10. **7.** You choose an odd number.

8. You choose an even number greater than 8.

Probability and Odds If you know the probability of an event, you can use the following formula to find the odds in favor of that event.

$$\text{Odds} = \frac{\text{Probability event will occur}}{\text{Probability event will not occur}} = \frac{\text{Probability event will occur}}{1 - \text{Probability event will occur}}$$

EXAMPLE 3 Finding Odds Using Probability

Basketball Sean makes 65% of his free throws. What are Sean's odds in favor of making a free throw?

SOLUTION

$\text{Odds} = \frac{0.65}{1 - 0.65}$ Write percents as decimals.

$= \frac{0.65}{0.35}$ Subtract.

$= \frac{65}{35}$, or $\frac{13}{7}$ Multiply by $\frac{100}{100}$. Then simplify.

▶ **Answer** Sean's odds in favor of making a free throw are 13 to 7.

✓ GUIDED PRACTICE for Example 3

9. **What If?** In Example 3, suppose Sean makes 85% of his free throws. What are Sean's odds in favor of making a free throw?

12.7 EXERCISES

HOMEWORK KEY

★ = STANDARDIZED TEST PRACTICE Exs. 20, 32, 33, 35, and 45

○ = HINTS AND HOMEWORK HELP for Exs. 5, 9, 11, 15, 31 at classzone.com

SKILL PRACTICE

VOCABULARY **Copy and complete the statement.**

1. Find the ratio of the number of favorable outcomes to the number of unfavorable outcomes to find the __?__ of an event.

2. Two events are __?__ when one event or the other (but not both) must occur.

COMPLEMENTARY EVENTS **You are given the probability that event A will occur. Find the probability that event A will *not* occur.**

SEE EXAMPLE 1 on p. 685 for Exs. 3–6

3. $P(A) = 84\%$
4. $P(A) = \frac{2}{5}$
5. $P(A) = 0.37$
6. $P(A) = \frac{9}{10}$

MARBLES **You randomly choose a marble from the given group. Find the probability of choosing a red marble, and of *not* choosing a red marble. Then find the odds in favor of choosing a blue marble.**

SEE EXAMPLES 1 AND 2 on pp. 685–686 for Exs. 7–10

7. 3 red and 7 blue marbles
8. 4 red and 9 blue marbles
9. 6 red and 5 blue marbles
10. 6 red, 5 blue, and 3 green marbles

ODDS **You roll a number cube. Find the odds in favor of the given event.**

SEE EXAMPLE 2 on p. 686 for Exs. 11–15

(11.) Roll a 3.

12. Roll a number less than 6.

13. Roll a number greater than 2.

14. Roll an odd number less than 5.

(15.) **ERROR ANALYSIS** Describe and correct the error made in finding the odds in favor of rolling a number greater than 4 on a number cube.

> ✗ Odds $= \frac{4}{2} = \frac{2}{1}$
> The odds in favor are 2 to 1.

LETTERED TILES **You are randomly selecting lettered tiles. Use the given probability to find the odds in favor of selecting the letter.**

SEE EXAMPLE 3 on p. 687 for Exs. 16–20

16. $P(\text{letter I}) = 5\%$

17. $P(\text{letter E}) = 55\%$

18. $P(\text{letter S}) = 12\%$

19. $P(\text{letter R}) = 8\%$

20. ★ **MULTIPLE CHOICE** The probability of an event is 60%. What are the odds in favor of the event?

(A) 3 to 5 (B) 2 to 3 (C) 5 to 3 (D) 3 to 2

ODDS **Use the odds in favor of an event to find the probability of the event.**

21. 1 to 3

22. 1 to 1

23. 27 to 23

24. 7 to 13

25. xy **ALGEBRA** The odds in favor of an event are a to b. Write an expression for the probability of the event.

26. **CHALLENGE** You spin a spinner with n equal-sized sections numbered 1 through n. The probability of getting a number greater than 9 is 25%. What are the odds in favor of getting a number less than 5? *Explain.*

PROBLEM SOLVING

SEE EXAMPLE 1 on p. 685 for Exs. 27–28

27. **CLOTHING** You randomly pull a sock from a drawer with 4 patterned socks, 8 gym socks, 6 striped socks, and 2 red socks. What is the probability that you do *not* choose a gym sock?

PIZZA **Use the circle graph. It shows the number of pizza orders for each type of crust.**

28. What is the probability that a randomly chosen pizza order is *not* for thin crust?

What kind of crust?

Regular 52
Thin 28
Stuffed 20

SEE EXAMPLE 2 on p. 686 for Exs. 29–31

29. What are the odds in favor of a randomly chosen pizza order being for regular crust?

30. What are the odds in favor of a randomly chosen pizza order *not* being for stuffed crust?

(31.) **HOCKEY** A hockey goalie has a save percentage of 93%. What are the goalie's odds in favor of making a save?

SEE EXAMPLE 3 on p. 687 for Ex. 32

32. ★ **MULTIPLE CHOICE** The weather forecast says that there is a 30 percent probability of rain. What are the odds in favor of rain?

(A) 3 to 7 (B) 3 to 10 (C) 7 to 3 (D) 10 to 3

33. ★ **SHORT RESPONSE** Sam finds the probability of Event A is 0.2. Jan finds the odds in favor of Event A are 1 to 4. Are they both right? *Explain.*

ODDS AGAINST In Exercises 34 and 35, use the following information.

In this lesson, you learned how to find the *odds in favor* of an event. You can also find the *odds against* an event.

$$\text{Odds against} = \frac{\text{Number of unfavorable outcomes}}{\text{Number of favorable outcomes}}$$

34. You randomly choose a chip from a bag of 6 blue, 3 red, and 5 green chips. Find the odds in favor of choosing a green chip. Then find the odds against choosing a green chip.

35. ★ **WRITING** You hear a friend claim that "the odds that you get hit by lightning are a million to one." Is your friend talking about *odds in favor* or *odds against*? *Explain* your reasoning.

36. **MULTI-STEP PROBLEM** Assume that when an arrow hits the target shown at the right, the arrow is equally likely to hit any point on the target. The probability P that an arrow lands within the red bull's-eye circle is given by $P = \frac{\text{Area of bull's-eye}}{\text{Area of target}}$.

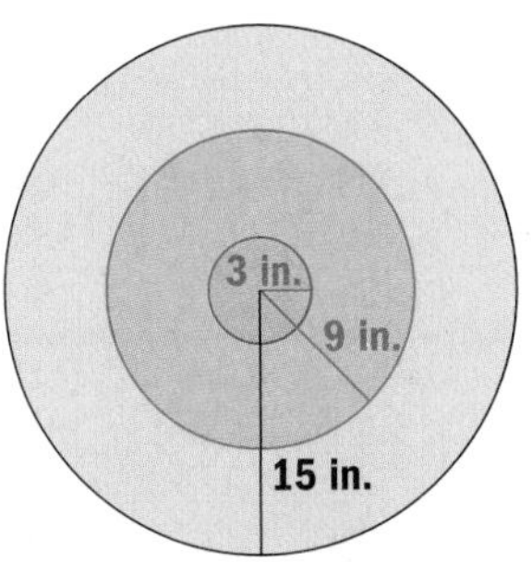

   a. **Geometry** What is the area of the bull's-eye? What is the total area of the target? Write your answers in terms of π.

   b. **Probability** What is the probability that an arrow hitting the target lands within the bull's-eye?

   c. **Odds** What are the odds that an arrow hitting the target lands on the blue region?

37. **CHALLENGE** Beverage A includes a bottle cap with 1 to 11 odds in favor of winning a free bottle. Beverage B's bottle cap includes an x% probability of winning. After opening 132 bottles of each drink, you win 1 more time with beverage B than with beverage A. Find x.

MIXED REVIEW

Prepare for Lesson 12.8 in Exs. 38–41

Find the product. *(p. 243)*

38. $\frac{1}{5} \cdot \frac{1}{5}$ 39. $\frac{3}{4} \cdot \frac{3}{4}$ 40. $\frac{5}{6} \cdot \frac{4}{5}$ 41. $\frac{4}{9} \cdot \frac{3}{8}$

Find the slope of the line passing through the points. *(p. 482)*

42. $(-8, 12), (9, 2)$ 43. $(7, 5), (-3, 6)$ 44. $(-1, -5), (-4, -10)$

45. ★ **MULTIPLE CHOICE** What is the length of the hypotenuse of a right triangle that has leg lengths of 24 inches and 45 inches? *(p. 612)*

   (A) 38 in. (B) 46 in. (C) 51 in. (D) 120 in.

Extension

Use after Lesson 12.7

Number Sets and Probability

GOAL Apply set theory to numbers and probability.

KEY VOCABULARY
- **set,** *p. 690*
- **element,** *p. 690*
- **empty set,** *p. 690*
- **universal set,** *p. 690*
- **union,** *p. 690*
- **intersection,** *p. 690*
- **complement,** *p. 690*

A **set** is a collection of distinct objects. Each object in a set is called an **element** or *member* of the set. You can use set notation to write a set by enclosing the elements of the set in braces. For example, the set A of positive even numbers less than 20 can be written as

$$A = \{2, 4, 6, 8, 10, 12, 14, 16, 18\}.$$

The **empty set** is the set with no elements and is written as $\varnothing$. The **universal set** is the set of all elements under consideration and is written as U. Sets can be related to one another in a variety of ways, as shown below.

KEY CONCEPT *For Your Notebook*

Union, Intersection, and Complement

The **union** of two sets A and B is the set of all elements in *either* A or B, and is written $A \cup B$.

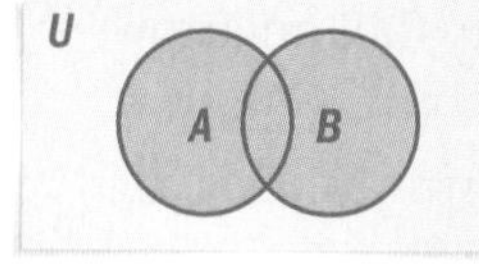

The **intersection** of two sets A and B is the set of all elements in *both* A and B, and is written $A \cap B$.

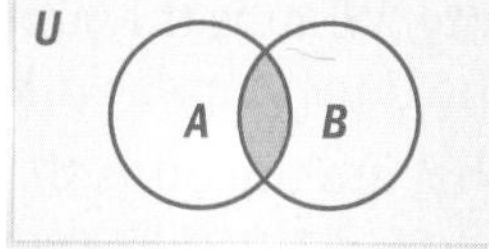

The **complement** of set A is the set of all elements in U that are *not* in A and is written $\sim A$.

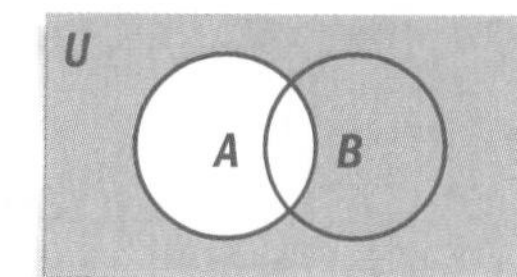

EXAMPLE 1 Finding Complements of Sets

Let U be the integers from 0 to 10. Let $A = \{1, 2, 3, 4, 5\}$ and $B = \{2, 4, 6, 8, 10\}$.

a. Find $\sim A$.

b. Find $\sim(A \cup B)$.

VENN DIAGRAMS
When drawing diagrams for the complement of a set, be sure to shade everything that is not included in the set.

SOLUTION

a. The set $\sim A$ consists of all the elements in U that are not in A.

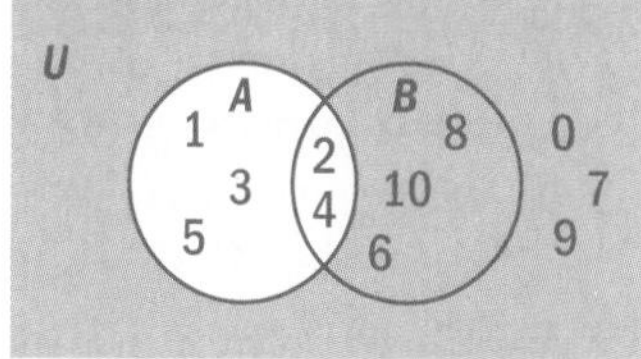

$\sim A = \{0, 6, 7, 8, 9, 10\}$

b. The complement of $A \cup B$ is the set of all elements in neither A nor B.

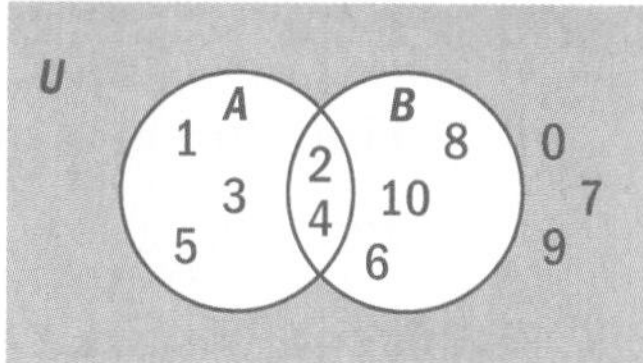

$\sim(A \cup B) = \{0, 7, 9\}$

Probability and Sets You can find the probability that an element of set A is in U as you did for other probabilities.

$$P(\text{set } A) = \frac{\textbf{Number of favorable outcomes}}{\textbf{Total number of outcomes}} = \frac{\textbf{Number of elements in set } A}{\textbf{Number of elements in } U}$$

EXAMPLE 2 Finding Probabilities for Complements of Events

Consider the universal set U to be the whole numbers from 15 to 25. Let A be the set of even numbers and B be the set of perfect squares. Find $P(\sim(A \cap B))$ and $P(\sim(A \cup B))$ when an element is chosen at random from U.

SOLUTION

STEP 1 **List** the elements of A and B.

$A = \{16, 18, 20, 22, 24\}$ $\qquad B = \{16, 25\}$

STEP 2 **Find** $\sim(A \cap B)$ and $\sim(A \cup B)$.

$A \cap B = \{16\}$, so $\sim(A \cap B) = \{15, 17, 18, 19, 20, 21, 22, 23, 24, 25\}$

$A \cup B = \{16, 18, 20, 22, 24, 25\}$, so $\sim(A \cup B) = \{15, 17, 19, 21, 23\}$

STEP 3 **Calculate** the probabilities.

$$P(\sim(A \cap B)) = \frac{\text{Number of elements in } \sim(A \cap B)}{\text{Number of elements in } U} = \frac{10}{11}$$

$$P(\sim(A \cup B)) = \frac{\text{Number of elements in } \sim(A \cup B)}{\text{Number of elements in } U} = \frac{5}{11}$$

EXERCISES

SEE EXAMPLE 1 on p. 690 for Exs. 1–8, 13

Let U be the set of integers from -7 to 7, A be the set of multiples of 3, and B be the set of whole numbers from 2 to 5. List the elements in the given set. Draw a Venn diagram to represent it.

1. $\sim A$ **2.** $\sim B$ **3.** $\sim(A \cup B)$ **4.** $\sim(A \cap B)$

5. $\sim A \cup B$ **6.** $A \cap \sim B$ **7.** $\sim A \cap \sim B$ **8.** $\sim A \cup \sim B$

SEE EXAMPLE 2 on p. 691 for Exs. 9–12

Let U, A, and B be the sets described for Exercises 1–8. Find the probability that an element chosen at random from U belongs to the set described.

9. $\sim A \cup B$ **10.** $A \cap \sim B$ **11.** $\sim A \cap \sim B$ **12.** $\sim A \cup \sim B$

13. Reasoning What is the intersection of a set A and its complement? What is the union of these two sets? *Justify* your reasoning.

CHALLENGE Two sets are equal if they contain the same elements. For example for every set A, $\sim(\sim A) = A$. Use a Venn diagram to show that the sets are equal for all sets A and B.

14. $\sim A \cup \sim B = \sim(A \cap B)$ **15.** $\sim A \cap \sim B = \sim(A \cup B)$

16. $A \cap \sim B = \sim(\sim A \cup B)$ **17.** $A \cup \sim B = \sim(\sim A \cap B)$

GOAL
Use a simulation to explore probability.

MATERIALS
- index cards
- calculator

12.8 Probability and Simulations

You can use a simulation to explore probability. A *simulation* is an experiment done to explore the probability of an event.

EXPLORE 1 Simulate a real-world situation.

Do a simulation to find an experimental probability that you and a friend are the 2 students randomly chosen from a group of 8 students.

STEP 1 **Label** eight index cards as shown. Use 1 to represent yourself, 2 to represent your friend, and 3, 4, 5, 6, 7, and 8 to represent the other students.

1	2	3	4
5	6	7	8

STEP 2 **Shuffle** the cards. Randomly draw a card, and then another, without replacing the first. Record your results. Decide whether or not the results represent you and your friend being chosen. Replace the cards.

STEP 3 **Repeat** drawing a pair of cards. Draw a total of 10 pairs. For each pair of cards drawn, record the results.

Use the ratio $\frac{\text{you and friend are chosen}}{\text{total number of pairs drawn}}$ to find the experimental probability that you and your friend are chosen.

Pair	Times Drawn
1, 4	I
7, 2	II
5, 8	I

PRACTICE

1. Use your results from the simulation above. Combine all the class results. Based on these results, what is the experimental probability that you and your friend are chosen?

2. The die at the right has 8 sides numbered 1–8. Each outcome is equally likely when the die is rolled. *Describe* how you can use this die to simulate the event above. *Explain* why each pair n, n must be disregarded.

EXPLORE 2 Use technology to simulate a real-world situation.

Use your calculator's random integer function to simulate randomly choosing 1 student from a group of 8. Find the experimental probability that any of the students is randomly chosen twice in a row.

STEP 1 **Use** 1, 2, 3, 4, 5, 6, 7, and 8 to represent the students.

STEP 2 **Clear** your calculator screen. Press MATH and choose the PRB menu. Select *randInt(*, the random integer function.

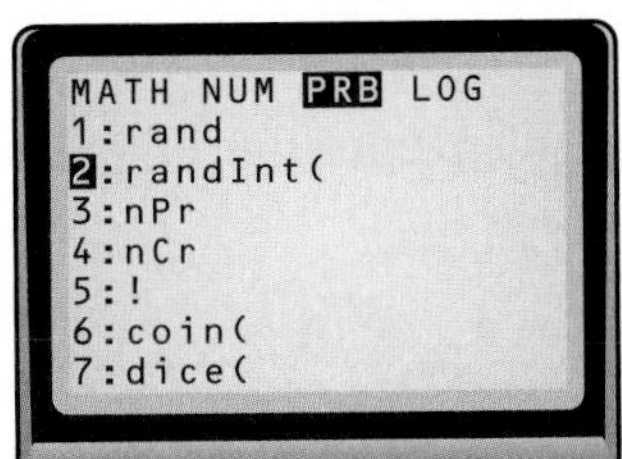

STEP 3 **Enter 1** , **8**) ENTER to select an integer at random from 1 to 8. Press ENTER again to simulate choosing a student again. Record whether your results represent a match.

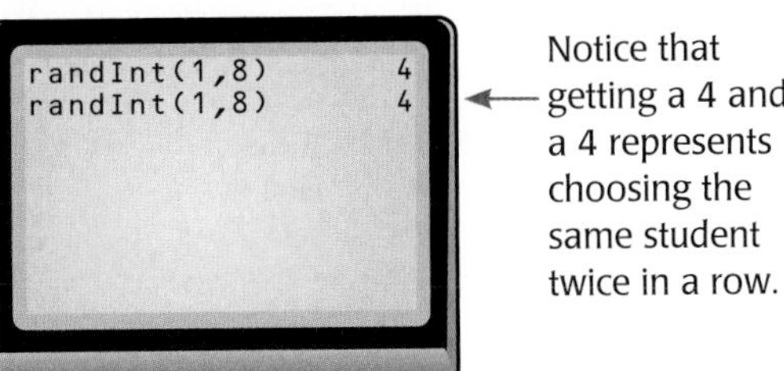

Notice that getting a 4 and a 4 represents choosing the same student twice in a row.

STEP 4 **Complete** the simulation a total of 10 times. Record your results. What is the experimental probability that any of the students is randomly chosen twice in a row?

PRACTICE Design a simulation of the situation.

3. You randomly choose to go to the library, from the choices mall, library, or bowling lanes.

4. You and your friend Chris are randomly chosen from a group of 10 team members to be co-captains.

DRAW CONCLUSIONS

5. **REASONING** Refer to Exercise 1 on page 692. Which results do you think are more likely to be closer to the theoretical probability that you and your friend are chosen, your results or the class results? *Explain.*

6. **WRITING** *Explain* how the simulation in Explore 2 above would be different if you wanted to find the probability that *you* are randomly chosen twice in a row from a group of eight people.

12.8 Independent and Dependent Events

Before You found the probability of an event.

Now You will study independent and dependent events.

Why? So you can find probabilities of games, as in Example 2.

KEY VOCABULARY
- **compound events,** *p. 694*
- **independent events,** *p. 694*
- **dependent events,** *p. 694*

When you consider the outcomes of two events, the events are called **compound events**. Compound events are **independent events** if the occurrence of one event does *not* affect the likelihood that the other event will occur. Compound events are **dependent events** if the occurrence of one event *does* affect the likelihood that the other will occur.

Suppose you randomly choose two gumballs one at a time from the jar below. The probability of choosing two red gumballs with replacement is different than the probability without replacement.

Independent Events

First Event

$P(\text{red}) = \frac{2}{5}$

Second Event

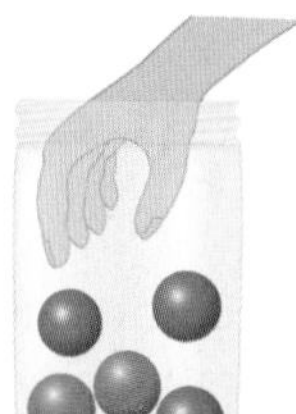

$P(\text{red}) = \frac{2}{5}$

If you replace the gumball, the probability of choosing a red one is the same each time.

Dependent Events

First Event

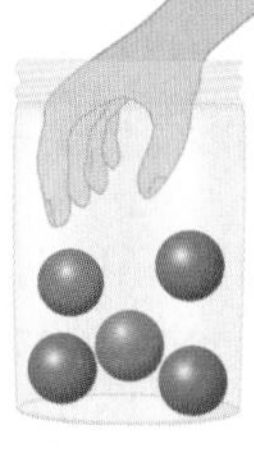

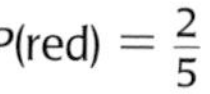

$P(\text{red}) = \frac{2}{5}$

Second Event

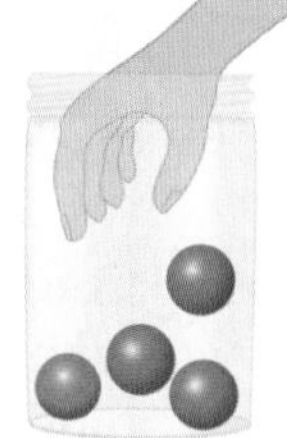

$P(\text{red}) = \frac{1}{4}$

If you don't replace the gumball after choosing, the probability changes.

EXAMPLE 1 Independent and Dependent Events

Tell whether the events are *independent* or *dependent*.

a. You roll a number cube. Then you roll the number cube again.

b. You randomly draw a number from a bag. Then you randomly draw a second number without putting the first number back.

SOLUTION

a. The result of the first roll does not affect the result of the second roll, so the events are independent.

b. There is one fewer number in the bag for the second draw, so the events are dependent.

Multiple Events To find the probability that Event A *and* Event B happen, you multiply probabilities. Because the occurrence of an event may affect the probability of another event, you should determine whether the events are independent or dependent before multiplying.

KEY CONCEPT *For Your Notebook*

Probability of Independent Events

Words For two independent events, the probability that both events occur is the product of the probabilities of the events.

Algebra If events A and B are independent, then $P(\text{A and B}) = P(\text{A}) \cdot P(\text{B})$.

EXAMPLE 2 Standardized Test Practice

School Fair Your class is raising money by operating a ball toss game. You estimate that about 1 out of every 25 balls tossed results in a win. What is the probability that someone will win on two tosses in a row?

Ⓐ $\frac{1}{625}$ Ⓑ $\frac{1}{50}$ Ⓒ $\frac{2}{25}$ Ⓓ $\frac{25}{2}$

ELIMINATE CHOICES
The probability of an event must be between 0 and 1. Choice D can be eliminated.

SOLUTION

The tosses are independent events, because the outcome of a toss does not affect the probability of the next toss resulting in a win.

So the probability of each event is $\frac{1}{25}$.

$$P(\text{win and win}) = P(\text{win}) \cdot P(\text{win}) = \frac{1}{25} \cdot \frac{1}{25} = \frac{1}{625}$$

▶ **Answer** The probability of two winning tosses in a row is $\frac{1}{625}$.
The correct answer is A. Ⓐ Ⓑ Ⓒ Ⓓ

✓ **GUIDED PRACTICE** for Examples 1 and 2

In Exercises 1 and 2, tell whether the events are *independent* or *dependent*. *Explain* your reasoning.

1. You toss a coin. Then you roll a number cube.
2. You randomly choose 1 of 10 marbles. Then you randomly choose one of the remaining 9 marbles.
3. You toss a coin twice. Find the probability of getting two heads.

Dependent Events If A and B are dependent events, the probability that B occurs given that A also occurs is not the same as the probability of B. So, you should use P(B given A) instead of P(B) to represent the probability that B occurs given that A also occurs.

KEY CONCEPT *For Your Notebook*

Probability of Dependent Events

Words For two dependent events, the probability that both events occur is the product of the probability of the first event and the probability of the second event given that the first event also occurs.

Algebra If events A and B are dependent, then $P(\text{A and B}) = P(\text{A}) \cdot P(\text{B given A})$.

EXAMPLE 3 Finding Probability of Dependent Events

Bingo You are playing the bingo card shown. The caller has 50 numbers left to call. What is the probability that you will get bingo with the next 2 numbers called?

SOLUTION

You need B7 and N44 for bingo. Find the probability of success when each of the next 2 numbers is drawn. Then multiply.

$P(\text{B7 or N44}) = \frac{2}{50} = \frac{1}{25}$ — There are 50 numbers left to call.

$P(\text{remaining number}) = \frac{1}{49}$ — There are 49 numbers left to call.

$P(\text{both numbers}) = \frac{1}{25} \cdot \frac{1}{49} = \frac{1}{1225}$ — Multiply the probabilities.

▸ **Answer** The probability that you will get bingo when the next 2 numbers are called is $\frac{1}{1225}$, or about 0.0008.

at classzone.com

✓ **GUIDED PRACTICE** for Example 3

4. **What If?** In Example 3, suppose 36 numbers are left to call. Find the probability.

5. **Prizes** You are randomly choosing 2 business cards from a dish with 40 cards, each from a different business, to win prizes. What is the probability you choose the cards for the dry cleaners and the hair salon?

12.8 EXERCISES

HOMEWORK KEY ★ = **STANDARDIZED TEST PRACTICE** Exs. 13, 15, 28, 29, 30, and 39

○ = **HINTS AND HOMEWORK HELP** for Exs. 3, 5, 9, 11, 25 at classzone.com

SKILL PRACTICE

VOCABULARY **Copy and complete the statement.**

1. When the occurrence of an event does not affect the probability of the next event, the events are _?_.

2. Two events are _?_ events if the occurrence of one event affects the probability that the other event will occur.

IDENTIFYING EVENTS **Tell whether the events are *independent* or *dependent*.**

SEE EXAMPLE 1 on p. 694 for Exs. 3–6

3. You randomly choose a marble from a jar. You replace the marble and randomly choose another marble.

4. Your teacher randomly chooses you to give a report. The teacher then randomly chooses Pam from the remaining students.

5. You randomly choose a password from a list of words. Then your friend randomly chooses a password from the remaining words.

6. You randomly draw a card from a deck of cards. You replace the card and then randomly draw another card.

FINDING PROBABILITIES **Events A and B are independent. Events C and D are dependent. Find the missing probability.**

SEE EXAMPLES 2 AND 3 on pp. 695–696 for Exs. 7–14

7. $P(\text{A}) = 0.4$
   $P(\text{B}) = 0.6$
   $P(\text{A and B}) = \underline{\ ?\ }$

8. $P(\text{A}) = 0.9$
   $P(\text{B}) = \underline{\ ?\ }$
   $P(\text{A and B}) = 0.09$

9. $P(\text{A}) = \underline{\ ?\ }$
   $P(\text{B}) = 0.6$
   $P(\text{A and B}) = 0.12$

10. $P(\text{C}) = 0.75$
    $P(\text{D given C}) = 0.5$
    $P(\text{C and D}) = \underline{\ ?\ }$

11. $P(\text{C}) = 0.8$
    $P(\text{D given C}) = \underline{\ ?\ }$
    $P(\text{C and D}) = 0.32$

12. $P(\text{C}) = \underline{\ ?\ }$
    $P(\text{D given C}) = 0.3$
    $P(\text{C and D}) = 0.039$

13. ★ **MULTIPLE CHOICE** You spin the spinner at the right twice. What is the probability of getting blue both times?

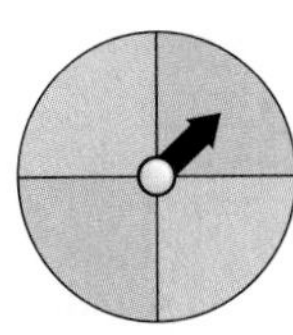

Ⓐ $\frac{1}{16}$ Ⓑ $\frac{1}{8}$ Ⓒ $\frac{1}{4}$ Ⓓ $\frac{1}{2}$

14. **ERROR ANALYSIS** Describe and correct the error made in finding $P(\text{A and B})$.

> ✗ $P(\text{A}) = 0.2$
> $P(\text{B given A}) = 0.25$
> $P(\text{A and B}) = 0.2 + 0.25 = 0.45$

15. ★ **OPEN-ENDED MATH** Create two probability problems, one for a situation involving independent events, and the other for a situation involving dependent events. Then calculate the probabilities. Show your work.

16. CHECKING REASONABLENESS A friend looks at the spinner and says that the probability of the spinner landing on the blue region and then the red region is about $0.5 \cdot 0.25$, or 0.125. Is this a reasonable estimate? *Explain.*

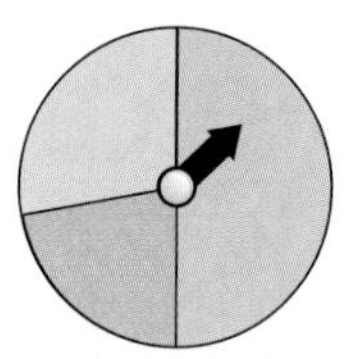

SELECTING LETTERS A bag contains 100 lettered tiles. The number of tiles that show various letters is given in the table. Find the probability of randomly choosing two letters with the given characteristics.

Letter	*Number of Tiles*
A	9
H	2
T	6

17. both A's if you replace the first before choosing the second

18. both A's without replacement

19. a T followed by an H, with replacement

20. a T followed by an H, without replacement

CHALLENGE Refer to the bag of 100 lettered tiles in Exercises 17–20.

21. The probability of choosing a D first and then an A without replacing the D is $\frac{1}{275}$. How many D's are in the bag?

22. The probability of choosing an E first, replacing it, and then choosing a T is $\frac{9}{1250}$. How many E's are in the bag?

PROBLEM SOLVING

In Exercises 23–25, tell whether the events are *independent* or *dependent*. Then find the probability.

SEE EXAMPLES 1, 2, AND 3 on pp. 694–696 for Exs. 23–25

23. BUTTONS You draw a button at random from the jar at the right. Without replacing the first button, you draw another. What is the probability that you draw a red button and then a yellow button? a yellow button and then a blue button?

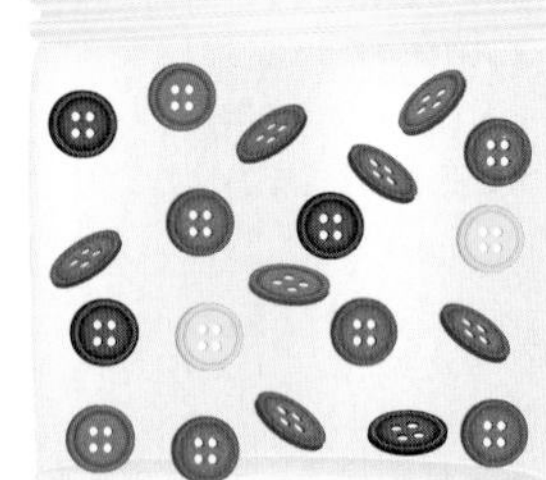

24. BANQUET At a banquet, you can order a main course of a chef's salad, salmon and potatoes, ham and beans, or steak and rice. You can drink water, juice, milk, coffee, or iced tea. All choices are equally likely. What is the probability that a randomly chosen person orders a chef's salad and juice?

25. BAKING You have a basket of rolls: 5 wheat, 6 sourdough, 8 sesame, and 9 cheese. You randomly choose a roll, keep it, and then choose another. What is the probability that you pick a sesame roll and then a cheese roll?

SEE EXAMPLES 2 AND 3 on pp. 695–696 for Exs. 26–28

26. LUCKY PLATE Each day, the person who gets the lucky plate wins a free snack from the school cafeteria. The cafeteria sells 127 lunches on Wednesday and 134 lunches on Thursday. You buy a lunch both days. What is the probability that you win on both days?

27. **ERROR ANALYSIS** A deck of 10 cards is numbered with the integers from 1 to 10. You randomly pick a card, and then another, without replacement. Describe and correct the error made in finding the probability of selecting 2 prime numbers.

$$P(A) = \frac{4}{10}$$
$$P(B \text{ given } A) = \frac{3}{10}$$
$$P(A \text{ and } B) = \frac{4}{10} \cdot \frac{3}{10} = \frac{12}{100} = \frac{3}{25}$$

28. ★ **SHORT RESPONSE** Your teacher is giving away two prizes by random drawing. She puts the class's 25 names into a hat. She draws the first name. Then she draws a second name without replacing the first name.

What is the probability that your name will be chosen first? Does the probability that your name will be chosen second depend on the first outcome? *Explain.*

29. ★ **EXTENDED RESPONSE** You are choosing an outfit at random. You can choose a red, blue, or green shirt as a top and jeans or khakis for pants.
    a. Make a tree diagram to find the number of possible outfits. *Describe* the relationship between the number of possible outfits and the probability of choosing one outfit.
    b. Find P(red shirt), P(jeans), P(red shirt and jeans).
    c. If $P(\text{red shirt and jeans}) = \frac{1}{10}$, how many shirts do you have to choose from if you still have only 2 pairs of pants? *Explain.*

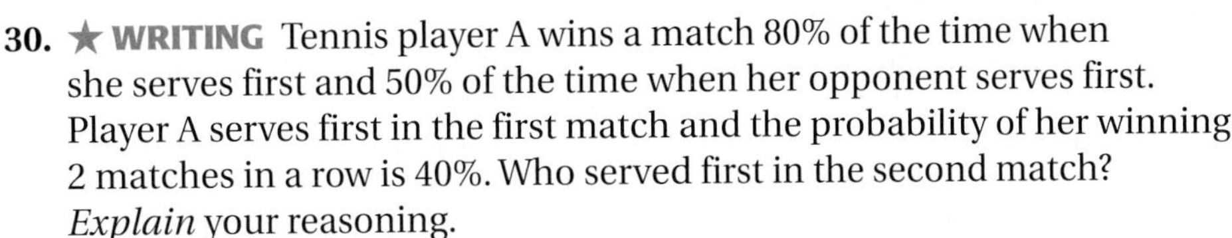

30. ★ **WRITING** Tennis player A wins a match 80% of the time when she serves first and 50% of the time when her opponent serves first. Player A serves first in the first match and the probability of her winning 2 matches in a row is 40%. Who served first in the second match? *Explain* your reasoning.

31. **REASONING** You toss a coin. What is the probability that you get heads 7 times in a row? Suppose you have already tossed heads 6 times in a row. What is the probability that you will get heads on the next toss? *Explain.*

32. **INVESTING** A brochure says, "If you invested money with us 5 years ago, that money grew by an average of 20%." The brochure also says, "Past performance is no guarantee of future results." Which statement leads you to think that investing money today is independent of past events? Which statements suggests the opposite? *Explain.*

33. **CHALLENGE** A town's election for mayor drew 75% of the town's 800 eligible voters. What is the probability that two different randomly selected people both voted in the election?

MIXED REVIEW

Get-Ready

Prepare for Lesson 13.1 in Exs. 34–37

Simplify the expression by combining like terms. *(p. 88)*

34. $a + 3a + 7a$

35. $11x + 2y + 6y + 2x$

36. $4b - a + 5c - 3c$

37. $2m + 5k + m + 2m - 3$

38. The table shows the amount of time in minutes that Cindy ran on the treadmill each day. Make a line graph of the data. *Predict* how long Cindy will run on Saturday. *Explain* your reasoning. *(p. 659)*

Monday	20
Tuesday	25
Wednesday	25
Thursday	35
Friday	41

39. ★ **MULTIPLE CHOICE** Which of the following relations is *not* a function? *(p. 583)*

(A) (2, 3), (4, 3), (6, 7), (9, 2)

(B) (2, 3), (4, 5), (6, 4), (5, 4)

(C) (−1, 8), (0, 11), (1, 8), (5, 4)

(D) (3, 5), (4, 3), (4, 6), (6, 9)

QUIZ *for Lessons 12.4–12.8*

1. **SHOES** You can buy sandals or sneakers in black, brown, tan, or white. Make a tree diagram to show the possible choices for shoes. *(p. 670)*

2. **CAMP** You are scheduling swimming, crafts, canoeing, and softball. How many different schedules of four different activities are possible? *(p. 675)*

3. **HOCKEY** Find the number of ways two players can be chosen from 20 team members. *(p. 675)*

4. **RAIN** The probability that it will rain today is 0.4. What are the odds in favor of rain? What is the probability that it will *not* rain? *(p. 685)*

Find the probability. *(p. 694)*

5. You roll a 5 on a 6-sided number cube. Then you roll another 5.

6. A bag holds 3 red and 5 blue tiles. You randomly draw a red tile, keep it, and then randomly draw a blue tile.

Brain Game

Lucky Numbers

Two balls will be randomly chosen without replacement from the bowl shown.

- Bo wins if the first ball is blue, and the next ball is a 3 or a 4.
- Sherry wins if the first ball is an even number and the next ball is green.
- Eva wins if both balls are red.

Who has the best chance of winning?

Use after Lesson 12.8

Samples

GOAL Identify biased samples and surveys.

KEY VOCABULARY
- **population,** *p. 701*
- **sample,** *p. 701*
- **random sample,** *p. 701*
- **biased sample,** *p. 701*

One way to collect data about a group is by doing a survey. A **population** is the entire group of people or objects that you want information about. When it is difficult to survey an entire population, a **sample**, or a part of the entire group, is surveyed.

The size of a sample affects the reliability of the results. Larger samples are considered to be more reliable than smaller samples. A larger sample size decreases the probability that you will get misleading results due to chance. For example, suppose you are flipping a coin. You will get 7 out of 10 heads more often than 70 out of 100 or 700 out of 1000.

In a **random sample**, each person or object has an equally likely chance of being selected. A non-random sample can result in a **biased sample** that is not representative of the population.

EXAMPLE 1 Identifying Potentially Biased Samples

Costume Dance The student council wants students to help decide on a theme for a costume dance. Students can choose one of the council's three ideas from the options listed at the right.

Which dance theme do you prefer?
Choose one:
☐ movies
☐ famous historical figures
☐ sports and games

Surveying all of the students will take too long, so a sample will be surveyed. Tell whether the survey method could result in a biased sample. *Explain* your reasoning.

a. Survey members of the movie club.

b. Survey students as they enter the school.

c. Survey students on the football team.

SOLUTION

a. This method could result in a biased sample because this group is more likely to favor the movie theme.

b. This method is not likely to result in a biased sample because a wide range of students will be surveyed.

c. This method could result in a biased sample because the football players are more likely to favor sports and games.

Continued on next page

Survey Questions When you create a survey, you need to phrase the questions so that the responses accurately reflect the views of the people surveyed. If not, the survey results may be misleading.

EXAMPLE 2 Identifying Potentially Biased Questions

Tell whether the question could produce biased results. *Explain.*

a. Do you support the unfair policy of requiring students to do a time-consuming community project? YES ☐ NO ☐

b. Do you like our new apple-nut yogurt flavor, now on sale in stores everywhere? YES ☐ NO ☐

SOLUTION

a. This question states that the policy is unfair and that the project is time-consuming. It encourages a response of *no*. So, the question could lead to biased results.

b. The question assumes that the person responding has tried the new yogurt flavor. Those who have not tried the new flavor may not give an accurate opinion. So, the question could lead to biased results.

EXERCISES

Stadiums **A city survey plans to ask residents whether they favor using public funds to pay for a new baseball stadium. Tell whether the method could result in a biased sample. *Explain.***

1. Ask people that call in to a sports radio talk show.
2. Ask every tenth person listed in the phone book.
3. Ask every fifth person who enters the sporting goods store in town.
4. **Menus** A restaurant wants to know what kinds of food to add to its menu to attract new customers. *Describe* a sampling method that the restaurant can use that is not likely to result in a biased sample.

Tell whether the survey question could produce biased results. *Explain* your reasoning.

5. Would you rather relax at home while reading a book, or go to a noisy, crowded mall?
6. Allowing messy, dangerous dogs into the park will cause safety and health problems. Will you vote to allow dogs into the park?
7. How often do you buy lunch in the school cafeteria?
8. Do you agree with this store's policy for returning purchases?

MIXED REVIEW *of Problem Solving*

Lessons 12.4–12.8

1. **MULTI-STEP PROBLEM** The probability that a person is a boy is 0.5. You have 4 cousins.
   a. Make a tree diagram to list all the possible outcomes for the 4 cousins.
   b. What is the probability that all 4 cousins are boys? *Explain* how you found your answer.
   c. What is the probability that all 4 cousins are *not* girls? *Describe* two ways to find the answer.

2. **SHORT RESPONSE** A group of 10 people travel in 2 cars with 5 people in each car. How many different groups can go in one car? How many ways can the group split into 2 cars? *Explain* your answers.

3. **GRIDDED ANSWER** The first team to win 3 out of 5 possible games will be the winner of a baseball tournament. In how many ways can a team win 3 out of 5 games?

4. **SHORT RESPONSE** The weather forecast says that there is a 40% probability of rain. Find the probability that it will *not* rain. Find the odds in favor of it *not* raining. *Explain* your reasoning.

5. **SHORT RESPONSE** What is the probability that when you roll a number cube 5 times, you roll a three 5 times in a row? If you have already rolled a three 4 times in a row, what is the probability that you will roll a three on the next roll? *Explain.*

6. **GRIDDED ANSWER** A CD case holds 30 CDs. How many groups of 3 CDs can you randomly select from the case?

7. **SHORT RESPONSE** A certain town can use the digits 0, 1, 2, 6, 7, and 8 for its telephone prefixes. How many three digit telephone prefixes are possible for this town if each digit can be used only once in a prefix and the first digit cannot be a 1 or a 0? *Explain* how you found your answer.

8. **EXTENDED RESPONSE** Zach goes to a restaurant for a sandwich. Each sandwich comes with one meat, one cheese, and one dressing.

Meat	*Cheese*	*Dressing*
Ham	American	Italian
Roast Beef	Mozzarella	Mayonnaise
Turkey	Provolone	Oil and Vinegar
	Swiss	Vinaigrette

   a. How many different kinds of sandwiches are possible?
   b. How many different kinds of sandwiches are possible if salami is added as a meat?
   c. How many different kinds of sandwiches are possible if mustard is added to the dressing choices instead of adding salami as a meat choice?
   d. Compare the results of parts (b) and (c). Do they produce the same number of possible sandwiches? *Explain.*

9. **GRIDDED ANSWER** There are 14 new DVD releases at the video store this week. You have a coupon to get 3 new releases for free. How many different groups of 3 DVDs can you get with the coupon?

12 CHAPTER REVIEW

@HomeTutor
classzone.com
Vocabulary Practice

REVIEW KEY VOCABULARY

- stem-and-leaf plot, *p. 649*
- box-and-whisker plot, *p. 654*
- lower quartile, *p. 654*
- upper quartile, *p. 654*
- lower extreme, *p. 654*
- upper extreme, *p. 654*
- circle graph, *p. 659*
- line graph, *p. 660*
- tree diagram, *p. 670*
- permutation, *p. 675*
- factorial, *p. 675*
- combination, *p. 680*
- complementary events, *p. 685*
- unfavorable outcome, *p. 686*
- odds, *p. 686*
- compound events, *p. 694*
- independent events, *p. 694*
- dependent events, *p. 694*

VOCABULARY EXERCISES

In Exercises 1–6, match the description with the correct vocabulary item from the list above.

1. An arrangement in which order is important
2. An arrangement in which order is *not* important
3. A graph that displays data in distinct categories
4. A graph used to display changes in a quantity over time
5. A plot used to order a data set
6. A plot that divides a data set into 4 quarters

REVIEW EXAMPLES AND EXERCISES

12.1 Stem-and-Leaf Plots

pp. 649–653

EXAMPLE

Make a stem-and-leaf plot of the data below:

24, 29, 35, 32, 22, 20, 43, 27, 41, 31, 26

STEP 1 **Record** the data set in an unordered stem-and-leaf plot.

Stem	Leaves
2	4 9 2 0 7 6
3	5 2 1
4	3 1

STEP 2 **Order** the leaves. Include a key.

Stem	Leaves
2	0 2 4 6 7 9
3	1 2 5
4	1 3

Key: 4 | 1 = 41

EXERCISES

Make an ordered stem-and-leaf plot of the data. Identify the interval that includes the most data values.

SEE EXAMPLES 1 AND 2 on pp. 649–650 for Exs. 7–10

7. 20, 25, 36, 16, 29, 32, 27, 42, 28, 31, 15, 19, 21, 37, 22

8. 11.2, 7.5, 15.1, 15.7, 15.0, 6.7, 11.3, 8.4, 7.3, 10.6, 9.2, 15.6, 11.9, 15.8

9. 81, 100, 94, 97, 86, 100, 97, 96, 84, 99

10. **Wind Speed** Make an ordered stem-and-leaf plot of the wind speed data, given in miles per hour: 9, 15, 8, 19, 11, 18, 11, 24, 7, 14, 21, 2, 7, 15, 12.

12.2 Box-and-Whisker Plots

pp. 654–658

EXAMPLE

Make a box-and-whisker plot of the data below:

70, 69, 75, 65, 64, 85, 61, 66, 73, 61, 84.

STEP 1 **Order** the data to find the median, quartiles, and extremes.

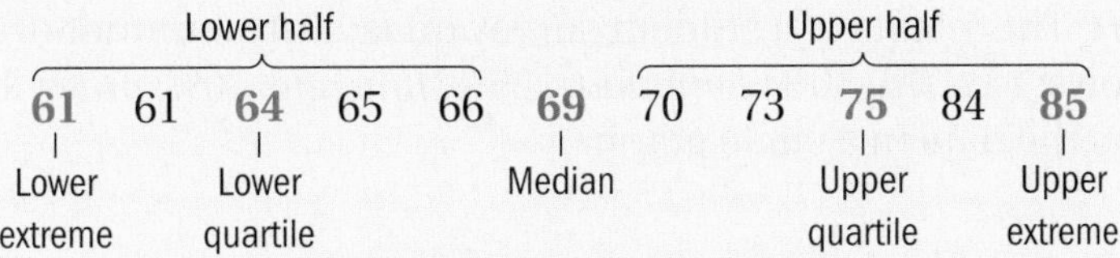

STEP 2 **Plot** these values below a number line.

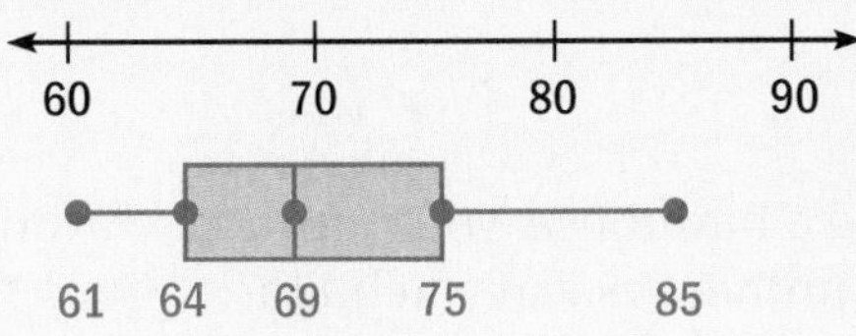

EXERCISES

Make a box-and-whisker plot of the data.

SEE EXAMPLES 1 AND 2 on pp. 654–655 for Exs. 11–13

11. 5, 13, 9, 31, 25, 21, 25, 18, 23, 14, 32, 3, 22, 11, 16

12. 62, 41, 65, 76, 68, 83, 81, 80, 70, 85, 79, 42, 61, 74, 68

13. **Chess** The prices of several chess sets are \$15, \$20, \$38, \$95, \$60, \$45, \$40, \$35, and \$50. Make a box-and-whisker plot of the data. *Describe* how the data are distributed.

12.3 Using Data Displays
pp. 659–664

EXAMPLE

Election A survey indicates 35% of students do not know who they will vote for in a school election, 38% will vote for Wong, and 27% will vote for Nelson. Display the data in a circle graph.

STEP 1 **Find** the number of degrees to use to represent each response as a section in a circle graph.

Not sure

$0.35(360°) = 126°$

Wong

$0.38(360°) \approx 137°$

Nelson

$0.27(360°) \approx 97°$

STEP 2 **Draw** a circle and use the angle measures to draw the sections.

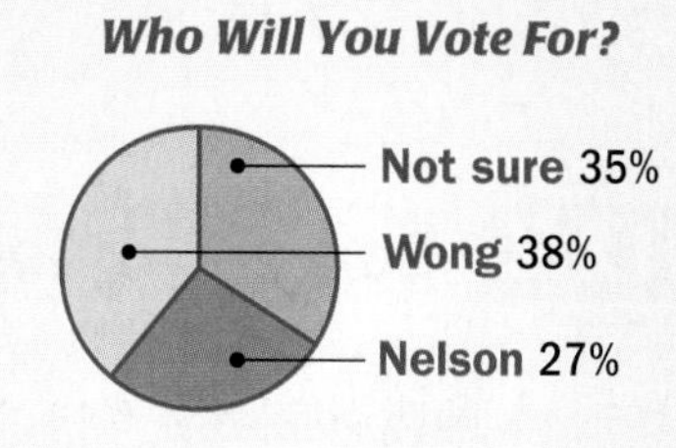

EXERCISE

SEE EXAMPLE 1 on p. 659 for Ex. 14

14. **Dessert** The results of a student survey on favorite summer drinks were as follows: *iced tea*, 50%; *lemonade*, 25%; *limeade*, 10%; *other*, 15%. Display the data in a circle graph.

12.4 Counting Methods
pp. 670–674

EXAMPLE

Construction To build a birdhouse, you can choose from 3 designs and 6 colors. How many different birdhouses can you build?

$3 \cdot 6 = 18$ **Counting principle**

designs ↗ colors ↖

▸ **Answer** You can build 18 different birdhouses.

EXERCISE

SEE EXAMPLES 1 AND 2 on pp. 670–671 for Ex. 15

15. **Clothing** You need to choose one of 4 hats and one of 3 shirts to wear. Make a tree diagram to find the number of different hat-shirt pairs. Use the counting principle to check your answer.

12.5 Permutations

pp. 675–679

EXAMPLE

Swimming At a swim meet, 10 swimmers are in an event. In how many ways can first, second, third, and fourth place medals be awarded?

$${}_{10}P_4 = \frac{10!}{(10-4)!} = \frac{10!}{6!}$$ **Use permutation formula.**

$$= \frac{10 \cdot 9 \cdot 8 \cdot 7 \cdot \cancel{6} \cdot \cancel{5} \cdot \cancel{4} \cdot \cancel{3} \cdot \cancel{2} \cdot \cancel{1}}{\cancel{6} \cdot \cancel{5} \cdot \cancel{4} \cdot \cancel{3} \cdot \cancel{2} \cdot \cancel{1}}$$ **Divide out common factors.**

$$= 5040$$ **Multiply.**

▸ **Answer** There are 5040 ways to award the medals.

EXERCISES

Find the number of permutations.

SEE EXAMPLE 3 on p. 676 for Exs. 16–20

16. ${}_8P_4$ **17.** ${}_{10}P_3$ **18.** ${}_{12}P_1$ **19.** ${}_{13}P_5$

20. The Griffiths have six children. In how many ways can they line up their children for a picture?

12.6 Combinations

pp. 680–684

EXAMPLE

Evaluate ${}_7C_5$.

$${}_7C_5 = \frac{{}_7P_5}{5!}$$ **Combination formula**

$$= \frac{7 \cdot 6 \cdot 5 \cdot 4 \cdot 3}{5!}$$ $${}_7P_5 = \frac{7!}{(7-5)!} = 7 \cdot 6 \cdot 5 \cdot 4 \cdot 3$$

$$= \frac{7 \cdot \overset{3}{\cancel{6}} \cdot \cancel{5} \cdot \cancel{4} \cdot \cancel{3}}{\cancel{5} \cdot \cancel{4} \cdot \cancel{3} \cdot \cancel{2} \cdot 1}$$ **Expand 5! Divide out common factors.**

$$= 21$$ **Simplify.**

EXERCISES

Find the number of combinations.

SEE EXAMPLES 2 AND 3 on pp. 681–682 for Exs. 21–25

21. ${}_9C_2$ **22.** ${}_6C_1$ **23.** ${}_9C_9$ **24.** ${}_{12}C_8$

25. MP3 Players Your MP3 player holds 15 songs and you have 30 songs in your collection. Can the number of possible groups of 15 songs be counted using a *permutation* or a *combination*? Find the number of groups possible.

12.7 Probability and Odds

pp. 685–689

EXAMPLE

Shopping Spree A customer is chosen at random from a group of 10 males and 15 females to win a shopping spree. What is the probability that the winner is *not* male? What are the odds in favor?

$$P(\text{not male}) = 1 - P(\text{male}) = 1 - \frac{10}{25} = \frac{15}{25}, \text{ or } \frac{3}{5}$$

$$\text{Odds} = \frac{\text{Number of favorable outcomes}}{\text{Number of unfavorable outcomes}} = \frac{\text{Number that are not male}}{\text{Number that are male}} = \frac{15}{10} = \frac{3}{2}$$

▶ **Answer** The probability that the winner is not male is $\frac{3}{5}$. The odds in favor of not choosing a male are 3 to 2.

EXERCISE

SEE EXAMPLES 1, 2, AND 3 on pp. 685–687 for Ex. 26

26. **Contest** The probability that you will win a contest is 76%. What is the probability that you will lose the contest? What are the odds in favor of losing the contest?

12.8 Independent and Dependent Events

pp. 694–699

EXAMPLE

Lettered Tiles Tiles with each of the 11 letters in PROBABILITY are in a bag. You randomly draw a tile, do not replace it, and then randomly draw a second tile. What is the probability that both tiles are I's?

$$P(\text{I and I}) = P(\text{I}) \cdot P(\text{I given I}) = \frac{2}{11} \cdot \frac{1}{10} = \frac{1}{55}$$

EXERCISES

SEE EXAMPLES 2 AND 3 on pp. 695–696 for Exs. 27–28

27. If you replace the first tile in the example above, what is the probability that the first tile is B and the second is L?

28. **Weather** A weather forecaster says there is a 60% chance that it will snow on Wednesday and a 25% chance that it will snow on Thursday. Find the probability that it will snow on both Wednesday and Thursday.

12 CHAPTER TEST

@HomeTutor
classzone.com
Chapter Test Practice

Make a stem-and-leaf plot of the data. Identify the interval that includes the most values. Then make a box-and-whisker plot.

1. 46 kg, 70 kg, 21 kg, 136 kg, 55 kg, 60 kg, 72 kg, 104 kg, 52 kg, 96 kg, 43 kg, 59 kg, 88 kg, 56 kg

2. 12.1 in., 13.5 in., 12.8 in., 10 in., 7 in., 11.2 in., 12.9 in., 11.1 in., 12 in., 13.7 in., 8.2 in., 10.1 in., 13.3 in., 12.5 in., 11.7 in.

Use the circle graph. It shows student replies to *Which animal career would you most enjoy?*

3. What is the probability that a randomly chosen student replied *rodeo star*?

4. What is the probability that a randomly chosen student did *not* reply *veterinarian*?

5. What are the odds in favor of a randomly chosen student replying *zookeeper*?

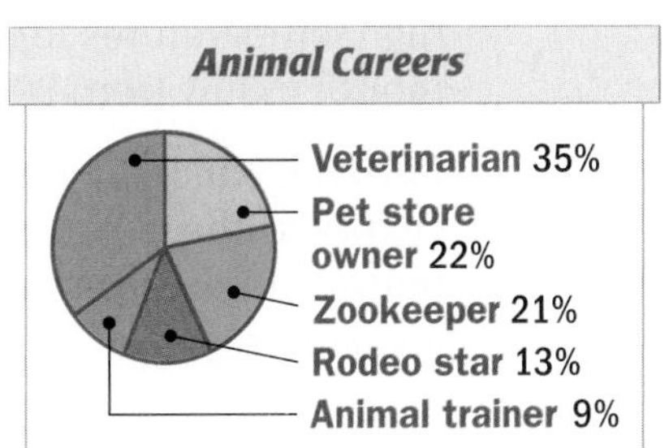

In Exercises 6 and 7, tell whether the events are *independent* or *dependent*. Then find the probability.

6. You roll a 6 on a number cube. Then you roll a 2.

7. You have 8 blue marbles and 12 red marbles in a bag. You randomly pick a blue marble on the first draw. Then you randomly pick another blue marble without replacing the first one.

8. **ACADEMY AWARDS** The lengths, in minutes, of the Best Picture Academy Award winning movies for the years 1990–1999 are 99, 118, 122, 131, 142, 160, 177, 183, 194, and 197. Make a box-and-whisker plot of the data. *Describe* how the data are distributed.

9. **TEMPERATURE** The record low temperatures in Miami, Florida, are given in the table. Display the data in an appropriate graph. *Justify* your choice of display.

Month	Ja	Fe	Mr	Ap	Ma	Jn	Jl	Au	Se	Oc	No	De
Temp (°F)	30	32	32	46	53	60	69	68	68	51	39	30

10. **MOVIES** You and four friends are going to a movie. In how many different orders can you pick your friends up? List all the possible orders.

11. **SCHOOL DANCE** You are making a banner for a school dance and have a choice of 8 colors. You want to use 4 different colors. How many different combinations are possible?

CONTEXT-BASED MULTIPLE CHOICE QUESTIONS

Some of the information you need to solve a context-based multiple choice question may appear in a table, a diagram, or a graph.

PROBLEM 1

The line graph shows a city's high temperatures for the month of July from 2000 to 2005.

Between which two consecutive years was the difference in high temperatures the greatest in absolute value?

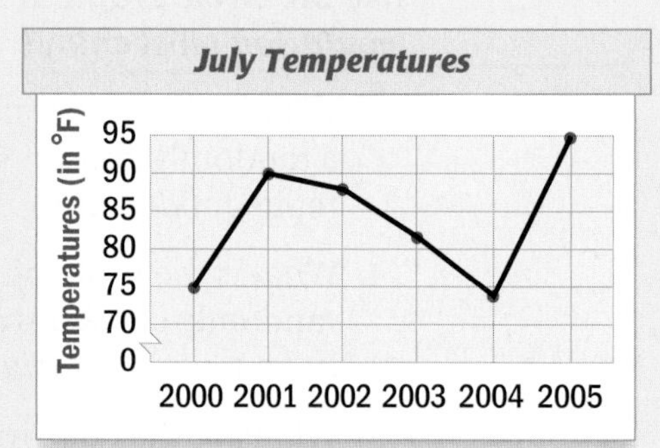

Ⓐ 2000–2001 Ⓑ 2002–2003 Ⓒ 2003–2004 Ⓓ 2004–2005

Plan

STEP 1 Read the problem carefully and make a plan.

INTERPRET THE GRAPH First determine the high temperature for each year. Then calculate the differences between the consecutive years. Find the difference with the greatest absolute value by comparing.

Solution

STEP 2 Determine the high temperature for each year.

The high temperatures for each year are as follows:

2000: 75°F	2001: 90°F	2002: 88°F
2003: 82°F	2004: 74°F	2005: 95°F

STEP 3 Find and compare the differences between years.

The differences between years are as follows:

2000–2001	$\lvert 90 - 75 \rvert = \lvert 15 \rvert = 15$
2001–2002	$\lvert 88 - 90 \rvert = \lvert -2 \rvert = 2$
2002–2003	$\lvert 82 - 88 \rvert = \lvert -6 \rvert = 6$
2003–2004	$\lvert 74 - 82 \rvert = \lvert -8 \rvert = 8$
2004–2005	$\lvert 95 - 74 \rvert = \lvert 21 \rvert = 21$

The difference with the greatest absolute value is 21°F, which occurs between 2004 and 2005. The correct answer is D. Ⓐ Ⓑ Ⓒ Ⓓ

PROBLEM 2

You randomly choose a mint from the jar shown. You eat the first mint that you choose and then choose another. What is the probability that you choose a green mint and then a yellow mint?

Ⓐ $\frac{1}{12}$ Ⓑ $\frac{2}{23}$

Ⓒ $\frac{7}{12}$ Ⓓ $\frac{55}{92}$

Plan

STEP 1 Read the problem carefully. Decide how you can use the given information to solve the problem.

INTERPRET THE DIAGRAM Count the number of green, yellow, and red mints in the jar. Then add to find the total number of mints in the jar.

For two dependent events, the probability that both events occur is the product of the probability of the first event and the probability of the second event given that the first event also occurs.

$P(\text{A and B}) = P(\text{A}) \cdot P(\text{B given A})$

Solution

STEP 2 Count the mints and find the probability of each event.

There are 6 green mints, 8 yellow mints, and 10 red mints in the jar. So, there are a total of 24 mints.

The probability of choosing a green mint is $\frac{6}{24}$, or $\frac{1}{4}$. The probability of choosing a yellow mint without replacing the green mint is $\frac{8}{23}$.

STEP 3 Find the probability of both events occurring.

The probability of both events occurring is $\frac{1}{4} \cdot \frac{8}{23} = \frac{2}{23}$.

The correct answer is B. Ⓐ Ⓑ Ⓒ Ⓓ

PRACTICE

1. In Problem 1, what is the median of the temperatures from 2000 to 2005?

   Ⓐ 21°F Ⓑ 84°F Ⓒ 85°F Ⓓ 95°F

2. In Problem 2, suppose that the first mint is returned to the jar before you choose the second mint. What is the probability of choosing a green mint and then a red mint?

   Ⓐ $\frac{5}{48}$ Ⓑ $\frac{5}{46}$ Ⓒ $\frac{2}{3}$ Ⓓ $\frac{189}{276}$

12 ★ Standardized TEST PRACTICE

MULTIPLE CHOICE

1. What does the bullet at 56 represent on the box-and-whisker plot?

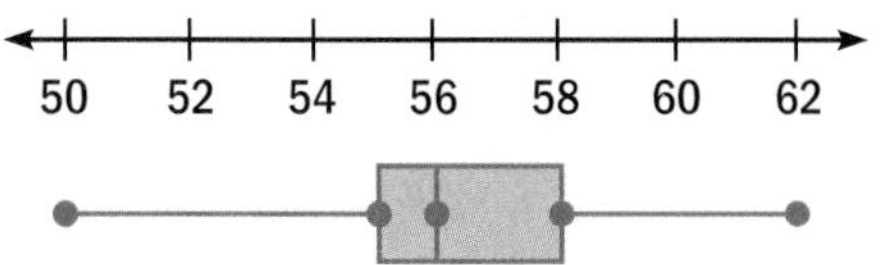

Ⓐ upper quartile Ⓑ median
Ⓒ lower quartile Ⓓ lower extreme

2. Which would be the most appropriate display for the data in the table below?

Sport	*Percent of students*
Football	17%
Baseball	28%
Basketball	39%
Soccer	8%

Ⓐ bar graph Ⓑ line graph
Ⓒ circle graph Ⓓ histogram

3. Your locker's unlocking code is made up of 3 numbers from 0 to 15. Each number must be different. How many codes are possible?

Ⓐ 45 Ⓑ 2730
Ⓒ 3360 Ⓓ 4096

4. You have 3 pairs of shoes, 6 pairs of pants, 4 shirts, and 3 belts. How many different combinations of shoes, pants, shirts, and belts can you make?

Ⓐ 16 Ⓑ 204
Ⓒ 216 Ⓓ 313

5. You roll a number cube once. What are the odds in favor of rolling a four?

Ⓐ $\frac{1}{6}$ Ⓑ $\frac{1}{5}$
Ⓒ $\frac{1}{4}$ Ⓓ $\frac{1}{3}$

6. The line graph shows the average number of geese in one area over seven months. What is the range of the data?

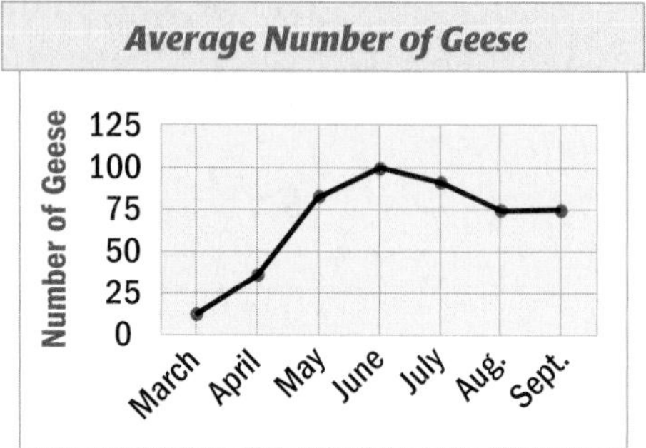

Ⓐ About 25 Ⓑ About 45
Ⓒ About 60 Ⓓ About 85

7. A bag holds 16 red balls and 24 white balls. You draw a ball at random, replace it, and draw a second ball. What is the probability of drawing a red ball and then a white ball?

Ⓐ $\frac{1}{384}$ Ⓑ $\frac{1}{4}$
Ⓒ $\frac{1}{6}$ Ⓓ $\frac{6}{25}$

Use the box-and-whisker plot below for Exercises 8 and 9. It displays data on prices (in dollars) for several stereo systems.

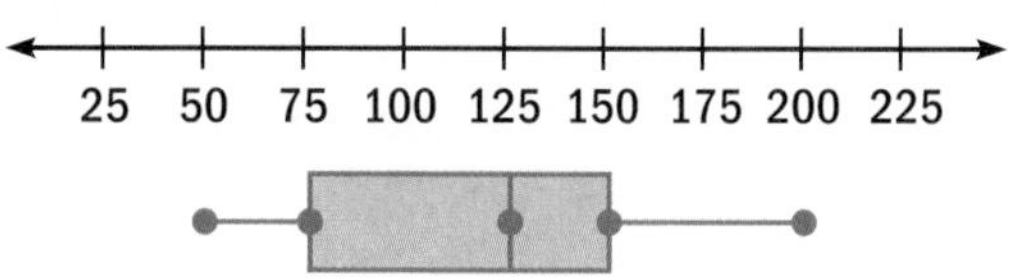

8. What is the least price for a stereo system?

Ⓐ \$25 Ⓑ \$50
Ⓒ \$75 Ⓓ \$125

9. What is the median price of the stereo systems?

Ⓐ \$75 Ⓑ \$100
Ⓒ \$125 Ⓓ \$150

GRIDDED ANSWER

10. Four cyclists are racing. Trophies are awarded to the people for first place and second place. In how many different ways can the trophies be awarded?

11. There are 14 small pepperoni pizzas and 12 small cheese pizzas in a freezer. Joey chooses a pizza at random. What is the probability that he will *not* choose a cheese pizza? Write your answer as a fraction.

12. A bag contains the 11 letters of the word MISSISSIPPI. You draw one letter at random, do not replace it, and then draw a second letter. What is the probability of drawing the letter I twice? Write your answer as a fraction.

13. A restaurant has 8 flavors of frozen yogurt. You would like a dish with 3 scoops of different flavors. How many different dishes can you choose?

SHORT RESPONSE

14. You roll two number cubes at the same time.

a. What is the probability that the sum of the numbers showing on the two cubes is less than or equal to 5? *Explain* how you found your answer.

b. What is the probability that the sum is greater than 5? *Explain* how you found your answer.

15. The players of a baseball team hit the following numbers of home runs during one season: 6, 17, 12, 11, 6, 21, 5, 12, 9, 14, 24, 4, 25, 14, 18.

a. Make a box-and-whisker plot of the data.

b. *Describe* what the plot shows.

EXTENDED RESPONSE

16. The double stem-and-leaf plot shows the heights of 15 football players and 15 basketball players.

Heights of football players (in.)		Heights of basketball players (in.)
9	6	8
3 3 2 2 1 1 0	7	3 5 6 6 6 7 8 9
8 7 6 4 1 0 0	8	4 5 6 6 7 7

Key: 0 | 7 | 3 represents 70 and 73

a. What is the height of the tallest football player?

b. How many basketball players are over 82 inches tall?

c. What is the median height of the football players? The basketball players?

d. In general, are the football players or the basketball players taller? *Explain* how you used the data display to make your conclusion.

13 Polynomials and Functions

Before

In previous chapters you've . . .

- Simplified expressions by combining like terms
- Graphed linear functions

Now

In Chapter 13 you'll study . . .

- 13.1 Polynomials
- 13.2 Adding polynomials
- 13.3 Monomials and powers
- 13.4 Multiplying binomials
- 13.5 Non-linear functions

Why?

So you can solve real-world problems about . . .

- treehouses, p. 723
- baseball, p. 737
- stage design, p. 737
- juggling, p. 739

at classzone.com

- Polynomials, p. 719
- Adding and Subtracting Polynomials, p. 722
- Multiplying Binomials, p. 733

Get-Ready Games

Review Prerequisite Skills by playing *Piñata Punch* and *Unmasking Expressions.*

PIÑATA PUNCH

$(5-11)^3 \cdot 2 \cdot (-6)^{-2}$

$\dfrac{4^7}{(9-5)^3}$

$3^{-3} \cdot 3^8 + 5$

$2^5 \cdot 7 \cdot 2^{-1}$

$\dfrac{(7+1)^6}{8^4}$

18, 12, 250, 112, 8, -64

Skill Focus: Using properties of exponents

To break open the piñata on your turn, you need to pick the right stick.

- Evaluate the expression under each stick.
- A stick breaks the piñata if it has the same value as one of the spots.
- Which stick breaks the piñata? Which spot should you hit?

Unmasking Expressions

$x - 4x + 3 + 9x$

$-7x + 8 - 2(3x + 4)$

$5(x - 6) + 10x - 3$

$8x - 3 - 4(2x + 3)$

$4 - (3x - 1) + x$

$17 - 4x - 13 + 2x$

John	Maria	Sam	Carol	Vincent	Sophie
$6x + 3$	$-2x + 4$	$-13x$	-15	$-2x + 5$	$15x - 33$

Skill Focus: Combining like terms

Find who is behind each of the masks.

- Match the expression under the mask with the correct simplified expression below a name.

Stop and Think

1. **WRITING** ***Explain*** **the steps for simplifying the expression that is given under the mask worn by Sam in** ***Unmasking Expressions.***
2. **CRITICAL THINKING** **Write another expression whose value would allow you to break the piñata in** ***Piñata Punch.***

13 Getting Ready

Review Prerequisite Skills

REVIEW WORDS

- **power,** *p. 19*
- **exponent,** *p. 19*
- **like terms,** *p. 89*
- **terms,** *p. 89*
- **coefficient,** *p. 89*
- **monomial,** *p. 178*
- **function,** *p. 583*

VOCABULARY CHECK

Copy and complete using a review word from the list at the left.

1. In the monomial $2x^3$, the 2 is the _?_ and the 3 is the _?_.
2. A relation that assigns exactly one output value to each input value is a(n) _?_.
3. A number, a variable, or a product of a number and one or more variables is a(n) _?_.

SKILL CHECK

Simplify the expression. ***(p. 88)***

4. $6x - 4 + 4x - 3$
5. $-5(2x + 3) - 4x$
6. $7(3x - 5) - (-x)$
7. $-2x - (-5x)$
8. $-2(-4x - 8)$
9. $-3(3x) + 18x$

Simplify. Write the expression using only positive exponents. ***(p. 208)***

10. $\frac{y^4}{y^6}$
11. $\frac{5^{37}}{5^{35}}$
12. $x^4 \cdot x^5$

List four solutions of the equation. ***(p. 593)***

13. $y = 3x - 5$
14. $y = -2x + 1$
15. $y = \frac{1}{2}x$

@HomeTutor Prerequisite skills practice at classzone.com

Notetaking Skills Summarizing Material

A summary of the property of exponents is shown at the right. In Chapter 13 you will apply the strategy of summarizing material to Example 1 on p. 734.

In your notebook, summarize the main ideas from each lesson. This will help you to see how key ideas are related.

Exponent Rules

Product of Powers

$x^2 \cdot x^3 = x^{2+3} = x^5$

Quotient of Powers ($x \neq 0$)

$\frac{x^5}{x^2} = x^{5-2} = x^3$

Zero Exponent ($x \neq 0$)

$x^0 = 1$

Negative Exponent ($x \neq 0$)

$x^{-4} = \frac{1}{x^4}$

13.1 Polynomials

Before You simplified expressions by combining like terms.
Now You will simplify polynomials by combining like terms.
Why? So you can apply polynomials, as with finding heights in Example 3.

KEY VOCABULARY
- **monomial,** *p. 178*
- **polynomial,** *p. 717*
- **binomial,** *p. 717*
- **trinomial,** *p. 717*
- **standard form,** *p. 717*

In Lesson 4.1 you were introduced to monomials. A **polynomial** is a monomial or a sum of monomials. Each monomial in a polynomial is called a *term*. Polynomials are classified by the number of their terms when they are in simplified form. If a polynomial has more than three terms, it is simply called a polynomial.

Monomial (1 term)	**Binomial** (2 terms)	**Trinomial** (3 terms)
$-2x$	$3x - 2$	$-2a^2 + 3a + 1$
4	$-s^4 + 6s^3$	$3 + 5r - 7r^2$

A polynomial in one variable is written in **standard form** if the exponents of the variable decrease from left to right.

Standard Form	**Not Standard Form**
$3x^3 - 2x^2 + 4$	$3 + 5y$
$-2m^6 + 5m^3 - m$	$7t^4 - t^7 - 2t^2 + 3t$

EXAMPLE 1 Writing Polynomials in Standard Form

Write the polynomial in standard form. Classify the polynomial.

a. $x - 9 + 5x^2 = x + (-9) + 5x^2$ Write subtraction as addition.

$= 5x^2 + x + (-9)$ Order terms with decreasing exponents.

Answer The polynomial $5x^2 + x - 9$ has 3 terms, so it is a trinomial.

b. $2x - 3x^3 = 2x + (-3x^3)$ Write subtraction as addition.

$= -3x^3 + 2x$ Order terms with decreasing exponents.

Answer The polynomial $-3x^3 + 2x$ has 2 terms, so it is a binomial.

AVOID ERRORS
If you do not see an exponent with a variable, then the exponent of the variable is 1.
$2x = 2x^1$

GUIDED PRACTICE for Example 1

Write the polynomial in standard form and classify it.

1. $4 + b^2 - 8b$ **2.** $11 + 2n^4 - 7n + 5n^2$ **3.** $-5 + 3x^2$

Simplifying Polynomials Remember that *like terms* have the same variables raised to the same powers. To simplify a polynomial, combine like terms by adding their coefficients.

EXAMPLE 2 Simplifying Polynomials

Simplify the polynomial and write it in standard form.

a. $3x^2 - 2x + 4x^2 - 3$

$= 3x^2 + 4x^2 - 2x - 3$ — **Group like terms.**

$= 7x^2 - 2x - 3$ — **Simplify.**

b. $x^2 + 2 + 4(x^2 - 2x)$

$= x^2 + 2 + 4(x^2) - 4(2x)$ — **Distributive property**

$= x^2 + 2 + 4x^2 - 8x$ — **Multiply.**

$= x^2 + 4x^2 + 2 - 8x$ — **Group like terms.**

$= 5x^2 + 2 - 8x$ — **Simplify.**

$= 5x^2 - 8x + 2$ — **Write in standard form.**

REVIEW LIKE TERMS
For help with like terms, see p. 88. Remember that $x^2 = 1x^2$.

EXAMPLE 3 Evaluating a Polynomial Expression

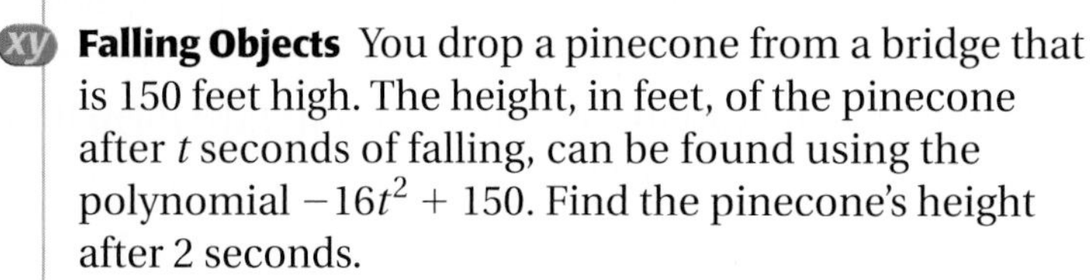

Falling Objects You drop a pinecone from a bridge that is 150 feet high. The height, in feet, of the pinecone after t seconds of falling, can be found using the polynomial $-16t^2 + 150$. Find the pinecone's height after 2 seconds.

SOLUTION

$-16t^2 + 150 = -16(2)^2 + 150$ — **Substitute 2 for *t*.**

$= -16(4) + 150$ — **Evaluate the power.**

$= -64 + 150$ — **Multiply.**

$= 86$ — **Add.**

▶ **Answer** The pinecone's height after 2 seconds is 86 feet.

✓ GUIDED PRACTICE for Examples 2 and 3

Simplify the polynomial and write it in standard form.

4. $7p + 5p^2 - 2 - 3p^2$

5. $10s^4 - 3s + s^4 - 1$

6. $2(a^2 + 3a - 1) + 2a^2$

7. $8x + 3(2x^2 - x + 1)$

8. $6d^3 - 4d - 4d^3 - 6d$

9. $-5x^2 + 7 + 2(-6 + 7x^2)$

Find the height of the pinecone in Example 3 after it falls for the given number of seconds.

10. 0.5 sec **11.** 1 sec **12.** 1.5 sec **13.** 3 sec

13.1 EXERCISES

HOMEWORK KEY
★ = STANDARDIZED TEST PRACTICE
Exs. 22, 36, 37, 41, and 49
○ = HINTS AND HOMEWORK HELP
for Exs. 7, 9, 13, 17, 33 at classzone.com

SKILL PRACTICE

VOCABULARY **Classify the polynomial.**

1. $x^2 + 3x - 7$
2. $y - 5$
3. $8s^2t$
4. $2a^2 + 9a^3 + a$

CLASSIFYING **Write the polynomial in standard form and classify it.**

SEE EXAMPLE 1 on p. 717 for Exs. 5–12

5. $7 + 3m$
6. $8 - n + 2n^2$
7. $5n - 1 - n^2$
8. $4b - 4 + 6b^3$
9. $2 - 5y + y^2$
10. $z^3 + 4z^2 + 7z^7$
11. $-13x^3 + 4x^{10}$
12. $3 - r^4 + r + 2r^3$

SIMPLIFYING **Simplify the polynomial and write it in standard form.**

SEE EXAMPLE 2 on p. 718 for Exs. 13–22

13. $2c^2 - c^2 + 5c$
14. $4q^3 - 7q^5 + 3q - q^3$
15. $g^3 - 10 + 2g^2 - 5g^3$
16. $1 + 12m^2 - 5m + 6m - 7$
17. $3x^2 + 5(x^2 - 3x + 6)$
18. $-6(2y^3 - 4y^2 + 1) + 10y^2$
19. $-4(t - 3t^2 + 8 - 4t) + 6t^2 - 5$
20. $-3(-s^4 + 2s - 6 - s) - 8s + s^4$
21. **ERROR ANALYSIS** Describe and correct the error made in simplifying the polynomial.

Animated Math at classzone.com

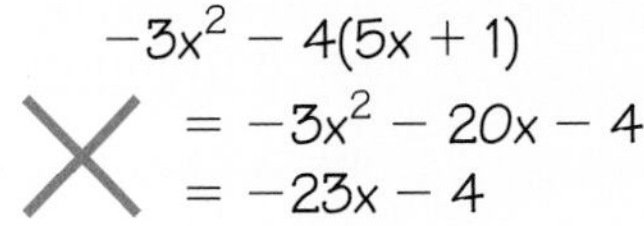

22. ★ **MULTIPLE CHOICE** Simplify the polynomial $5(x^2 - 2x - 3) - 9x^2$.

(A) $4x^2 + 10x - 15$
(B) $-4x^2 + 10x - 15$
(C) $-4x^2 - 15x - 10x$
(D) $-4x^2 - 10x - 15$

SIMPLIFYING POLYNOMIALS **Simplify the polynomial.**

23. $5a - 4(3b + 6) + 4b$
24. $-z^2 + 3z - 2(4y - 5z)$
25. $-3ab^2 + 2ab + 5a^2b^2 - 3ab^2 + 4ab$
26. $3xy + 2xy^2 - 5x^2y^2 + 3x^2y - 4xy - 7xy^2$
27. **EXAMPLES AND NONEXAMPLES** Give examples of three polynomials that are in standard form and three that are *not* in standard form.

GEOMETRY **Write an expression for the perimeter in standard form.**

28.
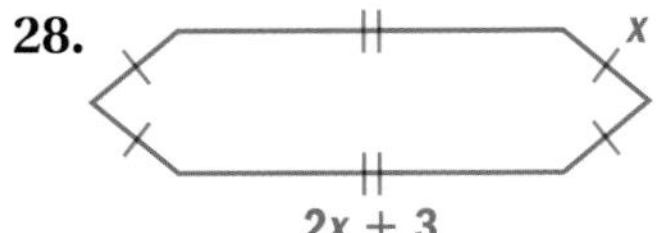

29.
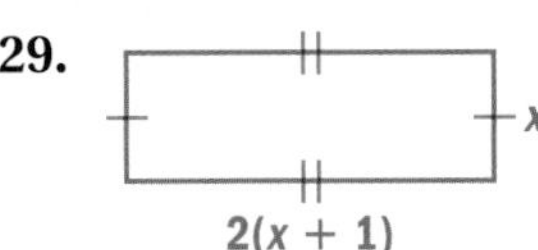

CHALLENGE **Find the expression that makes the equation true.**

30. $3xy + 6y - 2x^2 + 4 + \underline{\ ?\ } = 3x^2 - 5y - 7xy - 4x$
31. $4y^2 + 2x^2 + 9 + \underline{\ ?\ } = 3y^2 + x^2 + 5xy + 6$

PROBLEM SOLVING

BASEBALL Use the following information.

A player hits a ball 60 mi/h, or 88 ft/sec, upward. Evaluate $-16t^2 + 88t + 2$ to find the ball's height, in feet, after the given number of seconds.

SEE EXAMPLE 3 on p. 718 for Exs. 32–36

32. $t = 1.5$ 33. $t = 2$

34. $t = 2.5$ 35. $t = 3$

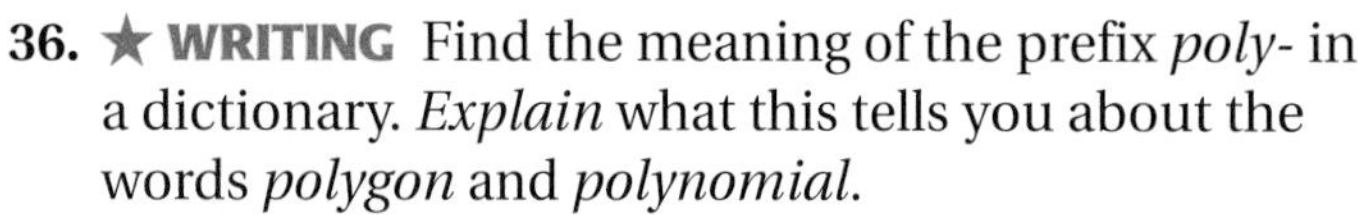

36. ★ **WRITING** Find the meaning of the prefix *poly-* in a dictionary. *Explain* what this tells you about the words *polygon* and *polynomial.*

37. ★ **MULTIPLE CHOICE** The height, in feet, of a falling pebble after t seconds of falling from a height of 45 feet can be found using the polynomial $-16t^2 + 45$. What is the pebble's height after 1.5 seconds?

Ⓐ 9 feet Ⓑ 21 feet Ⓒ 24 feet Ⓓ 36 feet

REASONING Tell whether the statement is *always, sometimes,* or *never* true. *Justify* your reasoning.

38. The terms of a trinomial are monomials.

39. A monomial has one factor.

40. A binomial has more than two terms.

41. ★ **SHORT RESPONSE** The longer leg of a right triangle is four more than twice the shorter leg. The hypotenuse is four less than three times the shorter leg. Write a simplified expression for the perimeter of the right triangle. Find the perimeter when the shorter leg is 10 inches long.

42. **REASONING** If a polynomial in one variable is written in standard form with all nonzero coefficients and it has n terms, what is the value of the greatest exponent? *Justify* your answer.

43. **CHALLENGE** Determine whether the equation $4g^2 + 3g = 7g^3$ is *always, sometimes,* or *never* true. *Explain* your reasoning.

MIXED REVIEW

Prepare for Lesson 13.2 in Exs. 44–47

Use the distributive property to simplify the expression. ***(p. 88)***

44. $8(3 + 9x)$ 45. $-3(11x - 4)$ 46. $-5x(7 + 2)$ 47. $12(6 - 1x)$

48. The letters in the word FUNCTION are put in a bag. You draw one letter randomly. Find the probability of drawing the letter N. ***(p. 381)***

49. ★ **MULTIPLE CHOICE** What is the volume of a cylinder with a radius of 4 meters and a height of 5 meters? ***(p. 554)***

Ⓐ $72\pi\text{ m}^3$ Ⓑ $80\pi\text{ m}^3$ Ⓒ $100\pi\text{ m}^3$ Ⓓ $320\pi\text{ m}^3$

13.2 Adding and Subtracting Polynomials

Before You simplified polynomials.

Now You'll add and subtract polynomials.

Why? So you can find the area of a surface, such as the floor space in Example 4.

KEY VOCABULARY

- **opposite,** *p. 58*
- **like terms,** *p. 89*

ACTIVITY

You can model polynomial addition with algebra tiles.

x^2-tile *x*-tile 1-tile

STEP 1 **Write** the two polynomials represented by the two groups of algebra tiles below.

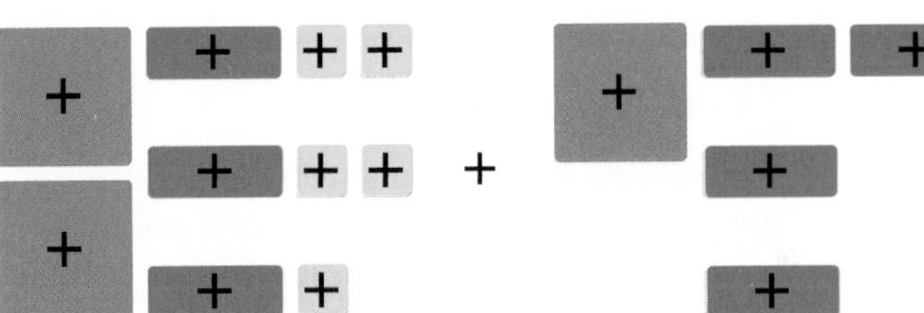

STEP 2 **Group** *like* algebra tiles to model the sum of the polynomials. Draw your model. Write the polynomial that your drawing represents.

STEP 3 **Use** algebra tiles to model the sum of the polynomials below. Write the polynomial that your model represents.

a. $(3x^2 + 6x + 1) + (x^2 + x)$ **b.** $(2x^2 + 3x + 1) + (4x^2 + x)$

In the activity, you used algebra tiles to add two polynomials. You add polynomials by combining like terms.

EXAMPLE 1 Adding Polynomials Vertically

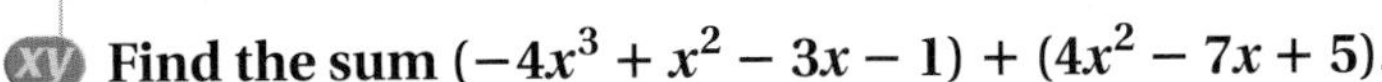

Find the sum $(-4x^3 + x^2 - 3x - 1) + (4x^2 - 7x + 5)$.

$$\begin{array}{r} -4x^3 + x^2 - 3x - 1 \\ +\quad 4x^2 - 7x + 5 \\ \hline -4x^3 + 5x^2 - 10x + 4 \end{array}$$

Write the second polynomial under the first.

Arrange like terms in columns.

Add like terms.

In Example 1, you combined like terms vertically. You can also add polynomials by combining like terms horizontally.

EXAMPLE 2 Adding Polynomials Horizontally

Find the sum $(2y^2 - 4y + 6) + (y^2 + 3y - 2)$.

SOLUTION

REGROUP TERMS
When you regroup terms, move a subtraction or addition sign with the term that follows it.

$(2y^2 - 4y + 6) + (y^2 + 3y - 2)$

$= 2y^2 + y^2 - 4y + 3y + 6 - 2$ **Group like terms.**

$= 3y^2 - y + 4$ **Combine like terms.**

Animated Math at classzone.com

✓ GUIDED PRACTICE for Examples 1 and 2

Find the sum.

1. $(6x^2 - 3x + 1) + (3x^3 + 4x^2 - 5x)$

2. $(5n^2 + 2n - 9) + (3n^2 - 4)$

3. $(y^2 - y + 1) + (-2y^2 + 2y - 1)$

4. $(3p^2 - p - 1) + (p^2 + p - 4)$

Subtracting Polynomials You can subtract a polynomial by adding its *opposite*. To find the opposite of a polynomial, multiply each of its terms by -1. You can subtract polynomials vertically or horizontally.

EXAMPLE 3 Subtracting Polynomials Vertically

Find the difference $(4x^3 + 5x^2 - 2x - 5) - (3x^3 - 4x + 2)$.

SOLUTION

AVOID ERRORS
Be sure to write the opposite of every term in the second polynomial, not just the first term.

STEP 1 **Find** the opposite of the second polynomial.

$-(3x^3 - 4x + 2) = -3x^3 + 4x - 2$

STEP 2 **Find** the sum $(4x^3 + 5x^2 - 2x - 5) + (-3x^3 + 4x - 2)$.

$4x^3 + 5x^2 - 2x - 5$ **Write the second polynomial under the first.**

$+ \ -3x^3 \qquad + 4x - 2$ **Arrange like terms in columns.**

$x^3 + 5x^2 + 2x - 7$ **Add like terms.**

✓ GUIDED PRACTICE for Example 3

Find the difference.

5. $(4r^2 - r + 8) - (r^2 + 6r - 1)$

6. $(6m^2 + 2m - 3) - (7m^2 + 4)$

EXAMPLE 4 Finding Area

Tree House The design for a tree house calls for a rectangular hole in the floor. Write a polynomial expression for the area of the tree house floor.

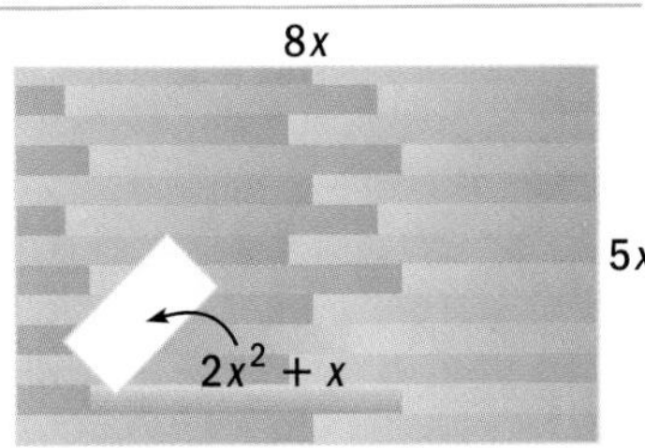

SOLUTION

To find the area of the floor, use the area of the two rectangles.

Area of Large Rectangle	**Area of Small Rectangle**
$8x \cdot 5x = 40x^2$	$2x^2 + x$

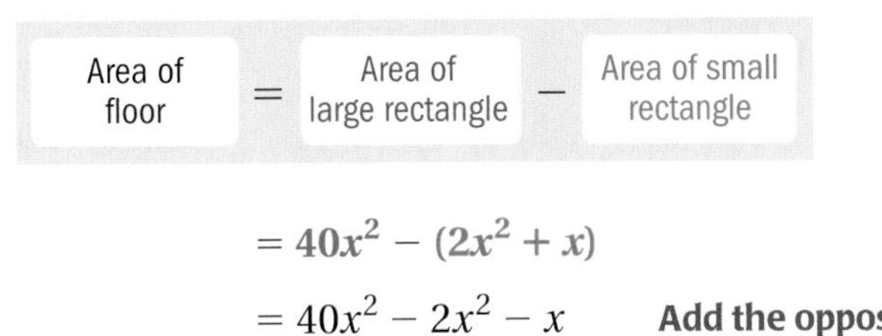

$= 40x^2 - (2x^2 + x)$

$= 40x^2 - 2x^2 - x$ **Add the opposite.**

$= 38x^2 - x$ **Combine like terms.**

AVOID ERRORS
Be sure to write the second polynomial in parentheses when subtracting.

▶ **Answer** A polynomial expression for the area of the floor is $38x^2 - x$.

GUIDED PRACTICE for Example 4

7. **What If?** Suppose the tree house in Example 4 has a length of $10x$ and a width of $6x$, and the area of the rectangular hole is $4x^2 - 2x$. Write a polynomial expression for the area of the tree house floor.

13.2 EXERCISES

HOMEWORK KEY
★ = **STANDARDIZED TEST PRACTICE** Exs. 12, 34, 35, 36, 37, 39, and 46
○ = **HINTS AND HOMEWORK HELP** for Exs. 3, 7, 13, 17, 33 at classzone.com

SKILL PRACTICE

VOCABULARY **Copy and complete the statement.**

1. To add polynomials, you should combine __?__.
2. To find the __?__ of a polynomial, multiply each of its terms by -1.

ADDING POLYNOMIALS **Find the sum.**

SEE EXAMPLES 1 AND 2 on pp. 721–722 for Exs. 3–10

3. $(8y + 5) + (4y - 3)$
4. $(x - 6) + (2x + 9)$
5. $(4x + 7) + (x - 3)$
6. $(-2a - 9) + (a + 4)$
7. $(-g^2 + g + 9) + (7g^2 - 6)$
8. $(3z^2 - 2z + 1) + (4z^3 + 3z)$
9. $(2k^2 + 5k) + (4k^2 - 5k)$
10. $(6x^3 - 12x + 1) + (8x^2 - 4)$

SEE EXAMPLES 1 AND 2 on pp. 721–722 for Exs. 11–12

11. **ERROR ANALYSIS** Describe and correct the error(s) in the solution.

$$\begin{array}{r} -4x^3 + 5x^2 - 7x + 2 \\ +\ \ 2x^3 - 6x + 10 \\ \hline -2x^3 - x^2 + 3x + 2 \end{array}$$

12. ★ **MULTIPLE CHOICE** Find the sum of the expressions $(-7x^3 + 4x^2 - 1)$ and $(x^3 - 9x + 3)$.

Ⓐ $-6x^3 + 4x^2 - 9x + 2$ Ⓑ $-8x^3 + 4x^2 - 9x - 4$

Ⓒ $-6x^3 + 5x^2 + 2$ Ⓓ $-8x^3 - 5x^2 + 4$

SUBTRACTING POLYNOMIALS **Find the difference.**

SEE EXAMPLE 3 on p. 722 for Exs. 13–20

13. $(7x + 10) - (x - 2)$
14. $(4p + 1) - (p - 7)$
15. $(-5d - 1) - (5d + 6)$
16. $(7y + 1) - (3y - 2)$
17. $(6r^2 + 2r - 5) - (3r^2 - 9)$
18. $(-4b^3 - 9b + 2) - (b^3 - b + 3)$
19. $(5a^2 + 3a + 8) - (2a^2 - 2a - 9)$
20. $(4p^3 + p^2 - 8) - (7p^3 + 2p + 5)$

SIMPLIFYING EXPRESSIONS **Simplify the expression.**

21. $(4n - 3) + (9n + 5) - (n - 1)$
22. $(-8m + 1) - (2m - 6) + 5m$
23. $-2(5y + 3) - 9(y + 1)$
24. $4(-3s^2 + s - 4) + (5s^2 + s + 7)$
25. $3(q^2 - q) + 2(7q^2 - 2q)$
26. $6(t^3 - t^2 + 3t) - 4(5t^3 + t^2 - t)$
27. $5(4x^3 - 2x^2 + 1) + 3(7x^2 - 5x)$
28. $-7(2v^4 + 3v^2 - 1) - 5(-3v^3 - 6)$

SOLVING EQUATIONS **Solve the equation.**

29. $(2x^2 - 3x + 4) - (x^2 - 3x + 13) = 0$
30. $(-6x^2 + 7x - 5) - (-6x^2 - 5x + 7) = 0$

31. **CHALLENGE** Let A and B represent polynomial expressions. Find A and B when $A + B = 5z - 4$ and $A - B = 3z + 10$. *Explain* your reasoning.

PROBLEM SOLVING

GEOMETRY **Write a polynomial expression for the perimeter of the figure. Simplify the polynomial.**

SEE EXAMPLE 4 on p. 723 for Exs. 32–35

32.

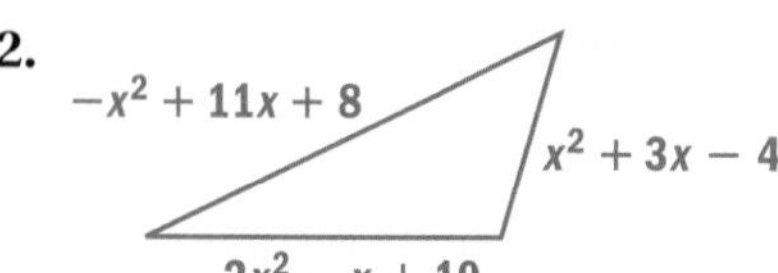

33.

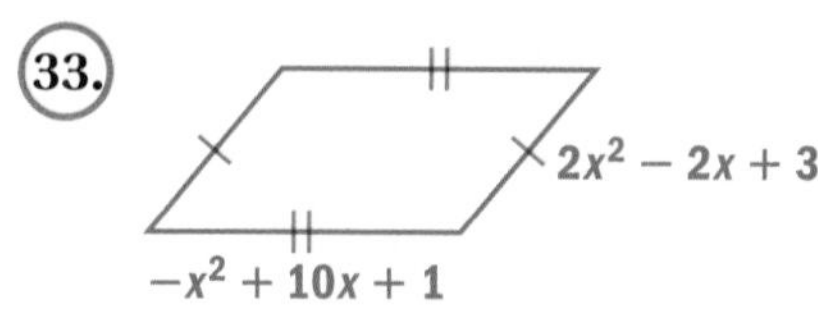

34. ★ **MULTIPLE CHOICE** The perimeter of the rectangle shown is 118 feet. What is the value of x?

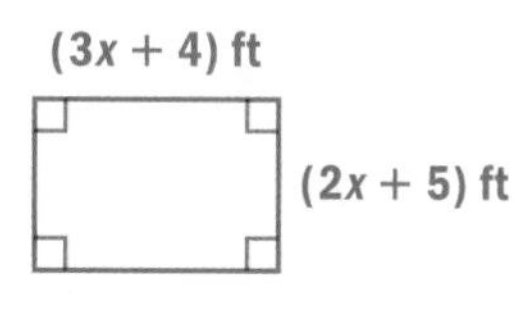

Ⓐ 10 Ⓑ 21.8

Ⓒ 29.5 Ⓓ 38

REVIEW FORMULAS
Need help with geometry formulas? See p. 142.

35. ★ **SHORT RESPONSE** *Explain* how to find the area of wallboard needed to cover the wall shown, not including the window. Then find the area as a polynomial in standard form.

7x
3x
$4x^2 + 2x$

36. ★ **OPEN-ENDED MATH** Give three examples of two trinomials in standard form whose sum is a binomial.

37. ★ **EXTENDED RESPONSE** To make a set of coasters, you cut identical circles out of a piece of clay rolled into a flat square.

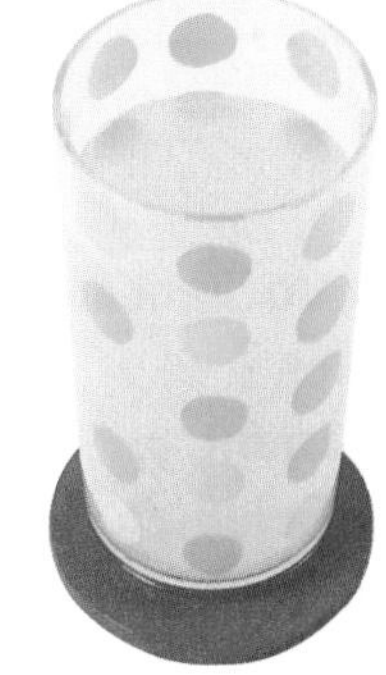

a. Write a polynomial expression for the area of clay that remains after you remove the circles as shown below.

b. Simplify the polynomial in part (a), using 3.14 for π.

c. Is there enough clay left over to make another coaster of the same radius and thickness? *Explain* your answer.

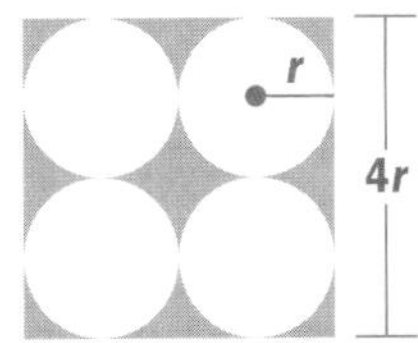

38. **GEOMETRY** You are constructing two wooden pyramids with square bases using the designs shown. Write a simplified polynomial expression for the total surface area of the two pyramids.

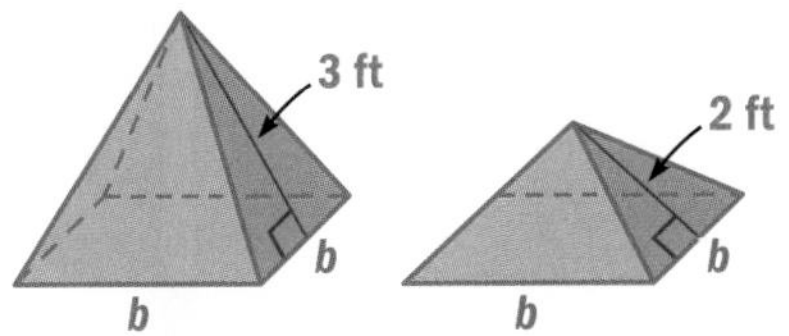

39. ★ **WRITING** *Describe* the similarities and differences between adding and subtracting integers and adding and subtracting polynomials.

40. **CHALLENGE** Find the values of x and y in the parallelogram. *Explain* the properties of the parallelogram you used to write your equations.

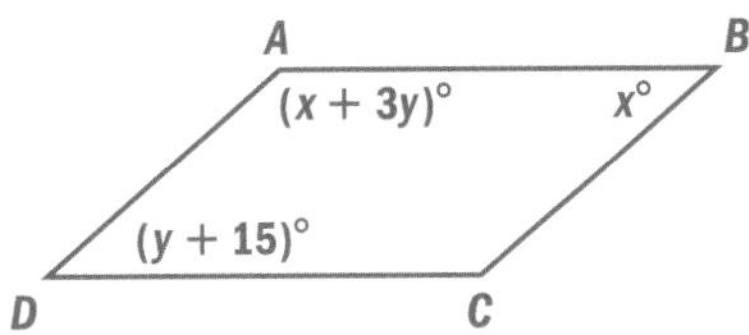

MIXED REVIEW

Prepare for Lesson 13.3 in Exs. 41–44

Simplify the expression. *(p. 202)*

41. $b^3 \cdot b^7$ **42.** $x^{12} \cdot x^2$ **43.** $m^4 \cdot m^5$ **44.** $a^3 \cdot a^6$

45. How many different passwords can be made using 4 different digits from 0 to 9? *(p. 670)*

46. ★ **MULTIPLE CHOICE** You roll a number cube. What is the probability that you roll a number greater than 4? *(p. 685)*

Ⓐ $\frac{1}{4}$ Ⓑ $\frac{1}{3}$ Ⓒ $\frac{1}{2}$ Ⓓ $\frac{2}{3}$

13.3 Monomials and Powers

Before You added and subtracted polynomials.

Now You will apply properties of exponents to monomials.

Why? So you can compare measures, such as volumes in Ex. 59.

KEY VOCABULARY
- **power,** *p. 19*
- **exponent,** *p. 19*
- **coefficient,** *p. 89*
- **monomial,** *p. 178*

ACTIVITY

You can use the properties of exponents to simplify monomials.

STEP 1 **Copy** and complete the table by expanding, regrouping, and simplifying each expression. What patterns do you notice?

Expression	Expand	Regroup	Simplify
$(3x)(4x^2)$	$3 \cdot x \cdot 4 \cdot x \cdot x$	$3 \cdot 4 \cdot x \cdot x \cdot x$	$12x^3$
$(-2x)(5x^4)$	?	?	?
$(xy)^3$	$xy \cdot xy \cdot xy$	$x \cdot x \cdot x \cdot y \cdot y \cdot y$	x^3y^3
$(4x)^2$	?	?	?
$(-3x)^3$	?	?	?

STEP 2 **Use** your results to simplify the expressions $(5x)(2x^3)$ and $(3pq)^2$.

REVIEW MULTIPLYING POWERS
Need help with rules of exponents? See p. 202.

In the activity, you expanded powers to multiply monomials. You can also multiply monomials by first multiplying their coefficients and then using the product of powers property to multiply variables.

EXAMPLE 1 Multiplying Monomials

Simplify the expression $(2x^3)(-3x)$.

$(2x^3)(-3x) = 2 \cdot x^3 \cdot (-3) \cdot x$ **Expand the expression.**

$= 2 \cdot (-3) \cdot x^3 \cdot x$ **Regroup factors.**

$= -6 \cdot x^3 \cdot x$ **Multiply coefficients.**

$= -6x^4$ **Product of powers property**

GUIDED PRACTICE for Example 1

Simplify the expression.

1. $4a(a^2)$ **2.** $(-2m)(7m^2)$ **3.** $(-x)(8x^2)$ **4.** $(y^5)(5y^3)$

Distributive Property You can use the distributive property and the properties of exponents to find the product of a monomial and a binomial.

EXAMPLE 2 Using the Distributive Property

Simplify the expression $2n(4n^2 - 5)$.

$2n(4n^2 - 5) = (2n)(4n^2) - (2n)(5)$	**Distributive property**
$= 8 \cdot n \cdot n^2 - 10 \cdot n$	**Multiply coefficients.**
$= 8n^3 - 10n$	**Product of powers property**

In the activity on page 726, you found powers of products. You can use the rule below to simplify a power of a product.

KEY CONCEPT — *For Your Notebook*

Power of a Product Property

Words To simplify a power of a product, find the power of each factor and multiply.

Algebra $(ab)^m = a^m \cdot b^m$ **Numbers** $(5 \cdot 2)^3 = 5^3 \cdot 2^3$

EXAMPLE 3 Simplifying a Power of a Product

TAKE NOTES

You will learn many new properties about exponents in this lesson. Be sure to write all the properties and a corresponding example of each in your notebook.

Container The radius of a container is twice its height. Write an expression for the volume of the container. Use the formula $V = \pi r^2 h$ in the table of formulas on p. 816.

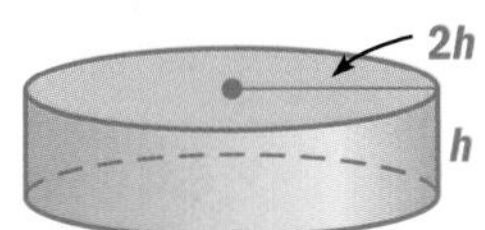

SOLUTION

$V = \pi(2h)^2 h$	**Substitute $2h$ for r.**
$= \pi(2^2 \cdot h^2)\, h$	**Power of a product property**
$= \pi \cdot 4 \cdot h^2 \cdot h$	**Evaluate each power.**
$= 4\pi h^3$	**Product of powers property**

▶ **Answer** An expression for the volume of the container is $4\pi h^3$.

✓ GUIDED PRACTICE for Examples 2 and 3

AVOID ERRORS

Remember that $(-x)^4 = (-1x)^4 = (-1)^4(x)^4$.

Simplify the expression.

5. $p(2p + 3)$ **6.** $-t^2(-2t + 8)$ **7.** $(5yz)^3$ **8.** $(-xy)^2$

9. What If? Suppose the radius of the container in Example 3 is three times its height. Write an expression for the volume of the container.

KEY CONCEPT — For Your Notebook

Power of a Power Property

Words To simplify a power of a power, multiply exponents.

Algebra $(a^m)^n = a^{mn}$ **Numbers** $(5^3)^2 = 5^{3 \cdot 2} = 5^6$

EXAMPLE 4 Simplifying a Power of a Power

ANOTHER WAY

You can also expand $(2y^2)^3$ by multiplying the monomial by itself 3 times.

$(2y^2)^3 = 2y^2 \cdot 2y^2 \cdot 2y^2$
$= 8y^6$

Simplify the expression $(2y^2)^3$.

$(2y^2)^3 = 2^3 \cdot (y^2)^3$ **Power of a product property**

$= 8 \cdot y^{2 \cdot 3}$ **Power of a power property**

$= 8y^6$ **Simplify.**

✓ GUIDED PRACTICE for Example 4

Simplify the expression.

10. $(2^4)^2$ **11.** $(x^6)^2$ **12.** $(5m^3)^2$ **13.** $(a^2b)^2$

13.3 EXERCISES

HOMEWORK KEY

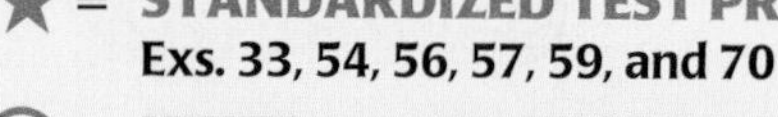

★ = **STANDARDIZED TEST PRACTICE** Exs. 33, 54, 56, 57, 59, and 70

○ = **HINTS AND HOMEWORK HELP** for Exs. 5, 13, 19, 29, 53 at classzone.com

SKILL PRACTICE

VOCABULARY **Match the expression with the property used to simplify it.**

1. $(2y)^5$ **A.** power of a power property

2. $(x^2)^7$ **B.** power of a product property

3. $3 \cdot x^4 \cdot x^6$ **C.** product of powers property

MULTIPLYING MONOMIALS **Simplify the expression by multiplying the monomials.**

SEE EXAMPLE 1 on p. 726 for Exs. 4–9

4. $(-4x)(5x^3)$ **5.** $(-16t)(-3t^9)$ **6.** $(-x^2)(-3x)$

7. $(3s)(-2s^3)$ **8.** $(-b^3)(-b^8)$ **9.** $(-y^2)(y^3)$

USING THE DISTRIBUTIVE PROPERTY **Simplify the expression by using the distributive property.**

SEE EXAMPLE 2 on p. 727 for Exs. 10–15

10. $2w(3w + 1)$ **11.** $-t(t^2 - 4)$ **12.** $-8x(x^5 + x)$

13. $3k^2(12 - k^5)$ **14.** $4q^3(3q + 6)$ **15.** $-7a^2(5a^3 - 9a)$

APPLYING POWER PROPERTIES **Simplify the expression by using the power of a product property or by using the power of a power property.**

SEE EXAMPLES 3 AND 4 on pp. 727–728 for Exs. 16–31

16. $(5z)^3$ **17.** $(xyz)^5$ **18.** $(2ab)^4$ **19.** $(-6z)^3$

20. $(-dt)^4$ **21.** $(3rs)^2$ **22.** $(-3xy)^3$ **23.** $(10bh)^5$

24. $(t^4)^2$ **25.** $(y^2)^2$ **26.** $(c^2)^9$ **27.** $(-x^2)^{10}$

28. $(ab^3)^2$ **29.** $(x^2y^2)^3$ **30.** $(3a^2)^2$ **31.** $(2r^3)^3$

32. ERROR ANALYSIS Describe and correct the error made in simplifying the expression.

$(3x^3)^2 = 3x^{3 \cdot 2}$
$= 3x^6$

33. ★ **MULTIPLE CHOICE** Simplify the expression $(-2b^4)^3$.

(A) $-8b^{12}$ (B) $-2b^{12}$ (C) $-8b^7$ (D) $-2b^7$

SCIENTIFIC NOTATION **Simplify the expression and write it in scientific notation.**

34. $(3 \times 10^4)^3$ **35.** $(9 \times 10^{10})^3$ **36.** $(5 \times 10^7)^4$

SIMPLIFYING EXPRESSIONS **Simplify the expression.**

37. $2(5mn^4)^3$ **38.** $-3a^{10}(a^4b^2c)^4$ **39.** $(-2x^4)^3(x^4yz^8)$

40. $3[(r^4s^3)^4 \cdot r^8s]^3$ **41.** $2[(c^2d)^3 \cdot (c^3d^4)^4]^2$ **42.** $\left(\frac{2x^2}{x}\right)^3$

43. $\left(\frac{9h^5}{h^7}\right)^2$ **44.** $\frac{(4x^2)^3}{(2x)^4}$ **45.** $\frac{(-3mn)^2}{(n^2)^3}$

CHALLENGE **Copy and complete the statement with a monomial.**

46. $8a^6 + 64a^3 = \underline{\ ?\ }(a^3 + 8)$ **47.** $12b^2 - 9b^2c^4 = \underline{\ ?\ }(4 - 3c^4)$

48. $18x^2y - 9xy^2 = \underline{\ ?\ }(2x - y)$ **49.** $12x^3y^6 + 20x^5y^2 = \underline{\ ?\ }(3y^4 + 5x^2)$

PROBLEM SOLVING

SEE EXAMPLES 1, 2, AND 3 on pp. 726–727 for Exs. 50–51

50. PHOTO ALBUMS You are making photo albums in different sizes. The photo area on each page is twice as long as it is wide and needs a 2 inch margin for binding. Write a polynomial expression for the total area of one page.

51. GEOMETRY A cube has side length of $5x$. Write an expression in simplest form for the volume of the cube.

52. GUIDED PROBLEM SOLVING Simplify the expression $\left(\frac{x}{y}\right)^4$.

a. Write the expression in expanded form.

b. Simplify by multiplying numerators and multiplying denominators.

c. Write a rule to simplify a quotient raised to a power.

SEE EXAMPLES 2 AND 3 on p. 727 for Exs. 53–54

53. **SEAT CUSHION** You need fabric for a window seat cushion. Use the trapezoid pattern shown to write a polynomial expression for the area of the top of the cushion. Simplify the expression.

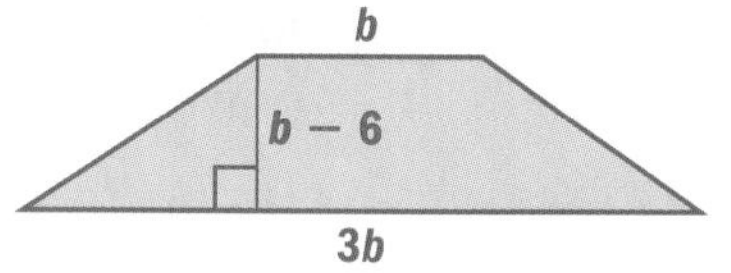

54. ★ **WRITING** *Explain* why $(4y)^2$ is different from $4y^2$.

55. **GEOMETRY** The volume of a cone is given by the expression $\frac{1}{3}\pi r^2 h$. Write the expression for the volume of a cone with twice the radius and *compare* it to the original expression.

56. ★ **SHORT RESPONSE** A circle has radius r and a square has a side length twice the radius of the circle. Write and simplify expressions for the areas of the figures. Then write and simplify a ratio comparing the area of the circle to the area of the square. Leave your answer in terms of π.

57. ★ **MULTIPLE CHOICE** The diameter of a cylindrical canister is four times its height h. Which expression represents its surface area?

(A) $4\pi h^2$ (B) $12\pi h^2$ (C) $16\pi h^2$ (D) $20\pi h^2$

58. **GEOMETRY** Write and simplify a polynomial expression for the volume of the square pyramid.

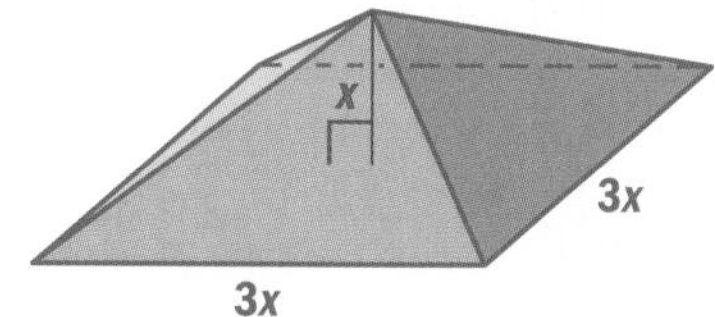

59. ★ **EXTENDED RESPONSE** You can use the formula for the volume of a sphere to approximate the volumes of spherical objects in our solar system. The volume V of a sphere is given by $V = \frac{4}{3}\pi r^3$.

a. **Calculate** The radius of Saturn is about 6.0×10^4 kilometers. Approximate the volume of Saturn. Write your answer in scientific notation.

b. **Calculate** The radius of Saturn's moon Dione is about 560 kilometers. Approximate the volume of Dione. Write your answer in scientific notation.

c. **Estimate** Write a ratio comparing the volume of Saturn to the volume of Dione. About how many times larger is Saturn than Dione?

60. **DECIBELS** A decibel (dB) is a measure of the intensity (or volume) of sound. For each increase in 10 dB, the intensity is 10 times as great. You are trying to have a conversation at a stadium where the noise level is 110 dB. Your conversation is at a volume of 60 dB. How many times greater is the volume of the crowd than the volume of your conversation? *Explain.*

61. **CHALLENGE** Use the properties of exponents to show that $\left(\frac{a}{b}\right)^m = \frac{a^m}{b^m}$ when b is a nonzero real number. (Hint: Use the definition of negative exponents). *Justify* each step.

MIXED REVIEW

Prepare for Lesson 13.4 in Exs. 62–65

Use the distributive property to simplify the expression. *(p. 88)*

62. $3(5x + 1)$ **63.** $-5(2x - 7)$ **64.** $-4(8 - x)$ **65.** $3(6x + 7y)$

Write the percent as a fraction in simplest form. *(p. 359)*

66. 55% **67.** 71% **68.** 29% **69.** 18%

70. ★ **OPEN-ENDED MATH** *Describe* a real-world event in which the odds in favor of the event are 1 to 3. *(p. 685)*

QUIZ *for Lessons 13.1–13.3*

Simplify the polynomial and write it in standard form. *(p. 717)*

1. $5x^2 + 4x - 3x^2 - 11x$ **2.** $-5k^3 - 2(3k^3 + k - 4)$

Find the sum or difference. *(p. 721)*

3. $(6n^3 - 2n^2) + (n^3 + 7n^2 - 4n)$ **4.** $(4b^2 - 3b + 8) - (2b^2 - 6)$

5. $(x^2 + 6x + 1) - (2x^2 - 8x + 4)$ **6.** $(3m^2 + m - 9) + (7m^2 + 2)$

7. AREA Write a polynomial expression for the area of the floor surrounding the rug in the diagram. Simplify the polynomial. *(p. 726)*

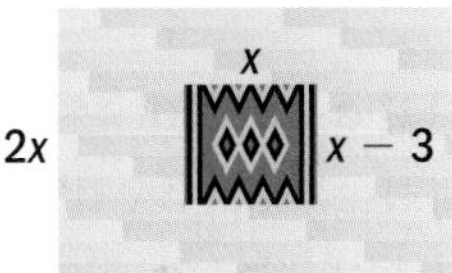

Simplify the expression. *(p. 726)*

8. $(3t^4)(4t^2)$ **9.** $(2c^3)^4$ **10.** $(-2y)^4$ **11.** $-5d(3d^2 + 2)$

Brain Game

Polynomial Potions

You need to make six perfumes using the six ingredients in the laboratory. Each perfume is made by adding two fragrances together. Use the ingredients listed below and the perfume labels to find the secret formulas.

Fragrance A	**Fragrance B**
$x^2 - 2x + 2$	$-x^2 - 6x - 2$
Fragrance C	**Fragrance D**
$2x^2 - 3x + 1$	$-3x^2 + 2x - 1$
Fragrance E	**Fragrance F**
$3x^2 + 5x - 4$	$-2x^2 + x - 3$

Lessons 13.1–13.3

1. **MULTI-STEP PROBLEM** A T-shirt company has operating expenses of \$3000 per month. The fabric for each shirt costs \$3, and each shirt is sold for \$12.
   a. Write an expression for the total cost of making x shirts in a month. Write an expression for the revenue (money collected) from selling x shirts in a month.
   b. Write an expression for the profit from selling x shirts. (*Hint*: Profit = Revenue − Cost.)
   c. The company sold 680 shirts last month. How much profit did it make?

2. **MULTI-STEP PROBLEM** Use the triangle below.

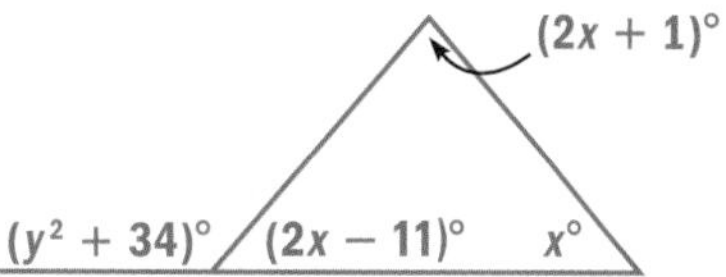

   a. Find the value of x.
   b. Find the measure of each angle inside the triangle.
   c. Find the value of y.

3. **EXTENDED RESPONSE** A restaurant sells half and whole submarine sandwiches. Each half sandwich costs \$1.50 to make and is sold for \$3. Each whole sandwich costs \$3 to make and is sold for \$5.
   a. Write an expression for the cost of making x half submarine sandwiches and y whole submarine sandwiches. Write an expression for the revenue (money collected) from selling x half sandwiches and y whole sandwiches.
   b. Write and simplify an expression for the profit from selling x half sandwiches and y whole sandwiches.
   c. The restaurant estimates it will sell 200 half submarine sandwiches this week. How many whole submarine sandwiches does it need to sell this week to have a profit of at least \$500? *Explain.*

4. **EXTENDED RESPONSE** For a spherical balloon with radius r, the surface area is given by the formula $S = 4\pi r^2$ and the volume is given by the formula $V = \frac{4}{3}\pi r^3$.

   a. Write and simplify expressions for the surface area of a sphere after doubling and after tripling the radius.
   b. Write and simplify expressions for the volume of a sphere after doubling and after tripling the radius.
   c. Write and simplify an expression for the ratio of the volume of a sphere (in cubic units) to its surface area (in square units). What is the ratio when the radius is 9 inches?

5. **SHORT RESPONSE** A walnut falls from a tree 75 feet off the ground. The polynomial $-16t^2 + 75$ gives the walnut's height, in feet, after t seconds of falling. Find its height after 1 second and after 2 seconds. Estimate how many seconds the walnut falls before hitting the ground. *Justify* your reasoning.

6. **OPEN-ENDED** *Describe* two separate figures, using at least two binomials for the sides, in which the perimeter can be written as $7x + 5$.

7. **GRIDDED ANSWER** The perimeter of a square kitchen floor is 36 feet. The length of each wall is 1 foot more than twice the length x, in feet, of the sink. How many feet long is the sink?

INVESTIGATION
Use before Lesson 13.4

GOAL
Multiply binomials using algebra tiles.

MATERIALS
- algebra tiles

13.4 Multiplying Binomials

You can model binomial multiplication with algebra tiles.

EXPLORE **Model the product $(x + 3)(3x + 2)$ with algebra tiles.**

STEP 1 **Model** each binomial with algebra tiles. Arrange the first binomial vertically and the second binomial horizontally, as shown.

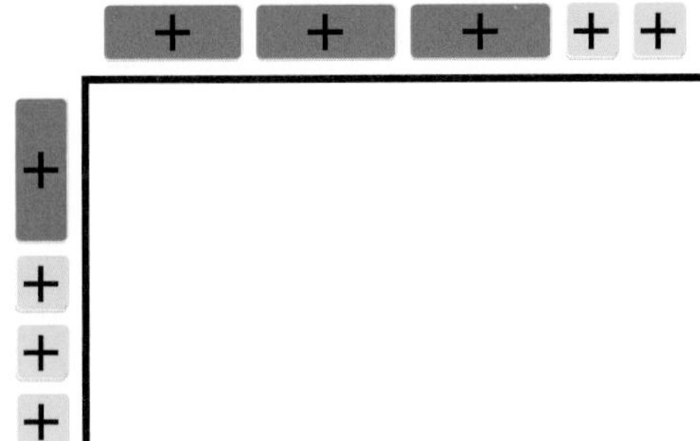

STEP 2 **Notice** that the binomials define a rectangular area with length $(3x + 2)$ units and width $(x + 3)$ units. Fill in the region with the appropriate tiles, as shown.

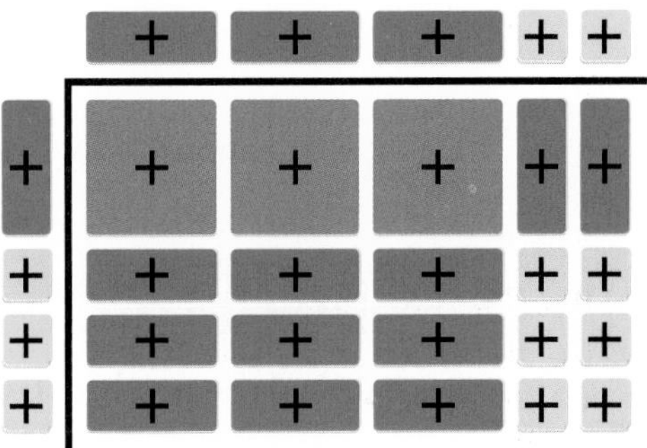

STEP 3 **Add** the areas of the rectangles on the inside of the model to see that the total area is $3x^2 + 11x + 6$. This is the product of the binomials.

PRACTICE **Find the product with algebra tiles. Draw your model.**

1. $(x + 1)(x + 2)$ **2.** $(x + 4)(x + 4)$ **3.** $(x + 2)(2x + 2)$

Animated Math at classzone.com

DRAW CONCLUSIONS

Model the expression with algebra tiles. Arrange the tiles in a rectangle. Find the two binomials that have this product.

4. $x^2 + 5x + 6$ **5.** $x^2 + 2x + 1$ **6.** $3x^2 + 8x + 4$

7. **REASONING** *Describe* how these models relate to the distributive property.

13.4 Multiplying Binomials

Before You multiplied monomials and polynomials.
Now You'll multiply binomials.
Why? So you can find the area of a surface, such as a stage in Ex. 48.

KEY VOCABULARY
- **polynomial,** *p. 717*
- **binomial,** *p. 717*

In the Investigation on page 733 you used a visual model to multiply binomials. The model below shows that $(x + 2)(3x + 1) = 3x^2 + 7x + 2$.

	x	x	x	1
x	x^2	x^2	x^2	x
1	x	x	x	1
1	x	x	x	1

Height: $x + 2$; width: $3x + 1$

You can multiply two binomials using a table or a vertical method.

EXAMPLE 1 Multiplying Binomials with a Table

Find the product $(-3x + 2)(8x + 7)$ and simplify.

TAKE NOTES
Summarizing key ideas about polynomials in your notebook will make these ideas easy to review.

Write the first polynomial on the left of the table.

Write the second polynomial above the table.

	$8x$	**7**
$-3x$	**$-24x^2$**	**$-21x$**
2	**$16x$**	**14**

Multiply to fill in the table.

The product is $-24x^2 - 21x + 16x + 14$. Combine like terms.

▶ **Answer** The product is $-24x^2 - 5x + 14$.

EXAMPLE 2 Multiplying Binomials Vertically

Find the product $(2x - 5)(3x + 4)$ and simplify.

$2x - 5$	**Write the first binomial.**
$\times \quad 3x + 4$	**Write the second binomial.**
$8x - 20$	**Multiply $4(2x - 5)$.**
$6x^2 - 15x$	**Multiply $3x(2x - 5)$. Line up like terms.**
$6x^2 - 7x - 20$	**Add $8x - 20$ and $6x^2 - 15x$.**

Distributive Property Another way to multiply binomials is to use the distributive property.

EXAMPLE 3 Multiplying Polynomials Horizontally

> **VOCABULARY**
> *Compound interest* is earned on the original amount of money in an account and on the interest already earned.

Banking You deposit \$1 into a savings account with interest compounded annually. The balance of the account after two years can be found using the expression $(1 + r)^2$, where r represents the annual interest rate. Expand this expression and simplify.

SOLUTION

To expand the expression, multiply two binomials.

$(1 + r)^2 = (1 + r)(1 + r)$	**$(1 + r)^2$ means $(1 + r)(1 + r)$.**
$= 1(1 + r) + r(1 + r)$	**Distributive property**
$= 1 + r + r + r^2$	**Distributive property**
$= 1 + 2r + r^2$	**Combine like terms.**
$= r^2 + 2r + 1$	**Write in standard form.**

The FOIL Method The letters in the word FOIL can help you remember how to multiply binomials. The letters should remind you to multiply the First pair, Outer pair, Inner pair, and Last pair.

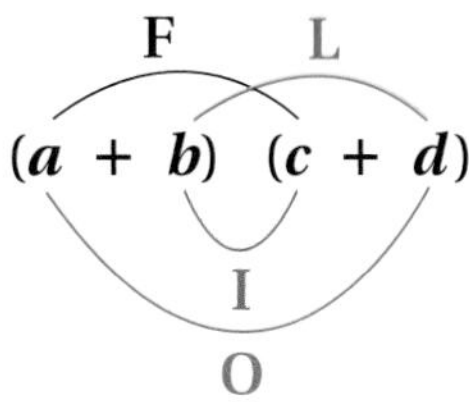

EXAMPLE 4 Multiplying with the FOIL Method

> **ANOTHER WAY**
> Another way to find the product in Example 4 is to either use a table or use the distributive property.

Find the product $(2x + 3)(3x - 1)$ and simplify.

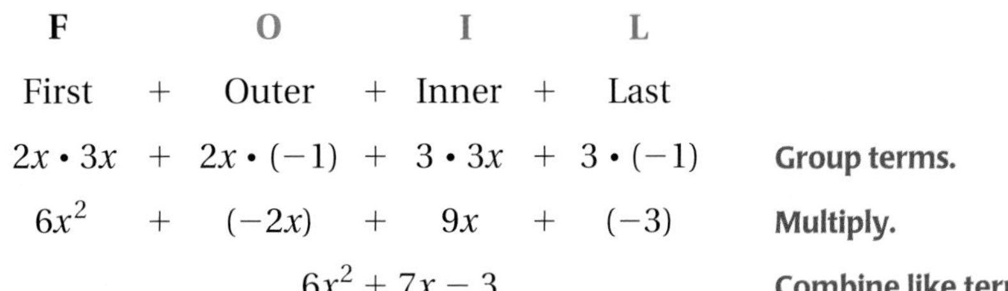

F		O		I		L	
First	+	Outer	+	Inner	+	Last	
$2x \cdot 3x$	+	$2x \cdot (-1)$	+	$3 \cdot 3x$	+	$3 \cdot (-1)$	**Group terms.**
$6x^2$	+	$(-2x)$	+	$9x$	+	(-3)	**Multiply.**
		$6x^2 + 7x - 3$					**Combine like terms.**

✓ GUIDED PRACTICE for Examples 1, 2, 3, and 4

Find the product and simplify.

1. $(x + 1)(x + 3)$
2. $(b - 4)(b - 3)$
3. $(3t - 4)(t + 2)$
4. $(d + 6)(d + 5)$
5. $(x - 3)(x - 1)$
6. $(5s + 3)(2s - 4)$

13.4 EXERCISES

HOMEWORK KEY

★ = **STANDARDIZED TEST PRACTICE**
Exs. 25, 40, 41, 43, 45, and 58

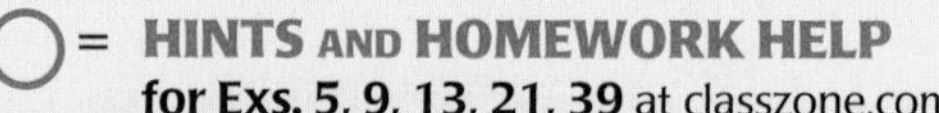

○ = **HINTS AND HOMEWORK HELP**
for Exs. 5, 9, 13, 21, 39 at classzone.com

SKILL PRACTICE

1. **VOCABULARY** Copy and complete: A polynomial with two terms is called a __?__.

2. **VOCABULARY** *Describe* the FOIL method in your own words.

SEE EXAMPLES 1 AND 2 on p. 734 for Exs. 3–8

MAKE A TABLE Use a table to find the product. Simplify the result. Then multiply vertically to check the result.

3. $(y - 4)(y + 1)$
4. $(g + 3)(g + 7)$
5. $(x - 4)(x + 4)$
6. $(2m + 3)(m - 7)$
7. $(3q - 1)(5q - 1)$
8. $(7b - 3)(9b + 4)$

MULTIPLYING BINOMIALS Find the product and simplify.

SEE EXAMPLES 1, 2, 3, AND 4 on pp. 734–735 for Exs. 9–25

9. $(x + 9)(x - 2)$
10. $(x + 3)(x - 3)$
11. $(a + 10)(a - 4)$
12. $(6r + 7)(r - 1)$
13. $(t - 1)(-3t - 4)$
14. $(-2x - 5)(11x - 12)$
15. $(3x + 1)(3x - 1)$
16. $(3x - 1)(5x - 4)$
17. $(2m + 7)(3m + 1)$
18. $(7b - 3)(-2b + 5)$
19. $(6z + 5)(6z + 5)$
20. $(2g + 9)(2g - 9)$
21. $\left(\frac{1}{2}x + 2\right)(4x - 6)$
22. $(9b - 12)\left(\frac{1}{3}b - 6\right)$
23. $(n^2 - 2)(n^2 + 1)$

24. **ERROR ANALYSIS** Describe and correct the error made in multiplying the binomials.

$$(x + 2)(x - 4) = x \cdot x + x \cdot 4 + 2 \cdot x + 2 \cdot (-4)$$
$$= x^2 + 4x + 2x - 8$$
$$= x^2 + 6x - 8$$

25. ★ **MULTIPLE CHOICE** What is the product $(x + 6)(x - 2)$?

Ⓐ $x^2 - 4x - 12$ Ⓑ $x^2 - 4x + 4$ Ⓒ $x^2 + 4x + 12$ Ⓓ $x^2 + 4x - 12$

MULTIPLYING TRINOMIALS Find the product and simplify.

26. $(x + 5)(2x^2 + 5x + 7)$
27. $(x - 4)(x^2 + 3x + 9)$
28. $(x + 6)(3x^2 - 4x + 1)$
29. $(2x + 1)(4x^2 - x + 5)$
30. $(3x + 2)(2x^2 + 6x - 4)$
31. $(4x - 3)(-x^2 - 5x - 6)$

MEASUREMENT Write the figure's area as a polynomial in standard form.

32.
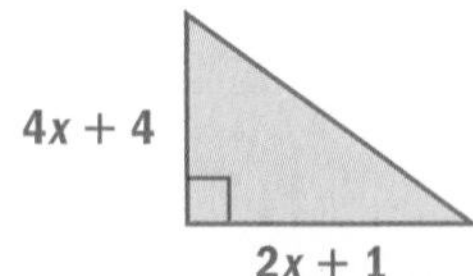

33.
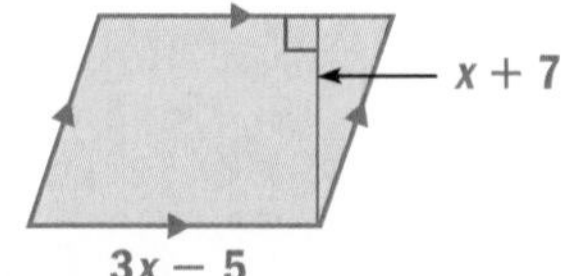

34.
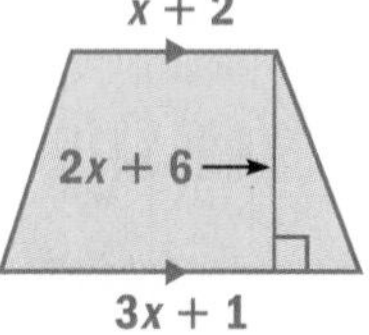

CHALLENGE Copy and complete the statement with the correct binomial.

35. $x^2 + 8x + 7 = (\underline{\ ?\ })(x + 7)$
36. $x^2 + 6x + 8 = (x + 2)(\underline{\ ?\ })$
37. $x^2 - 9x + 14 = (\underline{\ ?\ })(x - 2)$
38. $x^2 - 7x - 18 = (x - 9)(\underline{\ ?\ })$

PROBLEM SOLVING

SEE EXAMPLE 3 on p. 735 for Exs. 39, 47

39. **COMPOUND INTEREST** You deposit \$50 into a savings account with interest compounded annually. The expression $50(1 + r)^2$, where r is the interest rate, gives the account balance after 2 years. Expand this expression and simplify. Find the account balance when $r = 0.03$.

40. ★ **MULTIPLE CHOICE** Which product gives the area of the photograph and frame?

Ⓐ $(x + 18)(x + 8)$

Ⓑ $(2x - 18)(2x - 8)$

Ⓒ $(2x + 18)(2x + 8)$

Ⓓ $(x - 18)(x - 8)$

41. ★ **SHORT RESPONSE** *Describe* the pattern in the products of binomials like $(x - a)(x + a)$.

42. **REASONING** *Explain* why the expression $(x + 3)^2$ does not equal $x^2 + 9$. Include the correct simplification in your answer.

43. ★ **WRITING** How is finding the product of two binomials like finding the product of a monomial and a polynomial? How is it different?

44. **SWIMMING POOL** A swimming pool is surrounded by a walkway as shown. Write and simplify a polynomial expression for the area of the pool and walkway.

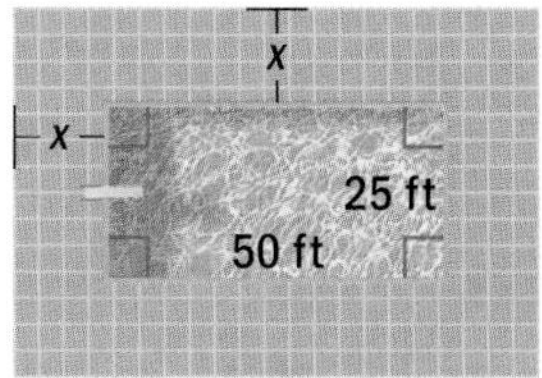

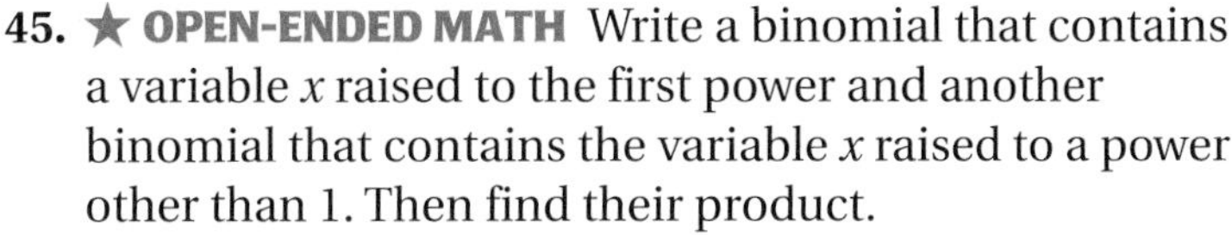

45. ★ **OPEN-ENDED MATH** Write a binomial that contains a variable x raised to the first power and another binomial that contains the variable x raised to a power other than 1. Then find their product.

46. **BASEBALL** The middle of a baseball is a sphere made of cork and two layers of rubber with a radius of 0.6875 inch. Use the surface area formula $S = 4\pi r^2$ to write a polynomial expression in terms of x for the amount of leather needed to cover the ball. Expand the expression and simplify.

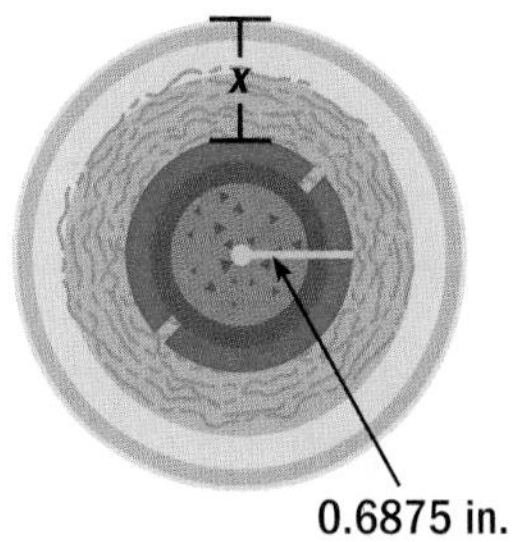

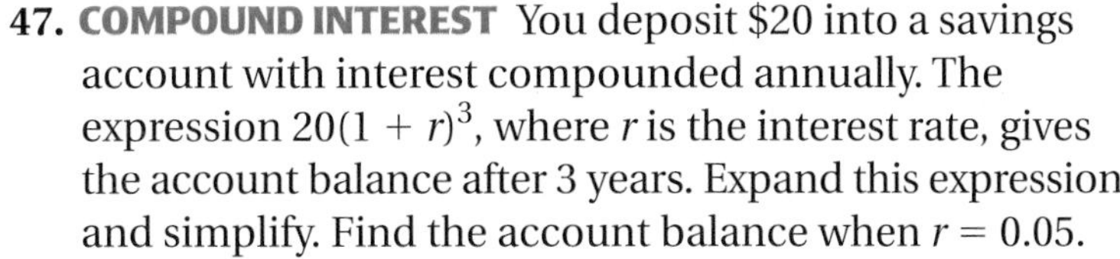

47. **COMPOUND INTEREST** You deposit \$20 into a savings account with interest compounded annually. The expression $20(1 + r)^3$, where r is the interest rate, gives the account balance after 3 years. Expand this expression and simplify. Find the account balance when $r = 0.05$.

48. **STAGE DESIGN** You are building a platform on a 30 foot by 20 foot stage for a school talent show as shown. Write and simplify a polynomial expression for the area of the platform using the design shown. Then find the area when x is 5 feet.

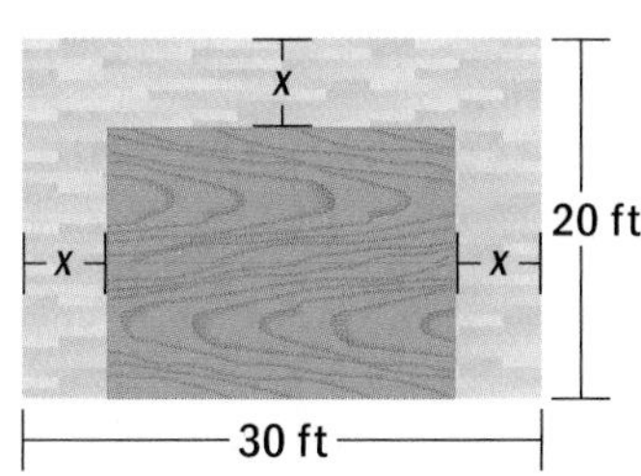

49. **GEOMETRY** The base of a triangle is 6 inches less than twice a number n. The height of the triangle is 6 inches more than 6 times the number n.

a. Write a simplified polynomial for the area of the triangle in terms of n.

b. If n is one fourth of the mean of the base and height, what is the area when the mean is 20 inches? Check the result.

50. **MULTI-STEP PROBLEM** You want to make a box with no lid out of a 17 inch by 11 inch piece of cardboard. You cut out squares of the same size from each corner. Then you fold the sides up and tape them together.

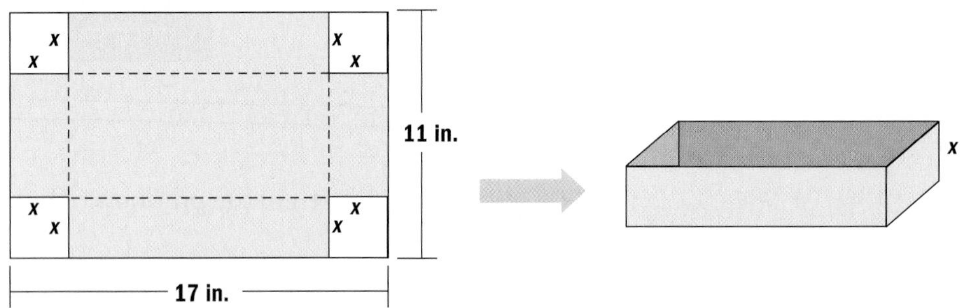

a. Write polynomials for the length, width, and height of the box.

b. Write a polynomial for the volume of the box in standard form.

c. Find the volume of the box for x values of 1 inch, 2 inches, 3 inches, and 4 inches. Which value gives the greatest volume?

d. Could a box be formed using cut out squares with side lengths of 6 inches? *Explain* why or why not.

51. **CHALLENGE** A rectangular house is twice as long as it is wide. It is surrounded by a lawn that extends 15 feet from the house on all sides. There is a 3 foot wide brick path from the street to the door.

a. Find and simplify expressions in terms of the width x, in feet, of the house for the total area of the house and yard, and for the area of the lawn.

b. Suppose the house is 60 feet long. Find the total area of the house and yard, and just the area of the lawn.

MIXED REVIEW

Get-Ready

Prepare for Lesson 13.5 in Exs. 52–54

Graph the linear equation. *(p. 598)*

52. $y = 6x - 4$

53. $y = x - 3$

54. $y = -2x + 7$

Find the product. *(p. 726)*

55. $-4r(r + 6)$

56. $3c(4c^2 + 2c)$

57. $-5x(-3x + 2)$

58. ★ **MULTIPLE CHOICE** So far this season, a baseball player has hit the ball 14 out of 21 times at bat. What are the odds in favor of the player hitting the ball the next time at bat? *(p. 685)*

Ⓐ $\frac{14}{35}$ Ⓑ $\frac{1}{2}$ Ⓒ $\frac{2}{3}$ Ⓓ $\frac{2}{1}$

13.5 Nonlinear Functions

Before You wrote function rules and graphed linear functions.
Now You'll use function notation and graph nonlinear functions.
Why? So you can write a function, as for e-mail sent in Ex. 49.

KEY VOCABULARY
- **function notation,** *p. 739*
- **vertical line test,** *p. 740*

In Lesson 11.1, you wrote functions as equations in x and y. You used x to name the input and y to name the output. Sometimes it is useful to use **function notation** instead. The symbol $f(x)$ is read as "the function of f at x" or "f of x."

function in x and y	function notation
$y = 3x - 4$	$f(x) = 3x - 4$
$y = 2x^2 + 2$	$f(x) = 2x^2 + 2$

EXAMPLE 1 Using Function Notation

Juggling You are juggling three balls. The height h, in feet, of the ball can be found using the equation $h = -16t^2 + 20t + 3$, where t is the number of seconds after you let go of the ball.

a. Write a function that models the height of a ball x seconds after you let go of it. Use function notation.

b. Evaluate for $x = 0.5$.

SOLUTION

a. Let $f(x)$ = height in feet and x = time in seconds.

$f(x) = -16x^2 + 20x + 3$ — **Write the height equation shown above in function notation.**

b. $f(0.5) = -16(0.5)^2 + 20(0.5) + 3$ — **Substitute 0.5 for x.**

$= -16(0.25) + 10 + 3$ — **Evaluate.**

$= 9$ — **Simplify.**

AVOID ERRORS
$f(x)$ does not mean "f times x." It means "the value of the function f at x."

▶ **Answer** The function is $f(x) = -16x^2 + 20x + 3$. The height of the ball 0.5 second after you let go of it is 9 feet.

GUIDED PRACTICE for Example 1

Rewrite using function notation. Evaluate for $x = 3$.

1. $y = x^2$ **2.** $y = 3x^2 + 4$ **3.** $y = -\frac{1}{2}x^2$

Graphing Functions The function in Example 1 is nonlinear. A nonlinear function has a graph that is not a straight line. In Lesson 11.4, you graphed linear functions using a table of values. You can also graph nonlinear functions by first making a table of values.

EXAMPLE 2 Standardized Test Practice

Which is the graph of the function $f(x) = x^2 - 1$?

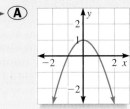

ELIMINATE CHOICES
You know that the graph passes through (0, −1). So, you can eliminate choice A.

Ⓐ
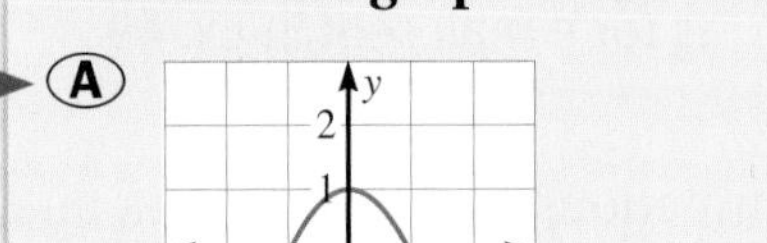

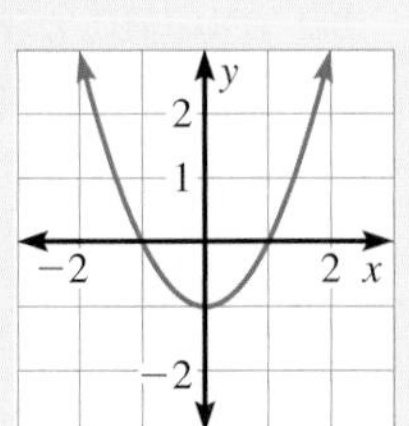

Ⓒ
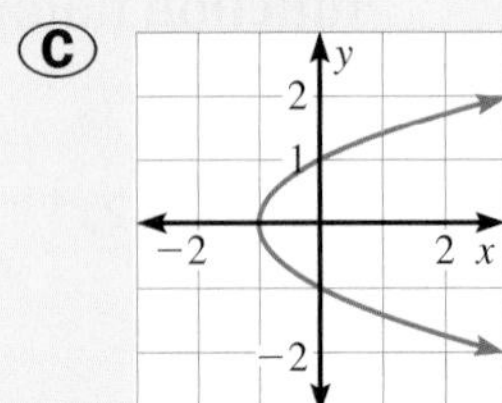

Ⓓ
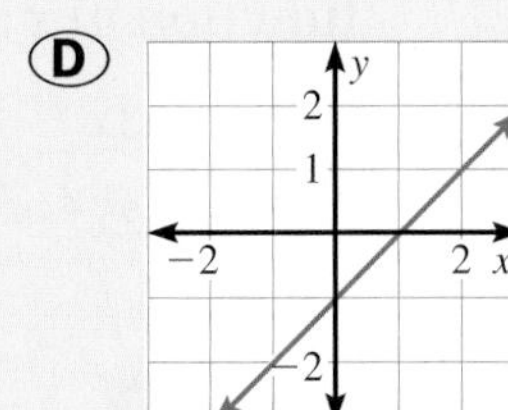

SOLUTION

STEP 1 **Choose** several x-values and make a table of values.

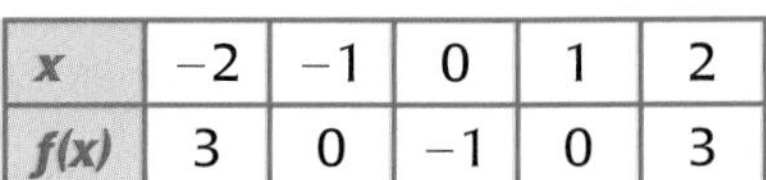

x	−2	−1	0	1	2
$f(x)$	3	0	−1	0	3

STEP 2 **List** the solutions as ordered pairs.
$(-2, 3), (-1, 0), (0, -1), (1, 0), (2, 3)$

STEP 3 **Plot** the ordered pairs. Then draw a smooth curve through the points, as shown.

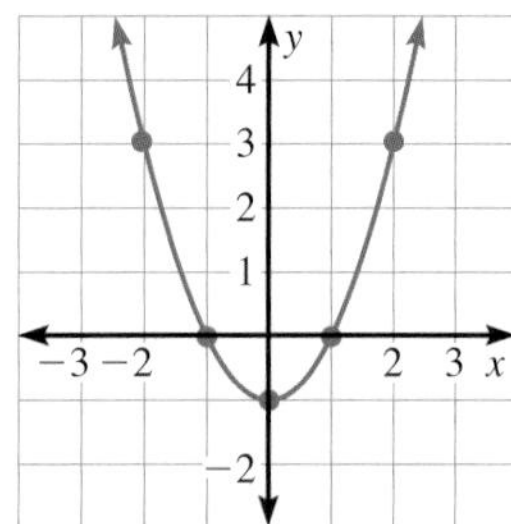

▶ **Answer** The graph that contains the points is graph B. The correct answer is B.
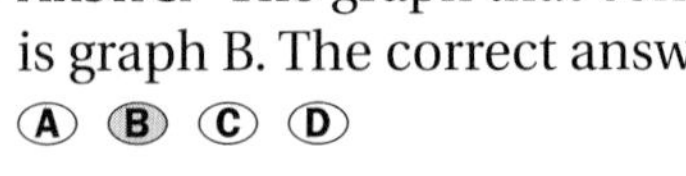

GUIDED PRACTICE for Example 2

Graph the function using a table of values.

4. $f(x) = -x^2 + 4$

5. $f(x) = x^2 + 1$

6. $f(x) = 2x^2$

Vertical Line Test You can use the **vertical line test** to tell whether a graph represents a function. If any vertical line intersects the graph at more than one point, then the graph does *not* represent a function. Remember, a function has exactly one output value for each input value.

EXAMPLE 3 Using the Vertical Line Test

 **Tell whether the graph represents a function.**

AVOID ERRORS

Consider *all* possible vertical lines by passing a straight edge across the entire graph. If any line intersects two or more points on the graph, the equation is not a function.

a.

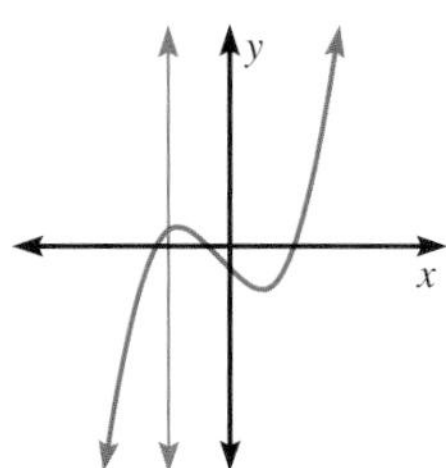

No vertical line intersects the graph at more than one point. So, the graph represents a function.

b.

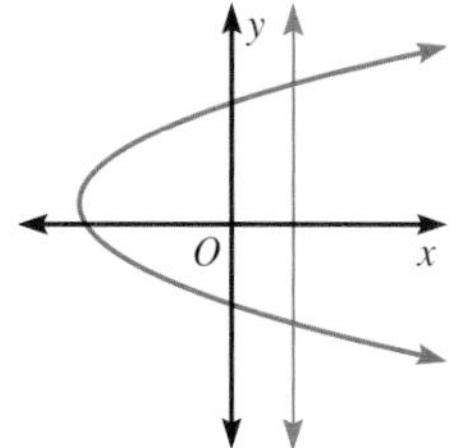

A vertical line intersects the graph at more than one point. So, the graph does *not* represent a function.

 **GUIDED PRACTICE** for Example 3

Tell whether the graph represents a function.

7.

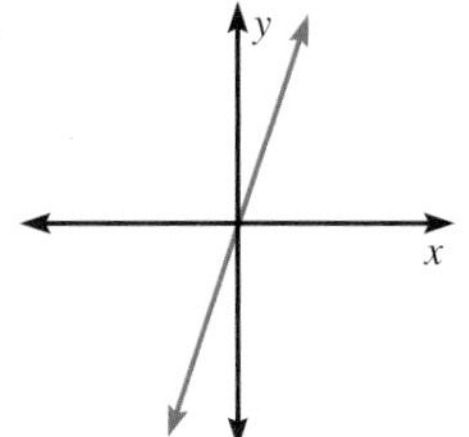

8.

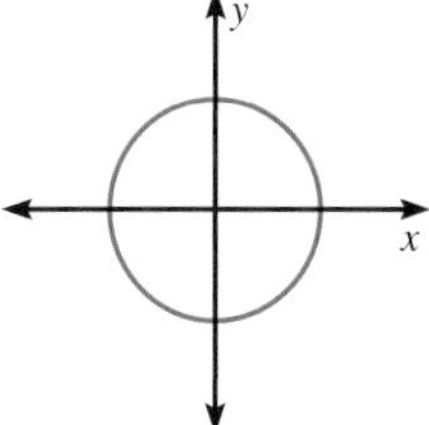

13.5 EXERCISES

HOMEWORK KEY

★ = **STANDARDIZED TEST PRACTICE** Exs. 10, 11, 42, 46, 47, 49, 51, and 65

○ = **HINTS AND HOMEWORK HELP** for Exs. 7, 13, 17, 21, 41 at classzone.com

SKILL PRACTICE

1. **VOCABULARY** *Explain* why $f = 2x + 4$ is not in function notation.

2. **VOCABULARY** Copy and complete: You can use the __?__ to determine whether a graph represents a function.

EVALUATING FUNCTIONS Rewrite the equation using function notation. Then evaluate the function for $x = -2, 0,$ and 2.

SEE EXAMPLE 1 on p. 739 for Exs. 3–9

3. $y = x^2$
4. $y = 4x^2$
5. $y = -3x^2$
6. $y = -x^2 + 10$
7. $y = x^2 - 5$
8. $y = 2x^2 - x$
9. **ERROR ANALYSIS** Describe and correct the error made in evaluating $f(x) = x^2 - 3$ for $x = -5$.

$f(-5) = -5^2 - 3$
$= -25 - 3$
$= -28$

SEE EXAMPLE 1 on p. 739 for Ex. 10

10. ★ **MULTIPLE CHOICE** Which equation is written in function notation?

(A) $2(f) + 4 = x$ (B) $f(x) = x^2 + 7$ (C) $y - 7 = x^2$ (D) $y = x^2 + 7$

SEE EXAMPLE 2 on p. 740 for Exs. 11–20

11. ★ **MULTIPLE CHOICE** Which is the graph of the function $y = \frac{1}{2}x^2$?

(A)
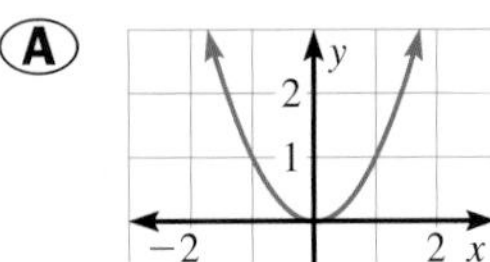

(B)
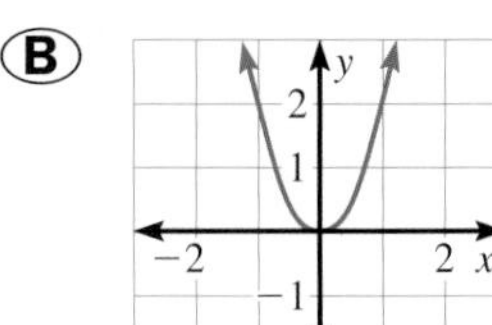

(C)
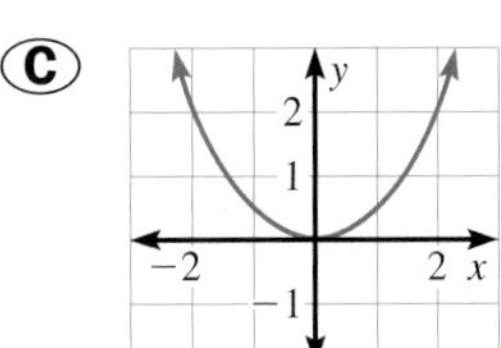

(D)
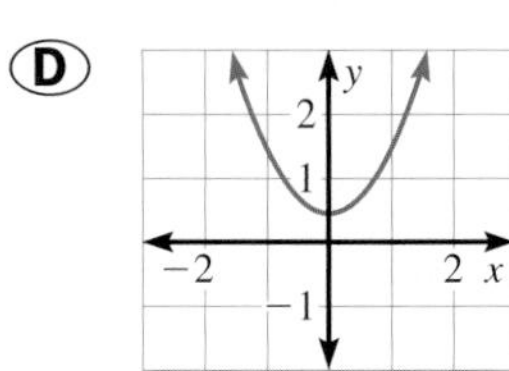

GRAPHING FUNCTIONS **Graph the function using a table of values with $x = -3, -2, -1, 0, 1, 2,$ and 3.**

12. $f(x) = 4x^2$ 13. $f(x) = x^2 + 8$ 14. $f(x) = -x^2 + 5$

15. $f(x) = -2x^2$ 16. $f(x) = 3x^2 - 4$ 17. $f(x) = -\frac{1}{2}x^2$

18. $f(x) = 5 - 5x^2$ 19. $f(x) = 4x^2 + x$ 20. $f(x) = x^2 - 3x$

VERTICAL LINE TEST **Tell whether the graph represents a function. Tell whether the graph is nonlinear.**

SEE EXAMPLE 3 on p. 741 for Exs. 21–24

21.
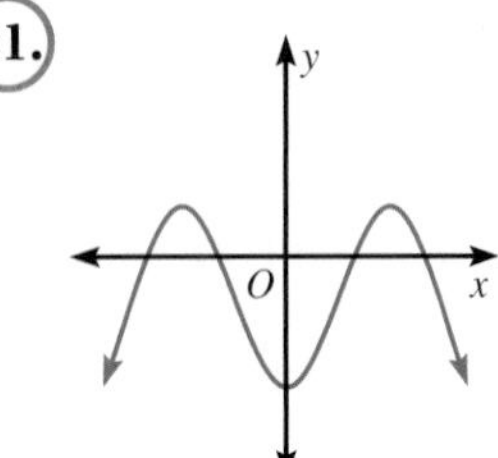

22.
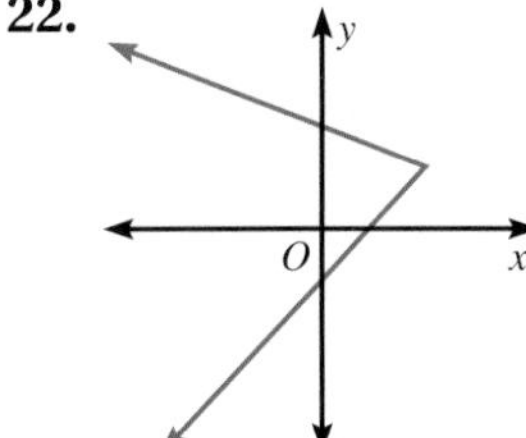

23.
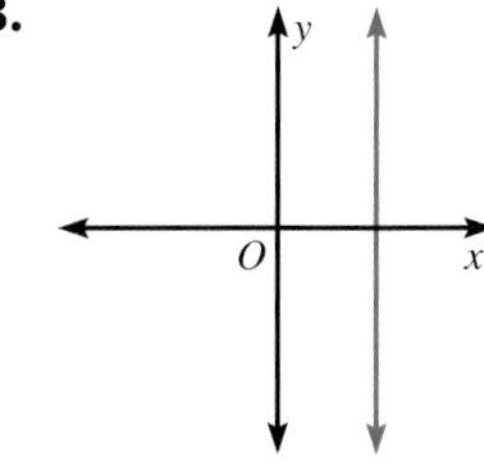

24. **WHICH ONE DOESN'T BELONG?** Which graph doesn't belong? *Explain.*

A.
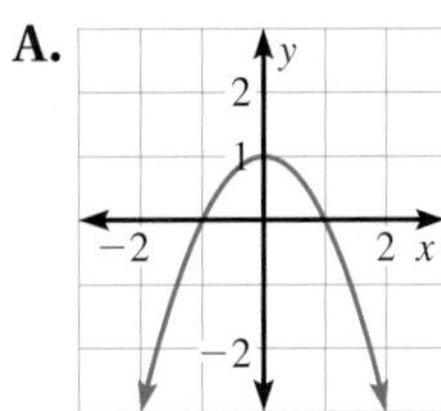

B.
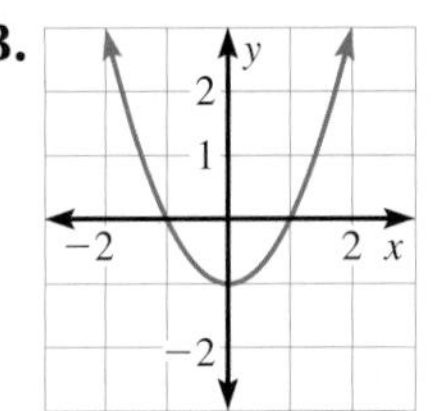

C.
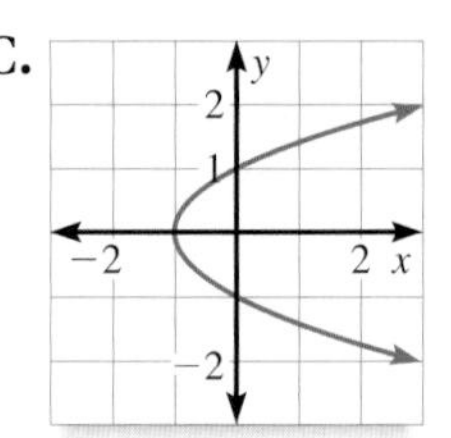

D.
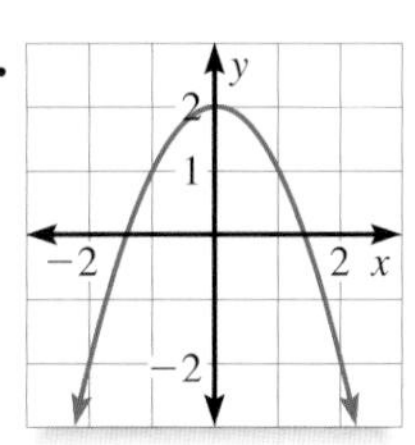

GRAPHING FUNCTIONS **Graph the function using a table of values.**

25. $f(x) = (x - 1)^2$ 26. $f(x) = (x + 2)^2$ 27. $f(x) = x^3 - 2$

28. $f(x) = 2x^3 - 3x$ 29. $f(x) = -x^4$ 30. $f(x) = 1 - \frac{1}{5}x^5$

SOLVING FOR X **Find the value(s) of x for which $f(x) = 4$.**

31. $f(x) = x^2$

32. $f(x) = 5x^2 - 6$

33. $f(x) = 8 - 4x^2$

34. $f(x) = (x + 7)^2$

35. $f(x) = (1 - x)^2$

36. $f(x) = x^3 + 4$

WORK BACKWARD **Write an equation in function notation for the given values.**

37.

x	−4	−2	0	2	4
$f(x)$	−64	−8	0	8	64

38.

x	−5	−2	0	3	6
$f(x)$	5	2	0	3	6

39. ROTATION Let c be a real number. Is the graph of $y = c$ a function? Is the graph a function after it is rotated 90° in either direction? *Explain.*

40. CHALLENGE Write an equation in function notation for the values in the table.

x	−2	−1	0	1	2
$f(x)$	−2	−5	−6	−5	−2

PROBLEM SOLVING

SEE EXAMPLE 1 on p. 739 for Exs. 41–43

41. REFLECTING POOL A rectangular reflecting pool is 50 feet long and 30 feet wide. The depth d, in feet, of the water is constant across the pool. Write a function that you can use to find the volume of water in the pool. Is the function *linear* or *nonlinear*?

42. ★ SHORT RESPONSE You drop a coin into a well. It hits water after 3 seconds. The elevation d, in feet, of the coin after it falls for t seconds in the air is given by $d = -16t^2 + 4$. Write the equation in function notation. How far does the coin fall before hitting the water? *Explain* your reasoning.

43. ACCOUNT BALANCES You deposit \$20 into a savings account that earns 2.4% interest compounded monthly. The expression $20(1.002)^t$ gives the account balance after t months. Write a function for the account balance, and find the balance after 1, 2, and 3 months.

SEE EXAMPLE 2 on p. 740 for Exs. 44, 45

44. DRAW A GRAPH Write a function for the area of the triangle shown at the right. Graph the function using a table of values. Estimate, to the nearest whole number, the value of x when the area of the triangle is 30 square inches.

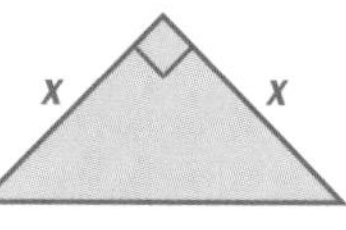

45. GEOMETRY Write in function notation an equation for the area of a circle with diameter x. Find the area when the diameter is 8 inches. Graph the equation.

SEE EXAMPLE 3 on p. 741 for Ex. 46

46. ★ WRITING *Describe* how to use the vertical line test and explain why it is used to determine whether a graph is a function.

47. ★ OPEN-ENDED MATH Write an equation for a nonlinear function. Graph the equation. Rotate the graph 90° clockwise and tell whether the rotated graph is a function.

SEE EXAMPLE 2 on p. 740 for Ex. 48

48. **GRAPH AND COMPARE** Graph the function $f(x) = x^3$ using a table of values. Be sure to include negative and positive x-values in your table. *Describe* how this graph is different from the graph of the function $f(x) = x^2$.

49. ★ **MULTIPLE CHOICE** You e-mail two copies of a joke on January 1. Each recipient e-mails two copies of the joke the day after receiving it. Which function gives the number of e-mails sent on day d, where $d = 1$ represents January 1, $d = 2$ represents January 2, and so on?

(A) $f(d) = 2d$ (B) $f(d) = 2^d$ (C) $f(d) = d^2$ (D) $f(d) = d + 2$

50. **MULTIPLE REPRESENTATIONS** In 2004, the United States population was about 292.8 million people and growing at 0.9% each year. You can predict the future population y with the equation $y = (292{,}800{,}000)(1.009)^t$, where t is the number of years since 2004.

  a. **Write a Function** Write the equation as a function.

  b. **Make a Table** Use the function in part (a) to create a table of values.

  c. **Draw a Graph** Draw a graph from the table in part (b). Predict the population of the United States in 2010.

51. ★ **EXTENDED RESPONSE** Graph the four functions below using tables of values and describe their differences. *Explain* the effect of a negative coefficient on a graph.

$f(x) = x^2$ $f(x) = -x^2$ $f(x) = \frac{1}{2}x$ $f(x) = -\frac{1}{2}x$

READING IN MATH **Read the information below for Exercises 52–54.**

Physics in Baseball The distance that a baseball flies in a home run is often estimated using physics, because using a measuring tape is often not reasonable. The major things that impact the distance that a hit baseball travels are the speed, the angle, and the height of the ball immediately after it leaves the bat. Because of other forces on the ball, the best angle to hit a home run has been proven to be about 35 degrees.

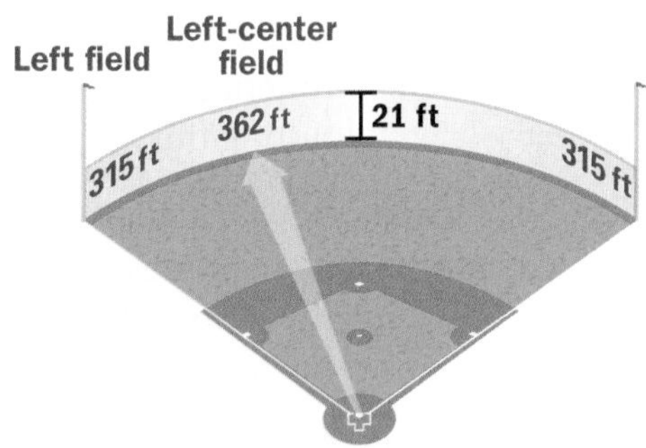

52. **Time** If a baseball were hit at a 35° angle and a speed of 110 feet per second from a height of 2.5 feet above the ground, it would travel about 90 feet per second horizontally. Write an equation in function notation for the horizontal distance traveled by the ball in x seconds.

53. **Distance** Under the conditions described in Exercise 52, the height of the ball is approximated by the function $f(x) = -16x^2 + 63x + 2.5$. When the ball is at a distance of 315 feet from the plate, is it high enough to go over the left field wall, shown above, and be a home run? *Explain.*

54. **Number Sense** *Describe* the domain of the function $f(t)$. Would this player have hit a home run if the ball had been hit to left-center field? *Explain.*

55. **CHALLENGE** Write a function for the area of the rectangle shown. Find the length and width of the rectangle when the area is *maximized*. *Explain* how you found your answers.

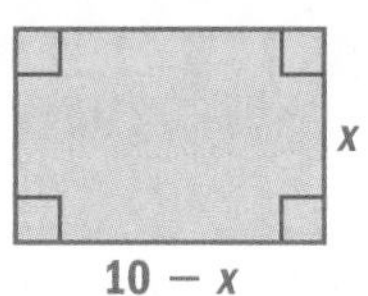

56. **CHALLENGE** Using tables of values, graph $f(x) = (x - 7)(x + 4)$, $g(x) = (x - 5)(x + 1)$, and $h(x) = (x - 2)(x + 3)$. Use your three graphs to predict the x-intercepts of the function $k(x) = (x - a)(x + b)$.

MIXED REVIEW

Solve the equation. *(p. 129)*

57. $3x + 1 = 7$
58. $2x + 5 = -17$
59. $-x + 1 = 2$
60. $-3x - 4 = 11$

CHOOSE A STRATEGY Use a strategy from the list to solve the following problem. *Explain* your choice of strategy.

61. You are saving pennies in a coffee can. On the first day, you put one penny in the can. On the second day, you put two more pennies in the can. On the third day, you put three more pennies in the can, and so on. How much money will be in the can on day 100?

Problem Solving Strategies
- Draw a Diagram *(p. 787)*
- Break into Parts *(p. 792)*
- Solve a Simpler Problem *(p. 793)*

Find the product and simplify. *(p. 734)*

62. $(x + 2)(x + 2)$
63. $(3z - 2)(2z - 1)$
64. $(5a - 1)(a + 3)$

65. ★ **MULTIPLE CHOICE** Which ordered pair is a solution of $2x + 4y = -12$? *(p. 593)*

Ⓐ $(-2, -2)$ Ⓑ $(-2, 2)$ Ⓒ $(2, -2)$ Ⓓ $(2, 2)$

QUIZ *for Lessons 13.4–13.5*

Find the product and simplify. *(p. 734)*

1. $(x - 1)(x + 9)$
2. $(a + 4)(a + 9)$
3. $(m - 2)(m - 8)$
4. $(4y + 5)(y - 2)$
5. $(b + 3)(4b - 3)$
6. $(3z - 2)(2z - 7)$

Rewrite using function notation. *(p. 739)*

7. $y = 3x + 9$
8. $y = -2x^2 - 4$
9. $y = 19 - x + x^2$

Evaluate the function for $x = -2, -1, 0, 1,$ and 2. *(p. 739)*

10. $f(x) = 2 - x^2$
11. $f(x) = \frac{1}{2}x^2 - 6$
12. $f(x) = x^2 + x$

Graph the function using a table of values. *(p. 739)*

13. $f(x) = -x^2 + 1$
14. $f(x) = \frac{1}{4}x^2$
15. $f(x) = -3x^2 - 4$

GOAL
Use a graphing calculator to graph nonlinear functions.

13.5 Graphing Nonlinear Functions

EXAMPLE **Use a graphing calculator to compare the functions.**

$y_1 = x^2$ $y_2 = 2x^2$ $y_3 = 3x^2$ $y_4 = 4x^2$

SOLUTION

Use the following keystrokes to enter the functions into a graphing calculator.

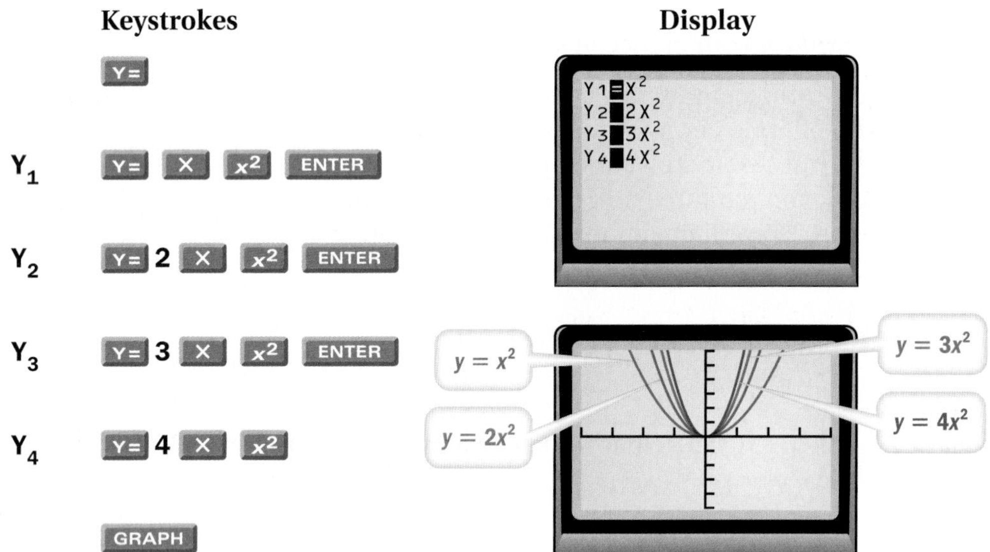

▸ **Answer** The graphs are curves, called *parabolas*, that pass through (0, 0). As the coefficient of x^2 increases, the curve gets narrower.

PRACTICE **Graph the functions using a graphing calculator. *Describe* the pattern in the graphs.**

1. $y = x^2 + 5$ **2.** $y = x^2 - 5$ **3.** $y = x^2 + 7$ **4.** $y = x^2 - 7$

GRAPH THE FUNCTIONS ***Compare*** **each graph to the graphs in the Example above.**

5. $y = -x^2$ **6.** $y = -2x^2$ **7.** $y = -3x^2$ **8.** $y = -4x^2$

9. $y = 3 - x^2$ **10.** $y = 3 + x^2$ **11.** $y = 8 - x^2$ **12.** $y = 8 + x^2$

Lessons 13.4 and 13.5

1. **MULTI-STEP PROBLEM** A cube has a side length of $x + 1$.
   a. Write the volume of the cube as a polynomial expression in standard form.
   b. A smaller cube has a side length of x. Write the volume of a cube with side length x as a monomial expression.
   c. The smaller cube is removed from the larger cube, as shown. Write a polynomial expression for the volume of the new solid in standard form.

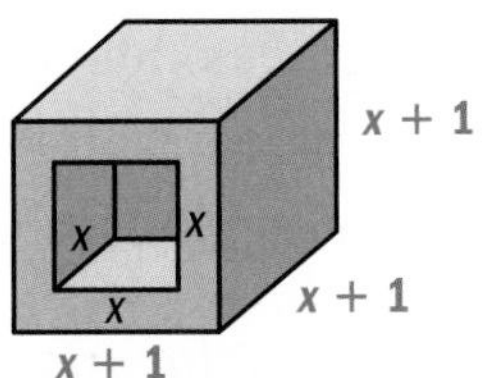

2. **GRIDDED ANSWER** The value, in dollars, of a \$2400 computer t years after buying it is $2400(0.5)^t$. If the computer was purchased in 2005, what is the first year that the value will be less than 5% of its original value?

3. **EXTENDED RESPONSE** Draw a square with length x, and cut out a triangle that shares one side of the square and has its two other sides in the interior of the square. The area of the figure can be modeled by $f(x) = x^2 - cx$, where c is half the height of the triangle. Graph the function for three values of c. *Compare* the graphs. Predict how the graph of the function $f(x) = x^2 - 25x$ will compare to your graphs.

4. **OPEN-ENDED** The height, in feet, of a thrown object is given by the function $f(x) = -16x^2 + vx + c$, where x is time in seconds, v is the initial upward speed in feet per second, and c is the initial height in feet. *Describe* a situation that this function could model and write a function to describe the height of an object.

5. **SHORT RESPONSE** A small business owner predicts that $P(t) = (5t - 3)^2 - 50$ models the profit, in thousands of dollars, for the next 5 years, while the accountant predicts the model is $P(t) = 16t^2 - 12t - 41$ if t is the number of years from today. Find an expression for the difference in the models. Evaluate this expression when $t = 4$. *Explain* the significance of your answer.

6. **EXTENDED RESPONSE** A vehicle is decelerating at a certain rate. The equation $f(x) = \sqrt{18x}$ describes the speed in miles per hour of the vehicle before the skid as a function of x, the skid length in feet.
   a. Copy and complete the table.

x	0	2	8	18	32	50
$f(x)$	?	?	?	?	?	?

   b. Use the table to estimate $f(7)$, $f(20)$, and $f(30)$. *Explain* your reasoning.
   c. Graph the function using the table of values in part (a). Is this graph linear? *Explain.*
   d. Use the graph in part (c) to estimate $f(11)$, $f(22)$, and $f(35)$.

7. **EXTENDED RESPONSE** A squirrel drops a nut from the top of a tree. The height of the nut can be modeled by $f(x) = -16x^2 + 90$, where x is the number of seconds after the nut is dropped.
   a. Copy and complete the table. Then graph the function.

x	0	0.5	1.0	1.5	2.0	2.5
$f(x)$	?	?	?	?	?	?

   b. Estimate the amount of time that passes before the nut hits the ground.
   c. From what height is the nut dropped? *Explain* your reasoning.

13 CHAPTER REVIEW

@HomeTutor
classzone.com
Vocabulary Practice

REVIEW KEY VOCABULARY

- polynomial, *p. 717*
- binomial, *p. 717*
- trinomial, *p. 717*
- standard form, *p. 717*
- function notation, *p. 739*
- vertical line test, *p. 740*

VOCABULARY EXERCISES

Copy and complete the statement.

1. The sum of two or more monomials is called a _?_.
2. The polynomial $x^3 - 2x + 1$ is a _?_.
3. A polynomial in one variable is written in _?_ if the exponents of the variable decrease from left to right.
4. You can use the _?_ to tell whether a graph represents a function.

Classify the polynomial as a *monomial*, a *binomial*, or a *trinomial*.

5. $5x^3 + 2x + 3$
6. $5a^3$
7. $5y + 3$
8. $-r + 3$

REVIEW EXAMPLES AND EXERCISES

13.1 Polynomials

pp. 717–720

EXAMPLE

Simplify the polynomial $4x^2 - 5(x^2 - x + 3 - 2x)$.

$4x^2 - 5(x^2 - x + 3 - 2x)$

$= 4x^2 - 5x^2 + 5x - 15 + 10x$ **Distributive property**

$= -x^2 + 15x - 15$ **Combine like terms.**

EXERCISES

Simplify the polynomial and write it in standard form.

SEE EXAMPLES 1, 2, AND 3 on pp. 717–718 for Exs. 9–15

9. $8k + 1 + 3k + k^2 - 4$
10. $5w - 2w + 2w^2 - 8$
11. $6p^2 + 9(2p^3 + 3 + p^2)$
12. $3x^2 + 4(7 - x^2 + 4x)$
13. $-8(2s - 3s^2 + 7) + 4s^3$
14. $4(5y - 2y^2 + 11) - 2y^2$
15. **Height** The height, in feet, of a falling acorn after t seconds of falling from a height of 70 feet can be found using the polynomial $-16t^2 + 70$. What is the acorn's height after 2 seconds of falling?

13.2 Adding and Subtracting Polynomials

pp. 721–725

EXAMPLE

Find the sum $(3x^2 - 2x + 7) + (5x - 9)$.

$$\begin{array}{r} 3x^2 - 2x + 7 \\ + \qquad 5x - 9 \\ \hline 3x^2 + 3x - 2 \end{array}$$

Write the second polynomial under the first.
Arrange like terms in columns.
Combine like terms.

EXERCISES

Find the sum or difference.

SEE EXAMPLES 1, 2, 3, AND 4 on pp. 721–723 for Exs. 16–20

16. $(10q^2 - 6) - (q^2 + 1)$

17. $(7y^2 + y - 4) + (y^2 - y - 1)$

18. $4(m^2 - 3m) + 5(2m^2 - m)$

19. $-2(v^3 - v^2 + v) - 3(v^3 + 4v^2)$

20. Perimeter Write a polynomial expression for the perimeter of the quadrilateral. Simplify the polynomial.

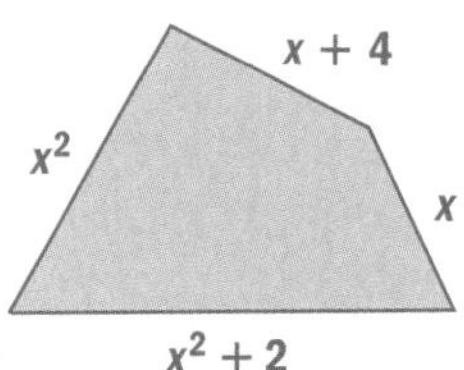

13.3 Monomials and Powers

pp. 726–731

EXAMPLE

Simplify the expression $(x^3)(3x)^2$.

$(x^3)(3x)^2 = x^3(3^2 \cdot x^2)$ **Power of a product property**

$= x^3 \cdot 9 \cdot x^2$ **Evaluate the power.**

$= 9x^5$ **Product of powers property**

EXERCISES

Simplify the expression.

SEE EXAMPLES 1, 2, 3, AND 4 on pp. 726–728 for Exs. 21–27

21. $(-6a^2b^4)^3$

22. $x^2(5x - 7)$

23. $-3a(a^2 - 2a)$

Write a polynomial expression for the area of the figure and simplify.

24.

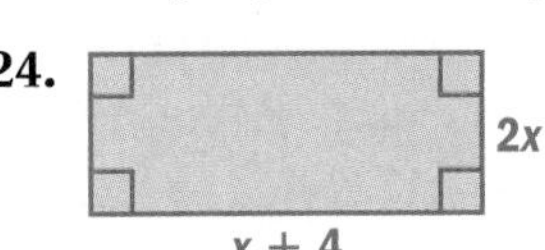

25. 3x + 9, 6x

26. x − 5, 4x

27. Volume Write the expression for the volume of a sphere with a radius of $3x$.

13.4 Multiplying Binomials

pp. 734–738

EXAMPLE

Find the product $(x + 3)(x + 2)$ and simplify.

$(x + 3)(x + 2) = x(x + 2) + 3(x + 2)$ **Distributive property**

$= x^2 + 2x + 3x + 6$ **Distributive property**

$= x^2 + 5x + 6$ **Combine like terms.**

EXERCISES

SEE EXAMPLES 1, 2, 3, AND 4 on pp. 734–735 for Exs. 28–30

Find the product and simplify.

28. $(t + 3)(t - 4)$ **29.** $(q - 7)(q - 9)$ **30.** $(2k - 9)(-4k - 1)$

13.5 Nonlinear Functions

pp. 739–745

EXAMPLE

Graph $f(x) = -2x^2 + 5$.

STEP 1 **Choose** several x-values and make a table of values.

x	−2	−1	0	1	2
$f(x)$	−3	3	5	3	−3

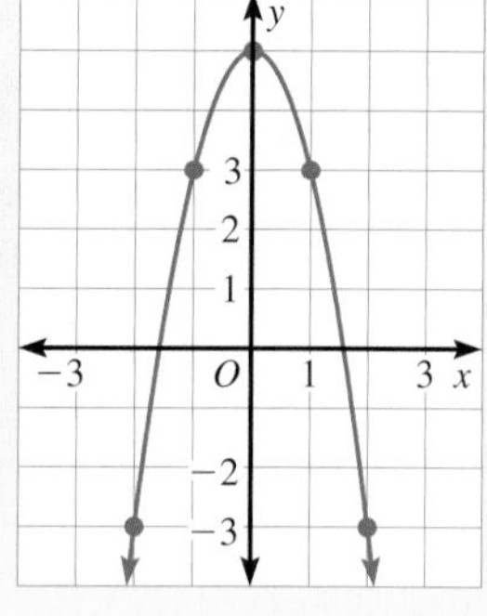

STEP 2 **List** the solutions as ordered pairs.
$(-2, -3), (-1, 3), (0, 5), (1, 3), (2, -3)$

STEP 3 **Graph** the ordered pairs. Draw a smooth curve through the points, as shown.

EXERCISES

Graph the function using a table of values.

SEE EXAMPLES 2 AND 3 on pp. 740–741 for Exs. 31–37

31. $f(x) = x^2 + 3$ **32.** $f(x) = 7 - x^2$ **33.** $f(x) = x^2 - 4$ **34.** $f(x) = 3x^2 + 1$

Tell whether the graph represents a function.

35.

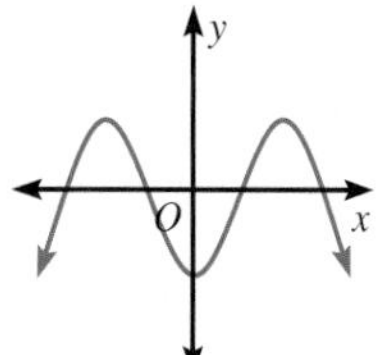

36.

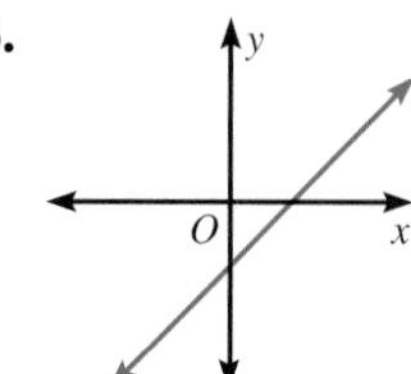

37.

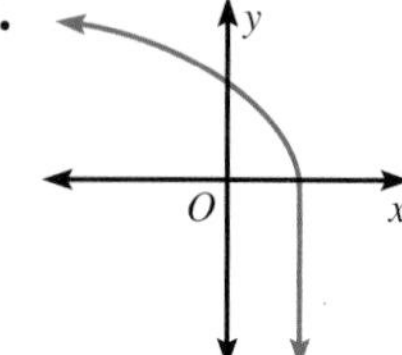

13 CHAPTER TEST

@HomeTutor
classzone.com
Chapter Test Practice

Simplify the polynomial and write it in standard form.

1. $10x - 7x + 4 + x^2 - 3x + 4$

2. $-y + 6(y^2 - y^3 + 1)$

Find the sum or difference.

3. $(3r^2 + 4r - 7) + (-r^2 - r + 11)$

4. $(4s^2 - 11s) - (s^2 - 6s + 21)$

5. $(4a^5 - a) + (-3a^5 + 1)$

6. $(-y^2 + 12) + (8y^2 - 10)$

7. $(5x^6 - 3x^2 + x) - (4x^2 + 2x)$

8. $(-7z^3 + z^2 - 5) - (z^3 - 3z^2 + 1)$

Simplify the expression.

9. $(3a^2)(5a^2b)$

10. $(9z)^2$

11. $(3d^2)^4$

12. $(-2w^4)^3$

13. $(-2p^2)^4$

14. $(x^4y)^8$

15. $(4n^2)(-3n)$

16. $(3r)^3(3r)$

Find the product and simplify.

17. $m(3m + 8)$

18. $7n(n^2 - 2)$

19. $3p(2p^2 + 3p)$

20. $(2x + 7)(3x + 2)$

21. $(4y + 12)(y - 3)$

22. $(z - 9)(5z + 8)$

23. $(4k + 5)(2k + 8)$

24. $(7b + 9)(b - 4)$

25. $(t - 6)(3t + 12)$

Graph the function using a table of values.

26. $f(x) = -5x^2$

27. $f(x) = x^2 + 3$

28. $f(x) = x^2 - 1$

Tell whether the graph represents a function.

29.

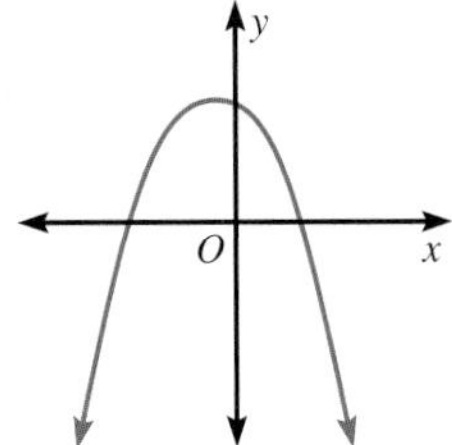

30.

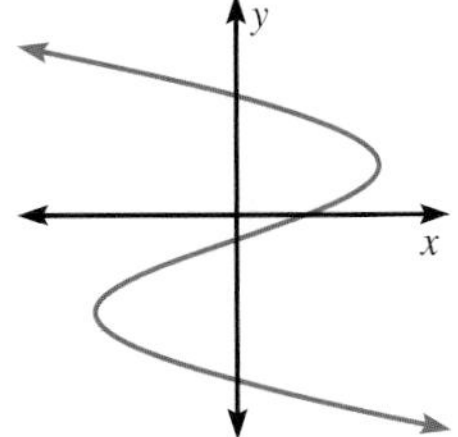

31.

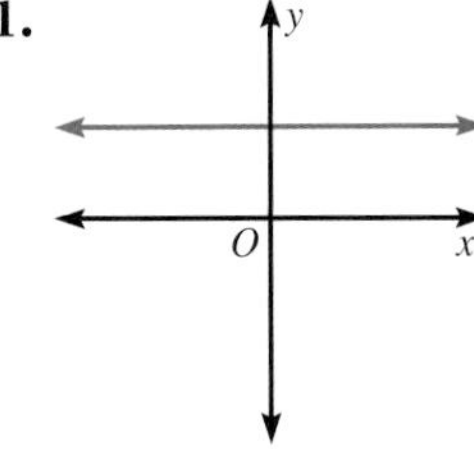

32. APPLE PICKING An apple falls from a 28 foot tall tree. The height, in feet, of the apple after t seconds of falling can be found using the polynomial $-16t^2 + 28$. Find the apple's height after 0.5 second.

33. PERIMETER Write a polynomial expression for the perimeter of the triangle. Simplify the polynomial.

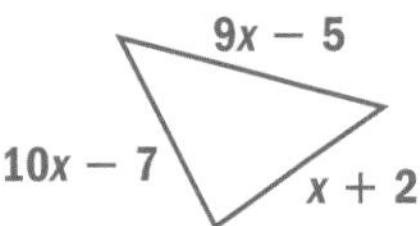

34. SPEED SKIING A speed skier is accelerating at a rate of a ft/sec^2 for a period of t seconds. The function $f(t) = \frac{1}{2}at^2$ models the distance, in feet, traveled by the skier. Graph the function that models an acceleration of 15 ft/sec^2.

13 ★ Standardized TEST PREPARATION

Scoring Rubric

Full Credit
- solution is complete and correct

Partial Credit
- solution is complete but errors are made, *or*
- solution is without error but incomplete

No Credit
- no solution is given, *or*
- solution makes no sense

SHORT RESPONSE QUESTIONS

PROBLEM

The polygon shown was created by removing a square from the corner of a rectangle. Write polynomial expressions for the area and the perimeter of the polygon. Then find the area and perimeter of the polygon when $x = 7$ inches. *Explain* your reasoning.

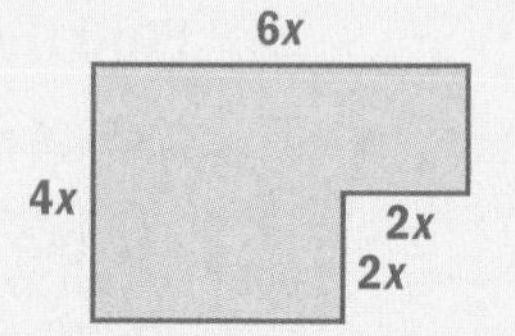

Below are sample solutions to the problem. Read each solution and the comments in blue to see why the sample represents full credit, partial credit, or no credit.

SAMPLE 1: Full Credit Solution

The steps are clearly stated and reflect correct mathematical reasoning.

To find the area of the polygon, subtract the area of the square that was removed from the area of the rectangle.

The area of the square removed is $(2x)(2x) = 4x^2$.

The area of the rectangle is $(4x)(6x) = 24x^2$.

Now, find the area of the polygon.

$$A = 24x^2 - 4x^2 = 20x^2$$

To find the perimeter of the polygon, add the side lengths.

$$P = 4x + 6x + 2x + 2x + 2x + 4x = 20x$$

The answer is correct.

When $x = 7$ inches, the area of the polygon is 980 square inches and the perimeter of the polygon is 140 inches.

SAMPLE 2: Partial Credit Solution

This reasoning is correct.

To find the area of the polygon, subtract the area of the square that was removed from the area of the rectangle.

The area of the polygon is $A = (4x)(6x) - (2x)(2x) = 24x^2 - 4x^2 = 20x^2$.

The perimeter is calculated incorrectly.

The perimeter of the polygon is $P = 4x + 6x + 2x + 2x = 14x$.

The answer is incorrect.

When $x = 7$ inches, the area of the polygon is 980 square inches and the perimeter of the polygon is 98 inches.

SAMPLE 3: Partial Credit Solution

This reasoning is correct.

To find the area of the polygon, subtract the area of the square that was removed from the area of the rectangle.

The area is calculated incorrectly.

The area of the polygon is $A = (4x)(6x) - (2x)(2x) = 24x - 4x = 20x$.

The perimeter of the polygon is $P = 4x + 6x + 2x + 2x + 2x + 4x = 20x$.

The answer is incorrect.

When $x = 7$ inches, the area of the polygon is 140 square inches and the perimeter of the polygon is 140 inches.

SAMPLE 4: No Credit Solution

The answer is incorrect and it is not justified.

The area of the polygon is 1176 square inches and the perimeter of the polygon is 140 inches.

PRACTICE Apply the Scoring Rubric

Score the solution to the problem below as *full credit, partial credit,* or *no credit*. *Explain* your reasoning.

PROBLEM An acorn falls from a tree 92 feet off the ground. The polynomial $-16t^2 + 92$ gives the acorn's height, in feet, after t seconds of falling. Find its height after 1 second and 2 seconds of falling. Estimate how many seconds the acorn falls before hitting the ground.

1. After 1 second, the acorn has a height of 76 feet. After 2 seconds, the acorn has a height of 60 feet. The acorn hits the ground after 5.75 seconds.

2. The height of the acorn after 1 second is:

$$-16t^2 + 92 = -16(1)^2 + 92 = 76 \text{ feet}$$

The height of the acorn after 2 seconds is:

$$-16t^2 + 92 = -16(2)^2 + 92 = 28 \text{ feet}$$

When the acorn hits the ground the height is zero, so:

$$-16t^2 + 92 = 0$$
$$t^2 = 5.75$$
$$t \approx 2.3979$$

The acorn hits the ground after about 2.4 seconds.

13 ★ Standardized TEST PRACTICE

SHORT RESPONSE

1. The function $S = 4\pi r^2$ gives the surface areas of a sphere with radius r. Write this equation in function notation. Graph the equation. Estimate the radius of a sphere that has a surface area of 50 square centimeters. Use 3.14 for π. *Explain* your steps.

2. The polygon shown was created by removing a square from the corner of a larger square. Write polynomial expressions for the area and the perimeter of the polygon. Then find the area and perimeter of the polygon when $x = 4$ meters. *Explain* your reasoning.

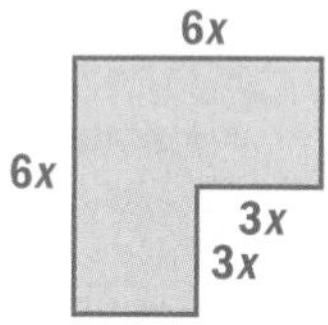

3. A ball is hit upward at a rate of 75 mi/h, or 110 ft/sec. The height, in feet, of the ball is given by the function $f(x)$, where $f(x) = -16x^2 + 110x + 3$ and x is the number of seconds after the ball is hit. Graph this function. Use the graph to estimate how many seconds will pass before the ball lands on the ground. *Explain* how you found your answer.

4. Write a polynomial expression for the area of each colored region of the figure shown. Write a polynomial expression for the sum of these areas. Write an expression for the area of the entire figure as a product of two binomials. *Explain* how you found the product.

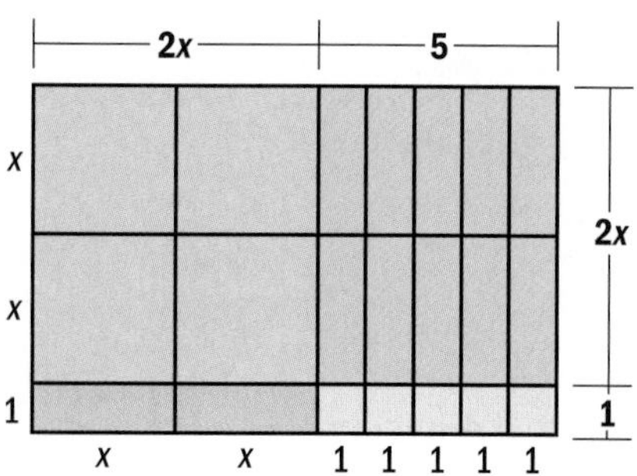

5. A farmer is enclosing a rectangular horse corral that connects to the side of a barn, as shown. You have 400 feet of fencing. Write a polynomial expression in terms of length l in standard form that represents the area of the corral. *Explain* how you found your answer.

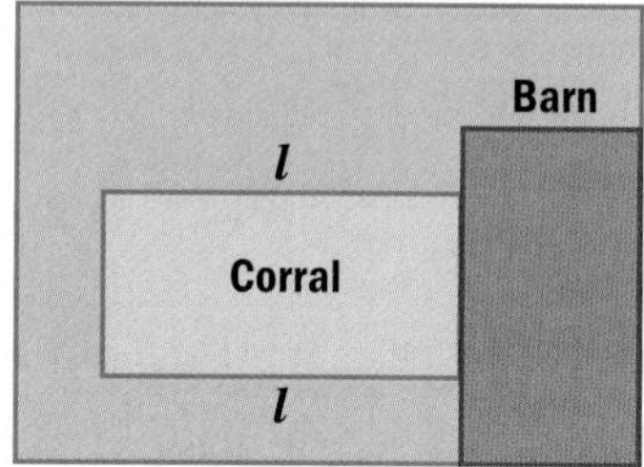

6. A ball falls from a ledge 100 feet off the ground. The polynomial $-16t^2 + 100$ gives the ball's height, in feet, after t seconds of falling. Find its height after 1 second and 2 seconds of falling. Estimate how many seconds the ball falls before hitting the ground.

7. The radius r of a cylinder is three times its height h. Write a polynomial expression for the surface area S of the cylinder using only the radius. Write a polynomial expression for the surface area of the cylinder using only the height. Use the formula $S = 2\pi r^2 + 2\pi rh$.

8. Write a polynomial equation for the perimeter of the trapezoid. Write a polynomial equation for the area of the trapezoid. Write the equations as functions. Are the functions linear? *Explain.*

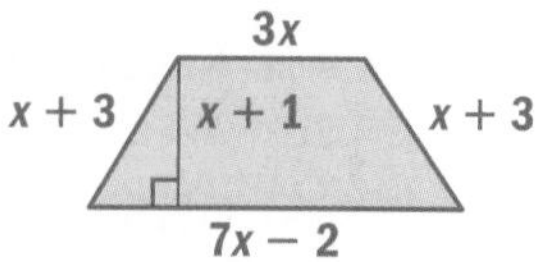

9. Graph $f(x) = 3x^2 - c$ for $c = 1, 3,$ and 5. *Explain* how the graphs are similar and how they are different. *Describe* the graph of the function $f(x) = 3x^2 - 100$.

MULTIPLE CHOICE

10. Simplify the expression $(3a^2)(4a + 1)$.

(A) $7a^2 + 3a$ (B) $7a^2 + 1$

(C) $12a^3 + 3a^2$ (D) $12a^3 + 3$

11. Find the product $(3x + 3)(2x - 2)$ and simplify.

(A) $6x^2 + 6$ (B) $6x^2 - 6$

(C) $6x^2 + 6x - 6$ (D) $6x^2 - 6x + 6$

12. The diameter of a cylinder is six times its height h. Which expression represents the volume of the cylinder?

(A) πh^3 (B) $9\pi h^3$

(C) $36\pi h^3$ (D) $144\pi h^3$

GRIDDED ANSWER

13. The perimeter of a square with a side length of $(4x + 1)$ feet is 52 feet. What is the value of x?

14. Find the value of the function $f(x) = 3x^2 + 14$ for $x = -2$.

15. A triangle has a height that is 5 more than 3 times the length of the base. The base is 4 inches. What is the area of the triangle, in square inches?

16. Jodi deposits \$40 into a savings account that earns 3% interest compounded monthly. The function $f(t) = 40(1.0025)^t$ gives the balance of the account after t months. What is the y-intercept of the graph?

EXTENDED RESPONSE

17. The position, in feet, of an object can be modeled by $f(t) = -16t^2 + 65$, where t is the number of seconds after the object is dropped.

a. Copy and complete the table. Then graph the function.

t	0	0.5	1	1.5	2	2.5
$f(t)$	?	?	?	?	?	?

b. Estimate the amount of time that passes before the object hits the ground.

c. From what height is the object dropped? What is the domain of the function? *Explain* your reasoning.

18. A store sells short-sleeve and long-sleeve T-shirts. Each short-sleeve T-shirt costs \$3 to make and is sold for \$6. Each long-sleeve T-shirt costs \$3.50 to make and is sold for \$8.

a. Write an expression for the cost of making x short-sleeve T-shirts and y long-sleeve T-shirts. Write an expression for the revenue from selling x short-sleeve T-shirts and y long-sleeve T-shirts.

b. Write an expression for the profit from selling x short-sleeve T-shirts and y long-sleeve T-shirts. (Hint: Profit = Revenue − Cost)

c. The store estimates it will sell 100 short-sleeve T-shirts this month. How many long-sleeve T-shirts does it need to sell this month to have a profit of at least \$1200? *Explain.*

13 CUMULATIVE REVIEW Chapters 1–13

Order the numbers from least to greatest.

1. $-45, 45, 43, -43, -43.5$ *(p. 57)*
2. $-25, -(-25), |35|, -|20|, |-16|$ *(p. 57)*
3. $2\frac{3}{10}, 2.32, \frac{11}{5}, 2.25, \frac{5}{2}$ *(p. 255)*
4. $0.45, \frac{3}{8}, 0.4, \frac{5}{12}, 0.46$ *(p. 255)*
5. $0.\overline{18}, 0.\overline{181}, 0.\overline{188}, 0.188$ *(p. 475)*
6. $2.\overline{7}, 2.\overline{72}, 2.\overline{727}, 2.72$ *(p. 475)*

Give the coordinates of the point. *(p. 94)*

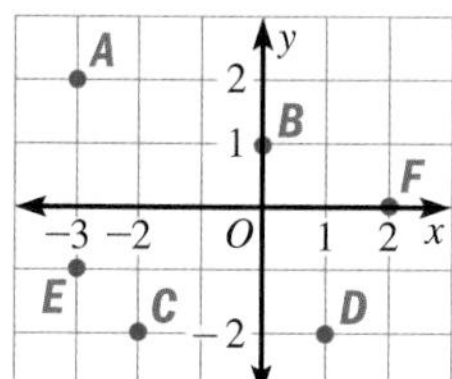

7. A
8. B
9. C
10. D
11. E
12. F

Evaluate the expression $\sqrt{x^2 - y^2}$ for the given values. *(p. 469)*

13. $x = 5, y = 3$
14. $x = 10, y = 8$
15. $x = 15, y = 12$

Find the perimeter of the triangle. *(p. 487)*

16.
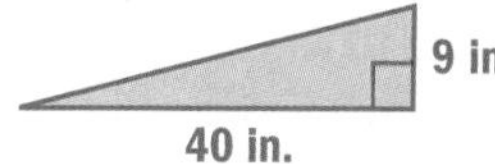

17.
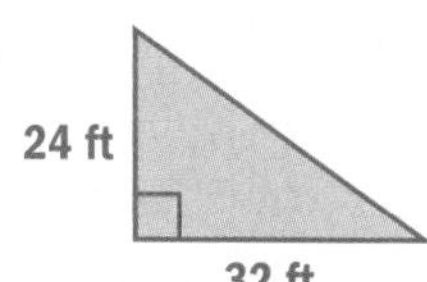

18.
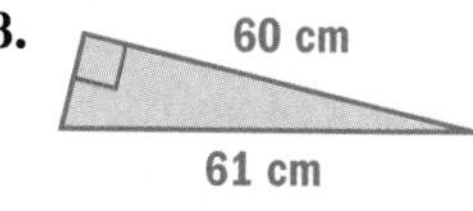

Graph the equation or inequality.

19. $y = 4 + \frac{2}{3}x$ *(p. 622)*
20. $x + y = 6$ *(p. 622)*
21. $2y + 6x = 10$ *(p. 622)*
22. $y < x - 4$ *(p. 622)*
23. $y \geq 2x - 3$ *(p. 629)*
24. $x + y > 6$ *(p. 629)*

Make a stem-and-leaf plot. Tell which stem includes the most values. Then make a box-and-whisker plot. *(pp. 649, 654)*

25. 46 kg, 70 kg, 21 kg, 136 kg, 55 kg, 60 kg, 72 kg, 104 kg, 52 kg
26. 12.1 in., 13.5 in., 12.8 in., 10 in., 7 in., 11.2 in., 12.9 in., 11.1 in., 12 in., 13.7 in.

Evaluate the expression.

27. ${}_{11}P_5$ *(p. 675)*
28. ${}_{13}P_4$ *(p. 675)*
29. ${}_{10}C_3$ *(p. 680)*
30. ${}_{12}C_7$ *(p. 680)*

Simplify.

31. $(10q^2 - 6) + (q^2 + 1)$ *(p. 721)*
32. $(7y^2 + y - 4) + (y^2 - y - 1)$ *(p. 721)*
33. $(3x^3 + 4x - 1) + (x^3 - x^2 - 8)$ *(p. 721)*
34. $(4x^2 - 2x + 5) - (x^2 - 6x + 8)$ *(p. 721)*
35. $(2xy)^3$ *(p. 726)*
36. $(7z)(-4z)^2$ *(p. 726)*
37. $(-c^3)(2c^4)$ *(p. 726)*
38. $-y^3(-y^2 + 11y)$ *(p. 726)*

39. **LANDSCAPING** A lawn cart can haul a maximum of 300 pounds. You are hauling logs across your yard for a landscaping project. Using 15 pounds as the average weight per log, write an inequality that models the situation. Solve the inequality and interpret the solution. ***(p. 154)***

40. **WALKING** You take a break after walking $3\frac{3}{4}$ miles of a 5 mile trail. How much of the trail is left? You walk $\frac{1}{2}$ of the remaining portion of the trail, then it starts to rain so you run to the end of the trail. How far did you run? ***(p. 238)***

41. **FUNDRAISER** At a school fundraiser, the science club made 58% of its money selling juice, 27% selling cookies, and 15% selling apples. The club made $87 selling juice. How much did the club make selling cookies? How much did it make selling apples? ***(p. 375)***

42. **BUILDINGS** The area of the square base of a building is 3721 square feet. Find the perimeter of the base of the building and the length of the diagonal of the base to the nearest foot. ***(p. 482)***

43. **DRAWING NETS** Draw a net for an octagonal pyramid. How many faces, edges, and vertices does the octagonal pyramid have? ***(p. 534)***

44. **BASEBALL** You have $60 to spend. Baseballs are $6 each and sunflower seeds are $3 per package. The number of each item you can buy is modeled by the equation $6x + 3y = 60$. Graph the equation and explain what the intercepts represent. ***(p. 606)***

45. **GROCERY SHOPPING** You have $20 to spend on peppers for a big pot of chili you are making. Jalapeno peppers cost $3.00 per pound and red bell peppers cost $4.00 per pound. The amount of each pepper you can buy is modeled by the inequality $3x + 4y \leq 20$ where x is the number of pounds of jalapeno peppers, and y is the number of pounds of red bell peppers. Graph the inequality. ***(p. 629)***

46. **PHOTOGRAPHY** You and six friends line up for a photograph in one row. In how many ways can you line up for the photograph? ***(p. 675)***

47. **SOFTBALL** A softball player has a batting average of .350, which means she gets a hit 35% of her times at bat. What are the odds that she will get a hit in her next at bat? ***(p. 685)***

48. **DISTANCE** The height, in feet, of a projectile t seconds after it was launched can be found by evaluating the expression $-16t^2 + 64t + 5$. Find the height of the projectile when $t = 1$ and $t = 3$. What do you notice? *Explain* how this is possible. ***(p. 717)***

49. **INTEREST** You deposit $25 into a savings account with interest compounded annually. The account balance after 2 years is given by the expression $25(r + 1)^2$. Expand this expression and simplify. ***(p. 734)***

Contents of Student Resources

Skills Review Handbook

Problem Solving Handbook: Strategy Review

Problem Solving Handbook: Strategy Practice

Extra Practice for Chapters 1–13

Tables

English-Spanish Glossary

Index

Credits

Selected Answers

Place Value

The **whole numbers** are the numbers 0, 1, 2, 3, ... A **digit** is any of the numbers 0, 1, 2, 3, 4, 5, 6, 7, 8, or 9. The decimals are numbers such as 121.32, 25.6, and 3.456. For example, the decimal 4.5 has the digits 4 and 5. The place value of each digit in a whole number or a decimal depends on its position within the number. For example, in the number 491,037.892, the 8 has a value of 0.8 or 8×0.1 because it is in the tenths' place.

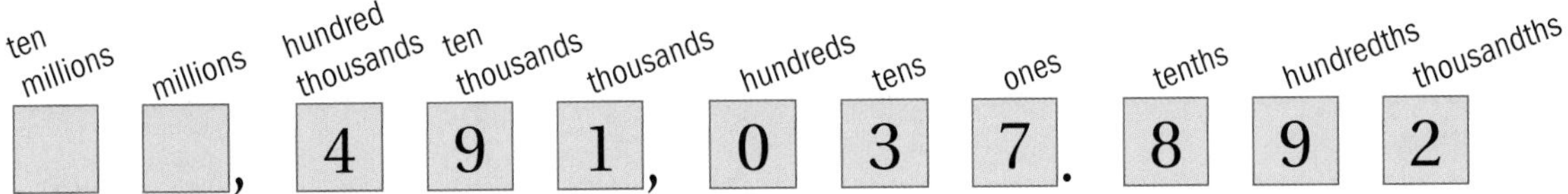

EXAMPLE 1

Write the number 27,037.6 in expanded form.

$27{,}037.6 = 20{,}000 + 7000 + 30 + 7 + 0.6$

$= 2 \times 10{,}000 + 7 \times 1000 + 3 \times 10 + 7 \times 1 + 6 \times 0.1$

The zero in the hundreds' position is a placeholder.

EXAMPLE 2

Write the number in standard form.

a. $4 \times 1000 + 5 \times 10 + 6 \times 0.1 + 8 \times 0.01$

b. Four million, sixty thousand, five and two thousandths

SOLUTION

a. $4 \times 1000 + 5 \times 10 + 6 \times 0.1 + 8 \times 0.01 = 4000 + 50 + 0.6 + 0.08$

$= 4050.68$

b. Write 4 in the millions' place, 6 in the ten thousands' place, 5 in the ones' place, and the 2 in the thousandths' place. Use zeros as placeholders for the other places. The answer is 4,060,005.002.

PRACTICE

Write the number in expanded form.

1. 56,809 **2.** 3.075 **3.** 1002.003 **4.** 306.405

Write the number in standard form.

5. $5 \times 100{,}000 + 6 \times 10 + 9 \times 1 + 7 \times 0.001$ **6.** Five million, ten and thirty-six thousandths

Rounding

To **round** a number means to approximate the number to a given place value. When rounding, look at the digit to the right of that place value. If the digit to the right is less than 5 (0, 1, 2, 3, or 4), round down. If the digit to the right is 5 or greater (5, 6, 7, 8, or 9), round up.

EXAMPLE 1

Round the number to the place value of the red digit.

a. 6932 **b.** 45.674

SOLUTION

a. Because the 9 is in the hundreds' place, round 6932 to the nearest hundred. Notice that 6932 is between 6900 and 7000, so it will round to one of these two numbers.

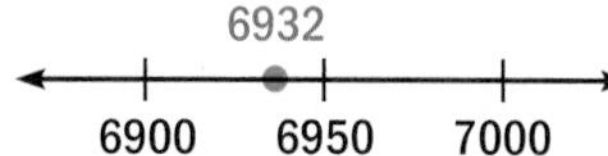

Notice that 6932 is closer to 6900 than to 7000.

The digit to the right of the 9 in the hundreds' place is the 3 in the tens' place. Because 3 is less than 5, round down.

▸ **Answer** 6932 rounded to the nearest hundred is 6900.

b. Because 6 is in the tenths' place, round 45.674 to the nearest tenth. Notice that 45.674 is between 45.6 and 45.7, so it will round to one of these two numbers.

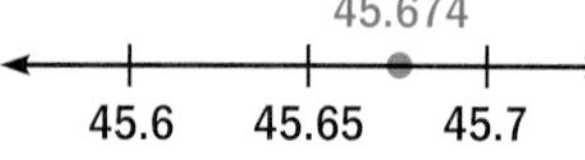

Notice that 45.674 is closer to 45.7 than to 45.6.

The digit to the right of the 6 in the tenths' place is the 7 in the hundredths' place. Because 7 is 5 or greater, round up.

▸ **Answer** 45.674 rounded to the nearest tenth is 45.7.

PRACTICE

Round the number to the place value of the red digit.

1. 1253
2. 57,309
3. 8.183
4. 32.76
5. 44,380
6. 12.535
7. 452.84
8. 998,543
9. 62.847
10. 640,796
11. 164.479
12. 1209.4
13. 52.961
14. 12,742.5
15. 3,501,652

Divisibility Tests

When two nonzero whole numbers are multiplied together, each number is a **factor** of the product. A number is **divisible** by another number if the second number is a factor of the first. For example, $2 \times 5 = 10$, so 2 and 5 are factors of 10, and 10 is divisible by both 2 and 5.

You can use the following tests to test a whole number for divisibility by 2, 3, 4, 5, 6, 8, 9, and 10.

Divisible by 2: The last digit of the number is 0, 2, 4, 6, or 8.
Divisible by 3: The sum of the digits of the number is divisible by 3.
Divisible by 4: The last two digits of the number are divisible by 4.
Divisible by 5: The last digit of the number is 0 or 5.
Divisible by 6: The number is divisible by both 2 and 3.
Divisible by 8: The last three digits of the number are divisible by 8.
Divisible by 9: The sum of the digits of the number is divisible by 9.
Divisible by 10: The last digit of the number is 0.

SKILLS REVIEW HANDBOOK

EXAMPLE 1

Test the number for divisibility by 2, 3, 4, 5, 6, 8, 9, and 10.

a. 2736 **b.** 74,420

SOLUTION

a. The last digit of 2736 is 6, so it is divisible by 2 but not by 5 or 10. The sum of the digits is $2 + 7 + 3 + 6 = 18$, so it is divisible by 3 and 9. The last two digits, 36, are divisible by 4, so 2736 is divisible by 4. Because 2736 is divisible by both 2 and 3, it is divisible by 6. The last three digits, 736, are divisible by 8, so 2736 is divisible by 8.

▶ **Answer** 2736 is divisible by 2, 3, 4, 6, 8, and 9.

b. The last digit of 74,420 is 0, so it is divisible by 2, 5, and 10. The sum of the digits is $7 + 4 + 4 + 2 + 0 = 17$, so it is not divisible by 3 or 9. The last two digits, 20, are divisible by 4, so 74,420 is divisible by 4. Because 74,420 is divisible by 2, but not by 3, it is not divisible by 6. The last three digits, 420, are not divisible by 8, so 74,420 is not divisible by 8.

▶ **Answer** 74,420 is divisible by 2, 4, 5, and 10.

PRACTICE

Test the number for divisibility by 2, 3, 4, 5, 6, 8, 9, and 10.

1. 34 **2.** 84 **3.** 285 **4.** 560 **5.** 972

6. 4210 **7.** 2815 **8.** 6390 **9.** 88,004 **10.** 75,432

Mixed Numbers and Improper Fractions

A **fraction** is a number of the form $\frac{a}{b}$ $(b \neq 0)$ where a is called the **numerator** and b is called the **denominator**.

A number $1\frac{3}{5}$, read as "one and three fifths," is a *mixed number*. A **mixed number** is the sum of a whole number part and a fraction part.

An **improper fraction**, such as $\frac{21}{8}$ is any fraction in which the numerator is greater than or equal to the denominator.

EXAMPLE 1

Write $3\frac{2}{5}$ as an improper fraction.

$3\frac{2}{5} = \frac{15+2}{5}$ 1 whole $= \frac{5}{3}$, so 3 wholes $= \frac{3 \times 5}{5}$, or $\frac{15}{5}$.

$= \frac{17}{5}$ Add.

EXAMPLE 2

Write $\frac{13}{4}$ as a mixed number.

1. Divide 13 by 4.

$$\begin{array}{r} 3\text{R}1 \\ 4\overline{)13} \\ \underline{12} \\ 1 \end{array}$$

2. Write the mixed number. $3 + \frac{1}{4} = 3\frac{1}{4}$

PRACTICE

Copy and complete the statement.

1. $7\frac{3}{5} = \frac{?}{5}$
2. $3\frac{1}{6} = \frac{?}{6}$
3. $\frac{23}{4} = 5\frac{?}{4}$
4. $\frac{17}{7} = 2\frac{?}{7}$

Write the mixed number as an improper fraction.

5. $3\frac{1}{2}$
6. $1\frac{5}{6}$
7. $4\frac{3}{8}$
8. $8\frac{5}{7}$
9. $10\frac{3}{4}$

Write the improper fraction as a mixed number.

10. $\frac{11}{4}$
11. $\frac{15}{2}$
12. $\frac{25}{6}$
13. $\frac{17}{3}$
14. $\frac{33}{8}$

Ratio and Rate

One way to compare numbers is to use a ratio. The **ratio** uses division to compare two numbers. You can write the ratio of a to b as $\frac{a}{b}$, as $a : b$, or as "a to b."

EXAMPLE 1

There are 15 boys and 17 girls in the band. Write the ratio of the number of boys to girls in the band in three ways.

$$\frac{\text{Number of boys}}{\text{Number of girls}} = \frac{15}{17} = 15 \text{ to } 17 = 15 : 17$$

A **rate** is a ratio of two quantities that have different units, such as $\frac{150 \text{ miles}}{3 \text{ hours}}$.

A **unit rate** is a rate with a denominator of 1 unit.

EXAMPLE 2

Write the rate $\frac{150 \text{ miles}}{3 \text{ hours}}$ as a unit rate.

$$\frac{150 \text{ mi}}{3 \text{ h}} = \frac{50 \text{ mi}}{1 \text{ h}} \quad (\div 3 \text{ top and bottom})$$

Divide 3 by 3 to get 1, so divide 150 by 3 also.

▸ **Answer** The unit rate is 50 miles per hour.

PRACTICE

The table shows the numbers of boys and girls in Mr. Smith's class and in Ms. Jung's class. Use the table to write the specified ratio.

1. Boys in Mr. Smith's class to girls in Mr. Smith's class
2. Boys in Mr. Smith's class to boys in Ms. Jung's class
3. Girls in Ms. Jung's class to all girls

	Boys	Girls
Mr. Smith's class	13	12
Ms. Jung's class	17	11

Write the rate and unit rate.

4. 8 feet in 2 seconds
5. \$24 for 8 pens
6. 333 miles in 6 hours
7. 280 words in 5 minutes
8. 3 quarts for \$2.50
9. 8 inches in 6 days

Adding and Subtracting Decimals

To add and subtract decimals, start with the digits in the place on the right. Moving to the left, add or subtract the digits one place value at a time, regrouping as needed.

EXAMPLE 1

Find the sum 0.157 + 0.663.

STEP 1 Add the thousandths. Regroup 10 thousandths as 1 hundredth and 0 thousandths.

$$\begin{array}{r} {\scriptstyle 1} \\ 0.157 \\ +\ 0.663 \\ \hline 0 \end{array}$$

STEP 2 Add the hundreths. Regroup 12 hundredths as 1 tenth and 2 hundredths.

$$\begin{array}{r} {\scriptstyle 11} \\ 0.157 \\ +\ 0.663 \\ \hline 20 \end{array}$$

STEP 3 Add the tenths. Place the decimal point in the answer.

$$\begin{array}{r} {\scriptstyle 11} \\ 0.157 \\ +\ 0.663 \\ \hline 0.820 \end{array}$$

EXAMPLE 2

Find the difference 30.7 − 3.8.

STEP 1 Start with the tenths. There are not enough tenths in 30.7 to subtract 8 tenths.

$$\begin{array}{r} 30.7 \\ -\ 3.8 \\ \hline \end{array}$$

STEP 2 Move to the ones. There are no ones in 30.7, so regroup 1 ten as 9 ones and 10 tenths.

$$\begin{array}{r} {\scriptstyle 9} \\ {\scriptstyle 2\,\not{10}\,17} \\ \not{3}\not{0}.\not{7} \\ -\ 3.8 \\ \hline \end{array}$$

STEP 3 Subtract. Place the decimal point in the answer.

$$\begin{array}{r} {\scriptstyle 9} \\ {\scriptstyle 2\,\not{10}\,17} \\ \not{3}\not{0}.\not{7} \\ -\ 3.8 \\ \hline 26.9 \end{array}$$

Check Because addition and subtraction are inverse operations, you can check your answer by adding: 26.9 + 3.8 = 30.7.

PRACTICE

Find the sum or difference.

1. 3.56 + 2.74 **2.** 12.7 + 93.8 **3.** 27.5 + 3.6 **4.** 0.923 + 0.179

5. 4.217 + 6.739 **6.** 9.3 − 2.8 **7.** 4.56 − 1.65 **8.** 13.64 − 5.85

9. 38.45 − 19.57 **10.** 741.52 − 48.66 **11.** 56.98 + 0.82 **12.** 100.476 − 4.989

13. 365.57 − 79.38 **14.** 49.86 + 2.65 **15.** 97.156 − 9.092 **16.** 232.543 − 209.692

Adding and Subtracting Fractions

To add two fractions with a common denominator, write the sum of the numerators over the denominator.

Numbers $\frac{2}{5} + \frac{1}{5} = \frac{3}{5}$ **Algebra** $\frac{a}{c} + \frac{b}{c} = \frac{a+b}{c}\ (c \neq 0)$

EXAMPLE 1

Find the sum $\frac{4}{7} + \frac{6}{7}$.

$\frac{4}{7} + \frac{6}{7} = \frac{4+6}{7}$ Write sum of numerators over denominator.

$= \frac{10}{7}$ Add.

$= 1\frac{3}{7}$ Write the improper fraction as a mixed number.

To subtract two fractions with a common denominator, write the difference of the numerators over the denominator.

Numbers $\frac{7}{9} - \frac{2}{9} = \frac{5}{9}$ **Algebra** $\frac{a}{c} - \frac{b}{c} = \frac{a-b}{c}\ (c \neq 0)$

EXAMPLE 2

Find the difference $\frac{10}{11} - \frac{4}{11}$.

$\frac{10}{11} - \frac{4}{11} = \frac{10-4}{11}$ Write difference of numerators over denominator.

$= \frac{6}{11}$ Subtract.

PRACTICE

Find the sum or difference.

1. $\frac{1}{3} + \frac{1}{3}$ **2.** $\frac{8}{9} + \frac{5}{9}$ **3.** $\frac{6}{7} - \frac{3}{7}$ **4.** $\frac{11}{12} - \frac{4}{12}$ **5.** $\frac{1}{8} + \frac{7}{8}$

6. $\frac{8}{11} + \frac{7}{11}$ **7.** $\frac{13}{15} - \frac{2}{15}$ **8.** $\frac{5}{6} - \frac{4}{6}$ **9.** $\frac{1}{9} + \frac{1}{9}$ **10.** $\frac{10}{11} - \frac{2}{11}$

11. $\frac{11}{12} + \frac{8}{12}$ **12.** $\frac{9}{10} - \frac{6}{10}$ **13.** $\frac{5}{9} - \frac{4}{9}$ **14.** $\frac{9}{16} + \frac{12}{16}$ **15.** $\frac{11}{14} - \frac{2}{14}$

16. $\frac{8}{15} - \frac{8}{15}$ **17.** $\frac{5}{12} + \frac{2}{12}$ **18.** $\frac{8}{10} + \frac{1}{10}$ **19.** $\frac{6}{7} + \frac{5}{7}$ **20.** $\frac{5}{8} - \frac{2}{8}$

Estimation in Addition and Subtraction

To **estimate** a solution means to find an approximate answer. When numbers being added have about the same value, you can use *clustering* to estimate their sum. Another way to estimate is to add the digits in the greatest place, then round the remaining parts of the numbers and add. Finally, add the sums together.

EXAMPLE 1

Estimate the sum 3836 + 4235 + 3982.

3836	4000	
4235	4000	**The numbers all cluster around the value 4000.**
+ 3982	+ 4000	
	12,000	

▸ **Answer** The sum 3836 + 4235 + 3982 is *about* 12,000.

To estimate a difference, first subtract the digits in the greatest place. Then round the remaining parts of the numbers and subtract the lesser number from the greater number. Finally, combine the two differences using addition or subtraction as shown below.

EXAMPLE 2

Estimate the difference 68,453 − 32,792.

STEP 1 First subtract the digits in the ten thousands' place.

68,453	60,000
− 32,792	− 30,000
	30,000

STEP 2 Then round the remaining digits to the nearest thousand. Subtract the lesser number from the greater number.

8,000
− 3,000
5,000

STEP 3 Because the greater remaining number was originally on the *top*, you *add* the differences.

30,000 + 5,000 = 35,000

Note that if the greater remaining number had originally been on the *bottom*, you would *subtract* the differences.

PRACTICE

Estimate the sum or difference.

1. 935 + 887 + 912

2. 4967 + 4802 + 5218

3. 5971 + 6032 + 7865

4. 8891 − 4932

5. 4373 − 2158

6. 449,739 − 285,921

Solving Problems Using Addition and Subtraction

You can use the following guidelines to tell whether to use addition or subtraction to solve a word problem.

- Use addition when you need to combine, join, or find a total.
- Use subtraction when you need to separate, compare, take away, find how many are left, or find how many more are needed.

EXAMPLE 1

You have 36 stamps in your stamp collection. You want to collect 18 more stamps. How many stamps will you have in all?

You need to combine, so you need to add.

$36 + 18 = 54$

▸ **Answer** You will have 54 stamps in your stamp collection.

EXAMPLE 2

Your total bill for lunch is \$4.78. You pay with a \$5 bill. How much change do you receive?

You need to take away, so you need to subtract.

$\$5.00 - \$4.78 = \$.22$

▸ **Answer** You receive $.22 in change.

PRACTICE

1. You spend $48 for a coat and $45 for a pair of shoes. How much do you spend in all?
2. You bought a box of 96 pencils. You gave 28 of the pencils to your friend. How many pencils do you have left?
3. You have $18. You buy a video for $15.99. How much money do you have left?
4. You have 24 country CDs and 18 pop CDs. How many country and pop CDs do you have in all?
5. You have 900 minutes a month on your cell phone plan. You have used 652 minutes so far this month. How many minutes do you have left?
6. You have $149. You make $24 babysitting. How much money do you have?

SKILLS REVIEW HANDBOOK

Multiplying Fractions

To multiply a fraction by a whole number, multiply the numerator of the fraction by the whole number and write the product over the denominator of the fraction. Simplify if possible.

EXAMPLE 1

Find the product.

a. $3 \times \frac{2}{7} = \frac{3 \times 2}{7}$ **Write the product of the whole number and the numerator over the denominator.**

$= \frac{6}{7}$ **Multiply.**

b. $\frac{3}{8} \times 5 = \frac{3 \times 5}{8}$ **Write the product of the whole number and the numerator over the denominator.**

$= \frac{15}{8}$, or $1\frac{7}{8}$ **Multiply. Then write as a mixed number.**

To multiply two fractions, write the product of the numerators over the product of the denominators. Simplify if possible.

$$\text{product of fractions} = \frac{\text{product of numerators}}{\text{product of denominators}}$$

EXAMPLE 2

Find the product.

$\frac{4}{5} \times \frac{2}{3} = \frac{4 \times 2}{5 \times 3}$ **Use rule for multiplying fractions.**

$= \frac{8}{15}$ **Multiply.**

PRACTICE

Find the product. Simplify if possible.

1. $6 \times \frac{2}{15}$ **2.** $2 \times \frac{6}{11}$ **3.** $4 \times \frac{5}{9}$ **4.** $8 \times \frac{5}{9}$ **5.** $\frac{3}{4} \times 7$

6. $\frac{4}{7} \times 5$ **7.** $\frac{6}{7} \times 3$ **8.** $\frac{3}{7} \times \frac{6}{11}$ **9.** $\frac{2}{3} \times \frac{4}{5}$ **10.** $\frac{3}{4} \times \frac{1}{7}$

11. $\frac{1}{8} \times \frac{3}{5}$ **12.** $\frac{7}{9} \times \frac{5}{8}$ **13.** $\frac{5}{9} \times \frac{2}{3}$ **14.** $\frac{3}{8} \times \frac{4}{5}$ **15.** $\frac{5}{12} \times \frac{5}{6}$

Multiplication of a Decimal by a Whole Number

To multiply a decimal by a whole number, multiply the entire first number (ignoring the decimal point) by the digit in each place value of the second number to get partial products. Add the partial products. Then place the decimal point in the answer, showing the same number of decimal places as in the decimal.

EXAMPLE 1

Find the product 31.5 × 206.

STEP 1 Multiply 31.5 by the ones' dig in 206. Ignore the decimal point.

$$\begin{array}{r} {}^{3} \\ 31.5 \\ \times\ 206 \\ \hline 1890 \end{array}$$

STEP 2 Skip the 0 in the tens' place, and multiply by the hundreds' digit. Start the partial product in the hundreds' place.

$$\begin{array}{r} {}^{1} \\ 31.5 \\ \times\ 206 \\ \hline 1890 \\ 630 \end{array}$$

STEP 3 Add the partial products. The decimal has one decimal place, so show one decimal place in the answer.

$$\begin{array}{r} 31.5 \\ \times\ 206 \\ \hline 1890 \\ 630 \\ \hline 6489.0 \end{array}$$

PRACTICE

Find the product.

1. 2.3 × 98
2. 0.62 × 46
3. 85 × 7.9
4. 0.56 × 63
5. 2.08 × 14
6. 6.52 × 36
7. 7.24 × 89
8. 8.35 × 16
9. 77.6 × 22
10. 3.45 × 105
11. 453 × 41.2
12. 614 × 6.71
13. 32.6 × 463
14. 71.8 × 934
15. 90.5 × 407
16. 15.36 × 123
17. 3.442 × 276
18. 93.08 × 306
19. 5.436 × 682
20. 60.97 × 708
21. 142.82 × 35
22. 25.987 × 76
23. 32.903 × 55
24. 243.72 × 38
25. 75.032 × 73
26. 380.77 × 114
27. 508.25 × 237
28. 15.456 × 591
29. 36.902 × 205
30. 8257.6 × 459

Dividing Decimals

In a division problem, the number being divided is called the **dividend** and the number it is being divided by is called the **divisor**. The result of the division is called the **quotient**. To **divide** two numbers, you start with the leftmost digit of the dividend and move to the right. Before you start dividing decimals, place the decimal point in the quotient.

EXAMPLE 1

Find the quotient 5.2 ÷ 8.

STEP 1

Place the decimal point in the quotient directly above the decimal point in the dividend. Then divide as with whole numbers. Because 8 is greater than 5, place a zero above the 5.

$$\text{divisor} \rightarrow 8\overline{)5.2} \leftarrow \text{dividend}, \quad \text{quotient } 0.$$

STEP 2

Because 8 × 6 = 48, estimate that 8 divides 52 about 6 times. Multiply 6 and 8. Then subtract 48 from 52. Be sure the difference is less than the divisor: 4 < 8.

$$\begin{array}{r} 0.6 \\ 8\overline{)5.2} \\ -\,48 \\ \hline 4 \end{array}$$

STEP 3

Add zero as a placeholder. Bring down the zero. Divide 40 by 8 to get 5. Multiply 5 and 8. Subtract 40 from 40. The remainder is zero.

$$\begin{array}{r} 0.65 \\ 8\overline{)5.20} \\ -\,48 \\ \hline 40 \\ -\,40 \\ \hline 0 \end{array}$$

EXAMPLE 2

Find the quotient 12 ÷ 2.8.

STEP 1

To multiply the divisor and the dividend by 10, move both decimal points 1 place to the right. Then divide as with whole numbers.

$$\text{divisor} \rightarrow 28\overline{)120} \leftarrow \text{dividend}$$

STEP 2

Because 28 × 4 = 112, estimate that 28 divides 120 about 4 times. Multiply 4 and 28. Then subtract 112 from 120.

$$\begin{array}{r} 4 \\ 28\overline{)120} \\ -\,112 \\ \hline 8 \end{array}$$

STEP 3

Be sure the difference is less than the divisor: 8 < 28. So 12 ÷ 2.8 is equal to $4\frac{8}{28}$, or $4\frac{2}{7}$.

$$\begin{array}{r} 4\text{R}8 \\ 28\overline{)120} \\ -\,112 \\ \hline 8 \end{array}$$

PRACTICE

Find the quotient.

1. 2.7 ÷ 6　**2.** 3.8 ÷ 4　**3.** 6.8 ÷ 8　**4.** 46.9 ÷ 7　**5.** 13.71 ÷ 3

6. 15 ÷ 2.5　**7.** 8 ÷ 1.3　**8.** 32 ÷ 5.46　**9.** 63 ÷ 7.12　**10.** 75 ÷ 6.357

Estimation in Multiplication and Division

One way to estimate a product or a quotient is to find a range for the product or quotient by finding a low estimate and a high estimate. A low estimate and a high estimate can be found by using *compatible numbers*, which are numbers that make a calculation easier.

EXAMPLE 1

Find a low and high estimate for the product 56 × 35 using compatible numbers.

For a low estimate, round both factors *down*. $50 \times 30 = 1500$

For a high estimate, round both factors *up*. $60 \times 40 = 2400$

▸ **Answer** The product 56 × 35 is between 1500 and 2400.

EXAMPLE 2

Find a low and high estimate for the quotient 23,400 ÷ 45 using compatible numbers.

When the divisor has more than one digit, round it.

For a *low* estimate, round the divisor *up* and choose a compatible dividend that is *lower* than the original dividend. $50\overline{)20{,}000}$ = 400

For a *high* estimate, round the divisor *down* and choose a compatible dividend that is *higher* than the original dividend. $40\overline{)24{,}000}$ = 600

▸ **Answer** The quotient 23,400 ÷ 45 is between 400 and 600.

PRACTICE

Find a low and high estimate for the product or quotient using compatible numbers.

1. 43 × 16	**2.** 359 × 28	**3.** 852 × 53	**4.** 734 × 76
5. 225 ÷ 6	**6.** 2795 ÷ 7	**7.** 17,934 ÷ 77	**8.** 41,042 ÷ 92
9. 326 × 48	**10.** 612 × 273	**11.** 745 × 158	**12.** 905 × 657
13. 625 × 28	**14.** 809 × 97	**15.** 742 ÷ 8	**16.** 231 ÷ 38
17. 5421 ÷ 7	**18.** 4972 ÷ 18	**19.** 1583 ÷ 82	**20.** 43,789 ÷ 64

Solving Problems Using Multiplication and Division

You can use the following guidelines to tell whether to use multiplication or division to solve a word problem.

- Use multiplication when you need to find the total number of objects that are in groups of equal size or to find a fractional part of another number.
- Use division when you need to find the number of equal groups or the number in each equal group.

EXAMPLE 1

You baked 48 muffins. You give $\frac{1}{3}$ of them to your friend. How many muffins did you give to your friend?

You need to find the fractional part of another number, so you need to multiply.

$$48 \cdot \frac{1}{3} = 16$$

▶ **Answer** You gave 16 muffins to your friend.

EXAMPLE 2

You bought 4 cans of soup for a total of \$3.56. How much did you pay for each can of soup?

You need to find the amount in each equal group, so you need to divide.

$$3.56 \div 4 = 0.89$$

▶ **Answer** You paid \$.89 for each can of soup.

PRACTICE

1. You bought 6 notebooks. Each notebook cost \$1.58. How much did you pay for all of the notebooks?
2. You have 92 baseball cards. You give $\frac{1}{4}$ of your cards to your friend. How many cards did you give your friend?
3. You have 12 flats of flowers. If each flat contains 48 flowers, how many flowers do you have?
4. You paid \$22.95 for the plates for your party. If you bought 9 packages of plates, how much did you pay for each package?

Points, Lines, and Planes

In geometry, a **point** is usually labeled with an uppercase letter, such as *A* or *B*. Points are used to name *lines, rays,* and *segments*. A **plane** is a flat surface that extends without end in all directions. You can represent a plane by a figure that looks like a floor or a wall.

Words	*Diagram*	*Symbols*
A **line** extends without end in two *opposite* directions.	X Y	$\overleftrightarrow{XY}$ or $\overleftrightarrow{YX}$
A **ray** has one **endpoint** and extends without end in *one* direction.	X Y	$\overrightarrow{XY}$
A **segment** has two endpoints.	X Y	$\overline{XY}$ or $\overline{YX}$

EXAMPLE 1

Identify and name the *line, ray,* or segment.

a. A B **b.** M N **c.** P Q

SOLUTION

a. The figure is a segment that can be named $\overline{AB}$.

b. The figure is a line that can be named $\overleftrightarrow{MN}$.

c. The figure is a ray that can be named $\overrightarrow{PQ}$.

PRACTICE

Match the name with the correct figure.

1. $\overline{CD}$ **2.** $\overleftrightarrow{CD}$ **3.** $\overrightarrow{CD}$

A. D C **B.** C D **C.**

In Exercises 4–7, use the diagram.

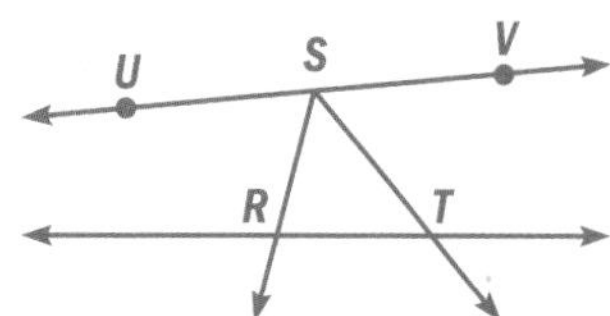

4. Name three points.

5. Name two rays.

6. Name two lines.

7. Name a segment that has *S* as an endpoint.

SKILLS REVIEW HANDBOOK

Angles

An **angle** is formed by two rays with the same endpoint. The endpoint is called the **vertex**. The symbol $\angle$ is used to represent an angle.

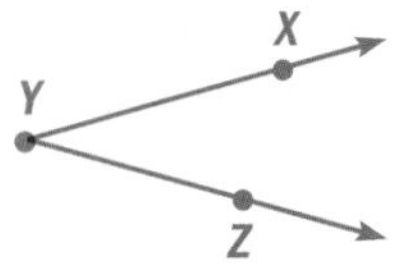

EXAMPLE 1

Name the angle above in three ways.

Name the angle by its vertex alone: $\angle Y$

Name the angle by its vertex and two points, with the vertex as the middle point: $\angle XYZ$

Name the angle by its vertex and two points, but reverse the order of the points: $\angle ZYX$

PRACTICE

Match the name with the correct angle.

1. $\angle ABC$
2. $\angle RST$
3. $\angle MNP$

A.

B.
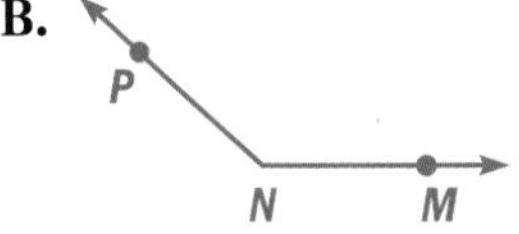

C.
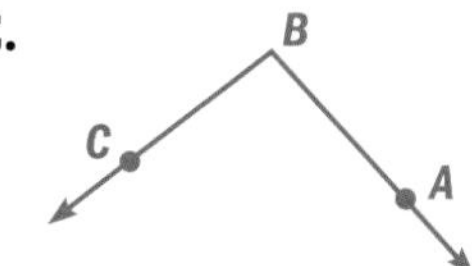

Name the angle in three ways.

4.
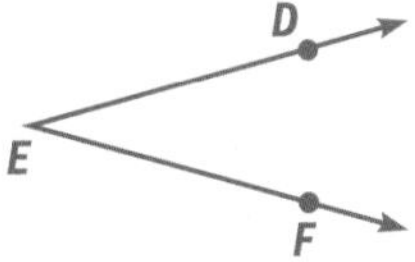

5.
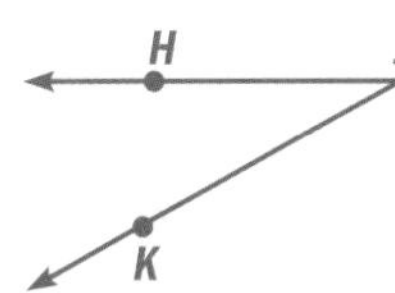

6.
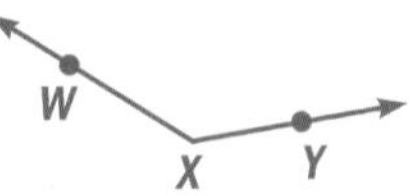

7.
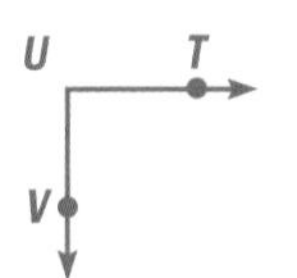

8.
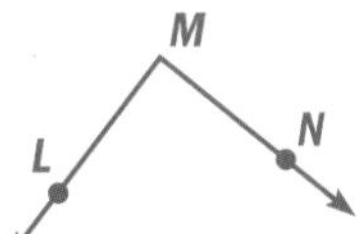

9.
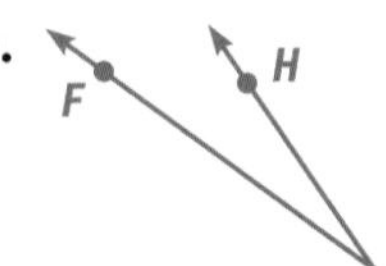

10. Draw a triangle with vertices *P*, *Q*, and *R*. Name each angle of the triangle in three ways.

Using a Ruler

An **inch ruler** has markings for inches, halves of an inch, fourths of an inch, eighths of an inch, and sixteenths of an inch. As the lengths get shorter, so do the markings.

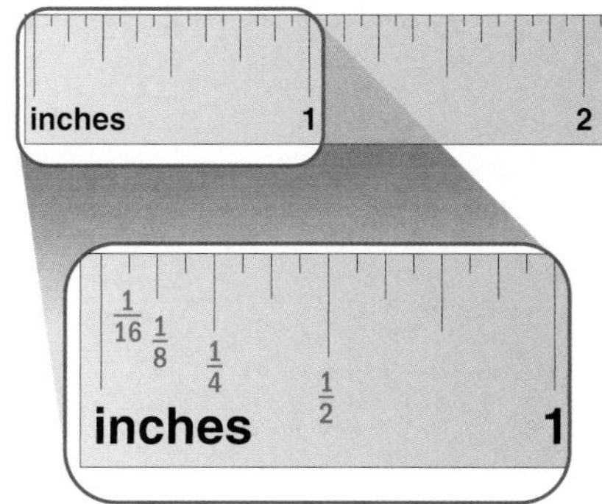

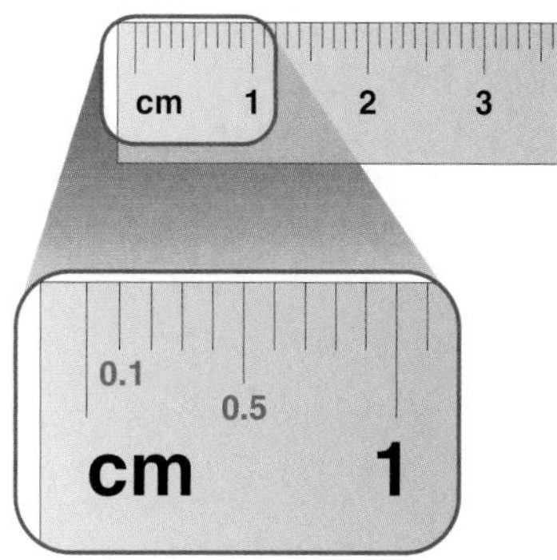

A **centimeter ruler** has markings for centimeters, halves of a centimeter, and tenths of a centimeter (also called *millimeters*). Like an inch ruler, as the lengths get shorter, so do the markings.

EXAMPLE 1

Use a ruler to draw a segment with the given length.

a. $2\frac{1}{8}$ inches

b. 3.8 centimeters

SOLUTION

a. Start at the leftmost mark on the ruler.

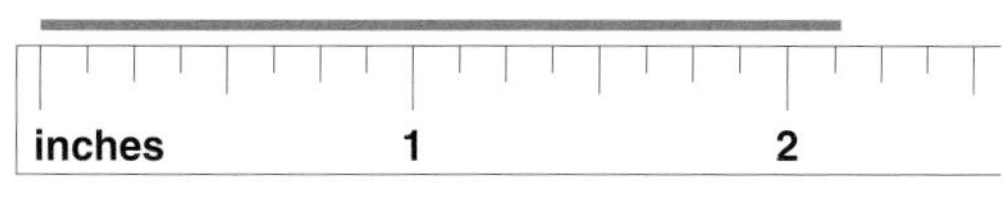

Draw a segment so that the other end is at the first $\frac{1}{8}$ in. mark after 2.

b. Start at the leftmost mark on the ruler.

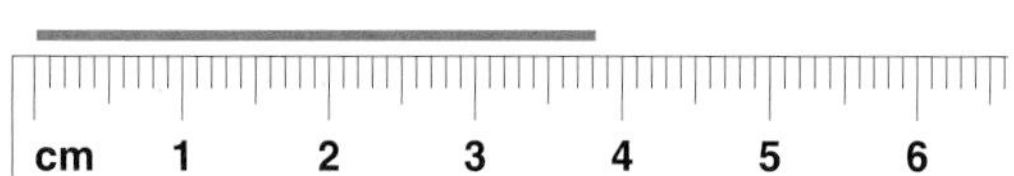

Draw a segment so that the other end is at the 3.8 cm mark.

PRACTICE

Use a ruler to draw a segment with the given length.

1. $\frac{7}{16}$ inch

2. $4\frac{5}{8}$ inches

3. 4.3 centimeters

4. 2.7 centimeters

5. $2\frac{5}{16}$ inches

6. 6.5 centimeters

7. 2.9 centimeters

8. $1\frac{1}{4}$ inches

Using a Protractor

A **protractor** is a tool you can use to draw and measure angles. A unit of measure for angles is the **degree** (°). To measure an angle, place the center of the protractor on the vertex of the angle and line up one ray with the 0° line. Then read the measure where the other ray crosses the protractor.

The measure of $\angle XYZ$ is 135°. You can write this as $m\angle XYZ = 135°$.

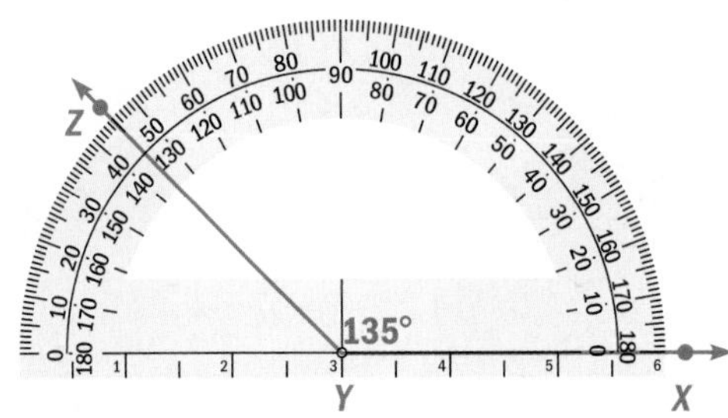

EXAMPLE 1

Use a protractor to draw an angle that has a measure of 48°.

STEP 1 Draw and label a ray.

STEP 2 Place the center of the protractor at the endpoint of the ray. Line up the ray with the 0° line. Then draw and label a point at the 48° mark on the inner scale.

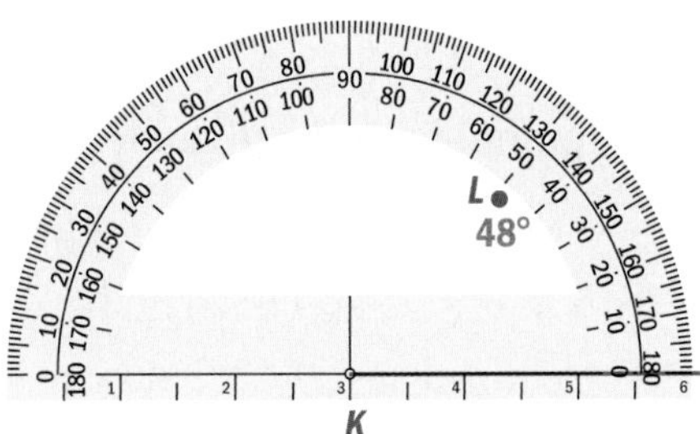

STEP 3 Remove the protractor and draw $\overrightarrow{KL}$ to complete the angle.

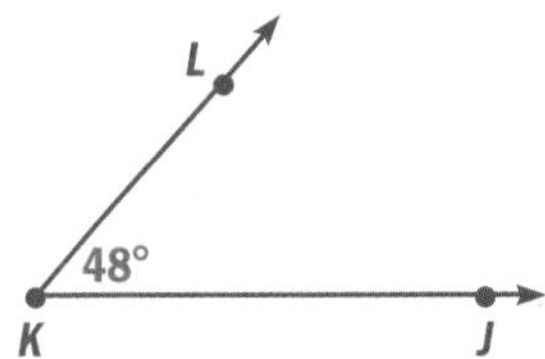

PRACTICE

Use a protractor to measure the angle.

1.

2.

3.

4. Use a protractor to draw angles measuring 46°, 125°, and 73°.

Using a Compass

A **compass** is an instrument used to draw circles. A **straightedge** is any object that can be used to draw a segment.

EXAMPLE 1

Use a compass to draw a circle with radius 3 cm.

Recall that the *radius* of a circle is the distance between the center of the circle and any point on the circle.

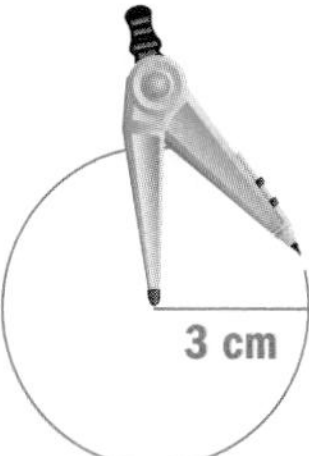

Use a metric ruler to open the compass so that the distance between the point and the pencil is 3 cm.

Place the point on a piece of paper and rotate the pencil around the point to draw the circle.

EXAMPLE 2

Use a straightedge and a compass to draw a segment whose length is the sum of *MN* and *PQ*.

M *N* *P* *Q*

SOLUTION

Use a straightedge to draw a segment longer than both given segments.

Open your compass to measure $\overline{MN}$. Using this compass setting, place the point at the left end of your segment and make a mark that crosses your segment.

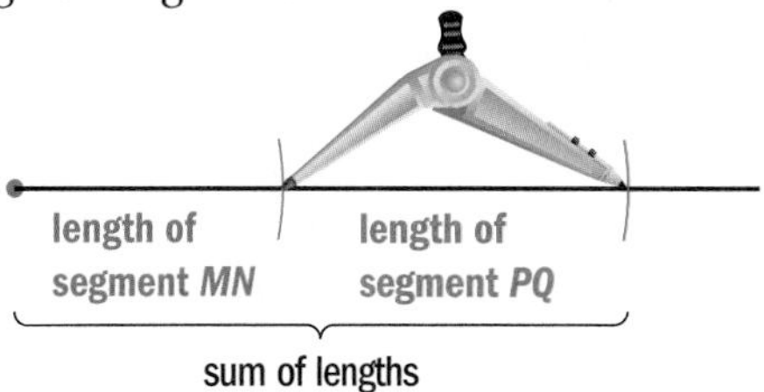

Then open your compass to measure $\overline{PQ}$. Using this compass setting, place the point at the first mark you made on your segment and make another mark that crosses your segment.

PRACTICE

1. Use a compass to draw a circle with radius 4 cm.
2. Use a straightedge and a compass to draw a segment whose length is the *sum* of the lengths of the two given segments.

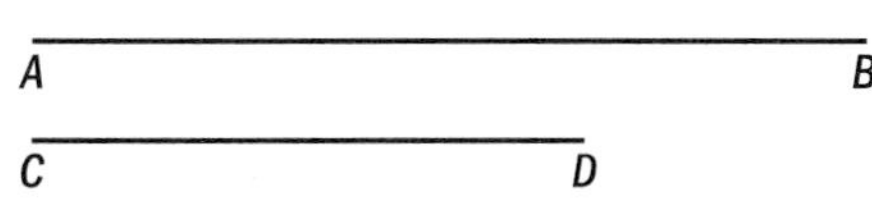

3. Use a straightedge and a compass to draw a segment whose length is the *difference* of the lengths of the two given segments in Exercise 2.

Solving Problems Involving Time

When you have a start time and an end time that are both before or both after noon, you can find the *elapsed time* by subtracting the start time from the end time. When you have a start time before noon and an end time after noon, you can find the elapsed time by adding 12 hours to the end time, then subtracting.

EXAMPLE 1

A seminar started at 8:30 A.M. and ended at 4:15 P.M. How long did the seminar last?

STEP 1 **Add** 12 to the later time.

$$\begin{array}{r} 4{:}15 \\ +\ 12{:}00 \\ \hline 16{:}15 \end{array}$$

STEP 2 **Subtract** to find the elapsed time.

You cannot subtract 30 from 15. Rename 1 hour as 60 minutes. Then subtract.

$$\begin{array}{r} \scriptstyle 15\ \ 75 \\ \not{1}\not{6}{:}\not{1}\not{5} \\ -\ 8{:}30 \\ \hline 7{:}45 \end{array}$$

▸ **Answer** The seminar lasted 7 hours 45 minutes.

EXAMPLE 2

Morgan spends 20 minutes on her math homework and studies 55 minutes for a science test. She starts at 4:45 P.M. When does she finish?

STEP 1 **Add** to find the elapsed time.

0:20	**Time for math**
+ 0:55	**Time for science**
0:75	**Elapsed time**
1:15	**Rewrite. 60 min = 1 h**

STEP 2 **Add** to find the end time.

4:45	**Start time**
+ 1:15	**Elapsed time**
5:60	**End time**
6:00	**Rewrite. 60 min = 1 h**

▸ **Answer** Morgan finished her math and science homework at 6:00 P.M.

PRACTICE

1. How long was a concert that started at 7:13 P.M. and ended at 9:24 P.M.?
2. How long was a school day that started at 8:10 A.M. and ended at 3:15 P.M.?
3. A soccer practice began at 2:45 P.M. The players warmed up for 10 minutes and scrimmaged for 40 minutes. What time did the practice end?
4. Jeff began watching a DVD at 7:25 P.M. He spent 1 hour 39 minutes watching the movie and 25 minutes watching the extra features on the DVD. What time did he finish watching the DVD?

Converting Customary Units

To convert customary units, multiply by a convenient form of 1. For example:

- To convert inches to feet, multiply by $\frac{1\text{ ft}}{12\text{ in.}}$.
- To convert feet to inches, multiply by $\frac{12\text{ in.}}{1\text{ ft}}$.

For a listing of customary units and time, see the Table of Measures on page 815.

EXAMPLE 1

Copy and complete the statement.

a. 13,200 ft = __?__ mi **b.** 6 c = __?__ fl oz **c.** 78 h = __?__ d

SOLUTION

a. $13{,}200\text{ ft} \times \frac{1\text{ mi}}{5280\text{ ft}} = \frac{\overset{5}{\cancel{13200}}\cancel{\text{ ft}} \times 1\text{ mi}}{\underset{2}{\cancel{5280}}\cancel{\text{ ft}}} = \frac{5}{2}\text{ mi, or } 2\frac{1}{2}\text{ mi}$ So, $13{,}200\text{ ft} = 2\frac{1}{2}\text{ mi}$.

b. $6\text{ c} \times \frac{8\text{ fl oz}}{1\text{ c}} = \frac{6\cancel{\text{ c}} \times 8\text{ fl oz}}{1\cancel{\text{ c}}} = 48\text{ fl oz}$ So, 6 c = 48 fl oz.

c. $78\text{ h} \times \frac{1\text{ d}}{24\text{ h}} = \frac{\overset{13}{\cancel{78}}\cancel{\text{ h}} \times 1\text{ d}}{\underset{4}{\cancel{24}}\cancel{\text{ h}}} = \frac{13}{4}\text{ d, or } 3\frac{1}{4}\text{ d}$ So, $78\text{ h} = 3\frac{1}{4}\text{ d}$.

EXAMPLE 2

Convert 82 ounces into pounds and ounces.

STEP 1 **Convert** 82 ounces to pounds.

$$82\text{ oz} \times \frac{1\text{ lb}}{16\text{ oz}} = \frac{\overset{41}{\cancel{82}}\cancel{\text{ oz}} \times 1\text{ lb}}{\underset{8}{\cancel{16}}\cancel{\text{ oz}}} = \frac{41}{8}\text{ lb, or } 5\frac{1}{8}\text{ lb}$$

STEP 2 **Convert** the fractional part from pounds to ounces.

$$\frac{1\text{ lb}}{8} \times \frac{16\text{ oz}}{1\text{ lb}} = \frac{1\cancel{\text{ lb}} \times \overset{2}{\cancel{16}}\text{ oz}}{\underset{1}{\cancel{8}}\cancel{\text{ lb}}} = 2\text{ oz}$$

▶ **Answer** So, 82 ounces = 5 lb 2 oz.

PRACTICE

Copy and complete the statement.

1. 23 yd = __?__ ft **2.** 4 lb = __?__ oz **3.** 42 qt = __?__ gal

4. 18 in. = __?__ yd **5.** 3 gal = __?__ pt **6.** 32 oz = __?__ lb

7. 26 fl oz = __?__ c __?__ fl oz **8.** 165 min = __?__ h **9.** 75 in. = __?__ ft __?__ in.

Converting Metric Units

The metric system is a base-ten system. Metric prefixes are associated with decimal place values.

thousands:	hundreds:	tens:	ones:	tenths:	hundredths:	thousandths:
kilo-	hecto-	deka-	meter, liter, gram	deci-	centi-	milli-

To convert from large to small metric units, multiply by a multiple of 10.

To convert from small to large metric units, divide by a multiple of 10.

For a listing of metric units, see the Table of Measures on page 815.

EXAMPLE 1

Copy and complete the statement.

a. 5.75 kg = ? g　　**b.** 44 m = ? cm　　**c.** 110 mL = ? L

SOLUTION

a. To convert from kilograms to grams, multiply by 1000.

$5.75 \times 1000 = 5750$, so 5.75 kg = 5750 g.

b. To convert from meters to centimeters, multiply by 100.

$44 \times 100 = 4400$, so 44 m = 4400 cm.

c. To convert from milliliters to liters, divide by 1000.

$110 \div 1000 = 0.11$, so 110 mL = 0.11 L.

EXAMPLE 2

Copy and complete using $<$, $>$, or $=$: 160 mg ? 16 g.

160 mg ? 16 g	**Strategy: Convert grams to milligrams.**
160 mg ? 16,000 mg	**16 × 1000 = 16,000, so 16 g = 16,000 mg.**
160 mg $<$ 16,000 mg	**Compare.**

▶ **Answer** 160 mg $<$ 16 g

PRACTICE

Copy and complete the statement.

1. 6.42 kL = ? L　　**2.** 4 cm = ? m　　**3.** 5.5 g = ? mg

Copy and complete the statement using $<$, $>$, or $=$.

4. 8 km ? 8000 m　　**5.** 1200 mg ? 12 g　　**6.** 9.2 L ? 0.0092 mL

Converting Between Metric and Customary Units

To convert between metric and customary units, use the approximate relationships shown below.

Length	***Capacity***	***Weight***
1 mm ≈ 0.0394 in.	1 mL ≈ 0.0338 fl oz	1 g ≈ 0.0353 oz
1 m ≈ 3.28 ft	1 L ≈ 1.06 qt	1 kg ≈ 2.2 lb
1 km ≈ 0.621 mi	1 kL ≈ 264 gal	

EXAMPLE 1

Copy and complete the statement. Round to the nearest whole number.

a. 127 km ≈ __?__ mi **b.** 116 lb ≈ __?__ kg **c.** 50 mL ≈ __?__ fl oz

SOLUTION

a. $127 \text{ km} \times \frac{0.621 \text{ mi}}{1 \text{ km}} = \frac{127 \cancel{\text{km}} \times 0.621 \text{ mi}}{1 \cancel{\text{km}}} = 78.867 \text{ mi} \approx 79 \text{ mi}$ So, 127 km ≈ 79 mi.

b. $116 \text{ lb} \times \frac{1 \text{ kg}}{2.2 \text{ lb}} = \frac{116 \cancel{\text{lb}} \times 1 \text{ kg}}{2.2 \cancel{\text{lb}}} = \frac{116}{2.2} \text{ kg} = 52.72 \text{ kg} \approx 53 \text{ kg}$ So, 116 lb ≈ 53 kg.

c. $50 \text{ mL} \times \frac{0.0338 \text{ fl oz}}{1 \text{ mL}} = \frac{50 \cancel{\text{mL}} \times 0.0338 \text{ fl oz}}{1 \cancel{\text{mL}}} = 1.69 \text{ fl oz} \approx 2 \text{ fl oz}$ So, 50 mL ≈ 2 fl oz.

EXAMPLE 2

Copy and complete using < or > =: 210 m _?_ 670 ft.

210 m _?_ 670 ft	**Strategy: Convert meters to feet.**
688.8 ft _?_ 670 ft	**210 × 3.28 = 688.8, so 210 m ≈ 688.8 ft.**
688.8 ft > 670 ft	**Compare.**

▶ **Answer** 210 m > 670 ft

PRACTICE

Copy and complete the statement. Round to the nearest whole number.

1. 80 kg ≈ __?__ lb **2.** 56 mi ≈ __?__ km **3.** 24 qt ≈ __?__ L

Copy and complete the statement using < or >.

4. 808 mm _?_ 33 in. **5.** 40 gal _?_ 0.5 kL **6.** 1 oz _?_ 20 g

Reading and Making Line Plots

A **line plot** uses a number line to show how often data values occur.

EXAMPLE

You surveyed 20 of your friends and asked them how many pets they have. Their responses were:

6, 2, 3, 1, 5, 0, 2, 4, 1, 1, 6, 2, 0, 3, 1, 4, 3, 2, 1, 1.

a. Make a line plot of the data. **b.** What was the most frequent response?

SOLUTION

a.

0 1 2 3 4 5 6

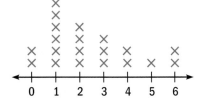

b. The greatest number of ×s is above 1, so 1 was the most frequent response.

PRACTICE

Make a line plot of the data.

1. In a survey, 15 people were asked how many TVs they own. Their responses were: 1, 2, 1, 4, 3, 2, 1, 5, 1, 2, 3, 1, 2, 1, 2.

2. In a survey, 18 people were asked how many times they eat out each week. Their responses were: 2, 4, 1, 3, 5, 6, 3, 7, 2, 1, 4, 8, 5, 4, 3, 4, 1, 2.

Use the line plot below. It shows the results of a questionnaire asking people how many hours they exercise each week.

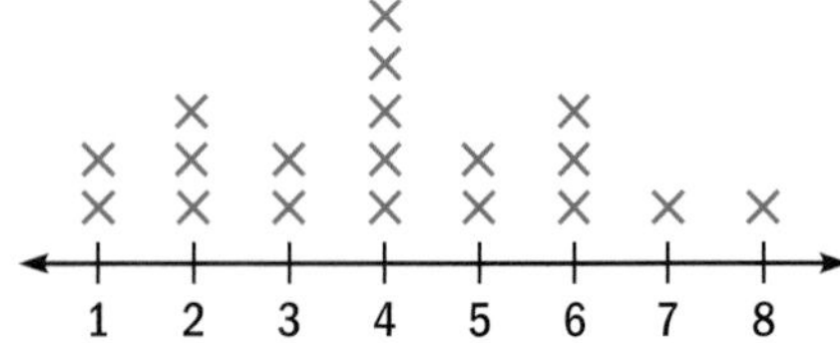

3. How many people completed the questionnaire?

4. How many more people exercise 4 hours each week than exercise 6 hours each week?

5. How many people exercise less than 3 hours each week?

Reading and Making Bar Graphs

Data are numbers or facts. A **bar graph** is one way to display data. A bar graph uses bars to show how quantities in categories compare.

EXAMPLE 1

The bar graph shows the results of a survey on favorite flavors of ice cream. Which flavor was chosen the most? Which flavor was chosen the least?

The longest bar on the graph represents the 11 people who chose chocolate. So, chocolate was chosen the most.

The shortest bar represents the 2 students who chose strawberry. So, strawberry was chosen the least.

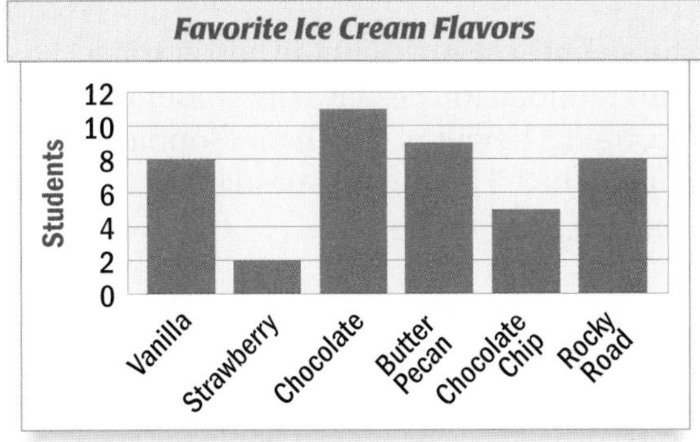

To make a bar graph, choose a title and a scale. Draw and label the axes. Then draw bars to represent the data given.

EXAMPLE 2

Draw a bar graph for the data given.

Subject	*Number of Students*
Math	8
English	15
History	20
Science	16

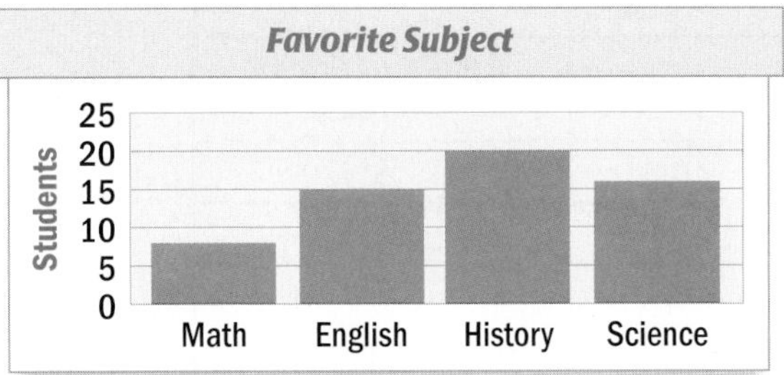

PRACTICE

In Exercises 1–3, use the bar graph of ice cream flavors above.

1. How many students chose butter pecan as a favorite ice cream flavor?
2. How many students chose vanilla as a favorite ice cream flavor?
3. Which two flavors were chosen by the same number of students?
4. Suppose 8 more students took the survey shown in the second example. Draw a new bar graph if 3 of the students chose math, 4 chose history, and 1 chose science.

Reading and Making Line Graphs

Another way to display data is to use a *line graph.* A **line graph** uses line segments to show how a quantity changes over time.

EXAMPLE 1

The line graph shows plant growth data collected by students every day for 7 days. The greatest increase in growth occurred between what two days? What was the amount of the increase?

The steepest segment in the line graph is from Monday to Tuesday. The students recorded a height of 1 inch on Monday and a height of 3.5 inches on Tuesday, for an increase of 2.5 inches.

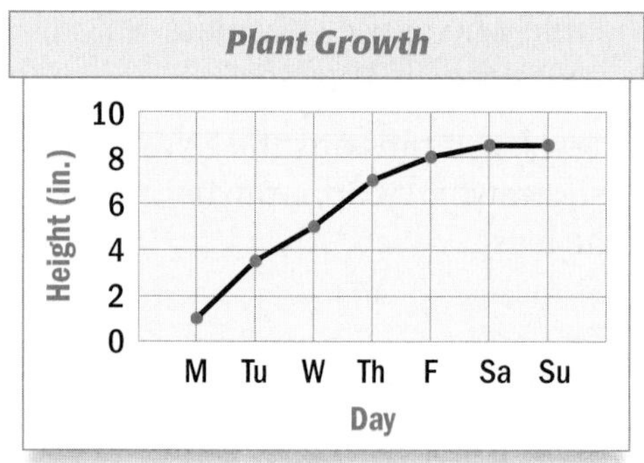

To make a line graph, choose a title and scales. Draw and label the axes. Then plot and connect points to represent the data given.

EXAMPLE 2

Draw a line graph for the data given.

Month	*Weight of Puppy (pounds)*
1	3
2	5.5
3	7
4	11

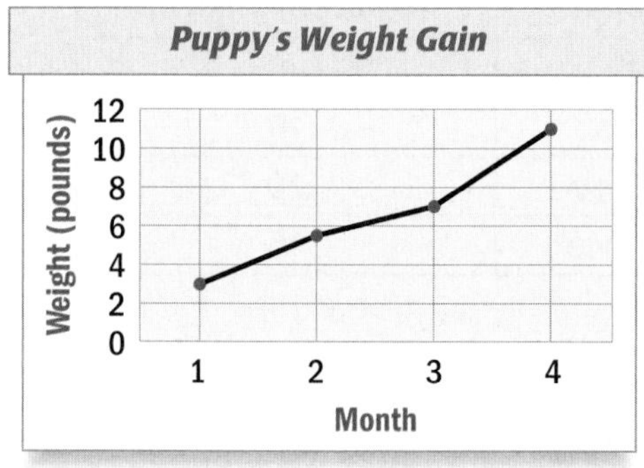

PRACTICE

In Exercises 1 and 2, use the plant growth line graph above.

1. Between which two days was the growth 1 inch?
2. Between which two days did the height remain the same?
3. Suppose in month 5 the puppy in the second example weighed 15 pounds. Copy the graph and add this data to it.

Venn Diagrams and Logical Reasoning

A **Venn diagram** uses shapes to show how sets are related.

EXAMPLE 1

Draw and use a Venn diagram.

a. Draw a Venn diagram of the whole numbers from 6 through 19 where set A consists of even numbers and set B consists of multiples of 5.

b. Is the following statement *true* or *false*? Explain. *No even whole number from 6 through 19 is a multiple of 5.*

c. Is the following statement *always, sometimes,* or *never* true? Explain. *A multiple of 5 from 6 through 19 is even.*

SOLUTION

a.

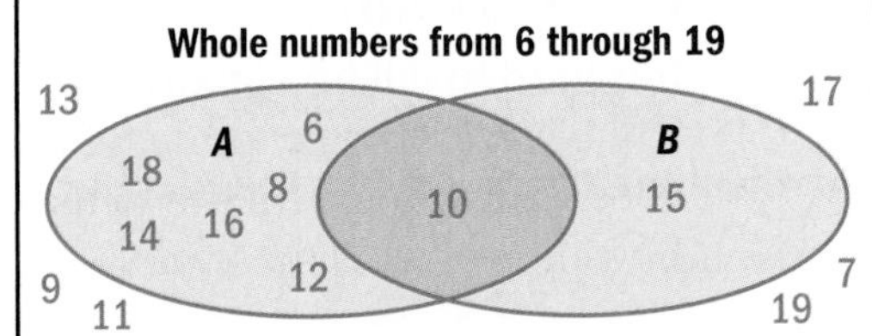

b. False. 10 is an even whole number that is a multiple of 5.

c. Sometimes. It is true that 10 is a multiple of 5 that is even, but 15 is a multiple of 5 that is odd.

PRACTICE

Draw a Venn diagram of the sets described.

1. Of the whole numbers less than 12, set A consists of numbers that are greater than 8 and set B consists of odd numbers.
2. Of the whole numbers less than 10, set C consists of multiples of 3 and set D consists of even numbers.

Use the Venn diagrams you drew in Exercises 1 and 2 to answer the question. Explain your reasoning.

3. Is the following statement *true* or *false*?
   There is only one odd number greater than 8 and less than 12.
4. Is the following statement *always, sometimes,* or *never* true?
   A whole number less than 10 is both a multiple of 3 and even.

SKILLS REVIEW HANDBOOK

Problem Solving Handbook
Problem Solving Strategy Review

Make a Model

Make a Model
Draw a Diagram
Guess, Check, and Revise
Work Backward
Make a List or Table
Look for a Pattern
Break into Parts
Solve a Simpler Problem
Use a Venn Diagram
Act It Out

Problem The width of a rectangular flag is $\frac{2}{3}$ its length. The flag is folded in half lengthwise. Then the flag is repeatedly folded into triangles, as shown, as many times as possible. How many layers thick will the resulting folded flag be?

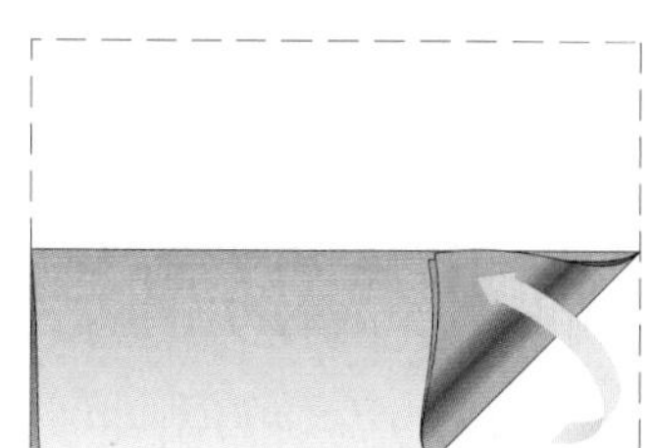

1 Read and Understand

You need to find the number of layers thick a flag will be when folded as described.

2 Make a Plan

It is hard to tell how many layers the flag will have. Making a model of the flag will allow you to perform the folds and count how many layers there are.

3 Solve the Problem

Cut a rectangle out of graph paper whose width is $\frac{2}{3}$ its length. Make the length of the rectangle 12 units and the width of the rectangle $\frac{2}{3} \cdot 12 = 8$ units.

Fold the rectangle in half lengthwise. Then repeatedly fold triangles.

Open the paper up and count the number of triangles. There are 12 small triangles, so the folded flag is 12 layers thick.

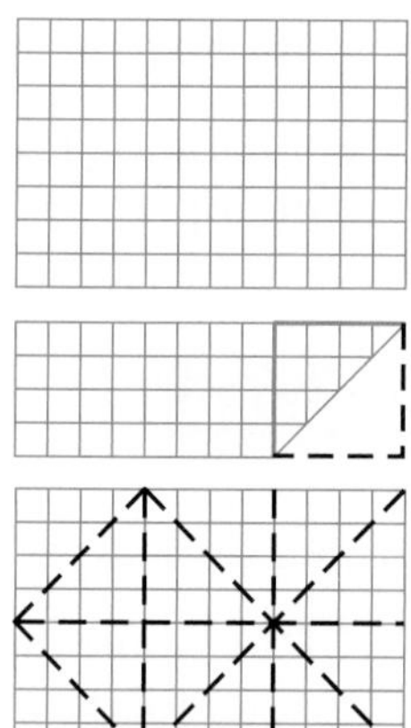

4 Look Back

Check your answer by making and folding another model for the flag, but one that has a different length and width.

Practice the Strategy

You are deciding between buying two frozen pizzas. One pizza is circular and has a diameter of 8 inches. The other pizza is rectangular with a length of 8 inches and a width of 5 inches. Without performing any calculations, tell which pizza has the greater area. *(See p. 796 for more practice.)*

Draw a Diagram

Problem Steve is hanging two large rectangular posters on one wall of his room. The width of the wall is $6\frac{1}{4}$ feet. Steve aligns the edge of one poster with the left edge of the wall. He aligns the edge of the other poster with the right edge of the wall. The posters overlap by 5 inches. If the posters are the same size and have the same orientation, what is the width of each poster?

- Make a Model
- **Draw a Diagram**
- Guess, Check, and Revise
- Work Backward
- Make a List or Table
- Look for a Pattern
- Break into Parts
- Solve a Simpler Problem
- Use a Venn Diagram
- Act It Out

1 Read and Understand

You need to find the width of each poster.

2 Make a Plan

Drawing a diagram can help you visualize how the posters are hung on the wall and how the given distances relate.

3 Solve the Problem

The outside edges of the posters align with the edges of the wall, and the posters overlap. Draw a diagram of this situation.

The length of the wall is $6\frac{1}{4}$ feet and the posters overlap by 5 inches. Label these distances. The diagram shows that the parts of the posters that do not overlap must measure $6\frac{1}{4}$ ft $-$ 5 in. $=$ 75 in. $-$ 5 in. $=$ 70 in.

The posters have the same width, so the part of each poster that does not overlap measures $70 \div 2 = 35$ in.

The width of each poster is $35 + 5 = 40$ in.

4 Look Back

Reread the problem and check that your diagram is consistent with each piece of the given information.

Practice the Strategy

In town, the post office is $1\frac{3}{8}$ miles south of the town hall. The town hall is $\frac{3}{4}$ mile north of the bank. How far and in what direction would you have to travel to get from the bank to the post office?
(See p. 796 for more practice.)

Guess, Check, and Revise

Problem In a certain arcade game, you roll each of 3 balls up a ramp and into rings of different sizes. For every 25 points you score, you get one ticket. In the first game you score 130 points by getting 2 balls in the inner ring and 1 ball in the outer ring. In the second game you score 110 points by getting 1 ball in the inner ring and 2 balls in the outer ring. How many points would you score by getting 3 balls in the inner ring?

1 Read and Understand

You need to find the points you would score by getting 3 balls in the inner ring. To find this, you first need to find the point value of the inner ring.

2 Make a Plan

You are given information about the combined number of points scored by getting balls in the two different rings. You are not given information on the individual point values of the rings. This suggests the strategy of guessing, checking, and then revising an answer.

3 Solve the Problem

Try guessing that the inner ring is worth 60 points and the outer ring is worth 10 points.

First game: $2(60) + 1(10) = 130$ ✓ **Second game:** $1(60) + 2(10) = 80$ ✗

Now try guessing 50 points for the inner ring and 30 points for the outer ring.

First game: $2(50) + 1(30) = 130$ ✓ **Second game:** $1(50) + 2(30) = 110$ ✓

The inner ring is worth 50 points and the outer ring is worth 30 points.

Since $3 \cdot 50 = 150$, getting 3 balls in the inner ring would result in a score of 150 points.

4 Look Back

Reread the problem to make sure that you answered the question being asked. Notice that the question asks for the points you would score by getting 3 balls in the inner ring, not the point values of the rings.

Practice the Strategy

The product of two numbers is 64. The difference of the same two numbers is 12. What is the sum of the two numbers? ***(See p. 797 for more practice.)***

Work Backward

Problem Kristin brought some picture frames to sell at a two-day craft fair. On the first day of the fair, Kristin sold $\frac{1}{4}$ of her picture frames. On the second day, Kristin sold $\frac{2}{3}$ of the remaining picture frames. If Kristin sold 30 picture frames on the second day of the fair, how many picture frames did she bring to sell at the craft fair?

1 Read and Understand

You need to find the number of picture frames that Kristin brought to the craft fair.

2 Make a Plan

You are given the number of frames sold during the second day of the fair, so you can work backward to find the number of frames remaining after the first day. Continue to work backward to find the number of frames brought to the fair.

3 Solve the Problem

Work backward from the 30 picture frames that were sold on the second day.

- Ask yourself: 30 is $\frac{2}{3}$ of what? Answer: 30 is $\frac{2}{3}$ of 45.

Work backward from the 45 picture frames remaining after the first day.

- Ask yourself: 45 is $\frac{3}{4}$ of what? Answer: 45 is $\frac{3}{4}$ of 60.

Kristin brought 60 picture frames to the craft fair.

4 Look Back

Work forward to check that your answer is correct. Kristin sold $\frac{1}{4} \cdot 60 = 15$ frames the first day. So she had $60 - 15 = 45$ remaining. She sold $\frac{2}{3} \cdot 45 = 30$ frames the second day.

Practice the Strategy

Mrs. O'Neil gives stickers to reward her students for good behavior. On Wednesday Mrs. O'Neil gave out 3 fewer stickers than on Tuesday. On Tuesday she gave out three times as many stickers as on Monday. If Mrs. O'Neil gave out 4 stickers on Monday, how many stickers did she give out on Wednesday?
(See p. 797 for more practice.)

Make a List or Table

- Make a Model
- Draw a Diagram
- Guess, Check, and Revise
- Work Backward
- **Make a List or Table**
- Look for a Pattern
- Break into Parts
- Solve a Simpler Problem
- Use a Venn Diagram
- Act It Out

Problem You get a haircut every 5 months. If you got a haircut in January of this year, in how many years will you next get a haircut in January? You get a haircut in January, in June, in November, and so on.

1 Read and Understand

You need to find how many years it will be until you again have a haircut in the month of January.

2 Make a Plan

You need to keep track of both the month in which you get a haircut and the number of years that have passed. Making a table is a good way to organize this information.

3 Solve the Problem

Make a table of the months in which you get a haircut. Remember that there are 4 months between months in which you get a haircut. Use a new column for each new year.

Year 1	Year 2	Year 3	Year 4	Year 5	Year 6
January	April	February	May	March	January
June	September	July	October	August	June
November		December			November

1 year 2 years 3 years 4 years 5 years

Your next haircut in January will take place in 5 years.

4 Look Back

Make sure that your answer seems reasonable. Since you get a haircut every 5 months, the total number of months between January haircuts should be divisible by 5. There are 12 months in a year, so there are $5 \cdot 12 = 60$ months in 5 years. Since 60 is divisible by 5, the answer seems reasonable.

Practice the Strategy

Sam does his laundry every 5 days. If he does his laundry on Tuesday of this week, in how many weeks will he next do his laundry on a Tuesday?
(See pp. 797–798 for more practice.)

Look for a Pattern

Problem A landscaper charges the prices shown in the table for mowing lawns of different sizes. How much would you expect the landscaper to charge for mowing a lawn that is 55,000 square feet?

Lawn size	Cost
10,000 ft²	$20
20,000 ft²	$28
30,000 ft²	$36
40,000 ft²	$44

LEN'S LAWN CARE

Make a Model
Draw a Diagram
Guess, Check, and Revise
Work Backward
Make a List or Table
Look for a Pattern
Break into Parts
Solve a Simpler Problem
Use a Venn Diagram
Act It Out

1 Read and Understand

You need to predict the cost of mowing a lawn with an area of 55,000 square feet.

2 Make a Plan

Since you are not given any information about the cost of mowing a lawn that is 55,000 square feet in size, you have to look for a pattern in the costs of the lawn sizes you are given.

3 Solve the Problem

Look for a pattern in the way the cost increases as the lawn size increases.

Lawn Size	*Cost*	
10,000 ft^2	$20	
20,000 ft^2	$28	+ $8
30,000 ft^2	$36	+ $8
40,000 ft^2	$44	+ $8

For each additional 10,000 square feet, the cost of mowing the lawn increases by $8. It can be expected that the cost of mowing a lawn that is 50,000 square feet will be $52 and the cost of mowing a lawn that is 60,000 square feet will be $60. Since 55,000 is halfway between 50,000 and 60,000, the cost of mowing 55,000 square feet should be halfway between $52 and $60.

You can expect the cost of mowing 55,000 square feet to be $56.

4 Look Back

Make sure that you performed your calculations correctly and that you answered the question being asked.

Practice the Strategy

Roland teaches piano lessons. All the lessons are the same length. On Saturday, the first lesson starts at 9:15 A.M., the second lesson starts at 9:50 A.M., the third lesson starts at 10:25 A.M., and the fourth lesson starts at 11:00 A.M. At what time will Roland begin teaching the seventh lesson?

(See p. 798 for more practice.)

PROBLEM SOLVING HANDBOOK

Break into Parts

Problem Dara is planning to wallpaper one wall of her living room. A diagram of her living room is given at the right. How many square feet of wallpaper will Dara need?

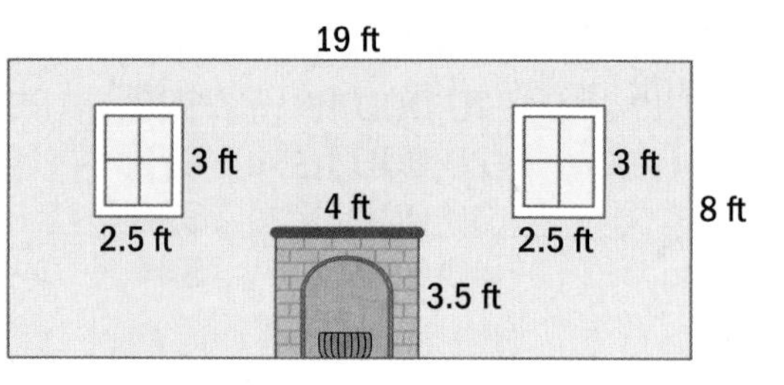

- Make a Model
- Draw a Diagram
- Guess, Check, and Revise
- Work Backward
- Make a List or Table
- Look for a Pattern
- **Break into Parts**
- Solve a Simpler Problem
- Use a Venn Diagram
- Act It Out

1 Read and Understand

You need to find the area of Dara's living room wall.

2 Make a Plan

Since wallpaper will not be placed everywhere, break the problem into parts by finding the overall area and subtracting the area of the windows and fireplace.

3 Solve the Problem

The overall area of the living room wall is:

$8(19) = 152$ square feet.

The area that will not be covered with wallpaper is:

$(2.5)(3) + (3.5)(4) + (2.5)(3) = 7.5 + 14 + 7.5 = 29$ square feet.

The area that will be covered with wallpaper is $152 - 29 = 123$ square feet.

4 Look Back

Check for reasonableness by estimating. The overall area of the living room is about $8(20) = 160$ square feet.

The area that will not be covered with wallpaper is about $3(3) + 4(4) + 3(3) = 34$ square feet.

The answer is reasonable since $160 - 34 = 126$.

Practice the Strategy

Rockford Middle School is organizing a 3-hour ice-skating dance for its 280 students. Ice skates will be provided for every student. The costs associated with having an ice-skating dance are given. How much will the dance cost?

Rink rental	$125 an hour
Dj	$80 an hour
Skate rental	$2 per person

(See p. 799 for more practice.)

Solve a Simpler Problem

Problem The Rios family is having a family reunion with 40 families. The first family to arrive puts 2 dimes in a jar to be given to a charity. The second family puts in 4 dimes, the third family puts in 6 dimes, and so on. The last family to arrive puts in 80 dimes. How much money is given to the charity?

1 Read and Understand

You need to find the sum of the even numbers from 2 though 80 and find the value of that number of dimes.

2 Make a Plan

To solve the problem, you could add every even number from 2 through 80, but this would take a long time. Instead, you can look for a simpler problem whose solution can help you find an answer.

3 Solve the Problem

Solve a simpler problem by grouping the even numbers from 2 through 80 into pairs of numbers whose sum is 82.

$$2 + 80 = 82$$

$$2 + 4 + 6 + \ldots + 76 + 78 + 80$$

$$4 + 78 = 82$$

The last pair of numbers is 40 and 42.

Since the numbers are even only, this means that there must be $40 \div 2 = 20$ pairs of numbers. So the sum of the even numbers from 2 through 80 is $20 \cdot 82 = 1640$. The amount of money given to charity is $1640 \times \$.10 = \$164$.

4 Look Back

Check that your answer is reasonable. There are a total of 40 numbers. Since the middle number is about 40, you can expect that the sum of the numbers would be about $40 \cdot 40 = 1600$. The answer is reasonable.

Practice the Strategy

A caterer uses square tables for dinner events. Each table can seat 4 people, with one person on each side. Tables can also be pushed together to seat more people. If the caterer needs to create one long table that can seat 30 people for dinner, how many square tables does he need to use?

(See p. 799 for more practice.)

Use a Venn Diagram

Problem In a survey about phone service, 205 people said they have a home phone only, and 40 said they have a cell phone only. 173 people said they have both a home phone and a cell phone, but no beeper, and 20 said they have a home phone, a cell phone, and a beeper. 24 people said they have a home phone and a beeper, but no cell phone, and 36 said they have a cell phone and a beeper, but no home phone. How many of the people surveyed have a cell phone?

- Make a Model
- Draw a Diagram
- Guess, Check, and Revise
- Work Backward
- Make a List or Table
- Look for a Pattern
- Break into Parts
- Solve a Simpler Problem
- **Use a Venn Diagram**
- Act It Out

1 Read and Understand

You need to find the number of people surveyed who have a cell phone.

2 Make a Plan

The answer is not obvious because some people have more than one type of service. Use a Venn diagram to organize the information.

3 Solve the Problem

Draw a Venn diagram to represent the given information.

The diagram shows that 269 people have cell phones.

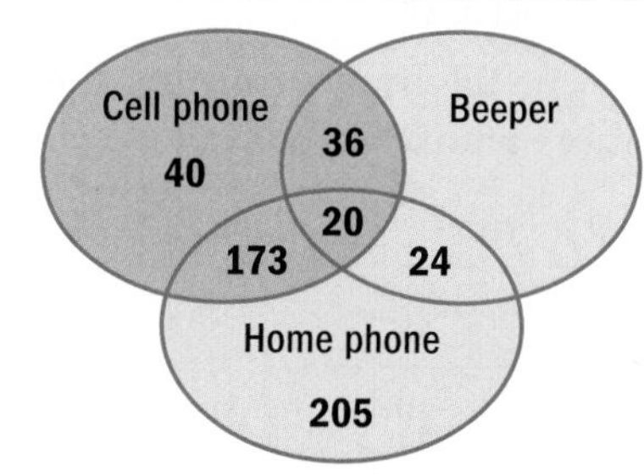

$40 + 36 + 20 + 173 = 269$

4 Look Back

Make sure that you placed the numbers in the correct places in the Venn diagram. Also check your addition.

Practice the Strategy

The tulips in a garden are yellow, white, red, or a mixture of these colors. There are 20 yellow tulips, 15 white tulips, and 12 red tulips. There are 8 yellow and white tulips, 10 yellow and red tulips, and 5 tulips with all three colors. There are no red and white tulips. How many tulips have at least some red?
(See pp. 799–800 for more practice.)

Act It Out

Problem You are in a lunch line with 4 students in front of you and 6 students behind you. You let a friend into the line in front of you, who then lets 2 students get in line behind her. Then 2 students join the end of the lunch line. How many students are now in the lunch line? What is your new position in the lunch line?

1 Read and Understand

You need to place a number of people in a line. Find the number of people in line and your place in line after people have joined the line.

2 Make a Plan

You can solve the problem by using slips of paper to represent people. Then follow the directions in the problem.

3 Solve the Problem

Begin by placing a slip of paper labeled with your name on it, then placing 4 slips to the left of it and 6 slips to the right of it.

Start of line [ ] [ ] [ ] [ ] [you] [ ] [ ] [ ] [ ] [ ] [ ]

Then place 3 slips to the left of the one representing you and two slips at the end of the line.

Start of line [ ] [ ] [ ] [ ] [ ] [ ] [ ] [you] [ ] [ ] [ ] [ ] [ ] [ ] [ ] [ ]

▸ **Answer** There are 16 people in line, and you are eighth in line.

4 Look Back

You can solve the problem a different way. Draw a diagram of the line as it is. Add to the diagram to show people joining it. Then count to find how many people are in line and what your position is.

Practice the Strategy

You have 8 quarters, 10 dimes, and 7 nickels. You give half your dimes and 2 nickels to a friend. Then you spend one fourth of your quarters and one nickel. How much money do you have left?

(See p. 800 for more practice.)

Problem Solving Strategy Practice

Solve the problem and show your work.

Make a Model

1. Each page of a photo album is 8 inches wide by 12 inches long. You have photos that are 4 inches wide by 6 inches long that you want to display in the album. Can you display 4 photos vertically on a single page? Can you display 3 photos horizontally? Can you display 2 photos vertically and 1 photo horizontally? *(Problem Solving Strategy Review, p. 786)*

2. Joe is making cellophane wrappers for pieces of his homemade saltwater taffy. He has 3 sheets of cellophane wrap that are each 9 inches wide and 10 inches long. How many 3 inch by 2 inch wrappers can Joe make? *(Problem Solving Strategy Review, p. 786)*

3. Elizabeth is making a 16 page booklet. She takes a piece of paper and folds it in half three times, as shown. Elizabeth then plans to staple the paper on the left edge, and trim the top and side of the booklet with scissors. She first wants to unfold the paper and number the pages of the book. Show how she should do this so that each page number appears in the lower right-hand corner of every page after the book is made. *(Problem Solving Strategy Review, p. 786)*

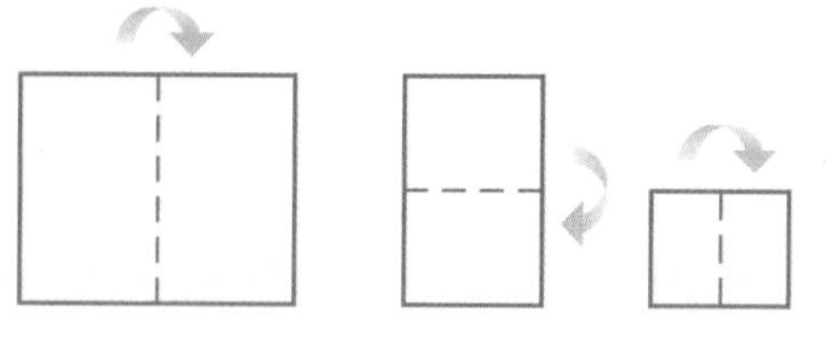

Draw a Diagram

4. Andy hung two dartboards directly across from each other on opposite walls in his basement. The walls are 15 feet apart. A toe line is a line marking where a player should stand to throw darts. Andy wants to mark a toe line exactly 7 feet $9\frac{1}{4}$ inches from the base of the wall on which each dartboard is hung. How far apart will the two toe lines be? *(Problem Solving Strategy Review, p. 787)*

5. Thomas is covering the wall area above his kitchen stove with square ceramic tiles. The square tiles have side lengths of 4 inches. The wall area above Thomas's stove is 2 feet by $2\frac{1}{2}$ feet. Thomas can cut tiles for an exact fit. What is the least number of tiles Thomas needs to cover the wall? *(Problem Solving Strategy Review, p. 787)*

6. You are making a beaded bracelet that is 7 inches long. You have 7 beads that you want to place on the bracelet. Each bead is $\frac{1}{2}$ inch long. You want equal amounts of space between each of the beads and between the end of the bracelet and the first bead and the end of the bracelet and the last bead. How far apart should the beads be? *(Problem Solving Strategy Review, p. 787)*

7. Marco and Ali deliver newspapers in the same neighborhood. Both start their paper routes at home. Marco's route takes him 2 blocks north, 3 blocks west, and then 5 blocks south. Ali's route takes her 4 blocks west, 3 blocks north, and then 5 blocks east. Marco lives 2 blocks north of Ali. How many times do their routes cross? *(Problem Solving Strategy Review, p. 787)*

Solve the problem and show your work.

Guess, Check, and Revise

8. The sum of two three-digit numbers is 534. Each number contains the digits 1, 2, and 3. What are the numbers? *(Problem Solving Strategy Review, p. 788)*

$$\begin{array}{r} \boxed{?}\ \boxed{?}\ \boxed{?} \\ +\ \boxed{?}\ \boxed{?}\ \boxed{?} \\ \hline 5\ \ \ 3\ \ \ 4 \end{array}$$

9. Seven children in a neighborhood are riding bicycles and tricycles. If there are a total of 17 wheels, how many children are riding each type of cycle? *(Problem Solving Strategy Review, p. 788)*

10. Dina bought a small plant, a medium plant, and a large plant for $37.50. The medium plant cost $5.00 more than the small plant, and the large plant cost $5.00 more than the medium plant. How much did the small plant cost? *(Problem Solving Strategy Review, p. 788)*

11. Consecutive numbers are numbers that follow one after another. The numbers 1, 2, and 3 are consecutive numbers. The sum of three consecutive numbers is 66. What are the numbers? *(Problem Solving Strategy Review, p. 788)*

12. You are playing a game where you collect blue chips and green chips. For every blue chip you get one point. For every green chip you lose a point. You have a total of 20 chips and 14 points. How many blue chips do you have? How many green chips do you have? *(Problem Solving Strategy Review, p. 788)*

Work Backward

13. Mr. Sanchez drove a rental car on a 3 day vacation. He drove twice as many miles on the first day as he drove on the second day. He drove 7 more miles on the second day than he drove on the third day. Mr. Sanchez drove 12 miles on the third day. How many miles did he drive during his vacation? *(Problem Solving Strategy Review, p. 789)*

14. Aisha runs every 3 days. She also does sit-ups every other day. If today is Tuesday and Aisha both ran and did sit-ups, on what day of the week did Aisha last do both activities on the same day? *(Problem Solving Strategy Review, p. 789)*

15. A dance company held auditions to fill 3 spots in the company. After the first round of auditions, $\frac{2}{3}$ of the dancers were cut. After the second round of auditions, $\frac{1}{4}$ of the remaining dancers were asked back for the third round. Five dancers made it to the third round of auditions. How many dancers were there in the first round of auditions? *(Problem Solving Strategy Review, p. 789)*

16. Andrew works out at a gym three times a week. He always starts with 15 minutes of stretching, followed by 50 minutes of cardiovascular exercise, and then 35 minutes of weightlifting. Andrew finishes his workouts at 7:15 P.M. What time does he start his workouts? *(Problem Solving Strategy Review, p. 789)*

17. At the beginning of the school year, your class was divided into seven equal groups. Later in the year, your group joined another group, and then two students left your group. Now there are four students in your group. How many students were in your class at the beginning of the year? *(Problem Solving Strategy Review, p. 789)*

Make a List or Table

18. Amy calls a store to order a tote bag with her initials ABC embroidered on it. The store employee she talks to later forgets the order of the initials. How many bags would the employee have to make to be sure that one bag has the initials in the correct order? *(Problem Solving Strategy Review, p. 790)*

Continued

Solve the problem and show your work.

19. Ben has a $5 bill and a $10 bill. He decides to buy 2 souvenirs at an airport shop. The prices of various souvenirs are given below. Ben has $5.50 after his purchase. Which souvenirs did he buy? ***(Problem Solving Strategy Review, p. 790)***

Souvenir Price List

Pen	$2.50
Keychain	$4.75
Hat	$6.25

20. Six cheerleaders form a pyramid. Suzie is always on the top, Diane and Avril are always in the middle row, and Monique, Olivia, and Tyra are always in the bottom row. How many different ways can the six cheerleaders form a pyramid? ***(Problem Solving Strategy Review, p. 790)***

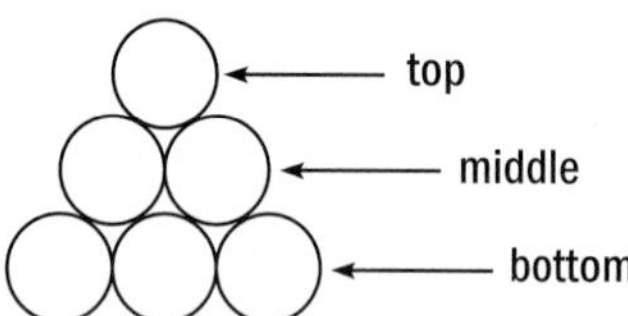

Look for a Pattern

21. Two grocery stores send discount coupons through the mail. Store A sends a $5 off coupon every other week. Store B sends a $10 off coupon every third week. Veronica does her weekly grocery shopping at whichever store has the better coupon. If both stores send coupons the first week of the year, how much will Veronica save with the coupons that year? ***(Problem Solving Strategy Review, p. 791)***

22. At track practice, the girls and the boys do a "leapfrog" drill. Six girls run in a single-file line next to 8 boys in a single-file line. Every quarter-lap around the track, the last runner in each line sprints to the front of the line. At the start of the drill, Mara is in the front of the girls' line and Dan is in the front of the boys' line. After how many laps will Mara and Dan both start sprinting at the same time? ***(Problem Solving Strategy Review, p. 791)***

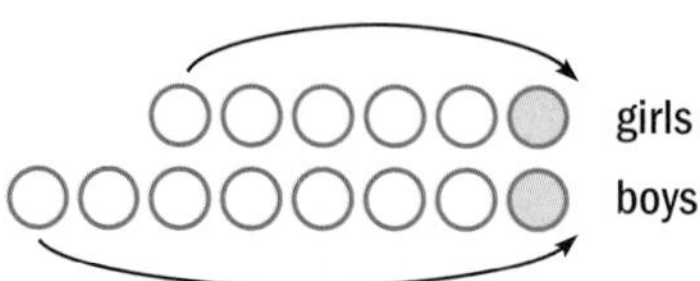

23. A commuter rail has its fares based on the number of zones traveled. The individual and family fares for a one-way ride within the first four numbers of zones are given in the table. The individual fare for traveling 6 zones is $4.50. What is the family fare for traveling 6 zones? If a family of 3 people is traveling on the commuter rail, is it cheaper for them to pay the individual fares or the family fare? ***(Problem Solving Strategy Review, p. 791)***

Number of zones	*Individual fare*	*Family fare*
1	$2.25	$9.00
2	$2.50	$10.00
3	$3.25	$13.00
4	$3.50	$14.00

24. Manny is stacking wooden crates to make a staircase, as shown below. He keeps adding crates to increase the height of the staircase. Each crate has a height of 1 foot. How many crates will Manny use to make a staircase that reaches a height of 9 feet? ***(Problem Solving Strategy Review, p. 791)***

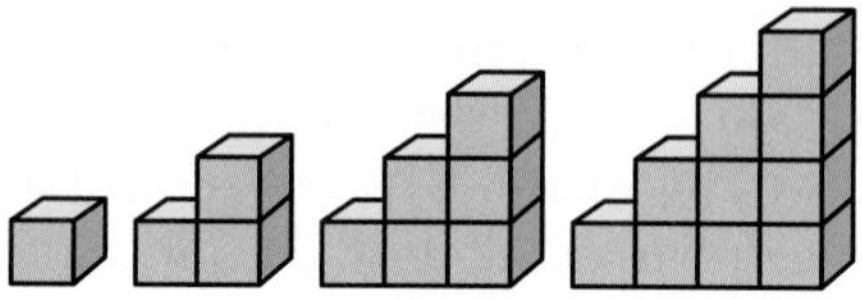

Solve the problem and show your work.

Break Into Parts

25. Auditions are being held for the school play. It takes 5 minutes to audition for an acting part and 3 minutes to audition for a chorus part. Only one student can audition at a time. There are 22 students auditioning for a chorus part and 25 students auditioning for an acting part. How long, in hours and minutes, will the auditions last? ***(Problem Solving Strategy Review, p. 792)***

26. How many different rectangles are in the figure below? ***(Problem Solving Strategy Review, p. 792)***

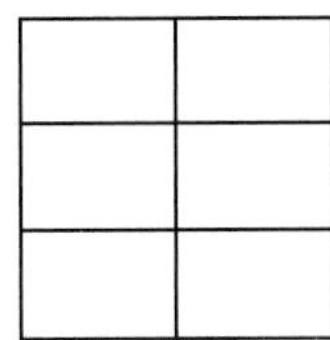

27. Your school is having a party. The party costs are given below. If 150 people are expected, how much will the party cost? ***(Problem Solving Strategy Review, p. 792)***

Decorations	$42
Appetizers	$5 per person
Drinks	$1.75 per person

Solve a Simpler Problem

28. Bridget decides to do her summer reading in the following way.

- The first day she will read 2 pages.
- The second day she will read 4 pages.
- The third day she will read 6 pages.

If Bridget continues increasing reading until she reads 100 pages in one day, how many pages will she read in all? ***(Problem Solving Strategy Review, p. 793)***

29. Matt is making confetti to throw at a surprise party. He uses a hole punch to punch holes that are $\frac{1}{4}$ inch in diameter. About how many holes can be punched out of one sheet of $8\frac{1}{2}$ inch by 11 inch paper? ***(Problem Solving Strategy Review, p. 793)***

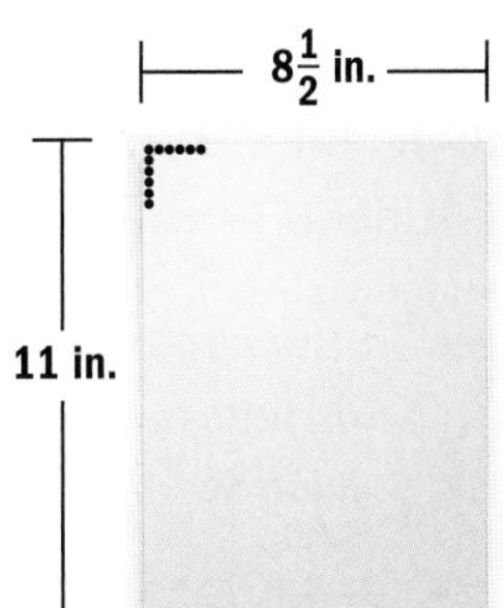

30. Jorie Middle School is having a slide show during the final assembly of the year. The slide show will have 200 photos taken throughout the year. The first photo will be of eighth graders, the second of sixth graders, the third of eighth graders, the fourth of seventh graders, the fifth of eighth graders, and so on. How many of the 200 photos will be of sixth graders? ***(Problem Solving Strategy Review, p. 793)***

31. The manager of an apartment complex is painting parking space numbers in the parking lot. The manager lost the stencil for the number 2. Instead of buying a new stencil, the manager decides to use the stencil for the number 5 and flip it upside down. The parking spaces are numbered from 1 to 300. How many times will the manager need to use the number 5 stencil? ***(Problem Solving Strategy Review, p. 793)***

Use a Venn Diagram

32. Of the 500 people with cameras at a high school graduation, 120 people used both a digital camera and a film camera. There were 208 people who used a film camera, but not a digital camera. How many people used only a digital camera? ***(Problem Solving Strategy Review, p. 794)***

Continued

Solve the problem and show your work.

33. On Saturday, several people fished from one pier. There were 11 people who caught only brown trout. There were 7 people who caught both brown trout and rainbow trout, and 13 people who caught only rainbow trout. How many people caught rainbow trout that day? ***(Problem Solving Strategy Review, p. 794)***

34. There are 18 students in your class. Eight students have a cat and five students have a dog. Two students have both a cat and a dog. How many students have neither a cat nor a dog? ***(Problem Solving Strategy Review, p. 794)***

35. At one high school there are 45 teachers who teach freshmen and sophomores, and 39 teachers who teach juniors and seniors. If there are 77 teachers at the high school, how many of them teach students in all four grade levels? ***(Problem Solving Strategy Review, p. 794)***

36. Twenty-four cats are in a shelter. Ten cats are black, and six cats have short tails. Three cats are black and have short tails. How many cats are neither black nor have short tails? ***(Problem Solving Strategy Review, p. 794)***

Act It Out

37. Justin, Bob, Kelly, Michelle, and Rebecca are all different heights. Kelly is taller than Michelle and Justin. Rebecca is shorter than Justin but taller than Michelle. Bob is the tallest of the five. List the students in order from tallest to shortest. ***(Problem Solving Strategy Review, p. 795)***

38. Four sets of twins are at a party. Each person shakes hands one time with every other person except his or her twin. How many handshakes take place? ***(Problem Solving Strategy Review, p. 795)***

39. The area of a poster board is 1000 square inches. You cut it in half repeatedly, setting aside one half each time. How many cuts will you make before the area of the remaining piece is less than 1 square inch? ***(Problem Solving Strategy Review, p. 795)***

40. You are dividing a sheet of paper into rectangles by folding it in thirds. You fold the paper 3 times into thirds without opening it. How many rectangles do you have? How many rectangles will you have if you fold the paper in thirds one more time? ***(Problem Solving Strategy Review, p. 795)***

41. Three boxes of different sizes are stacked on a table, with the largest box on the bottom and the smallest box on the top. You need to move the whole stack of boxes onto another table, but you can only move one box at a time. Also, no box can touch the floor, and no box can support a larger box without breaking. In addition to the table the boxes will be moved to, there is one other table in the room. All the tables are just large enough to hold the stack of boxes. List the moves it takes you to transfer the boxes. ***(Problem Solving Strategy Review, p. 795)***

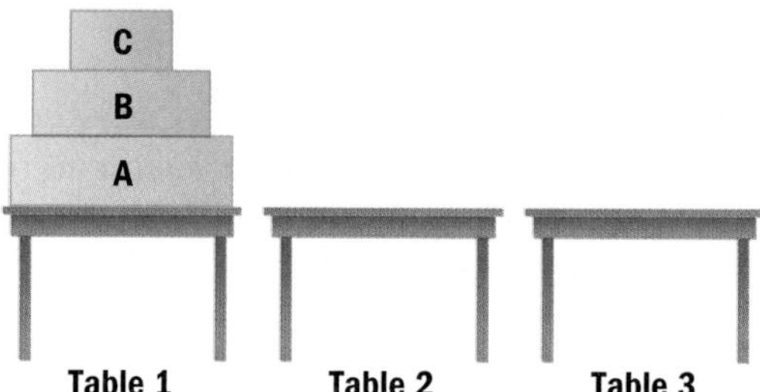

42. You have an ATM card for your savings account, but you forgot your four-digit personal identification number (PIN). You know that the first digit is a 4 and the last three digits include a 4, a 2, and a 6. How many possibilities are there for your PIN? ***(Problem Solving Strategy Review, p. 795)***

43. Darryl, Carlene, Tyrone, and Penelope are in line in that order for lunch at the cafeteria. Carlene lets Penelope cut in front of her. Darryl lets Tyrone cut in back of him. Tyrone then lets Carlene cut in front of him. In what order are they now? ***(Problem Solving Strategy Review, p. 795)***

Extra Practice

Chapter 1

1.1 The frequency table shows the heights of 30 students.

Height (inches)	54–55.9	56–57.9	58–59.9	60–61.9	62–63.9	64–65.9	66–67.9	68–69.9
Frequency	1	2	4	5	7	6	3	2

1. Make a histogram of the data shown in the frequency table.
2. Which height interval has the greatest number of students?
3. Can you use the histogram to determine the number of students who are between 60 and 69.9 inches tall? *Explain.*

1.2 Evaluate the expression.

4. $15 - 3 \cdot 2 + 4$
5. $42 \div [(5 - 2) \cdot (1 + 1)]$
6. $2 + \frac{100 - 36}{7 + 9}$
7. $4 \cdot 7 - 8 \cdot 3$
8. $3 + 10 \cdot 5 \div 2$
9. $(11 - 56 \div 8) \cdot 9$

1.3 Evaluate the expression when $r = 1.5$ and $s = 2.4$.

10. $10r + s$
11. $\frac{7s}{r + 0.5}$
12. $8rs$
13. $3(r + s)$

1.4 Evaluate the expression.

14. $24 - (2^3 + 1) \cdot 2$
15. $6^3 \div (2 + 1)^2 + 3$
16. $(8 - 5)^4 + 7 \cdot 5^2$

1.5 In Exercises 17–24, solve the equation using mental math.

17. $5n = 35$
18. $\frac{60}{t} = 4$
19. $12 + w = 75$
20. $41 - a = 23$
21. $9 + b = 17$
22. $63 - c = 10$
23. $6x = 54$
24. $\frac{m}{12} = 9$

1.6

25. Find the perimeter and area of a rectangular garden with a length of 13 feet and a width of 8 feet.
26. Ramon jogs at a rate of 5 miles per hour. How far does he jog in 1.5 hours?
27. Find the side length of a square that has a perimeter of 32 centimeters.

1.7

28. You do 5 hours of yard work each day for 4 days and earn \$6 per hour. Then you buy 2 concert tickets for \$12 each. Use the problem solving plan to find how much money you have left.

Chapter 2

2.1 **Use a number line to order the integers from least to greatest.**

1. 33, −24, −43, 7, 19, −2

2. −230, 157, −68, −146, 5, 94

Write the opposite and the absolute value of the integer.

3. −25

4. 467

5. 0

6. $|-2|$

2.2 **Find the sum.**

7. 342 + (−751)

8. −147 + 71

9. −89 + 268

10. −29 + (−51) + 36

11. −78 + 65 + 13

12. 93 + (−57) + (−102)

2.3 **Find the difference.**

13. −12 − 4

14. 10 − 13

15. 34 − (−17)

16. −18 − (−17)

17. 23 − 38

18. 81 − (−16)

19. −9 − (−77)

20. −63 − 19

2.4 **Find the product.**

21. (−7)(−50)

22. 25(−7)

23. −4(16)

24. (−12)(−21)

25. −95(0)(−58)

26. 54(−1)(5)

27. 8(−2)(−3)(5)

28. (−14)(4)(6)(9)

2.5 **In Exercises 29–32, find the quotient.**

29. $\frac{96}{-8}$

30. $\frac{-48}{-12}$

31. $\frac{0}{4}$

32. $\frac{-80}{5}$

33. Find the mean of the data: −8, 6, 3, −20, −9, 4.

2.6 **Evaluate the expression. Justify each step.**

34. −28 + (74 − 32)

35. $7\left(2 \cdot \frac{3}{7}\right)$

36. (−7.2 + 3.5) + (−3.5)

2.7 **Use the distributive property to evaluate or simplify the expression.**

37. −5(−3 + 8)

38. $3(m - 4)$

39. $-1(4 + 9r)$

40. $8(-4j - 3)$

Simplify the expression by combining like terms.

41. $-x + 3y - 5y + 6x$

42. $2(3k - 6) + 4 + 5k$

43. $5a - 3(2a + b) - 7b$

2.8 **Plot the point in a coordinate plane and describe its location.**

44. $A(3, -2)$

45. $B(5, 1)$

46. $C(0, -4)$

47. $D(-1, -3)$

Chapter 3

3.1 **Solve the equation. Check your solution.**

1. $n - 3 = 5$
2. $36 = p + 20$
3. $-4 = h - 9$
4. $27 + z = 51$

3.2 **Solve the equation. Check your solution.**

5. $32 = \frac{x}{2}$
6. $11k = -55$
7. $76 = 19r$
8. $\frac{y}{-1.4} = -5$

3.3 **Solve the equation. Check your solution.**

9. $5a - 2 = 33$
10. $\frac{d}{3} + 8 = -6$
11. $-1 = 14 - 2h$
12. $84 - z = 96$
13. $\frac{c}{4} + 7 = 12$
14. $47 = -6y + 5$
15. $73 = 15 - b$
16. $55 = 7t - 8$

3.4 **In Exercises 17 and 18, translate the statement into an equation. Then solve the equation.**

17. Five less than the product of 6 and a number is 13.
18. The sum of 5 and the quotient of a number and 3 is -1.
19. An auto repair shop charges \$48 per hour for labor plus the cost of parts. Your car needs new parts that cost \$129, and the total cost is \$201. How much time is required to repair the car?

3.5 **Find the area and perimeter of the triangle.**

20. 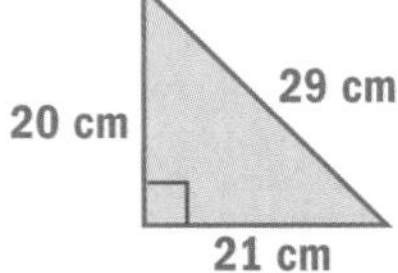

21. 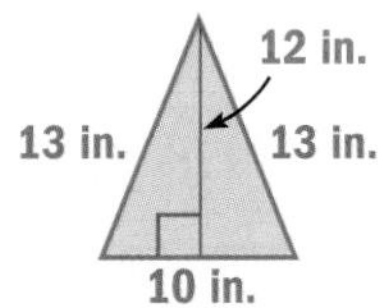

22. 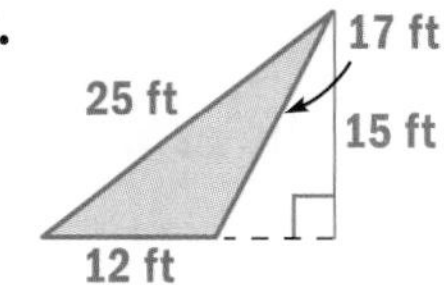

23. A rectangle has an area of 60 square meters and a length of 12 meters. What is the width of the rectangle? What is the perimeter?
24. A square has an area of 81 square feet. What is the length of each side?

3.6 **Solve the inequality. Then graph its solution.**

25. $4 + j \geq -1$
26. $0 < m - 6$
27. $z + 4.5 \leq 2$
28. $-38 > t - 46$

3.7 **Solve the inequality. Then graph its solution.**

29. $5x < -25$
30. $3 \leq -\frac{1}{3}y$
31. $2 \geq \frac{s}{4}$
32. $-13k > -65$

EXTRA PRACTICE

Chapter 4

4.1 **Write the prime factorization of the number.**

1. 72 **2.** 65 **3.** 153 **4.** 196

Factor the monomial.

5. $25pq$ **6.** $7a^3$ **7.** $22xy^2$ **8.** $54s^2t$

4.2 **Find the greatest common factor of the numbers or monomials.**

9. 45, 75 **10.** 108, 162

11. $6bc, 35abc^2$ **12.** $4p^2, 18qr$

13. $21mn, 9km^2$ **14.** $14x^2y^3, 28xy^2$

15. $34w^2z^2, 51w^5z^4$ **16.** $abcdf, a^2d^3gh$

4.3 **Write the fraction in simplest form.**

17. $\frac{32}{64}$ **18.** $\frac{-15}{39}$ **19.** $\frac{-22}{77}$ **20.** $\frac{17}{51}$

21. $\frac{10x}{45xy}$ **22.** $\frac{-16mn}{40mn}$ **23.** $\frac{-6ab}{4bc}$ **24.** $\frac{28rs}{7rst}$

4.4 **Find the least common multiple of the numbers or monomials.**

25. 30, 60 **26.** $4x, 18xy^2$

27. $5ab^2, 3bc^2$ **28.** $12x^3y, 8x^2y^4$

4.5 **Copy and complete the statement with <, >, or =.**

29. $\frac{7}{8} \underline{?} \frac{9}{11}$ **30.** $3\frac{3}{5} \underline{?} \frac{11}{3}$ **31.** $\frac{17}{6} \underline{?} 2\frac{13}{18}$ **32.** $1\frac{10}{15} \underline{?} \frac{35}{21}$

33. $\frac{11}{10} \underline{?} 1\frac{1}{8}$ **34.** $\frac{4}{5} \underline{?} \frac{6}{11}$ **35.** $\frac{50}{9} \underline{?} 5\frac{2}{7}$ **36.** $\frac{63}{15} \underline{?} 4\frac{5}{12}$

4.6 **Simplify the expression. Write your answer as a power.**

37. $z^5 \cdot z$ **38.** $5^8 \cdot 5^4$ **39.** $(-7)^6 \cdot (-7)^3$ **40.** $a^2 \cdot a^4$

41. $\frac{6^9}{6^5}$ **42.** $\frac{(-8)^{12}}{(-8)^2}$ **43.** $\frac{(-v)^7}{(-v)^4}$ **44.** $\frac{c^9}{c}$

4.7 **Simplify. Write the expression using only positive exponents.**

45. $6k^{-1}$ **46.** $a^3 \cdot a^{-3}$ **47.** $\frac{s^{-3}}{s^4}$ **48.** $n^{-4} \cdot n^{-2}$

4.8 **Write the number in scientific notation.**

49. 124,000,000 **50.** 0.0000005 **51.** 0.0000791 **52.** 32,100

Write the number in standard form.

53. 2.7×10^{-3} **54.** 9.09×10^2 **55.** 5.88×10^{11} **56.** 6.2×10^{-8}

Chapter 5

5.1 Find the sum or difference.

1. $\frac{7}{8} + \frac{5}{8}$
2. $5\frac{1}{5} - 3\frac{4}{5}$
3. $-\frac{11m}{15} + \frac{m}{15}$
4. $-\frac{5a}{9b} - \frac{4a}{9b}$

5.2 Find the sum or difference.

5. $\frac{9}{10} - \frac{5}{6}$
6. $\frac{2}{5} - \frac{3}{7}$
7. $4\frac{1}{4} + 3\frac{7}{8}$
8. $-\frac{5}{12} + \frac{11}{16}$

5.3 Find the product.

9. $\frac{7}{8} \cdot \frac{3}{14}$
10. $5 \cdot \left(-3\frac{1}{4}\right)$
11. $-\frac{5}{18} \cdot 1\frac{1}{3}$
12. $-1\frac{3}{5} \cdot \left(-2\frac{1}{4}\right)$

5.4 Find the quotient.

13. $\frac{5}{9} \div 2$
14. $-\frac{7}{12} \div \frac{2}{3}$
15. $4\frac{1}{8} \div \left(-1\frac{1}{3}\right)$
16. $-2\frac{1}{2} \div (-10)$

5.5 Write the fraction or mixed number as a decimal. Write the decimal as a fraction or mixed number.

17. $-\frac{48}{125}$
18. $4\frac{11}{12}$
19. -0.28
20. $0.\overline{72}$
21. 0.006
22. -8.34
23. $3\frac{7}{8}$
24. $-\frac{16}{250}$

Order the numbers from least to greatest.

25. $-\frac{7}{3}, -2\frac{5}{12}, -2.43, -2.5, -2\frac{2}{5}$
26. $\frac{18}{5}, 3\frac{1}{3}, 3.8, 3.55, 3\frac{7}{12}$
27. $\frac{26}{5}, 5.3, 5\frac{2}{9}, 5.21, 5\frac{3}{8}$
28. $-4.2, -4\frac{1}{6}, -\frac{59}{14}, -4\frac{3}{7}, -4.04$

5.6 Find the sum or difference.

29. $7.21 + (-3.4)$
30. $-9.8 + (-3.7)$
31. $0.8 - (-12.3)$
32. $8.217 - 9.68$
33. $-10.2 + (-6.35)$
34. $-8.78 + 3.9$
35. $3.28 - 11.395$
36. $-0.04 - 5.789$

5.7 Find the product or quotient.

37. $-8.32 \cdot (-0.47)$
38. $-20.51 \cdot 3.14$
39. $0.435 \div 0.29$
40. $2.072 \div (-0.74)$
41. $4.7 \cdot (-6.78)$
42. $-0.14 \cdot (-9.43)$
43. $-19.27 \div 2.35$
44. $0.224 \div 5.6$

5.8 Find the mean, median, mode(s), and range of the data.

45. Finishing times for a race in minutes: 24, 37, 57, 81, 31, 25, 43, 39, 33, 40, 34, 65, 50
46. Daily low temperatures: −6°F, −7°F, −6°F, 5°F, 3°F, 0°F, −3°F
47. Grades on quizzes: 93, 84, 100, 95, 89, 78, 78, 85, 83, 95

Chapter 6

6.1 Solve the equation. Then check the solution.

1. $6k - 8 - 4k = 6$
2. $16 = 2(s + 9) - 4$
3. $5(n + 7) + 1 = -9$
4. $-8 = -3m + 2 + 5m$
5. $\frac{7a - 2}{3} = 4$
6. $2 = \frac{3 - 4t}{5}$

6.2 Solve the equation. Then check the solution.

7. $3a + 2 = 7a + 10$
8. $9y - 8 = 6y + 7$
9. $5x + 7 = 8(x - 1)$
10. $13v = 7(9 - v)$
11. $5(w + 3) = -10w$
12. $2(z + 5) = 3z + 14$

6.3 Solve the equation. Then check the solution.

13. $2.8y + 8.6 = 9.12 - 1.2y$
14. $7.25p - 3 + p = 14.325$
15. $7 - 2.65z = -4.4z$
16. $x - \frac{2}{3}x = \frac{3}{4}$
17. $\frac{9}{10}n + \frac{1}{5} = \frac{7}{10}n - \frac{3}{5}$
18. $\frac{6}{4}r - \frac{21}{8} = \frac{3}{4}r$

6.4 Find the indicated measurement, where r = radius, d = diameter, and C = circumference. Use 3.14 or $\frac{22}{7}$ for π. Explain your choice of value for π.

19. $r = \underline{\ ?\ }$

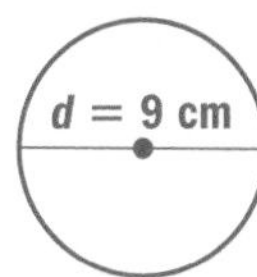

20. $C = \underline{\ ?\ }$

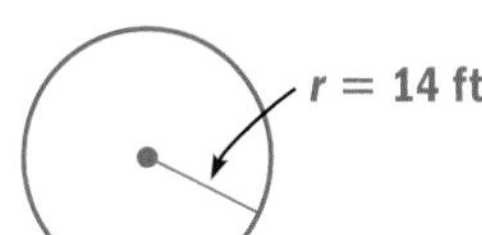

21. $r = \underline{\ ?\ }$

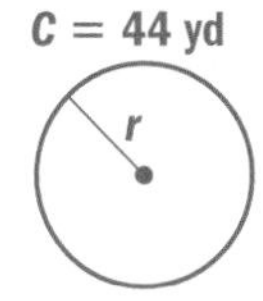

22. $d = \underline{\ ?\ }$

C = 15.7 in.

d

6.5 Solve the inequality. Then graph the solution.

23. $19 - 8c > 3$
24. $2(7 + n) \leq -10$
25. $5s + 3 \geq -7 - 5s$
26. $20 - 11x \geq -2$
27. $4(b - 3) > 20$
28. $-6y - 13 < 11 + 2y$

6.6 In Exercises 29–32, write the sentence as an inequality. Let n represent the unknown number. Then solve the inequality.

29. Twelve more than half a number is at most 8.
30. The difference of 3 times a number and 2 is greater than 7.
31. Four times a number is no less than 16.
32. The quotient of 18 and 6 times a number is less than 3.
33. You want to ride your bike for at least 28 miles. You have already biked for 10 miles. If you bike at a speed of 12 miles per hour, how much longer do you need to bike?
34. Nathan has $20 to spend at a carnival. The carnival has a $10 entrance fee. Ride tickets cost $.75 each. What number of tickets can Nathan buy?

Chapter 7

7.1 **A baseball team had 12 wins, 4 losses, and 2 ties in one season. Write the ratio as a fraction in simplest form and two other ways.**

1. wins to losses

2. losses to games played

3. wins to games played

Write the equivalent rate.

4. $\frac{9000 \text{ tickets}}{6 \text{ hours}} = \frac{? \text{ tickets}}{\text{hour}}$

5. $\frac{240 \text{ tickets}}{\text{hour}} = \frac{? \text{ tickets}}{\text{minute}}$

6. $\frac{7 \text{ meters}}{\text{second}} = \frac{? \text{ meters}}{\text{minute}}$

7.2 **Solve the proportion. Then check your solution.**

7. $\frac{x}{18} = \frac{25}{2}$

8. $\frac{4}{9} = \frac{5}{y}$

9. $\frac{3.6}{n} = \frac{4.8}{12.4}$

10. $\frac{m}{6} = \frac{35}{42}$

7.3 **Use a percent proportion.**

11. 9 is what percent of 75?

12. 42 is 25% of what number?

13. What number is 7% of 128?

14. 7 is what percent of 56?

7.4 **Write the decimal or fraction as a percent.**

15. 0.125

16. 1.42

17. $\frac{18}{25}$

18. $\frac{197}{200}$

Write the percent as a decimal and as a fraction.

19. 31%

20. 55%

21. 175%

22. 1.28%

7.5 **In Exercises 23–25, tell whether the change is an *increase* or *decrease*. Then find the percent of change.**

23. Original amount: 25
New amount: 28

24. Original amount: 144
New amount: 126

25. Original amount: 5000
New amount: 4950

7.6 **26.** A pair of shoes has a wholesale price of $28. The percent markup is 110%. What is the retail price?

27. Your food bill at a restaurant is $18.40. You leave a 15% tip. The sales tax is 5%. Find the total cost of the meal.

7.7 **Solve using the percent equation.**

28. What number is 121% of 412?

29. 13 is 15.6% of what number?

30. 57 is what percent of 76?

31. What number is 0.3% of 28?

7.8 **A bag contains 12 slips of paper numbered from 1 through 12. A slip of paper is chosen at random. Find the probability of the event.**

32. Drawing a number greater than 4

33. Drawing a number that is divisible by 5

Chapter 8

8.1 Find the measure(s) of the numbered angle(s).

1. 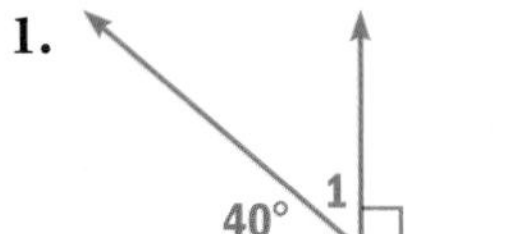

2. 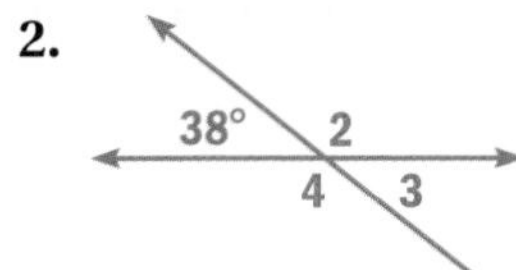

3. 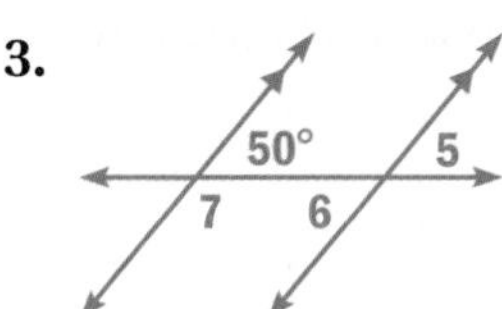

8.2 Find the value of *x*. Classify the triangle by its angles.

4. 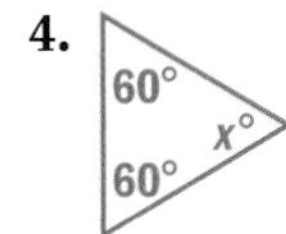

5. 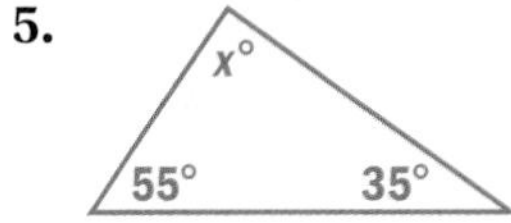

6. 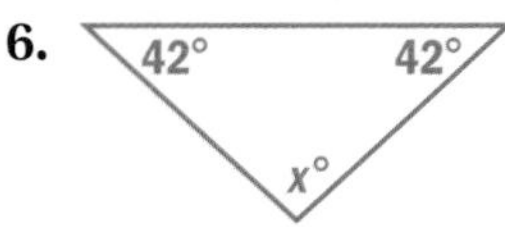

8.3 In Exercises 7–9, classify the quadrilateral.

7. 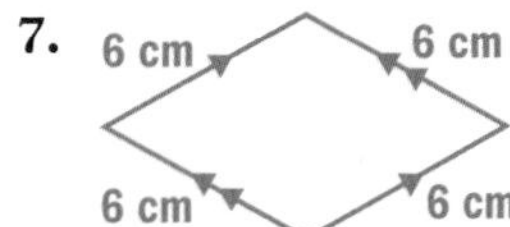

8. 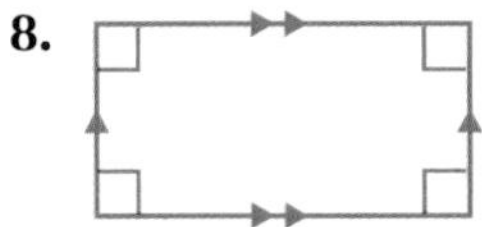

9. 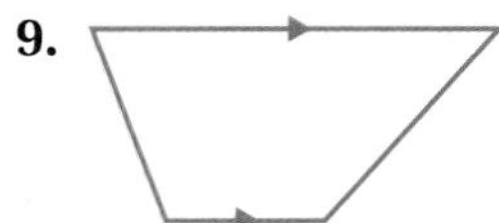

8.4 10. Find the sum of the angle measures in an 11-gon.

11. Find the measure of one angle in a regular 18-gon.

8.5 In Exercises 12–14, use the diagrams.

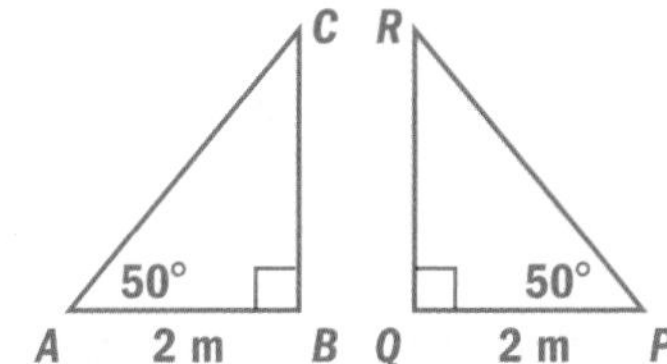

12. Name all pairs of congruent sides.

13. Name all pairs of congruent angles.

14. Explain how you know that $\triangle ABC \cong \triangle PQR$.

In Exercises 15–21, graph $\triangle ABC$ with vertices $A(-2, 4)$, $B(0, 2)$, and $C(-2, -6)$. Then graph its image after the given transformation.

8.6 15. Reflect $\triangle ABC$ in the x-axis.

16. Reflect $\triangle ABC$ in the y-axis.

8.7 17. Translate $\triangle ABC$ using $(x, y) \rightarrow (x - 1, y + 4)$.

18. Translate $\triangle ABC$ using $(x, y) \rightarrow (x + 2, y - 3)$.

19. Rotate $\triangle ABC$ 90° clockwise.

8.8 20. Dilate $\triangle ABC$ by a scale factor of 2.

21. Dilate $\triangle ABC$ by a scale factor of $\frac{1}{2}$.

Chapter 9

9.1 Use a calculator to approximate the square root. Round to the nearest tenth.

1. $\sqrt{52}$ **2.** $\sqrt{9.6}$ **3.** $-\sqrt{738}$ **4.** $-\sqrt{2037}$

Solve the equation. Check your solutions.

5. $k^2 = 900$

6. $h^2 - 5 = 44$

7. $153 + z^2 = 378$

8. $168 = v^2 - 1$

9. $a^2 + 7 = 88$

10. $m^2 = 3600$

11. $x^2 - 11 = 53$

12. $w^2 + 78 = 478$

9.2 In Exercises 13–16, graph the pair of numbers on a number line. Then copy and complete the statement with $<$, $>$, or $=$.

13. $\sqrt{18}\ \underline{?}\ 4$ **14.** $\sqrt{\frac{9}{16}}\ \underline{?}\ \frac{3}{4}$ **15.** $-8\ \underline{?}\ -\sqrt{70}$ **16.** $\frac{2}{3}\ \underline{?}\ \sqrt{\frac{1}{9}}$

17. Order the decimals 0.12, $0.\overline{1}$, $0.\overline{12}$, 0.123, and $0.\overline{123}$ from least to greatest.

18. Order the decimals 0.34, $0.\overline{3}$, $0.\overline{34}$, and 0.334 from least to greatest.

9.3 Let *a* and *b* represent the lengths of the legs of a right triangle, and let *c* represent the length of the hypotenuse. Find the unknown length.

19. $a = 21, b = 28, c = \underline{?}$

20. $a = \underline{?}, b = 63, c = 65$

21. $a = 56, b = \underline{?}, c = 65$

22. $a = 1.5, b = 3.6, c = \underline{?}$

23. $a = \underline{?}, b = 100, c = 125$

24. $a = 32, b = \underline{?}, c = 68$

9.4 Determine whether the numbers form a Pythagorean triple.

25. 40, 42, 58

26. 37, 39, 54

27. 15, 112, 113

28. 12, 35, 38

9.5 Find the values of the variables. Give exact answers.

29.

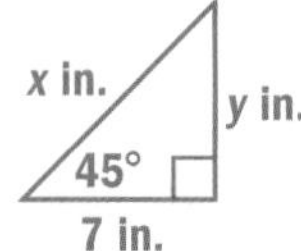

30.

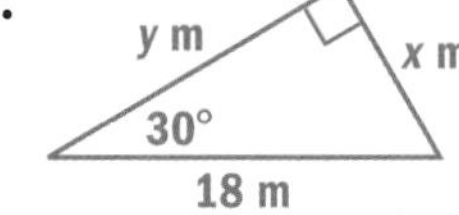

31.

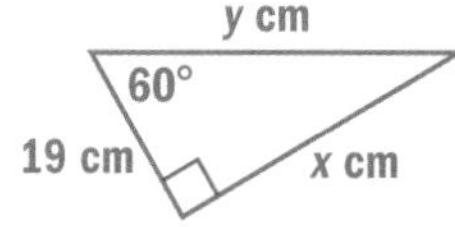

9.6 In $\triangle ABC$, write the sine, cosine, and tangent ratios for $\angle A$ and $\angle B$.

32.

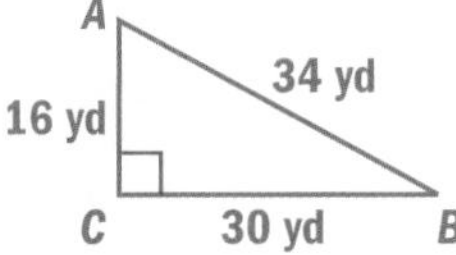

33.

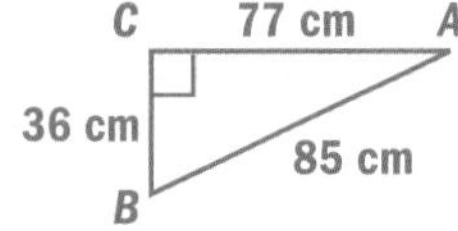

34.

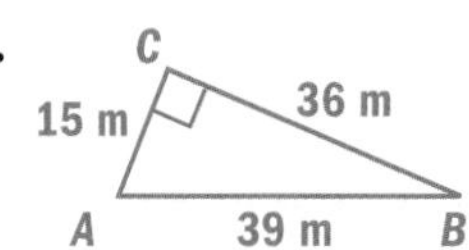

35. Use a calculator to approximate the sine, cosine, and tangent of 62°. Round your answers to four decimal places.

Chapter 10

10.1 **Sketch a parallelogram with base b and height h and find its area.**

1. $b = 15$ in., $h = 13$ in.
2. $b = 9.4$ ft, $h = 4.8$ ft
3. $b = 8\frac{1}{3}$ cm, $h = 1\frac{1}{5}$ cm

Sketch a trapezoid with bases b_1 and b_2 and height h and find its area.

4. $b_1 = 9$ m, $b_2 = 16$ m, $h = 18$ m
5. $b_1 = 40$ yd, $b_2 = 28$ yd, $h = 10.5$ yd

10.2 **In Exercises 6–13, find the area of the circle given its radius r or diameter d. Use 3.14 for π.**

6. $r = 18$ mi
7. $d = 80$ in.
8. $d = 11$ mm
9. $r = 2.9$ ft
10. $d = 7.8$ in.
11. $r = 0.3$ cm
12. $r = 11$ ft
13. $d = 16$ mi

10.3
14. How many faces, edges, and vertices does a hexagonal pyramid have?
15. Show two ways to represent a cylinder. Tell whether it is a polyhedron.

10.4 **Draw a net for the solid. Then find the surface area. Round to the nearest tenth.**

16. 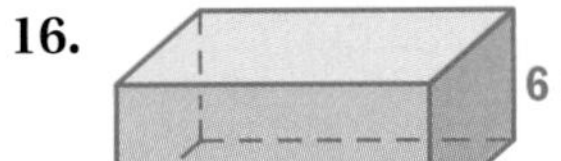

17. 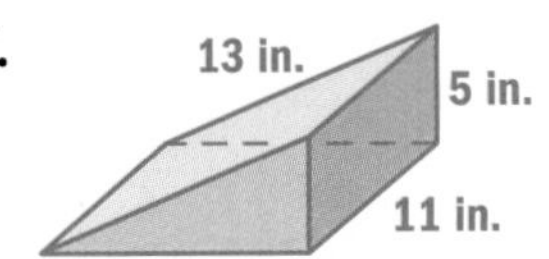

18.  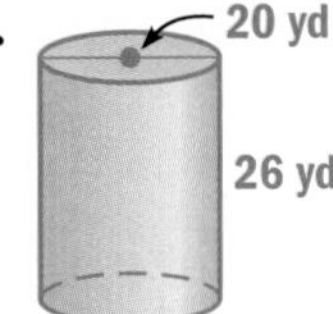

10.5 **Find the surface area of the solid. Round to the nearest tenth.**

19. A square pyramid with base side length 12 m and slant height 9 m
20. A cone with radius 8 cm and slant height 9 cm
21. A cone with diameter 15 m and slant height 8.2 m

10.6 **Find the volume of the solid. Round to the nearest tenth.**

22. The prism in Exercise 16
23. The prism in Exercise 17
24. The cylinder in Exercise 18

10.7 **Find the volume of the solid. Round to the nearest tenth.**

25. A square pyramid with base side length 10 ft and height 8 ft
26. A cone with radius 18 m and height 6 m
27. The triangular pyramid shown at the right

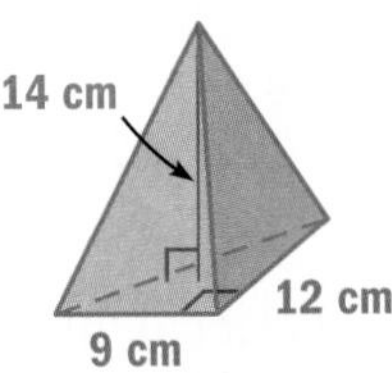

Chapter 11

11.1 **1.** Decide whether the relation (−3, 3), (−2, 2), (−1, 1), (0, 0), (1, 1) is a function. Explain your answer.

2. Make an input-output table for the function $y = 0.5x$. Use a domain of −4, −2, 0, 2, and 4. Identify the range.

3. Write a function rule that relates x and y.

Input x	−5	−3	−1	1
Output y	−6	−4	−2	0

11.2 **4.** Make a scatter plot of the data in Exercise 3. Describe the relationship between x and y.

11.3 **Tell whether the ordered pair is a solution of the equation.**

5. $y = 3x - 7$; (1, 4) **6.** $4x + y = 5$; (2, −1) **7.** $y = \frac{1}{2}x + \frac{1}{2}$; (−3, −1)

List four solutions of the equation.

8. $y = -x - 3$ **9.** $y = 7 + 2x$

10. $y = -\frac{2}{3}x$ **11.** $y = -x$

12. $-x + y = 1$ **13.** $3x + y = -2$

14. $x + 2y = 8$ **15.** $-3y + 4x = 7$

11.4 **Graph the linear equation.**

16. $y = -3$ **17.** $y = \frac{1}{4}x - 2$ **18.** $x = 4$ **19.** $3x + y = 4$

11.5 **In Exercises 20–23, find the intercepts of the graph of the equation.**

20. $y = -2x + 4$ **21.** $y = 5x - 1$ **22.** $x + 5y = -5$ **23.** $2x - 3y = 12$

24. Graph the line with an x-intercept of 4 and a y-intercept of −1.

25. Graph the line with an x-intercept of −2 and a y-intercept of 10.

11.6 **Find the slope of the line passing through the points.**

26. (−2, 3), (6, 1) **27.** (5, 0), (5, −9)

28. (6, −4), (2, −4) **29.** (7, −5), (−2, −14)

30. (−7, 8), (−9, 5) **31.** (−3, −2), (−7, 2)

32. (4, 9), (3, 13) **33.** (0, 7), (−3, −10)

11.7 **Find the slope and y-intercept of the graph of the equation.**

34. $y = 3x - 5$ **35.** $y = 2$ **36.** $y = -\frac{1}{3}x + 1$ **37.** $2x - y = 8$

11.8 **Graph the inequality.**

38. $y > -x - 3$ **39.** $6 \le 3y$ **40.** $5 + 2x > y$ **41.** $4x + 3y \le -12$

EXTRA PRACTICE

Chapter 12

In Exercises 1–3, use the following lengths, in inches, of alligators at an alligator farm: 140, 127, 103, 140, 118, 100, 117, 101, 116, 129, 130, 105, 99, 143.

12.1 1. Make an ordered stem-and-leaf plot of the data. Identify the interval that includes the most data values.

2. Find the median and range of the data.

12.2 3. Make a box-and-whisker plot of the data. What conclusions can you make?

12.3 4. In a survey about favorite kinds of movies, 20 people chose dramas, 4 chose horror movies, 8 chose science fiction, and 18 chose comedies. Represent the data in a circle graph.

5. You want to display the average monthly price of a stock for each month in 2001. What type of display would you use? Explain.

12.4 6. You can take one of three different classes in the morning or the afternoon. Make a tree diagram to find the number of choices that are possible.

7. A license plate has 3 digits followed by 3 letters. How many different license plates are possible?

12.5 **In Exercises 8–11, find the number of permutations.**

8. ${}_7P_2$ 9. ${}_{11}P_1$ 10. ${}_8P_5$ 11. ${}_{10}P_3$

12. There are 8 students in the school play. How many different ways can the cast be arranged in a row?

12.6 **In Exercises 13–16, find the number of combinations.**

13. ${}_5C_4$ 14. ${}_{20}C_2$ 15. ${}_6C_3$ 16. ${}_{12}C_9$

17. A CD case holds 30 CDs. How many ways can you select 3 CDs from the case?

12.7 18. A telephone number is chosen at random. Find the odds that the last digit is greater than 3.

12.8 19. You flip two coins. Find the probability that you do *not* get two heads.

20. You and two friends each roll a number cube. What is the probability that all of you roll a 3?

21. Ten slips of paper numbered 1 through 10 are placed in a bag. You draw a slip at random and draw another without replacing the first. Find the probability that both numbers are odd.

Chapter 13

13.1 **In Exercises 1–3, simplify the polynomial and write it in standard form.**

1. $3 + 5x - x^2 - 7x + 4$ **2.** $2t^4 + t^3 - 6 - 3t^3 + t^2$ **3.** $4(5 - k) + 4k - k^2 + 1$

4. The height, in feet, of a falling pebble after t seconds of falling from a height of 45 feet can be found using the polynomial $-16t^2 + 45$. Find the pebble's height after 1.5 seconds.

13.2 **Find the sum or difference.**

5. $(3x^2 + 5x - 4) + (-2x^3 + x^2 + 9x)$ **6.** $(-8x^2 - x + 1) - (7x^2 - 5x + 1)$

7. $(4x^3 - 8x^2 + 2) - (x^3 + x^2 - 6x + 5)$ **8.** $(-x^2 - 3x + 7) + (x^2 + 4x - 9)$

9. $(2x^3 - 2x^2 + 1) + (-x^3 + 9x + 5)$ **10.** $(3x^2 - 5x - 10) - (5x^3 + x - 2)$

13.3 **Simplify the expression.**

11. $(4z)(-7z^5)$ **12.** $(-r^2)(-3r^2)$

13. $-3n(2n - 5)$ **14.** $q^3(-q + 2)$

15. $(5ab)^3$ **16.** $(-rst)^4$

17. $(p^6)^4$ **18.** $(3y^5)^2$

13.4 **Find the product and simplify.**

19. $(2x + 1)(x - 5)$ **20.** $(m - 3)(-m + 4)$

21. $(d + 6)(d + 4)$ **22.** $(4y - 3)(4y + 3)$

23. $(a - 8)(a - 7)$ **24.** $(5x + 2)(2x - 1)$

13.5 **Rewrite using function notation.**

25. $y = 2x - 5$ **26.** $y = 3x^2$ **27.** $y = 5x^2 + 1$

Evaluate the function for $x = -2, -1, 0, 1,$ and 2.

28. $f(x) = 2x^2 + x$ **29.** $f(x) = \frac{1}{4}x^2$ **30.** $f(x) = \frac{1}{2}x^2 - x$

31. $f(x) = -3x^2 + 2x$ **32.** $f(x) = x^2 + 4x$ **33.** $f(x) = -x^2 - 3$

Graph the function using a table of values.

34. $f(x) = 3x^2$ **35.** $f(x) = -x^2 + 2$ **36.** $f(x) = 2x^2 - 4$

Tell whether the graph represents a function.

37.

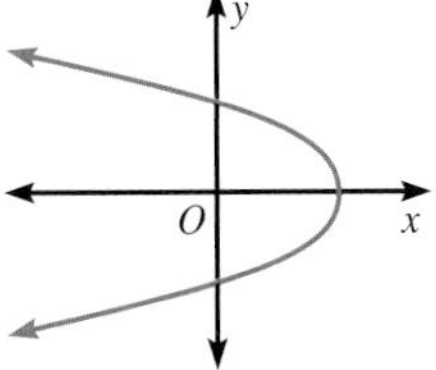

38.

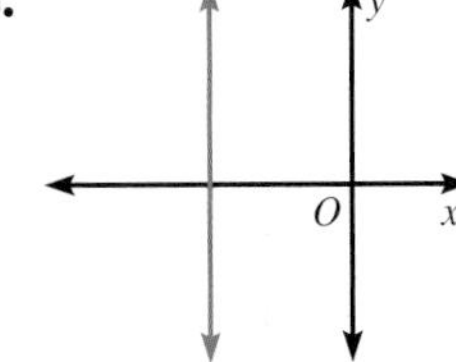

39.

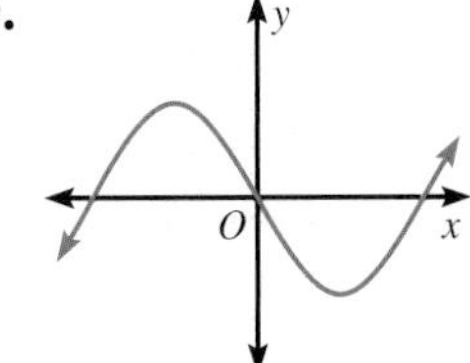

EXTRA PRACTICE

Tables

Table of Symbols

Symbol	Meaning	Page
26.10	decimal point	**2**
$=$	equals, is equal to	**8, 26**
$3 \cdot x$ $3(x)$ $3x$	3 times x	**8, 13**
$\frac{14}{2}$	14 divided by 2	**9**
( )	parentheses—a grouping symbol	**9**
[ ]	brackets—a grouping symbol	**9**
4^3	$4 \cdot 4 \cdot 4$	**19**
$\stackrel{?}{=}$	is equal to?	**27**
$\neq$	is not equal to	**27**
∟	right angle	**32, 403**
$\approx$	is approximately equal to	**38**
. . .	continues on	**57**
-3	negative 3	**57**
-3	the opposite of 3	**58**
$\lvert a \rvert$	the absolute value of a number a	**58**
(x, y)	ordered pair	**94**
$<$	is less than	**148, 324**
$>$	is greater than	**148, 324**
$\leq$	is less than or equal to	**148, 324**
$\geq$	is greater than or equal to	**148, 324**
$1.1\overline{6}$	repeating decimal 1.16666 . . .	**255**
π	pi—a number approximately equal to 3.14	**312**
$a:b, \frac{a}{b}$	ratio of a to b	**343**
%	percent	**354**
$^\circ$	degree(s)	**403, 776**
$\angle A$	angle with vertex point A	**403, 774**
$m\angle B$	the measure of angle B	**403**
$\perp$	is perpendicular to	**404**
$\parallel$	is parallel to	**405**
⟷ (two parallel arrows)	parallel lines	**405**
$\cong$	is congruent to	**427**
$\overline{AB}$	line segment AB	**427**
$\triangle ABC$	triangle with vertices A, B, and C	**428**
A'	the image of point A	**433**
$\sim$	is similar to	**447**
$\sqrt{a}$	the positive square root of a number a where $a \geq 0$	**469**
$\pm$	plus or minus	**471**
$\nleq$	is not less than or equal to	**629**
$3!$	3 factorial, or $3 \cdot 2 \cdot 1$	**675**
$f(x)$	the function of f at x	**739**
$\overleftrightarrow{AB}$	line AB	**773**
$\overrightarrow{AB}$	ray AB	**773**

Table of Measures

Time

60 seconds (sec) = 1 minute (min)
60 minutes = 1 hour (h)
24 hours = 1 day (d)
7 days = 1 week (wk)
4 weeks (approx.) = 1 month

365 days, 52 weeks (approx.), 12 months = 1 year
10 years = 1 decade
100 years = 1 century

Metric

Length

10 millimeters (mm) = 1 centimeter (cm)
100 cm, 1000 mm = 1 meter (m)
1000 m = 1 kilometer (km)

Area

100 square millimeters (mm^2) = 1 square centimeter (cm^2)
10,000 cm^2 = 1 square meter (m^2)
10,000 m^2 = 1 hectare (ha)

Volume

1000 cubic millimeters (mm^3) = 1 cubic centimeter (cm^3)
1,000,000 cm^3 = 1 cubic meter (m^3)

Liquid Capacity

1000 millimeters (mL), 1000 cubic centimeters (cm^3) = 1 liter (L)
1000 L = 1 kiloliter (kL)

Mass

1000 milligrams (mg) = 1 gram (g)
1000 g = 1 kilogram (kg)
1000 kg = 1 metric ton (t)

Temperature **Degrees Celsius (°C)**

0°C = freezing point of water
37°C = normal body temperature
100°C = boiling point of water

United States Customary

Length

12 inches (in.) = 1 foot (ft)
36 in., 3 ft = 1 yard (yd)
5280 ft, 1760 yd = 1 mile (mi)

Area

144 square inches ($in.^2$) = 1 square foot (ft^2)
9 ft^2 = 1 square yard (yd^2)
43,560 ft^2, 4840 yd^2 = 1 acre (A)

Volume

1728 cubic inches ($in.^3$) = 1 cubic foot (ft^3)
27 ft^3 = 1 cubic foot (yd^3)

Liquid Capacity

8 fluid ounces (fl oz) = 1 cup (c)
2 c = 1 pint (pt)
2 pt = 1 quart (qt)
4 qt = 1 gallon (gal)

Weight

16 ounces (oz) = 1 pound (lb)
2000 lb = 1 ton

Temperature **Degrees Fahrenheit (°F)**

32°F = freezing point of water
98.6°F = normal body temperature
212°F = boiling point of water

Table of Formulas

Geometric Formulas

Rectangle *(p. 32)*

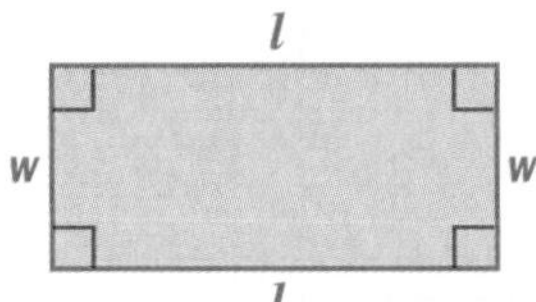

Area $A = lw$

Perimeter $P = 2l + 2w$

Square *(p. 32)*

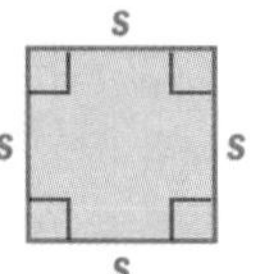

Area $A = s^2$

Perimeter $P = 4s$

Triangle *(p. 142)*

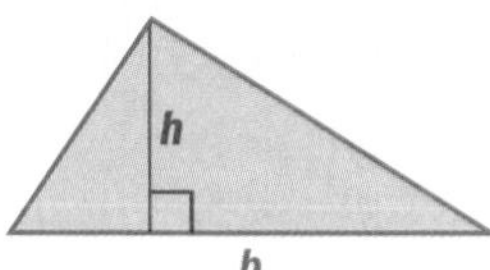

Area $A = \frac{1}{2}bh$

Parallelogram *(p. 521)*

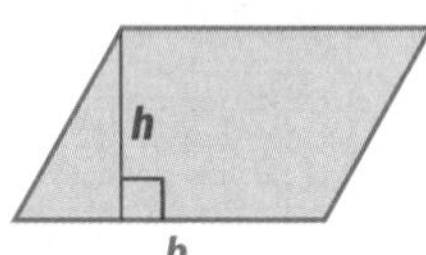

Area $A = bh$

Trapezoid *(p. 522)*

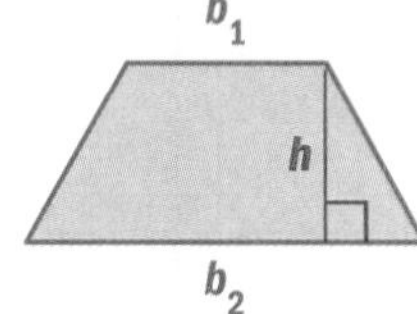

Area $A = \frac{1}{2}(b_1 + b_2)h$

Circle *(pp. 312, 527)*

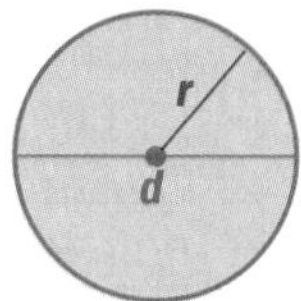

Area $A = \pi r^2$

Circumference $C = \pi d$ or $C = 2\pi r$

Prism *(pp. 543, 554)*

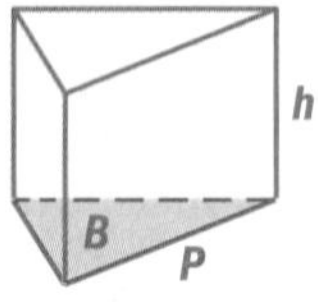

Surface Area $S = 2B + Ph$

Volume $V = Bh$

Cylinder *(pp. 544, 555)*

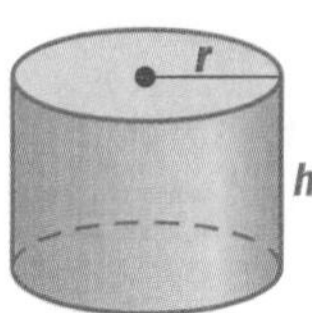

Surface Area $S = 2\pi r^2 + 2\pi rh$

Volume $V = \pi r^2 h$

Pyramid *(pp. 548, 561)*

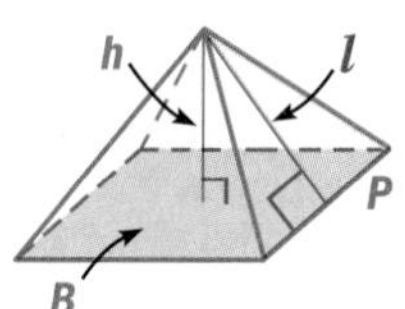

Surface Area $S = B + \frac{1}{2}Pl$

Volume $V = \frac{1}{3}Bh$

Cone *(pp. 550, 562)*

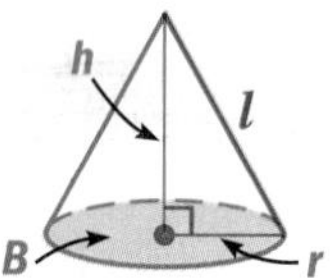

Surface Area $S = \pi r^2 + \pi rl$

Volume $V = \frac{1}{3}Bh = \frac{1}{3}\pi r^2 h$

Other Formulas

Distance traveled *(p. 33)*	$d = rt$ where d = distance, r = rate, and t = time
Simple interest *(p. 376)*	$I = Prt$ where I = simple interest, P = principal, r = annual interest rate, and t = time in years
Pythagorean theorem *(p. 482)*	In a right triangle, $a^2 + b^2 = c^2$ where a and b are the length of the legs, and c is the length of the hypotenuse.

Table of Properties

Number Properties

Identity Properties *(pp. 64, 74)*

Addition The sum of a number and the additive identity, 0, is the number.

Numbers $7 + 0 = 7$
Algebra $a + 0 = a$

Multiplication The product of a number and and the multiplicative identity, 1, is the number.

Numbers $3 \cdot 1 = 3$
Algebra $a \cdot 1 = a$

Inverse Properties *(pp. 64, 247)*

Addition The sum of a number and its additive inverse, or opposite, is 0.

Numbers $4 + (-4) = 0$

Algebra $a + (-a) = 0$

Multiplication The product of a nonzero number and its multiplicative inverse, or reciprocal, is 1.

Numbers $\frac{2}{3} \cdot \frac{3}{2} = 1$

Algebra $\frac{a}{b} \cdot \frac{b}{a} = 1 \ (a, b \neq 0)$

Commutative Property *(p. 83)*

Addition In a sum, you can add terms in any order.

Numbers $-2 + 5 = 5 + (-2)$
Algebra $a + b = b + a$

Multiplication In a product, you can multiply factors in any order.

Numbers $3(-6) = -6(3)$
Algebra $ab = ba$

Associative Property *(p. 84)*

Addition Changing the grouping of terms in a sum will not change the sum.

Numbers $(2 + 4) + 6 = 2 + (4 + 6)$
Algebra $(a + b) + c = a + (b + c)$

Multiplication Changing the grouping of factors in a product will not change the product.

Numbers $(6 \times 2.5) \times 4 = 6 \times (2.5 \times 4)$
Algebra $(ab)c = a(bc)$

Distributive Property *(p. 88)*

You can multiply a number and a sum by multiplying each term of the sum by the number and then adding these products. The same property applies to subtraction.

Numbers $3(4 + 6) = 3(4) + 3(6)$ $\quad 2(8 - 5) = 2(8) - 2(5)$
Algebra $a(b + c) = a(b) + a(c)$ $\quad a(b - c) = a(b) - a(c)$

Properties of Exponents *(pp. 202, 203)*

To find the *product of powers* with the same base, add their exponents

Numbers $5^2 \cdot 5^3 = 5^{2+3} = 5^5$
Algebra $a^b \cdot a^c = a^{b+c}$

To find the *quotient of powers* with the same nonzero base, subtract the denominator's exponent from the numerator's exponent.

Numbers $\frac{7^4}{7^2} = 7^{4-2} = 7^2$ **Algebra** $\frac{a^b}{a^c} = a^{b-c}$

Cross Products Property *(p. 349)*

The cross products of a proportion are equal.

Numbers Because $\frac{3}{4} = \frac{6}{8}$, $3 \cdot 8 = 4 \cdot 6$.

Algebra If $\frac{a}{b} = \frac{c}{d}$, then $ad = bc$, $b, d \neq 0$.

TABLES

Finding Squares and Square Roots

EXAMPLE 1 Finding a Square

Find 54^2.

Find 54 in the column labeled *No.* (an abbreviation for *Number*). Read across to the column labeled *Square*.

No.	*Square*	*Sq. Root*
51	2601	7.141
52	2704	7.211
53	2809	7.280
54	2916	7.348
55	3025	7.416

▸ **Answer** So, $54^2 = 2916$.

EXAMPLE 2 Finding a Square Root

Find a decimal approximation of $\sqrt{54}$.

Find 54 in the column labeled *No.* Read across to the column labeled *Sq. Root*.

No.	*Square*	*Sq. Root*
51	2601	7.141
52	2704	7.211
53	2809	7.280
54	2916	7.348
55	3025	7.416

▸ **Answer** So, to the nearest thousandth, $\sqrt{54} \approx 7.348$.

EXAMPLE 3 Finding a Square Root

Find a decimal approximation of $\sqrt{3000}$.

Find the two numbers in the *Square* column that 3000 is between. Read across to the column labeled *No.*; $\sqrt{3000}$ is between 54 and 55, but closer to 55.

No.	*Square*	*Sq. Root*
51	2601	7.141
52	2704	7.211
53	2809	7.280
54	2916	7.348
55	3025	7.416

▸ **Answer** So, $\sqrt{3000} \approx 55$. A more accurate approximation can be found using a calculator: 54.772256.

Table of Squares and Square Roots

No.	Square	Sq. Root	No.	Square	Sq. Root	No.	Square	Sq. Root
1	1	1.000	**51**	2601	7.141	**101**	10,201	10.050
2	4	1.414	**52**	2704	7.211	**102**	10,404	10.100
3	9	1.732	**53**	2809	7.280	**103**	10,609	10.149
4	16	2.000	**54**	2916	7.348	**104**	10,816	10.198
5	25	2.236	**55**	3025	7.416	**105**	11,025	10.247
6	36	2.449	**56**	3136	7.483	**106**	11,236	10.296
7	49	2.646	**57**	3249	7.550	**107**	11,449	10.344
8	64	2.828	**58**	3364	7.616	**108**	11,664	10.392
9	81	3.000	**59**	3481	7.681	**109**	11,881	10.440
10	100	3.162	**60**	3600	7.746	**110**	12,100	10.488
11	121	3.317	**61**	3721	7.810	**111**	12,321	10.536
12	144	3.464	**62**	3844	7.874	**112**	12,544	10.583
13	169	3.606	**63**	3969	7.937	**113**	12,769	10.630
14	196	3.742	**64**	4096	8.000	**114**	12,996	10.677
15	225	3.873	**65**	4225	8.062	**115**	13,225	10.724
16	256	4.000	**66**	4356	8.124	**116**	13,456	10.770
17	289	4.123	**67**	4489	8.185	**117**	13,689	10.817
18	324	4.243	**68**	4624	8.246	**118**	13,924	10.863
19	361	4.359	**69**	4761	8.307	**119**	14,161	10.909
20	400	4.472	**70**	4900	8.367	**120**	14,400	10.954
21	441	4.583	**71**	5041	8.426	**121**	14,641	11.000
22	484	4.690	**72**	5184	8.485	**122**	14,884	11.045
23	529	4.796	**73**	5329	8.544	**123**	15,129	11.091
24	576	4.899	**74**	5476	8.602	**124**	15,376	11.136
25	625	5.000	**75**	5625	8.660	**125**	15,625	11.180
26	676	5.099	**76**	5776	8.718	**126**	15,876	11.225
27	729	5.196	**77**	5929	8.775	**127**	16,129	11.269
28	784	5.292	**78**	6084	8.832	**128**	16,384	11.314
29	841	5.385	**79**	6241	8.888	**129**	16,641	11.358
30	900	5.477	**80**	6400	8.944	**130**	16,900	11.402
31	961	5.568	**81**	6561	9.000	**131**	17,161	11.446
32	1024	5.657	**82**	6724	9.055	**132**	17,424	11.489
33	1089	5.745	**83**	6889	9.110	**133**	17,689	11.533
34	1156	5.831	**84**	7056	9.165	**134**	17,956	11.576
35	1225	5.916	**85**	7225	9.220	**135**	18,225	11.619
36	1296	6.000	**86**	7396	9.274	**136**	18,496	11.662
37	1369	6.083	**87**	7569	9.327	**137**	18,769	11.705
38	1444	6.164	**88**	7744	9.381	**138**	19,044	11.747
39	1521	6.245	**89**	7921	9.434	**139**	19,321	11.790
40	1600	6.325	**90**	8100	9.487	**140**	19,600	11.832
41	1681	6.403	**91**	8281	9.539	**141**	19,881	11.874
42	1764	6.481	**92**	8464	9.592	**142**	20,164	11.916
43	1849	6.557	**93**	8649	9.644	**143**	20,449	11.958
44	1936	6.633	**94**	8836	9.695	**144**	20,736	12.000
45	2025	6.708	**95**	9025	9.747	**145**	21,025	12.042
46	2116	6.782	**96**	9216	9.798	**146**	21,316	12.083
47	2209	6.856	**97**	9409	9.849	**147**	21,609	12.124
48	2304	6.928	**98**	9604	9.899	**148**	21,904	12.166
49	2401	7.000	**99**	9801	9.950	**149**	22,201	12.207
50	2500	7.071	**100**	10,000	10.000	**150**	22,500	12.247

Equivalent Fractions, Decimals, and Percents

Fraction	*Decimal*	*Percent*
$\frac{1}{10}$	0.1	10%
$\frac{1}{8}$	0.125	$12\frac{1}{2}\%$
$\frac{1}{5}$	0.2	20%
$\frac{1}{4}$	0.25	25%
$\frac{3}{10}$	0.3	30%
$\frac{1}{3}$	$0.\overline{3}$	$33\frac{1}{3}\%$
$\frac{3}{8}$	0.375	$37\frac{1}{2}\%$
$\frac{2}{5}$	0.4	40%
$\frac{1}{2}$	0.5	50%
$\frac{3}{5}$	0.6	60%
$\frac{5}{8}$	0.625	$62\frac{1}{2}\%$
$\frac{2}{3}$	$0.\overline{6}$	$66\frac{2}{3}\%$
$\frac{7}{10}$	0.7	70%
$\frac{3}{4}$	0.75	75%
$\frac{4}{5}$	0.8	80%
$\frac{7}{8}$	0.875	$87\frac{1}{2}\%$
$\frac{9}{10}$	0.9	90%
1	1	100%

English-Spanish Glossary

A

absolute value (p. 58) The absolute value of a number a is the distance between a and 0 on a number line. The absolute value of a is written $|a|$.

valor absoluto (pág. 58) El valor absoluto de un número a es la distancia entre a y 0 en una recta numérica. El valor absoluto de a se escribe $|a|$.

$|4| = 4$ $\quad |-7| = 7$ $\quad |0| = 0$

---

acute angle (p. 411) An angle whose measure is less than 90°.

ángulo agudo (pág. 411) Un ángulo que mide menos de 90°.

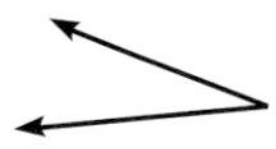

---

acute triangle (p. 411) A triangle with three acute angles.

triángulo acutángulo (pág. 411) Un triángulo que tiene tres ángulos agudos.

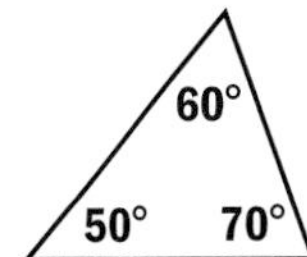

---

addition property of equality (p. 118) Adding the same number to each side of an equation produces an equivalent equation.

propiedad de igualdad en la suma (pág. 118) Al sumar el mismo número a cada lado de una ecuación se produce una ecuación equivalente.

If $x - 5 = 2$, then $x - 5 + 5 = 2 + 5$, so $x = 7$.
If $x - a = b$, then $x - a + a = b + a$.

Si $x - 5 = 2$, entonces $x - 5 + 5 = 2 + 5$, por lo tanto $x = 7$.
Si $x - a = b$, entonces $x - a + a = b + a$.

---

additive identity (p. 64) The number 0 is the additive identity because the sum of any number and 0 is the original number.

identidad de la suma (pág. 64) El número 0 es la identidad de la suma porque la suma de cualquier número y 0 es el número original.

$-7 + 0 = -7$
$a + 0 = a$

---

additive inverse (p. 64) The additive inverse of a number a is the opposite of the number, or $-a$. The sum of a number and its additive inverse is 0.

inverso aditivo (pág. 64) El inverso aditivo de un número a es el opuesto del número, o $-a$. La suma de un número y su inverso aditivo es 0.

The *additive inverse* of 6 is -6, so $6 + (-6) = 0$.

El *inverso aditivo* de 6 es -6, por lo tanto $6 + (-6) = 0$.

---

angle (p. 774) A figure formed by two rays that begin at a common point, called the vertex.

ángulo (pág. 774) Figura formada por dos semirrectas que comienzan en un punto común, llamado vértice.

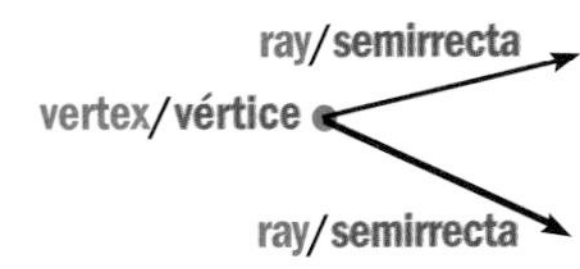

angle of rotation (p. 440) In a rotation, the angle formed by two rays drawn from the center of rotation through corresponding points on the original figure and its image.

ángulo de rotación (pág. 440) En una rotación, el ángulo formado por dos semirrectas trazadas desde el centro de rotación a través de puntos correspondientes en la figura original y su imagen.

See rotation.

Véase rotación.

---

annual interest rate (p. 376) In simple interest, the percent of the principal earned or paid per year.

tasa de interés anual (pág. 376) En interés simple, el porcentaje sobre el capital ganado o pagado por año.

See simple interest.

Véase interés simple.

---

area (p. 32) The number of square units covered by a figure.

área (pág. 32) La cantidad de unidades cuadradas que cubre una figura.

2 units/2 unidades

7 units/7 unidades

Area = 14 square units

Área = 14 unidades cuadradas

---

associative property of addition (p. 84) Changing the grouping of terms in a sum does not change the sum.

propiedad asociativa de la suma (pág. 84) Cambiar la manera en que se agrupan los términos en una suma no cambia la suma.

$(9 + 4) + 6 = 9 + (4 + 6)$

$(a + b) + c = a + (b + c)$

---

associative property of multiplication (p. 84) Changing the grouping of factors in a product does not change the product.

propiedad asociativa de la multiplicación (pág. 84) Cambiar la manera en que se agrupan los factores en un producto no cambia el producto.

$(2 \cdot 5) \cdot 3 = 2 \cdot (5 \cdot 3)$

$(ab)c = a(bc)$

B

bar graph (p. 3) A type of graph in which the lengths of bars are used to represent and compare data in categories.

gráfica de barras (pág. 3) Un tipo de gráfica en el que las longitudes de las barras se usan para representar y comparar datos.

Annual Sales at an Automobile Dealership
Ventas anuales en concesionario automotriz

Automobiles / Automóviles: 0, 100, 200, 300, 400

Cars / Carros; Trucks / Camiones; SUVs / SUVs

base of a parallelogram (p. 521) The length of any side of the parallelogram can be used as the base. **base de un paralelogramo** (pág. 521) La longitud de cualquier lado del paralelogramo puede usarse como la base.	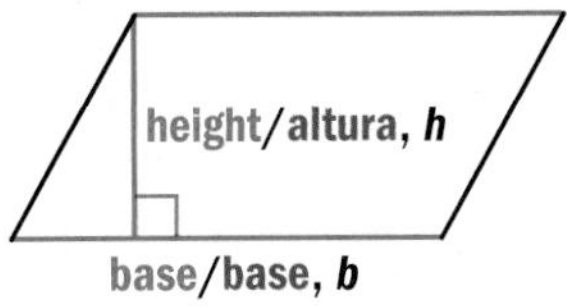 height/altura, h base/base, b
base of a power (p. 19) The number or expression that is used as a factor in a repeated multiplication. **base de una potencia** (pág. 19) El número o la expresión que se usa como factor en una multiplicación repetida.	In the power 5^3, the *base* is 5. La *base* de la potencia 5^3 es 5.
base of a triangle (p. 142) The length of any side of the triangle can be used as the base. **base de un triángulo** (pág. 142) La longitud de cualquier lado de un triángulo puede usarse como base.	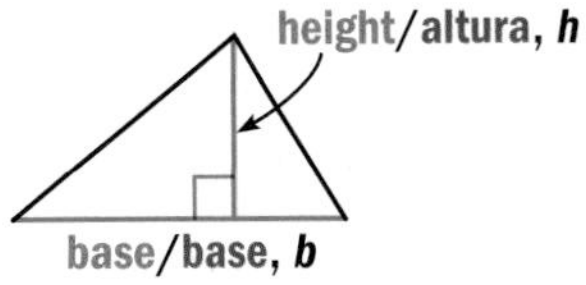 height/altura, h base/base, b
bases of a trapezoid (p. 522) The lengths of the parallel sides of the trapezoid. **bases de un trapecio** (pág. 522) Las longitudes de los lados paralelos de un trapecio.	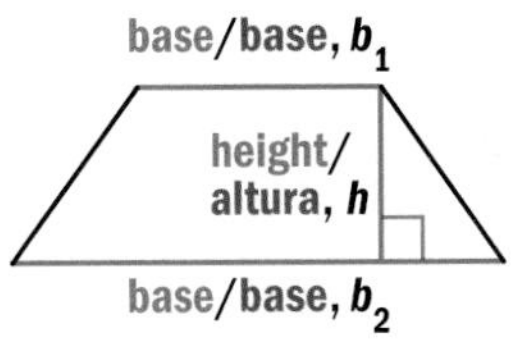 base/base, b_1 height/altura, h base/base, b_2
biased sample (p. 702) A sample that is not representative of the population from which it is selected. **muestra parcial** (pág. 702) Una muestra que no es representativa de la población de la cual fue seleccionada.	The members of a soccer team are a *biased sample* if you want to find the average time students spend playing sports each week. Los miembros de un equipo de fútbol son una *muestra parcial* para determinar la cantidad promedio de tiempo a la semana que los estudiantes practican deportes.
binomial (p. 717) A polynomial with two terms. **binomio** (pág. 717) Polinomio que tiene dos términos.	$7y^4 + 9$
box-and-whisker plot (p. 654) A data display that divides a data set into four parts using the lower extreme, lower quartile, median, upper quartile, and upper extreme. **diagrama de líneas y bloques** (pág. 654) Diagrama que divide un conjunto de datos en cuatro partes usando el extremo inferior, el cuartil inferior, la mediana, el cuartil superior y el extremo superior.	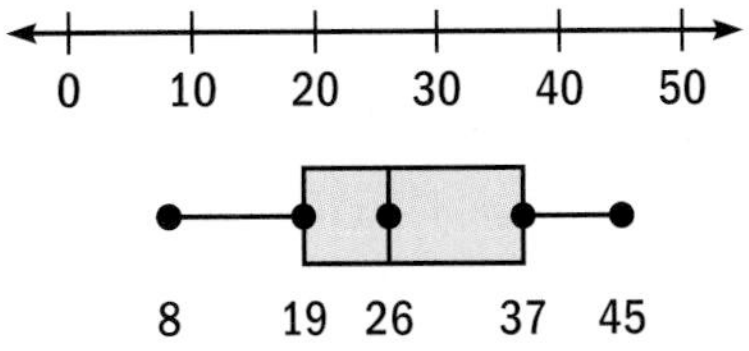 0 10 20 30 40 50 8 19 26 37 45

ENGLISH-SPANISH GLOSSARY

C

center of a circle (p. 312) The point inside the circle that is the same distance from all points on the circle. **centro de un círculo** (pág. 312) El punto en el interior del círculo que está a la misma distancia de todos los puntos del círculo.	*See* circle. *Véase* círculo.
center of a rotation (p. 440) The point about which a figure is turned when the figure undergoes a rotation. **centro de rotación** (pág. 440) El punto alrededor del cual gira una figura cuando la figura sufre una rotación.	*See* rotation. *Véase* rotación.
circle (p. 312) The set of all points in a plane that are the same distance, called the radius, from a fixed point, called the center. **círculo** (pág. 312) El conjunto de todos los puntos en un plano que están a la misma distancia, llamada radio, de un punto fijo, llamado centro.	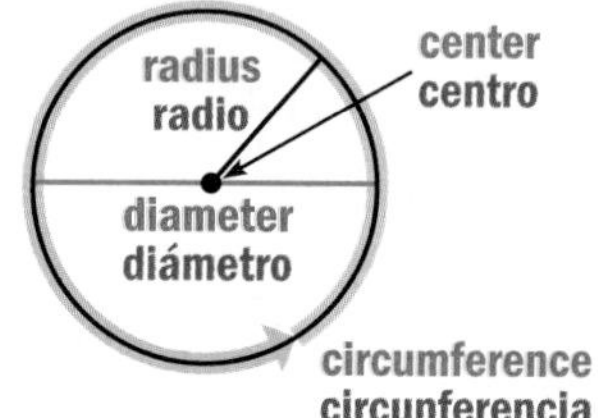
circle graph (p. 360, 659) A circle graph displays data as sections of a circle. The entire circle represents all the data. Each section is labeled using the actual data or using data expressed as fractions, decimals, or percents of the sum of the data. **gráfica circular** (pág. 360, 659) Una gráfica circular representa los datos como secciones de un círculo. El círculo completo representa todos los datos. Cada sección está rotulada con los datos reales o usando datos expresados como fracciones, decimales o porcentajes de la suma de los datos.	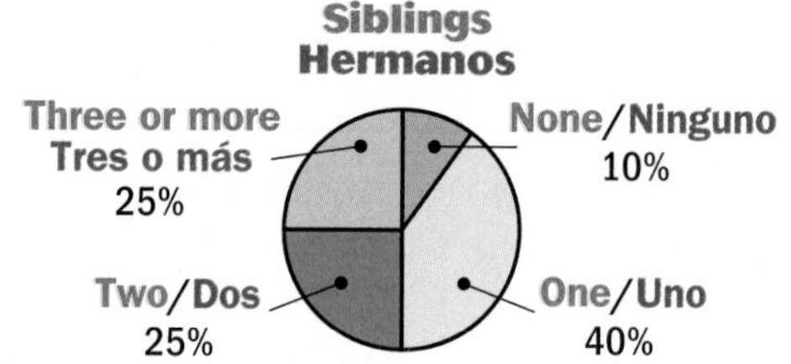
circumference (p. 312) The distance around a circle. **circunferencia** (pág. 312) La distancia alrededor de un círculo.	*See* circle. *Véase* círculo.
coefficient (p. 89) The number part of a term that includes a variable. **coeficiente** (pág. 89) La parte numérica de un término que incluye una variable.	The *coefficient* of $7x$ is 7. El *coeficiente* de $7x$ es 7.
combination (p. 680) A grouping of objects in which the order is not important. **combinación** (pág. 680) Agrupación de objetos en la que el orden no es importante.	There are 6 *combinations* of 2 letters chosen from VASE: VA VS VE AS AE SE Existen 6 *combinaciones* de 2 letras tomadas de la palabra VASO: VA VS VO AS AO SO

common factor (p. 181) A whole number that is a factor of two or more nonzero whole numbers.

factor común (pág. 181) Un número natural que es factor de dos o más números naturales distintos de cero.

The *common factors* of 8 and 12 are 1, 2, and 4.

Los *factores comunes* de 8 y 12 son 1, 2 y 4.

---

common multiple (p. 192) A multiple that is shared by two or more numbers.

múltiplo común (pág. 192) Un múltiplo compartido por dos o más números.

The *common multiples* of 4 and 6 are 12, 24, 36, ...

Los *múltiplos comunes* de 4 y 6 son 12, 24, 36, ...

---

commutative property of addition (p. 83) In a sum, you can add terms in any order.

propiedad conmutativa de la suma (pág. 83) En una suma, puedes sumar los términos en cualquier orden.

$4 + 7 = 7 + 4$

$a + b = b + a$

---

commutative property of multiplication (p. 83) In a product, you can multiply factors in any order.

propiedad conmutativa de la multiplicación (pág. 83) En un producto, puedes multiplicar los factores en cualquier orden.

$5(-8) = -8(5)$

$ab = ba$

---

complementary angles (p. 403) Two angles whose measures have a sum of 90°.

ángulos complementarios (pág. 403) Dos ángulos cuyas medidas suman 90°.

32° 58°

---

complementary events (p. 685) Two events are complementary when one event or the other (but not both) must occur.

eventos complementarios (pág. 685) Dos eventos son complementarios cuando un evento o el otro (no ambos) debe ocurrir.

When rolling a number cube, the events "getting an odd number" and "getting an even number" are *complementary events.*

Al lanzar un cubo numerado, los eventos "obtener un número par" y "obtener un número impar" y son *eventos complementarios* o *complementos.*

---

complement (p. 690) The set of all elements that are in universal set U that are not in set A, written as $\sim A$.

complemento (pág. 690) El conjunto de todos los elementos que están en el conjunto universal U y no están en el conjunto A, que se expresa como $\sim A$.

U A B

---

composite number (p. 177) A whole number greater than 1 that has positive factors other than 1 and itself.

número compuesto (pág. 177) Un número natural mayor que 1 que tiene factores positivos distintos a 1 y a sí mismo.

6 is a *composite number* because its factors are 1, 2, 3, and 6.

6 es un *número compuesto* porque sus factores son 1, 2, 3, y 6.

compound events (p. 694) Two or more events that can happen either at the same time or one after the other. **eventos compuestos** (pág. 694) Dos o más eventos que pueden ocurrir al mismo tiempo o uno después del otro.	*See* independent events *and* dependent events. *Véase* eventos independientes *y* eventos dependientes.
compound interest (p. 380) Interest earned on both the principal and on any interest that has already been earned. **interés compuesto** (pág. 380) Interés que se gana sobre el capital y sobre cualquier interés que ya se ha ganado.	You deposit \$250 in an account that earns 4% interest compounded yearly. After 5 years, your account balance is $y = 250(1 + 0.04)5 \approx \$304.16$. Depositas \$250 en una cuenta que gana 4% de interés compuesto anualmente. Después de 5 años, el balance de tu cuenta es $y = 250(1 + 0.04)5 \approx \$304.16$.
cone (p. 534) A solid with one circular base. **cono** (pág. 534) Un cuerpo geométrico que tiene una base circular.	base/base
congruent angles (p. 427) Angles that have the same measure. **ángulos congruentes** (pág. 427) Ángulos que tienen medidas iguales.	*See* congruent polygons. *Véase* polígonos congruentes.
congruent polygons (p. 427) Similar polygons that have the same size. For congruent polygons, corresponding angles are congruent and corresponding sides are congruent. The symbol $\cong$ indicates congruence and is read "is congruent to." **polígonos congruentes** (pág. 427) Polígonos similares que tienen el mismo tamaño. Para polígonos congruentes, los ángulos correspondientes son congruentes y los lados correspondientes son congruentes. El signo $\cong$ indica congruencia y se lee "es congruente con".	A B C E F D $\triangle ABC \cong \triangle DEF$
congruent segments (p. 427) Segments that have the same length. **segmentos congruentes** (pág. 427) Segmentos que tienen igual longitud.	*See* congruent polygons. *Véase* polígonos congruentes.
constant term (p. 89) A term that has a number but no variable. **término constante** (pág. 89) Un término que tiene un número pero no una variable.	In the expression $5y + 9$, the term 9 is a *constant term.* En la expresión $5y + 9$, el término 9 es un *término constante.*

converse (p. 483) An if-then statement where the hypothesis and conclusion of the original statement have been reversed.

Original: If you clean your room, then it will be neat.
***Converse*: If your room is neat, then you will clean it.**

recíproco (pág. 483) Un enunciado de tipo si-entonces en el cual la hipótesis y la conclusión del enunciado original se han intercambiado.

Original: Si ordenas tu habitación, entonces estará arreglada.
***Recíproco*: Si tu habitación está arreglada, entonces la arreglarás.**

coordinate plane (p. 94) A coordinate system formed by the intersection of a horizontal number line, called the x-axis, and a vertical number line, called the y-axis.

plano de coordenadas (pág. 94) Un sistema de coordinadas formado por la intersección de una recta numérica horizontal, llamada eje x, y una recta numérica vertical, llamada eje y.

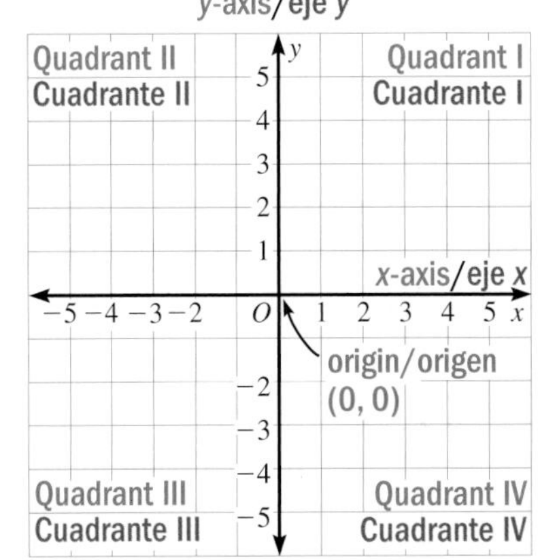

corresponding angles (p. 427) Angles that occupy corresponding positions when a line intersects two other lines.

ángulos correspondientes (pág. 427) Ángulos que ocupan posiciones correspondientes cuando una recta interseca otras dos rectas.

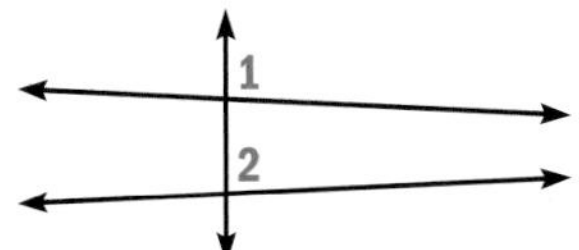

$\angle 1$ and $\angle 2$ are *corresponding angles*.

$\angle 1$ y $\angle 2$ son *ángulos correspondientes*.

corresponding parts (p. 427) Pairs of sides and angles of polygons that are in the same relative position.

elementos correspondientes (pág. 427) Pares de lados y ángulos de polígonos que están en la misma posición relativa.

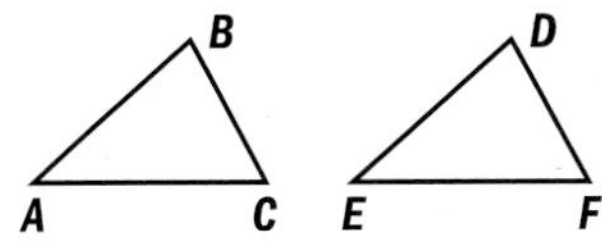

$\angle A$ and $\angle E$ are corresponding angles.
$\overline{AB}$ and $\overline{ED}$ are corresponding sides.

$\angle A$ y $\angle E$ son ángulos correspondientes.
$\overline{AB}$ y $\overline{ED}$ son lados correspondientes.

cosine (p. 500) The cosine of any acute angle A of a right triangle is the ratio of the adjacent leg to the hypotenuse.

coseno (pág. 500) El coseno de cualquier ángulo agudo A de un triángulo rectángulo es la razón entre el cateto adyacente y la hipotenusa.

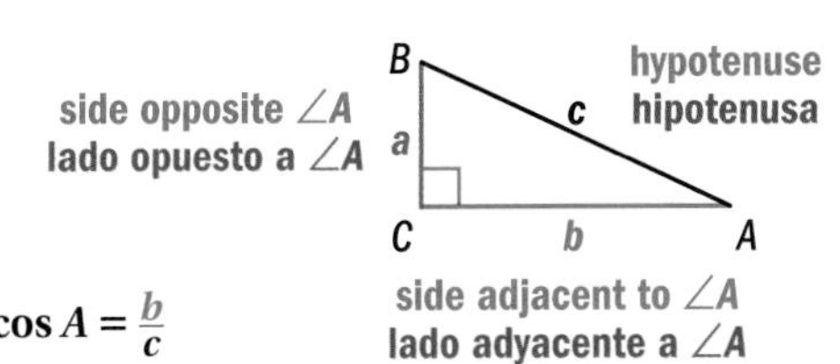

$\cos A = \frac{b}{c}$

counting principle (p. 671) If one event can occur in m ways, and for each of these a second event can occur in n ways, then the number of ways that the two events can occur together is $m \cdot n$. The counting principle can be extended to three or more events.

If a T-shirt is made in 5 sizes and in 7 colors, then the number of different T-shirts that are possible is $5 \cdot 7 = 35$.

principio de conteo (pág. 671) Si un evento puede ocurrir de m maneras, y para cada una de éstas un segundo evento puede ocurrir de n maneras, entonces el número de maneras en las que pueden ocurrir ambos eventos juntos es $m \cdot n$. El principio de conteo puede extenderse a tres o más eventos.

Si una camiseta se hace en 5 tallas y 7 colores, entonces el número de camisetas diferentes posibles es $5 \cdot 7 = 35$.

cross products (p. 349) For the proportion $\frac{a}{b} = \frac{c}{d}$, where $b \neq 0$ and $d \neq 0$, the cross product are ad and bc.

The *cross products* of the proportion $\frac{2}{3} = \frac{4}{6}$ are $2 \cdot 6$ and $3 \cdot 4$.

productos cruzados (pág. 349) Para la proporción $\frac{a}{b} = \frac{c}{d}$, donde $b \neq 0$ y $d \neq 0$, los productos cruzados son ad y bc.

Los *productos cruzados* de la proporción $\frac{2}{3} = \frac{4}{6}$ son $2 \cdot 6$ y $3 \cdot 4$.

cylinder (p. 534) A solid with two congruent circular bases that lie in parallel planes.

cilindro (pág. 534) Un cuerpo geométrico que tiene dos bases circulares congruentes que se ubican en planos paralelos.

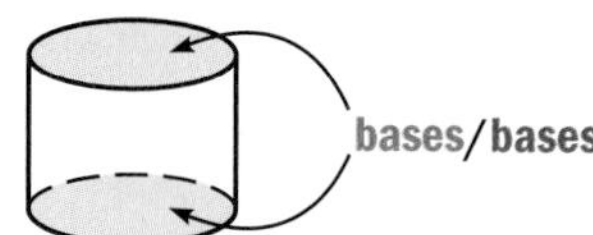

D

data (p. 3) Information, facts, or numbers that describe something.

Numbers of cars sold annually at a dealership: 340, 350, 345, 347, 352, 360, 365

datos (pág. 3) Información, hechos o números que describen algo.

Número de carros que se venden anualmente en el concesionario: 340, 350, 345, 347, 352, 360, 365

degrees (p. 776) Unit of measure for angles. The symbol for degrees is °. There are 360° in a circle.

grados (pág. 776) Unidad de medida para ángulos. El símbolo para los grados es °. Hay 360° en un círculo.

A 58°

dependent events (p. 694) Two events such that the occurrence of one affects the likelihood that the other will occur.

A bag contains 5 red and 8 blue marbles. You randomly choose a marble, do not replace it, then randomly choose another marble. The events "first marble is red" and "second marble is red" are *dependent events*.

eventos dependientes (pág. 694) Dos eventos tales que la ocurrencia de uno afecta la probabilidad de que ocurra el otro.

Una bolsa contiene 5 canicas rojas y 8 azules. Tomas una canica al azar y no la reemplazas, luego tomas otra canica al azar. Los eventos "primera canica es roja" y "segunda canica es roja" son *eventos dependientes*.

diagonal (p. 417) A segment, other than a side, that connects two vertices of a polygon. **diagonal** (pág. 417) Un segmento, distinto de un lado, que conecta dos vértices de un polígono.	diagonals/ diagonales
diameter of a circle (p. 312) The distance across the circle through the center. **diámetro de un círculo** (pág. 312) La distancia que atraviesa el círculo por el centro.	*See* circle. *Véase* círculo.
dilation (p. 449) A transformation that stretches or shrinks a figure. **dilatación** (pág. 449) Una transformación que estira o encoge una figura.	The scale factor is $\frac{1}{2}$. El factor de escala es $\frac{1}{2}$.
direct variation (p. 618) The relationship of two variables x and y if there is a nonzero number k such that $y = kx$ or $k = \frac{y}{x}$. **variación directa** (pág. 618) La relación entre dos variables x e y cuando hay un número k distinto de cero, de manera tal que $y = kx$ ó $k = \frac{y}{x}$.	$y = 5x$ $y = kx$
discount (p. 370) A decrease in the price of an item. **descuento** (pág. 370) Una disminución en el precio de un artículo.	The original price of a pair of jeans is \$42 but the store sells it for \$29.99. The *discount* is \$12.01. El precio original de un par de pantalones es \$42, pero la tienda los vende a \$29.99. El *descuento* es \$12.01.
distributive property (p. 88) For all numbers a, b, and c, $a(b + c) = ab + ac$ and $a(b - c) = ab - ac$. **propiedad distributiva** (pág. 88) Para todos los números a, b y c, $a(b + c) = ab + ac$ y $a(b - c) = ab - ac$.	$8(10 + 4) = 8(10) + 8(4)$ $3(4 - 2) = 3(4) - 3(2)$
division property of equality (p. 123) Dividing each side of an equation by the same nonzero number produces an equivalent equation. **propiedad de igualdad en la división** (pág. 123) Al dividir cada lado de una ecuación por el mismo número distinto de cero se obtiene una ecuación equivalente.	If $6x = 54$, then $\frac{6x}{6} = \frac{54}{6}$, so $x = 9$. If $ax = b$ and $a \neq 0$, then $\frac{ax}{a} = \frac{b}{a}$. Si $6x = 54$, entonces $\frac{6x}{6} = \frac{54}{6}$, por lo tanto $x = 9$. Si $ax = b$ y $a \neq 0$, entonces $\frac{ax}{a} = \frac{b}{a}$.

ENGLISH-SPANISH GLOSSARY

domain of a function (p. 584) The set of all possible input values for the function. **dominio de una función** (pág. 584) El conjunto de todos los valores de entrada posibles para la función.	*See* function. *Véase* función.

E

edge of a polyhedron (p. 534) A line segment where two faces of the polyhedron meet. **arista de un poliedro** (pág. 534) Un segmento de recta donde se encuentran dos caras del poliedro.	face cara edge arista vertex vértice
element (p. 690) An object in a set. **elemento** (pág. 690) Un objeto en un conjunto.	5 is an *element* of the set of whole numbers, $W = \{0, 1, 2, 3, 4, 5, \ldots\}$. 5 es un *elemento* en el conjunto de los números naturales $N = \{0, 1, 2, 3, 4, 5, \ldots\}$.
empty set (p. 690) The set with no elements, written as ∅. **conjunto vacío** (pág. 690) El conjunto que no tiene elementos, que se expresa como ∅.	The set of negative whole numbers = ∅. El conjunto de los números naturales negativos = ∅.
equation (p. 26) A mathematical sentence formed by setting two expressions equal. **ecuación** (pág. 26) Un enunciado matemático que se forma al establecer como iguales dos expresiones.	$3 \cdot 6 = 18$ and $x + 7 = 12$ are *equations.* $3 \cdot 6 = 18$ y $x + 7 = 12$ son *ecuaciones.*
equilateral triangle (p. 411) A triangle with three congruent sides. **triángulo equilátero** (pág. 411) Un triángulo que tiene tres lados congruentes.	
equivalent equations (p. 117) Equations that have the same solution(s). **ecuaciones equivalentes** (pág. 117) Ecuaciones que tienen la misma solución o soluciones.	$2x - 6 = 0$ and $2x = 6$ are *equivalent equations* because the solution of both equations is 3. $2x - 6 = 0$ y $2x = 6$ son *ecuaciones equivalentes* porque la solución de ambas ecuaciones es 3.
equivalent fractions (p. 187) Fractions that represent the same part-to-whole relationship. Equivalent fractions have the same simplest form. **fracciones equivalentes** (pág. 187) Fracciones que representan la misma relación entre la parte y el todo. Las fracciones equivalentes tienen la misma mínima expresión.	$\frac{6}{8}$ and $\frac{9}{12}$ are *equivalent fractions* that both represent $\frac{3}{4}$. $\frac{6}{8}$ y $\frac{9}{12}$ son *fracciones equivalentes* porque ambas representan $\frac{3}{4}$.

equivalent inequalities (p. 149) Inequalities that have the same solution. **desigualdades equivalentes** (pág. 149) Desigualdades que tienen la misma solución.	$3x \le 12$ and $x \le 4$ are *equivalent inequalities* because the solution of both inequalities is all numbers less than or equal to 4. $3x \le 12$ y $x \le 4$ son *desigualdades equivalentes* porque la solución de ambas desigualdades es todos los números menores que o iguales a 4.
equivalent ratios (p. 343) Ratios that have the same value. **razones equivalentes** (pág. 343) Razones que tienen el mismo valor.	$\frac{15}{12}$ and $\frac{25}{20}$ are *equivalent ratios* because $\frac{15}{12} = 1.25$ and $\frac{25}{20} = 1.25$. $\frac{15}{12}$ y $\frac{25}{20}$ son *razones equivalentes* porque $\frac{15}{12} = 1.25$ y $\frac{25}{20} = 1.25$.
evaluate (p. 8) To find the value of an expression with one or more operations. **hallar el valor** (pág. 8) Encontrar el valor de una expresión que tiene una o más operaciones.	$4(3) + 6 \div 2 = 15$
event (p. 381) A collection of outcomes of an experiment. **evento** (pág. 381) Un conjunto de resultados de un experimento.	An *event* for rolling a number cube is "getting a number divisible by 3." Al lanzar un cubo numerado, "obtener un número divisible por 3" es un *evento*.
experimental probability (p. 382) A probability based on a sample or repeated trials of an experiment. The experimental probability of an event is given by: $P(\text{event}) = \frac{\text{Number of favorable outcomes}}{\text{Number of trials or items in sample}}$ **probabilidad experimental** (pág. 382) Una probabilidad basada en el número de ensayos de un experimento. La probabilidad experimental de un evento se expresa: $P(\text{evento}) = \frac{\text{Número de resultados favorables}}{\text{Número de ensayos}}$	During one month, your school bus is on time 17 out of 22 school days. The *experimental probability* that the bus is on time is: $P(\text{bus is on time}) = \frac{17}{22} \approx 0.773$ Durante un mes, tu autobús llega a tiempo 17 de 22 días escolares. La *probabilidad experimental* de que el autobús llegue a tiempo es: $P(\text{autobús a tiempo}) = \frac{17}{22} \approx 0.773$
exponent (p. 19) A number or expression that represents how many times a base is used as a factor in a repeated multiplication. **exponente** (pág. 19) Un número o expresión que representa cuántas veces una base se usa como factor en una multiplicación repetida.	In the power 5^3, the *exponent* is 3. El *exponente* de la potencia 5^3 es 3.

F

face of a polyhedron (p. 534) A polygon that is a side of the polyhedron. **cara de un poliedro** (pág. 534) Un polígono que forma un lado del poliedro.	*See* edge of a polyhedron. *Véase* arista de un poliedro.

factor tree (p. 177) A diagram that can be used to write the prime factorization of a number. **árbol de factores** (pág. 177) Un diagrama que puede usarse para escribir la descomposición de un número en factores primos.	54 6 × 9 2 × 3 × 3 × 3
factorial (p. 675) The expression $n!$ is read "n factorial" and represents the product of all integers from 1 to n. **factorial** (pág. 675) La expresión $n!$ se lee "factorial n" y representa el producto de todos los números enteros desde 1 hasta n.	$4! = 4 \cdot 3 \cdot 2 \cdot 1 = 24$
favorable outcomes (p. 381) Outcomes corresponding to a specified event. **resultados favorables** (pág. 381) Los resultados correspondientes a un evento determinado.	When rolling a number cube, the *favorable outcomes* for the event "getting a number greater than 4" are 5 and 6. Al lanzar un cubo numerado, los *resultados favorables* para el evento "obtener un número mayor que 4" son 5 y 6.
formula (p. 32) An equation that relates two or more quantities such as perimeter, length, and width. **fórmula** (pág. 32) Una ecuación que relaciona dos o más cantidades tales como perímetro, longitud y ancho.	$P = 2l + 2w$
fraction (p. 762) A number of the form $\frac{a}{b}$ $(b \neq 0)$ where a is called the numerator and b is called the denominator. **fracción** (pág. 762) Un número de la forma $\frac{a}{b}$ $(b \neq 0)$ donde a es el numerador y b es el denominador.	$\frac{5}{7}$ and $\frac{18}{10}$ are *fractions*. $\frac{5}{7}$ y $\frac{18}{10}$ son *fracciones*.
frequency (p. 4) The number of data values that lie in an interval of a frequency table or histogram. **frecuencia** (pág. 4) El número de valores en un conjunto de datos que se ubican en un intervalo de una tabla de frecuencias o histograma.	*See* frequency table *and* histogram. *Véase* tabla de frecuencias *e* histograma.
frequency table (p. 4) A table used to group data values into intervals. **tabla de frecuencias** (pág. 4) Una tabla que se usa para agrupar valores de un conjunto de datos en intervalos.	(see table below)

Interval Intervalo	Tally Marca	Frequency Frecuencia
0–9	‖	2
10–19	‖‖	4
20–29	𝍸	5

front-end estimation (p. 261) A method for estimating the sum of two or more numbers. In this method, you add the front-end digits, estimate the sum of the remaining digits, and then add the results.

estimación por la izquierda (pág. 261) Un método para estimar la suma de dos o más números. En este método, se suman los dígitos de la izquierda, se estima la suma de los dígitos restantes y luego se suman los resultados.

To estimate $3.81 + 1.32 + 5.74$, first add the front-end digits: $3 + 1 + 5 = 9$.
Then estimate the sum of the remaining digits: $0.81 + (0.32 + 0.74) \approx 1 + 1 = 2$.
The sum is about $9 + 2 = 11$.

Para estimar la suma de $3.81 + 1.32 + 5.74$, suma primero los dígitos de la izquierda: $3 + 1 + 5 = 9$.
Luego estima la suma de los dígitos restantes: $0.81 + (0.32 + 0.74) \approx 1 + 1 = 2$.
La suma es aproximadamente $9 + 2 = 11$.

function (p. 583) A pairing of each number in a given set with exactly one number in another set. Starting with a number called an input, the function associates with it exactly one number called an output.

función (pág. 583) La asociación de cada número en un conjunto dado con exactamente un número de otro conjunto. Comenzando con un número llamado de entrada, la función asocia con él exactamente un número llamado de salida.

Input/Entrada, x	1	2	3	4
Output/Salida, y	2	4	6	8

The input-output table above represents a *function.*

La tabla anterior de entrada y salida representa una *función.*

function notation (p. 739) An equation that uses $f(x)$ to represent the output of the function f for an input of x.

notación de función (pág. 739) Una ecuación que usa $f(x)$ para representar la salida de la función f para una entrada de x.

$f(x) = 5x + 13$ is written using *function notation.*

$f(x) = 5x + 13$ está escrita según la *notación de función.*

G

graph of an inequality (p. 148) On a number line, the set of points that represents the solution of the inequality. (*See* half-plane.)

gráfica de una desigualdad (pág. 148) En una recta numérica, el conjunto de puntos que representa la solución de la desigualdad. (*Véase* semiplano.)

The *graph of the inequality* $x < 2$ is shown below.

La recta numérica es la *gráfica de la desigualdad* $x < 2$.

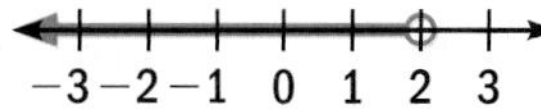

greatest common factor (GCF) (p. 181) The greatest whole number that is a factor of two or more nonzero whole numbers.

máximo común divisor (MCD) (pág. 181) El mayor número natural que es un factor de dos o más números naturales distintos de cero.

The *GCF* of 18 and 27 is 9.
The *GCF* of 48, 24, and 36 is 12.

El *MCD* de 18 y 27 es 9.
El *MCD* de 48, 24 y 36 es 12.

H

half-plane (p. 630) The graph of a linear inequality in two variables.

semiplano (pág. 630) La gráfica de una desigualdad lineal en dos variables.

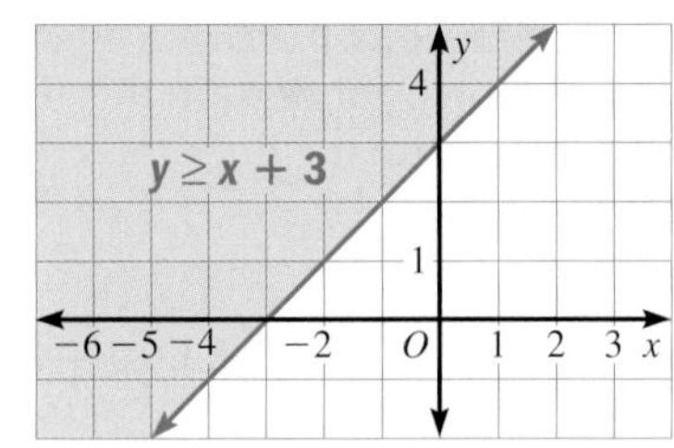

height of a parallelogram (p. 521) The perpendicular distance between the side whose length is the base and the opposite side.

See base of a parallelogram.

altura de un paralelogramo (pág. 521) La distancia perpendicular entre el lado cuya longitud es la base y el lado opuesto.

Véase base de un paralelogramo.

height of a trapezoid (p. 522) The perpendicular distance between the bases of the trapezoid.

See bases of a trapezoid.

altura de un trapecio (pág. 522) La distancia perpendicular entre las bases de un trapecio.

Véase bases de un trapecio.

height of a triangle (p. 142) The perpendicular distance between a side whose length is the base and the vertex opposite that side.

See base of a triangle.

altura de un triángulo (pág. 142) La distancia perpendicular entre el lado cuya longitud es la base y el vértice opuesto a esa base.

Véase base de un triángulo.

heptagon (p. 420) A polygon with seven sides.

heptágono (pág. 420) Polígono que tiene siete lados.

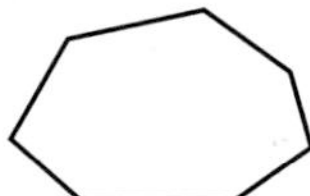

hexagon (p. 420) A polygon with six sides.

hexágono (pág. 420) Polígono que tiene seis lados.

histogram (p. 4) A graph that displays data from a frequency table. A histogram has one bar for each interval of the frequency table. The height of the bar indicates the frequency for the interval.

histograma (pág. 4) Una gráfica que muestra datos de una tabla de frecuencias. Un histograma tiene una barra para cada intervalo de la tabla de frecuencias. La longitud de la barra indica la frecuencia para el intervalo.

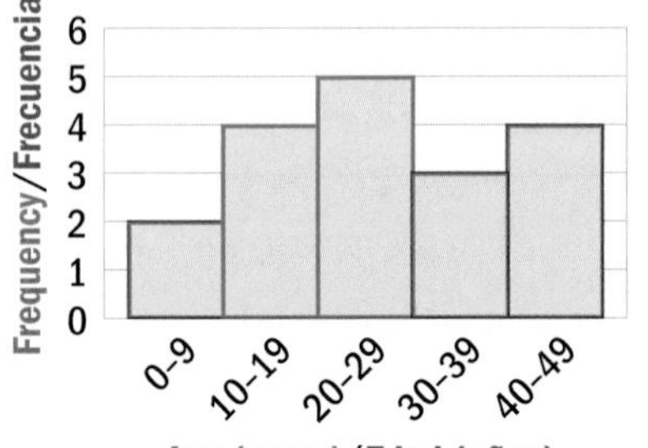

hypotenuse (p. 482) The side of a right triangle that is opposite the right angle. **hipotenusa** (pág. 482) El lado de un triángulo rectángulo que está opuesto al ángulo recto.	

I

identity property of addition (p. 64) The sum of a number and the additive identity, 0, is the number. **propiedad de identidad de la suma** (pág. 64) La suma de un número y la identidad de la suma, 0, es el mismo número.	$8 + 0 = 8$ $a + 0 = a$
identity property of multiplication (p. 74) The product of a number and the multiplicative identity, 1, is the number. **propiedad de identidad de la multiplicación** (pág. 74) El producto de un número y la identidad de la multiplicación, 1, es el mismo número.	$4 \cdot 1 = 4$ $a \cdot 1 = a$
image (p. 433) The new figure formed by a transformation. **imagen** (pág. 433) La figura nueva formada por una transformación.	*See* reflection, rotation, *and* translation. *Véase* reflexión, rotación *y* traslación.
improper fraction (p. 762) A fraction whose numerator is greater than or equal to its denominator. **fracción impropia** (pág. 762) Una fracción en la cual el numerador es mayor que el denominador o igual a él.	$\frac{8}{7}$ is an *improper fraction.* $\frac{8}{7}$ es una *fracción impropia.*
independent events (p. 694) Two events such that the occurrence of one does not affect the likelihood that the other will occur. **eventos independientes** (pág. 694) Dos eventos tales que la ocurrencia de uno no afecta la probabilidad de que ocurra el otro.	You toss a coin and roll a number cube. The events "getting heads" and "getting a 6" are *independent events.* Lanzas una moneda y después lanzas un cubo numerado. Los eventos "obtener cara" y "obtener 6" son *eventos independientes.*
inequality (p. 148) A mathematical sentence formed by placing an inequality symbol between two expressions. **desigualdad** (pág. 148) Un enunciado matemático formado colocando un símbolo de desigualdad entre dos expresiones.	$3 < 5$ and $x + 2 \geq -4$ are *inequalities.* $3 < 5$ y $x + 2 \geq -4$ son *desigualdades.*
input (p. 583) A number on which a function operates. An input value is in the domain of the function. **entrada** (pág. 583) Un número sobre el que opera una función. Un valor de entrada está en el dominio de la función.	*See* function. *Véase* función.

ENGLISH-SPANISH GLOSSARY

integers (p. 57) The numbers . . . , −4, −3, −2, −1, 0, 1, 2, 3, 4, . . . , consisting of the negative integers, zero, and the positive integers. **números enteros** (pág. 57) Los números ..., −4, −3, −2, −1, 0, 1, 2, 3, 4, ..., que constan de los números enteros negativos, cero y los números enteros positivos.	−8 and 14 are *integers*. $-8\frac{1}{3}$ and 14.5 are not *integers*. −8 y 14 son *números enteros*. $-8\frac{1}{3}$ y 14.5 no son *números enteros*.
interest (p. 376) The amount earned or paid for the use of money. **interés** (pág. 376) La cantidad ganada o pagada por el uso de dinero.	*See* simple interest. *Véase* interés simple.
interquartile range (p. 655) The difference between the upper and lower quartiles in a box-and-whisker plot. **rango entre cuartiles** (pág. 655) La diferencia entre los cuartiles superior e inferior en un diagrama de líneas y bloques.	0 10 20 30 40 50 8 19 26 37 45 The *interquartile range* is 37 − 19, or 18. El *rango entre cuartiles* es 37 − 19, ó 18.
intersection (p. 690) The set of all elements in *both* set *A* and set *B*, written as $A \cap B$. **intersección** (pág. 690) El conjunto de todos los elementos que están tanto en el conjunto *A* como en el conjunto *B*, que se expresa como $A \cap B$.	U A B
inverse operations (p. 117) Operations that "undo" each other. **operaciones inversas** (pág. 117) Operaciones que se "deshacen" mutuamente.	Addition and subtraction are *inverse operations*. Multiplication and division are also *inverse operations*. La suma y la resta son *operaciones inversas*. La multiplicación y la división también son *operaciones inversas*.
inverse property of addition (p. 64) The sum of a number and its additive inverse, or opposite, is 0. **propiedad inversa de la suma** (pág. 64) La suma de un número y su inverso aditivo u opuesto, es cero.	$5 + (-5) = 0$ $a + (-a) = 0$
inverse property of multiplication (p. 249) The product of a nonzero number and its multiplicative inverse, or reciprocal, is 1. **propiedad inversa de la multiplicación** (pág. 249) El producto de un número distinto de cero y su inverso multiplicativo, o recíproco, es 1.	$\frac{3}{4} \cdot \frac{4}{3} = 1$ $\frac{a}{b} \cdot \frac{b}{a} = 1 \quad (a, b \neq 0)$

inverse variation (p. 619) The relationship of two variables x and y if there is a nonzero number k such that $xy = k$ or $y = \frac{k}{x}$. **variación inversa** (pág. 619) La relación entre dos variables x e y cuando hay un número k distinto de cero, de manera tal que $xy = k$ ó $y = \frac{k}{x}$.	$\frac{x}{y} = k$ or $y = \frac{k}{x}$ $\frac{x}{y} = 8$ or $y = \frac{8}{x}$ $\frac{x}{y} = k$ ó $y = \frac{k}{x}$ $\frac{x}{y} = 8$ ó $y = \frac{8}{x}$
irrational number (p. 475) A real number that cannot be written as a quotient of two integers. The decimal form of an irrational number neither terminates nor repeats. **número irracional** (pág. 475) Un número real que no puede escribirse como un cociente de dos números enteros. La forma decimal de un número irracional no termina ni se repite.	$\sqrt{2}$ and 0.313113111... are *irrational numbers.* $\sqrt{2}$ y 0.313113111... son *números irracionales.*
isometric drawing (p. 539) A two-dimensional drawing of a three-dimensional figure that can be created using a grid of dots and a set of three axes that intersect to form 120° angles. **dibujo isométrico** (pág. 539) Un dibujo bidimensional de una figura tridimensional que se puede crear a partir de una cuadrícula de puntos y un conjunto de tres ejes para formar ángulos de 120°.	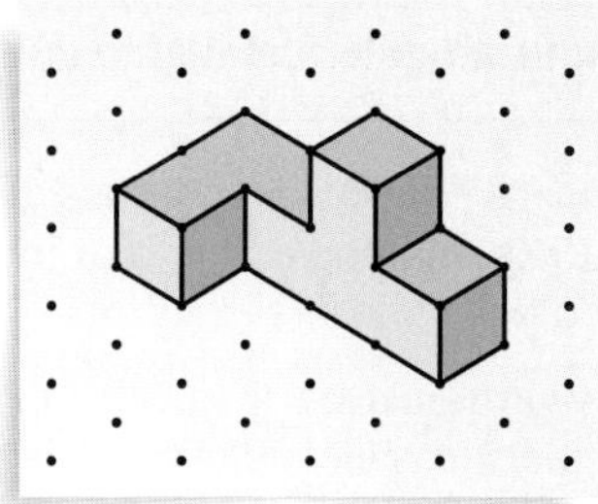
isosceles triangle (p. 411) A triangle with at least two congruent sides. **triángulo isósceles** (pág. 411) Un triángulo que tiene al menos dos lados congruentes.	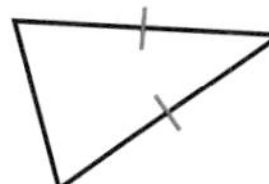

L

lateral surface area (p. 545) Surface area of a figure excluding the area of its base(s). **área de superficie lateral** (pág. 545) Área de la superficie de una figura que excluye el área de su(s) base(s).	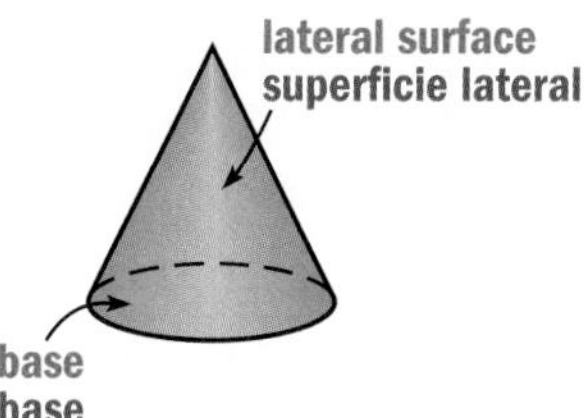
leading digit (p. 265) The first nonzero digit in a number. **dígito dominante** (pág. 265) El primer dígito distinto de cero en un número.	The *leading digit* of 725 is 7. The *leading digit* of 0.002638 is 2. El *dígito dominante* de 725 es 7. El *dígito dominante* de 0.002638 es 2.

ENGLISH-SPANISH GLOSSARY

least common denominator (LCD) (p. 198) The least common multiple of the denominators of two or more fractions. **mínimo común denominador (m.c.d.)** (pág. 198) El mínimo común múltiplo de los denominadores de dos o más fracciones.	The *LCD* of $\frac{7}{10}$ and $\frac{3}{4}$ is 20, the least common multiple of 10 and 4. El *m.c.d.* de $\frac{7}{10}$ y $\frac{3}{4}$ es 20, que es el mínimo común múltiplo de 10 y 4.
least common multiple (LCM) (p. 192) The least number that is a common multiple of two or more whole numbers. **mínimo común múltiplo (m.c.m.)** (pág. 192) El menor de los múltiplos comunes de dos o más números naturales.	The *LCM* of 4 and 6 is 12. The *LCM* of 3, 5, and 10 is 30. El *m.c.m.* de 4 y 6 es 12. El *m.c.m.* de 3, 5 y 10 es 30.
legs of a right triangle (p. 482) The two sides of a right triangle that form the right angle. **catetos de un triángulo rectángulo** (pág. 482) Los dos lados de un triángulo rectángulo que forman el ángulo recto.	*See* hypotenuse. *Véase* hipotenusa.
like terms (p. 89) Terms that have identical variable parts raised to the same power. (Two or more constant terms are considered like terms.) **términos semejantes** (pág. 89) Términos que tienen partes variables idénticas elevadas a la misma potencia. (Dos o más términos constantes se consideran términos semejantes.)	In the expression $x + 4 - 2x + 1$, x and $-2x$ are *like terms*, and 4 and 1 are *like terms.* En la expresión $x + 4 - 2x + 1$, x y $-2x$ son *términos semejantes*, y 4 y 1 son *términos semejantes.*
line (p. 773) A figure that extends without end in two opposite directions. **recta** (pág. 773) Una figura que se extiende infinitamente en dos direcciones opuestas.	X Y
line plot (p. 782) A number line diagram that uses X marks to show the frequencies of items or categories being tallied. **diagrama lineal** (pág. 782) Un diagrama de recta numérica que usa marcas X para mostrar las frecuencias con las que se marcan artículos o categorías.	0 1 2 3 4
linear equation (p. 598) An equation in which the variables appear in separate terms and each variable occurs only to the first power. **ecuación lineal** (pág. 598) Una ecuación en la que las variables aparecen en términos separados y cada variable se eleva sólo a la primera potencia.	$7y = 14x + 21$ is a *linear equation.* $7y = 14x + 21$ es una *ecuación lineal.*

linear function (p. 604) A function whose graph is a line or a part of a line.

función lineal (pág. 604) Una función cuya gráfica es una recta o parte de una recta.

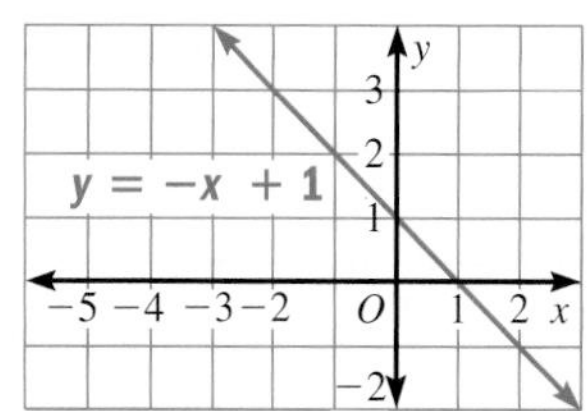

linear inequality (p. 629) An inequality in which the variables appear in separate terms and each variable occurs only to the first power.

desigualdad lineal (pág. 629) Una desigualdad en la que las variables aparecen en términos separados y cada variable se eleva sólo a la primera potencia.

$y \le 2x + 5$ is a *linear inequality.*

$y \le 2x + 5$ es una *desigualdad lineal.*

line graph (p. 660) A type of graph in which points representing data pairs are connected by line segments. A line graph is used to show how a quantity changes over time.

gráfica lineal (pág. 660) Un tipo de gráfica en la que los puntos que representan pares de datos se conectan por segmentos de recta. Se usa una gráfica lineal para mostrar cómo una cantidad cambia en el tiempo.

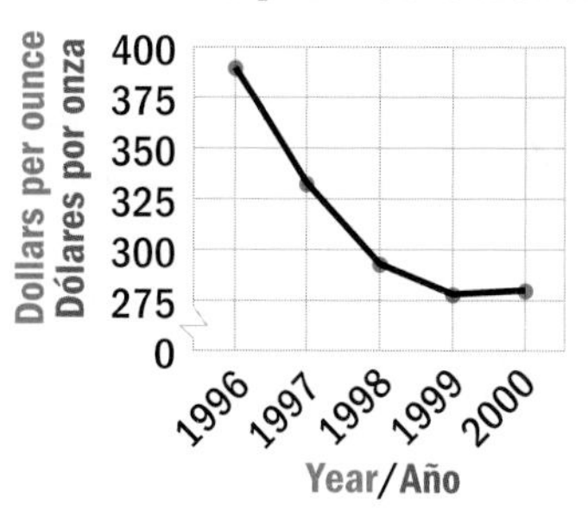

line of reflection (p. 434) The line over which a figure is flipped when the figure undergoes a reflection.

línea de reflexión (pág. 434) La recta sobre la que se invierte una figura cuando dicha figura se refleja.

See reflection.

Véase reflexión.

line of symmetry (p. 435) A line that divides a figure into two parts that are mirror images of each other.

línea de simetría (pág. 435) Una recta que divide una figura en dos partes que son imágenes reflejas entre sí.

See line symmetry.

Véase simetría lineal.

line symmetry (p. 435) A figure has line symmetry if it can be divided by a line, called a line of symmetry, into two parts that are mirror images of each other.

simetría lineal (pág. 435) Una figura tiene simetría lineal si puede dividirse por una recta, llamada línea de simetría, en dos partes que son imágenes reflejas entre sí.

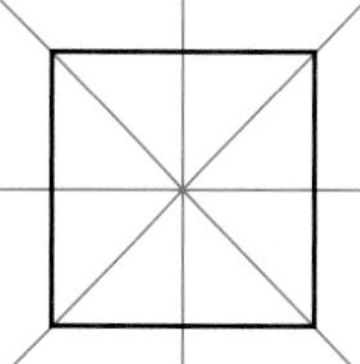

A square has 4 lines of symmetry.

Un cuadrado tiene 4 líneas de simetría.

ENGLISH-SPANISH GLOSSARY

lower extreme (p. 654) The least value in a data set. **extremo inferior** (pág. 654) El valor menor en un conjunto de datos.	*See* box-and-whisker plot. *Véase* diagrama de líneas y bloques.
lower quartile (p. 654) The median of the lower half of a data set. **cuartil inferior** (pág. 654) La mediana de la mitad inferior de un conjunto de datos.	*See* box-and-whisker plot. *Véase* diagrama de líneas y bloques.

M

markup (p. 370) The increase in the wholesale price of an item. **margen** (pág. 370) El aumento con respecto al precio de venta por mayor de un artículo.	The wholesale price of a loaf of bread is $1 but the store sells it for $1.59. The *markup* is $.59. El precio de venta al por mayor de una hogaza de pan es de $1, pero la tienda la vende a $1.59. El *margen* es de $.59.
mean (pp. 78, 272) The sum of the values in a data set divided by the number of values. **media** (págs. 78, 272) La suma de los valores en un conjunto de datos dividida por el número de valores.	The *mean* of the data set 85, 59, 97, 71 is $\frac{85 + 59 + 97 + 71}{4} = \frac{312}{4} = 78$. La *media* del conjunto de datos 85, 59, 97, 71 es $\frac{85 + 59 + 97 + 71}{4} = \frac{312}{4} = 78$.
median (p. 272) The middle value in a data set when the values are written in numerical order. If the data set has an even number of values, the median is the mean of the two middle values. **mediana** (pág. 272) El valor que está en el medio de un conjunto de datos cuando los valores están escritos en orden numérico. Si el conjunto de datos tiene un número par de valores, la mediana es la media de los dos valores que están en el medio.	The *median* of the data set 8, 17, 21, 23, 26, 29, 34, 40, 45 is the middle value, 26. La *mediana* del conjunto de datos 8, 17, 21, 23, 26, 29, 34, 40, 45 es 26, el valor que está en el medio.
mixed number (p. 762) A number that has a whole number part and a fraction part. **número mixto** (pág. 762) Un número que tiene una parte que es un número natural y una parte que es una fracción.	$3\frac{2}{5}$ is a *mixed number*. $3\frac{2}{5}$ es un *número mixto*.
mode (p. 272) The value in a data set that occurs most often. A data set can have no mode, one mode, or more than one mode. **moda** (pág. 272) En un conjunto de datos, el valor que ocurre con mayor frecuencia. Un conjunto de datos puede no tener moda, o puede tener una moda o más de una moda.	The *mode* of the data set 73, 42, 55, 77, 61, 55, 68 is 55 because it occurs most often. La *moda* del conjunto de datos 73, 42, 55, 77, 61, 55, 68 es 55 porque es el valor que aparece más veces.

monomial (p. 178) A number, a variable, or a product of a number and one or more variables.	**$3xy$, $8x^2$, x, and 14 are *monomials*.**
monomio (pág. 178) Un número, una variable o un producto de un número y una o más variables.	**$3xy$, $8x^2$, x y 14 son *monomios*.**
multiple (p. 192) A multiple of a number is the product of the number and any nonzero whole number.	**The *multiples* of 3 are 3, 6, 9, ...**
múltiplo (pág. 192) Un múltiplo de un número es el producto del número y cualquier número natural distinto de cero.	**Los *múltiplos* de 3 son 3, 6, 9, ...**
multiplication property of equality (p. 122) Multiplying each side of an equation by the same nonzero number produces an equivalent equation.	**If $\frac{x}{3} = 7$, then $3 \cdot \frac{x}{3} = 3 \cdot 7$, so $x = 21$. If $\frac{x}{a} = b$ and $a \neq 0$, then $a \cdot \frac{x}{a} = a \cdot b$.**
propiedad de igualdad en la multiplicación (pág. 122) Al multiplicar cada lado de una ecuación por el mismo número distinto de cero se obtiene una ecuación equivalente.	**Si $\frac{x}{3} = 7$, entonces $3 \cdot \frac{x}{3} = 3 \cdot 7$, por lo tanto $x = 21$. Si $\frac{x}{a} = b$ y $a \neq 0$, entonces $a \cdot \frac{x}{a} = a \cdot b$.**
multiplication property of zero (p. 74) The product of a number and 0 is 0. **propiedad del cero de la multiplicación** (pág. 74) El producto de un número y 0 es 0.	**$-4 \cdot 0 = 0$ $a \cdot 0 = 0$**
multiplicative identity (p. 74) The number 1 is the multiplicative identity because the product of any number and 1 is the original number. **identidad de la multiplicación** (pág. 74) El número 1 es la identidad de la multiplicación porque el producto de cualquier número y 1 es el número original.	**$9 \cdot 1 = 9$ $a \cdot 1 = a$**
multiplicative inverse (p. 247) The multiplicative inverse of a number $\frac{a}{b}$ ($a, b \neq 0$) is the reciprocal of the number, or $\frac{b}{a}$. The product of a number and its multiplicative inverse is 1.	**The *multiplicative inverse* of $\frac{3}{2}$ is $\frac{2}{3}$, so $\frac{3}{2} \cdot \frac{2}{3} = 1$.**
inverso multiplicativo (pág. 247) El inverso multiplicativo de un número $\frac{a}{b}$ ($a, b \neq 0$) es el recíproco de dicho número, es decir $\frac{b}{a}$. El producto de un número y su inverso multiplicativo es 1.	**El *inverso multiplicativo* de $\frac{3}{2}$ es $\frac{2}{3}$, por lo tanto $\frac{3}{2} \cdot \frac{2}{3} = 1$.**

N

negative integers (p. 57) The integers that are less than zero.	**The *negative integers* are $-1, -2, -3, -4, \ldots$.**
números enteros negativos (pág. 57) Números enteros menores que cero.	**Los *números enteros negativos* son $-1, -2, -3, -4, \ldots$**

net (p. 542) A two-dimensional representation of a solid. This pattern forms a solid when it is folded. **red** (pág. 542) Representación bidimensional de un cuerpo geométrico. Este patrón forma un cuerpo geométrico cuando se dobla.	
numerical expression (p. 8) An expression consisting of numbers and operations. **expresión numérica** (pág. 8) Una expresión compuesta por números y operaciones.	$4(3) + 24 \div 2$

O

obtuse angle (p. 411) An angle whose measure is greater than 90° and less than 180°. **ángulo obtuso** (pág. 411) Un ángulo cuya medida es mayor que 90° y menor que 180°.	
obtuse triangle (p. 411) A triangle with one obtuse angle. **triángulo obtusángulo** (pág. 411) Triángulo que tiene un ángulo obtuso.	120° 35° 25°
octagon (p. 420) A polygon with eight sides. **octágono** (pág. 420) Polígono que tiene ocho lados.	
odds in favor of an event (p. 686) The ratio of favorable outcomes to unfavorable outcomes. **probabilidades a favor de un evento** (pág. 686) La razón entre los resultados favorables y los resultados desfavorables.	The odds of rolling an even number on a six sided number cube is $\frac{3}{3}$, or 1. Las probabilidades de obtener un número par en un cubo numerado de seis lados son $\frac{3}{3}$, ó 1.
opposites (p. 58) Two numbers that are the same distance from 0 on a number line but are on opposite sides of 0. **opuestos** (pág. 58) Dos números que están a la misma distancia de 0 en una recta numérica pero en lados opuestos de 0.	-3 and 3 are *opposites*. -3 y 3 son *opuestos*.
order of operations (p. 8) A set of rules for evaluating an expression involving more than one operation. **orden de las operaciones** (pág. 8) Conjunto de reglas para hallar el valor de una expresión que tiene más de una operación.	To evaluate $3 + 2 \cdot 4$, you perform the multiplication before the addition: $3 + 2 \cdot 4 = 3 + 8 = 11$ Para hallar el valor de $3 + 2 \cdot 4$, haz la multiplicación antes que la suma: $3 + 2 \cdot 4 = 3 + 8 = 11$

ordered pair (p. 94) A pair of numbers (x, y) that can be used to represent a point in a coordinate plane. The first number is the x-coordinate, and the second number is the y-coordinate.

par ordenado (pág. 94) Un par de números (x, y) que se puede usar para representar un punto en un plano de coordenadas. El primer número es la coordenada x y el segundo número es la coordenada y.

(−2, 1)

origin (p. 94) The point (0, 0) where the x-axis and the y-axis meet in a coordinate plane.

origen (pág. 94) El punto (0, 0) donde se encuentran el eje x y el eje y en un plano de coordenadas.

See coordinate plane.

Véase plano de coordenadas.

outcomes (p. 381) The possible results when an experiment is performed.

resultados (pág. 381) Resultados posibles cuando se realiza un experimento.

When tossing a coin, the *outcomes* are heads and tails.

Al lanzar una moneda, los *resultados* son cara y cruz.

output (p. 583) A number produced by evaluating a function using a given input. An output value is in the range of the function.

salida (pág. 583) Número producido al hallar el valor de una función utilizando una entrada dada. Un valor de salida está dentro del rango de la función.

See function.

Véase función.

P

parallel lines (p. 405) Two lines in the same plane that do not intersect. The symbol ∥ is used to indicate parallel lines.

rectas paralelas (pág. 405) Dos rectas en el mismo plano que no se intersecan. Se usa el símbolo ∥ para indicar rectas paralelas.

$a \parallel b$

parallelogram (p. 416) A quadrilateral with both pairs of opposite sides parallel.

paralelogramo (pág. 416) Un cuadrilátero que tiene dos pares de lados opuestos paralelos.

pentagon (p. 420) A polygon with five sides.

pentágono (pág. 420) Polígono que tiene cinco lados.

percent (p. 354) A ratio whose denominator is 100. The symbol for percent is %.

porcentaje (pág. 354) Razón cuyo denominador es 100. El símbolo de porcentaje es %.

$$\frac{17}{20} = \frac{17 \cdot 5}{20 \cdot 5} = \frac{85}{100} = 85\%$$

ENGLISH-SPANISH GLOSSARY

percent of change (p. 366) A percent that shows how much a quantity has increased or decreased in comparison with the original amount: Percent of change $p = \frac{\text{Amount of increase or decrease}}{\text{Original amount}}$	The *percent of change p* from 15 to 19 is: $p = \frac{19 - 15}{15} = \frac{4}{15} \approx 0.267 = 26.7\%$
porcentaje de cambio (pág. 366) Porcentaje que muestra cuánto ha aumentado o disminuido una cantidad en comparación con la cantidad original: Porcentaje de cambio $p = \frac{\text{Cantidad de aumento o disminución}}{\text{Cantidad original}}$	El *porcentaje de cambio p* de 15 a 19 es: $p = \frac{19 - 15}{15} = \frac{4}{15} \approx 0.267 = 26.7\%$
percent of decrease (p. 366) The percent of change in a quantity when the new amount of the quantity is less than the original amount.	*See* percent of change.
porcentaje de disminución (pág. 366) Porcentaje de cambio en una cantidad cuando el valor nuevo de una cantidad es menor que la cantidad original.	*Véase* porcentaje de cambio.
percent of increase (p. 366) The percent of change in a quantity when the new amount of the quantity is greater than the original amount.	*See* percent of change.
porcentaje de aumento (pág. 366) Porcentaje de cambio en una cantidad cuando el valor nuevo de una cantidad es mayor que la cantidad original.	*Véase* porcentaje de cambio.
perfect square (p. 470) A number that is the square of an integer.	49 is a *perfect square* because $49 = (\pm 7)^2$.
cuadrado perfecto (pág. 470) Un número que es el cuadrado de un número entero.	49 es un *cuadrado perfecto* porque $49 = (\pm 7)^2$.
perimeter (p. 32) The distance around a figure. For a figure with straight sides, the perimeter is the sum of the lengths of the sides.	7 ft/7 pies 4 ft/4 pies 4 ft/4 pies 7 ft/7 pies *Perimeter* = 22 ft
perímetro (pág. 32) La distancia alrededor de una figura. Para una figura de lados rectos, el perímetro es la suma de las longitudes de los lados.	*Perímetro* = 22 pies
permutation (p. 675) An arrangement of a group of objects in a particular order.	There are 6 *permutations* of the 3 letters in the word CAT: CAT ACT TCA CTA ATC TAC
permutación (pág. 675) Disposición de un grupo de objetos en un orden particular.	Hay 6 *permutaciones* de las 3 letras de la palabra MAR: MAR AMR RMA MRA ARM RAM

perpendicular lines (p. 404) Two lines that intersect to form a right angle. The symbol ⊥ is used to indicate perpendicular lines. **rectas perpendiculares** (pág. 404) Dos rectas que se intersecan formando un ángulo recto. El símbolo ⊥ se usa para indicar rectas perpendiculares.	a b $a \perp b$
pi (π) (p. 312) The ratio of the circumference of a circle to its diameter. **pi** (π) (pág. 312) La razón entre la circunferencia de un círculo y su diámetro.	You can use 3.14 or $\frac{22}{7}$ to approximate π. Puedes usar 3.14 ó $\frac{22}{7}$ como el valor aproximado de π.
plane (p. 773) A plane can be thought of as a flat surface that extends without end. **plano** (pág. 773) Se puede pensar en un plano como una superficie plana que se extiende infinitamente.	
point (p. 773) A figure without dimensions that is represented by a dot. **punto** (pág. 773) Una figura sin dimensiones que se representa con un punto.	A
polygon (p. 420) A closed geometric figure made up of three or more line segments that intersect only at their endpoints. **polígono** (pág. 420) Figura geométrica cerrada compuesta de tres o más segmentos de recta que se intersecan sólo en sus extremos.	Polygon Polígono Not a polygon No polígono
polyhedron (p. 534) A solid that is enclosed by polygons. **poliedro** (pág. 534) Cuerpo geométrico encerrado por polígonos.	
polynomial (p. 717) A monomial or a sum of monomials. **polinomio** (pág. 717) Un monomio o una suma de monomios.	*See* binomial, trinomial, monomial. *Véase* binomio, trinomio, monomio.
population (p. 702) In statistics, the entire group of people or objects about which you want information. **población** (pág. 702) En estadística, todo el grupo de personas u objetos sobre los que se busca información.	If a biologist wants to determine the average age of the elephants in a wildlife refuge, the *population* consists of every elephant in the refuge. Si un biólogo quiere determinar la edad promedio de los elefantes de un santuario animal, la *población* consiste en cada elefante del santuario.

positive integers (p. 57) The integers that are greater than zero. **números enteros positivos** (pág. 57) Números enteros mayores que cero.	The *positive integers* are 1, 2, 3, 4, ... Los *números enteros positivos* son 1, 2, 3, 4, ...
power (p. 19) A product formed from repeated multiplication by the same number or expression. A power consists of a base and an exponent. **potencia** (pág. 19) Producto que se obtiene de la multiplicación repetida por el mismo número o expresión. Una potencia está compuesta de una base y un exponente.	2^4 is a *power* with base 2 and exponent 4. $2^4 = 2 \cdot 2 \cdot 2 \cdot 2 = 16$ 2^4 es una *potencia* con base 2 y exponente 4. $2^4 = 2 \cdot 2 \cdot 2 \cdot 2 = 16$
prime factorization (p. 177) Expressing a whole number as a product of prime numbers. **descomposición en factores primos** (pág. 177) Expresar un número natural como producto de números primos.	The *prime factorization* of 54 is $2 \times 3 \times 3 \times 3 = 2 \times 3^3$. La *descomposición en factores primos* de 54 es $2 \times 3 \times 3 \times 3 = 2 \times 3^3$.
prime number (p. 177) A whole number greater than 1 whose only positive factors are 1 and itself. **número primo** (pág. 177) Un número natural mayor que 1 cuyos únicos factores positivos son 1 y él mismo.	5 is a *prime number* because its only positive factors are 1 and 5. 5 es un *número primo*, porque sus únicos factores que son números naturales son 1 y 5.
principal (p. 376) An amount of money that is deposited or borrowed. **capital** (pág. 376) Una cantidad de dinero que se deposita o se solicita en préstamo.	*See* simple interest. *Véase* interés simple.
prism (p. 534) A solid, formed by polygons, that has two congruent bases lying in parallel planes. **prisma** (pág. 534) Cuerpo geométrico formado por polígonos, que tiene dos bases congruentes ubicadas en planos paralelos.	
probability of an event (p. 381) A number from 0 to 1 that measures the likelihood that the event will occur. **probabilidad de un evento** (pág. 381) Número de 0 a 1 que mide la posibilidad de que ocurra un evento.	*See* experimental probability *and* theoretical probability. *Véase* probabilidad experimental *y* probabilidad teórica.
proportion (p. 348) An equation stating that two ratios are equivalent. **proporción** (pág. 348) Una ecuación que establece que dos razones son equivalentes.	$\frac{3}{5} = \frac{6}{10}$ and $\frac{x}{12} = \frac{25}{30}$ are *proportions.* $\frac{3}{5} = \frac{6}{10}$ y $\frac{x}{12} = \frac{25}{30}$ son *proporciones.*

pyramid (p. 534) A solid, formed by polygons, that has one base. The base can be any polygon, and the other faces are triangles. **pirámide** (pág. 534) Cuerpo geométrico, formado por polígonos, que tiene una base. La base puede ser cualquier polígono y las otras caras son triángulos.	base/base
Pythagorean theorem (p. 482) For any right triangle, the sum of the squares of the lengths a and b of the legs equals the square of the length c of the hypotenuse: $a^2 + b^2 = c^2$. **teorema de Pitágoras** (pág. 482) Para cualquier triángulo rectángulo, la suma de los cuadrados de las longitudes a y b de los catetos es igual al cuadrado de la longitud c de la hipotenusa: $a^2 + b^2 = c^2$.	15, 25, 20 $15^2 + 20^2 = 25^2$
Pythagorean triple (p. 488) A set of three positive integers a, b, and c such that $a^2 + b^2 = c^2$. **triple de Pitágoras** (pág. 488) Conjunto de tres números enteros positivos a, b y c de modo que $a^2 + b^2 = c^2$.	5, 12, and 13 is a *Pythagorean triple.* 5, 12 y 13 es un *triple de Pitágoras.*

Q

quadrant (p. 94) One of the four regions that a coordinate plane is divided into by the x-axis and the y-axis. **cuadrante** (pág. 94) Una de las cuatro regiones en las que el eje x y el eje y dividen un plano de coordenadas.	*See* coordinate plane. *Véase* plano de coordenadas.
quadrilateral (p. 416) A closed geometric figure made up of four line segments, called sides, that intersect only at their endpoints; a polygon with four sides. **cuadrilátero** (pág. 416) Figura geométrica cerrada formada por cuatro segmentos de recta, llamados lados, que se intersecan sólo en sus extremos; polígono de cuatro lados.	

R

radical expression (p. 469) An expression involving a radical sign, $\sqrt{\ }$. **expresión radical** (pág. 469) Expresión que tiene un signo radical, $\sqrt{\ }$.	$\sqrt{3(22 + 5)}$ is a *radical expression.* $\sqrt{3(22 + 5)}$ es una *expresión radical.*
radius of a circle (p. 312) The distance between the center and any point on the circle. **radio de un círculo** (pág. 312) Distancia entre cualquier punto del círculo y su centro.	*See* circle. *Véase* círculo.

random sample (p. 702) A sample selected in such a way that each member of the population has an equally likely chance to be part of the sample. **muestra aleatoria** (pág. 702) Muestra seleccionada de tal manera que cada miembro de la población tiene la misma probabilidad de formar parte de la muestra.	A *random sample* of 5 eighth graders can be selected by putting the names of all eighth graders in a hat and drawing 5 names without looking. Una *muestra aleatoria* de 5 estudiantes de octavo grado puede seleccionarse colocando los nombres de todos los alumnos de octavo grado en un sombrero y sacando 5 nombres sin mirar.
range of a data set (p. 273) The difference of the greatest and least values in the data set. **rango de un conjunto de datos** (pág. 273) La diferencia entre el valor mayor y el valor menor en un conjunto de datos.	The *range of the data set* $60, 35, 22, 46, 81, 39$ is $81 - 22 = 59$. El *rango del conjunto de datos* $60, 35, 22, 46, 81, 39$ es $81 - 22 = 59$.
range of a function (p. 584) The set of all possible output values for the function. **rango de una función** (pág. 584) Conjunto de todos los valores de salida posibles para la función.	*See* function. *Véase* función.
rate (p. 344) A ratio of two quantities measured in different units. **tasa** (pág. 344) Razón entre dos cantidades medidas en unidades diferentes.	An airplane climbs 18,000 feet in 12 minutes. The airplane's *rate* of climb is $\frac{18{,}000 \text{ ft}}{12 \text{ min}} =$ 1,500 ft/min. Un avión asciende 18,000 pies en 12 minutos. La *tasa* de ascenso del avión es $\frac{18{,}000 \text{ pies}}{12 \text{ min}} =$ 1,500 pies/min.
rate of change (p. 619) A comparison of a change in one quantity with a change in another quantity. In real-world situations, you can interpret the slope of a line as a rate of change. **tasa de cambio** (pág. 619) Una comparación entre un cambio en una cantidad y un cambio en otra cantidad. En situaciones reales, puedes interpretar la pendiente de una recta como una tasa de cambio.	You pay \$7 for 2 hours of computer use and \$14 for 4 hours of computer use. The *rate of change* is $\frac{\text{change of cost}}{\text{change in time}} = \frac{14 - 7}{4 - 2} = 3.5$ or \$3.50 per hour. Pagas \$7 por usar la computadora durante 2 horas y \$14 por usar la computadora por 4 horas. La *tasa de cambio* es $\frac{\text{cambio en el costo}}{\text{cambio en el tiempo}} = \frac{14 - 7}{4 - 2} = 3.5$ o \$3.50 por hora.
ratio (p. 343) A comparison of two numbers using division. The ratio of a to b (where $b \neq 0$) can be written as a to b, as $\frac{a}{b}$, or as $a : b$. **razón** (pág. 343) Comparación entre dos números usando la división. La razón de a a b (donde $b \neq 0$) puede escribirse como a a b, como $\frac{a}{b}$ o como $a : b$.	The *ratio* of 17 to 12 can be written as 17 to 12, as $\frac{17}{12}$, or as $17 : 12$. La *razón* de 17 a 12 puede escribirse como 17 a 12, como $\frac{17}{12}$ o como $17 : 12$.

rational number (p. 255) A number that can be written as $\frac{a}{b}$ where a and b are integers and $b \neq 0$. **número racional** (pág. 255) Un número que se puede escribir como $\frac{a}{b}$ donde a y b son números enteros y $b \neq 0$.	$6 = \frac{6}{1}, -\frac{3}{5} = \frac{-3}{5}, 0.75 = \frac{3}{4}$, and $2\frac{1}{3} = \frac{7}{3}$ are all *rational numbers.* $6 = \frac{6}{1}, -\frac{3}{5} = \frac{-3}{5}, 0.75 = \frac{3}{4}$ y $2\frac{1}{3} = \frac{7}{3}$ son todos *números racionales.*
ray (p. 773) A figure that has one endpoint and extends without end in one direction. **semirrecta** (pág. 773) Una figura con un extremo que se extiende infinitamente en una dirección.	B A
real numbers (p. 475) The set of all rational numbers and irrational numbers. **números reales** (pág. 475) Conjunto de todos los números racionales e irracionales.	$0, -\frac{5}{9}, 2.75$, and $\sqrt{3}$ are all *real numbers.* $0, -\frac{5}{9}, 2.75$ y $\sqrt{3}$ son todos *números reales.*
reciprocals (p. 247) Two nonzero numbers whose product is 1. **recíprocos** (pág. 247) Dos números distintos de cero cuyo producto es 1.	$\frac{2}{3}$ and $\frac{3}{2}$ are *reciprocals.* $\frac{2}{3}$ y $\frac{3}{2}$ son *recíprocos.*
reflection (p. 433) A transformation that creates a mirror image of each point of a figure; also known as a *flip.* **reflexión** (pág. 433) Transformación que crea una imagen refleja de cada punto de una figura; también llamada *inversión.*	y flip inversión O x reflection in the y-axis reflexión en el eje y
reflex angle (p. 415) An angle greater than 180° but less than 360°. **ángulo cóncavo** (pág. 415) Un ángulo mayor que 180° pero menor que 360°.	210°
regular polygon (p. 420) A polygon with all sides equal in length and all angles equal in measure. **polígono regular** (pág. 420) Un polígono cuyos lados tienen igual longitud y cuyos ángulos tienen la misma medida.	Regular pentagon Pentágono regular
relation (p. 583) A set of ordered pairs. **relación** (pág. 583) Conjunto de pares ordenados.	(5, 7), (6, 5), (0, 5), (6, 0) is a *relation.* (5, 7), (6, 5), (0, 5), (6, 0) es una *relación.*

relative frequency (p. 382) The ratio of number of favorable outcomes to the total number of times the experiment was performed. **frecuencia relativa** (pág. 382) La razón entre el número de resultados favorables y el número de veces que se llevó a cabo un experimento.	*See* experimental probability. *Véase* probabilidad experimental.
relatively prime numbers (p. 182) Two or more nonzero whole numbers whose greatest common factor is 1. **números relativamente primos** (pág. 182) Dos o más números naturales distintos de cero cuyo máximo común divisor es 1.	9 and 16 are *relatively prime* because their GCF is 1. 9 y 16 son *relativamente primos* porque su MCD es 1.
repeating decimal (p. 255) A decimal that has one or more digits that repeat without end. **decimal periódico** (pág. 255) Decimal que tiene uno o más dígitos que se repiten infinitamente.	0.7777... and $1.\overline{29}$ are *repeating decimals.* 0.7777... y $1.\overline{29}$ son *decimales periódicos.*
rhombus (p. 416) A parallelogram with four congruent sides. **rombo** (pág. 416) Paralelogramo que tiene cuatro lados congruentes.	
right angle (p. 403) An angle whose measure is exactly 90°. **ángulo recto** (pág. 403) Un ángulo que mide exactamente 90°.	
right triangle (p. 411) A triangle with one right angle. **triángulo rectángulo** (pág. 411) Un triángulo que tiene un ángulo recto.	50° 40°
rise (p. 612) The vertical change between two points on a line. **distancia vertical** (pág. 612) El cambio vertical entre dos puntos en una recta.	*See* slope. *Véase* pendiente.
rotation (p. 440) A transformation that rotates a figure through a given angle, called the angle of rotation, and in a given direction about a fixed point, called the center of rotation; also known as a *turn*. **rotación** (pág. 440) Transformación que rota una figura por un ángulo dado, llamado ángulo de rotación, en una dirección dada alrededor de un punto fijo, llamado centro de rotación; también se conoce como *giro*.	center of rotation centro de rotación y O x turn/giro

rotational symmetry (p. 443) A figure has rotational symmetry if a turn of 180° or less produces an image that fits exactly on the original figure. **simetría de rotación** (pág. 443) Una figura tiene simetría de rotación si un giro de 180° o menor produce una imagen que es igual a la figura original.	90° 180° A square has *rotational symmetry.* Un cuadrado tiene *simetría de rotación.*
run (p. 612) The horizontal change between two points on a line. **distancia horizontal** (pág. 612) El cambio horizontal entre dos puntos en una recta.	*See* slope. *Véase* pendiente.

S

sample (p. 702) A part of a population. **muestra** (pág. 702) Una parte de una población.	To predict the results of an election, a survey is given to a *sample* of voters. Para predecir los resultados de unas elecciones, se encuesta a una *muestra* de votantes.
scale (p. 350) In a scale drawing, the scale gives the relationship between the drawing's dimensions and the actual dimensions. **escala** (pág. 350) En un dibujo a escala, la escala muestra la relación entre las dimensiones del dibujo y las dimensiones reales.	The *scale* "1 in. : 10 ft" means that 1 inch in the scale drawing represents an actual distance of 10 feet. La *escala* "1 pulg. : 10 pies" significa que una pulgada en el dibujo a escala representa una distancia real de 10 pies.
scale drawing (p. 347) A diagram of an object in which the dimensions are in proportion to the actual dimensions of the object. **dibujo a escala** (pág. 347) Un diagrama de un objeto cuyas dimensiones están en proporción con las dimensiones reales del objeto.	1 cm : 12 m
scale factor (p. 449) The ratio of corresponding side lengths of a figure and its image after dilation. **factor de escala** (pág. 449) La razón entre las longitudes de los lados correspondientes de una figura y su imagen después de una dilatación.	*See* dilation. *Véase* dilatación.
scale model (p. 350) A model of an object in which the dimensions are in proportion to the actual dimensions of the object. **modelo a escala** (pág. 350) Un modelo de un objeto cuyas dimensiones están en proporción con las dimensiones reales del objeto.	A *scale model* of the White House appears in Tobu World Square in Japan. The scale used is 1 : 25. En Tobu World Square, en Japón, hay un *modelo a escala* de la Casa Blanca. La escala utilizada es de 1 : 25.

scalene triangle (p. 411) A triangle with no congruent sides. **triángulo escaleno** (pág. 411) Un triángulo cuyos lados no son congruentes.	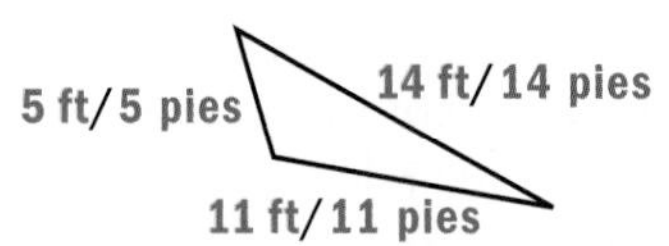
scatter plot (p. 588) The graph of a set of data pairs (x, y), which is a collection of points in a coordinate plane. **diagrama de dispersión** (pág. 588) La gráfica de un conjunto de pares de datos (x, y), que es un grupo de puntos en un plano de coordenadas.	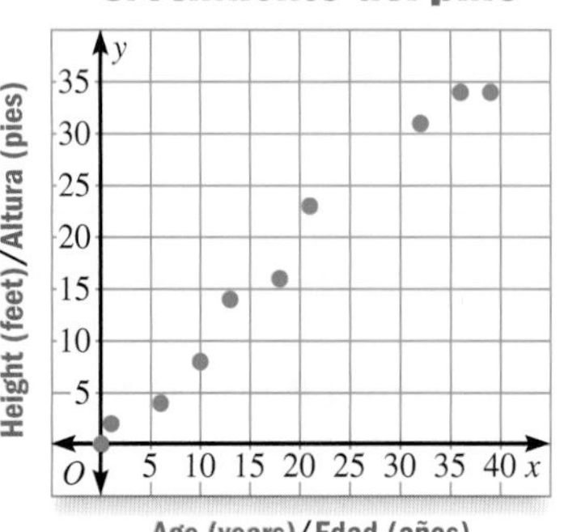
scientific notation (p. 212) A number is written in scientific notation if it has the form $c \times 10^n$, where c is greater than or equal to 1 and less than 10, and n is an integer. **notación científica** (pág. 212) Un número está escrito en notación científica si tiene la forma $c \times 10^n$ donde c es mayor que o igual a 1 y menor que 10, y n es un número entero.	In *scientific notation*, 328,000 is written as 3.28×10^5, and 0.00061 is written as 6.1×10^{-4}. En *notación científica*, 328,000 se escribe como 3.28×10^5 y 0.00061 se escribe como 6.1×10^{-4}.
sequence (p. 585) An ordered list of numbers. **secuencia** (pág. 585) Una lista ordenada de números.	1, 2, 3, 4, . . . is a *sequence*. 1, 2, 3, 4, ... es una *secuencia*.
set (p. 688) A collection of distinct objects. **conjunto** (pág. 688) Una agrupación de objetos particulares.	The set of whole numbers is $W = \{0, 1, 2, 3, 4, 5, \ldots\}$. El conjunto de los números naturales es $N = \{0, 1, 2, 3, 4, 5, \ldots\}$.
similar polygons (p. 447) Polygons that have the same shape but not necessarily the same size. Corresponding angles of similar polygons are congruent, and the ratios of the lengths of corresponding sides are equal. The symbol ~ is used to indicate that two polygons are similar. **polígonos semejantes** (pág. 447) Polígonos que tienen la misma forma pero no necesariamente el mismo tamaño. Los ángulos correspondientes de los polígonos semejantes son congruentes y las razones de las longitudes de los lados correspondientes son iguales. Se utiliza el símbolo ~ para indicar que dos polígonos son semejantes.	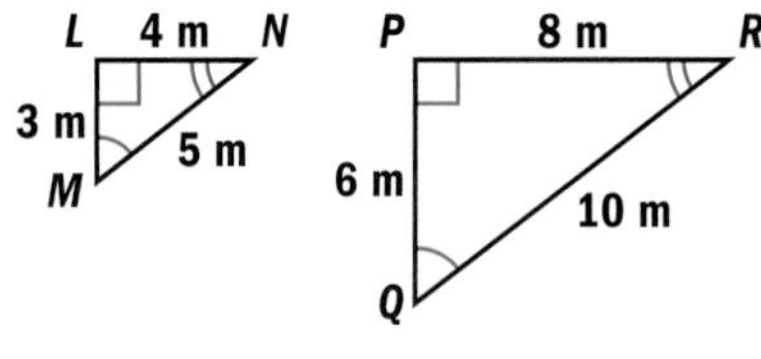 $\triangle LMN \sim \triangle PQR$

simple interest (p. 376) Interest that is earned or paid only on the principal. The simple interest I is the product of the principal P, the annual interest rate r written as a decimal, and the time t in years: $I = Prt$.

You deposit \$700 in a savings account that pays a 3% *simple annual interest* rate. After 5 years, the interest is $I = Prt = (700)(0.03)(5) = \$105$, and your account balance is $\$700 + \$105 = \$805$.

interés simple (pág. 376) El interés ganado o pagado sólo sobre el capital. El interés simple I es el producto del capital P, la tasa de interés anual r escrita en forma decimal y el tiempo t en años: $I = Prt$.

Depositas \$700 en una cuenta de ahorros que genera un *interés anual simple* del 3%. Después de 5 años, el interés es $I = Prt = (700)(0.03)(5) = \$105$, y el saldo de tu cuenta es $\$700 + \$105 = \$805$.

simplest form of a fraction (p. 187) A fraction is in simplest form if its numerator and denominator have a greatest common factor of 1.

The *simplest form of the fraction* $\frac{6}{8}$ is $\frac{3}{4}$.

mínima expresión de una fracción (pág. 187) Una fracción está en su mínima expresión si el máximo común divisor del numerador y del denominador es 1.

La *mínima expresión de la fracción* $\frac{6}{8}$ es $\frac{3}{4}$.

sine (p. 500) The sine of any acute angle A of a right triangle is the ratio of the opposite leg to the hypotenuse.

seno (pág. 500) El seno de cualquier ángulo agudo A de un triángulo rectángulo es la razón entre el cateto opuesto y la hipotenusa.

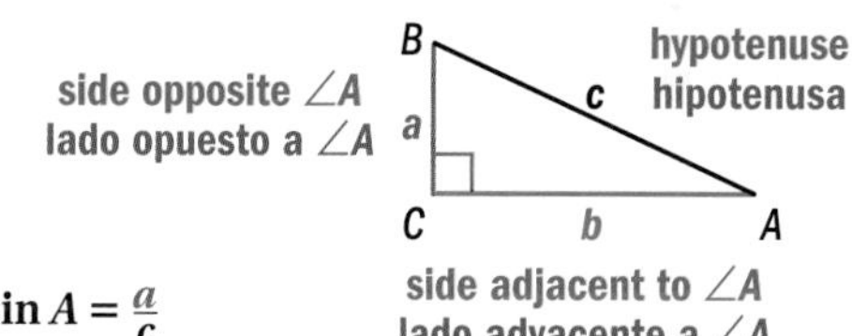

$\sin A = \frac{a}{c}$

slant height (p. 548) The height of any face that is not the base of a regular pyramid.

altura inclinada (pág. 548) En una pirámide regular, la altura de cualquier cara que no sea la base.

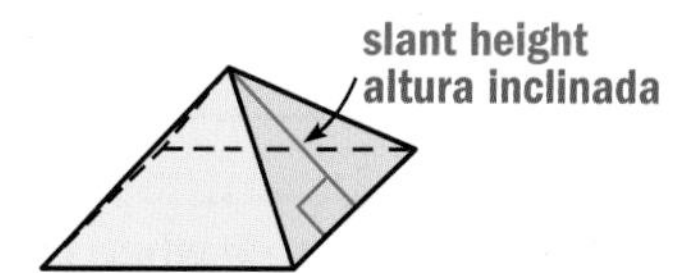

slope (p. 612) The slope of a nonvertical line is the ratio of the rise (vertical change) to the run (horizontal change) between any two points on the line.

pendiente (pág. 612) La pendiente de una recta no vertical es la razón entre la distancia vertical (cambio vertical) y la distancia horizontal (cambio horizontal) entre dos puntos cualesquiera de la recta.

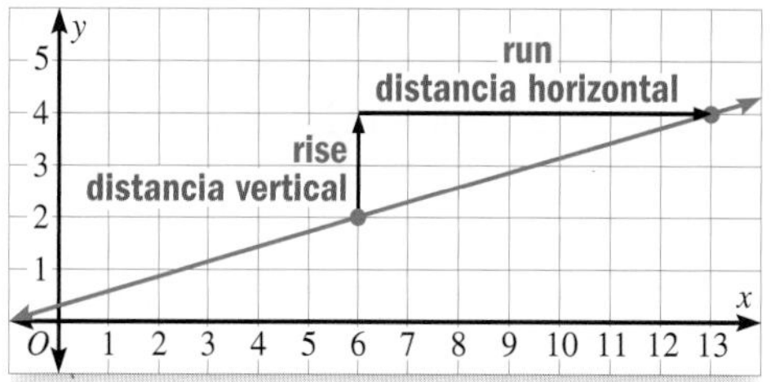

The *slope* of the line above is:

$$\text{slope} = \frac{\text{rise}}{\text{run}} = \frac{2}{7}$$

La *pendiente* de la recta anterior es:

$$\text{pendiente} = \frac{\text{distancia vertical}}{\text{distancia horizontal}} = \frac{2}{7}$$

slope-intercept form (p. 622) The form of a linear equation $y = mx + b$ where m is the slope and b is the y-intercept.

$y = 6x + 8$ is in *slope-intercept form*.

forma de pendiente e intersección (pág. 622) La forma de una ecuación lineal $y = mx + b$, donde m es la pendiente y b es la intersección en y.

$y = 6x + 8$ está en la *forma de pendiente e intersección*.

solid (p. 534) A three-dimensional figure that encloses a part of space. **cuerpo geométrico** (pág. 534) Figura tridimensional que encierra una parte del espacio.	*See* cone, cylinder, prism, pyramid, *and* sphere. *Véase* cono, cilindro, prisma, pirámide *y* esfera.
solution of a linear system (p. 627) An ordered pair that is a solution of each equation in a system of linear equations. **solución de un sistema lineal** (pág. 627) Un par ordenado que es la solución de cada ecuación en un sistema de ecuaciones lineales.	The *solution of the linear system* below is (3,3). $3y - x = 6$ $3y + 2x = 15$ La *solución del sistema lineal* a continuación es (3,3). $3y - x = 6$ $3y + 2x = 15$
solution of an equation (p. 26) A number that makes the equation true when substituted for the variable in the equation. **solución de una ecuación** (pág. 26) Número que hace verdadera la ecuación cuando sustituye la variable en la ecuación.	The *solution of the equation* $n - 3 = 4$ is 7. La *solución de la ecuación* $n - 3 = 4$ es 7.
solution of an equation in two variables (p. 593) An ordered pair (x, y) that makes the equation true when the values of x and y are substituted into the equation. **solución de una ecuación con dos variables** (pág. 593) Un par ordenado (x, y) que hace verdadera la ecuación cuando se sustituyen los valores de x e y en la ecuación.	(3, 8) is a *solution* of $y = 3x - 1$. (3, 8) es una *solución* de $y = 3x - 1$.
solution of an inequality (p. 148) The set of all numbers that make the inequality true when substituted for the variable in the inequality. **solución de una desigualdad** (pág. 148) Conjunto de todos los números que hacen verdadera la desigualdad cuando sustituyen la variable en la desigualdad.	The *solution of the inequality* $y + 2 > 5$ is $y > 3$. La *solución de la desigualdad* $y + 2 > 5$ es $y > 3$.
solution of a linear inequality (p. 629) An ordered pair (x, y) that makes the inequality true when the values of x and y are substituted into the inequality. **solución de una desigualdad lineal** (pág. 629) Un par ordenado (x, y) que hace verdadera la desigualdad cuando los valores de x e y se sustituyen en la desigualdad.	A *solution* of $y \geq 2x - 9$ is (5, 1). La *solución* de $y \geq 2x - 9$ es (5, 1).
solving an equation (p. 26) Finding all solutions of the equation by using mental math or the properties of equality. **resolver una ecuación** (pág. 26) Hallar todas las soluciones de la ecuación usando el cálculo mental o las propiedades de igualdad.	To *solve the equation* $4x = 20$, find the number that can be multiplied by 4 to equal 20; $4(5) = 20$, so the solution is 5. Para *resolver la ecuación* $4x = 20$, halla el número que multiplicado por 4 sea igual a 20; $4(5) = 20$, por lo tanto la solución es 5.

sphere (p. 534) A solid formed by all points in space that are the same distance from a fixed point called the center.

esfera (pág. 534) Cuerpo geométrico formado por todos los puntos en el espacio que se encuentran a la misma distancia de un punto fijo llamado centro.

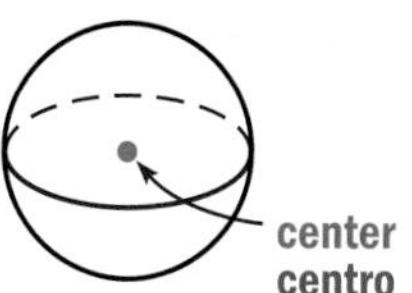

square root (p. 469) A square root of number n is a number m which, when multiplied by itself, equals n.

raíz cuadrada (pág. 469) La raíz cuadrada de un número n es un número m, el cual, cuando se multiplica por sí mismo, es igual a n.

The *square roots* of 81 are 9 and −9 because $9^2 = 81$ and $(-9)^2 = 81$.

Las *raíces cuadradas* de 81 son 9 y −9 porque $9^2 = 81$ y $(-9)^2 = 81$.

standard form (p. 717) A polynomial written with the exponents of the variable decreasing from left to right.

forma estándar (pág. 717) Polinomio escrito con los exponentes de la variable en orden descendente de izquierda a derecha.

$3x^5 - 8x^3 + 5x^2 + x - 2$ is in *standard form.*

$3x^5 - 8x^3 + 5x^2 + x - 2$ está en *forma estándar.*

stem-and-leaf plot (p. 649) A data display that helps you see how data values are distributed. Each data value is separated into a leaf (the last digit) and a stem (the remaining digits). In an ordered stem-and-leaf plot, the leaves for each stem are listed in order from least to greatest.

diagrama de tallo y hojas (pág. 649) Diagrama que muestra cómo se distribuyen los valores en un conjunto de datos. Cada valor está separado en una hoja (el último dígito) y un tallo (los dígitos restantes). En un diagrama de tallo y hojas ordenado, las hojas para cada tallo están en orden de menor a mayor.

stems/tallos	leaves/hojas
10	8
11	2 2 5
12	1 3

Key/Clave: 10 | 8 = 108

straight angle (p. 403) An angle whose measure is exactly 180°.

ángulo llano (pág. 403) Ángulo que mide exactamente 180°.

subtraction property of equality (p. 117) Subtracting the same number from each side of an equation produces an equivalent equation.

propiedad de igualdad en la resta (pág. 117) Al restar el mismo número de cada lado de la ecuación se obtiene una ecuación equivalente.

If $x + 7 = 9$, then $x + 7 - 7 = 9 - 7$, so $x = 2$.
If $x + a = b$, then $x + a - a = b - a$.

Si $x + 7 = 9$, entonces $x + 7 - 7 = 9 - 7$, por lo tanto $x = 2$.
Si $x + a = b$, entonces $x + a - a = b - a$.

supplementary angles (p. 403) Two angles whose measures have a sum of 180°.

ángulos suplementarios (pág. 403) Dos ángulos cuyas medidas suman 180°.

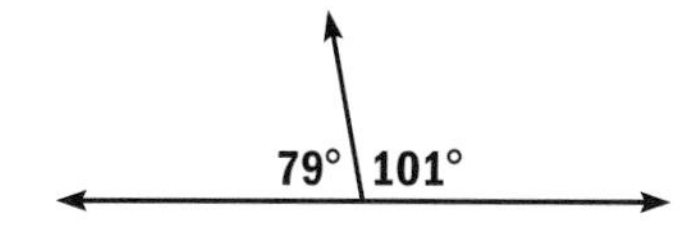

surface area of a polyhedron (p. 543) The sum of the areas of the faces of the polyhedron. **área de la superficie de un poliedro** (pág. 543) La suma de las áreas de las caras del poliedro.	3 in./3 pulg. 4 in./4 pulg. 6 in./6 pulg. *Surface area* $= 2(6)(4) + 2(6)(3) + 2(4)(3)$ $= 108$ in.^{2} *Área de la superficie* $= 2(6)(4) + 2(6)(3) + 2(4)(3)$ $= 108$ pulg.^{2}
system of linear equations (p. 627) A set of two or more linear equations with the same variables. **sistema de ecuaciones lineales** (pág. 627) Un conjunto de dos o más ecuaciones lineales con las mismas variables.	$3y - x = 6$ $3y + 2x = 15$

T

tangent (p. 500) The tangent of any acute angle A of a right triangle is the ratio of the opposite leg to the adjacent leg. **tangente** (pág. 500) La tangente de cualquier ángulo agudo A de un triángulo rectángulo es la razón entre el cateto opuesto y el cateto adyacente.	B, C, A, a, b, c side opposite $\angle A$ lado opuesto a $\angle A$ hypotenuse hipotenusa side adjacent to $\angle A$ lado adyacente a $\angle A$ $\tan A = \frac{a}{b}$
terminating decimal (p. 255) A decimal that has a final digit. **decimal exacto** (pág. 255) Decimal que tiene un dígito final.	0.4 and 3.6125 are *terminating decimals.* 0.4 y 3.6125 son *decimales exactos.*
terms of an expression (p. 89) The parts of an expression that are added together. **términos de una expresión** (pág. 89) Las partes de una expresión que se suman entre sí.	The *terms* of $2x + 3$ are $2x$ and 3. Los *términos* de $2x + 3$ son $2x$ y 3.
tessellation (p. 445) A covering of a plane with congruent copies of the same pattern so that there are no gaps or overlaps. **teselado** (pág. 445) La cobertura de un plano con copias congruentes del mismo patrón de modo que no haya huecos o superposiciones.	

theoretical probability (p. 381) When all outcomes are equally likely, the theoretical probability of an event is the ratio of the number of favorable outcomes to the number of possible outcomes. **probabilidad teórica** (pág. 381) Cuando todos los resultados son igualmente probables, la probabilidad teórica de un evento es la razón entre el número de resultados favorables y el número de resultados posibles.	A bag of 20 marbles contains 7 red marbles. The *theoretical probability* of randomly choosing a red marble is: $P(\text{red}) = \frac{7}{20} = 0.35$ Una bolsa de 20 canicas contiene 7 canicas rojas. La *probabilidad teórica* de tomar al azar una canica roja es: $P(\text{roja}) = \frac{7}{20} = 0.35$
transformation (p. 433) An operation that changes a figure into another figure, called the image. **transformación** (pág. 433) Operación que convierte una figura en otra figura, llamada imagen.	*See* translation, reflection, *and* rotation. *Véase* traslación, reflexión *y* rotación.
translation (p. 439) A transformation that moves each point of a figure the same distance in the same direction; also known as a *slide*. **traslación** (pág. 439) Transformación que mueve cada punto de una figura la misma distancia en la misma dirección.	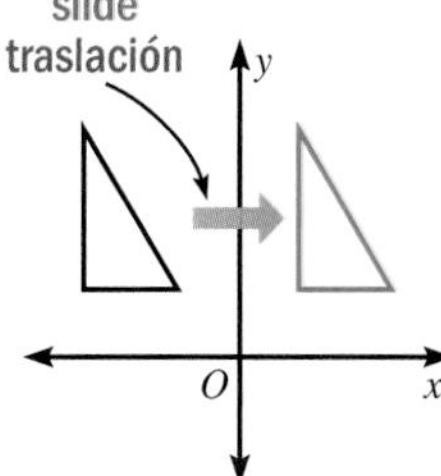
trapezoid (p. 416) A quadrilateral with exactly one pair of parallel sides. **trapecio** (pág. 416) Cuadrilátero que tiene exactamente un par de lados paralelos.	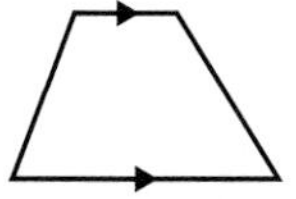
tree diagram (p. 670) A branching diagram that shows all the possible choices or outcomes of a process carried out in several stages. **diagrama de árbol** (pág. 670) Diagrama ramificado que muestra todas las opciones o resultados posibles de un proceso llevado a cabo en varias etapas.	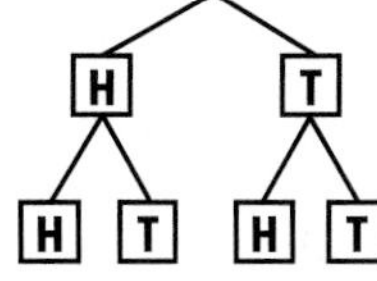 Outcomes: HH, HT, TH, TT Resultados: HH, HT, TH, TT
trigonometric ratio (p. 500) A ratio of the lengths of two sides of a right triangle. **razón trigonométrica** (pág. 500) Razón entre las longitudes de dos lados de un triángulo rectángulo.	*See* sine, cosine, *and* tangent. *Véase* seno, coseno *y* tangente.
trinomial (p. 717) A polynomial with three terms. **trinomio** (pág. 717) Polinomio que tiene tres términos.	$3x^2 + 2x - 4$

ENGLISH-SPANISH GLOSSARY

U

unfavorable outcome (p. 686) An outcome that is not a favorable outcome. **resultado desfavorable** (pág. 686) Resultado que no es un resultado favorable.	*See* favorable outcome. *Véase* resultado favorable.
union (p. 690) The set of all elements in *either* set A or set B, written as $A \cup B$. **unión de conjuntos** (pág. 690) El conjunto que incluye todos los elementos del conjunto A y el conjunto B, que se expresa como $A \cup B$.	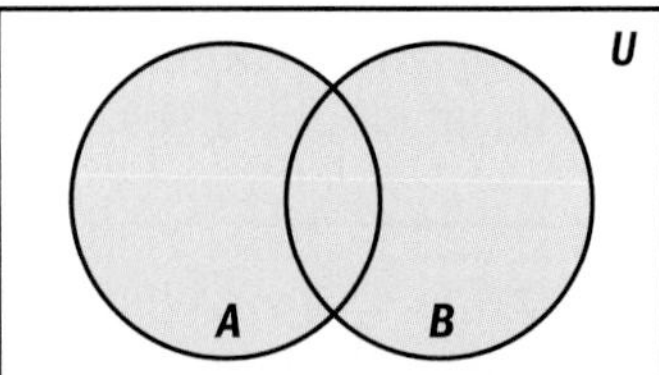
unit analysis (p. 39) Evaluate expressions with units of measure and check that your answer uses correct units. **análisis de unidades** (pág. 39) Hallar el valor de expresiones con unidades de medida y comprobar que la respuesta usa unidades correctas.	$\frac{\text{miles}}{\cancel{\text{hour}}} \cdot \cancel{\text{hours}} = \text{miles}$ $\frac{\text{millas}}{\cancel{\text{hora}}} \cdot \cancel{\text{horas}} = \text{millas}$
unit rate (p. 344) A rate that has a denominator of 1 unit. **tasa unitaria** (pág. 344) Una tasa cuyo denominador es 1 unidad.	$9 per hour is a *unit rate.* $9 por hora es una *tasa unitaria.*
universal set (p. 688) The set of all elements under consideration, written as U. **conjunto universal** (pág. 688) El conjunto de todos los elementos bajo consideración que se expresa como U.	If the universal set is the set of positive integers, then $U = \{1, 2, 3, \ldots\}$. Si el conjunto universal es el conjunto de los números enteros positivos, entonces $U = \{1, 2, 3, \ldots\}$.
upper extreme (p. 654) The greatest value in a data set. **extremo superior** (pág. 654) El valor mayor en un conjunto de datos.	*See* box-and-whisker plot. *Véase* diagrama de líneas y bloques.
upper quartile (p. 654) The median of the upper half of a data set. **cuartil superior** (pág. 654) La mediana de la mitad superior de un conjunto de datos.	*See* box-and-whisker plot. *Véase* diagrama de líneas y bloques.

V

variable (p. 13) A symbol, usually a letter, that is used to represent one or more numbers. **variable** (pág. 13) Símbolo, usualmente una letra, que se usa para representar uno o más números.	In the expression $m + 5$, the letter m is the *variable.* En la expresión $m + 5$, la letra m es la *variable.*

variable expression (p. 13) An expression that consists of numbers, variables, and operations. **expresión variable** (pág. 13) Expresión compuesta de números, variables y operaciones.	$n - 3, \frac{2s}{t}$, and $x + 4yz + 1$ are *variable expressions.* $n - 3, \frac{2s}{t}$ y $x + 4yz + 1$ son *expresiones variables.*
Venn diagram (p. 785) A diagram that uses shapes to show how sets are related. **diagrama de Venn** (pág. 785) Un diagrama que usa formas para mostrar cómo se relacionan los conjuntos.	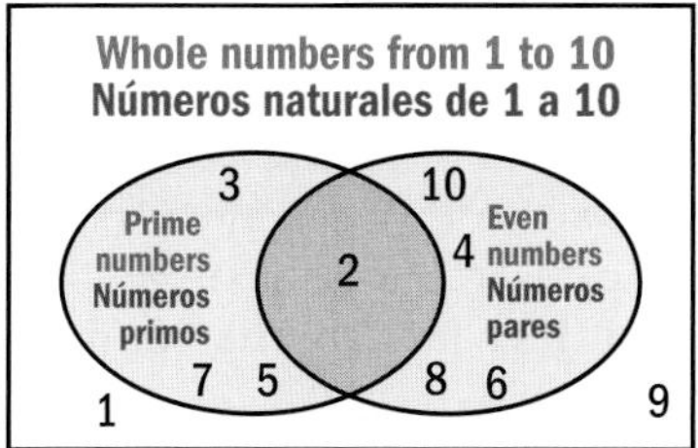
verbal model (p. 9) A word equation that represents a real-world situation. **modelo verbal** (pág. 9) Ecuación en palabras que representa una situación de la vida real.	Distance traveled = Speed of car · Time traveled Distancia recorrida = Velocidad del carro · Tiempo de viaje
vertex (p. 759) The endpoint of the rays that form an angle. **vértice** (p. 759) El extremo de las semirrectas que forman un ángulo.	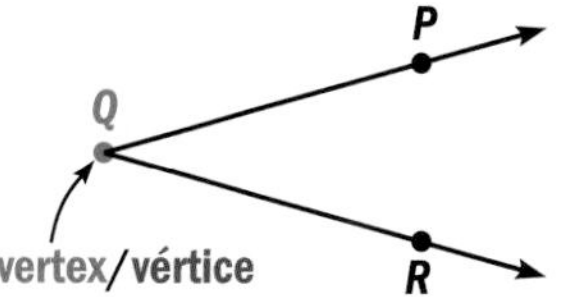
vertex of a polyhedron (p. 534) A point at which three or more edges of a polyhedron meet. **vértice de un poliedro** (pág. 534) Punto en el que se juntan tres o más aristas de un poliedro.	*See* edge of a polyhedron. *Véase* arista de un poliedro.
vertical angles (p. 404) A pair of opposite angles formed when two lines meet at a point. **ángulos opuestos por el vértice** (pág. 404) Par de ángulos opuestos entre sí formados por dos rectas que se intersecan.	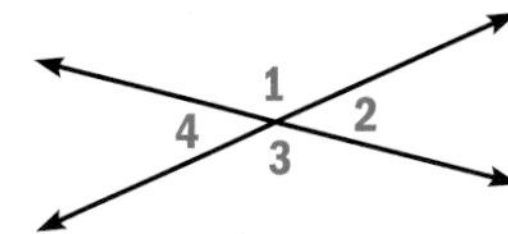 $\angle 1$ and $\angle 3$ are *vertical angles.* $\angle 2$ and $\angle 4$ are also *vertical angles.* $\angle 1$ y $\angle 3$ son *ángulos opuestos por el vértice.* $\angle 2$ y $\angle 4$ también son *ángulos opuestos por el vértice.*
vertical line test (p. 740) If the vertical line intersects a graph at more than one point, then the graph does not represent a function. **prueba de la línea vertical** (pág. 740) Si una recta vertical interseca una gráfica en más de un punto, entonces la gráfica no representa una función.	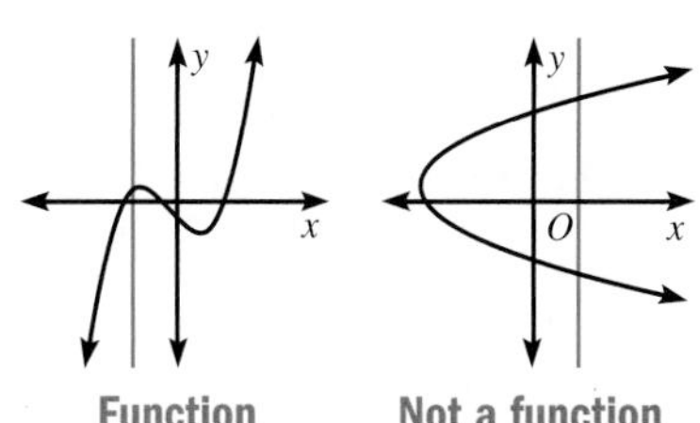

ENGLISH-SPANISH GLOSSARY

volume of a solid (p. 554) The amount of space the solid occupies.

volumen de un cuerpo geométrico (pág. 554) Cantidad de espacio que ocupa un cuerpo geométrico.

2 m

3 m

Volume $= \pi r^2 h \approx (3.14)(2)^2(3) \approx 37.7 \text{ m}^3$

Volumen $= \pi r^2 h \approx (3.14)(2)^2(3) \approx 37.7 \text{ m}^3$

W

whole numbers (p. 759) The numbers 0, 1, 2, 3, . . .

números naturales (pág. 759) Los números 0, 1, 2, 3, ...

X

***x*-axis** (p. 94) The horizontal number line in a coordinate plane.

eje *x* (pág. 94) La recta numérica horizontal en un plano de coordenadas.

See coordinate plane.

Véase plano de coordenadas.

***x*-coordinate** (p. 94) The first number in an ordered pair representing a point in the coordinate plane.

coordenada *x* (pág. 94) El primer número en un par ordenado que representa un punto en un plano de coordenadas.

The *x-coordinate* of the ordered pair $(-2, 1)$ is -2.

La *coordenada x* del par ordenado $(-2, 1)$ es -2.

***x*-intercept** (p. 606) The *x*-coordinate of the point where the graph intersects the *x*-axis.

intersección en *x* (pág. 606) La coordenada *x* del punto donde la gráfica interseca el eje *x*.

The *x*-intercept is **4**.
La intersección en *x* es **4**.

Y

***y*-axis** (p. 94) The vertical number line in a coordinate plane.

eje *y* (pág. 94) La recta numérica vertical en un plano de coordenadas.

See coordinate plane.

Véase plano de coordenadas.

***y*-coordinate** (p. 94) The second number in an ordered pair representing a point in a coordinate plane.

coordenada *y* (pág. 94) El segundo número en un par ordenado que representa un punto en un plano de coordenadas.

The *y-coordinate* of the ordered pair $(-2, 1)$ is 1.

La *coordenada y* del par ordenado $(-2, 1)$ es 1.

y-intercept (p. 606) The y-coordinate of the point where the graph intersects the y-axis.

intersección en y (pág. 606) La coordenada y del punto donde la gráfica interseca el eje y.

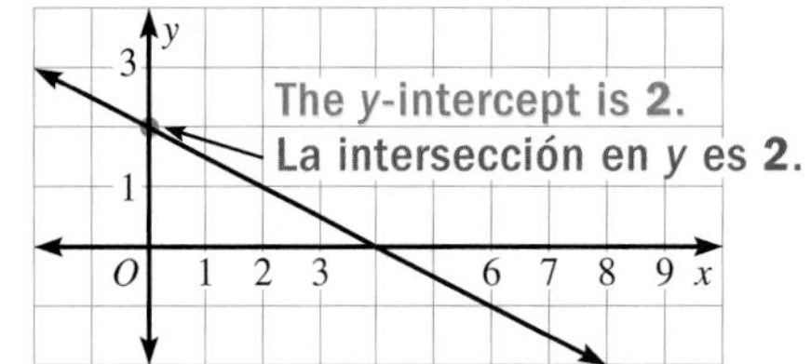

ENGLISH-SPANISH GLOSSARY

Index

A

INDEX

B

INDEX

C

D

E

G

H

I

INDEX

J

K

L

N

O

P

INDEX

S

Z

INDEX

Contents of Appendices

Appendix 1 Use after Lesson 8.5

KEY VOCABULARY
- **midpoint,** *p. 883*
- **segment bisector,** *p. 883*
- **perpendicular bisector,** *p. 883*
- **angle bisector,** *p. 885*

More Constructions

GOAL Construct geometric figures.

You can use a compass and straightedge to make a copy of a segment. This construction is shown in the following example.

EXAMPLE 1 Copying a Segment

STEP 1 **Draw** any segment AB. Then draw a ray with endpoint C.

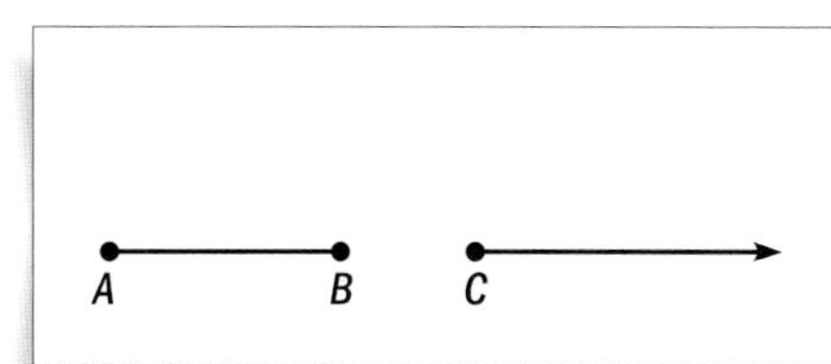

STEP 2 **Draw** an arc with center A that passes through B. Using the same compass setting, draw an arc with center C as shown. Label D. $\overline{CD}$ and $\overline{AB}$ have the same length.

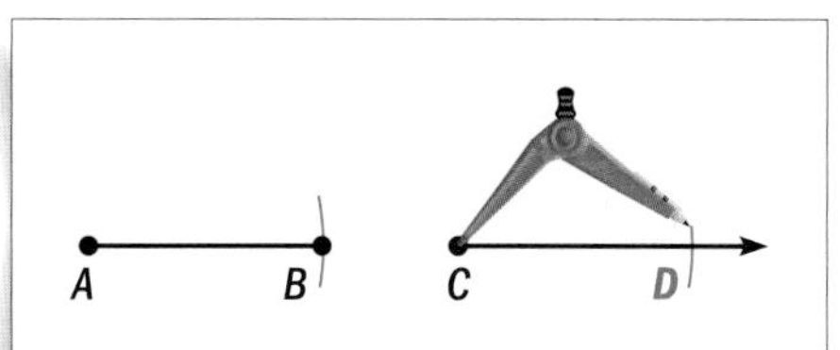

Midpoints and Bisectors The **midpoint** of a segment is the point that divides the segment into two congruent segments. A **segment bisector** is a segment, ray, line, or plane that intersects a segment at its midpoint. A segment bisector that is perpendicular to a segment is called a **perpendicular bisector**.

EXAMPLE 2 Constructing a Perpendicular Bisector

STEP 1 **Draw** any segment AB. Using a compass setting greater than half the length of $\overline{AB}$, draw an arc with center A.

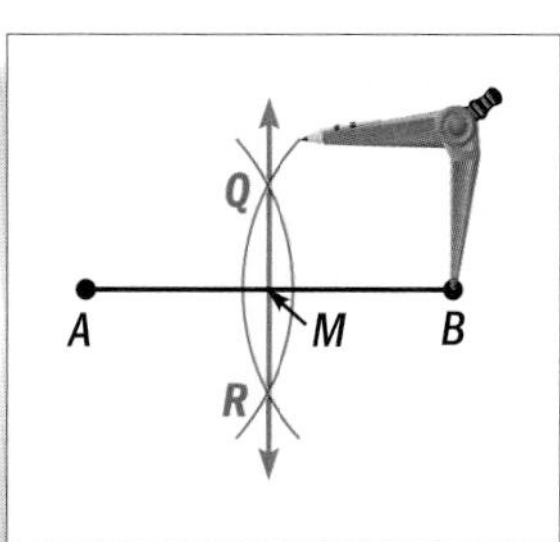

STEP 2 **Keep** the same compass setting. Draw an arc with center B so that it intersects the first arc two times. Label the intersections Q and R.

STEP 3 **Draw** $\overleftrightarrow{QR}$. This line is perpendicular to $\overline{AB}$ and bisects $\overline{AB}$ at M, the midpoint of $\overline{AB}$. $\overleftrightarrow{QR}$ is a perpendicular bisector of $\overline{AB}$.

Check Use a protractor to check that $m\angle QMB = 90°$. Use a ruler to check that $AM = MB$.

APPENDIX 1

Drawing Any Bisector Once you have found the midpoint M of a segment using the process from Example 2, you can draw *any* bisector of the segment, including bisectors that are not perpendicular to the segment. In the diagram shown at the right, for example, $\overline{XY}$, $\overleftrightarrow{KP}$, and $\overrightarrow{ML}$ are all segment bisectors of $\overline{AB}$.

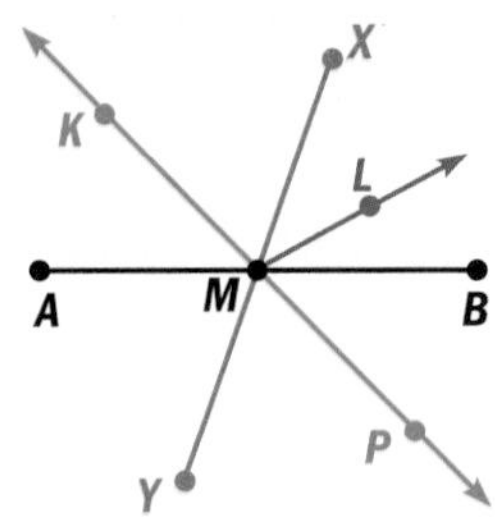

Using Technology In addition to using a compass and straightedge to perform constructions, you can also use geometry drawing software on a graphing calculator or computer.

EXAMPLE 3 Constructing a Perpendicular Through a Point

METHOD 1 ***Using Compass and Straightedge***

STEP 1 **Draw** a line and a point P on the line. Draw an arc with center P that intersects the line twice. Label A and B. Using a compass setting greater than AP, draw arcs with centers A and B.

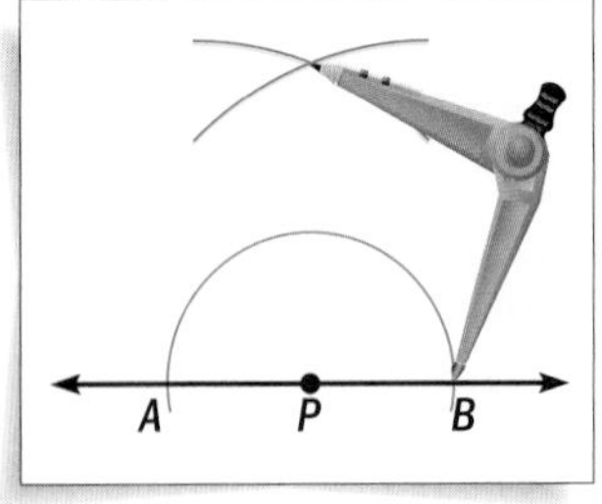

STEP 2 **Label** the point Q where the last two arcs intersect. Draw a line through P and Q. Lines PQ and AB are perpendicular.

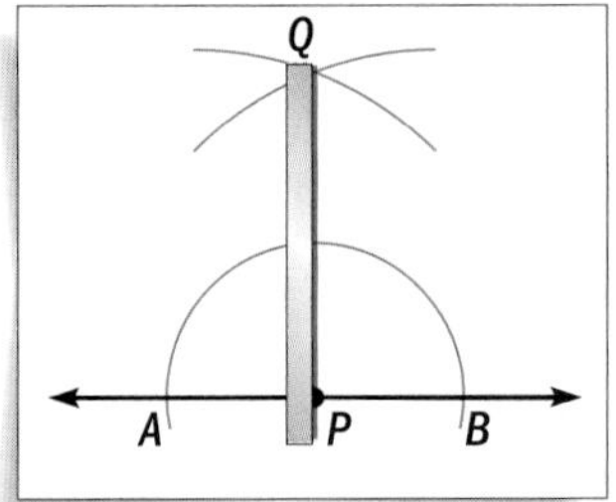

METHOD 2 ***Using Technology***

Note: The directions shown use Cabri® Jr. software on a graphing calculator.

STEP 1 **Use** the F2 menu to draw a *Line.* Choose *Point on* from the F2 menu and select the line to add a point on your line. Label the point A.

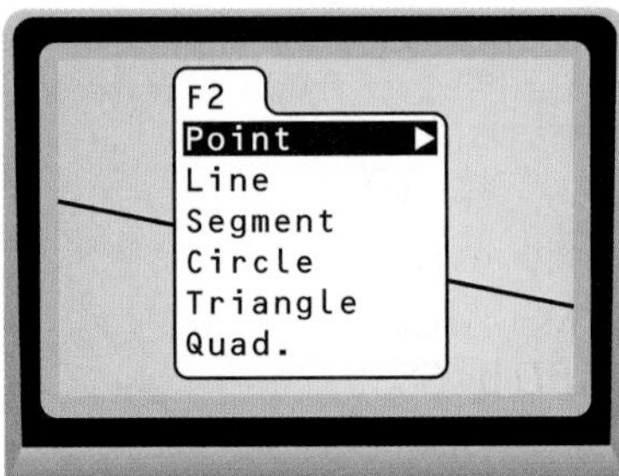

STEP 2 **Choose** *Perp.* from the F3 menu and select the line and then point A. The line constructed will be perpendicular to your line and pass through point A.

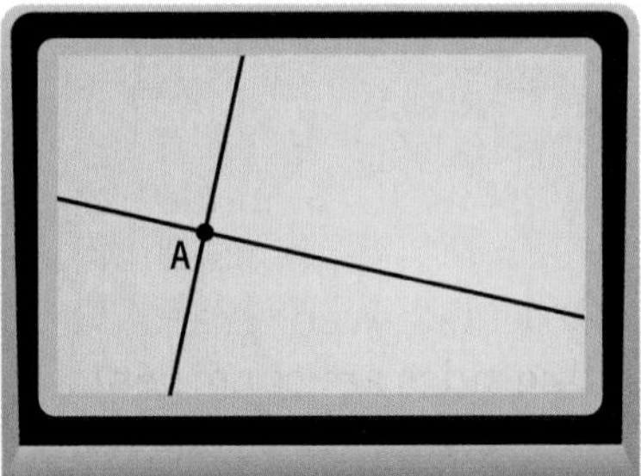

Angle Bisectors An **angle bisector** is a ray that divides an angle into two adjacent angles that are congruent. *Adjacent angles* are angles that share a common side and vertex but have no common interior points.

EXAMPLE 4 Constructing an Angle Bisector

STEP 1 **Draw** any angle A. Using any compass setting, draw an arc with center A that intersects the sides of $\angle A$ as shown. Label B and C.

STEP 2 **Use** any compass setting to draw an arc with center B. Using the same compass setting, draw an arc with center C that intersects the first arc as shown. Label the intersection D.

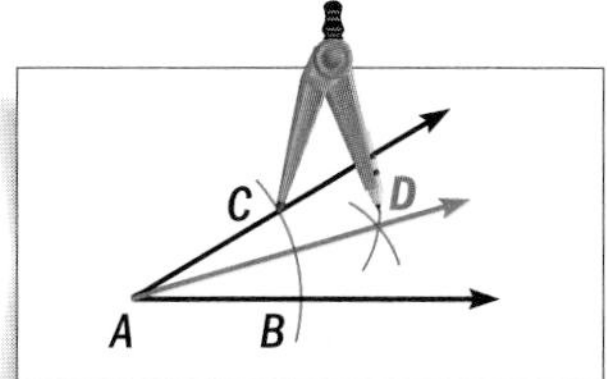

STEP 3 **Draw** a ray through A and D. This is the angle bisector. $\overrightarrow{AD}$ bisects $\angle A$, so $\angle CAD \cong \angle BAD$.

Triangles and Constructions In many of the constructions in this book, you created some sort of figure involving three points: for example, the vertex of an angle and two points along the angle's sides, or the two endpoints of a segment and a third point above or below the segment. These three points form an actual or possible triangle.

In some cases, you have used the same sequence of compass settings to create two (or more) congruent triangles. Recall that you can use Side-Side-Side (SSS), Side-Angle-Side (SAS), and Angle-Side-Angle (ASA) to tell whether two triangles are congruent. (See page 428 for more explanation.)

EXAMPLE 5 Using Congruent Triangles

Look back at the construction of an angle bisector in Example 4 above. Identify two congruent triangles in Step 3 of the construction and explain how you know they are congruent. Use the congruent triangles to verify that the ray constructed is the angle bisector.

SOLUTION

In Step 3 of Example 4 above, two triangles can be drawn: $\triangle ACD$ and $\triangle ABD$. You used one arc with center A to mark both points C and B, so $\overline{AB} \cong \overline{AC}$. You used the same compass setting to draw arcs from C and B to mark point D, so $\overline{BD} \cong \overline{CD}$. A side is congruent to itself, so $\overline{AD} \cong \overline{AD}$. So, three pairs of corresponding sides are congruent, and $\triangle ACD \cong \triangle ABD$ by SSS. Because all corresponding parts of congruent triangles are congruent, you can conclude that $\angle CAD \cong \angle BAD$ and so $\overrightarrow{AD}$ does bisect $\angle A$.

PRACTICE

Trace $\overline{AB}$. Then use a compass and straightedge to copy $\overline{AB}$. Construct (a) the perpendicular bisector of $\overline{AB}$ and (b) a segment bisector of $\overline{AB}$ that is not perpendicular to $\overline{AB}$. Identify the midpoint as M.

1. 

2. 

Trace $\overline{WX}$. Then use a compass and straightedge to copy $\overline{WX}$, and draw a point P on $\overline{WX}$. Then construct a line that passes through P and is perpendicular to $\overline{WX}$.

3. W P X

4. 

Trace the angle. Then use a compass and straightedge to copy the angle. Then construct its angle bisector.

5. 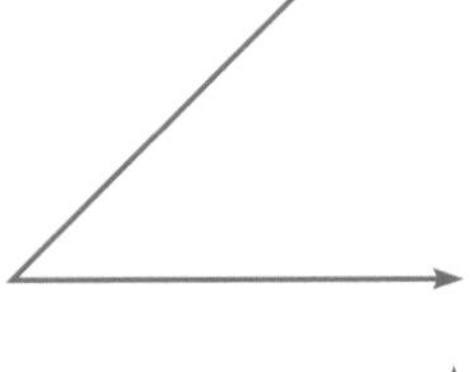

6. 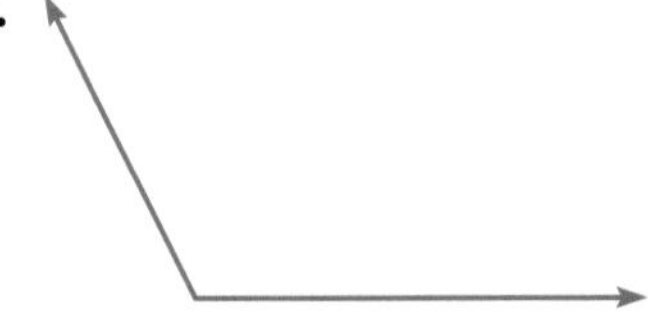

7. 

8.

9. Look back at the construction for copying an angle in Example 1 in the Extension on page 409.
   a. Identify any congruent triangles in Step 4.
   b. *Explain* how you know that they are congruent.

10. Look back at the construction of a perpendicular bisector in Example 2 on page 883.
    a. Identify two possible triangles in Step 3 that are congruent.
    b. *Explain* how you know that they are congruent.
    c. Are there any other pairs of congruent triangles in this situation? *Explain* your reasoning.

11. **TECHNOLOGY** Look back at the construction of parallel lines in Example 3 on page 410.
    a. *Describe* the steps you would take to draw two parallel lines using technology instead of a compass and straightedge.
    b. What are the advantages of each method? *Explain* your reasoning.

Appendix 2 *Use after Lesson 8.8*

KEY VOCABULARY
- **scale factor,** *p. 887*

Scale Factors, Similarity, and Congruence

GOAL Understand the relationship between similarity and congruence. Understand the relationships among scale factors, length ratios, and area ratios.

In Chapter 8, you learned that congruent polygons have the same shape and same size, and that similar polygons have the same shape but not necessarily the same size. So, you can see that congruence is a special case of similarity.

EXAMPLE 1 Distinguishing Between Similarity and Congruence

Tell whether the polygons are *similar, congruent,* or *both.*

a.

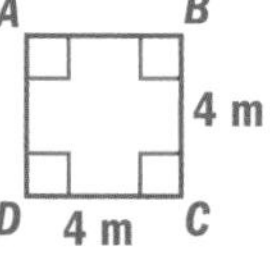

E F
8 m
H 8 m G

b.

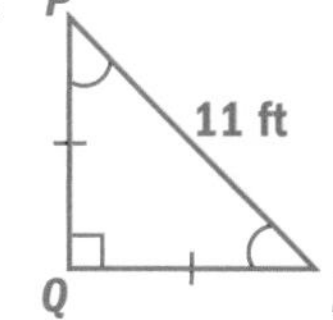

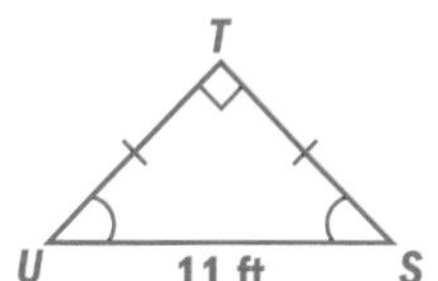

SOLUTION

a. The squares have the same shape. Their side lengths are different, so they do not have the same size. So, *ABCD* and *EFGH* are similar but not congruent.

b. The right triangles have the same shape and the same size. So, $\triangle PQR$ and $\triangle STU$ are both congruent and similar.

Scale Factors If two polygons are similar, then the ratio of the lengths of corresponding sides is called the **scale factor**. Scale factors are written in simplest form.

EXAMPLE 2 Finding a Scale Factor

What is the scale factor of the similar squares in Example 1?

SOLUTION

In part (a) of Example 1, the scale factor of *ABCD* to *EFGH* is $\frac{1}{2}$, because any ratio of corresponding side lengths $\left(\frac{AB}{EF}, \frac{BC}{FG}, \frac{CD}{GH}, \text{ or } \frac{DA}{HE}\right)$ is $\frac{4}{8} = \frac{1}{2}$.

EXAMPLE 3 Finding a Side Length

Two triangles *JKL* and *MNP* are similar with scale factor $\frac{2}{3}$. If $MP = 9$ feet, what is the length of $\overline{JL}$?

SOLUTION

The triangles are similar, so the ratio of any pair of corresponding side lengths will equal the scale factor. Because $\triangle JKL \sim \triangle MNP$, $\overline{JL}$ and $\overline{MP}$ are corresponding sides. You can draw a diagram of the situation.

$\frac{JL}{MP} = \frac{2}{3}$ **Write a proportion.**

$\frac{JL}{9} = \frac{2}{3}$ **Substitute 9 for MP.**

$JL = 6$ **Solve the proportion.**

▶ **Answer** The length of $\overline{JL}$ is 6 feet.

Area Ratios The ratio of the areas of two similar figures is related to the scale factor of the figures.

KEY CONCEPT *For Your Notebook*

Areas of Similar Polygons

Words The ratio of the areas of two similar polygons is the square of the scale factor.

Algebra If two polygons are similar with the lengths of corresponding sides in the ratio of $a : b$, then the ratio of their areas is $a^2 : b^2$.

EXAMPLE 4 Using Area Ratios

Look back at part (a) of Example 1. Verify that the area ratio relationship above is true for the similar squares.

SOLUTION

The area of square *ABCD* is $A = s^2 = 4^2 = 16$.

The area of square *EFGH* is $A = s^2 = 8^2 = 64$.

Recall from Example 2 that the scale factor of the squares is $\frac{1}{2}$.

The ratio of the areas of the squares is $\frac{16}{64} = \frac{1}{4}$, or $\frac{1^2}{2^2}$. ✓

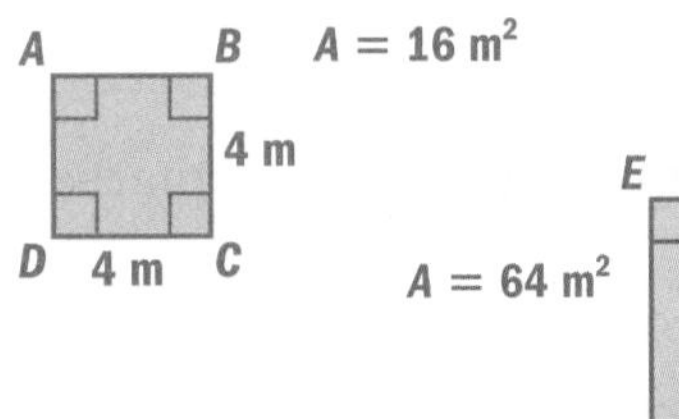

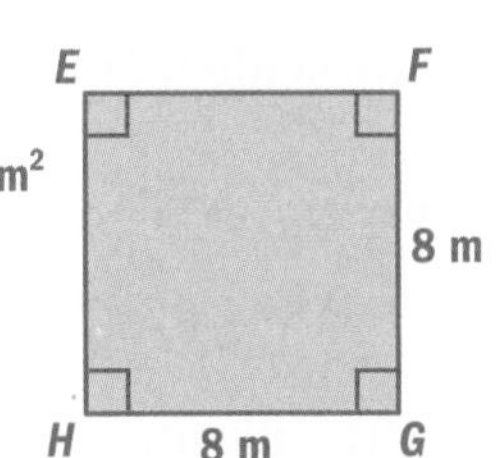

Finding Unknown Areas You can use the area of similar polygons ratio to find an unknown area, as shown in Example 5.

EXAMPLE 5 Finding an Area

Flower Gardens In a city park, one flower bed is a triangle with base 8 yards and area 144 square yards. Another flower bed is a similar triangle with base 6 yards. What is the area of the second garden?

SOLUTION

First draw a diagram to represent the problem. Label any known areas or dimensions.

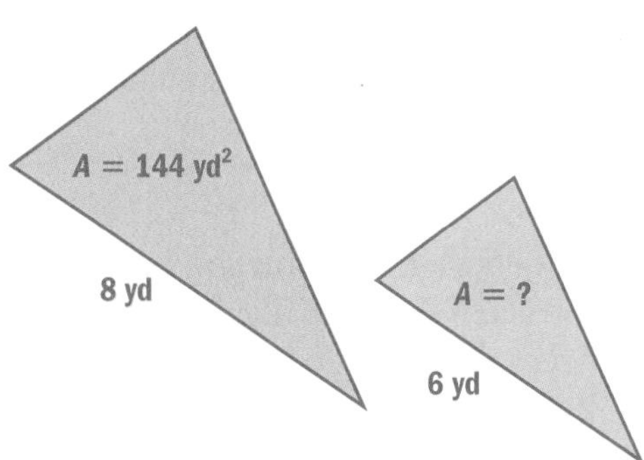

The triangles are similar, so the ratio of their areas is the square of the scale factor. The ratio of corresponding side lengths is 8 : 6, or 4 : 3. So, the ratio of the areas will be $4^2 : 3^2$, or 16 : 9.

$$\frac{\text{Area of larger triangle}}{\text{Area of smaller triangle}} = \frac{16}{9}$$ **Write ratio of areas.**

$$\frac{144}{x} = \frac{16}{9}$$ **Substitute.**

$$x = 81$$ **Solve for *x*.**

▸ **Answer** The area of the smaller flower bed is 81 square yards.

EXAMPLE 6 Using an Area Ratio

Two rectangles are similar, with areas 7 square meters and 28 square meters. The length of the smaller rectangle is 4 meters. What is the length of the larger rectangle?

SOLUTION

The rectangles are similar, so the ratio of their areas is the square of the scale factor. The ratio of the areas is 7 : 28, or 1 : 4. This ratio can be written as $1^2 : 2^2$, so the ratio of corresponding side lengths will be the square root, or 1 : 2.

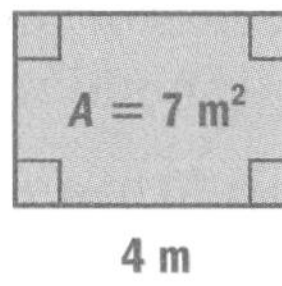

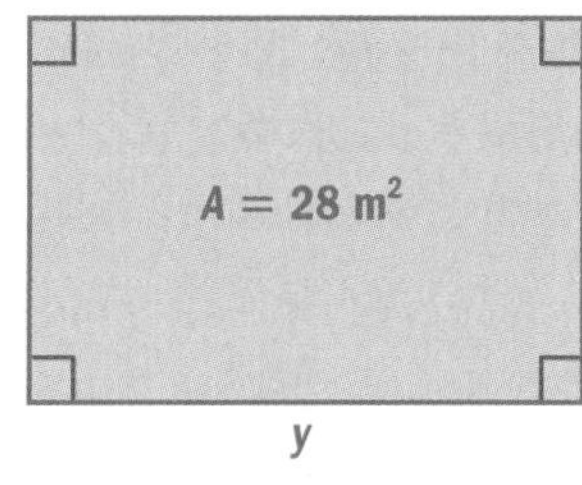

$$\frac{\text{Length of smaller rectangle}}{\text{Length of larger rectangle}} = \frac{1}{2}$$ **Write ratio of lengths.**

$$\frac{4\text{ m}}{y} = \frac{1}{2}$$ **Substitute.**

$$y = 8\text{ m}$$ **Solve for *y*.**

▸ **Answer** The length of the larger rectangle is 8 meters.

APPENDIX 2

PRACTICE

In Exercises 1–3, draw and label a pair of figures that fit the description. If not possible, explain why not.

1. two triangles that are similar, but not congruent
2. two rectangles that are congruent, but not similar
3. two pentagons that are both congruent and similar

In Exercises 4 and 5, copy and complete the statement with *always, sometimes,* or *never. Explain* your reasoning.

4. Two congruent polygons are ___?___ similar.
5. Two similar polygons are ___?___ congruent.
6. **WRITING** A dilation of a polygon produces a congruent polygon. What is the scale factor of the dilation? Give an example to support your answer.

Corresponding lengths in similar figures are given. Find the ratios (red to blue) of the lengths and areas. Then find the unknown area.

7. 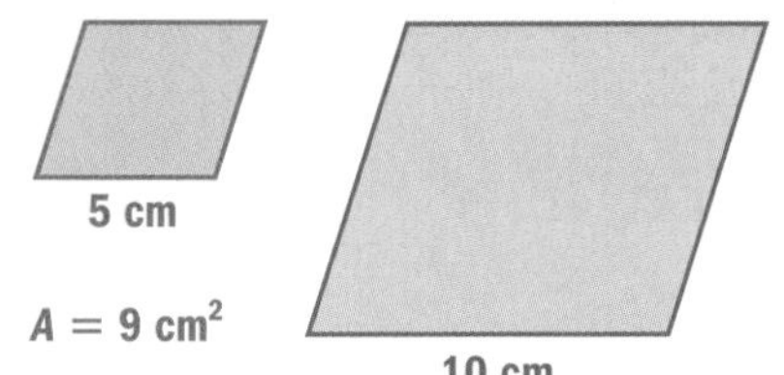

8. 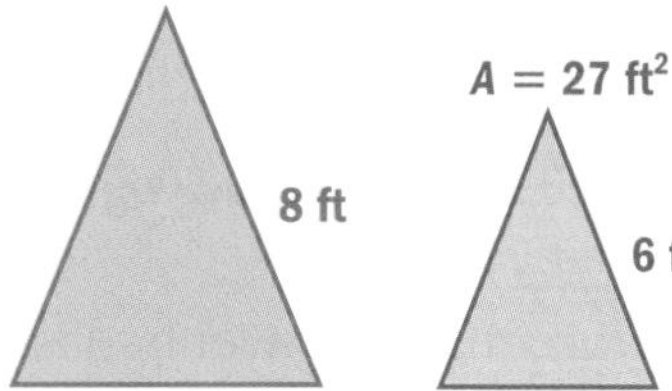

9. 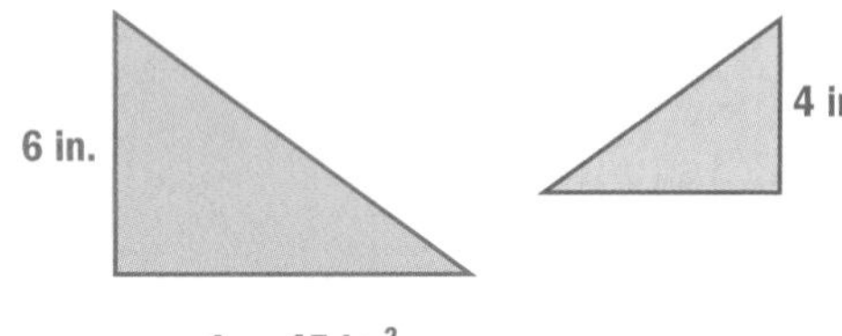

10. 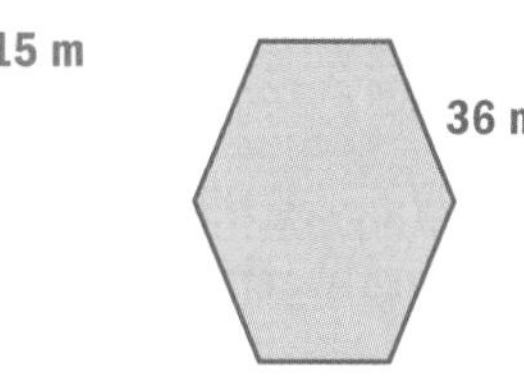

In Exercises 11–13, the ratio of the areas of two similar figures is given. Write the ratio of the lengths of corresponding sides.

11. Ratio of areas $= 4:25$
12. Ratio of areas $= 49:100$
13. Ratio of areas $= 121:9$
14. *Explain* how the ratio of the perimeters of two similar figures is related to the scale factor of the figures. Give an example to support your answer.
15. The radius of one circle is 3 times the radius of another circle. The area of the first circle is 63 square centimeters. What is the area of the second circle?
16. The area of the floor in one rectangular classroom is 320 square feet and the width of the room is 16 feet. The rectangular floor in another classroom is similar to the floor in the first classroom. The area of the floor in the second classroom is 180 square feet. What is the width of the second classroom?

KEY VOCABULARY
- **cross section,** *p. 892*

Solids and Cross Sections

GOAL Describe the formation of solid figures and their cross sections.

In Lesson 10.3, you classified and sketched solids. In the next two examples, you will see how to form solids by translating or rotating a plane figure in space.

EXAMPLE 1 Translating to Form a Solid

Sketch and describe the solid formed by translating the pentagon along the line.

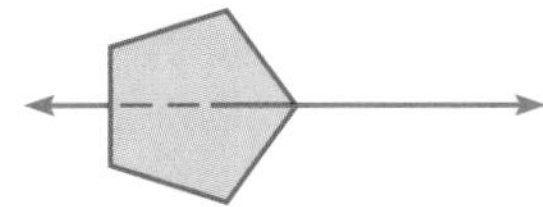

SOLUTION

STEP 1 **Draw** other possible locations where the pentagon could appear after being translated.

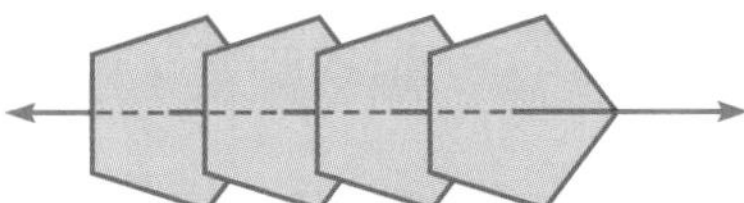

STEP 2 **Use** the drawings in Step 1 to sketch the solid formed by the translated pentagon.

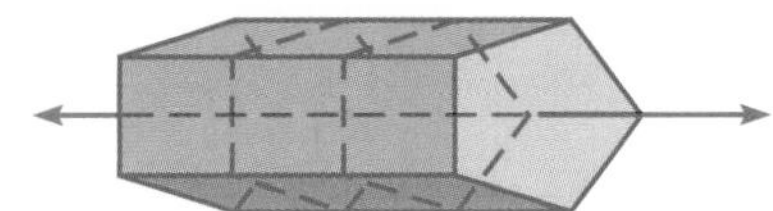

▸ **Answer** The solid formed by translating the pentagon along the line is a pentagonal prism.

EXAMPLE 2 Rotating to Form a Solid

Sketch and describe the solid formed by rotating the square around the line.

SOLUTION

Draw other possible locations where the square could appear after being rotated. Then sketch the solid formed by rotating the square.

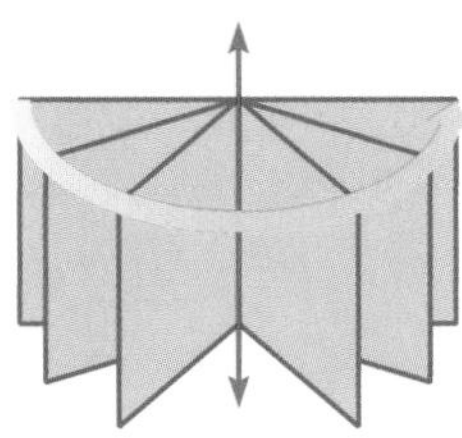

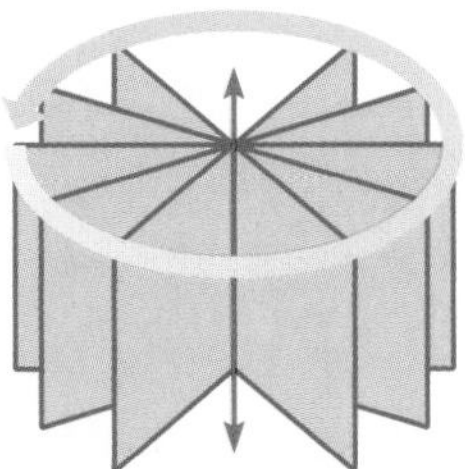

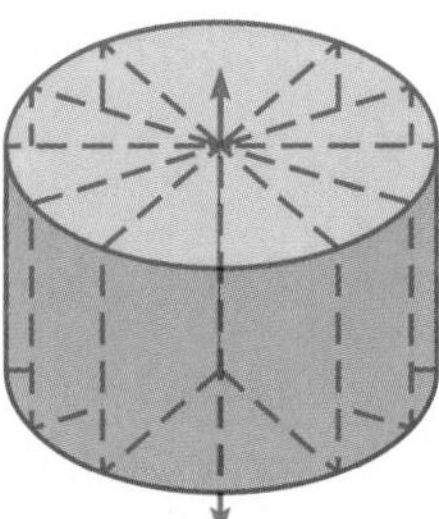

▸ **Answer** The solid formed by rotating the square around the line is a cylinder.

Cross Sections Imagine a plane slicing through a solid. The intersection of the plane and the solid is called a **cross section**. For example, the intersection of the plane and the sphere shown at the right is a circle.

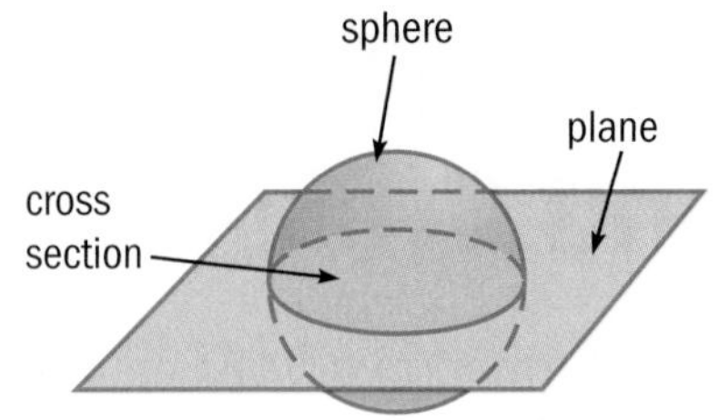

EXAMPLE 3 Describing Cross Sections

Describe the shape formed by the intersection of the plane and the solid.

a.

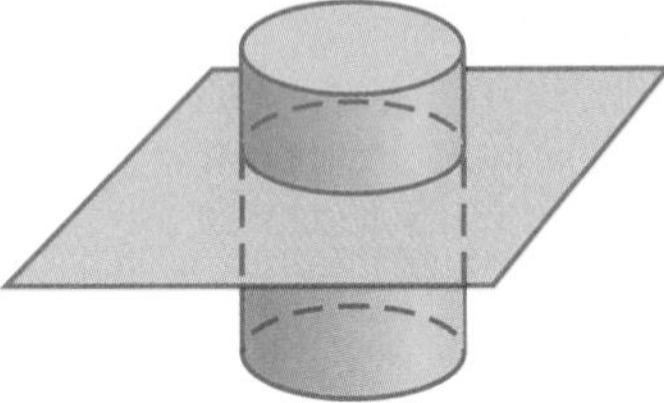

b.

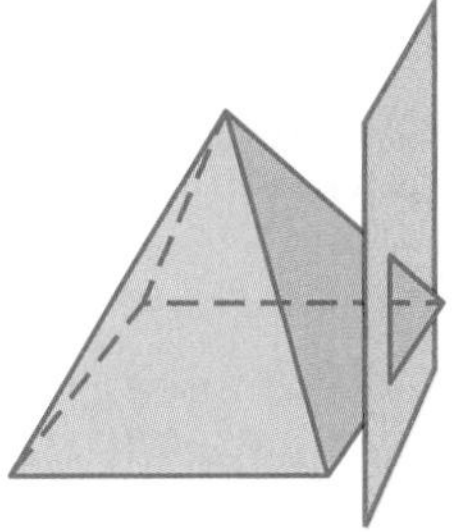

c.

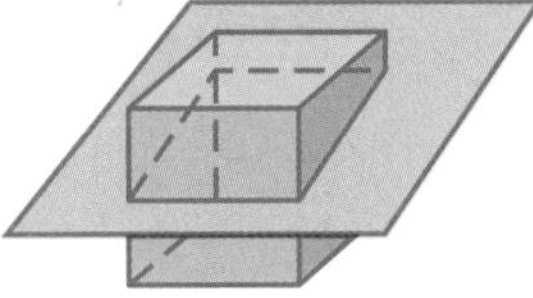

d.

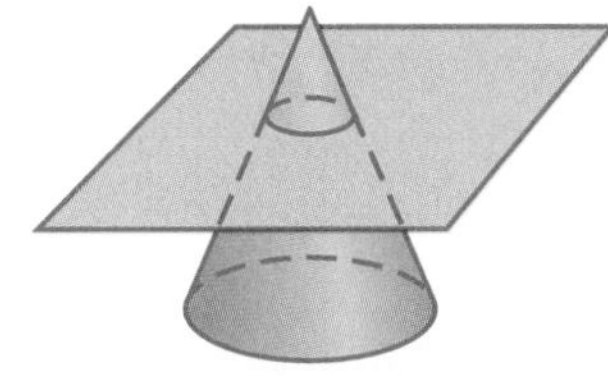

SOLUTION

a. The cross section is a circle.

b. The cross section is a triangle.

c. The cross section is a rectangle.

d. The cross section is a circle.

EXAMPLE 4 Sketching Cross Sections

Sketch the cross section formed by a vertical plane intersecting the front and left faces of a cube. Describe the shape formed.

SOLUTION

STEP 1 **Sketch** the solid. Locate vertices of a possible cross section.

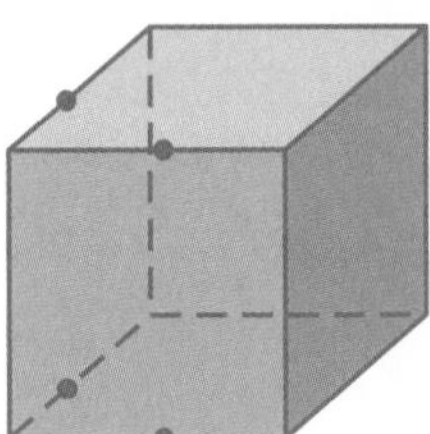

STEP 2 **Draw** the sides of the polygon.

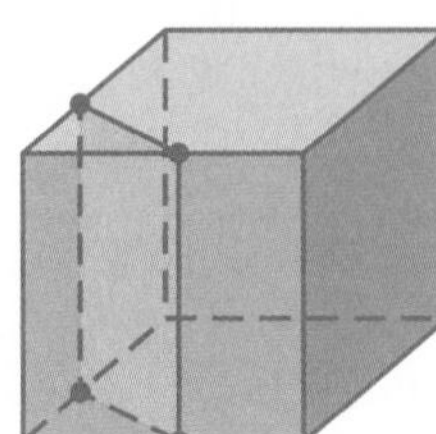

▸ **Answer** The intersection of the plane and cube shown is a rectangle.

PRACTICE

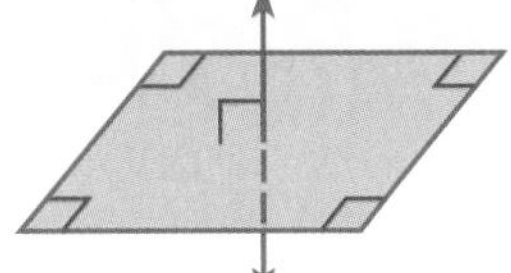

1. Sketch and describe the solid formed by translating the rectangle along the line shown at the right.

2. Are all solids formed by translating a plane figure along a line polyhedrons? *Explain* why or why not.

3. Sketch and describe the solid formed by rotating the triangle around the line shown at the right.

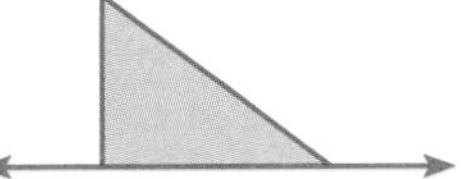

4. In Example 2, you saw that the rotation of a square around a line created a cylinder. Will every square that is rotated around a line form a cylinder? Support your answer with an example.

5. Describe how you can form a sphere by rotating a circle around a line. What must be special about the line?

6. Can you form a pyramid by rotating a plane figure around a line or by translating a plane figure along a line? *Explain* your reasoning.

In Exercises 7–9, describe the shape formed by the intersection of a vertical plane and the solid, through the red point.

7. 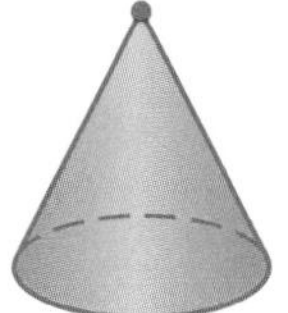

8. 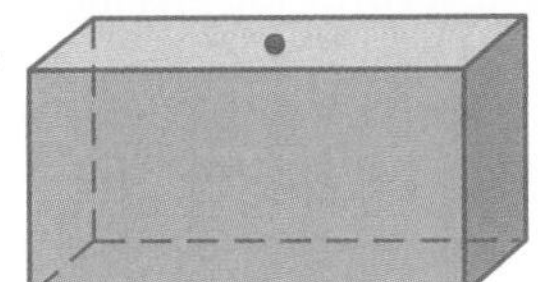

9. 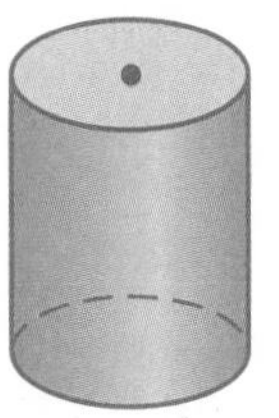

10. Name two shapes that can represent the cross section of a plane and a cone. *Explain* how the shape is formed.

11. Can the cross section of a plane and a polyhedron be a circle? *Explain* your reasoning.

12. *Explain* why the cross sections of the cylinders in Example 3 on page 892 and in Exercise 9 above are different.

13. A plane is parallel to the base of a pyramid and intersects the pyramid's vertex. Sketch and describe the cross section formed.

14. Is it possible for the cross section of a plane and a solid to be a line segment? Support your answer with examples.

Sketch the intersection of a plane and a cube so that the cross section is the given shape.

15. a square

16. a triangle

17. a rectangle that is not a square

18. a point

Appendix 4 *Use after Lesson 12.2*

KEY VOCABULARY
- **pictograph,** *p. 894*
- **line plot,** *p. 895*

Analyzing Pictographs and Line Plots

GOAL Analyze data from pictographs and line plots.

A **pictograph** is a way to display data using pictures. In a pictograph, an appropriate symbol is used to represent the type of data items. The graph includes a key to show the amount of data represented by each whole symbol.

EXAMPLE 1 Analyzing a Pictograph

Cellular Phones Each person in a History class was asked the number of cellular phone calls they made daily from Friday through Sunday. The information collected for the class was totaled and is shown in the pictograph below. How many calls were made each day? Did twice as many calls get made on one day than on another?

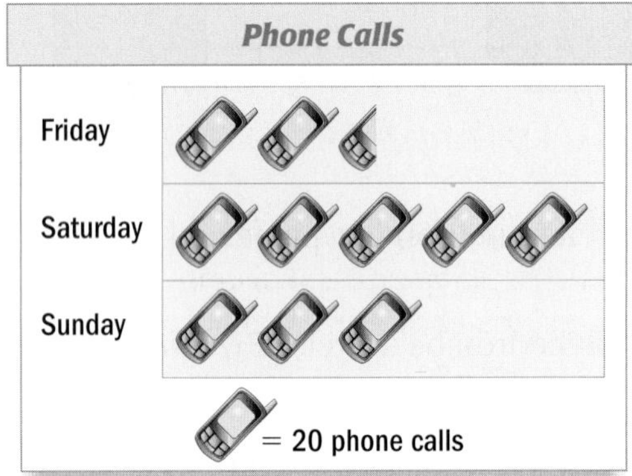

SOLUTION

Each whole symbol of a cellular phone represents 20 phone calls. So the half-symbol on Friday represents $\frac{1}{2} \cdot 20 = 10$ calls.

Day	Friday	Saturday	Sunday
Total number of calls	50	100	60

From the pictograph, you can see that there are twice as many symbols for Saturday (5 symbols) than for Friday ($2\frac{1}{2}$ symbols). The table also shows that twice as many calls were made on Saturday (100 calls) than on Friday (50 calls).

Line Plots A **line plot** is a way to show the frequency of a data value. You use a number line to visually display how often data values occur.

EXAMPLE 2 Making Conclusions from a Line Plot

Sleeping You asked 30 students how many hours they slept last Tuesday night. The information you collected is shown below.

Hours	5	6	7	8	9	10
Tally	I	IIII	卌	IIII	卌 IIII	卌 II
Frequency	1	4	5	4	9	7

a. Make a line plot of the data.

b. Make a conclusion about the data.

SOLUTION

a. Make a number line to indicate the number of hours spent sleeping on Tuesday night. Use X marks above the number line to show the frequency.

b. *Sample conclusion:* The total number of X marks above the numbers 8 and 9 is thirteen, so thirteen students spent 8 or 9 hours sleeping on Tuesday.

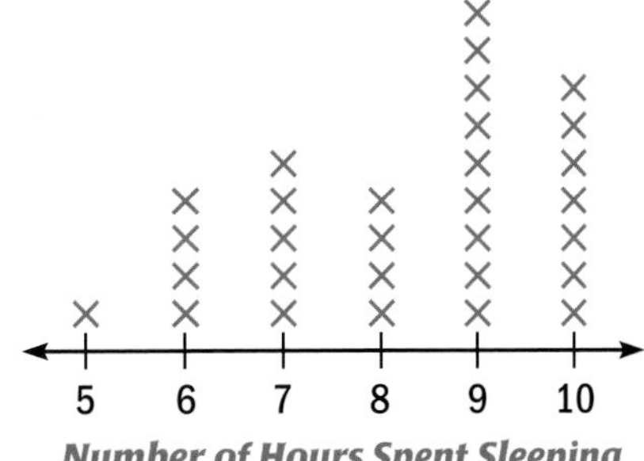

Number of Hours Spent Sleeping

Misleading Graphs A pictograph, line plot, or other data display may be misleading if the information is represented in a confusing or inconsistent manner. The display may lead to incorrect conclusions about the data.

EXAMPLE 3 Correcting a Misleading Line Plot

Movies The line plot shows data about the number of movies 11 people saw last month: 3 people saw 4 movies, 2 people saw 6 movies, and 5 people saw 9 movies. Explain why the line plot is misleading. Then redraw the line plot.

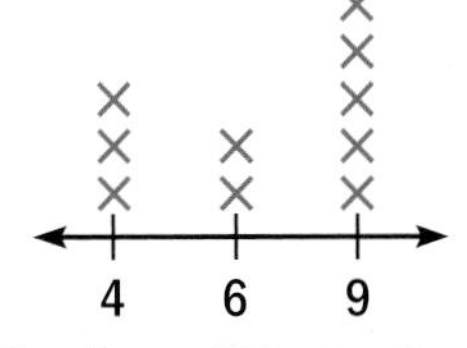

Number of Movies Seen

SOLUTION

Line plots use number lines, in which consecutive numbers should be evenly spaced. The line plot above does not accurately represent the range of the data. Redraw the line plot with all of the numbers from 4 to 9 to show the data more accurately.

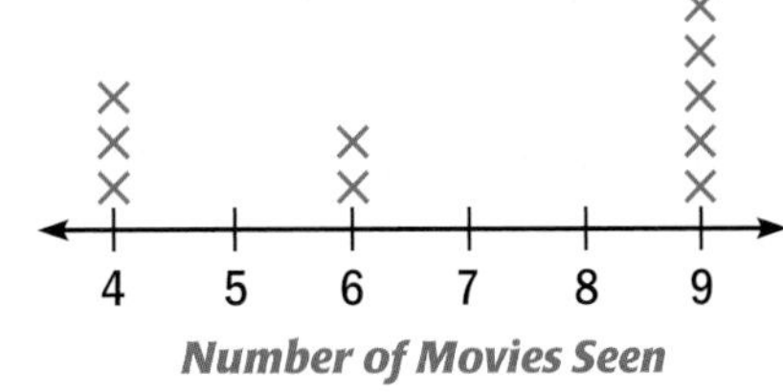

Number of Movies Seen

APPENDIX 4

PRACTICE

1. **LIMOUSINES** You asked 36 adults the number of times they have ridden in a limousine. The information you collected is shown below.

Number of times	0	1	2	3	4	5	6	7
Tally	𝍸 III	𝍸 𝍸 II	IIII	I	IIII	𝍸		II

   a. Make a line plot of the data.

   b. Make a conclusion about the data.

2. **MISLEADING GRAPHS** You asked 55 people how many pairs of shoes each owns. The results are shown in the table below. The data is then used to make the pictograph shown.

   a. Look at the partial symbols in the 1–5 pairs and 6–10 pairs rows in the pictograph. Do these symbols represent the same values? *Explain* why the pictograph is misleading.

   b. *Describe* how to redraw the graph so that is not misleading.

Pairs of shoes	*Number of people*
1–5	22
6–10	23
11+	10

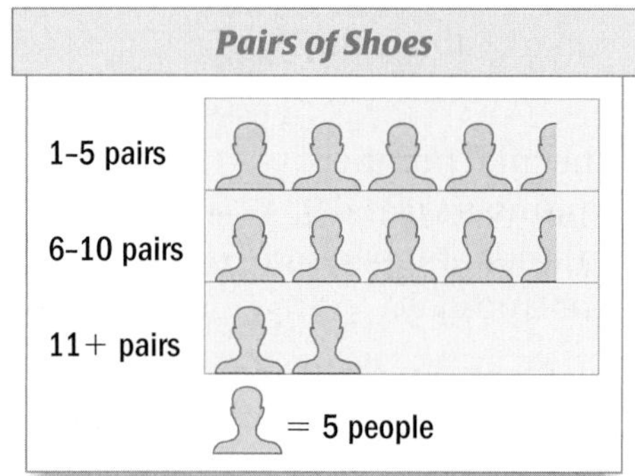

3. **OPEN-ENDED** Look back at the pictograph you drew in part (b) of Exercise 2 above. Make a conclusion about the data in the pictograph.

4. **OPEN-ENDED** Look back at the line plot in the Solution in Example 3 on page 895. Make a conclusion about the data in the line plot.

5. **REASONING** The table below shows the number of students in a dance class who are different ages.

   a. Can you make a pictograph from the data shown in the table? *Explain* why or why not.

   b. Can you make a line plot from the data? *Explain* why or why not.

Age of dancers	5–8	9–12	13–16
Tally	𝍸 𝍸 II	𝍸 III	III
Frequency	12	8	3

KEY VOCABULARY
- **census,** *p. 897*

Comparing a Sample and a Census

GOAL Compare survey results from samples of different sizes.

Recall from Extension 12.8 that a *population* is an entire group of people or objects that you want information about and a *sample* is a part of the population. A **census** is an official survey conducted on a regular basis (such as the U.S. Census) to gather information about an entire population.

Sample Sizes It may be difficult to survey an entire population, however, so information is often gathered about samples instead and then used to describe the entire population. Examples 1 and 2 show that the size of the sample used in a survey may affect how close the results match the actual information for the population.

EXAMPLE 1 Making Conclusions About Data from a Survey

Student Ages An adult education program offers evening courses for 600 students. One of the classes has 30 students. The teacher asks the age of each of the students in the class. The data is shown below.

40, 33, 73, 51, 40, 69, 43, 37, 37, 58, 42, 35, 26, 53, 48,
45, 58, 67, 28, 66, 54, 58, 54, 28, 69, 61, 67, 42, 52, 75

a. Look at students 1–7. What is the median age of the data in this sample?

b. Now look at students 1–15. What is the median age of the data in this second sample?

c. Now look at the class as a whole. What is the median age of the 30 students?

SOLUTION

a. Write the first seven ages in order from least to greatest.

33, 40, 40, 43, 51, 69, 73

The median age for this sample is 43.

b. Write the first 15 ages in order from least to greatest.

26, 33, 35, 37, 37, 40, 40, 42, 43, 48, 51, 53, 58, 69, 73

The median age for this sample is 42.

c. Write the class ages in order from least to greatest.

26, 28, 28, 33, 35, 37, 37, 40, 40, 42, 42, 43, 45, 48, 51,
52, 53, 54, 54, 58, 58, 58, 61, 66, 67, 67, 69, 69, 73, 75

The median age for this sample is 51.5 years.

EXAMPLE 2 Comparing Census and Survey Results

Suppose the median age of all 600 students in the adult education program in Example 1 on page 897 is 51 years old. Which sample in parts (a)–(c) of Example 1 comes closest to this actual value? Explain.

SOLUTION

The largest sample, in part (c) of Example 1, comes closest to the median age for the whole school. As the sample size increases, the statistics about the sample are more representative of the statistics about the entire population.

PRACTICE

1. **MEASURES OF CENTRAL TENDENCY** Look back at Example 1. What is the mean (to the nearest tenth of a year) of the sample in part (a)? in part (b)? in part (c)? Which of these means is closest to the mean of the ages of all 600 students in the program, 50.5 years?

2. **OPEN-ENDED** Conduct your own survey of a population of 30 people or more. Choose a question for your survey that will have a numerical answer.
   - **a.** What question did you choose to ask?
   - **b.** Make a list or table of the results. Find a measure of central tendency for your population.
   - **c.** Choose a few samples of different sizes from your population. Verify that as the sample size gets larger, the values of the measure of central tendency you chose approaches the value for the entire population.

3. **U.S. CENSUS** The U.S. Census Bureau has reported that 2,405,000 teenagers between the ages of 12–17 played golf in a recent year.
   - **a.** There were a total of 24,264,000 teenagers from 12–17 questioned for the survey. Approximately what percent of these teenagers played golf that year?
   - **b.** If you asked 10 of your friends if they played golf in the past year, would you expect the percent in the group who said yes to be close to the percent in part (a)? What would you expect to happen if you asked 20 teenagers the same question? 50 teenagers? *Explain.*

4. **RESEARCH** Use an encyclopedia or a statistics textbook.
   - **a.** Look up *random number generator. Explain* how to use a table or a graphing calculator to randomly generate a group of numbers.
   - **b.** Use a group of 30 or more randomly generated numbers. Find their mean, median, and mode.
   - **c.** Consider different sample sizes from your group of randomly generated numbers. Verify that larger sample sizes result in statistics that are closer to the statistics for the entire population.

Credits

Cover Yellow Dog Productions/Image Bank/Getty Images; **v** *top* Meridian Creative Group, *top center* Robert C. Jenks, Jenks Studio, *bottom center* McDougal Littell, *bottom* Jerry Head Jr.; **ix** PunchStock; **x** Associated Press, Rockwell; **xi** John Warden/Getty Images; **xii** Getty Images; **xiii** Peter Adams/Index Stock Imagery/PictureQuest; **xiv** Alan Schein Photography/Corbis; **xv** David Kelly Crow/PhotoEdit; **xvi** Royalty-Free/Corbis; **xvii** Craig Tuttle/Corbis; **xviii** Mark Antman/The Image Works; **xix** Myrleen Ferguson Cate/PhotoEdit; **xx** Paul Nicklen/National Geographic/Getty Images; **xxi** Getty Images; **xxii** Royalty-Free/Corbis; **xxiv** Corbis; **1** *left* PhotoDisc/Getty Images, *right* Royalty-Free/Corbis; **3** Diaphor Agency/Index Stock Photography, Inc.; **4** Alan Schein/Corbis/Stock Market; **7** The Press-Enterprise, Silvia Flores/AP Wide World Photos; **8** Getty Images; **11** Columbus Telegram/Julie Blum/AP Wide World Photos; **13** *top* PunchStock, *center* Zefa Visual Media—Germany/Index Stock Photography, Inc.; **15** Gérard Villaréal/Photo Researchers, Inc.; **17** James Meyer/The Image Bank/Getty Images; **18** Creatas; **19** Greer & Associates, Inc./Superstock Inc.; **20** Ron Watts/Corbis; **22** Bob Krist/Corbis; **23** Getty Images; **25** Nancy Sheehan/PhotoEdit; **26** Esteban Cobo/AFP/Getty Images; **27** Reuters Newmedia, Inc./Corbis; **29** Lenard Sanders; **30** Getty Images; **32** Gunter Marx Photography/Corbis; **34** Barbara Strnadova/Photo Researchers, Inc.; **35** Larry West/Photo Researchers, Inc.; **37** Kevork Djansezian/AP Wide World Photos; **38** Ted S. Warren/AP Wide World Photos; **41** Tony Freeman/PhotoEdit; **44** David Young-Wolff/PhotoEdit; **57** Associated Press, Rockwell; **58** Artville, LLC.; **60** Ken O'Donoghue; **61** Bob Daemmrich/The Image Works; **63** Bob Daemrich/PictureQuest; **65** Kwame Zikomo/Superstock Inc.; **67** Gianni Dagli Orti/Corbis; **68** Tim Haske/Index Stock Imagery; **71** Jeff Hunter/The Image Bank/Getty Images; **72** Arthur Morris/Corbis; **73** Stephen Frink/Corbis; **76** *left* PhotoDisc, *right* Corbis: Destination Tropics (vol. 112); **77** PhotoDisc; **78** Dean Conger/Corbis; **81** Paul A. Souders/Corbis; **82** Caron P./Corbis Sygma; **83** *top* Steve Casimiro/Allsport Concepts/Getty Images, *center* School Division/Houghton Mifflin; **86** Steven Senne/AP Wide World Photos; **87** PhotoDisc; **88** Jim Schwabel/Index Stock Photography, Inc.; **91** Ken O'Donoghue; **94** PhotoDisc Green/Getty Images; **97** Masterfile (RM); **101** Rafael Macia/Photo Researchers, Inc.; **112** NASA; **113** *left* NASA, *right* Corbis; **117** Bobby Model/National Geographic/Getty Images; **120** Ken O'Donoghue; **121** Darryl Torckler/Stone/Getty Images; **122** G.D.T./The Image Bank/Getty Images; **123** Peter Hvizdak/The Image Works; **129** Dennis O'Clair/Getty Images; **132** Colin Young-Wolff/PhotoEdit; **134** Getty Images; **135** Gabe Palmer/Corbis; **137** Syracuse Newspapers/The Image Works; **138** *top* Getty Images, *center* Ken O'Donoghue; **141** Index Stock; **142** John Warden/Stone/Getty Images; **148** Kurt Wittman/Corbis; **150** Ken O'Donoghue; **152** Adrian Weinbrecht/Getty Images; **153** Getty Images; **154** Art Wolfe/Stone/Getty Images; **157** Pablo Corral V/Corbis; **158** Tom Prettyman/PhotoEdit; **160** Richard Hutchings/PhotoEdit; **172** Alistair Corwin/Index Stock; **173** *background* Benelux Press/Index Stock, *top left* Stephen Simpson/Taxi/Getty Images, *top right* Tom Stewart/Corbis, *bottom left* Benelux Press/Index Stock; **176** Phil Schermeister/Corbis; **179** School Division/Houghton Mifflin; **180** Tom Carter/PhotoEdit; **181** Masterfile (RM); **182** School Division/Houghton Mifflin; **184** Bob Torrez/Stone/Getty Images; **185** Corbis; **187** *top* Erich Lessing/Art Resource, NY, *ruby, sapphire, spinel, emerald* Christie's Images, *pearl* Eric Kamp/Index Stock Photography, Inc.; **191** Claus Meyer/Minden Pictures; **192** Guy Cali/PictureQuest; **195** David Young-Wolff/PhotoEdit; **196** Mark Richards/PhotoEdit; **197** Getty Images; **198** Steve Miller/AP Wide World Photos; **199** Konrad Wothe/Minden Pictures; **201** Tom Stewart/Corbis; **202** Corbis; **206** H. Mark Helfer/NIST; **208** *top* M. Hans/Vandystadt/Photo Researchers, Inc., *bottom* Roger Holden/Index Stock/PictureQuest; **211** Microfield Scientific Ltd./Photo Researchers, Inc.; **212** Getty Images; **213** Doug Campbell/ImageState; **215** NASA; **216** SuperStock, Inc./SuperStock; **219** *left* Artville, *right* Pho/AP Wide World Photos; **230** David Brooks/Corbis; **231** *left* Don Mason/Corbis, *right* School Division/Houghton Mifflin; **233** Donna Day/Stone/Getty Images; **234** Shawn Lockhart, courtesy of Southwest Wisconsin Reptiles; **237** David Madison/Stone/Getty Images; **238** Ryan McVay/PhotoDisc; **239** Ken O'Donoghue; **241** AP Photo/Todd Bissonette; **243** PhotoDisc; **244** PhotoDisc Blue/Getty Images; **246** Gianni Cigolini/Image Bank/Getty Images; **247** Phil Schermeister/Corbis; **249** Tom Stewart/Corbis; **254** Getty Images; **255** G.K. & Vikki Hart/The Image Bank/Getty Images; **256** Steve Maslowski/Photo Researchers, Inc.; **259** Tom Bean/Stone/Getty Images; **260** Chuck Savage/Corbis; **261** Ken O'Donoghue; **263** Peter Adams/Index Stock Imagery/PictureQuest; **265** Bruce Leighty/Index Stock Photography, Inc.; **268** Michael K. Nichols/National Geographic/Getty Images; **269** G. Brad Lewis/ImageState; **272** Ralph White/Corbis; **275** PhotoDisc; **276** Kevin Schafer/The Image Bank/Getty Images; **277** Jon Feingersh/Corbis; **279** VStock/Alamy/Greg Stott/Masterfile; **291** Ken O'Donoghue; **293** *both* Ken O'Donoghue; **295** Getty Images; **296** Neo Vision/Photonica; **297** Ken O'Donoghue; **298** ThinkStock/SuperStock; **300** Stockbyte; **303** *top* Gary Bell/Taxi/Getty Images, *center* Georgette Douwma/Taxi/Getty Images; **306** Tony Anderson/Taxi/Getty Images; **309** Index Stock; **310** Ken O'Donoghue; **311** *top left and top center* Ken O'Donoghue, *top right* PhotoDisc, *bottom left and bottom right* Ken O'Donoghue, *bottom center* Jupiter Images; **312** Alan Schein Photography/Corbis; **314** Jonathan Nourok/PhotoEdit; **316** Getty Images; **317** NASA/USGS/Stockli, Nelson, Hasler/Laboratory for

Atmospheres/Goddard Space Flight Center; **318** Charles Krupa/AP Wide World Photos; **319** Jupiter Images; **321** Brooklyn Productions/The Image Bank/Getty Images; **324** Duomo/Corbis; **326** Ken O'Donoghue; **327** Bob Daemmrich/The Image Works; **328** Josef Peter Fankhauser/The Image Bank/Getty Images; **330** *left* Paul A. Souders/Corbis, *right* Fernando Bengoechea/Beateworks/Getty Images/Dorling Kindersley; **341** Ken O'Donoghue; **343** Tom Vezo/Minden Pictures; **347** Photo-Disc; **348** Wolfgang Kaehler/Corbis; **350** Courtesy of the City of Strawberry Point, Iowa; **352** age fotostock/SuperStock; **354** *top* Lee Celano/AP Wide World Photos, *bottom* PhotoDisc; **357** Kelvin Aitken/Peter Arnold, Inc.; **359** Phillip Lee Harvey/Stone/Getty Images; **361** Getty Images; **363** David Young-Wolff/PhotoEdit; **365** Getty Images; **366** *top* Nik Wheeler/Corbis, *bottom* PhotoDisc; **368** Patrik Giardino/Corbis; **370** *top* Richard Heinzen/SuperStock, *center* Darrell Gulin/Stone/Getty Images; **372** Horst Herget/Masterfile **373** Ken O'Donoghue; **374** Daniel Allan/Taxi/Getty Images; **375** *top* David Young-Wolff/Photo Edit, *center* PhotoDisc; **376** Photo-Disc; **378** Inga Spence/Index Stock Photography, Inc.; **381** David Young-Wolff/PhotoEdit; **382** Ken O'Donoghue; **385** Don Smetzer/Stone/Getty Images; **387** Larry Miller/Photo Researchers, Inc.; **401** Ken O'Donoghue; **403** Mike Chew/Corbis; **407** Ken O'Donoghue; **408** Index Stock; **409** Ken O'Donoghue; **411** Dean Conger/Corbis; **415** Index Stock; **416** Nikreates/Alamy; **420** Inga Spence/Visuals Unlimited; **421** *top* Ken O'Donoghue, *bottom* PhotoDisc; **425** *top* Stockfolio/Alamy, *bottom* Alan Schein Photography/Corbis; **427** Richard Cummins/Corbis; **431** Courtesy of Michigan State University, Department of Crop and Soil Sciences; **432** Sanford Ponder www.thepod.net; **433** Ken O'Donoghue; **435** *all* PhotoDisc; **439** Michael Newman/PhotoEdit; **443** *top* Ken O'Donoghue, *bottom left* Masterfile (RM), *bottom center* Royalty-Free/Corbis, *bottom right* Age fotostock/SuperStock; **445** Ken O'Donoghue; **447** *top* Frank Siteman, *screens* Frank Siteman, *televisions* PhotoDisc; **453** *top* EPA/Wayne Conradie/Landov, *bottom* PhotoDisc; **455** Masterfile (RM); **465** PhotoDisc; **466** *top left* Tony Denim/ImageState, *center* PhotoDisc/Ken O'Donoghue; **467** *top left* Joe McBride/Stone/Getty Images, *top right* PhotoDisc/Getty Images, *center* PhotoDisc, *bottom right* Royalty-Free/Corbis; **469** Getty Images; **471** Eunice Harris/Photo Researchers, Inc.; **473** Ed Elberfeld/Index Stock Photography, Inc.; **474** Jerry and Marcy Monkman/EcoPhotography.com/Alamy; **475** Goran Stenberg/AP Wide World Photos; **477** Craig Tuttle/Corbis; **479** Getty Images; **480** Ken O'Donoghue; **482** Royalty-Free/Corbis; **487** Tony Freeman/PhotoEdit; **490** Royalty-Free/Corbis; **492** Index Stock; **493** Cleve Bryant/PhotoEdit; **497** Superstock Inc./Superstock; **500** Jeff Greenberg/eStock Photography/PictureQuest; **504** Harvey Lloyd/Taxi/Getty Images; **521** Royalty-Free/Corbis; **522** Arcaid/Alamy; **527** Mark Antman/The Image Works; **530** John Carnemolla/Australian Picture Library/Corbis; **534** Index Stock; **536** *all* Ken O'Donoghue; **537** *left* Royalty-Free/Corbis, *second and third from left* Food Pix/Picture Quest; **541** Stephen Vowles/Alamy; **542** Royalty-Free/Corbis; **543** Ken O'Donoghue; **547** Dave G. Houser/Post-Houserstock/Corbis; **548** Kevin Bartram/The Galveston County Daily News/AP Wide World Photos; **551** *left and center* Corbis: Sports Objects (vol. 174), *right* PhotoDisc; **552** Royalty Free/Corbis; **554** Mark Gibson/Corbis; **561** PhotoDisc Blue/Getty Images; **565** Ace Stock Limited/Alamy; **568** David Young-Wolff/PhotoEdit; **581** *left* Jason Hindley/Stone/Getty Images, *right* Ken O'Donoghue; **583** Lonely Planet Images; **586** Peter Beck/Corbis; **588** Bill Aron/PhotoEdit; **591** Charles Gupton/Corbis; **593** Merritt Vincent/PhotoEdit; **596** Ken O'Donoghue; **597** Index Stock; **598** Corbis: Destination Tropics (vol. 112); **602** Antonio Mo/Taxi/Getty Images; **603** Getty Images; **605** West Rock/Taxi/Getty Images; **606** Myrleen Ferguson Cate/PhotoEdit; **609** Tom Stewart/Corbis; **612** Jim Schwabel/Index Stock Photography, Inc.; **616** Nancy R. Cohen/PhotoDisc/Getty Images; **617** Michael Newman/PhotoEdit; **622** RO-MA Stock/IndexStock; **625** J. H. Robinson/Photo Researchers, Inc.; **626** Ken O'Donoghue; **629** Michael Booth/Alamy; **631** Ken O'Donoghue; **633** Scott Spiker/ImageState; **635** Getty Images; **646–647** Frans Lanting/Minden Pictures; **647** *left* Tui De Roy/Minden Pictures, *center* Michio Hoshino/Minden Pictures, *right* Franz Lanting/Minden Pictures; **649** David Young Wolff/PhotoEdit; **653** Getty Images; **654** Paul Nicklen/National Geographic/Getty Images; **657** Associated Press, AP Photographer Victoria Arocho, Staff; **658** The Time Herald, Tony Pitts/AP Wide World Photos; **659** A. H. Rider/Photo Researchers, Inc.; **669** Marc Romanelli/The Image Bank/Getty Images; **670** David Young-Wolff/PhotoEdit; **673** Jeff Greenberg/The Image Works; **674** Billy Hustace/Stone/Getty Images; **675** Masterfile (RM); **678** *top* Antonio Mo/Taxi/Getty Images, *center* PhotoDisc; **680** *top* Index Stock, *center row* Ken O'Donoghue; **683** Ken O'Donoghue; **685** David Gray/Reuters; **689** Stephen Simpson/Taxi/Getty Images; **694** *top* Jeff Greenberg/PhotoEdit, *bottom* School Division/Houghton Mifflin; **698** David Young-Wolff/PhotoEdit; **699** Frank Siteman; **701** Ken O'Donoghue; **703** Marvin E. Newman/The Image Bank/Getty Images; Jeremy Woodhouse/Masterfile **714** *both* Ken O'Donoghue; **715** Comstock; **717** Matthias Clamer/Stone/Getty Images; **718** Masterfile; **720** Getty Images; **721** Royalty-Free/Corbis; **725** Ken O'Donoghue; **726** SPL/Photo Researchers, Inc.; **729** Getty Images; **730** Reuters/Corbis; **732** Royalty-Free/Corbis; Michael Newman/Photo Edit **734** Tom Carter/PhotoEdit; **737** Royalty-Free/Corbis; **739** Getty Images; **743** M. Dillon/Corbis; All illustrations by Morgan Cain Associates/McDougal Littell/Houghton Mifflin Co. and McDougal Littell/Houghton Mifflin Co.

Chapter 1

1.1 Skill Practice (p. 5) **1.** intervals **3.** restaurant **5.** about 9 more stores

7. a.

Hours spent on the Internet	Frequency
0-1.9	4
2-3.9	6
4-5.9	9
6-7.9	5
8-9.9	4
10-11.9	2

b.

Hours spent on the Internet	Frequency
0-2.9	7
3-5.9	12
6-8.9	7
9-11.9	4

c. Part (a); The intervals are smaller.

9.

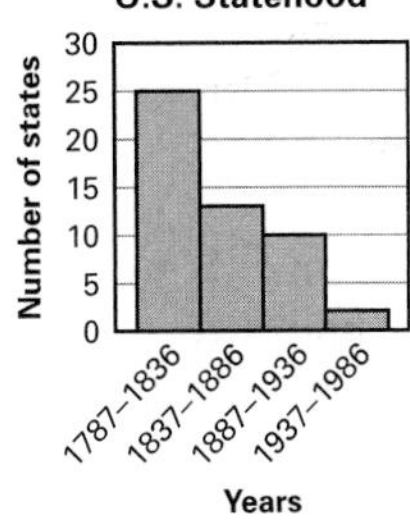

1.1 Problem Solving (pp. 6 – 7) **11. a.** 355, 385, 415, 445, 475, 505

b.

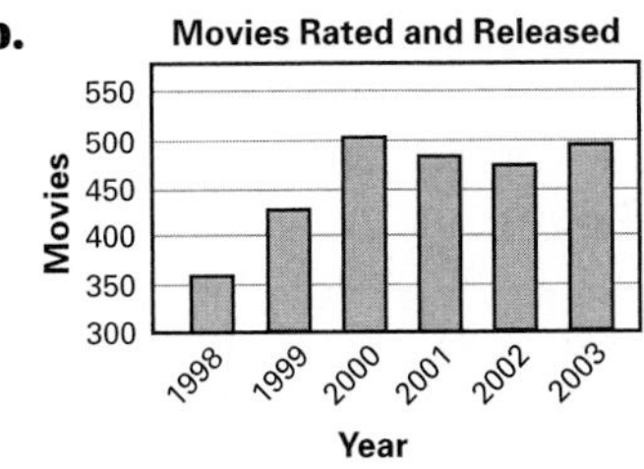

c. *Sample answer:* Overall the number of movies has increased but not at a consistent rate. **15.** 50 years **17.** No, there does not appear to be a pattern. **19.** frequency table; A frequency table gives exact numbers of high tides, whereas you have to estimate the number in a histogram.

1.2 Skill Practice (p. 10) **1.** Multiply 2 by 5. Add the result 10 to 8. Subtract 4 from this sum, 18, to obtain the final result, 14. **5.** 12 **7.** 18 **9.** 6 **11.** 4 **13.** 5 **15.** 12 **17.** 7 **19.** 30 **21.** 1.2 **23.** 3 **27.** $5 \cdot (2 + 3) - 8 = 17$ **29.** $13 - 5 \cdot (8 - 6) = 3$ **31.** $(12 \div 3) \cdot (4 + 1) = 20$

1.2 Technology Activity (p. 12) **1.** 106.8 **3.** 7 **5.** 5 **7.** 2 **9.** \$10.44 **11.** \$65.68

1.3 Skill Practice (pp. 15 – 16) **1.** variable; numerical **3.** 23 **5.** 15 **7.** 30 **9.** 28 **11.** 3 **13.** 4 must be multiplied by 7 before 5 is added; $5 + 28 = 33$ **15.** $10 - x$ **17.** $\frac{x}{7}$ **19.** $x - 15$ **21.** $22x$ **23.** 32.8; increased, $60.8 > 32.8$ **25.** 96; not changed, $96 = 96$ **27.** 1.6; increased, $29.6 > 1.6$ **29.** 10; decreased, $0.9 < 10$ **31.** 2.87 **33.** 3.74

1.3 Problem Solving (pp. 16 – 18) **39.** 31.5 mi **41.** $30x + 60y - 3z$ **43.** $20 - (2.75p + 2.5d)$; \$1.75 **49.** 1.8 cm; 3.6 cm **51.** *Sample answer:* The temperature of the room or the thickness of different parts of the sculpture could affect the melting rate.

1.4 Skill Practice (pp. 21 – 22) **1.** *Sample answer:* base 4^5 exponent **3.** 9^5; 9 to the fifth power **5.** n^6; n to the sixth power **7.** 1331 **9.** 64 **11.** 0 **13.** 121 **15.** 1000 **17.** 400 **19.** 16 **21.** 119 **23.** 432 **25.** 5 **27.** 221 **29.** 100 **31.** 49 **33.** 54 **35.** 7 **39.** $<$ **41.** $<$ **43.** $=$ **45.** 159.3 **47.** 2, 4, 8, 6; 4 **49.** 4, 16, 64, 256, 1024, 4096; 6, 4; The pattern is 6 and 4 alternating.

1.4 Problem Solving (pp. 22 – 23) **53.** 289 in.^{2} **55. a.** No, the diver has fallen only 64 ft. **b.** 80 ft; After 3 sec the diver has fallen 144 ft. The difference of 144 and 64 is 80. **57.** n^2 **61.** 48 mi/h **65.** 1; 1; $x^1 = x$ and $\frac{x}{x} = 1$, so $x^0 = 1$.

1.5 Skill Practice (pp. 28 – 29) **1.** solving an equation **3.** 22 **5.** 11 **7.** 11 **9.** 29 **11.** 2 **13.** 15 **15.** 17 **17.** 2 **19.** no **21.** no **23.** yes **27.** 24 divided by what number is 8? 3 **29.** 24 times what number is equal to 8? $\frac{1}{3}$ **31.** 3 **33.** 1 **35.** 4

1.5 Problem Solving (pp. 29 – 30) **45.** $14 + x = 43$; 29 in. **47.** $5033 + b = 5396$; 363 lb 53. $8h = 200 - 80$; 15 h

1.6 Skill Practice (pp. 34 – 35) **1.** Area is the surface a figure covers, while perimeter is the distance around the figure. **3.** $P = 30$ yd, $A = 54$ yd^2 **5.** $P = 20$ m, $A = 25$ m^2 **7.** The units should be square meters; $A = s^2 = (4)^2 = 16$ m^2 **9.** 6 m **11.** 324 in.^{2} **13.** 11 in. **15.** 5 mi **17.** 8 sec **19.** 15 ft/sec **21.** $P = 48$ in., $A = 126$ in.^{2}

1.6 Problem Solving (pp. 35 – 36) **27.** 68° F **29.** about 4 h **31.** 1560 ft

1.7 Skill Practice (p. 40) **1.** Read and Understand, Make a Plan, Solve the Problem, Look Back **3.** You know the cost of lunch and the cost of the drink. You need to find out what the customer's change is. **5.** Find the total spent on hot dogs and add it to the ticket cost. Then compare the total to \$16. **7.** \$10 **9.** \$4; "Each pack of pens contains 12 pens" is unnecessary information. **11.** $69x^5$, $66x^6$

1.7 Skill Practice (pp. 41 – 42)

15. a. $\frac{\text{Number of peolpe who ride in one hour}}{5 \text{ cars} \cdot 4 \text{ passengers}}$ = Number of trains that run **b.** 45 trains **c.** $45 \cdot 5 \cdot 4 = 900$ **19.** 150 mi **23.** 16 pages **25.** 3 dimes, 7 quarters **27.** five 3 minute acts **29.** 8 and 13 **31.** 5.4 mi; 1.8 mi

Chapter Review (pp. 45 – 48)

1. histogram **3.** order of operations **5.** 35–44; 65+ **7.** 39 **9.** 22 **11.** 3 **13.** 21 **15.** 2.6 **17.** 70 **19.** $n + 12$ **21.** $2 \cdot 28.5 - 20$; \$37 **23.** 1024 **25.** 6561 **27.** 1260 **29.** 144 ft **31.** 7 **33.** no **35.** no **37.** 16 cm **39.** 150 mi

Chapter 2

2.1 Skill Practice (pp. 59 – 60)

1. absolute value **3.** > **5.** < **7.** > **9.** > **11.** −20, −10, 5, 13, 15, 27 **13.** −20, −12, 18, 44, 59, 64 **17.** 19; −19 **19.** 740; 740 **21.** B **23.** D **25.** 32 **27.** −29 **29.** 81 **31.** −3 **33.** = **35.** < **37.** $-|47|, -28, |-65|, -(-73), |95|$ **39.** $-14, -8, -|6|, |-1|, -(-5)$

2.1 Problem Solving (pp. 60 – 61)

45. Gieselmann Lake, Jones Lake, Craigs Pond, Silver Lake, Seneca Lake **49.** 0 **51.** If a and b are both positive, or if a is negative and b is positive, then $a < b$. If a and b are both negative, or if a is positive and b is negative, then $a > b$. **53.** methanol, ethanol, propanol, water; Water will remain because it will have been boiling for the shortest time.

2.2 Skill Practice (pp. 65 – 66)

1. absolute values **3.** −12 **5.** 0 **7.** −19 **9.** 2 **13.** −112 **15.** 0; Inv. Prop. of Add. **17.** −30 **19.** −8 **21.** −29 **23.** 7 **25.** −3 **27.** −37 **29.** 37 **31.** 51 **33.** −1207 **35.** −999 **37.** always; The sum will have the common sign, which is negative. **39.** sometimes; It will be negative if the number with the greater absolute value is negative. **41.** 194 **43.** −14

2.2 Problem Solving (pp. 66 – 67)

49. 0 **51.** +3 **55. a.** 900 **b.** 300 B.C. **c.** 1200 years **57.** above par; −2 or 2 under par

2.3 Skill Practice (p. 70)

1. −2 −6 **3.** −7 **5.** −4 **7.** 0 **9.** −8 **11.** −27 **13.** 44 **15.** 5 **17.** −71 **19.** −15 **21.** −5 **23.** −23 **25.** 13 **29.** 5 **31.** 8 **33.** −12 **35.** 101 **37.** yes; *Sample answer:* The distance between two numbers is the same regardless of the order in which you subtract them. However, the difference is positive if you start with the greater number and negative if you start with the lesser number. So, $x - y$ and $y - x$ are always opposite.

2.3 Problem Solving (pp. 71 – 72)

41. −1000 **45.** 43°F **49.** Jurassic Period; $\frac{64}{186}$ or about $\frac{1}{3}$ **51.** 41°F

2.4 Skill Practice (p. 75)

1. negative **3.** 28 **5.** −18 **7.** −42 **9.** 0; Mult. Prop. of Zero **11.** −18 **13.** 180 **15.** −6; Ident. Prop. of Mult. **17.** 270 **19.** 60 **21.** −280 **23.** The product of two integers with the same sign is positive; $-8(-12) = 96$ **25.** 49 **27.** −48 **29.** 196 **31.** 93 **33.** −53 **35.** 52 **37.** 224 **39.** 336 **41.** −4 **43.** −4 **45.** −10 **47.** −4 **49.** no; *Sample answer:* $(-3)^2 = (-3)(-3) = 9$ and $-3^2 = (-1)(3)(3) = -9$

2.4 Problem Solving (p. 76)

53. −96 in. **55.** $400 + 5(-125) = -225$ **57.** −10; 100; −1000; 10,000; −100,000; *Sample answer:* When the exponent is even, the sign is positive. When the exponent is odd, the sign is negative.

2.5 Skill Practice (p. 79)

1. mean **3.** 0 **5.** −5 **7.** −14 **9.** 19 **11.** undefined **13.** $\frac{1}{5}$ **15.** −1 **17.** $-\frac{16}{7}$ or about −2.29 **19.** −3 **21.** −3 **23.** −3 **25.** 4 **27.** 14 **29.** −4 **31.** 27 **33.** 19 **35.** A

2.5 Problem Solving (pp. 80 – 81)

43. points: 21; assists: 4; rebounds: 11; *Sample answer:* If the data values are not all the same, then the mean cannot be the highest value or the lowest value, so there are actual values in the data set that are above and below the mean. **45.** –29.2°F

2.6 Skill Practice (pp. 85 – 86)

1. E **3.** B **5.** D **7.** 45; Assoc. Prop. of Add.; Comm. Prop. of Add. **9.** −290; Assoc. Prop. of Mult.; Comm. Prop. of Mult. **11.** 21; Assoc. Prop. of Add. **13.** −140; Comm. Prop. of Mult.; Assoc. Prop. of Mult. **15.** −900; Comm. Prop. of Mult.; Assoc. Prop. of Mult. **17.** $16 \cdot 54$ **19.** $4 + (2 + 9)$ or $(9 + 2) + 4$ **21.** $(16 + 8) + 2$ or $2 + (8 + 16)$ **23.** 69; $45 - (-68) - 44 = 45 + 68 + (-44)$ [Change Sub. to Add.] $= (45 + 68) + (-44)$ [Comm. Prop. of Add.] $= 113 + (-44)$ [Add] $= 69$ [Add] **25.** 3; $(-26 + 33) + (-4) = 7 + (-4) = 3$ [Add] **27.** 6; $\left(\frac{2}{7} + 5\right) + \frac{5}{7} = \left(5 + \frac{2}{7}\right) + \frac{5}{7}$ [Comm. Prop. of Add.] $= 5 + \left(\frac{2}{7} + \frac{5}{7}\right)$ [Assoc. Prop. of Add.] $= 5 + 1$ [Add] $= 6$ [Add] **29.** 420; $12 \cdot (7 \cdot 1 \cdot 5) = 12 \cdot (7 \cdot 5)$ [Ident. Prop. of Mult.] $= 12 \cdot 35$ [Mult.] $= 420$ [Mult.] **31.** 57; $36 + 57 + (-36) = 36 + (57 + (-36))$ [Assoc. Prop. of Add.] $= 36 + (-36 + 57)$ [Comm. Prop. of Add.] $= (36 + (-36)) + 57$ [Assoc. Prop. of Add.] $= 0 + 57$ [Inv. Prop. of Add.] $= 57$ [Ident. Prop. of Add.] **33.** 10; $24 + (-12 - 8) + 6 = 24 + 6 + (-12 - 8)$ [Comm. Prop. of Add.] $= 30 + (-12 - 8)$ [Add] $= 30 + [-12 + (-8)]$ [Add Opposite] $= 30 + (-20)$ [Add] $= 10$ [Add] **35.** $70x$ **37.** $x + 70$

2.6 Problem Solving (pp. 86 – 87)

41. 15 in.³; *Sample answer:* The box is 2.5 in. · 1.5 in. · 4 in., so the unit is in. · in. · in. or in.³ **43.** no; *Sample answer:* The expressions do not have same terms; The difference is that the first expression has "−15" and the second has "+15". **47.** discount: \$15.75; purchase: \$31.50

2.7 Skill Practice (pp. 90 – 91)

1. −6 **3.** $-6y$ **5.** B **7.** A **9.** 28 + 32; 60 **11.** 15 + 18; 33 **13.** −30 + 60 + 12; 42 **17.** $-40 + 8x$ **19.** $95 + 19w$ **21.** $6 + 2x$ **23.** $16w + 12z$ **25.** $5x + 3y - 3$ **27.** $4r + s$ **29.** $11z$ **31.** $8c - 14$ **33.** $2a + 8b - 14$ **35.** $-5.6x + 4.4y + 4.4z$

39. *Sample answer:* 9(19) = 9(20 − 1) = 180 − 9 = 171
41. *Sample answer:* 65(24) = 65(10 + 10 + 4) = 650 + 650 + 260 = 1300 + 260 = 1560

2.7 Problem Solving (pp. 91 – 92) **47.** $786.24

2.7 Technology Activity (p. 93) **1.** −28,546 **3.** 11,009 **5.** −2,105,804 **7.** −262,890,144 **9.** −101 **11.** yes; *Sample answer:* The numbers of blueberries in your 3 packages are 170 − 12 = 158, 170 − 8 = 162, and 170 + 16 = 186. The average for your 3 packages is $\frac{158 + 162 + 186}{3} = 168\frac{2}{3}$. That is a little below the claimed average of 170, but 3 packages is a small sample.

2.8 Skill Practice (pp. 96 – 97)

1.

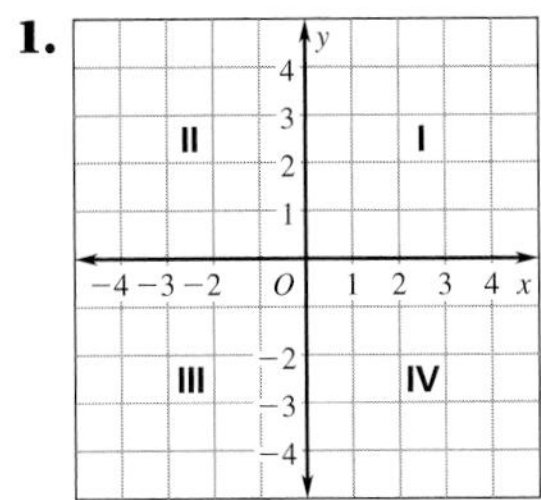

3. (−3, 3) **5.** (−5, 0) **7.** (0, −2) **9.** (−2.5, 2) *11–19. All descriptions start "Begin at the origin."* **11.** 4 to the right, 1 up; Quadrant I **13.** 3 to the left; on the *x*-axis **15.** 2 to the left, 3 up; Quadrant II **17.** 5 down; on the *y*-axis **19.** 8.2 to the left, 6.1 up; Quadrant II **21.** 2.4 to the right; on the *x*-axis **23.** The *x* and *y* coordinates are reversed. For *P*(2, 3), start at the origin, move 2 to the right, then 3 up. For *Q*(1, −1), start at the origin, move 1 to the right, 1 down.

25. square; 20 units

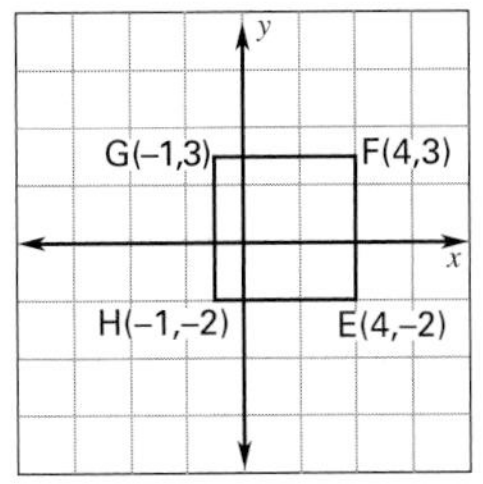

27. rectangle; 36 units

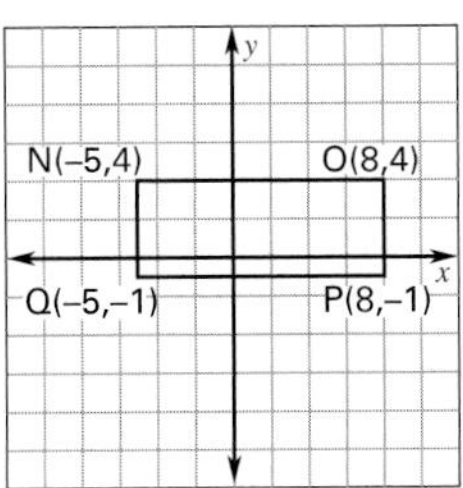

29. *P* = 20 units, *A* = 17 units²;

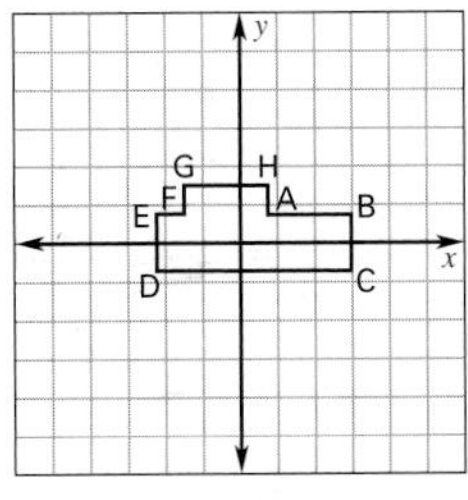

31. *P* = 25 units, *A* = 25 units²;

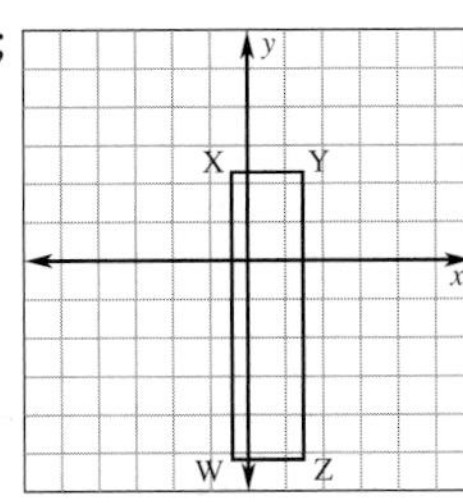

33. 11 units; (9, 12) and (2, 12); (9, −10) and (2, −10)

2.8 Problem Solving (pp. 97 – 99) **37.** (2, 5), (8, −1), (2, −7), (−4, −1) **39.** 2000 ft

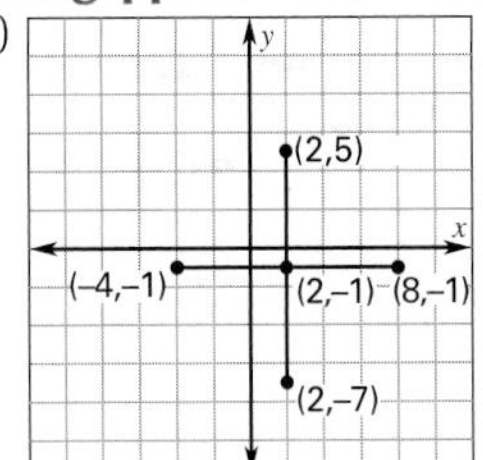

43. a. $.70; $1.40; $2.10 **b.**

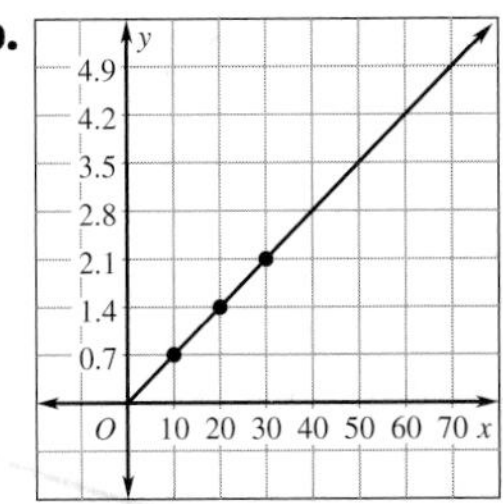

c. $4.20
45. *A*(−2, 6), *B*(1, 4), *C*(0, 1), *D*(−4, 1), *E*(−5, 4);

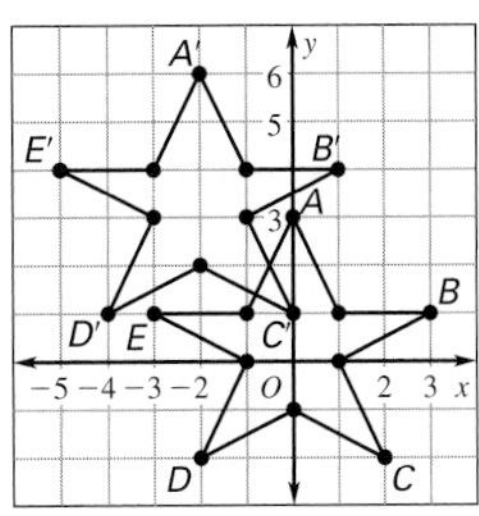

47. *Sample answer:* It is larger than the original; The perimeter of the second rectangle is twice the perimeter of the original rectangle.

49.

width *x* (cm)	1	2	3	4	5	6	7	8
Perimeter *P* (cm)	18	20	22	24	26	28	30	32

The ordered pairs lie on a line. (An equation of the line is $P = 2x + 16$.);

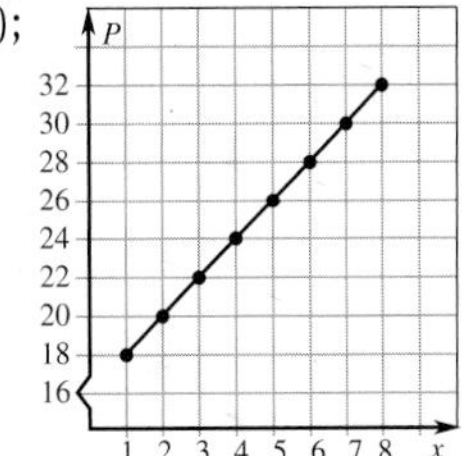

Chapter Review (pp. 102 – 106)

1. two; 15, −15 **3.** 4;

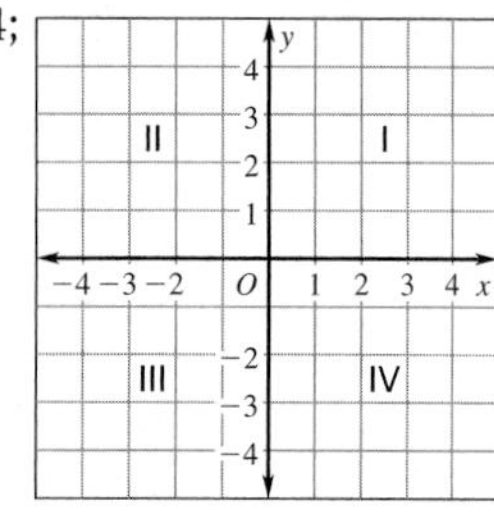

5. coordinate plane **7.** −42, −31, −5, 8, 11, 53 **9.** −22; 22 **11.** 512; 512 **13.** 92; 92 **15.** −147; 147 **17.** −172 **19.** 176 **21.** 401 **23.** −48 **25.** 34 **27.** −336 **29.** −86 **31.** 79 **33.** 137 **35.** −134 **37.** −54 **39.** 0 **41.** −192 **43.** −140 **45.** 56 **47.** 160 **49.** 152 ft **51.** 14 **53.** −9 **55.** −7 **57.** 3 **59.** 1 **61.** −3 **63.** −100; Comm. Prop. of Add., Assoc. Prop. of Add. **65.** 1900; Comm. Prop. of Mult., Assoc. Prop. of Mult. **67.** 1500; Assoc. Prop. of Mult. **69.** 3; Zero Prop. of Mult., Ident. Prop. of Add. **71.** $60x - 100$ **73.** $100z - 120$ **75.** $135 - 108t$ **77.** $7x - 2y$ **79.** $-4x - 6y$ **81.** $49a + b$ **83.** $84.50 **85.** (−4, 3) **87.** (−2, −3)

Chapter 3

3.1 Skill Practice (pp. 119 – 120)

1. inverse **3.** 6 **5.** 64 **7.** 7 **9.** 17 **11.** 40 **13.** −163 **15.** 1 **17.** 0.2 **19.** $\frac{1}{3}$ **21.** 1000 should be subtracted from both sides instead of added; $x + 1000 - 1000 = 5000 - 1000$; 4000 **23.** 8 **25.** −31 **27.** 35 **29.** $n + 12 = 25$; 13 **31.** $n - 3 = -16$; −13 **33.** $97 = 24 + 16 + k + 38$; 19 cm **35.** paper and pencil; 59 **37.** paper and pencil; 1173 **39.** negative; $-50 + 12 < 0$ **41.** 9 **43.** 3

3.1 Problem Solving (pp. 120 – 121)

47. a. tax **b.** $54.99 + x = 58.29$ **c.** $3.30 **49.** not correct; $t = 29 - 3$; 26°F **53.** $45 + x = 104$; 59 in. **55.** female: 8 in./year; male: 7 in./year; female

3.2 Skill Practice (pp. 124 – 125)

1. divide **3.** dividing by 5 **5.** subtracting −6 **7.** dividing by −3 **9.** 18 **11.** 13 **13.** 9 **15.** 10 **17.** 2.5 **19.** −2.1 **21.** 3 **23.** −6 **25.** −31.5 **31.** −8; simplify; divide each side by −1 **33.** 4; multiply each side by 6; simplify **35.** $12\frac{2}{3}$; multiply each side by 4; simplify

3.2 Problem Solving (pp. 125 – 126)

43. $1950 = 30x$; 65 **45.** $7a = 56$; $8 **49.** $100 = \frac{1}{5}t$; 500 m **51.** 22; 5

3.3 Skill Practice (pp. 131 – 132)

1. solution **3.** 3 **5.** 1 **7.** −8 **9.** 81 **11.** −5 **13.** 8 **15.** 30 **17.** 48.8 **19.** −12 **23.** equation; distributive property; subt. prop. of equality; simplify; division prop. of equality; simplify **25.** 2; Use Exercise 24 because 3 divides into 9 easily. **27.** 3; Use Exercise 23 because $6 \times \frac{1}{3}$ eliminates the fraction. **29.** $4x + 9 = 5$; −1; $3y - 10 = 2$; 4 **31.** $4h - 6 = -24$, undo division and simplify; $4h = -18$, undo subtraction and simplify; $h = -4.5$, undo multiplication and simplify **33.** $2w - 3 = 45$, undo division and simplify; $2w = 48$, undo subtraction and simplify; $w = 24$, undo multiplication and simplify **35.** $2(4t - 7) = -66$, undo division and simplify; $4t - 7 = -33$, undo multiplication and simplify; $4t = -26$, undo subtraction and simplify; $t = -6.5$, undo multiplication and simplify

3.3 Problem Solving (pp. 132 – 133)

39. 11 **43.** 19

3.4 Skill Practice (pp. 136 – 139)

1. equation **3.** D **5.** A **9.** $5n + 4 = 9$; 1 **11.** $-2n + 3.5 = 7.5$; −2 **13.** $\frac{|n|}{6} = 4$; 24, −24 **15.** $|n| + 6 = 12$; 6, −6

3.4 Problem Solving (pp. 136 – 139)

21. a. profit = cash taken in − expenses **b.** $93 = 6n - 15$ **c.** 18 **d.** $93 + 15 = 108$ and $108 \div 18 = 6$ **23.** 7 **25.** $7 **29.** 16 **31.** 29 **33.** 10 mi; no; $2 + 30 = 32$, $32 \neq 2 \times 17$ **35.** You need to know how many hours you worked.

3.5 Skill Practice (pp. 145 – 146)

1. base; height **3.** 12 cm²; 16 cm **5.** 30 ft²; 30 ft **7.** 3 ft **9.** 20 m **11.** 504 in.² **17.** 3 m **19.** $\frac{20}{w}$ in.

3.5 Problem Solving (pp. 146 – 147)

23. a. 42 yd² **b.** 9 yd² **c.** 51 yd² **29.** doubles **31.** quadruples

3.6 Problem Solving (pp. 150 – 152)

1. equivalent inequalities **3.** A **5.** D **7.** $x \geq -5$; all numbers greater than or equal to −5 **9.** $x < 6$; all numbers less than 6

11. $p < -5$;

13. $n > 9$;

15. $m \leq 11$;

17. $b < -9$;

19. $t > 4\frac{3}{4}$;

21. 1 through 9 **23.** 1 through 9 **29.** yes; When x is less than 2, 2 is greater than x. **35.** t is greater than or equal to 7 and less than 9; t is between 7 and 9, including 7.

3.6 Problem Solving (pp. 152 – 153)

37. a. 360 **b.** $x + 360 \geq 425$; $x \geq 65$ **c.**

39. $x + 57 > 93.5$; $x > 36.5$m **43.** $2.5 - x < 1.9$; $x > 0.6$ h; 37 min **45.** $T - 2200 \leq 2000$; $T \leq 4200$; one icon

3.7 Skill Practice (pp. 156 – 157)

1. reverse the direction of **3.** no **5.** yes **7.** $x \leq 32$; D 9. $x \geq -2$; A

11. $x < 8$;

13. $z \geq 3$;

15. $x > 4$;

17. $b \leq -360$;

19. $g < 6$; 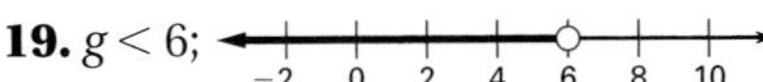

21. $c \geq -6$; −8 −6 −4 −2 0 2 4

23. $r > -56$; −70 −56 −42 −28 −14 0 14

25. $k \geq -3$; −6 −5 −4 −3 −2 −1 0

27. The inequality does not need to be reversed; $-3 < x$

31. $p \geq 2$; 0 1 2 3 4 5

33. $g < 2\frac{1}{4}$; $1\frac{3}{4}$ 2 $2\frac{1}{4}$ $2\frac{1}{2}$ $2\frac{3}{4}$ 3

35. $a \leq 36$; 33 34 35 36 37 38 39

39. $8 < n < 16$

3.7 Problem Solving (pp. 157 – 159) **43.** $5.5x \geq 275$; $x \geq 50$ **45.** You still have to isolate the variable by performing inverse operations. If multiplying or dividing by a negative number, you must reverse the direction of the inequality. **47. a.** $150p \leq 2000$ **b.** $p \leq 13.\overline{3}$ **c.** Up to 13 average sized people can ride the elevator together. **49.** $12l > 228$; $l > 19$ **51.** You can list all the solutions to an inequality used to find the possible measurements of the width of a pool. You cannot list all the solutions to an inequality used to find the number of people at the dance. **55.** $2w + 2(2w - 20) \geq 53$; $w \geq 15.5$; 16 in. by 11 in.

Chapter Review (pp. 161 – 164) **1.** addition and subtraction, multiplication and division; Inverse operations undo each other. **3.** equivalent **5.** −11 **7.** 12 **9.** −9 **11.** $\frac{4}{7}$ **13.** 14.8 **15.** 27 **17.** 55 **19.** 2 **21.** 9 **23.** −72 **25.** 27 **27.** $4p + 3 = 55$; 13 **29.** 12 **31.** 640 **33.** 9 ft **35.** $k \leq 10$; 7 8 9 10 11

37. $d \geq -6$; −8 −6 −4 −2 0 2 4

39. $b \leq -2$; -5 -4 -3 -2 -1 0 1

41. $p < 10.2$; 9 10 11

43. $d \leq 204$ **45.** $b > -4$ **47.** $k \geq 9$ **49.** $z < 2$

Chapter 4

4.1 Skill Practice (pp. 178 – 179) **1.** prime **3.** 1, 2, 3, 6, 9, 18 **5.** 1, 2, 17, 34 **7.** 1, 29 **9.** 1, 2, 3, 4, 6, 9, 12, 18, 27, 36, 54, 108 **11.** 1, 13, 23, 299 **13.** 1, 2, 4, 5, 8, 10, 16, 20, 25, 40, 50, 80, 100, 200, 400 **15.** composite **17.** prime **19.** 8, 2, 2, 2, 11; $2^3 \cdot 11$ **21.** 2, 2, 21, 5, 3, 7; $2 \cdot 3 \cdot 5 \cdot 7$ **23.** $5 \cdot 11$ **25.** $2^5 \cdot 3$ **27.** $2^2 \cdot 3^2 \cdot 11$ **29.** $2^4 \cdot 5^3$ **31.** $3 \cdot 5 \cdot c \cdot d$ **33.** $3 \cdot 3 \cdot x \cdot x \cdot y$ **35.** $2 \cdot 2 \cdot 2 \cdot 2 \cdot 3 \cdot n \cdot n \cdot n \cdot m \cdot m \cdot m$ **37.** $2 \cdot 2 \cdot 5 \cdot a \cdot b \cdot b \cdot b \cdot b \cdot c \cdot c$ **39.** 1 does not need to be included, 6 is not factored, and there are two factors of x; $18x^2y = 2 \cdot 3 \cdot 3 \cdot x \cdot x \cdot y$. **41.** $56 = 2 \cdot 2 \cdot 2 \cdot 7$; Find all other combinations of products of the prime factors. 2, $2 \cdot 2$, 7, $2 \cdot 2 \cdot 2$, $2 \cdot 7$, $2 \cdot 2 \cdot 7$. **43.** $225 = 3 \cdot 3 \cdot 5 \cdot 5$; Find all other combinations of products of the prime factors; 3, 5, $3 \cdot 3$, $3 \cdot 5$, $5 \cdot 5$, $3 \cdot 3 \cdot 5$, $3 \cdot 5 \cdot 5$. *45–47. Sample answers are given.* **45.** 3 + 13 **47.** 7 + 23

4.1 Problem Solving (pp. 179 – 180) **49. a.** 1, 2, 3, 4, 5, 6, 8, 10, 12, 15, 20, 24, 30, 40, 60, 120 **b.** 1 and 120, 2 and 60, 3 and 40, 4 and 30, 5 and 24, 6 and 20, 8 and 15, 10 and 12 **c.** 8 and 15, 10 and 12; *Sample answer:* The other arrangements would make an unreasonably long and narrow quilt.

4.2 Skill Practice (pp. 183 – 184) **1.** greatest common factor, or GCF **3.** 14 **5.** 4 **7.** 3 **9.** 1 **11.** The student forgot to include 2 as a factor twice; The GCF is $2 \cdot 2 \cdot 5 = 20$. **13.** no; 5 **15.** yes **17.** no; 18 **19.** yes **21.** $3x$ **23.** $5t^4$ **25.** $6s$ **27.** $3t$ **29.** 1 **35.** sometimes; For example, the GFC of 5 and 10 is 5. **37.** always; 1 is the only factor the two numbers share. **39.** Multiply the previous monomial by $4rs^2$; $256r^5s^7$, $1024r^6s^9$, $4096r^7s^{11}$; $4r^2s$

4.2 Problem Solving (pp. 184 – 185) **45.** *Sample answer:* The only factors of any prime number are 1 and itself, so the only common factor any two prime numbers can have is 1. For example, $5 = 1 \cdot 5$ and $7 = 1 \cdot 7$ have only 1 as a common factor, as do $43 = 1 \cdot 43$ and $79 = 1 \cdot 79$. **47.** The GCF of cx, cy, and cz is the product of c and the GCF of x, y, and z.

4.3 Skill Practice (pp. 189 – 190) **1.** simplest form **3.** $\frac{3}{7}$ **5.** $\frac{2}{3}$ **7.** $\frac{-5}{8}$, or $-\frac{5}{8}$ **9.** $\frac{3}{4}$ **11.** $\frac{-7}{8}$, or $-\frac{7}{8}$ **13.** yes **15.** yes **17.** no **19.** yes **21.** C *23–25. Sample answers are given.* **23.** $\frac{4}{9}, \frac{8}{18}$ **25.** $\frac{12}{35}, \frac{24}{70}$ **27.** $-\frac{2y}{5}$; −2 **29.** $\frac{x}{6}; \frac{1}{2}$ **31.** $\frac{5}{xy^2}; \frac{1}{15}$ **33.** $-\frac{5}{2x^2y^2}; -\frac{1}{90}$ **35.** 14 **37.** 24 **39.** no **41.** yes

4.3 Problem Solving (pp. 190 – 191) **45.** $\frac{6}{25}$ **47.** $\frac{13}{50}$

4.4 Skill Practice (pp. 194 – 195) **1.** common multiple **3.** 24 **5.** 40 **7.** 36 **9.** 24 **11.** 42 **13.** 165 **15.** 210 **17.** 420 **19.** 12 is the GCF, not the LCM; The LCM is $2 \cdot 2 \cdot 2 \cdot 3$, or 24. *21–27. Methods and explanations may vary.* **21.** mental math; 500 **23.** prime factorization; 90 **25.** prime factorization; 216 **27.** prime factorization; 630 **29.** $36y^4$ **31.** $35ab^2$ **33.** $36x^3y^5$ **35.** $120c^3d^6$

4.4 Problem Solving (pp. 195 – 196) **45.** 180 sec **49.** yes; The greater number is the LCM. **51.** 21; The color repeats every fourth figure, and the orientation repeats every fifth figure. The LCM of 4 and 5 is 20, and 20 figures after Figure 1 is 21.

4.5 Skill Practice (p. 200) **1.** least common multiple, or LCM **3.** 6 **5.** 24 **7.** < **9.** > **11.** > **13.** > **15.** You must first rewrite both fractions using the LCD and then compare numerators; $\frac{3}{5} = \frac{21}{35}$ and $\frac{4}{7} = \frac{20}{35}$. Because 21 > 20, $\frac{3}{5} > \frac{4}{7}$. **17.** $\frac{5}{4}, 1\frac{1}{2}, \frac{11}{6}$ **19.** $\frac{5}{9}, \frac{3}{4}, 1\frac{1}{3}$ **21.** $\frac{19}{12}, 1\frac{3}{5}, 2\frac{1}{4}, \frac{7}{3}$

SELECTED ANSWERS

23. $\frac{34}{3}, 11\frac{7}{12}, \frac{47}{4}$ **25.** = **27.** <

4.5 Problem Solving (p. 201) **37.** Sarah

4.6 Skill Practice (pp. 204 – 206) **1.** base **3.** 4^6 **5.** a^{12} **7.** u^8 **9.** b^{15} **11.** 3^7 **13.** $(-4)^5$ **15.** $9a^5$ **17.** $243x^9$ **19.** $25x^{16}$ **21.** $216x^6y^4$ **23.** 5^4 **25.** d^7 **27.** w^6 **29.** $(-7)^3$ **33.** z^5 **35.** $25n^3$ **37.** $2401r^4$ **39.** y^{10} **41.** When dividing monomials involving exponents, subtract the exponents; $\frac{x^{20}y^6}{x^5y^3} = x^{15}y^3$ **43.** $(-2)^6$ **45.** 2 **47.** $(-3)^5$ **49.** 1

51. $-4b^4$ **53.** $9n^3$ **55.** 8 **57.** 12 **59.** 4 **61.** 11 **63.** 8 **65.** 12 **67.** $3x - 3 = 12$; 5 **69.** $4x + 4 = 12$; 2 **71.** $x - 5 = 3$; 8 **73.** $2 = 4x - 2$; 1 **75.** 3^6; 729 **77.** 4^4; 256

4.6 Problem Solving (pp. 206 – 207) **83.** 10^{12} **85.** 10^{12} **87.** 10^6 **89. a.** 1 exameter **b.** 21 exameters **c.** 1,000,000,000 gigameters **d.** 21,000,000,000 gigameters **93.** 3^{16} mm²; 81; $(3^8 \cdot 9)(3^8 \cdot 9) = 3^{16} \cdot 81$

4.7 Skill Practice (p. 210) **1.** 1 **3.** $\frac{1}{81}$ **5.** $-\frac{1}{16}$ **7.** $\frac{1}{36}$ **9.** $-\frac{1}{625}$ **11.** 5^{-3} means $\frac{1}{5^3}$; $5^{-3} = \frac{1}{5^3} = \frac{1}{125}$ **13.** 1 **15.** $\frac{1}{c^7}$ **17.** $\frac{4}{z^6}$ **19.** $\frac{6}{r^9}$ **21.** 0 **23.** −5 **25.** −2 **27.** −7

29. always; A power with an exponent of zero is equal to 1, which is positive. **31.** sometimes; If the exponent is even, it will be positive.

4.7 Problem Solving (p. 211) **39.** 10^{11} **41.** 10^8

4.8 Skill Practice (pp. 214 – 215) **1.** yes; 9.32 is between 1 and 10, and 5 is an integer. **3.** yes; 7 is between 1 and 10, and −4 is an integer. **5.** 4.68×10^{-1} **7.** 8.92×10^{10} **9.** 2.13×10^6 **11.** 4.15×10^{-7} **15.** 4,350,000 **17.** 0.0871 **19.** 0.00000000176 **21.** 2,830,000,000,000 **23.** 6×10^8 **25.** 5.85×10^{-7} **27.** 6.552×10^{14} **29.** 1.066×10^5 **31.** 18.6 is not between 1 and 10, and when multiplying powers with the same base, you must add the exponents, not multiply; $(3 \times 10^2) \times (6.2 \times 10^3) = (3 \times 6.2) \times (10^2 \times 10^3) = 18.6 \times 10^5 = 1.86 \times 10^6$ **33.** > **35.** > **37.** 3.5×10^{11} **39.** 3.25×10^3

4.8 Problem Solving (pp. 215 – 217) **45. a.** 3.2 **b.** 10^2 **c.** 3.2×10^2 **47.** 1.5×10^7 **53.** 7.98×10^7; 4.161×10^9 **55.** \$8,600,000; \$60,200,000; \$3,139,000,000

4.8 Technology Activity (p. 218) **1.** 2.7115×10^{14} **3.** 1.584×10^{-11} **5.** 8.2×10^6 **7.** 4.02×10^{-7} **9.** 4.5×10^6 **11.** 1.4×10^{-9} **13.** about 7.7×10^{11} gal; about 4.015×10^{13} gal

Chapter Review (pp. 220 – 224) **1.** *Sample answer:* The greatest common factor is the largest number that is a factor of both numbers. The least common multiple is the smallest number that is a multiple of both numbers. **3.** *Sample answer:* abc, 5x, $12x^2y$ **5.** simplest form **7.** equivalent fractions **9.** composite **11.** prime **13.** 7 **15.** $2^3 \cdot 3 \cdot 5$ **17.** $2 \cdot 2 \cdot 7 \cdot x \cdot y \cdot y \cdot y$ **19.** $2 \cdot 2 \cdot 2 \cdot 2 \cdot 5 \cdot p \cdot p \cdot p \cdot p \cdot q \cdot q \cdot q$ **21.** 16 **23.** $7a$ **25.** 10 **27.** x **29.** yes **31.** no **33.** 30 baskets; 2 cans of cranberry sauce, 4 cans of canned fruit, 3 cans of corn, 2 boxes of muffin mix **35.** $\frac{3}{20}$ **37.** $\frac{n^2}{3}$ **39.** 270 **41.** $36n^3$ **43.** > **45.** = **47.** $\frac{5}{8}, \frac{7}{11}, \frac{2}{3}$ **49.** $\frac{17}{3}, 5\frac{7}{8}, \frac{53}{9}$ **51.** Joe; $\frac{1}{24}$ cup **53.** 9^9 **55.** a^{23} **57.** 5^3 **59.** b^7 **61.** y^8 **63.** x^3y^2 **65.** $\frac{1}{n^3}$ **67.** $\frac{3}{c^{13}}$ **69.** $\frac{3}{2z^2}$ **71.** 20 **73.** 9×10^{-7} **75.** 236,000,000 **77.** 0.0094 **79.** 1.612×10^9 **81.** 3.6624×10^9

Chapter 5

5.1 Skill Practice (pp. 235 – 236) **1.** denominator; numerator **3.** $\frac{7}{21}; \frac{1}{3}$ **5.** $\frac{2}{18}; \frac{1}{9}$ **7.** $-1\frac{4}{14}; -1\frac{2}{7}$ **9.** $-7\frac{7}{5}; -8\frac{2}{5}$ **11.** $-\frac{3n}{21}; -\frac{n}{7}$ **13.** $\frac{15}{a}$ **15.** $\frac{2a}{20b}; \frac{a}{10b}$ **17.** $\frac{4a}{2b}; \frac{2a}{b}$ **19.** $1\frac{1}{2}$ **21.** $1\frac{11}{18}$ **23.** $3\frac{1}{12}$ **25.** $-3\frac{3}{16}$ **27.** $\frac{1}{9}$ must be subtracted, not added; $1\frac{1}{3}$ **29.** $\frac{2}{17}$ **31.** $\frac{8}{9}$ **33.** 0 **35.** $\frac{8}{11}$ **37.** *Sample answer:* $1\frac{1}{5} + 2\frac{3}{5} = 3\frac{4}{5}$; $1\frac{1}{4} + \left(-1\frac{3}{4}\right) = -\frac{1}{2}$

5.1 Problem Solving (pp. 236 – 238) **41.** $18\frac{3}{4}$ in. **43.** $2\frac{1}{2}$ mm **45.** 1 ft $8\frac{1}{2}$ in.

5.2 Skill Practice (p. 240) **1.** least common multiple **3.** $\frac{5}{8}$ **5.** $\frac{13}{18}$ **7.** $-\frac{33}{40}$ **9.** $4\frac{4}{5}$ **11.** $11\frac{19}{36}$ **13.** $\frac{8}{11}$ **15.** $-\frac{33w}{40}$ **17.** $\frac{17s}{20}$ **19.** $-\frac{13}{50n}$ **21.** $\frac{54 + 11a}{21a}$

23–27. Methods will vary. **23.** true; paper and pencil **25.** false; estimation **27.** false; paper and pencil **29.** $3\frac{23}{70}$ **31.** $4\frac{1}{24}$

5.2 Problem Solving (pp. 241 – 242) **37.** $15\frac{3}{4}$ in. **41.** $x = 25\frac{1}{2} - 9\frac{1}{3} - 7\frac{5}{6}$; $8\frac{1}{3}$ ft

5.3 Skill Practice (p. 245) **1.** numerators; denominators **3.** $-1\frac{7}{8}$ **5.** $\frac{6}{25}$ **7.** $-\frac{25}{72}$ **9.** $4\frac{1}{2}$ **11.** $-19\frac{4}{5}$ **13.** −34 **15.** $-\frac{15}{16}$ **17.** $\frac{245}{288}$ **19.** $1\frac{7}{8}$ in.² **21.** $11\frac{113}{121}$ m² **23.** $-2\frac{1}{5}$ **25.** $1\frac{13}{72}$ **27.** $2\frac{3}{8}$ **29.** $4\frac{9}{16}$

5.3 Problem Solving (p. 246) **33.** $1\frac{2}{5}$ km **35.** $2\frac{1}{5}$ sec **37.** $13\frac{11}{18}$ ft²

5.4 Skill Practice (pp. 249 – 250) **1.** the reciprocal **3.** 6 **5.** $-2\frac{1}{2}$ **7.** $\frac{7}{9}$ **9.** $-5\frac{4}{7}$ **11.** $\frac{5}{12}$ **13.** $-\frac{3}{20}$ **15.** The wrong fraction was inverted; $-\frac{3}{10} \div \left(-\frac{4}{5}\right) = -\frac{3}{10} \times \left(-\frac{5}{4}\right) = \frac{3}{8}$ **17.** 8 **19.** $\frac{4}{9}$ **21.** $\frac{25}{36}$ **23.** 100 **25.** $2\frac{4}{49}$ **27.** $-7\frac{1}{12}$ **29.** $1\frac{3}{13}$ **31.** $3\frac{3}{5}$ **33.** $-1\frac{9}{14}$ **35.** $-5\frac{9}{10}$ **37.** $2 \div \frac{4}{5}$; $2\frac{1}{2}$

39.

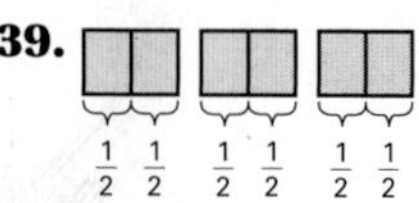

41. 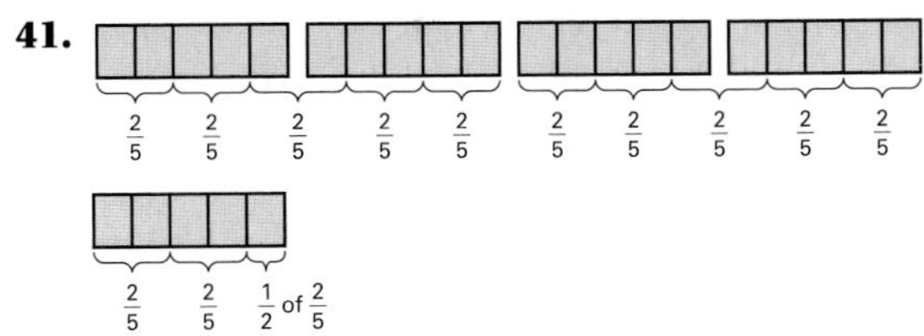

43. 20 **45.** $-5\frac{2}{3}$ **47.** 66 **49.** −8 **51.** yes; The *c* in the numerator and denominator will divide out.

5.4 Problem Solving (pp. 251 – 252) **53.** division because you are splitting 5 lb into $\frac{1}{4}$ lb sections; 20 **55.** addition because you are looking for a total of 3 different distances; $21\frac{7}{12}$ ft **57.** multiplication because you are adding the same number of pounds repeated times; 765 lb

5.4 Technology Activity (p. 253) **1.** $\frac{47}{55}$ **3.** $\frac{2}{3}$ **5.** $1\frac{1}{27}$ **7.** $\frac{2}{7}$ **9.** $11\frac{1}{5}$ **11.** $5\frac{1}{3}$ **13.** $374\frac{5}{8}$ lb

5.5 Skill Practice (pp. 257 – 258) **1.** rational, integer, whole **3.** rational, integer **5.** 0.75 **7.** −0.48 **9.** −0.16 **11.** 3.6875 **13.** $-0.\overline{42}$ **15.** $6.5\overline{3}$ **17.** $\frac{3}{10}$ has a decimal value of 0.3 not 0.03; 2.3 **19.** > **21.** > **23.** < **25.** = **27.** $-0.4, -\frac{2}{7}, 0.1, \frac{3}{10}, \frac{5}{6}$ **29.** $\frac{3}{5}$ **31.** $\frac{12}{25}$ **33.** $\frac{73}{200}$ **35.** $-5\frac{2}{625}$ **37.** $\frac{8}{9}$ **39.** $\frac{7}{33}$ **41.** $\frac{635}{999}$ **43.** $-\frac{7}{45}$ **45.** $1.\overline{21}$, 1.21, 3^{-2}, $\left(\frac{1}{3}\right)^3$ **47.** $0.\overline{4}, \frac{3}{7}, 4^{-2}, \left(\frac{1}{5}\right)^2$

5.5 Problem Solving (pp. 258 – 259) **49.** 0.66, 2^{-4}, $\frac{-1}{15}$, $-0.\overline{6}$ **51.** $\frac{x}{8}, \frac{x}{7}, \frac{x}{6}, \frac{x}{5}, \frac{x}{4}, \frac{x}{3}, \frac{x}{2}, x$; *x* continues to be divided by smaller and smaller numbers, resulting in greater values. **53.** 5

5.6 Skill Practice (pp. 262 – 263) **1.** 13; 11; 25 **3.** 3.093 **5.** −2.17 **7.** −10.89 **9.** −0.104 **11.** 59.61 **13.** −1.294 **15.** 32.15 **17.** The decimals are not lined up correctly; Line up the decimal points, 17.951. **19.** 2.4 **21.** 5.61 **23.** 7.31 **25.** −0.17 **27.** −6.347 **29.** 32 **31.** 60 **33.** 6.655 **35.** 0.1 **37.** 20.9 cm

39. 12.5 units; 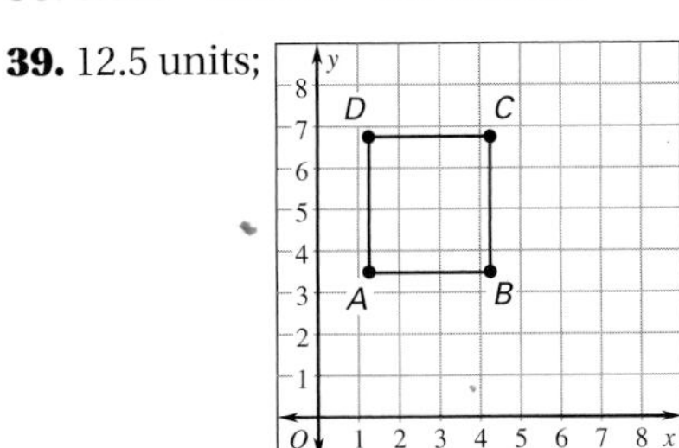

41. $6.\overline{224133}$ **43.** $11.\overline{1}$

5.6 Problem Solving (pp. 263 – 264) **45. a.** 1.96 m **b.** 1.31 m **47.** yes; The sum of the whole parts is 12. **49. a.** *Sample answer:* \$123 **b.** \$122.92 **c.** withdraw; \$21.67

5.7 Skill Practice (pp. 267 – 268) **1.** 7 **3.** 20.28 **5.** −5.74 **7.** 5 **9.** 12 **11.** 4 **13.** 2.5 **15.** about 1.89 **17.** −1.5 **19.** −8.7 **21.** about 290.41 **23.** The decimal in the answer was put in the wrong place; 33.252 **25.** D **27.** −8.1 **29.** −17.36 **31.** about 0.27 **33.** about −0.42 **35.** about −0.60 **37.** < **39.** 160.31 **41.** multiply by −0.5; 0.0625, −0.03125

5.7 Problem Solving (pp. 268 – 269) **47.** The decimals move one place to the left;

X	1	0.1	0.01	0.001	0.0001
87	87	8.7	0.87	0.087	0.0087
356	356	35.6	3.56	0.356	0.0356
1200	1200	120	12	1.2	0.12

51. 1; 2; 3; 7; Each factor has one decimal place, so the products have the number of decimal places equal to the exponent value. **53.** 87.6 mi/h; 1.2 **55.** 4548.12 ft^2

5.8 Skill Practice (pp. 274 – 275) **1.** mean **3.** range **5.** 5.875 km; 16 km; 16 km and 23 km; 17 km **7.** $\frac{1}{4}$; 0; 0; 7 **9.** 2013; 2000; no mode; 460 **11.** 19°; 13°; none; 83° **13.** 8 is also a mode; The modes are 5 and 8. **15.** mean, median **17.** mean **19.** with red: 30, 26, 16, 85; without red: $24\frac{1}{3}$, 24.5, 16, 23; The mean and range are much smaller without the 98. The mode is unchanged, and the median is slightly lower. **21.** 44; $58\frac{2}{7}$; 57; no mode **23.** 7; 8; no mode; 11 **25.** 38; 27.5; no mode; 25

5.8 Problem Solving (pp. 275 – 278) **31.** 52,327; 49,707; 49,646; mean; The mean takes into account the three dates with higher attendance. **35.** −97 m **37.** Jerry substituted the value of *a* and then found the mean using the numbers. Roberta found the mean before substituting the value; Both methods are correct; Roberta's method will save time, as it takes fewer calculations. **39.** You may not know if there are any very deep spots which would cause you to not be able to wade across. **41.** 9.625; 9.75; 9.675; Carl; Kurt; Isaac **43.** It removes the chance of an extremely high or low score affecting the mean.

Chapter Review (pp. 280 – 284) **1.** reciprocals; multiplicative inverses **3.** front-end estimation **5.** rational number **7.** $1\frac{3}{4}$ **9.** $1\frac{5}{7}$ **11.** $-\frac{n}{6}$ **13.** $-\frac{4n}{3}$ **15.** $\frac{17}{20}$ **17.** $\frac{37v}{15}$ **19.** $1\frac{5}{24}$ **21.** $-\frac{x}{34}$ **23.** $-\frac{1}{4}$ **25.** $-\frac{2}{21}$ **27.** −26 **29.** $-16\frac{1}{14}$ **31.** $\frac{13}{15}$ **33.** −4 **35.** $2\frac{1}{16}$ **37.** $-7\frac{7}{11}$ **39.** $1\frac{9}{16}$ **41.** −0.875 **43.** $3\frac{9}{20}$ **45.** $2\frac{65}{99}$ **47.** $-0.\overline{27}$ **49.** 42.598 **51.** 98.11 **53.** 0.803 **55.** −12.323 **57.** 3.0132 **59.** 2 **61.** $\frac{1}{8}$; 1; −7 and 2; 15 **63.** 8.25; 7; 4.8 and 7; 13.2

Chapter 6

6.1 Skill Practice (pp. 295 – 296) **1.** $5x, -9x; 6, -2$ **3.** 1 **5.** -6 **7.** 6 **9.** 4 **11.** -10 **13.** -1 **15.** -2 was not distributed correctly to -4; $3x - 2(x - 4) = 5$; $3x - 2x + 8 = 5$; $x = -3$ **17.** 1 **19.** -37 **21.** -22 **23.** -5 **25.** -2 **27.** -11 **29.** -21 **31.** $228 = \frac{1}{2}(x + 11)(19)$; 13 **33.** $x = 5, y = 8$; 34 units

6.1 Problem Solving (pp. 296 – 297) **35. a.** $8(70 + x) = 2560$ **b.** 250 tickets **37.** $P = 104$ mm; 34 **41.** $25 + (15 + 25)w - 10w = 235$; 7 weeks

6.2 Skill Practice (pp. 300 – 301) **1.** the distance all around the figure **3.** 7 **5.** 27 **7.** -8 **9.** 9 **11.** $\frac{1}{2}$ **13.** $3\frac{1}{2}$ **15.** 36 units **17.** 132 units **19.** -7 **21.** -3 **23.** -16 **25.** -7.5 **27.** true; $x + 8 = 6x - 7$, so $x = 3$ and all 4 sides are 11. **29.** C

6.2 Problem Solving (pp. 301 – 302) **33.** 5 tickets **35.** \$.80; \$60; *Sample answer:* If the cost of a balloon alone is x, then $7 \cdot 8 + 5x = 75x$, and the solution is 0.8 or \$.80. So $7 \cdot 8 + 5x = 56 + 4 = \$60$.

6.3 Skill Practice (pp. 305 – 306) **1.** least common denominator **3.** -4 **5.** -0.34 **7.** 3.4 **9.** 0.5 **11.** $\frac{7}{13}$ **13.** 1 **15.** 20 **17.** $-\frac{5}{4}$ or $-1\frac{1}{4}$ **19.** Some of the terms were multiplied by 10 and some by 100; $1.5x + 0.25 = 1.6x$; $150x + 25 = 160x$; $25 = 10x$; $x = 2.5$ **21.** 1000; 2.5 **23.** 45; $\frac{8}{57}$ **25.** 10; $\frac{45}{4}$ or $11\frac{1}{4}$ or 11.25 **27.** 8 or 1000; $\frac{64}{9}$ or $7\frac{1}{9}$ or $7.\overline{1}$ **29.** *Answers may vary. Sample answer:* $5x - 3 = 18$; $5x = 21$; $x = 4\frac{1}{5}$

6.3 Problem Solving (pp. 306 – 307) **35.** $3.96x + 4.76x = 13.08$; 1.5 lb **41.** 4950 ft^2; 44 ft

6.4 Skill Practice (pp. 314 – 316)

1.

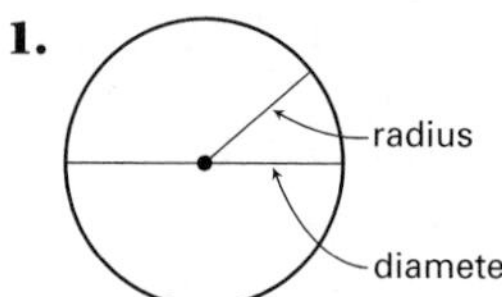

3. 62.8 mm; I used 3.14 because 10 is not a multiple of 7. **5.** 314 cm; I used 3.14 because 100 is not a multiple of 7. **7.** 44 in.; I used $\frac{22}{7}$ because 14 is a multiple of 7. **9.** 198 mm; I used $\frac{22}{7}$ because 63 is a multiple of 7. **11.** 264 ft; I used $\frac{22}{7}$ because 42 is a multiple of 7. **13.** 21 in. **15.** 10.5 km **17.** 1.5 cm **19.** 25 yd **21.** 7 m **23.** 2 cm; 6.28 cm **25.** 17 mm; 106.76 mm **27.** 21.42 ft **29.** $\frac{C}{d}$ by the Div. Prop. of Eq. **31.** $\frac{C}{2\pi}$ by the Div. Prop. of Eq.

6.4 Problem Solving (pp. 316 – 317) **37.** 22 in.; 66 in.; The larger is 3 times as great. **39.** about 23 ft **45.** *Sample answer:* 13 and 37; 13, because the square is closer in size to the small circle.

6.5 Skill Practice (pp. 320 – 321) **1.** less than, greater than, less than or equal to, greater than or equal to

3. $a \geq 1$;

5. $p \leq 6$;

7. $w > 2$;

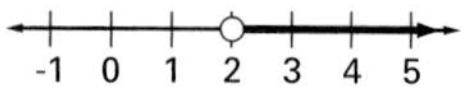

9. $c < \frac{1}{3}$;

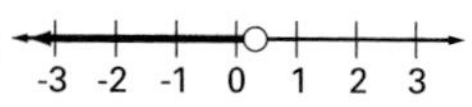

11. $z < -4$;

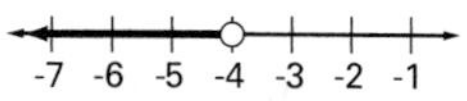

13. $n \leq -2$;

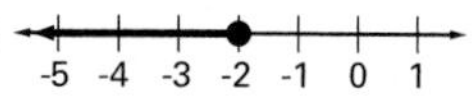

15. $a > -2$;

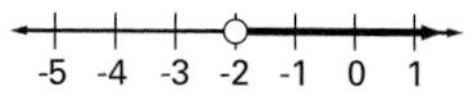

17. $k \geq 1$;

21. 21; $y \geq -10.5$ **23.** 6; $m < 24$ **25.** 100; $y < 5.1$ **27.** 100; $x \leq 49.3$ **29.** $-3 < x < 4$;

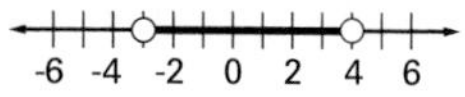

31. $-3 \leq x < 6$;

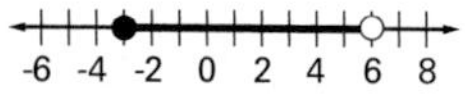

6.5 Problem Solving (pp. 321 – 322) **33. a.** $925 + 25p \geq 2500$ **b.** $p \geq 63$; You need at least 63 more pledges. **35.** $16{,}000 + 150n > 18{,}550$; $n > 17$; You have to catch more than 17 discs to have a new high score. **39.** $h < 6000$; The base height of a *Strato* cloud is less than 6000 ft. **41.** $6000 < h < 20{,}000$ **43.** You cannot buy a negative number of soft drinks.

6.5 Technology Activity (p. 323) **1.** $y < 13$ **3.** $n \leq -1$ **5.** $t > -3$ **7.** at most 16 pencils

6.6 Skill Practice (pp. 326 – 327) **1.** yes; It uses *at least.* **3.** no; It would be an equation. **5.** $x + 2 \leq 6$; $x \leq 4$ **7.** $x - 6 > 14$; $x > 20$ **9.** $x + 12 < 4$; $x < -8$ **13.** A number of ride tickets must be a whole number. **15.** A number of hot dogs must be a whole number.

6.6 Problem Solving (pp. 327 – 329) **21.** $30 + 4n < 6n$; $n > 15$; You have to attend more than 15 dances. **25.** $\frac{90 + 92 + 115 + x}{4} \geq 100$; $x \geq 103$ **27.** $6x + 30 + 24 \leq 108$; $x \leq 9$; no more than 9 boxes

Chapter Review (pp. 331 – 334) **1.** circle **3.** B **5.** C **7.** 6 **9.** 5 **11.** -4 **13.** 2 **15.** -7 **17.** -4 **19.** 2.25 **21.** $-\frac{5}{12}$ **23.** 16 **25.** \$.33/can **27.** 20 mm **29.** 21 ft **31.** 3.14 mi **33.** 140 m **35.** 279.46 ft **37.** $m < 9$ **39.** $14 - 3x \leq 11$; $x \geq 1$ **41.** at least 67 tickets

Chapter 7

7.1 Skill Practice (p. 345) **1.** A rate is a ratio of two quantities that have different units. **3.** $\frac{3}{2}$, 3 to 2, 3 : 2 **5.** $\frac{9}{14}$, 9 to 14, 9 : 14 **7.** $\frac{3}{1}$, 3 to 1, 3 : 1 **9.** $\frac{14}{3}$, 14 to 3, 14 : 3 **11.** 1 **13.** 1.75 **15.** 3000 **17.** 0.25 **19.** $\frac{4 \text{ adults}}{1 \text{ car}}$ **21.** $\frac{3 \text{ degrees}}{1 \text{ min}}$ **23.** $\frac{10 \text{ oz}}{1 \text{ serving}}$ **25.** $\frac{-4.25\text{m}}{1 \text{ sec}}$ **27.** Your friend should have multiplied by $\frac{7 \text{ days}}{1 \text{ week}} \cdot \frac{14 \text{ times}}{\text{day}} \cdot \frac{7 \text{ days}}{1 \text{ week}} = \frac{98 \text{ times}}{\text{week}}$. **29.** no **31.** yes **33.** 10 **35.** 3 **37.** 8 **39.** 6

7.1 Problem Solving (p. 346) **43.** 672 times

7.2 Skill Practice (pp. 350 – 351) **1.** Find the cross products and solve the resulting equation to solve the proportion. **3.** 3 **5.** 9 **9.** no **11.** yes **13.** 2 **15.** 9 **17.** 8 **19.** 0.06 **21.** 38.5 **23.** 1513 **25.** 6 in. **27.** 18.96 in. **29.** 1 **31.** 23 **33.** 2.5 **35.** $x = -3$, $y = -10.5$ **37.** $n = 16$, $p = 15$

7.2 Problem Solving (pp. 352 – 353) **39.** 2640 ft **41.** If you write 10 lb to \$16 as a fraction $\left(\frac{10}{16}\right)$ and write an equivalent fraction with 5 in the numerator, the denominator is 8, because $\frac{10}{16} = \frac{5}{8}$, so you can see that 5 lb of pasta costs \$8. **43. a.** 5.375 in., 1.9 in., 1.35 in. **47.** $\approx \frac{1 \text{ cm}}{450 \text{ ft}}$ **49.** *Sample answer:* \$72,800

7.3 Skill Practice (p. 356) **1.** percent **3.** $\frac{209}{b} = \frac{38}{100}$; 550 **5.** $\frac{5}{125} = \frac{p}{100}$; 4% **7.** $\frac{a}{245} = \frac{45}{100}$; 110.25 **9.** 90% **11.** 540 **13.** 135% **15.** 2.52 **21.** $<$ **23.** $>$ **25.** $=$ **27.** $5y$

7.3 Problem Solving (pp. 357 – 358) **31.** 81.8% **33.** 45 lb **35.** 16 ft **37.** 60% **41. a.** Mary Anne has mowed 960 ft^2 so far, and Josefina has mowed 1044 ft^2 so far. **b.** Mary Anne **c.** 1762.2 ft^2; about 51.8%

7.4 Skill Practice (pp. 361 – 362) **1.** 100; 1 **3.** 0.125 **5.** 1.1 **7.** 0.4455 **9.** 0.0078 **11.** 0.0008 **13.** 127% **15.** 210% **17.** 51% **19.** 5.7% **21.** 0.4% **23.** $\frac{4}{10}$ **25.** $\frac{13}{40}$ **27.** $1\frac{6}{25}$ **29.** $\frac{21}{500}$ **31.** $\frac{803}{10{,}000}$ **33.** 62.5% **35.** 1.25% **37.** 310% **39.** 8% **41.** 43.75% **43.** $<$ **45.** $>$ **47.** $>$ **49.** $=$ **51.** $>$ **53.** 6.5%, $\frac{9}{50}$, 0.5, 0.65, 66% **55.** $\frac{21}{100}$, 0.212, $\frac{21}{10}$, 212%, 21.2 **57.** 4.8%, $\frac{12}{25}$, 0.484, 480%, 4.84 **59.** A

61.

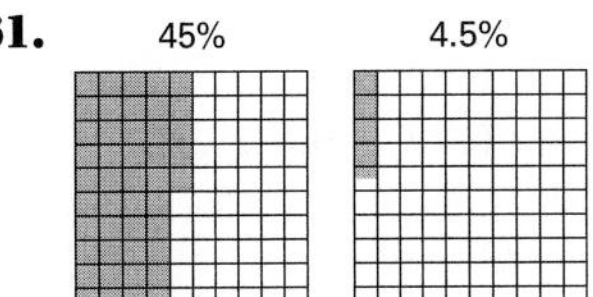

63.

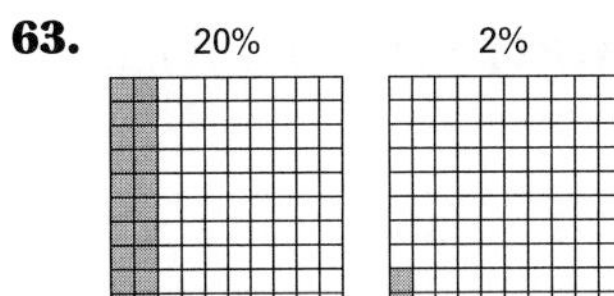

7.4 Problem Solving (pp. 363 – 364) **67.** 5% **69.** 31% **73.** $\frac{19}{50}$, $\frac{1}{2}$, 0.7, 79%, $\frac{17}{20}$

7.5 Skill Practice (p. 368) **1.** increase **3.** decrease; 2% **5.** increase; 14% **7.** increase; 20% **9.** 1144 **11.** 12.8 **13.** 77,000 **15.** Your friend did not add the increase to the original number. Multiplying a number by 5 and adding the product to the original number is a 500% increase. **17.** 50% **19.** 50% **21.** 50% **23.** 25%

7.5 Problem Solving (pp. 368 – 369) **25. a.** 219,700 **b.** 19,773 **c.** 239,473 **31.** 9 in. by 6 in.; The increase in area will be greater than 50%. The original area is 24 in.^{2}. The area of the enlargement is 54 in.^{2}. This is a 125% increase.

7.6 Skill Practice (pp. 372 – 373) **1.** markup **3.** \$51 **5.** \$41.25 **7.** \$29.40 **11.** \$61.61 **13.** \$274.98 **15.** \$22.50 **17.** discount; 25%; \$72 **19.** markup; 75%; \$168 **21.** markup; 80%; \$172.80

7.6 Problem Solving (pp. 373 – 374) **27.** \$37.80 **33.** \$21 **35.** 35%; \$38.35

7.7 Skill Practice (pp. 377 – 378) **1.** interest **3.** 414 **5.** 550 **7.** 66 **9.** 250 **11.** 78 **13.** 0.5% **15.** When using 60% in an equation, the decimal needs to be moved two places to the left; $54 = 0.60b$; $90 = b$ **17.** \$82.25 **19.** 40 **21.** 1 **25.** 2 yr **27.** \$2000

7.7 Problem Solving (pp. 378 – 379) **29. a.** $I = Prt$ **b.** $100 = P(0.03)(0.5)$ **c.** \$6,666.67 **33.** \$142.50; \$1342.50 **37.** 1.1; 3.3; 2.5; 5; 7.5; 3.8; 7.6; 11.4; *Sample answer:* 5% of a number is half of 10% of a number. 15% of a number is the sum of 5% and 10% of a number.

7.7 Technology Activity (p. 380) **1.** \$7577.03 **3.** \$3744.89 **5.** Your account balance is greater than your sister's by \$195.39 after 10 years.

7.8 Skill Practice (pp. 383 – 384) **1.** 2, 4, and 6 **3.** $\frac{1}{3}$ **5.** $\frac{11}{30}$ **7.** $\frac{0}{30}$ **9.** 20% **11.** 48% **13.** 100% **15.** 40 **17.** 0 **21.** $\frac{2}{3}$ **23.** $\frac{1}{8}$

7.8 Problem Solving (pp. 384 – 386) **27. b.** white: $\frac{1}{6}$; black: $\frac{1}{2}$; brown: $\frac{1}{3}$ **29.** 46% **31.** about 8 times **33. b.** *Sample answer:* Using the name Smith, the experimental probability of choosing the first letter was $\frac{2}{20}$; 10 times **35.** 50 children;

100 children; 300 children; 450 children
39. 25 times; There are 4 possible outcomes, choosing two girls, choosing two boys, choosing a girl and a boy, and choosing a boy and a girl. So, there is a 1 to 4 probability that you would choose two boys. Out of 100 times, 25 of them should be two boys.

Chapter Review (pp. 388 – 392) **1.** unit rate **3.** favorable outcomes; outcomes **5.** discount **7.** B **9.** $\frac{1}{1}$ **11.** $\frac{7.5 \text{ ft}}{1 \text{ sec}}$ **13.** $\frac{18 \text{ people}}{1 \text{ group}}$ **15.** $\frac{14 \text{ ft}}{1 \text{ sec}}$ **17.** $\frac{44.5 \text{ km}}{1 \text{ h}}$ **19.** Megan **21.** $5.\overline{3}$ **23.** 9 **25.** \$20 **27.** 6% **29.** 54.1% **31.** 0.038, $\frac{19}{500}$ **33.** 1.3, $\frac{13}{10}$ **35.** 250% **37.** 1860% **39.** 30% decrease **41.** 23% **43.** \$59.04 **45.** 96 **47.** \$48.30 **49.** red, 47%; yellow, 29%; blue, 24% **51.** 68%

Chapter 8

8.1 Skill Practice (pp. 406 – 407) **1.** supplementary **3.** supplementary **5.** 34° **7.** 158° **11.** m 2 = m 3 = 100°, m 1 = 80° **13.** m 1 = m 3 = m 5 = m 8 = m 9 = m 11 = 74°, m 2 = m 4 = m 6 = m 7 = m 10 = 106° **15.** B *17–19. Types may vary.* **17.** 115°; supplementary angles and corresponding angles **19.** 115°; supplementary angles and alternate interior angles **21.** sometimes; *Sample answer:* 150° + 30° = 180°, but 150° + 20° ≠ 180°. **23.** always; *Sample answer:* Perpendicular lines form a right angle, and angles that are supplementary to and vertical to a right angle are right angles. **25.** $y = \frac{16}{7}$; m $6 = 77\frac{1}{7}°$, m $3 = 102\frac{6}{7}°$

8.1 Problem Solving (pp. 407 – 408) **29.** 6 pairs; *Sample answer:* At each of the three parallel lines, 2 pairs of vertical angles are formed, so the total is 6 pairs. *Example:* See the diagram for Exercise 13 on page 406.

35.

105° 75°
75° 105°

37. Each is 67.5°; The vertical support at the peak divides the 135° angle in half, or 67.5°, and each of 1, 2, and 3 is a corresponding angle with the 67.5° angle.
39. 4 angles

8.1 Extension (p. 410)

1.

3.

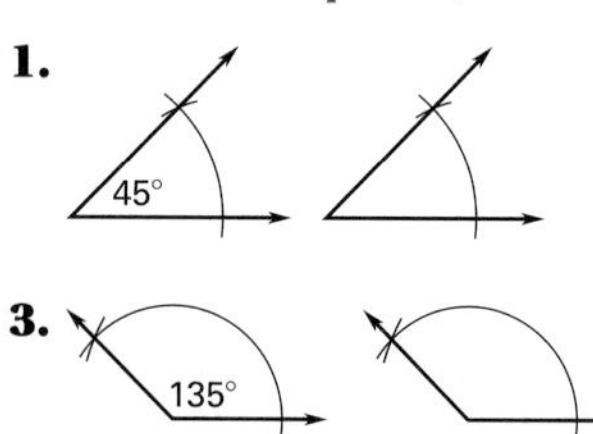

5.

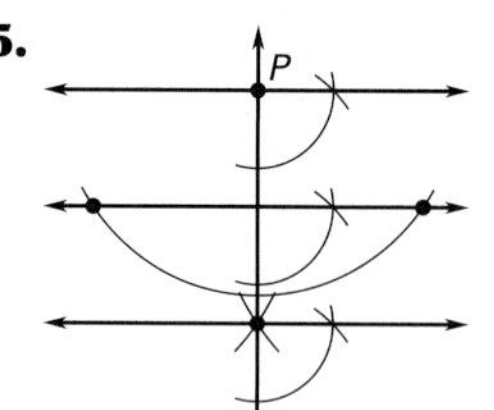

7.

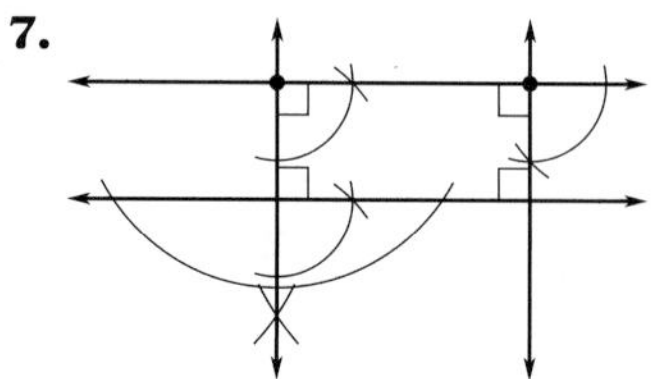

8.2 Skill Practice (pp. 413 – 414) **1.** scalene **3.** acute **5.** obtuse **7.** equilateral **9.** isosceles **11.** scalene **13.** 58; acute **15.** 32; obtuse **17.** No, the sum must be 180°, not 181°. **19.** Yes, the sum is 180°. **21.** 70°, 70°; acute **23.** 20°, 70°, 90° **25.** 60°, 60°, 60°

8.2 Problem Solving (pp. 414 – 415) **29.** 60°, 60°, 60° **31.** no; *Sample answer:* The sum of the measures of all three angles is 180°. If two angles are supplementary, then the measure of the third angle would have to be 0°, and there would not be a triangle. **35.** 295; reflex angle **37.** 250; reflex angle

8.3 Skill Practice (pp. 417 – 418) **1.** trapezoid **3.** trapezoid **5.** rhombus *7. Measurements may vary. Sample measurements are given.* **7.** 1.6 cm; rhombus **9.** $x = 109$ **11.** $x = 65$ **13.** $x = 65$, $y = 115$ **15.** A diagonal is not a side; diagonals of $ABCD$: $\overline{AC}$, $\overline{BD}$ **17.** $x = 5$; m $E = 121°$, m $H = 119°$ **19.** always; *Sample answer:* A rhombus is a parallelogram with four equal sides. **21.** always; *Sample answer:* A square is a parallelogram with 4 equal sides and 4 right angles. **23.** never; A trapezoid has exactly one pair of parallel sides, and a parallelogram has 2 pairs of parallel sides.

8.3 Problem Solving (p. 419) **27.** 2 diagonals; *Sample answer:*

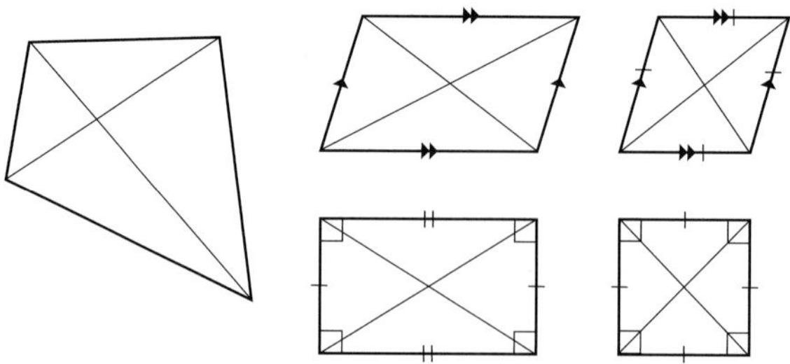

31. no; *Sample answer:* If the measures of three angles were 60°, then the measure of the fourth angle would have to be 360° − 3(60°) = 180°, so the figure would not have 4 distinct sides.

8.4 Skill Practice (pp. 422 – 423) **1.** polygon **3.** polygon **5.** regular polygon **7.** 2520° **9.** 3240° **11.** 144° **13.** 156° **15.** $x = 72$; m $R = m$ $N = 72°$, m $L = m$ $M = m$ $P = m$ $Q = 144°$ **17.** $x = 45$; m $A = m$ $D = m$ $C = 90°$, m $E = m$ $ABC = 135°$ **19.** 13-gon **21.** 18-gon

8.4 Problem Solving (pp. 423 – 424) **25.** not a polygon; The sides are not segments. **27.** *Answers may vary. Sample answer:* Some of the rocks are pentagons and hexagons. **29.** *Answers may vary. Sample answer:* Cut off the vertices without intersecting the cuts. **33.** 2, 5, 9, ...; 14 diagonals; **35.** regular 10-gon

8.5 Skill Practice (pp. 429 – 430) **1.** congruent **3.** *K*, *S*; *L*, *P*; *M*, *Q*; *N*, *R* **5.** 12 in. **7.** 80° **9.** 100° **11.** *ABC* *LKM* by SAS; *GJH* *PNQ* by SSS **15.** ASA; $2x + 6 = 32$, $x = 13$ **17.** *Answers may vary. Sample answers:*

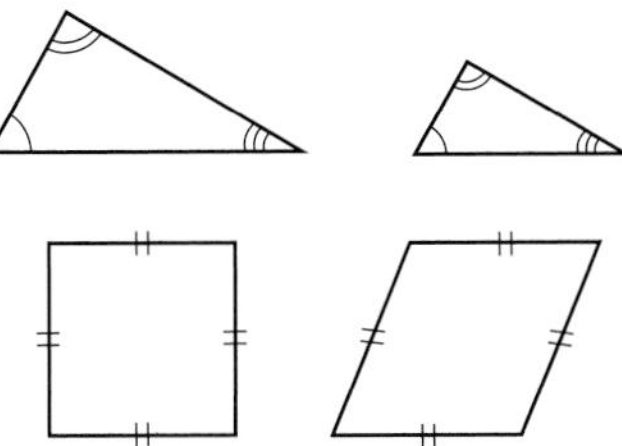

8.5 Problem Solving (pp. 431 – 432) **19.** Corresponding sides are equal, and corresponding angles are equal. **21.** The triangles are congruent by SSS. **23.** 127.5° **27.** no; *ABC* is not necessarily congruent to *XYZ*, so no other pairs of angles must be congruent. **29.** *Sample answer:* You can show the triangles are congruent if you know that the third sides of the two triangles are congruent or if you know that the angles between the two 7 ft sides in each triangle are congruent.

8.6 Skill Practice (pp. 435 – 436) **1.** reflection **3.** no **5.** no **7.**

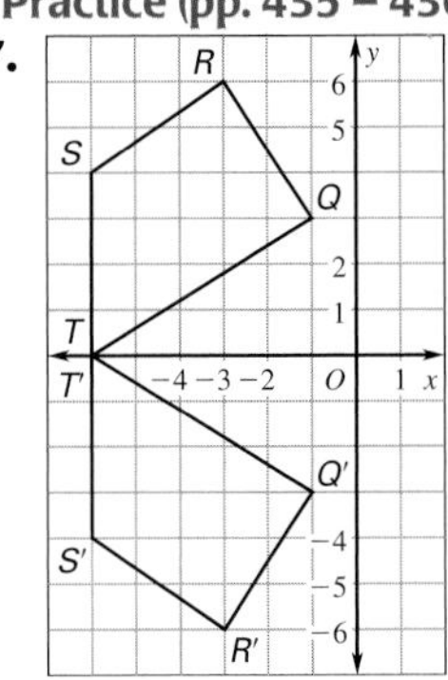

9. The image coordinates given are those for a reflection in the *y*-axis. The reflection of (x, y) in the *x*-axis is $(x, -y)$; Original: $A(4, 5)$, $B(2, 0)$, $C(6, 2)$; Image: $A'(4, -5)$, $B'(2, 0)$, $C'(6, -2)$ **13.** 6 lines of symmetry **15.** *Sample answer:* obtuse scalene triangle; yes, any scalene triangle;

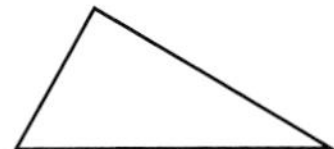

17. *Sample answer:* rectangle; yes, rhombus;

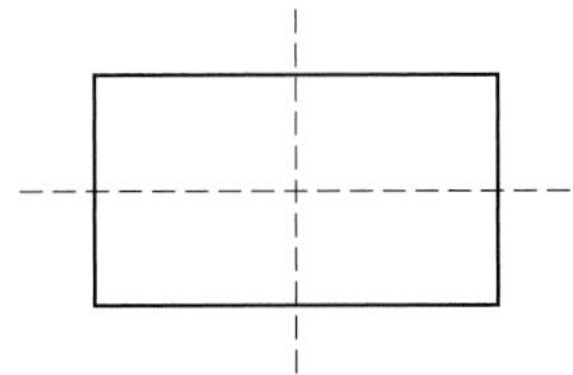

19.

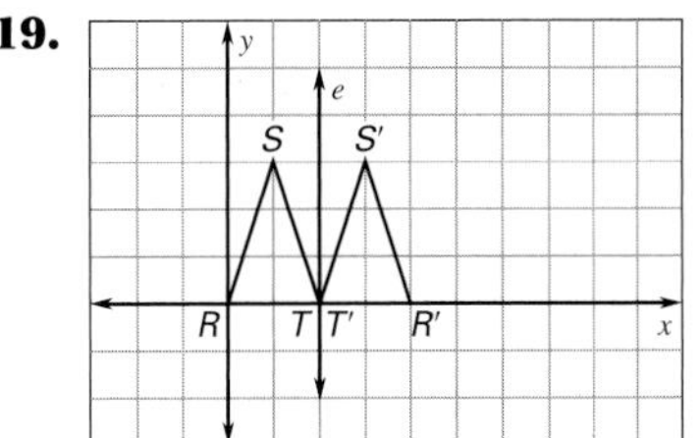

21.

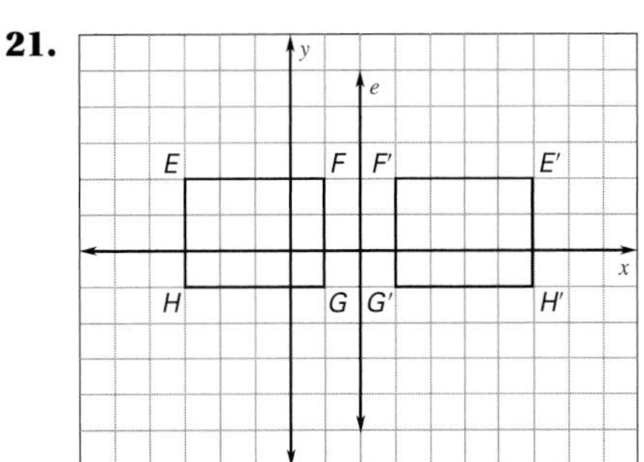

8.6 Problem Solving (pp. 437 – 438) **29.** *Answers may vary. Sample answer:* This method can be used in miniature golf, where you have to bounce the ball against a wall in order to go around an obstacle;

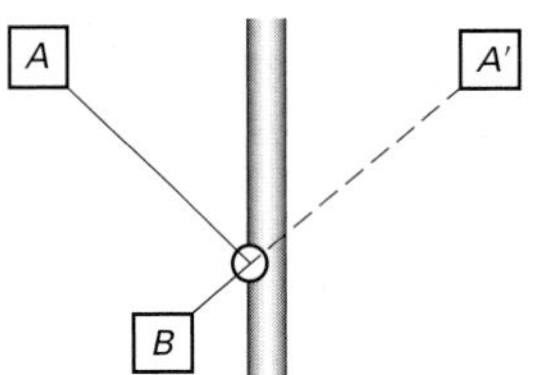

31. The figure has 1 line of symmetry, the *y*-axis;

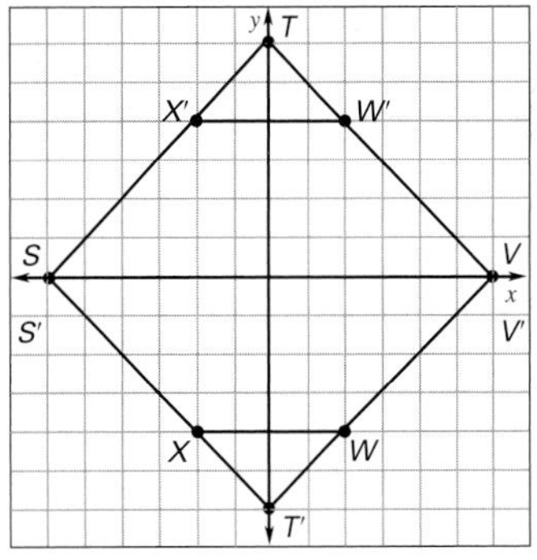

8.7 Skill Practice (pp. 441 – 443) **1.** reflection **3.** rotation **5.** $(x, y) \rightarrow (x - 5, y + 3)$ **7.** $L'(5, -4)$, $M'(1, -3)$, $N'(2, -5)$;

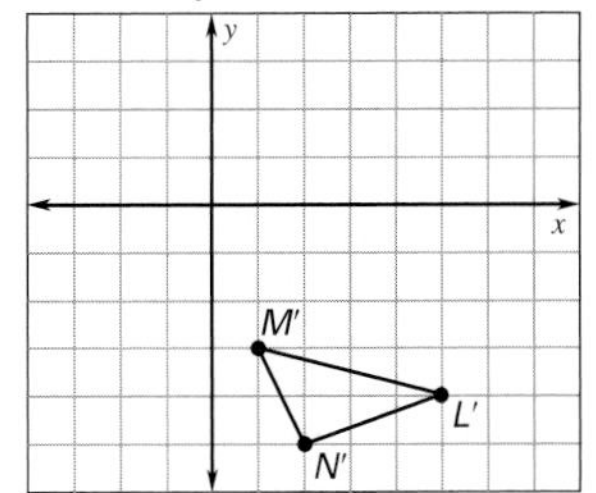

9. a., c.

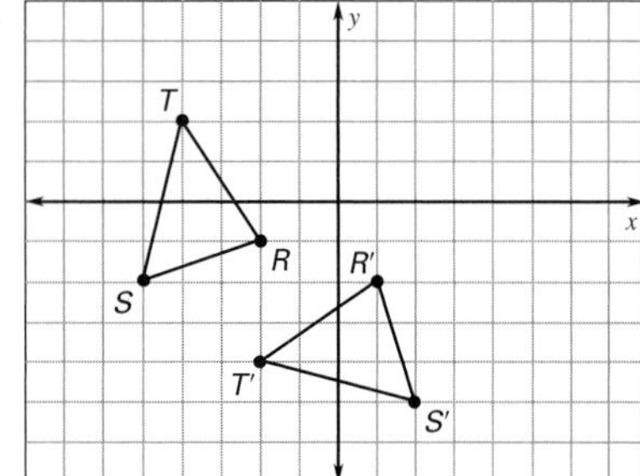

b. $R'(1, -2)$, $S'(2, -5)$, $T'(-2, -4)$

11.

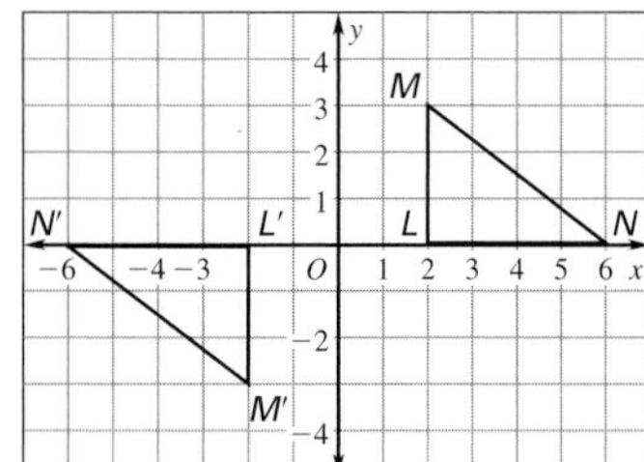

13.

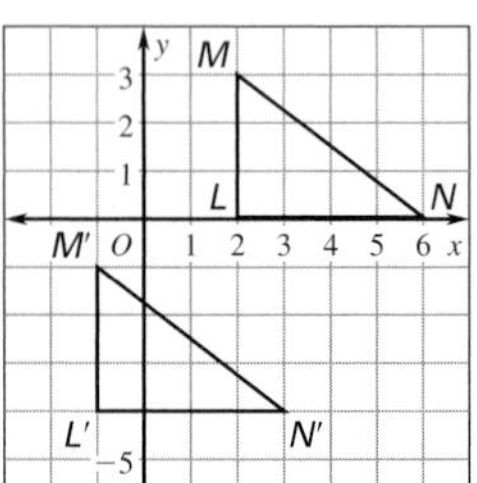

15.

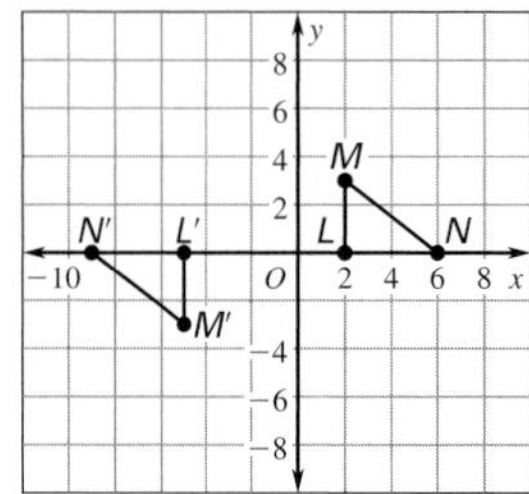

17. *Blue to red* translation: $(x, y) \to (x + 4, y - 4)$; reflection: in line $y = x$; rotation: 180°; *Red to blue* (1) Reflect in x-axis then reflect in y-axis; (2) Make two 90° clockwise rotations; (3) Make two 90° counterclockwise rotations.

8.7 Skill Practice (pp. 443 – 444) **19.** rotations of 45°, 90°, 135°, 180°, 225°, 270°, or 315° in the clockwise or counterclockwise direction **21.** reflection **23.** translation **25.** rotation **27.** left to right; yes, 60°; yes, 72°; yes, 40° **29.** Yes; *Sample answer:* The origami pinwheel in Exercise 19 has rotational symmetry but not line symmetry.

8.7 Extension (p. 446) **1.** no **3.** no
7. translation;

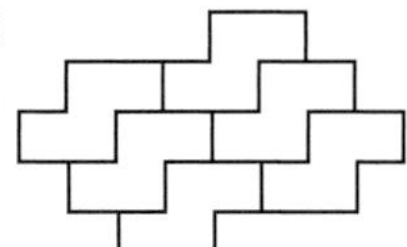

9. *Sample answer:*

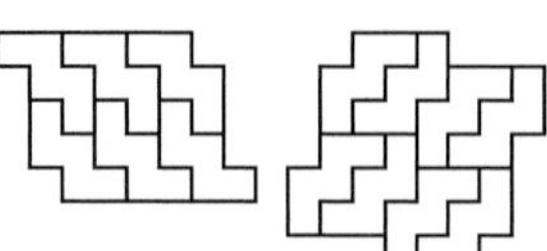

8.8 Skill Practice (pp. 450 – 452) **1.** scale factor **3.** yes; All regular triangles are similar. **5.** yes; Corresponding angles are congruent and $\frac{10}{5} = \frac{8}{4} = \frac{6}{3}$. **7.** 4 in. **9.** $\frac{9}{4}$ ft

11.

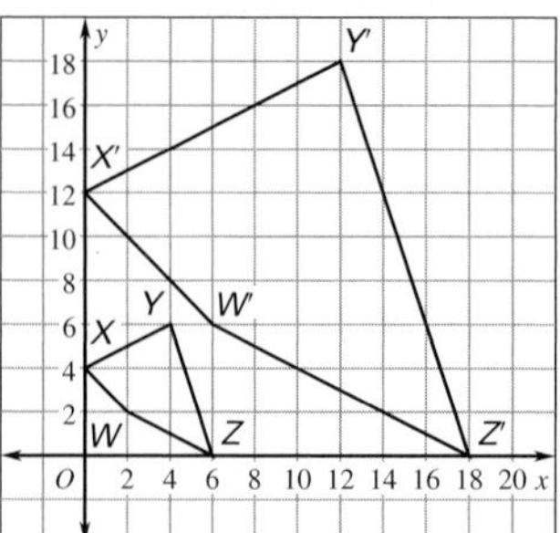

13.

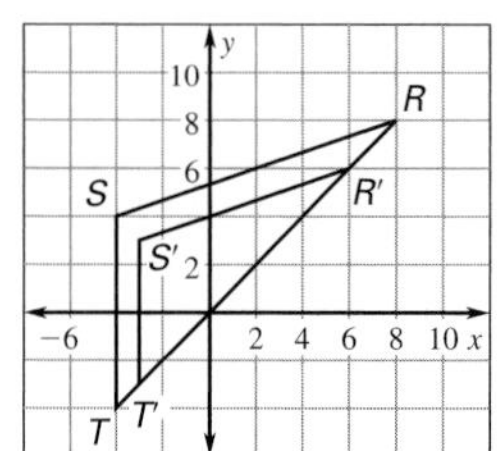

15.

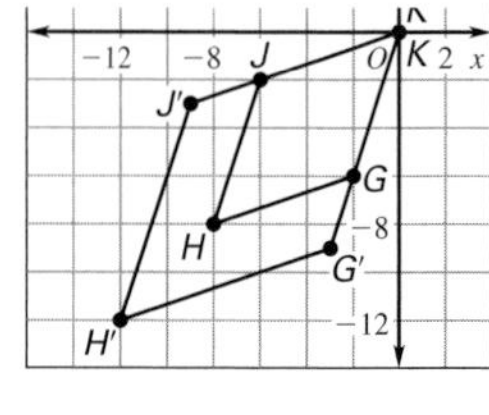

17. The student did not multiply the y values by 3;

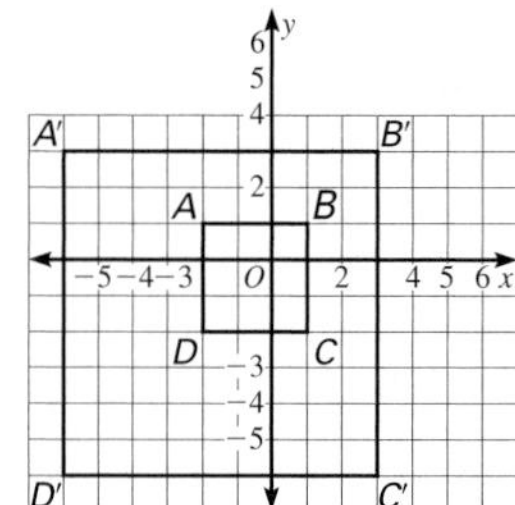

19. scale factor: $\frac{1}{2}$;

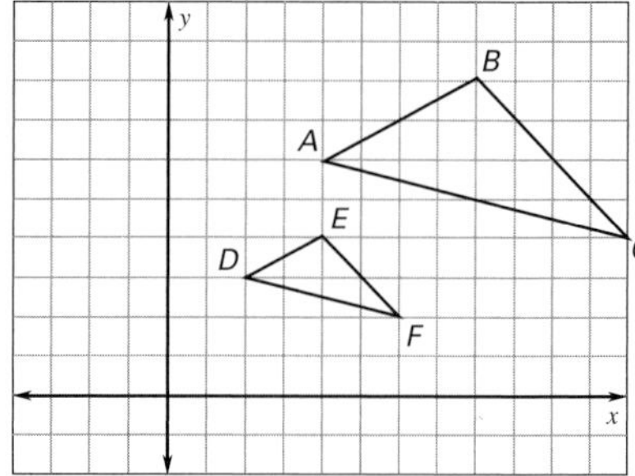

21. scale factor: 2;

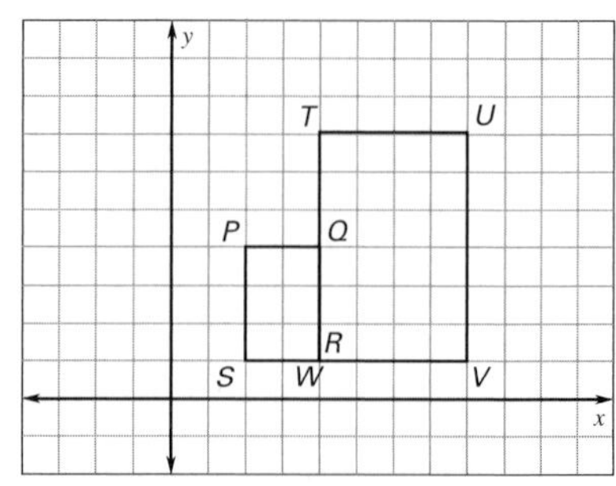

23. $x = 54$, $y = 6.75$ cm

8.8 Skill Practice (pp. 452 – 454) **25.** $\frac{4}{1}$; 14 units; the same **31.** identical; *Sample answer:* If the scale factor is 1, then the length of each edge of the second polygon will be 1 times the length of the corresponding edges of the first polygon. **33.** *Sample answer:* The area of *ABCD* is

80 in.^{2} so $AD = 80 \div 10 = 8$ in. The scale factor is $\frac{5}{10} = \frac{1}{2}$, so $WY = \frac{1}{2}AD = \frac{1}{2}(8) = 4$ in. Then the area of $WXYZ$ is (5 in.)(4 in.) = 20 in.^{2} **35.** $\frac{25}{6}$ **37.** *ABDF* ~ *CDFH* ~ *EFHJ* ~ *GHJL* ~ *IJLK* ~ *LKMN* ~ *OKMP*. They are all similar because all of their angles are equal and the sides of every rectangle are in the ratio 8 : 5.

Chapter Review (pp. 456 – 460) **1.** D **3.** B **5.** complementary **7.** heptagon **9.** 109° **11.** 25° **13.** 26; right triangle **15.** 88; acute triangle **17.** 60; parallelogram **19.** 150° **21.** *ABC* *GFH*; SAS **23.** *LMN* *PQR*; SAS

25.

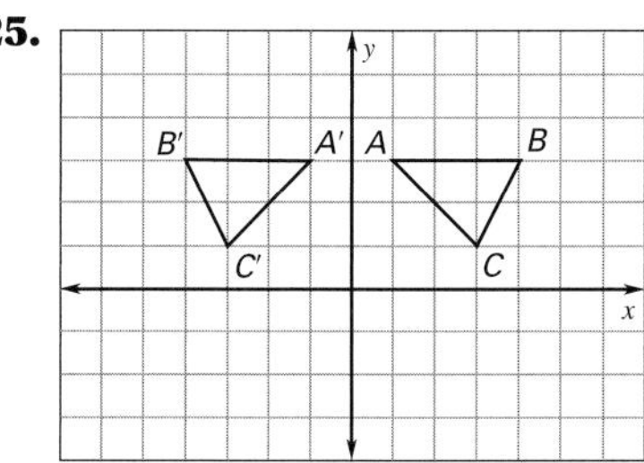

27. 5 **29.** $K'(1, 2)$, $L'(-1, 5)$, $M'(1, 4)$ **31.** 48 ft

Chapter 9

9.1 Skill Practice (pp. 472 – 473) **1.** $b^2 = c$ **3.** –1 **5.** 12 **7.** The answer is missing a negative sign; $-\sqrt{49} = -7$ **9.** 4 **11.** 7 **13.** 5 **15.** 11 **17.** 6.6 **19.** –78.8 **21.** 0 **23.** ±9 **25.** ±7 **27.** ±11 **29.** ±11.66 **31.** ±13.96 **33.** ±1.2 **35.** ±1.4 **37.** always **39.** 0 **41.** 9 **43.** $\frac{4}{5}$ **45.** $\frac{12}{13}$ **47.** 1.4 **49.** 3.4

9.1 Problem Solving (pp. 473 – 474) **57.** no; The tablecloth is $\frac{50}{12} = 4\frac{1}{6}$ ft by $4\frac{1}{6}$ ft. A side of the table is $\sqrt{21.5} \approx 4.6$ ft. The tablecloth is smaller than the table, so it will not cover the table. **59.** 24 ft; 9072 ft^2 **61.** 68.2 mi **63.** about 2212 ft

9.2 Skill Practice (pp. 477 – 479) **1.** irrational **3.** rational; It is a terminating decimal. **5.** rational; It is a repeating decimal. **7.** rational; $\sqrt{36} = 6$, which is a terminating decimal. **9.** irrational; $\sqrt{5}$ cannot be written as a quotient of two integers. **11.** rational; It is the quotient of two integers. **13.** rational; $\sqrt{\frac{100}{81}} = \frac{10}{9}$, which is the quotient of two integers. **15.** A; It is the only rational number in the group. **17.** > **19.** < **21.** < *23–39. Methods may vary.* **23.** >; estimation **25.** <; estimation **27.** =; mental math **29.** <; calculator **35.** $0.\overline{262}$, $0.\overline{26}$, 0.266, $0.2\overline{6}$ **37.** $0.\overline{39}$, 0.399, $0.3\overline{9}$, $\sqrt{0.17}$ **39.** –9, $\sqrt{81}$, 10.3, $\sqrt{220}$ **41.** $\frac{2}{5}$, 1.02, $\sqrt{1.25}$, $\sqrt{2.5}$ **43.** 3.6; irrational **45.** 3; rational **47.** 8.1; irrational **49.** irrational; The sum of an irrational number and an integer is irrational. **51.** irrational; The product of an integer and an irrational number is irrational. **53.** $\sqrt{13}$; 5; never **55.** 6; 6; always; $(\sqrt{ac})^2 = (\sqrt{ac})(\sqrt{ac}) = ac$ and $(\sqrt{a} \cdot \sqrt{c})^2 = (\sqrt{a})^2 \cdot (\sqrt{c})^2 = ac$ **57.** 3; 1; sometimes; They are equal when $a = d$. **59.** sometimes **61.** sometimes

9.2 Skill Practice (pp. 479 – 480) **67.** 20 stencils. **69.** no; The minimum wind speed required to fly the kite is $5\sqrt{\frac{19.6}{11.71}} \approx 6.5$ mi/h. A wind speed of 6 mi/h is not enough. **71.** no; *Sample answer:* The decimal shown on the calculator screen could terminate at a higher level of accuracy, or there might be a repeating pattern in the decimal that takes more decimal places to identify than are shown.

9.3 Skill Practice (pp. 484 – 485) **1.** hypotenuse **3.** 34 ft **5.** 104 m **7.** 120 cm **9.** 19.6 ft **11.** no **13.** yes **15.** yes **17.** 2 **19.** 5.3 **21.** 3 **23.** 20 **25.** 5 **27.** 4.24 ft

9.3 Problem Solving (pp. 485 – 486) **33.** 22.0 m

9.4 Skill Practice (pp. 489 – 490) **1.** Pythagorean triple **3.** 15 ft; 60 ft, 150 ft^2 **5.** 6 in.; 14.4 in., 8.64 in.^{2} **7.** 44 m; 286 m, 2574 m^2 **9.** 20 yd, 60 yd, 150 yd^2 **11.** The hypotenuse was used in the area formula instead of the missing leg; $a^2 + 2.1^2 = 5.3^2$, so $a \approx 4.9$ ft, and area $\approx \frac{1}{2}(4.9)(2.1) \approx 5.1$ ft^2 **13.** yes **15.** no **17.** 33 mi **19.** 5; 5; yes **21.** 2.5; 2.5, no **23.** $2a + a\sqrt{2}$; 30.7 units **25.** 12.2 **27.** 8.1 **29.** 9.5

9.4 Problem Solving (pp. 490 – 491)

31. a–b.

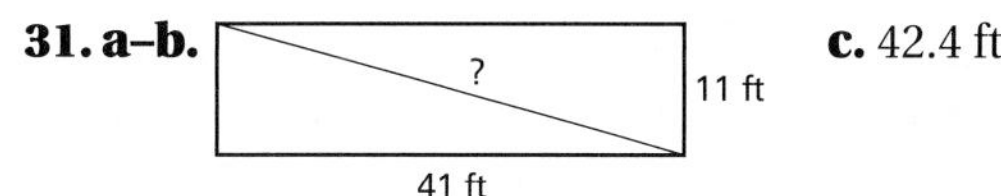

c. 42.4 ft

35. a.

	a	b	c	Perimeter	Area
ABC	3	4	5	12	6
DEF	6	8	10	24	24
TUV	9	12	15	36	54

b. By comparing the drawings, you can see that the perimeters are two and three times the original perimeter, but the areas are more than two and three times the original area.

9.5 Skill Practice (pp. 495 – 496) **1.** isosceles right **3.** 9 m **5.** $30\sqrt{2}$ ft **7.** 10 in. **9.** She multiplied by $\sqrt{3}$ instead of $\sqrt{2}$; hypotenuse = leg $\cdot \sqrt{2} = 8\sqrt{2}$ in. **11.** $x = 17$ cm, $z = 34$ cm **13.** $x = 8$ m, $y = 8\sqrt{3}$ m **15.** $x = 32\frac{1}{2}$ cm, $y = \frac{65\sqrt{3}}{2}$ cm **17.** 4 in. **19.** 16 mm

9.5 Skill Practice (pp. 496 – 497) **23.** 115 ft **27.** $12 + 6\sqrt{2}$ in., $48 + 24\sqrt{2}$ in.

9.6 Skill Practice (pp. 503 – 504) **1.** B **3.** C **5.** $\sin P = \frac{11}{61}$, $\cos P = \frac{60}{61}$, $\tan P = \frac{11}{60}$, $\sin R = \frac{60}{61}$, $\cos R = \frac{11}{61}$, $\tan R = \frac{60}{11}$ **9.** 0.9848 **11.** 0.2419 **13.** 13.197 cm **17.** 84.4 in. **19.** 119.0 ft **21.** $m\angle C = 60°$, $BC \approx 5$ in., $AC \approx 10$ in.; $\sin C = \frac{8.7}{10}$, $\cos C = \frac{1}{2}$, $\tan C = \frac{8.7}{5}$ **23.** $m\angle C = 70.3°$, $AB \approx 48.0$ cm, $BC \approx 17.2$ cm; $\sin C = \frac{48}{51}$, $\cos C = \frac{17.2}{51}$, $\tan C = \frac{48}{17.2}$

9.6 Problem Solving (pp. 504 – 505)

29. a. 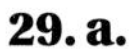

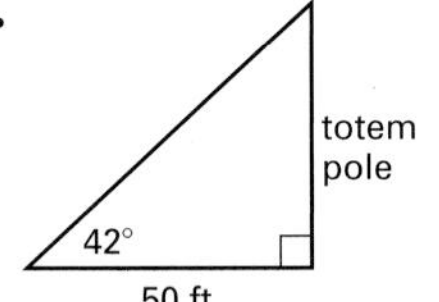

b. $\tan 42° = \frac{x}{50}$ **c.** 45 ft

31. 3.5 ft **33. a.** about 1813 m **b.** about 845 m **c.** less **37.** no; Use the tangent ratio to find the height of the office building, about 690 ft. If you assume that the angle to the top of the apartment building is 30°, then you can use the tangent ratio to find that the apartment building is about 231 ft tall. But 231 is not half of 690, so the angle must not be 30°. **39.** yes; for example, $\tan 60° \approx 1.7$ **41.** yes; $\cos 0° = 1$

9.6 Technology Activity (p. 507) **1.** 14.0° **3.** 42.6° **5.** 87.7° **7.** $\tan^{-1}(32.46)$; *Sample answer:* The greater the tangent of an angle, the larger the angle.

Chapter Review (pp. 509 – 512) **1.** A rational number can be written as the ratio of two integers, while an irrational number cannot. **3.** The sum of the squares of the lengths of the legs is equal to the square of the length of the hypotenuse. **5.** perfect square **7.** shortest **9.** converse **11.** −28 **13.** 30.7 **15.** −34.6 **17.** −17.5 **19.** ±11 **21.** ±6 **23.** ±4 **25.** ±12 **27.** 5.4 mi **29.** rational; It is a repeating decimal. **31.** irrational; $\sqrt{6}$ cannot be written as the quotient of two integers. **33.** rational; $\sqrt{\frac{27}{3}} = \sqrt{9} = 3$, which is a terminating decimal. **35.** irrational; $\sqrt{44}$ cannot be written as the quotient of two integers. **37.** < **39.** > **41.** 32 **43.** yes **45.** yes **47.** 216; 504 cm, 6804 cm² **49.** 55; 132 ft, 726 ft² **51.** $8\sqrt{2}$ in. **53.** $x = 6$ m, $y = 6\sqrt{3}$ m **55.** $\sin A = \frac{3}{5}$, $\cos A = \frac{4}{5}$, $\tan A = \frac{3}{4}$, $\sin B = \frac{4}{5}$, $\cos B = \frac{3}{5}$, $\tan B = \frac{4}{3}$ **57.** $\sin A = \frac{36}{85}$, $\cos A = \frac{77}{85}$, $\tan A = \frac{36}{77}$, $\sin B = \frac{77}{85}$, $\cos B = \frac{36}{85}$, $\tan B = \frac{77}{36}$

Chapter 10

10.1 Skill Practice (pp. 523 – 525) **1.** $A = bh$ **3.** $A = \frac{1}{2}(b_1 + b_2)h$ **5.** 130 cm² **7.** The height of the parallelogram is 5 inches, not 7 inches; $A = bh = 10(5) = 50$ in.² **9.** 96 sq units;

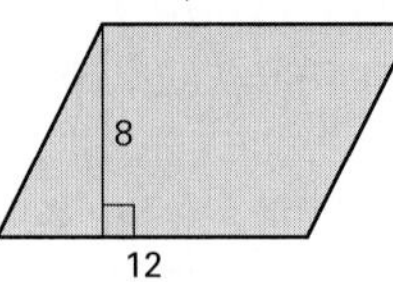

11. 220 sq units;

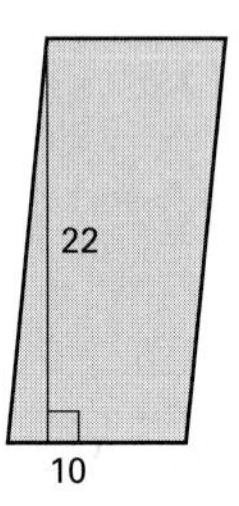

13. 16 sq units;

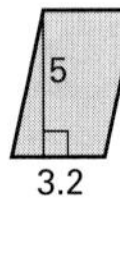

15. 162 in.² **17.** 480 m² **19.** 132 sq units;

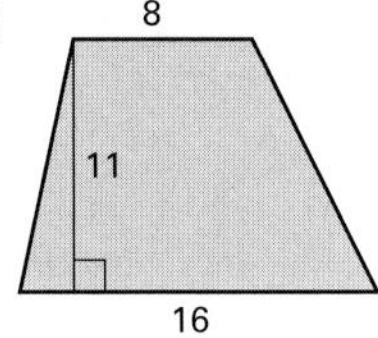

21. 52.4 sq units;

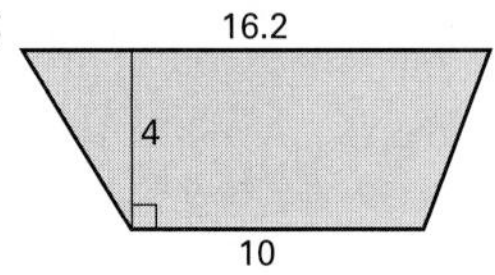

23. 12 ft²; 108 ft²; The area of *EFGH* is 9 times the area of *ABCD*. **25.** 360 ft² **27.** 30 sq units;

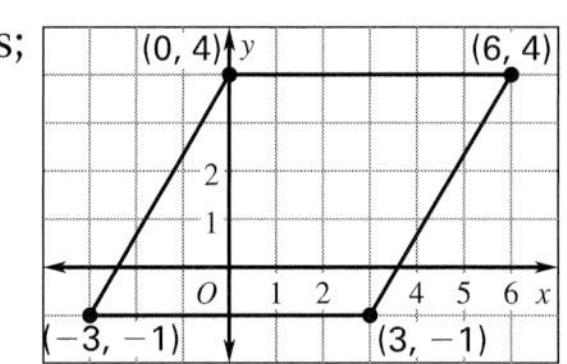

29. $84 = 12b$; 7 cm **31.** $100 = \frac{1}{2}(10 + 15)h$; 8 in. **33.** 270 in.² **35.** 1440 cm²

10.1 Problem Solving (pp. 525 – 526) **39.** 315 in.² **41.** $b = 26$ mm, $h = 13$ mm; $A = 338$ mm² **45.** *Sample answer:* about 43,750 mi²

10.2 Skill Practice (pp. 529 – 530) **1.** radius **3.** 12.56 ft² **5.** about 555.43 m² **7.** about 226.87 mm² **9.** The radius is 5.5 yd, not 11 yd; $A = \pi r^2 \approx (3.14)(5.5)^2 \approx 95.0$ yd² **11.** 907.46 ft² **13.** 615.44 mm² **15.** about 1268.59 in.² **17.** 1 m **19.** 6 in. **21.** 9 cm **23.** 36 cm **25.** 28.26 ft² **27.** 113.04 cm² **29.** 10 mm; 314 mm² **31.** 84 mm² **33.** 239.04 in.² **35.** 2 units; If $c = a$, then $2\pi r = \pi r^2$, and $r = 2$.

10.2 Problem Solving (pp. 530 – 532) **37.** 452.16 ft² **39.** about 4533.38 m² **41.** 10 ft²; $15 **43.** 4 yr **45. a.** about 192.33 in.²; 392.5 in.² **b.** 31 min

10.2 Technology Activity (p. 533) **1.** multiplied by 3 **3.** multiplied by 5 **5.** multiplied by $\sqrt{2}$; multiplied by $\sqrt{3}$; *Sample answer:* If the area of a circle is multiplied by n, then the radius is multiplied by $\sqrt{n}$.

10.3 Skill Practice (pp. 536 – 537) **1.** C **3.** B **5.** rectangular prism; yes **9.** octagonal prism; 10 faces, 24 edges, 16 vertices

11.

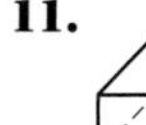

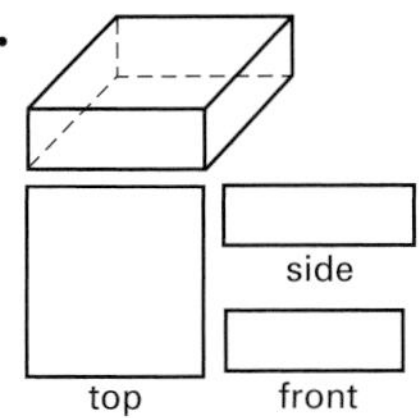

13.

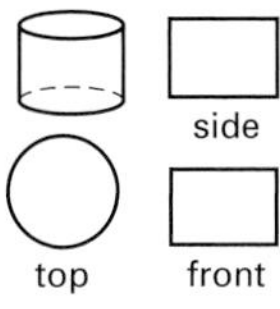

15. cylinder and cone **19.**

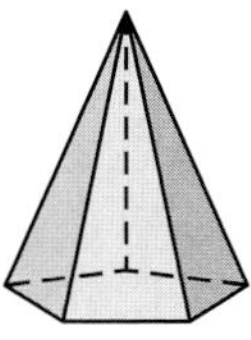

10.3 Extension (p. 540)

1.

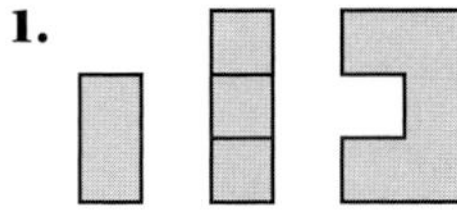

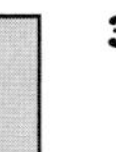

3.

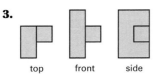

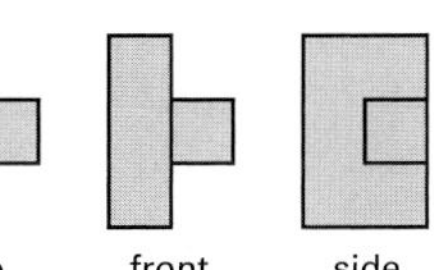

5.

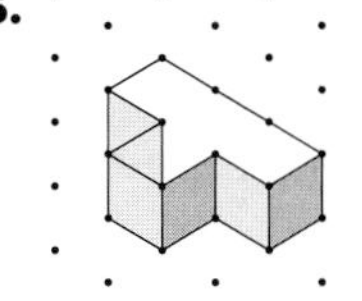

7.

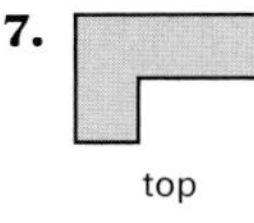

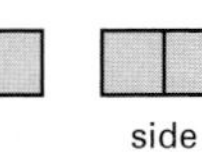

9.

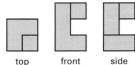

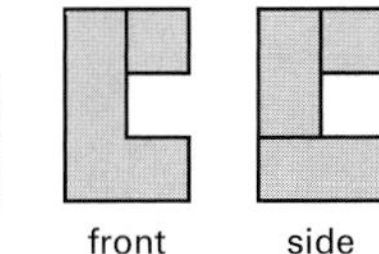

10.4 Skill Practice (pp. 545 – 546) **1.** *Sample answer:* Surface area is the sum of the areas of all the faces and lateral surfaces of a solid. **3.**

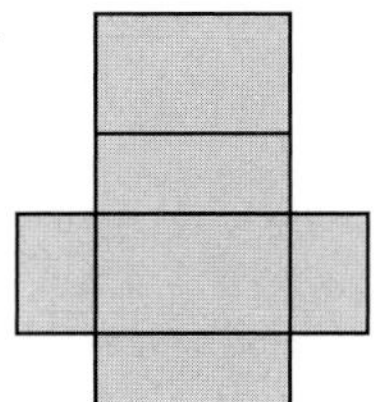

5.

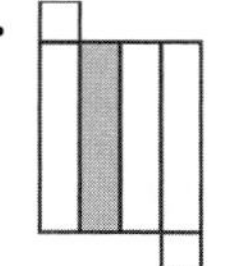

7. 1062 ft^2;

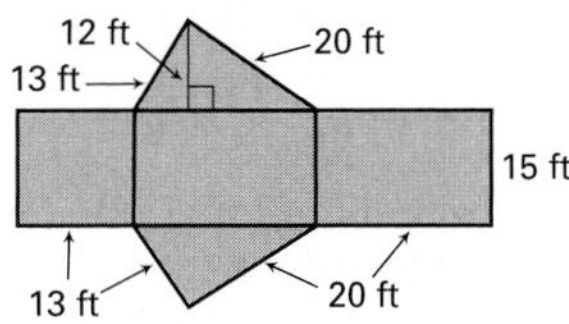

9. 48 in.^{2} **11.** 174 yd^2

15. 571.8 in.^{2}

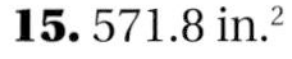

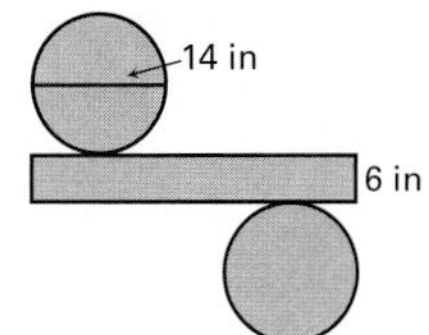

17. 301.6 m^2; 75.4 m^2;

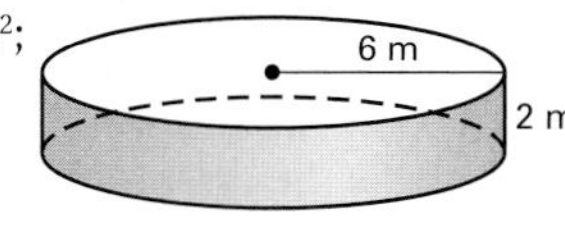

19. 1885.0 cm^2; 1256.6 cm^2;

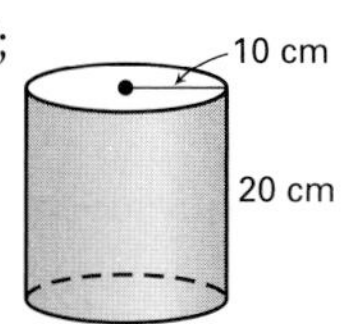

21. 150 ft^2 **23.** 204 cm^2 **25.** The lateral surface area does not include the area of the bases; lateral surface area = $2\pi rh = 2\pi(3)(7) \approx 131.9$ in.^{2}

10.4 Problem Solving (p. 547) **29.** 56,957.1 ft^2 **33.** 689.9 in.^{2}; **35.** $6s^2$

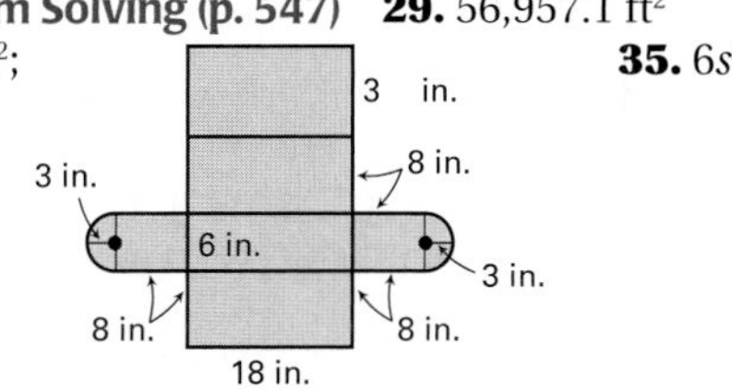

10.5 Skill Practice (pp. 550 – 551)

1.

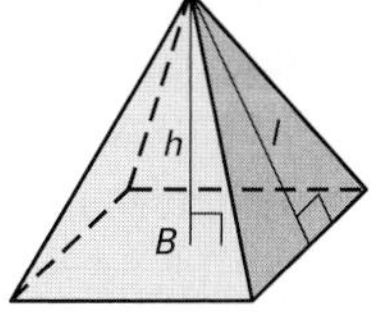

3–7. Sample nets are shown.

3. 36.9 ft^2;

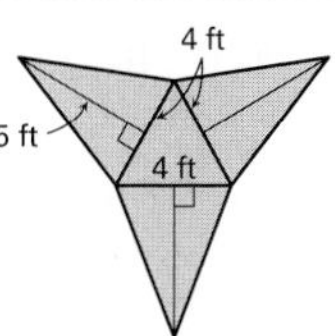

5. 301.6 cm^2;

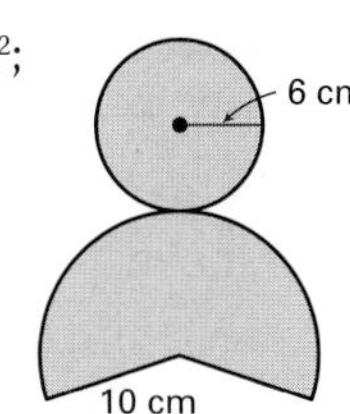

7. 150.8 in.^{2};

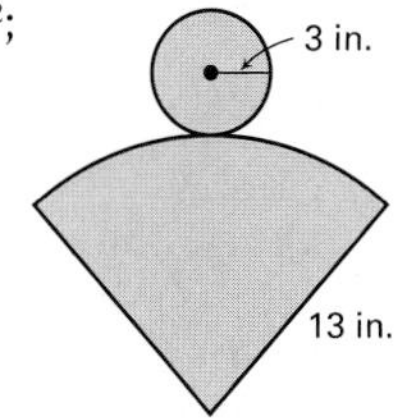

9. 67 cm^2 **11.** 697.4 m^2 **13.** The slant height l is 10 ft, not 8 ft; $S = \pi r^2 + \pi rl = \pi(6)^2 + \pi(6)(10) \approx 301.59$ ft^2

15. Use the Pythagorean Theorem to find the hypotenuse of a right triangle with legs 5 ft and 12 ft; 13 ft; 282.7 ft^2 **17.** 19.6 in.^{2} **19.** 153.9 in.^{2}

10.5 Problem Solving (pp. 551 – 552) **23.** 400 ft^2 **27.** 6π in.^{2} **29.** 54π in.^{2} **31.** When both r and l are multiplied by the same number, the surface area is multiplied by the square of that number; 150π in.^{2}

10.6 Skill Practice (pp. 557 – 558) **1.** *Sample answer:* Surface area is the two-dimensional space surrounding a solid, while volume is the three-dimensional space inside a solid. **3.** 132 m^3 **5.** 13.68 cm^3 **7.** 552.9 ft^3 **9.** 20.4 m^3 **11.** 2309.1 m^3 **13.** 64 yd^3 **15.** 1260 m^3 **17.** 339.3 cm^3 **19.** The area of the base is πr^2, not $2\pi r$; $V = Bh = \pi r^2 h = \pi(4^2)5 \approx 251.3$ m^3 **21.** 336 ft^3 **23.** 15 m; 30 m^3; 810 m^3; The volume of B is 27 times the volume of A.
25. doubling the radius; The effect is the same; In the volume formula for a cylinder, the radius is squared but the height is not; Since $V = lwh$ for a rectangular prism, if any dimension is doubled, the volume is doubled.

10.6 Problem Solving (pp. 558 – 559) **29.** surface area **31.** volume **33.** cylindrical; about 154.3 ft^3; The rectangular pool has a volume of 2560 ft^3, and the cylindrical pool has a volume of about 2714.3 ft^3. **35.** 10–11 times

10.7 Skill Practice (pp. 563 – 565) **1.** D **3.** A **5.** 12 in.^{3} **7.** 0.3 m^3 **9.** 144 yd^3 **11.** 2560 m^3 **13.** 247.5 ft^3 **15.** 95,425.9 ft^3 **19.** 506.8 ft^3 **21.** 2,019,960.3 cm^3 **23.** 70.7 ft^3 **25.** 93.6 m^2; 249.6 m^3 **27.** 13 yd **29.** 14 in. **31.** 904.8 cm^3 **33.** When you double the dimensions, you multiply the volume by 8. **35.** $V = lw(\frac{1}{3}h_1 + h_2)$

10.7 Problem Solving (pp. 565 – 566) **43. a.** 63.6 in.^{3} **b.** 1.06 in.^{3}/min **c.** about 17.8 min

10.7 Extension, p. 567 **1.** 33.5 ft^3 **3.** 4.2 yd^3 **5.** 904.8 m^3 **7.** $\frac{4}{3}\pi r^3$; $\frac{2}{3}\pi r^3$; $2\pi r^3$; volume of sphere = volume of cylinder − volume of cone

Chapter Review (pp. 569 – 572) **1.** B **3.** D **5.** 60 yd^2 **7.** 756 cm^2; 84 cm^2; The area of the smaller parallelogram is $\frac{1}{9}$ the area of the larger parallelogram. **9.** about 42.99 mi^2 **11.** 24 in. **13.** 9 yd **15.** cylinder; no **17.** 5 faces, 9 edges, 6 vertices **19.** 146 ft^2 **21.** 105 m^2 **23.** 56 in.^{2} **25.** 135 in.^{3} **27.** 126 cm^3 **29.** no; $\frac{1}{3}(3^2 \cdot 5) = 15 > 12$

Chapter 11

11.1 Skill Practice (pp. 585 – 586) **1.** domain; range **3.** is a function; Each input has exactly 1 output. **5.** not a function; The input −8 has 2 output values. **7.** not a function; The input 4 has 2 output values.

9. range: $-\frac{1}{2}, -\frac{1}{4}, 0, \frac{1}{4}, \frac{1}{2}$

x	−2	−1	0	1	2
y	$\frac{1}{2}$	$\frac{1}{4}$	0	$-\frac{1}{4}$	$-\frac{1}{2}$

11. range: 0, 1, 4

x	−2	−1	0	1	2
y	4	1	0	1	4

13. $y = x + 6$ **15.** $y = 3x - 2$ **17.** $A = 4n - 1$ **19.** *Answers may vary. Sample answer:* $y = 2x$;

x	−1	0	1	2	3
y	−2	0	2	4	6

11.1 Problem Solving (pp. 586 – 587) **21.** *Sample answer:* 15 lb;

p	12	13	14	15
E	4.8	5.2	5.6	6

23. $g = 2f$; 14 gal

11.2 Skill Practice (pp. 590 – 591) **1.** scatter plot
3.

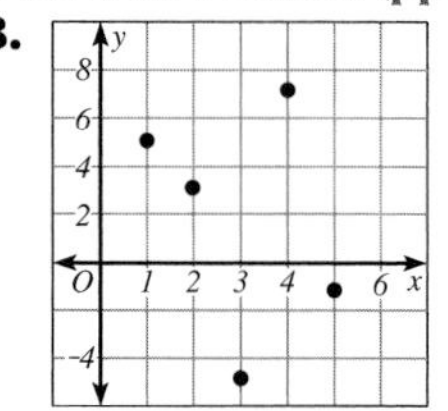

5. no relationship **7.** negative relationship **9.** positive relationship;

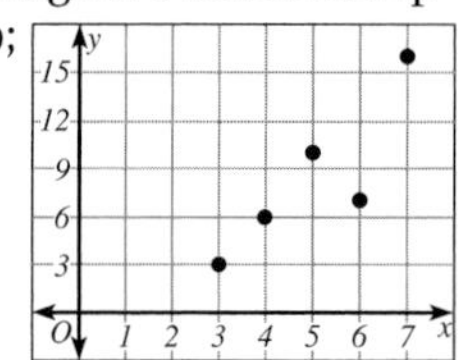

11. no relationship; *Sample answer:* A student's height is not related to the student's test score. **13.** negative relationship; If you have a loan, then as you pay off the loan the amount you still owe goes down. **17.** *Answers may vary. Estimate is given.* 11

11.3 Skill Practice (pp. 595 – 596) **1.** solution **3.** 3, 8, 13, 18 **5.** −25, −20, −15, −10 **7.** no **9.** yes **11.** yes *15–31. Answers may vary. Sample answers are given.* **15.** (−1, −45), (0, −51), (1, −57), (2, −63) **17.** (−1, 8), (0, 3), (1, −2), (2, −7) **19.** (−3, −6), (0, −5), (3, −4), (6, −3) **21.** $y = 42 - 4x$; (−1, 46), (0, 42), (1, 38), (2, 34) **23.** $y = 10 - 5x$; (−1, 15), (0, 10), (1, 5), (2, 0) **25.** $y = 2x + 19$; (−1, 17), (0, 19), (1, 21), (2, 23) **27.** $y = 2 - 3x$; (−1, 5), (0, 2), (1, −1), (2, −4) **29.** $y = 2x - \frac{5}{4}$; $(-1, -\frac{13}{4})$, $(0, -\frac{5}{4})$, $(1, \frac{3}{4})$, $(2, \frac{11}{4})$ **31.** $y = -\frac{15}{7}x + 6$; (−7, 21), (0, 6), (7, −9), (14, −24)

33. *Estimates may vary. Sample answers:* $9x = 21$; $8y = 5$; $9x + 8y$ is $21 + 5 = 26$, which is not equal to 16. *35–37. Answers may vary. Samples are given.*

35. $y = \frac{1}{2}x + 2$; (102, 53), (104, 54), (106, 55), (108, 56)

37. $y = \frac{1}{4}x + 6$; (104, 32), (108, 33), (112, 34), (116, 35)

11.3 Problem Solving (pp. 596 – 597) **43. a.** \$110 **b.** 7 sets **c.** No, the total cost will be \$350. The total cost includes \$14, which is charged only once. The shipping and handling does not double when the number of orders doubles. **49.** $10x + y = 120$; 40 min on games

11.4 Skill Practice (pp. 600 – 601) **1.** line **3.** yes **5.** yes

7.

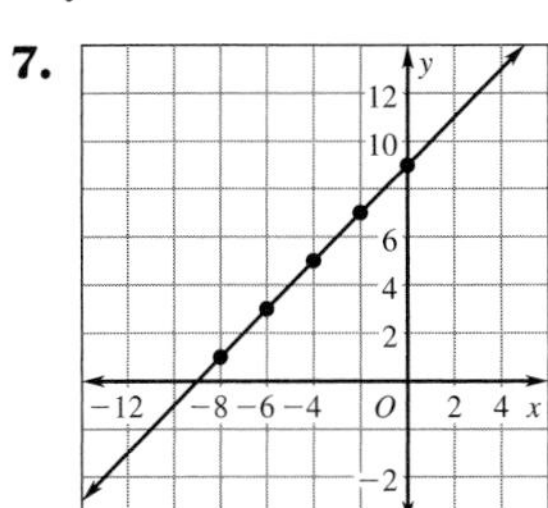

9.

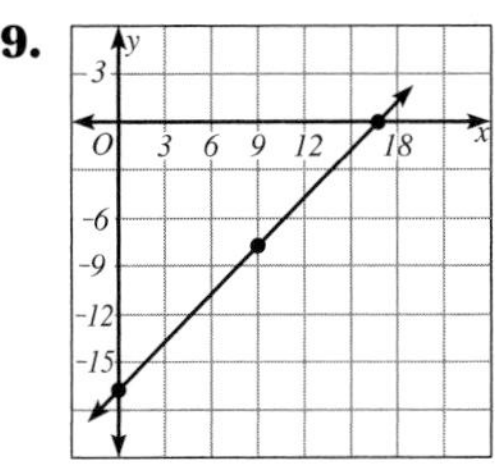

11.

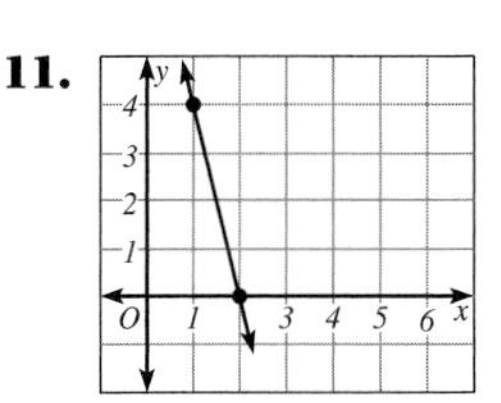

13.

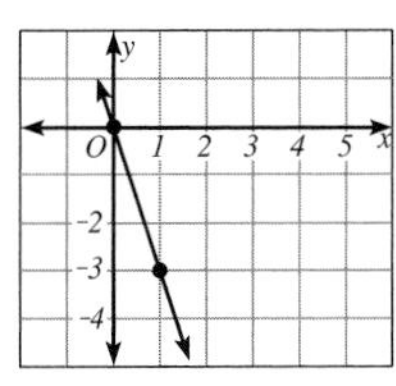

15.

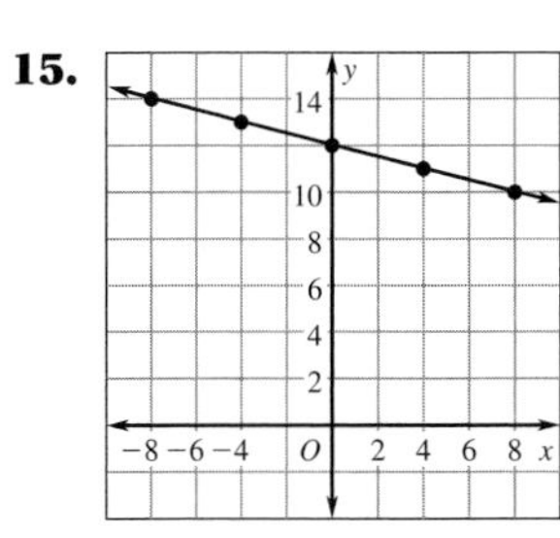

17.

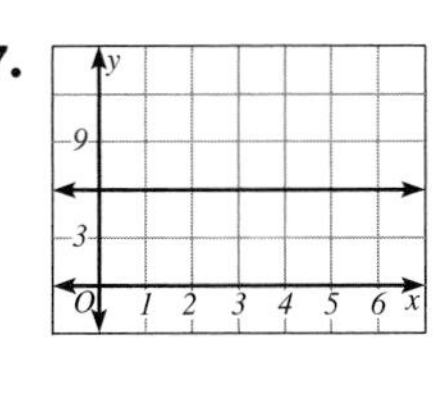

19.

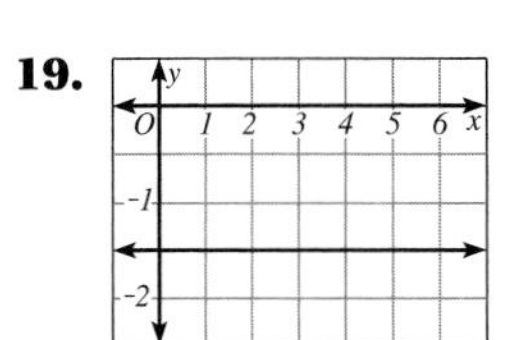

21.

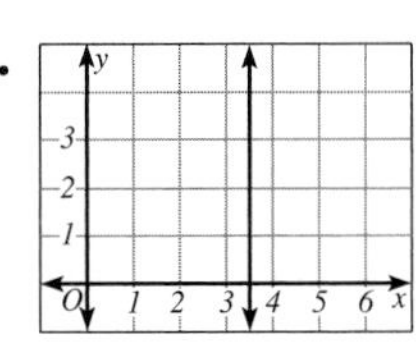

23. $y = 4x - 2$;

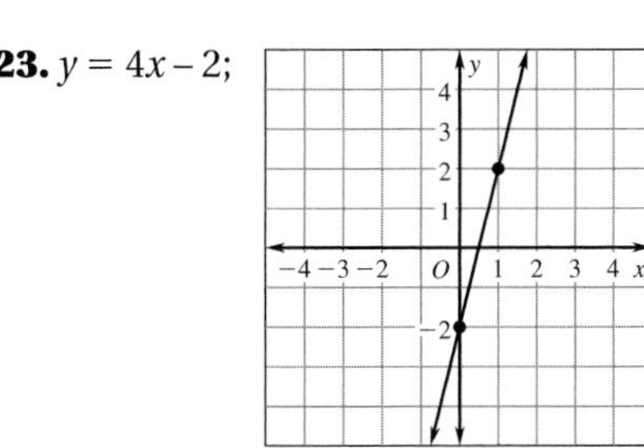

25. $y = -5x$;

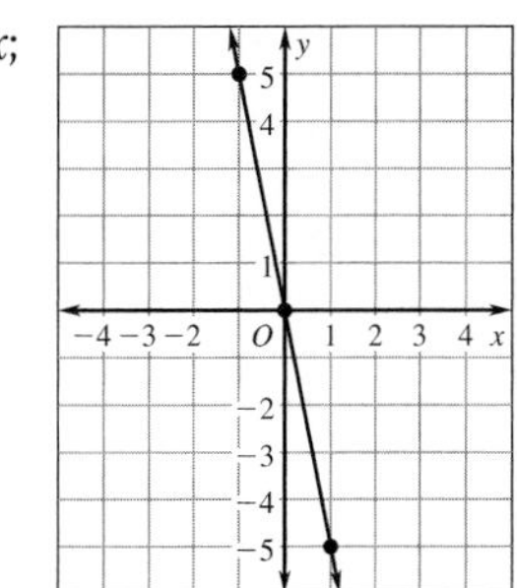

27. $x = 3$ **29–32.** *Sample answer:* All four lines are parallel; They cross the y-axis at different points;

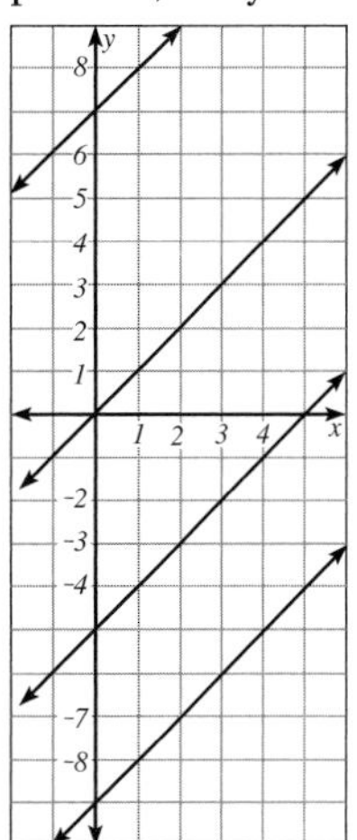

33–36. *Sample answer:* All four lines contain the origin; They have different "tilts";

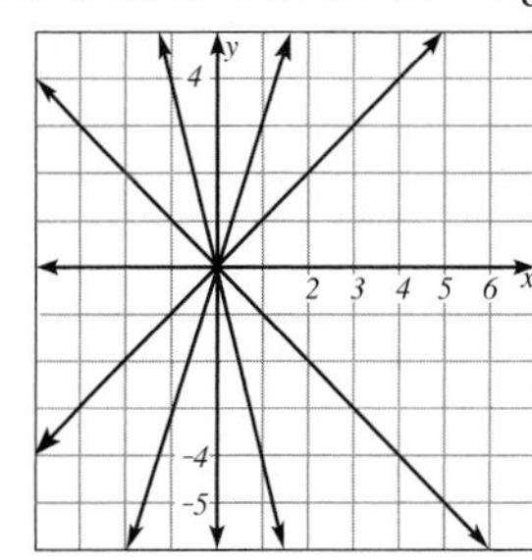

11.4 Problem Solving (pp. 602 – 603)

41. in 11 months;

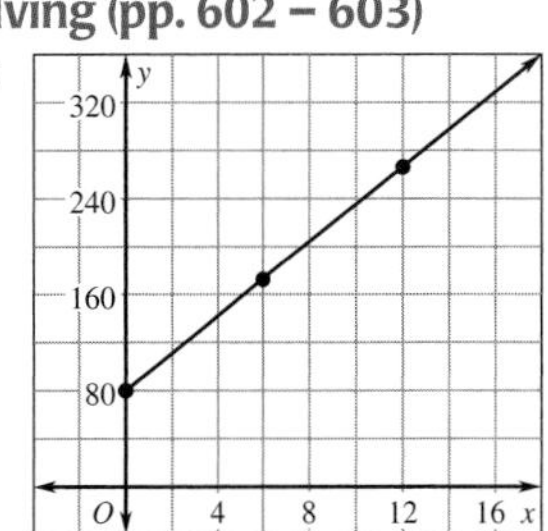

45. *Approximations may vary. Sample answer:* 37°C

47. a. $y = 2x + 1$ **b.** 6 months;

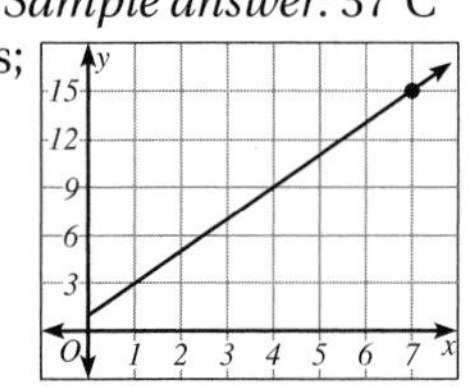

c. $2x + 1 = 13$, $2x = 12$, $x = 6$

SELECTED ANSWERS

11.4 Technology Activity (p. 604)

1.

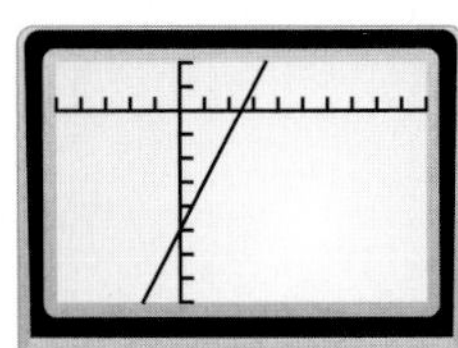

3.

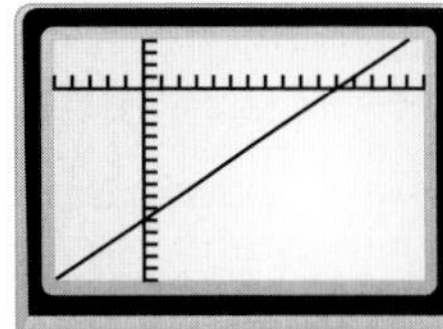

5. yes

11.5 Skill Practice (p. 608) **1.** x-intercept: 6; y-intercept: 1 **3.** x-intercept: $\frac{1}{2}$; y-intercept: –3 **5.** x-intercept: 2; y-intercept: –5 **7.** x-intercept: 5; y-intercept: 4

11.

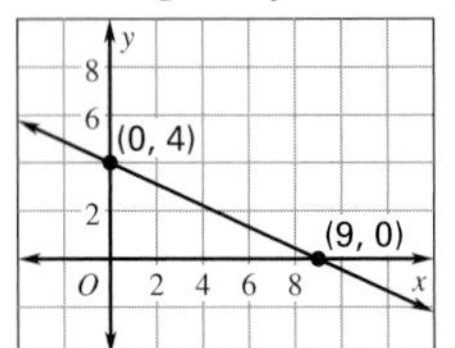

13.

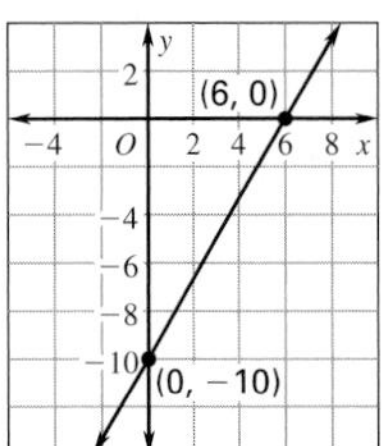

15. x-intercept: 3.5; y-intercept: 7;

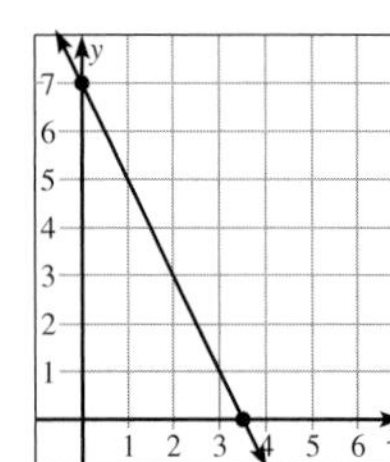

17. x-intercept: 2.6; y-intercept: 6.5;

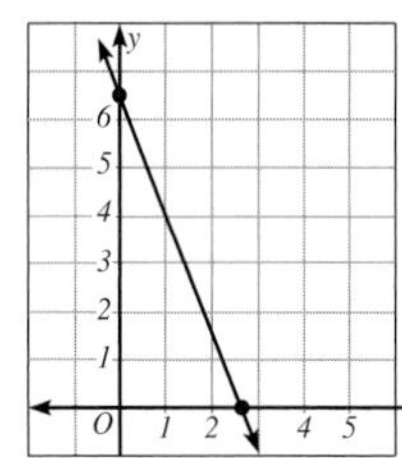

19. x-intercept: -2; y-intercept: 1;

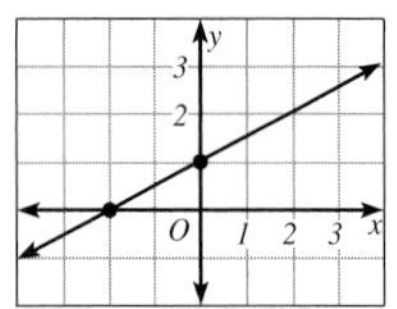

21. y-intercepts **23.** x-intercept: none; y-intercept: 9 **25.** x-intercept: 21; y-intercept: none

11.5 Problem Solving (p. 609) **29. a.** x and y represent the numbers of CDs and videos you can buy, respectively; **b.** x-intercept: 5; y-intercept: 6;

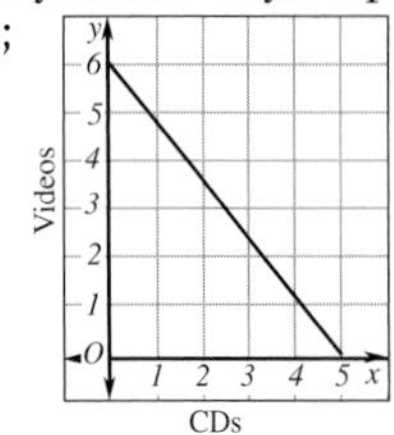

c. The intercepts indicate that you can buy 5 CDs and 0 videos or you can buy 0 CDs and 6 videos. **33.** It slants up; It goes through Quadrants I, III, and IV; *Sample answer:* Look at an example. If a line contains (1, 0) and (0, -1), it slants up from left to right and it goes through Quadrants I, III, and IV.

11.6 Skill Practice (pp. 614 – 615) **1.** rise **3.** slope **5.** (-2, 6), (1, 0); -2 **7.** $-\frac{1}{5}$ **9.** 0 **11.** undefined **13.** $-\frac{5}{12}$ **15.** $\frac{3}{32}$

17.

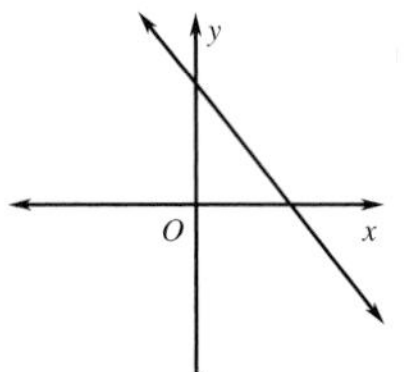

19.

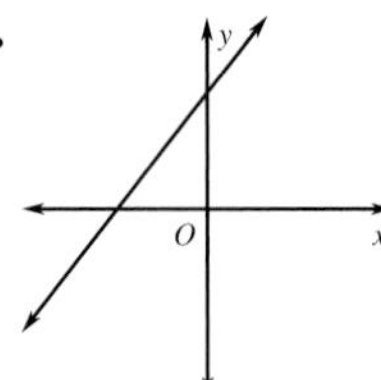

21. undefined, $-\frac{4}{3}$, 0;

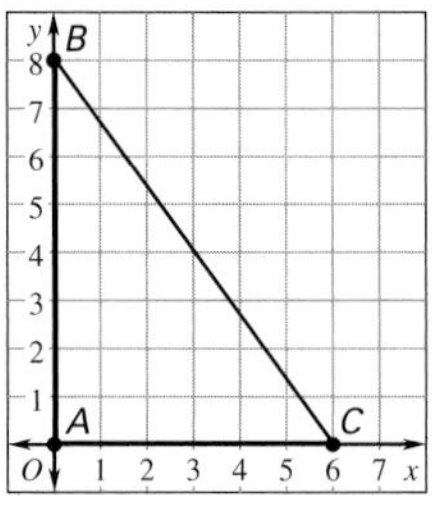

23. $-\frac{3}{2}$, 0, $\frac{3}{2}$;

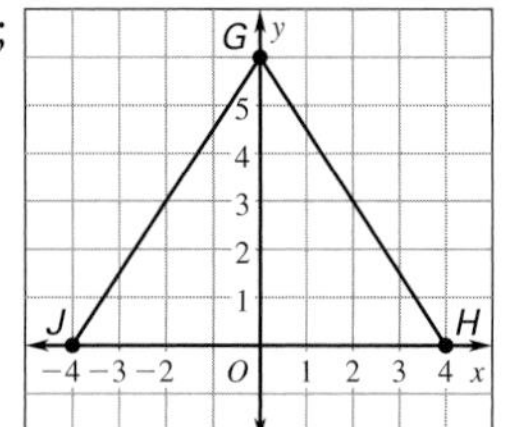

25. line a **29.** $y = 7$ **31.** right triangle; The slope of $\overline{RT}$ is $\frac{b-d}{a-c}$; the slope of $\overline{ST}$ is $\frac{b-d}{c-c}$, which is undefined; The slope of $\overline{RS}$ is $\frac{b-b}{a-c}$, which is 0.

11.6 Problem Solving (pp. 616 – 617) **35.** 3 **43.** 56,549 mm^3; 113,097 mm^3; 282,743 mm^3; 339,292 mm^3; The slope is about 2827 (which is the area of the base of the cylinder); The four points lie on a line, so any pair of points can be used to calculate the slope;

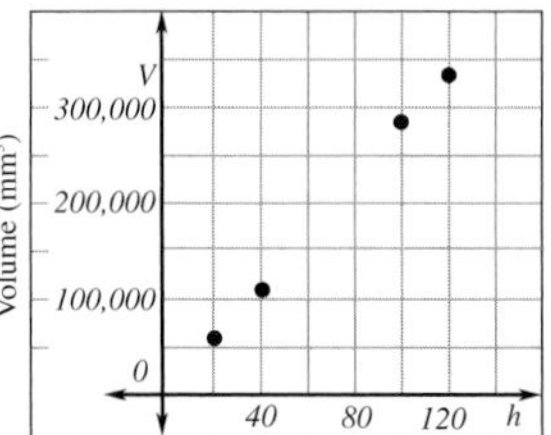

11.6 Extension (p. 619) **1.** neither; The data can be represented by $y = x + 1$, which is neither direct nor inverse variation. **3.** inverse variation; The data can be represented by $xy = 2$. **5.** direct variation; The equation can be written as $11x = 2.2y$ or $\frac{y}{x} = 5$. **7.** direct variation; The equation can be written as $y = (-\frac{1}{3})x$. **9.** neither; The equation can be written as $xy = -3 + x$, which is neither direct nor inverse variation. **11.** no; The equation in this case is $m = 4t + 20$. The variables m and t do not show direct variation because the ratio of m to t is not constant, due to the initial 20 dollars. Also, the equation cannot be written in the form $y = kx$. So, m and t are not directly proportional.

11.7 Skill Practice (pp. 624 – 625) **1.** slope **3.** $y = 2x - 5$ **5.** $y = x + 2$ **7.** slope: 1; y-intercept: 3 **9.** slope: 2; y-intercept: -1 **11.** slope: $-\frac{3}{4}$; y-intercept: 9 **13.** slope: 0; y-intercept: 3 **15.** slope: $\frac{13}{11}$; y-intercept: -13

17.

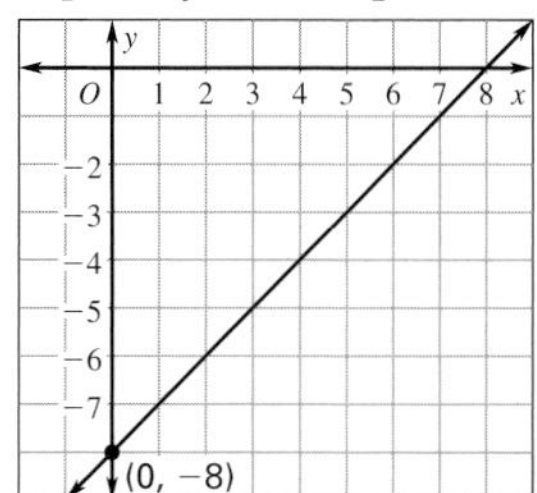

19.

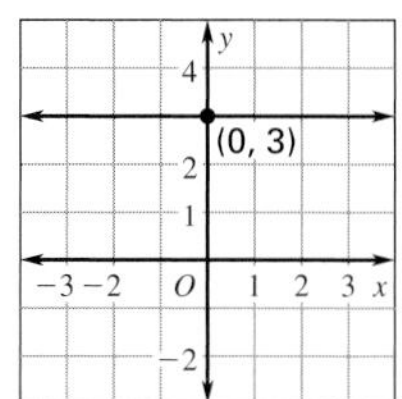

21.

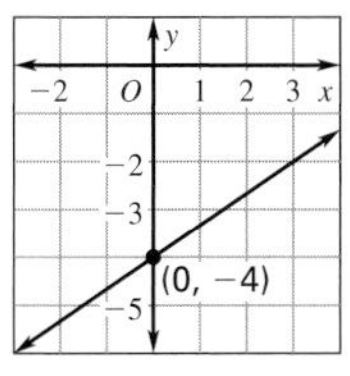

23. The student used the value of b as the x-intercept, not the y-intercept; The line should go through $(0, -1)$ and $(-1, 1)$. **25.** $y = -\frac{3}{2}x - 3$ **27.** $y = 3x - 1$ is steeper; Its slope is 3, and the slope of $y = 2x - 1$ is 2. **29.** -4; $y = -4$ **31.** 1; $y = -\frac{1}{2}x + 1$ **33.** 5; $y = 2x + 5$ **35.** $y = -\frac{2}{3}x + 14$

11.7 Problem Solving (pp. 625 – 626)

43. $y = -\frac{1}{2}x + 8$;

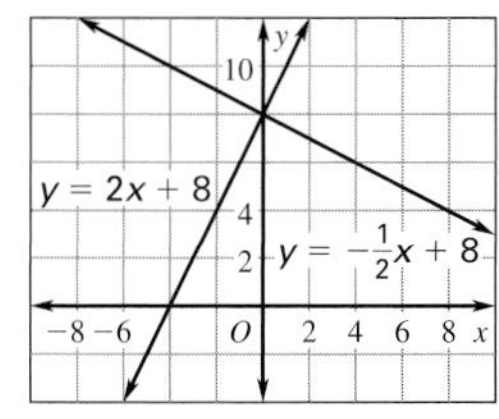

11.7 Extension (p. 628)

1. (1, 2);

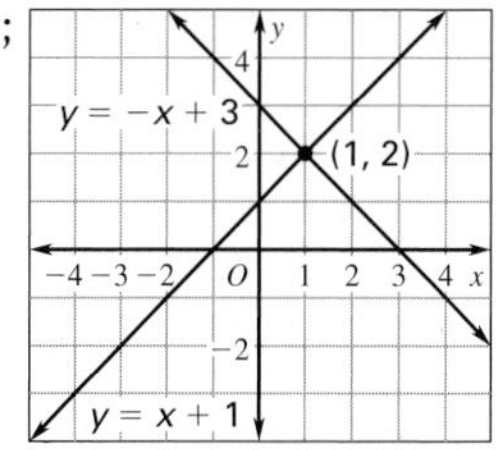

3. (6, −3);

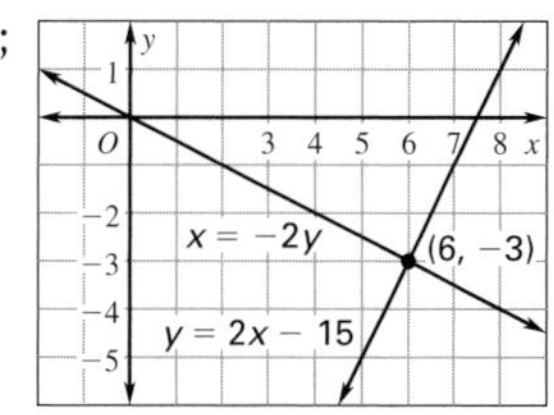

5. (−1, 5) **7.** There is no solution because the lines are parallel;

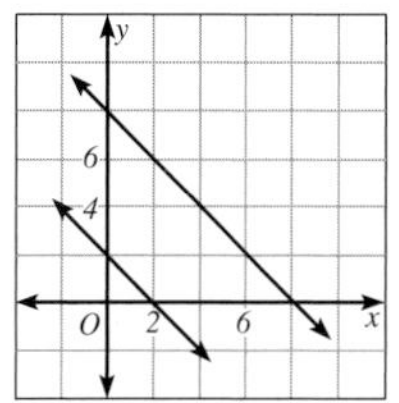

11.8 Skill Practice (pp. 631 – 632) **1.** half-planes **3.** yes **5.** no **7.**

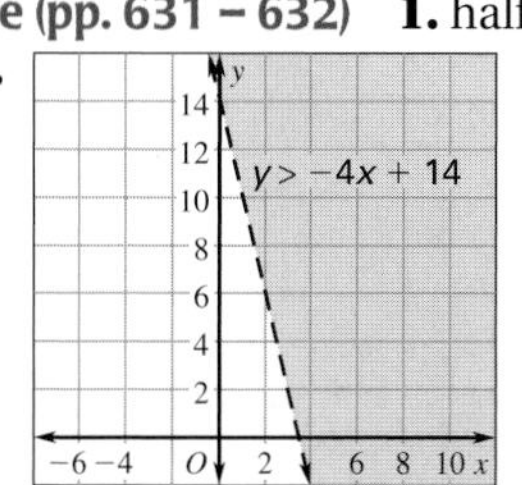

9.

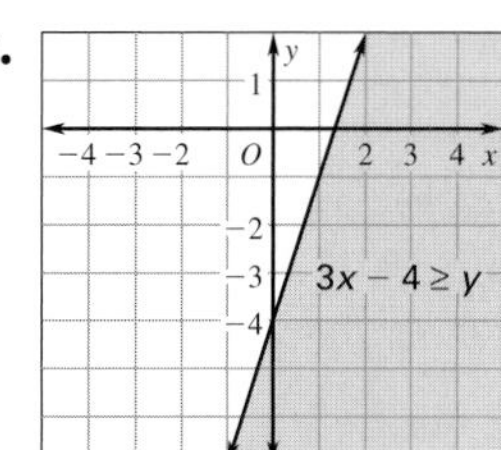

11.

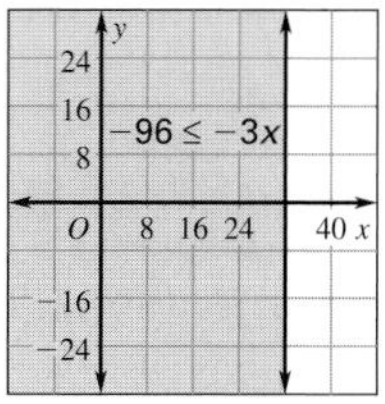

13.

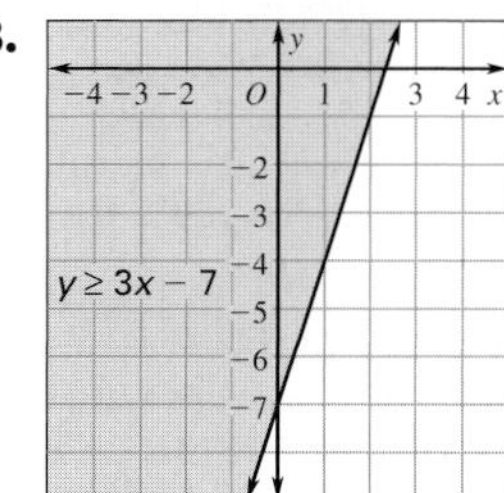

15.

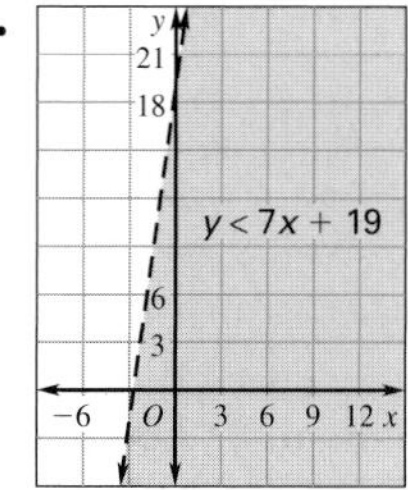

17. 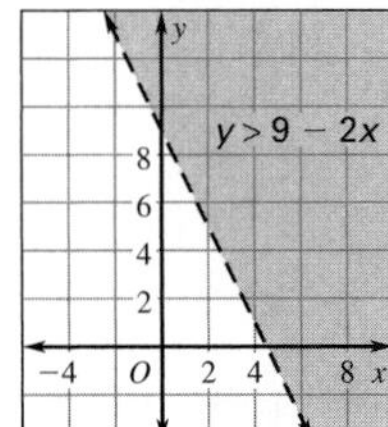

19. 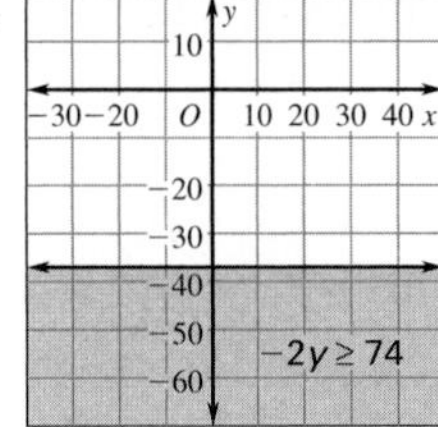

21. 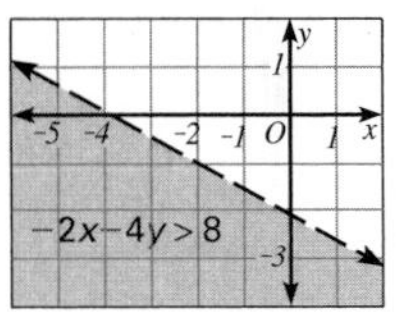

23. The symbol is $\leq$, but the graph uses a dashed line for the equation; The graph should use a solid line for the equation.

25. $x + y > 10$; 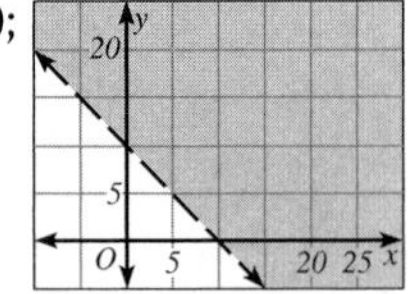

27. $x \geq 20$; 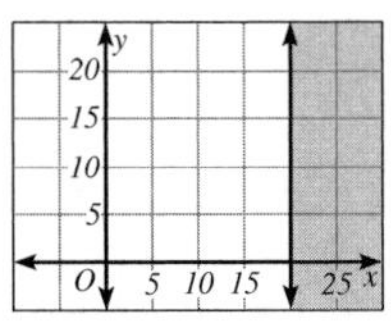

29. $y > 2x$; 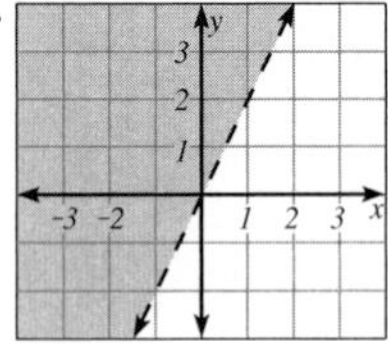

31. always **33.** never

11.8 Problem Solving (pp. 632 – 633) **35.** *Answers may vary. Sample answer:* 1.5 lb of peanuts and 2 lb of raisins; 0.75 lb of peanuts and 3 lb of raisins; 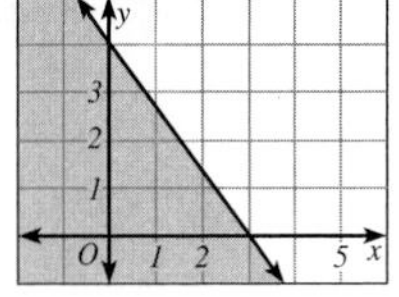

Chapter Review (pp. 636 – 640) **1.** function **3.** input; output **5.** To find the x-intercept, set $y = 0$ and solve for x. To find the y-intercept, set $x = 0$ and solve for y. **7.** *Sample answer:* Change the inequality symbol to =. Graph the equality, using a dashed line for $<$ or $>$ and a solid line for $\leq$ or $\geq$. Test a point in one of the half-planes. If it satisfies the inequality, shade that half-plane. If it does not satisfy the inequality, shade the other half-plane. **9.** yes; $y = x + 6$ **11.** yes; $y = -3x - 8$

13. The data represent indirect variation, with $st = 120$;

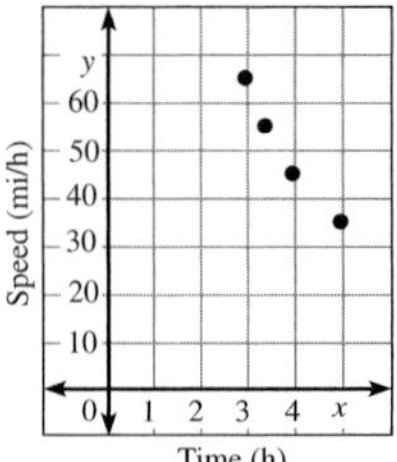

15. *Answers may vary. Sample answers:* $(-4, 5)$, $(0, 4)$, $(4, 3)$ **17.** 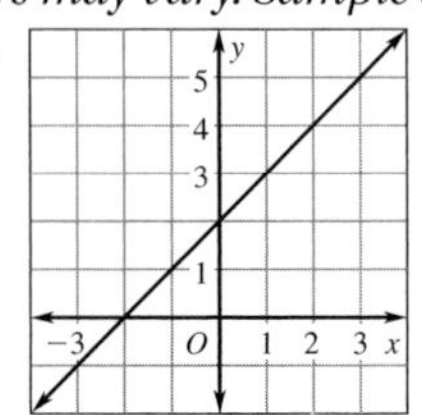 **19.** 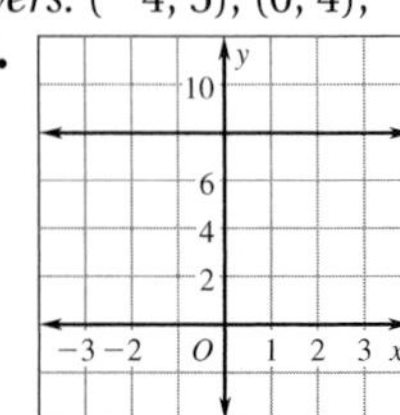

21. 488; The IRS collected $488 billion in 1980. **23.** *Answers may vary. Sample answers are given.* $(-3, 3)$, $(0, 3)$; 0 **25.** slope: $-\frac{2}{3}$; y-intercept: 4 **27.** $y = 4x + 10$; slope: 4; y-intercept: 10 **29.** $y = -\frac{3}{7}x - 3$; slope: $-\frac{3}{7}$; y-intercept: -3 **31.** 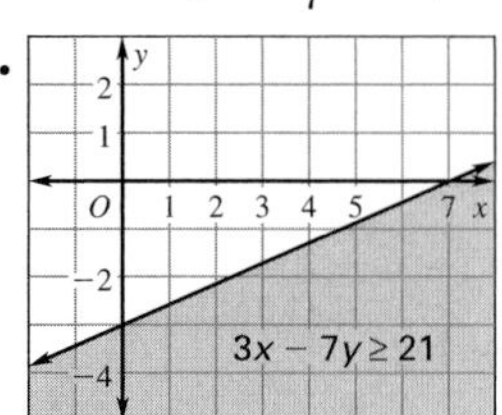

Chapter 12

12.1 Skill Practice (pp. 651 – 652) **1.** stem, leaf **3.** 8 | 0; stem: 8, leaf: 0 **5.** 12 | 9; stem: 12, leaf: 9

7. 60–69;

Stem	Leaves
4	0 5 8
5	0 2
6	1 3 5 6 7
7	4
8	2 4

Key: 5 | 0 = 50

9. 100–109;

Stem	Leaves
8	9
9	2 4 5
10	3 5 8 9
11	2 5

Key: 11 | 2 = 112

11. 18.0–18.9;

Stem	Leaves
18	1 3 4 6 7
19	
20	2
21	9
22	5 6 8

Key: 21 | 9 = 21.9

13. The bottom row on the stem-and-leaf plot should be two rows with stems 10 and 11, and the key is incorrect; The key should be 11 | 5 = 115.

Stem	Leaves
8	3
9	1 5
10	8
11	1 5

Key: 11 | 5 = 115

17.

Set C		Set D
	6	5
7 0	7	
	8	7 8
8 2	9	3 5
2	10	2
8 1	11	5

Key: 2 | 9 | 3 = 92 and 93

19.

Set C		Set D
7	4	
	5	5
8 3	6	8
7	7	8
8 0	8	
8	9	1 3 5
	10	0

Key: 8 | 9 | 1 = 9.8 and 9.1

21. 2.0; 2.0; 0.1, 2.0 and 2.8

12.1 Problem Solving (pp. 652 – 653)

25. 5 min, 45 min; 30–39 minute interval

27. \$62, \$53;

4	3 7
5	5 9
6	2 2
7	2 8
8	4 4
9	6

Key: 8 | 4 = 84

31. a. 13.7°F;

56	8 9
57	6
58	0
59	
60	1
61	6
62	7
63	
64	
65	7
66	8
67	
68	
69	1 9
70	5

Key: 56 | 8 = 56.8

b. 13.8, 14.2, 14.4, 15.6, 17.1, 18.7, 20.6, 21.4, 21.1, 19.3, 16.4, 13.8 **c.** *Sample answer:* The temperatures in degrees Celsius are lower than the temperatures in degrees Fahrenheit, and temperatures in degrees Celsius are distributed over a smaller range. This is because as temperatures change by 1 degree Celsius, they change by 1.8 degrees Fahrenheit;

13	8 8
14	2 4
15	6
16	4
17	1
18	7
19	3
20	6
21	1 4

Key: 14 | 2 = 14.2

12.2 Skill Practice (pp. 656 – 657)

1. lower quartile

3. **5.**

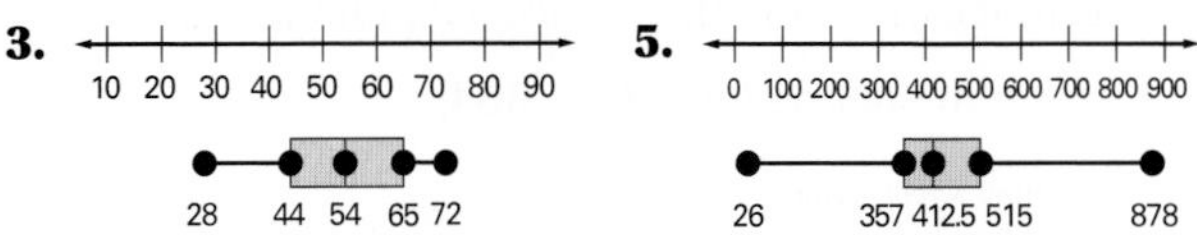

7. 35 is the upper extreme, not the upper quartile. 33 is the upper quartile. **9.** 11 in. **11.** 28 in. **13.** 25 and 50 **15.** D **17.** false; Both of these intervals include about one quarter of the data.

12.2 Problem Solving (pp. 657 – 658)

21. a. 210; 100 150 200 250 300 350

b. median: 251, lower quartile: 204, upper quartile: 301, extremes: 141 and 351 **c.** 100 150 200 250 300 350

141 204 251 301 351

23. *Sample answer:* Khalila has a higher median score than Tasha, 11 points versus 9 points, but her performance is much more variable. For Khalila, it took an interval of 7, from 7 to 14, to contain half of her point totals, but for Tasha, it took only an interval of 4, from 8 to 12, to contain half of her point totals, so Tasha's scoring is more consistent. This is also shown by the fact that the extremes for Tasha are between the extremes for Khalila. Also, the range for Tasha is only 8 points, but the range is 15 points for Khalila.

25. 371,000;

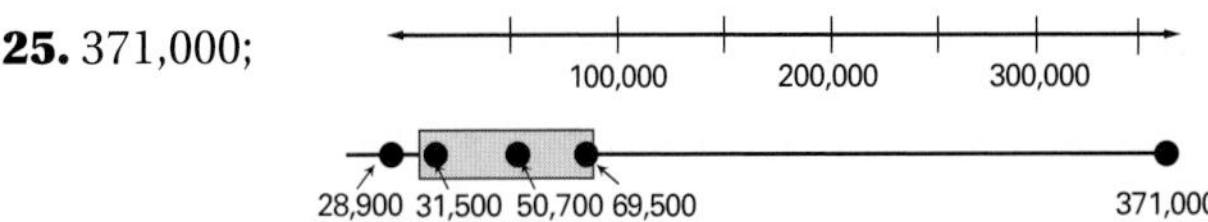

12.3 Skill Practice (pp. 661 – 662)

1. circle graph, line graph **3.** 135° **5.** 162°

7. How Often Do You Snack?

Never 0

Often 30

Rarely 50

Sometimes 120

9.

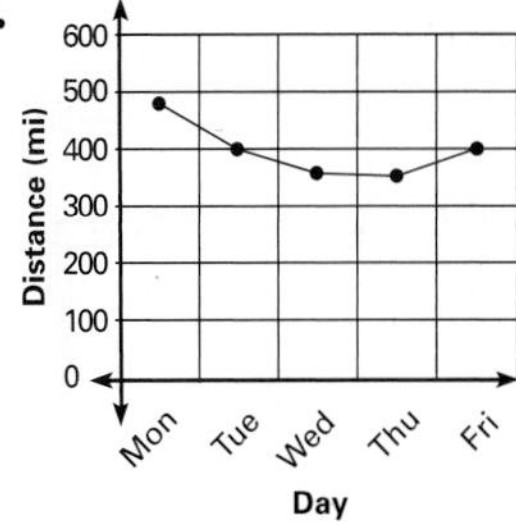

11.

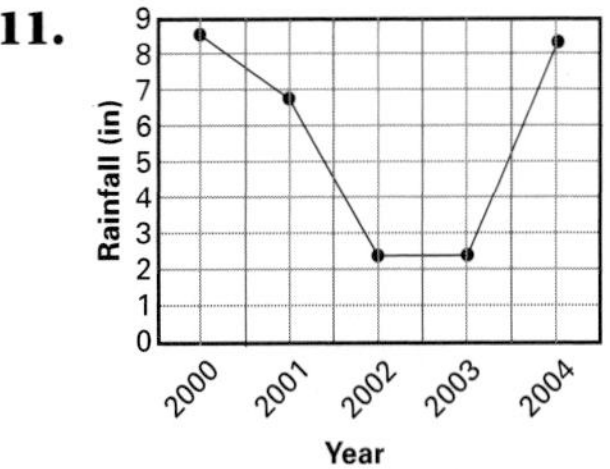

13. circle graph; The data represents parts of a whole. **17.** line graph; The data is collected over time.

SELECTED ANSWERS

19. *Sample answer:* histogram; The data is the frequency of occurrence in equal intervals for a certain range.

12.3 Problem Solving (pp. 663 – 664)

21.

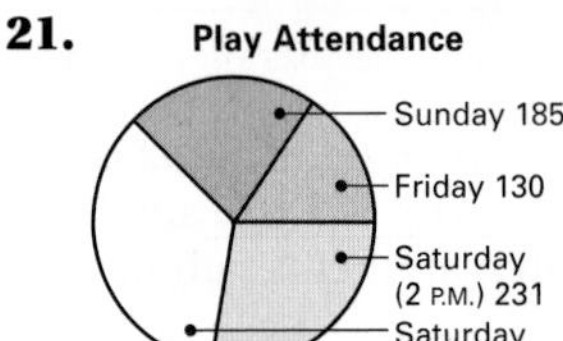

23. The Bronx: 14%, Queens: 36%, Brooklyn: 24%, Staten Island: 18%, Manhattan: 8%

27. The vertical axis is marked by 10,000's since the data is between 20,000 and 40,000.

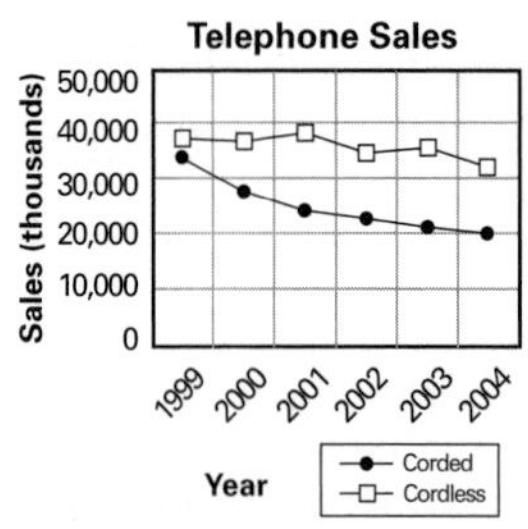

29. 2887 phones per year **31.** 1470; 2771; 4320; 5671; 6786; 8669; 10,170; 11,723; 13,777; 15,269 **33.** *Sample answer:* Subtract the total rushing yards in 1989 from the total rushing yards in 1993, and subtract the total rushing yards in 1994 from the total rushing yards in 1998. The larger number represents the interval during which Sanders accumulated more rushing yards.

12.3 Technology Activity (pp. 665 – 666)

1.

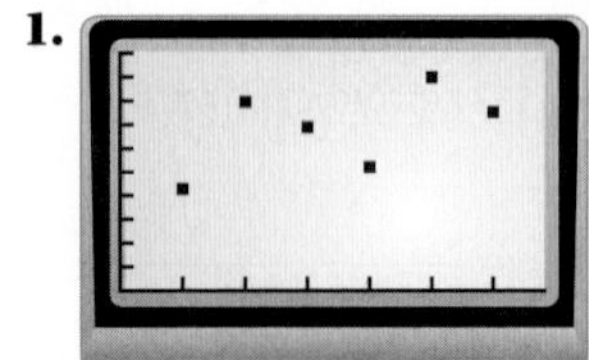

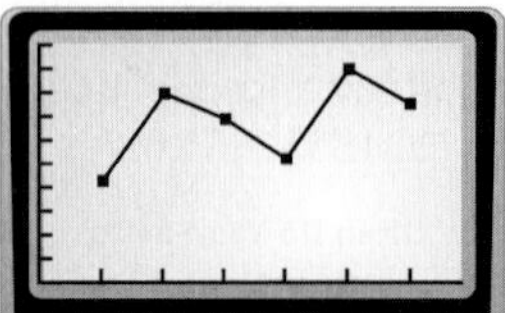

3.

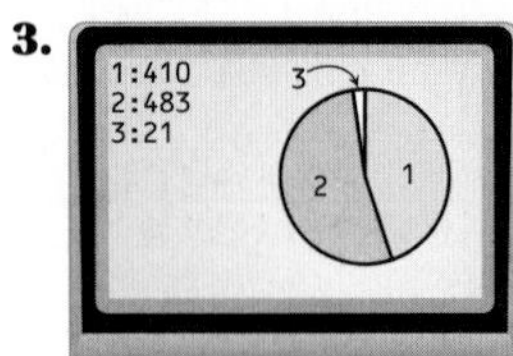

12.3 Extension (p. 668)

1. no; *Sample answer:* There is a break in the vertical scale, so the relative change is smaller than it appears;

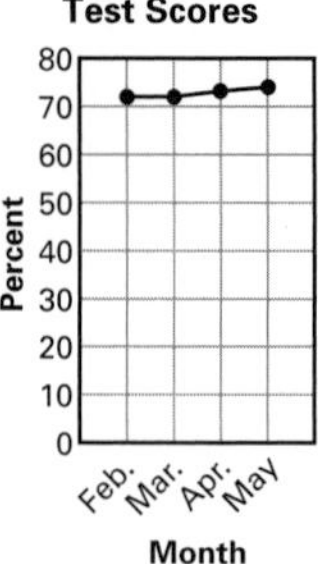

3. Pitcher Wins; Pitcher Losses

12.4 Skill Practice (pp. 672 – 673)

1. $m \cdot n$ **3.** 8 choices **5.** 6 choices **9.** $\frac{21}{26}$ **11.** $\frac{1}{456{,}976}$ **13.** 18 outcomes

12.4 Problem Solving (pp. 673 – 674)

17. *Sample answer:* Draw a tree diagram to list and then count all of the possibilities, or use the counting principle.
23. 64 symbols; 1 symbol; 1 symbol

12.5 Skill Practice (pp. 677 – 678)

1. ${}_{15}P_7$ **3.** 2 **5.** 5040 **7.** 12 **9.** 604,800 **11.** 665,280 **13.** 360,360
15. The denominator should be $(5 - 3)!$; ${}_5P_3 = \frac{5!}{(5-3)!} = \frac{5 \cdot 4 \cdot 3 \cdot 2 \cdot 1}{2 \cdot 1} = 5 \cdot 4 \cdot 3 = 60$ **17.** ${}_7P_7 = 5040$
19. ${}_{52}P_5 = 311{,}875{,}200$ **21.** ${}_{24}P_4 = 255{,}024$
23. $<$ **25.** $<$ **27.** $<$

12.5 Problem Solving (pp. 678 – 679)

29. 5040 permutations **33.** 210 permutations
35. 12 ways; Ed and Sue, Ed and Ty, Ed and Nestor, Sue and Ed, Ty and Ed, Nestor and Ed, Sue and Ty, Ty and Sue, Sue and Nestor, Nestor and Sue, Ty and Nestor, Nestor and Ty

12.6 Skill Practice (pp. 682 – 683)

1. 9; 5
3. 10 pairs;

1, 2	~~1, 3~~	~~1, 4~~	~~1, 5~~
~~2, 1~~	2, 3	~~2, 4~~	~~2, 5~~
3, 1	~~3, 2~~	3, 4	~~3, 5~~
4, 1	4, 2	~~4, 3~~	4, 5
5, 1	5, 2	5, 3	~~5, 4~~

5. 4 **7.** 7 **9.** 28 **11.** 45 **13.** 165 **15.** 36
17. Order is not important, so the possibilities can be counted by evaluating ${}_8C_2$, not ${}_8P_2$; ${}_8C_2 = \frac{{}_8P_2}{2!} = \frac{8 \cdot 7}{2 \cdot 1} =$ 28 possibilities **19.** permutation; 24 orders
21. combination; 10 groups

12.6 Problem Solving (pp. 683 – 684)
27. 15 combinations **29.** 792 teams **35. a.** 40,320 ways **b.** 45 ways **c.** 1,814,400 ways; Order is important, so evaluate $_{10}P_8$.

12.7 Skill Practice (pp. 687 – 688) **1.** odds in favor **3.** 16% **5.** 0.63 **7.** $\frac{3}{10}, \frac{7}{10}; \frac{7}{3}$ **9.** $\frac{6}{11}, \frac{5}{11}; \frac{5}{6}$ **11.** $\frac{1}{5}$ **13.** $\frac{2}{1}$ **15.** The student transposed the numerator and denominator; Odds $= \frac{2}{4} = \frac{1}{2}$, so the odds in favor are 1 to 2. **17.** $\frac{11}{9}$ **19.** $\frac{2}{23}$ **21.** $\frac{1}{4}$ **23.** $\frac{27}{50}$ **25.** $\frac{a}{a+b}$

12.7 Problem Solving (pp. 688 – 689) **27.** $\frac{3}{5}$ **29.** $\frac{13}{12}$ **31.** $\frac{93}{7}$

12.7 Extension, p. 691

1. $\{-7, -5, -4, -2, -1, 1, 2, 4, 5, 7\}$;

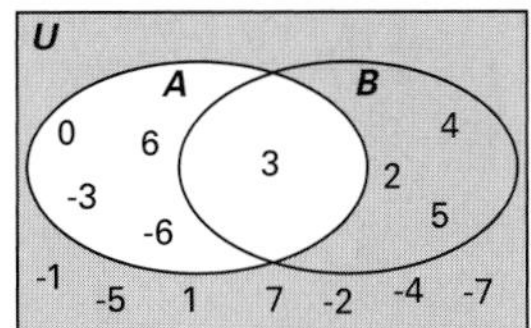

3. $\{-7, -5, -4, -2, -1, 1, 7\}$;

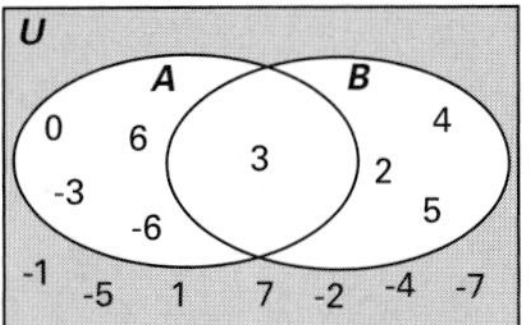

5. $\{-7, -5, -4, -2, -1, 1, 2, 3, 4, 5, 7\}$;

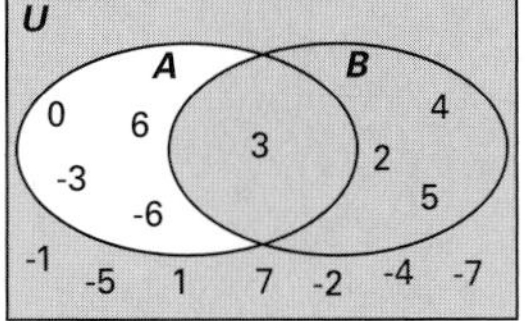

7. $\{-7, -5, -4, -2, -1, 1, 7\}$;

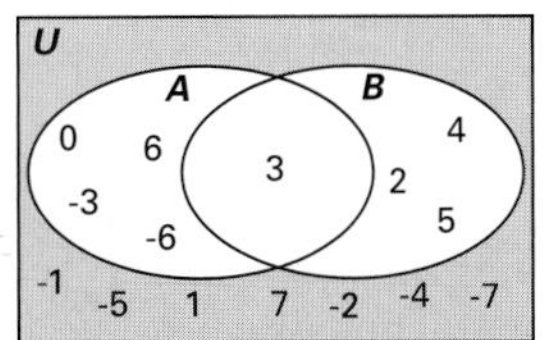

9. $\frac{11}{15}$ **11.** $\frac{7}{15}$ **13.** $\varnothing$; *U*; There are no elements that are both in *A* and not in *A*. The set of all elements in *A* or not in *A* is all the elements in *U*.

15.

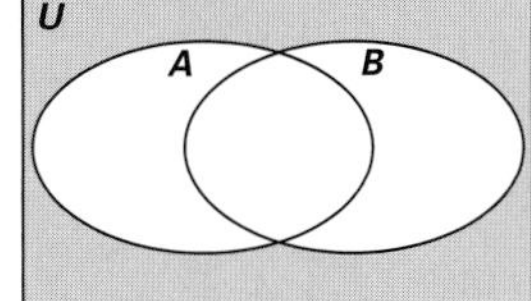

17.

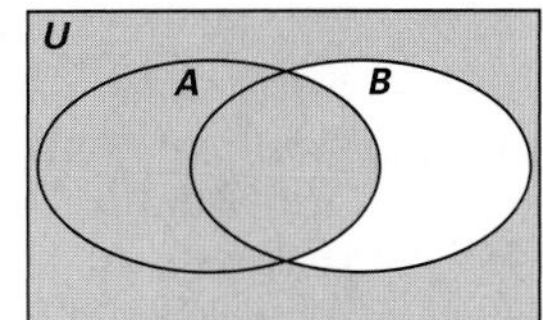

12.8 Skill Practice (pp. 697 – 698) **1.** independent **3.** independent **5.** dependent **7.** 0.24 **9.** 0.2 **11.** 0.4 **17.** $\frac{81}{10,000}$ **19.** $\frac{3}{2500}$

12.8 Problem Solving (pp. 698 – 700)

23. dependent; $\frac{1}{19}; \frac{2}{95}$ **25.** dependent; $\frac{2}{21}$ **27.** The probability of *B* given $A = \frac{3}{9}$, not $\frac{3}{10}$; $P(A \text{ and } B) = \frac{4}{10} \cdot \frac{3}{9} = \frac{12}{90} = \frac{2}{15}$ **31.** $\frac{1}{128}; \frac{1}{2}$; The probability of each toss is independent, so the probability that you will get heads is always $\frac{1}{2}$.

12.8 Extension, p. 702 **1.** yes; People who call in to a sports talk show are likely to favor sports. **3.** yes; People who enter a sporting goods store are likely to favor sports. *5–7. Sample explanations are given.* **5.** yes; This question suggests the mall is noisy and crowded. It encourages respondents to favor staying at home. So, the question could lead to biased results. **7.** no; This question is straightforward with no suggestions. It is not likely to lead to biased results.

Chapter Review (pp. 704 – 708) **1.** permutation **3.** circle graph **5.** stem-and-leaf plot

7. 20–29;

1	5 6 9
2	0 1 2 5 7 8 9
3	1 2 6 7
4	2

Key: 3 | 1 = 31

9. 90–99;

8	1 4 6
9	4 6 7 7 9
10	0 0

Key: 10 | 0 = 100

11.

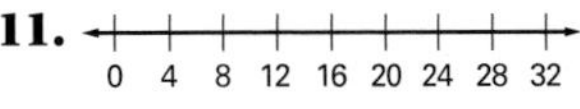

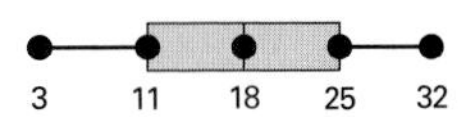

13. *Sample answer:* About half of the chess sets are priced between \$27.50 and \$55. The \$95 set lies well beyond the third quartile and appears to be an outlier;

15 30 45 60 75 90 105

15 27.5 40 55 95

15. 12 pairs;

H1 H2 H3 H4

S1 S2 S3 S1 S2 S3 S1 S2 S3 S1 S2 S3

17. 720 **19.** 154,440 **21.** 36 **23.** 1 **25.** combination; 155,117,520 groups **27.** $\frac{2}{121}$

SELECTED ANSWERS

Chapter 13

13.1 Skill Practice (p. 719) **1.** trinomial **3.** monomial **5.** $3m + 7$; binomial **7.** $-n^2 + 5n - 1$; trinomial **9.** $y^2 - 5y + 2$; trinomial **11.** $4x^{10} - 13x^3$; binomial **13.** $c^2 + 5c$ **15.** $-4g^3 + 2g^2 - 10$ **17.** $8x^2 - 15x + 30$ **19.** $18t^2 + 12t - 37$ **21.** $-3x^2$ and $-20x$ are not like terms; $-3x^2 - 20x - 4$ is the simplest form. **23.** $5a - 8b - 24$ **25.** $5a^2b^2 - 6ab^2 + 6ab$ **27.** *Answers may vary. Sample answer:* Standard form: $x + 1, x^2 + x + 1, 2x^3 + 3x^2 + 4x + 1$; Not standard form: $1 + x, x^2 + 1 + x, 1 + x + x^2$ **29.** $6x + 4$

13.1 Problem Solving (p. 720) **33.** 114 ft **35.** 122 ft **39.** sometimes; The monomial 1 has one factor, but the monomial $5x$ has two factors.

13.2 Skill Practice (pp. 723 – 724) **1.** like terms **3.** $12y + 2$ **5.** $5x + 4$ **7.** $6g^2 + g + 3$ **9.** $6k^2$ **11.** The terms were not aligned properly, and unlike terms were combined; $-2x^3 + 5x^2 - 13x + 12$ **13.** $6x + 12$ **15.** $-10d - 7$ **17.** $3r^2 + 2r + 4$ **19.** $3a^2 + 5a + 17$ **21.** $12n + 3$ **23.** $-19y - 15$ **25.** $17q^2 - 7q$ **27.** $20x^3 + 11x^2 - 15x + 5$ **29.** 3, -3

13.2 Problem Solving (pp. 724 – 725) **33.** $2(2x^2 - 2x + 3) + 2(-x^2 + 10x + 1)$; $2x^2 + 16x + 8$

13.3 Skill Practice (pp. 728 – 729) **1.** B **3.** C **5.** $48t^{10}$ **7.** $-6s^4$ **9.** $-y^5$ **11.** $-t^3 + 4t$ **13.** $36k^2 - 3k^7$ **15.** $-35a^5 + 63a^3$ **17.** $x^5y^5z^5$ **19.** $-216z^3$ **21.** $9r^2s^2$ **23.** $100{,}000b^5h^5$ **25.** y^4 **27.** x^{20} **29.** x^6y^6 **31.** $8r^9$ **35.** 7.29×10^{32} **37.** $250m^3n^{12}$ **39.** $-8x^{16}yz^8$ **41.** $2c^{36}d^{38}$ **43.** $\frac{81}{h^4}$ **45.** $\frac{9m^2}{n^4}$

13.3 Problem Solving (pp. 729 – 731) **51.** $125x^3$ **53.** $\frac{1}{2}(b - 6)(3b + b)$; $2b^2 - 12b$ **55.** $\frac{4}{3}\pi r^2h$; It is 4 times the original expression.

13.4 Skill Practice (p. 736) **1.** binomial **3.** $y^2 - 3y - 4$ **5.** $x^2 - 16$ **7.** $15q^2 - 8q + 1$ **9.** $x^2 + 7x - 18$ **11.** $a^2 + 6a - 40$ **13.** $-3t^2 - t + 4$ **15.** $9x^2 - 1$ **17.** $6m^2 + 23m + 7$ **19.** $36z^2 + 60z + 25$ **21.** $2x^2 + 5x - 12$ **23.** $n^4 - n^2 - 2$ **27.** $x^3 - x^2 - 3x - 36$ **29.** $8x^3 + 2x^2 + 9x + 5$ **31.** $-4x^3 - 17x^2 - 9x + 18$ **33.** $3x^2 + 16x - 35$

13.4 Problem Solving (pp. 737 – 738) **39.** $50 + 100r + 50r^2$; \$53.05 **47.** $20r^3 + 60r^2 + 60r + 20$; \$23.15 **49. a.** $6n^2 - 12n - 18$ **b.** 72 in.^{2}

13.5 Skill Practice (pp. 741 – 743) **1.** The left side should be $f(x)$, not just f. **3.** $f(x) = x^2$; 4, 0, 4 **5.** $f(x) = -3x^2$; -12, 0, -12 **7.** $f(x) = x^2 - 5$; -1, -5, -1 **9.** The square of -5 should be 25, not -25; $f(-5) = (-5)^2 - 3 = 25 - 3 = 22$

13.

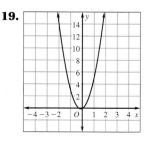

15.

17.

19.

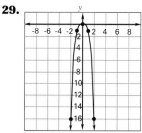

21. yes; yes **23.** no; no

25.

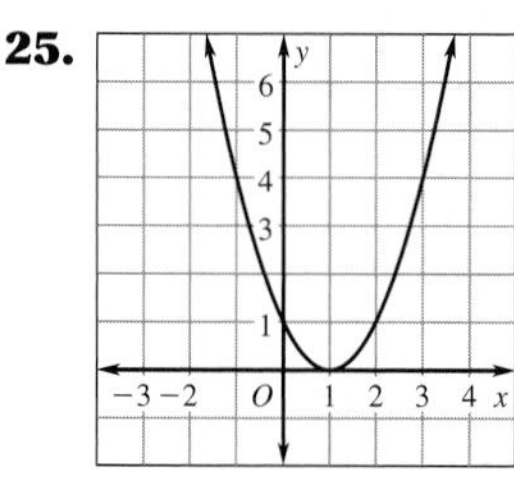

27.

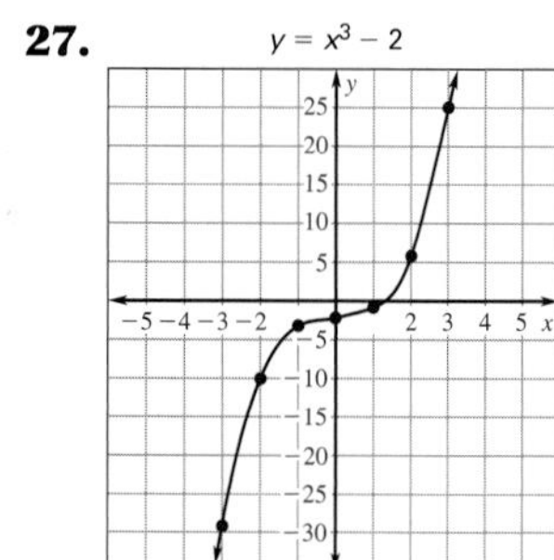

29.

31. 2, -2 **33.** 1, -1 **35.** -1, 3 **37.** $f(x) = x^3$ **39.** The graph of $y = c$ is a function because it is a horizontal line. If it is rotated 90°, it is a vertical line, so it would not represent a function.

13.5 Problem Solving (pp. 743 – 745) **41.** $f(d) = 1500d$; The function is linear. **43.** $f(x) = 20(1.002)^t$; \$20.04; \$20.08; \$20.12 **45.** $f(x) = \frac{\pi x^2}{4}$; 50.3 in.^{2};

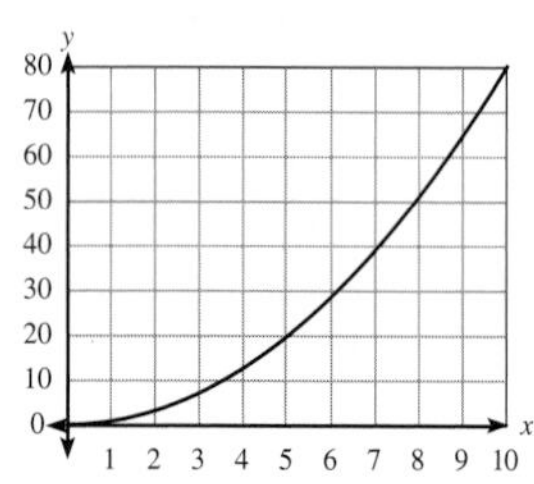

49. B **53.** yes; *Sample answer:* $f(x) = 90x$ describes the horizontal distance in terms of time. When the distance is 315 ft, then $315 = 90x$ and $x = \frac{315}{90} = 3.5$ s. Using $f(t) = -16t^2 + 63t + 2.5$ with $t = 3.5$, the height is $-16(3.5)^2 + 63(3.5) + 2.5 = 27$ ft. The height of the wall is 21 ft and $27 \geq 21$, so the hit will be a home run.

13.5 Technology Activity (p. 746) **1–4.** *Sample answer:* The graphs are all parabolas with the same shape and with vertices on the y-axis, but each graph moves up or down compared to the graph of $y = x^2$ by the number of units that are added to or subtracted from x^2. The graph moves up if this number is positive and down if this number is negative.

1.

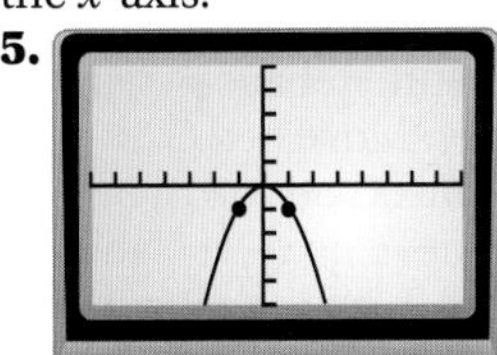

3.

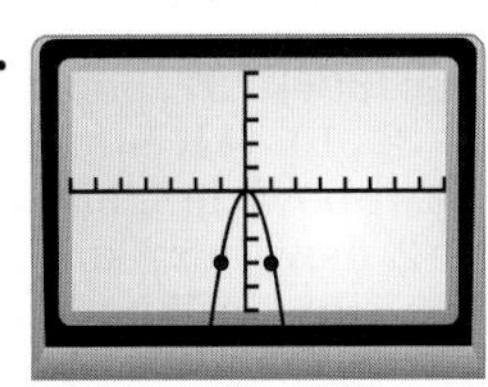

5–8. *Sample answer:* The graphs are the same as the graphs in the example, except they are reflected about the x-axis.

5.

7.

9. *Sample answer:* The graph is the same shape as the first graph in the example, reflected about the x-axis and shifted vertically 3 units;

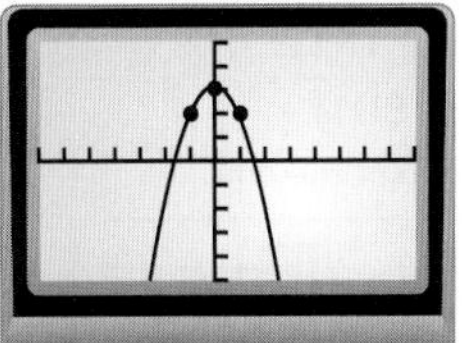

11. *Sample answer:* The graph is the same shape as the first graph in the example, reflected about the x-axis and shifted vertically 8 units;

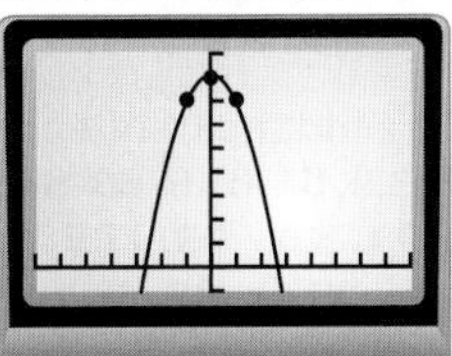

Chapter Review (pp. 748 – 750) **1.** polynomial **3.** standard form **5.** trinomial **7.** binomial

9. $k^2 + 11k - 3$ **11.** $18p^3 + 15p^2 + 27$ **13.** $4s^3 + 24s^2 - 16s - 56$ **15.** 6 ft **17.** $8y^2 - 5$ **19.** $-5v^3 - 10v^2 - 2v$

21. $-216a^6b^{12}$ **23.** $-3a^3 + 6a^2$ **25.** $\frac{1}{2}(6x)(3x + 9) = 9x^2 + 27x$ **27.** $36\pi x^3$ **29.** $q^2 - 16q + 63$

31.

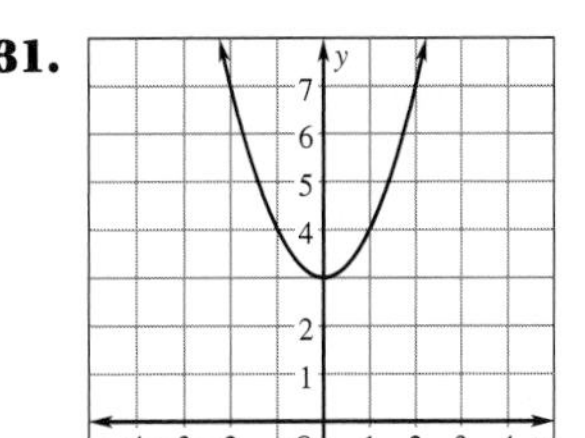

33.

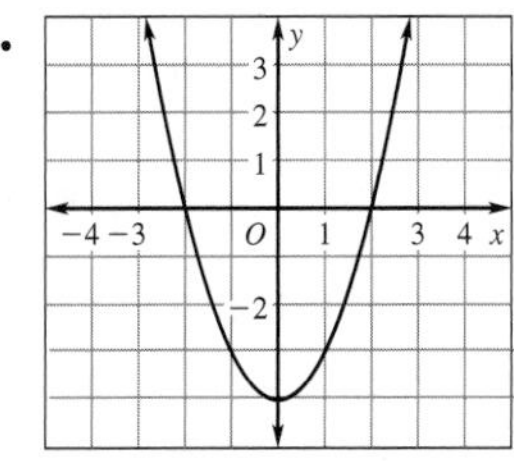

35. yes **37.** no

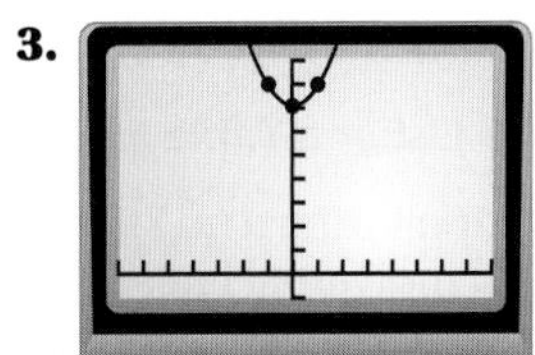

Skills Review Handbook

Place Value (p. 759) **1.** $5 \times 10{,}000 + 6 \times 1000 + 8 \times 100 + 9 \times 1$ **3.** $1 \times 1000 + 2 \times 1 + 3 \times 0.001$ **5.** 500,069.007

Rounding (p. 760) **1.** 1300 **3.** 8.2 **5.** 40,000 **7.** 450 **9.** 62.8 **11.** 164.5 **13.** 52.96 **15.** 3,501,700

Divisibility Tests (p. 761) **1.** 2 **3.** 3, 5 **5.** 2, 3, 4, 6, 9 **7.** 5 **9.** 2, 4

Mixed Numbers and Improper Fractions (p. 762)

1. 38 **3.** 3 **5.** $\frac{7}{2}$ **7.** $\frac{35}{8}$ **9.** $\frac{43}{4}$ **11.** $7\frac{1}{2}$ **13.** $5\frac{2}{3}$

Ratio and Rate (p. 763)

1. $\frac{13}{12}$, 13 to 12, 13 : 12 **3.** $\frac{11}{23}$, 11 to 23, 11 : 23 **5.** $\frac{\$24}{8 \text{ pens}} = \frac{\$3}{1 \text{ pen}}$ **7.** $\frac{280 \text{ words}}{5 \text{ min}} = \frac{56 \text{ words}}{1 \text{ min}}$ **9.** $\frac{8 \text{ in.}}{6 \text{ days}} = 1\frac{1}{3}$ in. per day

Adding and Subtracting Decimals (p. 764) **1.** 6.3 **3.** 31.1 **5.** 10.956 **7.** 2.91 **9.** 18.88 **11.** 57.8 **13.** 286.19 **15.** 88.064

Adding and Subtracting Fractions (p. 765) **1.** $\frac{2}{3}$ **3.** $\frac{3}{7}$ **5.** 1 **7.** $\frac{11}{15}$ **9.** $\frac{2}{9}$ **11.** $1\frac{7}{12}$ **13.** $\frac{1}{9}$ **15.** $\frac{9}{14}$ **17.** $\frac{7}{12}$ **19.** $1\frac{4}{7}$

Estimation in Addition and Subtraction (p. 766) *1–5. Estimates may vary.* **1.** 2700 **3.** 20,000 **5.** 2200

Solving Problems Using Addition and Subtraction (p. 767) **1.** \$93 **3.** \$2.01 **5.** 248 min

Multiplying Fractions (p. 768) **1.** $\frac{4}{5}$ **3.** $2\frac{2}{9}$ **5.** $5\frac{1}{4}$ **7.** $2\frac{4}{7}$ **9.** $\frac{8}{15}$ **11.** $\frac{3}{40}$ **13.** $\frac{10}{27}$ **15.** $\frac{25}{72}$

Multiplication of a Decimal by a Whole Number (p. 769) **1.** 225.4 **3.** 671.5 **5.** 29.12 **7.** 644.36 **9.** 1707.2 **11.** 18,663.6 **13.** 15,093.8 **15.** 36,833.5 **17.** 949.992 **19.** 3707.352 **21.** 4998.7 **23.** 1809.665 **25.** 5477.336 **27.** 120,455.25 **29.** 7564.91

Dividing Decimals (p. 770) **1.** 0.45 **3.** 0.85 **5.** 4.57 **7.** 6 R2 **9.** 8 R604

Estimation in Multiplication and Division (p. 771) *1–19. Estimates may vary.* **1.** 400 and 1000 **3.** 40,000 and 54,000 **5.** 30 and 40 **7.** 200 and 300 **9.** 12,000 and 20,000 **11.** 70,000 and 160,000 **13.** 12,000 and 21,000 **15.** 90 and 100 **17.** 700 and 800 **19.** 10 and 20

Solving Problems Using Multiplication and Division (p. 772) **1.** \$9.48 **3.** 576 flowers

Points, Lines, and Planes (p. 773) **1.** B **3.** A *5–7. Answers may vary.* **5.** $\overrightarrow{SR}$ and $\overrightarrow{ST}$ **7.** $\overline{SR}$

Angles (p. 774) **1.** C **3.** B **5.** $\angle HJK$, $\angle J$, $\angle KJH$ **7.** $\angle TUV$, $\angle U$, $\angle VUT$ **9.** $\angle FGH$, $\angle G$, $\angle HGF$

Using a Protractor (p. 776) **1.** 110° **3.** 88°

Using a Compass (p. 777) **1.** A good answer will show a circle with radius 4 cm. **3.** ————

Elapsed Time (p. 778) **1.** 2 hours 11 minutes **3.** 3:35 P.M.

Converting Customary Units (p. 779) **1.** 69 **3.** $10\frac{1}{2}$ **5.** 24 **7.** 3; 2 **9.** 6; 3

Converting Metric Units (p. 780) **1.** 6420 **3.** 5500 **5.** <

Converting Between Systems (p. 781) **1.** 176 **3.** 23 **5.** <

Reading and Making Line Plots (p. 782)

1.

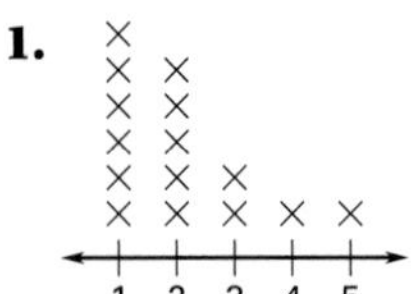

3. 19 people **5.** 5 people

Reading and Making Bar Graphs (p. 783) **1.** 9 students **3.** Vanilla and Rocky Road

Reading and Making Line Graphs (p. 784)

1. Thursday and Friday **3.**

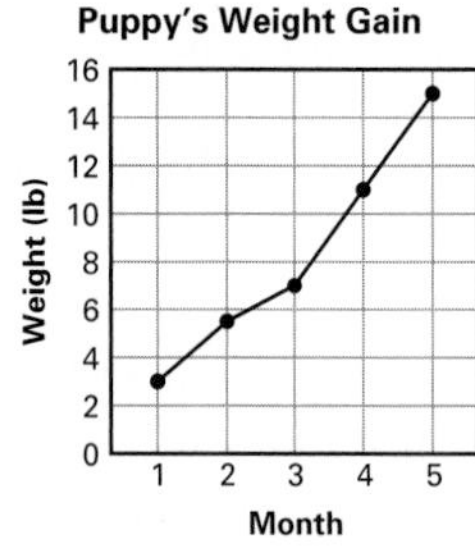

Venn Diagrams and Logical Reasoning (p. 785)

1.

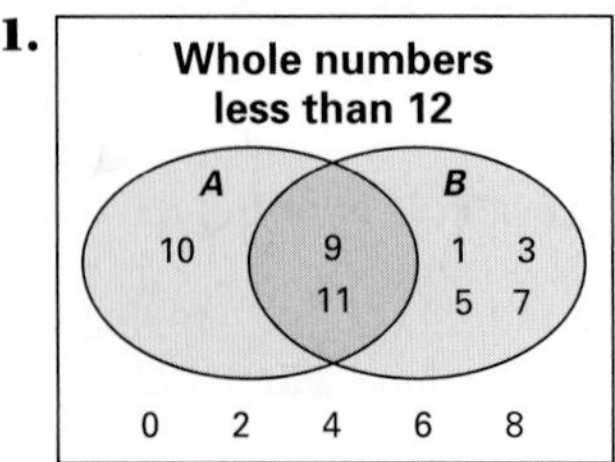

3. false; Both 9 and 11 are odd numbers greater than 8 and less than 12.

Problem Solving Practice

Make a Model (p. 796) **1.** yes; no; yes

3.

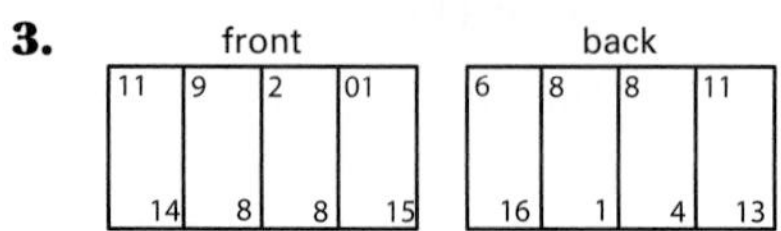

Draw a Diagram (p. 796) **5.** 45 **7.** 3

Guess, Check, and Revise (p. 797) **9.** 4 on bicycles, 3 on tricycles **11.** 21, 22, and 23

Work Backward (p. 798) **13.** 69 **15.** 60 **17.** 21

Make a List or a Table (pp. 797 – 798) **19.** 2 keychains

Look for a Pattern (p. 798) **21.** \$265 **23.** \$18; individual fares

Break into Parts (p. 799) **25.** 3 hours 11 minutes **27.** \$1054.50

Solve a Simpler Problem (p. 799) **29.** 1496 **31.** 220

Use a Venn Diagram (pp. 799 – 800) **33.** 20 **35.** 7

Act It Out (p. 800) **37.** Bob, Kelly, Justin, Rebecca, and Michelle **39.** 10 **41.** *Sample answer:* Move box C to Table 3, move box B to Table 2, stack box C on top of box B on Table 2, move box A to Table 3, move box C to Table 1, stack box B on top of box A on Table 3, and stack box C on top of boxes B and A on Table 3. **43.** Darryl, Carlene, Tyrone, and Penelope

Extra Practice

Chapter 1 (p. 801)

1.

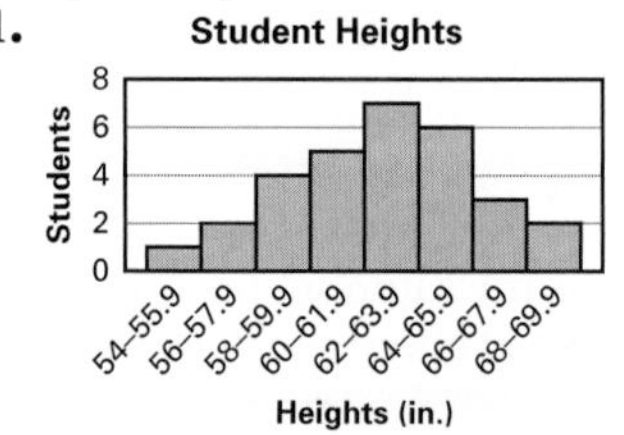

3. yes; You can add the frequencies for the intervals 60–61.9, 62–63.9, 64–65.9, 66–67.9, and 68–69.9. **5.** 7 **7.** 4 **9.** 36 **11.** 8.4 **13.** 11.7 **15.** 27 **17.** 7 **19.** 63 **21.** 8 **23.** 9 **25.** 42 ft; 104 ft^2 **27.** 8 cm

Chapter 2 (p. 802) **1.** −43, −24, −2, 7, 19, 33 **3.** 25; 25 **5.** 0; 0 **7.** −409 **9.** 179 **11.** 0 **13.** −16 **15.** 51 **17.** −15 **19.** 68 **21.** 350 **23.** −64 **25.** 0 **27.** 240 **29.** −12 **31.** 0 **33.** −4 **35.** $7(2 \cdot \frac{3}{7})$ [original expression] $= 7(\frac{3}{7} \cdot 2)$ [Comm. Prop. of Mult.] $= (7 \cdot \frac{3}{7}) \cdot 2$ [Assoc. Prop. of Mult.] $= 3 \cdot 2$ [Multiply 7 and $\frac{3}{7}$] $= 6$ [Multiply 3 and 2] **37.** $(-5)(-3) + (-5)(8)$; -25 **39.** $-4 - 9r$ **41.** $5x - 2y$ **43.** $-a - 10b$

44–47. 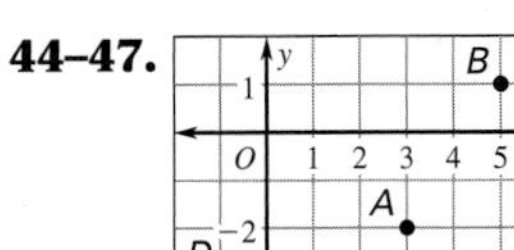

45. Quadrant I

47. Quadrant III

Chapter 3 (p. 803) **1.** 8 **3.** 5 **5.** 64 **7.** 4 **9.** 7 **11.** 7.5 **13.** 20 **15.** −58 **17.** $6n - 5 = 13$; 3 **19.** 1.5 h **21.** 60 in.^{2}; 36 in. **23.** 5 m; 34 m

25. $j \geq -5$;

27. $z \leq = -2.5$;

29. $x < -5$;

31. $s \leq = 8$;

Chapter 4 (p. 804) **1.** $2^3 \cdot 3^2$ **3.** $3^2 \cdot 17$ **5.** $5^2 \cdot p \cdot q$ **7.** $2 \cdot 11 \cdot x \cdot y \cdot y$ **9.** 15 **11.** bc **13.** $3m$ **15.** $17w^2z^2$ **17.** $\frac{1}{2}$ **19.** $-\frac{2}{7}$ **21.** $\frac{2}{9y}$ **23.** $-\frac{3a}{2c}$ **25.** 60 **27.** $15ab^2c^2$ **29.** > **31.** > **33.** < **35.** > **37.** z^6 **39.** $(-7)^9$ **41.** 6^4 **43.** $(-v)^3$ **45.** $\frac{6}{k}$ **47.** $\frac{1}{s^7}$ **49.** 1.24×10^8 **51.** 7.91×10^{-5} **53.** 0.0027 **55.** 588,000,000,000

Chapter 5 (p. 805) **1.** $1\frac{1}{2}$ **3.** $-\frac{2m}{3}$ **5.** $\frac{1}{15}$ **7.** $8\frac{1}{8}$ **9.** $\frac{3}{16}$ **11.** $-\frac{10}{27}$ **13.** $\frac{5}{18}$ **15.** $-3\frac{3}{32}$ **17.** −0.384 **19.** $-\frac{7}{25}$ **21.** $\frac{3}{500}$ **23.** 3.875 **25.** $-2.5, -2.43, -2\frac{5}{12}, -2\frac{2}{5}, -\frac{7}{3}$ **27.** $\frac{26}{5}, 5.21, 5\frac{2}{9}, 5.3, 5\frac{3}{8}$ **29.** 3.81 **31.** 13.1 **33.** −16.55 **35.** −8.115 **37.** 3.9104 **39.** 1.5 **41.** −31.866 **43.** −8.2 **45.** 43; 39; no mode; 57 **47.** 88; 87; 78 and 95; 22

Chapter 6 (p. 806) **1.** 7 **3.** −9 **5.** 2 **7.** −2 **9.** 5 **11.** −1 **13.** 0.13 **15.** −4 **17.** −4 **19.** 4.5 cm **21.** 7 yd; Use $\frac{22}{7}$ for π since 44 is divisible by 22.

23. $c < 2$;

25. $s \geq = -1$;

27. $b > 8$;

29. $\frac{1}{2}n + 12 \leq 8$; $n \leq -8$ **31.** $4n \geq 16$; $n \geq 4$

33. at least $1\frac{1}{2}$ h

Chapter 7 (p. 807) **1.** $\frac{3}{1}$, 3 : 1, 3 to 1 **3.** $\frac{2}{3}$, 2 : 3, 2 to 3 **5.** 4 **7.** 225 **9.** 9.3 **11.** 12% **13.** 8.96 **15.** 12.5% **17.** 72% **19.** 0.31; $\frac{31}{100}$ **21.** 1.75; $\frac{7}{4}$ **23.** increase; 12% **25.** decrease; 1% **27.** \$22.08 **29.** $83\frac{1}{3}$ **31.** 0.084 **33.** $\frac{1}{6}$

Chapter 8 (p. 808) **1.** $m\angle 1 = 50°$ **3.** $m\angle 5 = 50°$; $m\angle 6 = 50°$; $m\angle 7 = 130°$ **5.** $x = 90$; right **7.** rhombus **9.** trapezoid **11.** 160° **13.** $\angle A \cong \angle P$; $\angle B \cong \angle Q$; $\angle C \cong \angle R$

15. 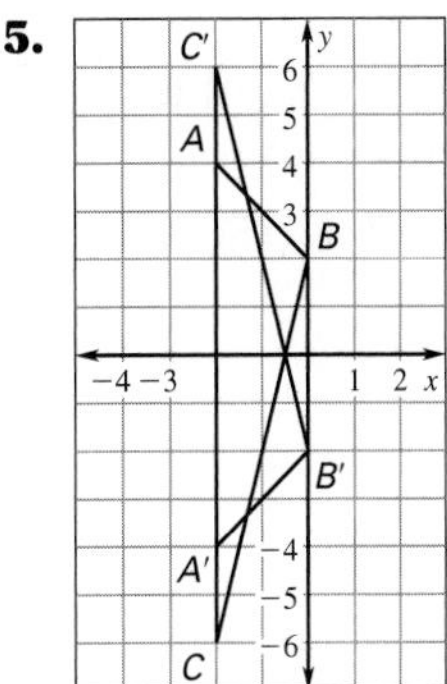

17. 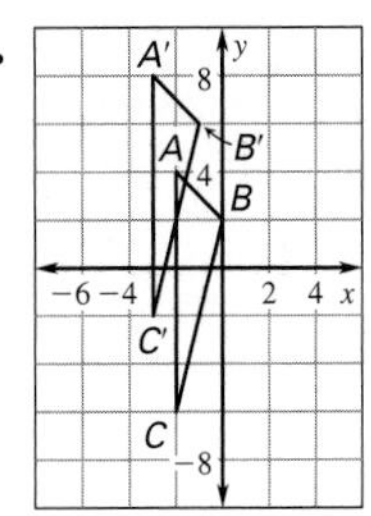

19. 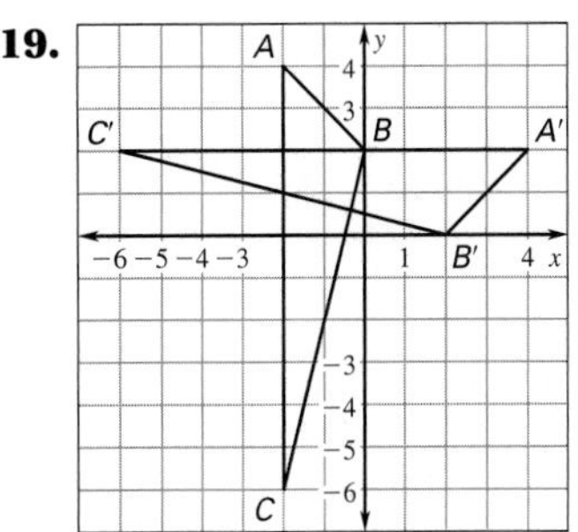

21. 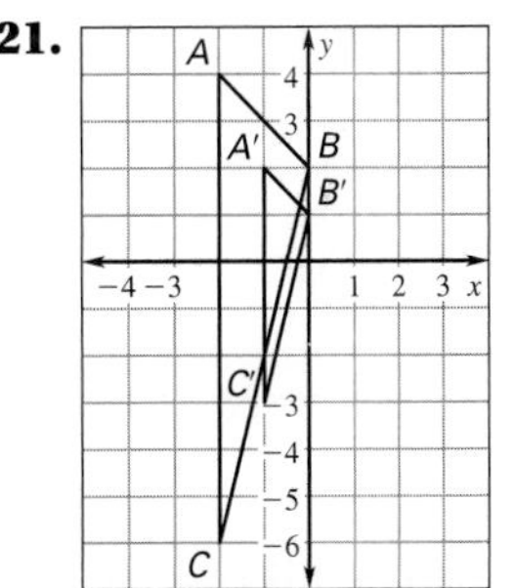

Chapter 9 (p. 809) **1.** 7.2 **3.** −27.2 **5.** 30, −30 **7.** 15, −15 **9.** 9, −9 **11.** 8, −8 **13.** > **15.** > **17.** $0.\overline{1}, 0.12, 0.\overline{12}, 0.123, 0.\overline{123}$ **19.** 35 **21.** 33 **23.** 75 **25.** yes **27.** yes **29.** $x = 7\sqrt{2}$; $y = 7$ **31.** $x = 19\sqrt{3}$; $y = 38$ **33.** $\sin A = \frac{36}{85}$; $\cos A = \frac{77}{85}$; $\tan A = \frac{36}{77}$; $\sin B = \frac{77}{85}$; $\cos B = \frac{36}{85}$; $\tan B = \frac{77}{36}$ **35.** $\sin 62° \approx 0.8829$; $\cos 62° \approx 0.4695$; $\tan 62° \approx 1.8807$

Chapter 10 (p. 810) **1.** 195 in.^{2}; 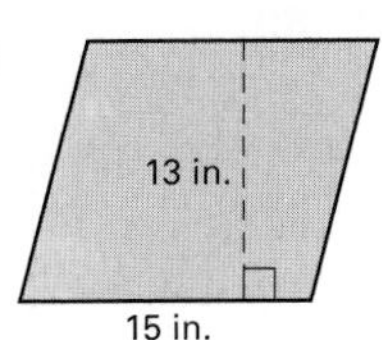

3. 10 cm^2; 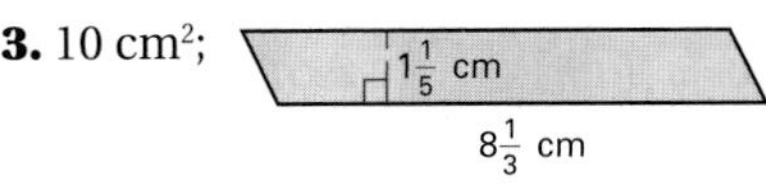

SELECTED ANSWERS

5. 357 yd^2;

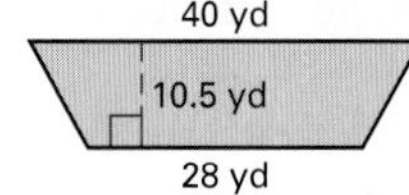

7. 5020 in.^{2} **9.** 26.4 ft^2 **11.** 0.283 cm^2 **13.** 201 mi^2
15. It is not a polyhedron because circles are not polygons;

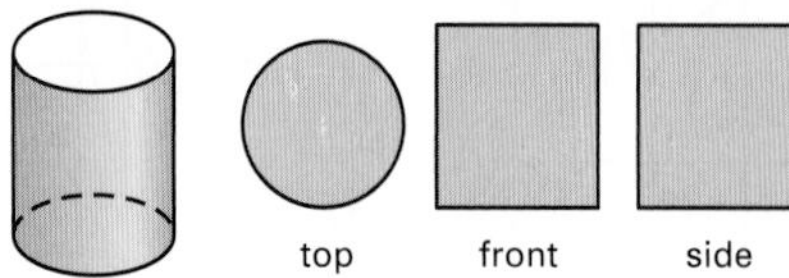

17. 390 in.^{2};

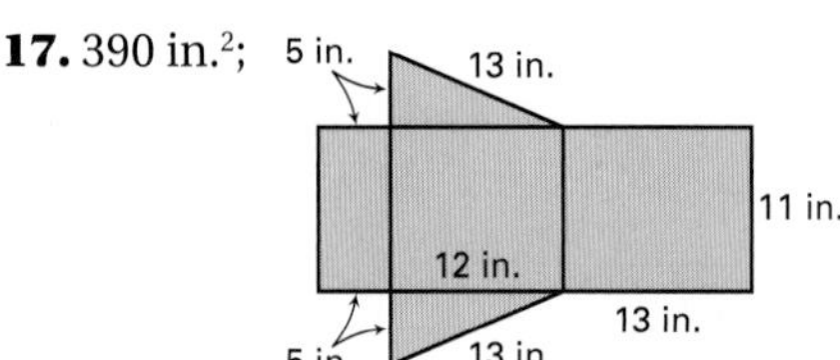

19. 360 m^2 **21.** 369.9 m^2 **23.** 330 in.^{3} **25.** 266.7 ft^3
27. 252 cm^3

Chapter 11 (p. 811)

1. yes; Each input has exactly one output. $y = x - 1$
5. no **7.** yes **9.** (–2, 3), (–1, 5), (0, 7), (1, 9)
11. (–2, 2), (–1, 1), (0, 0), (1, –1) **13.** (–2, 4), (–1, 1), (0, –2), (1, –5) **15.** (–2, –5), (1, –1), (4, 3), (7, 7)

17.

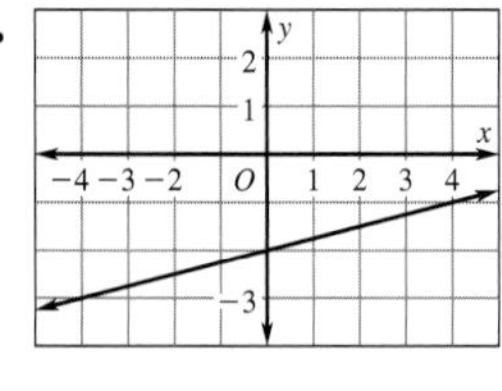

19.

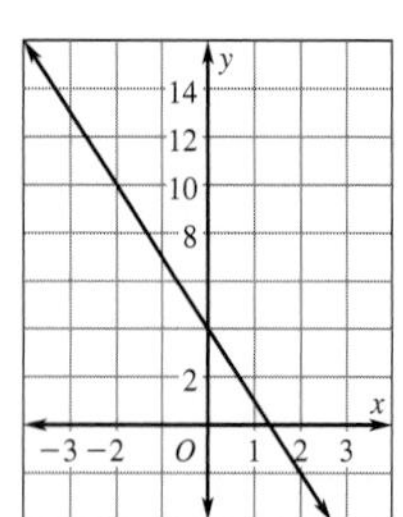

21. x-intercept, $\frac{1}{5}$; y-intercept, -1 **23.** x-intercept, 6; y-intercept, -4 **25.**

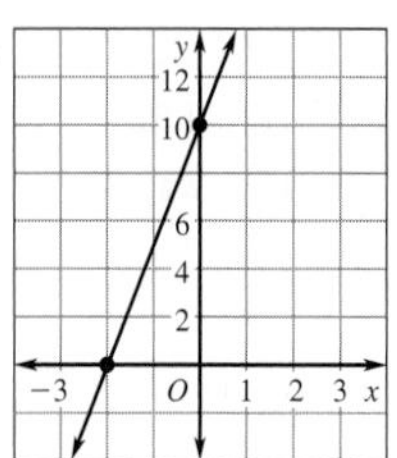

27. undefined **29.** 1 **31.** -1 **33.** $\frac{17}{3}$ **35.** 0; 2

37. 2; -8 **39.**

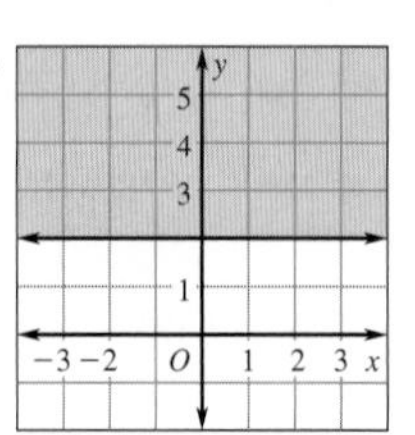

41.

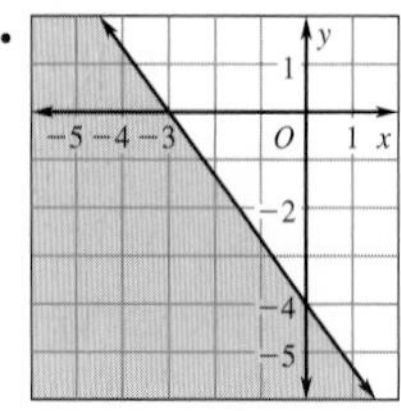

Chapter 12 (p. 812)

1. 100–109;

Stem	Leaves
9	9
10	0 1 3 5
11	6 7 8
12	7 9
13	0
14	0 0 3

Key: 13 | 0 = 130

3. *Sample answer:* About 50% of the lengths were between 103 in. and 130 in.;

100 110 120 130 140

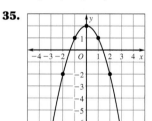

99 103 117.5 130 143

5. line graph; A line graph is used to represent data that change over time. **7.** 17,576,000 license plates
9. 11 **11.** 720 **13.** 5 **15.** 20 **17.** 4060 ways **19.** $\frac{3}{4}$
21. $\frac{2}{9}$

Chapter 13 (p. 813)

1. $-x^2 - 2x + 7$ **3.** $-k^2 + 21$
5. $-2x^3 + 4x^2 + 14x - 4$ **7.** $3x^3 - 9x^2 + 6x - 3$
9. $x^3 - 2x^2 + 9x + 6$ **11.** $-28z^6$ **13.** $-6n^2 + 15n$
15. $125\,a^3b^3$ **17.** p^{24} **19.** $2x^2 - 9x - 5$ **21.** $d^2 + 10d + 24$ **23.** $a^2 - 15a + 56$ **25.** $f(x) = 2x - 5$ **27.** $f(x) = 5x^2 + 1$ **29.** 1; $\frac{1}{4}$; 0; $\frac{1}{4}$; 1 **31.** -16; -5; 0; -1, -8
33. -7; -4; -3; -4; -7

35. [graph]

37. no **39.** yes

Mathematics – Grade 7

Numbers and Operations

Students will further develop their understanding of the concept of rational numbers and apply them to real world situations.

M7N1 Students will understand the meaning of positive and negative rational numbers and use them in computation.

a. Find the absolute value of a number and understand it as the distance from zero on a number line.

b. Compare and order rational numbers, including repeating decimals.

c. Add, subtract, multiply, and divide positive and negative rational numbers.

d. Solve problems using rational numbers.

Geometry

Students will further develop and apply their understanding of plane and solid geometric figures through the use of constructions and transformations. Students will explore the properties of similarity and further develop their understanding of 3-dimensional figures.

M7G1 Students will construct plane figures that meet given conditions.

a. Perform basic constructions using both compass and straight edge, and appropriate technology. Constructions should include copying a segment; copying an angle; bisecting a segment; bisecting an angle; constructing perpendicular lines, including the perpendicular bisector of a line segment; and constructing a line parallel to a given line through a point not on the line.

b. Recognize that many constructions are based on the creation of congruent triangles.

M7G2 Students will demonstrate understanding of transformations.

a. Demonstrate understanding of translations, dilations, rotations, reflections, and relate symmetry to appropriate transformations.

b. Given a figure in the coordinate plane, determine the coordinates resulting from a translation, dilation, rotation, or reflection.

M7G3 Students will use the properties of similarity and apply these concepts to geometric figures.

a. Understand the meaning of similarity, visually compare geometric figures for similarity, and describe similarities by listing corresponding parts.

b. Understand the relationships among scale factors, length ratios, and area ratios between similar figures. Use scale factors, length ratios, and area ratios to determine side lengths and areas of similar geometric figures.

c. Understand congruence of geometric figures as a special case of similarity: The figures have the same size and shape.

M7G4 Students will further develop their understanding of three-dimensional figures.

a. Describe three-dimensional figures formed by translations and rotations of plane figures through space.

b. Sketch, model, and describe cross-sections of cones, cylinders, pyramids, and prisms.

Algebra

Students will demonstrate an understanding of linear relations and fundamental algebraic concepts.

M7A1 Students will represent and evaluate quantities using algebraic expressions.

a. Translate verbal phrases to algebraic expressions.

b. Simplify and evaluate algebraic expressions, using commutative, associative, and distributive properties as appropriate.

c. Add and subtract linear expressions.

M7A2 Students will understand and apply linear equations in one variable.

a. Given a problem, define a variable, write an equation, solve the equation, and interpret the solution.

b. Use the addition and multiplication properties of equality to solve one- and two-step linear equations.

M7A3 Students will understand relationships between two variables.

a. Plot points on a coordinate plane.

b. Represent, describe, and analyze relations from tables, graphs, and formulas.

c. Describe how change in one variable affects the other variable.

d. Describe patterns in the graphs of proportional relationships, both direct $(y = kx)$ and inverse $\left(y = \frac{k}{x}\right)$.

Data Analysis and Probability

Students will demonstrate understanding of data analysis by posing questions, collecting data, analyzing the data using measures of central tendency and variation, and using the data to answer the questions posed. Students will understand the role of probability in sampling.

M7D1 Students will pose questions, collect data, represent and analyze the data, and interpret results.

- **a.** Formulate questions and collect data from a census of at least 30 objects and from samples of varying sizes.
- **b.** Construct frequency distributions.
- **c.** Analyze data using measures of central tendency (mean, median, and mode), including recognition of outliers.
- **d.** Analyze data with respect to measures of variation (range, quartiles, interquartile range).
- **e.** Compare measures of central tendency and variation from samples to those from a census. Observe that sample statistics are more likely to approximate the population parameters as sample size increases.
- **f.** Analyze data using appropriate graphs, including pictographs, histograms, bar graphs, line graphs, circle graphs, and line plots introduced earlier, and using box-and-whisker plots and scatter plots.
- **g.** Analyze and draw conclusions about data, including a description of the relationship between two variables.